Give your students choices.

Pearson's History titles are available in numerous formats to give you and your students more choices.

CourseSmart eTextbooks

offer the same content as the printed text in a convenient online format—with highlighting, online search, and printing capabilities. *60% off the list price of the traditional book.* www.coursesmart.com

MyHistoryLab

MyHistoryLab is a dynamic website that provides a wealth of resources geared to meet the specific teaching and learning needs of every instructor and student. **MyHistoryLab** includes an interactive eText—identical in content and design to the printed text—so students have access to their text wherever and whenever they need it. It also features unabridged audio files of the entire text, which enable students to learn and review in a new way. **MyHistoryLab** may be packaged with a printed text for no additional charge or purchased as a standalone eText. *35% off the net price of the traditional book.* www.myhistorylab.com

Books à la Carte editions

feature the exact same text in a convenient, three-hole-punched, loose-leaf version at a discounted price—allowing students to take only what they need to class. **Books à la Carte editions** are available both with and without access to **MyHistoryLab.** *35% off the net price of the traditional book.*

The Pearson Custom Library

The Pearson Custom Library lets you create a textbook that meets the specific needs of your course. Combine chapters from several best-selling Pearson textbooks and/or topical reading units in the sequence you want.

www.pearsonlearningsolutions.com

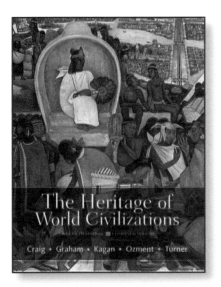

The Heritage of World Civilizations
Brief Fifth Edition

©2012

Albert M. Craig

William A. Graham

Donald Kagan

Steven M. Ozment

Frank M. Turner

CourseSmart eText
- ❏ *Combined Volume: 9780205052813*
- ❏ *Volume 1: 9780205052820*
- ❏ *Volume 2: 9780205052592*

MyHistoryLab with eText access card
- ❏ *Combined Volume:9780205054121*
- ❏ *Volume 1: 9780205053810*
- ❏ *Volume 2: 9780205053803*

Books à la Carte edition
(unbound, three-hole-punched version)
- ❏ *Volume 1: 9780205052264*
- ❏ *Volume 2: 9780205052561*

Books à la Carte edition (unbound,
three-hole-punched version) **plus MyHistoryLab**
- ❏ *Volume 1: 9780205218608*
- ❏ *Volume 2: 9780205218615*

Traditional printed text plus MyHistoryLab
- ❏ *Combined Volume: 9780205207572*
- ❏ *Volume 1: 9780205218608*
- ❏ *Volume 2: 9780205218615*

Traditional printed text
- ❏ *Combined Volume: 9780205835492*
- ❏ *Volume 1: 9780205835485*
- ❏ *Volume 2: 9780205835478*

Pearson Custom Library
Available Now

For more information, please visit
www.pearsonhighered.com/gomakehistory

19TH CENTURY U.S. HISTORY (AFTER 1865)

Levy Mark Twain: The Divided Mind of America's Best-Loved Writer
©2011, 9780205553754 / 0205553753
(Part of the Library of American Biography Series)

20TH CENTURY U.S. HISTORY (1945–PRESENT)

Brands Post-1945 America: American Dreams
©2011, 9780205568482 / 0205568483

Pelz Karl Marx
©2012, 9780321355836 / 0321355830
(Part of the Library of World Biography Series)

AMERICAN REVOLUTION

Offutt Patriots, Loyalists, and Revolution in New York, 1775-1776
©2011, 9780205785797 / 0205785794

THE COLD WAR

Judge & Langdon The Cold War: A Global History with Documents, 2/e
©2011, 9780205729111 / 0205729118

COLONIAL AMERICAN HISTORY (1492–1776)

Gallay Colonial and Revolutionary America: Text and Documents
©2011, 9780205809691 / 0205809693

Reich Colonial America, 6/e
©2011, 9780205743162 / 0205743161

HISTORIOGRAPHY

Hoefferle The Essential Historiography Reader
©2011, 9780321437624 / 0321437624

HISTORY OF AFRICAN AMERICANS

Carson, Lapsansky-Werner & Nash The Struggle for Freedom: A History of African Americans, 2/e, Combined Volume
©2011, 9780205832408 / 0205832407
Also available in Volumes I & II
(Penguin Academic Series)

Hine, Hine & Harrold The African-American Odyssey, 5/e, Combined Volume
©2011, 9780205728817 / 0205728812
Also available in Volumes I & II

HISTORY OF FILM

Pereboom History and Film: Moving Pictures and the Study of the Past
©2011, 9780131938465 / 0131938460

HISTORY OF MEXICAN AMERICANS

Acuña Occupied America: A History of Chicanos, 7/e
©2011, 9780205786183 / 0205786189

HISTORY OF NATIVE AMERICANS

Nicholas Sources in the Native American Past, Combined Volume
©2012, 9780205742516 / 0205742513
Also available in Volumes I & II

Townsend & Nicholas First Americans: A History of Native Peoples
©2012, 9780132069489 / 0132069482

HISTORY OF PENNSYLVANIA

Davis & Newman Pennsylvania History: Essays and Documents
©2011, 9780205701667 / 0205701663

HISTORY OF THE WEST

Anderson Will Rogers and "His" America
©2011, 9780205695065 / 020569506X
(Part of the Library of American Biography Series)

HISTORY OF WOMEN IN AMERICA

Skinner Women and the National Experience: Primary Sources in American History, 3/e, Combined Volume
©2011, 9780205743155 / 0205743153
Also available in Volumes I & II

THE SIXTIES (1960-1969)

Unger The Sixties
©2011, 9780132069557 / 0132069555

Primary Source Readers

Gorn, Roberts & Bilhartz Constructing the American Past: A Source Book of a People's History, 7/e
©2011, *Vol. I: 9780205773640 / 0205773648*
Vol. II: 9780205773633 / 020577363X

Merrell & Podair American Conversations
©2012, *Vol. I: 9780132446839 / 0132446839*
Vol. II: 9780131582613 / 0131582615

Unger & Tomes American Issues: A Primary Source Reader in United States History, 5/e
©2011, *Vol. I: 9780205803453 / 0205803458*
Vol. II: 9780205803446 / 020580344X

Secondary Source Readers

Youngs American Realities, 8/e
©2011, *Vol. I: 9780205764129 / 0205764126*
Vol. II: 9780205764136 / 0205764134

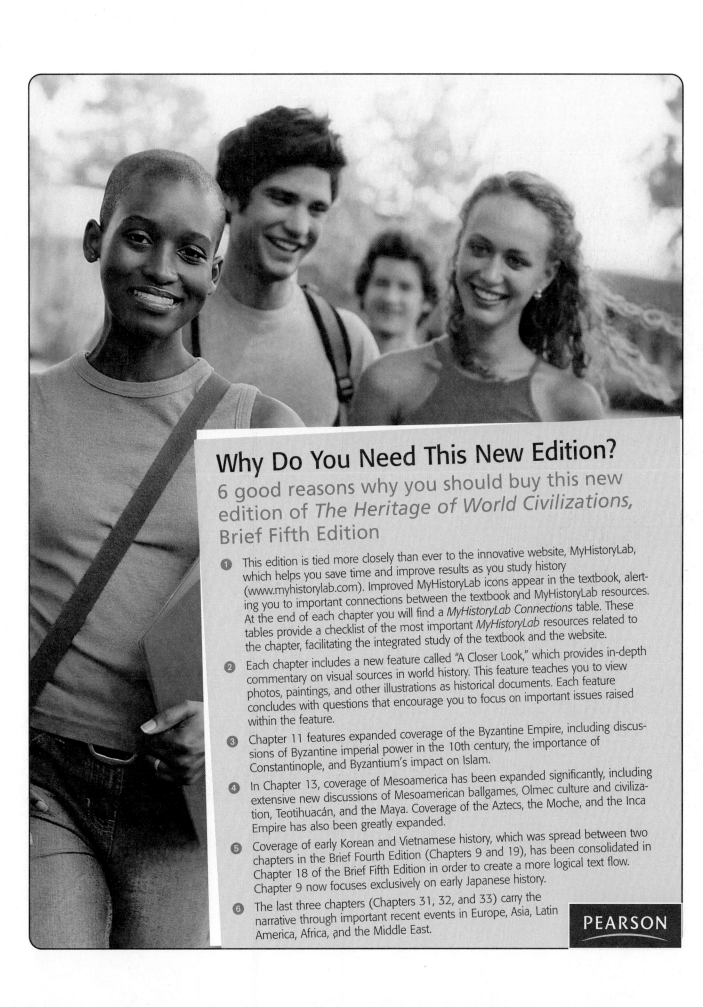

Why Do You Need This New Edition?

6 good reasons why you should buy this new edition of *The Heritage of World Civilizations,* Brief Fifth Edition

1. This edition is tied more closely than ever to the innovative website, MyHistoryLab, which helps you save time and improve results as you study history (www.myhistorylab.com). Improved MyHistoryLab icons appear in the textbook, alerting you to important connections between the textbook and MyHistoryLab resources. At the end of each chapter you will find a *MyHistoryLab Connections* table. These tables provide a checklist of the most important *MyHistoryLab* resources related to the chapter, facilitating the integrated study of the textbook and the website.

2. Each chapter includes a new feature called "A Closer Look," which provides in-depth commentary on visual sources in world history. This feature teaches you to view photos, paintings, and other illustrations as historical documents. Each feature concludes with questions that encourage you to focus on important issues raised within the feature.

3. Chapter 11 features expanded coverage of the Byzantine Empire, including discussions of Byzantine imperial power in the 10th century, the importance of Constantinople, and Byzantium's impact on Islam.

4. In Chapter 13, coverage of Mesoamerica has been expanded significantly, including extensive new discussions of Mesoamerican ballgames, Olmec culture and civilization, Teotihuacán, and the Maya. Coverage of the Aztecs, the Moche, and the Inca Empire has also been greatly expanded.

5. Coverage of early Korean and Vietnamese history, which was spread between two chapters in the Brief Fourth Edition (Chapters 9 and 19), has been consolidated in Chapter 18 of the Brief Fifth Edition in order to create a more logical text flow. Chapter 9 now focuses exclusively on early Japanese history.

6. The last three chapters (Chapters 31, 32, and 33) carry the narrative through important recent events in Europe, Asia, Latin America, Africa, and the Middle East.

PEARSON

COMBINED VOLUME

The Heritage of World Civilizations

Brief Fifth Edition

ALBERT M. CRAIG
Harvard University

WILLIAM A. GRAHAM
Harvard University

DONALD KAGAN
Yale University

STEVEN OZMENT
Harvard University

FRANK M. TURNER
Yale University

Prentice Hall
Boston   Columbus   Indianapolis   New York   San Francisco   Upper Saddle River
Amsterdam   Cape Town   Dubai   London   Madrid   Milan   Munich   Paris   Montréal   Toronto
Delhi   Mexico City   São Paulo   Sydney   Hong Kong   Seoul   Singapore   Taipei   Tokyo

Editorial Director: Craig Campanella
Executive Editor: Jeff Lasser
Editorial Project Manager: Rob DeGeorge
Editorial Assistant: Julia Feltus
Director of Marketing: Brandy Dawson
Senior Marketing Manager: Maureen E. Prado Roberts
Marketing Assistant: Samantha Bennett
Senior Managing Editor: Ann Marie McCarthy
Project Manager: Cheryl Keenan
Senior Manufacturing and Operations Manager for Arts & Sciences: Nick Sklitsis
Operations Specialist: Christina Amato
Brief Edition Editor: Katie Janssen
Manager, Visual Research and Permissions: Beth Brenzel
Senior Art Director: Maria Lange
Cover Designer: Bruce Killmer

Cover Art: Woodfin Camp & Associates, Inc./Diego Rivera (1866–1957), "The Great City of Tenochtitlan," 1945. (Detail) Mural, 4.92 × 9.71 m. Patio Corridor, National Palace, Mexico City, D.F., Mexico. © 2003 Banco de Mexico Diego Rivera & Fida Kahlo Museums Trust. Av. Cinco de Mayo No. 2, Col. Centro, Del. Cuauhtemoc 06059, Mexico, D.F. Reproduction authorized by the Instituto Nacional de Bellas Artes y Literatura.
AV Project Manager: Mirella Signoretto
Media Director: Brian Hyland
Media Project Manager: Tina Rudowski
Digital Media Editor: Alison Lorber
Composition and Full-Service Project Management: Linda Ruggeri, Prepare, Inc.
Printer/Binder: Webcrafters, Inc.
Cover Printer: Lehigh Phoenix Color
Text Font: 10/13 Goudy

Credits and acknowledgments borrowed from other sources and reproduced, with permission, in this textbook appear on appropriate page within text and on page C-1.

Library of Congress Cataloging-in-Publication Data

The heritage of world civilizations / Albert M. Craig ... [et al.]. -- Brief 5th ed.
    p. cm.
  Includes bibliographical references and index.
  ISBN 978-0-205-83549-2 (combined edition : alk. paper)
  ISBN 978-0-205-83548-5 (volume 1 : alk. paper)
  ISBN 978-0-205-83547-8 (volume 2 : alk. paper)
  1. Civilization--History--Textbooks. I. Craig, Albert M. II. Title.

CB69.H45 2011
909--dc22   2011005330

10 9 8 7 6 5 4 3 2 1

Combined Volume
ISBN-10: 0-205-83549-X
ISBN-13: 978-0-205-83549-2

Exam Copy
ISBN-10: 0-205-05254-1
ISBN-13: 978-0-205-05254-7

Volume 1
ISBN-10: 0-205-83548-1
ISBN-13: 978-0-205-83548-5

Volume 1 a la Carte
ISBN-10: 0-205-05226-6
ISBN-13: 978-0-205-05226-4

Volume 2
ISBN-10: 0-205-83547-3
ISBN-13: 978-0-205-83547-8

Volume 2 a la Carte
ISBN: 0-205-05256-8
ISBN: 978-0-205-05256-1

Prentice Hall is an imprint of

www.pearsonhighered.com

Brief Contents

Contents

Documents

Maps

The global financial crisis that commenced in 2008 has painfully sparked for this generation a new sense of the connectedness of international economic events and financial forces. The banking crisis in the United States, the burgeoning Chinese economy, the debt upheaval within the European Union, the rise and fall of commodity prices, and the entanglement of the flows of capital from one part of the developed world to another have painfully demonstrated how events and decisions in one nation or upon one continent can impact millions of people living far from the centers of those decisions. The economic crisis has followed fast upon a decade during which the military forces of the United States and Europe have invaded nations of the Middle East in response to terrorist attacks. Environmental crises, whether in the form of oceanic oil spills or volcanic eruption, can interfere with trade, commerce, and tourism, as can changes in the price and availability of oil on which the United States, Europe, Japan, China, and India—to mention only the largest industrial economies—are dependent from sources outside their borders and regions.

Economic and military interaction and environmental crises upon the global scene are the most dramatic and disruptive signs of the impact of globalization. However, more quietly but not less dramatically, for the past two decades, the steady growth of the Internet has created in a less dramatic and far more peaceful fashion a sense of world wide cultural and commercial interconnectedness. Whereas once undergraduates in American universities might have gone to a larger newspaper room in their college or university library to read newspapers from other countries several days or even weeks after they had been published, today's students can follow the press of countries around the world from smart phones, computers, and other electronic reading devices. The Internet permits students to view museum collections located on every continent. Books of great rarity and value once reserved for students in a few elite universities are now available electronically in all parts of the world. United States colleges and universities to an extent previously unimagined are establishing branches far beyond North America. Whereas American students as recently as the 1970s found almost half the world closed to travel, now they can travel globally with almost no barriers.

Today, the interconnectedness of cultures and peoples as well as of economies is inescapable. We certainly dwell in an era in which no active citizen or educated person can escape the necessity of understanding the past in global terms. Both the historical experience and the moral, political, and religious values of the different world civilizations now demand our attention and our understanding. It is our hope that in these new, challenging times *The Heritage of World Civilizations* will provide one path to such knowledge.

THE ROOTS OF GLOBALIZATION

Globalization—that is, the increasing interaction and interdependency of the various regions of the world—has resulted from two major historical developments: the closing of the European era of world history and the rise of technology.

From approximately 1500 C.E. to the middle of the twentieth century, Europeans, later followed by the United States, gradually came to dominate the world through colonization (most particularly in North and South America), state-building, economic productivity, and military power. That era of European dominance ended during the third quarter of the twentieth century after Europe had brought unprecedented destruction on itself during World War II, as the United States eventually confronted limitations in its post-war influence, and as the nations of Asia, the Near East, and Africa achieved new positions on the world scene. Their new political independence, their control over strategic natural resources, the expansion of their economies (especially those of the nations of the Pacific rim of Asia), and in some cases their access to nuclear weapons have changed the shape of world affairs.

Further changing the world political and social situation has been a growing discrepancy in the economic development of different regions that is often portrayed as a problem between the northern and southern hemispheres. Beyond the emergence of this economic disparity has been the remarkable advance of radical political Islamism during the past forty years. In the midst of all these developments, as a result of the political collapse of the former Soviet Union, the United States has emerged as the single major world power, though its position has been increasingly challenged by China, whose economic might now rivals that of the United States and whose military has embarked on a rapid buildup of its forces in Asia.

The second historical development that continues to fuel the pace of globalization is the advance of technology, associated most importantly with transportation, military weapons, and electronic communication. The advances in transportation over the past two centuries, including ships, railways, and airplanes, have made more parts of the world and its resources accessible to more people in ever shorter spans of time. Over the past century and a half, military weapons of increasingly destructive power enabled Europeans and then later the United States to dominate other regions of the globe. Now, the spread of these weapons means that any nation with sophisticated military technology can threaten other nations, no matter how far away. Furthermore, technologies that originated in the West from the early twentieth century to the present have been turned against the West. More recently, as already noted, the electronic revolution associated with computer technology and most particularly the Internet has sparked unprecedented speed and complexity in global communications. It is astonishing to recall that personal computers have been generally available for less than thirty-five years and the rapid personal communication associated with them has existed for less than twenty years.

Why not, then, focus only on new factors in the modern world, such as the impact of technology and the end of the European era? To do so would ignore the very deep roots that these developments have in the past. More important, the events of recent years demonstrate, as the authors of this book have long contended, that the major religious traditions continue to shape and drive the modern world as well as the world of the past. The religious traditions link today's civilizations to their most ancient roots. We believe this emphasis on the great religious traditions recognizes not only a factor that has shaped the past, but one that is profoundly and dynamically alive in our world today.

STRENGTHS OF THE TEXT

BALANCED AND FLEXIBLE PRESENTATION
In this edition, as in past editions, we have sought to present world history fairly, accurately, and in a way that does justice to its great variety. History has many facets, no one of which can account for the others. Any attempt to tell the story of civilization from a single perspective, no matter how timely, is bound to neglect or suppress some important part of that story.

Historians have recently brought a vast array of new tools and concepts to bear on the study of history. Our coverage introduces students to various aspects of social and intellectual history as well as to the more traditional political, diplomatic, and military coverage. We firmly believe that only through an appreciation of all pathways to understanding of the past can the real heritage of world civilizations be claimed.

The Heritage of World Civilizations, Brief Fifth Edition, is designed to accommodate a variety of approaches to a course in world history, allowing teachers to stress what is most important to them. Some teachers will ask students to read all the chapters. Others will select among them to reinforce assigned readings and lectures.

CLARITY AND ACCESSIBILITY   *The Heritage of World Civilizations*, Brief Fifth Edition, provides a powerful but concise narrative enriched by abundant illustrations, focused study tools, and critical-thinking questions that make the past come alive. Good narrative history requires clear, vigorous prose. Our goal has been to make our presentation fully accessible to students without compromising on vocabulary or conceptual level. We hope this effort will benefit both teachers and students.

CURRENT SCHOLARSHIP   As in previous editions, changes in this edition reflect our determination to incorporate the most recent developments in historical scholarship and the expanding concerns of professional historians. To better highlight the dynamic processes of world history, significant new and expanded coverage of the Byzantine Empire and the early civilizations of the Americas—particularly the civilizations of Mesoamerica and the Andes during the pre-colonial period—has been added to the Brief Fifth Edition.

CONTENT AND ORGANIZATION   The many changes in content and organization in this edition of *The Heritage of World Civilizations* reflect our ongoing effort to present a truly global survey of world civilizations that at the same time gives a rich picture of the history of individual regions:

- **Global Approach.** The Brief Fifth Edition continues to explicitly highlight the connections and parallels in global history among regions of the world. Each chapter begins with a "Global Perspective" essay that succinctly places in a wider, global framework the regions and topics that are to be discussed with an emphasis on the connections, parallels, and comparisons between and among different cultures.

- **Improved Organization.** Some chapters have been reorganized to improve narrative flow and to highlight important topics more clearly. At the suggestion of reviewers, Chapter 4 (Iran, India, and Inner Asia to 200 C.E.) and Chapter 10 (Iran and South Asia, 200 C.E.–1000 C.E.) in the Brief Fourth Edition have been consolidated into a single chapter in the Brief Fifth Edition: Chapter 4 (West Asia, Inner Asia, and South Asia to 1000 C.E.). Coverage of early Korean and Vietnamese history has been moved from Chapter 9 to Chapter 18, leaving Chapter 9 solely devoted to early Japan. Coverage of Korea and Vietnam has been consolidated in Chapter 18 with a far greater sense of continuity and a more effective and concise presentation.

- **New Design and Photo Program.** The entire text has been set in a crisp and engaging new design. Each of the 33 chapters includes photos never before included in previous editions of the text.

PEDAGOGICAL FEATURES

This edition retains many of the pedagogical features of previous editions, while providing increased assessment opportunities.

- **Global Perspective Essays** introduce the key problems of each chapter and place them in a global and historical context. Focus Questions prompt students to consider the causes, connections, and consequences of the topics they will encounter in the main narrative.
- **A Closer Look**—Each chapter includes this **new** feature, which provides in-depth commentary on visual sources in world civilization. This feature engages student visually with the textbook and encourages them to look at visuals as documents, not just as pictures. Each feature concludes with questions that encourage students to focus on important issues raised by the feature.
- **Religions of the World** essays examine the historical impact of each of the world's great religious traditions: Judaism, Christianity, Islam, Buddhism, and Hinduism.
- **Focus Questions,** organized by key subtopics, open each chapter and help students think about important topics for study and review. The focus questions are repeated at the appropriate sections in each chapter.
- **Overview Tables** summarize key concepts and reinforce material presented in the main narrative.
- **Chronologies** within each chapter help students situate key events in time.
- **Quick Reviews,** found at key places in the margins of each chapter, encourage students to review important concepts.
- **Documents,** including selections from sacred books, poems, philosophical tracts, political manifestos, letters, and travel accounts, expose students to the raw material of history, providing an intimate contact with peoples of the past. Questions accompanying the source documents direct students toward important, thought-provoking issues and help them relate the documents to the main narrative.
- **Visual Analysis Questions** ask students to consider photographs, fine art, and other illustrations as visual evidence.
- **Key Terms** are boldfaced in the text and are defined in the margin of the page.
- **Interactive Maps,** called "Map Explorations," prompt students to explore the relationship between geography and history in a dynamic fashion. There is at least one interactive map per chapter and all interactive maps can be found at *www.myhistorylab.com*
- **Chapter Summaries** conclude each chapter, organized by subtopic, and recap important points.
- **Chapter Review Questions,** organized by key subtopics, help students interpret the broad themes of each chapter.

NEW TO THIS EDITION

There is a new feature in the Brief Fifth Edition:

A Closer Look—*Each* chapter includes a new feature called "A Closer Look," which provides in-depth commentary on visual sources in world history. This feature teaches students to view photos, paintings, and other illustrations as historical documents. Each feature concludes with questions that encourage students to focus on important issues raised within the feature. See the Contents on page vi for the title of each of these new features.

Here are just some of the changes that can be found in the Brief Fifth Edition of *The Heritage of World Civilizations*:

Chapter 3, Greek and Hellenistic Civilization:
- A new document has been added: "The Delian League Becomes the Athenian Empire."

Chapter 4, West Asia, Inner Asia, and South Asia to 1000 C.E.:
- At the suggestion of reviewers, Chapter 4 (Iran, India, and Inner Asia to 200 C.E.) and Chapter 10 (Iran and South Asia, 200 C.E.–1000 C.E.) in the Brief Fourth Edition have been consolidated into a single chapter in the Brief Fifth Edition: Chapter 4 (West Asia, Inner Asia, and South Asia to 1000 C.E.).
- The Global Perspective feature is new.
- There is a new document, an excerpted letter from Tansar about the Shahanshah, titled "Tansar's Defense of His King, Ardashir I."
- Consolidation of the two chapters involved considerable rearranging, with coverage of Iran and Central Asia located in the first section of the consolidated chapter and coverage of India in the second section. These sections have been renamed as follows: "West and Inner Asia" and "South Asia."
- Coverage of caste has been improved.

Chapter 5, Africa: Early History to 1000 C.E.:
- Coverage of historians' and anthropologists' methods and crossovers has been expanded.

Chapter 6, Republican and Imperial Rome:
- A new document has been added on the ruin of the Roman family farm and the Gracchan reforms.

Chapter 8, Imperial China, 589–1368:
- Coverage of Empress Wu has been updated to reflect new biographical scholarship.

Chapter 9, Early Japanese History:
- Global Perspective feature has been rewritten.
- Coverage of early Korean and Vietnamese history has been moved from this chapter to Chapter 18, leaving Chapter 9 solely devoted to early Japan.
- Japanese Origins section and Jōmon subsection have been updated.
- Yayoi section has been updated with a discussion of new DNA findings.
- There is new coverage of Shōtoku and Kamatari in the section on Nara and Heian Japan.

[Note: Brief Fourth Edition Chapters 4 and 10 have been combined in the Brief Fifth Edition, causing all chapters that follow—Chapters 11–34 in the Brief Fourth Edition—to be renumbered in the Brief Fifth Edition.]

Chapter 11, The Byzantine Empire and Western Europe to 1000:

- Coverage of Byzantium has been greatly expanded, with new sections on Byzantine imperial power in the 10th century, Byzantium's impact on Islam, and the city of Constantinople.
- A new document has been added in response to reviewer suggestions: The Nicene Creed

Chapter 13, Ancient Civilizations of the Americas:

- Coverage of the Paleolithic and Archaic periods in the Americas has been greatly expanded.
- There is a more detailed discussion on the influence of the European perspective on how the history of the Americas in the pre-Columbian period has been written.
- Coverage of Mesoamerica has been expanded significantly, including extensive new discussions of Mesoamerican ballgames, Olmec culture and civilization, Teotihuacán, and the Maya.
- Coverage of the Aztecs, the Moche, and the Inca Empire has been greatly expanded.

Chapter 17, Conquest and Exploitation: The Development of the Transatlantic Economy:

- There is new coverage of the Indian Wars in the 17th century North American British colonies.
- There is new coverage of the alleged slave conspiracy in 1741 in New York City.

Chapter 18, East Asia in the Late Traditional Era:

- Coverage of Korea and Vietnam has been consolidated in Chapter 18 with a far greater sense of continuity and a more effective and concise presentation.
- The introduction to the Vietnam section contains a new overview of Southeast Asia.
- Coverage of the Choson dynasty in the Korean section has been revised and greatly improved.

Chapter 19, State Building and Society in Early Modern Europe:

- New coverage has been added on the Revolution of 1688.

Chapter 21, The Age of European Enlightenment:

- A new document has been added emphasizing the Enlightenment interest in technology and the mechanical arts.
- Coverage of technology has been emphasized to a greater extent throughout the chapter.
- Brief new commentary has been introduced on why the Enlightenment is unpopular in some Islamic circles.

Chapter 22, Revolutions in the Transatlantic World:

- A substantial new section has been added on the Haitian Revolution.
- Two new documents have been added: "Olympe de Gouges Issues a Declaration of the Rights of Woman" and "A Free Person of Color from St. Domingue Demands Recognition of His Status."

Chapter 23, Political Consolidation in Nineteenth-Century Europe and North America:

- A new document has been added: "Parnell Calls for Home Rule for Ireland."
- Coverage of race and Social Darwinism has been expanded.

Chapter 24, Northern Transatlantic Economy and Society, 1815–1914:

- A new document from "The Communist Manifesto" has been added.
- There is new coverage of child labor.

Chapter 25, Latin America from Independence to the 1940s:

- A new document has been added: "A Peruvian Commentator Decries Racial Thinking."

Chapter 26, India, the Islamic Heartlands, and Africa, 1800–1945:

- Chapter updated to include coverage of the British Zulu war.

Chapter 28, Imperialism and World War I:

- A new document has been added: "Social Darwinism and Imperialism."

Chapter 29, Depression, European Dictators, and the American New Deal:

- The following new documents have been added: "Stalin Calls for the Liquidation of the *Kulaks* as a Class" and "Mussolini Heaps Contempt on Political Liberalism."
- There is new coverage of forced starvation in the Ukraine by Stalin.
- New coverage has been added on FDR's failure to support anti-lynching legislation.

Chapter 30, World War II:

- A new document has been added: "Hitler States His Plans for Russia."

Chapter 31, The West Since World War II:

- Two new documents have been introduced: "The United States National Security Council Proposes to Contain the Soviet Union," and "Vladimir Putin Outlines a Vision of the Russian Future."
- The section on recent events in Russia has been significantly updated.

Chapter 32, East Asia: The Recent Decades:

- Coverage of China and Japan has been updated to reflect recent events.

Chapter 33, Postcolonialism and Beyond: Latin America, Africa, Asia, and the Middle East:

- Coverage of Latin America, Africa, Asia, and the Middle East has been updated to reflect recent events.

A NOTE ON DATES AND TRANSLITERATION

We have used B.C.E. (before the common era) and C.E. (common era) instead of B.C. (before Christ) and A.D. (anno domini, the year of our Lord) to designate dates.

Until recently, most scholarship on China used the Wade-Giles system of romanization for Chinese names and terms. China today, however, uses another system known as pinyin. Virtually all Western newspapers have adopted it. In order that students may move easily from the present text to the existing body of advanced scholarship on Chinese history, we now use the pinyin system throughout the text.

Also, we have followed the currently accepted English transliterations of Arabic words. For example, today Koran is being replaced by the more accurate Qur'an; similarly Muhammad is preferable to Mohammed and Muslim to Moslem. We have not tried to distinguish the letters 'ayn and *hamza*; both are rendered by a simple apostrophe (') as in Shi'ite. With regard to Sanskritic transliteration, we have not distinguished linguals and dentals, and both palatal and lingual *s* are rendered *sh*, as in Shiva and Upanishad.

MyHistoryLab (www.myhistorylab.com) *Save Time. Improve Results.* MyHistoryLab is a dynamic website that provides a wealth of resources geared to meet the diverse teaching and learning needs of today's instructors and students. MyHistoryLab's many accessible tools will encourage students to read their text and help them improve their grade in their course.

Instructor's Resource Manual Available at the Instructor's Resource Center, at **www.pearsonhighered.com/irc**, the Instructor's Resource Manual includes chapter outlines, overviews, key concepts, discussion questions, and suggestions for useful audiovisual resources.

Test Bank Available at the Instructor's Resource Center, at **www.pearsonhighered.com/irc**, the Test Bank includes approximately 1,500 test items (essay, multiple choice, true/false, and matching).

Instructor's Resource Center (www.pearsonhighered.com/irc) Text-specific materials, such as the Instructor's Resource Manual, Test Bank, map files, and PowerPoint™ presentations, are available for downloading by adopters.

MyTest Available at **www.pearsonmytest.com**, MyTest is a powerful assessment generation program that helps instructors easily create and print quizzes and exams. Questions and tests can be authored online, allowing instructors ultimate flexibility and the ability to efficiently manage assessment anytime, anywhere! Instructors can easily access existing questions and edit, create, and store using simple drag-and-drop and Word-like controls.

MyHistoryLab (www.myhistorylab.com) *Save Time. Improve Results.* MyHistoryLab is a dynamic website that provides a wealth of resources geared to meet the diverse teaching and learning needs of today's instructors and students. MyHistoryLab's many accessible tools will encourage you to read your text and help you improve your grade in your course.

CourseSmart www.coursemart.com CourseSmart is an exciting new choice for students looking to save money. As an alternative to purchasing the printed textbook, students can purchase an electronic version of the same content. With a CourseSmart eTextbook, students can search the text, make notes online, print out reading assignments that incorporate lecture notes, and bookmark important passages for later review. For more information, or to purchase access to the CourseSmart eTextbook, visit **www.coursesmart.com**

Books à la Carte Books à la Carte editions feature the exact same content as the traditional printed text in a convenient, three-hole-punched, loose-leaf version at a discounted price—allowing you to take only what you need to class. You'll **save 35% over the net price** of the traditional book.

***Primary Source: Documents in Global History* DVD** is an immense collection of textual and visual documents in world history and an indispensable tool for working with sources. Extensively developed with the guidance of historians and teachers, the DVD includes over 800 sources in world history—from cave art to satellite images of the Earth from space. More sources from Africa, Latin America, and Southeast Asia have been added to the latest version of the DVD. All sources are accompanied by head notes, focus questions, and are searchable by topic, region, or time period. The DVD can be bundled with *The Heritage of World Civilizations*, Brief Fifth Edition, at no charge. Please contact your Pearson representative for ordering information. (ISBN 0-13-178938-4)

Titles from the renowned **Penguin Classics** series can be bundled with *The Heritage of World Civilizations*, Brief Fifth Edition, for a nominal charge. Please contact your Pearson sales representative for details.

(continued)

SUPPLEMENTS FOR STUDENTS

Library of World Biography Series
www.pearsonhighered.com/educator/series/Library-of-World-Biography/10492.page   Each interpretive biography in the Library of World Biography Series focuses on a person whose actions and ideas either significantly influenced world events or whose life reflects important themes and developments in global history. Titles from the series can be bundled with *The Heritage of World Civilizations*, Brief Fifth Edition, for a nominal charge. Please contact your Pearson sales representative for details.

DK   *The Prentice Hall Atlas of World History*, **Second Edition**   Produced in collaboration with Dorling Kindersley, the leader in cartographic publishing, the updated second edition of *The Prentice Hall Atlas of World History* applies the most innovative cartographic techniques to present world history in all of its complexity and diversity. Copies of the atlas can be bundled with *The Heritage of World Civilizations*, Brief Fifth Edition, for a nominal charge. Contact your Pearson sales representative for details. (ISBN 0-13-604247-3)

Longman Atlas of World History   This atlas features carefully selected historical maps that provide comprehensive coverage of the major historical periods. Contact your Pearson sales representative for details. (ISBN 0-321-20998-2)

A Guide to Your History Course: What Every Student Needs to Know   Written by Vincent A. Clark, this concise, spiral-bound guidebook orients students to the issues and problems they will face in the history classroom. Available at a discount when bundled with *The Heritage of World Civilizations*, Brief Fifth Edition. (ISBN 0-13-185087-3)

A Short Guide to Writing about History, **Seventh Edition**   Written by Richard Marius, late of Harvard University, and Melvin E. Page, Eastern Tennessee State University, this engaging and practical text helps students get beyond merely compiling dates and facts. Covering both brief essays and the documented resource paper, the text explores the writing and researching processes, identifies different modes of historical writing, including argument, and concludes with guidelines for improving style. (ISBN 0-13-205-67370-8)

PEARSON myhistorylab™

FOR INSTRUCTORS AND STUDENTS

Save TIME. Improve Results.

MyHistoryLab is a dynamic website that provides a wealth of resources geared to meet the diverse teaching and learning needs of today's instructors and students. MyHistoryLab's many accessible tools will encourage students to read their text and help them improve their grade in their course.

Features of MyHistoryLab

- **Pearson eText**—An e-book version of *The Heritage of World Civilizations* is included in MyHistoryLab. Just like the printed text, students can highlight and add their own notes as they read the book online.
- **Audio Files**—Full audio of the entire text is included to suit the varied learning styles of today's students. In addition there are audio clips of speeches, readings, and music that provide another engaging way to experience history.
- **Pre-tests, Post-tests, and Chapter Reviews**—Students can take quizzes to test their knowledge of chapter content and to review for exams.
- **Text and Visual Documents**—A wealth of primary source documents, images, and maps are available organized by chapter in the text. Primary source documents are also available in the MyHistoryLibrary and can be searched by author, title, theme, and topic. Many of these documents include critical thinking questions.
- **History Bookshelf**—Students may read, download, or print 100 of the most commonly assigned history works like Homer's *The Iliad* or Machiavelli's *The Prince*.
- **Lecture and Archival Videos**—Lectures by leading scholars on provocative topics give students a critical look at key points in history. Videos of speeches, news footage, key historical events, and other archival videos take students back to the moment in history.
- **MySearchLab**—This website provides students access to a number of reliable sources for online research, as well as clear guidance on the research and writing process.

- **Gradebook**—Students can follow their own progress and instructors can monitor the work of the entire class. Automated grading of quizzes and assignments helps both instructors and students save time and monitor their results throughout the course.

NEW In-text References to MyHistoryLab Resources

Read, View, See, Watch, Hear, and **Study and Review Icons** integrated in the text connect resources on MyHistoryLab to specific topics within the chapters. The icons are not exhaustive; many more resources are available than those highlighted in the book, but the icons draw attention to some of the most high-interest resources available on MyHistoryLab.

Read the Document Primary and secondary source documents on compelling topics such as *Excerpts from Sundiata: An Epic of Old Mali, 1235* and *Tang Daizong on the Art of Government* enhance topics discussed in each chapter.

View the Image Photographs, fine art, and artifacts provide students with a visual perspective on topics within the chapters, underscoring the role of visuals in understanding the past.

See the Map Atlas and interactive maps present both a broad overview and a detailed examination of historical developments.

Watch the Video Video lectures highlight topics ranging from Agriculture in Africa, to Witch Hunts, to the Columbian Exchange, engaging students on both historical and contemporary topics. Also included are archival videos, such as *The Silk Road: 5,000 Miles and 1,500 Years of Cultural Interchange* and *Teotihuacán Ruins in Mexico*.

Hear the Audio For each chapter there are audio files of the text, speeches, readings, and other audio material that will enrich students' experience of social and cultural history.

Study and Review MyHistoryLab provides a wealth of practice quizzes, tests, flashcards, and other study resources available to students online.

NEW MyHistoryLab Connections

At the end of each chapter, a new section, MyHistoryLab Connections, provides a list of the references within the chapter and additional documents, maps, videos, or additional resources that relate to the content of the chapter.

ACKNOWLEDGMENTS

We are grateful to the many scholars and teachers whose thoughtful and often detailed comments helped shape this as well as previous editions of *The Heritage of World Civilizations*. The advice and guidance provided by Katie Janssen on the coverage of African history and Thomas M. Ricks on the coverage of Islam and the Middle East are especially appreciated. Steven Ozment would like to thank Ammanuel Gashaw Gebeyehu and Ece G. Turnator for their contributions to Chapter 11. Much of the coverage of the Byzantine Empire that is new to the Brief Fifth Edition was written by these two fine scholars.

REVIEWERS OF THIS EDITION

Wayne Ackerson, *Salisbury University*
Heather Barry, *St. Joseph's College*
Eric Martin, *Lewis-Clark State College*
Gary Paul Ritter, *Central Piedmont Community College*
Anthony R. Santoro, *Christopher Newport University*
Gilmar Visoni, *Queensborough Community College*
Kristen Post Walton, *Salisbury University*
William Zogby, *Mohawk Valley Community College*

REVIEWERS OF PREVIOUS EDITIONS

W. Nathan Alexander, *Troy University*
Jack Martin Balcer, *Ohio State University*
Charmarie J. Blaisdell, *Northeastern University*
Deborah Buffton, *University of Wisconsin at La Crosse*
Loretta Burns, *Mankato State University*
Gayle K. Brunelle, *California State University, Fullerton*
Douglas Chambers, *University of Southern Mississippi*
Chun-shu Chang, *University of Michigan, Ann Arbor*
Mark Chavalas, *University of Wisconsin at La Crosse*
Anthony Cheeseboro, *Southern Illinois University at Edwardsville*
William J. Courteney, *University of Wisconsin*
Samuel Willard Crompton, *Holyoke Community College*
James B. Crowley, *Yale University*
Bruce Cummings, *The University of Chicago*
Stephen F. Dale, *Ohio State University, Columbus*
Clarence B. Davis, *Marian College*
Raymond Van Dam, *University of Michigan, Ann Arbor*
Bill Donovan, *Loyola University of Maryland*
Wayne Farris, *University of Tennessee*
Anita Fisher, *Clark College*
Suzanne Gay, *Oberlin College*
Katrina A. Glass, *United States Military Academy*
Robert Gerlich, *Loyola University*
Samuel Robert Goldberger, *Capital Community-Technical College*
Andrew Gow, *University of Alberta*
Katheryn L. Green, *University of Wisconsin, Madison*
David Griffiths, *University of North Carolina, Chapel Hill*
Louis Haas, *Duquesne University*
Joseph T. Hapak, *Moraine Valley Community College*
Hue-Tam Ho Tai, *Harvard University*
David Kieft, *University of Minnesota*
Don Knox, *Wayland Baptist University*
Frederick Krome, *Northern Kentucky University*

Lisa M. Lane, *Mira Costa College*
Richard Law, *Washington State University*
David Lelyveld, *Columbia University*
Jan Lewis, *Rutgers University, Newark*
James C. Livingston, *College of William and Mary*
Garth Montgomery, *Radford University*
Richard L. Moore Jr., *St. Augustine's College*
Beth Nachison, *Southern Connecticut State University*
Robin S. Oggins, *Binghamton University*
George S. Pabis, *Georgia Perimeter College*
Louis A. Perez Jr., *University of South Florida*
Jonathan Perry, *University of South Florida*
Cora Ann Presley, *Tulane University*
Norman Raiford, *Greenville Technical College*
Norman Ravitch, *University of California, Riverside*
Thomas M. Ricks, *University of Pennsylvania*
Philip F. Riley, *James Madison University*
Thomas Robisheaux, *Duke University*
William S. Rodner, *Tidewater Community College*
David Ruffley, *United States Air Force Academy*
Dankwart A. Rustow, *The City University of New York*
James J. Sack, *University of Illinois at Chicago*
William Schell, *Murray State University*
Marvin Slind, *Washington State University*
Daniel Scavone, *University of Southern Indiana*
Linda B. Scherr, *Mercer County Community College*
Roger Schlesinger, *Washington State University*
Charles C. Stewart, *University of Illinois*
Nancy L. Stockdale, *University of Central Florida*
Carson Tavenner, *United States Air Force Academy*
Truong-bu Lam, *University of Hawaii*
Deborah Vess, *Georgia College and State University*
Harry L. Watson, *Loyola College of Maryland*
William B. Whisenhunt, *College of DuPage*
Paul Varley, *Columbia University*

Finally, we would like to thank the dedicated people who helped produce this revision: our editor, Jeff Lasser; editorial project manager Rob DeGeorge; Maria Lange, who created the handsome new design for this edition; Cheryl Keenan, our project manager; Christina Amato, our operations specialist, and Linda Ruggeri from Prepare, Inc, our production editor. We also owe a special thanks to Katie Janssen for her invaluable help in preparing this brief edition.

A.M.C

W.A.G

D.K

S.O

F.M.T

Albert M. Craig is the Harvard-Yenching Research Professor of History Emeritus at Harvard University, where he has taught since 1959. A graduate of Northwestern University, he received his Ph.D. at Harvard University. He has studied at Strasbourg University and at Kyoto, Keio, and Tokyo universities in Japan. He is the author of *Choshu in the Meiji Restoration* (1961), *The Heritage of Chinese Civilization*, Third Edition (2011), *The Heritage of Japanese Civilization*, Second Edition (2011), and, with others, of *East Asia: Tradition and Transformation* (1989). He is the editor of *Japan: A Comparative View* (1973) and co-editor of *Personality in Japanese History* (1970). At present he is engaged in research on the thought of Fukuzawa Yukichi. For eleven years (1976–1987) he was the director of the Harvard-Yenching Institute. He has also been a visiting professor at Kyoto and Tokyo universities. He has received Guggenheim, Fulbright, and Japan Foundation Fellowships. In 1988 he was awarded the Order of the Rising Sun by the Japanese government.

William A. Graham is Albertson Professor of Middle Eastern Studies in the Faculty of Arts and Sciences and O'Brian Professor and Dean of the Faculty of Divinity at Harvard University, where he has taught since 1973. He has directed the Center for Middle Eastern Studies and chaired Near Eastern Languages and Civilizations and the Study of Religion. He received his B.A. from the University of North Carolina, Chapel Hill, and the A.M. and Ph.D. from Harvard. He also studied in Göttingen, Tübingen, Lebanon, and London. He has chaired the (N. American) Council on Graduate Studies in Religion. In 2000 he received the quinquennial Award for Excellence in Research in Islamic History and Culture from the Research Centre for Islamic History, Art and Culture of the Organisation of the Islamic Conference. He has held Guggenheim and von Humboldt research fellowships and is a fellow of the American Academy of Arts and Sciences. He is the author of *Divine Word and Prophetic Word in Early Islam* (1977—ACLS History of Religions Prize, 1978), *Beyond the Written Word: Oral Aspects of Scripture in the History of Religion* (1987), *Islamic and Comparative Religious Studies* (2010), and, with others, of *Three Faiths, One God* (2003).

Donald Kagan is Sterling Professor of History and Classics at Yale University, where he has taught since 1969. He received the A.B. degree in history from Brooklyn College, the M.A. in classics from Brown University, and the Ph.D. in history from Ohio State University. During 1958–1959 he studied at the American School of Classical Studies as a Fulbright Scholar. He has received three awards for undergraduate teaching at Cornell and Yale. He is the author of a history of Greek political thought, *The Great Dialogue* (1965); a four-volume history of the Peloponnesian war, *The Origins of the Peloponnesian War* (1969); *The Archidamian War* (1974); *The Peace of Nicias and the Sicilian Expedition* (1981); *The Fall of the Athenian Empire* (1987); a biography of Pericles, *Pericles of Athens and the Birth of Democracy* (1991); *On the Origins of War* (1995); and *The Peloponnesian War* (2003). He is coauthor, with Frederick W. Kagan, of *While America Sleeps* (2000). With Brian Tierney and L. Pearce Williams, he is the editor of *Great Issues in Western Civilization*, a collection of readings. And with Gregory F. Viggiano, he is the editor of *Problems in the History of Ancient Greece: Sources and Interpretation* (2010). He was awarded the National Humanities Medal for 2002.

Steven Ozment is McLean Professor of Ancient and Modern History at Harvard University. He has taught Western Civilization at Yale, Stanford, and Harvard. He is the author of nine books. *The Age of Reform, 1250–1550* (1980), won the Schaff Prize, and was nominated for the 1981 National Book Award. Five of his books have been selections of the History Book Club: *Magdalena and Balthasar: An Intimate Portrait of Life in Sixteenth Century Europe* (1986), *Three Behaim Boys: Growing Up in Early Modern Germany* (1990), *Protestants: The Birth of A Revolution* (1992), *The Burgermeister's Daughter: Scandal in a Sixteenth Century German Town* (1996), and *Flesh and Spirit: Private Life in Early Modern Germany* (1999). Recent books include *Ancestors: The Loving Family of Old Europe* (2001), *A Mighty Fortress: A New History of the German People* (2004), and *The Serpent and the Lamb: When Lucas Cranach, the Elder Met Martin Luther* (2012).

Frank M. Turner was John Hay Whitney Professor of History at Yale University and Director of the Beinecke Rare Book and Manuscript Library at Yale University, where he served as University Provost from 1988 to 1992. He received his B.A. degree from the College of William and Mary and his Ph.D. from Yale. He received the Yale College Award for Distinguished Undergraduate Teaching. He directed a National Endowment for the Humanities Summer Institute. His scholarly research received the support of fellowships from the National Endowment for the Humanities, the Guggenheim Foundation, and the Woodrow Wilson Center. He is the author of *Between Science and Religion: The Reaction to Scientific Naturalism in Late Victorian England* (1974); *The Greek Heritage in Victorian Britain* (1981), which received the British Council Prize of the Conference on British Studies and the Yale Press Governors Award; *Contesting Cultural Authority: Essays in Victorian Intellectual Life* (1993); and *John Henry Newman: The Challenge to Evangelical Religion* (2002). He also contributed numerous articles to journals and served on the editorial advisory boards of *The Journal of Modern History*, *Isis*, and *Victorian Studies*. He edited *The Idea of a University*, by John Henry Newman (1996), *Reflections on the Revolution in France by Edmund Burke* (2003), and *Apologia Pro Vita Sua and Six Sermons* by John Henry Newman (2008). He served as a Trustee of Connecticut College from 1996–2006. In 2003, Professor Turner was appointed Director of the Beinecke Rare Book and Manuscript Library at Yale University.

1

The Birth of Civilization

((•─[Hear the **Audio** for Chapter 1 at www.myhistorylab.com

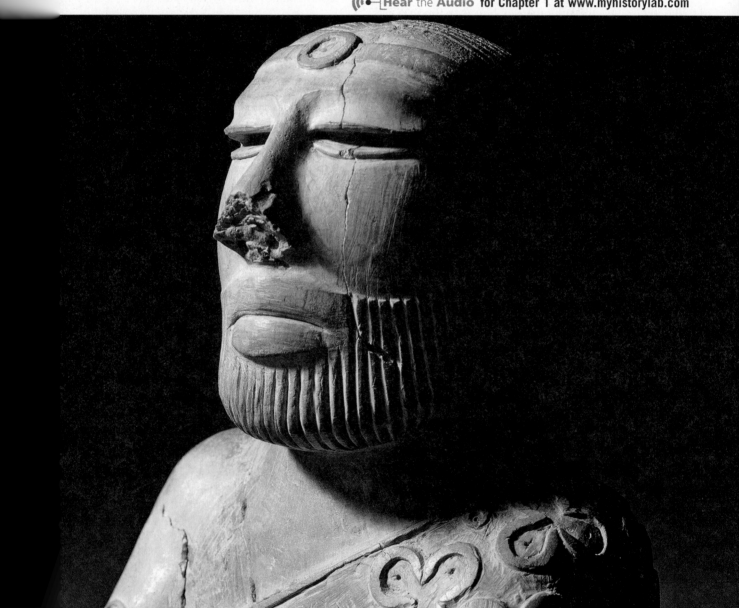

Mohenjo-Daro Figure. Scholars believe this limestone statue from about 2500 B.C.E. depicts a king or a priest from Mohenjo-Daro in the Indus valley in present-day Pakistan.

Does this figure seem to emphasize the features of a particular person or the attributes of a particular role?

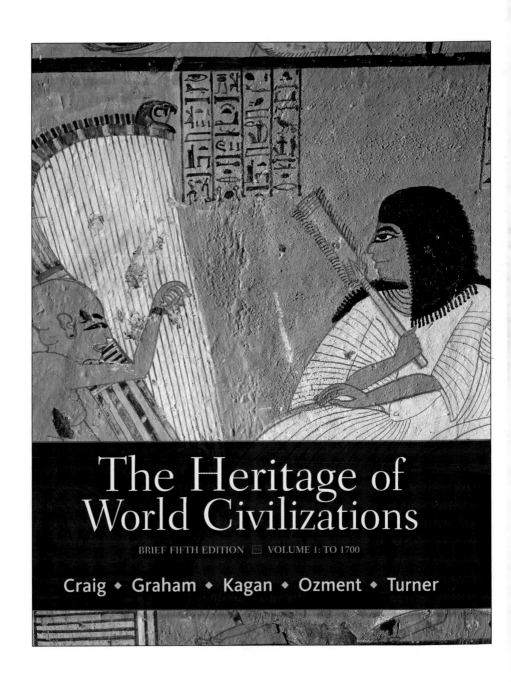

The Heritage of World Civilizations

BRIEF FIFTH EDITION ▦ VOLUME 1: TO 1700

Craig ◆ Graham ◆ Kagan ◆ Ozment ◆ Turner

To order, please request
Volume 1: To 1700, Chapters 1-17
ISBN-10: 0-205-83548-1 / ISBN-13: 978-0-205-83548-5

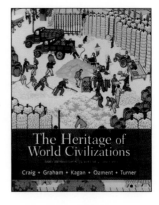

VOLUME 1: TO 1700
Chapters 1-17
ISBN-10: 0-205-83548-1
9-2   ISBN-13: 978-0-205-83548-5

VOLUME 2: SINCE 1500
Chapters 14-33
ISBN-10: 0-205-83547-3
ISBN-13: 978-0-205-83547-8

T he earliest humans lived by hunting, fishing, and collecting wild plants. Around 10,000 years ago, they learned to cultivate plants, herd animals, and make airtight pottery for storage. These discoveries transformed them from gatherers to producers, allowing them to grow in number and to lead a settled life. Beginning about 5,000 years ago, a far more complex way of life began to appear in some parts of the world. In these places humans learned how to increase harvests through irrigation and other methods. Much larger populations came together in towns, cities, and other centers, where they erected impressive structures and where industry and commerce flourished. They developed writing, enabling them to keep inventories of food and other resources. Specialized occupations emerged, complex religions took form, and social divisions increased. These changes marked the birth of civilization. ■

culture
The ways of living built up by a group and passed on from one generation to another.

EARLY HUMANS AND THEIR CULTURE

Humans are cultural beings. **Culture** is the sum total of the ways of living built up by a group and passed on from one generation to another. Culture includes behavior such as courtship or child-rearing practices; material things such as tools, clothing, and shelter; and ideas, institutions, and beliefs. Language, apparently a uniquely human trait, lies

WHY IS "culture" considered a defining trait of human beings?

1

GLOBAL PERSPECTIVE

CIVILIZATIONS

The way of life of prehistoric cave dwellers differed immensely from that of humans today. Yet the few millennia in which we have been civilized are but a tiny fraction of the long span of human existence. Especially during recent millennia, changes in our culture—our way of life—have far outpaced changes in our bodies. We retain the emotional makeup and motor reflexes of prehistoric men and women while living highly organized and often sedentary lives.

We might best view the early civilizations by asking how they fit into the sweep of history. One notable feature of human history is the acceleration in the pace of change. From the time that modern humans first appeared 100,000 years ago until 7000 B.C.E., few changes occurred. Humans migrated from Africa to other parts of the world and adapted to new climes. All lived by hunting, fishing, and gathering. The chief advance in technology during this longest span of human existence was from rough to smooth stone weapons and tools.

Then, from about 7000 B.C.E., innovations began. Humans learned to till the soil, domesticate animals, and make pots for the storage of food. A few millennia later, bronze was discovered and the so-called river valley civilizations formed along the Nile,

the Tigris-Euphrates, the Indus, and the Yellow rivers. Cities rose. Writing was invented. Societies divided into classes or castes: Most members engaged in farming, a few traded, and others assumed military, priestly, or governmental roles. As these civilizations expanded, they became richer, more populous, and more powerful.

The last millennium B.C.E. witnessed two major developments. One was the emergence, during 600–300 B.C.E., of the religious and philosophical revolutions that would indelibly mark their respective civilizations: monotheistic Judaism from which would later develop the world religions of Christianity and Islam; Hinduism and Buddhism in southern Asia; the philosophies of Greece and China. The second development was the rise of the Iron Age empires—the Roman, the Mauryan along the Ganges, the Han in China—during the centuries straddling the end of the millennium.

After the fall of these early empires, swift changes occurred. For a millennium, Europe and Byzantium fell behind, while China and the Middle East led in technology and the arts of government. But by 1500 Europe had caught up, and after 1700, it led. India had invented Arabic numerals, and Arab thinkers inspired

behind our ability to create ideas and institutions and to transmit culture from one generation to another. Our flexible and dexterous hands enable us to hold and make tools and so to create the material artifacts of culture. Because culture is learned and not inherited, it permits rapid adaptation to changing conditions, making possible the spread of humanity to almost all lands of the globe.

THE PALEOLITHIC AGE

Anthropologists designate early human cultures by their tools. The earliest period—the **Paleolithic Age** (from the Greek, "old stone")—dates from the earliest use of stone tools some 1 million years ago to about 10,000 B.C.E. During this immensely long period, people were hunters, fishers, and gatherers, but not producers, of food.

Paleolithic people learned to make increasingly sophisticated tools and to control fire, and they acquired language.

Evidence of religious faith and practice, as well as of magic, goes as far back as archaeology can take us.

Fear or awe, exultation, gratitude, and empathy with the natural world are reflected in the cave art and in the ritual practices, such as burial, found at the Paleolithic. The sense that there is more to the world than meets the eye—in other words, the religious response to the world—seems to be as old as humankind.

Paleolithic culture could support only a sparsely settled society. If hunters were too numerous, game would not suffice. Since labor appears to have been divided according to sex, it was probably women, gathering food, who discovered how to plant and care for seeds. This knowledge eventually led to agriculture and the Neolithic Revolution.

Paleolithic Age

The earliest period when stone tools were used, from about 1,000,000 to 10,000 B.C.E. From the Greek meaning "old stone."

•••Read the Document
From Hunter-gatherers to Food-producers-Overcoming Obstacles
at **myhistorylab.com**

•••Read the Document
The Development of Religion
at **myhistorylab.com**

•••Read the Document
The Toolmaker (3300 B.C.E.)
at **myhistorylab.com**

the Renaissance, but it was Europe that produced Copernicus and Newton.

The nineteenth century saw the invention of the steam engine, the steamship, the locomotive, the telegraph and telephone, and the automobile. After those inventions came electric lights, the radio, and, in the century that followed, the airplane.

In the twentieth century, invention and scientific discovery became institutionalized in university, corporate, and government laboratories. Ever increasing resources were committed to research. By the beginning of the twenty-first century man had walked on the moon, deciphered the human genome, and unlocked the power of the atom. Today, as discoveries occur ever more rapidly, we cannot imagine the science of a hundred years into the future.

If this process of accelerating change had its origins in 7000 B.C.E., what was the original impetus? Does the logic of nature dictate that once agriculture develops, cities will rise in alluvial valleys favorable to cultivation? Was it inevitable that the firing of clay to produce pots would produce metals from metallic oxides and lead to the discovery of smelting? Did the formation of aristocratic and priestly classes automatically lead to record keeping

and writing? If so, it is not at all surprising that parallel and independent developments should have occurred in regions as widely separated as China and the Middle East.

Or was the almost simultaneous rise of the ancient Eurasian civilizations the result of **diffusion**? Did migrating peoples carry seeds, new tools, and metals over long distances? The available evidence provides no definitive answer. Understanding the origins of the early civilizations and the lives of the men and women who lived in them from what is left of their material culture is like reconstructing a dinosaur from a broken tooth and a fragment of jawbone.

Focus Questions

◆ What were the processes behind the creation of early civilizations?

◆ What are the similarities and differences among the world's earliest civilizations?

◆ Why has the pace of change accelerated with time?

THE NEOLITHIC AGE

Anthropologists and archaeologists disagree as to why and how it happened, but around 10,000 years ago some groups in what we now call the Middle East began to change from a nomadic hunter-gatherer culture to a more settled agricultural one.

The shift to agriculture coincided with advances in stone tool technology, so this period is called the Neolithic Age (from the Greek, "new stone"). Productive animals, such as sheep and goats, were domesticated, as were food crops including wheat and barley.

Domestication allowed people to settle new areas. The invention of pottery enabled people to store, transport, and cook foods and liquids. People made cloth from flax and wool.

Because crops required constant care from planting to harvest, Neolithic farmers built permanent dwellings. Houses in a Neolithic village were normally all the same size, suggesting that most Neolithic villagers had about the same level of wealth and social status. Stones and shells were traded long distance, but Neolithic villages tended to be self-sufficient.

Two larger Neolithic settlements do not fit this village pattern. Çatal Hüyük, in a fertile agricultural region of present-day Turkey, was a large town with astonishingly diversified agriculture, arts, and crafts.

At an oasis near the Dead Sea, the town of Jericho was surrounded by a massive stone wall with at least one tower against the inner face. No other Neolithic settlement has been found with fortifications. These two sites show that the economies and settlement patterns of the Neolithic period may have been more complicated than scholars previously thought.

See the **Map**
The Beginnings of Food Production
at **myhistorylab.com**

Hear the **Audio**
at **myhistorylab.com**

Read the **Document**
Redefining Self—From Tribe to Village to City 1500 B.C.E. at **myhistorylab.com**

Çatal Hüyük. The illustration reconstructs part of Çatal Hüyük on the basis of archaeological findings.

What impression does this image give you of life in Çatal Hüyük?

•••[Read the Document
The Neolithic Village
at **myhistorylab.com**

Throughout the Paleolithic Age, the human population had been small and relatively stable. Over time, in the regions where agriculture and animal husbandry appeared, the number of human beings grew at an unprecedented rate. Farmers usually had larger families than hunters, and their children matured at a younger age than the children of hunters. But farmers had to work harder and longer than hunters did, and they had to stay in one place. Some scholars refer to the dramatic changes in subsistence, settlement, technology, and population of this time as the **Neolithic Revolution**. The earliest Neolithic societies appeared in the Middle East in about 8000 B.C.E., based on the cultivation of wheat and barley. In China, Neolithic agriculture based on millet and rice emerged around 4000 B.C.E. The Neolithic period began about 3600 B.C.E. in India, and Neolithic agriculture based on corn developed in Mesoamerica several millennia later.

THE BRONZE AGE AND THE BIRTH OF CIVILIZATION

Another major shift occurred first in the plains along the Tigris and Euphrates rivers in the region the Greeks and Romans called **Mesopotamia** (modern Iraq), later in the valley of the Nile River in Egypt, and somewhat later in India and the Yellow River basin in China. Towns grew alongside villages, and some towns then grew into much larger urban centers. The urban centers, or cities, usually had monumental buildings, such as temples and fortifications. These could be built only by the sustained effort of hundreds and even thousands of people over many years. Elaborate representational artwork appeared, sometimes made of rare and imported materials. New technologies, such as smelting and the manufacture of metal tools and weapons, were characteristic of urban life. Commodities such as pottery and textiles that had been made in individual houses in villages were mass-produced in cities, which also were characterized by social stratification—that is, different classes of people based on factors such as control of resources, family, religious or political authority, and personal wealth. The earliest writing is also associated with the growth of cities. Writing, like representational art, was a powerful means of communicating over space and time and was probably invented to deal with urban problems of management and record keeping. These attributes—urbanism; technological, industrial, and social change; long-distance trade; and new methods of symbolic communication—are defining characteristics of the form of human culture called **civilization**. At about the time the earliest civilizations were emerging, someone discovered how to combine tin and copper to make a stronger and more useful material—bronze. Archaeologists coined the term **Bronze Age** to refer to the period 3100–1200 B.C.E. in the Near East and eastern Mediterranean.

civilization
A form of human culture marked by urbanism, technological adaptation, social complexity, long-distance trade, and symbolic communication.

Bronze Age
The name given to the earliest civilized era, ca. 3100 to 1200 B.C.E. The term reflects the importance of the metal bronze, a mixture of tin and copper, for the peoples of this age for use as weapons and tools.

EARLY CIVILIZATIONS IN THE MIDDLE EAST TO ABOUT 1000 B.C.E.

By 4000 B.C.E., people had settled in large numbers in the river-watered lowlands of Mesopotamia and Egypt. By about 3000 B.C.E., when the invention of writing gave birth to history, urban life and the organization of society into centralized states were well established in the valleys of the Tigris and Euphrates rivers in Mesopotamia and the Nile River in Egypt.

Urban life is possible only when farmers and stockbreeders produce a substantial surplus beyond their own needs, so that city dwellers can eat. Water also has to be controlled. Mesopotamians had to build dikes to keep rivers from flooding their fields in the spring, and they had to store water for use in the autumn. In Egypt the Nile River flooded at the right moment for cultivation, so irrigation was simply a matter of directing the water to the fields.

HOW DID control over water resources influence early Middle Eastern civilizations?

●●●—Read the **Document**
Geography and Civilization: Egypt and Mesopotamia-Impact of Agriculture at **myhistorylab.com**

MESOPOTAMIAN CIVILIZATION

Mesopotamia is divided into two ecological zones, Assyria (roughly north of modern Baghdad) and Babylonia to the south. The oldest Mesopotamian cities seem to have been founded by the Sumerians during the fourth millennium B.C.E. in southern Babylonia. By 3000 B.C.E., the Sumerian city of Uruk was the largest city in the world (see Map 1–1 on page 6).

From about 2800 to 2370 B.C.E., during the Early Dynastic period, Sumerian city-states formed leagues among themselves that apparently had both political and religious significance. Quarrels over water and agricultural land led to incessant warfare, and in time, stronger towns and leagues formed kingdoms.

The people who occupied northern Mesopotamia and Syria spoke mostly Semitic languages (that is, languages in the same family as Arabic and Hebrew). Many of these Semitic peoples absorbed aspects of Sumerian culture, especially writing. The Mesopotamians believed that the large city of Kish, in northern Babylonia, had history's first kings.

In the east, a people known as the Akkadians established their own kingdom at a capital city called Akkad, under their first king, Sargon. The Akkadians conquered all the Sumerian city-states and invaded southwestern Iran and northern Syria. This was history's first empire, having a heartland, provinces, and an absolute ruler. It included numerous peoples, cities, languages, and cultures, as well as different ecological zones. Sargon's name became legendary as the first great conqueror of history. His grandson, Naram-Sin, ruled from the Persian Gulf to the Mediterranean Sea, with a standardized administration, vast wealth and power, and a grand style. Naram-Sin even declared himself a god. External attack and internal weakness destroyed the Akkadian Empire, but several smaller states survived independently.

●●●—Read the **Document**
Sumerian Law Code at **myhistorylab.com**

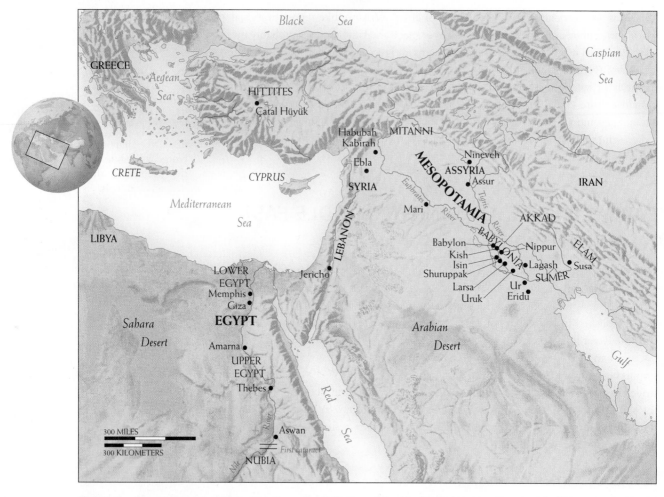

MAP 1-1. **The Ancient Near East.** Two river valley civilizations thrived in the Ancient Near East: Egypt, which was united into a single state, and Mesopotamia, which was long divided into a number of city-states.

What Factors in local geography might help explain the different political histories of Egypt and Mesopotamia?

◆●●▶ Read the Document
Two Accounts of an Egyptian Famine 2600s
B.C.E.: at **myhistorylab.com**

●●▶ View the Image
Hammurabi Receives His Law Code
from the Gods
at **myhistorylab.com**

cuneiform
A writing system invented by the Sumerians that used a wedge-shaped stylus, or pointed tool, to write on wet clay tablets that were then baked or dried (*cuneus* means "wedge" in Latin). The writing was also cut into stone.

chattel slavery
A form of slavery in which humans are owned as goods; the slave has no legal standing as a person and few, if any, rights.

In about 2125 B.C.E. the Sumerian city of Ur rose to dominance. Sumerian culture and literature flourished. Epic poems glorified the deeds of the ancestors of the kings of Ur. A highly centralized administration kept detailed records. After little more than a century, the Third Dynasty of Ur disintegrated in the face of famine and invasion. Elamites attacked from the east and captured the king. The Semitic-speaking Amorites invaded from the north and west, settling around the Sumerian cities and eventually founding their own dynasties. The Sumerians gradually disappeared as an identifiable group. The Sumerian language survived only in writing as the learned language of Babylonia taught in schools and used by priests and scholars.

The Amorite kings of Isin maintained relative peace until they were challenged by another Amorite dynasty at the city of Larsa, and a period of warfare began. A powerful new dynasty at Babylon defeated Isin, Larsa, and other rivals and dominated Mesopotamia for nearly 300 years. Its high point was the reign of its most famous king, Hammurabi (r. ca. 1792–1750 B.C.E.), best known today for the collection of laws that bears his name.

The Sumerians invented the writing system now known as **cuneiform** (from the Latin *cuneus*, meaning "wedge") because of the wedge-shaped marks they made by writing on clay tablets with a cut-reed stylus. The Sumerian writing system was hard to learn. It used several thousand characters, some of which stood for words and some for sounds. Literacy was restricted to an elite who could afford to go to school.

The Sumerians also began the development of mathematics. Before around 3000 B.C.E., people had not conceptualized the idea of numbers independently of counting specific things. Once an independent concept of number was established, mathematics developed rapidly. The Sumerian system was based on the number 60 (sexagesimal) rather than the number 10 (decimal). Sumerian counting survives in the modern 60-minute hour and the circle of 360 degrees. By the time of Hammurabi, the Mesopotamians were expert in many types of mathematics, including mathematical astronomy.

The Sumerians and their successors worshiped many gods and goddesses. These took human forms but differed from humans in their greater power, sublime position in the universe, and immortality. The Mesopotamians believed that the human race was created to serve the gods. The gods were considered universal but also as residing in specific places, usually one important god or goddess in each city. Mesopotamian temples were run like great households where the gods were fed lavish meals, entertained with music, and honored with devotion and ritual. The Mesopotamians were religiously tolerant and readily accepted the possibility that different people might have different gods.

The Mesopotamians had a vague and gloomy picture of the afterworld. The winged spirits of the dead were recognizable as individuals. They were confined to a dusty, dark netherworld, doomed to perpetual hunger and thirst unless someone offered them food and drink. There was no preferential treatment in the afterlife for those who had led religious or virtuous lives—everyone was in equal misery. Mesopotamian religion focused on problems of this world and how to lead a good life before dying.

The Mesopotamian peoples who came after the Sumerians believed that the gods revealed a person's destiny to those who could understand the omens, or indications of what was going to happen. The Babylonians therefore developed an elaborate science of divination based on chance observations, such as a cat walking in the street, and on ritual procedures, such as asking a question of the gods and then slaughtering a sheep to examine its liver and entrails for certain marks and features. Illness was blamed on witchcraft.

Religion played a large part in the literature and art of Mesopotamia. Epic poems told of the deeds of the gods, such as how the world was created and organized, of a great flood the gods sent to wipe out the human race, and of the hero-king Gilgamesh, who tried to escape death by going on a fantastic journey to find the sole survivor of the great flood.

The most imposing religious structure was the *ziggurat*, a tower in stages, sometimes with a small chamber on top. The terraces may have been planted with trees to resemble a mountain. Their precise purpose is not known. Through the Bible, they have entered Western tradition as the Tower of Babel.

Hundreds of thousands of cuneiform texts—royal letters, administrative records, and numerous documents belonging to private families—reveal how peoples in ancient Mesopotamia conducted their lives. Many of Hammurabi's laws deal with commerce, land tenure, and land rights. The subject that is most highly regulated in Hammurabi's code is the maintenance and protection of family, including marriage, inheritance, and adoption. Parents usually arranged marriages, and the bride usually left her own family to join her husband's. A marriage started out monogamous, but a husband whose wife was childless or sickly could take a second wife. Women could own property and conduct business independently.

There were two main types of slavery in Mesopotamia: **chattel slavery** and debt slavery. Chattel slaves were bought like any other piece of property and had no legal rights. They were often non-Mesopotamians bought from slave merchants

Akkadian Victory Stele.   The victory stele of Naram-Sin, king of Akkad, over the mountain-dwelling Lullubi, Mesopotamian, Akkadian period, ca. 2230 B.C.E. (pink sandstone). The king, wearing the horned helmet denoting divine power, strides forward at the head of his army. This is one of the finest sculptures to survive from the Akkadian period.

Louvre, Paris, France. The Bridgeman Art Library International Ltd.

How does this glorify the king? What makes him seem especially important?

QUICK REVIEW

Mesopotamian Religion

- ◆ Sumerians worshiped gods with human forms
- ◆ Babylonians sought evidence of divine action in movements of heavenly bodies
- ◆ Religion played an important part in Mesopotamian art and literature

•◆•🖳Read the Document
The Development of Religion in Primitive Cultures at **myhistorylab.com**

•◆•🖳Read the Document
Excerpts from *The Epic of Gilgamesh* at **myhistorylab.com**

A Closer Look

Babylonian World Map

Cartography was among the many intellectual achievements of the Babylonians. The map illustrated here was inscribed on a clay tablet in about 600 B.C.E., and appears to be the earliest surviving map of the world.

The Babylonians did not intend this map to be a precise or literal picture of the universe or even of the land on which human beings lived, for they omitted any representation of such important and numerous peoples as the Egyptians and Persians whom they knew very well.

There is a text written in cuneiform script above the picture and on the back of the tablet that helps make its identification as a map secure.

All the lands are encircled by a "Bitter River". Beyond that are seven islands arranged to form a seven-pointed star.

The tablet shows the world from a Babylonian point of view as flat and round, with Babylon sitting at its center on the Euphrates River.

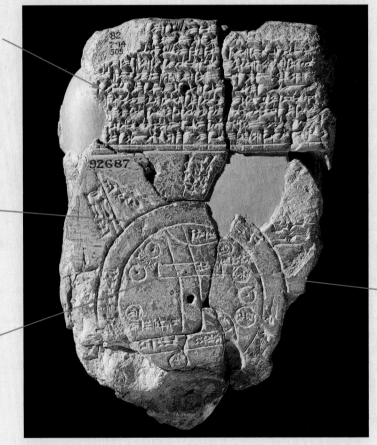

Surrounding Babylon are cities and lands, including Armenia and Assyria.

Courtesy of the Trustees of the British Museum. © The British Museum.

Questions

1. What can we learn from this map about how the Babylonians saw the world around them and their own place in it?

2. Why do you think this map locates some of the Babylonians' neighbors but ignores other important neighboring cultures?

3. Why has cartography remained so important throughout the ages?

4. Is the subjectivity reflected here confined to this map, or is it a general characteristic of cartography throughout history?

and were used in domestic service rather than in production. Chattel slaves were expensive luxuries. True chattel slavery did not become common until the Neo-Babylonian period (612–539 B.C.E.).

Debt slavery was more common. Rates of interest were high, as much as 33 $^1/_3$ percent, so people often defaulted on loans. If debtors had pledged themselves or members of their families as surety for a loan, they became the slave of the creditor; their labor went to pay the interest on the loan. Debt slaves could not be sold but could redeem their freedom by paying off the loan. Slaves and masters often labored side by side; little separated them except the misfortune of indebtedness.

CHRONOLOGY

KEY EVENTS AND PEOPLE IN MESOPOTAMIAN HISTORY

ca. 3500 B.C.E.	Development of Sumerian cities, especially Uruk
ca. 2800–2370 B.C.E.	Early Dynastic period of Sumerian city-states
ca. 2370 B.C.E.	Sargon establishes Akkadian Dynasty and Empire
ca. 2125–2027 B.C.E.	Third Dynasty of Ur
ca. 2000–1800 B.C.E.	Establishment of Amorites in Mesopotamia
ca. 1792–1750 B.C.E.	Reign of Hammurabi
ca. 1550 B.C.E.	Establishment of Kassite Dynasty at Babylon

EGYPTIAN CIVILIZATION

From its sources in Lake Victoria and the Ethiopian highlands, the Nile flows north some 4,000 miles to the Mediterranean. Ancient Egypt included the 750-mile stretch of smooth, navigable river from Aswan to the sea. South of Aswan the river's course is interrupted by several cataracts—rocky areas of rapids and whirlpools.

The Egyptians recognized two sets of geographical divisions in their country. Upper (southern) Egypt consisted of the narrow valley of the Nile. Lower (northern) Egypt referred to the broad triangular area, named by the Greeks after their letter *delta*, formed by the Nile as it branches out to empty into the Mediterranean. They also made a distinction between what they termed the "black land," the dark fertile fields along the Nile, and the "red land," the desert cliffs and plateaus bordering the valley.

The Nile alone made agriculture possible in Egypt's desert environment. Each year the rains of central Africa caused the river to rise over its floodplain. When the floodwaters receded, they left a rich layer of organically fertile silt. The construction and maintenance of canals, dams, and irrigation ditches to control the river's water, together with careful planning and organization of planting and harvesting, produced agricultural prosperity unmatched in the ancient world.

The Nile served as the major highway connecting Upper and Lower Egypt (see Map 1–2 on page 10). The cataracts, the desert, and the sea made Egypt relatively isolated. Egypt's security, along with the predictable flood calendar, gave its civilization a more optimistic outlook than that of Mesopotamia.

The 3,000-year span of ancient Egyptian history is traditionally divided into thirty-one royal dynasties, clustered into eight periods. During three so-called Intermediate periods, Egypt experienced political and social disintegration, and rival dynasties often set up separate power bases in Upper and Lower Egypt until a strong leader reunified the land. The unification of Egypt was vital, for it meant that the entire Nile valley could benefit from an unimpeded distribution of resources.

During the more than 400 years of the Old Kingdom (2700–2200 B.C.E.), Egypt enjoyed internal stability and great prosperity. The ruler, later given the title **pharaoh**, was a king who was also a god (the term comes from the Egyptian for "great house," much as we use "White House" to refer to the president). From his capital at Memphis, the god-king ruled Egypt according to principles that included *maat*, an ideal of order, justice, and truth.

In return for the king's building and maintaining temples, the gods preserved the equilibrium of the state and ensured the king's continuing power, which was absolute. Because the king was obligated to act infallibly in a benign and beneficent manner, the welfare of the people of Egypt was automatically guaranteed and safeguarded.

pharaoh
The god-kings of ancient Egypt. The term originally meant "great house" or palace.

•••—[Read the **Document**
Workings of Ma'at: "The Tale of the Eloquent Peasant" at **myhistorylab.com**

MAP EXPLORATION

To explore this map further, go to **http://www.myhistorylab.com**

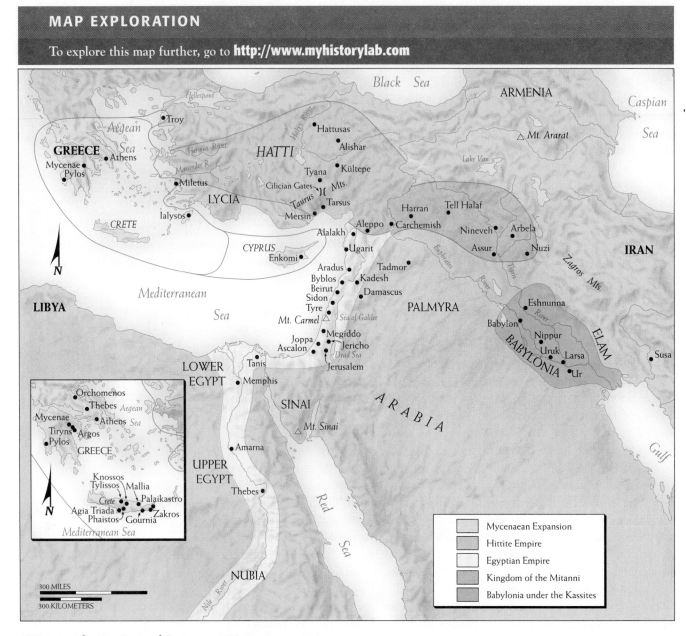

MAP 1–2. The Near East and Greece, ca. 1400 B.C.E.

About 1400 B.C.E., the Near East was divided among four empires. Egypt extended south to Nubia and north through Palestine and Phoenicia. Kassites ruled in Mesopotamia, Hittites in Asia Minor, and the Mitannians in Assyrian lands. In the Aegean, the Mycenaean kingdoms were at their height.

Do Certain empires seem more geographically "natural" to you than others? Besides coastal access and rivers, what physical factors might help unify some of these empires?

QUICK REVIEW

Egyptian Kingship

♦ Egyptian kings were considered gods

♦ Kings were the direct source of law and justice

♦ Egyptian government was an aspect of religion

Nothing better illustrates the nature of Old Kingdom royal power than the pyramids built as pharaonic tombs. Beginning in the Early Dynastic period, kings constructed increasingly elaborate burial complexes in Upper Egypt. Djoser, a Third Dynasty king, was the first to erect a monumental six-step pyramid of hard stone. Subsequent pharaohs built other stepped pyramids until Snefru, the founder of the Fourth Dynasty, converted a stepped pyramid to a true pyramid over the course of putting up three monuments.

Djoser's son Khufu (Cheops in the Greek version of his name) chose the desert plateau of Giza, south of Memphis, as the site for the largest pyramid ever constructed. Its dimensions are prodigious: 481 feet high, 756 feet long on each side, and its base covering 13.1 acres. The pyramid is made of 2.3 million stone blocks averaging 2.5 tons each. It is also a geometrical wonder, barely deviating from absolutely level and square.

Khufu's successors, Khafre (Chephren) and Menkaure (Mycerinus), built equally perfect pyramids at Giza, and together the three constitute one of the most extraordinary achievements in human history. Khafre also built the huge composite creature, part lion and part human, which the Greeks named the Sphinx. Recent research has shown that the Sphinx played a crucial role in the solar cult aspects of the pyramid complex.

The pyramids are remarkable not only for the great technical skill they demonstrate, but also for the concentration of resources they represent. They are evidence that the pharaohs controlled vast wealth and had the power to focus and organize enormous human effort over the years it took to build each pyramid. They also provide a visible indication of the nature of the Egyptian state: The pyramids, like the pharaohs, tower above the land, while the low tombs at their base, like the officials buried there, seem to huddle in relative unimportance.

In about 2200 B.C.E. the Old Kingdom collapsed and gave way to the decentralization and disorder of the First Intermediate period (2200–2025 B.C.E.). Later, Middle Kingdom (2025–1630 B.C.E.) pharaohs sought to evoke the past by building pyramid complexes like those of the later Old Kingdom rulers. Yet the events of the First Intermediate period had irrevocably changed the nature of Egyptian kingship. Gone was the absolute, distant god-king; the king was now more directly concerned with his people. In art, instead of the supremely confident faces of the Old Kingdom pharaohs, the Middle Kingdom rulers seem thoughtful, careworn, and brooding.

Egypt's relations with its neighbors became more aggressive during the Middle Kingdom. To the south, royal fortresses were built to control Nubia and the growing trade in African resources. To the north and east, Syria and Palestine increasingly came under Egyptian influence, even as fortifications sought to prevent settlers from the Levant from moving into the Delta.

The western Delta established an independent dynasty, ushering in the Second Intermediate period (1630–1550 B.C.E.). The eastern Delta came under the control of the Hyksos. Much later sources describe the Hyksos as ruthless invaders from parts unknown, but they were almost certainly Amorites from the Levant, part of the gradual infiltration of the Delta during the Middle Kingdom. After nearly a century of rule, the Hyksos were expelled, and the New Kingdom (1550–1075 B.C.E.) was established. During the Eighteenth Dynasty, Egypt pursued foreign expansion with renewed vigor. Military expeditions reached as far north as the Euphrates in Syria with frequent campaigns in the Levant. To the south, major Egyptian temples were built in the Sudan. Egypt's economic and political power was at its height.

Egypt's position was reflected in the unprecedented luxury and cosmopolitanism of the royal court and in the ambitious palace and temple projects undertaken throughout the country. The Eighteenth Dynasty pharaohs were the first to cut their tombs deep into the rock cliffs of a desolate valley in Thebes, known today as the Valley of the Kings. To date, only one intact royal tomb has been discovered there, that of the young Eighteenth Dynasty king Tutankhamun, and even it had been disturbed shortly after his death. The thousands of goods buried with him, many of them marvels of craftsmanship, give a glimpse of Egypt's material wealth during this period.

Following the premature death of Tutankhamun in 1323 B.C.E., a military commander named Horemheb assumed the kingship, which passed in turn to his own army

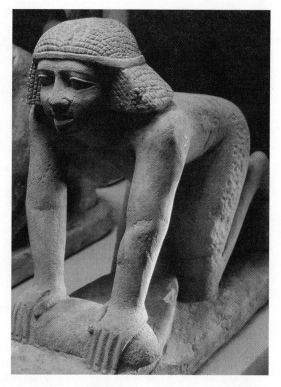

Making Bread. A hallmark of the early river civilizations was the development of techniques to increase harvests. This statue from the Old Kingdom in Egypt (ca. 2700–2200 B.C.E.) shows a woman kneading dough for bread.

What clues does this sculpture offer about this woman's quality of life?

View the Image
The Pyramids at Giza
at **myhistorylab.com**

View the Image
The Sphinx at **myhistorylab.com**

See the Map
Egypt in the Middle Kingdom
at **myhistorylab.com**

Pyramids at Giza. The three largest pyramids of Egypt, located at Giza, near Cairo, are the colossal tombs of pharaohs of the Fourth Dynasty (ca. 2640–2510 B.C.E.): Khufu (right), Chafre (center), and Menkaure (left). The small pyramids and tombs at their bases were those of the pharaohs' queens and officials.

What does the relative size of these pyramids suggest about the distribution of power in ancient Egypt?

View the Image
at **myhistorylab.com**

View the Image
Great Temple of Abu Simbel
at **myhistorylab.com**

See the Map
Egypt in the New Kingdom
at **myhistorylab.com**

hieroglyphs

The complicated writing script of ancient Egypt. It combined picture writing with pictographs and sound signs. Hieroglyph means "sacred carvings" in Greek.

commander, Ramses I. The Ramessides of Dynasty 19 undertook numerous monumental projects, among them Ramses II's rock-cut temples at Abu Simbel, south of the First Cataract, which had to be moved to a higher location when the Aswan High Dam was built in the 1960s. There and elsewhere, Ramses II left textual and pictorial accounts of his battle in 1285 B.C.E. against the Hittites at Kadesh on the Orontes in Syria. Sixteen years later, the Egyptians and Hittites signed a formal peace treaty, forging an alliance against an increasingly volatile political situation in the Middle East and the eastern Mediterranean during the thirteenth century B.C.E.

Merneptah, one of the hundred offspring of Ramses II, held off a hostile Libyan attack, as well as incursions by the Sea Peoples, a loose coalition of Mediterranean raiders who seem to have provoked and taken advantage of unsettled conditions. One of Merneptah's inscriptions commemorating his military triumphs contains the first known mention of Israel.

Despite Merneptah's efforts, by the end of the Twentieth Dynasty, Egypt's period of imperial glory had passed. The next thousand years witnessed a Third Intermediate period, a Saite renaissance, Persian domination, conquest by Alexander the Great, the Ptolemaic period, and finally, defeat at the hands of the Roman emperor Octavian in 30 B.C.E.

Writing first appears in Egypt about 3000 B.C.E. The writing system, dubbed **hieroglyphs** ("sacred carvings") by the Greeks, was highly sophisticated, involving hundreds of picture signs that remained relatively constant in the way they were rendered for over 3,000 years. Texts were usually written horizontally from right to left but could be written from left to right, as well as vertically from top to bottom in both horizontal directions. Egyptian literature includes narratives, myths, books of instruction in wisdom, letters, religious texts, and poetry, written on papyri, limestone flakes, and potsherds. The Egyptian language, part of the Afro-Asiatic (or Hamito-Semitic) family, evolved through several stages— Old, Middle, and Late Egyptian, Demotic, and Coptic— and has a history of continuous recorded use well into the medieval period.

The Egyptian gods, or pantheon, defy neat categorization, in part because of the common tendency to combine the character and function of one or more

CHRONOLOGY

MAJOR PERIODS IN ANCIENT EGYPTIAN HISTORY (DYNASTIES IN ROMAN NUMERALS)

3100–2700 B.C.E.	Early Dynastic period (I–II)
2700–2200 B.C.E.	Old Kingdom (III–VI)
2200–2025 B.C.E.	First Intermediate period (VII–XI)
2025–1630 B.C.E.	Middle Kingdom (XII–XIII)
1630–1550 B.C.E.	Second Intermediate period (XIV–XVII)
1550–1075 B.C.E.	New Kingdom (XVIII–XX)

gods. Amun, one of the eight entities in the Hermopolitan cosmogony, provides a good example. Thebes, Amun's cult center, rose to prominence in the Middle Kingdom. In the New Kingdom, Amun was elevated above his seven cohorts and took on aspects of the sun god Re to become Amun-Re.

Not surprisingly in a nearly rainless land, solar cults and mythologies were highly developed. Much thought was devoted to conceptualizing what happened as the sun god made his perilous way through the underworld in the night hours between sunset and sunrise. Three long texts trace Re's journey as he vanquishes immense snakes and other foes.

The Eighteenth Dynasty was one of several periods during which solar cults were in ascendancy. Early in his reign, Amunhotep IV promoted a single, previously minor aspect of the sun, the Aten ("disc") above Re himself and the rest of the gods. He declared that the Aten was the creator god who brought life to humankind and all living beings, with himself and his queen Nefertiti the sole mediators between the Aten and the people. He went further, changing his name to Akhenaten ("the effective spirit of the Aten"), building a new capital called Akhetaten ("the horizon of the Aten") near Amarna north of Thebes and chiseling out the name of Amun from inscriptions everywhere. Shortly after his death, Amarna was abandoned and partially razed. A large diplomatic archive of tablets written in Akkadian was left at the site, which give us a vivid, if one-sided, picture of the political correspondence of the day. During the reigns of Akhenaten's successors, Tutankhamun (born Tutankhaten) and Horemheb, Amun was restored to his former position, and Akhenaten's monuments were defaced and even demolished.

In representations, Egyptian gods have human bodies, possess human or animal heads, and wear crowns, celestial discs, or thorns. The lone exception is the Aten, made nearly abstract by Akhenaten, who altered its image to a plain disc with solar rays ending in small hands holding the hieroglyphic sign for life to the nostrils of Akhenaten and Nefertiti. The gods were thought to reside in their cult centers, where, from the New Kingdom on, increasingly ostentatious temples were built and staffed by full-time priests. At Thebes, for instance, for over 2,000 years successive kings enlarged the great Karnak temple complex dedicated to Amun.

Though the ordinary person could not enter a temple precinct, great festivals took place for all to see. During Amun's major festival of Opet, the statue of the god traveled in a divine boat along the Nile, whose banks were thronged with spectators.

The Egyptians thought that the afterlife was full of dangers, which could be overcome by magical means, among them the spells in the *Book of the Dead*.

The goals were to join and be identified with the gods, especially Osiris, or to sail in the "boat of millions." Originally only the king could hope to enjoy immortality with the gods, but gradually this became available to all. Since the Egyptians believed that the preservation of the body was essential for continued existence in the afterlife, early on they developed mummification, a process that by the New Kingdom took seventy days.

It is difficult to assess the position of women in Egyptian society because our pictorial and textual evidence comes almost entirely from male sources. Women's prime roles were connected with the management of the household. They could not hold office, go to scribal schools, or become artisans. Nevertheless, women could own and control property, sue for divorce, and, at least in theory, enjoy equal legal protection. Royal women often wielded considerable influence. The most remarkable was Hatshepsut, who ruled as pharaoh for nearly twenty years.

Seated Egyptian Scribe. One of the hallmarks of the early river valley civilizations was the development of writing. Ancient Egyptian scribes had to undergo rigorous training but were rewarded with a position of respect and privilege. This statue from the Fifth Dynasty (ca. 2510–2460 B.C.E.) is of painted limestone and measures 21 inches (53 cm) in height.

Musée du Louvre, Paris, © Giraudon/ Art Resource, New York.

What clues does this sculpture offer about this man's quality of life?

Watch the **Video**
The Temple of Karnak
at **myhistorylab.com**

Read the **Document**
Papyrus of Ani, The Egyptian Book of the Dead c. 1200 B.C.E. at **myhistorylab.com**

View the **Image**
Scene from the Egyptian Afterlife
at **myhistorylab.com**

Scene from the *Book of the Dead*. The Egyptians believed in the possibility of life after death through the god Osiris. Before the person could be presented to Osiris, forty-two assessor-gods tested aspects of the person's life. In this scene from a papyrus manuscript of the *Book of the Dead*, the deceased and his wife (on the left) watch the scales of justice weighing his heart (on the left side of the scales) against the feather of truth. The jackal-headed god Anubis also watches the scales, while the ibis-headed god Thoth keeps the record.

What does the presence of so many gods at a person's judgment ceremony suggest about the Egyptians' sense of an individual's significance?

View the Image
Egyptian Relief of Anubis
at **myhistorylab.com**

Watch the Video
Ramses II's Abu Simbel
at **myhistorylab.com**

QUICK REVIEW

Women in Ancient Egypt

◆ Household management was women's responsibility

◆ In theory women had legal rights equal to men's

◆ Royal women could hold great power

In art, both royal and nonroyal women are conventionally shown smaller than their husbands or sons, yet it is probably of greater significance that they are so frequently depicted in such a wide variety of contexts. Much care was lavished on details of their gestures, clothing, and hairstyles. With their husbands, they attend banquets, boat in the papyrus marshes, make and receive offerings, and supervise the myriad affairs of daily life.

Slaves did not become numerous in Egypt until the growth of Egyptian imperial power in the Middle Kingdom and the imperial expansion of the New Kingdom. Black Africans from Nubia to the south and Asians from the east were captured in war, branded, and brought back to Egypt as slaves. Sometimes an entire people were enslaved, as the Hebrews were, according to the Bible. Slaves in Egypt performed many tasks. Egyptian slaves could be freed, although manumission seems to have been rare. Nonetheless, former slaves were not set apart and could expect to be assimilated into the mass of the population.

ANCIENT NEAR EASTERN EMPIRES

HOW DID conquest and trade shape early empires in the Near East?

In the time of the Eighteenth Dynasty in Egypt, new groups of peoples had established themselves in the Near East: the Kassites in Babylonia, the Hittites in Asia Minor, and the Mitannians in northern Syria and Mesopotamia (see Map 1–2). The Kassites and Mitannians were warrior peoples who ruled as a minority over more civilized folk and absorbed their culture. The Hittites established a kingdom of their own and forged an empire that lasted some 200 years.

THE HITTITES

The Hittites were an Indo-European people, speaking a language related to Greek and Sanskrit. By about 1500 B.C.E., the Hittites had established a strong, centralized government with a capital near Ankara, the capital of modern Turkey. Between 1400 and 1200 B.C.E., they contested Egypt's control of Palestine and Syria. They played an important role in transmitting the ancient cultures of Mesopotamia and Egypt to the Greeks, who lived on their western frontier. The government of the Hittites was different from that of Mesopotamia in that Hittite kings did not claim to be divine or even to be the chosen representatives of the gods. In the early period, a council of nobles limited the king's power, and the assembled army had to ratify his succession to the throne.

Read the Document
Hittite Law Code: excerpts from *The Code of the Nesilim* at **myhistorylab.com**

By 1200 B.C.E., the Hittite Kingdom disappeared, swept away in invasions and the collapse of Middle Eastern nation-states at that time. Successors to the empire, called the Neo-Hittite states, flourished in southern Asia Minor and northern Syria until the Assyrians destroyed them in the first millennium B.C.E.

An important technological change took place in northern Anatolia, somewhat earlier than the creation of the Hittite Kingdom, but perhaps within its region. This was the discovery of how to smelt iron and the decision to use it rather than copper or bronze to manufacture weapons and tools. Archaeologists refer to the period after 1100 B.C.E. as the Iron Age.

THE KASSITES

The Kassites were a people of unknown origin who spoke their own language and who established at Babylon a dynasty that ruled for nearly 500 years. The Kassites were organized into large tribal families and carved out great domains for themselves in Babylonia. They promoted Babylonian culture, and many of the most important works of Babylonian literature were written during their rule. They supported a military aristocracy based on horses and chariots, the prestige weaponry of the age.

THE MITANNIANS

The Mitannians belonged to a large group of people called the Hurrians, some of whom had been living in Mesopotamia and Syria in the time of the kings of Akkad and Ur. Their language is imperfectly understood, and the location of their capital city, Washukanni, is uncertain. The Hurrians were important mediators of Mesopotamian culture to Syria and Anatolia. They developed the art of chariot warfare and horse training to a high degree and created a large state that reached from the Euphrates to the foothills of Iran. The Hittites destroyed their kingdom, and the Assyrian Empire eventually incorporated what was left of it.

THE ASSYRIANS

The Assyrians were originally a people living in Assur, a city in northern Mesopotamia on the Tigris River. They spoke a Semitic language closely related to Babylonian. They had a proud, independent culture heavily influenced by Babylonia. Assur had been an early center for trade but emerged as a political power during the fourteenth century B.C.E., after the decline of Mitanni. The first Assyrian Empire spread north and west against the neo-Hittite states but was brought to an end in the general collapse of Near Eastern states at the end of the second millennium. A people called the Arameans, a Semitic nomadic and agricultural people originally from northern Syria who spoke a language called Aramaic, invaded Assyria. Aramaic is still used in parts of the Near East and is one of the languages of medieval Jewish and Middle Eastern Christian culture.

THE SECOND ASSYRIAN EMPIRE

After 1000 B.C.E., the Assyrians began a second period of expansion, and by 665 B.C.E. they controlled all of Mesopotamia, much of southern Asia Minor, Syria, Palestine, and Egypt to its southern frontier.

They succeeded thanks to a large, well-disciplined army and a society that valued military skills. Some Assyrian kings boasted of their atrocities, so that their names inspired terror throughout the Near East. They constructed magnificent palaces at Nineveh and Nimrud (near modern Mosul, Iraq), surrounded by parks and gardens.

Assyrian Palace Relief. This eighth-century B.C.E. relief of a hero gripping a lion formed part of the decoration of an Assyrian palace. The immense size of the figure and his powerful limbs and muscles may well have suggested the might of the Assyrian king.

Gilgamesh. Relief from the Temple of Saragon II, Khorsabad. Assyrian, 8th century B.C.E. Giraudon/Art Resource, New York.

What else besides size and muscles suggests the power of this king?

●●●—[Read the Document
Empire of Assiria, ca. 1800 B.C.E.
at **myhistorylab.com**

The Assyrians systematically exploited their empire. They used various methods of control, collecting tribute from some regions, stationing garrisons in others, and sometimes pacifying districts by deporting and scattering their inhabitants.

The empire became too large to govern efficiently. The last years of Assyria are obscure, but civil war apparently divided the country. The Medes, a powerful people from western and central Iran, had been expanding across the Iranian plateau. They were feared for their cavalry and archers, against which traditional Middle Eastern armies were ineffective. The Medes attacked Assyria and were joined by the Babylonians, who had always been restive under Assyrian rule, under the leadership of a general named Nebuchadnezzar. In 612 B.C.E., they so thoroughly destroyed the Assyrian cities, including Nineveh, that Assyria never recovered. The ruins of the great Assyrian palaces lay untouched until archaeologists began to explore them in the nineteenth century.

THE NEO-BABYLONIANS

👁 See the Map
The Neo-Babylonian Empire, ca. 580 B.C.E.
at **myhistorylab.com**

The Medes did not follow up on their conquests, so Nebuchadnezzar took over much of the Assyrian Empire. Under him and his successors, Babylon grew into one of the greatest cities of the world.

The Greek traveler Herodotus described its wonders, including its great temples, fortification walls, boulevards, parks, and palaces, to a Greek readership that had never seen the like. Babylon prospered as a center of world trade, linking Egypt, India, Iran, and Syria–Palestine by land and sea routes. For centuries, an astronomical center at Babylon kept detailed records of observations that were the longest running chronicle of the ancient world. Nebuchadnezzar's dynasty did not last long, and the government passed to various men in rapid succession. The last independent king of Babylon set up a second capital in the Arabian Desert and tried to force the Babylonians to honor the moon god above all other gods. He allowed dishonest or incompetent speculators to lease huge areas of temple land for their personal profit. These policies proved unpopular—some said that the king was insane—and many Babylonians may have welcomed the Persian conquest that came in 539 B.C.E. After that, Babylonia began another, even more prosperous phase of its history as one of the most important provinces of another great Eastern empire, that of the Persians. We shall return to the Persians in Chapter 4.

EARLY INDIAN CIVILIZATION

WHAT INFLUENCES did the first Indus valley civilization have on later Indian religious and social practices?

To the east of Mesopotamia, beyond the Iranian plateau and the mountains of Baluchistan, the Asian continent bends sharply southward below the Himalayan mountain barrier to form the Indian subcontinent (see Map 1–3 on page 17). Several sizable rivers flow west and south out of the Himalayas in Kashmir and the Punjab (*Panjab*, "five rivers"), merging into the single stream of the Indus River in Sind before emptying into the Indian Ocean. The headwaters of South Asia's other great river system—the Ganges and its tributaries—are also in the Himalayas but flow south and east to the Bay of Bengal on the opposite side of the subcontinent.

MAP 1–3.   Indus and Vedic Aryan Cultures.

Indus culture likely influenced the Vedic Aryans, although the influence cannot be proved. Some scholars surmise, for example, that the fortified Aryan city of Hariyupiya, mentioned in later texts, may have been the same site as the older Indus city of Harappa.

What Geographical features appear to have influenced the size and shape of regions dominated by different cultures?

The subcontinent's earliest literate, urban civilization arose in the valley of the Indus River sometime after 2600 B.C.E. and by about 2300 B.C.E. was trading with Mesopotamia. Known as the **Harappan** or Indus civilization, it lasted only a few centuries. The region's second identifiable civilization dates to about 1500 B.C.E. and is known as the Vedic Aryan civilization—after the nomadic Indo-European immigrant people, or **Aryans**, who founded it, and their holy texts, or **Vedas**. This civilization endured for nearly 1,000 years without cities or writing, but its religious and social traditions commingled with older traditions in the subcontinent to form the Indian civilization as it has developed over the past 2,500 years.

Harappan
Term used to describe the first civilization of the Indus valley.

Aryans
The Indo-European speakers who invaded India and Iran in the second and first millennia B.C.E.

Vedas
The sacred texts of the ancient Aryan invaders of India. The Rig-Vedas are the oldest materials in the Vedas.

THE INDUS CIVILIZATION

Archaeologists discovered the existence of the Indus culture at the site of Harappa in the 1920s. Since then, some seventy cities, the largest being Harappa and Mohenjo-Daro, have been identified. This urban civilization had bronze tools, writing, covered drainage systems, and a diversified social and economic organization. Because its writing is still undeciphered, it remains the least understood of the early river valley civilizations. Archaeological evidence and inferences from later Indian life, however, allow us to reconstruct something of its highly developed and once thriving culture.

The Indus culture covered a huge area, yet it was remarkably homogeneous. City layouts, building construction, weights and measures, seal inscriptions, patterned pottery and figurines, and even the burnt brick used for buildings and flood walls are unusually uniform in all Indus towns, suggesting an integrated economic system and good internal communications.

Indus culture was also remarkably constant over time. Because the main cities and towns lay in river lowlands subject to flooding, they were rebuilt often, with each reconstruction closely following the previous pattern. Similarly, the Indus script, known from more than 2,000 stamp seals and apparently using both pictographic and phonetic symbols, shows no evidence of change over time. This evidence of stability, regularity, and traditionalism has led scholars to speculate that a centralized government, perhaps a conservative (priestly) theocracy, controlled this far-flung society.

Both Harappa and Mohenjo-Daro apparently had populations of more than 35,000 and were meticulously designed on a similar plan. To the west of each town stood a large, walled citadel on a raised rectangular platform. The town proper was laid out on a grid of main avenues, some as wide as 30 feet. The "blocks" formed by the main avenues were crisscrossed by small, less rigidly planned lanes, off which opened private houses, sometimes of more than one story. The typical house was built around a central courtyard and presented only blank walls to the lanes or streets outside, an arrangement still common in many Near Eastern and South Asian cities.

Ancient Mohenjo-Daro. Like most cities of the Indus valley civilization, Mohenjo-Daro was built principally of mud brick. The structures are laid on straight lines; streets cross each other at right angles. The impression is one of order, prosperity, and civic discipline.

Borromeo/Art Resource, New York.

How do the uniformity and regular placement of bricks influence your reaction to this site?

Perhaps the most striking feature of these cities was a complex system of covered drains and sewers. Private houses were serviced by wells, bathrooms, and latrines, and the great bath at Mohenjo-Daro was filled from its own large well. The drainage system that served these facilities was an engineering feat unrivaled until the time of the Romans, nearly 2,000 years later.

The economy of the Indus state or states was based on agriculture. Wheat and barley were the main crops. The Indus valley people wove cloth from cotton, made metal tools, and used the potter's wheel. Evidence points to trade between the Indus culture and Mesopotamia. Metals and semiprecious stones were apparently imported into the Indus region from present-day Iran and Afghanistan, as well as from Central Asia, from farther south on the Indian peninsula, and perhaps from Arabia. Similarities in artistic styles suggest that trade contacts resulted in cultural borrowings.

Among the most striking accomplishments of the Indus culture are fine bronze and stone sculptures. Other evidence of the skill of Indus artisans includes copper and bronze tools and vessels, black-on-red painted pottery, dressed stonework, stone and terra-cotta figurines and toys, silver vessels and ornaments, gold jewelry, and dyed woven fabric.

The elaborate bath facilities suggest that ritual bathing and water purification rites were important, as they still are in India today. The stone images from the so-called temples of Mohenjo-Daro and the more common terra-cotta figurines from other sites also suggest links to later Indian religious practices and symbols. The many images of male animals such as the humped bull might be symbols of power and fertility or might indicate animal worship. A recurring image of a male figure with leafy headdress and horns, often seated in a posture associated later in India with yogic meditation, has been likened to the Vedic Aryan "Lord of All Creatures." Terra-cotta figurines of females, often pregnant or carrying a child, are similar to female images in several prehistoric cultures. As possible precursors of Shiva's consort, they too may represent an element of pre-Aryan religion that reemerged later to figure in "Hindu" culture. Other aspects of Indus religion—burial customs, for example—are not clearly related to later Indian practices.

Sometime between 1800 and 1700 B.C.E., Indus civilization disappeared. Aryan invaders, changes in the course of the Indus, or a long period of dessication might have contributed to the Indus culture's demise. This civilization remains too shadowy for us to measure its influence, but Harappan predecessors of the Aryans likely contributed to later life in the subcontinent in ways that we have yet to discover.

THE VEDIC ARYAN CIVILIZATION

We know more about the Aryan culture that effectively "refounded" Indian civilization around 1500 B.C.E. Yet unlike Indus civilization, it was not urban and left neither city ruins nor substantial artifacts beyond tools, weapons, and pottery. Virtually our only source of knowledge about ancient Aryan life are the words of the Vedas, the Aryan sacred texts—hence we know the culture as "Vedic." Although the latest Vedic texts date from perhaps 500 B.C.E., the earliest may go back to 1700 B.C.E. Transmitted orally through the centuries, the Vedas were not written down until writing was reintroduced to India sometime after 700 B.C.E. The Vedas are priestly works, not histories; they reveal little about events but do offer insight into the religion, society, values, and thought of early Aryan India.

Veda, which means "knowledge," is the collective term for the texts still recognized today by most Indians as the holiest sources of their tradition. For Hindus, Veda is the eternal wisdom of primordial seers preserved for thousands of years in an unbroken oral tradition. The Vedas are the four major compilations of Vedic ritual, explanatory, and speculative texts. The collection of 1,028 religious hymns known as the *Rig-Veda* represents the oldest materials of the Vedas. The latest of these hymns date from about 1000 B.C.E., the oldest from perhaps 1700–1200 B.C.E., when the Aryans spread across the northern plains to the upper reaches of the Ganges.

Aryan is a different kind of term. The second-millennium invaders of northern India called themselves *Aryas* as opposed to the peoples whom they conquered. Vedic Sanskrit, the language of the invaders, gave this word to later Sanskrit as a term for "noble" or "free-born" (*arya*). The word is found also in old Iranian, or Persian, texts, and even the term *Iran* is derived from the Old Persian equivalent of *arya*. The peoples who came to India are more precisely designated Indo-Aryans, or Vedic Aryans.

In the nineteenth century, *Aryan* was the term applied to the widespread language group known today as **Indo-European**. This family includes Greek, Latin, the Romance and Germanic languages, the Slavic tongues, and the Indo-Iranian languages, including Persian and Sanskrit and their derivatives. The Nazis perversely misused "Aryan" to refer to a white "master race." Today most scholars use *Aryan* only to

Indus Stamp Seal. Note the familiar humped bull of India on this stone stamp seal.

© Scala/Art Resource, New York.

What impression does the level of detail in this depiction give you?

Indo-European

A widely distributed language group that includes most of the languages spoken in Europe, Persian, Sanskrit, and their derivatives.

identify the Indo-European speakers who invaded India and the Iranian plateau in the second millennium B.C.E. and the Indo-Iranian languages.

The Vedic Aryans were seminomadic warriors who reached India in small tribal groups through the mountain passes of the Hindu Kush. They were horsemen and cattle herders rather than farmers and city builders. They left their mark not in material culture but in the changes that their conquests brought to the regions they overran: a new language, social organization, techniques of warfare, and religious forms and ideas.

The early Aryans penetrated first into the Punjab and the Indus valley around 1800–1500 B.C.E., presumably in search of grazing lands for their livestock. Their horses, chariots, and copper-bronze weapons likely gave them military superiority over the Indus peoples or their successors. Rig-Vedic hymns echo these early conflicts. One late hymn praises the king of the *Bharatas*, giving us the Indian name for modern India, *Bharat*, "land of the Bharatas."

During the Rig-Vedic age (ca. 1700–1000 B.C.E.), the newcomers settled in the Punjab and beyond, where they took up agriculture and stockbreeding. Then, between about 1000 and 500 B.C.E., the *Late Vedic Age*, these Aryan Indians spread across the plain between the Yamuna and the Ganges and eastward. They cleared (probably by burning) the heavy forests that covered this region and then settled there. They also moved farther northeast to the Himalayan foothills and southeast along the Ganges, in what was to be the cradle of subsequent Indian civilization. The late Vedic period is also called the Brahmanic Age because it was dominated by the priestly religion of the Brahman class, as evidenced in commentaries called the *Brahmanas* (ca. 1000–800 or 600 B.C.E.). It is also sometimes called the Epic Age because it provided the setting for India's two classical epics, the **Mahabharata** and the **Ramayana**.

Both epics reflect the complex cultural and social mixing of Aryan and other earlier subcontinent peoples.

By about 200 CE, this mixing produced a distinctive new "Indian" civilization over most of the subcontinent. Its basis was clearly Aryan, but its language, society, and religion incorporated many non-Aryan elements. Harappan culture vanished, but both it and other regional cultures contributed to the formation of Indian culture as we know it.

Aryan society was apparently patrilineal—with succession and inheritance in the male line—and its gods were likewise predominantly male. Marriage appears to have been monogamous, and widows could remarry. Related families formed larger kin groups. The largest social grouping was the tribe, ruled by a chieftain or **raja** ("king" in Sanskrit), who shared power with a tribal council. In early Vedic days the ruler was chosen for his prowess; his chief responsibility was to lead in battle, and he had no priestly function or sacred authority. A chief priest looked after the sacrifices on which religious life centered. By the Brahmanic age the king, with the help of priests, had assumed the role of judge in legal matters and become a hereditary ruler claiming divine qualities. The power of the priestly class had also increased.

Although there were probably subgroups of warriors and priests, Aryan society seems originally to have had only two basic divisions: noble and common. The Dasas—the darker, conquered peoples—came to form a third group (together with those who intermarried with them) of the socially excluded. Over time, a more rigid scheme of four social classes (excluding the non-Aryan Dasas) evolved. By the late Rig-Vedic period, religious theory explicitly sanctioned these four divisions, or *varnas*—the priestly (*Brahman*), the warrior/noble (*Kshatriya*), the peasant/tradesman (*Vaishya*), and the servant (*Shudra*). Only the members of the three upper classes participated fully in social, political, and religious life. This scheme underlies the rigid caste system that later became fundamental to Indian society.

Mahabharata and Ramayana
The two classical Indian epics.

••• Read the Document
Excerpt from Mahábhárata
(1000–600 B.C.E.) at **myhistorylab.com**

raja
An Indian king.

OVERVIEW   The First Civilizations

Civilization is a form of human culture usually marked by the development of cities, the ability to make and use metal tools and instruments, and the invention of a system of writing. The first civilizations appeared in the Middle East between 4000 and 3000 B.C.E., and by the second millennium B.C.E., there were civilized societies in Eurasia, China, and the Americas.

Mesopotamia	Sumerians arrive in the Tigris-Eurphrates River valley, ca. 3500 B.C.E., and establish the first city-states, ca. 2800 B.C.E.
Egypt	Egyptian civilization develops along the Nile River, ca. 3100 B.C.E. Egypt becomes a unified state, ca. 2700 B.C.E.
Indus Valley	Flourishing urban civilization develops in northern India along the Indus River, ca. 2250 B.C.E.
China	City-states appear in the Yellow River basin, ca. 1766 B.C.E.
Americas	Agricultural surplus gives rise to the first cities in Mesoamerica, ca. 1500 B.C.E., and to the first Andean civilization in South America, ca. 2750 B.C.E.

The early seminomadic Aryans lived simply in wood-and-thatch or, later, mud-walled dwellings. They measured wealth in cattle and were accomplished at carpentry and bronze working (iron probably was not known in India before 1000 B.C.E.). They used gold for ornamentation and produced woolen textiles. They also cultivated some crops, especially grains, and were familiar with intoxicating drinks, including soma, used in religious rites, and a kind of mead. Music and gambling with dice appear to have been popular.

The Brahmanic Age left few material remains. Urban culture remained undeveloped, although mud-brick towns appeared as new lands were cleared for cultivation. Established kingdoms with fixed capitals now existed. Trade grew, especially along the Ganges, although there is no evidence of a coinage system. Later texts mention specialized artisans, including goldsmiths, basket makers, weavers, potters, and entertainers. Writing had been reintroduced to India around 700 B.C.E., perhaps from Mesopotamia along with traded goods.

Vedic India's main identifiable contributions to later history were religious. The central Vedic cult—controlled by priests serving a military aristocracy—remained dominant until the middle of the first millennium B.C.E. By that time other, perhaps older, religious forms were evidently asserting themselves among the populace. The increasing ritual formalism of Brahmanic religion provoked challenges both in popular practice and in religious thought that culminated in Buddhist, Jain, and Hindu traditions of piety and practice (see Chapter 2).

The earliest Indo-Aryans seem to have worshiped numerous gods, most of whom embodied or were associated with powers of nature. (See Document, "Hymn to Indra" on page 22.) The Rig-Vedic hymns are addressed to anthropomorphic deities linked to natural phenomena such as the sky, the clouds, and the sun. These gods are comparable to those of ancient Greece (see Chapter 3) and are apparently distantly related to them through the Indo-European heritage the Greeks and Aryans shared. The name of the Aryan father-god Dyaus, for example, is linguistically related to the Greek Zeus. The Vedic hymns praise each god they address as possessing almost all powers, including those associated with other gods.

Ritual sacrifice was the central focus of Vedic religion, its goal apparently being to invoke the presence of the gods to whom an offering was made rather than to expiate sins or express thanksgiving. Drinking soma juice was part of the ritual. A recurring

DOCUMENT

Hymn to Indra

This hymn celebrates the greatest deed ascribed to Indra, the slaying of the dragon Vritra to release the waters needed by people and livestock (which is also heralded at one point in the hymn as the act of creation itself). These waters are apparently those of the dammed-up rivers, but possibly also the rains as well. This victory also symbolizes the victory of the Aryans over the dark-skinned Dasas. Note the sexual as well as water imagery. The kadrukas may be the bowls used for soma in the sacrifice. The vajra is Indra's thunderbolt; the name Dasa for the lord of the waters is also that used for the peoples defeated by the Aryans and for all enemies of Indra, of whom the Pani tribe is one.

- **WHAT** are the main kinds of imagery used for Indra and his actions in the hymn? What divine acts does the hymn ascribe to Indra?

Indra's heroic deeds, indeed, will I proclaim, the first ones which the wielder of the vajra accomplished. He killed the dragon, released the waters, and split open the sides of the mountains.

He killed the dragon lying spread out on the mountain; for him Tvashtar fashioned the roaring vajra. Like bellowing cows, the waters, gliding, have gone down straightway to the ocean.

Showing off his virile power he chose soma; from the three kadrukas he drank of the extracted soma. The bounteous god took up the missile, the vajra; he killed the first-born among the dragons.

When you, O Indra, killed the first-born among the dragons and further overpowered the wily tricks (maya) of the tricksters, bringing forth, at that very moment, the sun, the heaven and the dawn—since then, indeed, have you not come across another enemy. Indra killed Vritra, the greater enemy, the shoulderless one, with his mighty and fatal weapon, the vajra. Like branches of a tree lopped off with an axe, the dragon lies prostrate upon the earth. . . .

Over him, who lay in that manner like a shattered reed flowed the waters for the sake of man. At the feet of the very waters, which Vritra had [once] enclosed with his might, the dragon [now] lay [prostrate]. . . .

With the Dasa as their lord and with the dragon as their warder, the waters remained imprisoned, like cows held by the Pani. Having killed Vritra, [Indra] threw open the cleft of waters which had been closed.

You became the hair of a horse's tail, O Indra, when he [Vritra] struck at your sharp-pointed vajra—the one god [eka deva] though you were. You won the cows, O brave one, you won soma; you released the seven rivers, so that they should flow. . . .

Indra, who wields the vajra in his hand, is the lord of what moves and what remains rested, of what is peaceful and what is horned. He alone rules over the tribes as their king; he encloses them as does a rim the spokes.

—*Rig-Veda 1.32*

Source: From *Sources of Indian Tradition* by William Theodore de Bary. Copyright © 1988 by Columbia University Press. Reprinted with permission of the publisher.

---

theme of the Vedic hymns that accompanied the rituals is the desire for prosperity, health, and victory. The late Vedic texts emphasize magical and cosmic aspects of ritual and sacrifice. Indeed, some of the *Brahmanas* maintain that only exacting performance of the sacrifice can maintain the world order.

The word *Brahman*, originally used to designate the ritual utterance or word of power, came to refer also to the generalized divine power present in the sacrifice. In the **Upanishads**, some of the latest Vedic texts and the ones most concerned with speculation about the universe, *Brahman* was extended to refer to the Absolute, the transcendent principle of reality. As the guardian of ritual and the master of the sacred word, the priest was known throughout the Vedic Aryan period by a related word, *Brahmana*, for which the English is *Brahman*. Echoes of these associations were to lend force in later Hindu tradition to the special status of the Brahman caste groups as the highest social class (see Chapter 4).

Upanishads

The Upanishads, which date to about the seventh century B.C.E., have been perennial sources of spiritual knowledge for Hindus. The word *upanishad* means "secret and sacred knowledge." This word occurs in the Upanishads themselves in more than a dozen places in this sense. The word also means "texts incorporating such knowledge." There are ten principal Upanishads.

CHRONOLOGY

ANCIENT INDIA

ca. 2250–1750 (2500–1500?) B.C.E.	Indus (Harappan) civilization (written script still undeciphered)
ca. 1800–1500 B.C.E.	Aryan peoples invade northwestern India
ca. 1500–1000 B.C.E.	Rig-Vedic period: composition of Rig-Vedic hymns; Punjab as center of Indo-Aryan civilization
ca. 1000–500 B.C.E.	Late Vedic period: Doab as center of Indo-Aryan civilization
ca. 1000–800/600 B.C.E.	Composition of Brahmanas and other Vedic texts
ca. 800–500 B.C.E.	Composition of major Upanishads
ca. 700–500 B.C.E.	Probable reintroduction of writing
ca. 400 B.C.E.–200 C.E.	Composition of great epics, the *Mahabharata* and Ramayana

EARLY CHINESE CIVILIZATION

NEOLITHIC ORIGINS IN THE YELLOW RIVER VALLEY

Agriculture began in China in about 4000 B.C.E. in the basin of the southern bend of the Yellow River. This is the northernmost of eastern Asia's four great river systems, all of which drain eastward into the Pacific Ocean. In recent millennia, the Yellow River has flowed through a deforested plain, cold in winter and subject to periodic droughts. But in 4000 B.C.E., its climate was warmer, with forested highlands in the west and swampy marshes to the east.

The chief crop of China's agricultural revolution was millet. A second agricultural development focusing on rice may have occurred on the Huai River. In time, wheat entered China from the west. The early Chinese cleared land and burned its cover to plant millet and cabbage and, later, rice and soybeans. When the soil became exhausted, fields were abandoned, and sometimes early villages were abandoned, too. Pigs, sheep, cattle, dogs, and chickens were domesticated, but hunting continued to be important to the village economy. Grain was stored in pottery, and stone tools included axes, hoes, spades, and sickle-shaped knives.

The earliest cultivators lived in wattle-and-daub pit dwellings with wooden support posts and sunken, plastered floors. Their villages were located in isolated clearings along slopes of river valleys. Archaeological finds of weapons and remains of earthen walls suggest tribal warfare between villages. Little is known of the religion of these people, although some evidence suggests the worship of ancestral spirits. They practiced divination by applying heat to a hole drilled in the shoulder bone of a steer or the undershell of a tortoise and then interpreting the resulting cracks in the bone. They buried their dead in cemeteries with jars of food. Tribal leaders wore rings and beads of jade.

EARLY BRONZE AGE: THE SHANG

The traditional history of China tells of three ancient dynasties: Xia (2205–1766 B.C.E.), Shang (1766–1050 B.C.E.), and Zhou (1050–256 B.C.E.).

WHY DID large territorial states arise in ancient China?

See the **Map**
Ancient China at **myhistorylab.com**

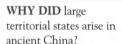 Hear the **Audio**
at **myhistorylab.com**

See the **Map**
The Shang Kingdom
at **myhistorylab.com**

View the **Image**
An Inscribed Oracle Bone
at **myhistorylab.com**

Until early in the twentieth century, historians thought the first two were legendary. Then, in the 1920s, archaeological excavations near present-day Anyang uncovered the ruins of a walled city that had been a late Shang capital.

Other Shang cities have been discovered more recently. The ruins contained the archives of the department of divination of the Shang court, with thousands upon thousands of "oracle bones" incised with archaic Chinese writing.

The names of kings on the bones fit almost perfectly those of the traditional historical record. This evidence that the Shang actually existed has led historians to suggest that the Xia may also have been an actual dynasty.

The characteristic political institution of Bronze Age China was the city-state. The largest was the Shang capital, which, frequently moved, lacked the monumental architecture of Egypt or Mesopotamia. The walled city contained public buildings, altars, and the residences of the aristocracy; it was surrounded by a sea of Neolithic tribal villages. The military aristocracy went to war in chariots, supported by levies of foot soldiers. The Shang fought against barbarian tribes and, occasionally, against other city-states in rebellion against Shang rule. Captured prisoners were enslaved.

The three most notable features of Shang China were writing, bronzes, and the appearance of social classes. Scribes at the Shang court kept records on strips of bamboo, but these have not survived. What have survived are inscriptions on bronze artifacts and the oracle bones. Some bones contain the question put to the oracle, the answer, and the outcome of the matter. Representative questions were: Which ancestor is causing the king's earache? If the king goes hunting at Qi, will there be a disaster? Will the king's child be a son? If the king sends his army to attack an enemy, will the deity help him? Was a sacrifice acceptable to ancestral deities?

What we know of Shang religion is based on the bones. The Shang believed in a supreme "Deity Above," who had authority over the human world. Also serving at the court of the Deity Above were lesser natural deities—the sun, moon, earth, rain, wind, and the six clouds. Even the Shang king sacrificed not to the Deity Above but to his ancestors, who interceded with the Deity Above on the king's behalf. Kings, while alive at least, were not considered divine but were the high priests of the state.

In Shang times, as later, religion in China was closely associated with cosmology. The Shang people observed the movements of the planets and stars and reported eclipses. Celestial happenings were seen as omens from the gods. The chief cosmologists also recorded events at the court. The Shang calendar had a month of 30 days and a year of 360 days. Adjustments were made periodically by adding an extra month. The king used the calendar to tell his people when to sow and when to reap.

Bronze appeared in China in about 2000 B.C.E., 1,000 years later than in Mesopotamia and 500 years later than in India. Because Shang casting methods were more advanced than those of Mesopotamia and because the designs on Shang bronzes continued those of the preceding black pottery culture, the Shang probably developed its bronze technology independently.

Among the Shang, as with other early river valley civilizations, the increasing control of nature through agriculture and metallurgy was accompanied by the emergence of a rigidly stratified society in which the many were compelled to serve the few. A monopoly of bronze weapons enabled aristocrats to exploit other groups. Nowhere was the gulf between the royal lineage and the baseborn more apparent than it was in the Shang institution of human sacrifice. When a king died, hundreds of slaves or prisoners of war, sometimes together with those who had served the king during his lifetime, might be buried with him. Sacrifices also were made when a palace or an altar was built.

Oracle Bone. Inscribed oracle bone from the Shang Dynasty city of Anyang.

Does the quality of the inscriptions on this bone make you think the bone is more a symbolic object or a tool?

LATE BRONZE AGE: THE WESTERN ZHOU

To the west of the area of Shang rule, in the valley of the Wei River, lived the warlike Zhou people. The last Shang kings were weak, cruel, and tyrannical. By 1050 B.C.E., they had been debilitated by campaigns against nomads in the north and rebellious tribes in the east. Taking advantage of this opportunity, the Zhou made alliances with disaffected city-states and swept in, conquering the Shang.

In most respects, the Zhou continued the Shang pattern of life and rule. The agrarian-based city-state continued to be the basic unit of society, and the Zhou social hierarchy was similar to that of the Shang. The Zhou assimilated Shang culture, continuing without interruption the development of China's ideographic writing. The Zhou also maintained the practice of casting bronze ceremonial vessels, but their vessels lacked the fineness that set the Shang above the rest of the Bronze Age world.

The Zhou kept their capital in the west but set up a secondary capital at Luoyang, along the southern bend of the Yellow River. They appointed their kinsmen or other aristocratic allies to rule in other city-states. Blood or lineage ties were essential to the Zhou pattern of rule.

One difference between the Shang and the Zhou was in the nature of the political legitimacy each claimed. The Shang kings, descended from shamanistic (priestly) rulers, had a built-in religious authority and needed no theory to justify their rule. But the Zhou, having conquered the Shang, needed a rationale for why they were now the rightful rulers. Their argument was that Heaven (the name for the supreme being that gradually replaced the Deity Above during the early Zhou), appalled by the wickedness of the last Shang king, had withdrawn its mandate to rule from the Shang, awarding it instead to the Zhou. This concept of the **Mandate of Heaven** was subsequently invoked by every dynasty in China down to the twenty-first century.

IRON AGE: THE EASTERN ZHOU

In 771 B.C.E. the Wei valley capital of the Western Zhou was overrun by barbarians. The heir to the throne, with some members of the court, escaped to the secondary capital at Luoyang, 200 miles to the east and just south of the bend in the Yellow River, beginning the Eastern Zhou period.

The first phase of the Eastern Zhou lasted until 481 B.C.E. The Zhou kings at Luoyang were unable to reestablish their old authority. By the early seventh century B.C.E., Luoyang's political power was nominal, although it remained a center of culture and ritual observances. During the seventh and sixth centuries B.C.E., the political configuration was an equilibrium of many small principalities on the north-central plain surrounded by larger, wholly autonomous territorial states along the borders of the plain (see Map 1–4 on page 26). The larger states consolidated the areas within their borders, absorbed tribal peoples, and expanded by conquering states on their periphery.

The second phase of the Eastern Zhou is known as the Warring States period, after a chronicle of the same name treating the years from 401 to 256 B.C.E. By the fifth century B.C.E., all defensive alliances had collapsed. Strong states swallowed their weaker neighbors. The border states grew in size and power. Interstate stability disappeared. By the fourth century B.C.E., only eight or nine great territorial states remained as contenders. The only question was which one would defeat the others and go on to unify China.

Mandate of Heaven
The Chinese belief that Heaven entrusts or withdraws a ruler's or a dynasty's right to govern.

CHRONOLOGY	
EARLY CHINA	
4000 B.C.E.	Neolithic agricultural villages
1766 B.C.E.	Bronze Age city-states, aristocratic charioteers, pictographic writing
771 B.C.E.	Iron Age territorial states
500 B.C.E.	Age of philosophers
221 B.C.E.	Unification of China

MAP 1–4. Early Iron Age Territorial States in China during the Sixth Century B.C.E..

After the fall of the Western Zhou in China in 771 B.C.E., large territorial states formed that became increasingly independent of the later Zhou kings.

Which States appear strongest in this period?

Three basic changes in Chinese society contributed to the rise of large territorial states. One was the expansion of population and agricultural lands. The walled cities of the Shang and Western Zhou had been like oases in the wilds, bounded by plains, marshes, and forests. But as population grew, wilds began to disappear, and the economy became almost entirely agricultural. Friction arose over boundaries as states began to abut. After the start of the Iron Age, farmers used iron tools to clear new lands and plow deeper, raising yields and increasing agricultural surpluses. Irrigation and drainage canals became important for the first time. Serfs gave way to independent farmers, who bought and sold land. By the third century B.C.E., China had about 20 million people, making it the most populous country in the world, a distinction it has never lost.

A second development was the rise of commerce. Roads built for war were used by merchants. Copper coins joined bolts of silk and precious metals as media of exchange. Rich merchants rivaled in lifestyle than landowning lower nobility. Bronze bells and mirrors, clay figurines, lacquer boxes, and musical instruments found in late Zhou tombs show that China's material and artistic culture leaped ahead during this period.

A third change that doomed the city-state was the rise of a new kind of army. The war chariots of the old aristocracy, practical only on level terrain, gave way to cavalry armed with crossbows. Most of the fighting was done by conscript foot soldiers. Armies numbered in the hundreds of thousands. The old nobility gave way to professional commanders. The old aristocratic etiquette, which governed behavior even in battle, gave way to military tactics that were bloody and ruthless. Prisoners were often massacred.

Change also affected government. Lords of the new territorial states began to style themselves as kings, taking the title that previously only Zhou royalty had enjoyed. To survive, new states had to transform their agricultural and commercial wealth into military strength. To collect taxes, conscript soldiers, and administer the affairs of state required records and literate officials. Academies were established to fill the need. Beneath the ministers, a literate bureaucracy developed. Its members were referred to as *shi*, a term that had once meant "warrior" but gradually came to mean "scholar-bureaucrat." The *shi* were of mixed social origins, including petty nobility, literate members of the old warrior class, landlords, merchants, and rising commoners. From this class, as we will see in Chapter 2, came the philosophers who created the "one hundred schools" and transformed the culture of China.

Bronze Vessel from the Shang Dynasty.
The little elephant on top forms the handle of the lid. Wine was poured through the spout formed by the big elephant's trunk.

What do you observe about the craftsmanship with which this vessel was created? What does this suggest about the situations in which it might have been used?

THE RISE OF CIVILIZATION IN THE AMERICAS

During the last Ice Age, the Bering region between Siberia and Alaska was dry land. Humans crossed this land bridge from Asia to the Americas, probably in several migrations, and moved south and east over many centuries. From these peoples a wide variety of original American cultures and many hundreds of languages arose.

The earliest immigrants to the Americas, like all Paleolithic peoples, lived by hunting, fishing, and gathering. At the time of the initial migrations, herds of large game animals were plentiful. By the end of the Ice Age, however, mammoths and many other forms of game had become extinct in the Americas. Where fishing or small game was insufficient, people had to rely on protein from vegetable sources. American production of plants providing protein far outpaced that of European agriculture. One of the most important early developments was the cultivation of maize (corn). The cultivation of maize appears to have been in place in Mexico by approximately 4000 B.C.E. Other important foods were potatoes (developed in the Andes), manioc, squash, beans, peppers, and tomatoes. Many of these foods entered the diet of Europeans, Asians, and other peoples after the European conquest of the Americas in the sixteenth century C.E.

Eventually four areas of relatively dense settlement emerged in the Americas. One of these, in the Pacific Northwest in the area around Puget Sound, depended on the region's extraordinary abundance of fish rather than on agriculture; this area did not develop urbanized states. Another was the Mississippi valley, where, based on maize agriculture, the inhabitants developed a high level of social and political integration that had collapsed several centuries before European contact. The other two, Mesoamerica and the Andean region of South America, saw the emergence of strong, long-lasting states. In other regions with maize agriculture and settled village life—notably the North American Southwest—food supplies might have been too insecure to support the development of states.

Mesoamerica, which extends from the central part of modern Mexico into Central America, is a region of great geographical diversity, ranging from tropical rain forest to semiarid mountains (see Map 1–5 on page 28). Archaeologists traditionally divide its preconquest history into three broad periods: pre-classic or formative (2000 B.C.E.–150 C.E.), classic (150–900 C.E.), and post-classic (900–1521). The earliest Mesoamerican civilization, that of the Olmecs, arose during the pre-classic period on the Gulf Coast beginning approximately 1500 B.C.E. The Olmec centers at San Lorenzo (ca. 1200–ca. 900 B.C.E.) and La Venta (ca. 900–ca. 400 B.C.E.) exhibit many of the characteristics of later Mesoamerican cities, including the symmetrical arrangement of large platforms, plazas, and other monumental structures along a central axis and possibly courts for the ritual ball game played throughout Mesoamerica at the time of the Spanish conquest. Writing developed in Mesoamerica during the late formative period. As we will see in Chapter 14, succeeding civilizations—including the classic period civilization of Teotihuacán, the post-classic civilizations of the Toltecs and Aztecs, and the classic and post-classic civilization of the Mayas—created large cities, developed sophisticated calendar systems, and were organized in complex social and political structures.

The Andean region is one of dramatic contrasts. Along its western edge, the narrow coastal plain is one of the driest deserts in the world. The

HOW DID agriculture influence the development of civilizations in Mesoamerica?

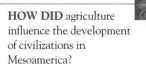

((•─[Hear the **Audio**
at **myhistorylab.com**

Mesoamerica
The part of North America that extends from the central part of modern Mexico to Central America.

CHRONOLOGY

EARLY CIVILIZATIONS OF MESOAMERICA

1500–400 B.C.E.	The Olmecs
200–750 C.E.	The Classic period in central Mexico. Dominance of Teotihuacán in the Valley of Mexico and Monte Alban in the Valley of Oaxaca
150–900 C.E.	The Classic period of Mayan civilization in the Yucatán and Guatemala

MAP 1–5. Civilization in Mesoamerica and the Andes.
Both Mesoamerica and the Andean region of South America saw the development of a series of civilizations beginning between 1500 and 1000 B.C.E.

What Geographical features do these civilizations have in common? How do they differ?

Olmec Head. This colossal Olmec head, now in the Museo Nacional de Antropologia in Mexico City, was excavated at San Lorenzo. Carved of basalt, it may be a portrait of an Olmec ruler. Olmec civilization thrived between 1500 and 800 B.C.E.

Compare this head to the statue from Mohenjo-Daro at the beginning of this chapter. How does this head's projection of power differ from the other statue's?

Andes rise abruptly from the coastal plain and then descend gradually into the Amazon basin to the east. Agriculture is possible on the coast only in the valleys of the many rivers that flow from the Andes into the Pacific. The earliest monumental architecture in the Andean region, built on the coast at the site of Aspero by people who depended on a combination of agriculture and the Pacific's rich marine resources, dates to about 2750 B.C.E., contemporary with the Great Pyramids of Egypt's Old Kingdom.

From 800 to 200 B.C.E. a civilization associated with the site of Chavín de Huantar in the highlands of Peru exerted great influence in the Andes. Artifacts in the distinctive Chavín style can be found over a large area dating to this period, which archaeologists call the Early Horizon. In many areas, this was a time of technical innovation, including pottery, textiles, and metallurgy. Whether the spread of the Chavín style represents actual political integration or the influence of a strong religious center is not known. The period following the decline of Chavín, which archaeologists call the Early Intermediate period, saw the development of distinc-

EARLY CIVILIZATION OF THE ANDES

ca. 2750 B.C.E.?	Monumental architecture at Aspero
800–200 B.C.E.?	Chavín (Early Horizon)
200 B.C.E.–600 C.E.	Early Intermediate period (Moche on the northern coast of Peru, Nazca on the southern coast)

tive cultures in several regions. Notable among these are the Moche culture on the northern coast of Peru and the Nazca culture on the southern coast. A second period of transregional integration—called the Middle Horizon—occurred around 600 C.E., this time probably associated with empires centered on the highland sites of Huari and Tiahuanaco. The succeeding Late Intermediate period was dominated on the northern coast of Peru by the Chimu successors of the Moche state. This period ended with the founding of the vast, tightly controlled empire of the Incas in the fourteenth and fifteenth centuries C.E.

SUMMARY

 WHY IS "culture" considered a defining trait of human beings?

Early Humans and Their Culture. Language facilitates the transmission of culture—the lifeways of a group—from one generation to the next. Cultural adaptation has allowed humans to spread around the globe. Beginning in 10,000 B.C.E., human beings shifted from a hunter-gatherer way of life to one marked by settled agriculture and the domestication of animals—a shift known as the Neolithic Revolution. Between 4000 and 3000 B.C.E., civilization began to appear in the Tigris and Euphrates valleys in Mesopotamia, then along the Nile River in Egypt, and somewhat later in the Indus valley in India and the Yellow River basin in China. Each of these early civilizations developed urban centers, monumental architecture, a hierarchical society, and a system of writing. The period is known as the Bronze Age because it coincided with the discovery of the technique for making bronze tools and weapons. *page 1*

 HOW DID control over water resources influence early Middle Eastern civilizations?

Early Civilizations in the Middle East to about 1000 B.C.E. The Sumerians founded the oldest

Mesopotamian cities around 3000 B.C.E. Beginning around 2370 B.C.E., the Sumerian city-states were conquered and absorbed in turn by the Akkadian, Babylonian, and Assyrian empires. The Sumerians passed much of their civilization down to their successors: a system of writing on clay tablets called *cuneiform*, the worship of gods based on natural forces, semidivine kings, and a highly developed bureaucracy. Watered by the Nile River and protected by deserts and the sea, Egyptian civilization was more secure and peaceful than that of Mesopotamia. Egypt became a unified kingdom around 2700 B.C.E. Religion dominated Egyptian life. The kings, or pharaohs, were considered gods on whom the lives and prosperity of their people depended. Egyptian history is divided into three main periods: Old Kingdom (2700–2200 B.C.E.), Middle Kingdom (2025–1630 B.C.E.), and New Kingdom (1550–1075 B,C.E.). Under the New Kingdom, Egypt contended for mastery of the Near East with the Hittite Empire. *page 5*

 HOW DID conquest and trade shape early empires in the Near East?

Ancient Near Eastern Empires. The Hittites, based in what is now Turkey between 1400 B.C.E. and 1200 B.C.E., helped transmit Mesopotamian and

Egyptian culture to the Greeks. They were also early smelters of iron. The Kassites, with their military aristocracy, helped preserve Babylonian culture. The Mitannians were horse-based warriors. The Assyrians were significantly influenced by Babylonian culture. By 665 B.C.E., thanks to military conquest, they controlled a vast territory. The Assyrian Empire fell to Nebuchadnezzar in 612 B.C.E., and the neo-Babylonians built their empire on trade. *page 14*

 WHAT INFLUENCES did the first Indus valley civilization have on later Indian religious and social practices?

Early Indian Civilization. By 2300 B.C.E. at least seventy Indus cities, the largest being Harappa and Mohenjo-Daro, had developed a sophisticated urban culture. Between 1800 and 1700 B.C.E., Indus civilization disappeared for unknown reasons. In its place, Indo-European (or Aryan) invaders established the Vedic culture, named after the ritual writings known as the Vedas. In turn, Vedic culture evolved into a "new" Indian civilization that spread over the whole subcontinent. *page 16*

 WHY DID territorial states arise in ancient China?

Early Chinese Civilization. The Shang Dynasty (1766–1050 B.C.E.) founded the earliest known Bronze Age civilization in China. The Shang and their successors, the Zhou (1050–256 B.C.E.), ruled as warrior aristocrats from city-states that fought outsiders and each other. By the fourth century B.C.E., as population and commerce expanded, rulers needed bigger armies to defend their states and trained bureaucrats to administer them. The result was the consolidation of many petty states into a few large territorial units. *page 23*

 HOW DID agriculture influence the development of civilizations in Mesoamerica?

The Rise of Civilization in the Americas. The first civilizations in the Americas arose in places that produced an agricultural surplus. In Mesoamerica (central Mexico and Central America) this was based on the cultivation of maize (corn). In the Andes valleys, it was based on a combination of agriculture and the rich marine resources of the Pacific. The Olmecs (1500–400 B.C.E.) established the first civilization in Mesoamerica, whereas the first monumental architecture appeared in the Andes region around 2750 B.C.E. *page 27*

KEY TERMS

Aryans (AIR-ee-uhns) (p. 17)
Bronze Age (p. 5)
chattel slavery (SHAT-1) (p. 7)
civilization (p. 5)
culture (p. 1)
cuneiform (koo-NAY-form) (p. 6)
diffusion (p. 3)
Harappan (huh-RAHP-uhn) (p. 17)
hieroglyphs (p. 12)
Indo-European (p. 19)
Mahabharata (muh-HAH-BAHR-uh-tuh) and *Ramayana* (RAH-MAH-yuh-nuh) (p. 20)

Mandate of Heaven (p. 25)
Mesoamerica (p. 27)
Mesopotamia (p. 4)
Neolithic Revolution (p. 4)
Paleolithic Age (p. 2)
pharaoh (p. 9)
raja (rah-JAH) (p. 20)
Upanishads (oo-PAHN-ee-shahdz) (p. 22)
Vedas (vay-DAHZ) (p. 17)

REVIEW QUESTIONS

1. How was life during the Paleolithic Age different from that in the Neolithic Age? What advances in agriculture and human development had taken place by the end of the Neolithic era? Is it valid to speak of a "Neolithic Revolution"?

2. What defines civilization? What are the similarities and differences among the world's earliest civilizations?

3. What general conclusions can you draw about the differences in the political and intellectual outlooks of the civilizations of Egypt and Mesopotamia?

4. Why were the Assyrians so successful in establishing their Near Eastern empire? How did their empire differ from that of the Hittites or Egyptians? In what ways did this empire benefit the Near East? Why did the Assyrian Empire ultimately fail to survive?

5. How does the early history of Indian civilization differ from that of the river valley civilizations of China, Mesopotamia, and Egypt? What does the evidence suggest were the social, economic, and political differences between the Indus civilization and the Vedic Aryan civilization?

6. What were the stages of early Chinese history? What led each to evolve toward the next?

7. What does the story of the appearance of civilization in the Americas tell us about the development of civilization generally? In what ways did the development of Mesoamerican civilizations follow patterns similar to those of early civilizations in the Middle East, the Near East, India, or China? In what ways did it differ?

Note: To learn more about the topics in this chapter, please turn to the Suggested Readings at the end of the book. For additional sources related to this chapter please see www.myhistorylab.com

PEARSON
myhistorylab Connections

Reinforce what you learned in this chapter by studying the many documents, images, maps, review tools, and videos available at **www.myhistorylab.com**

Read and Review

✓●—Study and Review Chapter 1

●●—Read the Document *From Hunter-gatherers to Food-producers–Overcoming Obstacles, p. 2*
The Development of Religion, p. 2
The Toolmaker (3300 B.C.E.), p. 2
Redefining Self—From Tribe to Village to City
1500 B.C.E., p. 3
The Neolithic Village, p. 4
Sumerian Law Code: The Code of Lipit-Ishtar, p. 5
Geography and Civilization: Egypt and
Mesopotamia–Impact of Agriculture, p. 5
Two Accounts of an Egyptian Famine 2600s B.C.E., p. 6
The Development of Religion in Primitive Cultures, p. 7
Excerpts from The Epic of Gilgamesh, p. 7
Workings of Ma'at: "The Tale of the Eloquent Peasant",
p. 9
The Report of Wenamun
Papyrus of Ani, The Egyptian Book of the Dead
c. 1200 B.C.E., p. 13
Hittite Law Code: excerpts from The Code of the Nesilim,
p. 14
Excerpt from Mahábhárata (1000-600 B.C.E.), p. 20
"Hou-Shih, from the Shih-Ching," p. 25

👁—See the Map *The Beginnings of Food Production, p. 3*
Egypt in the Middle Kingdom, p. 11
Egypt in the New Kingdom, p. 12
Empire of Assiria, ca. 1800 B.C.E., p. 15
The Neo-Babylonian Empire, ca. 580 B.C.E., p. 16
The Shang Kingdom, p. 24

👁—View the Image *Hammurabi Receives His Law Code from*
the Gods, p. 6
The Pyramids at Giza, p. 11

The Sphinx, p. 11
Egyptian Throne of Tutankhamun, 1333–1323 B.C.E.
Great Temple of Abu Simbel, p. 12
Scene from the Egyptian Afterlife, p. 13
Egyptian Relief of Anubis, p. 14
An Inscribed Oracle Bone, p. 24

👁—Watch the Video *The Temple of Karnak, p. 13*
Ramses II's Abu Simbel, p. 14

Research and Explore

👁—See the Map *Prehistoric Human Migration Patterns:*
From 1 million to 15,000 years ago

👁—See the Map *Ancient China on page 23*

●●—**Hear** the **Audio**

Hear the audio file for Chapter 1
at **www.myhistorylab.com**

2

Four Great Revolutions in Thought and Religion

((●●━[Hear the Audio for Chapter 2 at www.myhistorylab.com

The Way. Detail from a twelfth-century Daoist scroll, showing the feats of the "Eight Immortals," the most famous characters in Daoist folklore.
How does this landscape evoke the ineffability and mystery of Dao, or "the way"?

ll human cultures develop religious or philosophical systems. Some scientists have even debated whether humans are biologically "hard-wired" for religious beliefs. Certainly religion and philosophy meet profound human psychological needs, offering explanations of life's meaning. ■

COMPARING THE FOUR GREAT REVOLUTIONS

The most straightforward case is that of China. Both geographically and culturally, its philosophical breakthrough grew directly out of the earlier river valley civilization. No such continuity existed elsewhere in the world. In India, for example, the great tradition of Indian thought and religion emerged after 600 B.C.E. out of the Ganges civilization of Indo-Aryan warriors who had swept in from the northwest. Absorbing many particulars from the earlier Indus civilization, which had collapsed, the Aryans built a new civilization on the plains farther east along the mighty Ganges River. The transition was even more complex along the shores of the Mediterranean. No direct line of development can be traced from the Nile civilization of ancient Egypt or the civilizations of the Tigris-Euphrates River valley to Greek philosophy or to Judaic monotheism. Rather, the ancient river valley civilizations evolved into a complex amalgam that included diverse older religious, mythical, and cosmological traditions, as well as newer mystery cults. Judaic monotheism and Greek philosophy—representing different

WHAT ARE the fundamental beliefs or worldviews that were expressed in the four great revolutions in thought that occurred between 800 and 300 B.C.E.?

GLOBAL PERSPECTIVE

PHILOSOPHY AND RELIGION

Between 800 and 300 B.C.E, four philosophical or religious revolutions shaped the subsequent history of the world. The names of many of the figures involved in these revolutions are world-famous—Confucius, the Buddha, Abraham, Socrates, Plato, and Aristotle. All the revolutions occurred in or near the four heartland areas in which the river valley civilizations (described in Chapter 1) had appeared fifteen hundred or more years earlier. The transition from the early river valley civilizations to the intellectual and spiritual breakthroughs of the middle of the first millennium B.C.E. is schematized in Figure 2–1 on page 48.

Before considering each of the original breakthroughs that occurred between 800 and 300 B.C.E., we might ask whether they have anything in common. Five points are worth noting.

1. All the philosophical or religious revolutions occurred in or near the original river valley civilizations. These areas contained the most advanced cultures of the ancient world. They had sophisticated agriculture, cities with many literate inhabitants, and specialized trades and professions. In short, they had the material preconditions for breakthroughs in religion and thought.

2. Each of the revolutions in thought and ethos was born of a crisis in the ancient world. The appearance of iron meant better tools and weapons and, by extension, greater riches and more powerful armies. Old societies began to change and then to disintegrate. Old aristocratic and priestly codes of behavior broke down, producing a demand for more universalized rules of behavior, in other words, for ethics. The very relation of humans to nature or to the universe seemed to be changing. This predicament led to new visions of social and political order. The similarity between the Jewish Messiah, the Chinese sage-king, and Plato's philosopher-king is more than accidental. Each was a response to a crisis in a society of the ancient world. Each would reconnect ethics to history and restore order to a troubled society.

3. The number of philosophical and religious revolutions can be counted on the fingers of one hand. The reason is not that humans' creativity dried up after 300 B.C.E., but that subsequent breakthroughs and advances tended to occur within the original traditions, which, absorbing new energies, continued to evolve.

outgrowths of this amalgam—were each important in their own right. But their greatest influence occurred centuries later when they helped shape first Christianity and then Islam. (See Overview Figure 2–1 on page 48.)

PHILOSOPHY IN CHINA

WHY WAS the revolution in Chinese thought more similar to that in Greek thought than to Indian religion or Judaic monotheism?

Of the four great revolutions in thought of the first millennium B.C.E., the Chinese was closer to the Greek than to the Indian religious transformations or to Judaic monotheism. Just as Greece had a gamut of philosophies, so in China there were the "one hundred schools." But whereas Greek thought was speculative and concerned with the world of nature, Chinese thought was sociopolitical and practical. The background of the philosophical revolution in China was the disintegration of the old Zhou society (see Chapter 1). Thinkers searched for new principles by which to re-create a peaceful society. Even the Daoist sages, who were inherently apolitical, found it necessary to offer a political philosophy. Chinese thought also had far greater staying power than Greek thought, which only a few centuries after the glory of Athens was submerged by Christianity and did not reemerge as an independent force until the Renaissance. Chinese philosophy, though challenged by Buddhism, remained dominant until the early twentieth century. How were these early philosophies able to maintain such a grip on China when the cultures of every other part of the world fell under the sway of religions?

Part of the answer is that most Chinese philosophy had a religious dimension. But it was a religion with assumptions different from those with Judaic roots. In the Christian or Islamic worldview, there is a God who, however concerned with humankind, is not of this world. This worldview leads to dualism, the distinction between an otherworld, which is supernatural, and this world, which is natural.

••• Read the Document
Origins of the Chinese Civilization – Confucianism, Daoism or Legalism? at **myhistorylab.com**

4. After the first- and second-stage transformations, much of the cultural history of the world involves the spread of cultures derived from these original heartlands to ever-wider spheres. Christianity spread to northern and eastern Europe, the Americas, and parts of Asia and Africa; Buddhism to central, southeastern, and eastern Asia; Confucianism to Korea, Vietnam, and Japan; and Islam to Africa, southeastern Europe, and southern, central, and southeastern Asia. Sometimes the spread was the result of movements of people; other areas were like dry grasslands needing only the spark of the new ideas to be ignited. Typically, the process spread out over centuries.

5. Once a cultural pattern was set, it usually endured. Each major culture was resistant to the others and was only rarely displaced. Even in modern times, although the culture of modern science, and the learning associated with it, has penetrated every cultural zone, it has reshaped—and is reshaping, not displacing—the major cultures. Only Confucianism, the most secular of the traditional cultures, crumbled at the touch of science, and even its ethos remains a potent force in East Asian societies. These major cultures endured because they were not only responses to particular crises, but also attempts to answer universal questions concerning the human condition: What are human beings? What is our relation to the universe? How should we relate to others?

Focus Questions

◆ Why do you think so many revolutionary philosophical and religious ideas emerged at about the same time in many different regions? Do these ideas share any fundamental concerns?

◆ Why is this period in Eurasian history sometimes referred to as the "axial age"?

In the Chinese worldview, the two spheres are not separate: The cosmos is single, continuous, and nondualistic. It includes heaven, earth, and humanity. Heaven is above; earth is below. Humans, ideally guided by a wise and virtuous ruler, stand in between and regulate or harmonize the cosmological forces of heaven and earth through virtue and ritual sacrifices.

CONFUCIANISM

Confucius was born in 551 B.C.E. in a minor state in northeastern China. He probably belonged to the lower nobility or the knightly class, because he received an education in writing, music, and rituals. His father died when Confucius was young, so he may have known privation. He made his living by teaching. He traveled with his disciples from state to state, seeking a ruler who would put his ideas into practice. Although he may once have held a minor position, his ideas were rejected as impractical. He died in 479 B.C.E., honored as a teacher and scholar but having failed to find a ruler to advise. The name *Confucius* is the Latinized form of *Kong Fuzi*, or *Master Kong*, as he is known in China.

We know of Confucius only through the *Analects*—sayings collected by his disciples. They are mostly in the form of "The Master said," followed by his words. The picture that emerges is of a man of moderation, propriety, optimism, good sense, and wisdom. In an age of cruelty and superstition, he was humane, rational, and upright, demanding much of others and more of himself. Asked about death, he replied, "You do not understand even life. How can you understand death?"[1]

QUICK REVIEW

Confucius

◆ Born in 551 B.C.E. in northeastern China

◆ Probably belonged to the lower nobility or knightly class

◆ Made his living as a teacher and a scholar

---

[1] All quotations from Confucius in this passage are from Confucius, *The Analects*, trans. by D. C. Lau (Penguin Books, 1979).

•••⟩Read the Document
Confucianism: Government and the
Superior (551–479 B.C.E.)
at **myhistorylab.com**

•••⟩Read the Document
Confucian Political Philosophy:
An Excerpt from Mencius
at **myhistorylab.com**

Confucius. The master is shown here wearing the robes of a scholar of a later age.

Collection of the National Palace Museum, Taipei, Taiwan.

What clues does this image offer about the personality of Confucius?

CHRONOLOGY

CHINA

551–479 B.C.E.	Confucius
370–290 B.C.E.	Mencius
Fourth century B.C.E.	Laozi
221 B.C.E.	Qin unifies China

Confucius described himself as a conservator and transmitter of tradition. He idealized the early Shang and Zhou kings as paragons of virtue and particularly saw early Zhou society as a golden age. He sought the secrets of this golden age in its writings. Some of these writings, along with later texts, became the Confucian classics, which through most of Chinese history had an authority not unlike Scripture in the West.

Confucius proposed to resolve the turmoil of his own age by a return to the good old ways. When asked about government, he said, "Let the ruler be a ruler, the subject a subject, the father a father, the son a son." (The five Confucian relationships were ruler–subject, father–son, husband–wife, older brother–younger brother, and friend–friend.) If everyone fulfilled the duties of his or her status, then harmony would prevail. Confucius understood that the well-being of a society depends on the morality of its members.

But China was undergoing a dynamic transition, and it was not enough to stress basic human relationships. The genius of Confucius was to transform the old aristocratic code into a new ethic that any educated Chinese could practice. His reinterpretation of tradition can be seen in the concept of the *junzi*. This term literally meant "the son of the ruler" (or the aristocrat). Confucius redefined it to mean one of noble behavior, a person with the inner virtues of humanity, integrity, righteousness, altruism, and loyalty, and an outward demeanor and propriety to match. This redefinition was not unlike the change in the meaning of *gentleman* in England, from "one who is gentle-born" to "one who is gentle-behaved." But whereas *gentleman* remained a fairly superficial category in the West, in China *junzi* went deeper. Confucius saw ethics as grounded in nature. The true gentleman was in tune with the cosmic order.

Good government for Confucius depended on the appointment to office of good men, who would serve as examples for the multitude: "Just desire the good yourself and the common people will be good. The virtue of the gentleman is like wind; the virtue of the small man is like grass. Let the wind blow over the grass and it is sure to bend." Beyond the gentleman was the sage-king, who possessed an almost mystical virtue and power.

Confucianism was not adopted as the official philosophy of China until the Han Dynasty (202 B.C.E.–9 C.E.; see Chapter 7). But two other important Confucian philosophers had appeared in the meantime. Mencius (370–290 B.C.E.) represents the idealistic extension of Confucius's thought. He is famous for his argument that humans tend toward the good just as water runs downward. The role of education is to uncover and cultivate that innate goodness. Moreover, just as humans tend toward the good, so does Heaven possess a moral will. The will of Heaven is that a government should see to the education and well-being of its people. The rebellion of people against a government is the primary evidence that Heaven has withdrawn its mandate. At times in Chinese history, concern for the people was given only lip service. In fact, rebellions occurred more often against weak governments than against harsh ones. But the idea that government ought to care for the people became an intrinsic part of the Confucian tradition.

The other influential Confucian philosopher was Xunzi (300–237 B.C.E.), who represents a tough-minded extension of Confucius's thought. Xunzi felt Heaven was amoral, indifferent to whether China was ruled by a tyrant or a sage. He believed that human desires and emotions, if unchecked and unrefined, led to social conflict. So he emphasized etiquette and education as restraints on an unruly human nature, and good institutions, including punishments and rewards, as a means for shaping behavior. These ideas influenced the thinkers of the Legalist school.

DAOISM

It is often said that the Chinese have been Confucian while in office and Daoist in their private lives. **Daoism** offered a refuge from the burden of social responsibilities. The classics of the school are the *Laozi*, dating from the fourth century B.C.E., and the *Zhuangzi*, dating from about a century later.

The central concept of Daoism is the *Dao*, or Way. It is mysterious, ineffable, and cannot be named. It is the creator of the universe, the sustainer of the universe, and the process or flux of the universe. The *Dao* functions on a cosmic, not a human, scale. As the *Laozi* put it, "Heaven and Earth are ruthless, and treat the myriad creatures as straw dogs; the sage (in accord with the *Dao*) is ruthless, and treats the people as straw dogs."[2]

A sage joins the rhythms of nature by regaining an original simplicity. Various similes describe this state: "to return to the infinite," "to return to being a babe," or "to return to being the uncarved block." To attain this state, one must "learn to be without learning." Knowledge creates distinctions and interferes with participation in the *Dao*. One must also learn to be without desires beyond the immediate and simple needs of nature: "The nameless uncarved block is but freedom from desire." The sage acts without acting, and "when his task is accomplished and his work is done, the people will say, 'It happened to us naturally.' "

Beyond becoming one with the *Dao* are two other assumptions or principles. One is that any action pushed to an extreme will initiate a reaction to the opposite extreme. The other is that too much government, even good government, can become oppressive by its very weight. As the *Laozi* put it, "Govern a large state as you would cook small fish," that is, without too much stirring.

LEGALISM

A third great current in classical Chinese thought, and the most influential in its own age, was **Legalism**. Legalists were also concerned with ending the wars that plagued China. True peace, they believed, required a united country and a strong state. The Legalists did not seek a model in the distant past; different conditions require new principles of government. Nor did the Legalists model their state on a heavenly order of values. Human nature is selfish, argued both of the leading Legalists, Han Feizi (d. 233 B.C.E.) and Li Si (d. 208 B.C.E.). It is human to like rewards or pleasure and to dislike punishments or pain. If laws are severe and impartial, if what strengthens the state is rewarded and what weakens the state is punished, then a strong state and a good society will ensue.

Legalism was the philosophy of the state of Qin, which destroyed the Zhou in 256 B.C.E. and unified China in 221 B.C.E. Because Qin laws were cruel and severe, and because Legalism put human laws above an ethic modeled on Heaven, later generations of Chinese have denounced its doctrines. Yet its legacy of administrative and criminal laws became a vital part of subsequent dynastic China.

Laozi. The founder of Daoism, as imagined by a later artist.
Courtesy of the Freer Gallery of Art, Smithsonian Institution, Washington, DC (72.1).

What might be the significance of showing Laozi in the middle of a large, apparently empty space?

Daoism
A Chinese philosophy that teaches that wisdom lies in becoming one with the Dao, the "way," which is the creative principle of the universe.

Legalism
The Chinese philosophical school that argued that a strong state was necessary in order to have a good society.

•••—Read the Document
Laozi, excerpt from Tao Te Ching, "The Unvarying Way" at **myhistorylab.com**

•••—Read the Document
Daoism: The Classic of the Way and Virtue (500s-400s B.C.E.) at **myhistorylab.com**

•••—Read the Document
The Way of the State (475-221 B.C.E.) Legalism at **myhistorylab.com**

•••—Read the Document
Li Si and the Legalist Policies of Qin Shihuang (280-208 B.C.E.) at **myhistorylab.com**

---

[2] All quotations from the Laozi are from *Tao Te Ching*, trans. by D. C. Lau (Penguin Books, 1963).

RELIGION IN INDIA

WHAT FUNDAMENTAL institutions and ideas form the basis of Indian religion?

By 400 B.C.E., new social and religious forms took shape on the Indian subcontinent. This tradition took its classical "Indian" shape in the early first millennium C.E. Despite staggering internal diversity and divisions, and long periods of foreign rule, this Indian culture has survived for over 2,000 years.

"HINDU" AND "INDIAN"

Hindu

Term applied to the diverse social, racial, linguistic, and religious groups of India.

Indian culture and tradition include more than what the word **Hindu** commonly implies today. Earlier, *Hindu* simply meant "Indian." Outsiders used "Hindu" to characterize religious and social institutions of India as a whole, such as the concept of transmigration, the sacredness of the Vedas and the cow, worship of Shiva and Vishnu, and caste distinctions. *Hindu* is not a term for any single or uniform religious community.

Indian, on the other hand, commonly refers today to all native inhabitants of the subcontinent, whatever their beliefs. In this book we shall generally use the term *Indian* in this inclusive sense. For the period before the arrival of Muslim culture (ca. 1000 C.E.), we will use *Indian* also to refer to the tradition of thought and culture that began around the middle of the first millennium B.C.E. and achieved its classical formulation in the Hindu society and religion of the first millennium C.E.

HISTORICAL BACKGROUND

Chapter 1 showed how, in the late Vedic or Brahmanic period, a priest-centered cult dominated the upper classes of Aryanized northern Indian society. By the sixth century B.C.E., this had become an elite, esoteric cult. Elaborate animal sacrifices on behalf of Aryan rulers were an economic burden on the peasants, whose livestock provided the victims. During the seventh and sixth centuries B.C.E., skepticism in religious matters accompanied social and political upheavals.

Brahmanas

Texts dealing with the ritual application of the Vedas.

The latest Vedic texts themselves reflected a reaction against excessive emphasis on the power of sacrifice and ritual, accumulation of worldly wealth and power, and hope for an afterlife in a paradise. The treatises of the **Brahmanas** (ca. 1000–800 B.C.E.) dealt with the ritual application of the old Vedic texts, the explanation of Vedic rites and mythology, and the theory of the sacrifice. Early on they focused on controlling the sacred power (*Brahman*) of the sacrificial ritual, but they gradually stressed acquiring this power through knowledge instead of ritual.

This tendency became central in the Upanishads (ca. 800–500 B.C.E.). The Upanishadic sages and the early Jains and Buddhists (fifth century B.C.E.) shared certain revolutionary ideas and concerns. Their thinking and piety influenced all later Indian intellectual thought and also, through the spread of the Buddhist tradition, much of the intellectual and religious life of East and Southeast Asia as well. Thus, the middle centuries of the first millennium B.C.E. in India began a religious and philosophical revolution that ranks as a turning point in the history of civilization.

QUICK REVIEW

Sacred Texts

- Latest Vedic texts were a reaction against excessive emphasis on ritual and sacrifice
- *Brahmanas* dealt with ritual application of Vedic texts
- Upanishads were an extended reflection on meaning of ritual and nature of *Brahman*

THE UPANISHADIC WORLDVIEW

The Upanishads emphasize knowledge over ritual and stress immortality in terms of escape from existence itself. These ideas were already evident in two sentences from the prayer of an early Upanishadic thinker who said, "From the unreal lead me to the Real. . . . From death lead me to immortality." The first sentence points to knowledge, not the sacred word or act, as the ultimate source of power. The second sentence reflects a new concern with life after death. The old Vedic ideal of living a full and upright life so as to attain an afterlife among the gods no longer appears adequate. Immortality is now interpreted in terms of escape from mundane existence in any form. These two Upanishadic emphases changed the shape of Indian thought forever and provide the key to its basic worldview.

The quest for knowledge by the Upanishadic sages focused on the nature of the individual self (*atman*) and its relation to ultimate reality (*Brahman*). The gods are now merely part of the total scheme of things, subject to the laws of existence, and not to be put on the same plane with the transcendent Absolute. Prayer and sacrifice to particular gods for their help continue, but the higher goal is realization of *Brahman* through mental action alone, not ritual performance.

The culmination of Upanishadic speculation is the recognition that the way to the Absolute is through the self. Through contemplation, **atman-Brahman** is recognized not as a deity but as the principle of reality itself: the unborn, unmade, unitary, unchanging infinite. Of this reality, all that can be said is that it is "neither this nor that," because the ultimate cannot be conceptualized or described in finite terms. Beneath the impermanence of ordinary reality is the changeless *Brahman*, to which every being's immortal self belongs and of which it partakes. The difficulty is recognizing this self, and with it the Absolute, while one is enmeshed in mortal existence.

A second, related focus of Upanishadic inquiry was the nature of "normal" existence. The realm of life is impermanent, ever changing. What seem to be "solid" things—the physical world, our bodies and personalities, worldly success—are revealed in the Upanishads as insubstantial. Even happiness is transient. Existence is neither satisfying nor lasting. Only *Brahman* is eternal and unchanging. This perception prefigures the Buddhist emphasis on impermanence and suffering as the fundamental facts of existence.

The Upanishadic conception of existence as a ceaseless cycle, a never-ending alternation between life and death, became the basic assumption of all Indian thought and religious life. The endless cycle of existence, or *samsara*, is the key to understanding reality. The terrifying prospect of endless "redeath" as the normal lot of all beings in this world, whether animals, plants, humans, or gods, is the fundamental problem for all later Indian thought.

The Indian tradition developed two approaches to the problem of *samsara*. These two characteristic Indian responses to the problem posed by *samsara* underlie the fundamental forms of Indian thought and piety that took shape in the middle to late first millennium B.C.E. Both depend on **karma**, which in Sanskrit literally means "work" or "action." *Karma* is the concept that every action has its inevitable effects; as long as there is action of mind or body, there is continued effect and hence continued existence.

The first strategy for dealing with *samsara* has been characterized as the "ordinary norm," life lived according to *dharma*. Although **dharma** has many meanings, it most commonly means "the right (order of things)," "moral law," "right conduct," or even "duty." It includes the cosmic order (compare the Chinese *Dao*) as well as right action and individual moral responsibility. For the masses of Hindus, Buddhists, and Jains—those we might call the laity, as distinguished from monks and ascetics—life according to *dharma* demands acceptance of the responsibilities appropriate to one's sex, class and caste group, stage in life, and other life circumstances. It also allows for legitimate self-interest: one's duty is to do things that acquire merit for one's eternal *atman* and to avoid those that bring evil consequences. Rebirth in paradise is the highest goal attainable through the life of *dharma*, but all achievement in the world of *dharma* is ultimately impermanent and subject to change. (See Document, "The 'Turning of the Wheel of the Dharma': Basic Teachings of the Buddha" on page 40.)

The "extraordinary norm" is a more radical solution, seeking "liberation" (*moksha*) from existence: escaping all karmic effects by escaping action itself. Nonaction

atman-Brahman The unchanging, infinite principle of reality in Indian religion.

samsara
The endless cycle of existence, of birth and rebirth.

karma
The Indian belief that every action has an inevitable effect. Good deeds bring good results; evil deeds have evil consequences.

dharma
Moral law or duty.

DOCUMENT

The "Turning of the Wheel of the Dharma": Basic Teachings of the Buddha

Following are selections from the sermon said to have been the first preached by the Buddha. It was directed at five former companions with whom he had practiced extreme austerities. When he abandoned asceticism to meditate under the Bodh tree, they had become disillusioned and left him. This sermon is said to have made them the first to follow him. Because it set in motion the Buddha's teaching, or Dharma, on earth, it is usually described as "setting in motion the wheel of Dharma." The text is from the Dhammacakkappavattanasutta.

- **WHAT** extremes does the Middle Path try to avoid? What emotion drives the chain of suffering? How does the "knowledge" that brings salvation compare to the knowledge sought in the Hindu tradition?

Thus have I heard. The Blessed One was once living in the Deer Park at Isipatana (the Resort of Seers) near Baranasi (Benares). There he addressed the group of five *bhikkhus*.

"Bhikkhus, these two extremes ought not to be practiced by one who has gone forth from the household life. What are the two? There is devotion to the indulgence of sense-pleasures, which is low, common, the way of ordinary people, unworthy and unprofitable; and there is devotion to self-mortification, which is painful, unworthy and unprofitable.

"Avoiding both these extremes, the Tathagata has realized the Middle Path: it gives vision, it gives knowledge, and it leads to calm, to insight, to enlightenment, to Nibbana. And what is that Middle Path? It is simply the Noble Eightfold Path, namely, right view, right thought, right speech, right action, right livelihood, right effort, right mindfulness, right concentration. This is the Middle Path realized by the Tathagata, which gives vision, which gives knowledge, and which leads to calm, to insight, to enlightenment, to Nibbana. . . .

"The Noble Truth of suffering (*Dukkha*) is this: Birth is suffering; aging is suffering; sickness is suffering; death is suffering; sorrow and lamentation, pain, grief and despair are suffering; association with the unpleasant is suffering; dissociation from the pleasant is suffering; not to get what one wants is suffering—in brief, the five aggregates of attachment are suffering.

"The Noble Truth of the origin of suffering is this: It is this thirst (craving) which produces re-existence and re-becoming, bound up with passionate greed. It finds fresh delight now here and now there, namely, thirst for nonexistence (self-annihilation)."

"The Noble Truth of the Cessation of suffering is this: It is the complete cessation of that very thirst, giving it up, renouncing it, emancipating oneself from it, detaching oneself from it."

"The Noble Truth of the Path leading to the Cessation of suffering is this: It is simply the Noble Eightfold Path. . . ."

" 'This is the Noble Truth of Suffering (*Dukkha*)': such was the vision, the knowledge, the wisdom, the science, the light, that arose in me with regard to things not heard before. 'This suffering, as a noble truth, should be fully understood.' "

" 'This is the Noble Truth of the Cessation of suffering': such was the vision, 'This Cessation of suffering, as a noble truth, should be realized.' "

" 'This is the Noble Truth of the Path leading to the Cessation of suffering': such was the vision, 'This Path leading to the Cessation of suffering, as a noble truth, has been followed (cultivated).' "

"As long as my vision of true knowledge was not fully clear regarding the Four Noble Truths, I did not claim to have realized the perfect Enlightenment that is supreme in the world with its gods, in this world with its recluses and brahmanas, with its princes and men. But when my vision of true knowledge was fully clear regarding the Four Noble Truths, then I claimed to have realized the perfect Enlightenment that is supreme in the world with its gods, in this world with its recluses and brahmanas, with its princes and men. And a vision of true knowledge arose in me thus: My heart's deliverance is unassailable. This is the last birth. Now there is no more re-becoming (rebirth)."

This the Blessed One said. The group of five bhikkhus was glad, and they rejoiced at his words.

—*Samyutta-nikaya, LVI, II*

Source: From What the Buddha Taught by Walpola Rahula. Copyright © 1974 by W. Rahula, pp. 92–94. Used by permission of Grove Atlantic Inc.

is achieved only by withdrawal from "normal" existence. The person seeking release has to move beyond the usual responsibilities of family and society. Most often, this involves becoming a "renouncer" (*sannyasi*)—whether a Hindu hermit, yogi, or wanderer, or a Jain or Buddhist monk. The highest goal is not rebirth in heaven but permanent liberation (*moksha*) from all rebirth and redeath. The ideas that led individuals to seek the extraordinary norm were first fully elaborated in the Upanishads. Increasing numbers of people abandoned both the ritualistic religious practices and the society of class distinctions and material concerns around them. Many of these seekers were of warrior-noble (*Kshatriya*), not Brahmanic, birth. They took up the wandering or hermitic existence of the ascetic, seeking spiritual powers in yogic meditation and self-denial or even self-torture. Such seekers wanted to transcend bodily existence to realize the Absolute.

In the sixth century B.C.E., teachers of new ideas appeared, especially in the lower Ganges basin, in the area of Magadha (modern Bihar). Most of them rejected traditional religious practices as well as the authority of the Vedas in favor of ascetic discipline as the true spiritual path. The ideas and practices of two of these teachers became the foundations of new and lasting traditions of piety and faith, those of the Jains and the Buddhists.

MAHAVIRA AND THE JAIN TRADITION

The **Jains** are an Indian community that traces its tradition to Vardhamana, known as Mahavira ("the great hero"), who is traditionally believed to have lived from about 540 to 468 B.C.E. The Jains consider Mahavira as the final *Jina* ("victor" over *samsara*) or *Tirthankara* ("ford maker," one who finds a way across the waters of existence), in a line of twenty-four great teachers. The Jains (or *Jainas*, "adherents of the *Jina*") see in Mahavira not a god, but a human teacher who found and taught the way to extricate the soul from the bonds of the material world and its karmic accretions.

In the Jain view, there is no beginning or end to phenomenal existence, only ceaseless cycles of generation and degeneration. The universe is alive from end to end with an infinite number of souls, all immortal, omniscient, and pure in their essence. But all are trapped in *samsara*, whether as animals, gods, humans, plants, or even inanimate stones or fire. *Karma* here takes on a quasi-material form: Any thought, word, or deed attracts karmic matter that clings to and encumbers the soul. The greatest amounts come from evil acts, especially those done out of hate, greed, or cruelty.

Mahavira's path to release focused on eliminating evil thoughts and acts, especially those harmful to others. His radical ascetic practice aimed at destroying karmic defilements and, ultimately, all actions leading to further karmic bondage. At the age of 30, Mahavira began practicing the radical self-denial of a wandering ascetic, eventually even giving up clothing. After twelve years of self-deprivation and yogic meditation, he attained enlightenment. Then, for some thirty years, he went about teaching his discipline to others. At the age of 72 he chose to fast to death to burn out the last karmic residues, an action that some of the most advanced Jain ascetics have emulated down to the present day.

It would, however, be wrong to think of the Jain tradition in terms only of the extreme ascetic practices of some Jain mendicants. Jain monks are bound basically by the five great vows they share with other monastic traditions like the Buddhist and the Christian: not to kill, steal, lie, engage in sexual activity, or own anything.

Most Jains are not monks. Today there is a thriving lay community of perhaps 3 million Jains, most in western India. Laypersons have close ties to the monks and nuns, whom they support with gifts and food. Many Jain laypersons spend periods of their lives in retreat with monks or nuns. They are vegetarians and regard *ahimsa* ("noninjury") to any being as paramount. Compassion is the great virtue

Jains
An Indian religious community that teaches compassion for all beings.

◆◆◆—Read the Document
Selections from the Rig Veda
at **myhistorylab.com**

◆◆◆—Read the Document
Jainism: Selections from The Book of Sermons and The Book of Good Conduct 6th century B.C.E.-5th century C.E.
at **myhistorylab.com**

CHRONOLOGY

INDIA	
ca. 800–500 B.C.E.	The Upanishads
540–ca. 468 B.C.E.	Mahavira, the Jina/Vardamana
ca. 566–ca. 486 B.C.E.	Siddhartha Gautama, the Buddha

Jain Nuns. Jain pilgrims attend the Mahamastak Abhisheka ceremony in Shravanabelagola, India. During this ceremony, which takes place once every twelve years, the statue of Jain sage Gomateswara is bathed with milk, yogurt, saffron, gold coins, and religious items. This statue is thought to be the world's largest monolith.

What is noteworthy about these women's clothing? What questions would you like to ask them?

◉ View the Image
Buddhist Religious Site
at **myhistorylab.com**

◆◆ Read the Document
Rise of Buddhism–Forces for Social
Change? at **myhistorylab.com**

◆◆ Read the Document
Siddhartha Gautama
at **myhistorylab.com**

◆◆ Read the Document
Buddha's Sermon at Benares - The Edicts of
Ashoka (530 B.C.E., 268-233 B.C.E.)
at **myhistorylab.com**

◆◆ Read the Document
Vardhamana Mahariva, selections from
Akaranga-sutra, "Jain Doctrines and
Practices of Nonviolence."
at **myhistorylab.com**

QUICK REVIEW

Siddhartha Gautama

◆ Great Renunciation: at age 29 left home
to seek answers to eternal questions

◆ Unsatisfied with study with renowned
teachers

◆ Achieved status as the Buddha through
yogic meditation

for them, as for Buddhists. The merit of serving the extraordinary-norm seekers who adopt the mendicant life and of living a life according to the high standards of the community provides a goal even for those who as laypersons are following the ordinary norm.

THE BUDDHA'S MIDDLE PATH

It can be argued that India's greatest contribution to world civilization was the Buddhist tradition. It ultimately faded out in India, but it left its mark on Hindu and Jain religion and culture. Like the two other great universalist traditions, Christianity and Islam, it traces its origins to a single figure who for centuries has loomed larger than life for the faithful.

This figure is Siddhartha Gautama, known as the Buddha, or "Enlightened/ Awakened One." A contemporary of Mahavira, Gautama was also born (ca. 566 B.C.E.) in comfortable circumstances. At the age of 29, Gautama first perceived the reality of aging, sickness, and death as the human lot. He abandoned his home and family to seek an answer to the dilemma of the endless cycle of mortal existence. After this Great Renunciation, he studied with renowned teachers and later took up extreme ascetic disciplines of penance and self-mortification. He turned finally to intense yogic meditation under a Bodhi tree in the place known as Gaya. In one historic night, he moved through different levels of trance, during which he realized all of his past lives, the reality of the cycle of existence of all beings, and how to stop the karmic outflows that fuel suffering. Thus he became the Buddha; that is, he achieved full enlightenment—the omniscient consciousness of reality as it truly is. He pledged himself to achieving release for all beings.

Gautama devoted himself to teaching others his Middle Path between asceticism and indulgence. This path has been the core of Buddhist faith and practice ever since. It begins with realizing the Four Noble Truths: (1) All life is *dukkha*, or suffering; (2) the source of suffering is desiring; (3) the cessation of desiring is the way to end suffering; and (4) the path to this end is eightfold: Right Understanding, Right Thought, Right Speech, Right Action, Right Livelihood, Right Effort, Right Mindfulness, and Right Concentration. The key idea of the Buddha's teaching, or *dharma*, is that everything in the world of existence is causally linked. The essential fact of existence is *dukkha*: No pleasure—however great—is permanent (here we see the Buddhist variation on the central Indian theme of *samsara*).

Thus, Buddhist discipline focuses on the moral Eightfold Path, and the cardinal virtue of compassion for all beings, as the way to eliminate the selfish desiring that is the root of *samsara* and its unavoidable suffering. The Buddha himself had attained this goal; when he died (ca. 486 B.C.E.) after a life of teaching others how to master desiring, he passed from the round of existence forever. In Buddhist terminology, he attained nirvana, the extinguishing of karmic bondage. This attainment became the starting point for the growth and eventual spread of the Buddhist *dharma*, which was to assume new and diverse forms in its long history.

Buddhist tradition, like that of the Jains, encompassed from the outset seekers of both the extraordinary and the ordinary norms in their present lives. This dual community has remained characteristic of all forms of Buddhism wherever it is practiced. The fundamental vision has persisted of a humanly attainable wisdom that leads to compassion and release.

The later emergence of "Hindu" tradition drew on all three of these revolutionary strands in Indian thought—Upanishadic, Jain, and Buddhist—and integrated parts of their fundamental ideas about the universe, human life, morality, and society into the cultic and mythic strands of both Brahmanic and popular Indian practice.

A Closer Look

Statue of Siddhartha Gotama as Fasting Ascetic (Second Century C.E.)

This Gandharan statue represents Siddhartha Gotama before his enlightenment and achievement of Buddhahood, when he spent six years practicing ascetic austerities of extreme fasting and self-denial—an experience that he abandoned for what became his "Middle Path" teaching and practice. The Kushan Dynasty (first to seventh century C.E.) of NW India and modern Pakistan and Afghanistan (see Chapter 4) patronized art and architecture that seem to have had their formative patronage from the Buddhist Kushan king, Kanishka, in the early second century C.E. in the region of Gandhara (in present-day Pakistan). Gandharan art developed from the Kushana's employment of foreign artisans trained in Roman styles, leading to an art that fused Greco-Roman with Indian and Central Asian styles to produce one of the great cross-cultural traditions of art history. In its heyday, down to roughly the early third century C.E., Gandhara produced some of the most remarkable Buddhist art ever, influencing not only Buddhist but also Indian art long after.

Note the highly realistic depiction of bone structure and sinew on the emaciated ascetic figure. Not only is the Gandharan School credited with the first anthropomorphic depictions of the Buddha, but these depictions were done in highly realistic style, likely influenced by Roman realism.

The drapery style of the Gandharan figures is clearly derived from Roman style of the Imperial Period, which derives in turn from Greek styles.

The proportions of the body have a 1:5 relation of head-to-body height (more evident in standing statues), which is exactly that of late Roman and early Christian sculptures. Note the nimbus behind the realistic head; this motif may have originated in Central Asia and diffused east to China and west to the Mediterranean, but the earliest evidence for Buddhist use is in Kushan sculpture from the late first and second centuries.

Borromeo, EPA/Art Resource, New York.

Question

1. What might the various indications of Greco-Roman influence in this south-central Asian Buddhist sculpture suggest about the permeability of political and cultural boundaries from the Mediterranean to South and Central Asia in the early centuries C.E.?

2. The nimbus or halo of light behind the head here is widely attested in various forms across Asia as well as in the Mediterranean, in Hellenistic, Greek, Roman, Christian, Buddhist, and Hindu art. Why might this be so attractive, and what particular purposes would you think it serves in this or other figures in various traditions?

3. Most religious traditions have strands of piety within them that emphasize ascetic renunciation of worldly things, often involving extreme renunciation involving fasting (even to death in a few cases), sexual and other kinds of abstinence, and refusal to have any "possessions." In the Buddha's teaching, why is extreme renunciation and asceticism rejected? Can you compare these ideas to those in another tradition with which you are familiar?

 To examine this image in an interactive fashion, please go to **www.myhistorylab.com**

THE RELIGION OF THE ISRAELITES

HOW WAS the Hebrew concept of God and religion distinctive?

The ancient Near East was a **polytheistic** world; its people worshiped many gods. Local or regional gods and goddesses were represented largely as capricious, amoral beings, unaffected by the actions of humans. The major traditions of religious thought in Egypt and Mesopotamia did not offer comprehensive interpretations that linked humans to a transcendent realm.

Out of this pluralistic and religiously fragmented world came the great tradition of monotheistic faith represented historically in the Jewish, Christian, and Islamic communities. This tradition traces its origin to the small nation of the Israelites, or Hebrews. **Monotheism**, faith in a single, all-powerful God as the sole creator, sustainer, and ruler of the universe, may be older than the Hebrews, but its first clear historical manifestation was with them. It was among the Hebrew tribes that emphasis on the moral demands and responsibilities that the one God placed on individual and community was first definitively linked to human history itself, and history in turn was linked to a divine plan. This is the tradition of ethical monotheism.

FROM HEBREW NOMADS TO THE ISRAELITE NATION

The history of the Hebrews, later known as Israelites, must be pieced together from various sources, including the Hebrew Bible (the "Old Testament" in Christian terminology). Scholars once tended to disregard the Bible as a historical source, but the trend today is to take it seriously while using it cautiously.

According to tradition, Abraham came from Ur in southern Mesopotamia and wandered west with his Hebrew clan to tend his flocks in the land later known as Palestine. Such a movement would be in accord with what we know of a general westward migration of seminomadic tribes from Mesopotamia after about 1950 B.C.E. Some of Abraham's people settled in the Palestinian region, but others apparently wandered farther into Egypt. By about 1400 B.C.E., they had become a settled but subjected, even enslaved, people there. Under Moses, some of the Egyptian Israelites fled Egypt to find a new homeland to the east. They may then have wandered in the Sinai Desert and elsewhere for several decades before reaching Canaan, the province of Palestine that is described in the Bible as their promised homeland. This experience is the key event in biblical Israel's history: the forging of the covenant, or mutual pact, between God, or Yahweh, and his people. The Israelites emerged from the Exodus as a nation, a people with a sense of community and common faith.

The nation reached its peak as a kingdom under David (r. ca. 1000–961 B.C.E.) and Solomon (r. ca. 961–922 B.C.E.). But in the ninth century B.C.E., the kingdom split into two parts: Israel in the north and Judah, with its capital at Jerusalem, in the south (see Map 2–1). The rise of great empires around them brought disaster to the Israelites. The

MAP EXPLORATION

To explore this map further, go to
http://www.myhistorylab.com

MAP 2–1. Ancient Palestine.

The Hebrews established a unified kingdom under Kings David and Solomon in the tenth century B.C.E. After Solomon, the kingdom was divided into Israel in the north and Judah, with its capital, Jerusalem, in the south. North of Israel were the great commercial cities of Phoenicia.

How might the proximity of trade routes have influenced the development of Hebrew culture and belief?

Northern Kingdom fell to the Assyrians in 722 B.C.E.; its people were scattered and, according to tradition, lost forever—the so-called ten lost tribes. Only the kingdom of Judah, with its seat at Jerusalem, remained, and after that we may call the Israelites Jews. In 586 B.C.E., Judah was defeated by the Neo-Babylonian king Nebuchadnezzar II (d. 562 B.C.E.). He destroyed the great Temple built by Solomon and sent the Jewish nation into exile in Babylon. There, in the "Babylonian captivity," the Jews clung to their traditions and faith. After the Achaemenids defeated the Babylonians in 539 B.C.E., the Jews were allowed to return to their homeland. By about 516 B.C.E. they erected a second temple in a restored Jerusalem.

The new Judaic state was dominated for centuries by foreign peoples, but it maintained its religious and national identity. It was again destroyed and its people dispersed after the Romans' destruction of Jerusalem in 70 C.E., and yet again in 132 C.E. By this era, however, the Jews had developed a religious worldview that would long outlive any Judaic national state.

THE MONOTHEISTIC REVOLUTION

This small nation developed a tradition of faith that amounted to a revolution in ways of thinking about the human condition, the meaning of life and history, and the nature of the Divine. The revolutionary character of this interpretation lay in its uniquely moralistic understanding of human life and history and the uncompromising monotheism on which it was based.

At the root of this monotheistic tradition stands the figure of Abraham. Jews, Christians, and Muslims all look to him as the symbolic founder of their monotheistic faith. Abraham probably conceived of his Lord simply as his chosen deity among the many divinities who might be worshiped. Yet for the strength of his faith in his God, the biblical account recognizes him as the "Father of the Faithful," the first of the Hebrew patriarchs to make a **covenant** with the God who would become unique and supreme. In this, Abraham promised to serve only him, and his God promised to bless his descendants and guide them as his special people.

After Abraham, the next major step came with Moses. It is difficult to say how much the Mosaic covenant at Sinai actually marked the achievement of an exclusively monotheistic faith. Certainly, the covenant event was decisive in uniting the Israelites as a people with a special relationship to God. At Sinai, they received both God's holy Law (the Torah) and his promise of protection and guidance as long as they kept the Law. This was the pivotal moment in the monotheistic revolution.

After the bipartite division of the Israelite kingdom in 922 B.C.E., the *prophets* arose. These men and women believed they were messengers inspired by God to call their people back from immorality and the worship of false gods. The activity of the prophets was closely linked to the saga of Israelite national success, exile, and return in the mid-first millennium B.C.E. In the biblical interpretation of these events, we can see the progressive consolidation of the Judaic religion. The prophets' concern with purifying Jewish faith and with morality focused in particular on two ideas that proved central to Judaic monotheism. The first was the significance of history in the divine plan. Calling on the Jews' awareness of the Sinai covenant, the prophets saw in Israel's past and present

polytheistic
The worship of many gods.

monotheism
The worship of one universal God.

covenant
A solemn and formal pledge between two or more parties, usually to perform particular actions.

God the Sole Creator. The British poet and artist William Blake (1757–1827) envisions God.

What makes this God seem powerful? What relationship, if any, does this God seem to have with the human realm?

CHRONOLOGY

THE ISRAELITES

ca. 1000–961 B.C.E.	Reign of King David
ca. 961–922 B.C.E.	Reign of King Solomon
722 B.C.E.	Assyrian conquest of Israel (Northern Kingdom)
586 B.C.E.	Destruction of Jerusalem; fall of Judah (Southern Kingdom); Babylonian captivity
539 B.C.E.	Restoration of Temple; return of exiles

⊙ See the **Map**
Israel and Judah, Eighth Century B.C.E.
at **myhistorylab.com**

◉ Watch the **Video**
The Old City of Jerusalem
at **myhistorylab.com**

Messiah
The redeemer whose coming Jews believed would establish the kingdom of God on earth. Christians consider Jesus to be the Messiah (*Christ* means "Messiah" in Greek).

troubles God's punishment for failing in their covenant duties. The prophets saw Israel as the "suffering servant" among the nations, the people who would purify other nations and bring them ultimately to God. Here the nationalistic, particularistic focus of previous Israelite religion gave way to a universalist monotheism: Yahweh was now God of all, even the Babylonians or Assyrians. The second central idea emphasized the nature of Yahweh. The prophets saw in him the transcendent ideal of justice and goodness. God was a righteous God who expected righteousness from human beings. A corollary of God's goodness was his love for his people. However much he might have to punish them for their sins, God would finally lead them back to his favor.

The crux of the breakthrough to ethical monotheism lay in linking the Lord of the Universe to history and morality. The Almighty Creator was seen as actively concerned with the actions and fates of his human creatures as exemplified in Israel. God's involvement in history took on transcendent meaning; humankind was involved in the fulfillment of God's divine purpose.

Even after the exile, however, the realization of the prophesied days of peace and blessedness under God's rule clearly still had not come. This led to the concept that history's culmination would come in a future Messianic age; later, the idea that a Day of Judgment would cap the golden age of the **Messiah**, the redeemer who Jews believed would establish the kingdom of God on earth, became popular. Some of these ideas might have come from the Jews' encounter with Zoroastrian traditions during the exile, and they later influenced Christian and Muslim beliefs.

Another key element in the monotheistic revolution of the Jews was the Law itself. The Law is embodied in the five books of the Torah (the Pentateuch, or "five

Exile of the Israelites. In 722 B.C.E. the northern part of Jewish Palestine, the kingdom of Israel, was conquered by the Assyrians. Its people were driven from their homeland and exiled all over the vast Assyrian Empire. This wall carving in low relief comes from the palace of the Assyrian king Sennacherib at Nineveh. It shows the Jews with their cattle and baggage going into exile.

Erich Lessing/Art Resource, New York.

What seems to be important to these people as they go into exile?

books": Genesis, Exodus, Leviticus, Numbers, and Deuteronomy). Observation of the Torah allowed Jews to keep their faith even while in exile or without a temple. A holy, authoritative, divinely revealed scripture as an element of Judaic monotheism had revolutionary consequences, not only for Jews but also for Christians and Muslims.

For the first time, a nation defined itself not primarily by dynastic, linguistic, or geographic considerations but by shared religious faith and practice. Ethical monotheism was later to have still greater effects when not only Judaic but also Christian and Muslim traditions would change the face of much of the world.

GREEK PHILOSOPHY

Greek ideas had much in common with the ideas of earlier peoples. The Greek gods had most of the characteristics of the Mesopotamian deities; magic and incantations played a part in Greek lives, and their law was usually connected with divinity. But surprisingly, some Greeks developed ideas that were strikingly different and, in so doing, set a part of humankind on an entirely new path. As early as the sixth century B.C.E., Greeks living in the Ionian cities of Asia Minor raised questions and suggested answers about nature that produced an intellectual revolution. Their speculations about the nature of the world and its origin were completely naturalistic and included no reference to supernatural powers. One historian of Greek thought, discussing the views of Thales (624–545 B.C.E.), the first Greek philosopher, put the case particularly well:

> In one of the Babylonian legends it says: "All the lands were sea. Marduk bound a rush mat upon the face of the waters, he made dirt and piled it beside the rush mat." What Thales did was to leave Marduk out. He, too, said that everything was once water. But he thought that earth and everything else had been formed out of water by a natural process, like the silting up of the Delta of the Nile. It is an admirable beginning, the whole point of which is that it gathers together into a coherent picture a number of observed facts without letting Marduk in.[3]

By putting the question of the world's origin in a naturalistic form, Thales may have initiated both Western philosophy and Western science. This rational approach was applied even to the gods themselves. In the same century as Thales, Xenophanes of Colophon expressed the opinion that humans think of the gods as resembling themselves. Thus, Africans believed in flat-nosed, black-faced gods, and the Thracians in gods with blue eyes and red hair.[4] In the fifth century B.C.E. Protagoras of Abdera (ca. 490–420 B.C.E.) went so far in the direction of agnosticism as to say, "About the gods I can have no knowledge either that they are or that they are not or what is their nature."[5]

Rationalism and skepticism carried over into practical matters as well. The school of medicine led by Hippocrates of Cos (ca. 400 B.C.E.) attempted to understand, diagnose, and cure disease without recourse to supernatural forces or beings. One of the Hippocratics wrote of the mysterious disease epilepsy:

The Fall. The German artist Albrecht Dürer (1471–1528) engraved this image of the biblical first humans whose creation and fall are recounted in Genesis. God's covenant with humankind is central to his divine plan. However much he might punish people for their sins, God would finally lead them back to his favor.

How does Dürer's depiction highlight the special status of humans in God's creation?

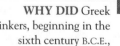

WHY DID Greek thinkers, beginning in the sixth century B.C.E., produce an intellectual revolution?

---

[3] Benjamin Farrington, *Greek Science* (London: Penguin Books, 1953), p. 37.
[4] Frankfort et al., *Before Philosophy* (1949), pp. 14–16.
[5] Hermann Diels, *Fragmente der Vorsokratiker*, 5th ed., ed. by Walther Kranz (Berlin: Weidmann, 1934–1938), Frg. 4.
[6] Ibid., Frgs. 14–16.

OVERVIEW Four Great Systems of Thought and Religion

In the accompanying flowchart, note the river valleys in which the original civilizations arose. Each was characterized by cities, writing systems, agriculture, and so on. (The Mississippi, Amazon, and Congo lacked such developments.) During the axial age from 500 to 200 B.C.E., the same areas saw the birth of the world religions of Hinduism, Buddhism, and Judaism, and the world philosophies of China and Greece. Each continued to develop, and in the Middle East, by a combination of Judaic and Greek elements, there occurred the rise of Christianity and Islam.

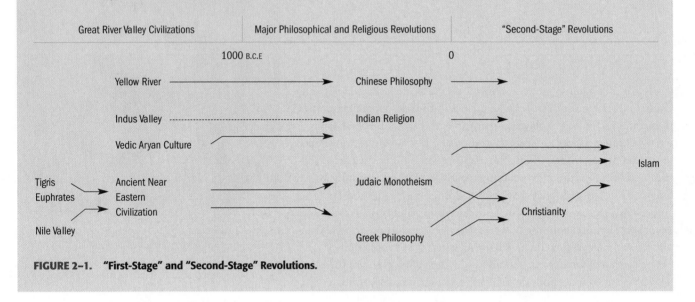

FIGURE 2–1. "First-Stage" and "Second-Stage" Revolutions.

It seems to me that the disease is no more divine than any other. It has a natural cause, just as other diseases have. Men think it divine merely because they do not understand it. But if they called everything divine which they do not understand, why, there would be no end of divine things.[6]

By the fifth century B.C.E., the historian Thucydides (ca. 460–400 B.C.E.) was analyzing and explaining the behavior of humans in society completely in terms of human nature and chance, leaving no place for the gods or supernatural forces. The relative unimportance of divine or supernatural forces also characterized Greek views of law and justice. Most Greeks, especially in the democratic states, understood that laws were made by humans and should be obeyed because they represented the expressed consent of the citizens.

These ideas are different from any that came before, and they are still relevant to major concerns in the modern world: What is the nature of the universe and how can it be controlled? Are there divine powers, and if so, what is humanity's relationship to them? Are law and justice human, divine, or both? What is the place in human society of freedom, obedience, and reverence?

REASON AND THE SCIENTIFIC SPIRIT

The rational spirit characteristic of Greek culture blossomed in the sixth century B.C.E. into what we call *philosophy*. The first steps were taken in Ionia on the coast of Asia Minor, on the fringe of the Greek world and in touch with the learning of the East (see

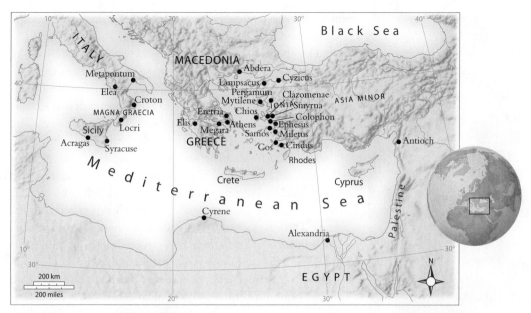

MAP 2–2.   Centers of Greek Philosophy.

Why are many centers of Greek philosophy located on the periphery of the Greek civilization?

Map 2–2). The Ionians were among the first to recognize that the Greek account of how the world was created and maintained and of the place of humans in it was not universally accepted. Perhaps this realization helped spark the first attempts at disciplined philosophical inquiry.

Thales of Miletus believed that the earth floated on water and that water was the primary substance. Thales observed that water has many forms: liquid, solid, and gaseous. He saw that it could "create" land by alluvial deposit and that it was necessary for all life. He used reason to organize these observations into a single explanation that accounted for many phenomena without any need for the supernatural. Thales of Miletus thus set the tone for future investigations: Greek philosophers assumed that the world was knowable, rational, and simple.

Another Milesian, Anaximander (ca. 611–546 B.C.E.), imagined that the basic element was something undefined, "unlimited." The world emerged from this basic element as the result of an interaction of opposite forces—wet and dry, hot and cold. Anaximander pictured the universe in eternal motion. Heraclitus of Ephesus, who lived near the end of the sixth century B.C.E., carried the dialogue further. He famously claimed, "All is motion." Yet Heraclitus also believed that the world order had a guiding principle, the *Logos*, and that though phenomena changed, the *Logos* did not. *Logos* has several meanings, among them "word," "language," "speech," and "reason." So when Heraclitus said that the physical world was governed by *Logos*, he implied that it could be explained by reason. Speculations about the physical world, what we would call natural science, thus led to even more difficult philosophical speculations about language, human thought, and knowledge itself.

In opposition to Heraclitus, the fifth century B.C.E. philosopher Parmenides of Elea and his pupil Zeno argued that change was only an illusion. Reason and reflection showed that reality was fixed and unchanging because it seemed evident that nothing could be created out of nothingness. Empedocles of Acragas (flourished [fl.] ca. 450 B.C.E.) spoke of four basic elements: fire, water, earth, and air. Like Parmenides, he thought reality was permanent but not immobile, for the four elements were moved by two

"The School of Athens." In this painting, the great Italian Renaissance painter Raphael portrayed the ancient Greek philosopher Plato and his student, Aristotle, engaged in debate. Plato, who points to the heavens, believed in a set of ideal truths that exist in their own realm distinct from the earth. Aristotle urged that all philosophy must be in touch with lived reality and confirms this position by pointing to the earth.

Does Raphael seem to endorse the position of either Plato or Aristotle, or does he seem to respect the ideas of each one equally?

atomists
School of ancient Greek philosophy founded in the fifth century B.C.E. by Leucippus of Miletus and Democritus of Abdera. It held that the world consists of innumerable, tiny, solid, indivisible, and unchangeable particles called atoms.

Sophists
Professional teachers who emerged in Greece in the mid-fifth century B.C.E. who were paid to teach techniques of rhetoric, dialectic, and argumentation.

polis
The basic Greek political unit, usually, but incompletely, translated as "city-state." The Greeks thought of the *polis* as a community of citizens theoretically descended from a common ancestor.

primary forces, Love and Strife, or, as we might say, attraction and repulsion.

This theory was a step on the road to the atomic theory of Leucippus of Miletus (fl. fifth century B.C.E.) and Democritus of Abdera (ca. 460–370 B.C.E.). They believed that the world consisted of innumerable tiny, solid particles (atoms) that could not be divided or modified and that moved about in the void. The size of the atoms and the ways they were arranged produced the secondary qualities that the senses could perceive, such as color and shape. Anaxagoras of Clazomenae (ca. 500–428 B.C.E.) had previously spoken of tiny fundamental particles called *seeds* that were put together on a rational basis by a force called *nous*, or "mind." Thus, Anaxagoras suggested a distinction between matter and mind. But the **atomists** regarded "soul," or "mind," as material and believed that everything was guided by purely physical laws. In the arguments of Anaxagoras and the atomists, we have the beginning of the philosophical debate between materialism and idealism that has continued through the ages. (See Document, "The Atomists' Account of the Origin of the World Order.")

POLITICAL AND MORAL PHILOSOPHY

Most Greeks were suspicious of metaphysical speculations. A far more influential debate was begun by a group of professional teachers who emerged in the mid-fifth century B.C.E. Called **Sophists**, they traveled about and received pay for teaching practical techniques of persuasion, such as rhetoric, which were highly valued in democracies like Athens. Some claimed to teach wisdom and even virtue. They applied reasoned analysis to human beliefs and institutions. They analyzed the tension and even the contradiction between nature and custom, or law. The more traditional among them argued that law itself was in accord with nature, and this view fortified the traditional beliefs about the *polis*, the Greek city-state (see Chapter 3). Others argued that laws were merely the result of an agreement among people, a way to prevent people from harming each other. The most extreme Sophists argued that law was contrary to nature, a trick whereby the weak controlled the strong. Critias (ca. 460–403 B.C.E.) went so far as to say that the gods themselves had been invented by some clever man to deter people from doing what they wished. Such ideas attacked the theoretical foundations of the *polis*.

The Greek concern with ethical, political, and religious issues is expressed brilliantly in the philosophical tradition that began with Socrates in the latter half of the fifth century B.C.E. That tradition continued with Socrates' pupil Plato and with Plato's pupil Aristotle. Aristotle also made great contributions to the scientific understanding of the physical world, but he is perhaps more important for his impact on later Western and Islamic metaphysics.

The starting point for the three giants of Hellenic moral and political philosophy was the social and political reality of the Greek city-state, or *polis*. The greatest crisis for the *polis* was the Great Peloponnesian War (435–404 B.C.E.), which is discussed in Chapter 3. Probably the most complicated response to this crisis may be found in the life and teachings of Socrates (469–399 B.C.E.). He wrote nothing, so our knowledge of him comes from his disciples Plato and Xenophon (ca. 435–354 B.C.E.) and from later tradition.

DOCUMENT

The Atomists' Account of the Origin of the World Order

Leucippus and Democritus were Greek thinkers of the fifth century B.C.E. who originated the theory that the world is entirely material, made up of atoms and the void, moving through space without external guidance. As these selections show, they provided a fundamental explanation of things that was purely natural, without divine or mythical intervention. Their view was passed on and later influenced such Renaissance scientists as Galileo.

- Compare the atomists' explanation of the origins of the world with that presented in the box entitled "Hymn to Indra" in Chapter 1. How do these explanations of the nature of things and how they got that way differ from those offered by different civilizations and by the Greeks before the sixth century B.C.E.? What are the consequences and significance of this new way of looking at the universe?

1. The world-orders arise in this way. Many bodies of all sorts of shapes "split off" from the infinite into a great void where, being gathered together, they give rise to a single vortex, in which, colliding and circling in all sorts of ways, they begin to separate apart, like to like. Being unable to circle in equilibrium any longer because of their congestion, the light bodies go off into the outer void like chaff, while the rest "remain together" and, becoming entangled, unite their motions and produce first a spherical structure. This stands apart like a "membrane," containing in itself all sorts of bodies; and, because of the resistance of the middle, as these revolve the surrounding membrane becomes thin as contiguous bodies continually flow together because of contact with the vortex. And in this way the earth arose, the bodies which were carried to the middle remaining together. Again, the surrounding membrane increases because of the acquisition of bodies from without; and as it moves with the vortex, whatever it touches it adds to itself. Certain of these, becoming entangled, form a structure at first very watery and muddy; but afterward they dry out, being carried about with the rotation of the whole, and ignite to form the substance of the heavenly bodies.

2. Certainly the atoms did not arrange themselves in order by design or intelligence, nor did they propound what movements each should make. But rather myriad atoms, swept along through infinite time or myriad paths by blows and their own weight, have come together in every possible way and tried out every combination that they could possibly create. So it happens that, after roaming the world for aeons of time in making trial of every combination and movement, at length they come together—those atoms whose sudden coincidence often becomes the origin of mighty things: of earth and sea and sky and the species of living things.

Source: The first selection is from Diogenes Laertius 9.31; the second is from Lucretius, De Rerum Naturae 5.419–431. Both selections from John Mansley Robinson, An Introduction to Early Greek Philosophy. Copyright © 1968 by John Mansley Robinson. Used with permission of the author.

Socrates was committed to the search for truth and for the knowledge about human affairs that he believed reason could reveal. His method was to question and cross-examine fellow Greeks. The result was always the same: Those he questioned might have technical information and skills but seldom had any knowledge of the fundamental principles of human behavior. Unlike the Sophists, Socrates did not accept pay for his teaching; he professed ignorance and denied that he taught at all. His individualism, moreover, was unlike the worldly hedonism of some of the Sophists. It was not wealth or pleasure or power that he urged people to seek, but "the greatest improvement of the soul." Contrary to the more radical Sophists, he thought that the *polis* and its laws had a legitimate claim on the citizen. But he was contemptuous of democracy, which seemingly relied on ignorant amateurs to make important political

QUICK REVIEW

Socrates and Athens

- Socrates distrusted democracy
- Athenians thought Socrates undermined the *polis*
- An Athenian jury sentenced Socrates to death

◆●◆–|Read the **Document**
Aristotle, excerpts from Physics and Posterior Analytics at **myhistorylab.com**

QUICK REVIEW

Plato and the *Polis*

- Plato hoped to reform the *polis*
- The *polis* could mold good men
- A philosopher-king would be the ideal ruler

decisions without any certain knowledge. Athenians thought Socrates was undermining the beliefs and values of the *polis*, and his dialectical inquiries had angered many important people. Socrates' insistence on the primacy of his own individualism and his determination to pursue philosophy even against the wishes of his fellow citizens created hostility. In 399 B.C.E., Socrates was condemned to death by an Athenian jury on the charges of bringing new gods into the city and of corrupting its youth. He was given a chance to escape, but in Plato's *Crito* we are told of his refusal to do so because of his veneration of the laws.

Socrates' career set the stage for later responses to the travail of the *polis*. Socratic beliefs were distorted almost beyond recognition by the Cynic school. The most famous Cynic was Diogenes of Sinope (ca. 400–325 B.C.E.). Socrates disparaged wealth and worldly comfort, so Diogenes wore rags and lived in a tub. As Plato said, Diogenes was Socrates gone mad. The Cynics moved even further from Socrates by abandoning the concept of the *polis* entirely. When Diogenes was asked about his citizenship, he answered that he was *kosmopolites*, a citizen of the world.

Plato (429–347 B.C.E.), the most important of Socrates' associates, is a perfect example of the pupil who becomes greater than his master. He was a writer of genius, leaving us twenty-six philosophical discussions, mostly in the form of dialogues. In 386 B.C.E., Plato founded the Academy, a center of philosophical investigation and a school for training statesmen and citizens that had a powerful impact on Greek thought and endured until the sixth century C.E.

Like Socrates, Plato firmly believed in the *polis* and its virtues of order, harmony, and justice. Unlike the radical Sophists, Plato thought that the *polis* was in accord with nature, and that one of its main objects was to produce good people. He accepted Socrates' doctrine of the identity of virtue and knowledge, or *episteme*, a body of true and unchanging wisdom. Only the few philosophers whose training, character, and intellect allowed them to see reality were qualified to rule; they themselves would prefer the life of pure contemplation but would accept their responsibility and take their turn as philosopher-kings. According to Plato's definition of justice, each man should do only that one thing to which his nature was best suited. The individual was subordinated to the community.

Plato understood that the *polis* of his day suffered from terrible internal stress, class struggle, and factional divisions. Redemption of the *polis* was at the heart of Plato's system of philosophy. He began by asking the traditional questions: What is a good man, and how is he made? Because goodness depended on knowledge of the good, it required a theory of knowledge. Even when the philosopher knew the good, the question remained of how the state could bring that knowledge to its citizens. That answer required a theory of education. Even purely logical and metaphysical questions, therefore, were subordinate to the overriding political questions. Plato's need to find a satisfactory foundation for the beleaguered *polis* thus contributed to the birth of systematic philosophy.

Aristotle (384–322 B.C.E.) was a pupil of Plato, but his different experience and cast of mind led him in new directions. As a young man, he came to study at the Academy, where he stayed until Plato's death. Later, he carried on research in marine biology, and biological interests played a large part in all his thoughts. In 342 B.C.E., Philip, the king of Macedon, appointed him tutor to his son, the young Alexander (see Chapter 3). In 336 B.C.E. he returned to Athens, where he founded his own school, the Lyceum. On the death of Alexander in 323 B.C.E., the Athenians rebelled against Macedonian rule, and Aristotle found it wise to leave Athens. He died the following year.

Aristotle studied an astonishing range of subjects including logic, physics, astronomy, biology, ethics, rhetoric, literary criticism, and politics. In each field, his method was the same. Aristotle began with observation of the empirical evidence, whether it was physical or common opinion. He applied reason and discovered inconsistencies or difficulties, then introduced metaphysical principles to explain the problems or to reconcile the inconsistencies. His view on all subjects, like Plato's, was teleological; that is, he recognized purposes apart from and greater than the will of the individual human being. Plato's purposes, however, were contained in the Ideas, or Forms—transcendental concepts outside the experience of most people. For Aristotle, the purposes of most things were easily inferred by observing their behavior in the world.

Aristotle's most striking characteristics are his moderation and common sense. His epistemology finds room for both reason and experience; his metaphysics gives meaning and reality to both mind and body; his ethics aims at the good life, which is the contemplative life, but recognizes the necessity for moderate wealth, comfort, and pleasure.

All these qualities are evident in Aristotle's political thought. Like Plato, he opposed the Sophists' assertion that the *polis* was the result of mere convention. Aristotle applied to politics the teleology that he saw in all nature. The *polis* made individuals self-sufficient and allowed them to realize their potential. It was therefore natural. It was also the highest point in the evolution of the social institutions: marriage, household, village, and finally, *polis*. For Aristotle, the purpose of the *polis* was neither economic nor military but moral: "The end of the state is the good life," the life lived "for the sake of noble actions," a life of virtue and morality.[7]

Characteristically, Aristotle was less interested in the best state—the utopia that required philosophers to rule it—than in the best state practically possible, one that would combine justice with stability. The constitution for that state was not the best constitution, but the next best, the one most possible for most states. Its quality was moderation, and it naturally gave power to neither the rich nor the poor but to the middle class, which also had to be the most numerous. The middle class possessed many virtues: It was free of the arrogance of the rich and the malice of the poor. One of its main objects was to produce good people. It was also the most stable class. The stability of the constitution came from being a mixed constitution, blending in some way the laws of democracy and those of oligarchy. Aristotle's scheme was unique because of its realism and the breadth of its vision.

All the political thinkers of the fourth century B.C.E. recognized that the *polis* was in danger and hoped to save it. All recognized the economic and social troubles that threatened it. It is ironic that the ablest defense of the *polis* came soon before its demise.

QUICK REVIEW

Aristotle and Moderation

- Aristotle balanced idealism and practicality
- The middle class was virtuous
- A mixed constitution fostered stability

---

[7]Aristotle, *Politics*, 1280b, 1281a.

SUMMARY

 WHAT ARE the fundamental beliefs or worldviews that were expressed in the four great revolutions in thought that occurred between 800 and 300 B.C.E.?

Comparing the Four Great Revolutions. Between 800 and 300 B.C.E., four philosophical and religious revolutions occurred. Chinese philosophy, Indian religion, Hebrew monotheism, and Greek philosophy have shaped world history ever since they emerged. *page 33*

 WHY WAS the revolution in Chinese thought more similar to that in Greek thought than to Indian religion or Judaic monotheism?

Philosophy in China. Traditional Chinese philosophical thought, which took shape with the teachings of Confucius in the sixth century B.C.E., remained dominant in China until the early twentieth century. It was concerned with social and political issues and sought to teach human beings how to live harmoniously and ethically under Heaven by prescribing correct relationships between people. Confucianism became China's official philosophy in the second century B.C.E. Other Chinese philosophies were Daoism and Legalism. As in Greece, there were many competing schools of thought in China. *page 34*

 WHAT FUNDAMENTAL institutions and ideas form the basis of Indian religion?

Religion in India. Hinduism, the dominant Indian religious tradition, took shape by 400 B.C.E. In Indian religion, existence was an endless alternation between life and death (*samsara*). The escape from this dilemma lay in the concept of *karma*, the idea that good actions (*dharma*) could lead to rebirth as a higher being, even a god, or to escape the cycle entirely and cease to exist entirely (*moksha*). Other religious traditions that originated during this period in India include Jainism and Buddhism. *page 38*

 HOW WAS the Hebrew concept of God and religion distinctive?

The Religion of the Israelites. Monotheism is the faith in a single, all-powerful God as the sole creator, sustainer, and ruler of the universe. The Hebrews were the first people to emphasize the moral demands that the one God, Yahweh, placed on the individual and the community and to see history as the unfolding of a divine plan. The Hebrews, or Jews, were also the first people in history to be defined by shared religious faith and practice. Through the Christian and Muslim traditions, Judaic monotheism would change the face of much of the world. *page 44*

 WHY DID Greek thinkers, beginning in the sixth century B.C.E., produce an intellectual revolution?

Greek Philosophy. The Greeks were the first to initiate the unreservedly rational investigation of the universe. They are the forerunners of Western philosophy and science. In the sixth and fifth centuries B.C.E., Greek thinkers sought to explain natural phenomena without recourse to divine intervention. In the later fifth century and the fourth century B.C.E., Socrates, Plato, Aristotle, and others applied the same rational, inquisitive approach to the study of moral and political issues in the life of the Greek city-state, or *polis*. *page 46*

KEY TERMS

atman-Brahman (AHT-muhn BRAH-mahn) (p. 39)
atomists (p. 50)
Brahmanas (p. 38)
covenant (p. 45)
Daoism (daow-ihzm) (p. 37)
dharma **(DAHR-muh)** (p. 39)
Hindu (p. 38)
Jains (p. 41)
karma (KAHR-muh) (p. 39)

Legalism (p. 37)
Messiah (p. 46)
monotheism (MAH-nah-THEE-iz-im) (p. 44)
polis **(POH-lihs)** (p. 50)
polytheistic (p. 44)
samsara **(suhm-SAHR-ah)** (p. 39)
Sophists (p. 50)

REVIEW QUESTIONS

1. Is your own outlook on life closer to Confucianism, Daoism, or Legalism? What specifically makes you favor one over the others?

2. Which fundamental assumptions about the world, the individual, and reality do the Jain, Hindu, and Buddhist traditions share? How do these assumptions compare with those that underlie Chinese philosophy, Jewish religious thought, and Greek philosophy?

3. In what sense is Buddhism the "Middle Path"? Buddha filled his own life with extreme asceticism; do you think this distorted his perspective on human suffering, or did it allow him to gain a true understanding of suffering?

4. What makes the monotheism of the Hebrews unique? To what extent did their faith bind the Jews politically? Why was the concept of monotheism so radical for Near Eastern civilization?

5. Describe the covenant between Jews and God. Could a polytheistic people have a covenant with one or more of their gods?

6. In what ways did the ideas of the Greeks differ from those of other ancient peoples? How do Aristotle's political and ethical ideas compare with those of Confucius? What were Socrates' contributions to the development of philosophy?

Note: To learn more about the topics in this chapter, please turn to the Suggested Readings at the end of the book. For additional sources related to this chapter please see www.myhistorylab.com

PEARSON myhistorylab Connections

Reinforce what you learned in this chapter by studying the many documents, images, maps, review tools, and videos available at **www.myhistorylab.com**

Read and Review

✓●─[**Study** and **Review** Chapter 2

●─[Read the Document *Origins of the Chinese Civilization–Confucianism, Daoism or Legalism?, p. 34*
Confucious, selections from the Analects, p. 35
Confucianism: Government and the Superior (551–479 B.C.E.), p. 36
Confucian Political Philosophy: An Excerpt from Mencius, p. 36
Laozi, excerpt from Tao Te Ching, "The Unvarying Way," p. 37
Daoism: "The Classic of the Way and Virtue (500s–400s B.C.E.)," p. 37
The Way of the State (475–221 B.C.E.) Legalism, p. 37
Li Si and the Legalist Policies of Qin Shihuang (280–208 B.C.E.), p. 37
Selections from the Rig Veda, p. 41
Jainism: Selections from The Book of Sermons and The Book of Good Conduct 6th century B.C.E.–5th century C.E., p. 41
Vardhamana Mahariva, selections from Akaranga-sutra, "Jain Doctrines and Practices of Nonviolence," p. 42
Buddha's Sermon at Benares—The Edicts of Ashoka (530 B.C.E., 268–233 B.C.E.), p. 42
Rise of Buddhism–Forces for Social Change?, p. 42
Siddhartha Gautama, p. 42
Aristotle, excerpts from Physics and Posterior Analytics, p. 52

●─[Watch the Video *The Old City of Jerusalem, p. 46*

Research and Explore

●─[View the Image *Buddhist Religious Site, p. 42*

●─[See the Map *Israel and Judah, Eighth Century B.C.E. p. 46*

((●─[Hear the **Audio**

Hear the audio file for Chapter 2
at **www.myhistorylab.com**

JUDAISM

Monotheism, the belief in a unique God who is the creator of the universe and its all-powerful ruler, first became a central and lasting element in religion among the Hebrews, later called Israelites and also Jews. Their religion, more than the many forms of polytheistic worship that characterized the ancient world, demanded moral rectitude and placed ethical responsibilities both on individuals and on the community as a whole. Their God had a divine plan for human history, which was linked to the behavior of his chosen people. This vision of the exclusive worship of the true God, obedience to the laws governing the community that derive from him, and a strong ethical responsibility was connected to humanity's historical experience in this world. Ultimately it gave rise to three great universal monotheistic religions: Judaism, Christianity, and Islam.

At the beginning of this tradition stands Abraham, whom all three religions recognize as the founder. According to the Torah (the first five books of the Hebrew Bible; the Christian Old Testament), Abraham entered into a covenant with God in which he promised to worship only this God, who in turn promised to make Abraham's descendants his own chosen people—chosen to worship him, to obey his Laws, and to undertake a special set of moral responsibilities. God renewed the covenant with Moses at Mount Sinai when he freed the Israelites from Egyptian bondage. He promised them the land of Canaan (later called Palestine and part of which is now the state of Israel) and gave them the Law (the Torah), including the Ten Commandments, by which they were to

"In the Beginning." The Hebrew word *Beresheet*, which means "in the beginning," opens the Book of Genesis. The Jews are people of the Book, and foremost among their sacred writings is the Hebrew Bible.

How does the design of this page reflect the role of the Book in Jewish faith?

guide their lives. As long as they lived by his Law, God would give them his guidance and protection.

In time the Israelites formed themselves into a kingdom that remained unified from about 1000 to 922 B.C.E. In the period after its division, prophets emerged. Thought to be inspired by God, they chastised the Israelites for their lapses into idolatry and immorality. Even as the kingdom was disintegrating and the Israelites were falling under the control of alien empires, the prophets preached social reform and a return to God's laws. The prophets saw Israel's misfortune as punishment for failing to keep the covenant and predicted disaster if the Israelites did not change their ways. When disasters came—the Jewish kingdoms captured, the people enslaved and exiled—the prophets interpreted Israel's status as a chosen people to mean that their sufferings would make them "a light unto the nations," leading other nations to the true worship of one God.

The prophets also preached that God was righteous and demanded righteousness from his people. But he was also a God of justice; although he might need to punish his people for their sins, he would one day reward them with divine favor. Traditional Jewish belief expects that the Messiah, or Anointed One, will someday come and establish God's kingdom on earth. He will introduce an age of universal brotherhood in which all nations will acknowledge the one true God.

The Jews are people of the Book, and foremost among their sacred writings is the Hebrew Bible, consisting of the Five Books of Moses (the Torah), the books of the prophets, and other writings. The Torah is the source of Jewish Law. Over the centuries, new experiences required new interpretation of the Law, which was accomplished by the oral Law, no less sacred than the written Law. Compilations of interpretation and commentary by rabbis (wise and learned teachers) were brought together to form the Talmud.

The destruction of their temple in Jerusalem by the Romans in 70 C.E. hastened the scattering of the Jews throughout the empire. Thereafter almost all Jews lived in the Diaspora (dispersion), without a homeland, a political community, or a national or religious center. In the fifth and sixth centuries the decline of the Sassanid Empire in Iran and the collapse of the Western Roman Empire undermined the institutions in which the Jews had found a stable way of life. In the seventh and eighth centuries the missionary zeal of the Christian church also brought hard times for the Jews in western Europe and in the Byzantine East. In the West, their condition improved in the ninth century under Charlemagne and his successors.

Persecution of the Jews. This 1900 painting, *After the Pogrom*, by the Polish painter Maurycy Minkowski, shows a group of women and children in the aftermath of a pogrom, an organized persecution of Jews that was once common in eastern Europe and Russia. Pogroms often became massacres. Encouraged by the Russian government, pogroms were particularly brutal in the late nineteenth and early twentieth centuries.

What seems to have happened to these people as a result of a pogrom?

Gift of Mr. and Mrs. Lester Klien. Jewish Museum/Art Resource, New York.

Under Islam, Jews, like Christians, were tolerated as people of the Book. Jewish settlements flourished throughout the Islamic world. After the Islamic conquest of Spain in 711, the Jews there enjoyed an almost 300-year-long golden age. During this period of extraordinary intellectual and cultural accomplishment, Jews practiced their religion openly and flourished economically.

The beginning of the Crusades in the eleventh century brought renewed persecution of the Jews in both the Christian and Islamic worlds. In the wake of the Christian reconquest of Spain, Jews were persecuted, killed, forced to convert, and finally expelled in 1492.

By the Middle Ages, Jews had divided into two distinct branches: those who lived in Christian Europe, called *Ashkenazim*, and those in the Muslim world, particularly Spain, called *Sephardim*. The Sephardim, with greater opportunities, developed a more secular life. Their language, Ladino, combined Hebrew and Spanish elements. The Ashkenazim, scattered in tiny communities, were forced to turn inward. Centered in German lands, they developed Yiddish, a combination of Hebrew and German. In time Yiddish became the language of most Jews in northern Europe, although the Torah was always read and studied in Hebrew.

Two of the dominant influences on modern Judaism have been Zionism—the effort to found a Jewish nation—and the death of some 6 million Jews in the Holocaust of World War II. Bolstered by the determination of Jews never again to find themselves victimized by the forces of anti-Semitism, the Zionist movement culminated in the founding of the state of Israel in 1948.

The adherents of Judaism are divided into several groups—Reform, Reconstruction, Conservative, and Orthodox—each holding significantly different views about the place of tradition and the traditional law in the modern world. All, however, would give assent to the saying of Hillel, the great Talmudic teacher of the first century B.C.E.: "What is distasteful to you do not to your fellow man. This is the Law, all the rest is commentary. Now go and study."

◆ In what ways did Judaism differ from the polytheistic religions?

◆ What elements of the religion helped it persist through the ages?

3

Greek and Hellenistic Civilization

((•—Hear the Audio for Chapter 3 at www.myhistorylab.com

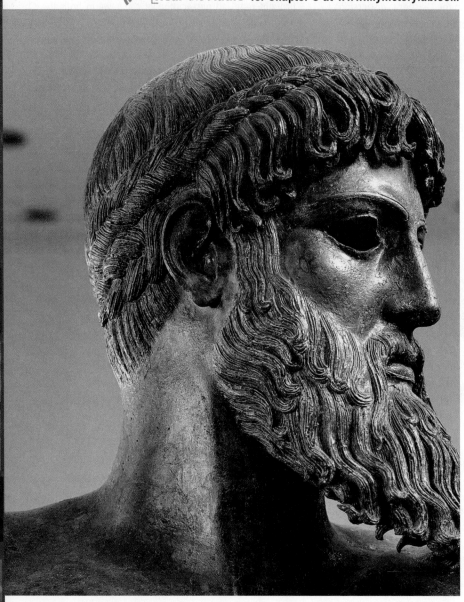

Bronze Statue. This striking bronze statue of Poseidon, created ca. 460 B.C.E. by the Greek sculptor Calamis, was found off the coast of Cape Artemision, Greece.

Is there anything about this statue that suggests it might have had a religious use?

bout 2000 B.C.E., *Greek-speaking peoples settled the lands surrounding the Aegean Sea, where they came into contact with the advanced civilizations of the Near East. The Greeks forged their own way of life, forming a set of ideas, values, and institutions that would spread far beyond their homeland. The foundation of this way of life was the independent city-state, or polis.*

Early in the fifth century B.C.E., *the great Persian Empire (see Chapter 4) threatened to extinguish Greek independence. Led by the city-states of Sparta and Athens, the Greeks won a remarkable victory over the Persians, securing a period of freedom and autonomy during which they realized their greatest political and cultural achievements. Athens developed an extraordinarily democratic constitution, but fears and jealousies created a split in the Greek world that led to a series of wars.*

In 338 B.C.E., *Philip of Macedon conquered the Greek states, ending the age of the polis. The conquests of Philip's son, Alexander, spread Greek culture far from its homeland. Preserved and adapted by the Romans, Greek culture influenced western Europe and the Byzantine Empire in the Middle Ages. In time the civilization emerging from the Greek and Roman experience crossed the Atlantic to the Western Hemisphere.* ■

⊙ **See the Map**
The Greek World at **myhistorylab.com**

GLOBAL PERSPECTIVE

THE ACHIEVEMENTS OF GREEK AND HELLENISTIC CIVILIZATION

Hellenic civilization lies at the root of Western civilization, and it has powerfully influenced the modern world. It emerged from the collapse of the Bronze Age Mycenaean civilization. However, it had little in common with Mycenaean civilization and the Bronze Age civilization of Crete or with other early civilizations—in Mesopotamia, Palestine-Syria, China, India, and elsewhere. These civilizations were characterized by strong, centralized monarchical governments ruling through tightly organized, large bureaucracies; hierarchical social systems; professional standing armies; and a regular system of taxation to support it all. To varying degrees, they all tended to cultural stability and uniformity. Hellenic civilization departed sharply from this pattern of development.

The crucial unit of the Greek way of life—forged in poverty and isolation following the Mycenaean collapse—was the *polis*, the Hellenic city-state. There were hundreds of *poleis*, ranging in size from a few thousand inhabitants to hundreds of thousands. Each evoked a kind of loyalty and attachment in its citizens that

made it unthinkable for them to allow it to be part of a larger political unit. The result was a dynamic, many-faceted, competitive, sometimes chaotic society in which rivalry for excellence and victory had the highest value. This competitiveness led to almost constant warfare, but it also inspired the Greeks' extraordinary achievements in literature and art.

In the Classical Age, which followed the Greeks' defeat of the powerful Persian Empire in the early sixth century B.C.E., while the rest of the world's civilizations remained monarchical, hierarchical, command societies, Athens, the seat of an Aegean empire, developed democratic government to an extent not seen again until modern times. Athenian citizenship—though limited to adult males of native parentage—granted full and active participation in every decision of the state without regard to wealth or class.

Despite the unique aspects of its culture, Greece was also deeply influenced by its neighbors, especially in its earliest stages. The influences of Egyptian art, for example, on early Greek sculpture are evident in the style and stance of statues, jewelry, and fig-

---

MINOANS, MYCENAEANS, AND THE GREEK "MIDDLE AGES" TO ca. 750 B.C.E.

WHAT WERE the defining qualities of Minoan, Mycenaean, and Homeric Greek society?

The large island of Crete was a cultural bridge between the older civilizations of Egypt and Asia and the new one of the Greeks.

THE MINOANS

In the third and second millennia B.C.E., a Bronze Age civilization arose on Crete that influenced the islands of the Aegean and the mainland of Greece (see Map 3–1 on page 62). This civilization is called **Minoan**, after Crete's legendary King Minos. Scholars have divided Minoan history into three major periods, Early, Middle, and Late Minoan. Dates for Bronze Age settlements on the Greek mainland, for which the term *Helladic* is used, are derived from the same chronological scheme.

The civilization of the Middle and Late Minoan periods in eastern and central Crete centered on several great palaces, the most important of which is Cnossus. The distinctive and striking art and architecture of these palaces reflect regional influences but are uniquely Cretan. Minoan cities lacked strong defensive walls, suggesting that they were not built for defense.

Along with palaces, paintings, pottery, and jewelry, excavations at Minoan sites have revealed clay writing tablets like those found in Mesopotamia. These tablets have three distinct kinds of writing on them, one of which is an early form of Greek. The tablets reveal a king who was supported by an extensive bureaucracy that kept remarkably detailed records. This sort of organization is typical of early civilizations in the Near East but, as we shall see, is nothing like that of the Greeks after the Bronze Age. The fact that some inventories were written in a form of Greek raises questions about the relationship between Crete and the Greek mainland during the Bronze Age.

Minoan

The Bronze Age civilization that arose in Crete in the third and second millennia B.C.E.

🔊 View the Image
The Toreador Fresco, Knossos, ca. 1500 B.C.E. Archeological Museum, Herakleion
at **myhistorylab.com**

urines. The Greeks adopted the Phoenician alphabet as the basis for their own. Nonetheless, as in the case of political development and the unique *polis*-centered way of life, the Greeks adapted and made uniquely their own the artistic styles, alphabet, and intellectual ideas they borrowed from their neighbors.

Even more significant, however, was the influence of Greek culture in world history. The culture of democratic yet imperial Athens gave rise to the greatest artistic, literary, and philosophical achievements of the Greek classical period, achievements that became integral to Roman culture and, via the Greco-Roman cultural synthesis, a pillar of European civilization. The conquests of Alexander and the Hellenistic states that followed in their wake spread Greek culture over a remarkably wide area and made a significant and lasting impression on the conquered societies and their neighbors. The Seleucid Dynasty ruled some parts of the Persian Empire for almost two centuries. As we will see in Chapter 4, a group of Greeks who broke away from the Seleucids carried Hellenistic culture even farther east, to the Indus valley in northwest India, creating the Indo-Greek Bactrian society. In art, Hellenistic influence reached even as far away as China. In the West, of course, the legacy of Hellenism was more substantial and enduring, powerfully shaping the culture of the Roman Empire that ultimately dominated the entire Mediterranean world.

Focus Questions

◆ Why are the achievements of Greek culture so fundamental to the development of Western civilization?

◆ In what ways was Greece influenced by neighboring civilizations? Which civilizations had the most influence on Greek culture, and why?

◆ How did the Hellenistic era differ from the Hellenic? What made Hellenistic culture more cosmopolitan than Hellenic culture?

THE MYCENAEANS

In the third millennium B.C.E., most of the Greek mainland was settled by people who used metal, built some impressive houses, and traded with Crete and the islands of the Aegean. They were not Greeks, and they spoke a language that was not Indo-European (the language family to which Greek belongs). The Late Helladic period began soon after 2000 B.C.E., when many of the Early Helladic sites show signs of invasion. These invasions probably signal the arrival of the Greeks.

Shaft graves cut into the rock at the royal palace-fortress of Mycenae show that by the Late Helladic period the conquerors had prospered. The whole mainland culture of the Late Helladic period goes by the name **Mycenaean**. Greek invaders also established themselves in a still flourishing Crete, making it part of the Mycenaean world. Mycenaean culture was very different from Minoan. Mycenaean cities were built on hills in positions commanding the neighboring territory. The Mycenaean people were

Mycenaean
The Bronze Age civilization of mainland Greece that was centered at Mycenae.

A Minoan Fresco. Acrobats leaping over a charging bull, from the east wing of the Minoan-period palace at Cnossus on the island of Crete. It is not known whether such acrobatic displays were for entertainment or were part of some religious ritual.

Scala/Art Resource, New York.

Why do you think the bull's power and size are emphasized in this image?

MAP 3–1.   The Aegean Area in the Bronze Age.   The Bronze Age in the Aegean area lasted from ca. 1900 to ca. 1100 B.C.E. Its culture on Crete is called Minoan and was at its height about 1900–1400 B.C.E. Bronze Age Helladic culture on the mainland flourished from ca. 1600 to 1200 B.C.E.

What geographic features of this area seem noteworthy to you?

warriors, led by strong kings who lived in palaces protected by defensive walls. Mycenaean palaces were adorned with murals, but instead of the peaceful scenery and games depicted on the Cretan murals, the Mycenaean murals depicted scenes of war and boar hunting.

About 1500 B.C.E. *tholos* tombs—large, beehivelike chambers cut into hillsides—replaced the earlier shaft graves. The *tholos* tombs, built of enormous, well-cut, fitted stones, were approached through an unroofed passage cut horizontally into the side of the hill. Only a strong king whose wealth was great, whose power was unquestioned, and who commanded the labor of many could undertake such a project.

The Mycenaean world was made up of a number of independent, powerful, and well-organized monarchies. At the height of their power (1400–1200 B.C.E.),

View the Image

Tomb Mask, Mycenaen
at **myhistorylab.com**

the Mycenaeans were prosperous and active traders. They are mentioned in the archives of the Hittite kings of Asia Minor and are named as marauders in Egyptian records. Sometime about 1250 B.C.E. they probably sacked Troy on the coast of northwestern Asia Minor, giving rise to the epic poems of Homer, the **Iliad** and the **Odyssey** (see Map 3–1). Around the year 1200 B.C.E., however, the Mycenaean world showed signs of great trouble; by 1100 B.C.E. it was gone. Its palaces were destroyed; many of its cities abandoned; and its art, its pattern of life, its system of writing buried and forgotten.

The reasons for the collapse of Mycenaean civilization are not known. Greek legends attribute it to the Dorians, a rude new wave of Greek speakers who invaded the Greek mainland from the north. Greece entered a dark "middle age" about which little is known. The Dorians, after occupying most of the Peloponnesus, swept south across the Aegean. Another group, known as the Ionians, spread east to what became Ionia.

These migrations made the Aegean a Greek lake. Trade, however, had ended with the fall of the region's advanced civilizations. Each Greek community was left largely to its own devices. The Near East was also in disarray at this time, so the Greeks had time to recover from their disaster and to create their unique style of life.

THE AGE OF HOMER

Homer provides the best picture of society in these "dark ages." His epic poems, the Iliad and the Odyssey, emerged from a tradition of oral poetry whose roots reached back to the Mycenaean Age. Through the centuries bards had sung tales of the heroes who had fought at Troy, preserving very old material by using verse arranged in rhythmic formulas to aid the memory. In the eighth century B.C.E., the oral poetry was reworked as the poems attributed to Homer. Although the poems tell of the deeds of Mycenaean heroes, the world they describe resembles that of the tenth and ninth centuries B.C.E.

See the Map

Mycenean Trade and Contacts at **myhistorylab.com**

The Iliad and the Odyssey

The epic poems by Homer about the "dark age" heroes of Greece who fought at Troy. The poems were written down in the eighth century B.C.E. after centuries of being sung by bards.

Read the Document

Homer, Debate Among the Greeks, from The Odyssey at **myhistorylab.com**

The Trojan Horse, Depicted on a Seventh-Century B.C.E. Greek Vase. According to legend, the Greeks finally defeated Troy by pretending to abandon their siege of the city, leaving behind a giant wooden horse. Soldiers hidden in the horse opened the gates of the city to their compatriots after the Trojans had brought it within their walls. Note the wheels on the horse and the Greek soldiers who are hiding inside it holding weapons and armor.

What is the general meaning of the metaphor "a Trojan horse"? Can you think of an example?

Kings in the Homeric poems have much less power than Mycenaean rulers had. Homeric kings were expected to consult their followers on important decisions. The right to speak in council was limited to noblemen, but common people could not be ignored. If a king planned a major change of policy, he would call the common soldiers to an assembly. They could not take part in debate, but they could express their feelings by acclamation. Homer shows that even in these early times Greeks practiced a form of constitutional government.

Homeric society was aristocratic. Noble status was hereditary and usually associated with wealth. Below the nobles were two other classes: *thetes* and slaves. Thetes were landless laborers, who endured the worst conditions in Homeric society. In a world where membership in a settled group provided the only security, free laborers were desperately vulnerable. Slaves—mostly women who served as maids and concubines—were attached to family households, so they were at least protected and fed. Throughout Greek history, agriculture mostly utilized free labor.

Homer's poems became the schoolbooks of the Greeks, who memorized his texts and emulated the behavior displayed in them. The values of the Homeric poems—physical prowess, courage, and fierce protection of family, friends, and property—reflected an aristocratic code that influenced all future Greek thought. Defense of personal honor and reputation was of supreme importance. The great hero of the *Iliad*, Achilles, withdraws from the field of battle at Troy and allows his fellow Greeks to be almost defeated when Agamemnon wounds his honor. He returns to the army not out of a sense of duty but to avenge the death of his friend Patroclus.

The highest virtue in Homeric society was *arete*: manliness, the excellence proper to a hero. Arete was best demonstrated by competing in a contest, an *agon*. Homeric battles are primarily individual matches between champions, and the major entertainment for Homer's heroes are athletic contests. The central ethical idea in Homer's epics is found in the instructions that fathers give their hero-sons: "Always be the best and distinguished above others"; "Do not bring shame on the family of your fathers." The chief aristocratic values of Homer's world—to vie for individual supremacy in *arete* and to defend and increase the honor of the family—would remain prominent Greek values long after Homeric society was only a memory.

THE *POLIS* IN THE EXPANDING GREEK WORLD

WHY WAS the *polis* the most characteristic Greek institution?

The characteristic Greek institution was the *polis*. The common translation of that word as "city-state" says both too much and too little. All Greek *poleis* began as agricultural villages or towns, and many stayed that way, so the word *city* is inappropriate. They were states, in the sense of being independent political units, but they were much more than that. The *polis* was thought of as a community of relatives; all its citizens, who were theoretically descended from a common ancestor, belonged to subgroups such as fighting brotherhoods (*phratries*), clans, and tribes. They worshiped the gods in common ceremonies.

Aristotle (see Chapter 2) argued that the *polis* was a natural growth and that the human being is by nature "an animal who lives in a *polis*." Humans alone have the power of speech and from it derive the ability to distinguish good from bad and right from wrong. Without law and justice, humans are the worst and most dangerous of the animals. With them they can be the best, and justice exists only in the *polis*.

DEVELOPMENT OF THE POLIS

Originally the word *polis* referred to a citadel, an elevated, defensible rock to which the farmers of the neighboring area could retreat when attacked. The **Acropolis** in Athens is an example. Gradually and without planning, towns grew up around these fortresses. For centuries they had no walls. The availability of farmland and of natural defenses determined where *poleis* sprang up. They were usually situated far enough away from the sea to avoid raids by pirates. Only later did an ***agora***—a marketplace and civic center—appear within the *polis*. The *agora* became the heart of the Greeks' remarkable social life, distinguished by conversation and argument carried on in the open air.

All the colonies established by the Greeks after 750 B.C.E. took the form of *poleis*; true monarchy disappeared. The original form of the *polis* was an aristocratic republic dominated by a council of nobles, who also monopolized political offices.

THE HOPLITE PHALANX

Crucial to the development of the *polis* was a new military technique. In earlier times the brunt of fighting had been carried on by small troops of cavalry and individual "champions" who first threw their spears and then came to close quarters with swords. Toward the end of the eighth century B.C.E., however, the **hoplite phalanx** came into being and remained the basis of Greek warfare thereafter.

A hoplite was a heavily armed infantryman who fought with a spear and a large shield. Hoplites were closely arrayed in a phalanx that was at least eight ranks deep. The success of a hoplite army depended on the discipline and courage of its individual soldiers: If they maintained formation, they were almost impossible to defeat, but if they broke ranks they were easily routed. Until the Roman legion appeared, the hoplite phalanx was the dominant military force in the Mediterranean.

The usual hoplite battle in Greece involved the armies of two *poleis* quarreling over a piece of land. One army invaded the territory of the other when its crops were almost ready for harvest. The defending army had to protect the fields. The farmer-soldier-citizen, who defended the *polis*, usually hoped to settle a dispute quickly by a single decisive battle and then get back to work. It was to the advantage of an agriculturally based society to keep wars short and limit their cost. Service in the phalanx created bonds between the aristocrats and the family farmers who fought side by side. This may explain why class conflicts were slow to develop, but it also meant that aristocratic monopolies of political power would eventually be challenged.

GREEK COLONIES

Between the eighth and the sixth century B.C.E., the Greeks vastly expanded the territory they controlled as well as their wealth and their contacts with other peoples. A burst of colonizing activity placed *poleis* from Spain to the Black Sea.

The Greeks settled the sparsely populated southern coast of Macedonia and the Chalcidian peninsula (see Map 3–2 on page 66). There were so many Greek colonies in Italy and Sicily that the Romans called the whole region **Magna Graecia** ("Great Greece"). The Greeks also put colonies in Spain and southern France. In the seventh century B.C.E. the Greeks had outposts throughout the Mediterranean world. Most colonies, though independent, were friendly with their mother cities. Each might ask the other for aid in time of trouble and expect to receive a friendly hearing, although neither was obliged to help.

Colonization had a powerful influence on Greek life. By relieving the pressure and land hunger of a growing population, it provided a safety valve that allowed the *poleis* to escape civil wars. Colonization also gave the Greeks a sense of cultural identity

---

Acropolis
The religious and civic center of Athens. It is the site of the Parthenon.

agora
The Greek marketplace and civic center. It was the heart of the social life of the *polis*.

hoplite phalanx
The basic unit of Greek warfare in which infantrymen fought in close order, shield to shield, usually eight ranks deep.

QUICK REVIEW

Greeks in Battle
- Hoplite: heavily armed infantryman
- Phalanx: close formation of hoplites at least eight ranks deep
- Most hoplite battles in Greece were between two *poleis* fighting over a piece of land

Magna Graecia Meaning "Great Greece" in Latin, it was the name given by the Romans to southern Italy and Sicily because there were so many Greek colonies in the region.

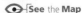 See the **Map**

Greece in the Archaic and Classical Ages, ca. 750–350 B.C.E. at **myhistorylab.com**

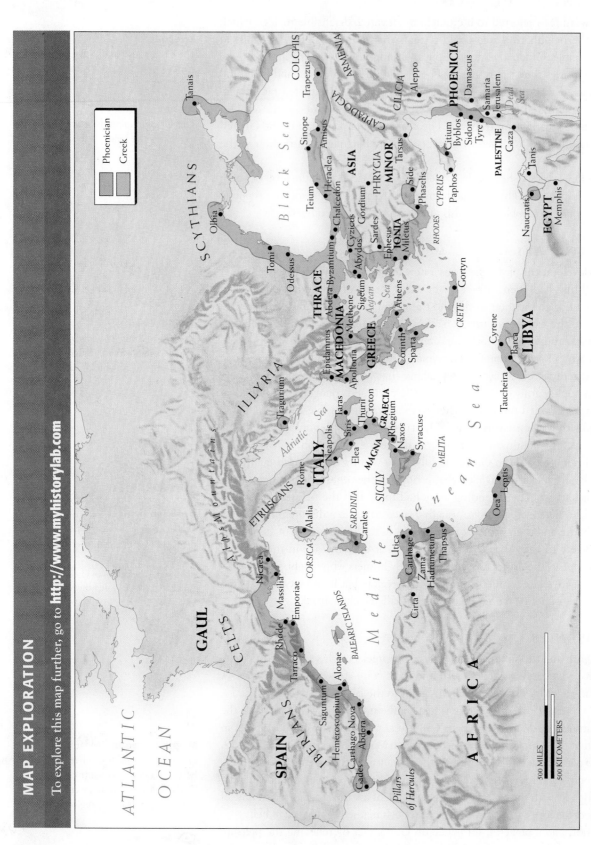

MAP 3–2. Phoenician and Greek Colonization.

Most of the coastline of the Mediterranean and Black seas was populated by Greek or Phoenician colonies. The Phoenicians were a commercial people who planted their colonies in North Africa, Spain, Sicily, and Sardinia, chiefly in the ninth century B.C.E. The height of Greek colonization came later, between ca. 750 and 550 B.C.E.

What impact did colonization have on Phoenician and Greek societies?

and fostered a **Panhellenic** ("all-Greek") spirit that led to the establishment of a number of religious festivals.

Panhellenic ("all-Greek")
The sense of cultural identity that all Greeks felt in common with each other.

Colonization also encouraged trade and industry. The influx of new wealth and the increased demand for goods stimulated a more intensive use of the land and an emphasis on crops for export, chiefly the olive and the wine grape. The manufacture of pottery, tools, weapons, fine metalwork, and perfumed oil was encouraged. The newly wealthy were not always aristocrats, and they resented their exclusion from political power, religious privileges, and social acceptance. In many states the resulting crises culminated, between 700 and 500 B.C.E., in the establishment of tyrannies.

THE TYRANTS (CA. 700–500 B.C.E.)

A tyrant was a monarch who had gained power in an unorthodox way and who exercised a strong one-man rule that might well be beneficent and popular. The founding tyrant, usually an aristocrat, typically sought the support of disgruntled elements within the *polis*: the politically powerless, newly wealthy, and poor farmers. He often expelled his aristocratic opponents and divided their land among his supporters. Tyrants presided over a period of population growth in the Greek world, and to maintain popular support they fostered trade and colonization. They sponsored programs of public works, founded new festivals, and provided patronage for the arts.

Tyranny, however, could turn oppressive, and it was inimical to the idea of the *polis*. The notion of the *polis* as a community for which each of its members was responsible, the connection of justice with that community, and the aristocratic hatred of monarchy all made tyranny seem alien and offensive to the Greeks. By the end of the sixth century B.C.E., tyranny had disappeared, and the last tyrants were remembered with bitterness. The tyrants had, however, helped secure the prosperity of Greece and had cultivated technology, the arts, and literature. Most importantly, they had broken the grip of the aristocracy on Greek society.

CHRONOLOGY	
RISE OF GREECE	
ca. 2900–1150 B.C.E.	Minoan period
ca. 1900 B.C.E.	Probable date of the arrival of the Greeks on the mainland
ca. 1600–1150 B.C.E.	Mycenaean period
ca. 1250 B.C.E.	Sack of Troy (?)
ca. 1200–1150 B.C.E.	Destruction of Mycenaean centers in Greece
ca. 1100–750 B.C.E.	Dark ages
ca. 750–500 B.C.E.	Major period of Greek colonization
ca. 725 B.C.E.	Probable date of Homer
ca. 700 B.C.E.	Probable date of Hesiod
ca. 700–500 B.C.E.	Major period of Greek tyranny

LIFE IN ARCHAIC GREECE

As the dark ages came to an end, the features that would distinguish Greek society took shape.

 WHAT FEATURES distinguished Archaic Greek society?

SOCIETY

Most people farmed the land, but the role of the artisan and the merchant grew increasingly important. Aristocrats led privileged lives.

Works and Days by the poet Hesiod (ca. 700 B.C.E.) gives a glimpse of a Greek farmer's life. His crops included grain (chiefly barley but some wheat), grapes for wine, olives for oil (used for cooking, lighting, and washing), green vegetables, and fruit. Sheep and goats provided milk and cheese, but farmers usually ate meat only when animals were sacrificed at religious festivals. Life was continual toil under the burning sun and in the freezing cold, and pleasures were few.

Attic Jar. From late in the sixth century B.C.E. this jar shows how olives, one of Athens's most important crops, were harvested.

Courtesy of the Trustees of the British Museum.

Why would olive harvesting be considered a suitable subject for illustrating a vase?

Most aristocrats employed hired laborers, sharecroppers, and sometimes slaves to work their lands. This gave them leisure for other activities. Aristocratic social life revolved around the drinking party, or **symposion**, a carefully organized activity for men only. Symposium guests might play games, enjoy professional entertainment, or amuse themselves with songs, poetry, or even philosophical disputes. Often their activities took the form of contests. Aristocratic values emphasized competition, the need to excel, and the desire to be recognized for one's achievements.

Athletic contests became especially popular in the sixth century B.C.E. The games included running events, boxing, wrestling, and the chariot race. Only the rich could afford racehorses, so the chariot race was a special preserve of aristocracy. Wrestling, however, was also favored by the nobility, and the *palaestra* where wrestlers practiced became an important social center. The contrast between the hard, drab life of the peasant and the leisured and lively one of the aristocrat could hardly be greater.

RELIGION

Like most ancient peoples, the Greeks were polytheists. A great part of Greek art and literature was closely connected with religion, as was the life of the *polis* in general. The Greek pantheon consisted of the following twelve gods who lived on Mount Olympus.

- Zeus, the father of the gods

- Hera, his wife

- Zeus's siblings:
  Poseidon, his brother, god of the seas and earthquakes
  Hestia, his sister, goddess of the hearth
  Demeter, his sister, goddess of agriculture and marriage

- Zeus's children:
  Aphrodite, goddess of love and beauty
  Apollo, god of the sun, music, poetry, and prophecy
  Ares, god of war
  Artemis, goddess of the moon and the hunt
  Athena, goddess of wisdom and the arts
  Hephaestus, god of fire and metallurgy
  Hermes, messenger of the gods, connected with commerce and cunning

The gods were assumed to behave like humans, from whom they differed primarily in strength and immortality. Like humans, the Olympians were believed to be subordinate to the Fates. Zeus was a defender of justice. Each *polis* honored one of the Olympians as its guardian deity, but all the gods were Panhellenic—they were worshiped throughout Greece. In the eighth and seventh centuries B.C.E., shrines were established at Olympia for the worship of Zeus, at Delphi for Apollo, and at Corinth for Poseidon. Each shrine held athletic contests in honor of its deity, to which all Greeks were invited and for which a sacred truce was declared.

The worship of the Olympian deities did not inspire intense emotion. Most Greeks seem to have thought that civic virtue consisted of worshiping the state deities in the traditional way, performing required public services, and fighting in defense of the state. Private ethics required only that one do good to one's friends and harm to one's enemies.

symposion
The carefully organized drinking party that was the center of Greek aristocratic social life. It featured games, songs, poetry, and even philosophical disputation.

In the sixth century B.C.E., the cult and oracle of Apollo at Delphi began to exercise great influence. The priests of Apollo urged self-control and warned that arrogance (*hubris*) caused moral blindness and invited divine vengeance. Famous mottos summed up their advice: "Know thyself," and "Nothing in excess."

Later, Greeks turned to deities who were worshiped with more emotional rites. Of these, the most popular was Dionysus, a god of nature and fertility, of the grape and drunkenness, and of ecstasy and sexual abandon.

THE ALPHABET

Early Greek traders in Syria had learned craft techniques and much more from the older civilizations of the Near East. About 750 B.C.E. they borrowed a writing system from one of the Semitic scripts and added vowels to create the first true alphabet. The new Greek alphabet was easier to learn than any earlier writing system, and Greece became a widely literate society.

POETRY

Changes in sixth-century B.C.E. Greek society were reflected in a new genre of poetry, the lyric. Sappho of Lesbos, Anacreon of Teos, and Simonides of Cous wrote on personal themes, often describing the pleasure and agony of love. The most interesting poet from a political point of view was Theognis of Megara, the spokesman for the old, defeated aristocracy of birth. He divided Greeks into two classes—the noble and the base. Only nobles could aspire to virtue, for he said that only they possessed critical moral and intellectual qualities. These prejudices remained strong in aristocratic circles throughout the next century and greatly influenced later thinkers, including Plato.

The God Dionysus Dances with Two Female Followers. The vase was painted in the sixth century B.C.E.

What do the women here appear to be doing?

THE *POLEIS* AND THE PERSIAN WARS

Each *polis* developed in unique ways. Sparta and Athens, which became the two most powerful Greek states, had particularly unusual histories. The Persian Wars of the sixth century B.C.E. brought an end to the fortunate isolation and freedom of the Greek cities on the coast of Asia Minor.

DEVELOPMENT OF SPARTA

About 725 B.C.E., population pressure and land hunger led the Spartans to conquer their western neighbor, Messenia. The Spartans won as much land as they would ever need. Because they reduced the Messenians to serfs, or **Helots**, they no longer had to work this land themselves. About 650 B.C.E., the Helots rebelled, and the Spartans faced a turning point. To keep down the Helots, who outnumbered them perhaps ten to one, they turned their city into a permanent military academy and camp.

The new system was designed to subordinate the natural feelings of devotion to family to a more powerful commitment to the *polis*. Privacy and comfort were sacrificed to produce the best soldiers in the world. Spartan officials decided which infants, male and female, were allowed to survive. At age 7, the Spartan boy was taken from his mother and trained in athletics and the military arts. He was enrolled in the army at age 20 and lived in barracks until he was 30. He could marry but could visit his wife only by stealth. At age 30 he became a full citizen and was allowed to live in his own

HOW WERE the Greeks able to defeat the Persians?

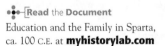

Read the **Document**
Education and the Family in Sparta, ca. 100 C.E. at **myhistorylab.com**

Helots
Hereditary Spartan serfs.

QUICK REVIEW

Spartan Society

- Spartan system controlled Spartan life from birth
- At age 7 Spartan boys began military training
- Spartan girls were also indoctrinated with idea of service to the state

Spartan Warrior. A bronze statuette from Corinth showing a warrior holding a Boeotian Shield ca. 500 B.C.E.

What is emphasized in this depiction of a warrior?

◆◆◆–⌐Read the **Document**

Plutarch on Life in Sparta (1st c. B.C.E.)
at **myhistorylab.com**

◉–⌐See the **Map**

Greece and Greek Colonies of the World,
ca. 431 B.C.E. at **myhistorylab.com**

Areopagus

The governing council of Athens, originally open only to the nobility. It was named after the hill on which it met.

house with his wife, although he took his meals at a public mess in the company of fifteen comrades. His simple food was provided by his own plot of land, worked for him by Helots. Only when he reached age 60 could the Spartan retire from military service.

Spartan girls were permitted greater freedom than other Greek females. Like their brothers, they were indoctrinated with the idea of service to Sparta. Nothing that might turn the mind away from duty was permitted.

Sparta was governed by two kings, a council of elders, and an assembly. The power of the kings was limited. The council of elders—twenty-eight men over age 60 who were elected for life—was consulted before any proposal was put before the assembly. The assembly, which consisted of all males over age 30, could only ratify, not debate, the decisions of magistrates, elders, and kings. Sparta also had a board of ephors, five men elected annually by the assembly. The ephors controlled foreign policy, oversaw the generalship of the kings, presided at the assembly, and guarded against rebellion by the Helots.

Suppression of the Helots required all the Spartans' effort and energy. They did not try to expand their borders, but they did force their neighbors to follow their lead in foreign affairs and supply them with troops. These alliances grew into the powerful Peloponnesian League led by Sparta. By 500 B.C.E., the Greeks had a force capable of facing mighty threats from abroad.

DEVELOPMENT OF ATHENS

In the seventh century B.C.E., Athens and the region of Attica constituted a typical aristocratic *polis*. The state was governed by the **Areopagus**, a council of nobles. Each year the council elected nine magistrates, called *archons*, who became members of the Areopagus after their year in office. A broad-based citizens' assembly represented the four tribes into which Attica's inhabitants were traditionally divided. The Areopagus, however, was the true master of the state.

Quarrels within the nobility and the beginnings of an agrarian crisis created pressure for socioeconomic change. A shift to more intensive agricultural techniques forced the less successful farmers to borrow from wealthy neighbors. Many defaulted and were enslaved for their debts. Some were sold abroad. The poor began to demand the abolition of debt and a redistribution of the land.

According to tradition, the Athenians elected the reformer Solon (ca. 639–559 B.C.E.) in 594 B.C.E. Solon immediately canceled debts, forbade debt slavery, and brought back Athenians enslaved abroad. He forbade the export of wheat, a food staple, but encouraged production of olive oil and wine for sale abroad. This nudged the Athenians toward a commercially based economy that utilized their land most efficiently for cash crops, such as olives and grapes. Solon changed the way Athens was governed. He expanded citizenship to include immigrant artisans and merchants and divided the citizenry into four classes on the basis of wealth. Only men of the wealthiest two classes could be *archons* and sit on the Areopagus. Men of the third class could be hoplites and serve on a council of 400 chosen by the assembly of all male citizens. The fourth class, the *thetes*, voted in the assembly and also sat on a new court of appeals.

Pisistratus (605?–527 B.C.E.) seized power in 546 B.C.E. and made himself the city's first tyrant. Pisistratus sought to increase the power of the central government at the expense of the nobles. He made no formal change in the institutions of government but saw to it that his supporters filled key offices. The unintended effect was to

CHRONOLOGY

KEY EVENTS IN THE EARLY HISTORY OF SPARTA AND ATHENS

ca. 725–710 B.C.E.	First Messenian War
ca. 650–625 B.C.E.	Second Messenian War
ca. 600–590 B.C.E.	Solon initiates reforms at Athens
ca. 560–550 B.C.E.	Sparta defeats Tegea: beginning of Peloponnesian League
546–527 B.C.E.	Pisistratus reigns as tyrant at Athens (main period)
510 B.C.E.	Hippias, son of Pisistratus, deposed as tyrant of Athens
ca. 508–501 B.C.E.	Clisthenes institutes reforms at Athens

give more Athenians a taste for participatory government. The tyranny ended with Pisistratus's son, Hippias (r. 527–510 B.C.E.). When his rule became harsh and unpopular, his aristocratic opponents, with Sparta's help, rallied and drove him into exile (510 B.C.E.).

Some Athenian aristocrats tried to restore the dominance they had enjoyed before Solon. Their plans were upset by Clisthenes, an aristocrat whose program won the backing of the masses. Clisthenes replaced Attica's traditional four tribes with ten new tribes composed of units drawn from all parts of Attica. The new organization increased devotion to the *polis* by weakening regional loyalties; it also deprived the nobility of their traditional power base. Clisthenes vested final authority in the assembly of all adult male Athenian citizens. Debate in the assembly was free and open; any Athenian could submit legislation, offer amendments, or argue the merits of any question.

Solon, Pisistratus, and Clisthenes put a more centralized and united Athens well on the way to prosperity and democracy by the beginning of the fifth century B.C.E.

••◦—**Read** the **Document**

Aristotle, The Creation of the Democracy in Athens at **myhistorylab.com**

THE PERSIAN WARS

Greek cities on the coast of Asia Minor came under the control first of King Croesus of Lydia (r. ca. 560–546 B.C.E.), and then in 546 B.C.E. of the powerful Persian Empire (see Chapter 4). At first, the cities of Ionia prospered under Persian rule. An ambitious tyrant of Miletus named Aristagoras, however, ended this calm. Aristagoras had urged a Persian expedition against the island of Naxos. When it failed, he tried to avoid punishment from Persia by raising a rebellion in Ionia (499 B.C.E.). He turned to the mainland Greeks for help. In 498 B.C.E., the Athenians and their allies burned Sardis, the seat of the Persian governor. But after the Athenians withdrew, the Persians reimposed their will. In 494 B.C.E. they wiped out Miletus and put down the Ionian rebellion.

WAR COMES TO GREECE

In 490 B.C.E. the Persian king, Darius (r. 521–486 B.C.E.), sent an expedition to punish Athens. Miltiades (d. 489 B.C.E.) led the Athenian army to a confrontation with the invaders at Marathon, a plain north of Athens, and won a decisive victory. For the Persians, however, Marathon was only a temporary defeat. In 481 B.C.E., Darius's successor, Xerxes (r. 486–465 B.C.E.), gathered an army of at least 150,000 men and a navy of more than 600 ships for the conquest of Greece. By then, Themistocles (ca. 525–462 B.C.E.) had become Athens's leading politician. His policies were aimed at making

A Closer Look

The Trireme

The Greeks of the Classical Period owed their prosperity and their freedom to the control of the seas that surrounded their lands, for without the navies that defeated the Persian invaders in 480–479 B.C.E. their cities would have been conquered and their distinctive civilization smothered before it had reached its peak. The key to their naval supremacy was their dominant warship, the trireme. The trireme was the combat vessel that dominated naval warfare in the Mediterranean in the fifth and fourth centuries B.C.E. The naval battles of the Persian Wars and the Peloponnesian War were fought between fleets of triremes—light, fast, and maneuverable ships powered by oars. This is a picture of the *Olympias*, a modern reconstruction of an ancient trireme, commissioned by the Greek navy.

The mast supported a sail that could help propel the ship when the wind was favorable. During battle, however, the mast was taken down, and the trireme maneuvered by oars alone.

The principal armament of the trireme was a bronze-clad ram, which extended from the keel at or below the waterline and was designed to pierce the light hulls of enemy warships. The ship also carried spearmen and bowmen who sometimes attacked enemy crews and could be landed like today's marines to fight on shore.

The trireme was propelled by 170 rowers, usually free citizens of the lower classes, in three tiers along each side of the vessel: 31 in the top tier, 27 in the middle, and 27 in the bottom. It was about 120 feet long and 18 feet wide, with a hull that was made of a thin shell of planks joined edge-to-edge and then stiffened by a keel and light transverse ribs.

Questions

1. What advantages do you think the trireme had over other kinds of warships? What disadvantages can you think of?

2. What is the significance, military and political, of having these ships rowed by free citizens?

 To examine this image in an interactive fashion, please go to **www.myhistorylab.com**

Athens a major naval power, and by 480 B.C.E., when Xerxes invaded, Athens had more than 200 ships. It was the Athenian navy that defeated the Persians.

Darius had launched a naval attack on the Greek mainland, but Xerxes invaded by land. His huge army had to keep in touch with its fleet for supplies. Themistocles reasoned that if the Greeks could defeat the Persian navy, the Persian army would have to retreat. His strategy was to try to delay the advance of the Persian army until he could fight the kind of naval battle he might hope to win.

The Spartans led a Greek army that made a famous, but futile, attempt to block the Persian invasion at a place called Thermopylae. The fate of Greece was subsequently decided by the Athenians in a sea battle in the narrow straits to the east of the island of Salamis. When they destroyed more than half of Xerxes' fleet, he retreated to Asia with a good part of his army.

The Persian general Mardonius was left behind to continue the fight. The Spartan regent, Pausanias (d. ca. 470 B.C.E.), amassed the largest army of Greek allies yet assembled. In the summer of 479 B.C.E., the army killed Mardonius and routed the remaining Persian forces. Meanwhile, the Ionian Greeks urged King Leotychidas, the Spartan commander of the fleet, to fight the Persian fleet. At Mycale, near Samos, he destroyed the Persian camp and fleet, and the Persians withdrew from the Aegean and Ionia.

CHRONOLOGY

GREEK WARS AGAINST PERSIA

ca. 560–546 B.C.E.	Greek cities of Asia Minor conquered by Croesus of Lydia
546 B.C.E.	Cyrus of Persia conquers Lydia and gains control of Greek cities
499–494 B.C.E.	Greek cities rebel (Ionian rebellion)
490 B.C.E.	Battle of Marathon
480–479 B.C.E.	Xerxes' invasion of Greece
480 B.C.E.	Battles of Thermopylae, Artemisium, and Salamis
479 B.C.E.	Battles of Plataea and Mycale

CLASSICAL GREECE

The repulse of the Persians marked the beginning of the Classical period in Greece, 150 years of intense cultural achievement that has rarely, if ever, been matched anywhere since (see Map 3–3 on page 74). The Classical period was also a time of destructive conflicts among the *poleis* that in the end left them weakened and vulnerable.

THE DELIAN LEAGUE

Greek unity was short-lived. Within two years of the Persian retreat, two spheres of influence emerged, one dominated by Sparta, the other by Athens. Athens, as Greece's largest naval power, was best equipped to protect the Ionian Greeks and make sure that the Persians did not return to the Aegean.

In the winter of 478–477 B.C.E., Aegean islanders, Greeks from the coast of Asia Minor, and some from other Greek cities met with Athenians on the sacred island of Delos to swear a permanent alliance under Athenian leadership. This **Delian League** kept the Persians at bay and cleared the Aegean of pirates. To create a workable system, some Greek states were forced into the league, and some that wished to resign were prevented from doing so. (See Document, "The Delian League Becomes the Athenian Empire" on page 75.) The Delian League and Athens were led at this time by a statesman and soldier named Cimon (d. 449 B.C.E.). His policy was to aggressively attack Persia while maintaining friendly relations with Sparta. He worked within the constraints of the popular democratic constitution that Clisthenes had given Athens.

WHAT WERE the main cultural achievements of Classical Greece?

●◆●⌐Read the **Document**
Herodotus, Histories (400 B.C.E.)
at **myhistorylab.com**

Delian League
An alliance of Greek states under the leadership of Athens that was formed in 478–477 B.C.E. to resist the Persians.

MAP 3–3.   Classical Greece.   Greece in the Classical period (ca. 480–338 B.C.E.) centered on the Aegean Sea. Although there were important Greek settlements in Italy, Sicily, and all around the Black Sea, the area shown in this general reference map embraced the vast majority of Greek states.

Why were most Greek cities located close to the sea?

THE FIRST PELOPONNESIAN WAR

In 465 B.C.E., the island of Thasos rebelled against the league. Cimon's suppression of this rebellion began the transformation of the league into an Athenian empire. Despite his success abroad, at home Cimon faced challenges from a faction that included Pericles (ca. 495–429 B.C.E.). Although Pericles was a member of a distinguished Athenian family, he wanted to increase the power of ordinary Athenians and break with the Spartans, traditional allies of some Athenian aristocrats.

In 461 B.C.E. Cimon's opponents engineered his exile, and Athens allied with Argos, Sparta's enemy in the Peloponnese. Almost overnight, Cimon's domestic and foreign policies were overturned. The policies of Athens's new regime helped incite a

DOCUMENT

The Delian League Becomes the Athenian Empire

In the years after its foundation in the winter of 478-477 B.C.E., the Delian League gradually underwent changes that finally justified calling it the Athenian Empire. In the following selection, the historian Thucydides explains why the organization changed its character.

- **WHY** did some allies choose to pay money rather than supply ships and men? Since membership in the league was originally voluntary, why did the allies refuse to meet their obligations? Who was responsible for converting a voluntary league of allies into the Athenian Empire?

The causes which led to the defections of the allies were of different kinds, the principal being their neglect to pay the tribute or to furnish ships, and, in some cases, failure of military service. For the Athenians were exacting and oppressive, using coercive measures towards men who were neither willing nor accustomed to work hard. And for various reasons they soon began to prove less agreeable leaders than at first. They no longer fought upon an equality with the rest of the confederates, and they had no difficulty in reducing them when they revolted. Now the allies brought all this upon themselves; for the majority of them disliked military service and absence from home, and so they agreed to contribute a regular sum of money instead of ships. Whereby the Athenian navy was proportionally increased, while they themselves were always untrained and unprepared for war when they revolted.

Source: Thucydides, *The Peloponnesian War*, Vol. 1, trans, by Benjamin Jowett, in *The Greek Historians*, ed. by F. R. B. Godolphin (New York: Random House, 1942), p. 609.

---

conflict with Sparta known as the First **Peloponnesian War**. The Athenians made great gains during the war's early years. They seemed invulnerable, winning control of some neighboring states and dominating the sea.

In 454 B.C.E., however, the tide turned. An Athenian fleet, which was dispatched to help the Egyptians rebel against Persia, was destroyed, and revolts broke out within the Delian League. Athens agreed to a peace of thirty years with Sparta. Greece was divided into two blocs: Sparta and its allies on the mainland, and Athens and what had become its empire in the Aegean.

Peloponnesian Wars
The protracted struggle between Athens and Sparta to dominate Greece between 465 and Athens's final defeat in 404 B.C.E.

THE ATHENIAN EMPIRE AND DEMOCRACY

The Athenians moved the Delian League's treasury from Delos to Athens and began to keep one-sixtieth of the league's annual revenues for themselves. Athens gave up the pretext of being the leader of a free alliance; the league was now the Athenian Empire, the key to Athens's prosperity and security.

While the Athenians tightened their control over their subjects, they expanded democracy for themselves at home. Under the leadership of Pericles, they evolved the freest government the world had yet seen. Property qualifications for offices were removed, opening all offices to all adult male citizens. Pericles introduced pay for jury service, which

CHRONOLOGY

KEY EVENTS IN ATHENIAN HISTORY BETWEEN THE PERSIAN WAR AND THE GREAT PELOPONNESIAN WAR

478–477 B.C.E.	Delian League founded
ca. 474–462 B.C.E.	Cimon leading politician
467 B.C.E.	Victory over Persians at Eurymedon River
465–463 B.C.E.	Rebellion of Thasos
462 B.C.E.	Ephialtes murdered; Pericles rises to leadership
461 B.C.E.	Cimon ostracized
461 B.C.E.	Reform of Areopagus
ca. 460 B.C.E.	First Peloponnesian War begins
454 B.C.E.	Athens defeated in Egypt; crisis in the Delian League
449 B.C.E.	Peace with Persia
445 B.C.E.	Thirty Years' Peace ends First Peloponnesian War

allowed the poor to take time off from work to serve. Judges traveled circuits to provide swift impartial justice for the poor who were living in the countryside. As the privileges of Athenian citizenship grew, however, access to citizenship was sharply restricted. Only those who had two citizen parents could claim what had become a valuable commodity.

Athens was governed as a direct democracy. Every political decision had to be approved by the popular assembly—the people themselves, not their representatives. Every judicial decision was subject to appeal to a popular court chosen from the Athenian male population. Many officials were selected by lot, which made class irrelevant. Elected officials generally continued to be members of noble families and were almost always rich men, but the people were free to choose whomever they wanted. All public officials could be removed from office and were held to a compulsory accounting at the end of their terms. There was no standing army; no police force; and no way to coerce the people.

Pericles was elected to the generalship (a military office with important political influence) fifteen years in a row and thirty times in all. After the First Peloponnesian War, he instituted a conservative policy designed to preserve the empire in the Aegean and peace with Sparta.

WOMEN OF ATHENS

Greek society was dominated by men, and Athenian democracy did nothing to change that. Women were excluded from most aspects of public life. They could not vote, take part in political assemblies, or hold office. Their only public function—an important one—was participation in certain rituals and festivals of the state religion.

In private life, women were always under the control of a male guardian—a father, husband, or relative. Women married young, usually between the ages of 12 and 18, whereas men typically did not marry until the age of 30. Marriages were arranged. To obtain a divorce, a woman needed the approval of a male relative.

The main function of an Athenian woman of a citizen family was to produce male heirs for her husband's household (*oikos*). Because the pure and legitimate lineage of offspring was important for ensuring transmission of rights to citizenship, women were segregated from men outside the family and confined to women's quarters in their homes. Men spent most of their time outside the home and were free to seek whatever sexual gratification they wanted.

The role played by Athenian women may have been more complex than their legal status suggests, for myths, pictorial art, and the tragedies and comedies performed at Athenian religious festivals often feature women as central characters and powerful figures in both the public and the private spheres.

THE GREAT PELOPONNESIAN WAR

The Thirty Years' Peace of 445 B.C.E. only lasted ten years. About 435 B.C.E., Athens and Sparta plunged back into conflict. This new war, long and disastrous, shook the foundations of Greek civilization.

The Spartan strategy was traditional: to invade the enemy's country and threaten the crops, forcing the enemy to defend them in a hoplite battle. The Athenian strategy was to retreat to their impregnable city, allow the devastation of their land, and raid the Peloponnesian coast to put pressure on Sparta by harassing its allies. The

---

QUICK REVIEW

Athenian Women

- Greek society was dominated by men
- Women were always under control of a male guardian
- Main function of Athenian women was to produce male heirs

CHRONOLOGY

THE GREAT PELOPONNESIAN WAR

435 B.C.E.	Civil war at Epidamnus
432 B.C.E.	Sparta declares war on Athens
431 B.C.E.	Peloponnesian invasion of Athens
421 B.C.E.	Peace of Nicias
415–413 B.C.E.	Athenian invasion of Sicily
405 B.C.E.	Battle of Aegospotami
404 B.C.E.	Athens surrenders

Read the Document
The Peloponnesian War
at **myhistorylab.com**

OVERVIEW   Greek Civilization

Historians divide ancient Greek civilization into periods marked by different forms of social and political organizations and by significant cultural achievements.

Minoan Based on the island of Crete, ca. 2900–1150 B.C.E., sea-based power, probably ruled by kings. Palace architecture, vivid frescoes.

Mycenaean Mainland Greece, ca. 1600–1150 B.C.E., city-states ruled by powerful kings assisted by an elaborate bureaucracy. Monumental architecture, gold- and bronzework.

Archaic Colonization from Greece to Asia Minor, southern Italy, and the coasts of the Black Sea, 700–500 B.C.E. Characteristic form of government was the *polis*, a city-state dominated by landholding aristocrats or ruled by tyrants. Lyric poetry, natural philosophy.

Classical Golden age of Athenian civilization, fifth century B.C.E. Athens and other *poleis* became much more democratic. Drama, sculpture in marble and bronze, architecture (the Acropolis), philosophy, history.

Hellenistic Conquests of Alexander the Great (356–323 B.C.E.) spread Greek culture to Egypt and as far east as the Indus Valley. Decline of the *polis*. Domination of the Greek world by large monarchical states. Stoic and Epicurean philosophy, realistic sculpture, advances in mathematics and science.

Athenian plan required restraint, which was abandoned after Pericles died in 429 B.C.E. After ten years of fruitless fighting, the war ended in stalemate.

In 415 B.C.E., Alcibiades (ca. 450–404 B.C.E.), a young and ambitious kinsman of Pericles, persuaded the Athenians to invade Sicily. When the entire expedition was destroyed, Athens's power and prestige were greatly diminished. Subjects of Athens's empire rebelled, and Sparta reopened the war—with Persian aid.

The Athenians fought on and won several important victories at sea, but their resources steadily diminished. When their fleet was destroyed at Aegospotami in 405 B.C.E., they could not rebuild it. The Spartans, under Lysander (d. 395 B.C.E.), blockaded Athens and cut off its food supply. In 404 B.C.E., Athens surrendered unconditionally.

STRUGGLE FOR GREEK LEADERSHIP

The collapse of the Athenian Empire opened the way for Spartan dominance of the Aegean. Lysander installed boards of ten local oligarchs loyal to him and supported by Spartan garrisons in most of the cities along the European coast and the islands of the Aegean. These tributaries brought Sparta almost as much revenue as the Athenians had collected.

Some of Sparta's allies, especially Thebes and Corinth, were alienated by Sparta's increasingly arrogant policies. The oligarchic government that Lysander installed in Athens in 404 B.C.E. came to be called the "Thirty Tyrants" by Athenians who resented its heavy-handed policies. When supporters of democracy fled to Thebes and Corinth and recruited an army to challenge the oligarchs' hold on Athens, Sparta's conservative king, Pausanias, arranged a peaceful settlement and the restoration of democracy. Thereafter, Athenian foreign policy remained under Spartan control, but otherwise Athens was free.

In 405 B.C.E. Greek mercenaries recruited with Spartan help intervened in Persia on behalf of Cyrus the Younger, who was contesting the accession to the Persian throne of his brother Artaxerxes II (r. 404–358 B.C.E.). The Greeks marched inland to

((•─[**Hear** the **Audio**

The Persian and Peloponnesian War 492–404 B.C.E. at **myhistorylab.com**

((•─[**Hear** the **Audio** at **myhistorylab.com**

View the Image
The Parthenon at **myhistorylab.com**

Read the Document
Greece and Persia: The Treaty of
Antalcides, 387 B.C.E.
at **myhistorylab.com**

Study and Review
Comparing Athens and Sparta
(5th century B.C.E.) at **myhistorylab.com**

Mesopotamia, defeating the Persians at Cunaxa in 401 B.C.E. Cyrus was killed, however, and the Greeks marched back to the Black Sea and safety. Their success revealed the potential weakness of the Persian Empire.

The Greeks of Asia Minor had supported Cyrus and were now afraid of Artaxerxes' revenge. The Spartans accepted their request for aid and sent an army into Asia, attracted by the prospect of prestige, power, and money. In 396 B.C.E. the command of this army was given to Sparta's new king, Agesilaus (444–360 B.C.E.), whose aggressive policy was to dominate Sparta until his death.

The Persians responded to Agesilaus's plundering army by seeking assistance among Greek states disaffected with Spartan domination, offering them money and other support. Thebes forged an alliance with Argos, Corinth, and Athens and engaged Sparta in the Corinthian War (395–387 B.C.E.), ending Sparta's Asian adventure. In 394 B.C.E. the Persian fleet destroyed Sparta's maritime empire. Athens, meanwhile, had rebuilt its walls, resurrected its navy, and recovered some of its lost empire. The Persians, who dictated the terms of the peace that ended the Corinthian War to the exhausted Greeks, were alarmed by this Athenian recovery and turned the management of Greece over to Sparta.

Sparta's actions grew increasingly arrogant and lawless. Agesilaus broke up all alliances except the Peloponnesian League and put friends in power in several Greek cities. In 382 B.C.E. Sparta seized Thebes during peacetime without warning or pretext. In 379 B.C.E. a Spartan army made a similar attempt on Athens. That action persuaded the Athenians to join with Thebes, which had rebelled from Sparta a few months earlier. In 371 B.C.E. the Thebans defeated the Spartans at Leuctra. They then encouraged the Arcadian cities of the central Peloponnesus to form a federal league and freed the Helots, helping them found a city of their own. Sparta's population had been shrinking so that it could field an army of fewer than 2,000 men at Leuctra. Now, hemmed in by hostile neighbors, deprived of much of its farmland and of the slaves who had worked it, Sparta ceased to be a first-rank power. Its aggressive policies had led to ruin.

For a short time, Thebes held power, thanks to its democratic constitution, its control over Boeotia, and two outstanding generals, Pelopidas (d. 364 B.C.E.) and Epaminondas (d. 362 B.C.E.). Under their leadership Thebes challenged the reborn Athenian Empire in the Aegean. But by 362 B.C.E. Thebes faced a Peloponnesian coalition as well as Athens. When Epaminondas was killed in battle, Theban dominance came to an end.

In 378 B.C.E. Athens organized a second confederation aimed at resisting Spartan aggression in the Aegean. The collapse of Sparta and Thebes removed the rationale for membership, so Athens's allies revolted. By 355 B.C.E. Athens had to abandon most of the empire. After two centuries of almost constant warfare, the Greeks returned to the chaotic disorganization that had characterized the era before the founding of the Peloponnesian League.

CLASSICAL CULTURE

The term *classical* often suggests calm and serenity, but the word that best describes Greek life, thought, art, and literature during the Classical period is *tension*. Among the achievements of this era (discussed in Chapter 2) were the philosophical works

CHRONOLOGY

SPARTAN AND THEBAN HEGEMONIES

404–403 B.C.E.	Thirty Tyrants rule at Athens
401 B.C.E.	Expedition of Cyrus, rebellious prince of Persia; Battle of Cunaxa
400–387 B.C.E.	Spartan War against Persia
398–360 B.C.E.	Reign of Agesilaus at Sparta
395–387 B.C.E.	Corinthian War
382 B.C.E.	Sparta seizes Thebes
378 B.C.E.	Second Athenian Confederation founded
371 B.C.E.	Thebans defeat Sparta at Leuctra; end of Spartan hegemony
362 B.C.E.	Battle of Mantinea; end of Theban hegemony

of Socrates (469–399 B.C.E.), Plato (ca. 427–347 B.C.E.), and Aristotle (384–322 B.C.E.). The same curiosity about the nature and place in the universe of human beings that motivated the philosophers also animated the arts of the period.

Two sources of tension contributed to the artistic outpouring of fifth century B.C.E. Greece. One was the conflict between the Greeks' pride in their accomplishments and their concern that overreaching would bring retribution. The second was the conflict between the hopes and achievements of individuals and the claims and limits put on them by their fellow citizens in the *polis*. These tensions were felt throughout Greece. They had the most spectacular consequences, however, in Athens in its Golden Age between the Persian and Peloponnesian wars.

Nothing reflects these concerns better than Attic (Athenian) tragedy, which emerged in the fifth century B.C.E. The tragedies were selected in a contest and presented in a large theater as part of public religious observations in honor of the god Dionysus. Most Attic tragedy was based on mythological subjects and dealt solemnly with religion, politics, ethics, or morality. The plays of the dramatists Aeschylus (525–456 B.C.E.) and Sophocles (ca. 496–406 B.C.E.) follow this pattern. The later plays of Euripides (ca. 480–406 B.C.E.) are more concerned with individual psychology.

Comedy was introduced into the Dionysian festival early in the fifth century B.C.E. The great master of the genre called Old Comedy, Aristophanes (ca. 450–385 B.C.E.), wrote political comedies filled with scathing invective and political satire.

Beginning in 448 B.C.E., Pericles undertook a great building program on the Acropolis with funds from the empire. The new buildings visually projected Athenian greatness, emphasizing the city's intellectual and artistic achievements and providing tangible proof that Athens was the intellectual center of Greece.

The first prose history ever written was a description of the Persian War by Herodotus (ca. 484–ca. 425 B.C.E.), "the father of history." His account attempts to explain human actions and draw instruction from them. He claimed that the Greek *polis* inspired voluntary obedience to the law in its citizen soldiers, whereas fear of punishment motivated the Persians.

Thucydides, the historian of the Peloponnesian War, was born about 460 B.C.E. and died about 400 B.C.E. He believed that human nature was essentially unchanging, so that a wise person, equipped with an understanding of history, might foresee events and guide them.

As the power of the *poleis* waned after the Great Peloponnesian War, some Greeks tried to shore up its weakening institutions. Others looked for radical alternatives; and still others turned their back on public life altogether. All these attitudes are reflected in the literature, philosophy, and art of the period.

View the **Image**
The Athenian Acropolis at **myhistorylab.com**

Read the **Document**
Antigone (442 B.C.E.) and Drama: Antigone, by Sophocles, ca. 441 B.C.E. and Sophocles, from Antigone at **myhistorylab.com**

The tendency to forsake the public for the private sphere is clear in a new genre that emerged in the fourth century B.C.E.: Middle Comedy. Old Comedy had dealt amusingly with serious subjects, but the themes of Middle Comedy were ordinary daily life, intrigue, and domestic satire. This tendency was magnified in New Comedy, which focused entirely on domestic scenes, the foibles of ordinary people, and the travails of lovers. The art of tragedy declined, but the great works of the previous century were revived, and Euripides, who had explored the psyches of individual characters, found his most appreciative audiences.

Fourth-century sculpture reflects the same movement away from the grand, the ideal, and the general toward the ordinary, the real, and the individual.

EMERGENCE OF THE HELLENISTIC WORLD

WHY DID Alexander the Great become an almost mythological figure?

The term *Hellenistic* was coined in the nineteenth century to describe a period of three centuries during which Greek culture spread from its homeland to Egypt and far into Asia. The result was a new civilization that combined Greek and Asian elements. The Hellenistic world was larger than the world of classical Greece, and its major political units were much larger than the *poleis*, although these endured in modified forms. Hellenistic civilization had its roots in the rise to power of a dynasty in Macedonia whose armies conquered Greece and the Persian Empire in the space of two generations.

MACEDONIAN CONQUEST

The kingdom of Macedon, north of Thessaly, had long served as a buffer between the Greek states and barbarian tribes farther to the north. The Macedonians were of the same stock as the Greeks and spoke a Greek dialect. By Greek standards, however, Macedon was semibarbaric. Constant internal conflict prevented Macedon from playing much of a part in Greek affairs up to the fourth century B.C.E., but once Macedon was unified under a strong king, that changed.

Philip II of Macedon (r. 359–336 B.C.E.), like many of his predecessors, admired Greek culture. He was talented in war and diplomacy and had boundless ambition. After he won control of a lucrative gold and silver mining region, he used his resources to turn his army into the finest fighting force in the world.

In 340 B.C.E., Philip besieged Perinthus and Byzantium, the lifeline of Athenian commerce. The Athenian fleet saved both cities, so Philip instead marched directly into Greece, and in 338 B.C.E., he defeated Athens and Thebes in Boeotia. Freedom and autonomy ended for the Greek *polis*. *Poleis* retained their institutions and control over their internal affairs for some time, but new political realities began to chart Greece's future.

ALEXANDER'S CONQUESTS

Philip was assassinated in 336 B.C.E., as he prepared to invade Persia. Philip's son, Alexander III (356–323 B.C.E.), later called Alexander the Great, succeeded his father at the age of 20 and inherited his plans for the conquest of Persia.

CHRONOLOGY

RISE OF MACEDON

359–336 B.C.E.	Reign of Philip II
338 B.C.E.	Battle of Chaeronea; Philip conquers Greece; founding of League of Corinth
336–323 B.C.E.	Reign of Alexander III, the Great
334 B.C.E.	Alexander invades Asia
333 B.C.E.	Battle of Issus
331 B.C.E.	Battle of Gaugamela
330 B.C.E.	Fall of Persepolis
327 B.C.E.	Alexander reaches Indus valley
323 B.C.E.	Death of Alexander

The usurper Cyrus and his Greek mercenaries had shown the vast and wealthy Persian
Empire to be vulnerable when they penetrated
deep into its interior early in the fourth century B.C.E. In 334 B.C.E. Alexander crossed the
Hellespont into Asia. His army consisted of
about 30,000 infantry and 5,000 cavalry; he
had no navy and little money. Consequently
he sought quick and decisive battles to gain
money and supplies from the conquered territory. To neutralize the Persian navy he moved
along the coast, depriving it of ports.

Alexander met the Persian forces of
Asia Minor at the Granicus River (see Map
3–4 on page 82), where he won a smashing

Alexander and Darius. King Darius III
looks back in distress as Alexander advances against his vanguard during the
battle of Issus, as depicted in a Roman
mosaic from the first century B.C.E.

**Do you think a Persian king with a different
personality could have resisted Alexander?**

victory in characteristic style: He led a cavalry charge across the river into the teeth of the
enemy on the opposite bank, almost losing his life in the process and winning the devotion of his soldiers. With the coast of Asia Minor now open, Alexander captured the
coastal cities, denying them to the Persian fleet.

In 333 B.C.E. Alexander marched inland to Syria, meeting the main Persian army
under King Darius III (r. 336–330 B.C.E.) at Issus. Alexander himself led the cavalry
charge that broke the Persian line and sent Darius fleeing to the east. Alexander continued along the coast and captured previously impregnable Tyre after a long and ingenious siege, putting an end to the threat of the Persian navy. He took Egypt with
little trouble and was greeted as liberator, pharaoh, and son of the Egyptian god Re.
While Alexander was at Tyre, Darius offered him his daughter and his entire empire
west of the Euphrates River in exchange for an alliance and an end to the invasion. But
Alexander wanted the whole empire and probably whatever lay beyond that.

In the spring of 331 B.C.E. Alexander marched into Mesopotamia. At
Gaugamela, near the ancient Assyrian city of Nineveh, he met Darius, ready for a last
stand. Once again, Alexander's tactical genius and personal leadership carried the day.
The Persians were broken and Darius fled once more. Alexander entered Babylon,
again hailed as liberator and king. In January of 330 B.C.E. he came to Persepolis, the
Persian capital, which held splendid palaces and the royal treasury. This bonanza ended
his financial troubles and put a vast sum of money into circulation, with economic
consequences that lasted for centuries. After a stay of several months, Alexander
burned Persepolis to dramatize the destruction of the native Persian Dynasty and the
completion of Hellenic revenge for the earlier Persian invasion of Greece.

Setting off after Darius, Alexander found him, dead, just south of the Caspian
Sea. He had been murdered and replaced by his relative Bessus, with the support of the
Persian nobility. Alexander soon captured Bessus. This pursuit, and his own great cu-
riosity and desire to see the most distant places, took Alexander to the frontier of India.

Near Samarkand, in the land of the Scythians, he founded the city of Alexandria
Eschate ("Furthest Alexandria"), one of the many cities bearing his name that he
founded as he traveled. As a part of his grand scheme of amalgamation and conquest,
he married the Bactrian princess Roxane and enrolled 30,000 young Bactrians to be
trained for his army.

In 327 B.C.E. Alexander took his army through the Khyber Pass to conquer the
lands around the Indus River (modern Pakistan). Reducing the region's king, Porus, to

•◆•⌐Read the **Document**
Plutarch on Alexander the Great (1st century B.C.E.) at **myhistorylab.com**

MAP 3–4. Alexander's Campaigns. The route taken by Alexander the Great in his conquest of the Persian Empire, 334–323 B.C.E. Starting from the Macedonian capital at Pella, he reached the Indus valley before being turned back by his own restive troops. He died of fever in Mesopotamia.

What are some factors that contributed to the breaking up of Alexander's empire after his death?

vassalage, he pushed on in the hope of reaching the river called Ocean that the Greeks believed encircled the world. Finally his weary men refused to go on. By the spring of 324 B.C.E. the army was back at the Persian Gulf, celebrating Macedonian style with a wild spree of drinking.

DEATH OF ALEXANDER

Alexander had great plans for the future: for the consolidation and organization of his empire; for geographic exploration; for new cities, roads, and harbors; perhaps even for further conquests in the West. There is some evidence that he asked to be deified and worshiped as a god. But in June 323 B.C.E. he got sick and died in Babylon at the age of 33. He quickly entered myth and legend, and a debate began about his goals, his personality, and his achievements that has continued to the present day.

Alexander was childless, and he made no arrangements for a successor. After prolonged warfare, three of his generals founded dynasties that continued the spread of Hellenistic culture:

- Ptolemy I, ca. 367–283 B.C.E.; founder of the Thirty-First Dynasty in Egypt, the Ptolemies, of whom Cleopatra, who died in 30 B.C.E., was the last

- Seleucus I, ca. 358–280 B.C.E.; founder of the Seleucid Dynasty in Mesopotamia

- Antigonus I, 382–301 B.C.E.; founder of the Antigonid Dynasty in Asia Minor and Macedon

For seventy-five years or so, the world ruled by Alexander's successors enjoyed prosperity. The vast sums of money he and they had put into circulation increased economic activity. The opening of vast new territories to Greek trade and the increased demand for Greek products helped stimulate commerce. The new prosperity, however, was not evenly distributed. The urban Greeks, the Macedonians, and the Hellenized natives who made up the upper and middle classes lived in comfort and even luxury, but native peasants did not.

Eventually, war and inflation produced economic crises. The kings bore down heavily, but the middle classes skillfully avoided their exactions, and peasants and city laborers reacted by slowing work and striking. In Greece, economic pressures led to civil wars. These internal difficulties made the Hellenistic kingdoms vulnerable to attack, and by the middle of the second century B.C.E. Rome had absorbed all of them except for Egypt. The two centuries of Hellenistic rule had, however, promoted economic and cultural cohesion throughout the eastern Mediterranean coast, Greece, Egypt, Mesopotamia, and the old Persian Empire.

HELLENISTIC CULTURE

Alexander's conquests and the establishment of the successor kingdoms, by ending the central role of the *polis* in Greek life and thought, marked a significant turning point in Greek literature, philosophy, religion, and art.

Deprived of control of their foreign affairs, their important internal arrangements determined by a foreign monarch, the postclassical cities lost the kind of political freedom that was basic to the old outlook. They were cities, but not *poleis*. As time passed they lost their sovereignty, becoming municipalities within military empires. For the most part, the Greeks after Alexander turned inward, away from politics, to address their hopes and fears. The confident, sometimes arrogant, humanism of the fifth century B.C.E. gave way to a kind of resignation to fate, a recognition of helplessness before forces too great for humans to manage.

QUICK REVIEW

Alexander's Leadership

- Alexander displayed tactical genius in military conflict
- Alexander's charisma attracted followers
- Marriage to a Bactrian princess exemplified Alexander's policies for integrating conquered peoples
- Alexander died without an heir or a plan for his successor

Read the **Document**

Descriptions of Alexandria, Egypt (1st century C.E.) at **myhistorylab.com**

See the **Map**

The Conquests of Alexander the Great at **myhistorylab.com**

HOW DID the Hellenistic world influence Western culture?

PHILOSOPHY

These developments are noticeable in the changes that overtook the established schools of philosophy as well as in the emergence of two new and influential groups of philosophers, the Epicureans and the Stoics.

Plato's Academy and Aristotle's Lyceum (see Chapter 2) continued to operate, reinforcing Athens's position as the center of philosophical studies. The Lyceum turned gradually away from Aristotle's universal investigations to become a center of literary and historical studies. The Academy turned even further from its founder's tradition, adopting the philosophical approach known as skepticism, established by Pyrrho of Elis (ca. 365–275 B.C.E.). The Skeptics thought that nothing could be known and so consoled themselves by suggesting that nothing mattered. It was easy for them, therefore, to accept conventional morality and the world as it was. The Cynics continued to denounce convention and to advocate a crude life in accordance with nature. Neither of these views had much appeal to the middle-class city dweller of the third century B.C.E., who sought some basis for choosing a way of life now that the *polis* no longer provided one ready-made.

Epicurus of Athens (342–271 B.C.E.), who founded a school in that city in 306 B.C.E., formulated a philosophy in keeping with the new mood. The goal of this philosophy was not knowledge but happiness, which Epicurus believed could be achieved through a life based on reason. Accepting the description of the physical universe proposed by the atomists Democritus and Leucippus (see Chapter 2), the **Epicureans** took sense perception to be the basis of all human knowledge. According to Epicurus, atoms were continually falling through the void and giving off images in direct contact with the senses. These falling atoms could swerve in an arbitrary, unpredictable way to produce the combinations seen in the world. When a person died, the atoms that composed the body dispersed so that the person had no further existence or perception and therefore nothing to fear after death. The gods, according to Epicurus, took no interest in human affairs. This belief amounted to a practical atheism, and the Epicureans were often thought to be atheists.

The purpose of Epicurean physics was to liberate people from the fear of death, the gods, and the supernatural. Epicurean ethics were hedonistic, identifying happiness with pleasure. But *pleasure* for Epicurus was chiefly negative: the absence of pain and trouble. The goal of the Epicureans was *ataraxia*, the condition of being undisturbed, without trouble, pain, or responsibility. To achieve it, one should ideally have sufficient means to withdraw from worldly affairs; Epicurus even advised against marriage and children. He preached a life of genteel, restrained selfishness, which might appeal to intellectuals of means but was not calculated to be widely attractive.

The Stoic school, established by Zeno of Citium (335–263 B.C.E.) soon after Epicurus began teaching, took its name from the Stoa Poikile, or Painted Portico, in the Athenian Agora, where Zeno and his disciples met. Like the Epicureans, the **Stoics** sought the happiness of the individual; but unlike Epicurean philosophy, Stoic philosophy was almost indistinguishable from religion. The Stoics believed that god and nature are the same and that humans must live in harmony within themselves and with nature. The guiding principle in nature is divine reason, (**logos**), or fire. Every human has a spark of this divinity, and after death it returns to the eternal Divine

One of the Masterpieces of Hellenistic Sculpture, the *Laocoön*. This is a Roman copy. According to legend, Laocoön was a priest who warned the Trojans not to take the Greeks' wooden horse within their city. This sculpture depicts his punishment. Great serpents sent by the goddess Athena, who was on the side of the Greeks, devoured Laocoön and his sons before the horrified people of Troy.

Laocoön, Vatican Museums, Vatican State. Copyright Giraudon/Art Resource, New York.

What message do you think a viewer was meant to take from looking at this statue?

Epicureans

School of philosophy founded by Epicurus of Athens (342–271 B.C.E.). It sought to liberate people from fear of death and the supernatural by teaching that the gods took no interest in human affairs and that true happiness consisted in pleasure, which was defined as the absence of pain.

Stoics

A philosophical school founded by Zeno of Citium (335–263 B.C.E.) that taught that humans could be happy only with natural law.

logos

Divine reason, or fire, which according to the Stoics, was the guiding principle in nature.

Spirit. From time to time the world is destroyed by fire, from the ashes of which a new world arises.

Human happiness, according to the Stoics, lies in the virtuous life, lived in accordance with natural law, in which "all actions promote the harmony of the spirit dwelling in the individual man with the will of him who orders the universe."

Only the wise—who know what is good, what is evil, and what is "indifferent"—can live such a life. Good and evil are dispositions of the mind or soul. Thus prudence, justice, courage, and temperance are good, whereas folly, injustice, and cowardice are evil. Life, health, pleasure, beauty, strength, wealth, and so on are neutral—morally "indifferent." The source of misery is passion, a disease of the soul and an irrational mental contraction that arises from morally indifferent things. The goal of the wise is *apatheia*, or freedom from passion.

With their striving for inner harmony and a life lived in accordance with the Divine Will, their fatalistic attitude, and their goal a form of apathy, the Stoics fit the post-Alexandrian world well. The spread of Stoicism eased the creation of a new political system that relied on the docile submission, not the active participation, of the governed.

LITERATURE

The literary center of the Hellenistic world in the third and second centuries B.C.E. was Alexandria, Egypt. There, Egypt's Hellenistic rulers, the Ptolemies, had founded a museum—a great research institute where royal funds supported scientists and scholars—and a library with almost half a million books. The library housed much of the great body of past Greek literature, most of which has since been lost. Alexandrian scholars had what they judged to be the best works copied, editing and criticizing them from the point of view of language, form, and content, and writing biographies of the authors. It is to this work that we owe the preservation of most of what remains to us of ancient literature.

The scholarly atmosphere of Alexandria stimulated the study of history and its ancillary discipline, chronology. Eratosthenes (ca. 275–195 B.C.E.) developed a chronology of important events since the Trojan War, and others undertook similar tasks. Contemporaries of Alexander, such as Ptolemy I (d. 284 B.C.E.), Aristobulus, and Nearchus, wrote apparently sober, factual accounts of his career. The fragments we have of the work of most Hellenistic historians suggest that they emphasized sensational and biographical detail over the rigorous, impersonal analysis characteristic of Thucydides.

ARCHITECTURE AND SCULPTURE

The Hellenistic monarchies greatly increased the opportunities open to architects and sculptors. Money was plentiful, rulers sought outlets for conspicuous display, new cities needed to be built and beautified, and the well-to-do created an increasing demand for objects of art. New cities were usually laid out on the grid plan introduced in the fifth century B.C.E. by Hippodamus of Miletus. Temples were built on the classical model, and the covered portico, or *stoa*, became a very popular addition to Hellenistic agoras.

Reflecting the cosmopolitan nature of the Hellenistic world, leading sculptors accepted commissions wherever they were attractive. The result was a certain uniformity, although Alexandria, Rhodes, and the kingdom of Pergamum in Asia Minor developed distinctive styles. In general, Hellenistic sculpture continued the trend that emerged in the fourth century B.C.E. toward the sentimental, emotional, and realistic

•••◖Read the **Document**

The Conquests of Alexander the Great
(1st century B.C.E.) at **myhistorylab.com**

A Page from *On Floating Bodies.*
Archimedes' work was covered by a tenth-century manuscript, but ultraviolet radiation reveals the original text and drawings underneath.

What scientific documents from our time do you think will be preserved?

and away from the balanced tension and idealism of the fifth century B.C.E. The characteristics of Hellenistic sculpture are readily apparent in the *Laocoön*, carved at Rhodes in the second century B.C.E.

MATHEMATICS AND SCIENCE

Among the most spectacular intellectual accomplishments of the Hellenistic Age were those in mathematics and science. Indeed, Alexandrian scholars were responsible for most of the scientific knowledge available to the West until the scientific revolution of the sixteenth and seventeenth centuries C.E.

Euclid's *Elements* (written early in the third century B.C.E.) is still the foundation for courses in plane and solid geometry. Archimedes of Syracuse (ca. 287–212 B.C.E.), who also made advances in geometry, established the theory of the lever in mechanics and invented hydrostatics.

Advances in mathematics, when applied to Babylonian astronomical tables available to Hellenistic scholars, spurred great progress in astronomy. As early as the fourth century B.C.E. Heraclides of Pontus (ca. 390–310 B.C.E.) had argued that Mercury and Venus circulate around the sun and not the Earth. He appears to have made other suggestions leading in the direction of a **heliocentric theory** of the universe. Aristarchus of Samos (ca. 310–230 B.C.E.) asserted that the sun, along with the other fixed stars, did not move and that the Earth revolved around the sun in a circular orbit and rotated on its axis while doing so. The heliocentric theory, however, did not take hold. Hipparchus of Nicaea (b. ca. 190 B.C.E.) constructed an ingenious and complicated geocentric model of the universe that did a good job of accounting for the movements of the sun, the moon, and the planets. Ptolemy of Alexandria (second century C.E.) adopted Hipparchus's system with a few improvements, and it remained dominant until the work of Copernicus, in the sixteenth century C.E.

Hellenistic scientists made progress in mapping the Earth as well as the sky. Eratosthenes of Cyrene (ca. 275–195 B.C.E.) accurately calculated the circumference of the Earth and wrote a treatise on geography based on mathematical and physical reasoning and the reports of travelers. Eratosthenes' map was in many ways more accurate than a later one, created by Ptolemy, which became standard during the Middle Ages.

heliocentric theory
The theory, now universally accepted, that the Earth and the other planets revolve around the sun. First proposed by Aristarchos of Samos (310–230 B.C.E.).

SUMMARY

 WHAT WERE the defining qualities of Minoan, Mycenaean, and Homeric Greek society?

Minoans, Mycenaeans, and Greek "Middle Age" to ca. 750 B.C.E. In the Minoan and Mycenaean periods, the Greek states were ruled by powerful kings supported by elaborate bureaucracies. The Mycenaean culture was militaristic, in contrast to that of the Minoans. Invaders from the north destroyed Mycenaean civilization around 1150 B.C.E. Homer's epic poems describe a society that emphasized honor. *page 60*

 WHY WAS the *polis* the most characteristic Greek institution?

The *Polis* in the Expanding Greek World. By 750 B.C.E., during the Archaic period, Greek society took its characteristic form: the *polid* (plural *poleis*), a self-governing city-state. The Greek innovations that continue to influence our world, including democracy and Greek philosophy, developed in the *poleis*. The most important *poleis* were Athens and Sparta. At first governed by landowning aristocrats, then by tyrants, many *poleis* evolved more democratic forms of government by 500 B.C.E. In an effort to avoid the pressures of overpopulation and land hunger, the Greeks established colonies around the shores of the Mediterranean and Black seas. *page 64*

 WHAT FEATURES distinguished Archaic Greek society?

Life in Archaic Greece. Most Greeks were hardworking farmers, a way of life described by Hesiod. The Greeks were polytheists who worshiped a pantheon of twelve gods. Cults gained importance. Literacy and poetry were important elements of Archaic culture. *page 67*

 HOW WERE the Greeks able to defeat the Persians?

Sparta and Athens. The policies and conflicts of Greece's two most significant *poleis*, Sparta and Athens, shaped Greek history. Alliances and military actions—the Persian War, the Peloponnesian Wars, and other conflicts—interacted with the internal politics and the social development of Greek states. Naval battles were decisive in defeating the Persians. *page 69*

 WHAT WERE the main cultural achievements of Classical Greece?

Classical Greece. After defeating two Persian attempts to conquer them in the early fifth century B.C.E., the Greeks entered their Golden Age. Among the accomplishments of Greek artists, writers, and thinkers were tragedy and comedy, secular history, and systematic logic, all of which still influence Western art and thought. *page 73*

 WHY DID Alexander the Great become an almost mythological figure?

Emergence of the Hellenistic World. Macedon under Philip II (r. 359–336 B.C.E.) and Alexander the Great (r. 336–323 B.C.E.) came to dominate first Greece and then all the Near East from Asia Minor to northern India. Daring and dashing, Alexander conquered vast territories. He died while he was still formulating plans for how to administer his empire, leaving his legacy open to interpretation. *page 80*

HOW DID the Hellenistic world influence Western culture?

Hellenistic Culture. Alexander's conquests spread Greek culture over a wide area and ushered in the Hellenistic era. Hellenistic scholars made Greek literature and science available to many different peoples who adopted it as their own. The Romans spread Hellenistic culture across the Mediterranean world and transmitted it to later generations in the West. *page 84*

KEY TERMS

Acropolis (uh-KRAH-puh-liss) (p. 65)

agora (AG-ehr-uh) (p. 65)

Areopagus (are-ee-OH-pag-uhs) (p. 70)

Delian (DEEL-yuhn) League (p. 73)

Epicureans (ehp-ih-KYOOR-ee-uhns) (p. 84)

heliocentric theory (p. 86)

Helots (HEH-lohtz) (p. 69)

hoplite phalanx (HOP-lahyt FAY-langks) (p. 65)

the *Iliad* (ILL-ee-uhd) and the *Odyssey* (p. 63)

logos (LOW-gos) (p. 84)

Magna Graecia (MAHG-nuh GREE-shuh) (p. 65)

Minoan (mih-NOH-uhn) (p. 60)

Mycenaean (mahy-sin-NEE-uhn) (p. 61)

Panhellenic (*PAN-huh-LAYN-ick*) (p. 67)

Peloponnesian (PEL-uh-puh-NEE-zhun) War (p. 75)

Stoics (*STOW-icks*) (p. 84)

symposion (sihm-POE-see-ON) (p. 68)

REVIEW QUESTIONS

1. Describe the Minoan civilization of Crete. How did the later Bronze Age Mycenaean civilization differ from the Minoan civilization in political organization, art motifs, and military posture? How valuable are the Homeric epics as sources of early Greek history?

2. Define the concept of *polis*. What role did geography play in its development, and why did the Greeks consider it a unique and valuable institution?

3. Compare the fundamental political, social, and economic institutions of Athens and Sparta about 500 B.C.E. Why did Sparta develop its unique form of government? What were the main stages in the transformation of Athens from an aristocratic state to a democracy between 600 and 500 B.C.E.?

4. Why did the Greeks and Persians go to war in 490 and 480 B.C.E.? What benefit could the Persians have derived from conquering Greece? Why were the Greeks able to defeat the Persians, and how did they benefit from the victory?

5. How was the Delian League transformed into the Athenian Empire during the fifth century B.C.E.? Did the empire offer any advantages to its subjects? Why was there such resistance to Athenian efforts to unify the Greek world in the fifth and fourth centuries B.C.E.?

6. Why did Athens and Sparta come to blows in the Great Peloponnesian War? What was each side's strategy for victory? Why did Sparta win the war?

7. Using examples from art, literature, and philosophy, explain the tension that characterized Greek life and thought in the Classical period.

8. Between 431 and 362 B.C.E. Athens, Sparta, and Thebes each tried to impose hegemony over the city-states of Greece, but none succeeded for long. Why did each state fail? How was Philip II of Macedon able to conquer Greece? Does more of the credit for Philip's success lie in Macedon's strength or in the weakness of the Greek city-states? What does your analysis reveal about the components of successful rule?

9. What were the major consequences of Alexander's death? Assess the achievements of Alexander. Was he a conscious promoter of Greek civilization or just an egomaniac drunk with a lust for conquest?

Note: To learn more about the topics in this chapter, please turn to the Suggested Readings at the end of the book. For additional sources related to this chapter please see www.myhistorylab.com

PEARSON
myhistorylab Connections

Reinforce what you learned in this chapter by studying the many documents, images, maps, review tools, and videos available at **www.myhistorylab.com**

Read and Review

✓•-[Study and Review   Chapter 3

•••-[Read the Document   *Homer, Debate Among the Greeks, from The Odyssey, p. 63*
Education and the Family in Sparta, ca. 100 C.E., p. 69
Plutarch on Life in Sparta (1st century B.C.E.), p. 70
Aristotle, The Creation of the Democracy in Athens, p. 71
Herodotus, Histories (400 B.C.E.), p. 73
Plutarch on Alexander the Great (1st century B.C.E.), p. 81
Greece and Persia: The Treaty of Antalcides, 387 B.C.E., p. 78
Antigone (442 B.C.E.) and Drama: Antigone, by Sophocles, ca. 441 B.C.E. and Sophocles, from Antigone, p. 79
Descriptions of Alexandria, Egypt (1st century C.E.), p. 83
The Conquests of Alexander the Great (1st century B.C.E.), p. 85

👁-[See the Map   *The Greek World, p. 59*
Mycenean Trade and Contacts, p. 63
Greece in the Archaic and Classical Ages, ca. 750–350 B.C.E., p. 65
The Peloponnesian War, p. 76
The Conquests of Alexander the Great, p. 83

☀-[View the Image   *The Toreador Fresco, Knossos, ca. 1500 B.C.E. Archeological Museum, Herakleion, p. 60*
Tomb Mask, Mycenaen, p. 62
The Parthenon, p. 78
The Athenian Acropolis, p. 79

((•●-[Hear the Audio   *The Persian and Peloponnesian War 492–404 B.C.E., p. 77*

✓-[Study and Review   *Comparing Athens and Sparta (5th c. B.C.E.), p. 78*

Research and Explore

👁-[See the Map   *Greece and Greek Colonies of the World, ca. 431 B.C.E., p. 70*

👁-[See the Map   *Greek and Phoenician Colonies and Trade*

((•●-[Hear the **Audio**

Hear the audio file for Chapter 3
at **www.myhistorylab.com**

4

West Asia, Inner Asia, and South Asia to 1000 C.E.

((•─┤Hear the **Audio** for Chapter 4 at www.myhistorylab.com

The Bodhisattva Avalokiteshvara. Detail of a Buddhist wall painting from the cave shrines at Ajanta (Maharashtra, India), Gupta period, ca. 475 C.E. Avalokiteshvara (known in China as Kwan-yin and in Japan as Kannon) is the bodhisattva of infinite mercy.

Why were *bodhisattvas* important to Mahayana Buddhists?

WEST AND INNER ASIA

WHAT WERE the main teachings of Zoroaster, and how did Zoroastrianism influence other traditions?

HOW DID the steppe peoples act as vehicles for cultural exchange?

HOW DID the Sasanids build a strong state?

SOUTH ASIA

HOW WAS the Maurya Empire created?

WHAT ROLES did Buddhism play in post-Maurya Indian culture?

WHY IS the Gupta Empire considered a high point of Indian civilization?

From the Mediterranean to China, the period from about 600 B.C.E. to the rise of Islam in the seventh century C.E. saw centralized empires flourish on an unprecedented scale—a development in which Iran and India preceded both China and the Roman West. Starting in the third millennium B.C.E., the Elamites (ca. 2700–639 B.C.E.), Achaemenids (ca. 539–330 B.C.E.), Seleucids (312–125 B.C.E.), Arsacids (c. 247 B.C.E.–233 C.E.), and Sasanids (224–651 C.E.) incorporated the Iranian plateau in their domains. Farther east, the Mauryas founded the first great Indian Empire (ca. 321–185 B.C.E.), followed by the Guptas (ca. 320–550 C.E.). Many of these empires built sophisticated bureaucracies, professional armies, and strong communication systems; they also facilitated or contributed to new cultural, political, and religious developments in their domains.

INDO-IRANIAN ROLES IN THE EURASIAN WORLD BEFORE ISLAM

The period of more than a millennium before the rise of Islam in the central lands of the Eurasian world is often thought of as dominated by the great empires of the Roman-Byzantine world and Han China. In global perspective, however, they had worthy counterparts in four empires in the Indo-Iranian world of West, Inner (Central), and South Asia between the Mediterranean and East Asia. In their heydays, the Achaemenids and Sasanids in Iran and the Mauryas and Guptas in India displayed the cultural vibrancy, economic prosperity, and wide dominion historically characteristic of all powerful imperial dynasties. They also built impressive road systems and played important roles in both linking the Roman, Byzantine, and African worlds with those of East and Southeast Asia, and in spreading Manichaean, Nestorian Christian, and, most importantly, Buddhist traditions across Asia.

In the West, Roman civilization had, by the third century C.E., its chief locus in regions east and south of Rome, while in Europe it endured more as a legacy coexisting uneasily with traditions of Germanic invaders. Roman imperial power had shifted east to Byzantium, where political and cultural traditions were under marked influences from Africa and West Asia. Alexandria, at the mouth of the Nile, was long the center of Hellenistic civilization, and the major Christian doctrinal coun-

cils were held in Asia. The post-Alexander states of West and Inner Asia and northwest India were important cultural melting pots and loci of contacts with the Greco-Roman "West," the Mesopotamian-Iranian world, the rest of India, and the Chinese "East." Other developments of major global importance also had their origin or locus in the Indo-Iranian world in these centuries: the Sasanid revival of imperial power and Zoroastrian religion, the rise and spread from North Africa to western China of the Manichaean movement, the completion of world masterpieces in the Sanskrit epics of the *Mahabharata* and *Ramayana*, Gandharan and then Guptan art, Indian religious, literary, mathematical, and scientific thought, and the spread of Mahayana Buddhist traditions over Tibet and Central Asia, and to China and ultimately Japan.

In Asia this was also an era in which influential, lasting religious traditions came of age. Some spread and took root far from their regions of origin—the Christian, Buddhist, and Confucian, as well as Judaic and Hindu traditions, for example. Others, such as Zoroastrianism, never attracted a wide following outside of their homelands. Zoroastrianism, however, was especially attractive to merchants, who carried it throughout Central Asia in their travels along the old Silk Road. It won converts among other merchants from elsewhere in Asia, and, more importantly, it influenced

Three noteworthy developments characterize this period. First, the era saw sustained contact among the major centers of culture from the Mediterranean to China. Trade drove much of the contact: large-scale empires created new markets for diverse goods, both material and human (such as slaves, soldiers, and artisans).

Alexander the Great's conquest (334–323 B.C.E.) of the Persian Empire and the regions eastward to North India provided the impetus for the era's second characteristic— dramatically increased contact among diverse cultures, races, and religious traditions. Although Alexander's empire was ephemeral, his conquests ended the Achaemenid Dynasty and allowed the rising Maurya power to extend across North India. The Hellenes and steppe peoples of northeastern Iran and Central (Inner) Asia, who ruled first post-Alexandrine Iran and then post-Maurya India down to the third century C.E., inherited a much wider world than those of their original homelands.

A third characteristic of this period was the rise of major religious traditions that would influence history from Africa to China. Judaism, Christianity, Hellenistic cults, Han Confucianism and classical Daoist thought, Zoroastrianism, the Hindu tradition, and Buddhism all developed in significant ways during this period. ◼

WEST AND INNER ASIA

"Iran" designates the massive expanse of Southwest Asia bounded to the north by the Caspian and Aral seas and Jaxartes (Syr Darya) River, east by the Indus valley, south by the Arabian Sea and Persian Gulf, and west by the Tigris-Euphrates

Judaism through Babylonia (where the major recension of the Talmud was codified) and in varying degree other religious traditions of Asia and the Middle East, including the Christian, Islamic, and Buddhist.

All of these developments should indicate that the notion of the "rise of the West" as a keynote of history only holds at most for the past six centuries, not for the past three millennia. When we consider the expansion of lands, luxuries, and trade under the several Persian, Byzantine, and Indian, let alone the subsequent Islamic, empires, the European world in these centuries did not promise much as a future global center of political or cultural life. Progress and culture seemed best embodied either in Achaemenid, Maurya, Sasanid, Gupta, and Byzantine culture in West and South Asia, in China under the Han, Sui, and Tang dynasties, or in Japan in Nara and Heian times.

A more impartial perspective on these centuries identifies important centers of cultural, religious, economic, and political vitality around the globe—in West, South, and East Asia, and in Rome, Byzantium, and Aksumite Ethiopia. Societies in each of these regions, themselves products of a syncretic blending of multiple cultural traditions, were dynamic enough to influence neighboring peoples and in some cases to export their religious and cultural traditions far afield. Merchants and missionaries alike braved hazardous land and sea travel, carrying ideas as well as goods to remote lands. Wares and religious ideas passed from hand to hand and mouth to mouth on the roads and sea routes from Byzantium to China, and Africa and West Asia to India and Southeast Asia, as centers of civilization in Africa and Asia flourished.

Yet with the rise of the last monotheistic world religious tradition, Islam, Indo-Iranian lands soon faced far-reaching changes that would later come to North and East Africa and Central, South, and Southeast Asia. In the time of Chosroes Anoshirvan in the sixth century C.E., who could have suspected that within a few hundred years Persian culture would eventually be recast in Islamic forms?

Focus Questions

◆ Why is a European perspective not helpful for understanding the world in the first millennium C.E.? How does a global perspective offer a better understanding of the development of civilizations in this era?

◆ Why did this period see a significant increase in cross-cultural contacts? How were these contacts manifested? Who participated in these increased contacts?

basin and Armenia. The heart of this region is the vast Iranian plateau, bounded on all sides by great mountain ranges, and containing two large, uninhabitable salt deserts.

People clustered wherever rainfall or groundwater was plentiful and communication easiest, notably the slopes and lowlands between the Zagros, Persis (Pars, Persia), Media, Hyrcania, and Parthia. The great Asian trade routes put Iran at the heart of east–west interchange.

ANCIENT BACKGROUND AND THE FIRST PERSIAN EMPIRE IN THE IRANIAN PLATEAU (550–330 B.C.E.)

THE ELAMITES

The Elamites were a non-Semitic-speaking people who built a flourishing civilization on the eastern frontier of Mesopotamia. They were repeatedly at war with the Sumerians, Babylonians, and Assyrians from around 2700 B.C.E. until their destruction by the Assyrian emperor Asshurbanipal in 639 B.C.E., when their cities were ransacked and their soil sown with salt. Although we have tablets, monumental inscriptions, and brick imprints from Elamite remains, scholars have not determined the language group to which Elamite belongs. It did, however, long outlive the Elamite state and was one of the three official languages of the Persian Empire.

WHAT WERE the main teachings of Zoroaster, and how did Zoroastrianism influence other traditions?

Medes and Persians

- Both groups descended from Aryan pastoralists
- Medes controlled western Iran and beyond, ca. 600 B.C.E.
- Achaemenid Empire was ruled by Persians
- Achaemenid government used many Median institutions

Ahura Mazda

Supreme god in ancient Iranian religion, especially in the religious system of the Iranian prophet Zoroaster. Ahura Mazda was worshiped by the Persian king Darius I (reigned 522 B.C.E.–486 B.C.E.) and his successors as the greatest of all gods and protector of the just king.

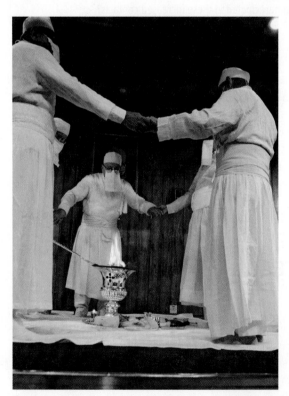

Zoroastrian priests hold hands around a devotional flame during a religious New Year's celebration in London in 1999.

What is the importance of fire in the Zoroastrian faith?

THE IRANIAN PEOPLES

The forefathers of the Iranian dynasts were Aryans. The oldest texts in ancient Persian dialects show that Aryan peoples settled on the Iranian plateau around 1100 B.C.E. Like their Vedic or Indo-Aryan relations in North India, these peoples were pastoralists—horse breeders—from the Eurasian or Central Asian steppes. The most prominent of these ancient Iranians were the Medes and the Persians. By the eighth century B.C.E., they had spread around the deserts of the plateau to settle and control its western and southwestern reaches, to which they gave their names, Media and Persis (Pars, and later Fars).

The Medes developed a tribal confederacy in western Iran and were the predecessors of today's Kurds. By 612 B.C.E., they and the Neo-Babylonians had defeated the mighty Assyrians and broken their hold on the Fertile Crescent. Persian power increased under the Achaemenid clan, starting in the seventh century B.C.E. Median supremacy on the Iranian plateau was over by the time of the Achaemenid ruler Cyrus the Great, around 550 B.C.E. Many of the institutions that developed in the ensuing empire were apparently based on Median practices; the Medes, in turn, had often drawn from Babylonian and Assyrian models. Part of the genius of the Achaemenids' unparalleled imperial success lay in their ability to use existing institutions to build their own state and to administer their far-flung dominions well.

ANCIENT IRANIAN RELIGION

Pre-Achaemenid texts suggest that old Iranian culture and religion were similar to those of the Vedic Aryans. The importance of water, fire, sacrifice, and the cow, as well as the names and traits of major divine beings and religious concepts, all have counterparts in Vedic texts. The emphasis was on moral order, or the "Right." The supreme heavenly deity was **Ahura Mazda**, the "Wise Lord."

ZOROASTER AND THE ZOROASTRIAN TRADITION

The first person who stands out in Iranian history was not Cyrus, the famous founder of the Achaemenid Empire, but the great prophet-reformer of Iranian religion, Zarathustra, commonly known in the West by the Greek version of his name, Zoroaster. Zoroaster probably lived in northeastern Iran, no later than 1000 B.C.E. Like the Hebrew prophets, the Buddha, and Confucius, Zoroaster presented a message of moral reform in an age of materialism, political opportunism, and ethical indifference.

Zoroaster was evidently trained as a priest in the old Iranian tradition, but his hymns, or *Gathas*, reflect his new religious vision. In these hymns we glimpse the values of a peasant-pastoralist society that was growing up alongside early urban trade centers in northeastern Iran. Zoroaster's personal experience of Ahura Mazda as the supreme deity led him to reinterpret the old sacrificial fire as Ahura's symbol. He called on people to abandon worship of all lesser deities, whom he identified as demons. He warned of a "final reckoning," when the good would be rewarded with "future glory" but the wicked with "long-lasting darkness, ill food, and wailing."

Zoroaster's preaching probably did not become an official "state" creed during his lifetime. But by the mid-fourth century B.C.E., the Zoroastrian reform had spread into western as well as eastern Iran. The quasi-monotheistic worship of Ahura Mazda, the Wise Lord, was rapidly accommodated to the veneration of older Iranian gods by the interpretation of these deities as secondary gods or even manifestations of the Wise Lord himself. The old Iranian priestly clan of the **Magi** may have integrated Zoroastrian ideas and texts into their older polytheistic tradition. Certainly the name "magi" was later used for the priests of the tradition that we call "Zoroastrian."

Zoroastrianism probably influenced not only Jewish, Christian, and Muslim ideas of angels, devils, messiah, last judgment, and afterlife, but also Buddhist concepts as well. Zoroastrianism was wiped out as a major force in Iran by the spread of Islam from the seventh and eighth centuries C.E. However, its tradition continues in the faith and practice of the Parsis, a community today of perhaps 100,000 people, most of them in western India.

THE ACHAEMENIDS

In October 1971 C.E., the Iranian monarch Muhammad Reza Shah (r. 1941–1979) hosted a lavish pageant amid the ruins of the ancient Persian capital, Persepolis, to commemorate the 2,500-year anniversary of the beginning, under Cyrus the Great, of "the imperial glory of Iran." The shah felt his modern secularist regime had re-created traditional Iranian glory. Although the Iranian revolution of 1978 ended his heavy-handed dictatorship, modern Iran does have a dual heritage: that of the rich Iranian Islamic culture and that of the far older, Indo-Iranian, Zoroastrian, and imperial culture of pre-Islamic Iran. The latter began with the Persian Achaemenid Dynasty.

Achaemenid rule in southwestern Iran (Persis) went back at least to Cyrus I (d. 600 B.C.E.), but the rise of Iran as a major imperial civilization is usually dated from the reign of his grandson, Cyrus the Great (559–530 B.C.E.). Cyrus defeated the last Median king about 550 B.C.E., and the last Babylonian king in 539 B.C.E. This victory marks the beginning of the Achaemenid Empire, for it joined Mesopotamia and the Iranian plateau for the first time under one rule—a unity that would last for centuries (see Map 4-1 on page 96). One result was the end of the Babylonian Exile of the Jews, for Cyrus allowed the Jews to return to their Holy Land and rebuild their Jerusalem temple (see Chapter 2). His most notable legacy to his heirs was not only his conquests, but also his model of rule through local elites and institutions rather than imperial administrative superstructures.

Early in his career, Cyrus had moved his capital from Susa to the old Median capital of Ecbatana (later Hamadan). He and his successors adopted Median administrative practice, and many Medes served the new state. Thus the Bible and other sources refer to Achaemenids as "Medes and Persians."

The new Persian Empire became the most extensive the world had ever seen. Cyrus's successor, Cambyses (r. 529–522 B.C.E.) added Egypt to the Achaemenid dominions. Darius I (r. 521–486 B.C.E.) enjoyed a prosperous reign in which the empire reached its greatest extent—from Egypt northeast to southern Russia and Sogdiana (Transoxiana) and east to the Indus valley.

Magi
A tribe from ancient Media, who, prior to the conquest of the Medes by the Achaemenid Empire in 550 B.C.E., were responsible for religious and funerary practices. The best known Magi were the "Wise Men from the East" in the Bible.

Zoroastrianism
A quasi-monotheistic Iranian religion founded by Zoroaster, who preached a message of moral reform and exhorted his followers to worship only Ahura Mazda, the Wise Lord.

⟨●—Hear the **Audio**
at **myhistorylab.com**

CHRONOLOGY

IRAN TO THE THIRD CENTURY C.E.

ca. 2000–1000 B.C.E.	Indo-Iranian (Aryan) tribes move south into the Iranian plateau and the Punjab of India
Between 1400 and 1000 B.C.E.	Probable range of dates within which Zarathushtra (Zoroaster) lived, likely in eastern/northeastern Iran (perhaps originally in Herat?)
ca. 628–551 B.C.E.	Traditional dating of the life of Zoroaster
559–530 B.C.E.	Reign of Cyrus the Great, Persian Achaemenid ruler
539–330 B.C.E.	Achaemenid Empire
331–330 B.C.E.	Alexander the Great (d. 323 B.C.E.) conquers Achaemenid Empire
312–63 B.C.E.	Seleucids rule in eastern territories of Achaemenid realm
ca. 248 B.C.E.–224 C.E.	Parthian Empire of the Arsacids in Iran, Babylonia

MAP EXPLORATION

To explore this map further, go to **http://www.myhistorylab.com**

MAP 4–1. The Achaemenid Persian Empire.

The empire created by Cyrus had reached its fullest extent under Darius when Persia attacked Greece in 490 B.C.E. It extended from the subcontinent of India to the Aegean Sea, and even into Europe, encompassing the lands formerly ruled by Egyptians, Hittites, Babylonians, and Assyrians.

Why were the Persians able to govern such a large empire for so long?

The next five rulers (486–359 B.C.E.) fared less well, and after 478 B.C.E., the Persians found themselves militarily inferior to the Greeks. Although they kept the divided Greeks at bay by clever diplomacy, Greek cultural influence grew in Asia Minor. Egyptian rebellions, succession struggles, conflict with Scythian steppe tribes, and poor leadership plagued Achaemenid rule, which was ended by Alexander the Great (see Chapter 3).

THE ACHAEMENID STATE

Perhaps the Achaemenids' greatest achievement was the relative stability of their rule. To justify their sovereignty—and the title of **Shahanshah**, "king of kings"—they claimed that Ahura Mazda had entrusted them with universal sovereignty, which they earned through justice and uprightness. The ruler became priest and sacrificer in the court rituals; a royal fire that burned throughout his reign symbolized his role as cosmic ruler. The success of the early Achaemenids strengthened their claim to divinely sanctioned royal status.

Shahanshah

"King of kings," the title of the Persian ruler.

The Achaemenids were tolerant of other cultural and religious traditions in ways earlier empires had not been. In part, the sheer size of their realms demanded it, but the contrast to later Roman imperial practice is striking. Even Darius's emphasis on Zoroastrian ritual and theology did not bring forced conformity or conversion to the "state cult," as his leniency toward the Jews shows (see Chapter 2).

The Achaemenids built a powerful army, but much of their success lay in their administrative abilities and willingness to borrow from predecessors. Most of their leaders were adept at conciliation and worked to establish their special *pax Achaemenica*. They maintained continuity as their state evolved from a tribal confederation into a sophisticated monarchy. Cyrus's state, with its largely Iranian troops and tribute system of revenue, was replaced by a monarchy supported by a noble class, professional armies (led by Persian elite troops), an administrative system of provinces ruled by governors called **satraps**, and fixed levies of revenue.

The excellence of Achaemenid administration can be seen in their communication and propaganda systems. Couriers linked imperial outposts with the heartlands over well-kept highways, which also facilitated rapid troop deployment. Herodotus called the greatest of these, from Sardis to Susa, "the King's Road" (see Map 4-1). A network of observers and royal inspectors kept the court abreast of activities outside the capital. An efficient chancery with large archives and numerous scribes served administrative needs. The Achaemenid bureaucracy's adoption of Aramaic, which had become the common language of the Near East under the Assyrians, helped link East and West. The Achaemenids never had a single fixed capital; they moved the court as needed. Although *satraps* were powerful princes in their own right, the power of the "king of kings" held together the diverse *satrapies* and tributary states.

THE ACHAEMENID ECONOMY

Economic life from Greece to India profited substantially from Achaemenid success. Although Croesus had introduced a coin-based monetary system in Lydia (sixth century B.C.E.), the Achaemenids greatly expanded on this. Coinage was used to pay part of the workers' wages in the construction of Persepolis and displaced in-kind payment altogether under Darius. Coinage stimulated banking operations, which had declined since the heyday of Mesopotamian rule in the previous millennium. The Achaemenids taxed diverse sources of income—estates, livestock, mines, trade, and production. They regulated wages and established money-goods equivalences (thus a sheep might be set at three shekels).

Agriculture remained the basic industry and normal occupation of free men. Serfs and slaves, both chattel and domestic, formed most of the labor force. Work animals were bred, bees colonized, and grapes, wheat, barley, and olives cultivated widely. Where water was scarce, the government dug irrigation canals. Rulers such as Darius mandated the transfer of fruit trees and other plants to different parts of the empire; thus from the east pistachio cultivation came to Aleppo, rice to Mesopotamia, and sesame to Egypt.

Fishing, timbering, and mining were fundamental to the economy. Some industries, such as those producing clothing, shoes, and furniture, developed alongside the older luxury crafts for the wealthy. The unprecedented volume of trade in Achaemenid times included large quantities of everyday household products that were now widely exchanged where earlier only luxury goods had been traded over long distances. Goods from India crossed paths with those of the Rhine valley; it was a prosperous era, marked by expanding markets—into southern Europe especially—and increased foreign travel, exploration, and investment.

The empire's stability laid the cosmopolitan basis for the coming Hellenic influences in western Asia in the wake of Alexander's conquests.

satraps
Governors of provinces in the Persian Empire.

See the **Map**
The Persian Empire at Its Greatest Extent at **myhistorylab.com**

Daric. A gold coin first minted under Darius I of Persia, fourth century B.C.E.
© Ashmollean Museum, Oxford, England, UK.

What are some important features of the Achaemenid economy?

HOW DID the steppe peoples act as vehicles for cultural exchange?

QUICK REVIEW

Alexander's Successors in Achaemenid Lands

◆ General Seleucus and his heirs ruled most of the Achaemenid realm

◆ Alexander's "new" cities served as bases for Seleucid control

◆ Seleucids maintained control with mercenary troops

Parthian Warrior. The Parthians were superb fighters and were particularly noted for the "Parthian shot," firing arrows backward while mounted on a galloping horse.

How would you imagine foot soldiers reacting to swift and mobile cavalry fighters like this?

steppe peoples
Nomadic tribespeople who dwelled on the Eurasian plains from eastern Europe to the borders of China and Iran. They frequently traded with or invaded more settled cultures.

SUCCESSOR STATES AND STEPPE PEOPLES

THE SELEUCID SUCCESSORS TO ALEXANDER IN THE EAST (ca. 312–63 B.C.E.)

Alexander's successors in Achaemenid lands, the Greek general Seleucus and his heirs (see Chapter 3) ruled much of the former Achaemenid realm from Babylon between about 312 and 246 B.C.E. They lost Babylonia to the Iranian Parthians in 140 B.C.E. Their capital moved from Babylon to Antioch during their long decline, until Pompey finally ended the much-reduced Seleucid kingdom in 63 B.C.E.

Alexander's policies of Hellenic-Persian fusion—the appointment of Iranians and Greeks as *satraps*, as well as large-scale Greek and Persian intermarriage—helped make Seleucid rule viable in many eastern areas. As a foreign minority, the Seleucids had to maintain control with mercenary troops. Always at war, neither Seleucus (r. 311–281 B.C.E.; see Chapter 3) nor the greatest of his successors, Antiochus the Great (r. 223–187 B.C.E.), ever matched the sustained power and scale of Achaemenid rule.

In the end, Alexander's policy of linking Hellenes with Iranians in political power, marriage, and culture bore fruit more lasting than empire. The Seleucid emphasis on building Greek-style cities stimulated the Hellenization process. During the second century B.C.E., Hellenistic culture and law became new ideals among Seleucid elites. The Seleucids welcomed into the ruling classes those non-Hellenes willing to become Hellenized. Aramaic, though declining in eastern Iran, remained the common tongue from Syria to the Hindu Kush. Greek culture penetrated but did not displace local social and cultural forms.

Zoroastrian religious tradition declined with the loss of its imperial-cult status. Syncretic cults of the Mediterranean Hellenistic world made inroads even in the East in Seleucid and, later, Parthian times (see below). Mystery and savior cults were becoming more popular in East and West. Hellenistic urban centers provided an environment in which the individual was less rooted in established traditions. This may have enhanced the attraction of the individual salvation promised by some Hellenistic cults and the emerging Christian, Mahayana Buddhist, Manichaean, and Hindu traditions.

THE PARTHIAN ARSACID EMPIRE (ca. 247 B.C.E.–223 C.E.)

The history of the Iranian plateau (and North India) was dominated from about 250 B.C.E. to 300 C.E. by incursions of Iranian tribal peoples originally from the Central Asian steppes. These were neither the first nor last such invasions from the steppe. Commonly ignored, these pastoral **steppe peoples** have been a major force in Eurasian history.

The Parni, said to be related to the Scythians, were probably the major group of Iranian steppe peoples who first settled the area south of the Aral Sea and Oxus. In late Achaemenid times, they moved south into Parthia and adopted its dialect; thereafter we call them Parthians. Stating around 247 B.C.E., the dynastic family of the Arsacids controlled first Parthia, and then expanding portions of the Iranian plateau. Under Mithradates I (ca. 171–138 B.C.E.) they emerged as a new Eurasian imperial force and true Achaemenid successors who were able to extinguish Seleucid power east of the Euphrates by 129 B.C.E.

Under the Parthians, trade apparently increased, especially north over the Caucasus, on the "Silk Road" to China, and along the Indian Ocean coast. Culturally, the Parthians were oriented toward the Hellenistic world of their Seleucid predecessors until the mid-first century C.E., after which they seem to have experienced a kind of Iranian revival that laid the groundwork for the nationalistic emphases of subsequent centuries. Despite their religious tolerance, the Parthians upheld such Zoroastrian traditions as maintenance of a royal sacred fire. The increasing popularity of Christianity and Buddhism in border areas may have stimulated Parthian attempts to collect the largely oral Zoroastrian textual heritage.

The Parthian Arsacids' imperial borders varied, but from their victory over the Romans at Carrhae in 53 B.C.E. (see Chapter 6) until their fall in 224 C.E., they were the major Eurasian power alongside Rome. Eventually the constant Roman wars of their last century and the pressure of the Kushan Empire in the east weakened them sufficiently for a new Persian dynasty, the Sasanids, to replace them.

THE INDO-GREEKS

The farthest reach of Hellenization in the East came with the **Indo-Greek** rulers of Bactria. About 246 B.C.E., Bactria's Greek *satrap* broke away from the Seleucids. His successors controlled territory that expanded into northern India. Most of the Indo-Greeks were Indian in language, culture, and religion, as their coins and inscriptions show. Before their demise at the hands of invading steppe peoples (ca. 130–100 B.C.E.), these Indo-Greeks left their mark on civilization in all the areas around their Bactrian center. Bactria was a major source of the later Greco-Buddhist art of Gandhara, one of history's remarkable examples of cross-cultural influence. The Indo-Greeks also probably helped spread Buddhism from India to Central Asia. The most famous of the Bactrian rulers, Menander, or Milinda (r. ca. 155–130 B.C.E.), is depicted as a Buddhist convert in a later Buddhist text, *The Questions of King Milinda*.

SCYTHIANS AND KUSHANS

The successors of the Indo-Greeks were steppe peoples who reflect the cosmopolitan nature of the world of Central Asia, eastern Iran, and northwestern India at this time.

Beginning about 130 B.C.E., Scythian, or Saka, tribes from beyond the Jaxartes (Syr Darya) overran northeastern Iran, taking Sogdiana's Hellenic cities and then Bactria. One group of Scythians extended their domain from Bactria into North India. Another went southwest into Herat and Sistan, where they encroached on Parthian territories. In northwestern India the Sakas were defeated by invading Iranians known as the Pahlavas, who went on to rule in northwestern India in the first century C.E. Still, Saka dynasties continued to rule in parts of northwestern and western India through the fourth century C.E.

The Sakas had been displaced earlier in Sogdiana by another steppe people, known from Chinese sources as the Yuezhi, from western China. These peoples, led by the Kushan tribe, drove the Sakas out of Bactria in the mid-first century B.C.E. About 100 years later, they swept over the mountains into northwestern India, ending Pahlava rule. The Kushans founded a long-lived Indian dynasty that controlled a relatively stable empire from the upper Oxus regions through Bactria, Gandhara, Arachosia, the Punjab, and over the Ganges plains as far as Varanasi (Banaras).

Indo-Greeks
Bactrian rulers who broke away from the Seleucid Empire to found a state that combined elements of Greek and Indian civilizations.

Greco-Buddhist Art. A sculpted head of the Buddha, second century B.C.E. Hellenistic influences are evident in the realistic modeling and sculptural plasticity.

Sculpted head of Buddha, from Gandhara, second century B.C. Paris, Musee Guimet. RMN: Reunion Musees Nationaux/Art Resource.

In what ways does this sculpture seem to be a portrayal of a real person? In what ways does it seem to be an idealized representation?

The Kushan kingdom of India was—along with Rome, China, and the weakened Parthian Empire of Iran—one of four major centers of civilization in Eurasia around 100 C.E. Its greatest ruler, Kanishka, was a great patron of Buddhism, and Kushan power in Central Asia facilitated the missionary activity that carried Buddhism across the steppes into China. The Kushan rulers had diplomatic contacts with Han China, Iran, and Rome. Greco-Buddhist art was fostered in Gandhara by Kanishka and his successors.

THE SASANID EMPIRE (224–651 C.E.)

HOW DID the Sasanids build a strong state?

See the Map
Arabia Before the Prophet, ca. 250–600 C.E.
at **myhistorylab.com**

THE SASANIDS

The Sasanids were a Persian dynasty who claimed to be the rightful Achaemenid heirs. They championed Iranian legitimacy and tried to brand their predecessor Parthians as outside invaders. The first Sasanid king, Ardashir (r. 224–ca. 239 C.E.), was a Persian warrior noble. He and his son, Shapur I (r. ca. 239–272), built a strong internal administration. Under Shapur's long rule, the Persian Empire grew. Shapur defeated three Roman emperors, even capturing one of them, Valerian (r. 253–260). Thus he could justifiably claim to be a restorer of Iranian glory and a "king of kings," or *shahanshah*. He also centralized and rationalized taxation, the civil ministries, and the military, although neither he nor his successors could fully contain the growing power of the nobility.

With the shift of the Roman Empire east to Byzantium in the early fourth century C.E., the West Asian stage was set for the next 350 years of conflict between the Byzantines based in Constantinople on the Bosphorus, and the Sasanids based in Ctesiphon on the Tigris. These two imperial centers were home to the two mightiest thrones of Eurasia until the coming of the Arabs. Each side won victories over the other and championed a different religious orthodoxy, but neither could completely subdue the other. In the sixth century each produced its greatest emperor: the Byzantine Justinian (r. 527–565) and the Sasanid Chosroes Anosharvan

Sasanid victory. Cliff-cut tombs at Nagsh-i Rustam, Iran. Stone relief depicts Philip the Arab in Roman dress kneeling before the third-century Persian King Shapur I on horseback wearing royal armor and crown, who grasps with his right hand the uplifted arms of the Byzantine Emperor Valerian. Located at the tombs of the Achaemenids, in Istakhr, Iran.

What major empires were in conflict during the Sasanid period?

("Chosroes of the Immortal Soul," r. 531–579). Yet, less than a century after their deaths, the new Arab power to the south reduced one empire dramatically and destroyed the other. Byzantium survived with the loss of most of its territory for another 800 years, but the Sasanid imperial order was swept away entirely in 651. Memory of the Sasanids did not, however, die. Chosroes became a legendary model of greatness for Persians and a symbol of imperial splendor among the Arabs. The Pahlavi monarchy in twentieth-century Iran attempted to use the historical memory of the Sasanids to legitimize its rule.

SOCIETY AND ECONOMY

Sasanid society was largely like that of earlier times. The extended family was the basic social unit. Zoroastrian orthodoxy recognized four classes: priests, warriors, scribes, and peasants. However, a great divide separated the royal house, the priesthood, and the warrior nobility from the common people (artisans, traders, and the rural peasantry).

The basis of the economy remained agriculture, but land became increasingly concentrated in the hands of an ever-richer minority of the royalty, nobility, and Zoroastrian priesthood. The burden of land taxation, like that of conscript labor and army duty, hit hardest those least able to afford it. This eventually produced a popular reaction, as shown by the Mazdakite movement discussed below.

The Sasanids taxed the lucrative caravan and sea trade in their territory (see Map 4-2). The empire's many urban centers and its foreign trade relied on a money system. It was from Jewish bankers in Babylonia and their Persian counterparts that Europe got the use of bills of exchange (the term *check* comes from a Pahlavi word).

Sasanid aristocratic culture drew on diverse traditions. The Sasanid heyday was the reign of Chosroes. Indian influences—not only religious, as in the case of Buddhist ideas, but also artistic and scientific—were especially strong. Indian medicine and mathematics were notably in demand and transmitted west by way of the Persian Gulf and Indian Ocean maritime routes. Hellenistic culture was also revived in the academy at Jundishapur, where Nestorian Christian scholars fleeing Byzantine persecution brought many Greco-Roman philosophical, scientific, and literary texts with them.

QUICK REVIEW

Sasanid Economy

◆ Based on agriculture

◆ Four classes, according to Zoroastrian orthodoxy

◆ Increasing gap between the rich and the poor

◆ Heavy taxes on trade

◆ Money system, including checks

MAP EXPLORATION

To explore this map further, go to **http://www.myhistorylab.com**

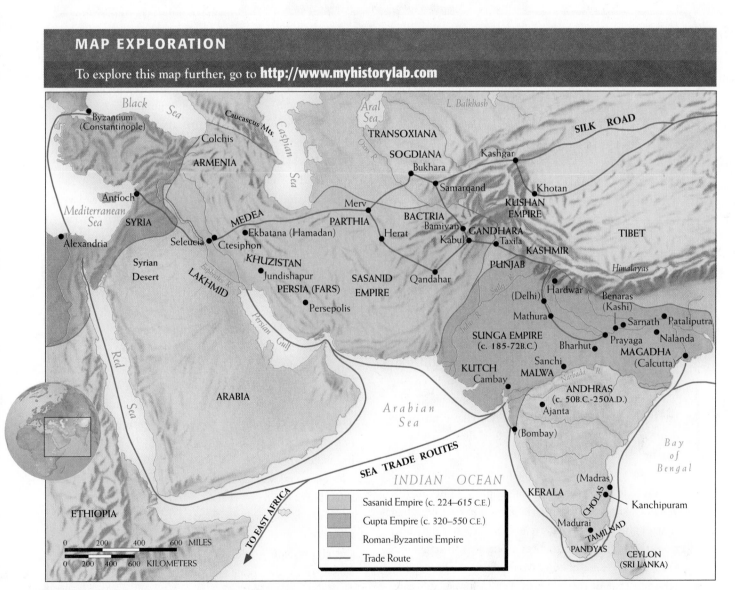

MAP 4-2.   International Trade Routes in Gupta and Sasanid Times.

This map shows the Gupta and Sasanid empires and the trade routes that linked them to each other and to other areas of the world.

How did the Indian Ocean facilitate trade between different regions?

RELIGION

The Sasanids institutionalized Zoroastrian ritual and theology as state orthodoxy. The first chief priest (*mobad*) of the empire, Tansar (or Tosar) began to compile an authoritative, written scriptural canon known as the *Avesta*; these texts include the hymns and sayings of Zarathushtra. He may also have instituted a calendar reform and replaced all images in the temples with the sacred altar fires of Zoroastrian tradition. (See Document, "Tansar's Defense of His King, Ardashir I.")

The most influential figure in Sasanid religious history was Tansar's successor, Kartir (or Kirdir) (ca. 239–293). After the death of the religiously tolerant Shapur, Kartir tried to convert not only pagans, but also Christians, Buddhists, and others. His

---

DOCUMENT

Tansar's Defense of His King, Ardashir I

The following is a brief excerpt from what is probably at base an actual letter of the Zoroastrian high priest, Tansar (third century C.E.) to a conquered vassal of the Sasanid Shahanshah, Ardashir I, which was revised in the sixth century for Sasanid propaganda purposes. The letter argues in general that religious norms had been restored by Ardashir after their collapse in Arsacid times. The text comes from a thirteenth-century Muslim history of Tabaristan in a Persian translation of an Arabic translation of the original.

- **WHY** might Tansar be an apologist for Anushirvan I? What can be inferred about the relationship between religious and imperial authority under the Sasanids?

The chief herbad, Tansar, has received the letter of Gushnasp, prince and king of Tabaristan and Parishwar.... You declared: "There is much talk about the blood shed by the king and people are dismayed." The answer is that there are many kings who have put few to death, yet have slain immoderately if they have killed but ten; and there are many who if they put men to death in their thousands would slay still more, being driven to it at the time by their people.... Punishments, you must know, are for three kinds of transgressions; first that of the creature against his God... when he turns from the faith and introduces a heresy into religion.... For (this) the King of kings has established a law far better than that of the ancients. For in former days any man who turned from the faith was swiftly... put to death.... The King of kings has ordered that such a man should be imprisoned, and that for the space of a year learned men should summon him at frequent intervals and advise him and lay arguments before him and destroy his doubts. If he become penitent and contrite and seek pardon of God, he is set free. If obstinacy and pride hold him back, then he is put to death. Next for what you said, that the King of kings has taken away fires from the fire temples, extinguished them and blotted them out, and that no one has ever before presumed so far against religion; know that the case is not so grievous but has been wrongly reported to you. The truth is that after Darius (III) each of [the Parthians' vassal kings] built his own [dynastic] fire temple. This was pure innovation, introduced by them without the authority of kings of old. The King of kings has razed the temples, and confiscated the endowments, and had the fires carried back to their places of origin.... Then you said: "He has exacted money from men of wealth and merchants".... The idea that the king of the day should seek help for the common people from the superfluity of the wealthy is a religious principle and clearly justified in reason.... The King of kings has cast the shadow of his majesty over all who have acknowledged his preeminence and service and have sent him tribute.... In the space of fourteen years, he thus brought it about that he made water flow in every desert and established towns and created groups of villages.... Good order in the affairs of the people affects him more than the welfare of his own body and soul....

Source: From Mary Boyce, ed. and trans., *Textual Sources for the Study of Zoroastrianism* (Manchester, England: Manchester University Press, 1984), pp. 109–110.

chief opponents were the Manichaeans, whom he considered Zoroastrian heretics, much as Christian groups, such as the Nestorians, saw them as Christian heretics.

The founder of the faith that bears his name, Mani (216–277 C.E.) preached a message both similar to and sharply divergent from its Zoroastrian, Judaic, and Christian forerunners. **Manichaeism** centered on a radically dualistic and moralistic view of reality in which good and evil, spirit and matter, always warred. These ideas are now commonplace in the major monotheistic religions. He sought to convert others to his views, which he presented as the culmination and restoration of the original unity of Zoroastrian, Christian, and Buddhist teachings. Mani may have been the first person in history to consciously "found" a new religious tradition or to seek to create a "scripture" for his followers.

Kartir eventually had Mani executed as a heretic in 277, but Mani's movement had great consequences. It spread westward to challenge the Christian church and eastward along the Silk Road to Central Asia and China to vie with Buddhist and Nestorian Christian traditions. Its ideas figured even centuries later in both Christian and Islamic heresies. Its adherents probably carried the Western planetary calendar to China, where in some areas it was used for centuries.

Despite the persistence of challenges such as Mani's, Kirdir had firmly grounded Zoroastrian orthodoxy, which became the backbone of Sasanid culture. Throughout Sasanid times, the priesthood increased its power as the jurists and legal interpreters of the land. With increasing endowments of new fire temples, the church establishment also eventually controlled much of Iran's wealth.

Nestorius (ca. 386–ca. 451), the Patriarch of Constantinople, had taught that the human and divine natures of Jesus Christ were distinct and separate, not unified in one person. Nestorius was condemned as a heretic at the Council of Ephesus in 431. The Sasanid kings, who were at war with the Byzantines, saw an opportunity: They supported the Nestorian Christians and opened schools to Nestorian scholars. Indeed, the Nestorian Church flourished in Persia, producing many missionaries who preached throughout Persia and Central and East Asia in the seventh and eighth centuries, reaching China in 635.

LATER SASANID DEVELOPMENTS

Despite the high Zoroastrian moral intent of many of their rulers, the Sasanid ideal of justice did not include equal distribution of the empire's bounty. The radical inequalities between the aristocracy and the masses erupted at least once in conflict with the Mazdakite movement at the end of the fifth century. Its leader, Mazdak, preached ideas drawn

CHRONOLOGY	
SASANID IRAN	
216–277 C.E.	Mani
223–224	Ardashir (r. 224–ca. 239) defeats the last Arsacid ruler, becomes *shahanshah* of Iran
ca. 225–ca. 239	Tansar chief priest (*mobad*) of the realm
239–272	Reign of Shapur I; expansion of the empire east and west
ca. 239–293	Kartir chief priest of the realm
ca. 307–379	Reign of Shapur II
488–531	Reign of Kavad I; height of Mazdakite movement
528	Mazdak and many of his followers massacred
531–579	Reign of Chosroes Anosharvan at Ctesiphon
651	Death of last Sasanid; Arabs conquer Persian Empire

Manichaeism
One of the major dualistic religions in ancient Persia, in which good and evil were constantly at odds with one another.

Manichaean Priests. This leaf from a Manichaean book (ca. eighth–ninth century C.E.) shows priests in white robes and tall hats kneeling in front of low desks. Each has a sheet of white paper, and some hold pens. Works such as this are an important source for our knowledge of Manichaean communities.

A leaf from a Manchurian book, Roko, Templek (MIK III 6368), eighth–ninth century, a manuscript painting 17.2 × 11.2 cm. Bildarchiv Preussischer Kulturbesitz/Art Resource, New York.

What are the basic beliefs of Manichaeism?

QUICK REVIEW

Mani (216–277 C.E.)
- Born of a noble Parthian family
- Mani's message similar to Zoroastrian, Judaic, and Christian forerunners
- Executed as a heretic in 277

ultimately from Manichaeism and the need for a more equal distribution of society's goods. This appealed primarily to the oppressed classes, although even one Sasanid ruler, Kavad I (r. 488–531), was sympathetic for a time. In 528 Kavad's son, the future Chosroes Anosharvan, massacred Mazdak and his followers. Although this finished the Mazdakites, the name was still used later, in Islamic times, for various Iranian popular revolts.

SOUTH ASIA

Large-scale imperial expansion came much later to the South Asian, or Indian, subcontinent than to the Iranian plateau. A cultural and religious heritage going back to the Aryan invaders of North India influenced the subsequent history of the vast and diverse subcontinent. Political unity has been rare. Today's division into India, Pakistan, and Bangladesh is merely the most recent. Only four times has much of the whole come under one rule: in the Maurya, Gupta, Mughal, and British imperial epochs. We look now at the first two of these.

THE FIRST INDIAN EMPIRE: THE MAURYAS (321–185 B.C.E.)

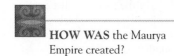

HOW WAS the Maurya Empire created?

Alexander the Great conquered the Achaemenids' northwest Indian provinces of Gandhara and the Indus valley in 327 B.C.E. The conquest had little or no impact on the Indian subcontinent except in Gandhara, where Greek and Indian cultural interpenetration increased. Only with the Mauryas was much of North India and the Deccan incorporated into the first true Indian Empire.

POLITICAL BACKGROUND

The basis for empire in North India was the rise of regional states and commercial towns between the seventh and fourth centuries B.C.E. The most powerful of these were the monarchies of the Ganges plains. North and northwest, in the Himalayan foothills and in the Punjab, tribal republics were more common. The Buddha and Mahavira came from two of these republics (see Chapter 2), although both spent much of their lives in the two most powerful Gangetic monarchies, Kosala and Magadha.

THE MAURYAS

Chandragupta Maurya (r. ca. 321–297 B.C.E.), an adventurer who seized Magadha and the Ganges basin in about 324 B.C.E., established the first true Indian Empire (see Map 4-3). Marching westward into the vacuum created by Alexander's departure (326 B.C.E.), he brought the Indus region and much of west-central India under his control. A treaty with the invading Seleucus added Gandhara and Arachosia to his empire and led to much Seleucid–Maurya contact thereafter.

Chandragupta's fame as the first Indian empire builder is rivaled by that of his Brahman minister, Kautilya, who may have been the actual architect of Maurya rule. However, even though it is ascribed to him, he probably did not write the *Arthashastra*, the most famous Indian treatise on the arts of governing. Chandragupta's son and successor, Bindusara (r. ca. 297–272 B.C.E.), conquered the Deccan, the great plateau that covers central India.

Read the Document
Kautilya, from Arthashastra, "The Duties of Government Superintendents"
at **myhistorylab.com**

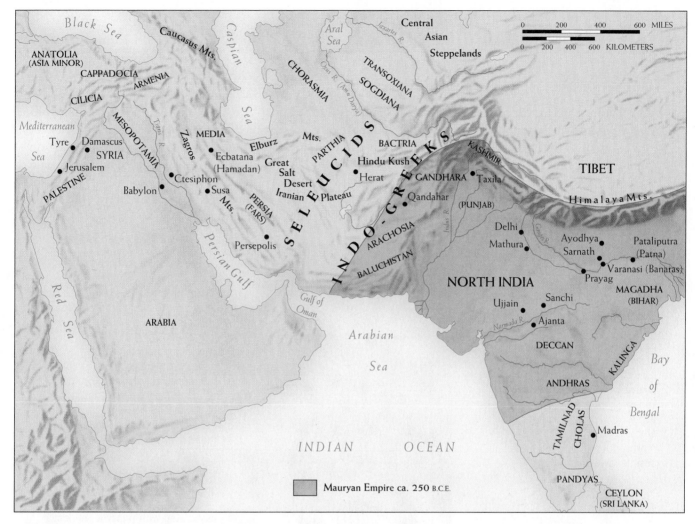

MAP 4–3.   Southwest Asia and India ca. 250 B.C.E.   This map shows not only the major cities and regions of the Iranian lands and the Indian subcontinent, but also the neighboring eastern Mediterranean world. Although the Mediterranean was closely tied to the Iranian plateau from Achaemenid times onward, its contacts with India in the wake of the conquests of Alexander the Great were many and varied.

Which states helped spread Greek culture from the Mediterranean to northern India?

The third and greatest Maurya, Ashoka (r. ca. 272–232 B.C.E.), left us numerous rock inscriptions. From Ashoka's edicts, we can piece together much of his reign and glimpse his character. In his first years as king, he conquered Kalinga, thus extending Maurya control over all the subcontinent except the far south.

Apparently revolted by the bloody Kalinga war, Ashoka underwent a religious conversion. Thereafter he pursued the Buddhist Middle Path as his ideal in both personal and state relations. He did not abandon all warfare, but he did eschew aggression in favor of "conquest by righteousness (*dharma*)." His edicts show that he pursued the laity's norm of the Buddhist *dharma*, striving to attain heaven by the merit of good actions. Ashoka eased some burdens imposed on the populace by earlier governments, and he instituted many beneficial public works. Ashoka provided the model of the ideal king for later Hindu and Buddhist thought—the *chakravartin*, or universal monarch who rules with righteousness, justice, and wisdom. He is a symbol of enlightened rule with few equals in history.

See the **Map**

Ashoka's Empire
at **myhistorylab.com**

QUICK REVIEW

Ashoka

- Considered a model ruler
- Rock inscriptions of his edicts are oldest deciphered Indian writings
- Converted to Buddhism after Kalinga war
- Appointed "*dharma* officials"

A Closer Look

Lion Capital of Ashoka at Sarnath

This sculpture, carved from a single sandstone block, sat originally (c. 250 B.C.E.) atop the Ashoka pillar or column at Sarnath, close by Varanasi (Banares) in present-day Uttar Pradesh, India. The base of the column is still in its original place (where it commemorated the Buddha's first sermon), but the lion capital resides in Sarnath Museum. The heads of the four Asiatic lions on the Ashoka column are said to have originally carried a large *dharmachakra* (now lost) above them. Used by Ashoka as the emblem of his rule, it was also adopted in 1950 as the Indian national emblem or seal and set, minus the lotus, over Sanskrit words from the Mundaka Upanishad, "Truth alone triumphs."

The *chakra*, or (chariot) wheel, was originally the prime Buddhist symbol, the "wheel of the Dharma" (*dharmachakra*), signifying the Buddha's teaching (*dharma*), often with eight spokes for the eightfold path, but here with twenty-four said to symbolize the Buddhist twelve laws of dependent origination and twelve of dependent cessation. Today the *dharmachakra*, or *ashokachakra*, is also the central emblem on the flag of India, representing the eternal wheel of cosmic law (Dharma).

The three visible and fourth (unseen here) lions sit on an abacus of circular *chakra* shape, on which an encircling frieze is emblazoned with four *chakras* alternating with four animals that may have represented four periods of the Buddha's life. The Indian national emblem interprets them as guardians of the four directions: the lion (north), elephant (east), horse (south), and bull (west). Some have seen Achaemenid Persian influence on these figures and the lions above.

The Ashoka capital rests on a bell-shaped lotus blossom in bloom, associated with purity in ancient Hindu and Buddhist lore, and sometimes said to represent the fountainhead of life and creativity.

The Great Stupa at Sanchi. This is an outstanding example of early Buddhist relic mounds. The mound, seated on an Ashokan foundation, was added to over the centuries. Magnificent carvings adorn its stone railing and gateways, one of which is shown in the left foreground. Sanchi is located in north-central India.

How does the worship of relics reflect Hindu influence on Buddhist practice?

Questions

1. Why might Ashoka have chosen the elements used in this capital as emblematic of his rule? Draw on what you know of his reign and life.

2. Why might independent India have decided on this royal emblem of an ancient Buddhist ruler as its national emblem? How does its symbolism transcend its possible original Buddhist symbolism?

3. How can the *chakra* be an apposite symbol both in Ashokan usage and in modern Indian usage?

By the end of Ashoka's reign, however, the empire's size hampered effective administration, and under his successors, Maurya rule disintegrated. Neither Ashoka's Buddhism nor his rejection of aggression was the cause of decline; more likely factors were economic strains and increased bureaucratic corruption, as well as his heirs' inability to claim the personal allegiances he had maintained. After his death local dynasties seized power in many areas.

In its heyday, Maurya bureaucracy was marked by centralization, standardization, and efficiency in long-distance communications; civil and military organization; tax collection; and information gathering. The fundamental unit of government was the village. Groups of villages formed districts within the larger provincial unit. Governors sent from the capital controlled most provinces.

The administration of the empire depended primarily on the king himself. Each of the three great Maurya kings was associated with one of the "new" religious movements of the age: Chandragupta with the Jains (see Chapter 2), his son with an ascetic tradition known as that of the Ajivikas, and Ashoka with the Buddhists. Such links must have strengthened Maurya claims to righteous leadership.

Revenues in the Maurya Empire came primarily from taxing the produce of the land, which was regarded as the king's property. Urban trade and production were also taxed heavily. The Maurya economic system also involved slavery, although most of it was domestic labor, often a kind of temporary indentured service.

Cities thrived across the empire. They were centers for arts, crafts, industry, literature, and education. Ashokan stone buildings and sculpture reflect sophisticated aesthetics and technique, as well as strong Persian and Greek influence.

An imperial ideal, a strengthened Buddhist movement, and strong central administration were among the Mauryas' gifts to Indian culture. They also left behind new cosmopolitan traditions of external relations and internal communication. Their many contacts with the West reflect their international perspective. The edicts suggest that writing and reading had become common. The Mauryas' excellent road system would later serve as routes for Buddhism's spread to Central Asia and China, as well as corridors for successive invaders moving in the opposite direction.

QUICK REVIEW

The Maurya State

◆ Government was centralized, standardized, and efficient

◆ The fundamental unit of government was the village

◆ Administration depended on the king

✓●⎯Study and Review
at **myhistorylab.com**

◉⎯See the Map
India at the Time of Ashoka, ca. 268–237 B.C.E. at **myhistorylab.com**

CHRONOLOGY

INDIA FROM THE SIXTH CENTURY B.C.E. **to the End of Maurya Rule**

ca. 600–400 B.C.E.	Late Upanishadic age: local/regional kingdoms and tribal republics along the Ganges and in Himalayan foothills, the Punjab, and northwestern India
ca. 550–324 B.C.E.	Regional empire of Maghadan kings
ca. 540–ca. 468 B.C.E.	Vardhamana Mahavira, Jain founder
ca. 537–ca. 486 B.C.E.	Siddhartha Gautama, the Buddha
330–325 B.C.E.	Alexander campaigns in Indus valley, Sogdiana, Bactria, and Punjab
324–ca. 185 B.C.E.	Maurya Empire controls most of northern India and the Deccan
ca. 272–232 B.C.E.	Reign of the Maurya emperor Ashoka

THE CONSOLIDATION OF INDIAN CIVILIZATION (ca. 200 B.C.E.–300 C.E.)

WHAT ROLES did Buddhism play in post-Maurya Indian culture?

In the post-Maurya period, the history of North India was dominated by the influx of various foreign peoples. In the rest of the subcontinent, indigenous Indian dynasties held sway, establishing a general pattern of regional and local political autonomy. Religiously and culturally, however, the centuries between the Mauryas and the Gupta Dynasty saw the consolidation of transregional patterns that permanently shaped Indian and, through the diffusion of Buddhism, Asian civilization.

THE ECONOMIC BASE

Although agriculture remained the basis of the post-Maurya economy, India's merchant classes prospered. The fine Maurya road system facilitated trade throughout India. India became a center of world trade largely because of Chinese and Roman demand for Indian luxury goods—jewels, semiprecious stones, sandalwood, teak, spices, cotton and silk textiles, exotic animals, and slaves. Within India, guild organizations flourished and provided technical education in skilled crafts. Coin minting increased after Maurya times, and banking flourished.

HIGH CULTURE

The great achievements of the post-Maurya arts were primarily Buddhist in inspiration. The Gandharan school of Buddhist art emerged in northwestern India. In Gandharan sculpture, Hellenistic naturalism of form joined with the more recent Indian tradition of Buddha images, producing sculptural figures with flowing draped garments through which the muscular lines of the human body are discernible. In central India as early as the first century B.C.E., artists were producing stone-relief sculpture with the naturalistic, yet flowing, human and animal forms that would become earmarks of the "classical" style of Indian art. The finest surviving examples are at the great Buddhist *stupas* (shrines) of Bharhut and Sanchi.

Language and literature during this period rested on the sophisticated Sanskrit grammar of Panini (ca. 300 B.C.E.?), which remains standard even today. Two Sanskrit masterpieces, the epics of the *Mahabharata* and the *Ramayana*, probably took shape by 200 C.E. The first is a composite work concerned largely with the nature of *Dharma* (the moral and cosmic Law; see Chapter 2). Included in its earlier, narrative portions are systematic treatments of *Dharma*, such as the Bhagavad Gita, or "Song of the Blessed Lord," the most influential of all Indian religious texts.

RELIGION AND SOCIETY

Brahmans continued to dominate Vedic learning and ritual. The major developments shaping "Hindu" tradition were (1) the consolidation of the caste system, Brahman ascendancy, and the "high" culture of Sanskrit learning; (2) the increasing dominance of theistic devotionalism (especially the cults of Vishnu and Shiva); and (3) the intellectual reconciliation of these developments with the older ascetic and speculative traditions deriving from the Upanishadic age. These social and religious developments would continue and solidify in the Gupta era and beyond.

Indian Buddhist monastic communities prospered under mercantile and royal patronage, especially in or near urban centers. Buddhist lay devotion figured prominently in Indian religious life. It was, however, a different tradition from the Buddhism of the theological texts, which focuses on the quest for *nirvana* and the "extraordinary norm"

✓•—Study and Review at **myhistorylab.com**

(see Chapter 2). The Buddha and Buddhist saints were naturally identified with popular Indian deities, and Buddhist worship easily assimilated to common Indian patterns of theistic piety. One reason that Buddhist tradition remained only one among many Indian religious paths was its absorption into the religious variety that then and now typifies the Hindu religious scene.

THE GOLDEN AGE OF THE GUPTAS (ca. 320–550 C.E.)

Indians have always considered the Gupta era a golden age of civilization in the subcontinent. Historians have seen it as the source of "classical" norms for Hindu religion and Indian culture—the symbolic equivalent of Periclean Athens, Augustan Rome, Sasanid Persia, or Han China. Most of the Guptas's reign was marked by relative peace and stability.

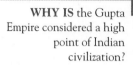

WHY IS the Gupta Empire considered a high point of Indian civilization?

Read the **Document**
Excerpt from Kama Sutra (1883)
Vatsayayana at **myhistorylab.com**

GUPTA RULE

The first Gupta king was Chandragupta (r. 320–ca. 330 C.E.), who became prominent in the whole Ganges basin after he married Princess Kumaradevi, daughter of a powerful tribal leader. Their son, Samudragupta (r. ca. 330–375), and especially their grandson, Chandragupta II (r. 375–415), turned kingdom into empire (see Map 4-2). Gupta splendor and power had no rival. Under Chandragupta II, India was arguably the most civilized and peaceful country in the world.

By about 500 a new wave of steppe nomads, the Huns, had overrun western India. This contributed to the collapse of the Gupta Empire in about 550.

GUPTA CULTURE

The Gupta era's claim to being India's golden age of culture could be sustained solely by its magnificent sculpture, the wall paintings of the Ajanta caves, and Kalidasa's matchless

Gupta Sculpture. Fifth-century C.E. statue of Lokanatha from Sarnath, which, despite damage, shows the fine sculptural work of the important school of Gupta artists at Sarnath and the influence on them of both Greco-Roman antecedents and native Indian traditions and conventions.

What are some of the details visible in this sculpture?

CHRONOLOGY

INDIA FROM THE GUPTA AGE TO ca. 1000 C.E.

320–550 C.E.	Gupta period
320–330	Reign of Chandragupta, first Gupta king
376–454	Reigns of Chandragupta II and Kumaragupta: Kalidasa flourishes; heyday of Gupta culture
399–414	Chinese Buddhist monk Faxien travels in India
ca. 440-500	Hun invasions from Central Asia into North India; Gupta decline, especially after Skandagupta's death in 467
550–ca. 1000	Regional Indian kingdoms in north and south; major Puranas composed; age of first great Vaishnava and Shaivite devotional poets in southern India
616–657	Reign of Harsha; revival of Gupta splendor and power
820	Death of Shankara, Vedantin philosopher-theologian

QUICK REVIEW

"Golden" Gupta Culture

♦ Kalidasa, the "Shakespeare" of Sanskrit letters

♦ Sarnath sculpture

♦ Ajanta cave-shrine

View the Image
Closer Look Ch. 4
at **myhistorylab.com**

dharma
Moral law or duty.

varnas
The four main classes that form the basis for Hindu caste relations.

jatis
The many subgroups that make up the Hindu caste system.

drama and verse. The "Shakespeare" of Sanskrit letters, Kalidasa flourished in the time of Chandragupta II and his successor.

We can see the depth of Gupta culture in its emphasis on education. In addition to religious texts, typical subjects included rhetoric, prose and poetic composition, grammar, logic, medicine, and metaphysics. Using an older Indian number system that the Arabs transmitted to Europe as "Arabic numerals," Gupta scholars cultivated mathematics especially.

Even in handwork and luxury crafts, Gupta products achieved new levels of quality and were in great demand abroad: silks, muslin, linen, ivory and other carvings, bronze metalwork, gold and silver work, and cut stones, among others.

RELIGION AND SOCIETY

The hierarchical character of Hindu/Indian society was formalized. The oldest manual of legal and ethical theory, the *Dharmashastra* of Manu, dates from about 200 C.E. Based on Vedic tradition, it treats the **dharma** appropriate to one's class and stage of life, rules for rites and study of the Veda, pollution and purification measures, dietary restrictions, royal duties and prerogatives, and other legal and moral questions.

In the *Dharmashastra* we find the classic statement of the four-class theory of social hierarchy. This traditional construct rests on the principle that every person is born into a particular station in life (as a result of *karma* from earlier lives), and every station has its particular *dharma*, or appropriate duties and responsibilities, from the lowest servant to the highest prince or Brahman. The Brahmans' ancient division of Aryans into the four **varnas**, or classes, of *Brahman* (priest), *Kshatriya* (noble/warrior/ruler), *Vaishya* (tradesperson/merchant etc.), and *Shudra* (servant/worker) provides a schematic structure. Although class distinctions had already hardened before 500 B.C.E., the classes were, in practice, somewhat fluid.

Much smaller and far more numerous subgroups, or **jatis**, are the units to which our English term *caste* best refers. These divisions (most representing originally occupational groups) were already the primary units of social distinction in Gupta times. *Jati* groupings are hereditary and distinguished essentially on principles of purity and pollution, which are expressed in three kinds of regulation: (1) commensality (one may take food only from or with persons of the same or a higher group); (2) endogamy (one may marry only within the group); and (3) trade or craft limitation (one must practice only the trade of one's group).

The caste system has been the basis of Indian social organization for at least two millennia. It enabled Hindus to accommodate foreign cultural, racial, and religious communities within Indian society by treating them as new caste groups. It permitted everyone to tell by dress and other marks how to relate to another person or group, thus giving stability and security to the individual and to society. It also represented the logical extension of the doctrine of *karma* into society—whether as justification, result, or partial cause of the system itself (see Chapter 2).

The Guptas' support of Brahmanic traditions and Vaishnava devotionalism reflected the waning of Buddhist traditions in the mainstream of Indian religious life. Devotional cults continued to grow in popularity. After Vishnu (especially in his form as the hero-savior Krishna) and Shiva (originally a fertility god), the chief focus of devotion came to be the Goddess in one of her many forms, such as Parvati, Shakti, Durga, or Kali.

Indian reverence for all forms of life and stress on *ahimsa*, or "noninjury" to living beings (see Chapter 2), are most vivid in the sacredness of the cow, a mainstay of life in India. In the development of Hindu piety and practice, a major strand was the tradition

The Buddhist temple of Borobodur, with tiers of stupas looking out over the island of Java. Built out of a half million blocks of stone, it represents a schema of the Buddhist cosmos. Construction began late in the eighth century; the temple was intended originally to be a Hindu sanctuary. **What is the relationship between Hinduism and Buddhism?**

of ardent theism known as *bhakti*, or "loving devotion." *Bhakti* was already evident in the Bhagavad Gita's treatment of Krishna. Gupta and later times saw the rise, especially in the Tamil-speaking south, of schools of bhakti poetry and worship. Also of major importance to devotional piety was the development in this era of the Puranas—epic, mythological, and devotional texts. They are still the functional sacred scriptures of grass-roots Hindu religious life, the Vedic texts remaining the special preserve of the Brahmans.

Whatever god or goddess a Hindu worships, it is usual to also pay homage on proper occasions to other appropriate deities. Most Hindus view one deity as their Supreme Lord but see others as manifestations of the Ultimate at lower levels. Hindu polytheism vividly affirms the infinite forms that transcendence takes in this world. The sense of the presence of the Divine everywhere is evident in the importance attached to sacred places.

The intellectual articulation of Hindu polytheism and relativism found its finest expression in post-Gupta formulations of Vedanta ("the end of the Veda"). The major Vedantin thinker, Shankara (d. 820), stressed a strict "nonduality" of the Ultimate, teaching that Brahman was the only Reality behind the "illusion" (*maya*) of the world of sense experience. Yet he accepted the worship of a lesser deity as appropriate for those who could not follow his extraordinary norm—the intellectual realization of the formless Absolute beyond all "name and form."

QUICK REVIEW

Bhakti

- *Bhakti*, or loving devotion, evident in the Bhagavad Gita's treatment of Krishna
- Derives in part from Tamil and other vernacular poets
- Through *bhakti*, pre-Aryan religious sensibilities reasserted themselves

Mahayana
The "Great Vehicle" for salvation in Buddhism. It emphasized the Buddha's infinite compassion for all beings.

Theravada
The "Way of the Elders." A school of Buddhism that emphasized the monastic ideal.

bodhisattva
A "Buddha to be" who postpones his own nirvana until he has helped all other beings become enlightened.

Within the Buddhist tradition, the major developments of these centuries were (1) the solidification of the two main strands of Buddhist tradition, the **Mahayana** and the **Theravada**, and (2) the spread of Buddhism abroad from its Indian homeland. The Mahayana ("Great Vehicle [of salvation]") arose in the first century B.C.E. Its proponents differentiated it sharply from the older, more conservative traditions of monk-oriented piety, which they labeled the Hinayana ("Little Vehicle"). In Mahayana speculation Buddhas were seen as manifestations of a single principle of "Ultimate" Reality, and Siddhartha Gautama was held to be only one Buddha among many. The Mahayana stressed the model of the Buddha's infinite compassion for all beings. The highest goal was not a *nirvana* of "selfish" extinction but the status of a **bodhisattva**, or "Buddha-to-be," who postpones his own nirvana until he has helped all other beings become enlightened.

MAP 4-4. Spread of Buddhist Traditions throughout Southeast Asia. By the twelfth century C.E., Buddhist traditions had taken root in many parts of Southeast Asia, often blending with local customs, as well as Hindu traditions that had been introduced earlier.

How did the spread of Buddhism in Southeast Asia replicate the earlier spread of Hindu traditions? Were there differences in the ways Hindu traditions spread and the ways Buddhism spread?

The *bodhisattva* can offer this aid because his long career of self-sacrifice has gained him infinite merit. Salvation becomes possible not only through individual merit, but also through devotion to the Buddhas and *bodhisattvas*. At the popular level, this idea translated into devotional cults of transcendent Buddhas and *bodhisattvas* conceived as cosmic beings. One of the most important of these beings was the Buddha Amitabha, who personifies infinite compassion. Amitabha presides over a Western Paradise, or Pure Land, to which all who have faith in him have access. (See Chapter 9 on Pure Land Buddhism in Japan.)

The older, more conservative "Way of the Elders" (Theravada) always focused on the monastic community but taught that service and gifts to the monks were a major source of merit for the laity. It emphasized gaining merit for a better rebirth through righteous conduct, lay devotion to the Buddha, and pilgrimage to his relics at various shrines, or **stupas**. The basis of Theravada piety and practice was the scriptural collection of traditional teachings ascribed to the Buddha, as reported by his disciples.

stupa
A Buddhist shrine.

Indian culture experienced little new outside influence from the Gupta era until Islamic times (after about 1000 C.E.). India's chief contacts were now with Southeast Asia and China, and most of the cultural transmission was from India eastward, not vice versa. India gave Theravada Buddhism to Ceylon, Burma, and parts of Southeast Asia (see Map 4-4). Mahayana Buddhism predominated in Central Asia and China, from which it spread in the fifth through eighth centuries to Korea and Japan. Tantric Buddhism, an esoteric Mahayana tradition heavily influenced by Hinduism, entered Tibet from North India in the seventh century and became the dominant tradition there.

SUMMARY

WHAT WERE the main teachings of Zoroaster, and how did Zoroastrianism influence other traditions?

Ancient Background and the First Persian Empire in the Iranian Plateau (550–330 B.C.E.). Ancient Iranian traditions had much in common with Vedic Aryan beliefs. Zarathustra (known in Greek as Zoroaster) spread a message of moral reform and emphasized a single supreme deity, Ahura Mazda. Zoroaster's teachings influenced later monotheistic religions, as well as Buddhism. The Persian Achaemenid Empire, based in Iran, established two centuries of tolerant, stable, prosperous rule from Egypt to the borders of India. Although the Achaemenid regime was tolerant of diverse religious traditions, the rulers practiced Zoroastrianism. *page 93*

HOW DID the steppe peoples act as vehicles for cultural exchange?

Successor States and Steppe Peoples. The Hellenic Empire of the Seleucids, starting around 312 B.C.E., permitted trade and culture to flourish from the Mediterranean to India. Seleucid rule fostered Greek culture in Western Asia. The Parthians (247 B.C.E.–223 C.E.) continued many Achaemenid traditions. They were religiously tolerant but supported Zoroastrianism, and laid much of the groundwork for later Persian nationalism. The Indo-Greeks of Bactria helped spread Greek ideas and aesthetics, while also helping Buddhism spread beyond India. Steppe peoples—particularly the Scythians and Kushans—fostered cross-cultural contact throughout the Iranian and Indian realms. *page 98*

HOW DID the Sasanids build a strong state?

The Sasanid Empire. The Sasanids sought to restore the glory of the ancient Achaemenid Persian Empire and promoted native Persian culture. They based their rule on orthodox Zoroastrianism and suppressed the Manichaeans as heretics. Although foreign trade flourished, Sasanid rulers favored the landed aristocracy at the expense of the peasantry, who were heavily taxed. Long wars with Rome and Byzantium ultimately sapped Sasanid strength and left the empire vulnerable to Islamic Arab invasion in the seventh century. *page 100*

 HOW WAS the Maurya Empire created?

The First Indian Empire: The Mauryas (321–185 B.C.E.). The Mauryas created the first true empire in India, starting around 321 B.C.E., using conquest, treaties, and possibly marriage to gain territory. The third Maurya ruler, Ashoka, has served as a universal model of enlightened rule. The strong and cosmopolitan Maurya Empire absorbed cultural influences from the Persians and the Greeks, among others. Buddhism flourished. *page 104*

 WHAT ROLES did Buddhism play in post-Maurya Indian culture?

The Consolidation of Indian Civilization (ca. 200 B.C.E.–300 C.E.). Trade was important in post-Mauryan India. Both Buddhist and Hindu devotional cults gained popularity. The arts were heavily influenced by Buddhism. *page 108*

 WHY IS the Gupta Empire considered a high point of Indian civilization?

Golden Age of the Guptas. The Gupta period (320–467 C.E.) is considered one of the highlights of Indian civilization. Indian civilization took on its enduring "Hindu" social, religious, and cultural shape. The fundamentally hierarchic nature of the caste system solidified. Hindu piety emphasized devotional cults to deities, especially Vishnu and Shiva. Indian Buddhism developed two main schools, the Mahayana and the Theravada, which spread to other parts of Asia. *page 109*

KEY TERMS

Ahura Mazda (ah-HOO-rah MAHZ-dah) (p. 94)
bodhisattva (p. 112)
dharma (p. 110)
Indo-Greeks (p. 99)
jatis (p. 110)
Magi **(MEY-jeye)** (p. 95)
Mahayana (p. 112)
Manichaeism (p. 103)
satrap **(sah-TRAP)** (p. 97)
Shahanshah (p. 96)
steppe peoples (p. 98)
stupa (p. 113)
Theravada (p. 112)
varna (p. 110)
Zoroastrianism (p. 95)

REVIEW QUESTIONS

1. Why was the Achaemenid Empire successful for so long? What was the political basis for Achaemenid power?

2. How was the Maurya Empire created? What role did Greeks play in its creation? How did Ashoka develop Maurya power and prestige?

3. How did the role of religion in the Achaemenid Empire compare to its role in the Maurya Empire?

4. Compare the historical importance of the Achaemenid and the Maurya empires. How does each compare to the empires of Rome and Han China?

5. Compare the major features of the Hindu and Buddhist traditions. Why do you think Buddhism and not Hinduism spread to much of Asia?

6. How did the Kushans, Scythians, and other inner Asian groups play important roles in world history?

7. What are the key elements of Manichaean religion? How was it related to Christian and Zoroastrian traditions?

8. How did the Sasanid Empire develop after the fall of the Parthians? What were the principal economic bases of the Sasanid state?

9. What were the major religious issues in the Sasanid Empire? What role did Zoroastrian "orthodoxy" play in Sasanid affairs?

10. How did new religious ideas come to Central Asia and China in these centuries?

11. In what sense can the high Gupta period (ca. 320–450 C.E.) be considered a "golden age"? What was the extent of the empire? Why did it collapse?

12. What factors in Persia and India in the seventh century might have made the Arab invasions possible?

13. What major affinities and differences do you see between the classical Buddhist and Hindu traditions that had crystallized by 500 C.E.?

Note: To learn more about the topics in this chapter, please turn to the Suggested Readings at the end of the book. For additional sources related to this chapter please see www.myhistorylab.com

PEARSON
myhist⌀rylab Connections

Reinforce what you learned in this chapter by studying the many documents, images, maps, review tools, and videos available at **www.myhistorylab.com**

Read and Review

✓● Study and Review Chapter 4

•••● Read the Document *Kautilya, from Arthashastra, "The Duties of Government Superintendents," p. 104*
Excerpt from Kama Sutra (1883) Vatsayayana, p. 109

👁● See the Map *Ashoka's Empire, p. 105*
Arabia Before the Prophet, ca. 250–600 C.E, p. 100
India at the Time of Ashoka, ca. 268–237 B.C.E., p. 107

●● View the Image *Closer Look, p. 106*

Research and Explore

👁● See the Map *The Persian Empire at Its Greatest Extent, p. 97*

●● Watch the Video *The Aryans in India*

(¡●● Hear the Audio

Hear the audio file for Chapter 4
at **www.myhistorylab.com**

HINDUISM

The term *Hinduism* is our modern word for the whole of the diverse religious traditions of India. Until the word was coined in the nineteenth century, it (like *Buddhism*) was not even a concept in the West, let alone in India. In contemporary usage, it has become a catchall term for all the Indian religious communities that look upon the texts of the Vedas (see Chapter 1) as eternal, perfect truth.

The historical beginnings of the varied Hindu traditions can be traced to the ancient Aryan migrations into southern Asia in the second millennium B.C.E. During this era the Vedic hymns were composed. They describe a pantheon of gods not unlike that among the Greeks, the Romans, the Iranians, and other Indo-European peoples. Centered on a sacrificial cult of these gods, Vedic religion increasingly became the preserve of the Brahman priestly class of early Indian society. The Brahmans gradually elaborated a cult characterized by sacrificial rituals, purificatory rules, and fixed distinctions of birth on which India's later caste system was based (see Chapter 4). These developments are mirrored in the later Vedic, or Brahmanical, texts (ca. 1000–500 B.C.E.) that provide commentary on and instructions for ritual use of the Vedic hymns.

After about 700 B.C.E. new developments emerged. North India produced a series of religious reformers, some of whom broke with Vedic tradition and championed knowledge and ascetic discipline over purity and ritual action. Of these, the most famous were Siddhartha Gautama (the Buddha, b. ca. 563 B.C.E.) and Mahavira Vardhamana (founder of the Jain tradition, b. ca. 550 B.C.E.). Other religious leaders reinterpreted the older sacrifice as an inner activity and deepened its spiritual dimensions. Their thinking is represented especially in the Upanishads, which many Hindus consider the most sublime philosophical texts in the Indian tradition.

Developed so long ago, such notions have been part of the complex vision of existence that lies behind the myriad forms of religious life known to us as Hinduism. In this vision the immortal part of each human being, the *atman*, is enmeshed in existence, but not ultimately of it. The nature of existence is *samsara*, a

Dancing Shiva. A magnificent South Indian bronze of Shiva. The fluid, balanced image depicts the so-called dancing Shiva engaged in his dance of simultaneous destruction and creation of the universe, an artistic-mythical rendering of the eternal flux of all worldly existence (13th century; bronze; 33.5 × 24.8 cm).

© The Nelson-Atkins Museum of Art, Kansas City, MO. (Purchase: Nelson Trust) 50-20.

In what ways is the circle an appropriate symbol for Hindu beliefs?

ceaseless round of cause and effect determined by the inescapable consequences of *karma*, or "action." The doctrine of *karma* is a moral as well as physical economy in which every act has unavoidable results; as long as mental or physical action occurs, life and change go on repeatedly. Birth determines one's place and duties in the traditional Indian caste system. Caste is the most visible and concrete reminder of the pervasiveness of the Hindu concept of absolute causality that keeps us enmeshed in existence. The final goal is to transcend this cycle, or *samsara*, in which we are all caught. The only way out of this otherwise endless becoming and rebirth is *moksha*, which may be gained through knowledge, action, or devotion.

On the popular level, the period after about 500 B.C.E. is most notable in Indian religious life for two developments. Both took place alongside the ever deeper entrenchment in society of caste distinctions and a supporting ethic of obligations and privileges. The first was the elaboration of ascetic traditions of inner quest and self-realization, such as that of yoga. The second was the rise of devotional worship of specific gods and goddesses who were seen by their worshipers as identical with the Ultimate—in other words, as supreme deities for those who served them. The latter development was of particular importance for popular religion in India. Evident in the famous and beloved Hindu devotional text, the Bhagavad Gita, it reached its highest level after 500 B.C.E. in the myriad movements of fervent, loving devotionalism, or *bhakti*, many of which remain important today. A striking aspect of Hindu piety has been its willingness to accommodate the focus on one "chosen deity" who is worshiped as supreme to a worldview that holds that the Divine can and does take many forms. Thus most Hindus worship one deity, but they do so in the awareness that faith in other deities can also lead one to the Ultimate.

The period between about 500 B.C.E. and 1000 C.E. saw the rise to special prominence of two gods, Vishnu and Shiva, as the primary forms in which the Supreme Lord was worshiped. Along with the mother-goddess figure, who takes various names and forms (Kali and Durga, for example), Vishnu and Shiva have remained the most important manifestations of the Divine in

Purification rituals in the waters of the holy Ganges. Purification rituals are part of the obligatory daily rituals of all "twice-born" Hindus. The morning purificatory-bathing rituals performed by the women here in the Ganges include greeting the sun with recitation and prayer.

Can you think of similar water-based rituals in other faiths?

India. Their followers are known as Vaishnavas and Shaivas, respectively. A few recurring phenomena and ideas can suggest something of Indian religiousness in practice.

Hindu practice is characterized especially by temple worship (*puja*), in which worshipers bring offerings of flowers, food, and the like. They especially seek out temple images for the blessing that the sight of these images brings. Another important part of Hindu devotionalism is the recitation of sacred texts, many of which are vernacular hymns of praise to a particular deity. *Mantras*, or special recitative texts from the Vedas, are thought to have extraordinary power and are used by many Hindus in their original Sanskrit form. Pilgrimage to sacred sites, especially rivers, mountains, and famous shrines, is a prominent part of Hindu religious life. India's landscape is filled with sacred sites and sacred pilgrim routes, both local and national in reputation. A prominent feature of Hindu life is preoccupation with purity and pollution, most evident in the food taboos associated with caste groupings.

The ascetic tendency in India is also highly developed. Although only a tiny minority of Indians take up a life of full renunciation, they are influential. Ascetic worshipers do not settle in one place, acquire possessions, or perform regular worship. Rather, they wander about in search of teachers and devote themselves to meditation and self-realization. Even though most Hindus have families and work at their salvation through *puja* and moral living, the ascetic ideal has an important place in the overall Indian worldview. It stands as a constant reminder of the deeper reality beyond the everyday world and any individual life.

◆ Compared to other faiths that have expanded globally, such as Christianity and Islam, why has Hinduism been largely confined to India?

◆ How has Hinduism accommodated and absorbed different beliefs and value systems?

5

Africa: Early History to 1000 C.E.

Rock Art from Tassili n'Ajjer National Park in Algeria, a UNESCO World Heritage Site. This painting might represent women gathering grain. It is one of a large group of works created between approximately 8000 B.C.E. and the early part of the Common Era. Now part of the Sahara Desert, at the time this area was much wetter and supported populations of large animals (other paintings show giraffes, elephants, and other animals) and humans.

Henri Lhote Collection. Musée de l'Homme, Paris, France/© Erich Lessing/Art Resource, New York.

How did changes in the climate of the Sahara influence settlement patterns and trade?

e now turn from the ancient societies that emerged in the Persian, Greek, and Hellenistic worlds to the world's second-largest continent—Africa. East Africa was the original home for the human species. In the ancient world, pharaonic Egypt, the Kushite kingdoms of Napata and Meroe, and the Ethiopian state of Aksum were all major powers with highly complex cultures in regular interchange with other civilizations from Rome to India and beyond. The Bantu expansion is one of the epic migrations of human history. The myriad ways Africans have adapted to various challenging environments provide invaluable information about human societies. Finally, the difficulties of writing African history have encouraged scholars to cross traditional disciplinary boundaries, bringing important new perspectives and tools to the repertoire of all historians.

119

"TRADITIONAL" PEOPLES AND NONTRADITIONAL HISTORIES

People in early African societies, like people everywhere, had definite ideas about what was important in their past—they had histories. What most of them did not have was writing, and historians have built their craft around interpretation of written records. African histories were generally transmitted in performance: in songs, poems, dances, rituals, and other activities that symbolically reenacted events from the past. Before the twentieth century, such performances and the artifacts they left behind (such as masks and costumes, rock paintings, ceremonial sites) lay outside historians' purview. Growing discontent with the privileging of the affairs and interests of societal elites—emphasis on ruling dynasties, wars, exploration, and invention, at the expense of the lives of ordinary people—eventually led historians to experiment with different types of source material and to subject traditional documentary sources to new types of analysis.

Historians of Africa arguably have to work harder than specialists in other regions to gather the information they need, but they also have unusually rich opportunities to collaborate with scholars in other disciplines. They often call themselves "Africanists" or "African Studies" scholars, to reflect their necessary expertise in fields such as paleontology, archaeology, anthropology, linguistics, demography, and oral literature. In their typically cross-disciplinary work, they are similar to Classicists, whose training may incorporate history, ancient languages, archaeology, art history, and other fields, or Environmental Historians, who highlight the role of nature in historical narratives, and whose backgrounds might include study in history, climatology, geography, biology, and other fields.

Academic research in African history is still an amazingly recent phenomenon. In the academic year 1958–1959, of 1,735 history graduate students in the United States, precisely one was concentrating on African history.[1] Within the past century,

[1] Steven Feierman, "African Histories and the Dissolution of World History," in R. Bates et al., eds., *Africa and the Disciplines* (Chicago: University of Chicago Press, 1993), p. 168.

ISSUES OF INTERPRETATION, SOURCES, AND DISCIPLINES

WHAT ARE the sources and techniques used for studying African history?

THE QUESTION OF "CIVILIZATION"

In Chapter 1 we defined "civilization" in terms of a cluster of attributes that relate to social complexity and technological development. In that sense the term identifies some common characteristics of the ancient societies that emerged in the valleys of the Nile, Mesopotamia, the Indus and Ganges, and China, and also of more recent societies. The term *civilization* is also associated more broadly with the sophistication of a people's intellectual, cultural, and artistic traditions. Too often we assume that societies that lack writing, cities, or a state bureaucracy are "uncivilized." Most historical African societies—indeed, most societies anywhere for most of history—may not have been civilizations in the narrow sense, but they were civilized in the broader sense. Like other continents, Africa has been home to both "civilizations"—large-scale states with writing, cities, and technology—and "civilized" societies that relied on rich traditions for their identities while adapting to changing circumstances and shaping their own histories.

SOURCE ISSUES

African history has matured in recent decades, but there is still much we do not know. Written documents, the evidence historians are most comfortable using, are minimal for much of sub-Saharan African history. Local oral traditions provide one valuable source of information (see Document, "Origins of the Gikuyu" on page 122). But oral traditions can give us access only to relatively recent history. Another source for African history is archaeology. The tropical climate that prevails in much of sub-Saharan Africa unfortunately destroys many types of artifacts that survive in drier regions. Nonetheless, archaeological scholarship has brought to light many formerly unknown intellectuals in Europe and America (not coincidentally, the same parts of the world where governments held colonies and legislated race-based discrimination) widely considered Africans to be "primitives" whose lives were governed by ancestral traditions and whose cultures were static, largely untouched by historical processes. Twentieth-century events—most visibly the wave of decolonization that swept Africa after World War II—demonstrated that Africans had a role in world history. The development of African universities and the internationalization of Western academia have created a small cadre of Africanists. These scholars have done important work, some of which has influenced historical study of other parts of the world; still, many questions in African history remain unanswered. Fifty years ago textbooks like this one insisted that "civilization" required not only population density, political organization, and writing, but also the plow. In the intervening decades, researchers in Africa and elsewhere have proven that in many places, plows quickly destroy the soil; some peoples' use of hoes instead of plows does not signal technological backwardness, but intelligent adaptation to local conditions. Consequently, this and other textbooks now consider metallurgy, not the use of plows, a hallmark of civilization. Some historians—including Africanists, as well as many who study women, peasants, and other groups whose members were generally illiterate—now question whether even writing is a necessary attribute of civilization.

Focus Questions

◆ What are the advantages and disadvantages of using written texts as primary sources for history?

◆ Think about the histories of other regions you have studied. Have you noticed historians using sources other than documents in these histories? If so, what kinds of sources?

◆ For histories of what other regions, peoples, or topics (e.g., history of science, art history, history of religion) can scholars make good use of nonwritten sources?

cultures. The Nok and Zimbabwean cultures, for example, left impressive but hard-to-decipher remains. Reports from outside observers are another source. It is only after about 950 C.E., however, that Islamic (and later, European) historians, geographers, and travelers provide detailed descriptions of the vast reaches of Africa beyond Egypt, Ethiopia, and North Africa. These outside records are of mixed value, since most authors brought strong biases to their assessments of this vast, diverse continent.

HISTORY AND DISCIPLINARY BOUNDARIES

History as we know it came of age in tandem with European nation-states. As the modern university emerged—with knowledge departmentalized into disciplines—Europe's global technological and economic dominance was immense. Around the time of the nineteenth-century European "Scramble for Africa" (see Chapter 26), racism combined with colonial self-interest caused many Western intellectuals to assume that Africans (and other "primitive" peoples) lived outside of historical time: Their lives were the same as their ancestors' lives, no matter how many generations into the past one looked—they had no history. According to European nationalism, one of the criteria for nationhood was that a people have a shared history (see Chapter 23). Conveniently, Africans and others who lacked history were incapable of forming their own nations.

There were interesting features of these peoples' lives, however, and academics who wanted to study them. Thus was born the discipline of anthropology. Anthropology has changed considerably over the past century, but in the nineteenth and early twentieth centuries it strove to give formal structure to observations of the "Other," people whose lives were imagined as utterly different from—and fundamentally unconnected to—those of contemporary Westerners.[2]

---

[2]See Sally Falk Moore, "Changing Perspectives on a Changing Africa: The Work of Anthropology," in Bates et al., *Africa and the Disciplines*.

DOCUMENT

Origins of the Gikuyu

This version of the creation story of the Gikuyu in Kenya was published by Jomo Kenyatta in 1938. Kenyatta was a Gikuyu (nowadays more frequently written as "Kikuyu") who studied in London under one of the foremost anthropologists of the day, Bronislaw Malinowski. Kenyatta was a leader in political organizations opposed to British colonial rule in Kenya. When Kenya became independent in 1963, Kenyatta was the first prime minister, and he led the country until his death in 1978.

- **DOES** anything in the style or content of this written document suggest that it is based on an oral tradition?

- In what ways might authoring this text have elevated Kenyatta's stature within Kenya? Can you imagine any potentially negative consequences for Kenyatta's authorship of this text?

- Do you notice similarities to other creation stories?

. . . According to the tribal legend, we are told that in the beginning of things, when mankind started to populate earth, the man Gikuyu, the founder of the tribe, was called by the Mogai (the Divider of the Universe), and was given as his share the land with ravines, the rivers, the forests, the game, and all the gifts that the Lord of Nature (Mogai) bestowed on mankind. At the same time Mogai made a big mountain which he called Kere-Nyage (Mount Kenya). . . . He then took the man Gikuyu to the top of the mountain of mystery, and . . . pointed out to the Gikuyu a spot full of fig trees (*mikoyo*), right in the centre of the country. [T]he Mogai . . . commanded him to descend and establish his homestead on the selected place. . . .

Gikuyu did as was commanded by the Mogai, and when he reached the spot, he found that the Mogai had provided him with a beautiful wife whom Gikuyu named Moombi (creator or moulder). Both lived happily, and had nine daughters and no sons.

Gikuyu was very disturbed at not having a male heir. In his despair he called upon the Mogai, [who] told Gikuyu not to be perturbed. . . . He then commanded him, saying, "Go and take one lamb and one kid from your flock. Kill them under the big fig tree (*mokoyo*) [then] burn the meat as a sacrifice to me, your benefactor. When you have done this, take home your wife and daughters. After that go back to the sacred tree, and there you will find nine handsome young men who are willing to marry your daughters under any condition that will please you and your family."

Gikuyu did as he was directed. . . . [W]hen Gikuyu returned to the sacred tree, there he found the promised nine young men who greeted him warmly. . . . [H]e took the nine youths to his homestead and introduced them to his family.

The strangers were entertained and hospitably treated according to the social custom. A ram was killed and a millet gruel prepared for their food. While this was being made ready, the youths were taken to a stream nearby to wash their tired limbs. After this, they had their meal, and conversed merrily with the family and then went to bed.

Early the next morning Gikuyu rose and woke the young men to have their morning meal with him. When they finished eating, the question of marriage was discussed. Gikuyu told the young men that if they wished to marry his daughters he could give his consent only if they agreed to live in his homestead under a matriarchal system.

The young men agreed to this condition, for they could not resist the beauty of the Gikuyu daughters, nor the kindness which the family had showed them. . . . [A]fter a short time all of them were married, and soon established their own family sets. . . . Thus the nine principal Gikuyu *meherega* clans were founded.

Source: From *Facing Mountain Kenya*, by Jomo Kenyatta, Vintage Books copyright © 1965. Published by William Heinemann Ltd., a division of Random House, Inc. Used by permisson of Alfred A. Knopf, a division of Random House, Inc.

While historians have traditionally concentrated on the use of documentary sources, anthropologists developed techniques for analyzing cultures based on either archaeological study of past societies or direct observation of present societies. In recent decades, however, historians and anthropologists have increasingly shared each others' concerns and techniques. In attempting to understand Africans and their histories, historians have moved beyond colonial-era paradigms, often collaborating with anthropologists and scholars in other disciplines.

PHYSICAL DESCRIPTION OF THE CONTINENT

Africa is three and a half times the size of the continental United States and second only to Asia in total area (see Map 5–1 on page 124). Because steep escarpments surmount most of its narrow coasts, Africa has few natural harbors, and communication between the coast and the interior is difficult. Of Africa's major rivers (the Niger, Congo, Nile, Zambezi, and Orange), only the Nile has a relatively long navigable reach below its **cataracts** in upper Egypt. The continent's vast size and sharp physical variations, from high mountains to swamplands, tropical forests, and deserts, have channeled long-distance communication and movement along certain corridors including the Rift Valley of East Africa, the coastal reaches of East or North Africa, the Niger or Zambezi River valley, and the sahelian savannahs bordering the great equatorial forest.

The characteristics of different regions derive largely from Africa's position astride the equator. As a whole, its climate is unusually hot. Climate bands north and south of the equator roughly mirror each other. Along the equator, dense rain forests dominate a west–east band of tropical woodland. North and south of this band, the lush rain forests give way to **savannah**—open woodlands and grassy plains. Savannah in turn passes into steppe, semidesert, and finally true desert as one moves farther from the equator. In the north, the semidesert is known as the **Sahel**. The adjoining **Sahara** ("the Desert"; Arabic *al-Sahrá*) is the world's largest desert. In southwestern Africa the **Kalahari** Desert partially cuts off the southern plateau and coastal regions from central Africa.

Other natural factors are important to Africa's history. Soils across Africa are typically tropical in character: They are low in hummus and are not highly productive for

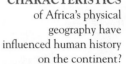

WHICH CHARACTERISTICS of Africa's physical geography have influenced human history on the continent?

cataract
A waterfall or steep rapids. Major cataracts on the Nile River are numbered.

savannah
An area of open woodlands and grassy plains.

Sahel
An area of steppe and semidesert that borders the Sahara.

Sahara
The world's largest desert. It extends across Africa from the Atlantic to the eastern Sudan. Historically, the Sahara has hindered contact between the Mediterranean and sub-Saharan Africa.

Kalahari
A large desert in southwestern Africa that partially isolates southern Africa from the rest of the continent.

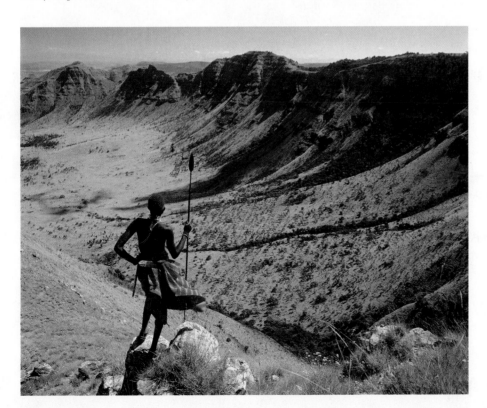

Great Rift Valley. A Samburu warrior stands before the eastern scarp of the Great Rift Valley in northern Kenya. This is believed to be the region where modern humans originated sometime before 100,000 B.C.E.

What are the noteworthy features of African geography?

MAP 5–1. Africa: Physical Features and Early Sites.   This map shows the major physical features of the continent and Iron Age sites of the western and central Sudan.

What patterns can you identify in Africa's physical features? Consider comparisons and contrasts north and south of the equator and between the eastern and western portions of the continent.

long. Water is scarce in most of Africa. Crop pests and insects such as the tsetse fly, mosquito, and locust have hampered farming and pastoralism in Africa. Still, abundant animal life has made hunting and fishing important means of survival in most of Africa. Africa also has great mineral wealth. Salt, iron, copper, and gold have been major trade goods from ancient times.

Africa is often discussed in terms of seven major regions: *North Africa*, the Mediterranean coastal regions from modern Morocco through Libya and including the northern Sahara; **Nilotic Africa**, roughly comprising the modern states of Egypt and Sudan; the **Sudan**, the broad belt of Sahel and savannah below the Sahara, stretching across the entire continent; *West Africa*, including the woodland coastal regions from Cape Verde to Cameroon and the western desert, Sahel, and savannah as far east as the Lake Chad basin; *East Africa*, from the Ethiopian highlands (a high, fertile plateau with steppe, Sahel, and desert to north and south) south over modern Kenya and Tanzania, an area split north to south by the Great Rift Valley; *central Africa*, the region north of the Kalahari, from the Chad basin across the Congo basin and southeast to Lake Tanganyika and south to the Zambezi River; and *southern Africa*, from the Kalahari Desert and Zambezi south to the Cape of Good Hope.

AFRICAN PEOPLES

AFRICA AND EARLY HUMAN CULTURE

Paleontological research indicates that our hominid ancestors evolved in the Great Rift Valley of highland East Africa at least 1.5 million years ago. Sometime before 100,000 B.C.E., modern humans—the species *Homo sapiens* (*sapiens*)—appeared and moved out to populate the world.

Archaeology documents substantial internal movements of peoples—and hence languages, cultures, and technologies—both north–south and east–west within the continent in ancient times. African goods circulated through Indian Ocean as well as Mediterranean trade. Nilotic Egypt served as a bridge between the rest of Africa and the Mediterranean and Near East. Well before the Common Era, the peoples of the upper Nile, Ethiopian highlands, and coastal areas of East Africa maintained contacts with Egypt, south Arabia, and probably India and Indonesia, via the Indian Ocean. Like Egypt, the North African coast engaged in Mediterranean trade throughout antiquity. Africa's Mediterranean littoral was a place where Berber speakers mixed with other Mediterraneans such as the Phoenicians. Here the powerful Carthaginian Punic state arose in the mid-first millennium, only to fall prey to Rome (see Chapter 6).

DIFFUSION OF LANGUAGES AND PEOPLES

Cultural and linguistic diffusion shows that, despite the continent's natural barriers, Africans have moved extensively. Between 1,000 and 3,000 languages are found in Africa, depending on how one distinguishes languages from dialects. They can be roughly divided into four major indigenous families (the Afro-Asiatic, the Nilo-Saharan, the Niger-Kongo, and the Khoisan), plus two later arrivals (the **Austronesian** language of Madagascar, and Indo-European languages from western Europe).

The Africanist scholar Roland Oliver has linked the development of language families to population growth that brought larger communities and extended movements of peoples.[3] After about 8000 B.C.E., **Afro-Asiatic** languages from the Jordan and Nile valleys spread to Arabia and across North Africa. Two southward extensions of these languages, from North Africa across the Sahara to the Chad basin, and from Egypt into the Ethiopian highlands and the Horn, likely occurred after 4000 B.C.E., possibly through the movement of sheep and cattle herders.

---

[3]For the discussion of language here and below, we rely on the summary and analysis of R. Oliver, *The African Experience* (Boulder, CO: Westview Press, 1991), pp. 38–50, and of E. Gilbert and J. Reynolds, *Africa in World History* (Upper Saddle River, NJ: Pearson Prentice Hall, 2008), especially Chapters 2 and 3.

QUICK REVIEW

Regions in Africa

- North Africa: Mediterranean coast, Sahara
- Nilotic Africa: lands surrounding Nile River
- The Sudan: Sahel/savannah band south of Sahara
- West Africa: coast, desert, Sahel, and savannah of the western Sudan
- East Africa: Ethiopian highlands, south to Tanzania
- Central Africa: Chad basin, Zaïre basin, south to Zambezi River
- Southern Africa: Cape of Good Hope, north to Kalahari Desert and Zambezi River

WHY ARE ideas about race not useful in understanding the histories of different groups in Africa?

Nilotic Africa
The lands along the Nile River.

Sudan
The broad band of Sahel and savannah that crosses the African continent south of the Sahara.

Austronesian
A widely dispersed language family with origins in the Pacific. Malagasy, spoken in Madagascar, is an Austronesian language.

Afro-Asiatic
A language family that includes Semitic languages, Kushitic, and others.

Nilo-Saharan
A language family concentrated in the band between the Nile and Rift highlands of Morocco.

Niger-Congo
A language family that originated in the savannah and woodlands of west and south-central Africa.

Bantu
A large subgroup of the Niger-Congo language family; also, the people who speak Bantu languages.

Khoisan
The language group spoken by the Khoikhoi, the San, and other peoples; also, the Khoikhoi and San peoples.

The **Nilo-Saharan** languages may have originated among fishing and cereal-growing societies in the Nubian region of the Nile and spread before 5000 B.C.E. west into the Sahara. Later they were largely displaced there by the southward extension of Afro-Asiatic languages into the Sahara through their pastoralist carriers. Nilo-Saharan languages must also have spread southeast with fisherman-farmers as far as the lakes region of the Great Rift Valley, where they were later partially displaced by Kushitic-speaking pastoralists or farmers.

The **Niger-Kongo** family had its homeland in the woodland savannah and equatorial forests of West and central Africa. Spoken by fisherfolk who may also have turned to farming, this group spread to the Atlantic coast from the Senegal River to the Cameroon mountains. Its largest subgroup, the **Bantu** speakers, later spread southward into the equatorial forestlands (largely as agriculturalists) and around the rain forests of central Africa (as herders and farmers) until they entered the eastern and southern savannahs (see Map 5–2).

The fourth language family, nowadays called **Khoisan**, apparently covered most of the southern half of the African continent by late Neolithic times but was largely displaced by the migration of Niger-Kongo Bantu speakers. The varied peoples who were ancestors of today's Khoisan speakers were probably primarily hunter-gatherers at this time. Eventually, most of these peoples adopted the languages of the immigrant Bantu-speaking agriculturalists and pastoralists.

The development of the complex language map of present-day Africa can thus be seen in terms of ancient developments in food production and movement of peoples within the continent.

"RACE" AND PHYSIOLOGICAL VARIATION

As recently as the late twentieth century, some interpreters attempted to link color or racial differences to the development of everything—from language and food production, to ironworking and state building—in Africa. None of these theories is tenable, however, because race itself is such a problematic concept, both historically and biologically. In the 1990s, there was a running dispute about whether ancient Egyptians were more "black" or "white," an argument in which skin pigmentation was meant to signal other attributes. (If Egyptians were black, they were assumed to be somehow more African than they already were simply by being in Africa, whereas white Egyptians would somehow have been more Mediterranean than African.) In reality, ancient Egypt was a multiethnic society, and ancient Egyptians seem to have been a people of many hues.

San Hunters, Southern Africa. There are many groups in Africa with different typical physiologies, skin pigmentation, and lifeways. As with all humans, however, there are more genetic differences between individuals than between groups.

Has race been a helpful concept for historians trying to understand African cultures?

The Greeks called all the dark-skinned peoples they were aware of in Africa *Ethiopians*, "those with burnt skins." The Arabs termed all of Africa south of the Sahara and Egypt *Bilad al-Sudan*, "Land of the Blacks" (from this we get the term *Sudan*). Although ancient writers observed variations in skin tone, it is important to avoid assuming that we understand what they meant in their observations. As with all historical records, these documents need to be read with attention to the authors' contexts and intentions.

MAP EXPLORATION

To explore this map further, go to **http://www.myhistorylab.com**

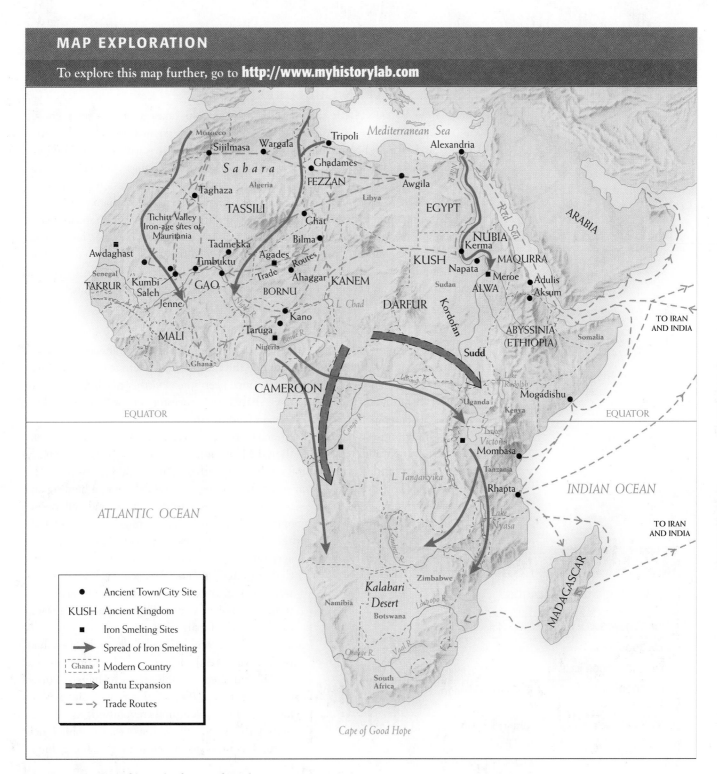

MAP 5–2. Ancient African Kingdoms and Empires.

What effect did the migrations of people and the spread of technology have on early African history?

Meanwhile, although skin color and other physiological characteristics are partially determined by genes, current research has found no genetic basis for the racial categories that humans have invented. There are more genetic differences between individuals than between groups.[4]

---

[4]See Gilbert and Reynolds, *Africa in World History*, Chapters 1–4.

THE SAHARA AND THE SUDAN TO THE BEGINNING OF THE COMMON ERA

WHAT EVIDENCE is there that early African cultures were in contact with each other?

EARLY SAHARAN CULTURES

Until about 2500 B.C.E. the Sahara was arable land with lakes and rivers, trees, grasses, and a reasonable climate. Animal, fowl, reptile, and fish populations allowed riparian (river- and lakeside) communities of considerable size to live with ease off the land. Then, from about 2500 B.C.E., climatic changes caused the Sahara to undergo a relatively rapid dessication, and the riparian communities of this vast territory disappeared.[5] By 1000 B.C.E., the dessication process had rendered the Sahara an immense, largely uninhabitable desert separating most of Africa from its Mediterranean coastal rim and the Near Eastern centers of early civilization. Even then, however, regular contacts between sub-Saharan Africa and the Mediterranean continued. Various north–south routes across the western and central Sahara were traversed by horses and carts or chariots and by migrating peoples long before the coming of the camel.

NEOLITHIC SUDANIC CULTURES

From the first millennium B.C.E., preliterate but complex agricultural communities of Neolithic and Early Iron Age culture dotted the central and western reaches of the sub-Saharan Sudan. These peoples may have once been spread farther north, in the then-arable Saharan lands they would have shared with ancestors of the Berber-speaking peoples of contemporary west-Saharan and North Africa.

This hypothesis has been bolstered by the excavation of town cultures from the mid-fifth millennium B.C.E. in Mali and Mauritania. In inland Mauritania, remains of an ancient but later agricultural civilization with as many as 200 towns have also been found. These reflect the transition from a hunting and fishing to a herding and rudimentary agricultural society. The progressive dessication of the second millennium B.C.E. may have forced these peoples farther south. These migrants carried with them both languages and techniques of settled agriculture. They domesticated new crops using their old techniques. Assisted by knowledge of ironworking, they effected an agricultural revolution. This meant considerable population growth in the more fertile Sudanic regions, especially near the Niger and Senegal rivers and Lake Chad. (A similar spread of agricultural techniques and cattle- and sheep-raising seems to have occurred down the Rift Valley of the East African highlands.) This agricultural revolution, completed during the first millennium B.C.E., enabled new cultural centers to develop in the sub-Saharan regions.

In the first millennium B.C.E. the Sudanic peoples carried their agricultural techniques and their languages eastward through the savannahs and southward, largely along the rivers, into the tropical rain forests of central and West Africa.

CHRONOLOGY	
EARLY AFRICAN CIVILIZATIONS	
ca. 7500–2500 B.C.E.	"Wet Holocene" period
ca. 2500 B.C.E.	Rapid dessication of Saharan region begins
ca. 2000–1000 B.C.E.	Increasing Egyptian influence in Nubia
ca. 1000–900 B.C.E.	Kushite kingdom with capital at Napata becomes independent of Egypt
751–663 B.C.E.	Kushite kings Piankhi and Taharqa rule all Egypt
ca. 600–500 B.C.E.	Meroe becomes new Kushite capital
ca. 500 B.C.E.–330 C.E.	Meroitic kingdom of Kush (height of Meroitic Kushite power ca. 250 B.C.E.–50 C.E.)
ca. 500 B.C.E.–500 C.E.?	Nok culture flourishes on Jos plateau in western Sudan (modern central Nigeria)

---

[5]Oliver, *The African Experience*, pp. 31–37.

This changed the face of sub-Saharan Africa, where previously small groups of hunter-gatherers had predominated. With the advent of iron smelting, these settled peoples were able to develop larger, more complex societies than their predecessors.

THE EARLY IRON AGE AND THE NOK CULTURE

Features of iron-smelting furnaces from widely scattered sites from the seventh century B.C.E. to the fourth century C.E. suggest that smelting was both introduced to Africa from the Near East, via Egypt, and independently invented within the continent, probably in the Great Lakes region. Thence it likely spread southward into western, central, and eastern parts of the continent.

Some of the most significant Iron Age sites have been found in what is today northeastern Nigeria on the Jos plateau. Here archaeological digs have yielded evidence of an early Iron Age people labeled the **Nok** culture (see Map 5–1). Excavations at Nok sites have yielded stone tools, iron implements, and sophisticated terra-cotta sculptures dating from about 900 B.C.E. to 200 C.E. Scholars date the introduction of iron smelting there to about the sixth century B.C.E. The Nok people cleared substantial woodlands from the plateau and combined agriculture with cattle herding. The continuities between the Nok culture's extraordinary sculptural art—especially magnificent burial or ritual masks—and later West African sculptural traditions suggest that this culture influenced later central and West African life. Ancient communities laid a foundation on which later and better-known Sudanic civilizations may have built.

A Terra-Cotta Head. This is from the Iron Age Nok culture, which occupied what is today northeastern Nigeria from about 900 B.C.E. to about 200 C.E.

© Werner Forman Archive/Art Resource, New York/Jos Museum, Nigeria.

What is the significance of continuities between Nok culture and later Sudanic civilizations?

Nok
A West African Iron Age culture renowned for its artistry.

NILOTIC AFRICA AND THE ETHIOPIAN HIGHLANDS

THE KINGDOM OF KUSH

The lower Nubian land of **Kush** lies in the upper Nile basin, just above the first cataract (see Map 5–2). There an Egyptianized segment of Nilo-Saharan-speaking Nubians built the second (after pharaonic Egypt) literate and politically unified civilization in Africa. As early as the fourth millennium B.C.E., the Old Kingdom pharaohs had subjugated and colonized Nubia. In the early second millennium B.C.E., however, an independent kingdom arose in Kush in the broad floodplain just above the third cataract of the Nile. As early as 2000 B.C.E., its capital, Kerma, had been a major trading outpost for Middle Kingdom Egypt, sending building materials, ivory, slaves, mercenaries, and gold north down the Nile.

The early Kushite kingdom achieved its greatest wealth and prosperity between the Middle and New Kingdoms of Egypt (ca. 1700–1500 B.C.E.). Finds in the royal palace fortress ruins and tombs suggest that its kings may have taken the gold mines of lower Nubia from the weakened Egyptian state in the Intermediate period. After the Hyksos invasions, with Egypt's recovery (from about 1500 B.C.E.), Kush came once more under Egyptian colonial rule and stronger Egyptian cultural influence. Then, sometime after 1000 B.C.E., as Egypt's New Kingdom floundered, a new Kushite state reasserted itself and by about 900 B.C.E. conquered both lower and upper Nubia, regaining independence and wealth from the Nubian gold mines.

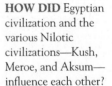

HOW DID Egyptian civilization and the various Nilotic civilizations—Kush, Meroe, and Aksum—influence each other?

Kush
An ancient Nubian kingdom that in some periods dominated, and in others was dominated by, pharaonic Egypt.

QUICK REVIEW

The Early Kushite Kingdom
- Located just above first cataract of the Nile
- Capital Kerma was a major trading outpost as early as 2000 B.C.E.
- It reached its zenith between 1700 and 1500 B.C.E.

THE NAPATAN EMPIRE

This new Kushite Empire was centered first at Napata, just below the fourth Nile cataract. The royal line that ruled at Napata saw themselves as Egyptian. They practiced the pharaonic custom of marrying their sisters, a practice known in many kingship institutions around the world. They buried their royalty embalmed in traditional Egyptian-style pyramids. In the eighth century B.C.E., they conquered Egypt and ruled it for about a century as the Twenty-fifth pharaonic dynasty. This Kushite Dynasty was driven out of Egypt proper by Assyria around 650 B.C.E.

THE MEROITIC EMPIRE

Forced back above the lower cataracts of the Nile by the Assyrians and kept there by the Persians, the Napatan kingdom became increasingly isolated and developed in its own distinctive ways. When an Egyptian army sacked Napata in 591 B.C.E., the capital was relocated farther south in the prosperous city of **Meroe**, bringing the seat of rule closer to the geographic center of the Kushite domains. Meroe was the center of a flourishing iron industry, from which iron smelting may have spread south and west. The Meroitic state was built on a staggeringly wide network of internal African and intercontinental trade. Its empire lasted until it was defeated and divided in the fourth century C.E. by Nuba peoples from west of the upper Nile.

In its heyday, from the mid-third century B.C.E. to the first century C.E., the Meroitic kingdom was "middleman" for varied African goods in demand in the Mediterranean and Near East: animal skins, ebony and ivory, gold, oils and perfumes, and slaves. The Kushites traded with the Hellenistic-Roman world, southern Arabia, and India. They shipped quality iron to Aksum and the Red Sea, and the Kushite lands between the Nile and the Red Sea were a major source of gold for Egypt and the Mediterranean world. Cattle breeding, cotton cultivation, and other agriculture were their economic mainstays.

This was an era of prosperity. Many monuments were built, including royal pyramids and the storied palace and walls of the capital. Fine pottery and jewelry were produced. Meroitic culture is especially renowned for its two kinds of pottery. The first, turned on wheels, was the product of an all-male industry attuned apparently to market demands; the second, made exclusively by hand by women, was largely for domestic use.

The political system of the Meroitic Empire had several features that distinguished it from its Egyptian models. The king seems to have ruled strictly by customary law, presumably as interpreted by whatever clerics served the state's needs. According to Greek accounts, firm taboos limited his actions; kings who violated those taboos could be forced to commit suicide. There was also a royal election system. The priests apparently considered the king a living god, an idea found in both ancient Egypt and many other African societies. Royal succession was often through the maternal rather than the paternal line (matrilineal succession was widespread in ancient Africa). The role of the queen mother in the election appears to have been crucial—another practice found elsewhere in Africa as well. By the second century B.C.E. a woman had become sole monarch, initiating a long line of queens, or "Candaces" (*Kandake*, from the Meroitic word for "queen mother"). The monarch seems to have presided over a central administration run by numerous high officials. The provinces were delegated to princes who must have enjoyed considerable autonomy, given the slow communications.

Beyond the ruling class, the few records available mention slaves, both female domestics and male laborers drawn largely from prisoners of war. Cattle breeders, farmers, traders, artisans, and minor government functionaries probably formed an

Meroe
The capital city of the ancient Napatan Empire, which at one time rivaled Aksum.

Meroitic Culture. The people of Meroe produced many examples of fine pottery. This fired clay jar is decorated with giraffes and serpents.

What were the two types of Meroitic pottery?

intermediate class between the slaves and the rulers. Kushite religious practices followed Egyptian traditions for centuries. By the third century B.C.E., however, gods unknown to Egypt became prominent. Most notable was Apedemak, a warrior god with a lion's head. The many lion temples associated with him (forty-six have been identified) reflect his importance. Such gods likely represented local deities who gradually took their places alongside the highest Egyptian gods.

THE AKSUMITE EMPIRE

A highland people who had developed their own commercially powerful trading state finished off the weakened Kushite Empire around 330 C.E. This was the newly Christianized state of **Aksum**, centered in the northern Ethiopian, or Abyssinian, highlands where the Blue Nile rises.

The peoples of Aksum descended from African Kushitic speakers and Semitic speakers from Yemenite southern Arabia. This mixing gave Aksum, and later Ethiopia, Semitic speech and script closely related to South Arabian. Greek and Roman sources tell of an Aksumite kingdom from at least the first century C.E.

In the first two centuries C.E., the kingdom's chief port of Adulis on the Red Sea made Aksum a strategic site on the increasingly important Indian Ocean trade routes that linked India and the East Indies, Iran, Arabia, and the East African coast with the Roman Mediterranean. Aksum also controlled trade between the African interior and the extra-African world, from Rome to Southeast Asia—notably exports of ivory, but also of elephants, obsidian, slaves, gold dust, and other inland products.

By the third century C.E., Aksum was one of the most impressive states of its age. A work attributed to the prophet Mani (ca. 216–277 C.E.) describes Aksum as one of the four greatest empires in the world. The Aksumites often held tributary territories across the Red Sea in southern Arabia. They also controlled northern Ethiopia and conquered Meroitic Kush. Thus they dominated some of the most fertile cultivated regions of the ancient world: their own plateau, the rich Yemenite highlands of southern Arabia, and much of the eastern Sudan across the upper Nile as far as the Sahara.

A king of kings in Aksum ruled this empire through tribute-paying vassal kings in the other subject states. By the sixth century the Aksumite king was even appointing southern Arabian kings himself. Aksum's gold, silver, and copper coins symbolized both its political and economic power. The Aksumites enjoyed a long-lived economic prosperity.

In religion, the pre-Christian paganism of Aksum resembled the pre-Islamic paganism of southern Arabia, with various gods and goddesses closely tied to natural phenomena. Jewish, Meroitic, and even Buddhist minorities lived in the major cities of Aksum—an index of the cosmopolitanism of the society and its involvement with the larger worlds beyond the Red Sea.

An inscription of the powerful fourth-century King Ezana tells of his conversion to Christianity, which led to the Christianizing of the kingdom as a whole. Subsequently, under Alexandrian influence, the Ethiopian church became **Monophysite** (that is, it adhered to the dogma of the single, unitary nature of Christ). In the fifth century C.E., the native Semitic language, Ge'ez, began to replace Greek in the liturgy, which proved a major step in the unique development of the Ethiopic or Abyssinian Christian church over the succeeding centuries.

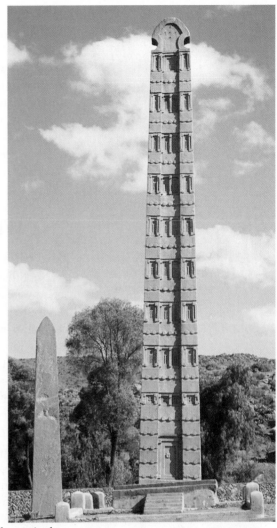

A Giant Stela at Aksum. Dating probably from the first century C.E., this giant carved monolith is the only one remaining of seven giant stelae—the tallest of which reached a height of 33 meters—that once stood in Aksum amidst numerous smaller monoliths. Although the exact purpose of the stelae is not known, the generally accepted explanation is that they were commemorative funerary monuments. Erecting them required engineering of great sophistication.
What does this stela suggest to you about Aksumite beliefs regarding death?

Aksum
A powerful Christianized trading state in the Ethiopian highlands.

Monophysite
Adhering to the dogma of the single, unitary nature of Christ (in opposition to the orthodox doctrine that Christ had two natures: human and divine).

ISOLATION OF CHRISTIAN ETHIOPIA

Aksumite trade continued to thrive through the sixth century. Aksumite power was eclipsed in the end by Arab Islamic power. Nevertheless, the Aksumite state continued to exist. Having sheltered a refugee group of Muhammad's earliest Meccan converts, the Aksumites enjoyed relatively cordial relations with Islamic domains. But Aksum became increasingly isolated. Its center of gravity shifted to the more rugged parts of the plateau, where a Monophysite Christian, Ge'ez-speaking culture emerged in the region of modern Ethiopia and lasted in relative isolation until modern times. Ultimately the whole Nubian region was Islamized, leaving Ethiopia the sole predominantly Christian state in Africa.

THE WESTERN AND CENTRAL SUDAN

WHAT ROLE did trade play in the rise of large political entities in the western and central Sudan?

AGRICULTURE, TRADE, AND THE RISE OF URBAN CENTERS

As Neolithic peoples moved southward, they discovered that Africa's equatorial rain forests were inhospitable to cows and horses, largely because of the animals' inability to survive the sleeping sickness (**trypanosomiasis**) carried by the tsetse fly. But the agriculturalists who brought their cereal grains and stone tools south found particularly good conditions in the savannah just north of the West African forests. By the first or second century C.E., settled agriculture, augmented by iron tools, had become the way of life of most inhabitants of the western Sudan; it had even progressed in the forest regions farther south. The savannah areas seem to have experienced a population explosion in the first few centuries C.E., especially around the Senegal River, the great northern bend in the Niger River, and Lake Chad. Villages, and chiefdoms of several villages, were the largest political units. As time went on, larger towns and political units developed in the western Sudan.

Trypanosomiasis

Sleeping sickness, a parasitic disease that is transmitted by tsetse flies. If untreated, it is fatal both to humans and animals.

Regional and interregional trade networks in the western and central Sudan date to ancient times; trans-Saharan trading routes were maintained throughout the first millennium B.C.E. Urban settlements—such as Gao, Kumbi (or Kumbi Saleh), and Jenne—emerged in the western Sahel. Excavations at Jenne in the upper Niger indicate that it dates from 250 B.C.E. and had a population of more than 10,000 by the late first millennium C.E.[6]

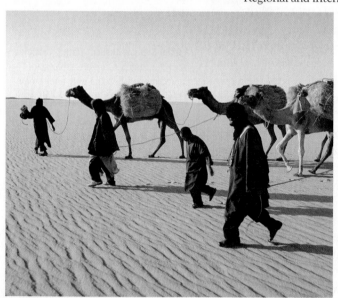

A Camel Caravan Crossing the Sahara.
Use of the camel as a beast of burden from the first century C.E. onward greatly increased trans-Saharan trade.

Why was the camel important to trade in Africa?

These and other early urbanized areas combined farming with fishing and hunting, and all developed in oasis or river regions rich enough to support dense populations and trade. The existence of relatively autonomous settlements made possible loose confederations or even imperial networks as time went on.

The introduction of the domesticated camel (the one-humped Arabian camel, or dromedary) from the East around the beginning of the Common Era increased trans-Saharan trade. By the early centuries C.E., the West African settled communities had developed important trading centers on their northern peripheries, in the Sahel near the edge of the true desert. The salt of the desert, needed in the settled savannah, and the gold of West Africa, coveted

[6]S. K. and R. J. McIntosh, *Prehistoric Investigations in the Region of Jenne, Mali* (Oxford: Oxford University Press, 1980), pp. 41–59, 434–461; and Oliver, *The African Experience*, p. 90. The ensuing discussion of West African urban settlement is taken primarily from Oliver's excellent summary, ibid., pp. 90–101.

MAP 5–3. Africa: Early Trade Routes and Early States of the Western and Central Sudan. This map shows some of the major routes of north–south trans-Saharan caravan trade and their links with Egypt and with Sudanic and forest regions of West Africa.

How did Africa's geography help determine its trade routes?

in the north, were prime trade commodities. Other items were also traded, including cola nuts, slaves, dates, and gum from West Africa, and horses, cattle, millet, leather, cloth, and weapons from the north. Towns such as Awdaghast, Walata, Timbuktu, Gao, Tadmekka, and Agades were the most famous southern terminals for this trade (see Map 5–3). These centers allowed the largely Berber middlemen who plied the desert routes to cross the perilous Sahara via oasis stations en route to the North African coasts or even Egypt. This was not an easy means of transporting goods; a typical crossing could take two to three months.

QUICK REVIEW

Trade

- Trade contributed to rise of larger political entities
- Regional and interregional trade networks date to ancient times
- Trade routes connected western and central Sudan with Egypt

FORMATION OF SUDANIC KINGDOMS IN THE FIRST MILLENNIUM

The growth of settled agricultural populations and the expansion of trade coincided with the rise of sizable states in the western and central Sudan. The most important states were located in Takrur on the Senegal River, from perhaps the fifth century, if not earlier; Ghana, between the northern bends of the Senegal and the Niger, from the fifth or sixth century; Gao, on the Niger southeast of the great bend, from before the eighth century; and Kanem, northeast of Lake Chad, from the eighth or ninth century. Although the origins of the major states in these areas are obscure, each represents the first of a series of large political entities in its region. All continued to figure prominently in subsequent West African history (see Chapter 14).

The states developed by the Fulbe people of Takrur and the Soninke people of Ghana depended on their ability to draw gold from the savannah region west of the upper Senegal into the trans-Saharan trade. Of all the sub-Saharan kingdoms of the late first millennium, Ghana was the most famous outside of the region, largely because of its control of the gold trade. Its people built a large regional empire centered at its capital, Kumbi Saleh. Inheriting his throne by matrilineal descent, the ruler was treated as a semidivine personage whose interaction with his subjects was mediated by a hierarchy of government ministers. He commanded a sizable army, including horsemen and archers, and was buried with his retainers under a dome of earth and wood. In contrast, the Songhai rulers of Gao had no gold trade until the fourteenth century. Gao was oriented in its forest trade toward the lower Niger basin and in its Saharan trade toward eastern Algeria. All of these states were based on agriculture and settled populations.

The power of Kanem originated with a nomadic federation of tribal peoples that merged to form a single people, the Kanuri. They took over the sedentary societies of Kanem, just east of Lake Chad, and later, Bornu, west of Lake Chad. By the thirteenth century the Kanuri had themselves become sedentary. Their kingdom controlled the southern terminus of perhaps the best trans-Saharan route—that running north via good watering stations to the oasis region of Fezzan in modern central Libya and thence to the Mediterranean. (We shall return to the later development of Kanem and the western Sudanic states in Chapter 14.)

CENTRAL, SOUTHERN, AND EAST AFRICA

WHY DID the coastal and inland regions of East Africa have different histories?

The African subcontinent is that part of central, southern, and East Africa that lies south of a line from roughly the Niger Delta and Cameroon to southern Somalia on the east coast.

BANTU EXPANSION AND DIFFUSION

In the southern subcontinent, most people speak one of more than 400 languages that belong to a single language group, Bantu, a subgroup of the Niger-Congo family. All Bantu languages are as closely related as are the Romance tongues of Europe. The proto-Bantu language probably arose south of the Benue River, in eastern Nigeria and modern Cameroon. Thence, during the latter centuries B.C.E. and the first century C.E., Bantu-speaking peoples apparently migrated in two basic directions: (1) south into the lower Congo basin and ultimately to the southern edge of the equatorial forest in present-day northern Katanga; and (2) east around the equatorial forests into the lakes of highland East Africa (see Map 5–3).

In all these regions, Bantu tongues developed and multiplied in contact with other languages. Likewise, Bantu speakers intermixed and adapted. Further migrations, from the first to as late as the eleventh century C.E., dispersed Bantu peoples more widely, into south-central Africa, coastal East Africa, and southern Africa. This dispersion led to the early civilization of "Great Zimbabwe" and Mapungubwe in the upper Limpopo region (treated in Chapter 14).

How the Bantu peoples managed to impose their languages on the earlier cultures of these regions, or intermix to produce hybrid-language cultures such as the Bantu-Arab Swahili (see Chapter 14), remains unexplained. The proto-Bantu had apparently been fishermen and hunters who also cultivated yams, date palms, and cereals. They raised goats and possibly sheep and cattle, but they did not bring cattle along in their migrations. Most of those migrating seem to have been cereal farmers whose basic political and social unit was the village. Perhaps they had unusually strong social cohesion, which allowed them to absorb other peoples; they were apparently not military conquerors. Possibly they simply had sufficient numbers to become dominant, or they may have brought diseases with them against which the aboriginals of the forests and southern savannah had no immunities. Bantu cultures became so fully interwoven with those of the peoples among whom they settled that we may never know the full story.

Bantu Languages and Group Distribution.
A Bantu-speaking mother with her child, photographed in South Africa around 1925. There are many distinct languages within the Bantu family distributed throughout Africa. Scholars use the relationships between these languages to trace the great Bantu migrations.

What kinds of factors might cause a group to develop a new dialect or new language?

Cave Painting from Namibia from at least 15,000 B.C.E., depicting rhinoceroses, giraffes, antelope, and zebra.

What do these images suggest to you about the importance of animals to the artist?

THE KHOISAN AND TWA PEOPLES

Alongside the Bantu-speaking majority in southern Africa is a minority who speak "Khoisan." The main two peoples that constitute the Khoisan speakers are the San and the Khoikhoi. (Westerners once referred to them as "Bushmen" and "Hottentots," names now considered offensive.) Formerly, observers believed the Khoikhoi and San could be distinguished from each other largely by their livelihood, the Khoikhoi labeled as herdsmen and the San as hunter-gatherers.[7] Both were seen as surviving representatives of a "primitive" stage of cultural evolution. More recent research has challenged these notions, and scholars now reject the very notion of cultural evolution. Much of the common wisdom about these peoples results from colonialist and postcolonial prejudice, which also accounts for the Khoisan's low socioeconomic status in contemporary Africa.

The San are likely the descendants of Neolithic and Early Iron Age peoples who created the striking prehistoric rock paintings of southern Africa. Today they are linguistically and culturally diverse subgroups throughout southern Africa who survive most prominently in the Kalahari region. The more homogeneous Khoikhoi were generally sheep- and cattle-herding pastoralists scattered across the south, yet speaking closely related Khoisan tongues. Their ancestors probably originated in northern Botswana. They were hunters who adopted animal herding from their Bantu-speaking neighbors, likely between 700 and 1000 C.E. They flourished as far south as the Cape of Good Hope as pastoralist clans, until their encounter with invading Dutch colonists in the mid-seventeenth century resulted in their demise as a distinct people.

In the central African rain forests, the Twa people commonly referred to in the West as "Pygmies" speak Bantu languages, but show other links to the Khoisan. Sandwe, a Khoisan language, is spoken by foraging groups in Tanzania, and small foraging groups in Kenya speak similar languages. They too are probably descendants of a population that preceded the Bantu migration.

EAST AFRICA

The history of pre-Islamic coastal East Africa differed from that of the inland highlands. Long-distance travel was easy and common along the seashore but less so inland. The coast was in contact with India, Arabia, and the Mediterranean via the Indian Ocean and Red Sea trade routes from at least the second century B.C.E. By contrast, we know little about the long-distance contacts of inland regions with the coastal areas until after 1000 C.E. Nonetheless, regional inland and coastal trade must also be ancient. Both coastal and overseas trade remained important and interdependent over the centuries because the Indian Ocean trade depended on the monsoon winds and could use only the northernmost coastal trading harbors of East Africa for round-trip voyages in the same year. The monsoon winds blow from the northeast December to March and thus can carry sailing ships south from Iran, Arabia, and India only during those months; they blow from the southwest April to August, so ships can sail from Africa northeast during those months. Local coastal shipping thus had to haul cargoes from south of Zanzibar and then transfer them to other ships for the annual round-trip voyages to Arabia and beyond.

---

[7]On distinctions between San and Khoikhoi, see Richard Elphick, *Kraal and Castle: Khoikhoi and the Founding of White South Africa* (New Haven, CT: Yale University Press, 1977), pp. xxi–xxii, 3–42; on the "construction" of their respective identities and for a summary of research on their antiquity and history, see E. N. Wilmsen, *Land Filled with Flies* (Chicago: University of Chicago Press, 1989). Note also that the once widely held notion that the Bantu and the Khoikhoi arrived in southern Africa at about the same time as the first European settlers was a fabrication to justify apartheid (see Chapter 34).

A Closer Look

Four Rock Art Paintings from Tassili n-Ajjer (4000–2000 B.C.E.)

These rock paintings from the central Saharan plateau of Tassili n-Ajjer in Algeria are four of hundreds of such paintings preserved from the late Neolithic period in Africa; on this plateau, paintings have been dated to the period 9000–1000 B.C.E. In the 4000–2000 B.C.E. period to which all four paintings here are dated, the art often depicts the cattle herded by pastoral nomads who spent the dry season largely sedentary on the plateau with their cattle, but it also depicts the animals hunted for food by the same peoples. Remember that this period coincided with the end of the long wet Neolithic or Holocene wet period (ca. 9000–2500 B.C.E.), when the Sahara had lakes and plains and dunes covered in places with grassland and populated by herds of elephants, giraffes, antelopes of various kinds, and other animals, such as the hippopotamus, that could not survive in the dessicated periods in the Sahara such as that which has prevailed since the late third millennium B.C.E. down to the present. These artists' keen observation of domesticated animals as well as varied wild animals is evident in these paintings, as is their ability to create striking and dramatic renderings of the human figure.

The magnificent artistry of this drawing of hippopotamuses reflects a keen aesthetic sensibility as well as a sharp observational capacity for the creatures these people encountered.

Here two antelopes are shown, again in highly artistic naturalistic rendering.

Both cattle and human figures are depicted here, without apparent linkage between the two. Note the elegant yet realistic rendering of both human and animal bodies and limbs.

Hunter with bow. Note the combination in the same figure of fidelity to life in the proportions and body parts of the hunter with the artistic rendering of motion and athletic grace that the figure displays.

Questions

1. Scholars have offered many differing interpretations—from magical efficacy of the images, to teaching images for youth, to simply rendering artistically scenes from daily life. What do you think might have been likely motivations for Neolithic nomadic peoples to create figural art on the rock walls near their dry-season camps?

2. Can you compare the relative simplicity or sophistication of these paintings with other examples of art in this book or with art that you know from other sources? How do these renderings change or reinforce your previous ideas about "prehistoric" African civilization or culture?

CHRONOLOGY

MOVEMENT AND CONTACT OF PEOPLES IN CENTRAL, SOUTHERN, AND EAST AFRICA

ca. 1300–1000 B.C.E.	Kushitic-speaking peoples migrate from Ethiopian plateau south along Rift Valley
ca. 400 B.C.E.–400 C.E.	Probable era of major Bantu migrations into central, East, and southeastern Africa
200–100 B.C.E.	East African coast becomes involved in Indian Ocean trade
ca. 100 B.C.E.	Probable time of first Indonesian immigration to East African coast
ca. 100–1500 C.E.	Nilotic-speaking peoples spread over upper Nile valley; Nilotic peoples spread over Rift Valley region

Long-distance trade came into its own in Islamic times—about the ninth century—as an Arab monopoly. Arab traders had settled in East African coastal towns for centuries. We can document Greco-Roman contact with East African trading centers as early as the first century C.E. Malagasy, the Austronesian language of Madagascar, points to the antiquity of contact with the East Indies. Southeast Asian crops including bananas and coconut palms spread across Africa as staple foods. East Africa also imported such items as Persian Gulf pottery, Chinese porcelain, and cotton cloth. The major African export around which east coast trade revolved was ivory, which was in perennial demand from Greece to India and even China. The slave trade was important, with African slaves exported to the Arab and Persian world, as well as to India or China. Gold became important in external trade only in Islamic times, from about the tenth century (see Chapter 14). With all this trade, ethnic and cultural mixing has long been the

Manyatta. Aerial view of a contemporary Maasai settlement, or *manyatta*, in Kenya.
What differentiates the Maasai from other groups living in the same region?

rule for the East African coast; even today, its linguistic and cultural traditions are rich and varied (see Chapter 14).

The history of inland East Africa south of Ethiopia is more difficult to trace, because of the absence of written sources. Linguistic and other clues indicate some key developments in the eastern highlands. These regions had seen an early infusion of peoples from the north, and over the centuries small groups continued to arrive. First came peoples speaking Kushitic languages of the Afro-Asiatic family, likely cattle herders and grain cultivators. Perhaps as early as 2000 B.C.E., they pushed from their homeland on the Ethiopian plateau down the Rift Valley as far as the southern end of Lake Tanganyika. They apparently displaced Neolithic hunter-gatherers possibly related to the Khoisan minorities of modern East and southern Africa.

Later, Nilotic-Saharan speakers moved from southwest of the Ethiopian plateau over the upper Nile valley by about 1000 C.E. Then they pushed east and south, following older Kushite paths, to spread over the Rift Valley and supplant the Kushites by the fifteenth century and subsequently cover much of the East African highlands in today's Uganda, Kenya, and Tanzania. Among these Nilotic peoples were the Luo and the Maasai. The Luo spread over a 900-mile-long swath of modern Uganda and parts of southern Sudan and western Kenya, adapting wherever they went. The Maasai, on the other hand, were and still are cattle pastoralists proud of their language, way of life, and cultural traditions. These distinguish them from the farmers or hunters whose settlements abut their pasturages at the top of the southern Rift Valley in modern Kenya and Tanzania. Here the Maasai have concentrated and remained.

These migrations and those of the Bantu, who entered the eastern highlands over many centuries, have made the highlands a melting pot of Kushitic, Nilotic, Bantu, and Khoisan groups. Today's populations here represent an immense linguistic and cultural diversity. Here as well as anywhere we see the myriad African peoples and cultures mirrored in a single region.

SUMMARY

 WHAT ARE the sources and techniques used for studying African history?

Issues of Interpretation, Sources, and Disciplines. Historians are challenged in their study of Africa by the paucity of written sources and by the European prejudices that have traditionally devalued African contributions to world culture. Africanists use cross-disciplinary methods and innovative scholarship to understand Africa's past. *page 120*

 WHICH CHARACTERISTICS of Africa's physical geography have influenced human history on the continent?

Physical Description of the Continent. Africa is large; much of it is at high elevation, and generally hot. Climate is very roughly symmetrical north and south of the equator. Communications and migrations are easiest

in a few channels. African soils must be nurtured to retain productivity. *page 123*

 WHY ARE ideas about race not useful in understanding the histories of different groups in Africa?

African Peoples. The human species, *Homo sapiens* (*sapiens*) originated in Africa. Archaeology reveals that there were extensive migrations of peoples across the continent from the earliest days of African history with widespread cross-cultural influences. Although many types of physiologies are visible in Africa, the concept of race does not help historians understand different groups. Migrations and cultural exchanges are not dependent on skin coloration, but many historical sources are distorted by discredited ideas about human characteristics. *page 125*

WHAT EVIDENCE is there that early African cultures were in contact with each other?

The Sahara and the Sudan. Neolithic agriculturalists spread south of the Sahara, bringing the agricultural revolution with them. Pottery styles and iron-smelting technologies spread between groups. The early Iron Age Nok culture is renowned for sophisticated sculpture. *page 128*

 HOW DID Egyptian civilization and the various Nilotic civilizations—Kush, Meroe, and Aksum—influence each other?

Nilotic Africa and the Ethiopian Highlands. Egypt had extensive interaction with the Nubian peoples to the south. Nubian kingdoms—Kush, Napata, Meroe, and Aksum (Ethiopia)—adopted many features of Egyptian civilization and sometimes dominated Egypt itself. Aksum adopted Christianity in the fourth century C.E. *page 129*

 WHAT ROLE did trade play in the rise of political entities in the western and central Sudan?

The Western and Central Sudan. Extensive trade across the Sahara between North Africa and the western and central Sudan enabled products and ideas from the Mediterranean to reach the African interior in exchange for African products, such as gold, ivory, and salt. Large, settled populations facilitated the development of states. *page 132*

WHY DID the coastal and inland regions of East Africa have different histories?

Central, Southern, and East Africa. The dominance of the Bantu language across the African subcontinent reflects ancient migration patterns. On the coast of East Africa, trade across the Red Sea and the Indian Ocean with Arabia and East Asia fostered a distinctive and sophisticated culture. *page 134*

KEY TERMS

Afro-Asiatic (p. 125)
Aksum (AHK-suhm) (p. 131)
Austronesian (p. 125)
Bantu (BAN-tu)
    (pp. 126)
cataract (p. 123)
Kalahari (p. 123)
Khoisan (KOI-sahn) (p. 126)
Kush (koosh) (p. 129)
Meroe (MEH-roh-ee)
    (p. 130)

Monophysite (moh-NOH-
    fiss-it) (p. 131)
Niger-Kongo (p. 126)
Nilo-Saharan (p. 126)
Nilotic Africa (p. 125)
Nok (p. 129)
Sahara (p. 123)
Sahel (p. 123)
savannah (p. 123)
Sudan (p. 125)
trypanosomiasis (p. 132)

REVIEW QUESTIONS

1. Why have historians generally paid more attention to pharaonic Egypt than to the societies of sub-Saharan Africa?

2. Summarize the argument for including writing among the necessary attributes of a "civilization." Summarize the argument against the writing requirement. Which argument do you find more compelling?

3. Discuss the strengths and weaknesses of the various sources and tools available to scholars of early African history.

4. What does the diffusion of peoples and languages in Africa tell us about early African history?

5. How does the political system of the Meroitic Empire compare to that of Egypt?

6. How did Aksum become a Christian state?

7. What were the most important goods for African internal trade? Which products were traded abroad? What can we learn from these trade patterns?

8. What was the role of geography in early African history? What about the specific case of Ghana? Of North Africa? Of the East African littoral? Of southern Africa?

9. Is the role of geography different in Africa than in the Near East or other regions you have studied? Explain.

10. What information presented in this chapter was most surprising to you, and why?

Note: To learn more about the topics in this chapter, please turn to the Suggested Readings at the end of the book. For additional sources related to this chapter please see www.myhistorylab.com

PEARSON
myhistorylab Connections

Reinforce what you learned in this chapter by studying the many documents, images, maps, review tools, and videos available at **www.myhistorylab.com**

Read and Review

✓—Study and **Review** Chapter 5

👁—See the **Map** *Kingdoms of the Upper Nile, p. 161*

Research and Explore

Watch the Video *Agriculture in Africa*
African Maps
Who were the Ancient Egyptians?
Ironworks in Africa

Watch the Video *West African States*

((•—Hear the Audio

Hear the audio file for Chapter 5
at **www.myhistorylab.com**

6

Republican and Imperial Rome

((•—[Hear the **Audio** for Chapter 6 at www.myhistorylab.com

Lady Playing the Cithara. This wall painting from the first century B.C.E. comes from the villa of Publius Fannius Synistor at Pompeii and shows a woman playing a cithara, a type of lyre. Behind her a child, presumably her daughter, provides support.

Roman. Paintings. Pompeian, Boscoreale. 1st Century B.C. "Lady playing the cithara." Wall painting from the east wall of large room in the villa of Publius Fannius Synistor. Fresco on lime plaster. H. 6 ft. 1/2 in. (187 × 187 cm.) The Metropolitan Museum of Art, Rogers Fund, 1903 (03.14.5) Photograph © 1986 The Metropolitan Museum of Art.

What were women's most important roles in ancient Rome?

T*he ancient Romans were responsible for one of the most remarkable achievements in history. From their city in central Italy, they conquered most of the Near East and much of Europe. They brought peace, prosperity, and unity to this vast region, a feat that has never been repeated.*

Rome's legacy is more than military prowess and superb political organization. The Romans transformed the intellectual and cultural achievements of the Greeks, creating the Greco-Roman tradition in literature, philosophy, and art. This tradition remains the heart of Western civilization. ■

GLOBAL PERSPECTIVE

REPUBLICAN AND IMPERIAL ROME

Despite the nearly continuous warfare that marked Roman history, including a long-lasting rivalry with the Sasanid Empire, it was primarily through trade that Romans came into contact with peoples beyond the borders of their empire.

Nonetheless, most Romans focused their energies on internal Roman territory, which expanded considerably during the late republic and the early empire to include much of the former Hellenistic kingdoms. Rome was a multicultural empire, encompassing territory and cultures in Africa and the Middle East, as well as northern and central Europe. Rome profited enormously from the territories it conquered in terms of material wealth, including foodstuffs, as Egypt quickly became the "breadbasket" of

the empire. It also realized cultural benefits, especially the blending of Greek and Asian culture that characterized the Hellenistic world. But the infusion of new ideas caused tension among Romans, as many conservative Romans objected to what they viewed as corrupting Asian influences from even the much admired, and copied, Greeks, which threatened to undermine traditional Roman values and strengths.

The conquest of a vast empire had moved the Romans away from their unusual historical traditions toward the more familiar path of empire trodden by rulers in Egypt, Mesopotamia, China, India, and Iran. It is especially instructive to look at Rome from the perspective of historians who discern a "dynastic cycle" in

---

ITALY BEFORE ROME

WHO WERE the early peoples of Italy?

In about 1000 B.C.E. bands of warlike peoples speaking a set of closely related languages we call Italic began to infiltrate Italy. By 800 B.C.E. they had occupied the highland pastures of the Apennines and soon challenged the earlier settlers for control of the western plains. The Romans would emerge from descendants of these tough mountain people.

Others who shaped the future of Italy included the Etruscans, the Greeks who colonized Sicily and southern Italy, and the Celts. Etruscan civilization, which was to have a powerful influence on the Romans, arose about 800 B.C.E. In the seventh and sixth centuries B.C.E. the Etruscans conquered Latium (which included Rome) and Campania, where they became neighbors of the Greeks of Naples. But after 500 B.C.E. Etruscan power rapidly declined. The Celts drove them from the Po valley about 400 B.C.E., and soon thereafter they lost control of their Etrurian heartland to an expanding Rome.

ROYAL ROME

WHAT PATTERNS of Roman governance were set in the royal period?

In the sixth century B.C.E. the town of Rome in Latium came under Etruscan control. Although it had been of little importance, it was a natural center for communication and trade. Led by Etruscan kings, the Roman army conquered most of Latium.

GOVERNMENT

imperium
"The power to command." The right of Roman kings to issue commands and to enforce them by fines, arrests, and physical punishment.

Roman kings had the awesome power of **imperium**—the right to issue commands and to enforce them by fines, arrests, and physical punishment, including execution. Although it tended to remain in families, kingship was elective. The Roman Senate approved the candidate for the office, and the Roman people, voting in assembly, formally granted the *imperium*. This procedure—the granting of great power to executive officers contingent on the approval of the Senate and ultimately the people—would remain a basic characteristic of Roman government.

The Senate met only when summoned by the king and then only to advise him. In reality its authority was great, for the senators, like the king, served for life. The Senate

((•—[**Hear** the **Audio**
at **myhistorylab.com**

China (see Chapter 7). The development of the Roman Empire, though by no means the same as the Chinese, fits the pattern fairly well. Like the former Han Dynasty in China, the Roman Empire in the West fell, leaving in its wake disunity, insecurity, disorder, and poverty. Like other similar empires in the ancient world, it had been unable to sustain what historian Edward Gibbon termed its "immoderate greatness."

- What was it about the period from the second century B.C.E. through the third century C.E. that allowed the opening of new routes by land and sea linking Europe to Central Asia, India, and China?

- Why did the Roman Empire decline in the West? Which of the problems that Rome faced were internal, and which were external? How were the two connected?

Focus Questions

- Why might we describe the Roman Empire as "multicultural"? What cultures most influenced Roman culture, and why?

---

had continuity and experience, and it was composed of the most powerful men in the state. It could not be ignored.

The third branch of government, the curiate assembly, was made up of all citizens and divided into thirty groups. The assembly also met only when summoned by the king. Voting was not by head but by group; a majority within each group determined its vote, and the decisions were made by majority vote of the groups. Group voting would be typical of all future forms of Roman assembly.

FAMILY

The center of Roman life was the family. At its head stood the father, whose power and authority resembled those of the king within the state. Over his children he held broad powers analogous to *imperium;* he could sell his children into slavery and might even kill them. Over his wife he had less power; he could not sell or kill her. In practice his

◆◆◆ Read the Document
Excerpt from *The Life of Cato the Elder* (2 C.E.) Plutarch at **myhistorylab.com**

Sarcophagus of an Etruscan Couple. Much of what we know of the Etruscans comes from their funerary art. This sculpture of an Etruscan couple is part of a sarcophagus.

© Erich Lessing/Art Resource, New York.

What continuities were there between Etruscan and Roman history?

power to dispose of his children was limited by other family members, by public opinion, and, most of all, by tradition. A wife could be divorced only for serious offenses. The Roman woman had a respected position and the main responsibility for managing the household. The father was the chief priest of the family, leading it in daily prayers to the dead that reflected the ancestor worship central to Roman culture.

CLIENTAGE

Clientage was one of Rome's most important institutions. The client was "an inferior entrusted, by custom or by himself, to the protection of a stranger more powerful than he, and rendering certain services and observances in return for this protection."[1] The client was said to be in the *fides*, or trust, of his patron, giving the relationship a moral dimension. The patron provided his client with physical and legal protection and economic support. In return the client would fight for his patron, work his land, and support him politically.

PATRICIANS AND PLEBEIANS

In the royal period Roman society was divided into two classes based on birth. The wealthy **patrician** upper class held a monopoly of power and influence. Its members alone could conduct state religious ceremonies, sit in the Senate, or hold office. They formed a closed caste by forbidding marriage outside their own group.

The **plebeian** lower class must have consisted originally of poor, dependent small farmers, laborers, and artisans, the clients of the nobility. As Rome grew, nonpatrician families acquired wealth. From early times, therefore, there were rich plebeians and patrician families that fell into poverty from incompetence or bad luck. The line between the classes and the monopoly of privileges nevertheless remained firm.

patricians
The hereditary upper class of early Republican Rome.

plebeians
The hereditary lower class of early Republican Rome.

THE REPUBLIC

WHAT CULTURES most influenced Roman culture, and why?

According to Roman tradition, the outrageous behavior of the last kings provoked the noble families to revolt in 509 B.C.E., leading to the creation of the republic.

CONSTITUTION

The Roman constitution was an unwritten accumulation of laws and customs. The Twelve Tables, the first attempt to codify Rome's harsh customs, was not published until 450 B.C.E.

The Romans granted consuls, their chief magistrates, the power of *imperium* that kings had exercised. Like the kings, the consuls led the army, had religious duties, and served as judges. But the power of the consul was kept in check in two ways. Two men held consulships simultaneously, and each could overrule the other. Both were limited to a term of only one year. Their *imperium* was also limited. Although the consuls had full powers of life and death in the field with the army, within the city of Rome, citizens could appeal to the popular assembly any cases involving capital punishment. Each consul also knew that, after one year in that role, he would spend the rest of his life as a member of the Senate, so only a reckless consul would ignore its advice. In serious crises, the consuls could, with the advice of the Senate, appoint a single *dictator*, who would hold *imperium* not subject to appeal both inside and outside the city for six months.

Read the Document
Livy: The Rape of Lucretia and the Origins of the Republic, ca. 10 B.C.E.
at **myhistorylab.com**

---

[1] E. Badian, *Foreign Clientelae (264–70 B.C.E.)* (Oxford: Oxford University Press, 1958), p. 1.

A Closer Look

Lictors

The lictors were attendants of the Roman magistrates who held the power of *imperium,* the right to command. In republican times these magistrates were the consuls, praetors, and proconsuls. The lictors were men from the lower classes—some were even former slaves. They constantly attended the magistrates when the latter appeared in public. The lictors cleared a magistrate's way in crowds, and summoned, arrested, and punished offenders for him. They also served as their magistrate's house guard.

After the establishment of the Roman Republic, the lictor and his fasces and axe were the symbols of those magistrates that held *imperium,* which means that they had the right to command. Twelve lictors accompanied each *consul* and a *praetor* had six. When a *dictator* was appointed during a crisis, he had an escort of twenty-four lictors to show that he was more powerful than both consuls.

The axe carried by the man on the left is a symbol of the magistrate's power, when he was acting as a military commander outside the city, to put a Roman citizen to death.

The bundle of sticks, called fasces, the other two lictors carry indicates the magistrate's right to employ corporal punishment, but their bindings symbolize the right of citizens not on military duty not to be punished without a trial.

The traditional dress of a lictor was a toga when in Rome, and a red coat called a *sagum* when outside the city or when taking part in a triumph.

Questions

1. Why do you think the Roman magistrates required such bodyguards?

2. What does their presence indicate about the nature of early Roman public life?

3. How does the presence of lictors suggest a different attitude toward public officials between the Roman and classical Athenian republics?

censor
A Roman official who counted the populace and drew up the citizen roles, thereby fixing taxation and status.

tribunes
Roman officials who had to be plebeians and were elected by the plebeian assembly to protect plebeians from the arbitrary power of the magistrates.

Punic Wars
Three wars between Rome and Carthage for dominance of the western Mediterranean that were fought from 264 B.C.E. to 146 B.C.E.

In 325 B.C.E. the Romans created the office of proconsul, which permitted a consul in the field to retain command during a long campaign. Another new office, that of praetor, was primarily judicial, but praetors also had *imperium* and served as generals. After the middle of the fifth century B.C.E., the job of identifying citizens and classifying them according to age and property was delegated to another new office, that of **censor**, a position that grew in power and prestige.

The Senate, composed of leading patricians, gained power when the monarchy ended. As the only ongoing deliberative body in the Roman state, it soon controlled finances and foreign policy.

The *centuriate assemble*, the early republic's most important popular assembly, was in a sense the Roman army acting in a political capacity. Its basic unit was the century, theoretically 100 fighting men who fought with the same kind of equipment. Because each man equipped himself, this organization divided the assembly into classes according to wealth.

THE STRUGGLE OF THE ORDERS

Patricians monopolized power in the early republic. Plebeians, however, made up much of the Roman army, and this gave them great political leverage. Their fight for political, legal, and social equality, the "struggle of the orders," lasted 200 years. They won the right to a plebeian tribal assembly led by elected officials called **tribunes**. A tribune could veto any action of a magistrate or any bill proposed in a Roman assembly or by the Senate. In 445 B.C.E. plebeians won the right to marry patricians, though not until 367 B.C.E. could they serve as consul. Gradually other offices, including the dictatorship and the censorship, opened to them. In 300 B.C.E. they were admitted to the most important priesthoods. In 287 B.C.E., plebeians secured the passage of a law making the decisions of the plebeian assembly binding on all Romans without the approval of the Senate.

The victory of the plebeians in the "struggle of the orders" primarily benefited wealthy plebeian families by allowing them to share the political privileges of the patrician aristocracy. The *nobiles*—a small group of wealthy families, both patrician and plebeian—dominated the Senate and controlled the highest offices of the state.

CONQUEST OF ITALY

By the beginning of the fourth century B.C.E., the Romans had become the chief power in central Italy. The city's Latin neighbors, the Latin League, sought to curtail Rome's expansion, but in 338 B.C.E. the Romans defeated the league and dissolved it.

The Romans did not destroy any conquered Latin cities. To some near Rome they granted full citizenship. To others farther away they granted municipal status, which included the right to local self-government and the right to trade and intermarry with Romans. Still other states became allies of Rome. The Romans established permanent colonies of veteran soldiers in conquered lands. The colonists remained Roman citizens and deterred rebellion. A network of durable roads—some still in use—connected the colonies to Rome.

Rome divided its enemies and extended its influence through military force and diplomatic skill. Rebels were punished harshly, but Rome was generous to those who submitted. Loyal allies could even gain full Roman citizenship. This policy gave allies a stake in Rome's future, and most remained loyal.

ROME AND CARTHAGE

In the ninth century B.C.E., the Phoenician city of Tyre had established the North African coastal colony of Carthage. In the sixth century B.C.E., Carthage became independent and expanded west and east. Carthage claimed an absolute monopoly on trade in the western Mediterranean (see Map 6–1).

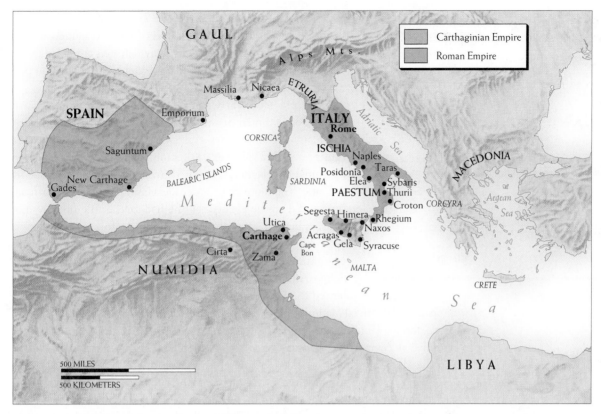

MAP 6–1.   The Western Mediterranean Area during the Rise of Rome.   This map covers the theater of the conflict between the growing Roman dominions and those of Carthage in the third century B.C.E. The Carthaginian Empire stretched westward from Carthage along the North African coast and into southern Spain.

Why did Rome repeatedly come into conflict with Carthage?

Sicily was strategically important to both Carthage and Rome. There, in 264 B.C.E., the two expanding powers first came to blows. Because the Romans called the Carthaginians Poeni or Puni (meaning "Phoenician"), the conflicts between them are called the **Punic Wars**.

Rome's strength was its army and Carthage's power was its navy, so at first neither side could make much progress against the other in the First Punic War. Once the Romans built a fleet, they were able to blockade the Carthaginian ports in Sicily. Carthage capitulated in 241 B.C.E., giving up Sicily and agreeing to pay a war indemnity. Neither side was to attack the allies of the other.

These terms were fair, but Rome broke them almost immediately. In 238 B.C.E., Rome seized Sardinia and Corsica, demanding an additional indemnity from Carthage. Carthage, meanwhile, was building a rich empire in Spain. In 221 B.C.E., Hannibal (247–182 B.C.E.) took command of Carthaginian forces in Spain. A few years earlier, Rome had received an offer of alliance from the Spanish town of Saguntum. The Romans accepted, and the Saguntines began to stir up Spanish tribes allied with Hannibal. Hannibal retaliated by seizing

A Roman Warship. Rome became a naval power late in its history, in the course of the First Punic War. Roman sailors initially lacked the skill and experience in sea warfare of their Carthaginian opponents, who could maneuver their oared ships to ram the enemy. To compensate for this disadvantage, the Romans sought to make a sea battle more like an encounter on land by devising ways to grapple enemy ships and board them with armed troops. In time they also mastered the skillful use of the ram. This picture shows a Roman ship, propelled by oars, with both ram and soldiers, ready for either kind of fight.

How did war with Carthage shape Roman history?

CHRONOLOGY

THE PUNIC WARS

264–241 B.C.E.	First Punic War
238 B.C.E.	Rome seizes Sardinia and Corsica
221 B.C.E.	Hannibal takes command of Punic army in Spain
218–202 B.C.E.	Second Punic War
216 B.C.E.	Battle of Cannae
202 B.C.E.	Battle of Zama
149–146 B.C.E.	Third Punic War
146 B.C.E.	Destruction of Carthage

Saguntum. Rome declared war in 218 B.C.E., but Hannibal struck first, marching overland from Spain to launch a swift and daring invasion of Italy. His army defeated the Romans in three battles, but his hopes for final victory depended on persuading Rome's allies to switch sides.

In 216 B.C.E., at Cannae, Hannibal destroyed a Roman army of 80,000 men. It was the worst defeat in Roman history, and many of Rome's allies went over to Hannibal. In 215 B.C.E., Philip V (r. 221–179 B.C.E.), king of Macedon, allied with Hannibal and launched a war to recover his influence on the Adriatic. For more than a decade Hannibal was free to roam Italy and do as he pleased, but he had neither the numbers nor the supplies to besiege the city of Rome itself.

The turning point in the conflict came when the Romans appointed Publius Cornelius Scipio (237–183 B.C.E.), later called Scipio Africanus, to the command in Spain. He was almost as talented as Hannibal. Within a few years Scipio had conquered all Spain and deprived Hannibal of help from that region. In 204 B.C.E., Scipio invaded Africa, forcing Hannibal to return to protect Carthage. In 202 B.C.E., Scipio defeated Hannibal at Zama. Carthage was stripped of its empire, and Rome emerged dominant over the Mediterranean from Italy westward.

Even so, some Romans refused to abandon their hatred of Carthage. Cato is said to have ended all his speeches in the Senate with the same sentence, "Besides, I think that Carthage must be destroyed." Eventually, the Romans took advantage of a technical breach of the peace to plow up the city's land, even putting salt in the furrows to ensure abandonment of the site. The Romans incorporated Carthage as the province of Africa.

The Roman conquest of overseas territory presented a new problem. The old practice of extending citizenship to defeated opponents stopped at the borders of Italy. The Romans made Sicily, Sardinia, and Corsica provinces. The governors of these provinces exercised an *imperium* free of the limits put on the power of officials in Rome. The natives of provinces became tribute-paying subjects of a Roman empire. Rome collected taxes by "farming them out," that is, by auctioning the right to collect taxes to the man who made the highest bid. The treasury got a guaranteed sum, and the tax collector made a profit by exploiting the provincials. Provincial government spread so much corruption that it threatened to destabilize the republic.

THE REPUBLIC'S CONQUEST OF THE HELLENISTIC WORLD

By the middle of the third century B.C.E., the eastern Mediterranean had reached a stable balance of power. That equilibrium was threatened by two aggressive monarchs, Philip V of Macedon and the Seleucid Antiochus III (223–187 B.C.E.). Philip and Antiochus moved swiftly, Antiochus against Syria and Palestine, Philip against Greek cities.

The threat that a more powerful Macedon might pose to Rome's friends, and perhaps even to Italy, persuaded the Romans to intervene. In 197 B.C.E., with Greek support, they defeated Philip in Thessaly. The Greek cities taken from Philip were made autonomous and declared free.

Soon after, Antiochus landed an army on the Greek mainland. The Romans drove him from Greece, and in 189 B.C.E. they crushed his army at Magnesia in Asia Minor. The Romans left Greek cities free, but they regarded Greece and Asia Minor as protectorates in which they could intervene as they chose.

QUICK REVIEW

Rome Conquers Greece

- Romans forbid interference in Greek cities by Macedonia
- Rome sees Greek cities as a kind of protectorate
- Rome responds with force to signs of anti-Roman feeling in Greek cities

What elements of Greek culture influenced Roman education?

In 179 B.C.E., Perseus (r. 179–168 B.C.E.) succeeded Philip V as king of Macedon. He tried to gain popularity in Greece by favoring the democratic and revolutionary forces in the cities. The Romans defeated him in 168 B.C.E. and divided Macedon into four separate republics. The new plan reflected a stern, businesslike policy promoted by the conservative censor Cato (234–149 B.C.E.). Leaders of anti-Roman factions in the Greek cities were punished severely, and in 146 B.C.E., the city of Corinth was destroyed. The Roman treasury benefited so much from these wars that Rome abolished direct property taxes on its citizens. Romans were learning that foreign campaigns could bring profit to the state, rewards to soldiers, and wealth, fame, and power to their generals.

GREEK CULTURAL INFLUENCE

Among the most important effects of Rome's expansion overseas were changes in the Roman style of life and thought. Roman aristocrats surrounded themselves with Greek intellectuals. Even conservatives, such as Cato, who spoke contemptuously of "Greeklings," learned Greek and absorbed Greek culture.

Almost from the beginning, the Romans identified their gods with Greek equivalents and incorporated Greek mythology into their own. In the third century B.C.E. important new cults were introduced from the East: the worship of Cybele, the Great Mother goddess from Asia Minor, and of Dionysus, or Bacchus. Interest in Babylonian astrology also grew.

Education was entirely the responsibility of the Roman family. It is not clear whether girls received any education in early Rome, although they did later on. Boys' education aimed at making them moral, pious, patriotic, law-abiding, and respectful of tradition. Contact with the Greeks of southern Italy produced momentous changes in Roman curricula. Greek teachers introduced the study of language, literature, and philosophy, as well as the idea of a liberal education, or what the Romans called *humanitas*—the root of our concept of the humanities.

The first need was to learn Greek, for Rome did not yet have a literature of its own. Schools were established in which the teacher, called a *grammaticus*, taught his students the Greek language and its literature, particularly the works of Homer. Thereafter, educated Romans were expected to be bilingual. Roman boys of the upper classes then studied rhetoric—the art of speaking and writing well—with Greeks who were expert in it. The Greeks considered rhetoric less important than philosophy. But the more practical Romans took to it avidly, for it was of great use in legal disputes and was becoming ever more valuable in political life. By the last century of the Roman Republic, the new Hellenized education had become dominant. Latin literature formed part of the course of study, but much of it was modeled after Greek examples. The number of educated people grew, extending beyond the senatorial class and outside the city of Rome.

Girls of the upper classes were educated similarly to boys. They were probably taught by tutors at home, although they were usually married by the age when men were pursuing higher education. Still, some women became prose writers or poets.

See the **Map**
The Roman Conquest of the Mediterranean During the Republic
at **myhistorylab.com**

Read the **Document**
Issue of the Day: Religion and Philosophy in the Roman Empire-Stoicism and Christianity? at **myhistorylab.com**

humanitas
The Roman name for a liberal arts education.

QUICK REVIEW

Roman Education

- Traditional Roman education was the responsibility of family
- Encounters with Greece changed form and content of education
- Schools established to teach Greek and Latin literature

MAP 6–2. Roman Dominions of the Late Republic.

This map shows the extent of the territory controlled by Rome at the time of Caesar's death in 44 B.C.E.

How did Rome's geographic location influence its growth?

A rich, socially ambitious Roman might support a Greek philosopher in his own home, so that through conversation his son could acquire the learning and polished thought necessary for the fully cultured gentleman. Some, like the great orator Cicero (106–43 B.C.E.), traveled to Greece to study with great teachers of rhetoric and philosophy. Education made the Romans part of the culture of the Hellenistic world, a world they dominated and, therefore, needed to understand.

ROMAN IMPERIALISM

WHY DID a growing gap between the wealthy and everyone else contribute to political instability?

Rome's expansion in Italy and overseas was accomplished without a plan. It brought the Romans an empire, and with it, power, wealth, and responsibilities (see Map 6–2).

AFTERMATH OF CONQUEST

War and expansion changed the economic, social, and political life of Italy. The Second Punic War damaged Italian farmland, and many veterans were unable to go back to their farms. Most became tenant farmers or hired hands. Often the land they abandoned was acquired by the wealthy, who converted these farms, later called *latifundia*, into large plantations.

Land was inexpensive, and slaves conquered in war provided cheap labor. By fair means and foul, large landholders obtained sizable quantities of public land and forced small farmers off it. These changes separated the people of Rome and Italy more sharply into rich and poor, the landed and the landless. The result was conflict that threatened the republic.

THE GRACCHI

By the middle of the second century B.C.E., the unintended consequences of Rome's rapid expansion troubled perceptive Roman nobles. The fall in status of the peasant farmers made it harder to recruit soldiers, and the patron's traditional control over his clients was weakened by their flight from their land.

Tiberius Gracchus (168–133 B.C.E.) became tribune in 133 B.C.E. on a program of land reform. (See Document, "The Ruin of the Roman Family Farm and the Gracchan Reforms" on page 154.) He had popular support but encountered political hostility. When another tribune twice vetoed his land reform bill, Tiberius had the offending tribune removed from office—in violation of the constitution. Tiberius then proposed and passed a bill that was even harsher than the first and more appealing to the people. Because no tribune dared to oppose him, he got his way. But the cost was the destruction of the Roman constitution.

Tiberius understood the danger to himself and to prospects for implementing his reforms once his term as tribune came to an end, so he announced his candidacy for a second successive term. This violated the term limits posed by the Roman constitution. Having no legal recourse, a mob of senators and their clients resorted to violence. They killed Tiberius and some 300 of his followers and threw their bodies into the Tiber River.

The Senate had put down the threat to its rule but at the price of the first internal bloodshed in Roman political history. Roman politics was changed irrevocably. Tiberius had demonstrated how to build a political career based on pressure from the people, not on aristocratic influence. In the last century of the republic, such politicians were called *populares*, whereas those who supported the traditional role of the Senate were called *optimates* ("the best men").

The tribunate of Gaius Gracchus (ca. 159–121 B.C.E.), brother of Tiberius, posed a greater threat to the Senate than that of Tiberius because all the tribunes supported Gaius. There would be no veto, and tribunes could now retain power through reelection. Gaius courted popularity by establishing colonies for landless veterans and passing a law stabilizing the price of grain in Rome. He also divided the wealthy by winning the backing of the equestrian order in his struggles with the Senate. The **equestrians** were rich men who supplied goods and services to the Roman state and collected taxes in the provinces. When Pergamum became the Roman province of Asia in 129 B.C.E., Gaius gave them the right to collect taxes there.

Gaius easily won reelection as tribune for 122 B.C.E., but then he made a misstep. He proposed giving citizenship to Italian allies, but the common people did not want to share the advantages of their Roman citizenship. Gaius lost his reelection campaign in 121 B.C.E., and a hostile consul provoked an incident that led to violence. Gaius was killed, and 3,000 of his followers were put to death without trial.

MARIUS AND SULLA

Before long the senatorial oligarchy faced a stronger opponent who got his start in a war with Jugurtha (d. 104 B.C.E.), king of Numidia. When the war dragged on, the people elected Gaius Marius (157–86 B.C.E.) to the consulship for 107 B.C.E. Later, when Rome faced threats from barbarians to the north, Marius served five consecutive terms

---

latifundia
Large plantations for growing cash crops owned by wealthy Romans.

populares
Roman politicians who sought to pursue a political career based on the support of the people rather than just the aristocracy.

equestrians
Literally "cavalrymen" or "knights." In the earliest years of the Roman Republic, those who could afford to serve as mounted warriors.

DOCUMENT

The Ruin of the Roman Family Farm and the Gracchan Reforms

The independent family farm was the backbone both of the Greek polis and of the early Roman Republic. Rome's conquests, the long wars that kept the citizen-soldier away from his farm, and the availability of great numbers of slaves at a low price, however, badly undercut the traditional way of farming and with it the foundations of republican society. In the following passage, Plutarch describes the process of agricultural change and the response to it of the reformer Tiberius Gracchus, tribune in 133 B.C.E.

- **WHY** did Roman farmers face troubles? What were the social and political consequences of the changes in agricultural life? What solution did Tiberius Gracchus propose? Why, besides selfishness and greed, did people oppose his plan?

Of the territory which the Romans won in war from their neighbours, a part they sold, and a part they made common land, and assigned it for occupation to the poor and indigent among the citizens, on payment of a small rent into the public treasury. And when the rich began to offer larger rents and drove out the poor, a law was enacted forbidding the holding by one person of more than five hundred [iugera] of land. For a short time this enactment gave a check to the rapacity of the rich, and was of assistance to the poor, who remained in their places on the land which they had rented and occupied the allotment which each had held from the outset. But later on the neighbouring rich men, by means of fictitious personages, transferred these rentals to themselves, and finally held most of the land openly in their own names. Then the poor, who had been ejected from their land, no longer showed themselves eager for military service, and neglected the bringing up of children, so that soon all Italy was conscious of a dearth of freemen, and was filled with gangs of foreign slaves, by whose aid the rich cultivated their estates, from which they had driven away the free citizens.

And it is thought that a law dealing with injustice and rapacity so great was never drawn up in milder and gentler terms. For men who ought to have been punished for their disobedience and to have surrendered with payment of a fine the land which they were illegally enjoying, these men it merely ordered to abandon their injust acquisitions upon being paid their value, and to admit into ownership of them such citizens as needed assistance. But although the rectification of the wrong was so considerate, the people were satisfied to let bygones be bygones if they could be secure from such wrong in the future; the men of wealth and substance, however, were led by their greed to hate the law, and by their wrath and contentiousness to hate the lawgiver, and tried to dissuade the people by alleging that Tiberius was introducing a redistribution of land for the confusion of the body politic, and was stirring up a general revolution.

Source: From Plutarch, "Tiberius Gracchus," in *Lives* 8–9, Vol. 10, trans. by Bernadotte Perrin and William Heinemann (London: G. P. Putnam's Sons, 1921), pp. 159-167.

from 104 B.C.E. until 100 B.C.E. He was a *novus homo* ("new man"), a political outsider, the first man from his family to win a consulship. He promised the voters that popular military reforms would lead to speedy victory. He eliminated the traditional property qualification for military service and opened the ranks to volunteers, mostly dispossessed farmers and rural proletarians. They enlisted for long terms of service, looked on the army as a career, and expected land as a bonus when they retired. They became semiprofessional clients of their general and backed the politician who seemed most likely to get them what they wanted. Marius had to obtain grants from the Senate to maintain his power and reputation. But with a large, loyal army behind him, he could frighten the Senate into doing his bidding. Marius's innovation created both the opportunity and the necessity for military leaders to challenge the authority of civilian government.

Marius quickly routed Jugurtha, but a guerrilla war dragged on. Finally, Marius's subordinate, Lucius Cornelius Sulla (138–78 B.C.E.), captured Jugurtha and ended the war. Marius, however, took the credit, leaving Sulla to plot his revenge.

WAR AGAINST THE ITALIAN ALLIES (90–88 B.C.E.)

For a decade Rome ignored Italian discontent. In frustration, the Italians revolted. The Romans immediately offered citizenship to those cities that remained loyal and soon made the same offer to the rebels if they laid down their arms. By 88 B.C.E. the war against the allies was over. All the Italians became Roman citizens, but they retained local self-government. Time blurred the distinction between Romans and Italians and forged them into a single nation.

SULLA'S DICTATORSHIP

Sulla was elected consul for 88 B.C.E. He backed the Senate in a war against Marius and his supporters, and following its victorious conclusion, he had himself appointed dictator. He used his power to restore the traditional Roman constitution and the power of the Senate. He could not, however, undo the effect of his example. Sulla had taken possession of Rome with its own army and led Romans in slaughtering Romans. Others soon followed suit.

ARTS AND LETTERS OF THE LATE REPUBLIC

The high point of Roman culture began in the last century of the republic, when art and writing show uniquely Roman qualities in spirit and sometimes in form.

The late republic's towering literary figure, Cicero (106–43 B.C.E.), is most famous for his orations. Together with his private letters, the speeches give us a clearer and fuller insight into his mind than the works of any other figure in antiquity. We see the political life of his period largely through his eyes. He also wrote treatises on rhetoric, ethics, and politics that put Greek philosophical ideas into Latin terminology, changing them to suit Roman conditions and values. Cicero believed in a world governed by divine and natural law that human reason could perceive. He looked to law, custom, and tradition to produce stability and liberty. His literary style, as well as his values and ideas, created an important legacy for the Middle Ages and, reinterpreted, for the Renaissance.

The period from the Gracchi to the fall of the republic was important for the development of Roman law. The edicts of the magistrates who dealt with foreigners developed the idea of a comprehensive *jus gentium*, or "law of peoples," as opposed to a law based strictly on Roman custom. In the first century B.C.E., under the influence of the Greeks, the *jus gentium* was equated with the *jus naturale*, or "natural law," taught by the Stoics.

Two of Rome's greatest poets, Lucretius and Catullus, were citizens of the late republic. The Hellenistic literary theorists believed that poetry should educate as well as entertain, a task Lucretius (ca. 99–ca. 55 B.C.E.) undertook in his epic poem *De Rerum Natura* (*On the Nature of Things*). It explained and advocated the scientific and philosophical theories of Epicurus and Democritus, which Lucretius believed would liberate people from superstition and the fear of death. Catullus's (ca. 84–ca. 54 B.C.E.) poems were personal. He wrote of the joys and pains of love and amused himself composing witty poetic exchanges. He illustrates the mind-set of the proud, independent, pleasure-seeking, late republican nobility.

Bust of Julius Caesar

What impression does this sculpture give you of Julius Caesar's personality?

THE FALL OF THE REPUBLIC AND THE AUGUSTAN PRINCIPATE

WHAT WERE the central features of Octavian rule?

POMPEY, CRASSUS, AND CAESAR

Marcus Licinius Crassus (115–53 B.C.E.) and Cnaeus Pompey (106–48 B.C.E.) won election to the consulship for the year 70 B.C.E. and repealed most of Sulla's laws. In 67 B.C.E., a special law gave Pompey *imperium* for three years over the entire Mediterranean and coastal lands to rid the area of pirates. When he returned to Rome in 62 B.C.E., he had more power, prestige, and popular support than any Roman in history. Crassus, though rich and influential, did not have a firm political base of his own or the kind of military glory needed to rival Pompey. During the 60s B.C.E., therefore, he allied himself with various popular leaders, the ablest of whom was Gaius Julius Caesar (100–44 B.C.E.).

FIRST TRIUMVIRATE AND THE DICTATORSHIP OF JULIUS CAESAR

To general surprise, Pompey disbanded his army and returned to Italy as a private citizen. But when the fearful Senate decided to try to turn his veterans against him by refusing to grant them land, he forged an alliance with Crassus and Caesar called the First Triumvirate.

Caesar was elected consul for 59 B.C.E. and enacted the Triumvirate's program. Caesar raised a great army for the conquest of Gaul, Crassus got a similar military command in the Middle East, and Pompey got land for his veterans and confirmation of his treaties from the Senate. By the time Caesar had conquered Gaul and was ready to return to Rome, the Triumvirate had dissolved. Crassus's invasion of Parthia had ended with his death at Carrhae in 53 B.C.E., and Pompey had allied with the Senate against Caesar.

●•◦—**Read the Document**
Excerpt from Life of Caesar (2nd century C.E.), Plutarch at **myhistorylab.com**

◉—**See the Map**
The Career of Julius Caesar at **myhistorylab.com**

Early in January of 49 B.C.E. the more extreme faction in the Senate ordered Pompey to defend the state and Caesar to lay down his command. For Caesar this meant exile or death, so he ordered his legions to cross the Rubicon River, the boundary of his province. This action was the first act of a civil war that ended in 45 B.C.E., when Caesar defeated forces under Pompey's sons.

Caesar made few changes in the government of Rome, but his monopoly of military power made a sham of the republic. His senatorial enemies conspired against him, and on March 15, 44 B.C.E., they stabbed him to death at a meeting of the Senate. The assassins expected his death to restore the republic, but instead thirteen more years of civil war eviscerated what was left of the republic.

CHRONOLOGY

THE FALL OF THE ROMAN REPUBLIC

133 B.C.E.	Tribunate of Tiberius Gracchus
123–122 B.C.E.	Tribunate of Gaius Gracchus
111–105 B.C.E.	Jugurthine War
104–100 B.C.E.	Consecutive consulships of Marius
90–88 B.C.E.	War against the Italian allies
70 B.C.E.	Consulship of Crassus and Pompey
60 B.C.E.	Formation of First Triumvirate
58–50 B.C.E.	Caesar in Gaul
53 B.C.E.	Crassus killed in Battle of Carrhae
49 B.C.E.	Caesar crosses Rubicon; civil war begins
46–44 B.C.E.	Caesar's dictatorship
45 B.C.E.	End of civil war
43 B.C.E.	Formation of Second Triumvirate
42 B.C.E.	Battle of Philippi
31 B.C.E.	Octavian defeats Antony at Actium

SECOND TRIUMVIRATE AND THE EMERGENCE OF OCTAVIAN

Caesar's heir was his grandnephew, Octavian (63 B.C.E.–14 C.E.). Marcus Antonius (Mark Antony) (ca. 83–30 B.C.E.) and Lepidus (d. 13 B.C.E.), two of Caesar's officers, joined Octavian in forming the Second Triumvirate, an alliance dedicated to punishing Caesar's assassins. The triumvirs defeated their enemy in 42 B.C.E. but soon quarreled among themselves. Octavian gained control of the western part of the empire. Antonius, together with Egypt's Queen Cleopatra (r. 51–30 B.C.E.), ruled the East. In 31 B.C.E., Octavian crushed the fleet and army of Antony and Cleopatra at Actium and ended the civil war. Octavian emerged in control of the Mediterranean world but faced the daunting challenge of restoring peace, prosperity, and confidence without making the mistake that had cost Caesar his life: He had to exercise the power of a king without appearing to threaten the republican traditions to which his fellow Romans were passionately attached.

THE AUGUSTAN PRINCIPATE

Octavian's constitutional solution was to drape a monarchy in republican trappings by apparently sharing authority with the Senate. All real power, however, lay with the ruler, whether he was called by the unofficial title of "first citizen" (*princeps*) like Octavian, or "emperor" (**imperator**) like those who followed. The outline of his plan emerged in 27 B.C.E.: He was to rule the provinces of Spain, Gaul, and Syria with proconsular power for military command and retain a consulship in Rome. The Senate would govern the other provinces. Twenty of Rome's twenty-six legions were stationed in Octavian's provinces, giving him effective control of the empire. The Senate, however, was grateful to him for establishing peace after Rome's long civil war, and it voted him many honors, including the semireligious title "**Augustus**," which connoted veneration, majesty, and holiness. Historians refer to Octavian in his role as Rome's first emperor as Augustus and characterize his regime as the Principate, a government that tried to conceal the naked power on which it rested.

AUGUSTAN ADMINISTRATION, ARMY, AND DEFENSE

Augustus made important administrative changes to reduce inefficiency and corruption, to eliminate the threat to peace and order by ambitious individuals, and to reduce the distinction between Romans and Italians, senators and equestrians. Augustus controlled the elections and saw to it that promising young men, whatever their origin, served the state. Equestrians and Italians who had no connection with the Roman aristocracy were admitted to the Senate, which Augustus treated with respect and honor.

The economy prospered, stimulated by wealth from newly conquered Egypt, by a general peace that stimulated commerce and industry, by a vast program of public works, and by a revival of small farming on the lands granted to Augustus's veterans.

Rome's soldiers became true professionals under Augustus. Enlistment was for twenty years, the pay was good, and there were bonuses and a pension on retirement. The citizen legions, together with auxiliary units staffed by provincials, stationed about 300,000 men on the empire's frontiers—barely enough to hold the line. The army in the provinces brought Roman culture to the natives. The soldiers spread their language and customs, often marrying local women and settling down there. They attracted merchants, who became the nuclei of new towns that became centers of Roman civilization. As time passed, the provincials on the frontiers became Roman citizens and helped strengthen Rome's defenses against the barbarians.

RELIGION AND MORALITY

A century of political strife and civil war had undermined traditional Roman society. Augustus undertook to preserve and restore family life by curbing adultery and divorce and encouraging early marriage and the procreation of legitimate children. He restored the dignity of formal Roman religion by building temples and reviving cults. Like Julius Caesar, he was deified after his death, and a state cult was dedicated to his worship.

Emperor Augustus (r. 27 B.C.E.–14 C.E.). This statue, now in the Vatican, stood in the villa of Augustus's wife Livia. The figures on the elaborate breastplate are all of symbolic significance. At the top, for example, Dawn in her chariot brings in a new day under the protective mantle of the sky god; in the center, Tiberius, Augustus's successor, accepts the return of captured Roman army standards from a barbarian prince; and at the bottom, Mother Earth offers a horn of plenty. **Why was symbolism particularly important to Augustus?**

Read the **Document**
Augustus on His Accomplishments (1st century C.E.) at **myhistorylab.com**

imperator
Under the Roman Republic, it was the title given to a victorious general. Under Augustus and his successors, it became the title of the ruler of Rome, meaning "emperor."

Augustus
The title given to Octavian in 27 B.C.E. and borne thereafter by all Roman emperors.

See the **Map**
Rome in the Age of Augustus, 31 B.C–A.D. 14 at **myhistorylab.com**

QUICK REVIEW

The Army under Augustus
- Augustus professionalized army
- 20-year enlistment with good pay and pension
- 300,000 men formed frontier army

THE GOLDEN AGE OF ROMAN LITERATURE

●◆●▢Read the Document
Augustus's *Moral Legislation: Family Values,*
18 B.C.E. at **myhistorylab.com**

Augustus replaced the complexity of republican patronage with a simple scheme in which all patronage flowed from the *princeps*. Two of the major poets of this time, Virgil and Horace, had lost their property during the civil wars. The patronage of the *princeps* allowed them the leisure and the security to write poetry and also made them dependent on him and limited their freedom of expression.

Virgil (70–19 B.C.E.) was the most important Augustan poet. His greatest work is the *Aeneid*, a long epic that linked the history of Rome with the Homeric tradition of the Greeks. Its hero, the Trojan Aeneas, personifies the ideal Roman qualities of duty, responsibility, serious purpose, and patriotism. Virgil celebrated the peace and prosperity Augustus established for the empire and supported Augustus's program for the revival of traditional Roman virtues.

●◆●▢Read the Document
Horace, "Dulce et Decorum Est Pro Patria
Mori" at **myhistorylab.com**

The great skills of the lyric poet Horace (65–8 B.C.E.) are best revealed in his *Odes*. Many of them glorify the new Augustan order, the imperial family, and the empire. Ovid (43 B.C.E.–18 C.E.) wrote entertaining love elegies that reveal the sophistication and the loose sexual conduct of the Roman aristocracy. His most popular work is *Metamorphoses*, a graceful, lively poem of epic length that retells Greek myths as charming stories. Ovid was exiled because his poetry did not conform to Augustan values.

The most important and influential prose writer of the time was Livy (59 B.C.E.–17 C.E.). His *History of Rome* traced the period from Rome's legendary origins until 9 B.C.E. Only one-fourth of his work survives. Livy's great achievement was the creation of a continuous, impressive narrative encompassing the full sweep of Roman history. Its purpose was to promote traditional morality and patriotism. He glorified Rome's greatness and, like Augustus, grounded it in Rome's hardy virtues.

Augustus was also a great patron of the visual arts. Augustus embarked on a building program that beautified Rome, glorified his reign, contributed to the general prosperity, and enhanced his popularity. The greatest sculptural monument of the age is the Altar of Peace (*Ara Pacis*), dedicated in 9 B.C.E. Its walls show a procession in which Augustus and his family appear to move forward, followed by the magistrates, the Senate, and the people of Rome. There is no better symbol of the new order.

PEACE AND PROSPERITY: IMPERIAL ROME

WHAT ROLE did cities play in the Roman Empire?

Augustus tried to cloak the monarchical nature of his government, but his successors soon abandoned all pretense. The rulers came to be called *imperator*—root of our word *emperor*—as well as *Caesar*. Augustus designated his heirs by giving them a share in the imperial power and responsibility (see Map 6–3). Tiberius (emperor

A Panel from the Ara Pacis (Altar of Peace).
The altar was dedicated in 9 B.C.E. It was part of a propaganda campaign—involving poetry, architecture, myth, and history—that Augustus undertook to promote himself as the savior of Rome and the restorer of peace. This panel shows the goddess Earth and her children with cattle, sheep, and other symbols of agricultural wealth.

Saturnia, Tellus, Goddess of Earth, Air and Water. Panel from the Ara Pacis. 13–9 B.C.E. Museum of the Ara Pacis, Rome. Nimatallah/Art Resource, New York.

Why would agricultural products make good symbols of peace?

MAP 6–3. Provinces of the Roman Empire to 117 C.E. The growth of the empire to its greatest extent is shown in three stages—at the death of Augustus in 14 B.C.E., at the death of Nerva in 98 C.E., and at the death of Trajan in 117 C.E. The division into provinces is also indicated. The inset outlines the main roads that tied the far-flung empire.

What trends can you observe in Roman expansion over time?

Relief from the Arch of Titus. Spoils from the Temple in Jerusalem were carried in triumphal procession by Roman troops. This relief from Titus's Arch of Victory in the Roman Forum celebrates his capture of Jerusalem in 70 C.E. after a two-year siege. The Jews found it difficult to reconcile their religion with Roman rule and frequently rebelled.

What are the most noticeable elements in this image? Why?

•••[Read the Document
Marcus Aurelius, *The Meditations*, Book Two (167 C.E.) at **myhistorylab.com**

●─[See the Map
The Roman Empire at Its Greatest Extent at **myhistorylab.com**

CHRONOLOGY

RULERS OF THE EARLY EMPIRE

27 B.C.E.–14 C.E.	Augustus
The Julio-Claudian Dynasty	
14–37 C.E.	Tiberius
37–41 C.E.	Gaius (Caligula)
41–54 C.E.	Claudius
54–68 C.E.	Nero
69 C.E.	Year of the four emperors
The Flavian Dynasty	
69–79 C.E.	Vespasian
79–81 C.E.	Titus
81–96 C.E.	Domitian
The "Good Emperors"	
96–98 C.E.	Nerva
98–117 C.E.	Trajan
117–138 C.E.	Hadrian
138–161 C.E.	Antoninus Pius
161–180 C.E.	Marcus Aurelius

14–37 C.E.), Gaius (Caligula, 37–41 C.E.), Claudius (41–54 C.E.), and Nero (54–68 C.E.) descended from Augustus's family. After their line died out in 68 C.E., various Roman armies marched on Italy and elevated four men in rapid succession to the throne. Vespasian (69–79 C.E.), the first emperor who did not come from the old Roman nobility, emerged victorious from the chaos, and his sons, Titus (79–81 C.E.) and Domitian (81–96 C.E.), carried forward the Flavian Dynasty.

The Flavian Dynasty ended with the assassination of Domitian. The Senate appointed Nerva (96–98 C.E.) emperor, and he became the first of the five "good emperors"; the others were Trajan (98–117 C.E.), Hadrian (117–138 C.E.), Antoninus Pius (138–161 C.E.), and Marcus Aurelius (161–180 C.E.). Until Marcus Aurelius, none of these men had sons, so they were each free to choose an able successor. The result was almost a century of excellent administration. This ended when Marcus Aurelius's incompetent son Commodus (180–192 C.E.) succeeded him.

ADMINISTRATION OF THE EMPIRE

The empire was a collection of cities and towns. Roman policy during the Principate was to raise urban centers to the status of Roman municipalities. The upper classes of the provinces were enlisted in the governments of their regions. This spread Roman culture and won the loyalty of influential people. As the imperial bureaucracy grew and became more efficient, however, the central administration took a greater role in local affairs and the municipalities lost autonomy. Efficient centralized control was obtained at the cost of the vitality of the cities.

Unlike most conquered peoples, the Jews found accommodation to Roman rule difficult. Their first rebellion was crushed by Vespasian's son, the future emperor Titus, in 70 C.E. At that time the Temple in Jerusalem was destroyed. A second revolt was put down in 117 C.E. Finally, when Hadrian ordered a Roman colony placed on the site of Jerusalem, Simon led a last uprising from 132 to 135 that was brutally suppressed.

Augustus and his successors had not tried to expand the empire, but Trajan launched a sustained offensive into neighboring territory. Between 101 and 106 C.E., he established the new province of Dacia north of the Danube. His intent was probably to defend the empire by driving wedges into enemy territory. The same strategy led him to invade the Parthian Empire in the East (113–117 C.E.). Hadrian kept Dacia but abandoned Trajan's eastern conquests. The Roman defense became rigid, and initiative passed to the barbarians. Marcus Aurelius spent most of his reign resisting attacks in the East and on the Danube frontier, and these attacks put enormous pressure on the empire's resources.

CULTURE OF THE EARLY EMPIRE

The prosperity and relative stability of the first two centuries of imperial Rome brought Roman architecture to full flower. Roman contributions to the building arts were largely advances in engineering that made huge structures feasible. To the basic post-and-lintel construction used by the Greeks, the Romans added the semicircular arch, borrowed from the Etruscans. When used internally in the form of vaults and domes, the arch permitted great buildings like the Roman baths. Romans also made good use of concrete, a building material first used by the Hellenistic Greeks. The Colosseum, an arena in Rome built by the Flavian emperors, is an excellent example of Roman architecture. The only major Roman temple to survive intact is the Pantheon, a building roofed by a great dome. Roman engineers also spread impressive bridges, roads, and aqueducts throughout the empire.

Pompeiian Woman. The Roman provincial city of Pompeii, near the Bay of Naples, was buried by an eruption of Mount Vesuvius in 79 C.E. As a result, the town, together with its private houses and their contents, was remarkably well preserved until recovery in the eighteenth century. Among the discoveries were a number of works of art, including pictorial mosaics and paintings. This depiction of a young woman, on a round panel from a house in Pompeii, is part of a larger painting that includes her husband holding a volume of Plato's writings. The woman is holding a stylus and a booklet of wax tablets and is evidently in the process of writing. Her gold earrings and hair net show that she is a fashionable person of some means.

Late first century C.E. Diameter 14 ⅝ inches. Sappho, idealized portrait of a girl posing as a poetess. Fresco from Pompeii, Insula occidentale. Museo Archeologico Nazionale, Naples, Italy, © Erich Lessing/Art Resource, New York.

What does this image suggest about the lives of well-to-do Roman women?

In Latin literature, the years between the death of Augustus and Marcus Aurelius are known as the Silver Age. Writers were gloomy, negative, and pessimistic, prone to criticism and satire. Historians of the era wrote about remote periods to avoid the risk of offending an emperor's sensibilities. Scholarship was encouraged, but we hear little of poetry. Romances written in Greek became popular as an escape from contemporary realities.

LIFE IN IMPERIAL ROME: THE APARTMENT HOUSE

The civilization of the Roman Empire was the product of the vitality of its cities. The typical city had about 20,000 inhabitants; Rome probably had in excess of half a million. Most of its residents were squeezed into tall apartment buildings, which the Romans called *insulae* ("islands"). The buildings, which were five or more stories tall, were uncomfortable and dangerous. Built cheaply, they were prone to collapse, and they were easily set on fire by the many torches, candles, oil lamps, and braziers their inhabitants used. They had no running water or other conveniences. Not surprisingly, Romans spent most of their time out of doors.

View the Image
Hadrian's Wall at **myhistorylab.com**

View the Image
Roman Coliseum at **myhistorylab.com**

View the Image
The Interior of the Dome of the Pantheon, Rome at **myhistorylab.com**

View the Image
Roman aqueduct at **myhistorylab.com**

A Roman Apartment House. This is a reconstruction of a typical Roman apartment house found at Ostia, Rome's port. The ground floor contained shops, and the stories above it held many apartments.

Gismondi (20th C). Museo della Civiltà Romana, Rome, Italy/© Scala/Art Resource, New York.

How do these buildings compare with the dwellings of other civilizations of this era?

THE RISE OF CHRISTIANITY

HOW DID Paul resolve the central dilemma of the relationship between Judaism and early Christianity?

"mystery" religions
The cults of Isis, Mithras, and Osiris, which promised salvation to those initiated into the secret or "mystery" of their rites.

✓•⎯Study and **Review**
The Roman and Christian Views of the Good Life at **myhistorylab.com**

•**•**•⎯Read the **Document**
Excerpt from The Gospel According to Luke (1st century C.E.) at **myhistorylab.com**

•**•**•⎯Read the **Document**
Excerpt from The Gospel According to Matthew (1st century C.E.) at **myhistorylab.com**

•**•**•⎯Read the **Document**
The Acts of the Apostles: Paul Pronounces the "Good News" in Greece, ca. 100 at **myhistorylab.com**

Pharisees
The group that was most strict in its adherence to Jewish law.

The story of how Christianity ultimately conquered the Roman Empire is one of the most remarkable in history. Christianity was opposed by the established religious institutions of its native Judaea and had to compete not only against the official cults of Rome and the sophisticated philosophies of the educated classes but also against **"mystery" religions** such as the cults of Mithra, Isis, and Osiris. Christians were also at times officially persecuted by the state. Despite all this, Christianity became the official religion of the empire.

JESUS OF NAZARETH

An attempt to understand the triumph of Christianity must begin with Jesus of Nazareth. The Gospel authors believed that Jesus was the son of God who came to redeem humanity and bring immortality to those who followed his teachings.

Jesus was born in Judaea in the time of Augustus and was an effective teacher in the tradition of the Jewish prophets. This tradition promised the coming of a Messiah (in Greek, *christos*—*Jesus Christ* means "Jesus the Messiah"), a redeemer who would make Israel triumph over its enemies and establish the kingdom of God on Earth. Jesus seems to have insisted that the Messiah would not establish an earthly kingdom but, at the Day of Judgment, God would reward the righteous and condemn the wicked. Until that day, which his followers believed would come soon, Jesus taught the faithful to abandon sin and worldly concerns; to follow the moral code described in the Sermon on the Mount, which preached love, charity, and humility; and to believe in him and his divine mission.

Jesus won a following, especially among the poor. This provoked the hostility of Jerusalem's religious leaders, who convinced the Roman governor that Jesus and his followers might be dangerous revolutionaries. Jesus was put to death in Jerusalem by the cruel and degrading method of crucifixion, probably in 30 C.E. His followers believed that he was resurrected on the third day after his death, and that belief became a critical element in their religion.

Although faith in Jesus as the Christ spread to some Jewish communities in Syria and Asia Minor, without Saint Paul it might have remained a small, heretical cult within Judaism.

PAUL OF TARSUS

Paul (?5–67 C.E.), whose Hebrew name was Saul, was born in Tarsus in Asia Minor. He had an excellent Hellenistic education and held Roman citizenship. He was also a **Pharisee**, a strict adherent of the Jewish law. He persecuted the early Christians until his own sudden conversion while traveling to Damascus about 35 C.E. The great problem facing the early Christians, like Paul, was their relationship to Judaism. If the new faith was a version of Judaism, then it must adhere to the Jewish law and seek converts only among Jews. James, called the brother of Jesus, held that view, whereas Hellenist Jews tended to see Christianity as a new and universal religion.

Paul supported the position of the Hellenists and soon won many converts among the gentiles. He believed that the followers of Jesus were called to be evangelists ("messengers") and to spread the gospel ("good news") of salvation during the short time that remained before Jesus returned for the Day of Judgment. Faith in Jesus as the Christ was necessary for salvation, but salvation was a gift of God's grace, not something earned by good works.

ORGANIZATION

The new religion had its greatest success in the cities and among the poor and uneducated. The rites of the early Christians appear to have been simple and few. Baptism by water removed original sin and permitted participation in the community and its activities. The central ritual was a common meal called the *agape* ("love feast"), followed by the ceremony of the *Eucharist* ("thanksgiving"), a celebration of the Lord's Supper in which unleavened bread was eaten and unfermented wine drunk. There were also prayers, hymns, and readings from works that eventually became the Christian scriptures.

At first the churches had little formal organization, but by the second century C.E., most cities had leaders called bishops. The doctrine of Apostolic Succession asserted that the message and authority Jesus had entrusted to his original disciples were passed on from bishop to bishop by the rite of ordination. The bishops maintained discipline within their churches and dealt with the civil authorities. In time they began meeting in councils to settle difficult questions, define orthodox belief, and expel those who would not accept it. Christianity could probably not have survived without such strong internal organization and government.

PERSECUTION OF CHRISTIANS

The new faith soon incurred the distrust of the pagan world and of the imperial government. The Christians' refusal to demonstrate their patriotism by worshiping the emperor was considered treason. By the end of the first century, membership in the Christian community had become a crime. Most persecutions during this period, however, were instituted not by the government but by mobs.

EMERGENCE OF CATHOLICISM

Most Christians held to traditional, simple, conservative beliefs. This body of majority opinion and the church that enshrined it came to be called **Catholic**, which means "universal." Its doctrines were deemed **orthodox**; those holding contrary opinions were called **heretics.**

By the end of the second century, an orthodox scriptural canon had emerged that included the Old Testament, the Gospels, and the Epistles of Paul. The orthodox drew up creeds, brief statements of faith to which true Christians should adhere. By the end of the second century, an orthodox Christian—that is, a member of the Catholic Church—had to accept its creed, its canon of holy writings, and the authority of the bishops.

ROME AS A CENTER OF THE EARLY CHURCH

The church in the city of Rome acquired special prominence. Rome benefited from the tradition that Jesus' apostles Peter and Paul were martyred there. Peter was thought to be the first bishop of Rome, and the Gospel of Matthew (16:18) reported Jesus saying to Peter, "Thou art Peter [in Greek, *Petros*] and upon this rock [in Greek, *petra*] I will build my church." Subsequent bishops of Rome claimed supremacy over the Catholic Church as heirs to the role Jesus granted to Peter.

Christian Martyr. Thrown to the lions in 275 C.E. by the Romans for refusing to recant his Christian beliefs, St. Mamai is an important martyr in the iconography of Georgia, a Caucasian kingdom that embraced Christianity early in the fourth century. This gilded silver medallion, made in Georgia in the eleventh century, depicts the saint astride a lion while he bears a cross in one hand, symbolizing his triumphant victory over death and ignorance.

agape
Meaning "love feast." A common meal that was part of the central ritual of early Christian worship.

Eucharist
Meaning "thanksgiving." The celebration of the Lord's Supper. Considered the central ritual of worship by most Christians. Also called Holy Communion.

See the **Map**
The Spread of Christianity
at **myhistorylab.com**

View the **Image**
Early Christian Symbols
at **myhistorylab.com**

Catholic
Meaning "universal." The body of belief held by most Christians enshrined within the church.

orthodox
Meaning "holding the right opinions." Applied to the doctrines of the Catholic Church.

heretics People who publicly dissent from officially accepted dogma.

QUICK REVIEW

Early Christian Rites
- Baptism by water to remove original sin, enter community
- *Agape*, a shared meal or "love feast"
- *Eucharist*, a thanksgiving celebration featuring unleavened bread and unfermented wine

THE THIRD AND FOURTH CENTURIES: CRISIS AND LATE EMPIRE

WHY DID the capital of the empire move from Rome to Constantinople, and what was the significance of this shift?

The prosperity created in Augustus's day by the end of the civil war and the influx of wealth from the East could not be sustained. Population seems to have declined. The cost of government, however, kept rising. Pressure on Rome's frontiers, meanwhile, reached massive proportions. In the East, by 224 C.E., a new Iranian dynasty, the Sasanids, reinvigorated Persia (see Chapter 4), recovered Mesopotamia, and raided deep into Roman territory. Germans, especially the Goths, threatened Rome's northern and western frontiers.

Read the **Document**
Jordanes, The Origin and Deeds of the Goths, Book twenty-six, at **myhistorylab.com**

MILITARY REORGANIZATION

Septimius Severus (r. 193–211 C.E.) and his successors transformed the character of the Roman army. Septimius was a military usurper who owed everything to the support of his soldiers. He was prepared to make Rome into an undisguised military monarchy. Septimius drew recruits for the army increasingly from peasants of the less civilized provinces, and the result was a barbarization of Rome's military forces.

ECONOMIC, SOCIAL, AND POLITICAL COSTS OF DEFENSE

Inflation had forced Commodus (r. 180–192 C.E.) to raise the soldiers' pay, but the Severan emperors had to double it to keep up with prices, which increased the imperial budget by as much as 25 percent. The emperors invented new taxes, debased the coinage, and even sold the palace furniture to raise money. Still, it was hard to recruit troops.

As external threats distracted the emperors, they were less able to preserve domestic peace. Piracy, brigandage, and the neglect of roads and harbors hampered trade. So, too, did inflation. As the money supply deteriorated, the government began to demand payment in food, supplies, and labor. Rebellions erupted in some provinces, and peasants and even town administrators fled to escape their burdens. The result was further weakening of the Roman economy.

The new conditions caused important changes in the social order. The state began to take on a military appearance. People's clothing became a kind of uniform that indicated their status. Titles were assigned to ranks in civilian society as to ranks in the army. The most important distinction was the one formally established by Septimius Severus between the *honestiores* (senators, equestrians, municipal aristocracy, and soldiers) and the lower classes, or *humiliores*. Septimius granted the *honestiores* legal privileges: lighter punishments, exemption from torture, and right of appeal to the emperor. It became more difficult to move from the lower order to the higher. Freedom and private initiative were suppressed as the state's needs forced it steadily to increase its control over its citizens.

By the mid-third century the empire seemed on the point of collapse, but two able soldiers, Claudius II Gothicus (r. 268–270 C.E.) and Aurelian (r. 270–275 C.E.), drove back the barbarians and stamped out disorder. Later emperors built defensive walls around Rome and other cities and hired Germanic mercenaries whose officers gave personal loyalty to the emperor rather than to the empire. These officers became a foreign, hereditary caste of aristocrats that increasingly supplied high administrators and even emperors. In effect, the Roman people succumbed to an army of mercenaries they themselves had hired.

PRESERVATION OF CLASSICAL CULTURE

The new ruling class thought of itself as effecting a great restoration, not a revolution. The new aristocracy sought order and stability—ethical, literary, and artistic—in the classical tradition. The great classical authors were reproduced in many copies, and their works were transferred from perishable and inconvenient papyrus rolls to sturdier codices, bound volumes that were as easy to use as modern books. Scholars digested long works like Livy's *History of Rome* into shorter versions and wrote learned commentaries and compiled grammars.

THE LATE EMPIRE: DIOCLETIAN TO CONSTANTINE

The period from Diocletian (r. 284–305 C.E.) to Constantine (r. 306–337 C.E.) was one of reconstruction and reorganization. The emperor Diocletian was a man of undistinguished birth who rose to the throne through the army. He concluded that the job of defending and governing the entire empire was too great for one man. He devised a new administrative system, a **tetrarchy**, to divide territorial responsibility for the empire among four men: two emperors and two assistants who were designated as their successors. This system seemed to promise orderly, peaceful transitions instead of assassinations, chaos, and civil war.

In 305 Diocletian retired and compelled his co-emperor to do the same. But his plan for a smooth succession failed. In 310 there were five competing emperors. Out of this chaos Constantine emerged as sole emperor in 324; he reigned until 337.

The emperor had now become almost unapproachable. Those admitted to his presence had to prostrate themselves before him and kiss the hem of his robe. He was addressed as *dominus* ("lord"), and he claimed a divine right to rule.

Constantine erected the new city of Constantinople on the site of ancient Byzantium on the Bosporus, which leads to both the Aegean and the Black seas, and made it the new capital of the empire. Its strategic location was excellent for protecting the eastern and Danubian frontiers, and, surrounded on three sides by water, it was easily defended.

The autocratic emperors governed through a civilian bureaucracy, which was kept separate from the army to divide power and reduce the temptation an official might have to challenge the emperor. The system was kept under surveillance by a network of spies and secret police, but they failed to eliminate corruption and inefficiency.

The cost of maintaining a 400,000-man army, a vast civilian bureaucracy, and an expensive imperial court strained an already weak economy. Peasants unable to pay their taxes and officials unable to collect them fled their posts. Wealthy individuals moved from cities to their rural estates, and many peasants sought protection from the government's tax collectors by becoming tenant farmers on these estates. They were tied to the land, as were their descendants, as a caste system hardened.

The peace and unity established by Constantine did not last. The Germans in the west attacked along the Rhine, but even greater trouble was brewing along the Danube where the Visigoths had been driven from their home in the Ukraine by the Huns. The Emperor Valentinian (r. 364–375) saw that he could not defend the empire alone and appointed his brother Valens (r. 364–378) as co-ruler in the East. The empire was again divided in two, and the cultures of the Latin West and the Greek East grew increasingly distinct. In 376, the Goths began to plunder the Balkan provinces. In 378, Valens met them in battle at Adrianople in Thrace, and he was cut down with most of the eastern army. Theodosius (r. 379–395), an able and experienced general, unified the empire, but at his death in 395 it was divided between his sons and never reunited again.

tetrarchy

Diocletian's (r. 284–305 C.E.) system for ruling the Roman Empire by four men with power divided territorially.

QUICK REVIEW

Constantinople

- Built on site of ancient Byzantium
- Established by Constantine
- On a peninsula, easily defended
- Access to Asia

MAP 6–4. **The Empire's Neighbors.** In the fourth century the Roman Empire was nearly surrounded by ever-more threatening neighbors. The map shows where these so-called barbarians lived and the invasion routes many of them took in the fourth and fifth centuries.

How did barbarian invasions transform the Roman world?

The West became increasingly rural as barbarian invasions grew (see Map 6–4). The villa, a fortified country estate, became the basic unit of society. *Coloni* (tenant farmers) served local magnates in return for economic assistance and protection. Cities were depopulated and shrank to tiny walled fortresses ruled by military commanders and bishops. The upper classes left the cities and moved to the country to escape the imperial authorities. The inability of the central authority to maintain and police roads curtailed trade and communications, and living conditions became increasingly primitive. By the fifth century, the West was devolving into rural enclaves ruled by independent aristocrats and worked by a dependent labor force. The only unifying institution was the Christian church. The pattern of life that was to prevail in the West during the early Middle Ages had been generally established.

The East was different. The Roman Empire, in altered form, persisted. Constantinople flourished as the "New Rome." Although its people continued to call themselves "Romans," their lifestyles were so different from those of ancient Rome that historians refer to them as subjects of the medieval *Byzantine* Empire. Constantinople's defensible location, the services of some skillful emperors, and the resources of its base in Asia Minor enabled the eastern empire to deflect and repulse barbarian attacks. A strong Byzantine navy allowed commerce to flourish and cities to prosper. Emperors generally kept the upper hand in dealing with restive aristocratic elements. Byzantine civilization was a unique combination of classical culture, Christian religion, Roman law, and eastern artistic influences. When historians speak of the decline and fall of the Roman Empire in the fourth and fifth centuries, they reference only the West. A form of classical culture persisted in Byzantium for another thousand years.

TRIUMPH OF CHRISTIANITY

In the troubled fourth and fifth centuries people sought the help of powerful, personal deities. It was by no means unusual for people to worship new deities alongside traditional ones and to intertwine features of several gods to create new ones, a phenomenon called **syncretism.** Christianity bore some resemblance to other new faiths of the period, but none of them developed its universal appeal.

In 303, Diocletian had launched the most serious persecution inflicted on the Christians in the Roman Empire. It failed to stem the Christian tide. Ancient states could not carry out a program of terror with the thoroughness of modern totalitarian governments, and the witness of Christian martyrs may have strengthened the faith. In short order, Christians witnessed a miraculous reversal of fortune.

The conversion of Diocletian's ultimate successor, Constantine, and his ascent as sole ruler of the empire transformed Christianity's prospects. Constantine provided lavish patronage for the church and encouraged widespread conversion. In 394, the emperor Theodosius forbade the celebration of pagan cults, and by the time he died, Christianity had become the official religion of the Roman Empire (see Map 6–5 on page 168).

Temptations of power and privilege constituted new threats to some Christians. State support for the faith threatened to subordinate the church to the state. In the East, that was generally the church's fate, but in the West, the weakness of emperors permitted church leaders to exercise independence. In 390, when Ambrose

•◆•⎯Read the **Document**
Eusebius on the Vision and Victory of Constantine I (The Great) (312) at **myhistorylab.com**

syncretism
Blending or fusion of different systems of religious or philosophical beliefs.

CHRONOLOGY

THE TRIUMPH OF CHRISTIANITY

ca. 4 B.C.E.	Jesus of Nazareth born
ca. 30 C.E.	Crucifixion of Jesus
64 C.E.	Fire at Rome: persecution by Nero
ca. 70–100 C.E.	Gospels written
ca. 250–260 C.E.	Major persecutions by Decius and Valerian
303 C.E.	Persecution by Diocletian
311 C.E.	Galerius issues Edict of Toleration
312 C.E.	Battle of Milvian Bridge; conversion of Constantine to Christianity
325 C.E.	Council of Nicaea
ca. 330 C.E.	Georgia and Armenia become first Christian kingdoms
395 C.E.	Christianity becomes official religion of Roman Empire

MAP EXPLORATION

To explore this map further, go to **http://www.myhistorylab.com**

(A) 200

Christian
Areas, 200

(B) 200 – 400

Christian
Areas, 200

Expansion,
200 – 400

(C) 400 – 600

Christian
Areas, 400

Expansion,
400 – 600

MAP 6–5. **The Spread of Christianity.**

Christianity grew swiftly in the third, fourth, fifth, and sixth centuries—especially after the conversion of the emperors in the fourth century. By 600, on the eve of the birth of the new religion of Islam, Christianity was dominant throughout the Mediterranean world and most of western Europe.

Which areas remained largely non-Christian at the end of the seventh century?

(ca. 339–397), bishop of Milan, excommunicated Emperor Theodosius, the emperor submitted to his authority and did penance. This set an important precedent for future assertions of the church's autonomy and authority.

The Christian emperors hoped to unify their increasingly decentralized realms by imposing Christianity as the only religion, but Christianity divided society in new ways. Safe from persecution, Christians engaged in doctrinal disputes among themselves, causing serious disturbances as Christians sought to distinguish orthodoxy from heresy. The most important controversy concerned **Arianism**, a debate begun by a priest named Arius of Alexandria (ca. 280–336). Arius's view that Jesus was not co-equal and co-eternal with God the Father was dismissed by his orthodox opponents, who argued that it undercut Jesus' power as savior. In 325, Constantine summoned the Council of Nicaea to settle the issue. The **Nicene Creed** issued by the council endorsed the doctrine of the Trinity: the belief that God is three persons (Father, Son, and Holy Spirit) who share one substance. Arianism, however, survived and spread and continued to create political difficulties for generations.

Arianism
The belief formulated by Arius of Alexandria (ca. 280–336 C.E.) that Jesus was a created being, neither fully man nor fully God, but something in between.

Nicene Creed
A statement of Christian belief, formulated by the council of Christian bishops at Nicaea in 324 C.E., that rejected Arianism in favor of the doctrine that Christ is both fully human and fully divine.

OVERVIEW   The Fall of the Roman Empire in the West

For centuries historians and social scientists have speculated why the ancient world collapsed. By contrast, the great English historian Edward Gibbon (1737–1794) wrote in his classic work *The Decline and Fall of the Roman Empire* that we should really ask not why Rome fell but why so vast an empire survived for so long. The following are some of the causes and explanations scholars have proposed for the fall of Rome. They range from the plausible to the ridiculous.

CAUSE	EXPLANATION
Climate change	A gradual drying and cooling climate destroyed the productivity of ancient agriculture on which the empire depended.
Soil exhaustion	Depleted soil around the Mediterranean no longer produced enough food to feed the population, which weakened and declined.
Lead poisoning	The use of lead pipes for drinking and cooking water led to widespread lead poisoning and sterility, especially among the upper classes who had the most access to running water.
Racial pollution	Eastern immigrants to Rome—Syrians, Greeks, and Jews—sapped the vitality of the Romans and destroyed their ability to rule and defend themselves.
Slavery	The prevalence of slavery made the Romans lazy and undercut free labor.
Intellectual stagnation	The failure to make advances in science and technology—to achieve a scientific revolution—led the empire to an intellectual and economic dead end.
Social disorder	The destruction of the middle class through civil war, invasion, and overtaxation wiped out the most productive and culturally aware part of the Roman population. Third-century emperors encouraged the rural poor to plunder the middle and upper classes.
Excessive government	Government exactions and regulations destroyed the operation of a market economy, which was the basis for prosperity.
Christianity	The adoption of Christianity as the official religion of the empire in the fourth century weakened the Roman state, diverted scarce resources to building and staffing churches and monasteries, and led large segments of the population to embrace pacifism.
Immorality	Gluttony, sloth, and sexual depravity replaced the old Roman virtues that had enabled Rome to conquer its empire.

CHRISTIAN WRITERS

Christianity inspired scholars who did important original work. Jerome (348–420), a Christian who had superb classical education, used his linguistic skills to create the Vulgate, a revised version of the Bible in Latin. It became the official version of the Bible used by the medieval Catholic Church.

In the East, Eusebius of Caesarea (ca. 260–ca. 340) attempted to develop a Christian theory of history as a working out of God's will in his *Ecclesiastical History*. All of history, he claimed, had divine significance and direction. Constantine's victory and the subsequent unity of empire and church was its culmination.

The closeness and complexity of the relationship between classical pagan culture and the Christianity of the late empire are exemplified in the career and writings of Augustine (354–430), bishop of Hippo in North Africa. His skill in pagan rhetoric and philosophy made him peerless among his contemporaries as a defender of Christianity and a theologian. His greatest works are his *Confessions*, an autobiography that describes his conversion, and *The City of God*. The latter was a response to Rome's sack by the Goths in 410. Augustine separated the fate of Christianity from that of the Roman Empire. He contrasted the secular world—the city of Man—with the spiritual—the City of God. The former was selfish and evil, the latter unselfish and good. All states, even a Christian Rome, were part of the City of Man and, therefore, corrupt and destined to pass away. Only the City of God was eternal and unaffected by earthly calamities.

Read the Document
St. Augustine of Hippo, *Theory of the "Just War"* at **myhistorylab.com**

SUMMARY

WHO WERE the early peoples of Italy?

Italy before Rome. Early and influential invaders of the Italian peninsula included the Etruscans, Greeks, and Celts. Starting around 800 B.C.E., the Etruscans established themselves as a military ruling class in northern Italy. *page 144*

WHAT PATTERNS of Roman governance were set in the royal period?

Royal Rome. Rome began as a small settlement in Latium in central Italy ruled by Etruscan kings. These kings, like later rulers of Rome, had the power of *imperium*. The importance of family, clientage, and the division of society into two broad classes were other enduring patterns that were set in this period. *page 144*

WHAT CULTURES most influenced Roman culture, and why?

The Republic. Rome became a republic in 509 B.C.E. The Roman constitution divided power between elected magistrates, the chief of whom were two consuls; an appointed Senate, whose members served for life; and popular assemblies. During the third century B.C.E., the aristocratic patricians were forced to share power with the common people, the plebeians. The institution of clientage by which clients pledged their loyalty to powerful patrons in return for legal and political protection was an important part of Roman political life. Rome expanded and engaged in the first of many conflicts with Carthage. In the third century B.C.E. Rome turned to the east and defeated the Hellenistic monarchies that had succeeded Alexander's empire. Macedon and Greece fell under Roman rule. This led to the adoption of Greek culture by the Roman aristocracy and the rapid Hellenization of Roman culture. *page 146*

WHY DID a growing gap between the wealthy and everyone else contribute to political instability?

Roman Imperialism. By the early fourth century, Rome had expanded to control all of Italy through a policy of conquest, alliances, colonies of Roman veterans, and generosity to foes who submitted. Between 264 and 146 B.C.E., Rome fought three wars with Carthage for control of the western Mediterranean. These Punic Wars ended with the destruction of Carthage but led to social and political disorder in Italy. Many small farmers lost their land, and efforts by the Gracchi brothers to resolve the problems ended in their murders. *page 152*

 WHAT WERE the central features of Octavian rule?

The Fall of the Republic and the Augustan Principate. The Roman Republic was destroyed by social unrest and rivalry among ambitious generals and politicians, the most successful of whom was Julius Caesar. After a civil war that followed Caesar's assassination in 44 B.C.E., his nephew Octavian emerged as the most powerful man in Rome. Under the title of Augustus, he set up a system that preserved the façade of republican institutions but was in fact a monarchy. *page 156*

 WHAT ROLE did cities play in the Roman Empire?

Peace and Prosperity: Imperial Rome. The Roman Empire stretched from Scotland to Iraq. Rome fostered the growth of cities, developed the rule of law, built a vast network of roads and other public works, and established peace and stability between 14 and 180 C.E. *page 158*

 HOW DID Paul resolve the central dilemma of the relationship between Judaism and early Christianity?

The Rise of Christianity. Christianity arose in the Roman province of Judaea in the first century C.E. Paul believed that Christianity was a universal religion that should be known beyond the Jewish community. Christianity spread throughout the empire despite occasional persecutions by the Roman state, which itself became Christian in the late fourth century. *page 162*

 WHY DID the capital of the empire move from Rome to Constantinople, and what was the significance of this shift?

The Third and Fourth Centuries: Crisis and Late Empire. In the third century C.E., the Roman peace collapsed under the pressure of invasions by barbarians in the West and the Sasanids in the East. Rival generals murdered emperors and usurped the throne. The economy declined. The state exacted more and more taxes and resources from its citizens. The emperors Diocletian and Constantine managed to halt the decline, but in the fifth century C.E. Roman authority in the West collapsed. In the East, however, a Christian Roman Empire based in the city of Constantinople survived and evolved into the Byzantine Empire that did much to preserve the Greek and Roman heritage for another thousand years. *page 164*

KEY TERMS

agape (ah-gah-PAY) (p. 163)
Arianism (p. 169)
Augustus (p. 157)
Catholic (p. 163)
censor (p. 148)
equestrians (p. 153)
Eucharist (p. 163)
heretics (p. 163)
humanitas (p. 151)
imperator (p. 157)
imperium (p. 144)
latifundia (lah-tee-foon-dee-ah) (p. 153)

"mystery religions" (p. 162)
Nicene Creed (p. 169)
orthodox (p. 163)
patrician (p. 146)
Pharisees (p. 162)
plebeian (p. 146)
populares (p. 153)
Punic Wars (p. 149)
syncretism (p. 167)
tetrarchy (p. 165)
tribunes (p. 148)

REVIEW QUESTIONS

1. How did the institutions of family and clientage and the establishment of patrician and plebeian classes contribute to the stability of the early Roman Republic? How important was education to the success of the republic?

2. Discuss Rome's expansion to 265 B.C.E. How was Rome able to conquer and control Italy? In their relations with Greece and Asia Minor in the second century B.C.E., were the Romans looking for security? Wealth? Power? Fame?

3. Explain the clash between the Romans and the Carthaginians in the First and Second Punic Wars. Could the wars have been avoided? How did Rome benefit from its victory over Carthage? What problems were created by this victory?

4. How did Greek culture influence Roman beliefs and practices?

5. What were the problems that plagued the Roman Republic in its final century? What caused these problems and how did the Romans try to solve them? To what extent was the republic destroyed by ambitious generals who loved power more than Rome itself?

172   **PART 2**   EMPIRES AND CULTURES OF THE ANCIENT WORLD, 1000 B.C.E. TO 500 C.E.

6. Discuss the Augustan constitution and government. What solutions did Augustus provide for the problems that had plagued the Roman Republic? Why was the Roman population willing to accept Augustus as head of the state?

7. Despite unpromising beginnings, Christianity was enormously popular by the fourth century C.E. Why were Christians persecuted by Roman authorities? What were the more important reasons for Christianity's success?

8. Consider three theories that scholars have advanced to explain the decline and fall of the Roman Empire. What are the difficulties involved in explaining the fall? What explanation would you give?

Note: To learn more about the topics in this chapter, please turn to the Suggested Readings at the end of the book. For additional sources related to this chapter please see www.myhistorylab.com

PEARSON

myhistorylab Connections

Reinforce what you learned in this chapter by studying the many documents, images, maps, review tools, and videos available at **www.myhistorylab.com**

Read and Review

✔•─Study and Review Chapter 6

•─Read the Document Excerpt from *The Life of Cato the Elder (2 C.E.)* Plutarch, p. 145

Livy: The Rape of Lucretia and the Origins of the Republic, ca. 10 B.C.E, p. 146

Issue of the Day: Religion and Philosophy in the Roman Empire-Stoicism and Christianity?, p. 151

Excerpt from Life of Caesar (2d century C.E.), Plutarch, p. 156

Augustus on His Accomplishments (1st century C.E.), p. 157

Augustus's Moral Legislation: Family Values, 18 B.C.E, p. 158

Horace, "Dulce et Decorum est Pro Patria Mori", p. 158

Marcus Aurelius, The Meditations, Book Two (167 C.E.), p. 160

Excerpt from The Gospel According to Luke (1st century C.E.), p. 162

Excerpt from The Gospel According to Matthew (1st century C.E.), p. 162

The Acts of the Apostles: Paul Pronounces the "Good News" in Greece ca. 100, p. 162

Jordanes, The Origin and Deeds of the Goths, Book twenty-six, p. 164

Eusebius on the Vision and Victory of Constantine I (The Great) (312), p. 167

St. Augustine of Hippo, Theory of the "Just War," p. 170

👁─See the Map *The Roman Conquest of the Mediterranean During the Republic,* p. 151

The Career of Julius Caesar, p. 156

Rome in the Age of Augustus, 31 B.C.–A.D. 14, p. 157

The Roman Empire at Its Greatest Extent, p. 160

The Spread of Christianity, p. 163

👁─View the Image Hadrian's Wall, p. 161

Roman Coliseum, p. 161

The Interior of the Dome of the Pantheon, Rome, p. 161

Roman aqueduct, p. 161

Early Christian Symbols, p. 163

✔•─Study and Review *The Roman and Christian Views of the Good Life,* p. 162

Research and Explore

•─Watch the Video *Defining Imperialism*

•─Watch the Video *Roman Roads*

─((•─Hear the Audio ─

Hear the audio file for Chapter 6
at **www.myhistorylab.com**

China's First Empire, 221 B.C.E.–589 C.E.

((•─ **Hear** the **Audio** for Chapter 7 at www.myhistorylab.com

Han Dynasty aristocrat out driving in his horse cart. Bronze relic excavated from a tomb in Kansu in northwestern China in 1969. Grave goods were a part of Chinese tradition for centuries.

What might this relic suggest about the social status of the individual buried in the tomb where this was found?

One hallmark of Chinese history is its striking continuity of culture, language, and geography. The Shang and Zhou dynasties were centered in north China along the Yellow River or its tributary, the Wei. The capitals of China's first empire were in exactly the same areas, and north China would remain China's political center up to the present. If Western civilization had experienced similar continuity, it would have progressed from Thebes in the valley of the Nile to Athens on the Nile; Rome on the Nile; then, in time, to Paris, London, and Berlin on the Nile; and each of these centers of civilization would have spoken Egyptian and written in Egyptian hieroglyphics.

These continuities do not mean that China was unchanging. One key turning point came in the third century B.C.E., when the old, quasi-feudal, multistate Zhou system gave way to a centralized bureaucratic government. The new centralized state built an empire stretching from the steppe in the north to Vietnam in the south.

The history of the first empire is composed of three segments: the Qin Dynasty, the Former Han Dynasty, and the Later Han Dynasty. The English word China is derived from the name of the first dynasty. The Qin overthrew the previous Zhou Dynasty in 256 B.C.E. and went on to unify China in 221 B.C.E. In reshaping China, the Qin developed such momentum that it became overextended and collapsed a single generation after the unification. The succeeding Han dynasties each lasted about 200 years, the Early Han from 206 B.C.E. to 8 C.E., the Later Han (founded by a descendant of the Former Han rulers) from 25 to 220 C.E. Historians usually treat each of the Han dynasties as a separate period of rule, although they were nearly continuous and shared many institutions and cultural traits. So deep was the impression left by these two dynasties on the Chinese that even today they call themselves the "Han people"—in contrast to Mongols, Manchus, Tibetans, and other minorities—and they call their ideographs "Han writing." ■

QIN UNIFICATION OF CHINA

Among the territorial states of the Late Zhou era, none was more innovative and ruthless than Qin (pronounced "chin"). Its location on the Wei River in northwest China—the same area from which the Zhou had launched their expansion a millennium

HOW DID the Qin unify China?

GLOBAL PERSPECTIVE

CHINA'S FIRST EMPIRE

Were there world-historical forces that produced great empires in China, India, and the Mediterranean at roughly the same time? Certainly these empires had similar features. All three came after revolutions in thought. The Han built on Zhou thought (it would be hard to imagine the Han bureaucratic state without Legalism and Confucianism), just as Rome used Greek thought, and the Mauryan Empire, Buddhist thought. In each case, the conception of universal political authority sustaining the empire derived from earlier philosophies. All three were Iron Age empires, joining their respective technologies with new organizational techniques to create superb military forces. All three had to weld together diverse regions into a single polity. All three created legacies that continued long after the empire had disappeared.

The differences between the empires are also instructive. Consider China and Rome. In China the pervasive culture—the only higher culture in the area—was Chinese, even before the first empire arose. This culture had been slowly spreading for centuries and in places outran the polity. Even the Ch'u people south of the Yangzi, while viewed as "semibarbarian" by northern Chinese, had a variation of the same common culture. Thus cultural unity had paved the way for political unity. In contrast, the polyglot empire of Rome encompassed quite different peoples, including older civilizations. The genius of Rome, in fact, was to fashion a government and a set of laws that could contain and reconcile its diverse cultures.

Geographically, however, Rome had an easier time of it, for the Mediterranean offered direct access to most parts of the empire and was a thoroughfare for commerce. In contrast, China was largely landlocked. It was composed of several regional economic units, each of which, located in a segment of a river basin separated from the others by natural barriers, looked inward. It

earlier—gave it strategic advantages: It controlled the passes leading out onto the Yellow River plain, so it was easy to defend and was a secure base from which to attack other states. From the late fourth century B.C.E., the Qin conquered a part of Sichuan and thus controlled two of the most fertile regions of ancient China. It welcomed Legalist administrators, who developed policies for enriching the country and strengthening its military. Despite its harsh laws, farmers moved to Qin from other areas, attracted by the order and stability of its society. Its armies had been forged by centuries of warfare against the nomadic raiders whose lands half encircled it. To counter these raiders, its armies adopted nomadic skills, developing cavalry in the fourth century. Other states regarded the Qin as tough, crude, and brutal but recognized its formidable strengths.

In 246 B.C.E. the man who would unify China succeeded to the Qin throne at the age of 13. He grew to be vigorous, ambitious, intelligent, and decisive. He is famous as a Legalist autocrat, but he was well liked by his ministers, whose advice he usually followed. (See Chapter 2 for a description of Legalism.) In 232 B.C.E., he began the campaigns that destroyed the six remaining territorial states. On completing his conquests in 221 B.C.E., to raise himself above the kings of the former territorial states, he adopted the glorious title that we translate as "emperor"—a combination of ideographs hitherto used only for gods or mythic heroes. Then, aided by talented officials, this First Qin Emperor set about applying to all of China the reforms that had been effective in his own realm. His accomplishments in the eleven years before his death, in 210 B.C.E., were stupendous.

Having conquered the civilized world of north China and the Yangzi River basin, the First Emperor sent his armies to conquer new lands. They reached the northern edge of the Red River basin in what is now Vietnam. They occupied China's southeastern coast and the area encompassing the present-day city of Guangzhou (see Map 7–1). In the north and the northwest, the emperor's armies fought against the Xiongnu, Altaic-speaking Hunnish nomads. During the previous age, northern border states had built long walls to protect settled lands from incursions by horse-riding raiders. The

View the Image
The Great Wall of China
at **myhistorylab.com**

was the genius of Chinese administration to overcome physical and spatial barriers and integrate the country politically.

A second difference was that government in Han China was more orderly, more complex, and more competent than that of Rome. For example, civil officials controlled the Chinese military almost until the end, whereas in later Roman times, emperor after emperor was set on the throne by the army or the Praetorian Guard. The Roman Empire was not a Chinese-type, single-family dynasty.

A third difference was in the military dynamics of the two empires. Roman power was built over centuries. Its history is the story of one state growing in power by steady increments, imposing its will on others, and gradually piecing together an empire. Not until the early centuries C.E. was the whole empire in place. China, in contrast, remained a multistate system right up to 232 B.C.E. and then, in a sudden surge, was unified by one state in eleven years. The greater dynamism of China during the first

empire can be explained, perhaps, by the greater military challenge it faced across its northern border: an immense Xiongnu nomadic empire. Because the threat was more serious than that any European barbarian enemy posed to Rome, the Chinese response was correspondingly massive. (Some historians say that Chinese expansion to the north and northwest drove the Xiongnu—the Huns—westward, displacing Germanic tribes that flooded into Europe and pressed against Roman frontiers.)

Focus Questions

◆ What challenges did the Roman, Han, and Mauryan empires face in conquering and integrating new territories? How did they meet these challenges?

◆ Compare and contrast the Roman and Han empires. What qualities did they have in common? How did they differ?

Qin emperor had them joined into a single Great Wall that extended 1,400 miles from the Pacific Ocean into Central Asia. Construction of the Great Wall cost the lives of vast numbers of conscripted laborers—by some accounts, 100,000; by others, as many as 1 million.

The most significant reform, carried out by the Legalist minister Li Si, extended the Qin system of bureaucratic government to the entire empire. Li Si divided China into forty prefectures, which were further subdivided into counties. The county heads were responsible to prefects, who, in turn, were responsible to the central government. Officials were chosen by ability. Bureaucratic administration was impersonal, based on laws to which all were subject. No one, for example, escaped taxation. This kind of bureaucratic centralism broke sharply with the old Zhou pattern of establishing dependent principalities for members of a ruler's family.

Furthermore, to ensure the smooth functioning of local government offices, former aristocrats of the territorial states were removed from their lands and resettled in the capital, near present-day Xian. They were housed in mansions on one side of the river, from which they could gaze across at the enormous palace of the First Emperor.

Other reforms further unified the First Emperor's vast domain. Roads were built radiating out from the capital city. The emperor decreed a system of uniform weights and measures. He unified the Chinese writing system, establishing standard ideographs. He established uniform axle lengths for carts. Even ideas did not escape the drive toward uniformity. Following the precepts of Legalism, the emperor and his advisers launched a campaign for which they have subsequently been

MAP 7–1. The Unification of China by the Qin State.
Between 232 and 221 B.C.E. the Qin state expanded and unified China.

Why did Qin expansion fail to move westward?

✓•⎰Study and Review
at **myhistorylab.com**

QUICK REVIEW

Qin Reforms

◆ Extension of Qin bureaucracy to entire empire

◆ Building of roads

◆ Creation of a unified writing system

◆ Creation of unified system of weights and measures

View the Image

Qin Shihuang's Terra-Cotta Soldiers
at **myhistorylab.com**

denounced: They collected and burned the books of Confucianism and other schools, and were said to have buried alive scholars opposed to the Legalist philosophy. Only useful books on agriculture, medicine, or Legalist teachings were spared.

But the Qin had changed too much, too quickly. To pay for the roads, canals, and the Great Wall, burdensome taxes were levied on the people. Commoners hated conscription and labor service, and nobles resented their loss of status. Merchants were exploited; scholars, except for Legalists, were oppressed. After the First Emperor died, in 210 B.C.E., intrigues broke out at court, and rebellions arose in the land. At the end, the short-lived dynasty was destroyed by the domino effect of its own legal codes. When the generals sent to quell a rebellion were defeated, they joined the rebellion rather than returning to the capital and incurring the severe punishment decreed for failure. The Qin collapsed in 206 B.C.E.

In 1974 a farmer near Xian discovered the army of 8,000 life-size terra-cotta horses and soldiers that guarded the tomb of the First Emperor. The historical record tells us that in the tomb itself, under a mountain of earth, are a replica of his capital; a relief model of the Chinese world with quicksilver rivers; other warriors with chariots of bronze; and the remains of horses, noblemen, and criminals sacrificed to accompany in death the emperor whose dynasty was to have lasted for 10,000 generations.

FORMER HAN DYNASTY (206 B.C.E.–8 C.E.)

WHAT IS the dynastic cycle?

dynastic cycle
The term used to describe the rise, decline, and fall of China's imperial dynasties.

THE DYNASTIC CYCLE

Confucian historians have seen a pattern in every dynasty of long duration. They call it the **dynastic cycle**. The stages of the cycle are interpreted in terms of the "Mandate of Heaven." The cycle begins with internal wars that eventually lead to the military unification of China. Unification is proof that heaven has given the unifier the mandate to rule. The first ruler, strong and vigorous, restores peace and order to China. Economic growth follows, almost automatically. The peak of the cycle is marked by public works, energetic reforms, and aggressive military expansion. During this phase, China appears invincible. But then the cycle turns downward. The costs of expansion, coupled with increasing opulence at the court, place a heavy burden on tax revenues just as they are beginning to decline. The vigor of the monarchs wanes. Intrigues develop at court. Central controls loosen, and provincial governors and military commanders gain autonomy. Finally, public works fall into disrepair, floods and pestilence occur, rebellions break out, and the dynasty collapses. For Confucian historians, the last emperors in a cycle are not only politically weak but also morally culpable.

The Great Wall of China. It was originally built during the Qin Dynasty (256–206 B.C.E.), but what we see today is the wall as it was completely rebuilt during the Ming Dynasty (1368–1644 C.E.).

Paolo Koch/Photo Researchers, Inc.

What purpose was the original Great Wall built to serve?

EARLY YEARS OF THE FORMER HAN DYNASTY

The first sixty years of the Han were the early phase of its dynastic cycle. After the collapse of the Qin, one rebel general gained control of the Wei basin and went on to unify China. He became the first emperor of the Han Dynasty and is known by his posthumous title of Gaozu (r. 206–195 B.C.E.). He rose from plebeian origins to

A Closer Look

The Terra-Cotta Army of the First Qin Emperor

In 1974 a Xian farmer, drilling for water, discovered the tomb of the First Qin Emperor (256–210 B.C.E.). To date, 8,000 warriors, copper horses, and war chariots have been found. The emperor's 76-meter-high burial chamber, which according to the records of history has a starry firmament and rivers of mercury, has not yet been excavated.

Government workshops molded arms, legs, torsos, and heads, which were then assembled. Some warriors wore tunics, some breastplates, and others fish-scale armor. There were eight basic face masks, and after the molding, details, such as mustaches, were added with clay. No two faces are alike. The completed warrior was painted with lacquer, though most color has disappeared during the 2,300 years since the "army" was drawn up in formation.

The workers who buried the emperor were sealed in the tomb to keep its location a secret. But in vain. Early grave robbers stole the valuable weapons that the warriors held (note the cupped hands) but ignored the worthless clay statues. After that, its location was unknown for two millennia.

Questions

1. How did the legalism of the Qin state affect its armies?

2. Why did the emperor have this ghostly army fabricated? Did he plan to lead it in an afterlife?

 To examine this image in an interactive fashion, please go to **www.myhistorylab.com**

become emperor, which would happen only once again in Chinese history. Gaozu built his capital at Chang'an, not far from the capitals of the previous dynasties. It took the emperor and his immediate successors many years to consolidate their power because they consciously avoided actions that would remind the populace of the hated Qin despotism. They made punishments less severe and reduced taxes. Good government prevailed, the economy rebounded, granaries were filled, and the government accumulated vast cash reserves. Later historians often singled out the early Han rulers as model sage-emperors.

HAN WUDI

The second phase of the dynastic cycle began with the rule of Wudi (the "martial emperor"), who came to the throne in 141 B.C.E. at the age of 16 and ruled for fifty-four years (141–87 B.C.E.). Wudi was daring, vigorous, and intelligent but also superstitious, suspicious, and vengeful. He wielded tremendous personal authority.

Building on the prosperity achieved by his predecessors, Wudi initiated new economic policies. He had a canal built from the Yellow River to the capital in northwest China, linking the two major economic regions of north China. He established "ever-level granaries" throughout the country so that the surplus from bumper crops could be bought and then resold in time of scarcity. To increase revenues, he levied taxes on merchants, debased the currency, and sold some offices. Wudi also moved against merchants who had built fortunes in untaxed commodities by reestablishing government monopolies—a practice of the Qin—on copper coins, salt, iron, and liquor. For fear of Wudi, no one spoke out against the monopolies, but a few years after his death, a famous debate was held at the court.

The "Salt and Iron Debate" was frequently cited thereafter in China, and in Japan and Korea as well. On one side, quasi-Legalist officials argued that the state should enjoy the profits from the sale of salt and iron. On the other side, Confucians argued that these resources should be left in private hands, for the moral purity of officials would be sullied by dealings with merchants. The Confucian scholars who compiled the historical account of the debate presented themselves as the winners, but state monopolies became a regular part of Chinese government finance.

Wudi also aggressively expanded Chinese borders—a policy that would characterize every strong dynasty. His armies swept south into what is today northern Vietnam and northeast across Manchuria to establish a military outpost in northern Korea that would last until 313 C.E.

THE XIONGNU

Xiongnu
A tribal confederation of nomadic pastoralists who controlled vast territories northwest of the Han Empire; to Europeans, they were the Huns.

The principal threat to the Han was from the **Xiongnu**, a nomadic pastoral people who lived to the north. Their mounted archers could raid China and flee before an army could be sent against them. To combat them, Wudi employed the entire repertoire of policies that would become standard thereafter. When possible he made allies of border nomads, who would fight against more distant tribes. Allies were permitted to trade with Chinese merchants; they were awarded titles and honors; and their kings were sent Chinese princesses as brides. (See Document, "Chinese Women among the Nomads" on page 182.) When trade and titles did not work, he used force. Between 129 and 119 B.C.E. he sent several armies of more than 100,000 troops into the steppe, destroying Xiongnu power south of the Gobi Desert. To establish a strategic line of defense aimed at the heart of the Xiongnu Empire further to the west, Wudi then sent 700,000 Chinese colonists to the arid Kansu panhandle and extended the Great Wall

MAP EXPLORATION

To explore this map further, go to **http://www.myhistorylab.com**

MAP 7–2.   The Han Empire 206 B.C.E.–220 C.E.

At the peak of Han expansion, Han armies advanced far out into the steppe north of the Great Wall and west into Central Asia. The Silk Road to Rome passed through the Tarim Basin to the Kushan Empire, and on to western Asia and the Middle East.

Why did the Han seek to expand their empire to the west and south?

to the Yumen (Jade Gate) outpost at the eastern end of the Tarim basin. From this outpost, Chinese influence was extended over the rim oases of Central Asia, establishing the **Silk Road** that linked Chang'an with Rome (see Map 7–2).

GOVERNMENT DURING THE FORMER HAN

To demonstrate how different they were from the Qin, early Han emperors set up some Zhou-like principalities, small, semiautonomous states with independent lords. But this was a token gesture. The principalities were closely superintended and then curtailed after several generations. Despite repudiating the Qin, the Han basically

Silk Road

Trade route from China to the West that stretched across Central Asia.

DOCUMENT

Chinese Women among the Nomads

The first of these selections is the lament of Xijun, a Chinese lady sent by Wudi in about 105 B.C.E. to be the wife of a nomad king of the Wusun people of Central Asia. Once there, she found her husband to be old and decrepit. He saw her only once or twice a year, when they drank a cup of wine together. They could not converse, as they had no language in common. The second selection, written centuries later, is by the Tang poet Du Fu, who visited the village of another woman sent to be the wife of a nomad king.

- **WHAT** does the fate of the women in these poems suggest about the foreign policy of the rulers of ancient China?

1.

My people have married me
In a far corner of Earth;
Sent me away to a strange land,
To the king of the Wu-sun.
A tent is my house,
Of felt are my walls;
Raw flesh my food

With mare's milk to drink.
Always thinking of my own country,
My heart sad within.
Would I were a yellow stork
And could fly to my old home!

2.

Ten thousand ranges and valleys approach the Ching Gate
And the village in which the Lady of Light was born and bred. She went out from the purple palace into the desert-land; She has now become a green grave in the yellow dusk. Her face!—Can you picture a wind of the spring? Her spirit by moonlight returns with a tinkling Telling her eternal sorrow.

[1] *Source:* From *Chinese Poems* by Arthur Waley. Copyright © 1946 by George Allen and Unwin Ltd., an imprint of HarperCollins Publishers Ltd. Reprinted by permission of the Arthur Waley Estate.

[2] *Source:* From *The Jade Mountain* translated by Witter Bynner, Copyright 1929 and renewed 1957 by Alfred A. Knopf, a division of Random House, Inc. Used by permission of Alfred A. Knopf, a division of Random House, Inc.

continued the Qin form of centralized bureaucratic administration. Officials were organized by grades and were paid salaries in grain, plus cash or silk. They were recruited by sponsorship or recommendation: Provincial officials had the duty of recommending promising candidates. A school established at Chang'an was said to have 30,000 students by the Later Han. Bureaucracy grew until, by the first century B.C.E., there were more than 130,000 officials—perhaps not too many for a population that had reached 60 million.

During the Han Dynasty, this "Legalist" structure of government became partially Confucianized. It did not happen overnight. The first Han emperor despised Confucians as bookish pedants—he once urinated in the hat of a scholar. But Confucian ideas proved useful. The Mandate of Heaven provided an ethical justification for dynastic rule. A respect for old records and the written word fit in well with the vast bookkeeping the empire entailed. Gradually the Confucian classics were accepted as the standard for education. Confucianism was seen as shaping moral men who would be upright officials, even in the absence of external constraints. Increasingly, laws were interpreted and applied by men with a Confucian education.

The court during the Han Dynasty exhibited features that would appear in later dynasties as well. All authority centered on the emperor, the all-powerful "son of heaven." When the emperor was weak, however, or ascended to the throne when still a child, others competed to rule in his name. Four contenders for this surrogate role appeared and reappeared through Chinese history: court officials, the empress dowager, court eunuchs, and military commanders.

Court officials were selected for their ability to govern: They staffed the apparatus of government and advised the emperor directly. Apart from the emperor himself, they were usually the most powerful men in China, yet their position was often precarious. Few officials escaped being removed from office or banished once or twice during their careers. Of the seven prime ministers who served Wudi, five were executed.

Of the emperor's many wives, the empress dowager was the one whose child had been named as the heir to the throne. Her influence sometimes continued even after her child became an adult emperor. But she was most powerful as a regent for a child emperor. On Gaozu's death in 195 B.C.E., for example, the Empress Lu became the regent for her child, the new emperor. Aided by her relatives, she seized control of the court and murdered a rival, and when her son was about to come of age, she had him killed and a younger son made the heir, thus continuing her rule as regent. When she died in 180 B.C.E., loyal adherents of the imperial family who had opposed her rule massacred her relatives.

Court eunuchs came mostly from families of low social status. They were brought to the court as boys, castrated, and assigned to work as servants in the emperor's harem. They were thus in contact with the future emperor from the day he was born, became his childhood confidants, and often continued to advise him after he had gained the throne. Emperors found eunuchs useful as counterweights to officials. But to the scholars who wrote China's history, the eunuchs were greedy half-men, given to evil intrigues.

Military leaders, whether generals or rebels, were the usual founders of dynasties. In the later phase of most dynasties, regional military commanders often became semi-independent rulers. A few even usurped the throne. Yet they were less powerful at the Chinese court than they were, for example, in imperial Rome, partly because the military constituted a separate category, lower in prestige than the better-educated civil officials. It was also partly because the court took great pains to prevent its generals from establishing a base of personal power. Appointments to command a Han army were given only for specific campaigns, and commanders were appointed in pairs so that each would check the other.

Another characteristic of government during the Han and subsequent dynasties was that its functions were limited. It collected taxes, maintained military forces, administered laws, supported the imperial household, and carried out public works that were beyond the powers of local jurisdictions. But government in a district that remained orderly and paid its taxes was left largely in the hands of local notables and large landowners. This pattern was not, to be sure, unique to China. Most premodern governments, even those that were bureaucratic, floated on top of their local societies and only rarely reached down and interfered in the everyday lives of their subjects.

THE SILK ROAD

Roman ladies loved diaphanous gowns of Chinese silk. Wealthy Chinese coveted Roman glass and gold. There was not a single camel train that traveled from Chang'an all the way to Rome. Instead, precious cargoes, moving more easily than persons, were passed across empires, like batons in relay races, from one network of merchants to another.

QUICK REVIEW

The Han Court

◆ Authority centered on the emperor

◆ When emperor was weak, others competed for power

◆ Court officials were chosen on the basis of their ability to govern

Funerary Figure. This kneeling figure is from the Han Dynasty.

Does this statue seem to represent a particular person? Why or why not?

During the Han and later dynasties, the route began with a network of Chinese or Central Asian traders that stretched from the Chinese capital to Lanzhou in northeastern China, through the Gansu corridor to Yumen or later Dunhuang. It then crossed the inhospitable Tarim basin, intermittently under Chinese military control, from oasis to oasis, to Kashi (Kashgar). From Kashi, the route continued in a northerly sweep to Tashkent, Samarkand, and Bukhara or in a southerly sweep to Teheran, Baghdad, and Damascus, and finally on to the Mediterranean ports of Tyre, Antioch, and Byzantium (Constantinople), which traded with Rome. (See Map 7–2.) Of the goods that departed Chang'an, only a minute portion reached Rome, which was not a destination as much as the center of the westernmost trade network. Only the thinnest trickle of Roman goods reached China.

The Silk Road, and the alternate oceanic route, point up China's isolation from other high centers of civilization. Goods were in transit more than half a year; the distance was measured in thousands of miles; camel caravans at times traveled as little as 15 miles a day. The route was hazardous, the climate extreme. Crossing deserts and mountain passes, travelers experienced cold, hunger, sandstorms, and bandits.

Most Chinese foreign trade was with their immediate steppe neighbors. The Chinese exported silk, lacquer, metal work, and later jewels, musk, and rhubarb (a digestive aid). They imported horses for their army, cattle, sheep, donkeys, and jade from Khotan and also woolens, medicines, indigo, and the occasional exotic animal. Only the most precious goods made their way to distant empires. Silk—light, compact, and valuable—was ideal. The Romans and Chinese had only the vaguest idea of where the other was located and knew nothing of the other's civilization. Romans thought silk came from a plant.

Exotic goods hawked in distant bazaars lend an aura of romance to the "Silk Road," but its true significance was as a transmission belt. In an early age China may have borrowed the chariot, compound bow, wheat, domesticated horses, and the stirrup from western Asia. Even the idea of mold-casting bronze may have come from beyond China's frontiers. Chinese technologies of paper making, iron casting, water-powered mills, and shoulder collars for draft animals, and later the compass and gunpowder, spread slowly from China to the West. Seeds of plants went in both directions, as did germs. During the Later Han, the Roman Empire lost a quarter of its population to an epidemic that, some say, appeared in China forty years later with equally dire results. During the fourteenth century, bubonic plague may have spread through the Mongol Empire from southwestern China to Central Asia to the Middle East, and then on to Europe as the Black Death. Missionary religions traveled east on the Silk Road: Buddhism toward the end of the Han Dynasty and Islam centuries later.

DECLINE AND USURPATION

During the last decade of Wudi's rule in the early first century B.C.E., military expenses ran ahead of revenues. His successor cut back on military costs, eased economic controls, and reduced taxes. But over the next several generations, large landowners began to use their growing influence in provincial politics to avoid paying taxes. State revenues declined. The tax burden on smaller landowners and free peasants grew heavier. In 22 B.C.E., rebellions broke out in several parts of the empire. At court, too, decline set in. There was a succession of weak emperors. Intrigues, nepotism, and factional struggles grew apace. Even officials began to sense that the dynasty no longer had the approval of heaven. The dynastic cycle approached its end.

Watch the *Video*
The Silk Road: 5,000 miles and 1,500 Years of Cultural Interchange
at **myhistorylab.com**

QUICK REVIEW

Decline of the Han

◆ Scheming, dissension, and violence in court

◆ Large landowners gained power

◆ Free farmers fled south

◆ Popular rebellions suppressed by generals, who then seized power

Many at the court urged Wang Mang, the regent for the infant emperor and the nephew of an empress, to become the emperor and begin a new dynasty. Wang Mang refused several times—to demonstrate his lack of eagerness—and then accepted in 8 C.E. He drew up a program of sweeping reforms based on ancient texts. He was a Confucian yet relied on new institutional arrangements rather than moral reform to improve society. He revived ancient titles, expanded state monopolies, abolished private slavery (about 1 percent of the population), made loans to poor peasants, and then moved to confiscate large private estates.

These reforms alienated many. Merchants disliked the monopolies. Large landowners resisted the expropriation of their lands. Nature also conspired to bring down Wang Mang: The Yellow River overflowed its banks and changed its course, destroying the northern Chinese irrigation system. Several years of poor harvests produced famines. The Xiongnu overran China's northern borders. In 18 C.E., a secret peasant society rose in rebellion. In 23 C.E., rebels attacked Chang'an, and Wang Mang was killed and eaten by rebel troops. He had tried to found a new dynasty from within a decrepit court without an independent military base. The attempt was futile. Internal wars continued in China for two more years until a large landowner, who had become the leader of a rebel army, emerged triumphant in 25 C.E. Because he was from a branch of the imperial family, his new dynasty was viewed as a restoration of the Han.

Chinese Galloping Horse. China traded with steppe merchants to obtain the horses needed to equip its armies against steppe warriors. Especially desired by the Chinese court were the fabled "blood-sweating" horses of far-off Ferghana (present-day Tajikistan). **How were horses used by the Chinese and by their neighbors?**

See the **Map**

China from the Later Zhou Era to the Han Era at **myhistorylab.com**

CHRONOLOGY

THE DYNASTIC HISTORY OF CHINA'S FIRST EMPIRE

256–206 B.C.E.	Qin Dynasty
206 B.C.E.–8 C.E.	Former Han Dynasty
25–220 C.E.	Later Han Dynasty

LATER HAN (25–220 C.E.) AND ITS AFTERMATH

FIRST CENTURY

WHY DID the Han Dynasty collapse?

The founder of the Later Han moved his capital east to Luoyang. Under the first emperor and his two successors, there was a return to strong central government and a laissez-faire economy. Agriculture and population recovered. By the end of the first century C.E., China was as prosperous as it had been during the good years of the Former Han. The shift from pacification and recuperation to military expansion came earlier than it had during the previous dynasty. During the reign of the first emperor, south China and Vietnam were retaken. Dissension among the Xiongnu enabled the Chinese to secure an alliance with some of the southern tribes in 50 C.E., and in 89 C.E. Chinese armies crossed the Gobi Desert and defeated the northern Xiongnu. This defeat sparked the migrations, some historians say, that brought those nomadic warriors to the southern Russian steppes and then, in the fifth century C.E., to Europe, where they were known as the Huns of Attila. In 97 C.E. a Chinese general led an army to the shores of the Caspian Sea. The Chinese expansion in inner Asia, coupled with more lenient government policies toward merchants, facilitated the camel caravans that carried Chinese silk across the Tarim basin and, ultimately, to merchants in Iran, Palestine, and Rome.

DECLINE DURING THE SECOND CENTURY

After 88 C.E. the emperors of the Later Han were ineffectual and short-lived. Empresses plotted to advance the fortunes of their families. Emperors turned for help to palace eunuchs. In 159 C.E. a conspiracy of eunuchs in the service of an emperor slaughtered the family of a scheming empress dowager and ruled at the court. When officials and students protested against the eunuch dictatorship, over a hundred were killed and over a thousand were tortured or imprisoned. In another incident in 190 C.E., a general deposed one emperor, installed another, killed the empress dowager, and massacred most of the eunuchs at the court.

In the countryside, large landowners grew more powerful. They harbored private armies. Farmers on the estates of the mighty were reduced to serfs. The landowners used their influence to avoid taxes. Great numbers of free farmers fled south for the same purpose. The remaining freeholders paid ever-heavier taxes and labor services. Many peasants turned to neo-Daoist religious movements that provided the ideology and organization to channel their discontent into action. In 184 C.E. rebellions organized by members of the religious movements broke out against the government. Han generals suppressed the rebellions but stayed on to rule in the provinces they had pacified. In 220 C.E. they deposed the last Han emperor.

A Green Glazed Pottery Model of a Later Han Dynasty Watchtower (87.6 x 35.6 x 38.1 cm). Note the resemblance to later Chinese Buddhist pagodas.

How might watchtowers have been used during the Later Han dynasty?

AFTERMATH OF EMPIRE

For more than three and a half centuries after the fall of the Han, China was disunited. For several generations it was divided into three kingdoms, whose heroic warriors and scheming statesmen were made famous by wandering storytellers. These figures later peopled the *Tale of the Three Kingdoms*, a great romantic epic of Chinese literature.

Chinese history during the post-Han centuries had two characteristics. The first was the dominant role played by the great aristocratic landowning families. With vast estates, huge numbers of serfs, fortified manor houses, and private armies, they were beyond the control of most governments. Because they took over many of the functions of local government, some historians describe post-Han China as having reverted to the quasi-feudalism of the Zhou. The second characteristic of these centuries was that northern and southern China developed in different ways.

In the south, a succession of six, ever-weaker states had their capital at Nanjing. Although these six southern states were called dynasties—and the entire period of Chinese history from 220 B.C.E. to 589 C.E. is called the Six Dynasties era after them—they were in fact short-lived kingdoms plagued by intrigues, usurpations, and coups d'état; frequently at war with northern states; and in constant fear of their own generals. The main developments in the south were (1) continuing economic growth and the emergence of Nanjing as a thriving center of commerce; (2) the ongoing absorption of tribal peoples into Chinese society and culture; (3) large-scale immigrations of Chinese fleeing the north; and (4) the spread of Buddhism and its penetration to the heart of Chinese culture.

In the north, state formation depended on the interaction of nomads and Chinese. During the Han Dynasty, Chinese invasions of the steppe had led to the incorporation of semi-Sinicized Xiongnu as the northernmost tier of the Chinese defense system—just as Germanic tribes had acted as the teeth and claws of the late Roman Empire. But as the Chinese state weakened, the highly mobile nomads broke loose, joined with other tribes, and began to invade China. The short-lived states that they formed are usually referred to as the "Sixteen Kingdoms." One kingdom was founded by invaders of Tibetan stock. Most spoke Altaic languages: the Xianbi (proto-Mongols), the Tuoba (proto-Turks), and the Ruan Ruan (who would later appear in eastern Europe as the Avars). But differences of language and ancestry were less important than these tribes' similarities:

1. All began as steppe nomads with a way of life different from that of agricultural China.

2. After forming states, all became at least partially Sinicized. Chinese from great families, which had preserved Han traditions, served as their tutors and administrators.

3. All were involved in wars—among themselves, against southern dynasties, or against conservative steppe tribes that resisted Sinicization.

4. Buddhism was as powerful in the north as in the south. As a universal religion, it acted as a bridge between "barbarians" and Chinese—just as Christianity was a unifying force in post-Roman Europe. The barbarian rulers of the north were especially attracted to its magical side. Usually Buddhism was made the state religion. Of the northern states, the most durable was the Northern Wei (386–534 C.E.), famed for its Buddhist sculpture.

HAN THOUGHT AND RELIGION

Poems describe the splendor of Chang'an and Luoyang: broad boulevards, tiled gateways, open courtyards, watchtowers, and imposing walls. Most splendid of all were the palaces of emperors, with their audience halls, vast chambers, harem quarters, and parks containing artificial lakes and rare animals and birds. But today little remains of the grandeur of the Han. Whereas Roman ruins abound in Italy and circle the Mediterranean, in China nothing remains above ground. Only the items buried in tombs— pottery, bronzes, musical instruments, gold and silver jewelry, lacquerware, and clay figurines—give a glimpse of the rich material culture of the Han period. Only the paintings on the walls of tombs tell us of its art. But a wealth of written records conveys the sophistication and depth of Han culture. Perhaps the two most important areas were philosophy and history.

WHAT WAS the extent of Buddhist influence under the Han?

HAN CONFUCIANISM

A major accomplishment of the early Han was the recovery of texts that had been lost during the Qin persecution of scholars. Some were retrieved from the walls of houses where they had been hidden; others were reproduced from memory by scholars. Debate arose regarding the relative authenticity of the old and new texts—a controversy that has continued until modern times. In 51 B.C.E. and again in 79 C.E. councils were held to determine the true meaning of the Confucian classics. In 175 C.E. an approved, official version of the texts was inscribed on stone tablets.

The first dictionary was compiled in about 100 C.E. Containing about 9,000 characters, it helped promote a uniform system of writing. In Han times, as today, Chinese from the north could not converse with Chinese from the southeastern coast, but a common written language bridged differences of pronunciation, contributing to Chinese unity. Scholars began writing commentaries on the classics, a major scholarly activity throughout Chinese history. Scholars learned the classics by heart and used classical allusions in their writing.

Han philosophers also extended Zhou Confucianism by adding to it the teachings of cosmological naturalism. Zhou Confucianists had assumed that the moral force of a virtuous emperor would not only order society but also harmonize nature. Han Confucianists explained why. Dong Zhongshu (ca. 179–104 B.C.E.), for example, held that all nature was a single, interrelated system. Just as summer always follows spring, so does one color, one virtue, one planet, one element, one number, and one officer of the court always take precedence over another. All reflect the systematic workings of yang and yin and the five elements. And just as one dresses appropriately to the season, so was it important for the emperor to choose policies appropriate to the sequences inherent in nature. If he was moral, if he acted in accord with Heaven's natural system, then all would go well. But if he acted inappropriately, then Heaven would send a portent as a warning—a blue dog, a rat holding its tail in its mouth, an eclipse, or a comet. If the portent was not heeded, wonders and then misfortunes would follow. It was the Confucian scholars, of course, who claimed to understand nature's messages and advised the emperor.

It is easy to criticize Han philosophy as a pseudoscientific or mechanistic view of nature, but it represented a new effort by the Chinese to encompass and comprehend the interrelationships of the natural world. This effort led to inventions like the seismograph and to advances in astronomy, music, and medicine. It was also during the Han that the Chinese invented paper, the wheelbarrow, the stern-post rudder, and the compass (known as the "south-pointing chariot").

HISTORY

The Chinese were the greatest historians of the premodern world. They wrote more history than anyone else, and what they wrote was usually more accurate. Apart from the *Spring and Autumn Annals* and the scholarship of Confucius himself, history writing in China began during the Han Dynasty. Why the Chinese were so history-minded has been variously explained: because the Chinese tradition is this-worldly; because Confucianists were scholarly and their veneration for the classics carried over to the written word; because history was seen as a lesson book (the Chinese called it a mirror) for statesmen, and thus a necessity for the literate men who operated the centralized Chinese state.

The practice of using actual documents and firsthand accounts of events began with Sima Qian (d. 85 B.C.E.), who set out to write a history of the known world from the most ancient times down to the age of the emperor Wudi. His *Historical Records* consisted of 130 substantial chapters (with a total of over 700,000 characters) divided into "Basic Annals"; "Chronological Tables"; "Treatises" on rites, music, astronomy, the calendar, and so on; "Hereditary Houses"; and seventy chapters of "Biographies," including descriptions of foreign peoples. A second great work, *The Book of the Han*, was written by Ban Gu (d. 92 C.E.). It applied the analytical schema of Sima Qian to a single dynasty, the Former Han, and established the pattern by which each dynasty wrote the history of its predecessor.

NEO-DAOISM

As the Han Dynasty waned, it became increasingly difficult to implement the Confucian ethic in the sociopolitical order. Some scholars abandoned Confucianism altogether in favor of **Neo-Daoism**, or "mysterious learning." A few wrote commentaries on the classical Daoist texts that had been handed down from the Zhou. The *Zhuangzi* was especially popular. Other scholars, defining the natural as the pleasurable, withdrew from society to engage in witty "pure conversations." They discussed poetry and philosophy, played the lute, and drank wine. The most famous were the Seven Sages of the Bamboo Grove of the third century C.E. One sage was always accompanied by a servant carrying a jug of wine and a spade—the one for his pleasure, the other to dig his grave should he die. Another wore no clothes at home. When criticized, he replied that the cosmos was his home, and his house his clothes. "Why are you in my pants?" he asked a discomfited visitor. Still another took a boat to visit a friend on a snowy night, but on arriving at his friend's door, turned around and went home. When pressed for an explanation, he said that it had been his pleasure to go, and that when the impulse died, it was his pleasure to return. This story reveals a scorn for convention coupled with an admiration for an inner spontaneity, however eccentric.

Another concern of what is called Neo-Daoism was immortality. Some sought it in dietary restrictions and yoga-like meditation, some in sexual abstinence or orgies. Others, seeking elixirs to prolong life, dabbled in alchemy, and although no magical elixir was ever found, the schools of alchemy to which the search gave rise are credited with the discovery of medicines, dyes, glazes, and gunpowder.

Meanwhile, popular religious cults arose among the common people. Since they included the Daoist classics among their sacred texts, these popular cults are also called Neo-Daoist. Like most folk religions, they contained an amalgam of beliefs, practices, and superstitions. They had a pantheon of gods and immortals and taught that the good or evil done in this life would be rewarded or punished in the innumerable heavens or hells of an afterlife. These cults had priests, shamans who practiced faith healing, seers, and sorceresses. For a time, they also had hierarchical church organizations, but these were smashed at the end of the second century C.E. Local Daoist temples and monasteries, however, continued until modern times. With many Buddhist accretions, they furnished the religious beliefs of the bulk of the Chinese population. Even in recent decades, these sects flourished in Taiwan and Chinese communities in Southeast Asia. They were suppressed in China in the Maoist era but were revived during the 1990s.

BUDDHISM

Central Asian missionaries, following the trade routes east, brought Buddhism to China in the first century C.E. It was at first viewed as a new Daoist sect, which is not surprising because early translators used Daoist terms to render Buddhist concepts. **Nirvana**, for example, was translated as "not doing" (*wuwei*). In the second century C.E., confusion about the two

Neo-Daoism
A revival of Daoist "mysterious learning" that flourished as a reaction against Confucianism during the Han Dynasty.

A Chinese Seismograph. The suspended weight swings in the direction of the earthquake. This moves a lever, and a dragon drops a ball into the mouth of one of the four waiting ceramic frogs.

How did the "mysterious learning" of Neo-Daoism contribute to science, technology, and medicine?

Nirvana In Buddhism the attainment of release from the wheel of *karma*.

religions led to the very Chinese view that Laozi had gone to India, where the Buddha had become his disciple, and that Buddhism was the Indian form of Daoism.

As the Han sociopolitical order collapsed in the third century C.E., Buddhism spread rapidly. (There are parallels to the spread of Christianity at the end of the Roman Empire.) Although an alien religion in China, Buddhism had some advantages over Daoism:

1. It was a doctrine of personal salvation, offering several routes to that goal.
2. It upheld high standards of personal ethics.
3. It had systematic philosophies, and during its early centuries in China, it continued to receive inspiration from India.
4. It drew on the Indian tradition of meditative practices and psychologies, which were the most sophisticated in the world.

◆▶─Read the Document
Faxien, Record of Buddhist Countries, Chapter Sixteen at **myhistorylab.com**

By the fifth century C.E. Buddhism had spread over all of China (see Map 7–3). Occasionally it was persecuted by Daoist emperors, but most courts supported Buddhism. The "Bodhisattva Emperor" Wu of the southern Liang Dynasty three times gave himself to a monastery and had to be ransomed back by his disgusted courtiers. Temples and monasteries abounded in both the north and the south. There were communities of women as well as of men. Chinese artists produced Buddhist painting and sculpture of surpassing beauty, and thousands of monk-scholars labored to translate sutras and philosophical treatises. Chinese monks went on pilgrimages to India. The record left by Fa Xian, who traveled to India overland and back by sea between 399 and 413 C.E., became a prime source of Indian history.

The Tang monk Xuanzang went to India from 629 until 645. Several centuries later, his pilgrimage was novelized as *Journey to the West*. The novel joins faith, magic, and adventure.

A comparison of Indian and Chinese Buddhism highlights some distinctive features of its spread. Buddhism in India had begun as a reform movement. Forget speculative philosophies and elaborate metaphysics, taught the Buddha, and concentrate on simple truths: Life is suffering, the cause of suffering is desire, death does not stop the endless cycle of birth and rebirth; only the attainment of *nirvana* releases one from the "wheel of *karma*." Thus, in this most otherworldly of the world's religions, all of the cosmic drama of salvation was compressed into the single figure of the Buddha meditating under the Bodhi tree. Over the centuries, however, Indian Buddhism developed contending philosophies and conflicting sects and, having become virtually indistinguishable from Hinduism, was largely reabsorbed after 1000 C.E.

In China, there were a number of sects with different doctrinal positions, but the Chinese genius was more syncretic. It took in the sutras and meditative practices of early Buddhism. It took in the Mahayana philosophies that depicted a succession of Buddhas, cosmic and historical, past and future, all embodying a single ultimate reality. It also took in the sutras and practices of Buddhist devotional sects. Finally, in the Tiantai sect, the Chinese joined together these various elements as different levels of a single truth. Thus the monastic routine of a Tiantai monk would include reading sutras, sitting in meditation, and also practicing devotional exercises.

Socially, too, Buddhism adapted to China. Ancestor worship demanded heirs to perform the sacrifices. Without progeny, ancestors might become "hungry ghosts." Hence, the first son was expected to marry and have children, whereas the second son, if he were

A mendicant friar of the Tang Dynasty. He is accompanied by a tiger, indicating the extent to which he has become one with nature and with his own true nature.

In what ways did the Chinese adapt Buddhism to fit their culture?

MAP 7–3.   The Spread of Buddhism and Chinese States in 500 C.E.
Buddhism originated in a Himalayan state in northwest India. It spread in one wave south to India and on to Southeast Asia as far as Java. But it also spread into northwest India, Afghanistan, Central Asia, and then to China, Korea, and Japan.

What is the relationship between the spread of Buddhism and trade?

so inclined, might become a monk. The practice also arose of holding Buddhist masses for dead ancestors. Still another difference between China and India was the more extensive regulation of Buddhism by the state in China. Just as Buddhism was not to threaten the integrity of the family, so Buddhism was not to reduce the taxes paid on land. As a result, limits were placed on the number of monasteries, nunneries, and monastic lands, and the state had to give its permission before men or women abandoned the world to enter a religious establishment—though these regulations were not always enforced.

SUMMARY

HOW DID the Qin unify China?

Qin Unification of China. The state of Qin unified China in 221 B.C.E. through military conquest. To the north it built the Great Wall to prevent incursions by the nomadic Xiongnu peoples. It ruled through a centralized bureaucracy in line with its Legalist philosophy. But the pace of its reform was so frenetic and its legal punishments were so harsh that it alienated its people. The Qin collapsed after the death of the First Emperor. *page 175*

WHAT IS the dynastic cycle?

Former Han Dynasty. China's pattern of dynastic cycles—military unification, consolidation, growth, reform, followed by decay and disintegration—began. The Former Han and Later Han, back-to-back dynasties, ruled China for more than four centuries (206 B.C.E.–220 C.E.). A pattern of centralized rule by officials educated in the Confucian classics was established. Ever since this period, the core Chinese population has referred to itself as the "Han people." *page 178*

WHY DID the Han Dynasty collapse?

Later Han and Its Aftermath. The Later Han established a new capital, but in most respects continued Former Han policies. Late in the first century C.E., the first in a line of weak emperors came to power, beginning the process of decline. After the fall of the Han, large landowners gained power and China was fragmented for several centuries. Northern and southern China developed differently. *page 185*

WHAT WAS the extent of Buddhist influence under the Han?

Han Thought and Religion. During long periods of peace and good government, literature, art, and history-writing flourished. Neo-Daoism partially eclipsed Confucianism. Buddhism entered China in the first century and spread rapidly in the third century, as the Han collapsed. *page 187*

KEY TERMS

dynastic cycle (p. 178)   **Silk Road** (p. 181)
Neo-Daoism (p. 189)   **Xiongnu** (p. 180)
Nirvana (p. 189)

REVIEW QUESTIONS

1. How did Legalism help the Qin unify China? What other factors played a part? What were the main features of Qin administration? Why did the Qin collapse?

2. What was the "dynastic cycle"? In what sense was it a Confucian moral rationalization? Was a cycle of administrative and military decline especially true of Chinese government, or can we see the same pattern elsewhere?

3. Who were the Xiongnu? How did Wudi respond to them?

4. How did the Silk Road work? What items were traded and on what route? What impact did this trade have on Chinese culture?

5. What challenges did the Han face in conquering and integrating new territories into the empire? How did they meet those challenges?

6. Compare and contrast the Roman and Han empires. What qualities did they have in common? How did they differ?

7. Who were the players who sought power at the Han court? Did the means they used reflect the differences in their positions?

8. What roles did Neo-Daoism have on elite Chinese culture and politics? What was its role among the larger populace?

9. Did Buddhism "triumph" in China in the same sense in which Christianity triumphed in the Roman world? Compare China to the Roman Empire. What problems did both empires face, and how did they try to resolve them?

Note: To learn more about the topics in this chapter, please turn to the Suggested Readings at the end of the book. For additional sources related to this chapter please see www.myhistorylab.com

PEARSON
myhistorylab Connections

Reinforce what you learned in this chapter by studying the many documents, images, maps, review tools, and videos available at **www.myhistorylab.com**

Read and Review

✓●─ **Study** and **Review** Chapter 7

●●●─ Read the **Document** *Li Si and the Legalist Policies of Qin Shihuang (280–208 B.C.E.), p. 177*
Sima Qian, The Life of Meng Tian, Builder of the Great Wall, p. 188
Faxien, Record of Buddhist Countries, Chapter Sixteen, p. 190

◉─ See the **Map** *China from the Later Zhou Era to the Han Era, p. 185*

◉─ Watch the **Video** *The Silk Road: 5,000 miles and 1,500 Years of Cultural Interchange, p. 184*

◉─ View the **Image** *The Great Wall of China, p. 176*
Qin Shihuang's Terra Cotta Soldiers, p. 178

Research and Explore

◉─ Watch the **Video** *Symbiosis in Central Asia*
Buddhism on the Silk Road
Central and Periphery
Kushan Empire
Silk Road

◉─ See the **Map** *Ancient China*

─── ((●─ **Hear** the **Audio** ───

Hear the audio file for Chapter 7
at **www.myhistorylab.com**

8

Imperial China, 589–1368

((•─Hear the Audio for Chapter 8 at www.myhistorylab.com

"Lady Wenji's Return to China: Wenji Arriving Home." Southern Song Dynasty. Circa 1150 C.E. Lady Wenji, who lived in the second century C.E., was the daughter of a high-ranking official who was abducted by the no-madic Xiongnu. She eventually married and bore two sons. After twelve years in captivity she was ransomed and returned to China, leaving her children behind. Wenji's ordeal became the subject of numerous poems and paintings, such as the one shown here.

Museum of Fine Arts, Boston.

What were some of the roles played by women in China in this period?

T*he Tang (618–907) is everyone's favorite dynasty: open, cosmopolitan, expansionist, exuberant, and creative. It was the example of Tang China that decisively influenced the formation of states and high cultures in Japan, Korea, and Vietnam. Poetry during the Tang attained a peak that has not been equaled since. The Song (960–1279) rivaled the Tang in the arts; it was China's great age of painting and the most significant period for Chinese philosophy since its origins in the Zhou. Although not militarily strong, the Song Dynasty also witnessed an important commercial revolution. The Yuan (1279–1368) was a short-lived dynasty of rule by Mongols during which China became the most important unit in the largest empire the world has yet seen.* ■

REESTABLISHMENT OF EMPIRE: SUI (589–618) AND TANG (618–907) DYNASTIES

HOW DID the Sui and Tang dynasties re-create China's empire?

In the period corresponding to the European Early Middle Ages, the most notable feature of Chinese history was the reunification of China, the re-creation of a centralized bureaucratic empire consciously modeled on the earlier Han Dynasty (206 B.C.E.–220 C.E.). Reunification, as usual, began in the north. The Northern Wei (386–534), the most enduring of the northern Sino-Turkic states, took the first steps. It moved its court south to Luoyang, made Chinese the language of the court, and adopted Chinese dress and surnames. It also used the leverage of its nomadic cavalry to impose a new land tax, mobilizing resources for state use. The Northern Wei was followed by several short-lived kingdoms. Because the emperors, officials, and military commanders of these kingdoms came from the same aristocratic stratum, the social distance between them was small, and the throne was often usurped.

THE SUI DYNASTY

Sui Wendi (d. 605), a talented general of mixed Chinese-Turkic ancestry, came to power in 581 and began the Sui Dynasty (589–618). He unified the north, restored the tax base, reestablished a centralized bureaucratic government, and went on to conquer

GLOBAL PERSPECTIVE

IMPERIAL CHINA

Rough parallels between China and Europe persisted until the sixth century C.E. Both saw the rise and fall of great empires. At first glance, the three and a half centuries that followed the Han Dynasty appear remarkably similar to the comparable period after the collapse of the Roman Empire: Central authority broke down, private armies arose, and aristocratic estates were established. Barbarian tribes once allied to the empires invaded and pillaged large areas. Otherworldly religions entered to challenge earlier official worldviews. In China, Neo-Daoism and then Buddhism challenged Confucianism, just as Christianity challenged Roman conceptions of the sociopolitical order.

But from the late sixth century C.E., a fundamental divergence occurred. Europe tailed off into centuries of feudal disunity and backwardness. A ghost of empire lingered in the European memory. But the reality, even after centuries had passed, was that tiny areas like France (one seventeenth the size of China), Italy (one thirty-second), or Germany (one twenty-seventh) found it difficult to establish an internal unity, much less re-create a pan-European or pan-Mediterranean empire. In contrast, China, which is about the size of Europe and geographically no

more natural a political unit, put a unified empire back together again, attaining new wealth, power, culture, and unified rule that has continued until the present. What explains the difference?

One reason China re-created its empire was that in China the victory of Buddhism was less complete than that of Christianity in Europe. Confucianism, and its conception of a unified empire, survived within the aristocratic families and at the courts of the Six Dynasties. It is difficult even to think of Confucianism apart from the idea of a universal ruler, aided by men of virtue and ability, ruling "all under Heaven" according to Heaven's Mandate. In contrast, the Roman concept of political order was not maintained as an independent doctrine. Moreover, empire was not a vital concept in Christian thought—except perhaps in Byzantium, where the empire lasted longer than it did in western Europe. The notion of a "Christian king" did appear in the West, but basically, the kingdom sought by Jesus was not of this world.

A second consideration was China's greater cultural homogeneity. It had a common written language that was fairly close to all varieties of spoken Chinese. Minority peoples and even barbarian conquerors—apart from the Mongols—were rapidly

QUICK REVIEW

Sui Wendi (d. 605)
- Founder of the Sui Dynasty (589–618)
- Talented ruler who unified China
- Grand Canal constructed and Great Wall rebuilt during his reign

See the Map
China during the Sui and Tang Dynasties
at **myhistorylab.com**

Chang'an
City in northern China, near present-day X'ian, that served as capital during the Sui and Tang dynasties.

Censorate The branch of the imperial Chinese government that acted as a watchdog, reporting instances of misgovernment directly to the emperor and remonstrating when it considered the emperor's behavior improper.

southern China and unify the country. During his reign, huge palaces arose in his Wei valley capital. The Great Wall was rebuilt. The Grand Canal was constructed, linking the Yellow and Yangzi rivers. This canal enabled the northern conquerors to tap the wealth of central and southern China. Peace was maintained with the Turkic tribes along China's northern borders. Eastern Turkic khans (chiefs) were sent Chinese princesses as brides.

The early years of the second Sui emperor were also constructive, but then Chinese attempts to meddle in steppe politics led to hostilities and wars. Hardships and casualties in campaigns against Korea and along China's northern border produced rising discontent. Natural disasters occurred. The court became bankrupt and demoralized. Rebellions broke out, and once again, there was a free-for-all among the armies of aristocratic military commanders. The winner, and the founder of the Tang Dynasty, was a relative of the Sui empress and a Sino-Turkic aristocrat of the same social background as those who had ruled before him.

Chinese historians often compare the short-lived Sui Dynasty with that of the Qin (256–206 B.C.E.). Each brought all of China under a single government after centuries of disunity. Each did too much, fell, and was replaced by a long-lasting dynasty. The Tang built on the foundations that had been laid by the Sui, just as the Han had built on those of the Qin.

THE TANG DYNASTY

The first Tang emperor took over the Sui capital, renamed it **Chang'an**, and made it his own. Within about a decade the new dynasty had extended its authority over all of China; tax revenues were adequate for government needs; and Chinese armies had begun the campaigns that would push Chinese borders out farther than ever

Sinicized. In contrast, after Rome the Mediterranean fell apart into its component cultures. Latin became the universal language of the Western church, but for most Christians it was a foreign language, a part of the mystery of the Mass, and even in Italy it became an artificial language, separate from the living tongue. European languages and cultures were divisive forces.

✓ ● Study and Review
China's Struggle for Cultural and Political Unity, 400 B.C.E.–A.D. 400 at **myhistorylab.com**

A third and perhaps critical factor was China's population density, which was at least fifteen times greater than that of France, Europe's most populous state. Population density explains why the Chinese could absorb barbarian conquerors so much more quickly than could Europe. More cultivators provided a larger agricultural surplus to the northern kingdoms than that enjoyed by comparable kingdoms in Europe. Greater numbers of people also meant better communications and a better base for commerce. To be sure, the centuries that followed the Han saw a decline in commerce and cities. In some areas barter or the use of silk as currency replaced money, but the economic level remained higher than in early medieval Europe. Several of the factors that explain the Sui–Tang regeneration of a unified empire apply equally well or better to the Song and subsequent dynasties. Comparisons across continents are difficult, but it seems likely that Tang and Song China had longer stretches of good government than any other part of the contemporary world. Not until the nineteenth century did comparable bureaucracies of talent and virtue appear in the West.

Focus Questions

◆ In what ways did China and Europe parallel each other in their development until the sixth century C.E.? How did they diverge after that?

◆ Why did China witness the reunification of empire after the fall of the Han Dynasty, whereas after the fall of Rome, Europe was never again united in a single empire?

◆ Why did Tang and Song China enjoy longer stretches of good government than anywhere else in the contemporary world during the same period?

(see Map 8–1 on page 198). Confucian scholars were employed at the court, Buddhist temples and monasteries flourished, and peace and order prevailed, especially from 624 to 755.

The first Tang emperor and his successors worked to reconcile conflicting interests. The emperor wanted a bureaucratic government in which authority was centralized in his own person, but at the same time he had to make concessions to the aristocrats—the dominant elements in Chinese society in the Late Han—who staffed his government and continued to dominate early Tang society.

The degree to which political authority was centralized was apparent in the formal organization of the bureaucracy. At the highest level were three organs: Military Affairs, the Censorate, and the Council of State (see Figure 8–1). Military Affairs supervised the Tang armies with the emperor, in effect, the commander in chief. The **Censorate** had watchdog functions: It reported instances of misgovernment directly to the emperor and could also remonstrate with the emperor when it considered his behavior improper. The Council of State was the most important body. It met daily with the emperor and was made up of the heads of the Secretariat, which drafted policies; the Chancellery, which reviewed them; and State Affairs, which carried them out.

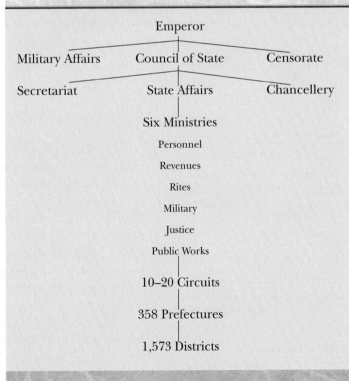

FIGURE 8–1. Tang Government Organization.

MAP EXPLORATION

To explore this map further, go to **http://www.myhistorylab.com**

MAP 8–1.   The Tang Empire at Its Peak During the Eighth Century.

The Tang expansion into Central Asia reopened trade routes to the Middle East and Europe. Students from Bohai, Silla (Korea), and Japan studied in the Tang capital of Chang'an and then returned, carrying with them Tang books and technology.

Why did the Chinese Empire continually seek to expand into Central Asia?

QUICK REVIEW

Centralization of Authority

◆ Three organs of bureaucracy: Military Affairs, Censorate, Council of State

◆ Council of State most important body

◆ Council of State met daily with the emperor

◆◆◆ Read the Document
Tang Daizong on the Art of Government
at **myhistorylab.com**

examination system

A method of selecting scholar-bureaucrats based on the results of a highly structured, and extremely competitive, series of tests.

Beneath State Affairs were the Six Ministries, which continued as the core of the central government down to the twentieth century; beneath them were the several levels of local administration.

Concessions to the interests of the aristocratic families were embodied in the tax system. All land was declared to be the property of the emperor and was then redistributed to able-bodied cultivators, who paid taxes in labor and grain. Because all able-bodied adult males received an equal allotment of land (women got less), the land-tax system was called the "equal field system." But the system was not egalitarian. Aristocrats enjoyed special exemptions and grants of "rank" and "office" lands that, in effect, confirmed their estate holdings.

Recruitment of officials also favored aristocrats, since most officials either were recommended for posts or received posts because their fathers had been high officials. Only a tiny percentage was recruited through the **examination system**. Those who passed the examinations had the highest prestige and were more likely to have brilliant careers. But only well-to-do families could afford the years of study needed to pass the rigorous examinations, so even the examination bureaucrats were usually aristocrats.

Women of the inner court continued to play a role in government. For example, Wu Zhao (626–ca. 706), a young concubine of the strong second emperor, married his weak heir. When the emperor suffered a stroke in 660, she dominated the court. After his death in 683 she ruled as regent and then, deposing her son, became emperor herself, the only woman in Chinese history to hold the title. She moved the court to Luoyang and proclaimed a new dynasty. A fervent Buddhist with an interest in magic, she saw herself as the incarnation of the messianic Buddha Maitreya and built temples throughout the land. Her sexual appetites were said to have been prodigious. She ruled China until she was 80; she was deposed in 705.

Surprisingly, Empress Wu's machinations may have strengthened the central government. In her struggle for power against the old northwestern Chinese aristocrats, she turned not to members of her family but to the products of the examination system and to a group known as the Scholars of the North Gate. This policy broadened the base of government by bringing in aristocrats from other regions of China. Her rule coincided with the maximal geographical expansion of Tang military power.

After a few years of tawdry intrigues, Xuan Zong came to the throne. In reaction to Empress Wu, he appointed government commissions headed by distinguished aristocrats to reform government finances. Examination bureaucrats lost power. The Grand Canal was repaired and extended. A new census extended the tax rolls. Wealth and prosperity returned to the court. His reign (713–756) was also culturally brilliant.

Chang'an was an imperial city, an administrative center that lived on taxes (see Map 8–2). It was designed to exhibit the power of the emperor and the majesty of his court. The city was laid out on a grid. At the far north of the city, the palace faced south, in keeping with Confucian tradition. In front of the palace was a complex of government offices from which an imposing 500-foot-wide avenue led to the main southern gate. Enclosed by great walls, the city covered 30 square miles. Its population was over 1 million: half within the walls, the other half in suburbs. It was the largest city in the world. (The population of China in the year 750 was about 50 million—about 4 percent of the country's present-day population.) Chang'an was also a trade center from which caravans set out across Central Asia. Merchants from India, Persia, Syria, and Arabia hawked the wares of the Near East and all of Asia in its two government-controlled markets.

THE TANG EMPIRE

A Chinese dynasty is like an accordion, first expanding into the territories of its neighbors and then contracting back to its densely populated core area. The principal threats to the Tang state were from Tibetans in the west, Turks in the northwest and north, and Khitan Mongols in Manchuria.

To protect its border, the Tang employed a four-tier policy. When nothing else would work, the Tang sent armies. But armies were expensive, and military solutions impermanent. For example, in 630 Tang armies defeated the eastern Turks; in 648 they took the Tarim basin, open-

◆◆◆▶ Read the **Document**

An Essay Question from the Chinese Imperial Examination System at **myhistorylab.com**

QUICK REVIEW

Chang'an

◆ Chang'an was an administrative center that lived on taxes

◆ Designed to show power and majesty of emperor and his court

◆ City was laid out on a grid

✓●▶ **Study** and **Review**

Comparative Case Study: Women in the Imperial Courts of China and Japan at **myhistorylab.com**

Chang'an

☐ Imperial building
■ Government building
▨ Upper-class district
▧ Middle-class district
▩ Working-class district

MAP 8–2. Chang'an. The great city of Chang'an had been a Chinese capital since the Han period. By the eighth century there were around a half-million people within the city walls, with the same number close by outside, making it the largest city in the world at the time. The rigorous grid structure accommodated a variety of districts, each with its own administration.

HOW DOES the layout of Chang'an exhibit the power of the emperor?

Relief of Tang Emperor's Horse. A bearded "barbarian" groom tends the charger of the second Tang emperor (r. 626–649). This stone relief was found on the emperor's tomb. Note the stirrup, a Chinese invention of the fourth century C.E.

A Relief of Emperor T'ai T'sung's Horse, "Autumn Dew." University of Pennsylvania Museum, Philadelphia (NEG.# S8-62840).

How might stirrups help horsemen? What kinds of activities would be easier with stirrups than without?

Uighur Turk

A pastoralist, Altaic-speaking group based in the plains northwest of China, south of Lake Baikal.

Read the Document
Chinese description of the Tibetans
at **myhistorylab.com**

CHRONOLOGY

IMPERIAL CHINA

589–618	Sui Dynasty
618–907	Tang Dynasty
960–1279	Song Dynasty
1279–1368	Yuan (Mongol) Dynasty

ing trade routes to western Asia for almost a century; and in 657 they defeated the western Turks and extended Chinese influence to petty states near Samarkand. By 698, however, the Turks were invading northeastern China again, and between 711 and 736 they were in control of the steppe from the Oxus River to China's northern frontier. Chinese efforts against Tibet were much the same. From 670 Tibet expanded and threatened China. In 679 it was defeated. In 714 it rose again, wars were fought from 727 to 729, and a settlement was reached in 730. But wars broke out anew. In 752 Tibet entered an alliance with the state of Nan Chao in Yunnan. In 763 Tibetan forces captured and looted Chang'an. They were driven out, but the point remains that no military victory was final.

The second tier of Chinese defenses was to use nomads against other nomads. The critical development for the Tang was the rise to power of the **Uighur Turks**. From 744 to 840, the Uighurs controlled Central Asia and were staunch allies of the Tang. Without their support, the Tang Dynasty would have ended sooner.

A third tier was the defense along China's borders, including the Great Wall. At mid-dynasty, whole frontier provinces in the north and the northwest were put under military commanders, who in time came to control the provinces' civil governments as well. The bulk of the Tang military was in such frontier commands. At times their autonomy posed as much of a threat to the Tang court as to the nomadic enemy.

The fourth line of defense was to bring the potential enemy into the empire as a tributary. The Tang definition of "tributary" included principalities truly dependent on China; Central Asian states conquered by China; enemy states, such as Tibet or the Thai state of Nan Chao in Yunnan, when they were not actually at war with China; the Korean state of Silla, which had unified the peninsula with Tang aid but had then fought Tang armies to a stalemate when they attempted to impose Chinese hegemony; and wholly independent states, such as Japan. All sent embassies bearing gifts to the Tang court, which housed and fed them and sent back costly gifts in return.

For some countries these embassies had a special significance. As the only "developed nation" in eastern Asia, China was a model for countries still emerging as states. An embassy gained access to the entire range of Tang culture and technology. In 640 there were 8,000 Koreans, mostly students, in Chang'an. China was able to exert great influence on its neighbors during their formative stages.

Within China, signs of decline began to appear around the mid-eighth century. China's frontiers started to contract. Tribes in Manchuria became unruly. Tibetans threatened China's western border.

In 751, an overextended Tang army was defeated by Arabs near Samarkand, closing China's caravan trade with the West for more than five centuries. Meanwhile, in 755 a Sogdian general, An Lushan, who commanded three Chinese provinces on the northeastern frontier, led his 160,000 troops in a rebellion that swept across northern China, capturing Luoyang and then Chang'an. The emperor fled to Sichuan—apparently all for love, which was soon lost: Ten years earlier the emperor Xuan Zong had taken a young woman, Yang Guifei, from the harem of his son. So infatuated was he that he neglected to govern. This was fine for a while, because his chief minister governed instead. When the minister died, though, Xuan Zong appointed his concubine's second cousin to the post, initiating a chain of events that

OVERVIEW   Chinese Policy toward Barbarians

For much of the history of the Chinese Empire, nomadic peoples from the west and north, whom the Chinese considered to be barbarians, posed a recurrent threat. The imperial Chinese government adopted a variety of strategies for dealing with this threat.

Armies	When nothing else worked, the Chinese went on the offensive and sent armies against the nomads. But armies were expensive, and victories over nomads were transitory. Within a few years the tribes would regroup and menace China anew.
Nomads against nomads	A second strategy was to obtain allies from the nomads along China's borders and use them against more distant nomads. To win over neighboring tribes, a variety of bribes was employed.
Border defense	In the north, an inner line of defense was the Great Wall. Also, late in dynasties, northern provinces were often placed under military governors.
Diplomacy	China sought to neutralize its neighbors by loosely attaching them to its empire. Nomadic tribes, Central Asian states, and Korea became "tributaries" of the emperor. Their rulers sent embassies bearing gifts ("tribute") to the imperial court, which fed and housed them, and sent them home with even costlier gifts and reports of China's power, wealth, splendor, and cultural achievements.

resulted in rebellion. En route to Sichuan, Xuan Zong's soldiers, blaming Yang Guifei for their plight, strangled her.

After a decade of wars and much devastation, a new emperor restored the dynasty with the help of the Uighur Turks, who looted Chang'an as part of their reward. The century of relative peace and prosperity that followed illustrates the resilience of Tang institutions. China was smaller, but military governors maintained the diminished frontiers. Provincial governors were more autonomous, but taxes were still sent to the capital. Occasional rebellions were suppressed. Most of the emperors were weak, but three strong emperors carried out reforms. The most important reform was that of the land system. The official census, on which land allotments and taxes were based, showed a drop in population from 53 million before the An Lushan rebellion to 17 million afterward. The government replaced the equal field system with a tax collected twice a year. The new system, begun in 780, lasted until the sixteenth century. Under it, a fixed quota of taxes was levied on each province. After the rebellion, government revenues from salt and iron surpassed those from land.

During the second half of the ninth century the government weakened further. Most provinces were autonomous, often under military commanders, and resisted central control. Wars, bandits, droughts, and peasant uprisings took their toll. By the 880s warlords had carved all of China into independent kingdoms, and in 907 the Tang Dynasty fell. But within half a century a new dynasty arose. The fall of the Tang did not lead to the centuries of division that had followed the Han. Something had changed within China.

TANG CULTURE

The creativity of the Tang period arose from the juxtaposition and interaction of cosmopolitan, medieval Buddhist, and secular elements. The rise of each of these cultural spheres was rooted in the wealth and the social order of the re-created empire.

Tang culture was cosmopolitan both because of its broad contacts with other cultures and peoples and because of its openness to them. Pilgrims, art, and philosophy flowed between India and China, so the voluptuousness of Indian painting and

View the Image
Court Lady Yang Guifei Mounting a Horse
at **myhistorylab.com**

Read the Document
Ibn Wahab, an Arab merchant, visits Tang
China at **myhistorylab.com**.

Tang Figurine. During the Tang Dynasty (618–907), well-to-do families placed glazed pottery figurines in the tombs of their dead. Perhaps they were intended to accompany and amuse the dead in the afterlife. Note the fancy chignon hairstyle of this female flutist, one figure in a musical ensemble. Today these figurines are sought by collectors around the world.

What are some characteristics of Tang culture?

Amitabha Buddha
The Buddhist Lord of the Western Paradise, or Pure Land.

Zen
A form of Buddhism, which taught that Buddha was only a man and exhorted each person to attain enlightenment by his or her own efforts.

sculpture influenced the Tang representation of the *bodhisattva*. Commercial contacts were widespread; foreign goods were sold in Chang'an marketplaces, and Arab and Persian quarters grew up in the seaports of southeastern China. Merchants brought their religions with them. Nestorian Christianity, Zoroastrianism, Manichaeism, Judaism, and Islam entered China at this time. (Most were swept away in the persecutions of the ninth century.)

Central Asian music and musical instruments became so popular they almost displaced the native tradition. Tang ladies adopted foreign hairstyles. Dramas and acrobatic performances by western Asians could be seen in the streets of the capital. In Tang poetry, too, what was foreign was judged on its own merits.

The Tang Dynasty was the golden age of Buddhism in China. Patronized by emperors and aristocrats, the Buddhist establishment acquired vast landholdings and wealth. Temples and monasteries were constructed throughout China. Little of the beauty and sophistication of temple art and architecture has survived in China, except in the Caves of the Thousand Buddhas in China's far northwest, which were sealed during the eleventh century and not rediscovered until the twentieth century. Only during the Tang did China have a "church" establishment that was at all comparable to that of medieval Europe, and even then it was subservient to the state. Buddhist wealth and learning brought with them secular functions: Temples served as schools, inns, or even bathhouses; they lent money; priests performed funerals and dispensed medicines. Occasionally the state moved to recapture the revenues monopolized by temples. The severest persecution, which marked a turn in the fortunes of Buddhism in China, occurred from 841 to 845, when an ardent Daoist emperor confiscated millions of acres of tax-exempt lands, put 260,000 monks and nuns back on the tax registers, and destroyed 4,600 monasteries and 40,000 shrines.

During the early Tang, the principal Buddhist sect was the Tiantai, but after the mid-ninth-century suppression, other sects came to the fore:

1. One devotional sect focused on Maitreya, a Buddha of the future, who will appear and create a paradise on earth. Maitreya was a cosmic messiah, not a human figure. The sect's teachings often furnished the ideology for popular uprisings and rebellions like the White Lotus, which claimed that it was renewing the world in anticipation of Maitreya's coming.

2. Another devotional sect worshiped the **Amitabha Buddha**, the Lord of the Western Paradise or Pure Land. This sect taught that in the early centuries after the death of the historical Buddha, people could obtain enlightenment by their own efforts, but later the Buddha's teachings had become so distorted that humans could obtain salvation only by reliance on Amitabha. All who called on Amitabha with a pure heart and perfect faith would be saved. Amitabha Buddhism developed a congregational form of worship, became the largest sect in China, and deeply influenced Chinese popular religion.

3. A third sect, most influential among the Chinese elites, began in China, where it was known as Chan. In the West, it is better known by its Japanese name, **Zen**. Zen taught that the historical Buddha was only a man and exhorted each person to attain enlightenment by his or her own efforts. Although its monks were well-

learned, Zen was anti-intellectual in its emphasis on direct intuition into one's own Buddha-nature. Enlightenment was to be obtained by a regimen of physical labor and meditation. To jolt the monk into enlightenment, some Zen sects posed riddles: "If all things return to the One, what does the One return to?" "From the top of a hundred-foot pole, how do you step forward?" The psychological state of the adept attempting to deal with these problems is compared to that of "a mosquito biting an iron ball." The discipline of meditation, combined with a Zen view of nature, profoundly influenced the arts in China and subsequently in Korea and Japan as well.

A third characteristic of Tang culture was the reappearance of secular scholarship and letters. A scholarly bureaucratic complex emerged. Most men of letters were also officials, and most high-ranking officials painted or wrote poems. This secular stream of Tang culture did not oppose Buddhism. Officials were often privately sympathetic to Buddhism, but as men involved in the affairs of government, their values were this-worldly. Court historians revived the Han practice of writing an official history of the previous dynasty. Scholars compiled dictionaries and wrote commentaries on the Confucian classics. More paintings were Buddhist than secular, but Chinese landscape painting had its origins during the Tang. Nowhere, however, was the growth of a secular culture more evident than in poetry, the greatest achievement of Tang letters. An anthology of Tang poetry compiled during the Ming period (1368–1644) contained 48,900 poems by almost 2,300 authors.

The poet Li Bo (701–762) was neither wholly secular nor Buddhist; he might better be called Daoist. He was exceptional among Tang poets in never having sat for the civil service examinations. Large and muscular, he was a swordsman and a carouser. Of the 20,000 poems he is said to have composed, 1,800 have survived, and a fair number have titles like "Bring on the Wine" or "Drinking Alone in the Moonlight." According to legend, he drowned while drunkenly attempting to embrace the reflection of the moon in a lake. His poetry is clear, powerful, passionate, and always sensitive to beauty. It also contains a sense of fantasy, as when he climbed a mountain and saw a star-goddess, "stepping in emptiness, pacing pure ether, her rainbow robes trailed broad sashes." According to Li Bo, life is brief and the universe is large, but this view did not lead him to renounce the world. Rather, he exulted, identifying with the primal flux of yin and yang:

> I'll wrap this Mighty Mudball of a world all up in a bag
> And be wild and free like Chaos itself![1]

Du Fu (712–770), an equally famous Tang poet, was from a literary family. He failed the metropolitan examination at the age of 23 and spent years wandering, impoverished. He eventually got a government job but fell into rebel hands during the An Lushan rebellion. His poetry is less lyrical and more allusive than Li Bo's. It also reflects more compassion for human suffering: for the mother whose sons have been

Caravaneer on a Camel. The animal's shaggy mane indicates that it is a Bactrian camel from Central Asia.

How did trade influence culture during the Tang and Song dynasties?

●▶─Read the **Document**
T'ang Dynasty Poetry (8th century) Li Po at **myhistorylab.com**

●▶─Read the **Document**
Lu You, excerpt from Diary of a Journey to Sichuan at **myhistorylab.com**

───────

[1]S. Owen, *The Great Age of Chinese Poetry: The High T'ang.* © 1980 (New Haven, CT: Yale University Press), p. 125. Reprinted by permission.

A Closer Look

A Tang Painting of the Goddess of Mercy

At the beginning of the twentieth century a sealed cave filled with the arts and objects of Tang China was discovered at Dunhuang in northwestern China, a jumping-off city to the Central Asian Silk Road.

Guanyin, the bodhisattva of compassion and mercy. A bodhisattva is an enlightened being who has postponed entering nirvana until all sentient beings are saved.

"Guanyin" means "hearing sounds," that is to say, hearing the pleas of all supplicants. In India, this bodhisattva was known as Avalokiteshvara and was male. In China, it became a female deity, Guanyin. In Japan it was known as Kannon and was female. Women prayed to it for a safe childbirth.

The donor of the painting was well-to-do and of official rank. His family, in formal dress and poses of piety, is shown as they might have stood in the family ancestral hall, men on the right and women on the left. Younger sons, their wives, and children are in the lower tier.

Questions

1. What, do you imagine, was the purpose of this painting?   2. What social values does the painting depict?

conscripted and sent to war; for brothers scattered by war; for his own family, to whom he returned after having been given up for dead. Like Li Bo, he felt that humans are short-lived and that nature endures. Visiting the ruins of the palace of the second Tang emperor, he saw "Grey rats scuttling over ancient tiles." "Its lovely ladies are the brown soil" and only "tomb horses of stone remain." Unlike Li Bo, his response to this sad scene was to

> Sing wildly, let the tears cover your open hands.
> Then go ever onward and on the road of your travels,
> Meet none who prolong their fated years.[2]

TRANSITION TO LATE IMPERIAL CHINA: THE SONG DYNASTY (960–1279)

The Song fits the dynastic cycle model of Chinese history. It reunified China in 960, establishing its capital at Kaifeng on the Yellow River (see Map 8–3). Mobilizing its resources effectively, it ruled for 170 years; this period is called the Northern Song. Then it weakened, losing the north in 1127 but continuing to rule the south from a new capital at Hangzhou for another 150 years. The Southern Song fell to the Mongols in 1279.

But there is more to Chinese history than the inner logic of the dynastic cycle. Important longer-term changes cut across dynasties. One such set of changes began during the late Tang and continued into the Song period. Its effects on the economy, society, state, and culture help to explain why China after the Tang did not relapse into centuries of disunity as it had after the Han—and why China never again experienced more than brief intervals of disunity.

AGRICULTURAL REVOLUTION OF THE SONG: FROM SERFS TO FREE FARMERS

Landed aristocrats had dominated local society in China during the Sui and Tang periods. The tillers of their lands were little more than serfs. The aristocracy weakened, however, during and after the Tang. Estates shrank as they were divided among a man's sons after his death. As the aristocrats' landholdings diminished, they were attracted to the capital where they became a metropolitan elite. After the fall of the Tang, the estates were often seized by warlords.

The fading power of the aristocracy and changes in the land and tax systems worked in favor of those who tilled the soil. The end of the equal field system freed farmers to buy and sell land, and ownership of land as private property gave cultivators greater independence. Taxes paid in grain gave way during the Song to taxes in money. The commutation of the labor tax to a money tax gave farmers more control over their time. Conscription, the cruelest and heaviest labor tax of all, disappeared as the conscript armies of the early and middle Tang were replaced by professional soldiers. Changes in technology also benefited the cultivator. New strains of an early-ripening rice permitted double cropping, and new commercial crops were developed.

WHAT WAS the agricultural revolution that occurred during the Song Dynasty?

See the **Map**
China under Tang and Song Dynasties
at **myhistorylab.com**

Hear the **Audio**
at **myhistorylab.com**

QUICK REVIEW

Song Agricultural Revolution

- Aristocracy declined
- Money taxes replaced labor tax and conscription
- New crops and technologies increased productivity

---

[2]Owen, The Great Age of Chinese Poetry, pp. 223–224.

MAP 8–3. The Northern Song and Liao Empires (Top) and the Southern Song and Jin Empires (Bottom). During the Northern Song, the Mongol Liao Dynasty ruled only the extreme northern edge of China. During the Southern Song, in contrast, the Manchurian Jin Dynasty ruled half of China.

Why did the authority of the Song Dynasty not extend beyond southern China after 1279?

The disappearance of the aristocrats also increased the authority of the district magistrate, the sole local representative of imperial authority. But there were too many villages in his district for him to be involved regularly in their internal governance. As long as taxes were paid and order was maintained, affairs were left in the hands of the village elites.

One other development that began during the Song—and became vastly more important later—was the appearance of a scholar-gentry class. The typical gentry family contained at least one member who had passed the provincial civil service examination and lived in a district seat or market town. Socially and culturally, these gentry were closer to magistrates than to villagers, but since they usually owned land in the villages, they shared some interests with local landholders. At times they functioned as a buffer between the village and the magistrate's office.

COMMERCIAL REVOLUTION OF THE SONG

Demographic shifts, innovative technologies, the growth of cities, the spread of money, and rising trade all contributed to changes in the countryside. These developments varied by region, but overall the economy reached new prosperity as it underwent a **Song commercial revolution**.

Until late in the Tang, the north had been China's most populous and productive region. But starting in the late ninth century the center of gravity of China's population, agricultural production, and culture shifted to the lower and eastern Yangzi region. Between 800 and 1100 the population of the region tripled, as China's total population increased to about 100 million. Its rice paddies yielded more per acre than the wheat or millet fields of the north, making rice the tax base of the empire. Its wealth led to the establishment of so many schools that the government set regional quotas for the examination system.

Technological advances during the Song included the abacus, the use of gunpowder in grenades and projectiles, and improvements in textiles and porcelains. In north China, the world's most advanced coal and iron-smelting industry developed. Using coke and bellows to heat furnaces to the temperatures required for carbonized steel, it provided superior tools and weapons. Printing began in China with the use of carved seals. The earliest woodblock texts, mostly on Buddhist subjects, appeared in the seventh century. By the tenth century a complete edition of the classics had been published, and by the mid-Song books printed with movable type were fairly common.

Exchange during the Tang had been based largely on silk. During the Northern Song large amounts of copper cash were coined, but the demand rose more rapidly than the supply. Beginning in the Southern Song, silver was minted to complement copper cash.

Cities with more than 100,000 households almost quadrupled in number. The Northern Song capital at Kaifeng is recorded as having had 260,000 households—probably more than 1 million inhabitants—and the Southern Song capital at Hangzhou had 391,000 households. Compare these capitals to those of backward Europe: London during the Northern Song had a population of about 18,000; Rome during the Southern Song had 35,000; and Paris even a century later had fewer than 60,000. These Song capitals were open within and spread beyond their outer walls. Restaurants, theaters, wine shops, and brothels abounded.

Trade between regions during the Song was limited mainly to luxury goods such as silk, lacquerware, medicinal herbs, and porcelains. Only where transport was cheap—along rivers, canals, or the coast—was interregional trade in bulk commodities economical, and even then it was usually carried on only to make up for specific shortages.

Foreign trade reached new heights during the Song. In the north, Chinese traders bought horses from Tibetan, Turkic, and Mongol border states and sold silks and tea. Along the coast, Chinese merchants took over the port trade that during the Tang had been in the hands of Korean, Arab, and Persian merchants. The new hegemony of Chinese merchants was based on improved ships using both sail and oars and equipped with watertight compartments and better rudders. Chinese captains, navigating with the aid of the compass, came to dominate the sea routes from Japan in the north to Sumatra in the south. The content of the overseas trade reflected China's advanced economy: It imported raw materials and exported finished goods. Porcelains were sent to Southeast Asia and then were carried by Arab ships to medieval trading centers on the Persian Gulf and down the coast of East Africa as far south as Zanzibar.

GOVERNMENT: FROM ARISTOCRACY TO AUTOCRACY

The millennium of late imperial China after the Tang is often spoken of as the age of **imperial autocracy** or as China's age of absolute monarchy. Earlier emperors were often personally powerful, but changes during the Song made it easier for emperors to be autocrats.

Song emperors had direct personal control over more offices than their Tang predecessors. The central government was also better funded. Revenues in 1100 were three times the peak revenues of the Tang, partly because of the growth of population and agricultural wealth, and partly because of the establishment of government monopolies on salt, wine, and tea and various duties, fees, and taxes levied on trade. During the Northern Song, these commercial revenues rivaled the land tax; during the Southern Song, they surpassed it.

The disappearance of the aristocracy strengthened the emperors. During the Tang, the emperor had come from the same Sino-Turkic aristocracy as most of his principal ministers, and he ruled on behalf of this aristocracy. During the Song, in contrast, government officials were commoners, mostly products of the examination system. They were separated from the emperor by an enormous social gulf.

Irrigation Methods on a Farm in the Yangzi Valley. A farmer and his wife use their legs and feet to work the square-pallet chain pump, a boy drives a water buffalo to turn a water-pumping device, and another boy fishes.

© Photograph by Wan-go Weng/Collection of H. C. Weng.

What does this image suggest about the productivity of Chinese farms during the Song Dynasty?

Song commercial revolution
The growth in trade, population, technology, money supply, and other factors that reinforced one another to create cycles of commerce-driven economic growth during the Song Dynasty.

QUICK REVIEW

Song Commercial Revolution
- Yangzi basin gains population and power
- Steel, printing, and other technologies improve
- Cash and credit permeate the economy
- More cities have large populations
- Trade increases

Imperial autocracy
The governing style practiced by the Song emperors, in which the ruler exercises unlimited, personal authority.

The Song examination system was larger than that of the Tang, though smaller than it would be under later dynasties. Whereas only 10 percent of officials had been recruited by examination during the Tang, the Song figure rose to over 50 percent and included the most important officials. To pass the examinations, the candidate had to memorize the Confucian classics, interpret selected passages, write in the literary style, compose poems on themes given by the examiners, and propose solutions to contemporary problems in terms of Confucian philosophy. The quality of the officials produced by the Song system was impressive. The Chinese examination system that flourished during the Song continued, with some interruptions, into the twentieth century. The continuity of Chinese government rested on the examination elite with its common culture and values.

The social base for this examination meritocracy was triangular, consisting of land, education, and office. Landed wealth paid the costs of education. Without passing the examinations, an official position was out of reach. And without office, family wealth could not be preserved, since property was divided each time it was inherited. Merchants had wealth but were despised by scholar-officials as grubby profit-seekers and were barred from taking the examinations. Some merchants bought land, and their sons or grandsons became eligible to take the exams. Similarly, a small peasant might build up his holdings, become a landlord, and educate a son or grandson. The system was steeply hierarchical, but it was not closed nor did it produce a new, self-perpetuating aristocracy.

SONG CULTURE

Song culture retained some of the energy of the Tang while becoming more intensely and perhaps more narrowly Chinese. The preconditions for the rich Song culture were a rising economy, an increase in the number of schools and higher literacy, and the spread of printing. Song culture was closely associated with the officials and the scholar-gentry, who were both its practitioners and its patrons. The secular culture of Tang officials became dominant during the Song.

Chinese consider the Song Dynasty the peak of their traditional culture. It was, for example, China's greatest age of pottery and porcelains. High-firing techniques were developed, and kilns were established in every area. Song pottery, with its beautiful glazes and restrained, harmonious shapes, was unlike anything produced in the world before, and it made ceramics a major art form in East Asia. The Song was also an age of great historians. Sima Guang (1019–1086) wrote *A Comprehensive Mirror for Aid in Government*, which treated all Chinese history rather than a particular dynasty. His sophisticated work included a discussion of documentary sources and an explanation of why he chose to rely on one source rather than another.

The greatest achievements of the Song, however, were in philosophy, poetry, and painting. The Song was second only to the Zhou as a creative age in philosophy. A series of original thinkers culminated in the towering figure of Zhu Xi (1130–1200). Zhu Xi studied Daoism and Buddhism in his youth, along with Confucianism. During his thirties he focused on Confucianism, deepening and making more systematic its social and political ethics by joining Buddhist and native metaphysical elements to it. This new Confucianism became a viable alternative to Buddhism for Chinese intellectuals. Comparable figures in other traditions include Saint Thomas Aquinas (1224–1274) of medieval Europe or the Islamic theologian al-Ghazali (1058–1111), each of whom produced a new synthesis or worldview that lasted for centuries (see Chapters 15 and 12, respectively).

An Elegant Song Dynasty Wine Pot with green celadon glaze (24.8 cm high).

Ewer with carved flower sprays. Porcelain with molded and carved low-relief decoration in grayish-green glaze. Northern Song Dynasty (960–1000 © Gift of The Asian Art Museum Foundation).

In what ways is this wine pot "elegant"? Do you think it is an accurate representation of Song culture?

DOCUMENT

Su Dungpo Imagined on a Wet Day, Wearing a Rain Hat and Clogs

After Su's death, a disciple wrote these lines.

- **WHAT** does this poem suggest about the social and political roles played by scholars?

When with tall hat and firm baton he stood in council,
The crowds were awed at the dignity of the statesman
*   in him.*
But when in cloth cap he strolled with cane and sandals,
He greeted little children with gentle smiles.

Source: From *An Introduction to Sung Poetry*, by Kojiro Yoshikawa, trans. by Burton Watson (Cambridge, MA: Harvard University Press, 1967). Copyright © 1967 by the Harvard-Yenching Institute, Monograph Series, poem, p. 122, illustration located on un-numbered page opposite p. 65. Reprinted by permission of Harvard-Yenching Institute.

Zhu Xi's teachings became a new orthodoxy, maintained by the civil service examinations. Like the examination system, the imperial institution, the scholar-gentry class, and the land system, his interpretation of Confucianism contributed to continuity and impeded change.

The most famous poet of the Northern Song was Su Dungpo (1037–1101), a man who participated in the full range of the culture of his age: He was a painter and a calligrapher; he practiced Zen and wrote commentaries on the Confucian classics; he superintended engineering projects; and he was a connoisseur of cooking and wine.

Su, a conservative, rose through a succession of posts to become the governor of a province. Eight years later, when the reformers came to power, Su was arrested and spent 100 days in prison, awaiting execution on a charge of slandering the emperor. Instead, he was released and exiled. He wrote, "Out the gate, I do a dance, wind blows in my face; our galloping horses race along as magpies cheer."[3] In exile, he farmed a plot of land at the "eastern slope" from which he took his literary name, Dungpo. After 1086 Su resumed his official career. In 1094 another shift occurred, and Su was exiled to the distant southern island of Hainan. After yet another shift, Su was on his way back to the capital when he died, in 1101. (See Document, "Su Dungpo Imagined on a Wet Day, Wearing a Rain Hat and Clogs.")

---

[3]Yoshikawa, *An Introduction to Sung Poetry*, p. 117.

An ink on silk handscroll, Southern Song Dynasty. The vast expanse of nature is hardly affected by the human presence.

Xia Gui, Chinese (active 1180–after 1224), "Twelve Views of Landscape." Southern Song Dynasty, (1127–1279). Handscroll; ink on silk. 11" x 90 3/4" (28.0 x 230.5 cm) overall. The Nelson-Atkins Museum of Art, Kansas City, Missouri. Purchase: Nelson Trust, 32-159/2. Photograph by John Lamberton.

What evidence of humans is there in this image?

In China, calligraphy and painting were seen as related. The same qualities of line, balance, and strength needed for calligraphy carried over to painting. Chinese calligraphy is immensely pleasing even to the untutored Western eye, and it is not difficult to distinguish between the elegant strokes of Huineng, the last emperor of the Northern Song, and the powerful brushwork of the Zen monk Zhang Jizhi. Song painting was varied, but its crowning achievement was landscapes. Song paintings are different from those of the West. Each stroke of the brush was final; mistakes could not be covered up. Each element in a scene was presented in its most pleasing aspect; the painting was not constrained by single-point perspective. Paintings had no single source of illumination, but contained an overall diffusion of light. Space was an integral part of the painting. If the painting contained human figures at all, they were small in a natural universe that was very large. Chinese painting thus reflected the same worldview as Chinese philosophy or poetry. The painter sought to grasp the inner reality of the scene, and not be bound up in surface details. In paintings by monks or masters of the Zen school, the presentation of an intuitive vision of an inner reality was even more pronounced.

CHINA IN THE MONGOL WORLD EMPIRE: THE YUAN DYNASTY (1279–1368)

WHY WERE the Mongols able to establish such a vast empire?

The Mongols created the greatest empire in the history of the world. It extended from the Caspian Sea to the Pacific Ocean; from Russia, Siberia, and Korea in the north to Persia and Burma in the south. Invasion fleets were even sent to Java and Japan, though without success. Mongol rule in China is one chapter of this larger story.

RISE OF THE MONGOL EMPIRE

The Mongols, a nomadic people, roamed the grasslands north of China where they raised horses and herded sheep. They lived in felt tents, or yurts. Women performed much of the work and were freer than women in China. Families belonged to clans, and related clans made up tribes. Tribes would gather during the annual migration from the summer plains to winter pasturage. Chiefs were elected, chosen for their courage, military prowess, judgment, and leadership. Like Manchu or Turkic, the Mongol tongue was Altaic. The Mongols worshiped nature deities and a supreme sky god. They communicated with their gods through religious specialists called *shamans*. Politically divided, they traded and warred among themselves and with settled peoples on the borders of their vast grassland domains.

The founder of the Mongol Empire, Temujin, was born in 1167. His father, a tribal chief, was poisoned while Temujin was still a child. Temujin fled; years later, he returned to the tribe, avenged his father, and in time became chief himself. Through his shrewd policy of alliances and remarkable survival qualities, he had united all Mongol tribes and had been elected their great khan, or ruler, by the time he was 40. It is by the title *Genghis* (also spelled *Jenghiz* or *Chinggis*) *Khan* that he is known to history. Genghis possessed an extraordinary charisma, and his sons and grandsons also became wise and talented leaders. Why the Mongol tribes should have produced such leaders at this point in history is difficult to explain.

A second conundrum is how the Mongols, who numbered only about 1.5 million, created the army that conquered vastly denser populations. Part of the answer is institutional. Genghis organized his armies into "myriads" of 10,000 troops, with decimal subdivisions of 1,000, 100, and 10. Elaborate signals were devised so that in battle even large units could be manipulated like the fingers of a hand. Mongol tactics were superb: Units would retreat, turn, flank, and destroy their enemies. The historical record makes clear that Genghis's nomadic cavalry had a paralytic effect on the peoples they encountered. The Mongols were peerless horsemen, and their most dreaded weapon was the compound bow, short enough to be used from the saddle yet more powerful than the English longbow.

They were astonishingly mobile. Each man carried his own supplies and covered vast distances quickly. In 1241, for example, a Mongol army had reached Hungary, Poland, and the shore of the Adriatic and was poised for a further advance into western Europe. But when word arrived of the death of the great khan, the army turned and galloped back to Mongolia to help choose his successor.

The Mongol army learned the use of siege weapons from enemies it conquered. Chinese engineers were used in campaigns in Persia. The Mongols also used terror; inhabitants of cities that refused to surrender in the Near East and China were put to the sword. Descriptions of the Mongols by those whom they conquered dwell on their physical toughness and pitiless cruelty.

But the Mongols had strengths that went beyond the strictly military. Genghis opened his armies to recruits from the Uighur Turks, the Manchus, and other nomadic peoples. In 1206 Genghis promulgated laws designed to prevent warring between tribes that would undermine his empire. Genghis also obtained thousands of pledges of personal loyalty from his followers, and he appointed these "vassals" to command his armies and staff his government. This policy gave his forces an inner coherence that countered the divisive effect of tribal loyalties. Unabashedly frank words attributed to Genghis may reveal what lay behind the Mongol drive to conquest: "Man's highest joy is in victory: to conquer one's enemies, to pursue them, to deprive them of their possessions, to make their beloved weep, to ride on their horses, and to embrace their wives and daughters."[4]

---

[4]J. K. Fairbank, E. O. Reischauer, and A. M. Craig, *East Asia, Tradition and Transformation* (Boston: Houghton Mifflin, 1973), p. 164.

●●●[Read the Document
Giovanni Di Piano Carpini on the Mongols
at **myhistorylab.com**

QUICK REVIEW

Genghis Khan

◆ Named Temujin at birth, in 1167
◆ "Khan" means great ruler
◆ Exceptionally charismatic
◆ Structured army for easy control, cohesiveness
◆ Divided empire among four sons

◉[See the Map
The Mongol Empire of Chinggis Khan, ca.
1227, at **myhistorylab.com**

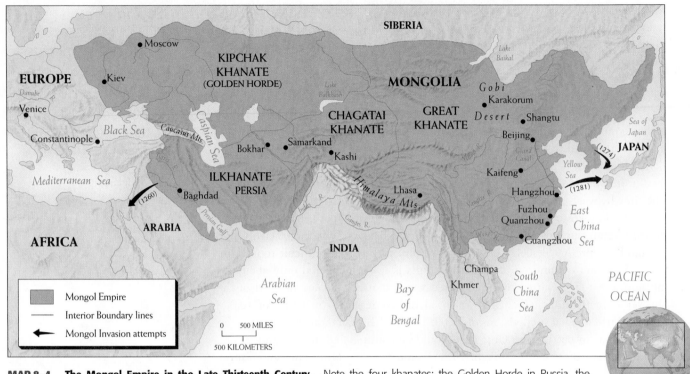

MAP 8–4. The Mongol Empire in the Late Thirteenth Century. Note the four khanates: the Golden Horde in Russia, the Ilkhanate in Persia, Chagatai in Central Asia, and the Great Khanate extending from Mongolia to southern China.

How did the Mongol Empire facilitate trade and communication?

Genghis divided his far-flung empire among his four sons. Over several generations, each of the four khanates became independent. The khanate of Chagatai was in Central Asia and remained purely nomadic. A second khanate of the Golden Horde ruled Russia from the lower Volga. The third was in Persia, and the fourth, led by those who succeeded Genghis as great khans, centered first in Mongolia and then in China (see Map 8–4).

MONGOL RULE IN CHINA

The standard theory used to organize Chinese history is the dynastic cycle, but a second theory explains Chinese history in terms of the interaction between the settled peoples of China and the nomads of the steppe. When strong states emerged in China, their wealth and population enabled them to expand militarily onto the steppe. But when China was weak, the steppe peoples overran China. To review briefly:

1. During the Han Dynasty (206 B.C.E.–220 C.E.), the most pressing problem in foreign relations was the Xiongnu Empire to the north.

2. During the centuries that followed the Han, various nomadic peoples invaded and ruled northern China.

3. The energy and institutions of these Sino-Turkic rulers of the northern dynasties shaped China's reunification during the Sui (589–618) and Tang (618–907) dynasties. The Uighur Turks also played a major role in Tang defense policy.

4. Northern border states became even more important during the Song. The Northern Song (960–1126) bought peace with payments of gold and silver to the Liao. The Southern Song (1126–1279), for all its cultural brilliance, was little more than a tributary state of the Jin Dynasty, which had expanded into northern China.

Kublai Khan. Wearing ermine coat, the Mongol emperor sits on a horse among Mongol warriors at the hunt. At his side is his consort, Chabi.

National Palace Museum, Taiwan, Republic of China.

How did the reign of Kublai Khan combine Mongol and Chinese elements?

From the start of the Mongol pursuit of world hegemony, the riches of China were a target. Genghis proceeded cautiously, determined to leave no enemy at his back. He first disposed of the Tibetan state to the northwest of China and then the Manchu state of Jin that ruled north China. Mongol forces took Beijing in 1227, the year Genghis died. They went on to take Luoyang and the southern reaches of the Yellow River in 1234, and all of north China by 1241. During this time, the Mongols were interested mainly in loot. Only later did Chinese advisers persuade them that more wealth could be obtained by taxation.

Kublai, a grandson of Genghis, was chosen as the great khan in 1260. In 1264 he moved his capital from Karakorum in Mongolia to Beijing. It was only in 1271 that he adopted a Chinese dynastic name, the Yuan, and, as a Chinese ruler, went to war with the Southern Song. Once the decision was made, the Mongols swept across southern China. The last Song stronghold fell in 1279.

Kublai Khan's rule in Beijing reflected the mixture of cultural elements in Mongol China. Kublai rebuilt Beijing as a walled city in the Chinese style. But Beijing was far to the north of any previous Chinese capital, away from centers of wealth and population; to provision it, the Grand Canal had to be extended. From Beijing, Kublai could look out onto Manchuria and Mongolia and maintain ties with the other khanates. The city proper was for the Mongols. Chinese were segregated in an adjoining walled city. The palace of the khan was designed by an Arab architect; its rooms were Central Asian in style. Kublai also maintained a summer palace at Shangdu ("Xanadu") in Inner Mongolia, where he could hawk and ride and hunt in Mongol style.

Early Mongol rule in northern China was rapacious and exploitative, but it later shifted toward Chinese forms of government and taxation, especially in the south and at the local level. Because it was a foreign military occupation, civil administration was highly centralized. Under the emperor was a Central Secretariat, and beneath it were ten "Moving Secretariats," which became the provinces of later dynasties. These highly centralized institutions and the arbitrary style of Mongol decision making accelerated the trend toward absolutism that had started during the previous dynasty.

About 400,000 Mongols lived in China during the Yuan period. For such a tiny minority to control the Chinese majority, it had to stay separate. One measure was to make military service a monopoly of Mongols and their nomadic allies. Garrisons were established throughout China with a strategic reserve on the steppe. Military officers were always regarded as more important than civil officials. A second measure was to use ethnic classifications in appointing civil officials. Mongols held the top civil and military posts. Persians, Turks, and other non-Chinese were given high civil posts. Northern Chinese, including Manchus and other border

214   **PART 3**   CONSOLIDATION AND INTERACTION OF WORLD CIVILIZATIONS, 500 C.E. TO 1500 C.E.

peoples, ranked above southern Chinese. Even when the examination system was sporadically revived after 1315, the Mongols and their allies took an easier examination; their quota was as large as that for Chinese, and they were appointed to higher offices.

The result was an uneasy symbiosis. Chinese officials directly governed the Chinese populace, collecting taxes, settling disputes, and maintaining the local order. Few of these officials ever learned to speak Mongolian, and Mongols usually did not bother to learn Chinese: Communication was through interpreters. Yet without the active cooperation of Chinese officials, Mongol rule in China would have been impossible.

FOREIGN CONTACTS AND CHINESE CULTURE

Diplomacy and trade within the greater Mongol Empire brought China into contact with other higher civilizations for the first time since the Tang period. Persia and the Arab world were especially important. Merchants, missionaries, and diplomats voyaged from the Persian Gulf and across the Indian Ocean to seaports in southeastern China; Arab communities in port cities grew. Camel caravans carrying silks and ceramics left Beijing for Baghdad. Chinese communities became established in Tabriz, the center of trading in western Asia, and in Moscow and Novgorod. Knowledge of printing, gunpowder, and Chinese medicine spread to western Asia. Chinese ceramics influenced those of Persia, while Chinese painting influenced Persian miniatures.

In Europe, knowledge of China was transmitted by the Venetian trader Marco Polo, who claimed to have served Kublai as an official between 1275 and 1292. His book, *A Description of the World*, was translated into most European languages. Many readers doubted that a land of such wealth and culture could exist so far from Europe, but the book excited an interest in geography. When Christopher Columbus set sail in 1492, his goal was to reach Polo's Zipangu (Japan).

The Moroccan Muslim scholar and explorer Ibn Battuta (1304–c. 1370) traveled throughout much of the Mongol world in the fourteenth century. In his account of his journeys, he described the Chinese as wealthy, but disinclined to flaunt their riches.

Mongol toleration encouraged contact across religions. Nestorian Christianity, spreading from Persia to Central Asia, reentered China; Kublai Khan's mother was a Nestorian Christian. Several papal missions were sent from Rome to the Mongol court, and an archbishopric was established in Beijing. Kublai sent a letter to the pope asking him to send a hundred educated men to his court. Tibetan Buddhism was the religion most favored by the Mongols, but Chinese Buddhism also flourished. Priests and monks of all religions were given tax exemptions. Half a million Chinese became Buddhist monks during the Mongol century. Islam made great gains, becoming permanently established in Central Asia and western China. Even Confucianism was regarded as a religion by the Mongols, and its teachers were exempted from taxes.

Despite these wide contacts with other peoples and religions, the high culture of China appears to have been influenced little—partly because China had little to learn from other areas, and partly because the centers of Chinese culture were in the south, the area least affected by Mongol rule. Overall, in reaction to the Mongol conquest, Chinese culture became conservative and turned in on itself.

The major contribution to Chinese arts during the Yuan was by dramatists, who combined poetic arias with vaudeville theater to produce a new operatic drama. Performed by traveling troupes, the operas relied on makeup, costumes, pantomime, and stylized gestures. The women's roles were usually played by men. Except for the

👁 See the **Map**

The Mongol Empire, 1206–1405 at **myhistorylab.com**

•••[Read the **Document**

Marco Polo at the Court of Kublai Khan, ca. 1300 at **myhistorylab.com**

•••[Read the **Document**

The Mongols: An excerpt from the Novgorod Chronicle, 1315 at **myhistorylab.com**

The Journey of Marco Polo. Marco Polo and companions en route to China on the Silk Road.

What role did travelers play in encouraging cross-cultural understanding or curiosity during the Yuan Dynasty?

arias—the highlights of the performance—the dramas used vernacular Chinese, appealing to a popular audience. Justice always triumphed, and the dramas usually ended happily. Yuan drama continued almost unchanged in later dynasties, and during the nineteenth century it merged with a form of southern Chinese theater to become today's Beijing Opera.

LAST YEARS OF THE YUAN

The Yuan was the shortest of China's major dynasties. Little more than a century elapsed between Kublai's move to Beijing in 1264 and the dynasty's collapse in 1368. After the rule of Kublai and his successor, a decline set in. By then, the Mongol Empire as a whole no longer lent strength to its parts. The khanates became separated by religion and culture as well as by distance. Tribesmen in Mongolia thought the great khans in Beijing had become too Chinese, while the court at Beijing never really gained legitimacy among the Chinese. When succession disputes, bureaucratic factionalism, and pitched battles between Mongol generals broke out, the Chinese showed little inclination to rally in support of the dynasty.

Problems arose in the countryside, too. Taxes were heavy, and some local officials were corrupt. The government issued excessive paper money and then refused to accept it in payment for taxes. The Yellow River changed its course, flooding the canals that carried grain to the capital. Further natural disasters during the 1350s led to popular uprisings. The White Lotus sect preached the coming of Maitreya. Regional military commanders, suppressing the rebellions, became warlords. Important economic regions were devastated and partially depopulated. At the end, a rebel army threatened Beijing, and the last Mongol emperor and his court fled on horses to Shangdu. When that city fell, they fled deeper into Mongolia.

SUMMARY

 HOW DID the Sui and Tang dynasties re-create China's empire?

Reestablishment of Empire: Sui (589–618) and Tang (618–907) Dynasties. The Sui and Tang dynasties (589–907) reunited China's empire through strong leadership and military conquest. Under the Tang, China expanded into Central Asia. Chang'an, the Tang capital, became the largest city in the world. Tang culture was rich and cosmopolitan, much influenced by its contacts with other cultures and immensely influential on the cultures of Japan, Korea, and Vietnam. The Tang Dynasty was also the golden age of Buddhism in China, and a variety of Buddhist sects flourished. *page 195*

 WHAT WAS the agricultural revolution that occurred during the Song Dynasty?

Transition to Late Imperial China: The Song Dynasty (960–1279). Under the Song Dynasty (960–1279), China experienced an agricultural revolution in which large aristocratic estates worked by serfs gave way to small landholdings owned by free farmers. New crops, water control, and fertilizers increased agricultural productivity. Advances in technology led to the invention of printing and the development of a coal and iron-smelting industry. The growth of a money economy encouraged the expansion of trade, both within China and with foreign countries. Song culture was particularly rich in philosophy, poetry, and painting. *page 205*

 WHY WERE the Mongols able to establish such a vast empire?

China in the Mongol World Empire: The Yuan Dynasty (1279–1368). After their unification by Genghis Khan (1167–1227), the Mongols created the greatest empire in history. The highly mobile Mongol cavalry overwhelmed Chinese armies. By 1279 the Mongols ruled all of China. But Mongol rule in China was short-lived and enjoyed only shallow Chinese support. Mongol rule in China ended in 1368. *page 210*

KEY TERMS

Amitabha Buddha (p. 202)
censorate (p. 197)
Chang'an (p. 196)
examination system (p. 198)
imperial autocracy (p. 207)
Song commercial revolution (p. 206)
Uighur Turks (p. 200)
Zen (p. 202)

REVIEW QUESTIONS

1. In what ways did China and Europe parallel each other in their development until the sixth century C.E.? How did they diverge after that?

2. Are there similarities between the Qin–Han transition and that of the Sui–Tang? Between Han and Tang expansion and contraction?

3. How did the Chinese economy change from the Tang to the Northern Song to the Southern Song? How did the polity change? How did China's relationships to surrounding states change?

4. What do Chinese poetry and art tell us about Chinese society? What position did poets occupy in Chinese society?

5. Briefly describe the "dynastic cycle" and the "settled Chinese/steppe nomads" theories of Chinese history. What are the strengths and weaknesses of each theory? Is one more useful than the other?

6. Summarize significant developments in Chinese Buddhism during this period. What was the relationship between Buddhism and the state at various times? Between Buddhism and the elite?

7. What drove the Mongols to conquer most of the known world? How could their military accomplish the task? Once they conquered China, how did they rule it? What was the Chinese response to Mongol rule?

Note: To learn more about the topics in this chapter, please turn to the Suggested Readings at the end of the book. For additional sources related to this chapter please see www.myhistorylab.com

myhistorylab Connections

Reinforce what you learned in this chapter by studying the many documents, images, maps, review tools, and videos available at **www.myhistorylab.com**

Read and Review

✓● Study and Review Chapter 8

Comparative Case Study: Women in the Imperial Courts of China and Japan, p. 199

●● Read the Document *Tang Daizong on the Art of Government, p. 198*

An Essay Question from the Chinese Imperial Examination System, p. 199

Chinese description of the Tibetans, p. 200

Ibn Wahab, an Arab merchant, visits Tang China, p. 201

T'ang Dynasty Poetry (8th century) Li Po, p. 203

Lu You, excerpt from Diary of a Journey to Sichuan, p. 203

Giovanni Di Piano Carpini on the Mongols, p. 211

Marco Polo at the Court of Kublai Khan, c. 1300, p. 214

The Mongols: An excerpt from the Novgorod Chronicle, 1315, p. 215

●● See the Map *China during the Sui and Tang Dynasties, p. 196*

China under Tang and Song Dynasties, p. 205

The Mongol Empire, 1206–1405, p. 214

●● View the Image *Court Lady Yang Guifei Mounting a Horse, p. 201*

Research and Explore

●● Watch the Video *Transit*

●● See the Map *The Mongol Empire of Chinggis Khan, ca. 1227, p. 211*

((●● Hear the Audio

Hear the audio file for Chapter 8
at **www.myhistorylab.com**

9

Early Japanese History

((•●┤Hear the Audio for Chapter 9 at www.myhistorylab.com

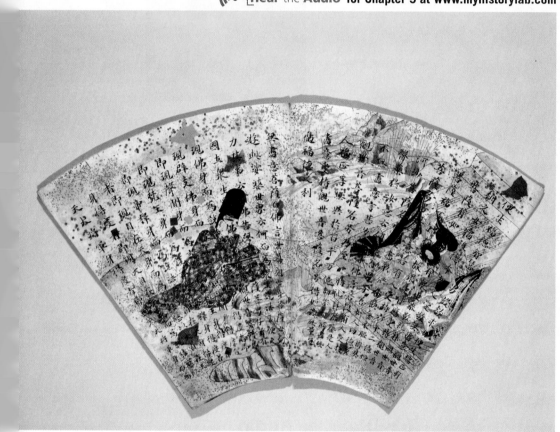

A twelfth-century Japanese fan. Superimposed on a painting of a gorgeously clad nobleman and his lady in a palace setting are verses in Chinese from a Buddhist sutra. The aesthetic pairing of sacred and secular was a feature of life at the Heian court. The fan could well have been used by a figure in Sei Shōnagon's *Pillow Book*.

What does the mix of cultural influences displayed here suggest about medieval Japan?

apanese history has three main turning points. Each was marked by a major influx of an outside culture, and each led to a massive restructuring of Japanese institutions. The first came during the third century B.C.E.*, when Old Stone Age Japan became an agricultural, metalworking society, similar to those on the Korean peninsula or in northeast Asia. The second came during the seventh and eighth centuries, when whole complexes of Chinese culture entered Japan directly. Absorbing these, archaic Japan made the leap to a higher historical civilization associated with the Chinese writing system, Chinese technologies and philosophies, and Chinese forms of Buddhism. Japan remained an independent part of this civilization for more than a millennium. The third turning point occurred in the nineteenth century, when Japan encountered the West.* ■

JAPANESE ORIGINS

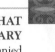

WHAT
REVOLUTIONARY
changes accompanied
the Yayoi?

THE JŌMON, JAPAN'S OLD STONE AGE

Japanese hotly debate their origins. New archaeological finds are front-page news. During the ice ages, Japan was connected by land bridges to Asia. Woolly mammoths entered the northern island of Hokkaido, and other continental fauna entered the lower islands. Did humans come, too? Because Japan's acidic volcanic soil eats up bones, there are no early skeletal remains. The earliest evidence of human habitation is finely shaped stone tools dating from about 30,000 B.C.E.

Then, from within this hunting and gathering society, in about 10,000 B.C.E., pottery developed. This is the oldest pottery in the world. Archaeologists are baffled by the appearance of pottery in an Old Stone Age hunting, gathering, and fishing society, when in all other early societies it developed along with agriculture as an aspect of New Stone Age culture. Japan's "Jōmon" society is named after the rope-like, cord-pattern (*jōmon*) designs on the pottery. Jōmon people lived in pit-dwellings with thatched roofs; population is extremely difficult to estimate, but there were probably about 200,000 of them.

THE YAYOI REVOLUTION

A second northeast Asian people began migrations down the Korean peninsula and across the Tsushima Straits to Japan from about 300 B.C.E. Their movement may have been caused by Chinese military activities. These people, called the Yayoi, were differ-

EAST ASIA

Heartland civilizations, as noted in Chapter 2, were few in number. Most of the world became "civilized" as the writing systems, philosophies, and technologies of the heartlands spread to adjacent areas. In East Asia, Chinese civilization spread to Japan, Korea, and Vietnam, just as in the West, the heartland civilization of the Middle East and Greece spread to Rome and Constantinople, and then to the rest of Europe. The transmission was faster in East Asia than in Europe because the early empire had been re-created by the Sui and Tang during the sixth century and was brilliantly vital, whereas the old Western Roman Empire lay in ruins.

When we speak of "East Asia," we refer as much to culture as to geography, to what Japan, Korea, and Vietnam had in common with China. They adopted Confucian and Buddhist teachings and with them conceptions of the universe, state, and human relations. They took in Chinese arts and technologies: painting, music, ceramics, criminal and civil law, medicine, and architecture. To the untutored Western eye, the paintings of China, Japan, and Korea often look much the same. They learned to write using Chinese characters. Since the languages of Japan, Korea, and Vietnam belonged to non-Chinese language families, it was initially as difficult for them to write in Chinese as it would be for us to write in Egyptian hieroglyphics.

We note, too, that Japan in the seventh and eighth centuries was not a blank slate onto which Chinese culture could be simply inscribed. Japan already had in place (and this is true for Korea and Vietnam as well) an agricultural economy, metalworking skills, settled village communities, and an archaic government. The appeal of Chinese civilization was irresistible, but specific needs and conditions shaped its adoption. For example, the archaic Yamato court found Chinese political institutions and tax systems useful in extending its control over outlying regions.

Mongolia, Central Asia, and Tibet stand in stark contrast to Japan, Korea, and Vietnam. Their climates were harsher, their agriculture more rudimentary, and their life-styles largely nomadic and pastoral. Despite their proximity to China and their frequent

Jōmon pottery figure. Did this bow-legged and somehow modern-looking statuette adorn an emperor's tomb in the period before 300 B.C.E.?

What is known about the Jōmon people?

ent from the Jōmon in language, appearance, and level of technology. There is no greater break in the entire Japanese record than that between the Jōmon and the Yayoi, for at the beginning of the third century B.C.E., the bronze, iron, and agricultural revolutions—which in the Near East, India, and China had been separated by thousands of years and each of which on its own had wrought profound transformations—entered Japan simultaneously.

It is uncertain whether the Yayoi came as a trickle and were absorbed—the predominant view in Japan—or whether they came in sufficient numbers to push back the indigenous Jōmon people. DNA studies suggest that modern Japanese and Koreans are closer to the Yayoi than to the Jōmon. In any case, Yayoi culture rapidly replaced that of the Jōmon as far east as the present-day city of Nagoya and diffused more slowly into eastern Japan, where conditions were less favorable for agriculture. Early Yayoi "frontier settlements" were located next to their fields. Their agriculture was primitive. By the first century C.E., the expanding Yayoi population led to wars for the best land. Villages were relocated to defensible positions on low hills away from the fields. A more peaceful order of regional tribal confederations and a ruling class of aristocratic warriors emerged. Late Yayoi excavations once again reveal villages alongside fields and far fewer stone axes.

During the third century C.E. a queen named Pimiko achieved a temporary hegemony over a number of regional tribal confederations. A Chinese chronicle describes Pimiko as a shaman, mature but unmarried. After Pimiko, references to Japan disappeared from the Chinese dynastic histories for a century and a half.

TOMB CULTURE, THE YAMATO STATE, AND KOREA

Emerging directly from Yayoi culture was an era (300–600 C.E.) characterized by giant tomb mounds. (They still dot the landscape near present-day Osaka.) The tombs, patterned on those in Korea, were circular mounds of earth built atop megalithic burial chambers. Like the Yayoi graves that preceded them, early tombs contained mirrors, jewels, and other ceremonial objects. Starting in the fifth century C.E., these objects were replaced by armor, swords, and military trappings, contacts with it, they were unable or unwilling to adopt its advanced civilization. In effect, on the steppe to the north and west, the Chinese seed fell upon stony places and was scorched or withered away. But in the agricultural lands of Japan, Korea, and Vietnam, it fell on good ground and brought forth fruit.

The difference had consequences. It seems paradoxical that Japan, Korea, and Vietnam, which took in Chinese civilization, became independent nations in recent times, whereas Tibet, Central Asia, and part of Mongolia, which refused Chinese civilization, eventually became a part of China. This is largely because they were at a lower level of development and unable to resist Chinese aggression. But also important is the fact that those countries that took in Chinese political culture used it to develop their own political identities. The self-awareness they developed as a people contributed to their emergence as independent nations. Their feelings toward China were also ambivalent—like those of Westernizing Third World countries toward the West.

Of the countries that took in Chinese civilization, Korea and Vietnam (which will be treated in Chapter 18) were closer to China for longer periods of time and had, as a result, a stronger Chinese imprint. Japan was the most distant, and also the largest and the most populous; consequently it became the most distinctive variant within East Asia. Its literature and arts were brilliant and diverse. Its history was a continuous progression, quite unlike the sequence of dynasties in China.

Focus Questions

◆ How does Japanese history illustrate the relationship between a "heartland civilization" and adjacent areas?

◆ Why did Korea, Vietnam, and Japan become independent nations in recent times? What other nations on the periphery of China did not?

reflecting a new wave of continental influences. The flow of people and culture from the Korean peninsula into Japan that began with Yayoi was continuous into historical times.

Japan reappeared in the Chinese chronicles in the fifth century C.E. This period was also covered in the earliest Japanese accounts of their own history, compiled in 712 and 720. These records describe regional aristocracies under the loose hegemony of the "great kings," whose courts were located on the fertile Yamato plain. Regional rulers held parallel political authority over their populations, as can be seen in the spread of tomb mounds for aristocrats throughout Japan. The court was the scene of incessant power struggles. Rebellions were frequent during the fifth and sixth centuries, and there were constant wars with "barbarian tribes" in southern Kyushu and eastern Honshu on the frontiers of "civilized" Japan.

The basic social unit of Yamato aristocratic society was the extended family (*uji*). Groups of specialist workers called *be* were attached to aristocratic families. There was a small class of slaves, but many peasants were neither slaves nor members of aristocratic clans or specialized workers' groups.

Relations with Korea were critical to the Yamato Court. During the fifth and sixth centuries, a three-cornered military balance developed on the Korean peninsula between the state of Paekche in the southwest, Silla in the east, and Koguryo in the north (see Map 9-1 on page 222). Japan was an ally of Paekche and maintained extensive trade and military relations with a weak southern federation known as the Kaya States. Imported iron weapons and tools gave the Yamato military strength. Korean immigrant artisans increased the court's wealth and influence. The first elements of Chinese culture entered Japan through Paekche: Chinese writing was adopted for the transcription of Japanese names during the fifth or sixth century; Confucianism entered in 513, when Paekche sent a "scholar of the Five Classics"; Buddhism arrived in 538 when a Paekche king sent a Buddha image, sutras, and possibly a priest.

CHRONOLOGY

EARLY JAPANESE HISTORY

8000–300 B.C.E.	Jōmon culture
Early Continental Influences	
300 B.C.E.–300 C.E.	Yayoi culture
300–680 C.E.	Tomb culture and the Yamato state
680–850 C.E.	Chinese Tang pattern in Nara and Early Heian Japan

MAP 9–1. Yamato Japan and Korea (ca. 500 C.E.) Paekche was Japan's ally on the Korean peninsula. Silla, Japan's enemy, was the state that would eventually unify Korea. (*Note*: Nara was founded in 710; Heian in 794.)

How did Japan's proximity to Korea and China influence its cultural development?

Eventually the political balance on the Korean peninsula shifted. In 532 Paekche turned against Japan. In 660 Silla, always hostile to Japan, unified the peninsula. But by this time Japan had established direct relations with China.

RELIGION IN EARLY JAPAN

The indigenous religion of the Yamato Japanese was an animistic worship of the forces of nature, later given the name of **Shintō**, or "the way of the gods," to distinguish it from Buddhism. Shintō probably entered Japan as part of Yayoi culture. The underlying forces of nature might be embodied in a waterfall, a twisted tree, a strangely shaped boulder, or a great leader who would be worshiped as a deity after his death. The more potent forces of nature became personified as deities. The sensitivity to nature and natural beauty that pervades Japanese art and poetry owes much to Shintō. Most villages had shamans, female or male religious specialists who, by entering a trance, could directly contact the inner forces of nature and gain the power to foretell the future or heal sickness.

Shintō

"The way of the gods." The animistic worship of the forces of nature that is the indigenous religion of Japan.

The Itsukashima Shrine. On the little island of Miyajima not far from Hiroshima is the lovely Itsukashima shrine dedicated to the daughters of the Shintō god of the moon and oceans. Its outer gate (*torii*) is constructed of camphor logs to resist the salt water. Originally built in the late sixth century, it was rebuilt in the sixteenth.

What does the location of this shrine suggest about how the shrine is meant to be used?

Early Shintō was connected with the state. Each clan had its own nature deity (*kami*) that it claimed as its original ancestor. When Japan was unified by the Yamato court, the myths of several clans were joined into a composite national myth. The deity of the Yamato great kings was the sun goddess, so she became the chief deity. The earliest Japanese histories, the earliest telling of the creation of Japan, switch mid-volume from stories of the gods, interspersed with the genealogies of noble families, to stories of early emperors and events in early Japan. The Japanese emperors, today the oldest royal family in the world, were viewed as the lineal descendants of the sun goddess and as "living gods." Other gods assumed lesser positions appropriate to the status of their clan. The Great Shrine of the sun goddess at Ise has always been the most important in Japan. (See Document, "Darkness and the Cave of High Heaven," on page 224.)

NARA AND HEIAN JAPAN

The second major turning point in Japanese history was the inflow of Chinese civilization between the seventh and twelfth centuries. Roughly speaking, until almost the end of the seventh century the Japanese studied China; during the eighth they implanted Chinese institutions; after that, they modified the institutions to meet Japanese needs. By the eleventh century the creative reworking of Chinese elements had led to distinctive Japanese forms, unlike those of China but equally unlike those of the earlier Yamato court.

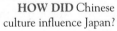

HOW DID Chinese culture influence Japan?

COURT GOVERNMENT

The regular embassies to the Tang court that began in 607 C.E. included traders, students, and Buddhist monks as well as representatives of the Yamato great kings. Like Third World students who study abroad today, Japanese who studied in China played key roles in their own government when they returned home. They brought back with them a quickening flow of technology, art, Buddhism, and knowledge of Tang legal and governmental systems. But for Yamato Japanese, the difficulties of mastering Chinese and China's philosophical culture were enormous. Prince Shōtoku (574–622) adopted the Chinese calendar and promulgated Chinese and Buddhist ideas. Fujiwara Kamatari (614–669) at mid-seventh century attempted more extensive reforms, though only a few were realized. Large-scale institutional changes using the Tang model began only in the 680s with the Emperor Temmu and his successor, the Empress Jitō (r. 686–697).

Temmu's life illustrates the interplay between Japanese power politics and the adoption of Chinese institutions. He usurped the throne from his nephew and then used

DOCUMENT

Darkness and the Cave of High Heaven

The younger brother of the sun goddess was a mischief-maker. Eventually the gods drove him out of heaven. On one occasion, he knocked a hole in the roof of a weaving hall and dropped in a dappled pony that he had skinned alive. One weaving maiden was so startled that she struck her genitals with the shuttle she was using and died.

- **Entering** a cave and then reemerging signifies death and rebirth in the religions of many peoples. What does this myth suggest regarding the social relations of the Shintō gods?

The Sun Goddess, terrified at the sight, opened the door of the heavenly rock cave, and hid herself inside. Then the Plain of High Heaven was shrouded in darkness, as was the Central Land of the Reed Plains [Japan]. An endless night prevailed. The cries of the myriad gods were like the buzzing of summer flies, and myriad calamities arose.

The eight hundred myriad gods assembled in the bed of the Quiet River of Heaven. They asked one god to think of a plan. They assembled the long-singing birds of eternal night and made them sing. They took hard rocks from the bed of the river and iron from the Heavenly Metal Mountain and called in a smith to make a mirror. They asked the Jewel Ancestor God to make a string of 500 curved jewels eight feet long. They asked other gods to remove the shoulder blade of a male deer, to obtain cherry wood from Mount Kagu, and to perform a divination. They uprooted a sacred tree, attached the string of curved jewels to its upper branches, hung the large mirror from its middle branches, and suspended offerings of white and blue cloth from its lower branches.

One god held these objects as grand offerings and another intoned sacred words. The Heavenly Hand-Strong-Male God stood hidden beside the door. A goddess bound up her sleeves with clubmoss from Mount Kagu, made a herb band from the spindle-tree, and bound together leaves of bamboograss to hold in her hands. Then she placed a wooden box face down before the rock cave, stamped on it until it resounded, and, as if possessed, she exposed her breasts and pushed her skirt-band down to her genitals. The Plain of High Heaven shook as the myriad gods broke into laughter.

The Sun Goddess, thinking this strange, opened slightly the rock-cave door and said from within: "Since I have hidden myself, I thought that the Plain of Heaven and the Central Land of the Reed Plains would all be in darkness. Why is it that the goddess makes merry and the myriad gods all laugh?"

The goddess replied: "We rejoice and are glad because there is here a god greater than you." While she spoke two other gods brought out the mirror and held it up before the Sun Goddess.

The Sun Goddess, thinking this stranger and stranger, came out the door and peered into the mirror. Then the heavenly Hand-Strong-Male God seized her hand and pulled her out. Another god drew a rope behind her and said: "You may not go back further than this."

So when the Sun Goddess had come forth, the Plain of High Heaven and the Central Land of the Reed Plains once again naturally shone in brightness.

Source: From the *Records of Ancient Matters (Kojiki)*, trans. by Albert Craig, with appreciation to Basil Hall Chamberlain and Donald L. Phillippi.

Tennō

"Heavenly emperor." The official title of the emperor of Japan.

Chinese systems to consolidate his power. He promulgated a Chinese-type law code that greatly augmented the powers of the ruler. He styled himself as the "heavenly emperor," or **tennō**, replacing the title of "great king."

Until the eighth century the capital was usually moved each time an emperor died. Then in 710 a new capital, laid out on a grid like the Chinese capital, Chang'an, was established at Nara. The capital was moved again in 784, and yet again in 794 to Heian (later Kyoto). This site remained the capital until the move to Tokyo in 1869. The superimposition of a Chinese-type capital on a still backward Japan produced a stark contrast. In the villages, peasants—who worshiped the forces in mountains and trees—lived in pit dwellings and either planted in crude paddy fields or used slash-and-burn techniques of dry-land farming. In the capital, pillared palaces housed the emperor and nobles, descended from the gods on high. They drank wine, wore silk, and enjoyed the paintings, perfumes, and pottery of the Tang. Clustered about the capital were Buddhist temples with soaring pagodas and sweeping tile roofs.

Governments at the Nara and Heian courts were headed by emperors, who were simultaneously Confucian rulers with the majesty accorded by Chinese law and Shintō rulers descended from the sun goddess. Protected by an aura of the sacred, their lineage retained power throughout the rest of Japanese history, though several emperors were killed and replaced by other family members.

Beneath the emperor, the same modified Chinese pattern prevailed. At the top was a Council of State, a powerful office from which leading clans sometimes manipulated authority. Beneath the council were eight ministries—two more than in China. (The extras were a Secretariat and the Imperial Household Ministry.) Local government was handled by sixty-odd provinces, which were further subdivided into districts and villages. In other respects, Japanese court government was unlike that of China. There were no eunuchs and little tension between the emperor and the bureaucracy— the main struggles were between clans. The Tang movement from aristocracy toward meritocracy was also absent in Japan. Family counted for more than grades. A feeble attempt to establish a Chinese-style examination elite failed.

Even during the Nara period the elaborate apparatus of Chinese government was too much. China had a population of 60 million; Nara Japan had 4 or 5 million. With fewer people to govern in Japan and no external enemies, court government focused on care of the imperial house. In the early Heian period, three new departments outside the Chinese system handled most of the functions of government: an office of auditors handled taxation, a bureau of archivists exercised executive power through the drafting of decrees, and police commissioners enforced laws and maintained order in the capital. Power shifted during the Heian period but always revolved around the emperor. Until the mid-ninth century, some emperors ruled directly. In 856, the northern branch of the Fujiwara clan began to establish a stranglehold on power that was not broken until the last half of the eleventh century. In 1072, the Emperor Shirakawa regained control of the government and strengthened the imperial family, but by then the capital was increasingly isolated, and threatening developments were taking place in the countryside.

PEOPLE, LAND, AND TAXES

The life of the common people of Japan remained harsh during the Nara and Heian periods. Estimates of the early Nara population suggest slightly more than 5 million persons; by the end of the Heian period, almost half a millennium later, the number had increased, scholars estimate, to only about 6 million. Why had population not grown more during these fairly peaceful centuries? One factor is that agricultural technology improved only slowly. Metals were still scarce, and wooden plow blades were still in use. Another factor was the frequency of droughts and famines. A third was the effect of continental germs—introduced by embassies or later commercial relations—on a previously isolated Japanese population that had not yet developed immunities. Periodic epidemics swept the court and village communities alike.

Taxes weighed heavily on village populations. In Nara and early Heian Japan, the economy was agricultural. The problem for peasants was to obtain land. The problem for the government, imperial family, nobles, and temples was to find labor to work their extensive landholdings. Japan attempted a solution, using China's so-called equal field system to distribute land to all able-bodied persons and collect from them three

Prince Shōtoku (574–622). A commanding figure at the pre-Nara Yamato court, Prince Shōtoku (shown here with two of his sons) promoted Buddhism and began regular embassies to China. "This world is a lie," he wrote, reflecting the Buddhist belief in an ultimate reality beyond.

How did embassies to China contribute to Japanese culture?

((•─[Hear the Audio
at **myhistorylab.com**

In the Heiji War of 1159–1160, regional samurai bands became involved in Kyoto court politics. This is a scroll painting of the burning of the Sanjō Palace.

Handscroll; ink and colors on paper. "Scroll w/depictions of the Night Attack on the Sanjō Palace" from Heiji monogatari emaki, 2nd half of the 13th century.Unknown. Japanese,Kamakura Period.Handscroll; ink & colors on paper.41.3 x 699.7 cm. Fenollosa-Weld C. Photograph © 2007 Courtesy Museum of Fine Arts, Boston.

Did the existence of samurai make Japan "feudal"?

samurai
Professional Japanese warriors.

QUICK REVIEW
___

Samurai

◆ Word comes from Japanese verb "to serve"

◆ Constituted Japan's military until fifteenth century

◆ Samurai were responsible for their own equipment and training

◆◆◆ Read the Document
Murasaki Shikibu, selections from the *Tale of Genji* at **myhistorylab.com**

taxes: a light tax of grain, a light tax of cloth or other local products, and a heavy tax of labor service. But this necessitated elaborate population and land registers. Even in China, with its sophisticated bureaucracy, the system broke down.

The Heian discarded the complex equal field system, and court officials simply gave each governor a quota of taxes to collect from his province. Each governor, in turn, gave quotas to the district magistrates. Governors and magistrates, when they could, collected more than their quotas and pocketed the difference. This surplus collection funded a new local ruling class.

Court nobles and powerful temples used their influence at court to obtain exemptions from taxation for their lands. About half the land in late Heian Japan was converted from tax-paying lands to tax-free estates. Even small landholders often commended their land to nobles, figuring they would be better off as serfs on tax-free estates than as free farmers subject to taxation. The pattern of commendations was random, resulting in estates composed of scattered parcels of land. Noble estate owners appointed stewards from among local notables to manage the land in exchange for a small slice of the cultivators' surplus. Stewards and district magistrates shared an interest in upholding the local order.

RISE OF THE SAMURAI

Nara Japan experimented with a Chinese military system based on conscription, but it proved inefficient. In 792, the court ended conscription and established a system of mounted warriors whose taxes were remitted in exchange for military service. They were stationed in the capital and in the provinces. The Japanese verb "to serve" is *samurau*, so those who served became known as **samurai**. Nonofficial private bands of local warriors replaced the official appointees in the mid-Heian period, and they constituted Japan's military until the fifteenth and sixteenth centuries, when foot soldiers became the core of the military.

Being a samurai was expensive. Horses, armor, and weapons were costly, and their use required long training. The primary weapon was the bow and arrow, used from the saddle. Most samurai were from well-to-do local families. Their initial function was to preserve local order and, possibly, to help with tax collection. But they contributed at times to disorder. From the second half of the ninth century there are accounts of district magistrates leading local forces against provincial governors, doubtless in connection with tax disputes.

Regional military coalitions or confederations first broke into history from 935 to 940, when a regional military leader, a descendant of an emperor, became involved in a tax dispute. He captured several provinces and called himself the new emperor. The Kyoto court responded by recruiting another military band to quell the rebellion. Other regional wars followed, and by the middle of the twelfth century there were regional military bands in every part of Japan. A power struggle at court in 1156 enabled a band led by Taira Kiyomori to seize control of Kyoto and the emperor. But, like the earlier Fujiwara family, he did not change the system. He only imposed a new stratum atop the many power centers already established at court.

ARISTOCRATIC CULTURE AND BUDDHISM

Shintō religious practices and village folkways, an extension of the culture of the late Yamato period, were among the most significant elements of the culture of Nara and early Heian Japan. The tiny aristocracy, about one-tenth of 1 percent of Japan's population, was encapsulated in the routines of court life, most of which had only recently with mystical powers. It is sometimes called esoteric Buddhism because it had secret teachings that were passed from master to disciple. In China, Shingon was persecuted and died out, but it was tremendously successful in Japan.

During the later Heian period, Buddhism began to be assimilated. Folk Shintō took in Buddhist elements, while in elite culture, Shintō was almost entirely absorbed by Buddhism. Shintō deities came to be seen as the local manifestations of universal Buddhas. Often great Buddhist temples had smaller Shintō shrines on their grounds. The Buddha watched over Japan and the cosmos; the shrine deity guarded the temple itself. Not until the mid-nineteenth century was Shintō disentangled from Buddhism, and then it occurred for political ends.

JAPAN'S EARLY FEUDAL AGE

The late twelfth century marked the shift from centuries of rule by a civil aristocracy to centuries of rule by military nobles. It saw the formation of the *bakufu* ("tent government"), a completely non-Chinese type of government. During this time the **shōgun** emerged as the de facto ruler of Japan, although in theory he was a military official of the emperor. New cultural forms emerged, along with changes in family and social organization.

THE KAMAKURA ERA

After Taira Kiyomori seized Kyoto in 1160, other bands still flourished elsewhere in Japan. The Taira, assuming their tutelage over the court would endure, embraced Kyoto's elegant lifestyle, but the Minamoto were rebuilding their strength in eastern Japan. In 1180 Minamoto Yoritomo (1147–1199) seized control of eastern Japan and began the war that ended in 1185 with the downfall of the Taira.

Yoritomo's victory was national. Warriors from every area vied to become his vassals. Yoritomo set up his headquarters at Kamakura, 30 miles south of present-day Tokyo, at the edge of his base of power in eastern Japan (see Map 9–2 on page 230). He called his government the *bakufu* in contrast to the civil government in Kyoto. The offices he established were few and practical and staffed by his vassals. The decisions of these offices were codified in 1232 as the Jōei Code. Yoritomo also appointed military governors in each province and military stewards on the former estates of the Taira and others who had fought against him. These appointments carried the right to some income from the land. The remainder of the income, as earlier, went to Kyoto as taxes or as revenues to the owners of the estates.

When Yoritomo died in 1199, his widow and her Hōjō kinsmen moved to usurp the power of the Minamoto house. The widow, having taken holy orders after her husband's death, was known as the Nun Shōgun. One of her sons was pushed aside. The other became shōgun but was murdered in 1219. After that, the Hōjō ruled as regents for a puppet shōgun, just as the Fujiwara had been regents for figurehead emperors. The Kyoto court led an armed uprising against Kamakura in 1221, but it was quickly suppressed. The Kamakura vassals had become loyal to the *bakufu*, which guaranteed their income from land; their personal loyalty to the Minamoto had ended with the death of Yoritomo.

THE MONGOLS

In 1266 Kublai Khan (see Chapter 8) sent envoys demanding that Japan submit to his rule. The Hōjō at Kamakura refused. The first Mongol invasion fleet arrived in 1274 with 30,000 troops but withdrew after initial victories. The Mongols again sent envoys; this time, they were beheaded. A second invasion of 140,000 troops, an amphibious

WHY CAN this period in Japan be described as feudal, and in what ways is this description misleading?

bakufu
"Tent government." The military regime that governed Japan under the shōguns.

shōgun
A military official who was the actual ruler of Japan in the emperor's name from the late 1100s until the mid-nineteenth century.

Minamoto Yoritomo. Founder of the Kamakura Shogunate. He is depicted here in court robes as a statesman and official though he was, above all, a warrior-general.

Why might Minamoto Yoritomo have wanted to present himself in civilian official dress?

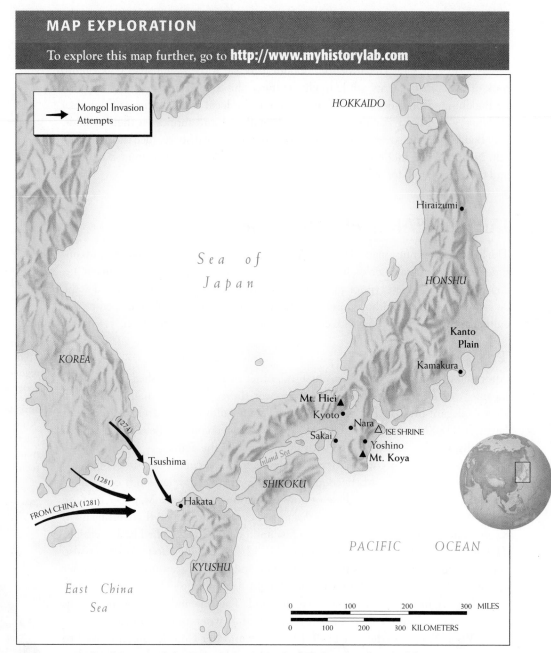

MAP EXPLORATION

To explore this map further, go to **http://www.myhistorylab.com**

MAP 9–2. **Medieval Japan and the Mongol Invasions.** The *bakufu* at Kamakura and the court at Kyoto were the two centers of power during the Kamakura period, 1185–1333. After 1336 the Ashika-ga *bakufu* was established in Kyoto, absorbing the powers of the court.

What geographic features do Kyoto and Kamakura share? From a geographic point of view, how do these locations differ?

See the Map

Medieval Japan and the Mongol Invasions at **myhistorylab.com**

kamikaze
"Divine winds" that sank a portion of the invading Mongol fleet in Japan in 1281.

force on a scale unprecedented in world history, arrived in 1281, two years after Kublai had completed his conquest of southern China. With gunpowder bombs and phalanx-es of archers protected by a forward wall of soldiers carrying overlapping shields, the Mongol forces overmatched the Japanese tactics of fierce individual combat. But a wall of stone had been erected along the curved shoreline of Hakata Bay in northwestern Kyushu, and the Mongols were held off for two months until **kamikaze**, or "divine winds," sank a portion of their fleet and forced the rest to withdraw. Preparations for a third expedition ended with Kublai's death in 1294. The burden of repelling the Mongols fell on Kamakura's vassals in Kyushu. But as no land was taken, there were few rewards for those who had fought, and dissatisfaction was rife.

THE QUESTION OF FEUDALISM

Scholars often contend that Yoritomo's rule marks the start of feudalism in Japan. Feudalism may be defined in terms of three criteria: lord–vassal relationships, fiefs given in return for military service, and a warrior ethic. Can Kamakura Japan be described in these terms?

Certainly, the mounted warriors who made up the armies of Yoritomo were predominantly his vassals, not his kin. As for fiefs, the answer is ambiguous. Kamakura vassals received rights to income from land in exchange for military service, but the income was usually a slice of the surplus from the estates of Kyoto nonmilitary aristocrats. Fiefs, as such, did not appear until the late fifteenth century.

There is no ambiguity, however, regarding the warrior ethic, which had been developing among regional military bands for several centuries before 1185. The samurai prized martial qualities such as bravery, cunning, physical strength, and endurance. They gave their swords names. Their sports were hunting, hawking, and archery. Warriors thought of themselves as a military aristocracy that practiced the "way of the bow and arrow."

But warrior bands were only part of society. Kamakura Japan still had two political centers: The *bakufu* had military authority, while the Kyoto court continued the late Heian pattern of civil rule. Yoritomo's vassal band was small, numbering perhaps 2,000 before 1221 and 3,000 thereafter, mostly concentrated in eastern Japan. The local social order of the late Heian era continued, and Kamakura vassals depended on the cooperation of existing power holders. In short, while the Kamakura vassals themselves could be called feudal, they were only a thin skin on the surface of a society constructed according to older principles.

THE ASHIKAGA ERA

At times, formal political institutions seem rocklike in their stability, and history unfolds within the framework they provide. Then, almost as if a kaleidoscope had been shaken, the old institutions collapse and are swept away. In their place appear new institutions and new patterns of personal relations that, often enough, had begun to take shape within the confines of the old. It is not easy to explain the timing of such upheavals, but they are easy to recognize. One occurred in Japan between 1331 and 1336.

By 1331, various tensions had developed within Kamakura society. Because the patrimony of a warrior was divided among his children, vassals became poorer over time. Kamakura vassals were dissatisfied with the Hōjō monopolization of key *bakufu* posts. While the ties of vassals to Kamakura weakened, the ties to other warriors within their region grew stronger until new regional bands were ready to emerge. The precipitating event was a revolt in 1331 by an emperor who thought emperors should actually rule. Kamakura sent Ashikaga Takauji (1305–1358), the head of a branch family of the Minamoto line, to put down the revolt; instead he joined it. Other regional lords then rose up and destroyed the Hōjō *bakufu* in Kamakura.

What emerged from the confusion of the period from 1331 to 1336 was a new *bakufu* in Kyoto and semiautonomous regional states in the rest of Japan.

CHRONOLOGY

GOVERNMENT BY MILITARY HOUSES

1160–1180	Taira rule in Kyoto
1185–1333 KAMAKURA *BAKUFU*	
1185	Founded by Minamoto Yoritomo
1219	Usurped by Hōjō
1221	Armed uprising by Kyoto court
1232	Formation of Jōei Code
1274 and 1281	Invasions by Mongols
1336–1467 ASHIKAGA *BAKUFU*	
1336-1392	Southern Court
1467	Start of Warring States period

QUICK REVIEW

Mongol Invasion

- 1266: Kublai Khan demands Japan submit to his rule
- 1274: Invasion fleet withdraws after initial victories
- 1281: Huge invasion force destroyed by *kamikaze*, or "divine winds"

Japanese Sword.
From medieval times, Japanese artisans have made the world's finest swords. They became a staple export to China. Worn only by samurai, they were also an emblem of class status, distinguishing the warriors from commoners.

Who were the samurai, and what roles did they play in Japanese history?

A Closer Look

The East Meets the East

Mongols invaded Japan in 1274 and 1281. Battles were fought. The invaders were eventually routed by typhoons known as kamikaze or "divine winds."

Takezaki Suenaga, one hand on the reins and one on his bow, fights bravely against the Mongol invaders. He wears armor of braided plates and helmet, and presses on despite the wounds suffered by his horse. (He later commissioned the scroll, as a record of his exploits, to be passed down to his descendants.)

Mongol warriors, bearing composite bows and spears, continue their attack, despite the shower of Japanese arrows. One Mongol, struck by an arrow, turns away.

"A bomb bursting in air." Gunpowder was invented in Song China in about 1000 C.E. and quickly gave rise to a variety of weapons. Song Chinese used these weapons when the Mongols invaded China, and the Mongols used them when they invaded Japan.

Questions

1. Why did the Mongols invade Japan?
2. How did the Japanese respond?
3. What does this picture reveal?

myhistorylab To examine this image in an interactive fashion, please go to **www.myhistorylab.com**

---

daimyo
Lords who owned vast estates and held regional power.

Each regional state was governed by a lord, now called a **daimyo**, and a small warrior band. The *bakufu* offices established by Ashikaga Takauji were simple and functional: a samurai office for police and military matters; an administrative office for financial matters; a documents office for land records; and a judicial board to settle disputes. They were staffed by Takauji's vassals. The *bakufu* also appointed vassals to watch over its interests in the far north, in eastern Japan, and in Kyushu.

The pattern of rule in the outlying regions was diverse. All regional lords or daimyo were the vassals of the shōgun, but the relationship was often nominal. The relationship between the *bakufu* and regional lords fluctuated from 1336 to 1467. The third shōgun, for example, tightened his grip on the Kyoto court, improved relations with the great Buddhist temples and Shintō shrines, and established ties with Ming China. His military campaigns dented the autonomy of regional lords. But even the third shōgun had to rely on his daimyo and their armies. To strengthen them for campaigns, he gave them new authority, which created problems for his successors. As ties of personal loyalty wore thin, new local warrior bands began to form.

WOMEN IN WARRIOR SOCIETY

The Nun Shōgun was one of a long line of important women in Japan. In Japanese mythology, the sun goddess ruled the Plain of High Heaven, while the late Yayoi shaman-ruler Pimiko was probably not an exceptional figure. Empresses ruled in Yamato and Nara courts, and they were followed by great women writers in the Heian period. Under the Kamakura *bakufu*, there was only one Nun Shōgun, but daughters as well as sons of warrior families often trained in archery and other military arts. As long as society was stable, women fared relatively well. But as fighting became more common in the fourteenth century, their position began to decline, and as warfare became endemic in the fifteenth, their status plummeted. The warrior's fief—his reward for serving his lord in battle and the lord's surety for his continuing service—became all important. To protect it, multigeniture, in which daughters as well as sons inherited property, gave way to unigeniture, inheritance by the most able son.

AGRICULTURE, COMMERCE, AND MEDIEVAL GUILDS

Population figures for medieval Japan are rough estimates at best, but recent scholarship suggests 6 million for the year 1200 and 15 million for 1600. Much of the increase occurred during the late Kamakura and Ashikaga periods, when the country was fairly peaceful. The increase was brought about by land reclamation and improvements in agricultural technology. Iron-edged tools became available to all. New strains of rice were developed. Irrigation and diking improved. Double cropping began with vegetables planted during the fall and winter in dry fields, which were flooded and planted with rice during the spring and summer.

In the Nara and early Heian periods, the economy was almost exclusively agricultural. Japan had no money, no commerce, and no cities—apart from Nara, which developed into a temple town living on assigned revenues, and Kyoto, where taxes were consumed. Following the example of China, the government had established a mint, but little money actually circulated. Taxes were paid in labor or grain. Commerce consisted of barter transactions, with silk or grain as the medium of exchange. Artisans produced for the noble households or temples to which they were attached. Peasants were economically self-sufficient.

From the late Heian period, partly as a side effect of fixed tax quotas, more of the growing agricultural surplus stayed in local hands, though not in the hands of the cultivators. This trend accelerated during the Kamakura and Ashikaga periods, as warriors took increasingly larger slices of the income of estates. As the income of civil nobles decreased, artisans detached themselves from noble households and began to produce for a wider market. Military equipment was an early staple of commerce, but gradually *sake*, lumber, paper, vegetable oils, salt, and products of the sea also became commercialized. A demand for copper coins appeared, and since they were no longer minted in Japan, huge quantities were imported from China.

During the Kamakura period, independent merchants appeared to handle the products of artisans. Some trade networks spread over all Japan. More often, artisan and merchant guilds, not unlike those of medieval Europe, paid a fee to obtain monopoly rights in a given area. Kyoto guilds paid fees to powerful nobles or temples, and later to the Ashikaga *bakufu*. In outlying areas guild privileges were obtained from the regional lords. From the Kamakura period onward, markets were held periodically in many parts of Japan, by a river or at a crossroads. Some place-names in Japan today reveal such an origin. Yokkaichi, today an industrial city, means "fourth-day market." It began as a place where markets were held on the fourth, fourteenth, and twenty-fourth days of each month. From the fifteenth century such markets were held with increasing frequency until, eventually, permanent towns were established.

View the Image
Japanese Court Ladies
at **myhistorylab.com**

Study and **Review**
Women in the Imperial Courts of China and Japan at **myhistorylab.com**

BUDDHISM AND MEDIEVAL CULTURE

The Nara and Heian periods are often referred to as Japan's classical age. The period that followed—say, from 1200 to 1600—is often called medieval. It was medieval in the root sense of the word in that it lay between the other two major spans of pre-modern Japanese history. It also shared some characteristics that we label medieval in Europe and China. However, there is one salient difference. Medieval Japanese culture was a direct outgrowth of the classical age; one can even say that during the early Kamakura there was an overlap. In contrast, Europe was torn by barbarian invasions, and a millennium separated the classical culture of Rome from high medieval culture. In China, too, the era of political disunity and barbarian invasions lasted 400 years, and it was during these years that its medieval Buddhist culture blossomed.

The results of the historical continuity in Japan are visible in every branch of its culture. The earlier poetic tradition continued with great vigor. The flat *Yamato-e* style of painting continued, as did artisanal production, using the same techniques. Just as Heian estates, and the authority of the court, continued into the Kamakura era, so did Heian culture extend into medieval Japan.

Nonetheless, medieval Japanese culture had some distinctly new characteristics. First, as the leadership of society shifted from court aristocrats to military aristocrats, new forms of literature appeared. The medieval military tales were as different from *The Tale of Genji* as the armor of the mounted warrior was from the no less colorful silken robes of the court nobility. Second, a new wave of culture entered from China. If the Nara and Heian had been shaped by Tang culture, medieval Japan—though not its institutions—was shaped by Song culture. The link is immediately apparent in the ink paintings of medieval Japan. Third, and most important, the medieval centuries were Japan's age of Buddhist faith. A religious revolution occurred during the Kamakura period and deepened during the Ashikaga.

JAPANESE PIETISM: PURE LAND AND NICHIREN BUDDHISM

Pure Land

In Buddhism, the celestial realm of the bodhisattva, Amida.

Among the doctrines of the Heian Tendai sect was the belief that the true teachings of the historical Buddha had been lost and that salvation could be had only by calling on the name of Amida, the Buddha who ruled over the Western Paradise, or **Pure Land**. The doctrine that the world had fallen on evil times and that only faith would suffice was given credence by earthquakes, epidemics, fires, and banditry in the capital, as well as wars throughout the land. During the tenth and eleventh centuries, itinerant preachers began to spread Pure Land doctrines and practices beyond the narrow circles of Kyoto.

Two early Kamakura figures stand out as religious geniuses who experienced the truth of Pure Land Buddhism within themselves. Hōnen (1133–1212) was perhaps the first to say that the invocation of the name of Amida alone was enough for salvation; faith, not works or rituals, was what counted. These claims brought Hōnen into conflict with the older Buddhist establishment and marked the emergence of Pure Land as a separate sect. Later, Shinran (1173–1262) taught that even a single invocation in praise of Amida, if done with perfect faith, was sufficient for salvation. But perfect faith was a gift from Amida and could not be obtained by human effort. Shinran taught that pride was an obstacle to purity of heart. One of his most famous sayings is "If even a good man can be reborn in the Pure Land, how much more so a wicked man"[1]—the wicked man is less inclined to assume that he is the source of his own salvation and therefore more apt to place his complete trust in Amida. Shinran broke with many of the practices of earlier Buddhism: He ate meat, married a nun, and taught that all occupations were equally "heavenly" if performed with a pure heart. Exiled from Kyoto, he traveled

---

[1]R. Tsunoda, W. deBary, and D. Keene, *Sources of Japanese Tradition* (New York: Columbia University Press, 1958), p. 217.

about Japan establishing "True Pure Land" congregations. (When the Jesuits arrived in Japan in the sixteenth century, they called this sect "the devil's Christianity.")

Pure Land Buddhism became the dominant form of Buddhism in Japan and remains so today. It was also the only sect in medieval Japan—apart from the Tendai sect on Mount Hiei—to develop political and military power. As a religion of faith, it developed a strong church as protection for the saved while they were still in this world. As peasants became militarized during the fifteenth century, some Pure Land village congregations created self-defense forces. At times they rebelled against feudal lords. In one instance, Pure Land armies ruled the province of Kaga for over a century. These congregations were smashed during the late sixteenth century, and the sect depoliticized.

A second devotional sect was founded by Nichiren (1222–1282), who believed that the Lotus Sutra perfectly embodied the teachings of the Buddha. He instructed his adherents to chant, over and over, "Praise to the Lotus Sutra of the Wondrous Law," usually to the accompaniment of rapid drumbeats. Like the repetition of "Praise to the Amida Buddha" in the Pure Land sect or comparable verbal formulas in other religions around the world, the chanting optimally induced a state of religious rapture. The goal of an internal spiritual transformation was common to both the devotional and the meditative sects of Buddhism. Nichiren was remarkable for a Buddhist in being both intolerant and nationalistic. He blamed the ills of his age on rival sects and asserted that only his sect could protect Japan. He predicted the Mongol invasions, and his sect claimed credit for the "divine winds" that sank the Mongol fleets. Even his adopted Buddhist name, the Sun Lotus, combined the character for the rising sun of Japan with that of the flower that had become the symbol of Buddhism.

Zen Buddhism

Meditation had long been a part of Japanese monastic practice. Zen teachings and meditation techniques were introduced by monks returning from study in Song China. Eisai (1141–1215) brought back the teachings of the Rinzai sect in 1191, and Dōgen (1200–1253) the Sōtō teachings in 1227. Eisai's sect was patronized by the Hōjō rulers in Kamakura and the Ashikaga in Kyoto. Dōgen established his sect on Japan's western coast, far from centers of political power.

Zen was a religion of paradox. Its monks were learned, yet it stressed a return to the uncluttered "original mind." Zen was punctiliously traditional, yet Zen was also iconoclastic. Its sages were depicted in paintings as tearing up sutras to make the point that it is religious experience and not words that count. Buddhism stressed compassion for all sentient beings, yet in Japan the Zen sect included many samurai whose duty it was to kill their lord's enemies.

Zen influenced the arts of medieval Japan. The most beautiful gardens were in Zen temples. The most famous, at Ryōanji, consists of fifteen rocks set in white sand. Zen monks, such as Josetsu, Shūbun (ca. 1415) and Sesshū (1420–1506), number among the masters of ink painting. Because the artist's creativity itself was seen as grounded in his experience of meditation, a painting of a waterfall was viewed as no less religious than a painting of the mythic Zen founder Bodhidharma.

Nō Plays

Another vital product of Ashikaga culture is the Nō play, a unique mystery drama that is the world's oldest living dramatic tradition. The play is performed on a simple wooden stage by male actors wearing robes of great beauty and carved, painted masks of enigmatic expressions. The text is chanted to the accompaniment of flute and drums. The language is poetic. The action is slow and highly stylized: Circling about the stage can represent a journey, and a vertical motion of the hand, the reading of a letter. At a

Kûya Invoking Buddha. The mid-Heian monk Kûya (903–972) preached Pure Land doctrines in Kyoto and throughout Japan. Little Buddhas emerge from his mouth.

Why does it make sense to depict a Pure Land monk with little Buddhas coming out of his mouth?

critical juncture in most plays, the protagonist is possessed by the spirit of another and performs a dance. Nō plays reveal a medley of themes present in medieval culture. Some pivot on incidents in the struggle between the Taira and the Minamoto. Buddhist ideas of impermanence, of this world as a place of suffering, and of the need to relinquish worldly attachments are found in many plays. Some plays are close to fairy tales, whereas some are based on stories from China.

SUMMARY

 WHAT REVOLUTIONARY changes accompanied the Yayoi?

Japanese Origins. Old Stone Age Japan became an agricultural, metalworking society when new technologies came to Japan from Korea in the third century B.C.E. By the fifth century C.E., the Yamato court ruled most of Japan. It was heavily influenced by Korea. Shintō nature worship was practiced in villages and associated with the government. *page* 219

 HOW DID Chinese culture influence Japan?

Nara and Heian Japan. In the seventh century, the second main turning point of their history, the Japanese began to adopt and adapt many features of Chinese culture, including Buddhism and Chinese writing, literature, and political institutions. Japan was ruled by a civil aristocracy under the emperor. An enormous gulf existed between aristocrats and commoners. Japanese government was heavily influenced by the Chinese imperial system. Japanese culture, however, was increasingly self-confident and was aristocratic in its tastes and forms of expression. Noblewomen wrote many of the great works of Japanese literature during this age. Buddhism became increasingly assimilated. *page* 223

 WHY CAN this period in Japan be described as feudal, and in what ways is this description misleading?

Japan's Early Feudal Age. In the eighth century mounted warriors called samurai began to dominate local society. By the late 1100s, power passed from the civil bureaucracy to military aristocrats. The shōguns' power was based on their ability to command the loyalty of military vassals. Minamoto Yoritomo's seizure of power in 1185 marked the beginning of Japan's feudal age. He established the *bakufu*, or "tent government," in Kamakura. In 1274 and 1281, Mongol invaders sent by Kublai Khan

retreated from Japan. In 1336, Ashitaga Takauji moved his *bakufu* to Kyoto. Women's status declined, while Buddhist sects reflected Japanese concerns. *page* 229

KEY TERMS

bakufu (bah-koo-foo) (p. 229)

daimyo (dye-myoh) (p. 232)

kamikaze (p. 230)

Pure Land (p. 234)

samurai (p. 226)

Shintō (p. 222)

shōgun (p. 229)

Tennō (ten-noh) (p. 224)

REVIEW QUESTIONS

1. In what sense was Japanese society during the Yayoi period defined by its eastern frontier? What changes in its early frontier society led to the building of tombs and the emergence of the Yamato great kings?

2. Discuss Japan's cultural ties with China during the Nara and Heian periods. How did Chinese culture affect Japanese government and religion? How did the Japanese change what they borrowed? Was the relation of Japanese culture to China like that of American culture to England?

3. Trace the rise in Japan of a society dominated by military lords and their vassals. Do the late Heian, Kamakura, and Ashikaga represent successive stages in the development of Japanese "feudalism"?

4. Compare and contrast Heian court culture with the "feudal" culture of the Kamakura and Ashikaga eras.

5. Trace the development of Japanese Buddhism. What sects emerged, and why?

6. What was the overall trajectory of the status of women in Japan, from the Yayoi period to the Ashikaga era? What caused changes in women's status?

Note: To learn more about the topics in this chapter, please turn to the Suggested Readings at the end of the book. For additional sources related to this chapter please see www.myhistorylab.com

myhistorylab Connections

Reinforce what you learned in this chapter by studying the many documents, images, maps, review tools, and videos available at **www.myhistorylab.com**

Read and Review

✓•─[Study and **Review**   Chapter 9

•ﾐ•─[Read the Document   *Murasaki Shikibu, selections from The Tale of Genji, p. 226*
Buddhism in Japan: The Taika Reform Edicts, p. 228

•ﾐ•─[View the Image   *Japanese Court Ladies, p. 233*

✓•─[Study and **Review**   *Women in the Imperial Courts of China and Japan, p. 233*

Research and Explore

👁•─[See the **Map**   *Medieval Japan and the Mongol Invasions, p. 230*

((•●─[Hear the **Audio**

Hear the audio file for Chapter 9
at **www.myhistorylab.com**

RELIGIONS OF THE WORLD

BUDDHISM

Hinduism, Buddhism, and Jainism all arose out of the spiritual ferment of Vedic India after 700 B.C.E. Buddhism shares a kinship with the other two religions much as Judaism, Christianity, and Islam have a relationship.

The founder of Buddhism, Siddhartha Gautama, was born about 563 B.C.E., a prince in a petty kingdom near what is now the border of India and Nepal. He was reared amid luxury and comforts, married at 16, and had a child. According to legend, at age 29 he saw a decrepit old man, sick and suffering, and a corpse. He suddenly realized that all humans would suffer the same fate. Gautama renounced his wealth and family and entered the life of a wandering ascetic. He visited famous teachers, for almost six years practiced extremes of ascetic self-deprivation, and finally discovered the Middle Path between self-indulgence and self-mortification. He attained *nirvana* at the age of 35, becoming the *Buddha*, or Enlightened One. The rest of his eighty years the Buddha spent teaching others the truths he had learned.

Basic to the Buddha's understanding of the human condition were the "Four Noble Truths": (1) All life is suffering—an endless chain of births and rebirths (*karma*); (2) the cause of the suffering is desire—it is desire that binds humans to the wheel of *karma*; (3) escape from suffering and endless rebirths can come only by the cessation of desire and the attainment of *nirvana*; (4) the path to *nirvana* is eightfold, requiring right views, thought, speech, actions, living, efforts, mindfulness, and meditation. Buddhists say that *nirvana* cannot be described: It is the ground of all existence, ineffable, and beyond time and space—an ultimate reality that may be experienced but not grasped intellectually.

The Buddha was a religious teacher, not a social reformer, yet his religious understanding led to ethical conclusions. He condemned the caste system that flourished in the India of his day. He denounced war, slavery, and the taking of life. He opposed appeals to miracles. He did not demand a blind faith in his doctrines: He told his followers to accept his teachings only after they had tested them against their own experience. He taught that poverty was a cause of immorality and that it was futile to attempt to suppress crime with punishments. He identified with all humanity, saying, "He who attends on the sick attends on me."

Because the goal of Buddhism is for all humans to become buddhas, some have called Buddhism the most contemplative and otherworldly of the great world religions. For the spiritually unprepared, and even for the historical Buddha, the way was not easy, and one lifetime was not enough.

Teenage Buddist monks walk past the ornate facade and towering stupa of Shwedagon Pagoda in Yangon, Myanmar (Burma).

William Waterfall/PacificStock.com

What is the role of monks in a Buddhist society?

Monks and nuns might practice the Eightfold Path, meditate for months and years, and experience an inner spiritual awakening, but only a few would gain enlightenment, the release from karmic causation. Most could only hope for a rebirth in a higher spiritual state—to begin again closer to the goal.

For laypeople the emphasis of Buddhism was on ethical living in human society as a preparation for a more dedicated religious quest in a future life.

Buddhism spread rapidly along the Ganges River and through northern India. In the time of King Ashoka (272–232 B.C.E.) of the Mauryas, it spread to southern India, Ceylon, and beyond. This was its great missionary age. As it spread throughout India its influence on religious practice at the village level was enormous, and its meditative techniques helped reshape Hindu yogic exercises. Eventually, however, Buddhism in India was re-Hinduized. It developed competing schools of metaphysics, a pantheon of gods and cosmic Buddhas, and devotional sects focusing on one or another of these cosmic figures. Its original character as a reform movement of Hinduism was lost, and between 500 and 1500 C.E. it was largely reabsorbed into Hinduism.

Beyond India, two major currents of Buddhism spread over Asia. One, known as the "Way of the Elders" (*Theravada*), swept

Two Seated Buddhas. This fifth- to sixth-century C.E. painting adorns a wall of a cave in Ajanta, India.

Borromeo/Art Resource, New York.

Why does Buddhist art sometimes show more than one Buddha?

Tibetan Buddhist nuns. The nuns belong to a Tibetan sect of the Mahayana (Greater Vehicle) Buddhism that swept north to Central Asia and Tibet, and then east to China, Korea, and Japan. Behind them, prayer flags blow in the wind.

What is the difference between Mahayana and Theravada Buddhism?

through continental Southeast Asia and the islands that are today Indonesia. The Theravada teaching was close to early Indian Buddhism and, as it spread, it carried with it other strands of Indian culture as well. Buddhism remains the predominant religion of Burma, Thailand, Cambodia, and Laos, although it must contend with more recent secular ideologies. In Thailand it remains the state religion: Thai kings rule as Buddhist monarchs; Thai boys spend short periods as Buddhist monks; and Thai temples (*wats*) continue as one center of village life. Before the spread of Islam, Buddhism also once flourished in Malaya, Sumatra, and Java.

The second major current, known as the "Greater Vehicle" (*Mahayana*), spread through northwest India to Afghanistan and Central Asia, and then to China, Tibet and Mongolia, Vietnam, Korea, and Japan. In each region the pattern that unfolded was different. In what is today Pakistan, Afghanistan, and Central Asia, Buddhism was overtaken and replaced by Islam. Mahayana doctrines entered Tibet during the sixth century C.E. and became firmly established several centuries later.

Today Tibetan Buddhism is the predominant religion of Tibet, Nepal, Sikkim, Bhutan, and Mongolia (although in Mongolia it is severely curtailed by Chinese authorities). In China, and then spreading from China to Korea, Vietnam, and Japan, Mahayana

Buddhism saw its fullest development. One key doctrine in this current was the ideal of the *bodhisattva*, a being who had gone all the way to *nirvana*, but held back in order to help others attain salvation.

Another Mahayana doctrine, that of the Chan (in China) or Zen (in Japan) sect, stressed meditation and perhaps was closer to the teachings of the historical Buddha.

In China, the Tang Dynasty (618–907) was the great Buddhist age, a time of unparalleled creativity in religious art, sculpture, and music. After that, although Buddhism continued to flourish at the village level, the governing scholar-gentry class shifted to the more worldly doctrines of Neo-Confucianism. In Vietnam, Korea, and Japan, the overall process replicated that of China, but the shift occurred later and with many local variations.

During modern times Buddhism—like all structures of faith—has struggled, with the secular doctrines of the scientific, and industrial, and communist revolutions exerting a powerful influence in the nineteenth and twentieth centuries. The future is unclear, but undoubtedly Buddhism will be powerfully affected by the ongoing transformations of Asian societies.

◆ Is Buddhism's relation to Hinduism parallel to Christianity's relation to Judaism?

◆ How do the teachings of the Buddha compare with Christian doctrine?

10

The Formation of Islamic Civilization, 622–1000

((•●[Hear the Audio for Chapter 10 at www.myhistorylab.com

Islamic Astronomy. Initially Muslim astronomers believed that the earth rested motionless at the center of a series of eight spheres, the last of which was studded with fixed stars revolving daily from east to west and at times from west to east. Muslim astronomers were influenced by and improved on Sanskrit, Sasanian, Syriac, and Greek texts on astronomy. *Rami*, the Sagittarius in this illustration from an eighteenth-century copy of a book by 'Abd al-Rahman ibn 'Ubmar al-Sufi (d. 986), has a set of twenty-nine gold spots that represent a stellar constellation.

How did Islam preserve Classical learning?

T*he diverse, but identifiable civilization that we call "Islamic" is the last great civilization to appear to date. The basic elements of the Islamic worldview derived from a single, prophetic-revelatory event, the Prophet Muhammad's proclamation of the Qur'an.[1] This event galvanized diverse, polytheistic Arabs into a new unity—the monotheistic, egalitarian community (umma) of* "submitters" (muslims) *to God.*

This community expanded far beyond Arabia; Persians, Indians, and others made it a great universalist tradition. Arab military prowess and cultural pride joined with a new religious orientation to initiate one of the most lasting revolutions in history, but peoples of the older Eurasian heartlands converted this revolution into a new civilization. Their acceptance of the Islamic vision of society (and reality) as more compelling than any older one—Jewish, Roman, Greek, Persian, Christian, or Buddhist—gave rise to a multifaceted Islamic civilization.

((•—[Hear the Audio
at **myhistorylab.com**

---

[1]*Qur'an* is a more accurate English transliteration of the Arabic word than *Koran*; similarly, *Muhammad* is preferable to *Mohammed, Muslim* to *Moslem, emir* to *amir,* and *ulama* to *ulema.*

THE EARLY ISLAMIC WORLDS OF ARAB AND PERSIAN CULTURES

The rise of Arabic, Persian, and Turkish Islamic cultures as core religious and cultural worlds of Islamic civilization is a pivotal moment in world history. In its first three centuries, the Islamic polity was arguably the most dynamic, multiethnic, multilingual imperial realm of its time. In the same age, Tang Chinese emperors renewed and restored the old Han imperium; Charlemagne and the Carolingians carved out a much smaller, more homogeneous empire in relatively underdeveloped western Europe; Byzantium fought to survive against Arab and Turkish arms and turned inward to conserve its traditions; and the regional kingdoms of post-Gupta India remained vulnerable to new forces (including Islamic ones) moving into northwestern India.

Only China compared favorably with the Islamic world during this period in political and military strength, cultural unity, creativity, and self-consciousness. The Tang and the Abbasids wielded commensurate power in their heydays, although the Chinese endured as a centralized state much longer than the Arab Islamic Empire. Certainly these were the era's greatest political

and cultural units. Each had one cultural language: Variations of Chinese were spoken by a large percentage of Chinese subjects, while Arabic became the administrative and religious *lingua franca* of the Islamic Empire, from Morocco to India, as the result of its status as the language of Qur'anic revelation and hence of learning. The two civilizations shared the use of pastoral cavalry as well as the adaptive ability to incorporate new peoples into their larger cultures—although Islamic civilization proved finally more flexible in this regard. Indeed, the great adaptability of Islamic religious traditions and their attendant social orders belie today's widespread misconception of Islamic traditions as inherently inflexible.

Islamic states were spread over vastly more culturally heterogeneous and widely dispersed geographical areas than was the Chinese Empire. Conquest initially fueled the economy of the new Islamic imperial state, but in the long run, trade, artisanal crafts, seafaring technology, and urban commercial centers became the backbone of the Islamic lands' prosperity, as well as the

ORIGINS AND EARLY DEVELOPMENT

WHAT WAS the Qur'anic message as expressed to Muhammad?

THE SETTING

By 600 C.E., the dominant Eurasian political powers, Christian Byzantium and Zoroastrian Sasanid Persia, had battled for West Asian political and cultural ascendancy for over four centuries. Then, in the wake of one final, mutually exhausting conflict (608–627), a new Arab power broke in from the south to weaken the first and destroy the second.

Pre-Islamic Arabia was not just a land of deserts, camels, and pastoralists. Byzantium and Persia had kept the nomads of the Syrian and northern Arabian steppe at bay by enlisting small Arab client kingdoms on the edge of the desert as buffer states. One of the biggest of these kingdoms was Christian in faith. Arab kingdoms had long flourished in the agriculturally rich highlands of southern Arabia, which had direct access to the international oceanic trade along its coasts (see Chapters 4, 5). Some of these kingdoms, including a Jewish one in the sixth century, were independent; others were under Persian or Abyssinian control. In the western Arabian highland of the Hijaz, astride its major trade route, the town of Mecca was a center of the caravan trade and a pilgrimage site because of its famous sanctuary, the **Ka'ba** (or Kaaba), where pagan Arab tribes enshrined gods. The settled Meccan Arabs ran a merchant republic in which tribal values were breaking down under the strains of urban commercial life. Still, these settled Arabs were not cut off from their nomadic relatives who lived on herding and by raiding settlements and caravans.

Ka'ba
A black meteorite in the city of Mecca that became Islam's holiest shrine.

The Arabic language, a Semitic tongue, defined and linked the Arab peoples, however divided they were by livelihood, religion, blood feuds, and tribal conflict. From the Yemen north to Syria-Palestine and Mesopotamia, Arabs shared a highly developed poetic idiom. Every tribe had a poet to exhort its warriors and insult its enemies before battle. Poetry contests were also held, often in conjunction with annual trade fairs that brought tribes together under a general truce.

QUICK REVIEW

Mecca
- Center of caravan trade
- Pilgrimage center because of presence of Ka'ba
- A merchant republic

See the **Map**
Expansion of Islam at
myhistorylab.com
prime means of disseminating Islamic concepts and traditions to new areas, as regional states replaced the centralized imperial state of the early caliphate.

This Islamic achievement was unique in that the peoples who built it did so by developing new religious, social, and political traditions rather than simply reviving old ones. In later centuries the early Arab impress on Islamic culture and religion was transformed by vast numbers of Persian- and Turkish-speaking Muslims and many regional cultural groups, from Swahili speakers in East Africa to multiple peoples of South and Southeast Asia. Yet in the midst of Islam's diversity, Arabic went abroad with the holy Qur'an as the sacred medium of God's revelation. Since Islam's earliest spread, individual Muslims worldwide have cultivated to some degree Arabic and the Arabic scripture and thus kept in touch with Islam's Arab origins.

This achievement was novel, at least in its global scale. Although the Muslim faith can be seen as a reformation of Jewish and Christian monotheism, it was directed not merely at reforming but subsuming the older Jewish and Christian traditions in a more comprehensive vision of God's plan on earth. And even as Islam can be seen as a reform of Semitic monotheism, Muslims also built on previous Persian, Turkish, and other traditions; they adopted and adapted elements of neighboring African, European, and Asian cultures. As a diverse, international civilization and religious tradition, Islam developed its own distinctive forms that persisted wherever Muslims extended the *umma*.

Focus Questions

◆ Why did only China compare favorably with the Islamic world during the first centuries after the birth of Islam? How were the two civilizations similar, and how were they different?

◆ What is unique about the Islamic achievement? In what ways was it built on the traditions of earlier religions?

Islam is not a "religion of the desert." It began in a commercial urban center and first flourished in an agricultural oasis and small merchant towns of the Hijaz. Its first converts were Meccan townsfolk and date farmers in Yathrib. Before becoming Muslims, most Arabs were animists; fewer were Jews or Christians. North–south caravans passed from Damascus through Mecca to Aden and the Indian Ocean, and no merchant involved in this traffic, as Muhammad himself was, could have been unfamiliar with the diverse cultures along the trade routes. Early Muslim leaders used Arab tribes as warriors and looked to Arab culture for their traditional roots long after the locus of Islamic power had left Arabia. But the empire and civilization they ultimately spawned were centered in the heartlands of Mediterranean and West Asian urban and rural cultures and based more on settled communal existence than on rural or desert tribal societies and economies.

MUHAMMAD AND THE QUR'AN

Muhammad (ca. 570–632) was raised an orphan in a commercial family of the old Meccan tribe of Quraysh. Later, in the midst of a successful business career made possible by his marriage to Khadija (d. ca. 619), an older, wealthy Meccan widow and entrepreneur, he became troubled by the idolatry, worldliness, and lack of social conscience around him. Such failings were equally offensive to sensitive Jewish or Christian morality, with which he was familiar, but these traditions had not displaced Arabian pagan traditions, despite the presence of some Jewish and Christian Arab tribes.

When he was about 40, Muhammad felt himself called by the one God, the God of Abraham, Moses, and Jesus, to "rise and warn" his fellow Arabs about their frivolous disregard for morality and worship of the Creator.

On repeated occasions revelation came to Muhammad through a messenger identified as God's angel, Gabriel. It took the form of a "reciting" (**qur'an**) of God's

Read the **Document**
Al-Tabari: Muhammad's Call to Prophecy
at **myhistorylab.com**

Qur'an
Meaning "a reciting." The Islamic bible, which Muslims believe God revealed to the Prophet Muhammad.

The Ka'ba in Mecca. In Muslim tradition, the Ka'ba (Arabic "cube") is the site of the first "house of God," founded by Adam, then rebuilt by Abraham and his son Ishmael at God's command. It is held to have fallen later into idolatrous use until Muhammad's victory over the Meccans and his cleansing of the holy house. The Ka'ba is the geographical point toward which all Muslims face when performing ritual prayer. It and the plain of Arafat outside Mecca are the two foci of the pilgrimage of Hajj that each Muslim aspires to make at least once in a lifetime.

The Five Pillars of Islam include the Hajj; what are the other four?

Islam
Meaning "submission." The religion founded by the Prophet Muhammad.

View the Image
The Qur'an at **myhistorylab.com**

Word—now rendered in "clear Arabic" for the Arabs, just as it had been given to previous prophets in Hebrew or other languages for their peoples.

The message of the Qur'an was clear: The Prophet is to warn his people against worshipping false gods and against all immorality, especially injustice to the poor, orphans, widows, and indeed all women. At the end of time, on Judgment Day, every person will be bodily resurrected to face what they have earned: eternal punishment in hellfire or eternal joy in paradise. The way to paradise lies in gratitude to God for His bounties, His revelatory guidance, and His readiness to forgive the penitent. It lies in social justice and obedient worship of God, and in recognition of God's transcendence. The proper human response to God is "submission" (*islam*) to His will, becoming *muslim* ("submissive") in one's worship and morality. All of creation naturally praises and serves God except humans, who can choose to obey or to reject him.

In this Qur'anic message, the ethical monotheism of Judaic and Christian tradition (probably reinforced by Zoroastrian and Manichaean influences) reaches fulfillment in a radically theocentric vision demanding absolute obedience to the Lord of the Universe. The Qur'anic revelations state that Muhammad is only the last in a series of prophets chosen to bring God's word: Noah, Abraham, Moses, Jesus, and nonbiblical Arabian figures like Salih had similar missions previously. The Qur'an is filled with stories of earlier biblical figures, especially Abraham and Moses. Most frequently mentioned from the Christian New Testament is Mary, mother of Jesus. Because the followers of earlier prophets neglected or altered their scriptures' teachings, Muhammad has been given one final reiteration of God's message. Jews, Christians, and pagans are summoned to heed this Qur'anic message.

The Prophet's preaching fell largely on deaf ears in the first years after his calling (traditionally dated to the year 610). A few followed the lead of his wife, Khadija, in recognizing him as a divinely chosen reformer. Some prominent Meccans joined him, but the merchant aristocracy as a whole resisted. His preaching against their gods and goddesses threatened their ancestral ways as well as the Ka'ba pilgrimage shrine and the lucrative trade it attracted. The Meccans began to persecute Muhammad's followers. After the deaths of Khadija and Muhammad's uncle and protector, Abu Talib, the situation worsened; the Prophet even had to send a small band of Muslims to Abyssinia for temporary refuge. Then, because of his growing reputation as a moral leader, Muhammad was called to Yathrib (an important agricultural oasis 240 miles north of Mecca) to arbitrate among its five quarreling tribes, three of which were Jewish. Having sent his Meccan followers ahead, Muhammad fled Mecca in July 622 for Yathrib, afterward known as Medina (*al-Madina*, "the City [of the Prophet]"). Some dozen years later, this "emigration," or **hegira** (in Arabic, *Hajj*), became the starting point for the Islamic calendar, the event marking the creation of a distinctive Islamic community, or **umma**.[2]

Muhammad quickly cemented ties between the Meccan emigrants and the Medinans, many of whom became converts. Raids on his Meccan enemies' caravans established his leadership. They reflect the economic dimension of the Medinan-Meccan struggle. The Arab Jews of Medina largely rejected his religious message and authority. They even made contact with his Meccan enemies, moving Muhammad to turn on them, kill or enslave some, banish others, and take their lands. Many of the Qur'anic revelations from this period pertain to communal order or chastise Jews and Christians who rejected Islam.

Muslim norms took shape in Medina: allegiance to the *umma*; honesty in all one's affairs; modesty in personal habits; abstention from alcohol and pork; fair division of inheritances; improved treatment of women, especially as to property and other rights in marriage; careful regulation of marriage and divorce; ritual ablution before any act of worship, be it reciting the Qur'an or prayer; three (later five) daily rites of worship facing the Meccan shrine of the Ka'ba; payment of a tithe to support less fortunate Muslims; annual daytime fasting for the month of Ramadan and, eventually, pilgrimage to Mecca at least once in a lifetime, if one is able. Five of these essential elements of Islamic became known as The Pillars: (1) *Shahada*, or the Muslim Creed ("There is no God but God and Muhammad is God's prophet"); (2) *Salat*, or prayer; (3) *Sawm*, fasting during Ramadan; (4) *Zakat*, or alms; and (5) **Hajj**, the pilgrimage.

Acceptance of Islamic political authority brought tolerance. A Jewish oasis yielded to Muhammad's authority and was allowed, unlike the resistant Medinan Jews, to keep its lands, practice its faith, and receive protection in return for paying a head tax. This practice was followed ever after for Jews, Christians, and other "people of Scripture" who accepted Islamic rule. After long conflict, the Meccans surrendered to Muhammad, and his acceptance of them into the *umma* set the pattern for the later Islamic conquests. Following age-old practice, Muhammad cemented many of his alliances with marriage (although while Khadija lived, he took no second wife). In the last years of the Prophet's life, the once tiny band of Muslims became the heart of a pan-Arabian tribal confederation, bound together by personal allegiance to Muhammad, submission (*islam*) to God, and membership in the *umma*.

hegira
The flight of Muhammad and his followers from Mecca to Medina in 622 C.E. It marks the beginning of the Islamic calendar.

umma
The Islamic community.

Hajj The pilgrimage to Mecca that all Muslims are enjoined to perform at least once in their lifetime.

---

[2]The twelve-month Muslim lunar year is shorter than the Christian solar year by about eleven days, a difference of about three years per century. Muslim dates are reckoned from the month in 622 in which Muhammad began his hegira (Arabic: *Hijra*). Thus Muslims celebrated the start of their lunar year 1401 in November 1980 (1979–1980 C.E. = A.H. [Anno Hegirae] 1400), whereas it was only 1,358 solar years from 622 to 1980.

WOMEN IN EARLY ISLAMIC SOCIETY

HOW DID the status of women improve under Islam?

The *umma* is a central concern in Islam, and the family is the core of the *umma*. Consequently, family law played a central role in the development of Islamic law. It is Islamic family law that stipulates the rights of women and men.

The Qur'an introduced into Arabian society radical new ideas that dramatically improved the status of women. For example, it prohibited the common practice of female infanticide, stating that all children should have the opportunity to live. The Qur'an recognizes a woman's right to contract her own marriage and stipulates that she, and not her male relatives, receives the dowry from her husband. Legally, a woman entering marriage was not an object to be bought and sold but rather a party to a negotiated contract. A woman was also guaranteed the right to inherit, own, and manage property.

Women are therefore afforded many rights in the Qur'an. Yet the Qur'an does not assume the full gender equality advocated in some modern societies in the twenty-first century. Islamic law stipulates that the father or senior male controls and guides the family unit. A male receives a larger share in inheritance and has fewer restrictions in initiating a divorce; also, a man's eyewitness testimony carries more weight in court than a woman's. Even though the Qur'an introduced many positive changes for women, it also presupposed and legitimated a patriarchal society and did not outlaw all customs that practically and symbolically kept women from full equality.

Polygamy is a practice often identified with Islam. The Qur'an tolerates this (preexisting) practice but seeks to control and regulate it. It states that a man can have up to four wives provided he can treat them all equally and fairly (Q. 4:3). Some Muslims interpret this verse as effectively prohibiting polygamy because it is manifestly impossible to treat and love two or more women "equally." And in fact, monogamy is globally the predominant Muslim marital practice.

Another practice commonly associated with Islam is female veiling, *hijab*, which is understood by Muslims as a practice of modesty. The veil is a generic term that applies to various types of body or facial covering, such as *chador* and *burqa*. Veiling of women was customary in a number of pre-Islamic societies, notably among upper-class women in the Byzantine and Sasanid empires. It was, and still is, common in parts of the Mediterranean. Islam did not invent the veil, nor does the Qur'an specifically stipulate veiling, let alone repression of women. Rather, it emphasizes that both men and women are responsible for their actions and should dress and act modestly. It does stipulate that women should guard their modesty and "draw their veils over their bosom and display their beauty only to their husbands and their fathers" (Q. 24:31).

As with many religious dictums, whatever their spirit, implementation has proven problematic. Though the original intention of veiling was to protect women and their honor, the veil and the derivative idea of seclusion often largely barred women from public life until the twentieth century. These and other Qur'anic verses have been used literally to justify patriarchy and keep women from exercising the full rights that the Qur'an affords them. With more modern education, many Muslim women have turned to the Qur'an to interpret these verses anew to stipulate practices that are both Islamic and compatible with modern ideas of equality. And of course different Islamic cultures, from Indonesia to North Africa to Europe and America, differ greatly in how literally or liberally they apply traditional practices and customs.

QUICK REVIEW

Women's Rights in the Qur'an

- Infanticide—commonly practiced on females—prohibited
- Women contract their own marriages, receive dowries
- Women can inherit, own, and manage property
- Society assumed to be patriarchal

Veiling. There are many different forms of veiling. These photos illustrate three. The left-hand photo shows a young woman dressed in contemporary clothing with just her head covered. The middle photo shows a Yemeni woman with all but her eyes covered. The right-hand photo shows an Afghani woman who is fully covered.

Why is there so much variation in veiling practices?

In early Islamic history, many women—such as the wives of Muhammad (Khadija and A'isha)—played influential roles. They were instrumental in defining certain aspects of Islamic law and even commanded troops in warfare. In medieval times, however, women were not, with a few notable exceptions, prominent in the public sphere. As in many other places around the world, women were largely cut off from public political, social, and educational activities. These negative effects are still visible today in many Middle Eastern, African, and Asian regions even as women generally are increasingly negotiating their way into the public sphere.

EARLY ISLAMIC CONQUESTS

WHY WAS Islam able to expand rapidly?

In 632 Muhammad died, leaving neither a son nor a designated successor. The new *umma* faced its first major crisis. A political struggle between Meccan and Medinan factions ended in a pledge of allegiance to Abu Bakr, the most senior of the early Meccan converts. Following old Arabian patterns, many tribes renounced allegiance to the Prophet after his death. Nevertheless, Abu Bakr's rule (632–634) as Muhammad's successor, or "caliph" (*khalifa*), reestablished Medinan hegemony and at least nominal religious conformity for much of Arabia. The Arabs were forced to recognize in the *umma* a new kind of supratribal community that demanded more than allegiance to a particular leader.

COURSE OF CONQUEST

Under the next two caliphs, Umar (634–644) and Uthman (644–656), Arab armies moved beyond the peninsula, intent on more than traditional bedouin booty raids. In one of history's most astonishing expansions, by 643 they had conquered the Byzantine and Sasanid territories of the Fertile Crescent, Egypt, and most of Iran. For the first time in centuries the lands from Egypt to Iran came under one rule. Finally, Arab armies swept west over the Byzantine-controlled Libyan coast and, in the east, pushed to the Oxus, defeating the last Sasanid ruler by 651.

An interlude of civil war followed during the contested caliphate of Muhammad's cousin and son-in-law Ali (656–661). Then the fifth caliph, Mu'awiya (661–680), directed further expansion and initiated the new Umayyad Dynasty, which survived despite a second civil war (680–692) until 750. In the Mediterranean, an Islamic fleet conquered Cyprus, plundered Sicily and Rhodes, and crippled Byzantine sea power. By 680 control of greater Persia was solidified by permanent Arab garrisoning of Khorasan, much of Anatolia was raided, Constantinople was besieged (but not taken), and Armenia was under Islamic rule.

Succeeding decades saw the eastern Berbers of Libyan North Africa defeated and converted to Islam in substantial numbers. With their help, "the West" (al-Maghrib, modern Morocco and Algeria) fell quickly. In 711 raids into Spain began (memory of the Berber Muslim leader of the first invaders, Tariq, lives on in the name of *Gibraltar*, from *Jabal Tariq*, "Mount Tariq"). By 716 the disunited Spanish Visigoth kingdoms had fallen, and much of Iberia was under Islamic control. Pushing north into France, the Arabs were finally checked by Charles Martel with a defeat at Tours (732). At the opposite end of the empire, buoyed by large-scale Arab immigration, Islamic forces consolidated their holdings as far as the Oxus River (Amu Darya) basin of Khorasan, and in 710 these forces reached the Indus region. Islamic power was supreme from the Atlantic to Central Asia (see Map 10–1).

FACTORS OF SUCCESS

This rapid expansion was possible because of the weakened military and economic condition of the Byzantines and Sasanids, the result of their chronic warfare with one another. The new Islamic vision of society and life also united the Arabs and attracted others. Its corollary was the commitment among the Islamic leadership to extend "the abode of submission" (*Dar al-Islam*) abroad. However, too much has been made of Muslim zeal for martyrdom. Assurance of paradise for those engaged in **jihad**, "just struggle (in the path of God)," is less likely to have motivated the average Arab tribesman—who, at least at the beginning, was usually only nominally Muslim—than did promise of booty. Life in the Peninsula was hard, so the hope of greater prosperity must have been compelling.

Still, religious zeal was important, especially as time went on. The early policy of sending Qur'an reciters among the Arab armies to teach essentials of Muslim faith and practice had its effects. Another factor was the leadership of the first caliphs and field generals, which, combined with Byzantine and Iranian weakness, gave Arab armies a distinct advantage. Some populations even welcomed Islamic rule as a relief from Byzantine or Persian oppression. Crucial here was Muslim willingness to allow Christian, Jewish, and even Zoroastrian groups to continue as minorities (with their own legal systems and no military obligations) under protection of Islamic rule. In return, they had to recognize Islamic political authority, pay a non-Muslim head tax (*jizya*), and not proselytize or interfere with Muslim religious practice. (Ironically, with time, the head tax and other strictures on non-Muslims encouraged many Christians and Jews to convert.)

Finally, the astute policies of the early leaders helped give the conquests overall permanence: relatively little bloodshed, destruction, or disruption in conquest; adoption of existing administrative systems (and personnel) with minimal changes; adjustment of unequal taxation; appointment of capable governors; and strategic siting of new garrison towns like Basra, Kufa, and Fustat (later Cairo).

jihad
"Struggle in the path of God." Although not necessarily implying violence, it is often interpreted to mean holy war in the name of Islam.

MAP EXPLORATION

To explore this map further, go to **http://www.myhistorylab.com**

MAP 10–1. Muslim Conquests and Domination of the Mediterranean to about 750 C.E. The rapid spread of the Islamic religious and political-military presence is shown here. Within 125 years of Muhammad's preaching, Muslim hegemony extended from Spain to Central Asia.

Why did so many subject peoples welcome Islamic rule?

THE NEW ISLAMIC WORLD ORDER

Although they were quick to adopt and adapt existing traditions in the lands they conquered, the Muslims brought with them a new worldview that demanded a new political, social, and cultural order, however long it might take to implement. Beyond military and administrative problems loomed the more important question of the nature of Islamic society. Under the Prophet the new community of the *umma* had replaced, at least in theory, the tribal, blood-based sociopolitical order in Arabia. Yet once the Arabs (most of whom became Muslims) had to rule non-Arabs and non-Muslims, new problems tested the ideal of an Islamic polity. Chief among these were leadership and membership qualifications, social order, and religious and cultural identity.

WHAT ROLES did the caliphate and the *ulama* play in Islamic states?

THE CALIPHATE

Allegiance to Muhammad had rested on his authority as divine spokesperson and gifted leader. His first successors were chosen much as were Arab *shaykhs* ("sheiks"), or tribal chieftains: by agreement of the leading elders, of the new religious "tribe" of

caliphate
The true line of succession to Muhammad.

imam
Islamic prayer leader.

emir
An Islamic military commander.

•◆•⊣Read the **Document**
Al-Tabari and Ibn Hisham, from
"The Founding of the Caliphate"
at **myhistorylab.com**

Muslims on the basis of superior personal qualities and the precedence in faith conferred by piety and association with the Prophet. The true line of succession to Muhammad was known as the **caliphate**, and the successors' titles were "successor" (*khalifa*, or caliph), "leader" (*imam*—literally, the one who stands in front to lead ritual worship), and "commander (*emir*) of the faithful." These names underscored religious and political authority, which most Muslims recognized in the caliphs Abu Bakr and Umar, and potentially in Uthman and Ali. Unfortunately, by the time of Uthman and Ali, dissension led to civil war. Yet the first four caliphs had all been close to Muhammad, and this gave their reigns a nostalgic aura of purity, especially as the later caliphal institution was based largely on sheer power legitimized by hereditary succession. (See Document, "Al-Mawardi and al-Hilli.")

The nature of Islamic leadership became an issue with the first civil war (656–661) and the recognition of Mu'awiya, a kinsman of Uthman, as caliph. He founded the first dynastic caliphate, that of his Meccan clan of Umayya (661–750). Umayyad descendants held power until they were ousted in 750 by the Abbasid clan, which based its legitimacy on descent from Abbas, an uncle of the Prophet. The Umayyads had the prestige of the office held by the first four, "rightly guided" caliphs. But many also deemed them to be worldly kings compared to the first four, "true" successors to Muhammad.

The Abbasids took the caliphate by open rebellion in 750, having exploited pious dissatisfaction with Umayyad worldliness, non-Arab Muslim resentment of Arab preference (primarily in Iran), and dissension among Arab tribal factions in the garrison towns. For all their stress on the Muslim character of their caliphate, the Abbasids were scarcely less worldly and continued the hereditary rule begun by the Umayyads. This they did well enough to retain control of most of the far-flung Islamic territories until 945, when the Shi'ite Buyid Dynasty took control in Baghdad and relegated the caliph to largely symbolic status. Thereafter, although their line continued until 1258, the caliphate was primarily a titular office representing an Islamic unity that existed largely in name only.

THE *ULAMA*

Although the caliph could exert his power to influence religious matters, he was never "emperor and pope combined," as European writers have claimed. Religious leadership in the *umma* devolved instead on another group. The functional successors of the Prophet in society at large were those Muslims recognized for piety and learning and as informal or even formal (as with state-appointed judges) authorities. Initially, they were the "Companions" (male and female) of Muhammad with greatest stature in the old Medinan *umma*—including the first four caliphs. This generation was replaced by those younger followers most concerned with preserving, interpreting, and applying the Qur'an and with maintaining the norms of the Prophet's original *umma*. Because the Qur'an contained few legal prescriptions, they had to draw on precedents from Meccan and Medinan practice, as well as oral traditions from and about the Prophet and Companions. They also had to standardize grammatical rules for a common Arabic language based on the Qur'an and pre-Islamic poetry. Furthermore, they had to improve the phonetic, cursive Arabic script, a task done so well that the script was gradually applied as the standard alphabetic script for other languages wherever Islamic culture became dominant: among Iranians, Turks, Indians, Indonesians, Malays, East Africans, and others. Along with these and other religious, intellectual, and cultural achievements, Muslim scholars developed an enduring pattern of education based on study under those persons highest in the unbroken cross-generational chain of trustworthy Muslims linking the current age with that of the earliest *umma*.

DOCUMENT

Al-Mawardi and al-Hilli

At his death, the Prophet left his followers without explicit instructions on leadership and governance of the umma. The question of political authority became hotly contested, which resulted ultimately in the major division between Sunni and Shi'i Muslims that has prevailed to this day. Below are two important later interpretations of political legitimacy by an influential Sunni official, al-Mawardi (974–1058), and a leading Shi'a theologian, al-Hilli (1250–1326).

- **WHAT** are the essential characteristics of a ruler according to both thinkers? What do these thinkers have in common, and what are their differences?

AL-MAWARDI

The *Imamate*: God, whose power be glorified, has instituted a chief of the Community as a successor to Prophethood and to protect the Community and assume the guidance of its affairs. Thus the *Imamate* is a principle on which stands the bases of the religious Community and by which its general welfare is regulated, so that the common good is assured by it. . . .

Thus the obligatory nature of the *Imamate* is established, and it is an obligation performed for all by a few, like fighting in a holy war, or the study of the religious sciences. . . .

As for those persons fitted for the *Imamate*, the conditions related to them are seven: . . . Justice in all its characteristics. . . . Knowledge requisite for independent judgment (*ijtihad*) about revealed and legal matters. . . . Soundness of the senses in hearing, sight, and speech, in a degree to accord with their normal functioning. . . . Soundness of the members from any defect that would prevent freedom of movement and agility. . . . Judgment conducive to the governing of subjects and administering matters of general welfare. . . . Courage and bravery to protect Muslim territory and wage the *jihad* against the enemy. . . . Pedigree: he must be of the tribe of Quraysh, since there has come down an explicit statement on this, and the consensus has agreed . . . .

He must maintain the Religion according to the principles established and agreed upon by the earliest . . . .

Al-Hilli

He who is worthy of the *Imamate* is a person appointed and specified by God and His Prophet, not any chance person; it is not possible that there be more than one person at any one period who is worthy . . . . Hence the *Imamate* is *lutf* [God's kindness to humans in guiding them]. . . .

It is necessary that the *Imâm* be immune to sin; otherwise he would need a Imâm, or spiritual guide, and that is impossible. And also if he committed sin, he would lose his place in men's hearts, and the value of his appointment would be nullified. And because he is the guardian of the law . . . he must be immune to sin . . . which no one perceives but God the most high. Hence . . . the *Imâm* must be appointed by God, not by the people.

Agreement has been reached that in appointing the *Imâm* the specification can be made by God and His Prophet, or by a previous *Imâm* . . . . [There is disagreement over] whether or not his appointment can be in a way that is other than specification (by God and the Prophet). He who knows the unseen make[s] it known. And that comes about in two ways: (1) by making it known to someone immune to sin, such as the Prophet, and then he tells us of the *Imâm*'s immunity to sin and of this appointment; (2) by the appearance of miracles wrought by his hand to prove his veracity in claiming the *Imamate*. Sunnis say that whenever the people [*umma*] acknowledge any person as chief, and are convinced of his ability and his power increases, he becomes the *Imâm*.

The *Imâm* [must] be absolutely the best of the people of his age, because he takes precedence over all. . . .

Source: From *The Middle East and Islamic World Reader* by Marvin Gettlemen and Stuart Schar © 2003 by Marvin Gettlemen and Stuart Schar. Reprinted by permission of Grove Press.

A Closer Look

The Dome of the Rock, Jerusalem (Interior)

The Dome of the Rock (completed in 691) is the earliest monumental structure of Islamic architecture. Apparently the earliest architectural and artistic project of the Ummayad Dynasty, it was constructed on the "Temple Mount" sacred site created in Herodian times. The best interpretation today is that it was built to signal prominently the success of Islam as the completion of Jewish and Christian monotheistic religion. Its magnificent mosaic tile ornamentation has been renewed on its exterior in Ottoman times (see exterior photograph on p. 253), but inside, as in this photograph, we see much of the original decoration in all its magnificence, along with the later marble covering sheathing walls, piers, and spandrels. The octagonal shape follows that of the Byzantine *martyria* and the wooden dome, stone and brick masonry, and careful symmetry of design derive from Byzantine church architecture.

The decorative mosaics display vegetal designs that are mixed with jewels, crowns, and breastplates, many from Sasanid and Byzantine insignia. The latter may well be regalia of kings defeated by the Muslims, while the trees depicted may recall Solomon's palace in Jerusalem, which is often referred to in early medieval traditions. Barely visible here are also bird wings, palmettes, and floral composites of Persian design that run around the interior.

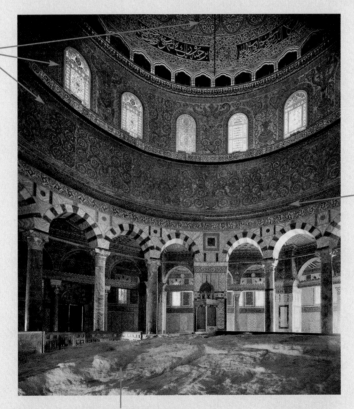

The long gold mosaic written inscription running completely around the building below the ceiling of the dome contains carefully chosen Qur'anic passages about Christ, none of which contradict Christian doctrine. This may be the earliest medieval use of writing in building decoration.

The rock over which the entire dome is built became in Muslim tradition the spot from which Muhammad's night ascension to the heavens (treated in the sources sometimes as visionary, sometimes as physical) began, although an older Muslim tradition marks it as the spot from which God returned to heaven after creating the earth.

Questions

1. Is the Dome of the Rock a late-antique Byzantine building (perhaps designed and built in part by Christian artisans), or a signal Muslim structure that uses pre-Islamic themes and motifs but combines them in novel ways to signal/symbolize Islam's reform of monotheism and the new Islamic imperium? Or could it be both? Discuss.

The Dome of the Rock in Jerusalem.
An early example of Islamic architecture, it dates from 685 and the first wave of Arab expansion. It is built over the rock from which Muslims believe Muhammad had a heavenly ascension experience and on which Jews believe Abraham prepared to sacrifice Isaac. The Dome of the Rock has symbolic significance for Muslims because the site is associated with the life of the Prophet. For a few years of Muhammad's time in Medina, Muslims even faced Jerusalem when they prayed, before a new Qur'anic revelation changed the direction to Mecca.

What are other examples of sites that are important, for different reasons, to two or more faiths?

These scholars came to be known as ***ulama*** ("persons of right knowledge"). Their personal legal opinions and collective discussions of issues, from theological doctrine to criminal punishments, established a basis for religious and social order. By the ninth century they had largely defined the understanding of the divine law, or *Shari'a*, that Muslims ever after have held to be definitive for legal, social, commercial, political, ritual, and moral concerns. This understanding and the methods by which it was derived form the Muslim science of jurisprudence (*fiqh*), the core discipline of Islamic learning.

The centers of *ulama* activity were Medina, Mecca, and especially Iraq (Basra and Kufa, later Baghdad), then Khorasan, Syria, North Africa, Spain, and Egypt. In Umayyad times, the *ulama* criticized caliphal rule when it strayed too far from Muslim norms. Gradually the *ulama* became a new elite identified with the upper class of each regional society under Islamic rule. Caliphs and their governors regularly sought their advice, but often only for moral or legal (the two are, in Muslim view, the same) sanction of a contemplated (or accomplished) action. Some *ulama* gave dubious sanctions and compromised themselves. Yet incorruptible *ulama* were seldom persecuted for their opinions (unless they supported sectarian rebellions), mostly because of their status and influence among rank-and-file Muslims.

Thus, without building a formal clergy, Muslims developed a workable moral-legal system based on a formally trained, if informally organized, scholarly elite and a

ulama

"Persons with correct knowledge." The Islamic scholarly elite who served a social function similar to the Christian clergy.

QUICK REVIEW

Religious Authority of the *Ulama*

- Opinions of *ulama* became the basis for religious and social order
- *Ulama* became a social and political elite
- *Ulama* were rarely prosecuted for their opinions

Ritual Worship. These illustrations show the sequence of movement prescribed for the ritual worship of *Salat* that each Muslim should perform five times a day. Various words of praise, prayer, and Qur'an recitation accompany each position and movement. The ritual symbolizes complete obedience to God as the one, eternal, omnipotent Lord of the universe.

How do the rituals depicted here convey an impression of submission?

tradition of concern with religious ideals in matters of public affairs and social order. If the caliphs and their deputies were seldom paragons of piety and were often ruthless, they had at least to act with circumspection and support pious standards publicly. Thus the *ulama* shared leadership in Muslim societies with the rulers, even if unequally—an enduring pattern in Islamic states.

THE *UMMA*

A strength of the Qur'anic message was its universality. By the time of the first conquests, the new state was already so rooted in Islamic ideals that non-Arab converts had to be accepted, even if it meant loss of tax revenue. The social and political status of new converts was, however, clearly second to that of Arabs. Umar had organized the army register, or **diwan**, according to tribal precedence in conversion to, or (for Christian Arab tribes) fighting for, Islam. The *diwan* served as the basis for distributing and taxing the new wealth, which perpetuated Arab precedence. The new garrisons, which rapidly became urban centers of Islamic culture, kept the Arabs enough apart that they were not simply absorbed into the cultural patterns or traditions of the new lands. The dominance of the Arabic language was ensured by the centrality of the Qur'an in Muslim life and the notion of its perfect Arabic form, together with the increasing administrative use of Arabic to replace Aramaic, Greek, Middle Persian, or Coptic.

Non-Arab converts routinely attached themselves to Arab tribes as "clients," which assured protection and a place in the *diwan*. Still, this meant accepting a permanent second-class citizenship. Although many non-Arabs, especially Persians, mastered Arabic and prospered, dissatisfaction among client Muslims led to uprisings against caliphal authority. Persian-Arab tensions were especially strong in Umayyad and early Abbasid times. Nevertheless, a Persian cultural renaissance eventually raised the Islamicized, or modern Persian language to high status in Islamic culture. Consequently, it profoundly affected Islamic religion, art, and literature.

Caliphal administration joined with the evolution of legal theory and practice and the consolidation of religious norms to give stability to the emerging Islamic society. So powerful was the Muslim vision of society that, upon the demise of a caliph, or even a dynasty such as the Umayyads, the *umma* and the caliphal office continued. There were, however, conflicting notions of that vision. In the first three Islamic centuries, two major interpretations crystallized that reflected idealistic interpretations of the *umma*, its leadership, and membership. When neither proved practical, they became minority visions that continued to fire the imaginations of some but failed to win broad-based support. A third, "centrist," vision found favor with the majority because it spoke to a wide spectrum and accommodated inevitable compromises in the cause of Islamic unity.

The most radical idealists traced their origin to the first civil war (656–661). They were the Kharijites, or "seceders" from Ali's camp, because, in their view, he compromised with his enemies. The Kharijites' demanded that the Muslim polity be based on strict Qur'anic principles. They espoused total equality of the faithful and held that the leader of the *umma* should be the best Muslim, whoever that might be. They took a rigorist view of membership in the *umma*: Anyone who committed a major sin was no longer a Muslim. Extreme Kharijites called on true Muslims to rebel against the morally compromised reigning caliph. The extremist groups were constant rallying points for opposition to the Umayyads and the Abbasids. More moderate Kharijites tolerated less-than-ideal Muslims and caliphs, yet they retained a strong sense of the moral imperatives of Muslim duty. Their ideals influenced wider Muslim pietism and even today moderate Kharijite groups survive in Oman and North Africa.

diwan
High governmental body in many Islamic states.

Ashura. As Shi'ites, Iranians stage elaborate passion plays, or *Taziyehs*, during the Ashura commemorations of the martyrdom of Imam Hussein b. 'Ali. These plays are performed annually during the first ten days of the Muslim lunar month of Muharram. Here is the culminating scene from a *Taziyeh* in Tehran on December 27, 2009, with one of the warriors of the Umayyad caliph Yazid standing over the body of the martyred Hussein, son of 'Ali and grandson of the Prophet Muhammad, who was slain at Kerbala on 10 Muharram, 680.

What are the basic beliefs of Shi'ites?

A second position was defined largely in terms of leadership of the *umma*. Muhammad had no surviving sons. Ali, who was both Muhammad's son-in-law and his cousin, claimed the caliphate in 656. Ali's blood tie with Muhammad was augmented, for many, by belief in the Prophet's designation of him as the next true Muslim leader, or *imam*. Ali's claim was contested by Mu'awiya in the first Islamic civil war. When Mu'awiya took over after a Kharijite murdered Ali in 661, many of Ali's followers felt that Islamic affairs had gone awry. The roots of the "partisans of Ali" (*Shi'at Ali*, or simply the **Shi'a**, or *Shi'ites*) go back to Ali's murder and especially to that of his son Husayn at Karbala, in Iraq, at the hands of Umayyad troops in 680.

Numerous rebellions in Umayyad times rallied around a person who claimed to be a true successor. The Abbasids based their right to the caliphate on membership in Muhammad's clan of Hashim. The major Shi'ite pretenders who emerged in the ninth and tenth centuries based their claims on both the Prophet's designation and their descent from Ali and Fatima, Muhammad's daughter. They also stressed the idea of a divinely inspired knowledge passed on by Muhammad to his designated heirs. Thus the true Muslim was the faithful follower of the *imams*, who carried Muhammad's blood and spiritual authority.

Shi'ites saw Ali's assassination and the massacre of Husayn and his family as proofs of the evil nature of this world's rulers, and as rallying points for true Muslims. Their martyrdom was extended to a line of Alid *imams* that varied among different groups of Shi'ites. True Muslims, like their *imams*, must suffer. But they would be vindicated by a *mahdi*, or "guided one," who would usher in a messianic age and judgment day that would see the faithful rewarded. (In the Sunni tradition, which we discuss next, similar "mahdist" movements arose occasionally as well.)

In later history Shi'ites did rule Islamic states, but only after 1500, in Iran, did Shi'ism prevail as the majority faith in a major state. The Shi'ite vision of the true *umma* has not been able to dominate the larger Islamic world.

Most Muslims ultimately accepted a third, less sharply defined position on leadership and membership in the *umma*. In part a compromise, it proved acceptable both to lukewarm Muslims or pragmatists and to persons of intense piety. To emphasize the correctness of their views, they eventually called themselves *Sunnis*—followers of the tradition (**sunna**) established by the Prophet and the Qur'an. Sunnis encompass a wide range of reconcilable ideas and groups. They have made up the broad middle spectrum of Muslims who tend to put communal solidarity and maintenance of the Islamic polity above purist adherence to particular tenets. They have been inclusivist rather than exclusivist, a trait that has typified the Islamic (unlike the Jewish or Christian) community through most of its history.

This centrist position provided the most workable basis for the new Islamic state. Its basic ideas were threefold: (1) The *umma* is theocratic, a state under divine authority, which translates into a nomocracy under the authority the Shari'a. The sources of guidance are, first, the Qur'an; second, Muhammad's precedent; and, third and fourth, the interpretive efforts and consensus of the Muslims (in practice, of the *ulama*). (2) The caliph is the absolute temporal ruler, charged with administering and defending the Abode of Islam and protecting

Shi'a
The minority of Muslims who trace their beliefs from the caliph Ali who was assassinated in 661 C.E.

sunna
Meaning "tradition." The dominant Islamic group whose followers are called Sunnis.

CHRONOLOGY

ORIGINS AND EARLY DEVELOPMENT OF ISLAM

ca. 570	Birth of Muhammad
622	The Hegira (*Hijra*, "emigration") of Muslims to Yathrib (henceforward *al-Madina*, "The City [of the Prophet]"); beginning of Muslim calendar
632	Death of Muhammad; Abu Bakr becomes first "successor" (*Khalifa*, caliph) to leadership, reigns 632–634
634–644	Caliphate of Umar; rapid conquests in Egypt and Iran
644–656	Caliphate of Uthman (member of Umayyad clan); more conquests; Qur'an text established; growth of sea power
656–661	Contested caliphate of Ali; first civil war
661–680	Caliphate of Mu'awiya; founding of Umayyad Dynasty (661–750); capital moved to Damascus; more expansion

Muslim norms; he possesses no greater authority than other Muslims in matters of faith. (3) A person who professes to be Muslim by witnessing that "There is no god but God, and Muhammad is his Messenger" should be considered a Muslim (because "only God knows what is in the heart"), and not even a mortal sin excludes such a person automatically from the *umma*.

Under increasingly influential *ulama* leadership, these and other basic premises of Muslim community became the theological underpinnings internationally of both the caliphal state and the majority Islamic social order.

THE HIGH CALIPHATE

WHY DID the caliphal empire decline?

•●•⌐Read the Document
Baghdad: City of Wonders
at **myhistorylab.com**

mamluk Slave soldiers who converted to Islam, the *mamluks* eventually became a powerful military caste and even governed Egypt from 1250 to 1517.

The consolidation of the caliphal institution began with the victory of the Umayyad caliph Abd al-Malik in 692 in a second civil war. The ensuing century and a half mark the era of the "high caliphate," the politically strong, culturally vibrant, wealthy, and centralized institution that flourished first under the Umayyads in Damascus and then in the Abbasid capital of Baghdad.[3] The "golden age" of caliphal power and splendor came in the first century of Abbasid rule, during the caliphates of the fabled Harun al-Rashid (786–809) and his son, al-Ma'mun (813–833).

THE ABBASID STATE

The Abbasids' revolution effectively ended Arab dominance as well as Umayyad ascendancy (except in Spain). The shift of the imperial capital from Damascus to the new "city of peace" built at Baghdad on the Tigris (762–766) symbolized the geographic shift in cultural and political orientation under the new regime. In line with this, more Persians entered the bureaucracy. The Abbasids' disavowal of Shi'ite hopes for a divinely inspired imamate reflected their determination to gain the support of a broad spectrum of Muslims, even if they still stressed their descent from al-Abbas (ca. 565–653), uncle of both Muhammad and Ali.

Whereas the Umayyads had relied on Syrian Arab forces, the Abbasids used Arabs and Persians as well as provincial mercenaries for their main troops. Beginning in the ninth century, they enlisted slave soldiers (**mamluks**), mostly Turks from the northern steppes, as their personal troops. The officers of these troops, themselves *mamluks*, soon seized positions of power in the central and provincial bureaucracies and the army. Eventually the caliphs were dominated by their *mamluk* officers. This domination led to increasing alienation of the Muslim populace from their own rulers. This was evident in Iraq itself, where unrest with his overbearing Turkish guard led the Abbasid caliph to remove the government from Baghdad to the new city of Samarra 60 miles up the Tigris, where it remained from 836 to 892 (see Map 10–2).

The Great Mosque of Samarra. Built in the mid-ninth century by the Abbasid caliph al-Mutawakkil, this Friday, or congregational, mosque has a prayer space larger than nine football fields, making it the largest such enclosed space in the Islamic world. The style of the minaret recalls the ziggurats of ancient Babylon.

Why was early Abbasid rule attractive to large numbers of people?

SOCIETY

The deep division between rulers and populace—the functionally secular state and its subjects—became typical of Islamic societies. However, even while provincial rulers' independence reduced Abbasid central power after the mid-ninth century, such rulers nominally recognized caliphal authority. This gave them legitimacy as guardians of the Islamic socioreligious order, which meanwhile found its real cohesiveness in the Muslim ideals being standardized and propagated by the *ulama*.

---

[3]This periodization of early Islamic government follows that of M. G. S. Hodgson, *The Venture of Islam*, Vol. 1 (Chicago: University of Chicago Press, 1984), pp. 217–236.

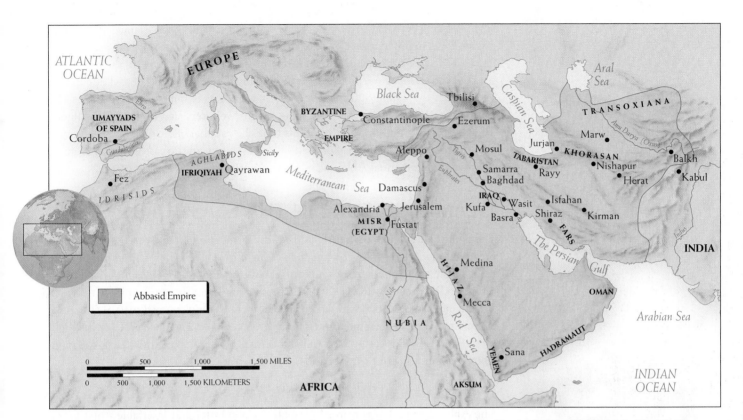

MAP 10–2. **The Abbasid Empire, ca. 900 C.E.** A great diversity of peoples and nations were united by the Abbasids. Their capital at Baghdad became the center of a trading network that linked India, Africa, and China.

Which Muslim regions were not part of the Abbasid Empire and why?

Full conversion of the populace of the Islamic Empire lagged behind centralization of political power and development of Islamic socioreligious institutions. Iraq and Iran saw the fullest Islamization of local elites before the mid-twelfth century, followed by Spain, North Africa, and Syria. Conversion and fuller Islamization increased Muslim self-confidence and diminished the need for centralized caliphal power.[4]

DECLINE

The eclipse of the caliphal empire was foreshadowed at the outset of Abbasid rule when one of the last Umayyads fled west to Spain, where he founded a Spanish Islamic state (756–1030) that produced the spectacular Moorish culture of Spain. The Spanish Umayyads grew so strong that they claimed the title of caliph in 929. In all the Abbasid provinces, regional governments were always potential independent states. In North Africa in 801 Harun al-Rashid's governor set up his own state in modern Tunisia. In Egypt, the Fatimids set up Shi'ite rule in 969 and claimed to be the only true caliphate.

In the East, Iranian lands grew harder for Baghdad to control. Beginning in 821 in Khorasan, Abbasid governors or rebels started independent dynasties repeatedly for the next two centuries, and the caliph usually had to recognize them. Among the longest-lived of these Iranian dynasties were the Samanids, who ruled at Bukhara as nominal Abbasid vassals from 875 until 999. They gave northeastern Iran a long period of economic and political security from Turkish steppe invaders. Under their

QUICK REVIEW

Abbasid State

- ◆ Ruled from Baghdad
- ◆ Arab dominance replaced by Eastern, especially Persian, influence
- ◆ Leaders of slave soldiers (*mamluks*) gained power
- ◆ Splendid court left rich cultural legacy

[4]Richard W. Bulliet, *Conversion to Islam in the Medieval Period* (Cambridge, MA: Harvard University Press, 1979), especially pp. 7–15, 128–138.

aegis, Persian poetry and Arabic scientific studies began a Persian Islamic cultural renaissance and an influential scientific tradition.

Of greatest consequence for the Abbasid caliphate was the rise in the mountains south of the Caspian of a Shi'ite clan, the Buyids, who took over Abbasid rule in 945. Henceforth the caliph and his descendants were largely puppets in the hands of a Buyid "commander" (*emir*). In 1055 the Buyids were replaced by the more famous, Turkish-speaking Seljuk **sultans**. By this time the caliphal office had long been under the control of the ruler in Baghdad, and this was to remain the case until the Mongols destroyed even nominal Abbasid caliphal authority in 1258 (see Chapter 12).

sultans Rulers who have almost complete sovereignty over a certain domain without claiming the title of caliph.

WHAT WERE the main achievements of "classical" Islamic culture?

ISLAMIC CULTURE IN THE CLASSICAL ERA

The pomp and splendor of the Abbasid court became the stuff of legends, such as those preserved much later in *A Thousand and One Nights*. Their rich cultural legacy was made possible by a strong army and central government and vigorous internal and external trade, probably stimulated by the prosperous Tang Chinese Empire with which Islamic lands had overland and maritime contact. Material factors, such as the introduction of paper manufacture from China through Samarkand about 750, or the flight of Byzantine scholars east to new Abbasid centers of learning, contributed to the intellectual vibrancy of the early Abbasid era.

INTELLECTUAL TRADITIONS

The Abbasid heyday was marked by sophisticated tastes and insatiable thirst for all knowledge. An Arab historian called Baghdad "the market to which the wares of the sciences and arts were brought, where wisdom was sought as a man seeks after his stray camels, and whose judgment of values was accepted by the whole world." Contacts (primarily among intellectuals) between Muslims and Christian, Jewish, Zoroastrian, and other "protected" communities contributed to the cosmopolitanism of the age. Some older intellectual traditions experienced a revival. Philosophy, astronomy, mathematics, medicine, and other natural sciences enjoyed strong interest and patronage. In Islamic usage, philosophy and the sciences were subsumed under *falsafa* (from Greek *philosophia*). Islamic culture took over the tradition of rational inquiry from the Hellenic world and preserved and developed it when Europe was a cultural backwater.

An Illustration from *The Maqamat* of al Hariri (d. 1122), a masterpiece of Arabic literature of the later Middle Ages. Its entertaining stories, written in rhymed prose, have passed into popular lore in the Islamic world.

What are some characteristics of Arabic literature?

C H R O N O L O G Y	
"CLASSICAL" PERIOD OF THE HIGH CALIPHATE	
786–809	Caliphate of Harun al-Rashid; apogee of caliphal power
813–833	Caliphate of al-Ma'mun; patronage of translations of Greek, Sanskrit, and other works into Arabic; first heavy reliance on slave soldiers (*mamluks*)
875	Rise of Samanid power at Bukhara; patronage of Persian poetry paves way for Persian literary renaissance
909	Rise of Shi'ite Fatimid Dynasty in North Africa
945–1055	Buyid emirs rule the eastern empire at Baghdad; Abbasid caliphs become largely figureheads
1055	Buyids replaced by Seljuk sultans as effective rulers at Baghdad and custodians of the caliphate

Arabic translations of Greek and Sanskrit works stimulated progress in astronomy and medicine. Translation reached its peak in al-Ma'mun's new academy headed by a Nestorian Christian, Hunayn ibn Ishaq (d. 873), noted for his medical and Greek learning. There were Arabic translations of everything from the Greek works of Galen, Ptolemy, Euclid, Aristotle, Plato, and the Neo-Platonists to Indian Sanskrit fables earlier translated into Middle Persian under the Sasanids. Such translations stimulated not only Arabic learning, but later also that of the less advanced European world.

LANGUAGE AND LITERATURE

Arabic language and literature developed greatly in the new empire. A significant genre of Arabic writing emerged. Known as *adab*, or "manners" literature, it included essays and didactic literature influenced by Persian letters. Poetry also flourished by building on the tradition of the Arabic ode, or **qasida**. Grammar was central to the interpretation of the Qur'an that occupied the *ulama* and undergirded an emerging religious-learning curriculum. Historical, geographical, and biographical writing became major Arabic genres. They owed much to the ancient accounts of "the battle days of the Arabs" but sought to record the lives of the Prophet and Companions, and then those of subsequent generations. Such records of persons were crucial to judging the reliability of the "chains" of transmitters accompanying each traditional report, or **hadith**. A *hadith* reports words or actions ascribed to Muhammad and the Companions; it became the chief source of Muslim legal and religious norms alongside the Qur'an, as well as the basic unit of most prose genres. The work of al-Shafi'i (d. 820) on legal reasoning was the shining exemplar of the many collections of the *hadith* that were mined by preachers and interpreters of the law.

qasida
Some of the most elaborate poems in the world, they generally run 50–100 lines, have a single, unifying theme, regular rhyme and meter, and speak in praise of a ruler or an idea.

hadith
A saying or action ascribed to Muhammad.

ART AND ARCHITECTURE

In art and architecture the Abbasid era saw the crystallization of a "classical" Islamic style by about 1000 C.E. Except for ceramics and calligraphy, most Islamic art and architecture had clear antecedents in Greco-Roman, Byzantine, or Persian art. But older forms and motifs were now used in new ways and combinations, and they spread to new locales—generally from east (especially the Fertile Crescent) to west (Syria, Egypt, North Africa, and Spain). Sasanid stucco decoration techniques and designs turned up, for example, in Egypt and North Africa. Chronologically, urban Iraq developed an Islamic art first, then made its influence felt east and west, whether in Bukhara or in Syria and North Africa. Also new were the combination and elaboration of discrete forms, as in the case of the colonnade (or hypostyle) mosque or complex arabesque designs.

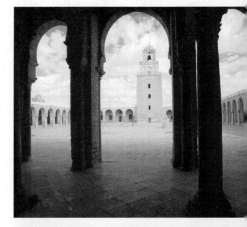

Muslims had reason to be self-confident about their faith and culture. Most monuments of the age express the distinctiveness they felt. Particular formal items, such as calligraphic motifs and inscriptions on buildings, came to characterize Islamic architecture and define its functions. Most striking was the avoidance of pictures or icons in

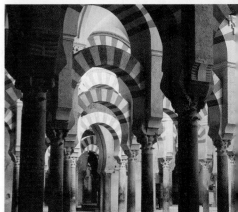

The Congregational Mosque. Two examples of the finest congregational mosques of the classical Islamic world. The large courtyards and pillared halls of these buildings were intended not only for worship, but also for mass community gatherings for official communications or mustering troops in time of war. Their splendor announced the presence and power of Islamic rule. The top photo shows the Great Mosque at Qayrawan in modern Tunisia, built during the eighth and ninth centuries. The bottom photo shows the Spanish Umayyad mosque in Córdoba, built in the eighth to tenth centuries in a series of roofed extensions—unlike the mosque of Qayrawan, which has only one great hall and covered colonnades around its central courtyard.

(A) Werner Forman Archive, Art Resource, New York; (B) Adam Lubroth, Art Resource, New York.

How does the layout of these mosques comment on the role of the community in early Islam?

The Qur'an. Gold-embellished page from an eighth- or ninth-century Qur'an in Kufic script (23.8 × 35.5 cm). The earliest Qur'ans were oriented horizontally and lettered in angular Kufic script (named for the city of Kufa in Iraq).

Arabic Manuscript: 30.60 Page from a Koran, 8th–9th century. Kufic script. H: 23.8 x W: 35.5 cm. Courtesy of the Freer Gallery of Art, Smithsonian Institution, Washington, DC: Purchase, F1930.60r.

Why would a Qur'an be written in an artful script, in a manuscript incorporating gold?

public art. This was, of course, in line with the Muslim aversion both to any hint of idolatry and to the strongly iconic Byzantine Christian art. Although this iconoclasm later diminished, it was a telling expression of the general thrust of Muslim faith and the culture it animated. Overall, the Muslims' artistic achievements before the year 1000 impress us with a quality that is distinctively and "classically" Islamic, whatever the details of particular examples.[5]

SUMMARY

 WHAT WAS the Qur'anic message as expressed to Muhammad?

Origins and Early Development. The Prophet Muhammad (ca. 570–632) was the founder of Islam. Born in the Arabian commercial city of Mecca, he was influenced by contact with Arab Christians and with Jews. At about age 40, he had a religious experience during which, Muslims believe, God's messenger angel Gabriel repeatedly performed recitation (*qur'an*) of God's word to him. The message of the Qur'an was (1) social justice and worship of the one true God are required of every person; (2) at the end of time, people will be resurrected and judged by God, who will reward or punish them according to how they have lived; and (3) the proper response to God is submission (*islam*) to his will by becoming a *muslim* ("one who submits"). *page 242*

 HOW DID the status of women improve under Islam?

Women in Early Islamic Society. Islamic law emphasizes community, and family is the foundation of community. The Qur'an recognizes many more rights for women than traditional Arabian custom permitted, but the social vision expressed in the Qur'an is still fundamentally patriarchal. *page 246*

 WHY WAS Islam able to expand rapidly?

Early Islamic Conquests. By the time of Muhammad's death, his followers had conquered all of Arabia. Under his successors, the caliphs, Muslim Arab armies conquered most of the Near East, North Africa, Spain, Sasanid Iran, and northwest India. Many of the peoples of these territories welcomed Islamic rule as liberation from Persian or Byzantine domination and eventually converted to Islam and became part of the *umma*, the community of Islamic believers. *page 247*

 WHAT ROLES did the caliphate and *ulama* play in Islamic states?

The New Islamic World Order. Disputes over the succession to the Prophet divided Muslims. The *ulama*, Islamic religious and legal scholars, played a prominent part in Islamic society as interpreters of Islamic tradition and law. Islamic unity and preservation of the community (*umma*) withstood the idealistic challenges of the Kharijites and the Shi'ites, largely thanks to the broad appeal of centrist Sunni interpretations of the faith. *page 249*

 WHY DID the caliphal empire decline?

The High Caliphate. Under the Abbasid caliphs who ruled from the city of Baghdad, the Islamic Empire began to splinter. Large parts of the empire—Spain, North Africa, Iran—seceded. Military commanders (*emirs*) in Baghdad reduced the caliphs to mere figureheads by the tenth century. *page 256*

[5]Grabar, *Formation of Islamic Art*, (New Haven: Yale University Press, 1973), pp. 1–103, 206–213.

WHAT WERE the main achievements of "classical" Islamic culture?

Islamic Culture in the Classical Era. Islamic culture enjoyed its "classical" phase under the Abbasids. Arabic translations of Greek and Sanskrit works stimulated progress in astronomy and medicine. Arabic literature and poetry flourished. As the sacred medium of God's final revelation, the Arabic language spread throughout the Islamic world. Arabic artists and architects built on Greco-Roman, Byzantine, and Persian traditions to develop a distinctive Islamic style in decoration, painting, and architecture. *page 258*

KEY TERMS

caliphate (KAY-liff-AYT) (p. 250)

diwan (dih-WAHN) (p. 254)

emir (ee-MEER) (p. 250)

hadith (ha-DEETH) (p. 259)

Hajj (HADJ) (p. 245)

hegira (hih-JEYE-rah) (p. 245)

imam (ih-MAHM) (p. 250)

islam (p. 244)

jihad (jih-HAHD) (p. 248)

Ka'ba (KAAH-ba) (p. 242)

mamluk (MAM-look) (p. 256)

qasida (kuh-SEE-duh) (p. 259)

qur'an (koh-RAN) (p. 244)

Shi'a (SHEE-ah) (p. 255)

sultans (p. 258)

sunna (SOO-nah) (p. 255)

ulama (OO-luh-MAAH) (p. 253)

umma (UHM-uh) (p. 245)

REVIEW QUESTIONS

1. Describe Arabian society before Islam. What were the prime targets of the Qur'anic message in that society?

2. What are the main features of the Islamic worldview? How do Islamic ideas about history, salvation, law, social justice, and other key issues compare to those of Christianity and Judaism?

3. What rights for women did the Qur'an support that were not widely accepted in Arab society? In what areas can the Qur'an be seen as limiting women's rights?

4. What were the primary kinds of leadership in the early Islamic polities? To what extent was political and religious leadership separated in different offices and functions?

5. Discuss the conversion of subject populations in the early centuries of Islamic empire. What were the incentives and obstacles to conversion?

6. As time passed after Muhammad's death and Muslim territory expanded, were Muslims successful in preserving the community envisioned in the Qur'an? Discuss why or why not.

7. Why were the initial Arab armies so successful?

8. Why was the imperial caliphal state eclipsed? What were some of the lasting accomplishments of the Umayyad and Abbasid empires?

9. What are the doctrinal differences between Kharijites, Shi'ites, and Sunnis? In what sense are Sunnis "centrist"?

10. Discuss the "classical" culture of the golden age of the caliphate. What role did foreign traditions play in it? What were some of its prominent achievements?

Note: To learn more about the topics in this chapter, please turn to the Suggested Readings at the end of the book. For additional sources related to this chapter please see www.myhistorylab.com

 myhistorylab Connections

Reinforce what you learned in this chapter by studying the many documents, images, maps, review tools, and videos available at **www.myhistorylab.com**

Read and Review

✓ **Study** and **Review** Chapter 10

Read the Document *Al-Tabari: Muhammad's Call to Prophecy, p. 243*

Al-Tabari and Ibn Hisham, from "The Founding of the Caliphate," p. 250

Baghdad: City of Wonders, p. 256

View the Image *The Qur'an, p. 244*

Research and Explore

See the Map *Expansion of Islam, p. 243*

 Hear the **Audio**

Hear the audio file for Chapter 10 at **www.myhistorylab.com**

11

The Byzantine Empire and Western Europe to 1000

((•—Hear the Audio for Chapter 11 at www.myhistorylab.com

Hagia Sophia. One of the greatest achievements of Byzantine civilization, Hagia Sophia (the Church of Holy Wisdom) was completed in 537 C.E. by Anthemius of Tralles and Isidore of Miletus. Circled with numerous windows, the great dome floods the hall with light and, together with the church's many other windows, mosaics, and open spaces, gives the interior a remarkable airiness and luminosity. After the Turkish conquest of Constantinople in 1453, Hagia Sophia was transformed into a mosque.

What impression do you get from looking at this space? Do you think the architects wished to convey this feeling?

The early Middle Ages (or early medieval period) marks the birth of Europe. Greco-Roman culture combined with Germanic culture and an evolving Christianity to create distinctive political and cultural forms. In government, religion, and language, what had been the northern and western provinces of the Roman Empire grew apart from the eastern Byzantine world and a Mediterranean-based Islamic Arabia.

German tribes had been settling peacefully around the Roman Empire since the first century B.C.E., but in the fourth century C.E. they began to migrate directly into it from the north and east. During the fifth century they turned fiercely against their hosts, largely because the Romans treated them so cruelly. To the south, Arab dominance transformed the Mediterranean and challenged Western trade with the East. Western Europe became insular. Forced to manage by themselves, western Europeans learned to develop their native resources. The reign of Charlemagne saw a modest renaissance of antiquity, aided by Byzantium and Arabia. The peculiar social and political forms that emerged during this period—manorialism and feudalism—successfully coped with unprecedented chaos on local levels, while nourishing the growth of distinctively Western institutions. ■

THE END OF THE WESTERN ROMAN EMPIRE

In the early fifth century, Italy and Rome suffered a series of devastating blows. In 410 the Visigoths sacked Rome. In 452 the Huns, led by Attila—known to contemporaries as the "scourge of God"—invaded Italy. And in 455 Rome was overrun by the Vandals.

By the mid-fifth century, power in western Europe had passed to barbarian chieftains. In 476, the traditional date given for the fall of the Roman Empire, the barbarian

HOW DID the Byzantine Empire continue the legacy of the Roman Empire?

THE EARLY MIDDLE AGES

In western Europe, the centuries between 400 and 1000 witnessed both the decline of Classical civilization and the birth of a new European civilization. Beginning with the fifth century, a series of barbarian invasions separated western Europe culturally from its Classical age. This prolonged separation was unique to western Europe. Along with the invasions themselves and the new cultural traits they brought into Europe, it was pivotal to the development of European civilization. Although some important works and concepts survived from antiquity due largely to the Christian church, Western civilization labored for centuries to recover its rich classical past in "renaissances" stretching into the sixteenth century. Out of this mixture of barbarian and surviving (or recovered) classical culture, Western civilization was born. With the aid of a Christian church eager to restore order and centralized rule, the Carolingians created a new, albeit fragile, imperial tradition. But Western society remained highly fragmented politically and economically during the Early Middle Ages. Meanwhile, many of the world's other great civilizations of the first millennium C.E. were peaking.

In China, particularly in the seventh and eighth centuries, Tang Dynasty rulers also sought ways to secure their borders against foreign expansion, mainly pastoral nomads. China at this time was far more cosmopolitan and politically unified than western Europe, and also centuries ahead in technology. By the tenth century, the Chinese were printing with movable type, an invention the West did not achieve until the fifteenth century, and then very likely borrowed in prototype from China. The effective authority of Chinese rulers extended far beyond their immediate centers of government. The Tang Dynasty held sway over their empire in a way Carolingian rulers could only imagine.

In Japan, the Yamato court (300–680), much like the court of the Merovingians and Carolingians, struggled to unify and control the countryside. Shintō, a religion friendly to royalty, aided the Yamato. As in the West, a Japanese identity evolved through struggle and accommodation with outside cultures, especially with the Chinese, the dominant influence on Japan between the seventh and twelfth centuries. But foreign cultural influence, again as in the West, never managed to eradicate the

Odovacer (ca. 434–493) deposed the last Western Roman emperor. The Eastern emperor Zeno (r. 474–491) recognized Odovacer's authority in the West, and Odovacer acknowledged Zeno as sole emperor, contenting himself to serve as Zeno's Western viceroy. By the end of the fifth century the Ostrogoths had settled in Italy, the Franks in northern Gaul, the Burgundians in Provence, the Visigoths in southern Gaul and Spain, the Vandals in Africa and the western Mediterranean, and the Angles and Saxons in England (see Map 11–1 on page 266).

The barbarians admired Roman culture and had no desire to destroy it. Except in Britain and northern Gaul, Roman law, government, and language (Latin) coexisted with the new Germanic institutions. Only the Vandals and the Anglo-Saxons refused to profess titular obedience to the emperor in Constantinople.

The Visigoths, the Ostrogoths, and the Vandals were Christians, which helped them accommodate to Roman culture, but they followed the Arian creed, which was considered heretical in the West. Around 500, the Franks converted to the Orthodox, or "Catholic," form of Christianity supported by the bishops of Rome. As we will see, the Franks ultimately dominated most of western Europe, helping convert the Goths and other barbarians to Roman Christianity.

A gradual interpenetration of two strong cultures—a creative tension—marked the period of the Germanic migrations. Despite the Western military defeat, the Goths and the Franks became far more romanized than the Romans were germanized. Latin language, Nicene Christianity, and eventually Roman law and government were to triumph in the West during the Middle Ages.

THE BYZANTINE EMPIRE

Imperial power shifted to the eastern part of the Roman Empire, whose center was the city of Byzantium (modern-day Istanbul). Between 324 and 330, Emperor Constantine the Great rebuilt and renamed the city after himself. Constantinople indigenous culture. By the ninth century a distinctive Sino-Japanese culture existed. Like western Europe, Japan remained a fragmented land during these centuries, despite a certain allegiance and willingness to pay taxes to an imperial court. Throughout Japan, as in western Europe, the basic unit of political control consisted of highly self-conscious and specially devoted armed retainers. A system of lordship and vassalage evolved around bands of local mounted warriors known as samurai. Through this system, local order was maintained in Japan until the fifteenth century. Like the Merovingian and Carolingian courts, the Japanese court had to tolerate strong and independent regional rulers.

While western Europe struggled for political and social order in the fourth and fifth centuries, Indian civilization basked in a golden age under the reign of the Guptas (320–467). In this era of peace and stability, when a vocationally and socially limiting caste system neatly imposed order on Indian society from Brahmans to outcasts, culture, religion, and politics flourished.

In the seventh century, Islamic armies emerged from the Arabian Peninsula, conquered territory from India to Spain by 710, and gave birth to a powerful new international civilization. Cosmopolitan and culturally vibrant, this civilization flourished despite the breakdown of Islamic political unity beginning in the ninth and tenth centuries. Islamic cultural strides in this era overshadowed the modest cultural renaissance in the West under Charlemagne.

Focus Questions

◆ What caused the prolonged separation of western European civilization from its Classical past? What were the consequences of this separation for western Europe?

◆ Which other society most resembled that of western Europe during this period? Why?

◆ While western Europe struggled to regain order, unity, and contact with its Classical past, what was happening in the other great civilizations of the world?

remained the capital of both the old Roman and the new Byzantine Empires until the eighth century, when Charlemagne reclaimed the Western Roman Empire's imperial title. The term *Byzantine* refers to the Greek, Hellenistic, Roman, and Judaic monotheistic elements that distinguish the culture of the East from the Latin West.

The history of the Byzantine Empire has three distinct periods:

1. From the rebuilding of Byzantium as Constantinople in 324, through an early period of expansion and splendor, to the beginning of the Arab expansion and the spread of Islam in 632.

2. A time of sustained contraction and splintering, from 632 to the conquest of Asia Minor by the Saljuq Turks in 1071 or, as some prefer, to the fall of Constantinople to the Western Crusaders in 1204.

3. From either 1071 or 1204 to the catastrophic fall of Constantinople to the Ottoman Turks in 1453, the end of the empire in the East.

THE REIGN OF JUSTINIAN

The first period of Byzantine history (324–632) was by far its greatest, and its pinnacle was the reign of the emperor Justinian (r. 527–565). He ruled with the assistance of his remarkable wife, Theodora. The daughter of a circus bear trainer, Theodora had allegedly been an entertainer and a prostitute

Justinian as Conqueror. A classical ivory carving of Justinian celebrating his conquests in Italy, North Africa, and West Asia, ca. 500 C.E.

What were some of Justinian's nonmilitary achievements?

MAP EXPLORATION

To explore this map further, go to **http://www.myhistorylab.com**

MAP 11–1.   Barbarian Migrations into the West in the Fourth and Fifth Centuries.

The forceful intrusion of Germanic and non-Germanic tribes into the empire from the last quarter of the fourth century through the fifth century made for a constantly changing pattern of movement and relations. The map shows the major routes taken by the usually unwelcome newcomers and the areas most deeply affected by the main groups.

Which part of the Roman Empire was least affected by barbarian migrations?

View the **Image**
Emperor Justinian at **myhistorylab.com**

Read the **Document**
Reign Justinian: Secret History, Procopius
at **myhistorylab.com**

Read the **Document**
Prologue, Corpus Civilis, ca. 530
at **myhistorylab.com**

QUICK REVIEW

Justinian Government

- *Corpus Juris Civilis* collated and revised Roman law
- Close ties between rulers and church
- Empire had many large cities and was the crossroads of Asian and European civilizations

in her youth. She equaled her husband in intelligence and exceeded him in toughness. In 532, when a riot threatened to overthrow their administration, he planned to flee. She convinced him to stay and put down the rebellion by ordering the slaughter of tens of thousands of protesters.

Under Justinian, the empire's strength lay in its more than 1,500 cities. Constantinople was the largest, with perhaps 350,000 inhabitants, and it was the crossroads of Asian and European cultures. Larger provincial cities had populations of approximately 50,000. These towns were administered at first by councils of wealthy local landowners, the *Decurions*. Being heavily taxed, these landowners were prone to rebellion. Consequently, by the sixth century the emperor had replaced them with governors chosen for their personal loyalty. Tighter central control was justified by the need to resist barbarian pressures from the north and east.

Justinian's policy—"one God, one empire, one religion"—was to centralize government by imposing legal and doctrinal conformity throughout his domain. To this end he ordered a codification of existing law. The result was the *Corpus Juris Civilis*, or "Body of Civil Law," organized in four parts. The *Code* revised imperial edicts issued by emperors since the reign of Hadrian (r. 117–138). The *Novellae*, or "New Things," dealt with decrees issued by emperors since 534, including Justinian.

OVERVIEW Barbarian Invasions of the Western Roman Empire

The Germanic tribes—the barbarians—who overran the Western Roman Empire had coexisted with the Romans for centuries in a relationship marked more by the commingling of cultures and trade than by warfare. The arrival of the Huns from the east in the late fourth century, however, caused many of the tribes, beginning with the Visigoths in 376, to flee westward and seek refuge within the empire. They found the western half of the empire weakened by famine, disease, high taxation, and an enfeebled military. The Romans lost control of their frontiers, and in the fifth century, the tribes overran the West and set up their own domains. The following is a list of the most important tribes and the areas they controlled by the year 500.

TRIBES	AREA OF CONTROL
Anglo-Saxons	Most of England
Franks	Northeast France
Burgundians	Eastern-central France
Alemanni	Switzerland
Visigoths	Most of Spain and southern France
Suevi	Northwest Spain
Vandals	North Africa
Ostrogoths	Italy, Austria, Croatia, Slovenia

The *Digest* organized opinions penned by famous jurists, and the *Institutes* was a kind of textbook for scholars. Because Roman law emphasized the authority of a single sovereign, later European rulers found Justinian's collection useful when they struggled to centralize power. Between the Renaissance and the nineteenth century, his code helped shape many governments.

Empress Theodora and her Attendants ca. 547 C.E. A mosaic from the Basilica of S. Vitale in Ravenna, Italy.

Was Theodora typical of powerful women in this era? Explain.

MAP 11–2.   The Byzantine Empire at the Death of Justinian.   The inset shows the empire in 1025, before its losses to the Seljuk Turks.

How did Justinian attempt to re-create the Roman Empire?

Justinian attempted to regain control of the Western Roman Empire, but his success was partial and temporary. He reoccupied Italy, North Africa, and parts of Spain but at a cost that his beleaguered empire could ill afford (see Map 11–2).

Nomadic Avars, Slavs, and Bulgars invaded the lands north and west of Constantinople in the sixth and seventh centuries. The Slavs were converted to Eastern Orthodoxy (Byzantine Christianity) by two learned missionaries sent from Constantinople: the future Saints Cyril and Methodius. They created a Greek-based alphabet adapted to writing the Slavic language. When the Bulgars conquered and absorbed the Slavs, this script was revised; it is now known as Cyrillic or Old Church Slavonic. It facilitated the spread of Byzantine Christianity and culture in eastern Europe and Russia.

During the reign of Emperor Heraclius (r. 610–641), the empire turned east. Heraclius spoke only Greek, not Latin. He spent his entire reign resisting Persian and Islamic invasions, the former successfully, the latter in vain. In 628 he defeated the Persian king Chosroes. After 632, Islamic armies progressively overran the empire. Not until the reign of Leo III of the Isaurian Dynasty (r. 717–740) did the Byzantines repel Arab armies and regain at least most of Asia Minor, but the larger Mediterranean empire was lost forever. The downsized empire was restructured by creating provincial strongholds under the direct authority of imperially appointed generals, allowing a more disciplined and flexible use of military power in time of crisis.

THE IMPORTANCE OF CONSTANTINOPLE

As the capital of the Eastern Roman Empire and an immense commercial network, Constantinople was vital to the Empire and featured prominently in the psyche of its neighbors and enemies. The Byzantines claimed that two-thirds of the world's wealth was concentrated in their capital.[1] Since all the city's economic activity was strictly regulated, a large bureaucratic corpus arose that featured its own aristocracy.[2] This class was soon influential at court and stood counter to the landed nobility, ensuring that the empire never became a feudal order.

Constantinople's riches attracted merchants from all over Europe and the Muslim world. By 1143, Constantinople contained Genoan, Pisan, French, Venetian, Jewish, and Muslim "quarters," or areas reserved for the homes and businesses of outsiders. The existence of such collectives meant that their sponsor nations developed an active interest in the economic affairs of the city, while native Byzantines felt betrayed by their government. This tension affected the political landscape of the entire region. For allowing the masses to exact bloody retribution on the merchant quarters, Andronicus I rose to power and eventually usurped the throne.[3] Constantinople's fame was far-reaching. The Varangian Guard, a fearsome force that served as palace bodyguards, was composed entirely of Scandinavian and English soldiers, young men who had left their homelands to seek their fortune in the "Empress of Cities." The city suffered numerous sieges in its history, with each failed attempt only adding to the perceived glory of success. Constantinople was such an object of fascination to Arab empires that mystical traditions proclaimed the Muslim conquest of Constantinople as one of the six portents of *ashrat al sa'a*, the end of the world.[4]

Ruins of Constantinople. The walls of the city of Constantinople were built in the fifth century and were expanded and improved until the fifteenth century.

What were some of the symbolic roles played by Constantinople?

⊙ See the **Map**

The Byzantine Empire under Justinian at **myhistorylab.com**

THE HEIGHT OF BYZANTINE IMPERIAL POWER IN THE TENTH CENTURY

The military reforms of the seventh and eighth centuries allowed the Byzantine Empire to deal more successfully with its enemies, leading to a period of stability and peace in the middle of the tenth century. Under rulers of the Macedonian Dynasty, founded by Basil I (867-886), the eastern Mediterranean was again under Byzantine control. Bulgarian advances into Byzantine territory were brought to a halt by the fiercest military emperor of the dynasty, Basil II (r. 976-1025), known as the "Bulgar-slayer."

The tenth century became a period of strong imperial rule. Macedonian rule brought forth a flourishing age of art, culture, and literature personified in the period's philosopher-king, Emperor Constantine VII *Porphyrogenitus* (i.e. "born in the 'imperial

[1] Robert de Claris, "La conquête de Constantinople," in *Three Old French Chronicles of the Crusades*, ed. Edward N. Stone (Seattle, WA, 1939), Chapter 81.

[2] George Ostrogorsky, *History of the Byzantine State* (New Brunswick, NJ: Rutgers University Press, 1999), p. 253.

[3] Charles M. Brand, *Byzantium Confronts the West 1180–1204* (Cambridge, MA: Harvard University Press, 1968), p. 41.

[4] Nadia Maria El-Cheikh, *Byzantium Viewed by the Arabs* (London, England: Harvard University Press, 2004), p. 67.

purple' ''), sole ruler from 945 to 959. The University of Constantinople and the intellectuals who attended this institution in the eleventh century were products of the Macedonian revival. They included, most famously, Michael Psellus, the author of *The Chronography*, an account of the reigns of fourteen Byzantine emperors and empresses. Economically speaking, the Macedonian rule was a period of "state-controlled" growth, when imperial legislation restrained the growth of large landowners in order to protect small landowners and peasants.

The military peace that made this revival possible began to dissolve with the loss of the last stronghold of the Byzantine Empire in the West: Bari, a town in southern Italy which fell to the Norman kings of France in 1071. In the same year, Muslim Saljuq Turks destroyed the imperial army at the battle of Manzikert in 1071 and overran Anatolia, the heartland from which Constantinople recruited its soldiers. Thereafter, the Byzantine Empire was forced to fight against enemies on two fronts, while it continued to serve as a bastion of the religious and cultural heritage of the West.

After two decades of steady Turkish advances, the Eastern emperor Alexius I Comnenus (r. 1081–1118) called for Western aid in 1092. Three years later, the West launched the first Crusade. A century later (1204), the Fourth Crusade stopped in Constantinople en route to Jerusalem, but not to rescue the Eastern capital; Latin Crusaders inflicted more damage on Eastern Christendom's holy city than all previous non-Christian invaders had done. (See Chapter 15.)

⊙ See the Map
Byzantium 1000–1100
at **myhistorylab.com**

THE RELIGIOUS DIVERSITY OF CHRISTENDOM

Religious belief alternately served and undermined imperial political unity. In 391, Christianity became the official faith of the Eastern Empire, while all other religions and sects were deemed "demented and insane." The patriarch of Constantinople crowned Byzantine emperors. Patriarchs in other cities received generous endowments of land and gold from rich donors, empowering the church to act as the state's welfare agency. Great wealth and prestige bound the clergy tightly to state service.

Christianity was the dominant faith, but large numbers of Jews lived within the Byzantine Empire. Roman law had protected them, so long as they did not proselytize Christians, but some Byzantine emperors tried to induce or to compel their conversion to Christianity. Neither approach was successful.

Although the state religion was Orthodox Christianity, some Christian heresies attracted large followings and occasionally received imperial support. Justinian, for instance, was passionately orthodox, but Theodora was a Monophysite, a variant of the faith that was popular in the East. Monophysites taught that Christ had a single, immortal nature and was not a union of eternal God and mortal man. Byzantine art portrays Christ, a self-same person with God, as impassive and transcendent, not as a suffering mortal man. The modern Coptic, Syrian, and Armenian churches endorse this belief. It was condemned as a heresy in the West in 451.

Eastern and Western theologians also disagreed on whether the Holy Spirit proceeded from both the Son and the Father. This dispute dates back to the first Ecumenical Council in Nicaea (modern Iznik, a city in western Turkey) convened in 325. There the council established 'The Orthodox Creed' also known as 'The Nicene Creed.' It was adopted with certain changes by the ecumenical council of Constantinople (381) and by subsequent ecumenical councils of the Eastern Orthodox Church. According to the Nicene-Constantinopolitan Creed, the Holy Spirit proceeded from the Father alone, unlike the post-sixth century versions accepted by the

Virgin and Child with Saints and Angels. A sixth-century icon of the Virgin and Child surrounded by warrior saints (Theodore on the left; George on the right) and wary angels. A rare survivor of eighth-century iconoclasm.

What is iconoclasm?

DOCUMENT

The Nicene Creed

The Nicene-Constantinopolitan Creed is the first official pronouncement of the Christian belief system and the first official definition of the Christian "orthodox" faith. As such, the creed distinguished orthodox belief or "correct" belief, from heretical versions.

- **THE NICENE** Creed emphasizes the two natures of Christ. Which "unorthodox" beliefs does this document aim to uproot? Historically, how did the controversy surrounding the term *filioque* arise? Please discuss the significance of the term starting from the Nicene Creed.

"We believe in one God, the Father Almighty, maker of all things visible and invisible; and in one Lord Jesus Christ, the Son of God, the only begotten of his Father, of the substance of the Father, God of God, Light of Light, very God of very God, begotten, not made, being of one substance with the Father. By whom all things were made, both which [are] in heaven and in earth. Who for us men and for our salvation came down [from heaven] and was incarnate and was made man. He suffered and the third day he rose again, and ascended into heaven. And he shall come again to judge both the quick and the dead. And [we believe] in the Holy Ghost. And whosoever shall say that there was a time when the Son of God was not, or that before he was begotten he was not, or that he was made of things that were not, or that he is of a different substance or essence [from the Father] or that he is a creature, or subject to change or [convert] - all that say so the Catholic and Apostolic Church anathematizes them.

Source: Philip Schaff and Henry Wace, eds., *The Seven Ecumenical Councils, vol. 14, A Select Library of Nicene and Post-Nicene Fathers of the Christian Church* (Grand Rapids, MI, 1957).

Western Church, which included the phrase "from the Son" (*filioque*). (See Document, "The Nicene Creed.")

Some scholars perceive here a hidden political concern: By protecting the unity and majesty of the Father, Eastern theology was safeguarding the unity and majesty of the emperor himself, from whom all power on earth was believed properly to flow. The Eastern emperors claimed absolute sovereignty, both secular and religious. They practiced Caesaropapism, or the emperor acting as if he held authority over the church as well as over his kingdom. By comparison, the West nurtured a separation of church and state that began to flower in the eleventh century.

A dispute over the use of sacred images (icons) in worship, which erupted in the eighth century, further divided the East and West. In 726, Emperor Leo III (r. 717–741) forbade the use of images and icons by all Christians. His intention may have been to weaken the monastic owners of popular icons and to court populations influenced by Muslim and Jewish contempt for image worshipers. At any rate, his attack on traditional practices shocked the West and helped drive the Roman popes into an alliance with Europe's strongest emerging rulers, the Frankish kings. Constantinople underwent a spate of iconoclasm (destruction of icons) but reversed itself in the mid-ninth century and restored respect for sacred images.

The Eastern church rejected several requirements of Roman Christianity. It denied the existence of Purgatory; permitted lay divorce and remarriage; allowed priests, but not bishops, to marry; and embraced vernacular liturgies in place of Greek and Latin. In these matters Eastern Christians gained opportunities and rights Christians in the West would not enjoy until at least the Protestant Reformation in the sixteenth century.

Having accumulated for centuries, differences between the Eastern and Roman churches finally resulted in a schism in 1054. The pope's envoy, Cardinal

•••⊣Read the Document
Epitome Iconoclastic Seventh Synod, 754
at **myhistorylab.com**

Humbertus, who was sent to Constantinople to try to resolve some of the points in contention, excommunicated his Eastern colleagues, and they in turn condemned the West. The result was a breach that remained until 1965, when a Roman pope and the patriarch of Constantinople met to revoke the mutual condemnations of 1054.

THE IMPACT OF ISLAM ON EAST AND WEST

HOW DID the Islamic world influence medieval Western civilization?

A new drama began to unfold in the sixth century with the rise of Islam (see Chapter 10). Emperors in Constantinople struggled with invading Arab armies. Unlike Germanic invaders, who absorbed and adapted Roman culture and religion, the Arabs ultimately imposed their own culture and religion on the lands they conquered.

An Arab-Berber army under Tariq ibn Ziyad (Gibraltar, "mountain of Tariq," is named after him) conquered Visigothic Spain in 711, beginning a 700-year reign in what is today Andalusia. By the middle of the eighth century Arabs were masters of the southern and eastern Mediterranean coastline, territories today held, for the most part, by Islamic states. Muslim armies also pushed north and east through Mesopotamia and Persia and beyond. The Muslim conquerors generally tolerated Christians and Jews, provided they paid taxes and made no efforts to proselytize Muslim communities. The Arabs forbade mixed marriages and any conscious cultural interchange. Special taxes on conquered peoples encouraged them to convert to Islam.

Assaulted from East and West, Christian Europe developed a lasting fear and suspicion of the Muslims. Eventually, Byzantine Emperor Leo III (r. 717–740) stopped Arab armies at Constantinople after a year's siege (717–718). In subsequent centuries the Byzantines further secured their borders and for a time expanded militarily and commercially into Muslim lands. In the West, the Franks under Charles Martel defeated a raiding party of Arabs on the western frontier of the Frankish kingdom near Tours (today in central France) in 732, ending the possibility of Arab expansion into the heart of Europe. The Mediterranean remained something of a "Muslim lake" during the High Middle Ages, and the center of the evolving western European civilization shifted north. Yet positive contact and influence continued between Muslims and Christians. Western trade with the East continued to be of great importance to the Carolingians.

BYZANTIUM'S CONTRIBUTION TO ISLAMIC CIVILIZATION

The Islamic Empire found itself face to face with Byzantium: An astonishingly vital, young phenomenon confronted what then seemed to be an exhausted, ancient empire. A sequence of Islamic invasions and sieges did not, however, destroy the Byzantines, and eventually borders between the two empires were more or less established.

With the slowdown of Muslim expansion, commerce and exchange with Byzantium intensified. The caliphates of Islam regarded Byzantium as a model. The splendor of court culture and ceremony was adopted from the Byzantines with the intent to intimidate and impress; Byzantine architecture and craftsmanship were much admired; and Byzantine art and iconography formed a foundation for later Arab illuminations and artwork.[5]

Arab empire-builders were curious about earlier peoples and wished to associate themselves with an older tradition of authority. In the Byzantines, they saw the greatest challenge to the legitimacy of the Islamic Empire. The Muslims also wanted to understand their faith in intellectual terms. From these diverse motives there developed considerable interest in Ancient Greek learning, particularly in works on logic, philosophy, and medicine. A great deal of translation was underway by the ninth century,

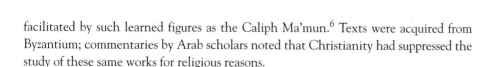

facilitated by such learned figures as the Caliph Ma'mun.[6] Texts were acquired from Byzantium; commentaries by Arab scholars noted that Christianity had suppressed the study of these same works for religious reasons.

THE WESTERN DEBT TO ISLAM

Arab invasions and presence in the Mediterranean area during the Early Middle Ages contributed both directly and indirectly to the formation of western Europe. They did so indirectly by driving west Europeans back onto their native tribal and inherited Judeo-Christian, Greco-Roman, and Byzantine resources, from which they created a Western culture of their own. Also, by diverting the attention and energies of the Byzantine Empire during the formative centuries, the Arabs prevented it from expanding into western Europe. That allowed two Germanic peoples to gain ascendancy: first the Franks and then the Lombards, who invaded Italy in the sixth century and settled in the Po valley.

Despite hostilities between the Christian West and the Muslim world, there was creative interchange between them, with the West having the most to gain. Arab civilizations were enjoying their golden age. Between the eighth and tenth centuries, Moorish Córdoba was a model multicultural city embracing Arabs, Berbers, Spanish Christian converts to Islam, and native Jews. The Arabs taught Western farmers how to irrigate fields and Western artisans how to tan leather and refine silk. The West also gained from its contacts with Arabic scholars. Ancient Greek works on astronomy, mathematics, and medicine became available in Latin translation, thanks to the Arabs. Down to the sixteenth century, the basic gynecological and child-care manuals guiding the work of Western midwives and physicians were compilations made by the Baghdad physician Al-Razi (Rhazes), the philosopher and physician Ibn-Sina (Avicenna) (980–1037), and Ibn Rushd (Averröes) (1126–1198), who was also Islam's greatest authority on Aristotle. Jewish scholars made important contributions; the great Moses Maimonides (1135–1204) wrote in both Arabic and Hebrew. The Arabs, exceptional poets, gave the West its most popular book, the folk tales of *The Arabian Nights*.

THE DEVELOPING ROMAN CHURCH

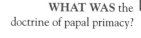

WHAT WAS the doctrine of papal primacy?

Throughout the period of imperial decline, Germanic invasions, and Islamic expansion, one Western institution remained firmly entrenched and gained in strength: the Christian church. The church sought to organize itself according to the centralized, hierarchical administrative structure of the empire, with strategically placed "viceroys" (bishops) in European cities who looked for spiritual direction to their leader, the bishop of Rome (later pope). As the Western Empire crumbled, local bishops and cathedral chapters (ruling bodies of clergy) filled the vacuum of authority. The local cathedral became the center of urban life and the local bishop the highest authority for those who remained in the cities. In Rome, on a larger and more fateful scale, the pope took control of the city as the Western emperors gradually departed and died out. Western Europe soon discovered that the Christian church was its best repository of Roman administrative skills and classical culture.

The Christian church had been graced with special privileges, great lands, and wealth by Emperor Constantine, whose Edict of Milan in 313 gave Christians a favored status within the empire. In 380 Emperors Theodosius I (r. ca. 379–395) and Gratian I

[5]El-Cheikh, *Byzantium Viewed by the Arabs*, pp. 154, 60, 194.

[6]Irfan Shahid, "Byzantium and the Islamic World," in *Byzantium, a World Civilization*, ed. Angeliki E. Laiou and Henry Maguire (Washington, DC: Dumbarton Oaks Research Library and Collection, © 1992), 51.

Religious Diversity. A Muslim and a Christian play the *ud* or lute together, from a thirteenth-century *Book of Chants* in the Escorial Monastery of Madrid. Medieval Europe was deeply influenced by Arab-Islamic culture, transmitted particularly through Spain. Some of the many works in Arabic on musical theory were translated into Latin and Hebrew, but the main influence on music came from the arts of singing and playing spread by minstrels.

A Moor and a Christian playing the lute, miniature in a book of music from the "Cantigas" of Alfonso X "the Wise" (1221–1284). Thirteenth century (manuscript). Monastero de El Escorial, El Escorial, Spain/index/bridgeman Art Library.

What kinds of exchanges took place between Muslims and western Europeans during the Middle Ages?

QUICK REVIEW

Monasticism

◆ First monks, like Anthony of Egypt, were hermits

◆ Basil the Great encouraged service

◆ Benedict of Nursia developed hierarchical, self-sufficient monasteries

◆ Monks were disciplined, respected by public

◆•◆—Read the Document
St. Benedict's Rules for Monks
at **myhistorylab.com**

apostolic primacy
The doctrine that the popes are the direct successors to the Apostle Peter and, as such, heads of the church.

(r. 367–383) raised Christianity to the official religion of the empire. Both Theodosius and his predecessors acted as much for political effect as out of religious conviction; in 313 Christians composed about one-fifth of the population of the empire, making Christianity the strongest among the empire's competing religions. Mithraism, a religion popular among army officers and restricted to males, was its main rival.

The church could act as a potent civilizing and unifying force. It had a religious message of providential purpose and individual worth that could give solace and meaning to life at its worst. It had a ritual of baptism and a creedal confession that united people beyond the traditional barriers of social class, education, and gender. And alone in the West, the church retained an effective hierarchical administration, staffed by the best educated minds in Europe and centered in emperorless Rome.

MONASTIC CULTURE

Monastic culture proved again and again to be the peculiar strength of the church during the Middle Ages. The first monks were hermits, such as Anthony of Egypt (ca. 251–356), who felt compelled to withdraw from society and give up all worldly attachments to pursue a purely spiritual life. So many people were attracted to the hermits' movement that communal organizations had to be devised to serve them. The monastic life, which was guided by the biblical "counsels of perfection" (chastity, poverty, and obedience), came to be regarded as the purest form of religious practice. Basil the Great (329–379), whose rule (regulations to govern a monastery) spread widely throughout the East, urged monks to leave their protected enclaves and serve the needs of others by caring for orphans, widows, and the infirm.

The great organizer of Western monasticism was Benedict of Nursia (ca. 480–547). In 529 he established a monastery at Monte Cassino, in Italy, founding the form of monasticism—Benedictine—that quickly came to dominate in the West. Benedict wrote a sophisticated *Rule for Monasteries*, a comprehensive plan that both regimented and enriched monastic life. Benedictine monasteries were hierarchically organized and directed by an abbot. Periods of study and religious devotion (about four hours each day of prayers and liturgical activities) alternated with manual labor (up to eight hours, including copying manuscripts)—a program that carefully promoted the religious, intellectual, and physical well-being of the monks. During the Early Middle Ages Benedictine missionaries Christianized both England and Germany. Their disciplined organization and devotion to hard work made the Benedictines an economic and political power as well as a spiritual force wherever they settled.

THE DOCTRINE OF PAPAL PRIMACY

Constantine and the Eastern emperors looked on the church as little more than a department of the state. The bishops of Rome, however, opposed royal intervention. Taking advantage of imperial weakness and distraction, they developed the doctrine of "papal primacy," which raised the bishop of Rome to an unassailable supremacy within the church. As the "pope," he was both head of the Roman Catholic Church and Christ's vicar on earth, continuing the line of Christ's apostles from St. Peter. The new title put him in a position to claim power within the secular world, giving rise to repeated conflicts between church and state throughout the Middle Ages.

Pope Damasus I (366–384) laid the foundation for papal claims to absolute authority by asserting Rome's **apostolic primacy**. He pointed to Jesus' words to Peter in the Gospel of Matthew (16:18): "Thou art Peter, and upon this rock I will build my church." Because tradition maintained that Peter was the first bishop of Rome and that he died there, Damasus insisted that Rome's popes, Peter's successors, were heirs to the role Jesus had decreed for Peter. Pope Leo I (440–461) assumed the title *pontifex maximus*—"supreme priest"—and laid claim to a "**plenitude of power**," supremacy over all other bishops in the church. Pope Gelasius I (492–496) stated that the authority of the clergy was "more weighty" than the power of kings, for priests were given charge over divine affairs.

DIVISION OF CHRISTENDOM

The division of Christendom into Eastern (Byzantine) and Western (Roman Catholic) churches has its roots in the Early Middle Ages and was due in part to linguistic and cultural differences. In East and West, church organization closely followed that of the secular state. A novel combination of Greek, Roman, and Asian elements shaped Byzantine culture, giving Eastern Christianity a stronger mystical dimension than Western Christianity. This difference in outlook may have predisposed Eastern patriarchs to submit more passively than Western popes ever could to royal intervention in their affairs.

Differences in doctrine and practice were exacerbated when the Eastern and Western churches both claimed jurisdiction over newly converted areas in the northern Balkans. Beyond these issues, three major factors lay behind the religious break between East and West. The first revolved around questions of doctrinal authority. The Eastern church put more stress on the authority of the Bible and the ecumenical councils of the church in the definition of Christian doctrine than on the counsel and decrees of the bishop of Rome. The claims of Roman popes to a special primacy of authority were unacceptable to the East, where regional churches were independent and autonomous. This basic issue of authority lay behind the mutual excommunication of Pope Nicholas I and Patriarch Photius in the ninth century, and that of Pope Leo IX (through his ambassador to Constantinople, Cardinal Humbert) and Patriarch Michael Cerularius in 1054.

A second major issue in the separation of the two churches was the Western addition of the *filioque* clause to the Nicene-Constantinopolitan Creed. According to this anti-Arian clause, the Holy Spirit proceeds "also from the Son" (*filioque*) as well as from the Father, making clear the Western belief that Christ was fully of one essence with God the Father and not a lesser being.

The third factor was the iconoclastic controversy of the first half of the eighth century. As noted earlier, after 725 the Byzantine emperor Leo III (r. 717–741) attempted to force Western popes to abolish the use of images in their churches. This stand met fierce official and popular resistance. To punish the West, Leo confiscated valuable papal lands. This direct challenge to the papacy coincided with a threat to Rome and the Western church from the Lombards of northern Italy. Assailed on two fronts, the Roman papacy seemed doomed. But the papacy has been one of the most resilient and enterprising institutions in Western history. In 754 Pope Stephen II (r. 752–757) formed an alliance with the Franks' ruler, Pepin III, to defend the church against the Lombards and to serve as a Western counterweight

plenitude of power
The teaching that the popes have power over all other bishops of the church.

•••⌐Read the **Document**
Pope Leo I on Bishop Hilary of Arles
at **myhistorylab.com**

CHRONOLOGY

MAJOR POLITICAL AND RELIGIOUS DEVELOPMENTS OF THE EARLY MIDDLE AGES

313	Emperor Constantine issues the Edict of Milan
325	Council of Nicaea defines Christian doctrine
410	Rome invaded by Visigoths under Alaric
413–426	Saint Augustine writes *The City of God*
451–453	Europe invaded by the Huns under Attila
476	Barbarian Odovacer deposes Western emperor and rules as king of the Romans
529	Saint Benedict founds monastery at Monte Cassino
533	Justinian codifies Roman law
732	Charles Martel defeats Arabs at Tours
754	Pope Stephen II and Pepin III ally

to the Eastern emperor. This marriage of religion and politics created a new Western church and empire and determined much of the course of Western history thereafter.

THE KINGDOM OF THE FRANKS

WHY DID
Charlemagne's empire break up after his death?

MEROVINGIANS AND CAROLINGIANS: FROM CLOVIS TO CHARLEMAGNE

Clovis and his successors gave the Franks a major role in the recovery of western Europe. The territory under their control included modern France, Belgium, the Netherlands, and western Germany. In attempting to govern this extensive kingdom, the Merovingians encountered the most persistent problem of medieval political history—the competing claims of the "one" and the "many," the struggle of a lone king to impose centralized government on local magnates.

The Merovingian kings addressed this problem by making pacts with the landed nobility and by creating the royal office of count. The counts were men without possessions to whom the king gave great lands in the expectation that they would be loyal officers. But once established in office, the Merovingian counts became territorial rulers in their own right. The Frankish kingdom progressively fragmented into independent regions and tiny principalities. The Frankish custom of dividing the kingdom equally among the king's legitimate male heirs only made matters worse. By the seventh century, the Frankish king lacked effective executive power. Real power was concentrated in the office of the Mayor of the Palace, who was the spokesman at the king's court for the great landowners. Through this office, the Carolingian dynasty rose to power.

The Carolingians took their name from the dynasty's greatest ruler, Carolus (later to be known as Charlemagne). They controlled the office of the Mayor of the Palace for over one hundred years, starting with Pepin I, who died in 639. Pepin II (d. 714) ruled in fact, if not in title, over the Frankish kingdom. His illegitimate son, Charles Martel ("the Hammer," d. 741), created a great cavalry by bestowing lands known as *benefices* or **fiefs** on powerful nobles, who, in return, agreed to be ready to serve as the king's army. It was such an army that checked the Arabs at Tours in 732. Then, with the enterprising connivance of the pope, the Carolingians simply expropriated the Frankish crown in 751.

The fiefs so generously bestowed by Charles Martel to create his army came in large part from landed property that he usurped from the church. His alliance with the landed aristocracy permitted the Carolingians to have some measure of political success where the Merovingians had failed. The Carolingians created counts almost entirely out of the landed nobility from which the Carolingians themselves had risen. The Merovingians, in contrast, had tried to compete directly with these great aristocrats by raising the landless to power. By playing to strength rather than challenging it, the Carolingians strengthened themselves, at least for the short term. The church, by this time dependent on the protection of the Franks against the Eastern emperor and the Lombards, had no choice but to tolerate the seizure of its lands. Later, the Franks partially compensated the church for the lands.

The church played a large and enterprising role in the Frankish government. By Carolingian times, monasteries were a dominant force. Their intellectual achievements made them respected repositories of culture. Their religious teaching and example imposed order on surrounding populations. Their relics and rituals made them magical shrines to which pilgrims came in great numbers. Thanks to their donated

QUICK REVIEW

Merovingians

- Frankish dynasty founded by Clovis
- Created royal office of count
- Fragmentation of kingdom
- Mayor of the Palace gained power

fief

Land granted to a vassal in exchange for services, usually military.

lands and serf labor, many had become very profitable farms and landed estates. By Merovingian times, the higher clergy were already employed in tandem with counts as royal agents. It was the policy of the Carolingians to use the church to pacify conquered neighboring tribes—Frisians, Thuringians, Bavarians, and especially the Franks' archenemies, the Saxons.

Conversion to Nicene Christianity became an integral part of the successful annexation of conquered lands and people; the cavalry broke bodies, while the clergy won hearts and minds. The Anglo-Saxon missionary Saint Boniface (b. Wynfrith, ca. 680–754) was the most important of the German clergy who served Carolingian kings in this way. Christian bishops in missionary districts and elsewhere became lords, appointed by and subject to the king—an ominous integration of secular and religious policy in which lay the seeds of the later Investiture Controversy of the eleventh and twelfth centuries (see Chapter 15).

The church helped the Carolingians with more than territorial expansion. Pope Zacharias (r. 741–752) sanctioned Pepin the Short's termination of the vestigial Merovingian Dynasty and the Carolingian accession to kingship of the Franks. According to legend, Saint Boniface annointed Pepin, thereby investing Frankish rule with a sacral character from the start.

Zacharias's successor, Pope Stephen II (r. 752–757), appealed directly to Pepin when he was driven from Rome in 753 by the Lombards. In 754 the Franks and the church formed an alliance against the Lombards and the Eastern emperor, whose power was greater than the Franks' power in central Italy at the time. Carolingian kings became the protectors of the Catholic Church and thereby "kings by the grace of God." Pepin gained the title *patricius Romanorum*, "father-protector of the Romans," a title heretofore borne only by the representative of the Eastern emperor. In 755 the Franks defeated the Lombards and gave the pope the lands surrounding Rome, creating what came to be known as the **Papal States**. During this time the papacy began to circulate a fraudulent document, *Donation of Constantine*, which was intended to prove to the Franks that the church was the heir to the legacy of Rome's empire. It was exposed as a forgery in the fifteenth century.

The papacy had looked to the Franks for an ally strong enough to protect it from the Eastern emperors. It is an irony of history that the church found in the Carolingian Dynasty a Western imperial government that drew almost as slight a boundary between state and church as did Eastern emperors. Although preferable to Eastern domination, Carolingian patronage of the church proved to be no less constraining.

REIGN OF CHARLEMAGNE (768–814)

Charlemagne, the son of Pepin the Short, continued the role of his father as papal protector in Italy and his policy of territorial conquest in the north. After defeating the Lombards of northern Italy in 774, Charlemagne took the title "King of the Lombards." He subjugated surrounding pagan tribes, foremost among them the Saxons, and brought the Danubian plains into the Frankish orbit by the virtual annihilation of the Avars, a tribe related to the Huns. The Arabs were chased beyond the Pyrenees. By the time of his death on January 28, 814, Charlemagne's kingdom embraced modern France, Belgium, Holland, Switzerland, almost the whole of Germany, much of Italy, a portion of Spain, and the island of Corsica (see Map 11–3, on page 278).

Encouraged by ambitious advisers, Charlemagne reached to be a universal emperor. His sacred palace city, Aachen (in French, Aix-la-Chapelle), was constructed in conscious imitation of the courts of the ancient Roman and the contemporary Eastern emperors. Although he permitted the church its independence, he looked after it paternalistically. He used the church above all to promote social stability and hierarchical

Papal States

Territory in central Italy ruled by the pope until 1870.

QUICK REVIEW

Church and State

- ◆ Church played a large role in the Frankish government
- ◆ Christian bishops became lords in service of the king
- ◆ Papacy looked to Franks for protection from the Eastern emperors

MAP 11–3.   The Empire of Charlemagne to 814.   Building on the successes of his predecessors, Charlemagne greatly increased the Frankish domains. Such traditional enemies as the Saxons and the Lombards fell under his sway.

How does the extent of Charlemagne's empire compare with that of the ancient western Roman Empire?

⊙-See the Map
Charlemagne's Empire, 814
at **myhistorylab.com**

order throughout the kingdom. Frankish Christians were ceremoniously baptized, professed the Nicene Creed (with the *filioque* clause), and learned in church to revere Charlemagne.

Charlemagne realized his imperial pretensions on Christmas Day 800, when Pope Leo III (795–816) crowned him emperor. This event created what would later be called the Holy Roman Empire, a revival, based after 870 in Germany, of the old Roman Empire in the West. The coronation benefited both the church and Charlemagne. Before his coronation, he had been a minor Western potentate in the eyes of Eastern emperors; afterward, Eastern emperors recognized his imperial dignity.

Charlemagne stood six feet, three and one half inches tall—a fact confirmed when his tomb was opened and exact measurements of his remains were taken in 1861. He was restless, ever ready for a hunt. Informal and gregarious, he insisted on the presence of friends even when he bathed and was widely known for his practical jokes, lusty good humor, and warm hospitality. People and gifts came to Aachen from all over the world; in 802, Charlemagne received a white elephant from the caliph of Baghdad, Harun-al-Rashid.

Charlemagne had five official wives in succession, and many mistresses and concubines, and he sired numerous children. This created problems. His oldest son by his first marriage, Pepin, was jealous of the attention Charlemagne showed to the sons of his second wife. Fearing the loss of paternal favor, Pepin joined a conspiracy against his father. He spent the rest of his life in confinement in a monastery after the plot was exposed.

Charlemagne governed his kingdom through counts, of whom there were perhaps as many as 250. Each count had three main duties: to maintain a local army loyal to the king, to collect tribute and dues, and to administer justice throughout his district. This last responsibility was undertaken through a district law court known as the *mallus*, which heard testimony from the parties involved in a dispute or crime, passed judgment, and assessed a monetary compensation to be paid to the injured party. In cases where guilt or innocence was unclear, recourse was often taken to judicial duels or "divine" tests and ordeals. Among these was the length of time a defendant's hand took to heal after immersion in boiling water.

As in Merovingian times, many counts used their official position and new judicial powers to their own advantage. As they grew stronger and more independent, they came to regard the land grants with which they were paid as hereditary positions rather than generous royal donations. This development signaled the impending fragmentation of Charlemagne's kingdom.

Charlemagne never solved the loyalty problem. Ecclesiastical agents proved no better than secular ones; except for their attendance to the liturgy and to church prayers, landowning bishops were largely indistinguishable from the lay nobility. Charlemagne sensed—rightly, as the Gregorian reform of the eleventh century would prove—that the emergence of a distinctive and reform-minded class of ecclesiastical landowners would be a danger to royal government. Charlemagne purposefully treated his bishops as he treated his counts, that is, as vassals who served at the king's pleasure.

Charlemagne used his wealth to attract Europe's best scholars to Aachen. Theodulf of Orleans (d. 821), Angilbert (d. 814), and Charlemagne's biographer Einhard (ca. 770–840) developed court culture and education. The renowned Anglo-Saxon master Alcuin of York (735–804), who became director of the king's palace school in 782, brought classical and Christian learning to Aachen and was handsomely rewarded for his efforts with several wealthy monastic estates. Although Charlemagne appreciated learning for its own sake, he also intended to upgrade the administrative skills of the royal bureaucracy. By preparing the sons of nobles to run the religious and secular offices of the realm, court scholarship served kingdom building. With its special concentration on grammar, logic, rhetoric, and basic mathematics, the school provided training in the basic tools of bureaucracy. Charlemagne's scholars created a new, clear style of handwriting—Carolingian minuscule—and fostered the use of accurate Latin in official documents, developments that helped increase lay literacy. Charlemagne's sister Gisela oversaw the copying of classical manuscripts, thereby preserving the treasures of antiquity. Through personal correspondence and visitations, Alcuin created a community of scholars and clerics at court and infused administration with a sense of comradeship and common purpose. A modest renaissance, or rebirth, of antiquity occurred in the palace school as scholars collected and preserved ancient manuscripts. Alcuin worked on a correct text of the Bible and made editions of the monastic *Rule* of Saint Benedict. These scholarly activities served official efforts to bring uniformity to church law and liturgy, educate the clergy, and improve moral life within the monasteries.

Charlemagne. An equestrian figure of Charlemagne (or possibly one of his sons) from the early ninth century.

Bronze equestrian statuette of Charlemagne, 3/4 view, from Metz Cathedral, ninth–tenth century. Louvre, Paris, France. Copyright Bridgeman-Giraudon/Art Resource, New York.

Would you consider Charlemagne a successful leader? Why or why not?

••• Read the Document
Life of Charlemagne (early ninth century)
Einhard, at **myhistorylab.com**

Plowing the Fields. The invention of the moldboard plow greatly improved farming. The heavy plow cut deeply into the ground and furrowed it. This illustration from the Luttrell Psalter (ca. 1340) also shows that the traction harness, which lessened the strangulation effect of the yoke on the animals, had not yet been adopted. Indeed, one of the oxen seems to be on the verge of choking.

What other improvements in farming practice occurred during this period?

manors

Village farms owned by a lord.

demesne

The part of a manor that was cultivated directly for the lord of the manor.

serfs

Peasants tied to the land they tilled.

QUICK REVIEW

Serfs

◆ Status varied: free and unfree
◆ All owed dues in kind to the lord of the manor
◆ Much discontent, many escaped

three-field system

A medieval innovation that increased the amount of land under cultivation by leaving only one-third fallow in a given year.

The agrarian economy of the Middle Ages was organized and controlled through village farms known as **manors**. Peasants labored as farmers in subordination to a lord, a more powerful landowner who gave them land and a dwelling in exchange for their services and a portion of their crops. That part of the land farmed by the peasants for the lord was the **demesne**, which on average made up about one-quarter to one-third of the arable land. All crops grown there were harvested for the lord.

Peasants were treated according to their social status and the size of their landholdings. A freeman—that is, a peasant with hereditary property (property free from the claims of an overlord)—became a **serf** by surrendering his property to a greater landowner (a lord) in exchange for protection and assistance. The free serf received his land back from the lord with a clear definition of his economic and legal rights. Although the land was no longer his property, he had full possession and use of it, and the number of services and amount of goods he was to supply to the lord were carefully spelled out. Peasants who entered the service of a lord with little real property to bargain with (perhaps only a few farm implements and animals) ended up as unfree serfs and were much more vulnerable to the lord's demands, spending up to three days a week working the lord's fields. Truly impoverished peasants who lived and worked on the manor as serfs had the lowest status and were the least protected.

Serfs were subject to so-called dues in kind: firewood for cutting the lord's wood, sheep for grazing their sheep on the lord's land, and the like. Thus the lord, who for his part furnished shacks and small plots of land from his vast domain, had at his disposal an army of servants who provided him with everything from eggs to boots. That many serfs were discontented is reflected in the high number of recorded escapes. An astrological calendar from the period marks the days most favorable for escaping. Fugitive serfs roamed the land as beggars and vagabonds, searching for new and better masters.

By the time of Charlemagne, the moldboard plow, which was especially needed in northern Europe where the soil was heavy, and the three-field system of land cultivation were coming into use. These developments greatly improved agricultural productivity. Unlike the older "scratch" plow, which crisscrossed the field with only slight penetration, the moldboard cut deep into the soil and turned it to form a ridge, providing a natural drainage system for the field as well as permitting the deep planting of seeds. Unlike the earlier two-field system of crop rotation, which simply alternated fallow with planted fields each year, the **three-field system** increased the amount of cultivated land by leaving only one-third fallow in a given year.

As owners of the churches on their lands, the lords had the right to raise chosen serfs to the post of parish priest, placing them in charge of the churches on the lords' estates. Church law directed the lord to set a serf free before he entered the clergy, but lords preferred a "serf priest," one who not only said the Mass on Sundays and holidays but also continued to serve his lord during the week. Like Charlemagne with his bishops, Frankish lords cultivated a docile parish clergy.

Ordinary people baptized themselves and their children, confessed the Creed Mass, tried to learn the Lord's Prayer, and received last rites from the priest when death approached. Local priests were no better educated than their congregations, and instruction in the meaning of Christian doctrine and practice remained minimal. People became particularly attached to the more tangible veneration of relics and saints. Charlemagne shared many of the religious beliefs of his ordinary subjects: He collected and venerated relics, made pilgrimages to Rome, frequented the church of Saint Mary in Aachen several times a day, and directed in his last will and testament that much of his great treasure be spent to endow Masses and prayers for his departed soul.

BREAKUP OF THE CAROLINGIAN KINGDOM

Late in life, an ailing Charlemagne knew that his empire was ungovernable. The seeds of dissolution lay in regionalism. In medieval society, a direct relationship existed between physical proximity to authority and loyalty to authority. Local people obeyed local lords more readily than they obeyed a glorious but distant king. Charlemagne had been forced to recognize and even to enhance the power of regional magnates in order to win needed financial and military support.

The Carolingian kings did not give up easily, however. Charlemagne's only surviving son and successor, Louis the Pious (r. 814–840), had three sons by his first wife. Louis acted early in his reign to break the tradition of dividing his kingdom equally among his sons. Instead, Louis made his eldest son, Lothar (d. 855), co-regent and sole imperial heir in 817. He gave Lothar's brothers important but much lesser assigned hereditary lands: Pepin (d. 838) became king of Aquitaine and Louis "the German" (d. 876) became king of Bavaria.

In 823 Louis's second wife, Judith of Bavaria, bore him a fourth son, Charles (d. 877). Determined that her son should receive more than just a nominal inheritance, the queen incited the brothers Pepin and Louis to war against Lothar and persuaded their father to divide the kingdom equally. As the bestower of crowns upon emperors, the pope had an important stake in the preservation of the revived Western Empire and the imperial title, so the pope condemned Louis and restored Lothar to his original magnificent inheritance. But this stirred the resentments of Lothar's brothers, including his half-brother, Charles, who joined in renewed war against him.

In 843, with the Treaty of Verdun, peace finally came to Louis's surviving heirs (Pepin had died in 838). The great Carolingian Empire was partitioned into three equal parts. Lothar received a middle section, which came to be known as Lotharingia and embraced roughly modern Holland, Belgium, Switzerland, Alsace-Lorraine, and Italy. Charles the Bald received the western part of the kingdom, or roughly modern France, and Louis the German came into the eastern part, or roughly modern Germany. Although Lothar retained the imperial title, the universal empire ceased to exist. Not until the sixteenth century, with the election in 1519 of Charles I of Spain as the Holy Roman Emperor Charles V, would the Western world again see a kingdom as vast as Charlemagne's.

Carolingian fragmentation continued. When Lothar died in 855, his kingdom was divided equally among his three surviving sons, leaving it much smaller and weaker than the kingdoms of Louis the German and Charles the Bald. Henceforth, western Europe would be divided into an eastern and a western Frankish kingdom—roughly Germany and France—at war over the fractionalized middle kingdom, a contest that has continued into modern times.

The political breakdown of the Carolingian Empire coincided with new external threats. In the late ninth and tenth centuries, successive waves of Normans (North men), better known as Vikings, swept into Europe from Scandinavia. *Vikings* was a catchall term for Scandinavian peoples who visited Europe alternately as gregarious traders and savage raiders, and their exploits have been preserved in sagas that reveal a cultural world filled with mythical gods and spirits. Taking to sea in oceangoing longboats of rugged, doubled-hulled construction, they terrified their neighbors to the south, invading and occupying English and European coastal and

QUICK REVIEW

Charlemagne's Successors

- Louis the Pious (r. 814–840) made his son Lothar sole imperial heir

- Civil war broke out between Lothar and Louis's other sons

- The Treaty of Verdun (843) divided the empire into three equal parts

A Closer Look

A Multicultural Book Cover

Carolingian education, art, and architecture served royal efforts to unify the kingdom by fusing inherited Celtic-Germanic and Greco-Roman-Byzantine cultures. Charlemagne, his son, and grandsons decorated their churches with a variety of art forms, among them illuminated manuscripts, such as the bejeweled metalwork that became the binding of the *Lindau Gospels* (ca. 870).

The Christ seen here reflects early Christian art and Byzantine theology, which did not endow divinity with human suffering. So impassive is this Christ that he seems almost to smile on the cross.

However, the surrounding panels show the angels in heaven and Christ's followers on earth writhing with grief.

Questions

1. Does the inclusiveness of this book cover suggest a shared heritage among the Celts, Germans, Greeks, Romans, and Byzantines?

2. How does this composite of cultures on the book cover compare with their actual historical relations in the ninth century?

3. Since the nonsuffering Christ on the book cover presents a distinctive Byzantine icon, does this suggest agreement among the parties over the portrayal of the Savior's crucifixion?

4. Do the agonizing figures on the book cover (both angels and humans) represent other religious traditions that prefer a suffering Christ upon the cross?

myhistorylab To examine this image in an interactive fashion, please go to **www.myhistorylab.com**

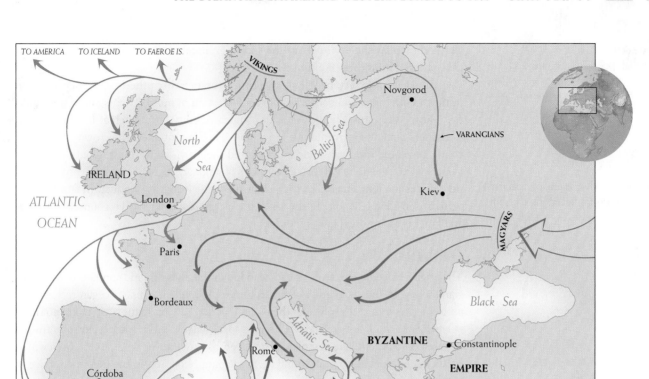

MAP 11–4.   Viking, Muslim, and Magyar Invasions to the Eleventh Century.   Western Europe was sorely beset by new waves of outsiders from the ninth to the eleventh century. From north, east, and south, a stream of invading Vikings, Magyars, and Muslims brought the West at times to near collapse and of course gravely affected institutions within Europe.

How did early medieval Europe respond to invasions?

river towns. In the ninth century, the Danes briefly besieged Paris, while other Vikings turned York into a major trading post for their woolens, jewelry, and ornamental wares. Erik the Red made it to Greenland, and his son Leif Erikson wintered in Newfoundland 500 years before Columbus. In the eleventh century Christian conversions and English defeat of the Norwegians effectively restricted Vikings to their Scandinavian homelands.

Magyars, or Hungarians, who were great horsemen, also swept into western Europe from the eastern plains, while Muslims made incursions across the Mediterranean from North Africa (see Map 11–4). The Franks built fortified towns and castles in strategic locations as refuges. When they could, they bought off the invaders with grants of land and payments of silver. In the resulting turmoil, local populations became more dependent than ever on local strongmen for life and livelihood, creating the essential precondition for the maturation of feudal society.

FEUDAL SOCIETY

The Middle Ages were characterized by a chronic absence of effective central government and the constant threat of famine, disease, and foreign invasion. In this state of affairs the weaker sought the protection of the stronger, and the true lords and masters became those who could guarantee immediate protection from rapine and starvation.

See the **Map**

Viking Muslim and Magyar Invasions 1000 at **myhistorylab.com**

Magyars
The majority ethnic group in Hungary.

WHAT IS a feudal society?

feudal society
The social, political, military, and economic system that prevailed in the Middle Ages and beyond in some parts of Europe.

vassal
A person granted an estate or cash payments in return for accepting the obligation to render services to a lord.

Read the **Document**
Feudalism, 1083, Archbishop of Cologne
at **myhistorylab.com**

fealty
An oath of loyalty by a vassal to a lord, promising to perform specified services.

The term **feudal society** refers to the social, political, military, and economic system that emerged from these conditions.

In a feudal society, people require firm assurance that others can be depended on in time of dire need. Feudalism is above all a system of mutual rights and responsibilities. During the Early Middle Ages, the landed nobility became great lords who ruled over their domains as miniature kingdoms. They maintained their own armies and courts, regulated local tolls, and even minted their own coins. Large groups of warrior **vassals** were created by extensive bestowals of land, and these developed into a prominent professional military class with its own code of knightly conduct. In feudal society, most serfs docilely worked the land, the clergy prayed and gave counsel, and lords and knights maintained law and order.

ORIGINS

The origins of feudal government can be found in the divisions and conflicts of Merovingian society. In the sixth and seventh centuries, individual freemen began to solve the problem of survival by placing themselves under the protection of more powerful freemen, who built up armies and became local magnates. Freemen who so entrusted themselves to others were described collectively as *vassi* ("those who serve"), from which evolved the term *vassalage*, meaning the placement of oneself in the personal service of another who promises protection in return.

Landed nobles, like kings, tried to acquire as many vassals as they could, because military strength in the Early Middle Ages lay in numbers. It proved impossible to maintain these growing armies within the lord's own household, which was the original custom, or to support them by special monetary payments, so the practice evolved of granting them land as a "tenement." Such land came to be known as a *benefice*, or a *fief*, and vassals were expected to dwell on it and maintain their horses and other accouterments of war in good order. Originally vassals, therefore, were little more than gangs-in-waiting.

VASSALAGE AND THE FIEF

Vassalage involved **fealty** to the lord. To swear fealty was to promise to refrain from any action that might threaten the lord's well-being and to perform personal services for him on his request. Chief among the expected services was military duty as a mounted knight. This could involve a variety of activities: a military expedition, escort duty, standing castle guard, or the placement of one's own fortress at the lord's disposal, if the vassal was of such stature as to have one. Continuous bargaining and bickering occurred over the terms of service.

Limitations were placed on the number of days a lord could require services from a vassal. In France in the eleventh century, about forty days of service per year were considered sufficient. It also became possible for vassals to buy their way out of military service by a monetary payment known as *scutage*. The lord, in turn, applied this payment to the hiring of mercenaries, who often proved more efficient than contract-conscious vassals. Beyond his military duty, the vassal was also expected to give the lord advice when he requested it and to sit as a member of his court when it was in session.

CHRONOLOGY

CAROLINGIAN DYNASTY (751–987)

750–800	Fraudulent Donation of Constantine created in an effort to counter Frankish domination of church
751	Pepin III "the Short" becomes king of the Franks
755	Franks drive Lombards out of central Italy; creation of Papal States
768–814	Charlemagne rules as king of the Franks
774	Charlemagne defeats Lombards in northern Italy
800	Pope Leo III crowns Charlemagne
814–840	Louis the Pious succeeds Charlemagne as "emperor"
843	Treaty of Verdun partitions the Carolingian Empire
870	Treaty of Mersen further divides Carolingian Empire
875–950	Invasions by Vikings, Muslims, and Magyars
962	Ottonian Dynasty succeeds Carolingian in Germany
987	Capetian Dynasty succeeds Carolingian in France

The lord's obligations to his vassals were very specific. He was, first of all, obligated to protect the vassal from physical harm and to stand as his advocate in public court. After fealty was sworn and homage paid, the lord provided for the vassal's physical maintenance by the bestowal of a benefice, or fief. The fief was simply the physical or material wherewithal to meet the vassal's military and other obligations. It could take the form of liquid wealth as well as the more common grant of real property. There were so-called money fiefs, which empowered a vassal to receive regular payments from the lord's treasury. Such fiefs created potential conflicts because they made it possible for one country to acquire vassals among the nobility of another. Normally, the fief consisted of a landed estate of anywhere from a few to several thousand acres, but it could also take the form of a castle.

In Carolingian times, a benefice, or fief, varied in size from one or more small villas to several *mansi*, which were agricultural holdings of 25 to 48 acres. The king's vassals received benefices of at least 30 and as many as 200 such mansi. Royal vassalage with a benefice understandably came to be widely sought by the highest classes of Carolingian society. As a royal policy, however, it proved deadly to the king. Although Carolingian kings jealously guarded their rights over property granted in benefice to vassals, resident vassals were still free to dispose of their benefices as they pleased. Vassals of the king, strengthened by his donations, in turn created their own vassals. These vassals, in turn, created still further vassals of their own—vassals of vassals of vassals—in a reverse pyramiding effect that fragmented land and authority from the highest to the lowest levels by the late ninth century.

Beginning with the reign of Louis the Pious (r. 814–840), bishops and abbots swore fealty and received their offices from the king as a benefice. The king formally invested these clerics in their offices during a special ceremony in which he presented them with a ring and a staff, the symbols of high spiritual office. This presumptuous practice of lay investiture, like the Carolingian confiscation of church land mentioned earlier, was a sore point for the church. In the eleventh and twelfth centuries it would provoke a great confrontation between church and state as reform-minded clergy rebelled against what they believed to be involuntary clerical vassalage.

FRAGMENTATION AND DIVIDED LOYALTY

In addition to the fragmentation brought about by the multiplication of vassalage, effective occupation of the land led gradually to claims of hereditary possession. Hereditary possession became a legally recognized principle in the ninth century and laid the basis for claims to real ownership. Further, vassal engagements came to be multiplied in still another way as enterprising freemen sought to accumulate as much land as possible. One man could become a vassal to several different lords. This development led in the ninth century to the concept of a "liege lord"—one master whom the vassal must obey even to the harm of the others, should a direct conflict among them arise.

The problem of loyalty was reflected not only in the literature of the period, with its praise of the virtues of honor and fidelity, but also in the development of the ceremonial acts by which a freeman became a vassal. In the mid-eighth century, an "oath of fealty" highlighted the ceremony. A vassal reinforced his promise of fidelity to the lord by swearing a special oath with his hand on a sacred relic or the Bible. In the tenth and eleventh centuries, paying homage to the lord involved not only the swearing of such an oath but also the placement of the vassal's hands between the lord's and the sealing of the ceremony with a kiss.

Despite their problems, feudal arrangements provided stability throughout the Early Middle Ages and aided the difficult process of political centralization during

Lord and Vassal. A seventh-century portrayal of a vassal, who kneels before his lord and inserts his hands between those of his lord in a gesture of mutual loyalty: the vassal promising to obey and serve his lord, the lord promising to support and protect his vassal.

Spanish School (seventh century). Lord and vassal, decorated page (vellum). Archivo de la Corona de Aragon, Barcelona, Spain/Index/Bridgeman Art Library.

What caused fragmentation in the feudal system?

286 **PART 3** CONSOLIDATION AND INTERACTION OF WORLD CIVILIZATIONS, 500 c.e. TO 1500 c.e.

the High Middle Ages. The genius of feudal government lay in its adaptability. Contracts of different kinds could be made with almost anybody, as circumstances required. The process embraced a wide spectrum of people, from the king at the top to the lowliest vassal in the remotest part of the kingdom. The foundations of the modern nation-state would emerge in France and England from the fine-tuning of essentially feudal arrangements as kings sought to adapt their goal of centralized government to the reality of local power and control.

SUMMARY

 HOW DID the Byzantine Empire continue the legacy of the Roman Empire?

The End of the Western Roman Empire. In the fifth century, Roman authority in the West collapsed under the impact of Germanic invasions. Imperial power shifted to the eastern part of the Roman Empire—known as the Byzantine Empire—with its capital at Constantinople. The Byzantine Empire would endure until the Ottoman Turks captured Constantinople in 1453. The peak of Byzantine power occurred during the reign of Justinian (527–565), whose achievements included the *Corpus Juris Civilis*, a codification of Roman law on which most European law was based until the nineteenth century. The Byzantine Empire helped protect medieval western Europe from Muslim invaders and preserved much of classical learning. *page 263*

 HOW DID the Islamic world influence medieval Western civilization?

The Impact of Islam on East and West. Islamic Arab armies conquered most of the Mediterranean rim. Christian Europe developed a lasting fear and suspicion of Muslims. Franks under Charles Martel defeated an Arab raiding party in central France in 732. Christian-Muslim trade continued, and the Islamic world acted as a conduit for classical learning to the West. Córdoba was a thriving multicultural city. *page 272*

WHAT WAS the doctrine of papal primacy?

The Developing Roman Church. The church was the strongest and most prestigious institution in early medieval Europe, where it filled the vacuum created by the collapse of Roman authority. Monastic culture was especially strong. The greatest organizer of Western monasticism was Saint Benedict of Nursia (480–547). Benedictine monasteries were an economic, political, and spiritual force throughout the West. With the collapse of imperial authority in the West, the bishops of Rome—the popes—developed the doctrine of papal primacy by which they claimed supreme authority over church doctrine and the clergy. These claims were unacceptable in the East, where a

separate Greek Orthodox Church developed under the control of the Byzantine emperors. *page 273*

 WHY DID Charlemagne's empire break up after his death?

The Kingdom of the Franks. The Frankish ruler Charlemagne (r. 768–814) sought to re-create a universal Western empire and was crowned emperor by the pope in 800. Charlemagne's realm embraced modern France, Belgium, Holland, and Switzerland, most of Germany, and parts of Italy and Spain. He formed a close alliance with the church and relied on churchmen as royal agents and administrators. His palace school at Aachen was the center of a modest renaissance of classical learning under scholars such as Alcuin of York (735–804). But Charlemagne's empire proved to be ungovernable. Charlemagne had increased the power of local lords whose support he needed to rule, but their power and wealth became so great that they were able to put their self-interest above royal authority. After Charlemagne's death, his empire dissolved amid quarrels among his heirs, the revolts of powerful nobles, and invasions by Vikings, Magyars, and Muslims. *page 276*

WHAT IS a feudal society?

Feudal Society. The Middle Ages were characterized by a chronic absence of central government and the constant threat of famine, disease, and invasion. Lords were those who could guarantee protection under these conditions. In feudal society, a local lord offered security in return for allegiance from his dependents or vassals. It was a system of mutual rights and responsibilities. Medieval vassals pledged fealty to their lord in return for a fief, or grant of land. They promised to support their "liege lord" with troops or money when he called on them for aid.

The feudal economy was organized and controlled through agrarian villages known as manors, worked by free peasants who had their own modest property and economic and legal rights, or by serfs, impoverished peasants who were bound to the land and obliged to provide their lords with an array of services, dues in kind, and products. *page 283*

KEY TERMS

apostolic primacy (p. 274)   **manors** (p. 280)
demesne (dih-MEEN) (p. 280)   **Papal States** (p. 277)
fealty (p. 284)   **plenitude of power** (p. 275)
feudal society (p. 284)   **serf** (p. 280)
fiefs (p. 276)   **three-field system** (p. 280)
Magyars (p. 283)   **vassals** (p. 284)

REVIEW QUESTIONS

1. Trace the history of Christianity to the reign of the emperor Charlemagne. How did the church become a political power in the Western Roman Empire?

2. How did the Franks become the dominant force in western Europe? What were the characteristics of Charlemagne's rule? Why did his empire break apart?

3. How did the Merovingians attempt to solve the problem of "the one versus the many"? To what extent did they succeed? How did the Carolingian approach differ? Was it more successful?

4. How and why was the history of the eastern or Byzantine half of the Roman Empire so different from the western half? What were the major political and religious differences? How would you compare Justinian to Charlemagne?

5. Compare and contrast the teachings of Islam, Roman Catholicism, and Byzantine or Orthodox Christianity. Are they irreconcilable?

6. Discuss the role of Islam in the cultural development of western Europe. What impacts, direct or indirect, of Islam would you characterize as positive, and why? What about negative impacts?

7. What were the defining features of feudalism? Is a feudal society a "backward" society?

8. Why were trust and loyalty such important issues in western Europe's feudal period? Can you think of a social structure in which trust and loyalty are more important than they are in feudal society? Can you think of one where trust and loyalty are less important?

Note: To learn more about the topics in this chapter, please turn to the Suggested Readings at the end of the book. For additional sources related to this chapter please see www.myhistorylab.com

PEARSON
myhistorylab Connections

Reinforce what you learned in this chapter by studying the many documents, images, maps, review tools, and videos available at **www.myhistorylab.com**

Read and Review

✓•⌐**Study** and **Review** Chapter 11

••⌐**Read** the **Document** *Reign Justinian: Secret History, Procopius, p. 266*

Prologue, Corpus Civilis, ca. 530, p. 266

Epitome Iconoclastic Seventh Synod 754, p. 271

St. Benedict's Rules for Monks, p. 274

Pope Leo I on Bishop Hilary of Arles, p. 275

Life of Charlemagne (early ninth century) Einhard, p. 279

Feudalism, 1083, Archbishop of Cologne, p. 284

◉⌐**See** the **Map** *Charlemagne's Empire, 814, p. 278*

Viking Muslim and Magyar Invasions, 1000, p. 283

◉⌐**View** the **Image** *Emperor Justinian, p. 266*

Research and Explore

◉⌐**See** the **Map** *The Byzantine Empire under Justinian, p. 269*

◉⌐**See** the **Map** *Byzantium, 1000–1100, p. 270*

((•⌐**Hear** the **Audio**

Hear the audio file for Chapter 11
at **www.myhistorylab.com**

12

The Islamic World, 1000–1500

((•●—[Hear the Audio for Chapter 12 at www.myhistorylab.com

Islamic World Map. The geographical treatise and collection of wondrous tales, *The Wonders of Creation*, was popular in medieval and early modern Islamic society. The map shown here portrays several creatures supporting the world in the firmament. North is oriented at the bottom. Africa is the large triangular landmass jutting upward.

How does the perspective of this world map comment on the worldview of Islam in this period?

THE ISLAMIC HEARTLANDS

HOW DID the Sunni, Shi'ite, and Sufi traditions develop between the years 1000 and 1500?

WHO WERE the Mamluks, and why were they able to withstand the Mongols?

WHAT WERE the main ways Islam spread beyond Eurasia?

ISLAMIC INDIA AND SOUTHEAST ASIA

HOW DID trade and Sufi orders spread Islam?

WHAT ALLOWED Muslim rulers eventually to dominate India?

HOW DID local traditional beliefs shape Muslim practice in Southeast Asia?

HOW DID Islam become an enduring part of Indian civilization?

WHAT WERE some characteristics of Hindu culture in this period?

C entralized caliphal power in the Islamic world had broken down by the mid-tenth century. Regional Islamic states with distinctive political and cultural identities dominated—a pattern that would endure to modern times (see Map 12–1 on page 292). Yet the diverse Islamic lands remained part of a larger civilization. Muslims from Córdoba in Spain could (and did) travel to Bukhara in Transoxiana or Zanzibar or Malaysia and feel at home. Regionalism and cosmopolitanism, diversity and unity, have characterized Islamic civilization ever since.

The next 500 years saw the growth of a truly international Islamic community, united by shared norms of communal order represented and maintained by Muslim religious scholars

THE EXPANSION OF ISLAMIC CIVILIZATION, 1000–1500

In Islamic and other Asian territories, the period from about 1000 to around 1500 is difficult to characterize simply. The spread of Islam to new peoples or their ruling elites is an obvious theme. However, the history of Islam in India, for example, is hardly the history of India as a whole. The vast conquests and movements of Mongols and Central Asian Turks out of inner Asia were among the most striking developments in this period. Their effects on the societies they conquered were often cataclysmic, whether in China, South Asia, West Asia, or eastern Europe. These conquests and migrations wiped out much of the existing orders and forced countless refugees to flee to new areas. After the initial conquests, however, the empires created by these pastoral warriors, or *ghazis,* of Central Asia helped facilitate the movement across the Eurasian continent of people, merchandise, ideas, and, in the fourteenth century, the Bubonic pandemic. They also contributed, even if unintentionally, new, often significant human resources to older civilizations, such as those of China, the Islamic heartlands, and South Asia.

In this era, Islam became a truly cosmopolitan tradition of religious, cultural, political, and social values and institutions.

This achievement was possible because Islamic culture was highly adaptable and open to "indigenization," or a syncretistic blending of cultural traits, even in seemingly hostile contexts of polytheistic Hindu, South Asian, and African societies. The ability to adapt while maintaining the core tenets of the Muslim faith enabled Islamic religion and culture to take root in many different regions of the globe. Also in this period, distinct traditions of art, language, and literature, for all their regional diversity, became part of a larger Muslim whole. Islamic civilization had none of the territorial contiguity or linguistic and cultural homogeneity of either Chinese or Japanese civilization. Nevertheless, the Islamic world did become a recognizable international reality, a true *Dar al-Islam,* or "House of Islam," in which a Muslim could travel among and exchange ideas and goods with Muslims of radically different backgrounds from Morocco to China and encounter them as brothers/sisters of the *umma.* Ibn Battuta (1304–c. 1370), a Moroccan jurist, traveled for thirty years through Egypt to India and then to parts of Southeast Asia and China before returning to dictate his *Travels in Asia and Africa, 1325–1354.* As an Islamic judge and Arabic speaker, he was able to journey the length

---

(ulama). *Sufism, the strand of Islam that stressed spirituality and allegiance to a spiritual master, gained popularity, especially after 1200. The growth of Sufi affiliations or brotherhoods influenced Muslim life everywhere, often countering the more legalistic aspects of ulama conformity. Shi'ite ideas offered another alternative vision. Movements loyal to Ali and his heirs challenged but failed to reverse centrist Sunni predominance among the majority of Muslims, even though Shi'ite dynasties ruled much of the Islamic heartlands in the tenth and eleventh centuries.*

A cultural renaissance fueled the spread of modern Persian as the major language of Islam alongside Arabic. The Persian-dominated Iranian and Indian Islamic world became more distinct from the western Islamic lands where Arabic prevailed.

Two Asian steppe peoples, the Mongols and the Turks, controlled much of the Islamic world in these centuries, but with different results. Turkish rulers—the Saljuq sultans in Iran and Anatolia, and the "slave-kings" of both the Mamluk sultanate in Egypt and the Delhi sultanate in north India—infused Islamic cultures with Turkish influence. The Mongols conquered much of the Islamic heartlands in the thirteenth century, but their culture and religion did not become dominant. Instead, in this age Islam became the major new influence in Central, South, and Southeast Asia, as well as sub-Saharan Africa. ■

THE ISLAMIC HEARTLANDS

RELIGION AND SOCIETY

HOW DID the Sunni, Shi'ite, and Sufi traditions develop between the years 1000 and 1500?

In this period Islamic society was shaped by the consolidation and institutionalization of Sunni legal and religious norms, Sufi traditions and personal piety, and Shi'ite legal and religious norms.

and breadth of the global Islamic world and feel himself still within the bounds of one civilization.

Indian traditional culture was not bound up with a missionary religious tradition like that of Islam, and the developing caste system closely associated with Hindu traditions was less adaptable and much more tied to its homeland. Yet in this age Hindu kingdoms flourished in Indonesia, although these kingdoms mostly rejected the caste system and thus accommodated Hinduism and Indian culture to local conditions. Buddhism, another highly adaptable religion, was expanding across much of Central and Eastern Asia, thereby solidifying its place as an international missionary tradition.

Christianity, by contrast, was not rapidly expanding in Africa, Asia, or Europe. The somewhat disastrous experience of the Crusades (see Chapter 15) brought Europeans into closer contact with the Islamic world than ever before but did not attract converts to Christianity or increase European power in the Mediterranean. In the year 1000 Europe was almost a cultural and political backwater compared to major Islamic or Hindu states, let alone China. By 1500, however, European Christianity was poised for internal revolution and international expansion. European civilization was riding the crest of a commercial and cultural renaissance, enjoying economic and political growth, and starting global exploration for gold and silver to trade with more prosperous and cultured Asian lands. The impact on the Indian Ocean and Chinese-Japanese trade and shipping entrepôts was not immediate; it was only after the mid–eighteenth century that European exploration and trade initiatives became full-scale imperial expansion and rule that changed the rest of the globe profoundly.

See the Map
The Spread of Islam
at **myhistorylab.com**

Focus Questions

◆ What impact did the Mongols and Central Asian Turks have on the Islamic world?

◆ Why were Muslims and Buddhists more successful than Hindus and Christians in spreading their faiths in this era? What does this suggest about the characteristics of a successful world religion?

CONSOLIDATION OF A SUNNI ORTHOPRAXY

The *ulama* (both Sunni and Shi'ite) gradually became entrenched religious, social, and political elites throughout the Islamic world, especially after the breakdown of centralized power in the tenth century. Their integration into local merchant, landowning, and bureaucratic classes led to stronger identification of these groups with Islam.

From the eleventh century, the *ulama*'s power and fixity as a class were expressed in the institution of the **madrasa**, or college of higher learning. On the one hand, the *madrasa* had grown up naturally as individual experts frequented a given mosque or private house and attracted students seeking to learn the Qur'an, the *hadith* ("Tradition"), jurisprudence, Arabic grammar, and the like. On the other hand, rulers endowed the *madrasas* with buildings, scholarships, and salaried chairs, so that they could control the *ulama* by appointing teachers and influencing the curriculum. In theory, such control might combat unwelcome sectarianism. Unlike the university, with its corporate organization and institutional degrees, the *madrasa* was a support institution for individual teachers, who personally certified students' mastery of particular subjects. It gave an institutional base to Islam's long-developed system of students seeking out the best teachers and studying texts with them until they received the teachers' formal certification, or "permission" to transmit and teach those same texts themselves.

Largely outside *ulama* control, popular "unofficial" piety flourished in local pilgrimages to saints' tombs, in folk celebrations of Muhammad's birthday and veneration of him in poetry, and in ecstatic chant and dance among Sufi groups. But the shared traditions of family and civil law, daily worship rituals, fasting in **Ramadan**, and the Hegira united almost all Muslims, even most Kharijites or Shi'ites. In the Christian world, theological dogmas determined sectarian identity. Muslims, however, tended to define Islam in terms of what Muslims do—by practice rather than by beliefs. The chief

madrasa
An Islamic college of higher learning.

Ramadan
The month each year when Muslims must fast during daylight hours.

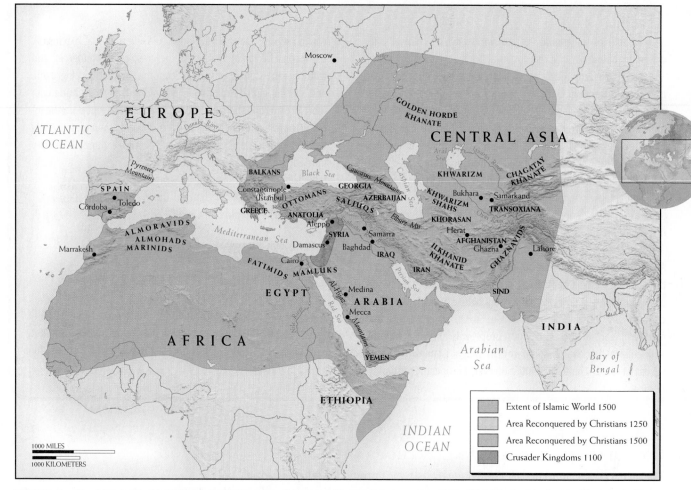

MAP 12–1.   The Islamic World, 1000–ca. 1500. Compare this map with Map 10–1 on page 249. Although the Muslim world expanded into Africa, India, and Central Asia, it also lost Spain to Christian reconquest.

Given the many Muslim states shown on this map, to what extent is it correct to speak of a single Islamic civilization?

arbiters of "normative" Sunni and Shi'ite Islam among the *ulama* were the *faqihs*, or legal scholars, not the theologians.

Sunni orthopraxy, or "correct religious practice," discouraged religious or social innovations. It was well established by the year 1000 as the dominant tradition, even though Shi'ite aspirations often made themselves felt either politically or theologically. The emergence of a conservative theological orientation tied to one of the four main Sunni legal schools, the Hanbalites (after Ibn Hanbal, d. 969) narrowed the scope for creative doctrinal change. The Hanbalites relied on a literalist reading of the Qur'an and the *hadith*. The *ulama* also became more socially conservative as they were integrated into social aristocracies. *Ulama* were often as committed to the status quo as rulers.

Sufi

Sufism is a mystic tradition within Islam that encompasses a diverse range of beliefs and practices dedicated to Divine love and the cultivation of the elements of the Divine within the individual human being. The chief aim of all Sufis is to let go of all notions of duality, including a conception of an individual self, and to realize the Divine unity.

SUFI PIETY AND ORGANIZATION

Sufi piety stresses the spiritual and mystical dimensions of Islam. The term **Sufi** apparently came from the Arabic *suf* ("wool"), based on the old ascetic practice of wearing only a coarse woolen garment. Sufi simplicity and humility had roots with the Prophet and Companions but developed as a distinctive tendency when, after about 700 C.E., male and female pietists emphasized a godly life over and above mere observance of Muslim duties. Some stressed ascetic avoidance of temptations, others loving devotion to God. Sufi piety bridged the abyss between human and Divine that Muslim insistence on an omniscient, omnipotent God implies. Socially, Sufi piety merged with folk piety in such popular practices as saint veneration, shrine pilgrimage, ecstatic worship, and seasonal festivals. Sufi writers collected stories of saints, wrote treatises on the Sufi path, and composed some of the world's finest mystical poetry.

Some Sufis were revered as spiritual masters and saints. Their disciples formed brotherhoods with their own distinctive mystical teaching, Qur'an interpretation, and devotional practice. These fraternal orders became the chief instruments of the spread of Muslim faith, as well as a locus of popular piety in almost all Islamic societies. Organized Sufism has always attracted members from the populace at large (in this, it differs from monasticism), as well as those dedicated to poverty or other radical disciplines. Indeed, Sufi orders became in this age one of the typical social institutions of everyday Islamic life. Whether Sunni or Shi'ite, many Muslims have ever since identified in some degree with a Sufi order.

CONSOLIDATION OF SHI'ITE TRADITIONS

Shi'ite traditions crystallized between the tenth and twelfth centuries. Many states now came under Shi'ite rulers, but only the Fatimids in Egypt established an important empire. A substantial Shi'ite populace developed only in Iran, Iraq, and the lower Indus (Sind).

Two Shi'ite groups emerged as the most influential. The first were the "Seveners," or "Isma'ilis," who recognized Isma'il (d. ca. 760), first son of the sixth Alid *imam*, as the seventh *imam*. Their thought drew on Gnostic and Neo-Platonic philosophy, knowledge of which they reserved for a spiritual elite. Isma'ili groups were often revolutionary.

By the eleventh century, however, the majority of Shi'ites accepted a line of twelve *imams*, the last of whom is said to have disappeared in Samarra (Iraq) in 873 into a cosmic concealment from which he will eventually emerge as the Mahdi, or "Guided One," to usher in the messianic age and final judgment. These "Twelvers" still focus on the martyrdom of the twelve *imams* and look for their intercession on the Day of Judgment. They have flourished best in Iran, home of most Shi'ite thought. The Buyids who took control of the Abbasid caliphate in 945 were Twelvers. The Safavids made Twelver doctrine the Iranian "state religion" in the sixteenth century (see Chapter 20).

REGIONAL DEVELOPMENTS

After the tenth century the western (or Mediterranean) half of the Islamic world had two regional foci: (1) Spain (*Al-Andalus*), Moroccan North Africa, and, to a lesser extent, West Africa; and (2) Egypt, Syria-Palestine, Anatolia, Arabia, and Libyan North Africa. The history of the eastern half of the Islamic world in the period between 1000 and 1500 was marked by the violent Mongol incursions of the thirteenth century.

SPAIN, NORTH AFRICA, AND THE WESTERN MEDITERRANEAN ISLAMIC WORLD

The grandeur of Spanish or Andalusian Islamic culture is visible still in Córdoba's Great Mosque and the remnants of the Alhambra Palace. In European tradition, the *Chanson de Roland* recalls Charlemagne's retreat through the Pyrenees after failing to check the first Spanish Umayyad's growing power. That ruler, Abd al-Rahman I (r. 756–788), was the founder of the cosmopolitan tradition of Spanish Umayyad culture at Córdoba, the cultural center of the Western world for the next two centuries. Renowned for medicine, science, literature, intellectual life, commercial activity, public baths and gardens, and courtly elegance, Córdoba reached its zenith under Abd al-Rahman III (r. 912–961),

Dancing Dervishes. This image from a 1552 Persian manuscript depicts a Sufi master dancing with his disciples. Sufis often use music and bodily movement to induce ecstatic experiences, which they feel bring them closer to God.

What role did Sufis play in the spread of Islam during this period?

QUICK REVIEW

Islamic Higher Education

- *Madrasa*: college of higher learning
- *Madrasas* were support institutions for individual teachers
- Operated within Islamic tradition of students seeking best teachers

WHO WERE the Mamluks, and why were they able to withstand the Mongols?

Al-Andalus
The Arabic name given to those parts of the Iberian Peninsula governed by Muslims, or Moors, at various times between 711 and 1492.

The Alhambra. Built in the fourteenth century, the Alhambra's serene, almost severe aspect belies its spectacular interior ornamentation. Considered one of the greatest examples of Islamic architecture and one of the most beautiful of all surviving medieval buildings, the Alhambra rises within its curtain walls above Granada, the last of the great Andalusian Moorish cities.

What were some highlights of Moorish culture?

•◄━|Read the Document
Ibn Rushd Averroes 12th century
at **myhistorylab.com**

Decorated Ceramic Bowl. A glazed ceramic bowl with a gazelle or antelope, symbolic of beauty and grace. From North Africa, Tunisian area, Fatimid (tenth–twelfth centuries).

Who were the Fatimids?

Reconquista
The Christian reconquest of Spain from the Muslims from 1000 to 1492.

who took the title of caliph in 929. His absolutist, but benevolent, rule saw a largely unified, peaceful Islamic Spain. The mosque-university of Córdoba that he founded attracted students from Europe as well as the Islamic world.

A sad irony of this cosmopolitan world was recurring religious exclusivism, as well as conflict among Muslims and Christians alike. Abroad, Abd al-Rahman III checked both Fatimid power in North Africa and northern Spain's Christian kingdoms, making possible a golden era of Moorish power and culture. After his death, fragmentation into warring Muslim principalities allowed a resurgence of Spain's Christian states from about 1000 until 1085, when the city of Toledo fell permanently into Christian hands.

Brief Islamic revivals in Spain and North Africa came under African reform movements of the Almoravids and Almohads. The Almoravids originated as a religious-warrior brotherhood among Berber nomads in West Africa. Having subdued northwestern Africa, in 1086 they carried their zealotry from their new capital of Marrakesh into Spain, reuniting its Islamic kingdoms. They persecuted arabized Christians (Mozarabs) as well as some Moorish Jews. Ensuing wars began the final major phase of the Spanish "Reconquest" (*Reconquista*), in which Christian rulers regained and Christianized Iberia. These conflicts are best known in the West for the exploits of El Cid (d. 1099), the mercenary adventurer who became the Spanish national hero.

The Almohads ended Almoravid rule in Morocco in 1147 and then conquered much of southern Spain. Before their demise (1225 in Spain; 1275 in Africa), they stimulated a brilliant revival of Moorish culture. During this era, paper manufacture reached Spain and then the rest of western Europe from the Islamic world. The westward odyssey of Indian fable literature through Iran and the Arab world ended in Spanish and Latin translations in thirteenth-century Spain. The greatest lights of this Spanish Islamic intellectual world were the major philosopher and physician Ibn Rushd (Averroës, d. 1189); the great Muslim mystical thinker Ibn al-Arabi (d. 1240); and the famous Jewish Arab philosopher Ibn Maymun (Maimonides, d. 1204).

EGYPT AND THE EASTERN MEDITERRANEAN ISLAMIC WORLD: THE FATIMIDS AND THE MAMLUKS

The major Islamic presence in the Mediterranean from the tenth to the twelfth centuries was that of the Shi'ite Fatimids, who claimed descent from Muhammad's daughter, Fatima. They began as a Tunisian dynasty, then conquered Morocco, Sicily, and Egypt (969), where they built their new capital, Cairo (*al-Qahira*, "the Victorious"). Their rule as Isma'ili Shi'ite caliphs (see Chapter 10) meant that for a time there were three "caliphates": in Baghdad, Córdoba, and Cairo. Content to rule a Sunni majority in Egypt, they sought recognition as true imams by other Isma'ili groups and were able briefly to take western Arabia and most of Syria from the Buyid "guardians" of the Abbasid caliphate (see Chapter 10).

Fatimid rule spawned two splinter groups that have played visible, if minor, roles in history. The Druze of modern Lebanon and Syria originated around 1020 with members of the Fatimid court who professed the divinity of one of the Fatimid caliphs. The tradition they founded is too far from Islam to be considered a Muslim sect. The Isma'ili Assassins, on the other hand, were a radical Muslim movement founded by a Fatimid defector in the Elburz Mountains of Iran around 1100. The name "Assassins" derives not from their infamous political assassinations, but from a European corruption of Arabic *Hashishiyyin* ("users of hashish"). This likely stemmed from the report that they used drugs to manipulate followers into undertaking usually suicidal assassination missions. Their movement was eradicated by the Mongols in the thirteenth century.

The Fatimids built the al-Azhar Mosque in Cairo as a center of learning, a role it maintains today, albeit for Sunni, not (as then) Shi'ite, scholarship. Fatimid rulers treated Egypt's Coptic Christians generally as well as they did their Sunni majority, and many Copts held high offices. Jews also generally fared well under Fatimid rule.

After 1100 the Fatimids weakened, falling in 1171 to Salah al-Din (Saladin, 1137–1193), a general and administrator under the Turkish ruler of Syria, Nur al-Din (1118–1174). Saladin, a Sunni Kurd, is well known in the West for his battles with the Crusaders, especially the retaking of Jerusalem (1187). After Nur al-Din's death, Saladin added Syria-Palestine and Mesopotamia to his Egyptian dominions and founded the Ayyubid Dynasty that, under his successors, controlled all three areas until Egypt fell to the Mamluks in 1250 and most of Syria and Mesopotamia to the Mongols by 1260.

Like Nur al-Din, and on the model of the Saljuks (see Chapter 10), Saladin founded *madrasas* to teach Sunni law. His and his Ayyubid successors' reigns in Egypt saw the entrenchment of a self-conscious Sunnism under a program of mutual recognition and teaching of all four Sunni schools of law. Henceforward Shi'ite Islam disappeared from Egypt.

The heirs of the Fatimids and Saladin in the eastern Mediterranean were the redoubtable Mamluk **sultans** ("[those with] authority"). The Mamluks were chiefly Circassians from the Caucasus, captured in childhood and trained as slave-soldiers. The first Mamluk sultan, Aybak (r. 1250–1257), and

CHRONOLOGY

WESTERN ISLAMIC LANDS

756–1021	Spanish Umayyad Dynasty
912–961	Rule of Abd al-Rahman III; height of Umayyad power and civilization
969–1171	Fatimid Shi'ite Dynasty in Egypt
ca. 1020	Origin of Druze community (Egypt/Syria)
1056–1275	Almoravid and Almohad dynasties in North and West Africa, Spain
1096–1291	Major European Christian crusades into Islamic lands; some European presence in Syria-Palestine
1171	Fatimids fall to Saladin, Ayyubid lieutenant of the ruler of Syria
1189	Death of Ibn Rushd (Averroës), philosopher
1204	Death of Musa ibn Maymun (Maimonides), philosopher, Jewish savant
1240	Death of Ibn al-Arabi, theosophical mystic
1250–1517	Mamluk sultanate in Egypt and (from late 1200s) Syria; claimed the Abbasid caliphate
1258	Hulagu Khan's Mongols sack Baghdad, ending Abbasid era
1260	Mamluk victory at Ain Jalut halts Mongol advance into Syria
ca. 1300	Ottoman state founded in western Anatolia
1406	Death of Ibn Khaldun, historian, social philosopher
1453	Byzantine empire ends with conquest of Constantinople by Ottoman forces under Sultan Mehmet I (1451–1481)

his successors were elite Turkish and Mongol slave-officers originally from the bodyguard of Saladin's dynasty. Seizing power in Egypt from the Ayyubids, they became the only Islamic dynasty to withstand the Mongols. Their victory at Ain Jalut in Palestine (1260) ended the Mongols' westward movement. The Mamluk state was based on a military fief system and total control by the slave-officer elite. Whereas the early Mamluks were often succeeded by sons or brothers, succession after 1400 was typically a survival of the fittest; no sultan reigned more than a few years.

The Mamluk sultan Baybars (r. 1260–1277), conqueror of the last Crusader fortresses, figures prominently in Arab legend. To legitimize his rule, he revived the Abbasid caliphate at least in name after Baghdad's devastation by the Mongols (1258) by installing an uncle of Baghdad's last Abbasid as caliph in Cairo. He made treaties with Byzantine and European sovereigns, and with the newly converted Muslim ruler, or *khan*, of the Golden Horde—the Mongol Tatars of southern Russia. His public works in Cairo were numerous, and he extended Mamluk rule south to Nubia and west among the Berbers.

As trade relations with Mongol domains improved after 1300, the Mamluks prospered, commanding a large empire. However, the Black Death epidemic of

sultans
Rulers who have almost complete sovereignty over a certain domain without claiming the title of caliph.

QUICK REVIEW

The Mamluks
- Only Islamic dynasty to withstand Mongols
- Based in eastern Mediterranean, Cairo
- Patronized scholars and artists

Mamluk Bottle. This elegant glass bottle was made in Mamluk workshops in Syria in the mid-fourteenth century for the Yemenite ruler.

John Tsantes/Courtesy of the Freer Gallery of Art, Smithsonian Institution, Washington, DC.

●●●⊷[Read the **Document**
al-Tha'Alibi, Recollections of Bukhara, at **myhistorylab.com**

QUICK REVIEW
───────────────

Ghaznavid Culture

◆ Mahmud of Ghazna supported Persian arts, scholarship

◆ Mathematician/scientist al-Biruni

◆ Poet Firdawsi helped establish "New Persian" language

Mamluk Trade. Trade in spices and other precious commodities between the Mamluks and western Europe was significant. In this painting from about 1500, we see Venetian ambassadors received by the governor of Damascus, who sits on a low platform wearing a distinctive, horn-shaped turban.

What kinds of goods were traded between Christian Europe and the Muslim Mediterranean?

1347–1348 in the Arab Middle East hurt the Mamluk and other regional states badly. Still, the Mamluks survived even the Ottoman conquest of Egypt in 1517 to continue there as Ottoman governors into the nineteenth century.

Architecture, much of which still graces Cairo, remains the major Mamluk bequest to posterity. In addition, mosaics, calligraphy, and metalwork were among the arts and crafts of special note. The Mamluks were great patrons of scholars who excelled in history, biography, astronomy, mathematics, and medicine. The most important of these was Ibn Khaldun (d. 1406). Born of a Spanish Muslim family in Tunis, he settled in Cairo as an adult. He is still recognized as the greatest Muslim social historian and philosopher of history.

THE ISLAMIC EAST: ASIA BEFORE THE MONGOL CONQUESTS

The Persian dynasties of the Samanids at Bukhara (875–999) and the Buyids at Baghdad (945–1055) were the major successors to eastern Abbasid dominion. Their successes epitomized the rise of regional states that undermined the caliphate from the ninth century onward. Similarly, their demise reflected another emerging pattern: the ascendancy of Turkish slave-rulers (like the Mamluks in the west) and Oghuz Turkish peoples, known as Turkomans. With the Saljuqs, what began with the use of Turkish slave troops in ninth-century Baghdad ended in the permanent presence of Turkish ruling dynasties in Islamic lands. As late converts, they became typically the most zealous of Sunni Muslims.

The rule of the Samanids in Transoxiana was ended by a Turkoman group in 999, but they had already lost eastern Iran south of the Oxus in 994 to one of their own slave governors, Subuktigin (r. 976–997). He set up his own state at Ghazna in modern Afghanistan, whence he and his son and successor, Mahmud of Ghazna (r. 998–1030), launched successful campaigns against his former masters. The Ghaznavids are notable for their patronage of Persian literature and culture and their conquests in northwestern India, which began a lasting Muslim presence in India. Mahmud was their greatest ruler. He is still remembered for his booty raids and destruction of temples in western India. At its peak, his empire stretched from western Iran to the Oxus and Indus.

Mahmud attracted to Ghazna numerous Khurasani Persian scholars and artists, notably the great scientist and mathematician al-Biruni (d. 1048), and the poet Firdawsi (d. ca. 1020). Firdawsi's *Shahnama* ("The Book of Kings") is the masterpiece of Persian literature, an epic of 60,000 verses that helped fix the "New Persian" language already developed especially by the earlier, prolific Khurasani poet, the Isma'ili Shi'ite Rudaki (d. ca. 941). It also helped revive pre-Islamic cultural traditions of the greater Iranian world, which became a hallmark of later Persian literature. After Mahmud the empire declined, although Ghaznavids ruled at Lahore until 1186.

The Saljuqs were the first major Turkish dynasty of Islam. They were a steppe clan who settled in Transoxiana, became avid Sunnis, and extended their sway over Khorasan in the 1030s. In 1055 they took Baghdad. As the new guardian of the caliphate and master of an Islamic empire, the Saljuq leader Tughril Beg (r. 1037–1063) took the title of *sultan* to signify his temporal authority. He and his early successors made various Iranian cities their capitals instead of Baghdad.

As new Turkish tribes joined their ranks, the Saljuqs brought Islamic rule for the first time into the central Anatolian plateau at Byzantine expense, even capturing the Byzantine emperor in their victory at

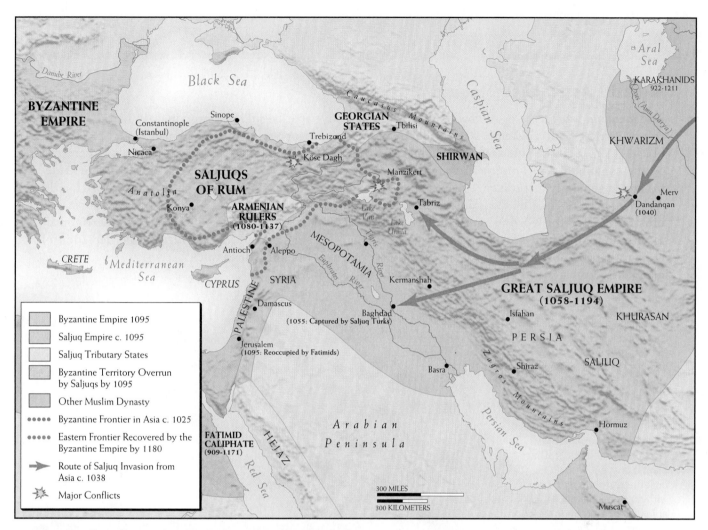

MAP 12–2. The Saljuq Empire, ca. 1095. By 1200, the Saljuqs had conquered Persia, Mesopotamia, and Syria and defeated Byzantine armies at Manzikert in 1071, altering the balance of power in the eastern Mediterranean and Near East.

How do the Saljuq conquests reveal the power of steppe peoples to overturn settled societies?

Manzikert, in Armenia, in 1071 (see Map 12–2). They also conquered much of Syria and wrested Mecca and Medina from the Shi'ite Fatimids. Turkish rule in Anatolia dates from 1077, when the Saljuq governor there formed a separate sultanate. Known as the Saljuqs of Rum ("Rome," i.e., Byzantium), these rulers were only displaced after 1300 by the Ottomans, another Turkish dynasty, who eventually conquered not only Anatolia but southeastern Europe (see Chapter 20).

The most notable Saljuq was the vizier Nizam al-Mulk, the real power behind two sultans from 1063 to 1092. In his time new roads and caravanserais (inns) for trade and pilgrimage were built, canals were dug, mosques and other public buildings were founded (including the first great Sunni *madrasas*), and science and culture were patronized. He also founded in 1067 what some contend was the first Muslim "university," the legal-theological *madrasa* of the Nizamiyyah in Baghdad. He subsequently established similar *madrasas* in Mesopotamia and Persia. He supported an accurate calendar reform and authored a major work on the art of governing, the *Siyasatnameh*. Before his murder by an Isma'ili assassin in 1092, he appointed as professor in the

QUICK REVIEW

Saljuq Culture

- Vizier Nizam al-Mulk established numerous *madrasas*
- Muhammad al-Ghazali, Muslim religious thinker
- Umar Khayyam, astronomer, mathematician, poet

A Closer Look

Al-Hariri, *Assemblies (Maqamat)*

The *maqama* was a type of rhymed Arabic prose narrative that began most prominently with the tenth-century writer Badi' al-Zaman al-Hamadhani and reached its apogee with Muhammad al-Hariri of Basra (1054–1122). Hariri's *Assemblies* is comprised of 50 rhetorically extravagant stories usually centered on the exploits of a picaresque trickster, Abu Zayd, who exposes the foibles of the powerful and prideful and is generally a confidence man who makes his way by his wits. The best illustrations of Hariri's *Assemblies* were done by the Iraqi miniature painter Yahya al-Wasiti in 1237. Here, one of al-Wasiti's illustrations for the 43rd *maqama* shows in realistic detail the arrival in a village of the narrator al-Harith and Abu Zayd on camels. Note that although Muslims have often avoided visual depiction of human beings as infringing on God's creativity, magnificent miniatures such as this were created in many different ages and places in the traditional Islamic world.

The village mosque's minaret is shown clearly here, with the rest of the village depicted as a line of houses along a street with glimpses of inhabitants engaged in everyday activities (spinning, talking, etc.) in the interior of the houses. The stylized layout and motifs (e.g., the plants) of the painting are nonetheless quite dynamic, with many people and animals engaged in different acts and activities.

Within the tightly composed picture there are various animals (goats, poultry, water buffalo) depicted, just as there are villagers, all subordinated to, and on a different plane from, the two arriving figures and the receiving villager in the foreground.

Questions

1. What kinds of activity and people can you pick out in the village? What sources of livelihood can you identify? What kinds of animals? How does the artist communicate so much activity and dynamism in such a small space?

2. Other than the minaret, what distinguishes the mosque from the rest of the village? What formal mechanisms does al-Wasiti use to make the scene dynamic despite the portrayal of characters in a stylized manner and layout?

Annotations by Susan Douglass.

Nizamiyyah Muhammad al-Ghazali (d. 1111), probably the greatest Muslim religious thinker. He also patronized the mathematician and astronomer Umar Khayyam (d. 1123), whose Western fame rests on the poetry of his "Quatrains," or *Ruba'iyat*.

Iranian Saljuq rule crumbled and by 1194 was wholly wiped away by another Turkish slave dynasty from Khwarizm in the lower Oxus basin. By 1200 these Khwarizm-Shahs had built a large, if shaky, empire and sphere of influence covering Iran and Transoxiana. In the same era the Abbasid caliph at Baghdad, al-Nasir (r. 1180–1225), established an independent caliphal state in Iraq. Neither his heirs nor the Khwarizm-Shahs were long to survive.

ISLAMIC ASIA IN THE MONGOL AGE

The building of a vast Mongol Empire spanning Asia from China to Poland in the thirteenth century proved momentous not only for eastern Europe and China (see Chapter 8), but also for Islamic Eurasia and India. A Khwarizm-Shah massacre of Mongol ambassadors brought down the full wrath of the Great Khan, Genghis (ca. 1162–1227), on the Islamic east. He razed entire cities from Transoxiana and Khorasan to the Indus (1219–1222). After his death, his empire's division into four khanates under his four sons gave the Islamic world respite. But in 1255 Hulagu Khan (r. 1256–1265), a grandson of Genghis, led a massive army again across the Oxus. Adding Turkish troops to his forces (Mongol armies typically included many Turks), he went from victory to victory, destroying every Iranian state. In 1258, when the Abbasid caliph refused to surrender, Hulagu's troops plundered Baghdad, killing at least 80,000 inhabitants, including the caliph and his sons.

Hulagu's wife, with Nestorian Christians and Buddhists in his inner circle, persuaded him to spare the Christians of Baghdad. He followed this policy in later conquests, including the sack of Aleppo—which, like Baghdad, resisted. Thus, when Damascus surrendered Western Christians had hopes of seeing Mamluk Cairo and Islamic power collapse, but Hulagu's drive west was delayed by rivalry with his kinsman Berke. A Muslim convert, Berke ruled the khanate of the Golden Horde, the southern-Russian Mongol state north of the Caucasus. He was in contact with the Mamluks, and some of his Mongols even helped them defeat Hulagu in Palestine (1260), stopping a Mongol advance into Egypt. A treaty in 1261 between the Mamluk sultan and Berke established an alliance confirming the breakup of Mongol unity and autonomy for the four khanates: in China (the Yuan Dynasty), Iran (the Ilkhans), Russia (the Golden Horde), and Transoxiana (the Chagatays).

Hulagu and his heirs ruled the old Persian Empire from Azerbaijan for seventy-five years as viceroys (Il-Khans) of the Great Khan of China's viceroys (*Il-Khans*). As elsewhere, the Mongols did not eradicate the society they inherited. Their native paganism and Buddhist and Christian leanings yielded to Muslim faith, although they practiced religious tolerance. After 1335 the Ilkhanid Empire broke up into provinces, and for fifty years Iran was again fragmented.

This situation prepared the way for a new Turko-Mongol conquest from Transoxiana, under Timur-i Lang ("Timur the Lame," or "Tamerlane," 1336–1405). Even Genghis Khan could not match Timur in the savagery of military campaigns. Timur's raiding between 1379 and 1405 was not aimed at empire-building, but sheer conquest. In successive campaigns he swept everything before him in a flood of devastation: eastern Iran (1379–1385); western Iran, Armenia, the Caucasus, and upper Mesopotamia (1385–1387); southwestern Iran, Mesopotamia, and Syria (1391–1393); Central Asia from Transoxiana to the Volga and as far as Moscow (1391–1395); North India (1398); and northern Syria and Anatolia (1400–1402). Timur's sole positive contributions seem to have been the buildings he sponsored at Samarkand, his capital. He left behind him ruins, death, disease, and political chaos across the entire eastern Islamic world, which did not soon recover. His was, however, the last great steppe invasion, for firearms soon destroyed the steppe horsemen's advantage.

Timur's sons ruled after him in Transoxiana and Iran (1405–1494). The most successful Timurid was Shahrukh (r. 1405–1447), who for a time controlled a united Iran. His capital, Herat, became an important center of Persian Islamic culture and Sunni piety. He patronized the famous Herat school of miniature painting as well as Persian literature and philosophy. The Timurids had to share Iran with Turkoman dynasties in western Iran, once even losing Herat to one of them. They and the Turkomans were the last Sunnis to rule Iran. Both were eclipsed at the end of the fifteenth century by the militant Shi'ite dynasty of the Safavids, who ushered in a new, Shi'ite era in the Iranian world (see Chapter 20).

THE SPREAD OF ISLAM BEYOND THE HEARTLANDS

WHAT WERE the main ways Islam spread beyond Eurasia?

The period from roughly 1000 to 1500 saw Islamic civilization spread to become a lasting religious, cultural, social, and political force in new regions (see Map 12–1). Expanding not only from Mesopotamia, Persia, and the Black Sea north to Moscow under the Golden Horde, but also west to the Balkans and the Danube basin under the Ottoman Turks, Islamic rule covered the greater part of Eurasia in this era (see Chapter 20). Meanwhile, India, Malaysia, Indonesia, inland West Africa, and coastal East Africa became major spheres of Islamic political, social, cultural, and commercial presence. In all these regions Sufi orders were most responsible for converting people and spreading Islamic cultural influences, though merchants, too, were major agents of cultural Islamization.

Conquest was a third (but demographically less important) means of Islamization (and either Arabization or Persianization) in these regions. Sometimes only ruling elites, sometimes wider circles, became Muslims, but in India, Southeast Asia, and sub-Saharan Africa much of the populace retained their languages, heritage, and religious traditions, while their elites learned Arabic and/or Persian as second or third languages. Nonetheless, in the most important of these regions, India, the coming of Islam brought epochal changes.

ISLAMIC INDIA AND SOUTHEAST ASIA

Indian Islamic civilization (like earlier Indian civilization) was formed by creative interaction between invading foreigners and indigenous peoples. The early Arab and Turkish invaders were a foreign Muslim minority; their heirs were truly "Indian" as well as Islamic, adding a new dimension to both Indian and Islamic civilization. From then on, Indian civilization would both include and enrich Islamic traditions.

THE SPREAD OF ISLAM TO SOUTH ASIA

HOW DID trade and Sufi orders spread Islam?

Well before the Ghaznavids came to the Punjab, Muslims were to be found even outside the original Arab conquest areas in Sind (see Map 12–3). Muslim merchants had settled in the port cities of Gujarat and southern India as diaspora communities to profit from internal Indian trade as well from trade with the Indies and China. Wherever Muslim traders went, converts to Islam were attracted by business advantages as well as by the

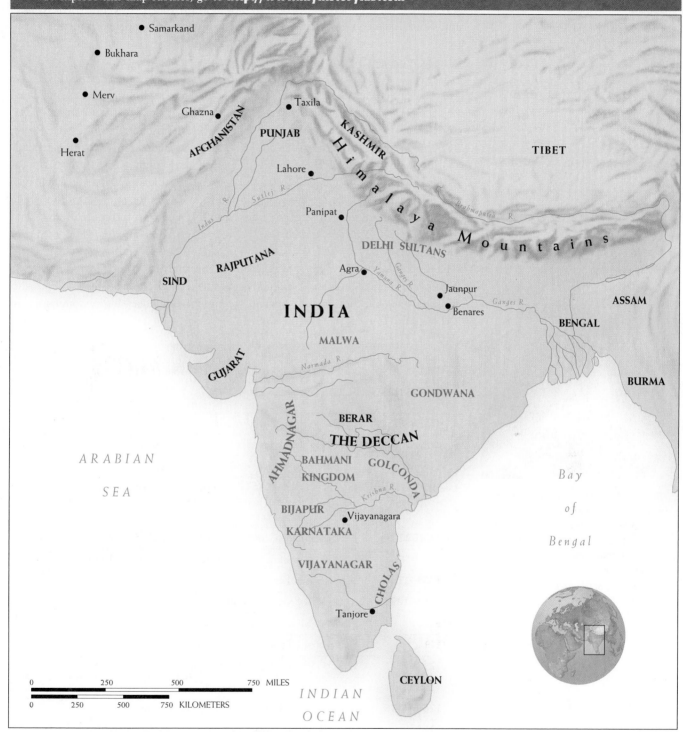

MAP 12–3. The Indian Subcontinent, 1000–1500.

Shown are major kingdoms and regions.

Where in India were the principal Islamic states located during this period?

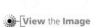
View the Image

The Indian Ocean Dhow Sailing Vessel,
at **myhistorylab.com**

Deccan
Large plateau with varying terrain that
constitutes most of southern India.

WHAT ALLOWED
Muslim rulers eventually
to dominate India?

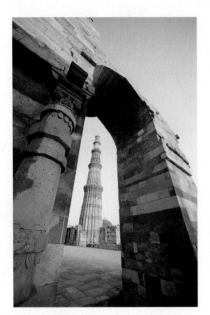

The Qutb Minar (Victory Tower) in Delhi is
an example of classic Indo-Muslim
architecture. Constructed in the twelfth
century, this soaring tower of red
sandstone commemorated Islamic
military victory.

**What features of this tower reflect Indian
cultural traditions?**

straightforward ideology and practice of Islam and its officially egalitarian, "classless" ethic. Sufi orders had gained a foothold in the central **Deccan** and in the south, giving today's south Indian Muslims old roots. Sufi piety also drew converts in the north, especially when the Mongol devastation of Iran in the thirteenth century sent refugees into North India. Muslim refugees strengthened Muslim life in the subcontinent.

MUSLIM-HINDU ENCOUNTER

From the outset Muslim leaders had to rule a land dominated by utterly different cultural and religious traditions. Much as early Muslim rulers in Iranian territories had given Zoroastrians legal status as "people of Scripture" (like Christians and Jews; see Chapter 10), the first Arab conquerors in Sind (711) had treated Hindus as "protected peoples" under Muslim sovereignty. These precedents gave Indian Muslim rulers a legal basis for co-existence with their Hindu subjects but did not remove Hindu resistance to Islamic rule.

The chief obstacle to Islamic expansion in India was the strength of the Hindu warrior class that emerged after the Hun and other Asian invasions of the fifth and sixth centuries. Apparently descended from invaders and the native Hindu warrior (Kshatriya) class, they were known from about the mid-seventh century as *Rajputs*. The Rajputs were a large group of northern Indian clans sharing a fierce warrior ethic and strong Hindu cultural and religious traditionalism. They fought the Muslims with great tenacity, but their inability to unite brought them under Muslim domination in the sixteenth century (see Chapter 20).

CHRONOLOGY	
EASTERN ISLAMIC LANDS	
875–999	Persian Samanid Dynasty, centered at Bukhara
ca. 941	Death of Rudaki, first Persian epic poet, father of "New Persian"
945–1055	Persian Buyid Shi'ite Dynasty in Baghdad controls caliphs
994–1186	Ghaznavid Dynasty in Ghazna (modern Afghanistan) and Lahore (modern Pakistan), founded by Subuktigin (r. 976–997) and his son, Mahmud of Ghazna (r. 998–1030)
ca. 1020	Death of Firdawsi, compiler of the Persian national epic, the *Shahnama*
ca. 1050	Death of al-Biruni, scientist, mathematician, and polyglot
1055–1194	Saljuq rule in Baghdad
1063–1092	Viziership of Nizam al-Mulk
1067	Nizam al-Mulk founds Nizamiyya Madrasa in Baghdad
1111	Death of al-Ghazali, theologian and scholar
1219–1222	Genghis Khan plunders eastern Iran to Indus region
1258	Hulagu Khan conquers Baghdad
1260–1335	Hulagu and his Il-Khanid successors rule Iran
1261	Mamluk-Mongol treaty halts westward Mongol movement
1379–1405	Campaigns of Timur-i Lang (Tamerlane) devastate entire Islamic East
1405–1447	Shahrukh, Timurid ruler at Herat, great patron of arts and philosophy
1405–1494	Timurids, successors of Tamerlane, rule in Transoxiana and Iran

ISLAMIC STATES AND DYNASTIES

A series of Turkish-Afghan rulers known as the "Slave Sultans of Delhi" extended and maintained Islamic power over North India for nearly a century (1206–1290). Such slave-soldiers, or **mamluks**, figured prominently in the leading elites of the new regime, much as they did in the Mamluk Dynasty in Egypt. Five descendants of Iltutmish ruled after him until 1266. The most vigorous of these was his daughter Raziyya, who ruled as sultana from 1237 to 1241.

Four later Muslim dynasties—the Khaljis, Tughluqs, Sayyids, and Lodis—continued the Delhi sultanate until nearly 1500. This run of Muslim dynasties was interrupted by Timur's Mongol-Turkish invasion and sack of Delhi in 1398, from which the city took decades to recover. However, even before this devastation—roughly from the mid-1300s—the sultanate's central authority waned. In the two centuries before the advent of the Mughals in the mid-sixteenth century, many regions became partially or wholly independent, smaller sultanates, Rajput kingdoms, or tiny Hindu or Muslim principalities. The sultanate was often only the most prominent among various kingdoms. Regional rule predominated across the subcontinent.

The most important independent Islamic state was that of the Bahmanids in the Deccan (1347–1527). These rulers were famous for architecture and the intellectual life of their court, as well as for containing the powerful South Indian Hindu state of Vijayanagar (1336–1565). (The first documented use of firearms in the subcontinent was in a Bahmani battle with the raja of Vijayanagar in 1366.) Most regional capitals fostered a rich cultural life. Jaunpur, to the north of Benares (Varanasi), for example, became an asylum for artists and intellectuals after Timur's sack of Delhi and boasted an impressive tradition of Islamic architecture. Kashmir, an independent sultanate from 1346 to 1589, was a literary center where many Indian texts were translated into Persian.

SOUTHEAST ASIA

Islam spread into Southeast Asia as a result of a natural extension of long-distance Islamic (Arab and Persian) and Indian trade across the Indian Ocean, land and sea migrations of scholars and merchants, and socialization of Indian peoples of South Asia. This extension of much older trade contacts eastward beyond the Indian subcontinent had unique characteristics of its own. Because of their geographic location, the islands in Southeast Asia readily connected India and China and thus became an important trade route by the fifteenth century. The spread of Islam in this region was not a steady, progressive development. Rather, the proliferation of Islam was idiosyncratic, and a number of distinct Islamic traditions emerged, centered largely around five areas: Java, Sumatra, Melaka, Acheh, and Moluccas (see Map 12–4 on page 304).

In some areas, such as the Moluccas, traditional Muslim beliefs coexisted with ancestor-worship, sorcery, or magic. Various central Islamic rites such as the pilgrimage (*Hajj*) were perceived to be an Arab custom and thus optional for "true" Muslims. Eventually, many political leaders adopted a more stringent Islamic practice, largely because this aided in greater centralization and consolidation of power.

One of the greatest sources of tension and conflict in this area was only tangentially related to distinct religious views: It was the struggle between the center and the periphery. Before the arrival of the Dutch in the early seventeenth century, the various urban rulers, typically located in port cities, benefited from the new global economy. They sought to subsume under their control the hereditary chiefs, who had also converted to Islam, by invoking Islam and their vision of a perfect society. The local

HOW DID local traditional beliefs shape Muslim practice in Southeast Asia?

mamluks
Slave-soldiers who converted to Islam, the mamluks eventually became a powerful military caste and even governed Egypt from 1250 to 1517.

MAP 12–4. **The Spread of Islam in Southeast Asia.**

What were the main reasons for the spread of Islam in Southeast Asia?

traditions proved to be durable, especially in the rural areas. Muslims in Southeast Asia therefore adapted Islam to their needs and customs rather than simply replacing the indigenous practices with the new universal and foreign religion.

RELIGIOUS AND CULTURAL ACCOMMODATION

HOW DID Islam become an enduring part of Indian civilization?

Despite the division of the subcontinent into multiple political units, the five centuries after Mahmud of Ghazna saw Islam become an enduring, influential element of Indian culture—especially in the north and the Deccan. The Delhi sultans were able, except for Timur's invasion, to fend off the Mongols, as had the Mamluks in Egypt. They thereby provided a political and social framework within which Islam could take root. Although a Muslim minority of Persianized Turks and Afghans continued to rule a Hindu majority, conversion went on at various levels of society. **Ghazis** ("warriors") carried Islam by conquest to pagan groups in eastern Bengal and Assam. Some Hindu converts came from the ruling classes serving Muslim overlords. Sufi orders converted many Hindus among the lower classes. The Muslim aristocracy, initially mostly foreigners, was usually treated in Indian society as a separate caste group. Lower class Hindu converts were assimilated into lower "Muslim castes," often identified by occupation. (See Document, "How the Hindus Differ from the Muslims" on page 306.)

Sanskrit had long been the common Indian scholarly language, but in this period regional languages, such as Tamil in the south, achieved literary and administrative status, and Persian became the intellectual and cultural language of the North Indian ruling elites. However, the infusion of substantial numbers of Muslims into the subcontinent produced a new language, **Urdu-Hindi**, with both Perso-Arabic and Indic ele-

ghazis
Warriors who carried Islam by force of arms to pagan groups.

Urdu-Hindi
A language that combines Persian-Arabic and native Indian elements. Urdu is the Muslim version of the language. Hindi is the Hindu version.

OVERVIEW   Major Islamic Dynasties, 1000s–1500s

DYNASTY	LOCATION	DYNASTY	LOCATION
(Spanish) Umayyads	Spain (756–1031)	"Great" Saljuqs Saljuqs (of Rum)	Iraq, Iran (1038–1194); Anatolia (1077–1307)
Almoravids	North Africa, Spain (1056–1147)	Abbasids	Based in Iraq (749–1258)
Almohads	North Africa, Spain (1130–1269)	Ghaznavids	Transoxiana, NW India (977–1186)
Fatimids	North Africa, then Egypt, Syria (909–1171)	Khwarizm-Shahs	Central Asia, Iran (c. 1077–1231)
Ayyubids	Egypt, Syria, Yemen (1169–late 1400s)	Ilkhanids	Iran (1256–1353)
Mamluks	Egypt, Syria (1250–1517)	Timurids	Transoxiana, Iran (1370–1506)
Samanids	Khurasan, Transoxiana (819–1005)	Delhi Sultans	Northern India (1206–1555)
Buyids	Iran, Iraq (932–1062)	Bahmanids and successors	Deccan/Central India (1347–1527)

ments. It began to take shape soon after the eleventh-century Muslim influx and developed in response to the increasing need of Hindus and Muslims for a shared language. It became the spoken idiom of the Delhi region and a literary language of North Indian and Deccan Muslims in the seventeenth and eighteenth centuries. Indo-European in grammar, it used Perso-Arabic vocabulary and script and was at first called *Hindi* ("Indian") or *Dakani* ("southern"), then in British times *Hindustani*. Eventually *Urdu* became the name for its Islamic version, based on its Perso-Arabic, Turkish heritage, and *Hindi* for the version associated with Hindu culture and its Sanskrit heritage. Ultimately, Urdu became the official national language of modern Pakistan, and Hindi, of modern India.

Indian Muslims, both immigrants and converts, were susceptible to Hindu influence (in language, marriage customs, and caste consciousness), much like Muslims in Africa and Asia. Unlike earlier immigrant elites, they were never utterly absorbed into Hindu culture but remained in some measure a group apart, proud to be distinct. The Muslim ruling classes saw themselves as protectors and propagators of Islam in India, and most of the Delhi sultans sought formal recognition for their rule from the nominal Abbasid caliphs in Baghdad or, in Mamluk times, in Cairo.

Nevertheless, the reciprocal influence of Muslims and Hindus was inevitable, especially in popular piety and among the masses as opposed to the ruling elites. Sufi devotion had an appeal similar to that of Hindu devotional, or **bhakti** movements (see Chapter 4), and each influenced the other. Some of India's most revered Sufi and *bhakti* saints date from the fourteenth and fifteenth centuries. During this period, various theistic mystics strove to transcend Hindu-Muslim antagonism and exclusivism. They typically preached devotion to a God who saves his worshipers without regard to either Hindu caste obligations or legalistic Muslim observance. The poet-saints Ramananda (d. after 1400) and Kabir (d. ca. 1518) were the two most famous such reformers.

bhakti
Hindu devotional movements.

DOCUMENT

How the Hindus Differ from the Muslims

Al-Biruni (d. ca. 1050), the greatest scholar-scientist of medieval Islam, was born in northeastern Iran. He spent much of his life at the court of Mahmud of Ghazna, whom he accompanied on expeditions into northwestern India. Alongside his scientific work, he learned Sanskrit, studied the Hindus, and wrote a History of India. *The following selections from this work illustrate the reach and sophistication of his mind.*

- **HOW DOES** the emphasis on purity and the impurity of foreigners that Biruni imputes to the Hindus compare with the attitudes of Islam? Other religions? Does this passage suggest why the Hindu tradition has remained largely an Indian one while Islam became international? To what might Biruni be referring in his comments on the relative absence of religious controversy among Hindus?

. . . The barriers which separate Muslims and Hindus rest on different causes.

First, they differ from us in everything which other nations have in common. And here we first mention the language, although the difference of language also exists between other nations. If you want to conquer this difficulty (i.e., to learn Sanskrit), you will not find it easy, because the language is of an enormous range, both in words and inflections, something like the Arabic, calling one and the same thing by various names, both original and derived, and using one and the same word for a variety of subjects, which, in order to be properly understood, must be distinguished from each other by various qualifying epithets. . . .

Secondly, they totally differ from us in religion, as we believe in nothing in which they believe, and vice versa.

On the whole, there is very little disputing about theological topics among themselves; at the utmost, they fight with words, but they will never stake their soul or body or their property on religious controversy. On the contrary, all their fanaticism is directed against those who do not belong to them—against all foreigners. They call them *mleecha*, i.e., impure, and forbid having any connection with them, be it by intermarriage or any other kind of relationship, or by sitting, eating, and drinking with them, because thereby, they think, they would be polluted. They consider as impure anything which touches the fire and the water of a foreigner; and no household can exist without these two elements. Besides, they never desire that a thing which once has been polluted should be purified and thus recovered, as, under ordinary circumstances, if anybody or anything has become unclean, he or it would strive to regain the state of purity. They are not allowed to receive anybody who does not belong to them, even if he wished it, or was inclined to their religion. This, too, renders any connection with them quite impossible, and constitutes the widest gulf between us and them.

In the third place, in all manners and usages they differ from us to such a degree as to frighten their children with us, with our dress, and our ways and customs, and as to declare us to be devil's breed, and our doings as the very opposite of all that is good and proper. By the by, we must confess, in order to be just, that a similar depreciation of foreigners not only prevails among us and the Hindus, but is common to all nations towards each other.

Source: From Edward C. Sachau, *Alberuni's India*, Vol. 1 (London: Kegan Paul, Trench, Truebner, 1910), pp. 17, 19, 20.

HINDU AND OTHER INDIAN TRADITIONS

WHAT WERE some characteristics of Hindu culture in this period?

The history of India from 1000 to 1500 was also important for the religious and cultural communities of India that as a whole vastly outnumbered the Muslims. The Jain tradition flourished, notably in Gujarat, Rajputana, and Karnataka. In the north Muslim conquests effectively ended Indian Buddhism—which had already been waning—by the eleventh century.

Hindu religion and culture flourished even under Muslim rule, as the continuing social and religious importance of the Brahmans and the popularity of *bhakti* movements throughout India attest. This was an age of Brahmanic scholasticism that produced many commentaries and manuals but few seminal works. *Bhakti* creativity was much greater. The great Hindu Vaishnava Brahman Ramanuja (d. 1137) reconciled *bhakti* ideas with the classical Upanishadic Hindu worldview in the Vedantin tradition. *Bhakti* piety permeates the masterpiece of Hindu mystical love poetry, Jayadeva's *Gita Govinda* (twelfth century), which is devoted to Krishna, the most important of Vishnu's incarnations.

The south continued to be the center of Hindu cultural, political, and religious activity. The major dynastic state in the south in this age was that of the Cholas, who flourished from about 900 to 1300 and patronized a famous school of bronze sculpture at their capital, Tanjore. Their mightiest successor, the kingdom of Vijayanagar (1336–1565), subjugated the entire south in the fourteenth century and resisted its Muslim foes longer than any other kingdom. Vijayanagar itself was one of India's most lavish cities and a center of the cult of Shiva before its destruction by the Deccan Bahmanid sultan.

Krishna Dancing on the Head of the Serpent Kaliya. This fifteenth-century bronze figure from Vijayanagar is based on the legend of how Kaliya infested the Jumna River's waters until Krishna leaped in and emerged dancing on the vanquished snake. Asian Art Museum of San Francisco. The Avery Brundage Collection B65B72. **How were Islam and Hinduism altered by their contact with each other?**

SUMMARY

 HOW DID the Sunni, Shi'ite, and Sufi traditions develop between the years 1000 and 1500?

Religion and Society. Between 1000 and 1500, the most important developments for the shape of Islamic society were of Sunni and Shi'ite legal and religious norms and of Sufi traditions and personal piety. Sunnism was the dominant tradition across the Islamic world. In both main branches of Islam, the *ulama* became the religious, social, and political elites and discouraged religious innovation. Shi'ism flourished in Iran under the Savafid rulers. Sufi piety stresses the spiritual and mystical dimensions of Islam. Sufi fraternal orders, whether Sunni or Shi'ite, became the chief instruments for spreading the Muslim faith in most Islamic societies. *page 290*

 WHO WERE the Mamluks, and why were they able to withstand the Mongols?

Regional Developments. Despite general religious tolerance and high cultural achievements, the Muslims were gradually pushed out of Spain by the Spanish Christian states between 1000 and 1492. In Egypt, the Shi'ite Fatamids established a separate caliphate from 969 to 1171.

 Read the Document
A Contemporary Describes Timur
at **myhistorylab.com**

The Mamluks, elite Turkish and Mongol slave-officers, were the only Muslim dynasty to withstand the Mongol invasions, thanks to military might and strong government. The Saljuqs, based in Anatolia and Iraq, were the first major Turkish dynasty of Islam. Other notable Islamic dynasties were the Ghaznavids in Transoxiana and the Khwarizm-Shahs in Persia. In 1255 the Mongols invaded the Muslim world and swept all before them, conquering Transoxiana, Persia, and Iraq, where they captured Baghdad and killed the last Abbasid caliph in 1258, before being defeated by the Mamluks in Syria in 1260. Thereafter, the Mongols established the Ilkhanid Dynasty in Persia and converted to Islam. Another wave of Turko-Mongol conquest under Timur-i Lang further devastated much of the Near East between 1379 and 1405. *page 293*

 WHAT WERE the main ways Islam spread beyond Eurasia?

The Spread of Islam beyond the Heartlands. Islamic rulers controlled most of Eurasia in the 1000–1500 period. Islam also gained influence in India, Malaysia,

Indonesia, and parts of West and East Africa. Trade and commerce, Sufi orders, and conquest were among the means by which Islam spread. *page 300*

 HOW DID trade and Sufi orders spread Islam?

The Spread of Islam to South Asia. Muslim traders, as well as Sufi brotherhoods, spread Islam in India, where it appealed to local needs and, for traders, seemed to offer business advantages. *page 300*

 WHAT ALLOWED Muslim rulers eventually to dominate India?

Muslim–Hindu Encounter. Hindus enjoyed protected status under Muslim rule in India, but they still resisted. Over time, lack of Hindu unity allowed Muslim rulers to increase their power. *page 302*

 HOW DID local traditional beliefs shape Muslim practice in Southeast Asia?

Islamic States and Dynasties. The Delhi sultanate, in which mamluks were prominent, maintained power in Northern India for much of this period. A variety of smaller, independent states emerged starting in the mid-1300s, including the Islamic Bahmanids in the Deccan. In Southeast Asia, Islam was spread by Muslim merchants and traders, as well as by Sufi brotherhoods, and wherever it took root, it blended with local customs. *page 303*

 HOW DID Islam become an enduring part of Indian civilization?

Religious and Cultural Accommodation. A new language, Urdu-Hindi, combined Persian-Arabic and indigenous Indian elements. There was reciprocal influence between Muslims and Hindus. *page 304*

WHAT WERE some characteristics of Hindu culture in this period?

Hindu and Other Indian Traditions. Buddhism all but disappeared from India during these years, but Hindu religion and culture flourished, even under Muslim control. Hindu devotional, or *bhakti*, movements were especially creative. *page 306*

KEY TERMS

Al-Andalus (p. 293)
bhakti (p. 305)
Deccan (p. 302)
ghazis (p. 305)
madrasa (p. 291)
mamluk (p. 303)

Ramadan (p. 291)
Reconquista (p. 294)
Sufi (soo-FEE) (p. 292)
sultans (p. 295)
Urdu-Hindi (p. 305)

REVIEW QUESTIONS

1. In the 1000–1500 period, why did no Muslim leader build a unified large-scale Islamic empire of the extent of the early Abbasids?

2. How were the *ulama* educated? What was their relationship to political leadership? What social roles did they play? What was the role of the *madrasas* in Islamic culture and civilization?

3. What was the impact of the institutionalization of Sufi piety and thought? What were the social and political roles of Sufism?

4. Discuss cultural developments in Spain before 1500. Why was Córdoba such a model of civilized culture? What were some of the distinguishing features of *al-Andalus*?

5. Why did Islam survive the successive invasions by steppe peoples (Turks and Mongols) from 945 on? What were the lasting results of these "invasions" for the Islamic world?

6. What were the primary obstacles to stable rule for India's Muslim invaders and immigrants? How did they deal with these obstacles?

7. What are some examples of reciprocal influence between Muslim and Hindu traditions in India?

8. What were noteworthy characteristics of the spread of Islam in Southeast Asia?

Note: To learn more about the topics in this chapter, please turn to the Suggested Readings at the end of the book. For additional sources related to this chapter please see www.myhistorylab.com

PEARSON
myhistorylab Connections

Reinforce what you learned in this chapter by studying the many documents, images, maps, review tools, and videos available at **www.myhistorylab.com**

Read and Review

✓● Study and Review Chapter 12

●●● Read the Document   *Al-Ghazali, excerpt from Confessions, p. 292*

Ibn Rushd Averroes 12th century, p. 294

al-Tha'Alibi, Recollection of Bukhara, p. 296

A Contemporary Describes Timur, p. 307

◉ View the Image   *The Indian Ocean Dhow Sailing Vessel, p. 302*

Research and Explore

👁 See the Map   *The Spread of Islam, p. 291*

👁 See the Map   *Delhi Sultanate, 1236 C.E.*

(((●● Hear the Audio

Hear the audio file for Chapter 12
at **www.myhistorylab.com**

13

Ancient Civilizations of the Americas

((•━│Hear the Audio for Chapter 13 at www.myhistorylab.com

A Mixtec View of Creation. In this manuscript, which predates the Spanish conquest, the Mixtec Indians of Oaxaca, Mexico, illustrate how their gods created the world. The complex narrative depicted here relates the creation of the Mother and Father of the gods by Lord and Lady One-Deer.

What is the connection between religious authority and political power in Native American civilizations, and how does this compare with other civilizations in the premodern period?

H umans first settled the American continents between 12,000 and 30,000 years ago. At that time glaciers locked up much of the world's water, lowering the sea level and opening a land bridge between Siberia and Alaska. The earliest undisputed archaeological evidence of humans in Tierra del Fuego, at the southern tip of South America, dates to 11,000 years ago, indicating that by then the immigrants' descendants had spread over all of both North and South America. When the glaciers receded the oceans rose, severing Asia from America. The inhabitants of the Americas were isolated from the inhabitants of Africa and Eurasia and would remain so until 1492.

Although isolated from one another, the peoples of the Americas, Africa, and Eurasia experienced similar cultural changes at the end of the Paleolithic. Some people shifted from

ANCIENT CIVILIZATIONS OF THE AMERICAS

Civilization in the Americas before 1492 developed independently of civilization in the Old World. As the pharaohs of Egypt were erecting their pyramid tombs, the people of the desert Pacific coast of Peru were erecting temple platforms. While King Solomon ruled in Jerusalem, the Olmec were creating their monumental stone heads. As Rome reached its apogee and then declined, so did the great city of Teotihuacán in the Valley of Mexico. As Islam spread from its heartland, the rulers of Tikal brought their city to its greatest splendor before its abrupt collapse. Maya mathematics and astronomy rivaled those of any other peoples of the ancient world. And as the aggressive nation-states of Europe were emerging from their feudal past, the Aztecs and Incas were consolidating their great empires. The agriculture, engineering, and public works of these states—as exemplified by the famous Aztec drainage systems, the floating gardens or *chiampas* of Lake Texcoco, and the Inca system of roads and their terraced agriculture—exquisitely demonstrate an ability to master the most challenging environments.

The encounter between Old World and New commencing at the close of the fifteenth century, however, proved devastating for American civilizations. The same naval and military technology that allowed Europeans to embark on the voyages of discovery and fight destructive wars among themselves caught the great native empires unprepared. More important, however, was what historian Alfred Crosby has called the "Columbian Exchange." The peoples of the New World exchanged trade goods, ideas, technology, and microbes among themselves, along north–south trade routes that linked the American Southeast and Southwest to Mesoamerica, and the peoples of the northern Andes to those of the central and southern regions, as well as east–west routes linking eastern North America with the Great Lakes region and beyond. The coming of the Spanish profoundly disturbed both the patterns of trade and the ecological balance. Most significant, the Spanish introduced new epidemic diseases against which the peoples of the New World did not possess immunity. During the first century after the encounter

hunting and gathering to an agricultural way of life. Scholars of the early Americas call this the Paleoindian period.

Between approximately 8000 B.C.E. and 2000 B.C.E., in what is termed the Archaic period, climatic changes occurred in Central America. Large animals, including mammoth, became extinct, altering humans' food supply. The diet of maize (corn), beans, and squash came to predominate. The domestication of new crops led to a much more sedentary life. New kinds of weapons and tools were developed to secure and process new foods.

After about 2000 B.C.E., during what is called the Formative period, remarkable civilizations emerged as societies grew increasingly stratified, villages coalesced into urban centers, monumental architecture was erected, and artistic traditions developed. The two most prominent centers of pre-Columbian American civilization—and the focus of this chapter—were Mesoamerica, in what is today Mexico and Central America, and the Andean region of South America. At the time of the European conquest of the Americas in the sixteenth century, two relatively recent, expansionist empires—the Aztecs, or Mexica, in Mesoamerica, and the Inca in the Andes—dominated their respective environments. Spanish conquerors obliterated both of these empires and nearly succeeded in obliterating native culture. But in both regions, Native American traditions have endured, overlaid and combined in complex ways with Spanish culture, to provide clues to the pre-conquest past. ■

RECONSTRUCTING THE HISTORY OF NATIVE AMERICAN CIVILIZATION

WHAT PROBLEMS do scholars face in reconstructing the history of Native American civilizations?

Andean civilizations in South America never developed writing, and in Mesoamerica much of the written record was destroyed by time and conquest. Archaeologists have been able to create a picture of the economic and social organization of ancient American civilizations, but archaeology alone cannot produce the kind of narrative history that thousands of years of written records have made possible for Eurasian civilizations.

these diseases, killing vast numbers of people and affording the Europeans a psychological edge, played a key role in the conquest of the peoples of the New World.

Equally important in understanding the ability of small numbers of Europeans to conquer these advanced civilizations, however, was the nature of the civilizations themselves. Neither the Americans nor their cultures were static or immobile; they were definitely not, in one historian's words, "a people without history," even if much of that history is lost to us because of the absence or destruction of written records. The European invaders succeeded most rapidly in toppling the most organized of the societies in the New World, the Aztecs and the Inca, precisely because these societies were organized, centralized, and hierarchical.

It is important to remember that the history of New World civilizations in the face of the encounter was tightly linked to internal developments before the arrival of Europeans. The Aztecs and Incas, in particular, ruled over different peoples, many of whom resented their subjugation and saw in the arrival of the Europeans an opportunity to assert their autonomy. Thus the Spanish in Mexico and, to a lesser extent, in Peru, found allies among the local peoples willing to do much of the fighting for them. When Hernán Cortés faced the Aztecs in the decisive battle for their capital city, Tenochtitlán, he did so with at least 30,000 indigenous warriors by his side. Consequently, the Spanish intruded into a political situation that was itself already in flux and prepared to respond to the introduction of new military and cultural forces.

Focus Questions

◆ Why is it important to bear in mind that the civilizations of the New World had long and rich histories before the arrival of Europeans? Why is it so difficult to discover the details of the history of the peoples of the Americas? What are our major sources of information?

◆ What role did the environment play in the formation of American civilizations?

However, from the ancient civilization of the Maya in Mesoamerica specimens of writing survive, and scholars have deciphered their script and attached names, dates, and events to silent ruins.

◉ View the Image
Mayan Ruins, at **myhistorylab.com**

We also have accounts of the history and culture of the Aztecs and Inca produced by Spanish missionaries and officials. Although these accounts are invaluable sources of information, they are also obviously biased. Scholars seeking to understand Native American civilization have had to rely on the language and categories of European thought to investigate peoples and cultures that had nothing to do with Europe. Columbus and other early explorers (see Chapter 17), believing they had reached the East Indies, called the people they met in the Caribbean "Indians." This misnomer stuck and extended to all Native American peoples who, of course, had other names for themselves. The name *America* itself is European, taken from Amerigo Vespucci (1451–1512), a Florentine who explored the coast of Brazil in 1501 and 1502.

MESOAMERICA: THE FORMATIVE PERIOD AND THE EMERGENCE OF MESOAMERICAN CIVILIZATION

Mesoamerica (meaning "middle America") extends from Central Mexico into Central America (see Map 13–1 on page 314). This is a region of great physical diversity, ranging from lowland tropical rain forests to temperate highlands with fertile basins and valleys. Lowland regions include the Yucatán Peninsula and the Gulf and Pacific coasts. Highland regions include Mexico's central plateau and the mountainous areas of Guatemala. Most of Mesoamerica's mineral resources are found in the highlands. The lowlands were the source of many important trading goods, including hardwoods, plant dyes, and the prized feathers of exotic birds.

WHAT GROUP dominated Olmec society?

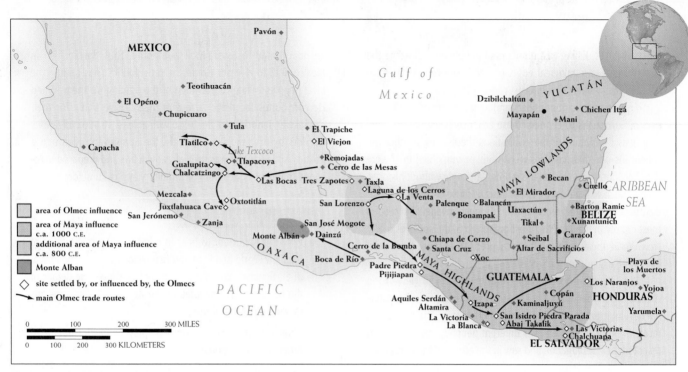

MAP 13–1. Mesoamerica: The Formative and Classic Periods.

What Role did trade play in the formation of Mesoamerican civilizations?

✓•⌐Study and Review
at **myhistorylab.com**

obsidian

A hard volcanic glass that was widely used in Mesoamerica.

Aztec Calendar Stone. When the Aztec "calendar" was unearthed in Mexico in 1790, it confirmed the greatness and complexity of the Americas' pre-Columbian civilizations.

What system was the basis for the Aztec calendar?

Mesoamerica also designates a distinctive cultural tradition that emerged in this region between 1000 and 2000 B.C.E., manifested itself in a succession of impressive states until the coming of European conquerors in the sixteenth century, and continues to express itself in the lives of indigenous peoples. Mesoamerica is not culturally homogeneous: The peoples of Mesoamerica were and are ethnically and linguistically diverse. There was no single Mesoamerican civilization, nor was there a single linear development of civilization in the region. Nonetheless, Mesoamerican civilizations shared many traits, including writing, a sophisticated calendrical system, many gods and religious ideas, a ritual ball game, and urban centers with religious and administrative buildings symmetrically arranged around large plazas.

Long-distance trade linked the peoples of Mesoamerica. Metallurgy came late to Mesoamerica, and it was used primarily for ceremonial objects rather than for weapons and tools. Mesoamericans made weapons and other tools from **obsidian**, a volcanic glass capable of holding a razor-sharp edge, and for that reason a valued trade commodity.

Mesoamerican history before the Spanish conquest is conventionally divided into four major periods: Archaic, Formative, Classic, and Post-classic. The term *Classic*, with its connotations of "best" or "highest," derives from European historical frameworks. It reflects the view of many early Mesoamericanists that the Classic period, which corresponds more or less to the time during which the Maya civilizations of the southern Yucatán erected dated stone monuments called stelae, was the high point of Mesoamerican civilization. Despite various controversies, this chronology continues to provide a useful framework.

The transition from hunting and gathering to settled village life occurred gradually in Mesoamerica during the Archaic period. The cornerstone of the process was the domestication of maize (corn) and other staple crops, including beans and squash. Other plants native to the Americas that were domesticated in this period include tomatoes, chili peppers, and avocado. Maize and beans were particularly important

Figure 13.1 Number of Domesticated Species Compared*

	Continent			
	Eurasia	**Sub-Saharan Africa**	**The Americas**	**Australia**
Domesticated Species	13	0	1	0

*A species is defined as a wild mammal weighing on the average over 100 pounds. Thirteen species were domesticated in Eurasia in antiquity: sheep, goats, cows, pigs, horses, Arabian camels, Bactrian camels, donkeys, reindeer, water buffalo, yak, Bali cattle, and mithan. Only one species was domesticated in the Americas: llamas (alpacas), which are found in the Andes.

Adapted from Jared Diamond, *Guns, Germs, and Steel* (New York: W. W. Norton, 1997).

because together they provide a richer source of protein than the grains that were the basis of the Neolithic revolution in the ancient Near East and China. Mesoamerica was poor in sources of animal protein, having only a few small domesticated animals—among them dogs and turkeys—and no large herd animals like the cattle, sheep, and goats of the Old World (see Figure 13–1).

The domestication of maize, beans, and other plants secured the people of Mesoamerica an adequate and dependable diet. Over time they devised myriad ways to prepare and store these staples. Since the conquest, maize has also been one of Mesoamerica's major contributions to the world.

Probably because they had no large draft animals, the people of the Americas never developed the wheel. (They did make wheeled toys, however.) In Mesoamerica, humans did all the carrying. And because there were neither horses nor chariots, wars in Mesoamerica—and in Andean South America—were fought by foot soldiers.

Between 5000 and 2500 B.C.E. villages began to appear in both highland and lowland regions of Mesoamerica. By about 2000 B.C.E. settled agricultural life had taken hold in much of the region. As in the Old World, people began to make fired clay vessels, and ceramic technology appeared. Nomadic hunter-gatherers have little need of storage, but farmers do, and clay vessels filled that need. Pottery is also a medium for artistic expression, and it played a role in religion and ritual observance.

MESOAMERICAN BALLGAMES

Peoples throughout ancient Mesoamerica played a complicated ball game that originated before 1700 B.C.E. Ruins of approximately 1,500 ball courts from different eras have been unearthed from the Southwest of the United States to the Amazon, as well as on Cuba. Early Spanish explorers and missionaries witnessed the game among the Aztecs and were fascinated.

The game involved multiple players—team sizes differed from area to area—contesting a hard rubber ball, apparently without using their hands. Courts were shaped in the form of an "I" and were usually at least as long as a modern football field. The goal was to move the ball to the opponents' end court. At some point in the Classic period, the game came to involve shooting the ball through a stone hoop.

The Mesoamerican ball game was very dangerous and often violent. The rubber balls were hard, so players wore elaborate protective headgear and padding for both arms and legs, as portrayed in ancient sculpture and paintings. Some sculptures

Ball Court at Monte Alban. Like most ball-game courts that have survived throughout Mesoamerica, the ball court at the Monte Alban Temple Complex in Oaxaca has an "I" shape with a long, narrow alley flanked on both sides by stone walls.

What purposes did Mesoamerican ball games serve?

••◄ Read the **Document**
Victory over the Underworld,
at **myhistorylab.com**

portray women in sports gear, though it is unclear whether women actually competed. The players, like modern sports figures, occupied prestigious positions in their societies.

Games often carried elaborate political and ritualistic overtones. Some accounts tell of political disputes being settled by playing a ball game instead of warfare. For some peoples, the game served to reenact major events recorded in mythology. (See p. 320 regarding the Maya ball games.) On other occasions the games were rigged to reenact past warfare, with the team of the side that had lost the war losing the game. In some cases, losers were sacrificed.

THE OLMEC

◄•◄ Hear the **Audio**
Early Americas
at **myhistorylab.com**

By about 1500 B.C.E. Mesoamerica's agricultural villages were beginning to coalesce into more complicated societies with towns, monumental architecture, class divisions, long-distance trade, and sophisticated artistic traditions (see Map 13–1). The most prominent Early Formative period culture is the Olmec, centered on the lowlands of Mexico's Gulf coast. Most knowledge about the Olmecs comes from the archaeological sites of San Lorenzo and La Venta. San Lorenzo, first occupied in about 1500 B.C.E., had developed into a prominent center by about 1200 B.C.E. It included public buildings, a drainage system linked to artificial ponds, and a ball court. The center flourished until about 900 B.C.E., and was abandoned by about 400 B.C.E. As San Lorenzo declined, La Venta rose to prominence, flourishing from about 900 to 400 B.C.E. La Venta's most conspicuous feature is the 110-foot Great Pyramid, which stands at one end of a group of platforms and plazas aligned along a north–south axis. Many artifacts were buried along the center line of this axis.

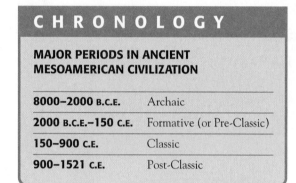

CHRONOLOGY

MAJOR PERIODS IN ANCIENT MESOAMERICAN CIVILIZATION

8000–2000 B.C.E.	Archaic
2000 B.C.E.–150 C.E.	Formative (or Pre-Classic)
150–900 C.E.	Classic
900–1521 C.E.	Post-Classic

The population of San Lorenzo and La Venta was never great, probably less than 1,000 people. The monumental architecture and sculpture at these sites—including massive stone heads, thought to be portraits of rulers, carved from basalt from quarries as much as 65 miles away—suggest that Olmec society was dominated by an elite class of ruler-priests able to command the labor of farmers who lived in outlying villages.

Among the most pervasive images in Olmec art is that of the were-jaguar, a half-human, half-feline creature. The were-jaguar may have been a divine ancestor figure, perhaps providing the elite with the justification for their authority. Similarities between the were-jaguar iconography and that of later Mesoamerican deities suggest some of the underlying continuities linking Mesoamerican societies over time.

The raw material for many Olmec artifacts, such as jade and obsidian, comes from other regions of Mesoamerica. Control of trade in such high-status materials by the Olmec elite contributed to their prestige and authority.

THE VALLEY OF OAXACA AND THE RISE OF MONTE ALBÁN

Olmec civilization had disappeared by about 200 B.C.E. Some of the most significant settlements in the Late Formative period were in the Valley of Oaxaca. Around 500 B.C.E., Monte Albán was built on a hill where three branches of the valley meet. Its population grew to about 5,000, and it emerged as the capital of a state that dominated the Oaxaca region. Carved images of bound prisoners imply that warfare played a role in establishing its authority. These images also suggest an early

Olmec Monument. A large carved monument from the Olmec site of La Venta with a naturalistically rendered human figure.

What does the size of Olmec carvings suggest about Olmec political power?

origin for the ritual human sacrifice that characterized most Mesoamerican cultures. Monte Albán maintained its independence against the growing power of the greatest city of the Classic period, Teotihuacán.

THE EMERGENCE OF WRITING AND THE MESOAMERICAN CALENDAR

The earliest evidence of writing and the Mesoamerican calendar has been found in the Valley of Oaxaca. The Mesoamerican calendar is based on two interlocking cycles, each with its own day and month names. One cycle, tied to the solar year, was of 365 days; the other was of 260 days. Combining the two cycles produced a "century" of 52 years, the amount of time required before a particular combination of days in each cycle would repeat itself. The hieroglyphs found in Oaxaca relate to the 260-day cycle. At the time of the Spanish conquest, all the peoples of Mesoamerica used the 52-year calendrical system.

THE CLASSIC PERIOD IN MESOAMERICA

The Classic period was a time of cultural florescence. In central Mexico, it saw the rise of Teotihuacán, a great city that rivaled the largest cities of the world at the time. The Maya, who built densely populated cities in the seemingly inhospitable rain forests of the southern Yucatán, developed a sophisticated system of mathematics and Mesoamerica's most advanced hieroglyphic writing. Indeed, urban life in Classic Mesoamerica was richer and grander than that of contemporaneous Europe north of the Alps.

Scholars have recently made enormous strides in understanding Classic civilization. Progress in deciphering Maya hieroglyphics has opened a window on politics and statecraft. Archaeological studies have broadened our understanding of Teotihuacán and Maya cities, providing clues to the lives of the people who lived in them.

Classic cities, with their many temples, plazas, and administrative buildings, were religious and administrative centers whose rulers combined secular and religious authority. Warfare was common, and Classic rulers did not hesitate to use force to expand their authority. Ritual sacrifice of captive enemies was widespread.

TEOTIHUACÁN

In the Late Formative period two centers competed for dominance over the rapidly growing population of the Valley of Mexico. Cuicuilco was located at the southern end of the valley, whereas Teotihuacán was located about 30 miles northeast of Mexico City. When a volcano destroyed Cuicuilco in the first century C.E., Teotihuacán grew into a great city, perhaps Mesoamerica's first city-state, dominating central Mexico for centuries and strongly influencing the rest of Mesoamerica.

Natural advantages contributed to Teotihuacán's rise. A network of caves recently discovered under its most prominent monument, the Pyramid of the Sun (the name by which the Aztecs knew it), may have been considered an entrance to the underworld. Stone quarried from the caves was used to construct the city, creating a symbolic link between the city's buildings and its sacred origins. Teotihuacán is also near a source of obsidian, and it straddled a trade route to the Gulf Coast and southern Mesoamerica. It was surrounded by fertile farmland.

At its height around 500 C.E., Teotihuacán extended over almost 9 square miles and had a population of more than 150,000, making it one of the largest cities in the world at the time. Its size and organization suggest that it was ruled by a powerful, centralized authority. It was laid out on a rigid grid plan dominated by a broad, 3-mile-long thoroughfare known as the Avenue of the Dead. Religious and administrative structures and a market occupy the center of the city. At one end of the Avenue of the Dead is the so-called Pyramid of the Moon, and near it, to one side, is the 210-foot-high

WHAT WERE some of the main achievements of the Classic period civilizations in Mesoamerica?

Watch the Video
Teotihuacán Ruins in Mexico
at **myhistorylab.com**

A Closer Look

The Pyramid of the Sun in Teotihuacán

Teotihuacán, located outside Mexico City, remains one of the most important and most mysterious of all the great pre-Columbian archaeological sites. It was a vast city with a population in the hundreds of thousands, flourishing at its height in about 500 C.E. and becoming abandoned about 800 C.E., hundreds of years before the rise of the Aztec Empire. Extremely little is actually known about this city, including the name it inhabitants gave it. The name "Teotihuacán," meaning Where the Gods Were Born, is the name that the Aztecs gave to it long after it had been abandoned. They also gave names to many of the surviving structures and streets in the city.

    The Pyramid of the Sun is the second largest pyramid on the American continents and the third in the world, being just over 200 feet high. It was constructed during the first two centuries C.E. The religious rituals for which it was intended are unclear, though human sacrifice appears to have occurred on it. The great structure, which was probably topped by a small frame temple, is located over a system of subterranean caves linked to the pyramid. This and other monuments in Teotihuacán were admired by the later peoples who lived in central Mexico who associated the site with their own myths. At the time Cortés arrived, the Aztec emperor Moctezuma visited the site, apparently hoping to receive guidance or wisdom from the ancients who had once inhabited it.

This somewhat romanticized painting by Jorge Pérez de Lara in 1878 indicates how the Pyramid of the Sun and the area surrounding it looked in the decades before formal archaeological excavations began in 1905 and the pyramid was restored in 1910 as part of the centennial of Mexican independence.

This photo illustrates how tourists encounter the site today, with the great pyramid having been reconstructed now for over a century. In ancient times, the pyramid was apparently covered by plaster and painted red. Much archaeological work remains to be carried out on the Pyramid of the Sun and Teotihuacán as a whole.

Picture Desk, Inc./Kobal Collection.

Questions

1. How might you imagine the reactions of successive generations of visitors to the ruins of the Pyramid of the Sun? For example, what were the reactions of the pre-Aztec peoples who encountered it as an abandoned site, the Aztecs who considered it a sacred place, the early Spanish who were amazed at the size of the edifice, later archaeologists, and still later tourists? How do differing expectations determine what people experience when visiting ancient sites? Why is it so difficult to imagine ancient urban sites, now abandoned with only monuments remaining, as places once inhabited by tens of thousands of people?

2. How does archaeological evidence, in the Americas or elsewhere in the world, differ from written records or the artistic record?

3. How could the restoration of the Pyramid of the Sun in 1910 be used to link modern and ancient Mexico? Do you know of other restorations of ancient sites carried out by modern governments?

Pyramid of the Sun. More than 2,000 residential structures surround the city center. The lavish homes of the city's elite lie nearest the center. Most of the city's residents lived in walled apartment compounds that were also centers of craft manufacture with neighborhoods devoted to pottery, obsidian work, and other specialties. Parts of the city were reserved for foreign traders. Murals adorned the interiors of many residences, of common people as well as the elite. The humble dwellings of poor farmers—who were apparently forced to abandon their villages and move to Teotihuacán—occupied the city's periphery.

Teotihuacán's influence extended throughout Mesoamerica. In the central highlands, dispersed settlements were consolidated into larger centers laid out similarly to Teotihuacán, suggesting conquest and direct control—a Teotihuacán empire. The city's influence in more distant regions may have reflected close trading ties. The city's obsidian and pottery were exchanged widely for items like the green feathers of the quetzal bird and jaguar skins, valued for ritual garments.

Among the deities of Teotihuacán are a storm god and his goddess counterpart, who may be linked to the Aztec's rain god. The people of Teotihuacán also worshiped a feathered serpent, recognizably antecedent to the god the Aztecs worshiped as Quetzalcoatl and the Maya as Kukulcan. Murals also suggest that the Teotihuacán elite, like the Maya and later Mesoamerican peoples, drew their own blood as a form of sacrifice to the gods. They also practiced human sacrifice.

After 500 C.E. Teotihuacán's influence began to wane, and in the eighth century its authority collapsed. A fire swept through the city, destroying the ritual center and the residences of the elite and hinting at an internal revolt. Although a substantial population remained, the city never regained its former status. It retained a hold on the imagination of succeeding generations of Mesoamericans, however, much as the ruins of ancient Greece and Rome influenced later Europeans. The name by which we know it, Teotihuacán, was given by the Aztecs and means "City of the Gods." It was still a revered pilgrimage site at the time of the Spanish conquest.

THE MAYA

Maya civilization arose in southern Mesoamerica. The earliest distinctively Maya urban sites date to around 800 B.C.E.. The most important of these is Nakbé. The pyramid structures so popularly identified with Mayan culture were fully developed between 300 B.C.E. and 300 C.E. During the later Classic period, Maya civilization experienced a remarkable florescence in the lowland jungles of the southern Yucatán. It is this last era about which scholars now possess the most knowledge, because of inscriptions on stone monuments. More scholarship and archaeological exploration have been devoted to the Mayan peoples than any other culture of Mesoamerica, and our understanding of Classic Maya civilization has changed radically in recent decades. The Maya have also entered the modern popular imagination.

All the pre-Spanish societies of Mesoamerica were literate, recording historical and religious information on scrolled or screenfold books made with deerhide or bark paper. Only a handful of these books, four of them Mayan, have survived. (Spanish priests, who viewed native religious texts as idolatrous, burned almost all of them.) The Maya of the Classic period, who developed Mesoamerica's most advanced writing system, were unique in the extent to which they inscribed writing and calendrical symbols in stone, pottery, and other imperishable materials.

Teotihuacán. Temple façade showing Quetzalcoatl, the feathered serpent, as well as the god Tlalc, with round eyes.

What were important features of religious belief in Teotihuacán?

QUICK REVIEW

Teotihuacán

- Population of more than 150,000 at its height
- Dominated by Avenue of the Dead
- Influence of city extended throughout Mesoamerica

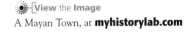

View the Image
A Mayan Town, at **myhistorylab.com**

Tikal, the largest city, probably had a population of between 50,000 and 70,000 at its height. Terracing, irrigation systems, and other agricultural technologies increased yields enough to support dense populations. Powerful ruling families and their elite retainers dominated cities, supported by a far larger class of farmer-commoners. Maya inscriptions mostly recount important events in the lives of rulers. Warfare between cities was chronic. As murals and sculptures show, captured prisoners were sacrificed to appease the gods and glorify the victorious ruler.

The Maya believed that the world had gone through several cycles of creation before the present one. They recognized no clear distinction between a natural and a supernatural world or between religious and political authority. Rulers claimed association with the gods to justify their authority. They wore special regalia and performed rituals—including bloodletting ceremonies, the sacrifice of captives, and ball games—to sustain the gods and the cosmic order.

The Classic Maya developed a sophisticated mathematics and were among the first peoples in the world to invent the concept of zero. In addition to the 52-year calendar they shared with other Mesoamerican societies, the Maya developed an absolute calendar, known as the **Long Count**. The Long Count calendar—like the Jewish, Christian, or Muslim calendars—was anchored to a fixed starting point in the past. The calendar had great religious as well as practical significance for the Maya. They viewed the movements of the celestial bodies to which the calendar was tied—including the sun, moon, and Venus—as deities. The complexity and accuracy of their calendar reflect Maya skills in astronomical observation. They adjusted their lunar calendar for the actual length of the lunar cycle (29.53 days) and may have had provisions like our leap years for the actual length of the solar year. The calendar's association with divine forces and the esoteric knowledge required to master it must have been important sources of prestige and power for its elite guardians.

During the Classic period many independent units, each composed of a capital city and smaller subject towns and villages, alternately vied and cooperated with each other, rising and falling in relative prominence. Tikal, at its height the largest Classic Maya city, is also one of the most thoroughly studied. The residential center covers more than 14 square miles and has more than 3,000 structures. The city follows the uneven terrain of the rain forest and is not laid out on a grid. Monumental causeways link the major structures of the site. Tikal benefited from its strategic position. It is located near a source of flint, valued as a raw material for stone tools, and swamps that with modification might have been agriculturally productive. It has access to river systems that lead both to the Gulf and the Caribbean coasts, giving it control of the trade between those regions.

A single dynasty of thirty-nine rulers reigned in Tikal from the Early Classic period until the eighth century. Early rulers in this Jaguar Paw line were buried in a structure known as the North Acropolis, and the inscriptions associated with their tombs provide details, including in many cases their names, the dates of their rule, and the dates of major military victories. Late in the fourth century links developed between Tikal and Teotihuacán. One ruler, Curl Nose, who ascended to the throne in 379, may have married into the ruling family from the Teotihuacán-dominated city of Kaminaljuyu in the southern highlands.

Long Count

A Mayan calendar that dated from a fixed point in the past.

Maya Calendar. This copy of a page from the Dresden codex shows detailed calendrical observations and astronomical predictions. The original calendar was inscribed on stone tablets.

How did the Mayan calendar relate to Mayan religious beliefs?

For about a hundred years beginning in the mid-sixth century, Tikal and most other lowland Maya sites lost much of their influence and may have suffered a serious defeat at the hands of the city of Caracol. Then in 682 the ruler Ah Cacau (r. 682–723?) ascended the throne and initiated a new period of vigor and prosperity for Tikal, again expanding its influence through conquest and strategic marriage alliances. Ah Cacau and his two immediate successors, Yax Kin (r. 734–?) and Chitam (r. 769–?), began an ambitious building program, creating most of Tikal's surviving monumental structures. Chitam was the last ruler in the Jaguar Paw Dynasty. After he died Tikal again declined, and, like other sites in the southern lowlands, it never recovered.

Similar dynastic histories have emerged from research at other Classic Maya sites. Inscriptions in the shrine above the tomb of Lord Pacal (r. 615–683), the greatest ruler of the city of Palenque, record the city's entire dynastic history back to mythic ancestors. Two of the rulers in this genealogy were women, including Pacal's mother, Lady Zac Kuk (r. 612–640).

Between 800 and 900 C.E. Classic civilization collapsed in the southern lowlands. The ruling dynasties all came to an end, the construction of monumental architecture and sculpture with Long Count dates ceased, and the great cities were virtually abandoned. The cause of the collapse is still unknown. Factors that may have contributed to it include intensifying warfare, population growth, and attempts to increase agricultural production that ultimately backfired.

The focus of Maya civilization shifted to the northern Yucatán. There the site of Chichén Itzá, located next to a sacred well, flourished from the ninth to the thirteenth centuries. Stylistic resemblances between Chichén Itzá and Tula, the capital of the Post-Classic Toltec Empire in central Mexico (discussed next), suggest ties between the two cities. After Chichén Itzá's fall, Mayapan became the main Maya center. By the time of the Spanish conquest it too had lost sway, and the Maya had divided into small, competing centers.

Mayan Mural. This reproduction of one of the remarkable murals found at the Maya site of Bonampak shows the presentation of captives to the city's ruler, Chan Muan.

What roles did captives play in Mayan society?

THE POST-CLASSIC PERIOD

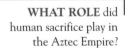

After Teotihuacán collapsed in the eighth century, warfare increased, and several smaller militaristic states emerged, centered around fortified hilltop cities. Interregional trade and market systems became increasingly important, and secular and religious authority began to diverge.

WHAT ROLE did human sacrifice play in the Aztec Empire?

THE TOLTECS

About 900 C.E. a people known as the Toltecs rose to prominence. Their capital, Tula, is located near the northern periphery of Mesoamerica. Like Teotihuacán, it lay close to an important source of obsidian. The Toltecs themselves were apparently descendants of one of many "barbarian" northern peoples (like the later Aztecs) who began migrating into Mesoamerica during the Late Classic period.

Later Aztec mythology glorified the Toltecs as the fount of civilization, attributing to them a vast and powerful empire to which the Aztecs were the legitimate heirs. Other Mesoamerican peoples at the time of the conquest also assigned legendary status to the

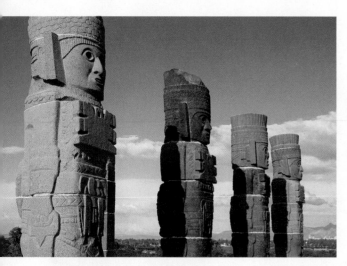

Tula Statuary. Tula, now Hidalgo, Mexico, was the capital of the Toltec civilization. These enormous statues, known as the Atlantes, stand atop the remains of the ancient Toltec pyramid raised in ancient Tula.

Why did the Aztecs claim links with the Toltecs?

Mexica
The Aztecs' name for themselves.

Toltecs. The archaeological evidence for a Toltec empire, however, is ambiguous. Tula, with 35,000 to 60,000 people, was never as large or as organized as Teotihuacán. Toltec influence reached many regions of Mesoamerica, and the city established extensive trade routes, especially for luxury goods. Archaeologists are uncertain whether that influence translated into political control. Toltec iconography, which stresses human sacrifice, death, blood, and military action, supports their warlike reputation. Their deities are clearly antecedent to those worshiped by the Aztecs, including the feathered serpent Quetzalcoatl and the warlike trickster Tezcatlipoca.

Whatever the reality of Toltec power, it was short-lived. By about 1100 Tula was in decline and its influence gone.

THE AZTECS

The people commonly known as the Aztecs referred to themselves as the **Mexica**, a name that lives on as *Mexico*. When the Spanish arrived in 1519, the Aztecs dominated much of Mesoamerica. Their capital city, Tenochtitlán, was the most populous yet seen in Mesoamerica. Built on islands and landfill in the southern part of Lake Texcoco in the Valley of Mexico, it was home to at least 200,000 people. It had great temples and palaces. Bearing tribute to its rulers and goods to its great markets, canoes crowded the city's canals, and pedestrians thronged its streets and the great causeways linking it to the mainland. The city's traders brought precious goods from distant regions; vast wealth flowed in constantly from subject territories. Yet the Aztecs were relative newcomers, the foundation of their power being less than 200 years old.

We have more information about the Aztecs than any other preconquest Mesoamerican people. Many of the Spanish conquistadors recorded their experiences, and postconquest administrators and missionaries collected valuable information. Although filtered through the bitterness of defeat for the Aztecs and the biases of the conquerors, these records nevertheless provide detailed information about Aztec society and Aztec history.

According to their own legends, the Aztecs were originally a nomadic people inhabiting the shores of a mythical Lake Aztlán northwest of the Valley of Mexico. At the urging of their patron god Huitzilopochtli, they began to migrate, arriving in the Valley of Mexico early in the thirteenth century. Scorned by the people of the cities and states already there, but prized and feared as mercenaries, they ended up in the marshy land on the shores of Lake Texcoco. They finally settled on the island that became Tenochtitlán in 1325 after seeing an eagle perched there on a prickly pear cactus, an omen Huitzilopochtli had said would identify the end of their wandering.

The Aztecs initially accepted a position as tributaries and mercenaries for Azcazpotzalco, then the most powerful state in the valley, but soon became trusted allies with their own tribute-paying territories and claims through marriage to descent from the Toltecs. In 1428, under their fourth ruler, Itzcoatl (r. 1427–1440), the Aztecs formed a triple alliance with Texcoco and Tlacopan, turned against Azcazpotzalco, and became the dominant power in the Valley of Mexico. Less than 100 years before the arrival of Cortés, the Aztecs began the aggressive expansion that brought them their vast tribute-paying empire (see Map 13–2).

Itzcoatl also laid the foundation of Aztec imperial ideology. He ordered the burning of all the ancient books in the valley, expunging any history that conflicted with Aztec pretensions, and restructured Aztec religion and ritual to support and justify Aztec preeminence. The Aztecs now presented themselves as the divinely ordained suc-

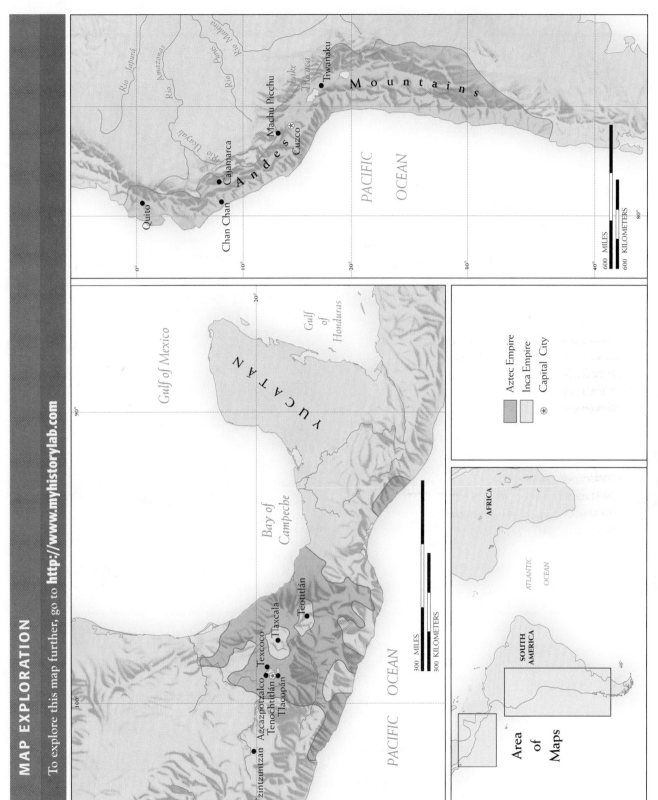

MAP EXPLORATION

To explore this map further, go to **http://www.myhistorylab.com**

MAP 13–2. The Aztec and Inca Empires on the Eve of the Spanish Conquest.
What were the chief differences between the Aztec and Inca empires?

DOCUMENT

Nezahualcoyotl of Texcoco Sings of the Giver of Life

Nezahualcoyotl, ruler of Texcoco, lived from 1402 to 1472 and was admired as a philosopher-king. In this poem he sings of the presence of the Giver of Life who invents himself and of the ability of human beings to invoke this divinity, but at the same time he emphasizes the impossibility of achieving any close relationship with the divinity.

- In what ways does this song remind you of the thought and religious traditions of the early civilizations of China, India, Egypt, and Greece? What are the characteristics of "He Who invents Himself"? What kind of relationship can human beings achieve with this being? Why does the singer compare seeking the Giver of Life with seeking someone among flowers?

In no place can be the house of He Who invents Himself.
But in all places He is invoked,
in all places He is venerated,
His glory, His fame are sought on the earth.
It is He Who invents everything
He is Who invents Himself: God.
In all places He is invoked,
in all places He is venerated,
His glory, His fame are sought on the earth.
No one here is able,
no one is able to be intimate
with the Giver of Life;
only He is invoked, at His side,

near to Him,
one can live on the earth.
He who finds Him,
knows only one thing; He is invoked,
at His side, near to Him,
one can live on the earth.
In truth no one is intimate with You,
O Giver of Life!
Only as among the flowers,
we might seek someone,
thus we seek You,
we who live on the earth,
while we are at Your side.
Our hearts will be troubled,
only for a short time,
we will be near You and at Your side.
The Giver of Life enrages us,
He intoxicates us here.
No one can be perhaps at His side,
be famous, rule on the earth.
Only You change things
as our hearts know it:
No one can be perhaps at His side,
be famous, rule on the earth.

Source: Excerpt (pp. 86–88) from *Fifteen Poets of the Aztec World*, by Miguel Leon-Portilla. Copyright © 1992 by Miguel Leon-Portilla. Reprinted by permission of University of Oklahoma Press.

cessors to the ancient Toltecs, and with each new conquest and the growing splendor of Tenochtitlán, they seemed to ratify that claim. (See Document, "Nezahualcoyotl of Texcoco Sings of the Giver of Life.")

Aztec conquests ultimately included almost all of central Mexico. To the west, however, they were unable to conquer the rival Tarascan Empire with its capital of Tzintzuntzan. And within the Aztec realm several pockets, most prominently Tlaxcala, remained unsubdued.

The Aztec Empire was extractive. After a conquest, the Aztecs usually left the local elite in power but demanded heavy tribute in goods and labor. Tribute included goods of all kinds, including agricultural products, fine craft goods, gold and jade, textiles, and precious feathers. This wealth underwrote the grandeur of Tenochtitlán, making it "a beautiful parasite, feeding on the lives and labour of other peoples and casting its shadow over all their arrangements."[1]

---

[1] Inga Clendinnen, *Aztecs: An Interpretation* (Cambridge: Cambridge University Press, 1991), p. 8.

Human sacrifice on a prodigious scale was central to Aztec ideology. The Aztecs believed that Huitzilopochtli, as sun god, required human blood to sustain him as he battled the moon and stars each night to rise again each day. The prime candidates for sacrifice were war captives, and the Aztecs often engaged in "flowery wars" with traditional enemies just to obtain captives. On major festivals, thousands of victims might perish. Led up the steps of the temple of Huitzilopochtli, a victim was thrown backward over a stone, his arms and legs pinned, while a priest cut out his heart. He would then be rolled down the steps of the temple, his head placed on a skull rack, and his limbs butchered and distributed to be eaten. Small children were sacrificed to the rain god Tlaloc, who was believed to be pleased by their tears.

Victims were also selected as stand-ins for particular gods, to be sacrificed after a series of rituals. For example, each year a beautiful male youth was chosen to represent the powerful god Tezcatlipoca. All year, the chosen one wandered through the city dressed as the god and playing the flute. A month before the end of his reign he was given four young women as wives. Twenty days before his death he was dressed as a warrior, and for a few days he virtually ruled the city. Then he was sacrificed.

No other Mesoamerican people practiced human sacrifice on the scale of the Aztecs. It must have intimidated subject peoples. It may also have reduced the population of fighting-age men from conquered provinces, and with it the possibility of rebellion. Together with the heavy burden of tribute, human sacrifice fed resentment and fear, which may help explain why so many subject peoples were willing to throw in their lot with Cortés when he challenged the Aztecs.

Three great causeways linked Tenochtitlán to the mainland. These met at the ceremonial core of the city, dominated by a double temple dedicated to Huitzilopochtli and Tlaloc. The palaces of the ruler and high nobles lay just outside the central precinct. The ruler's palace was the empire's administrative center, with government officials, artisans and laborers, gardens, and a zoo of exotic animals. The rest of the city was divided into four quarters, which were further divided into numerous wards (*calpulli*). Some *calpulli* were specialized, reserved for merchants (*pochteca*) or artisans. The city was laid out on a grid formed of streets and canals. Agricultural plots of great fertility known as *chinampas* bordered the canal and the lake shores. Aqueducts carried fresh water from springs on the lake shore into the city. A massive dike kept the briny water of the northern part of Lake Texcoco from contaminating the waters around Tenochtitlán.

Aztec society was hierarchical, authoritarian, and militaristic. It was divided into two broad classes, noble and commoner, with merchants and certain artisans forming an intermediate category. The nobility enjoyed great wealth and luxury. Laws and regulations relating to dress reinforced social divisions.

The Aztecs were morally austere. They valued obedience, respectfulness, discipline, and moderation. Laws were strict and punishment was severe. Standards for the nobility were higher than for commoners, and punishments for sexual and social offenses were more strictly enforced the higher one stood in the hierarchy. Drunkenness was frowned upon and harshly punished among the elite. Parents would even execute their own children for breaking moral laws and customs.

The Founding of Tenochtitlán. According to legend, the tribal god Huitzilopochtli led the Aztecs/Mexica to a spot where an eagle sat atop a prickly pear cactus (*tenochtli*) growing out of a rock and told them to build their capital there. This symbol now graces the Mexican flag. This image first appeared in the *Codex Mendoza*, a pictorial history of the Aztecs, presumably prepared for the first viceroy of New Spain, Antonio Mendoza, around 1541.

How did the Aztecs build their empire?

calpulli

The wards into which the Aztec capital, Tenochtitlán, was divided.

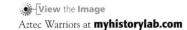

View the Image
Aztec Warriors at **myhistorylab.com**

Human Sacrifice. Illustration from a colonial-era manuscript volume, known as the Codex Magliabecchiano, presenting Aztec ritual sacrifice on a temple altar.

What role did human sacrifice play in Aztec society?

 See the **Map**

Pre-Columbian Civilization in Mesoamerica, at **myhistorylab.com**

The highest rank in the nobility was that of *tlatoani* (plural *tlatoque*), or ruler of a major political unit. The highest were the rulers of the three cities of the Triple Alliance; of them, the highest was the *tlatoani* of Tenochtitlán. Below them were the *tetcutin*, lords of subordinate units. And below them were the *pipiltin*, who filled the bureaucracy and the priesthood.

The bulk of the population was made up of commoners who farmed the *chinampas*, harvested fish from the lake, and provided labor for public projects. All commoners belonged to a *calpulli*, each of which had its own temple. Girls and boys alike received training in ritual and ideology in the song houses attached to these temples. Some criminal offenses were punished with enslavement, and serfs worked the estates of noblemen.

Professional traders and merchants—*pochteca*—were important figures in Aztec society. Their activities, backed by the threat of Aztec armies, were a key factor in spreading Aztec influence. Artisans of luxury goods—including lapidaries, feather workers, and goldsmiths—also had their own *calpulli* and enjoyed a special status.

Markets were central to Aztec economic life. The great market at Tlatelolco, adjacent to Tenochtitlán, impressed the Spaniards with its great size, orderliness, and variety of goods. More than 60,000 people went there daily. Market administrators, both women and men, regulated transactions. Cacao beans and cotton cloaks served as mediums of exchange.

Above all else, Aztec society was organized for war. Although there was no standing army as such, all young men received military training. Combat was a matter of individual contests, not the confrontation of massed infantry. A warrior's goal was to subdue and capture prisoners for sacrifice. Prowess in battle, as measured by the number of prisoners a warrior captured, was key to social advancement, and failure brought social disgrace.

Women could inherit and own property. They traded in the marketplace, and their craftwork could provide income. Women had access to priestly roles, although they were barred from high religious positions. In general, the Aztec emphasis on warfare left women excluded from positions of high authority. A woman's primary role was to bear children, and childbirth was compared to battle. Death in childbirth, like death in battle, guaranteed rewards in the afterlife.

ANDEAN SOUTH AMERICA: THE PRECERAMIC AND INITIAL PERIODS

HOW DID Andean peoples modify their environments?

The Andean region of South America—primarily modern Peru and Bolivia—also had a long history of indigenous civilization. This is a region of dramatic contrasts. South of the equator, a narrow strip of desert lines the Pacific coast. Beyond this strip the Andes Mountains rise abruptly. Small river valleys descend the western face of the mountains, cutting the desert plain to create a series of oases. The cold waters of the Humboldt Current sweep north along the coast from the Antarctic, carrying rich nutrients that support abundant sea life. Within the Andes are regions of high peaks and steep terrain, regions of grassland (*puna*), and deep, warm, fertile intermontane valleys. The eastern slopes of the mountains, covered with dense vegetation, descend into the great tropical rain forest of the Amazon basin (see Figure 13–2).

From ancient times, the people of the coast lived by exploiting the marine resources of the Pacific and by cultivating maize, beans, squash, and cotton. They also engaged in long-distance trade by sea along the Pacific coast.

The people of the highlands domesticated several plants native to the Andean region, including the potato, other tubers, and a grain called quinoa, which they cultivated on the high slopes of the Andes. In the intermontane valleys they cultivated maize. And in the *puna* grasslands they kept herds of llamas and alpacas for their fur and meat and as beasts of burden. Since ancient times, highland communities maintained access to the different resources available in different altitude zones. They share this adaptation, which anthropologists sometimes call *verticality*, with people in other mountainous regions, such as the Alps and the Himalayas.[2]

Andean civilization is conventionally divided into seven periods: Preceramic, Initial, Early Horizon, Early Intermediate, Middle Horizon, Late Intermediate, and Late Horizon. The Early, Middle, and Late Horizons are periods in which a homogeneous art style spread over a wide area. The Intermediate periods are characterized by regional stylistic diversity. Although there have been archaeological excavations of spectacular Andean sites, such as Machu Pichu, Andean archaeology has been less developed than that of other regions of pre-Columbian America, in large measure because of the difficulty of reaching the sites.

The earliest monumental architecture in Peru dates to the early third millennium B.C.E., roughly contemporary with the Great Pyramids of Egypt. Mostly near the shore, these earliest centers of Norte Chico civilization consist of ceremonial mounds and plazas and predate the introduction of pottery to Peru.

Coastal people at this time subsisted primarily on the bounties of the sea, supplemented with squash, beans, and chili peppers cultivated in the floodplains of the coastal rivers. They also cultivated gourds—for use as containers and utensils—and cotton. The cotton fishing nets and other textiles of this period represent the beginning of the sophisticated Andean textile tradition. The Norte Chico civilization appears to have been in decline by about 1800 B.C.E.

The earliest public buildings in the highlands date to before 2500 B.C.E. These are typically stone-walled structures enclosing a sunken fire pit used to burn ritual offerings. The distribution of these structures, first identified at the site of Kotosh, suggests that highland people shared a set of religious beliefs that archaeologists have called the *Kotosh religious tradition*. Highland people during the late preceramic period cultivated maize as well as potatoes and other highland tubers. Llamas and alpacas were fully domesticated by about 2500 B.C.E. There is little evidence of social stratification for

Grassy plain 13,000 ft. above sea level
Uplands: 10,500–12,500 ft. above sea level
Frost-free valleys 7,500–10,000 ft. above sea level
Lower slopes of mountains: 2,400–7,000 ft. above sea level
Dry coastal region: 2,400 ft. above sea level

FIGURE 13–2. The Andean environment packs tremendous ecological diversity into a small space.

CHRONOLOGY

PERIODS OF ANDEAN CIVILIZATION

ca. 3000–ca. 2000 B.C.E.	Preceramic
ca. 2000–ca. 800 B.C.E.	Initial
ca. 800–ca. 200 B.C.E.	Early Horizon
ca. 200 B.C.E.–ca. 600 C.E.	Early Intermediate
ca. 600–ca. 800/1000 C.E.	Middle Horizon
ca. 800/1000–ca. 1475	Late Intermediate
ca. 1475–1532	Late Horizon (Inca Empire)

---

[2]Michael Mosley, *The Incas and Their Ancestors* (New York: Thames and Hudson, 1992), p. 42.

the late preceramic period. The public structures of both the coast and the highlands appear to have been centers of community ritual for relatively egalitarian societies.

The introduction of pottery to Peru around 2000 B.C.E. corresponds to a major shift in settlement and subsistence patterns on the coast, marking the beginning of the Initial period. People became increasingly dependent on agriculture as well as on maritime resources. They moved their settlements inland, built irrigation systems, and began cultivating maize. They built large and impressive ceremonial centers, with forms that varied by region. Population grew and society became gradually but increasingly stratified. Incised carvings of bodies with severed heads at Cerro Sechín and Sechín Alto in the Casma suggest growing conflict. Centers apparently remained independent of one another.

CHAVÍN DE HUANTAR AND THE EARLY HORIZON

WHY DID Chavín influence spread?

The large coastal centers of the Initial period declined early in the first millennium B.C.E. At about the same time, beginning around 900 B.C.E., a site in the highlands, Chavín de Huantar, was growing in influence (see Map 13–3). Located on a trade route between the coast and the lowland tropical rain forest, Chavín was the center of a powerful religious cult with a population of perhaps 3,000 at its height. The architecture of its central temple complex reflects coastal influence. Its artistic iconography draws on many tropical forest animals, including monkeys, serpents, and jaguars. The structure known as the Old Temple is honeycombed with passageways and drains; archaeologists think water was channeled through these drains to produce a roaring sound. At the end of the central passageway is an imposing stela carved in the image of a fanged deity that combines human and feline features. A small hole in the ceiling above suggests that it may have been an oracle whose "voice" was that of a priest in the gallery above.

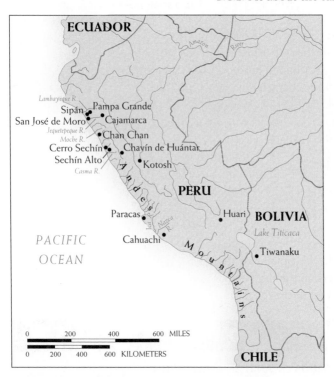

MAP 13–3. **Pre-Inca sites discussed in this chapter.**

What were the differences between highland and coastal cultures in early South American history?

Between about 400 and 200 B.C.E. Chavín influence spread widely throughout Peru, probably because of the prestige of its cult. The florescence of Chavín was marked by important technological innovations in ceramics, weaving, and metallurgy. Excavations at Chavín and other Early Horizon sites point to increasing social stratification. Examination of skeletal remains, for example, suggests that people who lived closer to the ceremonial center ate better than people living on the margins of the site.

THE EARLY INTERMEDIATE, MIDDLE HORIZON, AND LATE INTERMEDIATE PERIODS

HOW DO Tiwanaku and Huari foreshadow the achievements of the Inca?

Signs of increasing warfare accompany the collapse of the Chavín culture and the ideological unity it had brought to the Andes. During the Early Intermediate period, increasing regional diversity combined with increasing political centralization as the first territorial states emerged in the Andes. Among the best-known of these cultures are the Nazca on the south coast of Peru and the Moche on the north coast.

NAZCA

The Nazca culture, which flourished from about 100 B.C.E. to about 700 C.E., was centered in the Ica and Nazca valleys. The people of the Nazca valley built underground aqueducts to tap groundwater and divert it into irrigation canals. Cahuachi, the largest Nazca site, was empty most of the year, filling periodically with pilgrims during religious festivals. It may have been the capital of a Nazca confederation, with each of its many temple platforms representing a member unit.

The earlier Paracas culture on the south coast produced some of the world's finest, most intricate textiles. The Nazca, too, are renowned for their textiles and their polychrome pottery, elaborately decorated with images of Andean plants and animals. They may be most famous, however, for their colossal earthworks, or geoglyphs, the so-called Nazca lines. These were created by brushing away the dark gravel of the desert to reveal a lighter-colored surface. Some geoglyphs depict figures like hummingbirds, spiders, and killer whales that appear on Nazca pottery. These are usually located on hillsides visible to passersby. Others, usually consisting of radiating lines and geometric forms, are drawn on Nazca's pampa flats and are only visible from the air.

The Nazca Geoglyph located in the Peruvian desert depicts a vast hummingbird. The lines were constructed by the Nazca people probably sometime between 250 C.E. and 600 C.E. They appear to have been sacred paths walked by Nazca people perhaps somewhat as medieval Europeans walked a labyrinth. At the summer solstice the final parallel line points to the sun. The features of this and other geoglyphs can only be discerned from the air, and their exact purpose remains a matter of speculation.

How do these geoglyphs illustrate the connection between culture and the environment?

MOCHE

The Moche culture flourished from about 200 to 700 C.E. on the north coast of Peru. At its height it dominated all the coastal river valleys for 370 miles. The culture takes its name from the Moche valley, the site of two huge structures, the Pyramid of the Sun and the Pyramid of the Moon. The cross-shaped Pyramid of the Sun, the largest adobe structure in the Americas, was some 1,200 feet long by 500 feet wide and rose in steps to a height of 60 feet. It was made with more than 143 million adobe bricks, each of which had a mark that probably identified the group that made it. Archaeologists think the marks enabled Moche lords to be sure that subject groups fulfilled their tribute obligations. The Moche area may have been divided into northern and southern realms, with each valley ruled from its own center, Pampa Grande or Cerro Blanco.

The Moche were skilled potters, producing molded and painted vessels that reveal much about Moche life, religion, and warfare. Realistic portrait vessels may depict actual people. Other vessels provide evidence about the appearance of Moche architecture and the kind of regalia worn by the elite. The discovery in the late 1980s of the undisturbed tombs of Moche rulers suggests that a central theme in Moche iconography—the sacrifice ceremony—was an actual ritual. Depictions of the sacrifice ceremony show elaborately dressed figures drinking the blood of sacrificed prisoners. The Moche were also the most sophisticated metalsmiths in the Andes. They developed innovative alloys, cast weapons and agricultural tools, and used the lost-wax process to create small, intricate works. As with so many of the pre-Columbian peoples, the reason for the decline of the Moche is uncertain.

Moche Earspool. This magnificent earspool of gold, turquoise, quartz, and shell was found in the tomb of the Warrior Priest in the Moche site of Sipan, Peru, 300 C.E.

Courtesty of UCLA Fowler Museum of Cultural History/Susan Einstein/Christopher B. Donnan.

What processes did the Moche use in their metalwork?

TIWANAKU AND HUARI

In the fifth century C.E., as Teotihuacán was reaching its height in Mesoamerica, the first expansionist empires were emerging in the Andean highlands. One of these was centered at Tiwanaku in the Bolivian altiplano near the south shore of Lake Titicaca;

quipu
Knotted string used by Andean peoples for record keeping.

the other was at Huari, in the south-central highlands of Peru. Although they differ in many ways, both are associated with productive new agricultural technologies, and both show evidence of a form of statecraft that reflects Andean verticality and foreshadows the administrative practices of the later Inca Empire. The artistic symbolism of both also shares many features, suggesting a shared religious ideology. Archaeologists still do not have a firm grip on the chronology of Tiwanaku and Huari or the relationship between them.

Tiwanaku lies at more than 12,600 feet above sea level, making it the highest capital in the ancient world. Construction apparently began at the site in about 200 C.E. It began its expansionist phase from about 500 to 600 C.E. and collapsed 500 years later, in the eleventh century. The city occupied 1 to 2 two square miles and may have had a population of 20,000 to 40,000 people at its height. Laid out on a grid, it is dominated by several large and impressive public structures and ceremonial gateways. The enormous effort expended in transporting the stone for these monuments indicates the power of the Tiwanaku rulers over the labor of their subjects.

A system of raised-field agriculture on the shores of Lake Titicaca provided Tiwanaku with its economic base. This system involved farming on artificial platforms capped with rich topsoil and separated by basins of water. Experimental reconstructions have shown it to be extremely productive.

Tiwanaku dominated the Titicaca basin and neighboring regions. It probably exerted its influence through its religious prestige and by establishing colonies and religious-administrative structures in distant territories. As with other cultures in the region, human sacrifice played a part in Tiwanaku rituals.

The Huari Empire flourished from about 600 to 800 C.E., dominating the highlands from near Cuzco in the south to Cajamarca in the north. For a brief period it also extended a fortified colony into Tiwanaku territory. The capital, Huari, covers about 1.5 square miles. It consists of a sprawl of large, high-walled stone enclosures, and it had a population of 20,000–30,000.

Huari is located in an intermontane valley and its rise is associated with the development of techniques for terracing and irrigating the slopes of the valley to increase their productivity. The spread of this beneficial technology may have facilitated the expansion of the Huari Empire, explaining its acceptance without signs of military domination. Huari administrative centers were undefended and built in accessible places. Many archaeologists think they may have functioned like later Inca administrative centers, housing a small Huari elite that organized local labor for state projects. Again like the Inca, Huari administrators used **quipu** record-keeping devices made of string. Inca *quipu*, however, used knots, whereas Huari *quipu* used different colored string.

THE CHIMU EMPIRE

Although there is evidence of Huari influence on the Peruvian north coast, it is unlikely to have taken the form of direct political control. After the demise of Moche authority, two new states emerged on the north coast. One, named for the site of Sican, was centered in the Lambayeque valley. The central figure in Sican iconography, the Sican Lord, may have been a representation of a mythical founder figure named Nyamlap, mentioned in post-conquest Spanish chronicles. Like their Moche predecessors in the Lambayeque valley, the Sican people were skilled smiths who produced sumptuous gold objects.

The other new north coast state, known as Chimu, was centered in the Moche valley. In two waves of expansion the Chimu built an empire that incorporated the Lambayeque valley and stretched for 800 miles along the coast, from the border of Ecuador in the north to the Chillon valley in the south. The administrative capital of this empire, Chan Chan, was a vast city in the Moche valley. Its walls enclosed 8 square miles, and its central core covered over 2 square miles. Serving as the focus of the city were some ten immense adobe-walled enclosures known as *ciudadelas*. With their large open plazas, their administrative and storage facilities, and their large burial mounds, these probably housed the empire's ruling elite. Surrounding them were smaller compounds that probably housed the lesser nobility. And surrounding these were the homes and workshops of the artisans and workers who served the elite. Two areas were apparently transport centers, where llama caravans brought raw materials to the capital from the empire's territories. The total population of the city was between 30,000 and 40,000. Human sacrifice probably marked some Chimu ceremonies.

About 1470, only sixty years before the arrival of the Spaniards, the Chimu Empire was swept away by a powerful new state from the southern highlands of Peru, the Inca Empire.

Machu Picchu. The Inca city of Machu Picchu perches on a saddle between two peaks on the eastern slopes of the Andes.
Why would the Inca have situated Machu Picchu in such a remote location?

THE INCA EMPIRE

In 1532, when Francisco Pizarro encountered it, the Inca Empire was one of the largest states in the world. Its domains encompassed the area between the Pacific coast and the Amazon basin for some 2,600 miles, from southern Colombia to northern Chile (see Map 13–2). Its ethnically and linguistically diverse population numbered in the millions, with settlements linked by excellent roads. The Incas inhabited the lowland river valleys along the coast and the highlands, but did not settle in the Amazon rain forest.

The Inca themselves called their domain *Tawantinsuyu*, the Land of the Four Quarters. Their capital, Cuzco, lay at the intersection of these divisions. Home to the ruler (Inca) and the ruling elite, it was a city of great splendor and magnificence. Its principal temples, dedicated to the sun and moon, gleamed with gold and silver. Its outer boundaries had been drawn to resemble the shape of a vast puma.

The origins of the Inca are obscure. According to Inca traditions, expansion began in the fifteenth century in the wake of a revolt of the Chanca people that nearly destroyed Cuzco. Inca Yupanqui, son of the city's aging ruler, led a heroic resistance and crushed the revolt. Assuming the name Pachacuti, he laid the foundations of Inca statecraft; he and his successors expanded their domains to bring the blessings of civilization to the rest of the Andean world. There is clearly an element of imperial propaganda in this legend. The Inca did expand dramatically in the fifteenth century, but archaeological evidence suggests that they had been expanding their influence for decades and perhaps centuries before the Chanca revolt.

The Inca enlarged their empire through a combination of alliance and intimidation as well as conquest. They organized their realm into a hierarchical administrative structure and imposed a version of their language, **Quechua**, as the administrative language of the empire. (Quechua is still widely spoken in the Peruvian Andes.) The Inca emperorship was not conveyed by direct inheritance. A dispute over the royal succession was occurring at the time of the Spanish arrival and was exploited by the Spanish.

The Inca and the peoples they ruled were extremely devout in their religion. The Inca saw themselves in a profound relationship to their dead forebears; they

HOW DID the Inca enlarge and organize their empire?

Mummified remains. A mummy, exhumed at the cemetery at Puruchuco-Huaquerones, with a feathered headdress, thought to signify high status.
What kinds of bodies were most likely to be mummified in Inca culture?

Quechua
The Inca language.

mita
The Inca system of forced labor in return for gifts and ritual entertainments.

Mitimaqs
Communities whom the Incas forced to settle in designated regions for strategic purposes.

mamakuna
Inca women who lived privileged but celibate lives and had important economic and cultural roles.

chicha
A maize beer brewed by the *mamakuna* for the Inca elite.

The Inca *Quipumayoc*. The grand treasurer shown holding a *quipu*, a device made of knotted strings, used to record administrative matters and sacred histories. Information was encoded in the colors of the strings and the style of the knots.

How did the Inca organize their empire?

deeply honored their ancestors. Mummified bodies of ancestors were preserved, especially among the elite. Property of the dead was owned communally. Consequently, the property of a deceased Inca emperor was not inherited by his successor but by his descendants, a group known as a Panaca. When a new Inca emperor came to power, he had to undertake military expansion to provide property for his own descendants.

The official Inca religion was organized in a strongly hierarchical fashion, as were the gods being worshiped. Incas sacrificed animals to their gods and, on occasions of great communal difficulty, also sacrificed human beings, often children. Beyond the major population centers, religion was essentially folk worship of spirits rather than formal gods.

Unlike the Aztecs, who extracted primarily economic tribute from their subject peoples, the Inca relied on various forms of labor taxation. They divided agricultural lands into several categories, allowing local populations to retain some for their own support and reserving others for the state and the gods. In a system known as the **mita**, local people worked for the state on a regular basis, receiving in return gifts and lavish state-sponsored ritual entertainments. Men also served in the army and labored on the construction of vast public works projects, building cities and roads, and terracing hillsides. In a policy that reflects the Andean practice of colonizing ecologically varied regions, the Inca also designated entire communities as **Mitimaqs**, moving them about to best exploit the resources of their empire. They sometimes settled loyal people in hostile regions and moved hostile people to loyal regions.

The Inca employed several groups of people in what amounted to full-time state service. One of these, the **mamakuna**, consisted of women who lived privileged but celibate and carefully regulated lives in cities and towns throughout the empire. *Mamakuna* might also be given in marriage by Inca rulers to cement alliances. These so-called Virgins of the Sun played an important economic as well as religious role, weaving textiles and brewing the maize beer known as **chicha** for the Inca elite. Textiles were highly prized in Andean society. Cloth and clothing were not only a principal source of wealth and prestige in Inca society, they were also a means of communication. Complex textile patterns served as insignia of social status, indicating a person's rank and ethnic affiliation. *Chicha* had great ritual importance and was consumed at state religious festivals. Another group of full-time state workers, the *yanakuna*, were men whose duties included tending the royal llama herds.

The Incas made their presence felt in their empire through regional administrative centers and warehouses linked by a remarkable system of roads. The centers served to organize, house, and feed people engaged in *mita* labor service and to impress upon them the power and beneficence of the state with feasting and ritual. The wealth of the empire, collected in storehouses, sustained the *mita* laborers, fed and clothed the army, and enriched the Inca elite. Although the Inca lacked writing, they kept detailed administrative records on their string *quipu*.

To move their armies, administer their domains, and distribute the wealth of their empire efficiently, the Inca built more than 14,000 miles of road. These ranged from narrow paths to wide thoroughfares. Rope suspension bridges crossed gorges and rivers, and stairways eased the ascent of steep slopes. A system of relay runners sped messages to Cuzco from the far reaches of the empire. This road system later facilitated Spanish conquest of the empire.

Over their long history the people of the Andes adapted to their challenging environment in ways that allowed them to prosper, bringing more land under cultivation than is the case today. Building on ancient Andean traditions, the Inca engineered a productive economy that brought its people a measure of well-being that would not survive the destruction of the empire by Spanish invaders. When those invaders arrived in the 1530s, they found the Inca Empire in political strife as two brothers contested the title of Inca. The Spanish also confronted an Inca population that had been significantly lessened by a small pox epidemic during the previous decade. That disease, introduced to Mexico in 1520, had spread rapidly in the Americas and reached the Andes before the Europeans themselves. The Spanish conquest meant that the most extensive and administratively sophisticated empire of pre-Columbian America had endured less than a century.

SUMMARY

 WHAT PROBLEMS do scholars face in reconstructing the history of Native American civilizations?

Reconstructing History. Some Maya written accounts survive, but much of the history of Native Americans is reconstructed through archaeological evidence. Accounts written after the Spanish conquest can provide valuable information, but they must be interpreted carefully. *page 312*

WHAT GROUP dominated Olmec society?

Mesoamerica. Mesoamerica means "middle America." It extends from central Mexico to Central America. Although there was no single Mesoamerican civilization, the civilizations of the Olmecs, the peoples of Monte Albán and Teotihuácan, the Maya, the Toltecs, and the Aztecs shared many features: urban centers with monumental buildings arranged on large plazas, writing, a sophisticated calendrical system, religious ideas that included human sacrifice, and the cultivation of certain crops, especially maize and beans. The cities of Mesoamerica were also linked by trade. Elite ruler-priests dominated Olmec society, and probably other Mesoamerican societies. *page 313*

 WHAT WERE some of the main achievements of the Classic period civilizations in Mesoamerica?

The Classic Period. The great city of Teotihuacán influenced much of Mesoamerica. Maya civilization featured writing, sophisticated mathematics and astronomy, and religious ritual. *page 317*

 WHAT ROLE did human sacrifice play in the Aztec Empire?

The Post-Classic Period. Warfare increased, and secular and religious authority began to separate as the Classic period's political structures disintegrated. The brief era of

Toltec power was followed by the Aztecs, who established the largest Mesoamerican state before the coming of the Spanish in the sixteenth century. The Aztec Empire depended on tribute from conquered peoples. Aztec society was organized for war and was divided into nobles and commoners, with merchants and certain artisans forming intermediate categories. The Aztecs practiced wide-scale human sacrifice to provide blood to the sun god. Most of the victims were captured warriors, so the Aztecs went to war frequently. Women could own property and participate in trade but were subordinate to men and excluded from positions of high authority. *page 321*

 HOW DID Andean peoples modify their environments?

Andean South America. Monumental architecture and public buildings in Peru date from the third millennium B.C.E. When pottery first appeared in Peru, around 2000 B.C.E., a process of increasing reliance on agriculture began. This process was reinforced by expanding ceremonial centers and population growth. *page 326*

 WHY DID Chavín influence spread?

Chavín de Huantar. Chavín de Huantar was a trade center. It was also the home of a powerful religious cult that gained regional influence because of its prestige. *page 328*

 HOW DO Tiwanaku and Huari foreshadow the achievements of the Inca?

Early Intermediate, Middle Horizon, and Late Intermediate Periods. Territorial states including the Nazca and the Moche were followed by the expansionist Tiwanaku and Huari empires. Tiwanaku and Huari rulers, like the Incas later on, were able to mobilize large numbers of laborers for immense state projects. The Chimu Empire was swept away by the Incas. *page 328*

HOW DID the Inca enlarge and organize their empire?

The Inca Empire. The Incas built the most extensive Andean empire. It extended for 2,600 miles from Ecuador to Chile between the Pacific coast and the Amazon basin. Inca rule relied on conquest, intimidation, and alliances with other peoples. The Inca exacted taxation in terms of forced labor and constructed over 14,000 miles of roads and numerous rope bridges. Although the Inca lacked writing, they kept detailed accounts using knotted strings. *page 331*

KEY TERMS

calpulli (p. 325)

chicha (p. 332)

Long Count (p. 320)

Mexica **(meh-HEE-kah)** (p. 322)

mamakuna (p. 332)

mita (p. 332)

Mitimaqs (p. 332)

obsidian (p. 314)

Quechua **(KEHTCH-oo-ah)** (p. 331)

quipu **(KEE-poo)** (p. 330)

REVIEW QUESTIONS

1. What tools have historians used to study the early history of peoples in the Americas? How has understanding of Native American civilizations changed over time?

2. Describe the rise of civilization in Mesoamerica and Andean South America. What does it have in common with the rise of civilization elsewhere? In what ways was it unique?

3. What role did the environment play in the formation of American civilizations?

4. The appearance of monumental architecture in the ancient world was often associated with hierarchical agricultural societies. Was this the case for the Peruvian coast?

5. What were some of the accomplishments of the Classic civilizations of Mesoamerica? How do they compare with contemporary civilizations elsewhere in the world?

6. How was the Aztec Empire organized? How does it compare to the early empires of the ancient world in the Near East, Europe, and Asia?

7. How was the Inca Empire organized? How does it compare to the early empires of the ancient world in the Near East, Europe, and Asia?

8. Both the Aztec and Inca empires fell in the early sixteenth century when confronted with Spanish forces of a few hundred men. What factors might have contributed to their defeat?

Note: To learn more about the topics in this chapter, please turn to the Suggested Readings at the end of the book. For additional sources related to this chapter please see www.myhistorylab.com

myhistörylab Connections

Reinforce what you learned in this chapter by studying the many documents, images, maps, review tools, and videos available at **www.myhistorylab.com**

Read and Review

✓●⌐Study and Review   Chapter 13

••●⌐Read the Document   *Victory over the Underworld, p. 316*

●⌐View the Image   *Mayan Ruins, p. 313*
A Mayan Town, p. 319
Aztec Warriors, p. 325

●⌐Watch the Video   *Teotihuacán Ruins in Mexico, p. 317*

((●⌐Hear the Audio   *Early Americas, p. 316*

Research and Explore

👁⌐See the Map   *Pre-Columbian Civilization in Mesoamerica, p. 326*

👁⌐See the Map   *Civilizations in North America*

(((●⌐**Hear** the **Audio**

Hear the audio file for Chapter 13
at **www.myhistorylab.com**

14
Africa ca. 1000–1700

The Great Mosque at Kilwa, ca. 1100 C.E. The Swahili city of Kilwa, on the coast of present-day Tanzania, was likely founded by Muslim traders with strong links to the Indian Ocean world. The insides of its domes were lined with Chinese porcelain. Now in ruins, this large congregational mosque was probably in its day the largest fully enclosed structure in sub-Saharan Africa.

What characterizes Swahili culture?

D ifferent parts of the African continent had very different histories early in the second millennium C.E. Many regions had substantial interactions with the Islamic and European worlds; others engaged in trade and cultural exchanges within the continent.

The Atlantic slave trade affected almost all of Africa between the fifteenth and nineteenth centuries. This subject is treated in detail in Chapter 17, but here, we cannot overlook its importance in disrupting and reconfiguring African economies, social organization, and politics.

We begin with Africa above the equator, where Islam's influence increased and substantial kingdoms and empires flourished. Then we discuss West, East, central, and southern Africa and the effects of Arab-Islamic and European influence. ■

GLOBAL PERSPECTIVE

AFRICA, 1000–1700

Long-distance trade—the supply-and-demand-driven movement of goods, people, and cultural attitudes and practices—typically stimulates historical change. This was as true in Africa in the early second millennium as in the Americas, Europe, Asia, or anywhere in the world. Different regions in Africa were oriented differently in relation to trade routes and trading partners, and these regions developed in markedly different ways between 1000 and 1700.

The North African coast and the Sahel lay amidst trading networks linking the Mediterranean world, the growing **Dar al-Islam** ("House of Submission"–the Islamic realm), and the rich kingdoms of West Africa. The East African coast was integrated into the trading and cultural networks of the Indian Ocean basin and was firmly engaged with the Muslim world there. The rest of sub-Saharan Africa was culturally diverse; people here engaged primarily in intra-African trade with cultures that occupied other ecological niches. It is important to remember that Africa is a continent that is home to many societies with different histories, languages, religions, and cultures. In this way it is

See the Map
Trade Routes in Africa
at **myhistorylab.com**

similar to Europe, but Africa is also much larger than Europe and more ethnically and culturally diverse.

Along the Mediterranean, the key new factor in African history at this time was the Ottomans' imperial expansion into Egypt and the **Maghreb**. The long Ottoman hegemony altered the political configuration of the Mediterranean world. Merchants and missionaries carried Islam and Arabian cultural influences across the Sahara from North Africa and the Middle East to the western, central, and Nilotic Sudan, where Muslim conversion played a growing social and political role, especially among the ruling elites who profited most from brokering trade between their lands and the Islamic north. Islam provided a shared arena of expression for at least some classes and groups in societies over a vast area from Egypt to Senegambia. In Africa as elsewhere, new converts modified Islam through a process of syncretism. Distinctively African forms of Islam emerged, faithful to the central tenets of the religion, but differing in observances and customs from those of the Arabian cultural

See the Map
Discovery: The Maghrib
and West Africa,
Fourteenth Century
at **myhistorylab.com**

NORTH AFRICA AND EGYPT

HOW DID the Ottomans govern North Africa and Egypt?

Dar al-Islam
In Arabic, the "House of Submission," or Islamic world. This term has many shades of meaning, ranging from a place where the government is under Muslim control to a place where individuals are free to practice Islamic beliefs.

Maghreb
Literally, in Arabic, "place of sunset," or the west; refers to the northwest of Africa, and specifically what is now Morocco.

Sharifs
A term for leaders who are direct descendants of the Prophet Muhammad through his first grandson, Hasan ibn Ali.

Watch the Video
Piracy at **myhistorylab.com**

As we saw in Chapter 12, Egypt and other North African societies played a central role in Islamic and Mediterranean history after 1000 C.E. From Tunisia to Egypt, Sunni religious and political leaders and their Shi'ite, especially Isma'ili, counterparts struggled for the minds of the masses. By the thirteenth century, the Shi'ites had become a small minority among Muslims in Mediterranean Africa. In general, a feisty regionalism characterized states, city-states, and tribal groups north of the Sahara and along the lower Nile. No single power controlled them for long. Regionalism persisted even after 1500, when most of North Africa came under the influence—and often, direct control—of the Ottoman Empire centered in Istanbul.

By 1800 the nominally Ottoman domains from Egypt to Algeria were effectively independent. In Egypt the Ottomans had established direct rule after their defeat of the Mamluks in 1517, but by the seventeenth century power had passed to Egyptian governors descended from the Mamluks. The Mediterranean coastlands between Egypt and Morocco were officially Ottoman provinces, or regencies, but by the eighteenth century, Algiers, Tripoli (in modern Libya), and Tunisia had institutionalized their own political structures.

Morocco, ruled by a succession of **Sharifs** (leaders claiming descent from the family of the Prophet Muhammad), was the only North African sultanate to remain fully independent after 1700. The most important *Sharifian* Dynasty was that of the Sa'dis (1554–1659). One major reason for Morocco's independence was that its Arab and Berber populations united after 1500 to oppose the Portuguese and the Spaniards.

sphere, especially in attitudes toward women and relationships between the sexes.

South of the Sahara, dynamic processes of state-building and trade were the main forces for cultural change. In central and South Africa, except along the eastern coast, and in the West African forests, older African traditions held sway, and there was little or no evidence of Islam beyond individual Muslims involved in trade. On the eastern coast, however, Islam influenced the development of the Swahili culture and language, a unique blend of African, Indian, and Arabian traditions, and Islamic traders linked the region to India, China, and the Indies. In sub-Saharan Africa, the spread of Islam took place almost entirely through peaceful means.

Along the Atlantic and Indian Ocean coasts of Africa, the key development of the fifteenth century was the arrival of ships carrying traders and missionaries from Christian Europe. The strength of African societies and the biological dangers to Europeans venturing into the interior meant that most of the trade between the African interior and Europeans on both coasts remained under the control of Africans for generations. Even

before Europeans themselves reached the interior, however, the trade in slaves, weapons, and gold that they fostered greatly altered African political and social structures not only along the coasts but also in regions untouched by the outsiders. The European voyages of discovery of the fifteenth and sixteenth centuries presaged the African continent's involvement in a new, expanding, and, by the eighteenth century, European-dominated global trading system. This system generally exploited rather than bolstered African development, as the infamous Atlantic slave trade (see Chapter 17) and the South African experience illustrate.

((•─[**Hear** the **Audio**
Influences in Africa 2
at **myhistorylab.com**

Focus Questions

◆ Where in Africa was Islamic influence concentrated? How did Islam spread? What does this reveal about the relationship between commerce and cultural diffusion?

◆ Why did different regions in Africa develop in different ways between 1000 and 1700?

THE SPREAD OF ISLAM SOUTH OF THE SAHARA

Islamic influence in sub-Saharan Africa began as early as the eighth century. By 1800 it affected most of the Sudanic belt and the coast of East Africa. The process was generally peaceful, gradual, and partial. Conversion to Islam was rare beyond the ruling or commercial classes, and Islamic faith tended to coexist or blend with indigenous beliefs. Agents of Islam brought commercial and political changes as well as the Qur'an, new religious practices, and literate culture.

In East Africa, Muslim traders moving down the coastline with the ancient monsoon trade routes had begun to "Islamize" ports and coastal regions even before 800 C.E. From the thirteenth century on, Islamic trading communities and city-states developed along the coast from Mogadishu to Kilwa.

In the western and central parts of the continent, Islam was introduced primarily by traders from North Africa and the Nile valley. Berbers who plied the desert routes (see Chapter 5) to trading towns such as Awdaghast on the edge of the Sahel as early as the eighth century were Islam's chief agents. From there Islam spread south to centers such as Kumbi Saleh and beyond, southeast across the Niger, and west into Senegambia. Migrating Arab tribal groups that settled in the central sub-Saharan Sahel also helped spread Islam.

The year 985 marks the first time a West African royal court—that of the kingdom of Gao, east of the Niger bend—officially became Muslim (see Chapter 5), though Gao rulers did not try to convert their subjects.

By contrast, the rulers of the later kingdom of Ghana long maintained their indigenous traditions even though they traded with Muslims and had Muslim advisers.

HOW DID Islam spread south of the Sahara?

●─[See the **Map**
East African Coast to 1600
at **myhistorylab.com**

Starting in the 1030s zealous militants known as Almoravids (see Chapter 12) began a conversion campaign that eventually swept into Ghana's territory, taking first Awdaghast and later, in 1076, Kumbi Saleh. Thereafter, the forcibly converted Soninke ruling group of Ghana spread Islam among their own populace and farther south in the savannah. They converted Mande-speaking traders, who brought Islam south into the forests.

Farther west, the Fulbe rulers of Takrur became Muslim in the 1030s and propagated their new faith among their subjects. The Fulbe, or Fulani, remained important carriers of Islam over the next eight centuries as they migrated gradually into new regions as far east as Lake Chad, where some rulers were Muslim as early as 1100.

Major groups in West Africa strongly resisted Islamization, especially the Mossi kingdoms founded in the Volta region at Wagadugu around 1050 and Yatenga about 1170.

SAHELIAN EMPIRES OF THE WESTERN AND CENTRAL SUDAN

WHAT WERE the four most important states in the Sahel between 1000 and 1600?

As we noted in Chapter 5, substantial states had risen in the first millennium C.E. in the Sahel just south of the Sahara.[1] From about 1000 to 1600, four of these developed into relatively long-lived empires: Ghana, Mali, and Songhai in the western Sudan, and Kanem-Bornu in the central Sudan.

GHANA

Ghana established the model for later Sahelian empires in the western Sudan. Well north of modern Ghana (and unrelated to it except by name), it lay between the inland Niger Delta and the upper Senegal. A Ghanaian kingdom existed as early as 400–600 C.E., but Ghana emerged as a regional power only near the end of the first millennium to flourish for about two centuries. Its capital, Kumbi (or Kumbi Saleh), on the desert's edge, was well sited for the Saharan and Sahelian trade networks. Ghana's major population group was the Soninke; *Ghana* is the Soninke term for "ruler."

Ghanaian rulers were descended matrilineally (through the previous king's sister) and ruled through a council of ministers. Contemporaneous reports, especially from the eleventh-century Muslim writer al-Bakri, indicate that the king was supreme judge and held court regularly to hear grievances. The royal ceremonies held in Kumbi Saleh were embellished with the wealth and power befitting a king held to be divinely blessed, and perhaps semidivine.

Slaves were at the bottom of Ghana's hierarchical society; farmers and draftsmen above them; merchants above them; and the king, his court, and the nobility on top. Ghana's power rested on a solid economic base. Tribute from the empire's many chieftaincies and taxes on royal lands and crops supplemented duties levied on all incoming and outgoing trade. This trade—north–south between the Sahara and the savannah, and especially east–west through the Sahel between Senegambia and more easterly trading towns like Gao on the Niger Bend—involved a variety of goods. Imported salt, cloth, and metal goods such as copper from the north were probably exchanged for gold

---

[1]S. K. and R. J. McIntosh, *Prehistoric Investigations in the Region of Jenne, Mali* (Oxford: Oxford University Press 1980), pp. 41–59, 434–461; R. Oliver, *The African Experience* (New York: HarperCollins, 1991), pp. 90–101.

and kola nuts from the south. The regime apparently also controlled the gold (and, presumably, the slave) trade that originated in the savanna to the south and west.

Although the Ghanaian king and court did not convert to Islam, they made elaborate arrangements to accommodate Muslim traders and government servants in a separate settlement a few miles from Khumbi's royal preserve. Muslim traders were prominent at court, literate Muslims administered the government, and Muslim legists advised the ruler.

A huge, well-trained army secured royal control, enabling the kings to extend their sway in the late tenth century to the Atlantic shore and to the south (see Map 14–1 on page 342). In 992, Ghanaian troops wrested Awdaghast from the Berbers. The empire was, however, vulnerable to attack from the desert, as Almoravid Berber forces proved in 1054 when they took Awdaghast in a single raid.

Ghana's empire was probably destroyed in the late twelfth century by the anti-Muslim Soso people from the mountains southeast of Kumbi Saleh; they were a Malinke clan who had long been part of the Ghanaian Empire. Their brief ascendancy between 1180 and 1230 ended the once great transregional power centered at Kumbi Saleh.[2]

Mali

With Ghana's collapse and the Almoravids' focus on North Africa, the western Sudan broke up into smaller kingdoms. In the early twelfth century Takrur's control of the Senegal valley and the gold-producing region of Galam made it the strongest state in the western Sudan. Like Ghana, however, it was soon eclipsed, first by the brief Soso ascendancy and then by the rise of Mali.

In the mid-thirteenth century, the Keita ruling clan of Mali forged a new and lasting empire, built on monopolization of the lucrative north–south gold trade. The Keita kings dominated enough of the Sahel to control the flow of West African gold from the Senegal regions and the forestlands south of the Niger to the trans-Saharan trade routes and the influx of copper and salt in exchange. Based south of their Ghanaian predecessors, in the fertile land along the Niger, they controlled all trade on the upper Niger, as well as the Gambia and Senegal trade to the west. They used captives for plantation labor in the Niger inland delta to produce surplus food for trade.

Agriculture and cattle farming were the primary occupations of Mali's population. Rice was grown in the river valleys and millet in the drier parts of the Sahel. Together with beans, yams, and other agricultural products, this made for a plentiful food supply. Fishing flourished along the Niger and elsewhere. Cattle, sheep, and goats were plentiful. The chief craft specialties were metalworking (iron and gold) and weaving of cotton grown within the empire.

The Malinke, a southern Mande-speaking people of the upper Niger region, formed the core population of the new state. They apparently lived in walled urban settlements typical of the western savanna region. Each walled town held 1,000 to 15,000 people and was linked to neighboring cities by trade and intermarriage.

The Keita Dynasty had converted to Islam around 1100 C.E. Keita's rulers even claimed descent from Muhammad's famous **muezzin** Bilal ibn Ribah, a former black slave from Abyssinia whose son was said to have settled in the Mande-speaking region. During Mali's heyday in the thirteenth and fourteenth centuries, its kings often

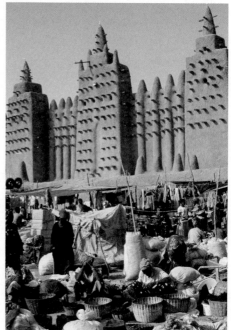

The Great Mosque at Jenne. Jenne was one of the important commercial centers controlled by the empire of Mali in the thirteenth and fourteenth centuries. The thriving market in front of the mosque reflects the enduring vitality of trade and commerce in the region.

How widely was Islam adopted in western Sudan?

muezzin
The leader of a mosque's call to prayers.

---

[2]D. Conrad and H. Fisher, "The Conquest That Never Was: Ghana and the Almoravids, 1076," *History in Africa* 9 (1982): 1–59; 10 (1983): 53–78.

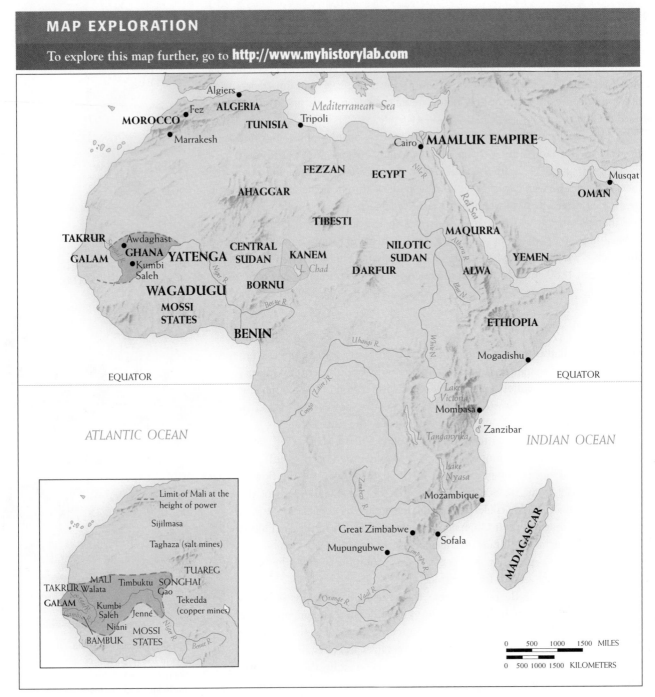

MAP EXPLORATION

To explore this map further, go to **http://www.myhistorylab.com**

MAP 14–1. **Africa ca. 900–1500.** Shown are major cities and states referred to in the text. The main map shows the region of West Africa occupied by the empire of Ghana from ca. 990 to ca. 1180. The inset shows the region occupied by Mali between 1230 and 1450.

Why was Ghana's location important for its prosperity?

◄◄◄─┤**Read the Document**
Excerpts from Sundiata: An Epic of Old Mali, 1235 at **myhistorylab.com**

made the pilgrimage to Mecca, bringing back with them military aids, such as Barbary war horses, and new ideas about political and military organization. Through Muslim traders' networks, Mali was connected to other areas of Africa, especially to the east.

Mali's imperial power was built largely by the Keita King Sundiata (or Sunjaata, r. 1230–1255). Sundiata and his successors exploited their agricultural resources, significant population growth, and Malinke commercial skills to build an empire even more powerful than that of Ghana. Sundiata extended his control west to the Atlantic coast and east beyond Timbuktu. By controlling the commercial entrepôts of Gao, Walata, and Jenne, he dominated the Saharan as well as the Niger trade. He built his capital, Niani, into a major city. Niani was located on a tributary of the Niger in the savannah at the edge of the forest in a gold- and iron-rich region. It had access to the forest trade products of gold, kola nuts, and palm oil; it was easily defended by virtue of its surrounding hills; and it was readily reached by river.

The empire that Sundiata and his successors built ultimately encompassed three major regions and language groups of Sudanic West Africa: (1) the Senegal region (including Takrur), populated by speakers of the West Atlantic Niger-Kongo language group; (2) the central Mande states between Senegal and Niger, occupied by the Niger-Kongo-speaking Soninke and Mandinke; and (3) the peoples of the Niger in the Gao region who spoke Songhai, the only Nilo-Saharan language west of the Lake Chad basin. Mali was less a centralized bureaucratic state than the center of a vast sphere of influence that included provinces and tribute-paying kingdoms. Many individual chieftaincies were independent but recognized the sovereignty of the supreme, sacred *mansa*, or "emperor," of the Malian realms.

The greatest Keita king was Mansa Musa (r. 1312–1337), famous for his pilgrimage through Mamluk Cairo to Mecca in 1324. He spent or gave away so much gold in Cairo alone that he started massive inflation lasting over a decade. He brought many Muslim scholars, artists, scientists, and architects back to Mali, where he consolidated his power and secured peace throughout his vast dominions. The devout ruler fostered the spread of Islam. Under Musa's rule, Timbuktu became famous for its *madrasas* and libraries, making it the leading intellectual center of sub-Saharan Islam and a major trading city of the Sahel—roles it retained long after Mali's empire declined.[3]

After Musa, rivalries for the throne diminished Mali's dominance. The empire slowly withered until a new Songhai power supplanted it after about 1450.

SONGHAI

There was a Songhai kingdom around Gao, on the eastern arc of the great bend of the Niger, as early as the eleventh or twelfth century. In 1325 Mansa Musa gained control of the Gao region. Mali's domination ended with the rise of a dynasty in Gao known as the Sunni or Sonni around 1375. The kingdom became an imperial power under the greatest Sunni ruler, Sonni Ali (r. 1464–1492). For more than a century the Songhai Empire was arguably the most powerful state in Africa (see Map 14–2 on page 344). With a strong military built around a riverboat flotilla and cavalry, Sonni Ali took Jenne and Timbuktu. He pushed the Tuareg Berbers back into the northern Sahel and Sahara and stifled threats from the southern forestland.

QUICK REVIEW

King Sundiata (r. 1230–1255)

◆ Built Mali's imperial power

◆ Mali's empire was more powerful than its Ghanaian predecessor

◆ Empire encompassed three major regions: Senegal, the central Mande states, and the peoples of Niger in the Gao region

● ● ●—Read the **Document**
The Travels of Ibn Battuta "Ibn Battuta in Mali" at **myhistorylab.com**

● ● ●—Read the **Document**
Al-Umari describes Mansa Musa of Mali at **myhistorylab.com**

mansa

Malian emperor, from Mandinka word meaning "king of kings."

Mansa Musa, King of Mali. The fourteenth-century Catalan Atlas shows King Mansa Musa of Mali, seated on a throne holding a nugget of gold. A camel rider approaches him.

Why would a fourteenth-century European atlas show Mansa Musa?

---

[3]For more on Mali, especially its wealth and Timbuktu's role as a center of scholarship, see E. Gilbert and J. T. Reynolds, *Africa in World History: From Prehistory to the Present* (Upper Saddle River, NJ: Prentice Hall, 2008), pp. 106-109.

MAP EXPLORATION

To explore this map further, go to **http://www.myhistorylab.com**

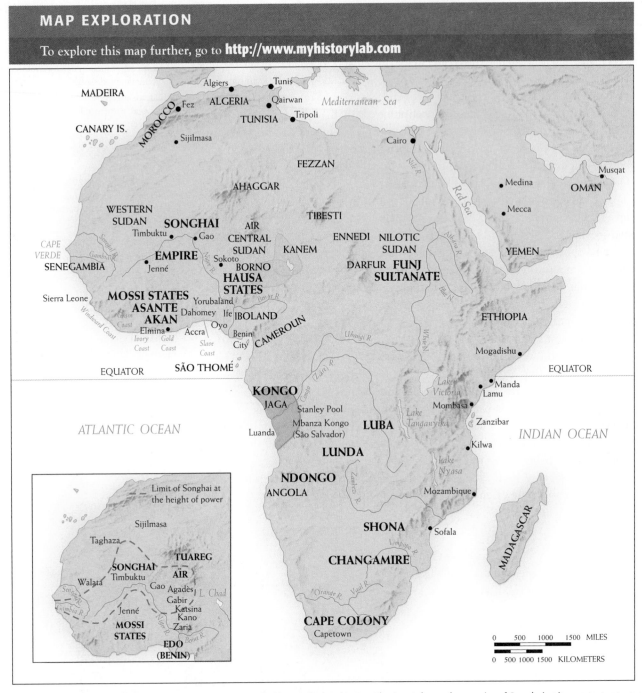

MAP 14–2. **Africa ca. 1500–1700.** Important towns, regions, peoples, and states. The inset shows the empire of Songhai at its greatest extent in the early sixteenth century.

What was Songhai's major source of wealth?

His successor Askia Muhammad al-Turi (r. 1493–1528) continued Sonni Ali's expansionist policies. Between them, these two rulers built an empire that stretched west nearly to the Atlantic, northwest into the Sahara, and east into the central Sudan. Like their Ghanaian predecessors, they took advantage of their control of access to gold and other West African commodities to cultivate and expand the caravan trade to the North African coast. This provided their major source of wealth.

Unlike Sonni Ali, who maintained his people's traditional faith, Askia Muhammad and his Askia successors were emphatically Muslim. At-Turi modeled the Songhai state on the Islamic empire of Mali. (See Document, "Muslim Reform in Songhai.") In his reign, many Muslim scholars came to Gao, Timbuktu, and Jenne. He appointed Muslim judges (*qadis*) throughout the empire and made Timbuktu a major intellectual and legal training center. He replaced native Songhais with Arab Muslim immigrants as government officials. Like Mansa Musa before him, Muhammad made a triumphal pilgrimage to Mecca, where he was hailed as "Caliph of the western Sahara." From his vast royal treasury he supported the poor and Sufi leaders, or **marabouts**, and built mosques throughout the realm. Nevertheless, he failed to Islamize the empire or to ensure a strong central state for his successors.

The last powerful Askia leader was Askia Dawud (r. 1549–1583), under whom Songhai prosperity and intellectual life reached its apogee. Both trans-Saharan trade and royal patronage of the arts rose to new levels. Still, difficulties mounted. The last Askias battled the Mossi to the south and Berbers from the north. Civil war broke out over the royal succession in 1586, dividing the empire. In 1591 an assay sent by the Sa'dis of Morocco used superior gunpowder weapons, coupled with the aid of disaffected Songhai princes, to defeat the last Askia of Gao, and the Gao Empire collapsed.

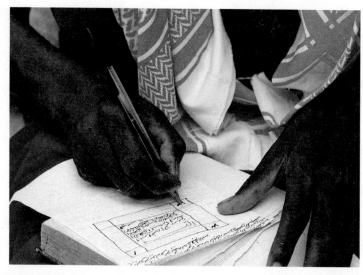

A Marabout Creates a *Grigri*. A verse from the Qur'an is copied onto a piece of paper, which will be folded and put in a leather pouch. The pouch is worn as an amulet, to protect the wearer from sickness, harm, or evil.

Are you aware of the use of amulets in non-Muslim religious traditions?

marabout

In Sunni Islam as practiced in West Africa, a *marabout* is a spiritual leader, versed in the Koran, who often guides the personal lives of his followers.

⊙ See the **Map**
African Empires in the Western Sudan at **myhistorylab.com**

KANEM AND KANEM-BORNU

A fourth sizable Sahelian Empire—this one in the central Sudan—arose after 1100. Called Kanem, it began as a southern Saharan confederation of the nomadic tribes known as Zaghawah. By the twelfth century a Zaghawah group, the Kanuri, had settled in Kanem. From there they began a campaign of military expansion during the thirteenth century. Their leader, Mai Dunama Dibbalemi (r. ca. 1221–1259), was a contemporary of Sundiata in Mali. Dibbalemi was a Muslim, and he used a synthesis of Islam and African traditions of sacred kingship to sanction his rule. Islam provided a rationale for expansion through *jihad*, or holy "struggle" against polytheists.

Dibbalemi and his successors extended Kanuri power north into the desert and northeast along the Sahelian-Saharan fringe. In both directions they controlled important trade routes—north to Libya and east to the Nile. The next two centuries saw the mixing of Kanuri and local Kanembu peoples. There was a corresponding transformation of the

CHRONOLOGY

SAHELIAN EMPIRES OF THE WESTERN SUDAN

ca. 990–ca. 1180?	Empire of Ghana
1076	Ghana loses Awdaghast to Almoravids
1180–1230	Soso clan controls old Ghanaian territories
ca. 1230–1450	Empire of Mali, founded by Sundiata
1230–1255	Reign of Sundiata
1312–1337	Reign of Mansa Musa
1340–1370s	Independent Songhai state emerges in Gao after throwing off Malian rule
ca. 1450–1591	Songhai Empire at Gao
1462–1492	Reign of Sonni Ali
1493–1591	Askia Dynasty rules Songhai Empire
1493–1528	Reign of Askia Muhammad al-Turi
1549–1583	Reign of Askia Dawud

DOCUMENT

Muslim Reform in Songhai

Around 1500 Askia Muhammad al-Turi, the first Muslim Songhai ruler, wrote to the North African Muslim theologian Muhammad al-Maghili (d. 1504) about proper Muslim practices. In these excerpts from al-Turi's seventh question, we glimpse the new convert's zeal for conformity to traditional religious norms, as well as the king's desire for bettering social order and his concern for justice. The answers from al-Maghili reflect the puritanical "official line" of the conservative ulama who did not want to allow syncretism to emerge among newly converted groups.

- **WHAT** are the problems and corresponding solutions described in the letters? Which problem did al-Maghili find most serious? Why? Which do you think would have been most serious? Why?

FROM ASKIA MUHAMMAD AL-TURI'S SEVENTH QUESTION

Among the people [of the Songhay Empire], there are some who claim knowledge of the supernatural through sand divining and the like, or through the disposition of the stars . . . [while] some assert that they can write (talismans) to bring good fortune . . . or to ward off bad fortune. . . . Some defraud in weights and measures. . . .

One of their evil practices is the free mixing of men and women in the markets and streets and the failure of women to veil themselves . . . [while] among the people of Djenné [Jenne] it is an established custom for a girl not to cover any part of her body as long as she remains a virgin . . . and all the most beautiful girls walk about naked . . . .

So give us legal ruling concerning these people and their ilk, and may God Most High reward you!

FROM MUHAMMAD AL-MAGHILI'S ANSWER

The answer—and God it is who directs to the right course—is that everything you have mentioned concerning people's behavior in some parts of this country is gross error. It is the bounden duty of the commander of the Muslims and all other believers who have the power to change every one of these evil practices.

As for any who claims knowledge of the supernatural in the ways you have mentioned . . . he is a liar and an unbeliever. . . . Such people must be forced to renounce it by the sword. Then whoever renounces such deeds should be left in peace, but whoever persists should be killed with the sword as an unbeliever; his body should not be washed or shrouded, and he should not be buried in a Muslim graveyard. . . .

As for defrauding in weights and measures it is forbidden (*haram*) according to the Qur'an, the Sunna and the consensus of opinion of the learned men of the Muslim community. It is the bounden duty of the commander of the Muslims to appoint a trustworthy man in charge of the markets, and to safeguard people's means of subsistence. He should standardize all the scales in each province. . . . Similarly, all measures both large and small must be rectified so that they conform to a uniform standard. . . .

Now, what you mentioned about the free mixing of men and women and leaving the pudenda uncovered is one of the greatest abominations. The commander of the Muslims must exert himself to prevent all these things. . . . He should appoint trustworthy men to watch over this by day and night, in secret and in the open. This is not to be considered as spying on the Muslims; it is only a way of caring for them and curbing evildoers, especially when corruption becomes widespread in the land as it has done in Timbuktu and Djenné . . . .

Source: From *The African Past*, trans. by J. O. Hunwick, reprinted in Basil Davidson (Grosset and Dunlap, The Universal Library), pp. 86–88. Reprinted by permission of Curtis Brown Ltd. Copyright © 1964 by Basil Davidson.

shaykh
Arabic word for a tribal elder or Islamic scholar; can also be rendered as sheikh, sheik, or cheikh.

Kanuri leader from nomadic **shaykh** to Sudanic king and of Kanem from a nomadic to a largely sedentary, quasi-feudal kingdom. Like Mali to the west, Kanem's dominion was of two kinds: direct rule over and taxation of core territories, and indirect control over and collection of tribute from a wider region of vassal chieftaincies. Islamic acculturation progressed most rapidly in the core territories.

Civil strife, largely over royal succession, weakened the Kanuri state. After 1400 the locus of power shifted from Kanem to Bornu, southwest of Lake Chad. Here, in the 1490s, a new Kanuri Empire arose almost simultaneously with the collapse of the Askia Dynasty of the Songhai Empire at Gao. Firearms and Turkish military instructors acquired after a pilgrimage to Mecca enabled the Kanuri leader Idris Alawma (r. ca. 1575–1610) to unify Kanem and Bornu. He set up an avowedly Islamic state and extended his rule as far as Hausaland, between Bornu and the Niger. The center of trading activity as well as political power now shifted from the Niger Bend east to Kanuri-controlled territory.

Deriving its prosperity from the trans-Saharan trade, Idris Alawma's regional empire survived for nearly a century. It was broken up by a long famine, Tuareg attacks, weak leadership, and loss of control over trade to smaller, better-organized Hausa states to the west. The ruling dynasty held out until 1846, but by 1700 its power had been sharply reduced.

CHRONOLOGY

CENTRAL SUDANIC EMPIRES

ca. 1100–1500	Kanuri Empire of Kanem
ca. 1220s–1400	Height of empire of Kanem
ca. 1221–1259	Reign of Mai Dunama Dibbalemi
ca. 1575–1610	Reign of Idris Alawma, major architect of the Kanem-Bornu state
ca. 1575–late 1600s (1846)	Kanuri Empire of Kanem-Bornu

THE EASTERN SUDAN

The Christian states of Maqurra and Alwa in the Nilotic Sudan, or Nubia, lasted for more than 600 years, beginning in the early seventh century. They maintained political, religious, and commercial contact with Egypt, the Red Sea world, and much of the Sudan.

After 1000 C.E. Maqurra and Alwa continued treaty relations with their more powerful northern Egyptian neighbors. However, the Mamluks intervened repeatedly in Nubian affairs, and Arab nomads constantly threatened the Nubian states. Both Maqurra and Alwa were subject to immigrating Muslim Arab tribesmen and to traders and growing Muslim minorities. Long-term intermingling of Arabic and Nubian cultures created a new Nilotic Sudanese people and culture.

A significant factor in the gradual disappearance of Christianity in Nubia was its elite character there and its association with the Egyptian world of Coptic Christianity. Maqurra became officially Muslim at the beginning of the fourteenth century, although Christianity persisted briefly. The Islamization of Alwa came later, under the long-lived Funj sultanate that replaced the Alwa state.

The Funj state flourished between the Blue and White Niles and to the north along the main Nile from just after 1500 until 1762. The Funj were originally cattle nomads who apparently adopted Islam soon after setting up their kingdom. During the late sixteenth and seventeenth centuries, the Funj developed an Islamic society whose Arabized character was unique in sub-Saharan Africa. A much reduced Funj state survived until an Ottoman Egyptian invasion in 1821.

WHY DID Christianity gradually disappear in Nubia?

THE FORESTLANDS—COASTAL WEST AND CENTRAL AFRICA

WEST AFRICAN FOREST KINGDOMS: THE EXAMPLE OF BENIN

Many states with distinct political, religious, and cultural traditions had developed in the southern and coastal regions of West Africa. The forest kingdom of Benin reflects the sophistication of West African culture before 1500; its art, in particular, is renowned for its enduring beauty.

 HOW DID the arrival of Europeans affect the peoples of West and central Africa?

oba

Title of the king of Benin.

uzama

An order of hereditary chiefs in Benin.

((•—Hear the **Audio**
Influences in Africa 2
at **myhistorylab.com**

The Edo speakers of Benin have occupied the southern Nigerian region between Yorubaland and the Ibo peoples east of the lower Niger for millennia. Traditional Edo society is organized according to a patrilineal system emphasizing primogeniture. The village is the fundamental political unit, and authority is built around the organization of males into age-grade units.[4]

Traditional Edo culture was closely linked to that of Ife, one of the most prominent Yoruba states northwest of Benin. A distinct kingdom of Benin existed as early as the twelfth century, and traditional accounts of both Ife and Edo agree that an Ife prince was sent to rule in Benin around 1300. The power of the **oba**, or king, was sharply limited by the Edo leaders who invited the foreign ruler. These leaders were known as the **uzama**, an order of hereditary chiefs. According to tradition, the fourth *oba* managed to wrest more control from these chiefs and expanded his ceremonial authority. In the fifteenth century, with King Ewuare, Benin became a royal autocracy and a large state of regional importance.

Ewuare rebuilt the capital—known today as Benin City—and named it and his kingdom Edo. He exercised his sweeping authority in light of the deliberations of a royal council. Ewuare formed this council not only from the palace *uzama* but also from the townspeople. He gave each chief specific administrative responsibilities and rank in the government hierarchy. Ewuare and his successors developed a tradition of military kingship and engaged in major wars of expansion, into Yorubaland to the west and Ibo country to the east, across the Niger River. They claimed for the office of *oba* an increasing ritual authority that presaged more radical developments in the king's role.

In the seventeenth century the *oba* was transformed from a military leader into a religious figure with supernatural powers. Human sacrifice, specifically of slaves, seems to have accompanied the cult of deceased kings and became even more frequent later in the nineteenth century. Succession by primogeniture was discontinued, and the *uzama* chose *obas* from any branch of the royal family.

Benin's court art—the splendid terra-cotta, ivory, and especially the famous brass sculpture of Ife-Benin—is among the glories of human creativity. Some scholars trace the artistic and technical lineage of these magnificent works to the sculptures of the Nok culture of ancient West Africa (see Chapter 5). Cast bronze plaques depicting legendary and historical scenes were mounted in the royal palace in Benin City before the sixteenth century. There are also brass heads, apparently of royalty, that resemble the many life-size terra-cotta and brass heads found at Ife. Similar sculptures have been found both to the north and in the Niger Delta.

EUROPEAN ARRIVALS ON THE COASTLANDS: SENEGAMBIA AND THE GOLD COAST

Along the coasts of West and central Africa, between 1500 and 1800, the changes wrought by the burgeoning Atlantic slave trade are notorious (see Chapter 17). But there were other significant developments. The introduction of food crops from the Americas—maize, peanuts, squash, sweet potatoes, cocoa, and cassava (manioc)—had far-reaching impacts. Africa's gradual involvement in the emerging global economic system paved the way for European colonial domination. The European names for segments of the coastline—the Grain (or Pepper) Coast, the Ivory Coast, the Gold Coast, and the Slave Coast—identify the main exports that could be extracted by ship.

CHRONOLOGY	
BENIN	
ca. 1100–1897	Benin state
ca. 1300	First Ife king of Benin state
1440–1475	Reign of Ewuare

---

[4]A. F. C. Ryder, *Benin and the Europeans, 1485–1897* (New York: Longman, 1969), p. 1. Ryder's work is a basic reference for the following brief summary about Benin.

A Closer Look

Benin Bronze Plaque with Chief and Two Attendants

BENIN ARTISTS AND ARTISANS produced spectacular sculptures from the late thirteenth century until the coming of the British in 1897. Their figures typically have the head-to-body proportions of this example, about one to four—perhaps emphasizing the head's importance as a marker of identity and behavior and a symbol of life. The details of the clothing might have been "readable" as to the wearer's rank and family. The stylized faces are typical of Benin bronzes (often actually of brass); dating the piece is hard, but given the two small European figures depicted in the upper field and the sophisticated detail, it is most likely sixteenth or seventeenth century.

The royal figure here has an elaborate headdress with two feathers on top and pendant plumes behind; two bead necklaces, one with leopard teeth mixed in; armlets and anklets; a loincloth; a leopard skin with fringe; a quadrangular bell on a double necklace; a spear with leaf-shaped blade; and an ornamented shield.

Two European figures, possibly Portuguese, are shown from the waist up; both have long moustaches, clublike weapons, plumed helmets, neck ruffs, and armor.

The two royal attendants are carrying round fans, wearing helmets, and adorned like the king with bracelets.

Benin Plaque. Brass. Lost wax. W. Africa 16th–17th century C.E. Hillel Burger/Peabody Museum, Harvard University © President and Fellows of Harvard College. All rights reserved.

Questions

1. The sophisticated Benin bronze artistry allowed for highly detailed sculpture that, for all its stylization, captured its subjects vividly and in great detail. What do you make of the differences between the depictions of the Benin Africans and the two European figures?

2. It has been speculated that this was a piece of court art and the depiction of the royal figure and attendants was intended to exalt royal power and prestige. Do you see evidence of this? If so, what is the evidence?

 To examine this image in an interactive fashion, please go to **www.myhistorylab.com**

Ife figure, ca. twelfth – fifteenth centuries C.E. The serene classicism of Ife art is equaled only by that of ancient Greece.

What other artistic traditions seem to be linked to Ife?

In West Africa, Senegambia—which takes its name from the Senegal and Gambia rivers—was one of the earliest regions affected by European trade. Senegambia's maritime trade with European powers, like the older overland trade from the interior, was primarily in gold and products such as salt, cotton goods, hides, and copper. For roughly a century Senegambian states also provided slaves for European purchase; perhaps a third of all African slaves exported during the sixteenth century came from Senegambia. Thereafter, however, the focus of the slave trade shifted south and east along the coast (see Chapter 17). Over time, Portuguese-Africans and the British came to control the Gambia River trade, while the French won the Senegal River markets.

The Gold Coast was another West African coastal district heavily affected by the arrival of international maritime trade. As the name suggests, after 1500 the region served as the outlet for the gold fields in the forestland of Akan. Beginning with the Portuguese at Elmina in 1481, but primarily after 1600, European states and companies built coastal forts to protect their trade and to serve as depots for inland goods. The trade in gold, kola nuts, and other commodities seems to have encouraged the growth of larger states, perhaps because they could better handle and control the overland commerce.

The intensive contact of the Gold Coast with Europeans also led to the importation and spread of American crops, notably maize and cassava. The success of these crops in West and central Africa likely contributed to substantial population growth in the sixteenth and seventeenth centuries. The Gold Coast was an importer of slaves until long after 1500. Slaves became major exports in the late seventeenth century, especially in the Accra region. The economy was so disrupted by the slave trade that gold mining declined sharply. Eventually more gold came into the Gold Coast from the sale of slaves than went out from its mines (see Chapter 17).

CENTRAL AFRICA: THE KONGO KINGDOM AND ANGOLA

Before 1500 natural barriers—including swamps in the north, coastal rain forests to the west, highlands to the east, and deserts in the south— impeded international contact and trade with the vast center of the continent. In tropical central Africa, there had long been regional interactions in movements of peoples and in trade and culture (see Chapter 5). Political, economic, and social units varied in size; peoples such as the Lunda and the Luba, on the southern savannah below the rain forest, carved out sizable kingdoms by the fifteenth century and expanded their control over neighboring areas into the eighteenth century.

The Portuguese came to the western coastal regions looking for gold and silver but found none. Ultimately, their main export was slaves. At first, slaves were taken for gang labor to the Portuguese sugar plantations on Sao Tomé island in the Gulf of Guinea and then, in vast numbers, to perform similar plantation labor in Brazil. In the 1640s the Dutch briefly succeeded the Portuguese as the major suppliers of African slaves to English and French plantations in the Caribbean.

The Kongo Kingdom was located on a fertile, well-watered plateau south of the lower Zaïre River valley. Astride the border between forest and grassland, the Kongo kings had built a central government based on a pyramid structure of tax or tribute collection, dating from the fourteenth century. The king's authority was tied to his role as a spiritual spokesman for the

CHRONOLOGY

CENTRAL AFRICA

1300s	Kongo Kingdom founded
1483	Portuguese come to central African coast
ca. 1506–1543	Reign of Affonso I as king of Kongo
1571	Angola becomes Portuguese proprietary colony

gods or ancestors. By 1600 Kongo was half the size of England and boasted a high state of specialization in weaving and pottery, salt production, fishing, and metalworking.

When the Portuguese came to central Africa in 1483, Kongo was the major state with which they dealt. The Portuguese brought Mediterranean goods, preeminently luxury textiles from North Africa, to trade; slaves became the primary export. Although imported luxuries augmented the prestige and wealth of the ruler and his elites, they did nothing to replace the labor pool lost to slavery. At first the Portuguese put time and effort into education and Christian proselytizing, but the desire for more slaves eventually outweighed these concerns. As demand grew, local rulers increasingly attacked neighbors to garner slaves for Portuguese traders (see Chapter 17).

The Kongo ruler Affonso I (r. ca. 1506–1543) was a Christian convert who initially welcomed Jesuit missionaries and supported conversion. But in time he broke with the Jesuits. Affonso had constant difficulty curbing the more exploitative slaving practices and independent-minded provincial governors, who undermined royal authority by dealing directly with the Portuguese. Affonso's successor finally restricted Portuguese activity to Mpinda harbor and the Kongo capital of Mbanza Kongo (São Salvador). A few years later, Portuguese attempts to name the Kongo royal successor caused a bloody uprising against them that led in turn to a Portuguese boycott on trade with the kingdom.

Thereafter, disastrous internal wars shattered the Kongo state. Slavery contributed to provincial unrest. Independent Portuguese traders and adventurers soon did their business outside government channels and tried to manipulate the Kongo kings.

Kongo, however, enjoyed renewed vigor in the seventeenth century. The Kongo kings ruled as divine-right monarchs at the apex of a complex sociopolitical pyramid. Royal power came to depend on hired soldiers armed with muskets. The financial base of the kingdom rested on tribute from officials and taxes and tolls on commerce. Christianity, the state religion, was accommodated to traditional beliefs. Sculpture, iron and copper technology, dance, and music flourished.

To the south, in Portuguese Angola, the experience was even worse than in Kongo. The Ndongo Kingdom flourished among the Mbundu people during the sixteenth century, though the Portuguese controlled parts of Angola as a proprietary colony (the first white colonial enterprise in black Africa). By the end of the 1500s Angola was exporting thousands of slaves yearly through the port of Luanda. In less than a century the hinterland had been depopulated. New internal trade in salt and the spread of American food crops such as maize and cassava (which became part of the staple diet of the populace) produced some positive changes in the interior, but in the coastal region the Portuguese brought catastrophe.

Queen Nzinga of Ndongo, who ruled from 1615 to 1660. This contemporary engraving shows her negotiating a treaty with the Portuguese. She is seated on the back of a slave.

Who seems to have the most power in this scene?

 Read the **Document**
Voyage from Lisbon
at **myhistorylab.com**

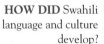 View the **Image**
Loango, the Capital of the Kingdom of the Congo at **myhistorylab.com**

EAST AFRICA

SWAHILI CULTURE AND COMMERCE

HOW DID Swahili language and culture develop?

The participation of East African port towns in the lucrative South Seas trade was ancient. Arabs, Indonesians, and even some Indians had been absorbed into what had become, during the first millennium C.E., a predominantly Bantu-speaking population from Somalia south. From the eighth century onward Islam traveled with Arab and Persian sailors and merchants to these southerly trading centers of what the Arabs called the land of the *Zanj*, or "Blacks" (hence "Zanzibar"). Conversion to Islam, however, occurred only along the coast. In the thirteenth century Muslim traders

◆◆◆ Read the Document
Descriptions of the cities of Zanj
at **myhistorylab.com**

Swahili
A language and culture that developed from the interaction of Africans and Arabs along the East African coast.

QUICK REVIEW

East African Port Towns

◆ Part of trade with Middle East, Asia, and India

◆ Tied together by common language, Swahili

◆ Swahili civilization reached its peak in the fourteenth and fifteenth centuries

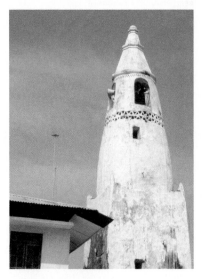

The Malindi Mosque on Zanzibar Island is an example of Islamic influence in Swahili culture.

What are some other examples of Islamic influence on Swahili culture?

Moors
The Spanish and Portuguese term for Muslims.

from Arabia and Iran began to dominate coastal cities from Mogadishu to Kilwa. By 1331 the traveler Ibn Battuta wrote of Islamic rulers, inhabitants, and mosques all along the coast.[5]

A shared language called **Swahili**, or Kiswahili (from the Arabic plural *sawahil*, "coastlands"), developed along the coast. Its structure is Bantu; its vocabulary is largely Bantu but incorporates many words with Arabic roots; it is written in Arabic script. Like the language, Swahili culture is basically African with a large contribution by Arab, Persian, and other extra-African elements. This admixture created a new consciousness and identity. Today, many coastal peoples who share the Swahili language join African to Persian, Indian, Arab, and other ancestries.

Like the Swahili language and culture, the spread of Islam was largely limited to the coastal civilization, with the possible exception of the Zambezi valley, where Muslim traders penetrated upriver. This contrasts with the Horn of Africa, where Islamic kingdoms developed both in the Somali hinterland and on the coast.

Swahili civilization reached its apogee in the fourteenth and fifteenth centuries. The harbor trading towns were the administrative centers of the local Swahili states, and most of them were sited on coastal islands or easily defended peninsulas. Merchants came from abroad and from the African hinterlands. These towns were impressive, with stone mosques, fortress-palaces, harbor fortifications, fancy residences, and commercial buildings combining African and Arabo-Persian elements.

The Swahili states' ruling dynasties were probably African in origin, though elite families often included Arab or Persian members. Swahili coastal centers boasted an advanced, cosmopolitan culture; by comparison, most of the populace in the small villages lived in mud or sometimes stone houses and earned their living farming or fishing. Society seems to have consisted of three principal groups: the local nobility, the commoners, and resident foreigners engaged in commerce. Slaves constituted a fourth class, although their local extent (as opposed to their sale) is disputed.

The flourishing trade of the coastal centers was based on ivory taken from inland elephants. Other exports included gold, slaves, turtle shells, ambergris, leopard skins, pearls, fish, sandalwood, ebony, and cotton cloth. The chief imports were cloth, porcelain, glassware, glass beads, and glazed pottery. Cowrie shells were a common currency in the inland trade, but coins minted at Mogadishu and Kilwa from the fourteenth century on were increasingly used in the trading centers.

THE PORTUGUESE AND THE OMANIS OF ZANZIBAR

The original Swahili civilization declined in the sixteenth century. Trade waned with the arrival of the Portuguese, who destroyed both the Islamic commercial monopoly on the oceanic trade and the main Islamic city-states along the coast. Decreases in rainfall or invasions of Zimba peoples from inland regions may also have contributed to the decline.

The Portuguese undoubtedly intended to gain control of the South Seas trade (see Chapter 17). In Africa, as everywhere, they saw the **Moors** (the Spanish and Portuguese term for Muslims) as their implacable enemies; they viewed the struggle to wrest the commerce and the ports of Africa and Asia from Islamic control as a Christian crusade.

---

[5]*Travels in Asia and Africa, 1325–1354*, trans. and selected by H. A. R. Gibb (New York: Robert M. McBride, 1929), pp. 110–113.

After the initial Portuguese victories along the African coast, there was no concerted effort to spread Christianity beyond fortified coastal settlements. Thus the long-term cultural and religious consequences of the Portuguese presence were slight. The Portuguese did, however, cause widespread economic decline. Inland Africans refused to cooperate with them, and Muslim coastal shipping from India and Arabia was reduced sharply. Ottoman efforts in the late sixteenth century failed to defeat the Portuguese, but after 1660 the strong eastern Arabian state of Oman raided the African coast with impunity. In 1698 the Omanis took Mombasa and ejected the Portuguese everywhere north of Mozambique.

Under the Omanis, Zanzibar became a new and major power center in East Africa. Control of the coastal ivory and slave trade fueled prosperity by the later eighteenth century. Zanzibar itself benefited from the introduction of clove cultivation in the 1830s; cloves became its staple export. (The clove plantations also became the chief market for a new internal slave trade.) Omani African sultans dominated the east coast until 1856, when Zanzibar and its coastal holdings became independent under a branch of the same family that ruled in Oman. Zanzibar passed eventually to the British in the late 1880s. Still, the Islamic imprint on the coast survives today.

CHRONOLOGY

EAST AND SOUTHEAST AFRICA

900–1500	"Great Zimbabwe" civilization
ca. 1200–1400	Development of Bantu Kiswahili language
ca. 1300–1600	Height of Swahili culture
1698	Omani forces take Mombasa, oust Portuguese from East Africa north of the port of Mozambique
1741–1856	United sultanate of Oman and Zanzibar

SOUTHERN AFRICA

SOUTHEASTERN AFRICA: "GREAT ZIMBABWE"

About the same time that the east coast trading centers were beginning to flourish, a different kind of civilization was thriving farther south, in the rocky, savannah-woodland watershed between the Limpopo and Zambezi rivers (now southern Zimbabwe). This civilization was sited far enough inland never to have felt the impact of Islam. It was founded in the tenth or eleventh century by Bantu-speaking Shona people, and it became a large and prosperous state between the late thirteenth and late fifteenth centuries. We know it only through the archaeological remains of approximately 150 settlements.

The most impressive of these ruins is the apparent capital known today as "Great Zimbabwe," a huge site encompassing two major building complexes. One, called the acropolis, is a series of stone enclosures on a high hill. It overlooks a larger enclosure that contains many ruins and a circular tower, all surrounded by a massive wall some 32 feet high and up to 17 feet thick. The acropolis complex may have contained a shrine, whereas the larger enclosure was apparently the royal palace and fort. The stonework reflects a

HOW DID slavery affect race relations in Cape Colony?

 See the **Map**

African Climate Zones and Bantu Migration Routes, ca. 3000 B.C.E. at **myhistorylab.com**

Great Zimbabwe. Ruins of the Conical Tower inside the Great Enclosure at Great Zimbabwe.

What were some probable sources of Great Zimbabwe's power?

prazeros
Portuguese and mixed-race owners of large estates in the Zambezi valley.

Carving from Great Zimbabwe. This soapstone carving of a bird comprises the top portion of a monolith from Great Zimbabwe, c. 1200 – 1400 C.E. [H: Bird—14 1/2″ (36.8 cm); H: Monolith—5′ 4 1/2″ (1.64 m).] Stone-carved birds are national emblems in Zimbabwe and were commonly found on walls and monoliths dating back to Great Zimbabwe in the eleventh century.

What is known about the culture at Great Zimbabwe?

wealthy and sophisticated society. Artifacts from the site include gold and copper ornaments, soapstone carvings, and imported beads, as well as glass and porcelain of Chinese, Syrian, and Persian origins.

The state seems to have partially controlled the gold trade between inland areas and the east coast port of Sofala. Its territory lay east and south of substantial gold-mining enterprises. This large settlement was probably home to the ruling elite of a prosperous empire. Its wider domain was made up mostly of smaller settlements whose inhabitants lived by subsistence agriculture and cattle raising.

Earlier Iron Age sites farther south suggest that other large state entities may have preceded Great Zimbabwe. The specific impetus for Great Zimbabwe may have been a significant immigration around 1000 C.E. of Late Iron Age Shona speakers who brought with them mining techniques and farming innovations, along with their ancestor cults. Improved farming and animal husbandry could have led to substantial population growth. The expanding gold trade linked the flourishing of Zimbabwe to that of the East African coast from about the thirteenth century.

We may never know why this impressive civilization declined after dominating its region for nearly 200 years. It appears that the northern and southern sectors of the state split up, and people moved away from Great Zimbabwe, probably because the farming and grazing land there was exhausted. The southern successor kingdom, Changamire, was powerful from the late 1600s until about 1830. The northern successor state, which stretched along the Zambezi, was known to the first Portuguese sources as the kingdom ruled by the Mwene Mutapa, or "Master Pillager," the title of its sixteenth-century ruler, Mutota, and his successors.

THE PORTUGUESE IN SOUTHEASTERN AFRICA

Portuguese attempts to obtain gold from the Zambezi region of the interior by controlling trade on the Swahili coast were failures. The Portuguese then established fortified posts up the Zambezi and meddled in Shona politics. In the 1690s the Changamire Shona Dynasty conquered the northern Shona territory and pushed the Portuguese out of gold country.

All along the Zambezi, a lasting consequence of Portuguese intrusion was the creation of quasi-tribal chiefdoms. These were led by ***prazeros***, interracial descendants of the area's first Portuguese estate holders, Africans, and Indian immigrants. By the end of the eighteenth century, they formed a few clanlike groups that controlled vast land-holdings and commanded armies, often made up largely of slaves. They functioned as warlords, too strong for either the Portuguese or the regional African rulers to control.

SOUTH AFRICA: THE CAPE COLONY

In South Africa the Dutch planted European colonials almost inadvertently, yet the consequences were far-reaching. The first Cape settlement was built in 1652 by the Dutch East India Company as a resupply point for Dutch vessels traveling between the Netherlands and the East Indies. The support station grew gradually, becoming by century's end a large settler community (the population of the colony in 1662, including slaves, was 392; by 1714 it had reached 3,878).[6] These settlers were the forebears of the Afrikaners of modern South Africa.

Local Khoikhoi people were gradually incorporated into the colonial economy. The Khoikhoi (see Chapter 5) were mostly pastoralists; they had neither traditions of strong political organization nor an economic base beyond their herds. At first they freely bartered livestock for iron, copper, and tobacco. However, when settlers began to

---

[6]R. Elphick and H. Giliomee, *The Shaping of South African Society, 1652–1820* (Cape Town: Longman, 1979), p. 4.

displace the Khoikhoi in the southwestern Cape, conflicts ensued. The results were the consolidation of European landholdings and a breakdown of Khoikhoi society. Dutch military success led to even greater control over the Khoikhoi by the 1670s. Treated as free persons, they became the chief source of colonial wage labor—labor that was in ever greater demand as the colony grew.

The colony also imported slaves from all along the South Seas trade routes, including India, East Africa, and Madagascar. Slavery set the tone for relations between the emergent, and ostensibly "white," Afrikaner population and the "coloreds" of other races. Free or not, the latter were eventually all too easily identified with slave peoples.

After the first settlers spread out around the company station, nomadic white livestock farmers, or **Trekboers**, moved more widely afield, leaving the richer but limited farming lands of the coast for the drier interior tableland. There they contested wider groups of Khoikhoi cattle herders for the best grazing lands. The Trekboers developed military techniques—notably the "commando," a collective civilian raid—to secure their way of life by force. Again the Khoikhoi were the losers. By 1700 they were stripped almost completely of their own pasturages, and their way of life was destroyed. Increasing numbers of Khoikhoi took up employment in the colonial economy. Others moved north to join with other refugees from Cape society (slaves, mixed bloods, and some freedmen) to form raiding bands operating along the frontiers of Trekboer territory close to the Orange River. The disintegration of Khoikhoi society continued in the eighteenth century, accelerated sharply by smallpox—a European import against which this previously isolated group had no immunity.

Cape society in this period was diverse. The Dutch East India Company officials (including Dutch Reformed ministers), the emerging Afrikaners (both settled colonists and Trekboers), the Khoikhoi, and the slaves played differing roles. Intermarriage and cohabitation of masters and slaves added to the social complexity, despite laws designed to check such mixing. Accommodation of nonwhite minority groups within Cape society proceeded; the emergence of **Afrikaans**, a new vernacular language of the colonials, shows that the Dutch immigrants themselves were subject to acculturation. By the time of English domination after 1795, the sociopolitical foundations of modern South Africa—and the bases of **apartheid**—were firmly laid.

Early European View of Khoikhoi. This seventeenth-century illustration of Khoikhoi reflects a European view of daily life near the Cape of Good Hope.
What economic role did the Khoikhoi play in the Cape Colony?

Trekboers
White livestock farmers in Cape Colony.

Afrikaans
The new language, derived from Dutch, that evolved in the seventeenth- and eighteenth-century Cape Colony.

apartheid
"Apartness," the term referring to racist policies enforced by the white-dominated regime that existed in South Africa from 1948 to 1992.

SUMMARY

 HOW DID the Ottomans govern North Africa and Egypt?

North Africa and Egypt. Developments in African history from 1000 to 1700 varied from region to region. In North Africa, the key new factor was the imperial expansion of the Ottoman Empire as far west as Morocco. But the development of independent regional rulers soon rendered Ottoman authority in North Africa purely nominal. *page 338*

 HOW DID Islam spread south of the Sahara?

The Spread of Islam South of the Sahara. Islam was introduced between the eighth century and 1800. In most cases, the process was slow, peaceful, and partial; ruling elites and traders were more likely to practice Islam, whereas most commoners followed traditional practices. *page 339*

WHAT WERE the four most important states in the Sahel between 1000 and 1600?

Sahelian Empires of the Western and Central Sudan. Several substantial states arose south of the Sahara: Ghana, Mali, Songhai, and Kanem. The ruling elites of these states converted to or were heavily influenced by Islam, although most of their populations practiced local religions or engaged in syncretism. Much of the wealth of these states was tied to their control of the trans-Saharan trade routes. *page 340*

 WHY DID Christianity gradually disappear in Nubia?

The Eastern Sudan. The Nubian Christian states of Maqurra and Alwa were gradually Islamized. *page 347*

 HOW DID the arrival of Europeans affect the peoples of West and central Africa?

The Forestlands: Coastal West and Central Africa. In the coastal forestlands of West Africa, a substantial kingdom arose in Benin, famous for its brass sculptures. Senegambia and the Gold Coast were influenced by contact with European traders and the introduction of food crops from the Americas. Social, political, and economic structures in Kongo and Angola were disrupted by Portuguese slave trading. *page 347*

 HOW DID Swahili language and culture develop?

East Africa. On the east coast, Islam influenced the development of the distinctive Swahili culture and language, and Islamic traders linked the region to India and East Asia. Omanis gained control of Zanzibar. *page 351*

 HOW DID slavery affect race relations in Cape Colony?

Southern Africa. The ruins at Great Zimbabwe leave many questions unanswered. The Portuguese followed the Zambezi to the gold fields that fed the trade at the Swahili coast, but they were unable to profit much. In southernmost Africa, Trekboers displaced Khoikhoi. The Trekboers imported slaves from India and other parts of Africa, and soon the master–slave relationship became their model for all interactions with nonwhites. *page 353*

KEY TERMS

Afrikaans (AF-rih-KAHNS) (p. 355)
apartheid (a-PART-HAYT) (p. 355)
Dar al-Islam (DAR-ahl-his-LAHM) (p. 338)
Maghreb (MUHG-RUHB) (p. 338)
mansa (MAHN-SAH) (p. 343)
marabouts (MAYR-uh-BOOZ) (p. 345)
Moors (p. 352)
muezzin (myoo-EHZ-ihn) (p. 341)
oba (OH-bah) (p. 348)
prazeros (p. 354)
Sharifs (shuh-REEFS) (p. 338)
shaykh (SHAYK) (p. 346)
Swahili (swah-HEE-lee) (p. 352)
Trekboers (TREHK-BORZ) (p. 355)
uzama (p. 348)

REVIEW QUESTIONS

1. Why did Islam succeed in the Sudanic belt and East Africa? What role did warfare play in its success? What role did trade have in it?

2. What is the importance of the empires of Ghana, Mali, and Songhai to world history? Why was the control of the trans-Saharan trade so important to these kingdoms? What was the importance of Islamic culture to them? Why did each of these empires break up?

3. What was the impact of the introduction of food crops from the Americas on various regions of Africa during this period?

4. How did Swahili culture form? Describe its defining characteristics. Why has its impact on the East African coast endured?

5. What was the impact of the Portuguese on East Africa and central Africa? How did European coastal activities affect the African interior?

6. Why did Ottoman influence decline in northern Africa in the eighteenth century?

7. How did the Portuguese and Dutch differ from or resemble the Arabs and other Muslims who came as outsiders to sub-Saharan Africa?

8. What is known about Great Zimbabwe? What questions remain? How might the remaining questions be answered?

9. Discuss the diversity of Cape society in South Africa before 1700. Who were the Trekboers, and what was their conflict with the Khoikhoi? How was the basis for apartheid formed in this period?

Note: To learn more about the topics in this chapter, please turn to the Suggested Readings at the end of the book. For additional sources related to this chapter please see www.myhistorylab.com

myhistorylab Connections

Reinforce what you learned in this chapter by studying the many documents, images, maps, review tools, and videos available at **www.myhistorylab.com**

Read and Review

✓●─|**Study** and **Review** Chapter 14

●●●─|Read the Document *Excerpts from Sundiata: An Epic of Old Mali, 1235,* p. 342
The Travels of Ibn Battuta "Ibn Battuta in Mali," p. 343
Al-Umari describes Mansa Musa of Mali, p. 343
Voyage from Lisbon, p. 351
Descriptions of the cities of Zanj, p. 352

👁─|See the Map *Trade Routes in Africa,* p. 338
Discovery: The Maghrib and West Africa, Fourteenth Century, p. 338
East African Coast to 1600, p. 339
African Empires in the Western Sudan, p. 345
African Climate Zones and Bantu Migration Routes, ca. 3000 B.C.E., p. 353

●─|View the Image *Loango, the Capital of the Kingdom of the Congo,* p. 351

((●─|Hear the Audio *Influences in Africa 2,* p. 339
Influences in Africa 2, p. 348

Research and Explore

●─|Watch the Video *Piracy,* p. 338

●─|Watch the Video *West African States*

((●─|Hear the Audio

Hear the audio file for Chapter 14
at **www.myhistorylab.com**

15

Europe to the Early 1500s: Revival, Decline, and Renaissance

((•—[Hear the Audio for Chapter 15 at www.myhistorylab.com

The Medieval Universe. In medieval Europe, the traditional geocentric or earth-centered universe was usually depicted by concentric circles. In this popular German work on natural history, medicine, and science, Konrad von Megenberg (1309–1374) depicted the universe in a most unusual but effective manner. The seven known planets are contained within straight horizontal bands that separate the earth below from heaven, populated by the saints, above.

Which realm seems more important to the artist, heaven or earth?

T he High Middle Ages (the eleventh through the thirteenth centuries in Europe) were a period of political expansion and consolidation and of intellectual flowering and synthesis. The Latin, or Western, church established itself as a spiritual authority independent of secular monarchies, which became more powerful and self-aggrandizing. The parliaments and popular assemblies that accompanied the rise of these monarchies laid the foundations of modern representative institutions.

An agricultural revolution increased food supplies and populations. Trade and commerce revived, towns expanded, banking and credit developed, and a "new rich" merchant class rose to power in Europe's cities. Universities were established. Contact with the Arab world gave access to the writings of the ancient Greek philosophers, which stimulated the great expansion of Western culture during the late Middle Ages and the Renaissance.

The late Middle Ages and the Renaissance, roughly from 1300 to 1500, were a time of both unprecedented calamity and bold new beginnings in Europe. France and England grappled with each other in a bitter conflict known as the Hundred Years' War (1337–1453). Bubonic plague (the "Black Death") killed as much as one third of the population in many regions between 1348 and 1350. A schism divided the church (1378–1417). And in 1453

GLOBAL PERSPECTIVE

THE HIGH MIDDLE AGES IN WESTERN EUROPE

With its borders finally secured, Western Europe during the High Middle Ages was able to concentrate on its political institutions and cultural development, which had been ignored during the early Middle Ages. For Western Europe, the High Middle Ages were a period of clearer self-definition during which individual lands gained much of the geographic shape we recognize today. Europe also began to escape its relative isolation from the rest of the world, which had prevailed since the early Middle Ages. Two factors contributed to this increased engagement: the Crusades and renewed trade along the Silk Road linking China and Europe, made possible by the Mongol conquests in Asia.

Under the Song Dynasty (960–1279), before Mongol rule, China continued its technological advance. In addition to the printing press, the Chinese invented the abacus and gunpowder. They also enjoyed a money economy unknown in the West. But culturally, these centuries between 1000 and 1300 were closed and narrow by comparison with those of the Tang Dynasty. Politically, the Song were far more autocratic. This was also an era of expansion for Chinese trade, and one of the few in Chinese history in which merchants as a group were able to advance in wealth and status. Although the imperial reach of the Song was limited, Chinese culture in this period was more open to outside influences than in any previous era.

In the late twelfth century Japan shifted from civilian to military rule; the Kamakura *bakufu* governed by mounted warriors who were paid with rights to income from land in exchange for their military services. This rise of a military aristocracy marked the beginning of Japan's "medieval," as distinct from its "classical," period. Three Mongol invasions in the thirteenth century also fostered a strong military to resist them. With a civilian court also in existence, Japan actually had a dual government (that is, two emperors and two courts) until the fourteenth century. However, this situation differed greatly from the deep and permanent national divisions developing at this time among the emerging states and autonomous principalities of Western Europe.

the Turks captured Constantinople. But at the same time, the late Middle Ages witnessed a rebirth that would continue into the seventeenth century. Scholars began criticizing medieval assumptions about the nature of God, humankind, and society. Printing was invented, and local languages—Europe's vernaculars—gained recognition. Patriotism and incipient nationalism became major forces in the independent nation-states of Europe. ■

REVIVAL OF EMPIRE, CHURCH, AND TOWNS

WHAT IMPACT did the Crusades have on medieval European society?

OTTO I AND THE REVIVAL OF THE EMPIRE

The fortunes of both the old empire and the papacy began to revive when the Saxon Henry I ("the Fowler"; d. 936) became the first non-Frankish king of Germany in 918. Henry rebuilt royal power. His son Otto I (r. 936–973) maneuvered his relatives into power in Bavaria, Swabia, and Franconia and then invaded Italy and proclaimed himself its king in 951. In 955 he defeated the Hungarians at Lechfeld, securing German borders against new barbarian attacks and earning the title "the Great."

Otto enlisted the help of the church in rebuilding his realm. He appointed bishops and abbots to administer his land, since these men possessed a sense of universal empire but they could not marry and found families to compete with his own. In 961, Otto responded to a call for help from Pope John XII (955–964), and in 962, Otto received in return an imperial coronation. The church was brought ever more under royal control, but it was increasingly determined to assert its independence.

THE REVIVING CATHOLIC CHURCH: THE CLUNY REFORM MOVEMENT AND THE INVESTITURE STRUGGLE

Otto's successors became so preoccupied with Italy that they allowed their German base to disintegrate. As the German Empire began to crumble in the eleventh century, the church, unhappy under imperial domination, declared its independence by embracing the Cluny reform.

The great monastery at Cluny had been founded in 910 in east-central France. The Cluny reformers maintained that clergy should not be subservient to kings; clergy should

Within the many developing autonomous Islamic lands at this time, the teachings of Muhammad created an international culture. Religious identity enabled Muslims to transcend their new and often very deep regional divisions. Similarly, Christianity allowed Englishmen, Frenchmen, Germans, and Italians to think of themselves as one people and to unite in crusades to the Holy Land. As these Crusades got under way in the late eleventh century, Islam too was on the march, penetrating Anatolia and Afghanistan and impinging upon India, where it met a new challenge in Hinduism.

The legacy of the Crusades was mixed. They accomplished few of the goals that originally motivated the European Crusaders; the Holy Land remained under Islamic control, the Crusader kingdoms there collapsed within a few generations of their founding, and the animosity toward Christians fostered by the Crusades resonates even today in the Middle East. Still, the Crusades brought Europeans into more direct and frequent contact with the non-European world than they had known since the heyday of the Roman Empire. Crusaders sampled and sent home products from the Middle East, Asia, and North Africa, creating new tastes in food, art, and even fashion. The resulting growth in demand for these products impelled rising numbers of European merchants to seek these products beyond Europe. Eventually Europeans sought to bypass the Islamic world entirely and secure supplies of Eastern products, especially spices, by going directly to the sources in India and East Asia. By such development European isolation was ended.

Focus Questions

◆ How did the High Middle Ages in Europe differ from the early Middle Ages?

◆ What was the legacy of the Crusades for Europe? In what ways did they signal the start of new relationships between Europe and the wider world?

serve under the direct authority of the pope. They denounced "secular" parish clergy, who lived with concubines in marriage-like relationships. Distinctive features of Western religion—separation of church and state, and the celibacy of the Catholic clergy—had their origins in the Cluny reform movement. From Cluny, reformers were dispatched throughout France and Italy, and in the late eleventh century the papacy embraced their proposals.

Pope Gregory VII (r. 1073–1085) advocated other reforms, too. In 1075, he condemned under penalty of excommunication the well-established custom of a king appointing bishops to administer his estates, "investing" them with the ring and staff that symbolized their ecclesiastical office. Emperor Henry IV of Germany saw this as a direct challenge to his authority. In contrast, Germany's territorial princes supported the pope, for they believed that anything that weakened the emperor strengthened them.

The lines of battle were quickly drawn. Henry assembled his loyal German bishops at Worms in January 1076 and had them proclaim their independence from Gregory. Gregory promptly excommunicated Henry and absolved all Henry's subjects from loyalty to him. The German princes were delighted, and Henry faced a general revolt. He had no choice but to come to terms with Gregory. In a famous scene, he prostrated himself outside the pope's castle in northern Italy in January 1077, reportedly standing barefoot in the snow off and on for three days before the pope gave him absolution. Papal power seemed to triumph, but the struggle was not yet over.

The Investiture Controversy was finally settled in 1122 with the Concordat of Worms in which the new Emperor Henry V (r. 1106–1125) agreed not to invest bishops with the ring and staff, and Pope Calixtus II (r. 1119–1124) recognized the emperor's right to grant bishops their secular fiefs. The emperor effectively retained the right to nominate or veto a candidate. The settlement created separate spheres of ecclesiastical and secular authority; it also set the stage for future conflicts between church and state.

THE CRUSADES

What the Cluny reform was to the clergy, the **Crusades** to the Holy Land were to the laity: an outlet for the heightened religiosity of the late eleventh and twelfth centuries.

QUICK REVIEW

Church and State

◆ Investiture crisis centered on authority to appoint and control clergy

◆ Pope Gregory excommunicated Henry IV when Henry proclaimed his independence from the papacy

◆ Crisis settled in 1122 with Concordat of Worms

Crusades

Religious wars directed by the church against "infidels" and "heretics."

MAP 15–1. **The Early Crusades.** Routes and several leaders of the Crusades during the first century of the movement are shown. The names on this map do not exhaust the list of great nobles who went on the First Crusade. The even showier array of monarchs of the Second and Third Crusades still left the Crusades, on balance, ineffective in achieving their goals.

What obstacles did the Crusaders encounter?

Late in the eleventh century, the Byzantine Empire was under severe pressure from the Seljuk Turks. The Eastern emperor, Alexius I Comnenus, appealed for Western aid. At the Council of Clermont in 1095, Pope Urban II responded by launching the First Crusade. Scholars debate the motives of the Crusaders. Genuine religious piety played a major part. The papacy promised Crusaders forgiveness for all their sins should they die in battle, and a crusade to the Holy Land was the ultimate religious pilgrimage. The pope and others may also have hoped to stabilize the West by sending large numbers of restless, feuding young nobles off to foreign lands. (About 100,000 took part in the First Crusade.) Younger sons of noblemen, for whom there were no estates at home, may have hoped that a crusade would make their fortunes. Urban also saw the Crusades as an opportunity to reconcile Eastern and Western Christianity.

Drawn by the dream of liberating the holy city of Jerusalem, which the Seljuk Turks had held since the seventh century, three great armies gathered in France, Germany, and Italy. As the Crusaders marched by different overland routes toward Constantinople, they seized the opportunity to rid Europe of Jews as well as Muslims. Jewish communities, especially in the Rhineland, suffered bloody pogroms (see Map 15–1).

The Eastern emperor was suspicious of the uncouth, spirited soldiers who gathered at his capital, and his subjects, whose villages the Westerners plundered, were openly hostile. Nevertheless, the Crusaders succeeded in doing what Byzantine armies had failed to do. They routed the Seljuks, and on July 15, 1099, they took the city of Jerusalem. They owed their success to their superior military discipline and weaponry and to the fact that the Muslims failed to unite to oppose them.

The victorious Crusaders set up a "kingdom of Jerusalem" composed of a number of tiny feudal states. These were tenuously held islands in a sea of Muslims intent on their destruction. As the Crusaders built castles for the defense of their new territories, their focus shifted from conquest to economic development. Some, like the military-religious order of the Knights Templar, acquired vast fortunes.

After about forty years, the Crusader states began to fall. The Second Crusade, preached by the Cistercian monk Bernard of Clairvaux (1091–1153), attempted a rescue but met with dismal failure. In October 1187, Saladin (r. 1138–1193), king of Egypt and Syria, reconquered Jerusalem, a victory so brilliant and unexpected that Pope Urban III was said to have dropped dead upon hearing about it. Save for a brief interlude in the thirteenth century, the holiest of cities remained in Islamic hands until the twentieth century.

The Third Crusade in the twelfth century (1189–1192) attempted to reclaim Jerusalem, under three of Europe's greatest rulers: Richard the Lion-Hearted of England, Frederick Barbarossa of the Holy Roman Empire, and Philip Augustus of France. Barbarossa died in an accident en route to the front, and Philip Augustus returned to France to prey on Richard's lands. Left alone, Richard could do little. On his way home, Richard was captured by Emperor Henry VI. England paid a huge ransom to win his release. Popular resentment at the failed, costly venture contributed to the events that produced the Magna Carta in 1215, an effort to curb the power of England's kings.

Politically and religiously the first three Crusades were a failure. But they stimulated Western trade with the East, as Venetian, Pisan, and Genoan merchants followed the Crusaders across Byzantium to lucrative new markets.

Venetian commercial ambitions shaped the Fourth Crusade. Thirty thousand Crusaders gathered in Venice in 1202, intending to sail to Egypt. When they could not raise the money to pay for their transport, they negotiated: In exchange for passage, they agreed to take the rival Christian port of Zara for Venice. Europe was stunned, but worse was to come. The Crusaders were next diverted to Constantinople, which fell to their assault in 1204. A Latin ascended the Byzantine throne, and Venice became the dominant commercial power in the eastern Mediterranean.

Pope Innocent III was chagrined by the misdirection of a Crusade he had authorized, but once Constantinople was in Latin hands, he changed his mind. The opportunity to bring Greek Christians under the control of the Latin church was too tempting. The Greeks, however, could not be reconciled to Latin rule, and in 1261 the man they recognized as their legitimate emperor, Michael Paleologus, recaptured the city. He had help from Venice's rival, Genoa. The Fourth Crusade did nothing to heal the political and religious divisions that separated East and West.

TOWNS AND TOWNSPEOPLE

In the eleventh and twelfth centuries, most towns were small. Only about 5 percent of western Europe's population were urban dwellers, but they were some of the most creative members of medieval society.

•••—Read the Document
Arab-Syrian Gentleman Discusses Franks
at **myhistorylab.com**

👁—See the Map
The Major Crusades
at **myhistorylab.com**

•••—Read the Document
The Magna Carta 1215
at **myhistorylab.com**

((•—Hear the Audio
at **myhistorylab.com**

CHRONOLOGY	
THE CRUSADES	
1095	Pope Urban II launches the First Crusade
1099	The Crusaders take Jerusalem
1147–1149	The Second Crusade
1187	Jerusalem retaken by the Muslims under Saladin
1189–1192	Third Crusade
1202–1204	Fourth Crusade

Foundry in Florence. Skilled workers were an integral component of the commerce of medieval towns. This scene shows the manufacture of cannons in a foundry in Florence.

What parts of this image are most detailed? Why?

A Closer Look

European Embrace of a Black Saint

St. Maurice, patron saint of Magdeburg, Germany, was a third-century Egyptian Christian, who commanded the Egyptian legion of the Roman army in Gaul. In 286 C.E. he and his soldiers were executed for impiety after refusing to worship the Roman gods. Maurice's cult began in 515, and he became a favorite saint of Charlemagne and other pious, warring German kings.

Portrayed as a white man for centuries, St. Maurice first appeared as a black man in the mid-thirteenth century. In the era of the Crusades, rulers had their eyes on new possessions in the Orient, and an Eastern-looking patron saint (Maurice) seemed the perfect talisman as Western merchants and armies ventured forth to trade and conquer. At this time, artists also began to paint as a black man one of the three Magi who visited baby Jesus on his birthday. The name Maurice was close to the German word for black dye ("Mauro") and later Moors ("Mohren"). Progressively, the third-century saint was transformed into a black African. By the fifteenth and sixteenth centuries, his head adorned the coats-of-arms of leading Nuremberg families who traded in the Near East, among them the Tuchers, Nuremberg's great cloth merchants, and Albrecht Dürer, Germany's most famous Renaissance artist.

Questions

1. Did Charlemagne and other German kings embrace Maurice as their favorite saint for mercenary, religious, or military motives?

2. Was racism behind the portrayal of Maurice as a white man for eleven centuries, before painters presented him as the black saint he had always been?

3. Why would some of Nuremberg's wealthy, leading families adorn their coats-of-arms with the head of an African saint?

myhistorylab To examine this image in an interactive fashion, please go to **www.myhistorylab.com**

Towns were dominated at first by the feudal lords whose charters guaranteed the towns' safety. The purpose of towns was originally to concentrate skilled laborers who could manufacture the finished goods desired by lords and bishops. As towns grew, they attracted serfs who used their skills and industriousness to raise themselves into higher social ranks. Lords in the countryside had to offer serfs better terms of tenure to keep them on the land, so the growth of towns improved conditions for all serfs.

The first merchants may have been enterprising serfs. Long-distance traders were often people who had nothing to lose and everything to gain from the enormous risks of foreign trade. They traveled together in armed caravans and convoys, buying goods and products as cheaply as possible at the source and selling them for all they could get in Western ports (see Map 15–2 on page 366). Merchants were outside the traditional social groups of nobility, clergy, and peasantry, but as they gained wealth, they gained respect and imitators. They also challenged traditional authority.

Townspeople needed simple, uniform laws and a government sympathetic to new forms of business activity. Commerce was incompatible with the fortress mentality of the lords of the countryside. Merchants especially wanted to end the arbitrary tolls and tariffs imposed by regional magnates. Small shopkeepers and artisans identified far more with merchants than with aloof lords and bishops. The lesser nobility (small knights) outside the towns also supported the new mercantile economy. During the eleventh and twelfth centuries, the burgher upper classes successfully challenged the old noble urban lords. Towns allied with kings against the nobility in the countryside, rearranging the centers of power and dissolving classic feudal government. Many towns in the High and Late Middle Ages formed their own independent communes.

With urban autonomy came new models of self-government. Around 1100 the old urban nobility and the new burgher upper class merged into an urban patriciate. From this new ruling class was born the aristocratic town council. Enriching and complicating the situation was the fact that small artisans and craftspeople slowly developed their own protective associations or **guilds** and began to gain a voice in government. The towns' opportunities for the "little person" had created the slogan "Town air brings freedom." Townspeople thought of themselves as citizens with basic rights, not subjects at the mercy of their masters' whim.

Towns became a major force in the transition from feudal societies to national governments. They were a ready source of educated bureaucrats and lawyers who knew Roman law, the tool for running the state. Money earned by townspeople enabled kings to hire their own armies, freeing them from dependence on the nobility. Towns, in turn, won royal political recognition and had their constitutions guaranteed. In France, towns became integrated early into royal government. In Germany, they fell under ever tighter control by the princes. In Italy, uniquely, towns became genuine city-states during the Renaissance.

Towns attracted Jews, who plied trades in small businesses. Many became wealthy as moneylenders to kings, popes, and businesspeople. Jewish intellectual and religious culture both dazzled and threatened Christians. Suspicion and distrust among Christians led to an unprecedented surge in anti-Jewish sentiment in the late twelfth and early thirteenth centuries.

In the twelfth century, translations and commentaries by Byzantine and Spanish Islamic scholars introduced western Europeans to the works of Aristotle, Euclid, and Ptolemy, the texts of Greek physicians and Arab mathematicians, and the corpus of Roman law. The resulting intellectual ferment gave rise to modern Western universities such as Bologna (established 1158) and the University of Paris.

In the High Middle Ages, people assumed that truth was already known and only needed to be properly organized, elucidated, and defended. Under this model of learning, known as **Scholasticism**, students summarized and compared the traditional authorities,

QUICK REVIEW

Town Charters
- Towns originally dominated by feudal lords
- Town charters granted townspeople safety and independence
- Growth of towns improved conditions for serfs generally

The University of Bologna in central Italy was distinguished as the center for the revival of Roman law. This carving on the tomb of a Bolognese professor of law shows students attending one of his lectures.

Why were universities important in medieval history?

guild
An association of merchants or craftsmen that offered protection to its members and set rules for their work and products.

Scholasticism
Method of study based on logic and dialectic that dominated the medieval schools. It assumed that truth already existed; students had only to organize, elucidate, and defend knowledge learned from authoritative texts, especially those of Aristotle and the Church Fathers.

MAP EXPLORATION

To explore this map further, go to **http://www.myhistorylab.com**

MAP 15–2.   Medieval Trade Routes and Regional Products.   Trade in Europe varied in intensity and geographical extent in different periods during the Middle Ages. The map shows some of the channels that came to be used in interregional commerce. Labels tell part of what was carried in that commerce.

How strong were the connections among Europe, the Middle East, and Africa at this time?

elaborated their arguments pro and con, and drew the logical conclusions. After Aristotle's works were popularized in the West, logic and dialectic became the new tools for disciplining thought and knowledge. Dialectic was the art of discovering a truth by pondering the arguments against it. Together with aspiring philosophers, theologians, and lawyers, even medical students learned their vocation by debating the authoritative texts in their field, not by clinical medical practice.

Peter Abelard (1079–1142) was the boldest advocate for the new Aristotelian learning. The leading philosopher and theologian of his day, he became Master of Students at Notre Dame. His thinking was unique in its appreciation of subjectivity. He claimed, for instance, that a person's motives determined whether the person's actions were good or evil, not the acts themselves. He also said that an individual's feeling of repentance was a more important factor in receiving God's forgiveness than the church's sacrament of penance.

His audacious logical critique of religious doctrine earned him powerful enemies. Abelard, as he laments in his autobiography, played into their hands by seducing Heloise, a young woman he was hired to tutor. She was the niece of a powerful church leader. After she became pregnant, Abelard wed her—but kept the marriage secret, for university teachers, like clergy, were required to be celibate. Her uncle hired men to castrate Abelard. Thereafter he became a monk, and she entered a convent. They exchanged letters in which he denigrated his love for her as wretched desire. Repentance failed to ingratiate him with the church authorities. In 1121, his works were burned, and in 1140, nineteen propositions that he had taught were condemned as heresies. Heloise outlived him by twenty years and won renown for her efforts to improve conditions for cloistered women.

Read the Document
Abelard Defends Himself
at **myhistorylab.com**

regular clergy
Monks and nuns who belong to religious orders.

secular clergy
Parish clergy who did not belong to a religious order.

MEDIEVAL SOCIETY

THE ORDER OF LIFE

In the art and literature of the Middle Ages, three basic social groups were represented: the landed nobility; the clergy; the peasantry and village artisans. After the eleventh century, long-distance traders and merchants emerged as a fourth social group.

No medieval social group was absolutely uniform. Noblemen formed a broad spectrum. Dignity and status within the nobility were directly related to the exercise of authority over others. By the Late Middle Ages, separate classes of higher and lower nobility had evolved in both town and country. The higher were the great landowners and territorial magnates, long the dominant powers in their regions; the lower were petty landlords, the descendants of minor knights, newly rich merchants, or wealthy farmers.

Waging war was the nobleman's sole profession. In the eighth century, the adoption of stirrups made mounted warriors Europe's most valued military assets. The chief virtues of these knights were physical strength, courage, and belligerency.

By the Late Middle Ages, several factors forced the landed nobility into a steep economic and political decline from which it never recovered. Climatic changes and agricultural failures created large famines, while the great plague (discussed later) brought about unprecedented population losses. Changing military tactics (the use of infantry and heavy artillery during the Hundred Years' War) made the noble cavalry nearly obsolete. And the alliance of wealthy towns with the king weakened the nobility. After the fourteenth century, land and wealth counted for far more than lineage as qualification for entrance into the highest social class.

Unlike the nobility or peasantry, one was not born into the clerical estate. It was acquired by religious training and ordination and was, in theory, open to anyone. There were two fundamental categories of clergy. The **regular clergy** were the monks who lived according to a special ascetic rule (*regula*) in cloisters apart from the world. In the thirteenth century, two new orders were sanctioned, the Franciscans and the Dominicans, whose members went out into the world to preach the church's mission and to combat heresy. The **secular clergy**, who lived and worked directly among the laity in the world (*saeculum*), formed a vast hierarchy. At the top were the wealthy cardinals, archbishops, and bishops. Below them were the urban priests, the cathedral canons, and the court clerks. Finally, there was the great mass of poor parish priests, who were neither financially nor intellectually much above the common people they served.

During most of the Middle Ages, the clergy were honored as the first estate, and theology was the queen of the sciences. There was great reverence for the clergy's function as mediators between God and humanity. The priest brought the Son of God down to

WHAT NEW group was
added to the three
traditional groups in
medieval society?

Dominicans (top) and Franciscans (bottom).
Unlike the other religious orders, the Dominicans and Franciscans did not live in cloisters but wandered about preaching and combating heresy. They depended for support on their own labor and the kindness of the laity.
Cliche Bibliothèque Nationale de France, Paris.

Why are books so prominent in both these images?

earth when he celebrated the sacrament of the Eucharist, and his absolution released penitents from punishment for sin. Mere laypeople did not presume to judge priests.

The largest and lowest social group in medieval society was one on whose labor the welfare of all others depended: the agrarian peasantry. Many peasants lived and worked on the manors of the nobility. The lord of the manor required a certain amount of produce (grain, eggs, and the like) and services from the peasant families, and he held judicial and police authority over them. The lord owned and operated the machines that processed crops into food and drink, and he had the right to subject his tenants to exactions known as *banalities*. He could, for example, force them to breed their cows with his bull, and pay for the privilege, or make their wine in his wine press. The lord also collected as an inheritance tax a serf's best animal. Without the lord's permission, a serf could neither travel nor marry outside the manor in which he served. Serfs were not chattel slaves, however. It was to a lord's advantage to keep his serfs healthy and happy; his welfare, like theirs, depended on a successful harvest. Serfs had their own dwellings and modest strips of land, and they lived off the produce of their own labor. They could sell any surpluses, and serfs could pass their property on to their children.

Two basic changes transformed the peasantry during the Middle Ages. The first was the increasing importance of single-family holdings: As families retained property from generation to generation, family farms replaced manorial units. The second was the conversion of the serf's dues into money payments, a change made possible by the revival of trade and the return of a monetary economy. By the thirteenth century, many peasants held their land as rent-paying tenants and no longer had servile status.

In the mid-fourteenth century, when the great plague and the Hundred Years' War created a labor shortage, nobles in England and France tried to turn back the clock by increasing taxes on the peasantry and restricting their migration to the cities. Their efforts triggered rebellions, which were brutally crushed. As growing national sentiment would break European society's political unity, and heretical movements end its nominal religious unity, the peasantry's revolts revealed the absence of medieval social unity.

MEDIEVAL WOMEN

The image of women in the Middle Ages was quite different than the reality of women's lives. The image was sketched by celibate male clergy who viewed virginity as morally superior to marriage and claimed that women were physically, mentally, and morally inferior to men. They defined only two respectable roles for women: subjugated housewife or confined nun. Many medieval women were neither.

The clerical view of women was contradicted both within the church itself and in secular society. During the twelfth and thirteenth centuries, the burgeoning popularity of the cult of the Virgin Mary, of chivalric romances, and of courtly love literature celebrated women as natural moral superiors of men. Peter Lombard (1100–1169), an influential theologian, taught that God created Eve from Adam's rib because God intended woman neither to rule nor to be ruled but to be at man's side as his partner in a mutual relationship.

Germanic law treated women better than Roman law had done, recognizing basic rights. German women could inherit, administer, and dispose of property, and they could take men to court and sue for bodily injury and rape. German women married husbands of similar age, and a German bride was entitled to a gift of property from her husband that she retained in case of his death.

The nunnery was an option for single women who could afford it: Entrance required a dowry. Within a nunnery a woman could rise to a position of leadership and exercise authority, but even cloistered women had to submit to supervision by male clergy. The number of women in cloisters was never very large; in late medieval England no more than 3,500 women entered the cloister.

Medieval Marketplace. A fifteenth-century rendering of an eleventh- or twelfth-century marketplace. Medieval women were active in all trades, but especially in the food and clothing industries.

© Scala/Art Resource, New York.

How did the realities of women's lives compare to the image cultivated by Christian clergy?

In the ninth century, the Carolingian monarchs obeyed the church and began to enforce monogamy. This was both a gain and a loss for women. Wives were accorded greater dignity and legal security, but their burdens as household managers and bearers of children multiplied. The life span of Frankish women decreased in the ninth century.

The vast majority of medieval women worked for income. Between the ages of 10 and 15, girls and boys were apprenticed to learn productive trades. Married women often operated their own shops or became partners in the shops of their husbands. Women appeared in virtually every "blue-collar" trade, from butcher to goldsmith, but mostly worked in the food and clothing industries. Women belonged to guilds, just like men, and they could become craftmasters, but they were paid less than men who did the same jobs. In the late Middle Ages, townswomen had some opportunities for schooling and to acquire **vernacular** literacy, but they were excluded from the learned professions of scholarship, medicine, and law.

vernacular
The everyday language spoken by the people, as opposed to Latin.

GROWTH OF NATIONAL MONARCHIES

ENGLAND: HASTINGS (1066) TO MAGNA CARTA (1215)

Medieval England's political destiny was determined by the response to the death of the childless Anglo-Saxon ruler Edward the Confessor (r. 1042–1066). Through a connection with Edward's mother, a Norman princess, Duke William of Normandy (d. 1087) laid claim to the English throne. The Anglo-Saxon assembly preferred a native nobleman, Harold Godwinsson (ca. 1022–1066). William invaded England, defeating Harold's army at Hastings on October 14, 1066. William I "the Conqueror" was crowned king of England in Westminster Abbey.

William established a strong monarchy but kept the Anglo-Saxon tax system, the practice of court writs (legal warnings) as a flexible form of central control over localities, and the Anglo-Saxon quasi-democratic tradition of frequent *parleying*—that is, the holding of conferences between the king and lesser powers who had vested interests in royal decisions. The result was a balancing of monarchical and parliamentary elements that continues to characterize English government today.

William's grandson, Henry II (r. 1154–1189), had large French holdings through inheritance and his marriage to Eleanor of Aquitaine (1122–1204). Henry II's increasing autocracy was met with strong political resistance from both the nobility and the clergy. Under Henry's successors, the brothers Richard the Lion-Hearted (r. 1189–1199) and John (r. 1199–1216), burdensome taxation turned resistance into rebellion. With the full support of the clergy and the townspeople, the barons forced King John to recognize the **Magna Carta** ("Great Charter") in 1215, a document that reaffirmed traditional rights and personal liberties. This famous cornerstone of modern English law put limits on royal power and secured the right of representation in government to the privileged.

HOW DID England and France develop strong royal governments by the thirteenth century?

Read the **Document**
The Battle of Hastings 1066
at **myhistorylab.com**

See the **Map**
England and France ca. 1180
at **myhistorylab.com**

Magna Carta
The "Great Charter" limiting royal power that the English nobility forced King John to sign in 1215.

Battle of Hastings. William the Conqueror on horseback urging his troops into combat with the English at the Battle of Hastings (October 14, 1066).

Detail from the Bayeux Tapestry, scene 51, c. 1073–1083. Musee de la Tapisserie, Bayeaux, France. Photo copyright Bridgeman-Giraudon/Art Resource, New York.

How did changes in military tactics influence relationships between monarchs and nobles in the Middle Ages?

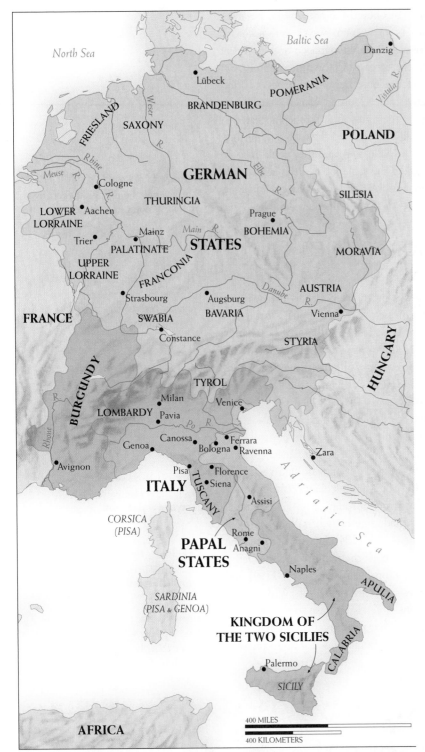

MAP 15–3.   Germany and Italy in the Middle Ages.   Medieval Germany and Italy were divided lands. The Holy Roman Empire (Germany) embraced hundreds of independent territories that the emperor ruled only in name. The papacy controlled Rome and tried to enforce its will in central Italy. Under the Hohenstaufens (mid-twelfth to mid-thirteenth century), internal German divisions and papal conflict reached new heights; German rulers sought to extend their power to southern Italy and Sicily.

Why were emperors unable to unite Germany and Italy in the Middle Ages?

FRANCE: BOUVINES (1214) TO THE REIGN OF LOUIS IX

Powerful feudal princes dominated France from the beginning of the Capetian Dynasty (987) until the reign of Philip II Augustus (1180–1223). During this period, the Capetian kings wisely concentrated their limited resources on securing the territory surrounding Paris, by then the center of French government and culture.

The Duke of Normandy, who after 1066 was master of England, was also a vassal of the French king. Philip Augustus acted decisively to maintain control over his Norman vassal: His armies occupied all the English territories on the French coast except for Aquitaine. At Bouvines on July 27, 1214, the French won handily over the English and their German allies. The victory unified France around the monarchy and thereby laid the foundation for French ascendancy in the Late Middle Ages.

Louis IX (r. 1226–1270), the grandson of Philip Augustus, embodied the medieval view of the perfect ruler. He inherited a unified and secure kingdom. Under him, the efficient French bureaucracy became an instrument of order and fair play in local government. He sent royal commissioners to monitor the local officials and act as champions of the people. Louis abolished private wars and serfdom within his own royal domain, gave his subjects the right of appeal from local to higher courts, and made the tax system more equitable. The French people came to associate their king with justice, and a unifying national identity grew strong.

During Louis's reign, French society and culture became an example to all of Europe, a pattern that continued into the modern period. Northern France became the showcase of monastic reform, chivalry, and Gothic art and architecture. It was the golden age of Scholasticism, and Europe's greatest thinkers converged on Paris.

THE HOHENSTAUFEN EMPIRE (1152–1272)

While stable governments developed in both England and France during the Middle Ages, the Holy Roman Empire fragmented (see Map 15–3). Frederick I Barbarossa (1152–1190), the first of the Hohenstaufens, reestablished imperial authority but also initiated a new phase in the contest between popes and emperors. In 1186 his son—the future Henry VI (r. 1190–1197)—married Constance, heiress to the kingdom of Sicily. The Papal States were now encircled, antagonizing the popes. When Henry VI died in 1197, Germany was thrown into civil war. Henry VI's four-year-old son, Frederick, had for his own safety been made a ward of Pope Innocent III (r. 1198–1215). Innocent had both the motive and the means to challenge the Hohenstaufens.

In December 1212, the pope supported his ward's coronation as Emperor Frederick II. But Frederick soon disappointed his papal sponsor by giving the German princes what they wanted—undisputed authority over their territories. Germany was fragmenting into petty kingdoms. The papacy punished Frederick by excommunicating him (four times) and leading German princes in revolt against him. This transformation of the papacy into a formidable political and military power made the church highly vulnerable to criticism from religious reformers and royal apologists.

When Frederick died in 1250, the German monarchy died with him. The princes established an electoral college in 1257 to pick the emperor, and the "king of the Romans" became their puppet.

POLITICAL AND SOCIAL BREAKDOWN

Hundred Years' War

The Hundred Years' War (1337–1453) started when the English king Edward III (r. 1327–1377), grandson of Philip the Fair of France (r. 1285–1314), claimed the French throne. But the war was more than a dynastic quarrel. England and France were territorial and economic rivals with a long history of animosity, making the Hundred Years' War a struggle for national identity.

France had three times the population of England, was far wealthier, and fought on its own soil. But most major battles were stunning English victories. Unlike England, France was still struggling to make the transition from a fragmented feudal society to a centralized modern state. France's defeats also resulted from incompetent leadership and English military superiority. The English infantry was more disciplined than the French, and English archers could fire six arrows a minute with enough force to pierce the armor of a knight at 200 yards. Eventually, thanks in part to the inspiring leadership of Joan of Arc (1412–1431) and a sense of national identity and self-confidence, the French were able to expel the English. By 1453, all that remained to the English was their coastal enclave of Calais.

The Hundred Years' War had lasting political and social consequences. It devastated France, but it also awakened French nationalism and hastened the country's transition from a feudal monarchy to a centralized state. In both France and England the burden of the war fell most heavily on the peasantry, who were forced to support it with taxes and services.

The Black Death

Agricultural improvements spurred population growth in the Late Middle Ages. Europe's population roughly doubled between the years 1000 and 1300. There were more people than there was food to feed them or jobs to employ them, and the average European faced the probability of extreme hunger at least once during his or her expected thirty-five-year life span. Between 1315 and 1317, for example, cold weather and crop failures produced a great famine. Decades of overpopulation, economic depression, famine, and bad health made Europeans vulnerable to a virulent plague that struck with full force in 1348.

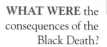

WHAT WERE the consequences of the Black Death?

⊙ See the **Map**
The Hundred Years' War
at **myhistorylab.com**

⊙ See the **Map**
The 100 Years' War
at **myhistorylab.com**

⊙ See the **Map**
Black Death and Peasant Revolts
at **myhistorylab.com**

•●• Read the **Document**
Black Death, 1349, Henry Knighton
at **myhistorylab.com**

MAP 15–4.   Spread of the Black Death.   Apparently introduced by sea-borne rats from areas around the Black Sea where plague-infested rodents have long been known, the Black Death had great human, social, and economic consequences. According to one of the lower estimates, it killed 25 million people in Europe. The map charts the spread of the plague in the mid-fourteenth century. Generally following trade routes, it reached Scandinavia by 1350, and some believe it then went on to Iceland and even Greenland. Areas off the main trade routes were largely spared.

What were some social and economic consequences of the plague?

Black Death

The bubonic plague that killed millions of Europeans in the fourteenth century.

The **Black Death**, so-called because it discolored the body, followed the trade routes from Asia into Europe. Appearing in Sicily in late 1347, it entered Europe through the port cities of Venice, Genoa, and Pisa in 1348, and swept rapidly northward. Areas outside the major trade routes, like Bohemia, remained virtually unaffected. Bubonic plague made numerous reappearances in succeeding decades. It is estimated that western Europe had lost as much as two-fifths of its population by the early fifteenth century (see Map 15–4).

The plague was transmitted by fleas and rats, but it also entered the lungs and could be spread by sneezes. Contemporary physicians had little understanding of how diseases worked. Popular wisdom held that bad air caused the disease. Some thought that earthquakes had released poisonous fumes. Psychological reactions varied tremendously. Some hoped that moderation and temperance would save them; some indulged in sexual promiscuity; some fled in panic; some developed a morbid religiosity. Parades of flagellants whipped themselves, hoping to induce God to show mercy and intervene. Jews were baselessly accused of spreading the disease, and pogroms flared. The church tried to maintain order, but across western Europe people developed an obsession with death and a deep pessimism that endured for decades.

Whole villages vanished. The labor supply shrank, so wages increased and those of skilled artisans soared. Many serfs substituted money payments for their labor services and pursued more rewarding jobs in the cities. Agricultural prices fell because of lowered demand, and the price of luxury and manufactured goods—the work of skilled artisans—rose. The noble landholders suffered the greatest decline in power. They were forced to pay more for finished products and for farm labor, while receiving a smaller return on their agricultural produce. Rents declined everywhere.

Some landowners converted arable land to sheep pasture, substituting more profitable wool production for labor-intensive grain crops. The propertied classes also used their political influence to pass repressive legislation that forced peasants to stay on their farms and froze wages at low levels. The result was an eruption of peasant rebellions in France and England.

Although the plague hit urban populations hard, cities recovered relatively quickly. Cities had always protected their interests by regulating competition and immigration from rural areas. After the plague, the reach of such laws was extended to include the lands of nobles and landlords, many of whom were now integrated into urban life. Guilds used their political influence to pass restrictive legislation that protected their markets. Master artisans wanted to keep their numbers low to limit competition, but the journeymen they employed wanted access to the guild so that they could set up shops of their own. To the old conflict between the urban patriciate and the guilds was now added a struggle within the guilds themselves.

There was gain as well as loss for the church, too. Many clergy died—up to one-third in places—as they dutifully ministered to the sick and dying. As a great landholder, the church's income and, therefore, its political influence declined. But it received new revenues from the vastly increased demand for religious services for the dead and the dying and from new gifts and bequests.

Watch the **Video**
at **myhistorylab.com**

QUICK REVIEW

The Black Death
- Popular name for bubonic plague
- High mortality
- Spread along trade routes
- Many contemporary theories about its causes and cure
- Altered fundamental socioeconomic relationships

Black Death. Men and women carrying plague victims in coffins to the burial ground in Tournai, Belgium, 1349.

How did the high mortality rates of the Black Death alter socioeconomic relationships?

Read the **Document**
Peasant Revolt in England
at **myhistorylab.com**

ECCLESIASTICAL BREAKDOWN AND REVIVAL: THE LATE MEDIEVAL CHURCH

BONIFACE VIII AND PHILIP THE FAIR

By the fourteenth century popes faced rulers far more powerful than themselves. When Pope Boniface VIII (r. 1294–1303) issued a bull, *Clericis Laicos*, which forbade lay taxation of the clergy without prior papal approval, King Philip the Fair of France (r. 1285–1314) unleashed a ruthless antipapal campaign. Boniface made a last-ditch stand against state control of national churches when he issued the bull *Unam Sanctam* in

WHY DID France's king support the Great Schism?

Read the **Document**
Unam Sanctam 1302, Pope Boniface VIII
at **myhistorylab.com**

Papal Authority. Pope Boniface VIII (r. 1294–1303), who opposed the taxation of the clergy by the kings of France and England, issued one of the strongest declarations of papal authority, the bull *Unam Sanctam*. This statue is in the Museo Civico, Bologna, Italy.

Scala/Art Resource, New York.

Why did royal power grow relative to papal power in this period?

Curia
The papal government.

Great Schism
The appearance of two, and at times three, rival popes between 1378 and 1415.

Holy Roman Empire
The revival of the old Roman Empire, based mainly in Germany and northern Italy, that endured from 870 to 1806.

1302, declaring that temporal authority was "subject" to the spiritual power of the church. The French responded with force. Philip sent troops that beat the pope badly and might even have executed him had not an aroused populace rescued him. No pope ever again seriously threatened kings and emperors. Future relations between church and state tilted toward state control of religion within particular monarchies.

THE GREAT SCHISM (1378–1417) AND THE CONCILIAR MOVEMENT TO 1449

Boniface VIII's successor, Clement V (r. 1305–1314), moved the papal court to Avignon on the southeastern border with France, where it remained until Pope Gregory XI (r. 1370–1378) reestablished the papacy in Rome in 1377. When Pope Urban VI (r. 1378–1389) proclaimed his intention to reform the papal government in the **Curia**, France's Charles V (r. 1364–1380) feared a loss of influence. Charles V supported the **Great Schism**, which began on September 20, 1378, when thirteen cardinals (twelve of whom were French) elected a cousin of the French king as Pope Clement VII (r. 1378–1397). Clement returned to Avignon. Allegiance to the competing papal courts divided along political lines. England and its allies—the **Holy Roman Empire** (based on the old Roman Empire, mostly Germany and northern Italy), Hungary, Bohemia, and Poland—retained their allegiance to Urban VI. France and its orbit—Naples, Scotland, Castile, and Aragon—supported Clement VII. In 1409 a council at Pisa deposed both the Roman and the Avignon popes and elected yet another pope, recognized by neither Rome nor Avignon. This intolerable situation lasted until November 1417, when a church legal council elected a new pope, Martin V (r. 1417–1431), and reunited the church.

The papacy regained much of its prestige and authority. But the recourse to church councils had planted the conviction that the leader of an institution must be responsive to its members.

THE RENAISSANCE IN ITALY (1375–1527)

 WHY WAS the Renaissance a transition from the medieval to the modern world?

Renaissance
The revival of ancient learning and the supplanting of traditional religious beliefs by new secular and scientific values that began in Italy in the fourteenth and fifteenth centuries.

The **Renaissance** is the term used to describe fourteenth- and fifteenth-century efforts to revive ancient learning. It marked a transition from the medieval to the modern world. Medieval Europe, especially before the twelfth century, had been a fragmented feudal society with an agricultural economy, its thought and culture dominated by the church. Renaissance Europe, especially after the fourteenth century, was characterized by growing national consciousness and political centralization, an urban economy based on organized commerce and capitalism, and ever greater secular control of thought and culture.

The distinctive features and achievements of the Renaissance are most striking in Italy from roughly 1375 to 1527, the year of the infamous sack of Rome by imperial soldiers. What was achieved in Italy during these centuries deeply influenced northern Europe.

THE ITALIAN CITY-STATE: SOCIAL CONFLICT AND DESPOTISM

The Renaissance began in the cities of late medieval Italy. Italy was the natural gateway between East and West; Venice, Genoa, and Pisa traded with the Middle East throughout the Middle Ages. During the thirteenth and fourteenth centuries, the trade-rich Italian cities became powerful city-states, dominating the political and economic life of their regions. By the fifteenth century, the great Italian cities had become the bankers for much of Europe. There were five major states in Italy: the duchy of Milan, the republics of Florence and Venice, the Papal States, and the kingdom of Naples.

Social strife and competition for political power were so intense within the cities that most had evolved into despotisms by the fifteenth century. Venice, ruled by a successful merchant oligarchy, was the notable exception. Elsewhere, the new social classes and divisions within society produced by rapid urban growth fueled chronic, near-anarchic conflict. In Florence, true stability was not established until the ascent to power in 1434 of the wealthy Cosimo de' Medici (1389–1464), who controlled the city from behind the scenes. His grandson Lorenzo the Magnificent (1449–1492, r. 1478–1492) ruled Florence in near-totalitarian fashion.

Despotism was less subtle elsewhere in Italy. Dominant groups in many cities co-operated in the hiring of a strongman, known as a *podesta*, to maintain law and order. Political turbulence and warfare also fostered diplomacy. City-states strove to stay abreast of foreign military developments and, if shrewd enough, gained power and advantage without actually going to war.

HUMANISM

Humanism was the scholarly study of the Latin and Greek classics and the ancient Church Fathers, both for their own sake and to promote a rebirth of ancient norms and values. Humanists advocated the *studia humanitatis*, a liberal arts program that embraced grammar, rhetoric, poetry, history, politics, and moral philosophy. The first humanists were orators and poets. They wrote original literature inspired by the newly discovered works of the ancients, and they taught rhetoric within the universities. They were sought as secretaries, speech writers, and diplomats in princely and papal courts.

Classical and Christian antiquity had been studied before, but the Italian Renaissance of the Late Middle Ages was more secular and lay dominated, had broader interests, recovered more manuscripts, and possessed far superior technical skills compared to earlier rebirths of antiquity. Unlike their Scholastic rivals, humanists drew their own conclusions after reading original sources in Latin or Greek. (See Document, "Pico della Mirandola States the Renaissance Image of Man" on page 376.)

Francesco Petrarch (1304–1374), the father of humanism, celebrated ancient Rome in his writings and tirelessly collected ancient manuscripts. His critical textual studies, elitism, and contempt for the allegedly useless learning of the Scholastics were shared by many later humanists. Dante Alighieri's (1265–1321) *Vita Nuova* and *Divine Comedy*—together with Petrarch's sonnets—form the cornerstones of Italian vernacular literature. Petrarch's student and friend Giovanni Boccaccio (1313–1375) wrote the *Decameron*, 100 bawdy tales told in various voices, and assembled an encyclopedia of Greek and Roman mythology.

The classical ideal of a useful education that produces well-rounded, effective people inspired far-reaching reforms. The most influential Italian Renaissance tract on education, Pietro Paolo Vergerio's (1349–1420) *On the Morals That Befit a Free Man*, was written directly from classical models. Vittorino da Feltre (d. 1446) directed his students to a highly disciplined reading of ancient authors, together with vigorous physical exercise.

Educated and cultured noblewomen had a prominent place at Renaissance courts, among them Christine de Pisan (1365–1434). She was an expert in classical, French, and Italian languages and literature whose most famous work, *The City of Ladies*, describes the accomplishments of history's great women.

humanism
The study of the Latin and Greek classics and of the Church Fathers both for their own sake and to promote a rebirth of ancient norms and values.

studia humanitatis
During the Renaissance, a liberal arts program of study that embraced grammar, rhetoric, poetry, history, philosophy, and politics.

Read the **Document**
Letters to Cicero, 14th c., Petrarch
at **myhistorylab.com**

Read the **Document**
Dante's Divine Comedy, 1321
at **myhistorylab.com**

DOCUMENT

Pico della Mirandola States the Renaissance Image of Man

One of the most eloquent Renaissance descriptions of the abilities of humankind comes from the Italian humanist Pico della Mirandola (1463–1494). In his famed Oration on the Dignity of Man (ca. 1486), Pico described humans as free to become whatever they choose.

- **In what** does the dignity of humankind consist? Does Pico reject the biblical description of Adam and Eve's fall? Does he exaggerate a person's ability to choose freely to be whatever he or she wishes? What inspired such seeming hubris during the Renaissance?

The best of artisans [God] ordained that that creature (man) to whom He [God] had been able to give nothing proper to himself should have joint possession of whatever had been peculiar to each of the different kinds of being. He therefore took man as a creature of indeterminate nature and, assigning him a place in the middle of the world, addressed him thus: "Neither a fixed abode nor a form that is thine alone or any function peculiar to thyself have we given thee, Adam, to the end that according to thy longing and according to thy judgment thou mayest have and possess what abode, what form, and what functions thou thyself shalt desire. The nature of all other beings is limited and constrained within the bounds of laws prescribed by Us. Thou, constrained by no limits, in accordance with thine own free will, in whose hand We have placed thee, shalt ordain for thyself the limits of thy nature. We have set thee at the world's center that thou mayest from thence more easily observe whatever is in the world. We have made thee neither of heaven nor of earth, neither mortal nor immortal, so that with freedom of choice and with honor, as though the maker and molder of thyself, thou mayest fashion thyself in whatever shape thou shalt prefer. Thou shalt have the power to degenerate into the lower forms of life, which are brutish. Thou shalt have the power, out of thy soul's judgment, to be reborn into the higher forms, which are divine." O supreme generosity of God the Father, O highest and most marvelous felicity of man! To him it is granted to have whatever he chooses, to be whatever he wills.

Source: From Giovanni Pico della Mirandola, *Oration on the Dignity of Man*, in *The Renaissance Philosophy of Man*, ed. by E. Cassirer et al., Phoenix Books, 1961, pp. 224–225. Reprinted by permission of The University of Chicago Press.

RENAISSANCE ART IN AND BEYOND ITALY

Throughout Renaissance Europe, the values and interests of the laity were less subordinated to those of the clergy than in previous centuries. In education, culture, and religion, the secular world's purely human pursuits were appreciated as ends in themselves.

This perspective is especially prominent in the painting and sculpture of the High Renaissance (late fifteenth and early sixteenth centuries), when Renaissance art reached its maturity. In imitation of Greek and Roman art, painters and sculptors created well-proportioned and even heroic figures. Whereas Byzantine and Gothic art had been religious and idealized, Renaissance art, especially in the fifteenth century, reproduced nature and human nature realistically in both its physical beauty and grotesqueness.

Italian artists led the way, taking advantage of new technical skills and materials developed during the fifteenth century: oil paints, the technique of shading to enhance realism (**chiaroscuro**), and sizing figures to convey to the viewer a feeling of continuity with a painting (linear perspective). Compared with their flat Byzantine and Gothic counterparts, Renaissance paintings seem filled with energy and life. The great masters of the High Renaissance include Leonardo da Vinci (1452–1519), Raphael (1483–1520), and Michelangelo Buonarroti (1475–1564). A modernizing, experimental style known as **Mannerism** followed, reaching its peak in the late sixteenth and early seventeenth centuries. Tintoretto (d. 1594) and the Spaniard El Greco (d. 1614) were Mannerism's supreme representatives.

View the Image
Da Vinci, Mona Lisa
at **myhistorylab.com**

View the Image
Michelangelo's David
at **myhistorylab.com**

chiaroscuro
The use of shading to enhance naturalness in painting and drawing.

Mannerism
A style of art in the mid- to late sixteenth century that permitted artists to express their own "manner" or feelings in contrast to the symmetry and simplicity of the art of the High Renaissance.

Watch the Video
at **myhistorylab.com**

ITALY'S POLITICAL DECLINE: THE FRENCH INVASIONS (1494–1527)

Italy's autonomous city-states had always cooperated to oppose foreign invaders. In 1494, however, Naples, supported by Florence and the Borgia pope Alexander VI (1492–1503), prepared to attack Milan. The Milanese despot Ludovico il Moro (r. 1476–1499) invited the French to revive their dynastic claim to Naples. Within five months the French king Charles VIII (r. 1483–1498) had crossed the Alps and raced as conqueror through Florence and the Papal States into Naples. Ferdinand of Aragon (r. 1479–1516), who was also king of Sicily, helped create a counteralliance, the League of Venice, which forced Charles to retreat. The French returned to Italy under Louis XII (r. 1498–1515), this time assisted by the Borgia pope Alexander VI (1492–1503). Alexander, probably the most corrupt pope in history, sought to secure a political base in Romagna, officially part of the Papal States, for his son Cesare. Seeing that a French alliance could allow him to reestablish control over the region, Alexander abandoned the League of Venice. Louis successfully invaded Milan in August 1499. In 1500 he and Ferdinand of Aragon divided Naples between themselves, while the pope and Cesare Borgia conquered the Romagna.

In 1503 Cardinal Giuliano della Rovere became Pope Julius II (1503–1513). He suppressed the Borgias and placed their newly conquered lands in Romagna under papal jurisdiction. After securing the Papal States with French aid, Julius changed sides and sought to rid Italy of the French invaders. Julius, Ferdinand of Aragon, and Venice formed a Holy League in October 1511, and soon Emperor Maximilian I (r. 1493–1519) and the Swiss joined them. By 1512 the French were in full retreat.

Jan van Eyck, "Adam and Eve" (1432). In the wings of the Dutch painter Jan van Eyck's earliest work, the Ghent Altarpiece, Adam and Eve appear after their fall. Unlike the Italian Renaissance masters, the Netherlandish master portrays them as true-to-life humans, not heroic, idealized figures. Above their heads their son Cain kills his brother Abel, a commentary on human behavior after the Fall.

Why would church paintings be important during this period?

⊙ See the **Map**
Empire and the Papacy in Italy
at **myhistorylab.com**

Michelangelo's "Creation of Adam." The High Italian Renaissance obsession with the muscular, robust, heroic body finds expression in Michelangelo's rendering of the "The Creation of Adam" in the Sistine Chapel.

What emotional responses does this image seem designed to elicit in viewers?

Niccolò Machiavelli. Santi di Tito's portrait of Machiavelli, perhaps the most famous Italian political theorist, who advised Renaissance princes to practice artful deception and inspire fear in their subjects if they wished to succeed.

Scala/Art Resource, New York.

Is Machiavelli's advice still relevant today?

Read the Document
The Prince, 1519, Machiavelli
at **myhistorylab.com**

WHAT WERE the bases for the rise of the modern sovereign state in the fifteenth century?

The French invaded Italy again under Francis I (r. 1515–1547). French armies massacred Swiss soldiers of the Holy League in 1515. That victory won from the Medici pope Leo X (r. 1513–1521) an agreement known as the Concordat of Bologna (1516), which gave the French king control over the French clergy and the right to collect taxes from them in exchange for French recognition of the pope's superiority over church councils. This helped keep France Catholic after the outbreak of the Protestant Reformation. But the new French entry into Italy also led to the first of four major wars with Spain in the first half of the sixteenth century, the Habsburg–Valois wars, none of which France won.

NICCOLÒ MACHIAVELLI

These invasions made a shambles of Italy. Niccolò Machiavelli (1469–1527) became convinced that Italian political unity and independence were ends that justified any means. Machiavelli admired the heroic acts of ancient Roman rulers, what Renaissance people called their *Virtù*. Juxtaposing the strengths of idealized ancient Romans with the failures of his contemporaries, Machiavelli became famously cynical. Only an unscrupulous strongman, he concluded, could impose order on so divided and selfish a people. Machiavelli hoped to see a strong ruler emerge from the Medici family. But the second Medici pope, Clement VII (r. 1523–1534), watched helplessly as Rome was sacked by the army of Emperor Charles V (r. 1519–1556) in 1527, the year of Machiavelli's death.

REVIVAL OF MONARCHY: NATION BUILDING IN THE FIFTEENTH CENTURY

After 1450, unified national monarchies progressively replaced fragmented and divisive feudal governance. The dynastic and chivalric ideals of feudalism did not disappear: Minor territorial princes survived, and representative assemblies even gained influence in some regions. But by the late fifteenth and early sixteenth centuries, the old problem of the one and the many was being decided in favor of monarchy.

In the feudal monarchy of the High Middle Ages, the basic powers of government were divided between the king and his semi-autonomous vassals. The nobility and the towns acted with varying degrees of success through such evolving representative bodies as the English Parliament, the French Estates General, and the Spanish Cortes to thwart the centralization of royal power. As a result of the Hundred Years' War and the schism in the church, however, the landed nobility and the clergy were in decline in the Late Middle Ages. Towns began to ally with the king, and townspeople staffed the royal offices. This new alliance between king and town slowly broke the bonds of feudal society and facilitated the rise of the modern sovereign state.

In a sovereign state, the powers of taxation, war making, and law enforcement are concentrated in the monarch and exercised by his chosen agents. Monarchies began to create standing national armies in the fifteenth century. As the noble cavalry receded and the infantry and the artillery became the backbone of armies, mercenary soldiers were recruited from Switzerland and Germany to form the mainstay of the "king's army." The growing cost of warfare increased the need to develop new national sources of royal income. The highest classes stubbornly believed they were immune from government taxation, so royal revenue grew at the expense of those least able to resist and least able to pay. Monarchs had several options. As feudal lords they could collect rents from their royal domain. They might also levy national taxes on basic

CHRONOLOGY

MAJOR POLITICAL EVENTS OF THE ITALIAN RENAISSANCE (1375–1527)

1378–1382	Ciompi revolt in Florence
1434	Medici rule in Florence established by Cosimo de' Medici
1454–1455	Treaty of Lodi allies Milan, Naples, and Florence (in effect until 1494)
1494	Charles VIII of France invades Italy
1495	League of Venice unites Venice, Milan, the Papal States, the Holy Roman Empire, and Spain against France
1499	Louis XII invades Milan (the second French invasion of Italy)
1500	The Borgias conquer Romagna
1512–1513	The Holy League (Pope Julius II, Ferdinand of Aragon, Emperor Maximilian I, and Venice) defeat the French
1513	Machiavelli writes *The Prince*
1515	Francis I leads the third French invasion of Italy
1516	Concordat of Bologna between France and the papacy
1527	Sack of Rome by imperial soldiers

food and clothing, such as the *gabelle* or salt tax in France and the *alcabala* or 10 percent sales tax on commercial transactions in Spain. Kings could also levy direct taxes on the peasantry and on commercial transactions in towns under royal protection. The French **taille** was such a tax. Sale of public offices and the issuance of high-interest government bonds were innovative fund-raising devices. Kings turned for loans to rich nobles and to the great bankers of Italy and Germany.

taille
A direct tax imposed by the French monarchy on land owned by non-nobles.

MEDIEVAL RUSSIA

In the late tenth century Prince Vladimir of Kiev (r. 972–1015), then Russia's dominant city, received delegations of Muslims, Roman Catholics, Jews, and Greek Orthodox Christians, each group hoping to win the Russians to its religion. Prince Vladimir chose Greek Orthodoxy, adding a new cultural bond to the long-standing commercial ties between Russia and the Byzantine Empire.

Vladimir's successor, Yaroslav the Wise (r. 1016–1054), developed Kiev into a magnificent political and cultural center, but after his death, rivalry among princes made it just one of several national centers.

Mongol (or Tatar) armies (see Chapters 8 and 12) invaded Russia in 1223, and Kiev fell in 1240. Russian cities became tribute-paying principalities of the segment of the Mongol Empire called the **Golden Horde**, which had its capital on the lower Volga. Mongol rule further separated Russia from the West but left Russian political institutions and religion largely intact. Thanks to their far-flung trade, the Mongolians brought most Russians greater peace and prosperity than they had enjoyed before. The princes of Moscow grew wealthy and expanded the principality. Ivan III, called Ivan the Great (d. 1505), brought all of northern Russia under Moscow's control and ended Mongol rule in 1480. By the last quarter of the fifteenth century, Moscow had replaced Kiev as the political and religious center of Russia. In Russian eyes it was destined to become the "third Rome" after the fall of Constantinople to the Turks in 1453.

Read the **Document**
Vladimir Kiev's Acceptance of Christianity
at **myhistorylab.com**

Golden Horde
Name given to the Mongol rulers of Russia from 1240 to 1480.

FRANCE

There were two cornerstones of French nation building in the fifteenth century: England's retreat from the continent following its loss of the Hundred Years' War, and the defeat of Charles the Bold (r. 1467–1477) and his duchy of Burgundy. The dukes of Burgundy were probably Europe's strongest rulers in the mid-fifteenth century, and they hoped to build a dominant middle kingdom between France and the Holy Roman Empire. Continental powers joined forces to oppose them, and Charles the Bold was killed in battle at Nancy in 1477.

The dissolution of Burgundy left Louis XI (r. 1461–1483) free to secure the monarchy in his expanded kingdom. Louis harnessed the nobility and expanded trade and industry. It was because Louis's successors inherited such a secure and efficient government that France was able to pursue Italian conquests in the 1490s and to fight a long series of losing wars with the Habsburgs in the first half of the sixteenth century. By the mid-sixteenth century France was again a defeated nation, almost as divided as it had been during the Hundred Years' War.

SPAIN

Spain, too, became a strong country in the late fifteenth century. Both Castile and Aragon had been poorly ruled kingdoms until the 1469 marriage of Isabella of Castile (r. 1474–1504) and Ferdinand of Aragon (r. 1479–1516). Castile was by far the richer and more populous of the two. Each retained its own government agencies and cultural traditions. Together, Isabella and Ferdinand were able to subdue their realms, secure their borders, and venture abroad militarily. Townspeople allied themselves with the crown and progressively replaced the nobility within the royal administration. The crown also extended its authority over the wealthy chivalric orders.

Spain had long been remarkable as a place where Islam, Judaism, and Christianity coexisted with a certain degree of toleration. This toleration ended decisively. Ferdinand and Isabella exercised almost total control over the Spanish church as they placed religion in the service of national unity. They appointed the higher clergy and the officers of the Inquisition. Spanish spiritual life became uniform and regimented, which is a major reason Spain became a base for Europe's Counter-Reformation in the sixteenth century.

See the Map
Spain 1491
at **myhistorylab.com**

The anti-French marriage alliances Isabella and Ferdinand arranged for their children influenced European history for decades. Their patronage of the Genoese adventurer Christopher Columbus (1451–1506) led to the creation of the Spanish Empire in the New World. Gold and silver from mines in Mexico and Peru helped make Spain Europe's dominant power in the sixteenth century.

ENGLAND

The last half of the fifteenth century was especially difficult for the English. Following the Hundred Years' War, civil war broke out in England between two rival branches of the royal family, the House of York and the House of Lancaster. This conflict, named the Wars of the Roses (York's symbol, according to legend, was a white rose, and Lancaster's a red rose), kept England in turmoil from 1455 to 1485.

The Lancastrian monarchy of Henry VI (r. 1422–1461) was challenged by the Duke of York and his supporters in prosperous southern towns. In 1461 Edward IV (r. 1461–1483), son of the Duke of York, seized power. His brother and successor was Richard III (r. 1483–1485), whose reign saw the growth of support for the exiled Lancastrian Henry Tudor. Henry returned to England to defeat Richard in 1485 and became King Henry VII (r. 1485–1509), founder of a Tudor dynasty that endured until 1603.

To bring the rival royal families together and give his offspring an incontestable hereditary claim to the throne, Henry married Edward IV's daughter, Elizabeth of York. With the aid of a much-feared instrument of royal power, the Court of Star Chamber, he imposed discipline on the English nobility. He shrewdly construed legal precedents to the advantage of the crown and used English law to further his own ends. He confiscated so much noble land and wealth that he was able to govern without depending on Parliament for grants. Henry constructed a powerful monarchy that became one of early modern Europe's most exemplary governments during the reign of his granddaughter, Elizabeth I (r. 1558–1603).

SUMMARY

 WHAT IMPACT did the Crusades have on medieval European society?

Revival of Empire, Church, and Towns. Germany's Otto I breathed new life into both empire and papacy. In the tenth century, the Cluny reform movement increased popular respect for the church and strengthened the clergy. In the Investiture Controversy, the papacy secured the independence of the clergy by enlisting the support of the German princes against the Holy Roman Emperors, thus weakening imperial power in Germany. The Crusades were based on the intense passions of popular piety. The rise of merchants, self-governing towns, and universities helped restructure power. By supporting rulers against the nobility, towns gave kings the resources to build national governments. *page 360*

 WHAT NEW group was added to the three traditional groups in medieval society?

Medieval Society. In theory, medieval society was divided into three main groups: clergy (those who prayed), nobility (those who fought as mounted warriors), and laborers (peasants and artisans). But merchants became a fourth group. Women faced constraints, but their lives were far richer and more varied than Christian imagery suggested. *page 367*

HOW DID England and France develop strong royal governments by the thirteenth century?

Growth of National Monarchies. Much of medieval history involved the struggle by rulers to assert their authority over powerful local lords and the church. In England and France, monarchs and nobles reached accommodation, and national identity was strengthened. The Holy Roman Empire, however, disintegrated. *page 369*

 WHAT WERE the consequences of the Black Death?

Political and Social Breakdown. Both the Hundred Years' War and the Black Death weakened the nobility. Bubonic plague devastated areas surrounding trade routes. Population loss had many consequences, including a shortage of labor and high demand for luxury goods leading to a rise in status for artisans. Cities and kings were, on balance, strengthened. *page 371*

 WHY DID France's king support the Great Schism?

Ecclesiastical Breakdown and Revival: The Late Medieval Church. By the end of the thirteenth century, kings had become more powerful than popes, and the French king, Philip the Fair, was able to defy the papacy. In the fourteenth century, the Great Schism further weakened papal prestige. The papacy never recovered its authority over national rulers. *page 373*

 WHY WAS the Renaissance a transition from the medieval to the modern world?

The Renaissance in Italy (1375–1527). The Renaissance, which began in the Italian city-states in the late fourteenth century, marks the transition from the medieval to the modern world. Humanism promoted a rebirth of ancient norms and values and the classical ideal of an educated, well-rounded person. The growth of secular values led to a great burst of artistic activity by artists such as Leonardo da Vinci, Raphael, and Michelangelo. The political weakness of the Italian states invited foreign intervention. The sack of Rome in 1527 marks the end of the Renaissance. *page 374*

WHAT WERE the bases for the rise of the modern sovereign state in the fifteenth century?

Revival of Monarchy: Nation Building in the Fifteenth Century. By the fifteenth century, England, France, and Spain had developed into strong national monarchies with centralized bureaucracies and professional armies. Although medieval institutions, such as the English Parliament, limited royal power in theory, in practice monarchs in these countries held unchallenged authority. In previous centuries, the Great Schism, the Hundred Years' War, and the Black Death weakened the church and the nobility. Townspeople supported the kings. A similar process was beginning in Russia, where the rulers of Moscow were extending their authority after throwing off Mongol rule. *page 378*

KEY TERMS

Black Death (p. 372)
chiaroscuro (KEY-ahr-uh-SKYOOR-oh) (p. 376)
Crusades (p. 361)
Curia (p. 374)
Golden Horde (p. 379)
Great Schism (p. 374)
guild (p. 365)
Holy Roman Empire (p. 374)
humanism (p. 375)
Magna Carta (p. 369)
Mannerism (p. 376)
regular clergy (p. 367)
Renaissance (p. 374)
Scholasticism (p. 365)
secular clergy (p. 367)
studia humanitatis (p. 375)
taille (p. 379)
vernacular (p. 369)

REVIEW QUESTIONS

1. How do you account for the success of the Cluny reform movement? Can major features of the modern Catholic Church be found in the Cluny reforms?

2. Was the Investiture Controversy a political or religious conflict? Summarize the respective arguments of Gregory VII and Henry IV. Is the conflict a precedent for the modern doctrine of the separation of church and state?

3. Why did Germany remain divided while France and England began to coalesce into reasonably strong states during the High Middle Ages?

4. How did the responsibilities of the nobility differ from those of the clergy and the peasantry during the High Middle Ages? How did each social class contribute to the stability of society?

5. Describe the circumstances that gave rise to towns. How did towns change traditional medieval society?

6. How did the Hundred Years' War, the Black Death, and the Great Schism in the church affect the course of history? Which had the most lasting effects on the institutions it touched?

7. Was the church an aggressor or a victim in the Late Middle Ages and the Renaissance? How successful was it in its confrontations with Europe's emerging dynastic states?

8. What was "reborn" in the Renaissance? Were the humanists the forerunners of modern secular education and culture or eloquent defenders of a still medieval Christian view of the world against the church's secular and pagan critics?

9. Historians find features of modern states developing in Europe during the Late Middle Ages and Renaissance. What modern features can you identify in the governments of the Italian city-states, the northern monarchies, and in Russia?

Note: To learn more about the topics in this chapter, please turn to the Suggested Readings at the end of the book. For additional sources related to this chapter please see www.myhistorylab.com

myhist🕰️rylab Connections

Reinforce what you learned in this chapter by studying the many documents,
images, maps, review tools, and videos available at **www.myhistorylab.com**

Read and Review

✓•─[Study and Review Chapter 15

•••─[Read the Document *Expulsion, Jews from France 12th
Century, p. 362*
Arab-Syrian Gentleman Discusses Franks, p. 363
The Magna Carta 1215, p. 363
Medieval Town Customs: Town, Chester, England, p. 365
Abelard Defends Himself, p. 367
The Battle of Hastings 1066, p. 369
Black Death, 1349, Henry Knighton, p. 371
Peasant Revolt in England, p. 373
Unam Sanctam 1302, Pope Boniface VIII, p. 373
Letters to Cicero, 14th c., Petrarch, p. 375
Dante's Divine Comedy, 1321, p. 375
The Prince, 1519, Machiavelli, p. 378
Vladimir Kiev's Acceptance of Christianity, p. 379

👁─[See the Map *The Major Crusades, p. 363*
England and France ca. 1180, p. 369
The Hundred Years' War, p. 371
100 Years' War, p. 371
Black Death and Peasant Revolts, p. 371
Empire and the Papacy in Italy, p. 377
Spain 1491, p. 380

•••─[View the Image *Da Vinci, Mona Lisa, p. 376*
Michelangelo's David, p. 376

Research and Explore

(•)•─[Watch the Video *Plague, p. 373*

👁─[See the Map *Medieval Manor*

(•••─[**Hear** the **Audio**

Hear the audio file for Chapter 15
at **www.myhistorylab.com**

16

Europe 1500–1650: Expansion, Reformation, and Religious Wars

((•–[Hear the **Audio** for Chapter 16 at www.myhistorylab.com

Allegory of the Jesuits and their missions in the four continents from the church of San Pedro, Lima, Peru. Anonymous painter (eighteenth century). St. Ignatius is flanked on his left by Francis Xavier, sporting a chasuble with Asian motifs. In the background, Jesuits living all over the world and occupying a variety of hierarchies within the church, including those wearing Chinese costumes and prelate robes, preside over the conversion of the faithful in India, China, Africa, and the Americas. Like Atlas, the Jesuits carry the globe on their shoulders.

Why do you think the peoples of India, China, Africa, and the Americas are shown smaller than the European missionaries in this painting?

F*or Europe the late fifteenth and sixteenth centuries were years of unprecedented territorial expansion. Permanent colonies were established in the Americas, and the exploitation of the New World's human and mineral resources began.*

Starting early in the sixteenth century, a powerful religious movement spread rapidly throughout northern Europe, altering society and politics as well as the spiritual lives of individuals. Attacking what they believed to be burdensome superstitions and corrupt practices, Protestant reformers led a revolt against the medieval church. Hundreds of thousands of people from all social classes set aside the beliefs of centuries and adopted a simplified religious practice.

The Protestant Reformation challenged aspects of the Renaissance, especially its tendency to follow classical sources in glorifying human nature and its loyalty to traditional religion. Protestants were more impressed by the human potential for evil than by the inclination to do good. But Protestants also embraced many Renaissance values, especially humanist educational reforms and the study of ancient languages, which gave them tools to master Scripture and challenge the papacy. Reform within the church (Counter-Reformation) gave birth to new religious orders and won many Protestant converts back to Catholicism.

As different groups identified their political and social goals with either Protestantism or Catholicism, bloody confrontations spread across Europe. During the Thirty Years' War (1618–1648), international armies of varying religious persuasions clashed in central and northern Europe. ■

EUROPEAN EXPANSION

The European turn to the Atlantic was a consequence of its weakness in the East due to Muslim domination there. However, a recovering Europe was now able to compete for access to valuable goods in Eastern markets by navigating the high seas. In the late fifteenth and the sixteenth centuries, Europeans sailed far from their own shores to Africa, southern and eastern Asia, and the New World of the Americas. From Japan to Peru, they directly confronted civilizations other than their own and that of Islam, with which they already had contact in the form of trade and, more often, by force of arms. A major motivation for the voyages, which began with a reconnaissance of the West African coast, was to circumvent the Muslim monopoly on the movement of spices from the Indian Ocean into Europe, a grip that had only strengthened with the rise of the Ottomans. A wealthier, more self-confident Europe, now recovered from the great plague-induced population decline of the fourteenth century—its taste for Asian spices long-since whetted during the Crusades—was ready to take those spices at their sources.

For much the same reasons (trade and self-aggrandizement) voyages of exploration also set forth from Ming China—especially between 1405 and 1433—reaching India, the Arabian Gulf, and East Africa. Had those voyages been followed up, they might have prevented Europeans from establishing a presence in the Indian Ocean. But the Chinese faced both serious pressures on their northern and western borders, and the problem of administrating a vast, multicultural empire stretching into Central Asia, where non-Chinese rivals had to be kept under control. Moreover, the dominant Neo-Confucian philosophy espoused by the scholar-bureaucrats in the imperial court disdained merchants and commerce, extolling instead a peasant agrarian economy.

These factors led the Chinese to turn inward and abandon overseas trade and exploration precisely at the moment when Europeans were exploring the coast of Africa on their way to the Indian Ocean. It was a fateful choice because it meant that the Asian power best able to resist the establishment of European commercial and colonial empires in the Indian Ocean had

THE DISCOVERY OF A NEW WORLD

WHY DID western Europeans start exploring, trading, and settling around the world in the fifteenth century?

The discovery of the Americas dramatically expanded the horizons of Europeans, both geographical and intellectual. Knowledge of the New World's inhabitants and exploitation of its mineral and human wealth set new cultural and economic forces in motion. Beginning with the voyages of the Portuguese and Spanish in the fifteenth century, commercial supremacy progressively shifted from the Mediterranean and Baltic seas to the Atlantic seaboard, and western Europe's global expansion began in earnest (see Map 16–1 on page 388).

THE PORTUGUESE CHART THE COURSE

《•●─Hear the Audio
at **myhistorylab.com**

Seventy-seven years before Columbus sailed under Spain's flag, Portugal's Prince Henry the Navigator (1394–1460) began exploration of Africa's Atlantic coast. The Portuguese first sought gold and slaves. During the second half of the fifteenth century, the Portuguese delivered 150,000 slaves to Europe. By the end of that century, they were hoping to find a sea route around Africa to spice markets in Asia.

Overland routes to India and China had long existed, but they were difficult, expensive, and monopolized by Venetians and Turks. The first exploratory voyages were slow and tentative, but they provided experience that taught sailors the skills needed to cross the oceans to the Americas and Asia.

In 1455, the pope gave the Portuguese rights to all the lands, goods, and slaves they might discover from the coast of Guinea to the Indies. The church hoped that conquests would be followed by mass conversions. The explorers also kept an eye out for "Prester John," rumored to be a potential Christian ally against the Muslims. Bartholomew Dias (d. 1500) opened the Portuguese Empire in the East when he rounded the Cape of Good Hope at the tip of Africa in 1487. A decade later, in 1498, abdicated that role, leaving a vacuum of power for Europeans to fill. Still, Chinese merchants continued to ply ocean trade routes and settle as far from home as the Philippines and, in later centuries, the west coasts of North and South America. Wherever there was commerce in Chinese goods, there were Chinese merchants, albeit now operating without support from their government.

Although parallels may be drawn between the court culture of the Forbidden Palace in Beijing and that of King Louis XIV in seventeenth-century France, the Chinese government, with its philosophy of Confucianism, remained more unified and patriarchal than its counterparts in the West. The Chinese, at first, tolerated other religions, warmly embracing Jesuit missionaries, in part because political power in China was not bound to a particular religion. The Japanese were also admirers of the Jesuits, who arrived in Japan with the Portuguese in 1543. The admiration was mutual, leading to 300,000 Christian converts by 1600. Tolerance of Christianity did not last as long

in Japan as in China. Hideyoshi, in his drive for internal unity, banned Christianity in the late sixteenth century. Nonetheless China and Japan, as well as many Islamic societies, including the Ottomans and the Mughals, demonstrated more tolerance for foreign religions, such as Christianity, than did the West for Islam, or Asian religious traditions.

Focus Questions

◆ Why did Europeans launch voyages of exploration in the fifteenth and sixteenth centuries? What role did the Crusades and the rise of the Ottoman Empire play in this enterprise?

◆ Why did the Chinese voyages of exploration under the Ming come to a halt? What were the consequences for world history?

◆ What was the biological impact of the European discovery of America?

Vasco da Gama (d. 1524) stood on the shores of India. When he returned to Portugal, his cargo was worth sixty times the cost of the voyage. Later, the Portuguese established colonies in Goa and Calcutta and successfully challenged the Arabs and the Venetians for control of the European spice trade.

While the Portuguese concentrated on the Indian Ocean, the Spanish set sail across the Atlantic, hoping to establish a shorter route to the East Indies. Rather than beat the Portuguese at their own game, however, Columbus unwittingly discovered the Americas.

Christopher Columbus in old age (d. 1506) by Sebastiano del Piombo.

What did Columbus intend to do when he sailed west across the Atlantic?

THE SPANISH VOYAGES OF CHRISTOPHER COLUMBUS

On October 12, 1492, after a thirty-three-day voyage from the Canary Islands, Columbus landed in San Salvador (Watlings Island) in the eastern Bahamas. He thought San Salvador was an outer island of Japan, for his knowledge of geography was based on Marco Polo's thirteenth-century account of his years in China and a global map by a Nuremberg mapmaker, which showed only ocean between the west coast of Europe and the east coast of Asia (see Map 16–2 on page 389).

Naked, friendly natives met Columbus and his crew. They were Taino Indians, who spoke a variant of the Arawak language. Believing he had landed in the East Indies, Columbus called these people Indians. The natives' generosity amazed Columbus, as they freely gave his men corn, yams—and many sexual favors. "They never say no," Columbus marveled, observing how easily they could be enslaved.

Soon Amerigo Vespucci (1451–1512), after whom America is named, and Ferdinand Magellan (1480–1521) carefully explored the coastline of South America. Their travels proved that the new lands were part of an entirely unknown continent that opened on the great Pacific Ocean.

◆◆◆ Read the Document
Duarte Barbosas to Africa, India
at **myhistorylab.com**

◆◆◆ Read the Document
Columbus journal and letter
at **myhistorylab.com**

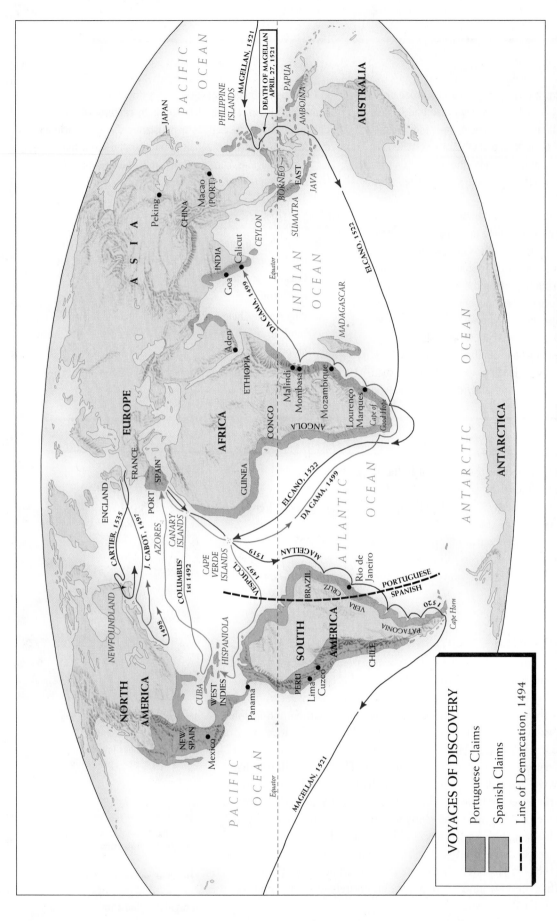

MAP 16–1. European Voyages of Discovery and the Colonial Claims of Spain and Portugal in the Fifteenth and Sixteenth Centuries. The map dramatizes Europe's global expansion in the fifteenth and sixteenth centuries.

Why did western Europeans want to find a sea route to Asia?

MAP 16–2. Martin Behaim's "Globe Apple." What Columbus knew of the world in 1492 was contained in this map by Nuremberg geographer Martin Behaim (1440–1507), creator of the first spherical globe of the earth. The ocean section of Behaim's globe is reproduced here. Departing the Canary Islands (in the second section from the right), Columbus expected his first major landfall to be Japan, or what he calls Cipangu (in the second section from the left). When he landed at San Salvador, he thought he was on an outer island of Japan; after reaching Cuba, he believed it to be Japan. Only slowly did it dawn on him that these new lands had never before been seen by Europeans.

From Admiral of the Ocean Sea by Samuel Eliot Morison. Copyright 1942 © renewed 1970 by Samuel Eliot Morison. By permission of Little, Brown and Company, Boston, MA.

How did this map influence Columbus's worldview?

IMPACT ON EUROPE AND AMERICA

Unbeknownst to those who undertook and financed it, Columbus's first voyage marked the beginning of more than three centuries of Spanish conquest, exploitation, and administration of a vast American empire. The wars Christian Aragon and Castile waged against the Islamic Moors had just ended, and the early Spanish explorers retained their zeal for converting non-Christians.

The voyages to the New World had important consequences for both Europe and America. They created Europe's largest and longest-surviving trading bloc and yielded great wealth for Spain. This wealth fueled European-wide economic expansion and spurred other European countries to undertake their own colonial ventures.

European expansion also had major consequences for ecosystems. Numerous species of fruits, vegetables, and animals were introduced to Europe from America and vice versa. European diseases also devastated America's natives. (See the discussion of the "Columbian Exchange" in Chapter 17.) Spain's imprint on the new territories—Roman Catholicism, economic dependence, and a hierarchical society—is still visible today (see Chapter 33).

QUICK REVIEW

Impact of Columbus's First Voyage on Europe and America

- ◆ Spurred other European nations to colonial expansion
- ◆ Financed Spain's role in the age's political and religious conflicts
- ◆ Brought disease, war, and destruction to native peoples

THE REFORMATION

The **Reformation** was a sixteenth-century religious movement that sought to reform the church. It led to the establishment of Protestantism and the religious division of Western Christendom.

WHO WERE the early Protestant leaders?

RELIGION AND SOCIETY

The Reformation broke out first in the free imperial cities of Germany and Switzerland. There were sixty-five such cities, each a small kingdom unto itself. Most had Protestant movements. Some turned Protestant and remained so, while others developed mixed confessions that allowed Catholics and Protestants to coexist.

Reformation

The sixteenth-century religious movement that sought to reform the Roman Catholic Church and led to the establishment of Protestantism.

Certain groups favored the Reformation more than others. In many places, trade guilds were in the forefront of the Reformation. Evidence suggests that people who felt bullied by either local or distant authority—a guild by an autocratic local government, a city by a prince or king—saw the Protestant movement as an ally.

Social and political experience thus coalesced with religious issues in both town and countryside. When Martin Luther wrote, preached, and sang about a priesthood of all believers and ridiculed papal laws as arbitrary human inventions, he touched political as well as religious nerves.

POPULAR MOVEMENTS AND CRITICISM OF THE CHURCH

The Protestant Reformation could not have occurred without the monumental crises of the late medieval church and the Renaissance papacy. Laity and clerics alike began to seek a more heartfelt, idealistic piety. The Late Middle Ages saw independent lay and clerical efforts to reform local religious practice.

A variety of factors contributed to lay criticism of the church. The laity in the cities was learning more about the world and those who controlled their lives. They traveled widely—as soldiers, pilgrims, explorers, and traders. New postal systems and the printing press increased the information at their disposal. The new age of books and libraries raised literacy and heightened lay curiosity, confidence, and criticism.

SECULAR CONTROL OVER RELIGIOUS LIFE

On the eve of the Reformation, Rome's international network of church offices began to be pulled apart by a growing sense of regional identity (incipient nationalism) and the increasing competence of local secular administrations. Rare was the late medieval German town that did not have complaints about the maladministration, concubinage, or fiscal misconduct of its clergy.

City governments also sought to restrict clerical privileges and to improve local religious life by bringing the clergy under the local tax code and by endowing new clerical positions for well-trained and conscientious preachers.

THE NORTHERN RENAISSANCE

The scholarly works of northern humanists created a climate favorable to religious and educational reforms. Northern scholars tended to come from more diverse social backgrounds and to be more devoted to religious reforms and new lay freedoms than were their Italian counterparts.

The growth of schools and lay education combined with the invention of cheap paper to create a mass audience for printed books. Johann Gutenberg (d. 1468) invented printing with movable type in the German city of Mainz around 1450. By 1500, printing presses operated in more than 200 cities throughout Europe, providing a new medium for politicians, humanists, and reformers alike.

The most famous northern humanist was Desiderius Erasmus (1466–1536). Idealistic and pacifistic, Erasmus aspired to unite the classical ideals of humanity and civic virtue with the Christian ideals of love and piety. He summarized his own beliefs with the phrase *philosophia Christi*, a simple, ethical piety in imitation of Christ, as opposed to what he saw as the dogmatic, ceremonial, and factious religious practice of his contemporaries. Erasmus edited the works of the Church Fathers and published a Greek edition of the New Testament (1516), which became the basis for a new, more accurate Latin translation (1519). Martin Luther later used both of these works as the basis for his famous German translation.

QUICK REVIEW

Criticism of the Church

◆ Many people did not see the church as a foundation for religious piety

◆ Laity and clerics were interested in alternatives and reform

◆ Laypersons were increasingly willing to take initiative

View the Image
Early Print Shop
at **myhistorylab.com**

QUICK REVIEW

Desiderius Erasmus (1466–1536)

◆ Most famous northern humanist

◆ Saw study of Bible and classics as best path to reform

◆ Edited the works of the Church Fathers and completed a Greek edition of the New Testament

The best known early English humanist was Sir Thomas More (1478–1535), a close friend of Erasmus. More's *Utopia* (1516), a criticism of contemporary society, depicts an imaginary society based on reason and tolerance that requires everyone to work and has rid itself of all social and political injustice. Although More himself remained staunchly Catholic, humanism paved the way for the English Reformation.

In Spain, humanism served the Catholic Church. Francisco Jiménez de Cisneros (1437–1517) was a confessor to Queen Isabella and, after 1508 Grand Inquisitor, a position from which he was able to enforce the strictest religious orthodoxy. Jiménez was a conduit for humanist scholarship and learning. He founded the University of Alcalá near Madrid, printed a Greek edition of the New Testament, and translated many religious tracts that aided clerical reform and control of lay religious life. His greatest achievement, taking fifteen years to complete, was the Complutensian Polyglot Bible, a six-volume work that placed the Hebrew, Greek, and Latin versions of the Bible in parallel columns.

The Gutenberg Bible.   Print and Protestantism would drive the history of the sixteenth century. Well established by the mid-fifteenth century, the printing press made possible the diffusion of both secular and religious learning. In addition to Humanistic scholarship, print also served the educational and propaganda campaigns of princes and religious reformers, increasing literacy in both Latin and vernacular languages. Among the printed works preparing the way none was more stimulating than Gutenberg's Latin Bible. In the mid-1520s Martin Luther made separate German translations of the New and the Old Testaments, henceforth to become the battering rams of the Protestant Reformation.

Why were Bibles printed in the vernacular particularly important to Protestants?

MARTIN LUTHER AND GERMAN REFORMATION TO 1525

Unlike France and England, late medieval Germany lacked the political unity to enforce "national" religious reforms during the Late Middle Ages. As popular resentment of clerical immunities and ecclesiastical abuses spread, opposition to Rome formed. German humanists had long voiced such criticism, and by 1517 it provided a solid foundation for Martin Luther's reform.

View the Image
Martin Luther
at **myhistorylab.com**

Luther (1483–1546) was educated by teachers who had been influenced by the Northern Renaissance. His family hoped he would study law, but instead he entered a monastery and was ordained in 1507. In 1510 he traveled to Rome and witnessed the abuses for which the papacy was being criticized. In 1511, he was transferred to the Augustinian monastery in Wittenberg, where he earned his doctorate in theology and became a leader within the monastery, the new university, and the spiritual life of the city.

Luther was plagued by the disproportion between his own sense of sinfulness and the perfect righteousness that God required for salvation according to medieval theology. Traditional church teaching and the sacraments were no consolation. Between 1513 and 1518 Luther gradually concluded that the righteousness God demands does not come from religious works but is present in full measure in those who believe and trust in the redemptive life and death of Christ. Luther's belief is known as "justification by faith alone."

The Electoral Princes of Saxony, by Lucas Cranach the Elder (ca. 1532). The three princes Luther served: Frederick the Wise, John the Constant, and John Frederick the Magnanimous.

Why did some German princes support Luther?

indulgence
Remission of the temporal penalty of punishment in purgatory that remained after sins had been forgiven.

Luther criticized the church practice of granting **indulgences**. According to medieval theology, God rightly imposed punishments for all sins. When a penitent received absolution from a priest for a mortal sin, God's eternal penalty was transformed into a temporal penalty, a "work of satisfaction" that could be performed in earthly time (for example, through prayers, fasting, almsgiving, and pilgrimages). Penitents who failed to complete their works of satisfaction would suffer in purgatory unless they received an indulgence, a remission of the temporal penalty. Originally, indulgences had been granted for significant self-sacrifice, such as going on a Crusade to the Holy Land.

In 1343, Pope Clement VI (r. 1342–1352) had proclaimed the existence of a "treasury of merit," an infinite reservoir of good works in the church's possession that could be dispensed at the pope's discretion. The church sold "letters of indulgence," which covered the works of satisfaction owed by penitents. By Luther's time, they were regularly dispensed for small cash payments and presented as remitting not only the donor's punishments but also those of their dead relatives presumed to be suffering in purgatory.

In 1517, an indulgence was preached on the borders of Saxony in the territories of Archbishop Albrecht of Mainz, who had large debts. The selling of the indulgence was a joint venture by Albrecht, German bankers, and Pope Leo X (r. 1513–1521), half the proceeds going to the pope and half to Albrecht and his creditors. The famous indulgence preacher John Tetzel (d. 1519) exhorted the crowds: "Don't you hear the voices of your dead parents and other relatives crying out, 'Have mercy on us, for we suffer great punishment and pain. From this you could release us with a few alms.' "[1]

•••—[Read the **Document**
Erasmus Julius Excluded Heaven
at **myhistorylab.com**

ninety-five theses
Document posted on the door of Castle Church in Wittenberg, Germany, on October 31, 1517, by Martin Luther protesting, among other things, the selling of indulgences.

When Luther, according to tradition, posted his **ninety-five theses** for reform on the door of Castle Church in Wittenberg, on October 31, 1517, he protested the impression that indulgences actually remitted sins and released the dead from punishment in purgatory. Luther believed such claims made salvation look like something that could be bought and sold.

Luther's proposals made him famous overnight. They were embraced by humanists, but the church began disciplinary proceedings. Emperor Maximilian I's death in January 1519 diverted official attention to the contest for a new emperor. Charles I of Spain, then 19 years old, succeeded his grandfather and became Emperor Charles V (r. 1519–1556). The electors won political concessions from Charles that prevented him from taking unilateral action against Germans, something for which Luther later had cause to be grateful. (See Map 16–3.)

•••—[Read the **Document**
Martin Luther's Ninety-Five Theses
1517 at **myhistorylab.com**

In a June 1519 debate with Professor John Eck (1486–1543), Luther challenged the infallibility of the pope and the inerrancy of church councils, arguing for the first time that Scripture held sole and sovereign authority over faith. He burned all his bridges to the old church when he defended John Huss, a condemned heretic. In 1520, Luther issued three pamphlets elaborating on his beliefs. In April 1521, Luther defended his religious teaching before the imperial **Diet of Worms**, over which newly elected Emperor Charles V presided. Ordered to recant, Luther declared that he could not act against Scripture, reason, and his own conscience. On May 26, 1521, he was placed under the imperial ban and became an "outlaw." Friends hid him in a secluded castle, where he spent almost a year translating the New Testament into German and attempting by correspondence to oversee the first stages of the Reformation in Wittenberg.

Diet of Worms
The meeting of the representative (diet) of the Holy Roman Empire presided over by the Emperor Charles V at the German city of Worms in 1521 at which Martin Luther was ordered to recant his ninety-five theses.

---

[1]*Die Reformation in Augenzeugen Berichten*, ed. by Helmar Judghans (Dusseldorf: Karl Rauch Verlag, 1967), p. 44.

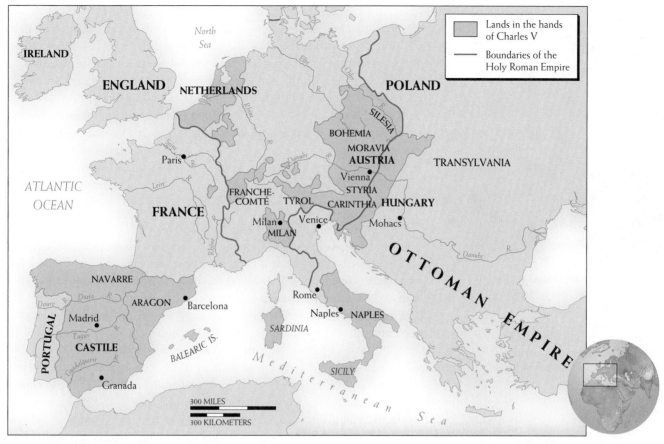

MAP 16–3.   The Empire of Charles V.   Dynastic marriages and good fortune concentrated into Charles's hands rule over the lands shown here, plus Spain's overseas possessions. Crowns and titles rained down on him; election in 1519 as emperor gave him new burdens and responsibilities.

What were the geographical advantages and disadvantages of the empire of Charles V?

The Reformation was greatly helped in these early years by the emperor's wars with France (the Habsburg-Valois Wars) and the advance of the Ottoman Turks into eastern Europe. Against both adversaries Charles V needed German troops, so he promoted friendly relations with the German princes. In 1526, each German territory was given freedom to enforce the Edict of Worms against Luther "so as to be able to answer in good conscience to God and the emperor." German princes effectively gained religious sovereignty. In 1555, the Peace of Augsburg enshrined local control over religion in imperial law.

In the late 1520s and the 1530s, Protestant preachers built sizable congregations in many cities that pressured urban governments to adopt religious reforms. Many magistrates had long pushed for reform and welcomed the preachers as allies. Religious reform became a territorial political movement as well, led by the elector of Saxony and the prince of Hesse. Like the urban magistrates, the princes recognized political and economic opportunities for themselves in the demise of the Roman Catholic Church, and they urged the reform on their neighbors. By the 1530s, there was a powerful Protestant alliance prepared for war with the Catholic emperor.

There were early divisions within the Protestant movement. German peasants, for example, had at first believed Luther to be an ally. They solicited his support of their political and economic rights, including their revolutionary request for release

View the Image
Martin Luther Statue in Hesse Germany
at **myhistorylab.com**

See the Map
Religious Divisions of Europe
at **myhistorylab.com**

Read the Document
Against Murderous Thieving Hordes
Peasants at **myhistorylab.com**

Execution of a Peasant Leader. The punishment of a peasant leader in a village near Heilbronn. After the defeat of rebellious peasants in and around the city of Heilbronn, Jacob Rorbach, a well-to-do peasant leader from a nearby village, was tied to a stake and slowly roasted to death.

Why did Luther not support rebellious peasants?

⊙ See the **Map**
The Swiss Confederation
at **myhistorylab.com**

transubstantiation
The doctrine that the entire substances of the bread and wine are changed in the Eucharist into the body and blood of Christ.

consubstantiation
The doctrine that the substances of both bread and wine, and the body and blood of Christ, are present in the Eucharistic offering.

⊙ View the **Image**
Anabaptist Torture in Muenster
at **myhistorylab.com**

from serfdom. But Lutherans were not social revolutionaries. Luther believed that Christian freedom was an inner release from guilt and anxiety, not the right to an egalitarian society. When the peasants revolted in 1524–1525, Luther condemned them as "unchristian" and urged the princes to crush their revolt without mercy. Tens of thousands of peasants died.

Luther also had a disturbing perspective on Jews. In 1523 he published the pamphlet, "Jesus Christ Was Born a Jew," in which he urged Christians to be kind to Germany's Jews in the hope that they might convert to reformed Christianity. But in the late 1530s and early 1540s, he urged German princes forcibly to remove nonconverting Jews to a land of their own, as France, Spain, and Bohemia had already done. Instead, the Jews found a protector in Emperor Charles V.

ZWINGLI AND THE SWISS REFORMATION

Switzerland was a loose confederacy of thirteen autonomous cantons or states and allied areas. Some became Protestant, some remained Catholic, and a few managed to compromise. The two preconditions of the Swiss Reformation were the growth of national sentiment and a desire for church reform.

Ulrich Zwingli (1484–1531), based in Zurich, was widely known for opposing superstition and the sale of indulgences. Zwingli's reform guideline was simple and effective: Whatever lacked literal support in Scripture was to be neither believed nor practiced. After a public disputation in January 1523, Zurich became effectively a Protestant city and the center of the Swiss Reformation. Its harsh discipline in pursuit of religious ideals made it one of the first examples of a "puritanical" Protestant city.

Landgrave Philip of Hesse (1504–1567) sought to unite Swiss and German Protestants in a mutual defense pact. His efforts were spoiled by theological disagreements between Luther and Zwingli over the nature of Christ's presence in the Eucharist. Zwingli maintained a symbolic interpretation of Christ's words, "This is my body," claiming that Christ was only spiritually present in the bread and wine of the Eucharist. Luther insisted that Christ's human nature shared the properties of his divine nature; where Christ was spiritually present, he could also be bodily present. For Luther, the Eucharistic miracle was not **transubstantiation**, as Rome taught, but "**consubstantiation**": Christ's body and blood being one with, but not of, the bread and wine of the Eucharist. Philip of Hesse brought Luther and Zwingli together in October 1529, but they were unable to work out their differences. The disagreement splintered the Protestant movement theologically and politically.

ANABAPTISTS AND RADICAL PROTESTANTS

Many people wanted a more rapid and thorough implementation of primitive Christianity. The most important of these radical groups were the Anabaptists, the sixteenth-century ancestors of the modern Mennonites and Amish. The Anabaptists rejected infant baptism, insisting that only the baptism of a consenting adult conforms to Scripture. (*Anabaptism* derives from the Greek word meaning "to rebaptize.") Anabaptists withdrew from society to form communities modeled on the example of the first Christians. Political authorities saw their separatism as a threat, and in 1529 rebaptism became a capital offense throughout the Holy Roman Empire.

JOHN CALVIN AND THE GENEVAN REFORMATION

Calvinism was the religious ideology that inspired or accompanied massive political resistance in France, the Netherlands, and Scotland. Believing in both divine predestination and the individual's responsibility to create a godly society, Calvinists were zealous reformers. In a famous and controversial study, *The Protestant Ethic and the Spirit of Capitalism* (1904), the German sociologist Max Weber argued that this peculiar combination of religious confidence and self-disciplined activism produced an ethic congenial to emergent capitalism.

On May 21, 1536, Geneva voted to adopt the Reformation: "to live according to the Gospel and the Word of God . . . without . . . any more masses, statues, idols, or other papal abuses." John Calvin (1509–1564), a reform-minded humanist and lawyer, arrived in Geneva soon thereafter. He wrote articles for the governance of the new church, as well as a catechism to guide and discipline the people. Calvin's measures were too strong for Genevans' tastes, however, and in February 1538 the reformers were exiled from the city.

Calvin then spent two years in Strasbourg, a model Protestant city. He married and wrote a second edition of his masterful *Institutes of the Christian Religion*, which many consider the definitive theological statement of the Protestant faith. Calvin was invited to return to Geneva in 1540.

Calvin and his followers thought the "elect" should live a manifestly God-pleasing life. The consistory, a judicial body composed of clergy and laity, enforced strict moral discipline and was unpopular with many Genevans. But after 1555 the city's magistrates were all devout Calvinists, and more than one-third of Geneva's population was Protestants who had been driven out of France, England, and Scotland, so Calvin had strong support.

Christ Blessing the Children, by Lucas Cranach the Elder (1538). This novel painting was a Lutheran protest against the Anabaptists, who refused to recognize the efficacy of infant baptism. Appealing to the example of Jesus, who had been baptized as an adult, Anabaptists (the name means "rebaptism") disavowed their infant baptism and sought another when they were old enough to grasp what it meant. Here, Jesus joins a throng of new mothers to caress, kiss, and commend their babies to God. After 1529, Anabaptism became a capital offense in the Holy Roman Empire.

Why were there early divisions within the Protestant movement?

•••─┤**Read** the **Document**
Calvin Ecclesiastical Ordinances
at **myhistorylab.com**

•••─┤**Read** the **Document**
Calvin on Predestination 16th century
at **myhistorylab.com**

CHRONOLOGY

PROGRESS OF PROTESTANT REFORMATION ON THE CONTINENT

1517	Luther posts ninety-five theses against indulgences
1519	Charles I of Spain elected Holy Roman emperor (as Charles V)
1519	Luther challenges infallibility of pope and inerrancy of church councils at Leipzig Debate
1521	Papal bull excommunicates Luther for heresy
1521	Diet of Worms condemns Luther
1521–1522	Luther translates the New Testament into German
1524–1525	Peasants' Revolt in Germany
1529	Marburg Colloquy between Luther and Zwingli
1530	Diet of Augsburg fails to settle religious differences
1531	Formation of Protestant Schmalkaldic League
1536	Calvin arrives in Geneva
1540	Jesuits, founded by Ignatius of Loyola, recognized as order by pope
1545–1563	Council of Trent institutes reforms and responds to the Reformation
1546	Luther dies
1547	Armies of Charles V crush Schmalkaldic League
1555	Peace of Augsburg recognizes rights of Lutherans to worship as they please

POLITICAL CONSOLIDATION OF THE LUTHERAN REFORMATION

In the 1530s German Lutherans formed regional consistories, which oversaw and administered the new Protestant churches. These consistories replaced the old Catholic episcopates. Under the leadership of Philip Melanchthon (1497–1560), educational reforms established compulsory primary education, schools for girls, a humanist revision of the school curriculum, and instruction of the laity in the new religion.

The Reformation also took root elsewhere. In Denmark, Lutheranism became the state religion under Christian III (r. 1536–1559). In Sweden, Gustavus Vasa (r. 1523–1560) confiscated church property and subjected the clergy to royal authority. The absence of a central political authority made Poland a model of religious pluralism and toleration in the second half of the sixteenth century.

Charles V attempted to enforce a compromise agreement between Protestants and Catholics in 1540–1541. Then he turned to a military solution: In 1547 imperial armies crushed the Protestant Schmalkaldic League. The emperor issued the Augsburg Interim, an order that Protestants everywhere must readopt Catholic beliefs and practices. But Protestants resisted fiercely, and the emperor relented. The Peace of Augsburg in September 1555 made the division of Christendom permanent by recognizing what had already been established in practice: *cuius regio, eius religio*, meaning that the ruler of a land would determine the religion of the land. Lutherans were permitted to retain all church lands forcibly seized before 1552. Those discontented with the religion of their region were permitted to migrate. Calvinism, however, was not recognized by the Peace of Augsburg. Calvinists organized to lead national revolutions throughout northern Europe.

THE ENGLISH REFORMATION TO 1553

Late medieval England had a well-earned reputation for defending the rights of the crown against the pope. The marriage of King Henry VIII (r. 1509–1547) finally precipitated England's break with the papacy.

Henry married Catherine of Aragon (d. 1536), a daughter of Ferdinand and Isabella of Spain and the aunt of Emperor Charles V, in 1509. By 1527 the union had produced only a single surviving child, Mary Tudor (d. 1558). Henry came to believe that his marriage was cursed because Catherine had briefly been the wife of his late brother, Arthur.

Henry wanted to marry Anne Boleyn (ca. 1504–1536), one of Catherine's young ladies in waiting. This required papal annulment of the marriage to Catherine, which Henry could not get. Henry's ministers proposed a simple solution: The king could declare his supremacy over English spiritual affairs, as he did over English temporal affairs. Then he could decide the status of his own marriage.

•••–[Read the Document
The Act of Supremacy (England), 1534
at **myhistorylab.com**

In 1529 Parliament convened for what would be a seven-year session. In 1533 the "Reformation Parliament" put the clergy under royal jurisdiction, and Henry wed the pregnant Anne Boleyn. Parliament's later Act of Supremacy declared Henry "the only supreme head on earth of the church of England."

Despite his political break with Rome, Henry continued to endorse Catholic doctrine in a country seething with Protestant sentiment. When Edward VI (r. 1547–1553), Henry's son by his third wife, Jane Seymour, became king at age 10, his regents enacted much of the Protestant Reformation. In 1553, when Mary Tudor succeeded to the throne, she restored Catholic doctrine and practice with a single-mindedness that rivaled that of her father. It was not until the reign of Anne Boleyn's daughter Elizabeth I (r. 1558–1603) that a lasting religious settlement was worked out in England.

•••–[View the Image
Thomas Cranmer's Execution
at **myhistorylab.com**

DOCUMENT

Ignatius of Loyola's "Rules for Thinking with the Church"

As leaders of the Counter-Reformation, the Jesuits attempted to live by and instill in others the strictest obedience to church authority. The following are some of the eighteen rules included by Ignatius in his Spiritual Exercises to give Catholics positive direction. These rules also indicate the Catholic reformers' refusal to compromise with Protestants.

- **Would** Protestants find any of Ignatius's "rules" acceptable? Might any of them be controversial among Catholic laity as well as among Protestant laity?

In order to have the proper attitude of mind in the Church Militant we should observe the following rules:

1. Putting aside all private judgment, we should keep our minds prepared and ready to obey promptly and in all things the true spouse of Christ our Lord, our Holy Mother, the hierarchical Church.

2. To praise sacramental confession and the reception of the Most Holy Sacrament once a year, and much better once a month, and better still every week. . . .

3. To praise the frequent hearing of Mass. . . .

4. To praise highly the religious life, virginity, and continence; and also matrimony, but not as highly. . . .

5. To praise the vows of religion, obedience, poverty, chastity, and other works of perfection and supererogation. . . .

6. To praise the relics of the saints . . . [and] the stations, pilgrimages, indulgences, jubilees, Crusade indulgences, and the lighting of candles in the churches.

7. To praise the precepts concerning fasts and abstinences . . . and acts of penance. . . .

8. To praise the adornments and buildings of churches as well as sacred images. . . .

9. To praise all the precepts of the church. . . .

10. To approve and praise the directions and recommendations of our superiors as well as their personal behaviour. . . .

11. To praise both the positive and scholastic theology. . . .

12. We must be on our guard against making comparisons between the living and those who have already gone to their reward, for it is no small error to say, for example: "This man knows more than St. Augustine"; "He is another Saint Francis, or even greater." . . .

13. If we wish to be sure that we are right in all things, we should always be ready to accept this principle: I will believe that the white that I see is black, if the hierarchical Church so defines it. For I believe that between . . . Christ our Lord and . . . His Church, there is but one spirit, which governs and directs us for the salvation of our souls.

Source: From *The Spiritual Exercises of St. Ignatius*, trans. by Anthony Mottola, pp. 139–141. Copyright © 1964 by Doubleday, a division of Bantam, Doubleday, Dell Publishing Group, Inc. Used by permission of Doubleday, a division of Random House, Inc.

CATHOLIC REFORM AND COUNTER-REFORMATION

The medieval church had already faced internal criticisms and efforts at reform before the **Counter-Reformation** was launched in reaction to Protestant successes.

Sixteenth-century popes had resisted efforts to change the laws and institutions of the church. Many new religious orders, however, led a broad revival of piety within the church. The Society of Jesus (the Jesuits) was instrumental in the success of the Counter-Reformation. Organized by Ignatius of Loyola in the 1530s, within a century the society had more than 15,000 members scattered throughout the world, including thriving missions in India, Japan, and the Americas.

Ignatius of Loyola (1491–1556) began his spiritual pilgrimage in 1521 while recuperating from battle wounds. Reading Christian classics, he was so impressed with the heroic self-sacrifice of the church's saints that he underwent a profound

Counter-Reformation

The sixteenth-century reform movement in the Roman Catholic Church in reaction to the Protestant Reformation.

 Watch the Video
at **myhistorylab.com**

QUICK REVIEW

The Jesuits

- The Society of Jesus founded in 1530s by Ignatius of Loyola

- Achieve spiritual self-mastery through discipline and passion for spirituality

The Miracle of St. Ignatius of Loyola, by Peter Paul Rubens. Here, the founder of the Society of Jesus, surrounded by angels and members of the new Jesuit Order, preaches to an aroused assembly.

What elements of this painting capture the spirit of the Counter-Reformation?

View the **Image**
Ignatius of Loyola,
at **myhistorylab.com**

Read the **Document**
Council of Trent 1545–1563
at **myhistorylab.com**

religious conversion. Ignatius devised a program of religious and moral self-discipline called the *Spiritual Exercises*, which outlined a path to absolute spiritual self-mastery. Ignatius believed that a person could shape his or her own behavior, even create a new religious self, through disciplined study and regular practice. Ignatius's exercises were intended to teach Catholics to submit to higher church authority and spiritual direction. (See Document, "Ignatius of Loyola's 'Rules for Thinking with the Church'" on page 397.) The potent combination of discipline, self-control, and passion for traditional spirituality and mystical experience helped counter the Reformation and won many Protestants back to Catholicism, especially in Austria and Germany.

Pope Paul III (r. 1534–1549) called a general council to reassert church doctrine. Three sessions, spread over eighteen years, met in the imperial city of Trent in northern Italy under firm papal control. The Council of Trent's most important reforms concerned internal church discipline. The selling of church offices was forbidden. The authority of local bishops was strengthened. Parish priests were required to be neatly dressed, educated, strictly celibate, and active among their parishioners. The council did not make a single doctrinal concession to the Protestants, instead reaffirming traditional beliefs and practices. Parish life revived under the guidance of a devout and better-trained clergy.

HOW DID family life change during the Reformation era?

THE REFORMATION AND DAILY LIFE

Although politically conservative, the Reformation brought about far-reaching changes in traditional religious practices and institutions.

RELIGION IN FIFTEENTH-CENTURY LIFE

In the fifteenth century, the church calendar regulated daily life. About one-third of the year was given over to some kind of religious observance or celebration. Clerics made up 6 to 8 percent of the total population of the great cities of central Europe, exercising considerable political as well as spiritual power.

Monasteries and nunneries were influential institutions. Local aristocrats were closely identified with particular churches and chapels. The Mass and liturgy were read entirely in Latin. Images of saints were regularly displayed, and on certain holidays their relics were paraded about and venerated. Pilgrims gathered by the thousands at religious shrines, searching for cures or seeking diversion. Several times during the year, special preachers appeared with letters of indulgence to sell. Many clergy lived openly with concubines and had children in relationships tolerated by the church if penitential fines were paid.

People complained about the clergy's exemption from taxation and, in many instances, also from the civil criminal code. People grumbled about having to support church offices whose occupants actually worked elsewhere, and many felt that the church had too much influence over education and culture.

RELIGION IN SIXTEENTH-CENTURY LIFE

In these same cities after the Reformation had firmly established itself, the same aristocratic families governed; the rich generally got richer and the poor poorer. But overall numbers of clergy fell by two-thirds and religious holidays shrank by one-third. Monasteries and nunneries were nearly absent, many having been transformed into hospices for the sick and poor or into educational institutions. In the churches, which had also been reduced in number by at least a third, worship was conducted almost completely in the vernacular. Local shrines were closed down, and anyone found openly venerating saints, relics, and images was subject to fine and punishment. Copies of Luther's translation of the New Testament, or excerpts from it, were in private homes. The clergy could marry, and most did. They paid taxes and were punished for their crimes in civil courts. Domestic moral life was regulated by committees composed of roughly equal numbers of laity and clergy, over whose decisions secular magistrates had the last word.

Not all Protestant clergy were enthusiastic about this new lay authority in religion, and the laity, too, was ambivalent about some aspects of the Reformation. Over half of the original converts returned to the Catholic fold before the end of the sixteenth century. Half of Europe's population was Protestant in the mid-sixteenth century, but by the mid-seventeenth century only a fifth remained Protestant.[2]

FAMILY LIFE IN EARLY MODERN EUROPE

Changes in the timing and duration of marriage, family size, and infant and child care suggest that social and economic pressures were influencing family life. The Reformation was only one factor in these changes.

Between 1500 and 1800, men and women in western Europe and England married at later ages than they had previously: men in their mid- to late twenties and women in their early to mid-twenties. After the Reformation, both Protestants and Catholics required parental consent and public vows in church before a marriage could be deemed fully licit. Late marriage in the West reflected the difficulty couples had supporting themselves independently. In the sixteenth century, one in five women never married, and an estimated 15 percent were widows. Women who bore children for the first time at advanced ages had higher mortality rates. Delayed marriage increased premarital sex and the number of illegitimate children.

Marriage tended to be "arranged" in the sense that the parents met and discussed the terms of the marriage. But the wealth and social standing of the bride and the bridegroom were not the only things considered. By the fifteenth century, it was usual for the future bride and bridegroom to have known each other, and their feelings were respected by parents.

The western European family was conjugal, or nuclear, consisting of two parents and two to four children who survived into adulthood. Infant mortality and child death were common. The family lived within a larger household, including in-laws, servants, laborers, and boarders.

Artificial birth control has existed since antiquity, but early birth control measures were not very effective, and for both historical and moral reasons the church opposed them. The church and physicians encouraged women to suckle their own newborns rather than hand them off to wet nurses (lactating women who sold their services). Because nursing has a contraceptive effect, some women nursed to space out their pregnancies, while those who wanted many children used wet nurses.

[2]Geoffrey Parker, *Europe in Crisis, 1598–1648* (Ithaca, NY: Cornell University Press, 1979), p. 50.

See the Map
Europe after the Reformation
at **myhistorylab.com**

QUICK REVIEW

Marriage, 1500–1800
- Couples married later in life
- 20 percent of women never married
- Couples had children every two years; many died
- "Wet nursing" was controversial
- Remarriage after death of a spouse was often quick

Portrait of His Wife and Two Elder Children, by Hans Holbein the Younger (1528). German-English painter Hans Holbein's painting of his wife and two of his children.

What was it like to be a child in early modern Europe?

A Closer Look

A Contemporary Commentary of the Sexes

G.1431: R8. MGVK⌀ Taming of the Lion [334 × 477] 1524 *Berlin*

Taming the Lion

A No man is ever so high or good
That he cannot be managed by a woman
Who does his will
In friendly love and service.

B Although he is tyranical wild,
He is soon calmed by a woman.
She boldly strokes his open mouth,
His anger fades, he does not bite.

C The lion, most lordly of beasts,
Famous for his strength and nobility,
Favors us women with heartfelt gifts
And good humor accompanies his kindness.

D How wonderfully you reflect
Your taming at woman's hand,
Bearing patiently what another
Does to you against your will.

E O powerful king and greatest lord
Your equal is neither near nor far.

Excelling all, both large and small,
Upon your head should lie a crown.

F Lord lion, although you are feared by all,
A woman knows how to saddle you,
Bending you to her will by love.
True love finds a home with a good man.

G How well you have been groomed!
Now how lively and cheerful!
One so spirited
May have the company of women.

H Lord lion, you may have your every wish.
Cover your trail with your tail
And you will not be tracked down.
Those who love in secret know this well.

Lion I let the women amuse themselves by serving me.
What harm can they possibly do me?
If I want, I can suddenly turn fierce again.
He is a fool who lets himself be taught by women.

Questions

1. In the scene above, who controls the relationship between the sexes? Is the lion a truly forbidding patriarch, or is the matriarch the one on top?

2. How does this artistic portrayal of womankind compare with the lives of historical women featured in the chapter?

3. Compare the scene with: "Christ Blessing the Children" (p. 395); Holbein's portrait of his wife and children (p. 399); and Hans Baldung Grien's portrayal of witches (p. 406).

4. What general conclusions can be drawn about the relationship of the sexes?

myhistorylab To examine this image in an interactive fashion, please go to **www.myhistorylab.com**

Family life had features that seem cold and distant to us today. Children between the ages of 8 and 13 were sent from their homes into apprenticeships, school, or employment. Widowers and widows often remarried within a few months of a spouse's death, and marriages with extreme disparity in age between partners also suggest limited affection. In response to such modern-day criticism, it must be remembered that a well-apprenticed child was a self-supporting child, and hence one with a future. Given the primitive living conditions, contemporaries appreciated the utilitarian and humane side of marriage and understood when widowers and widows quickly remarried.

◆◆◆ **Read** the **Document**
Office and Dutie Husband Juan Luis Vives at **myhistorylab.com**

THE WARS OF RELIGION

After the Council of Trent adjourned in 1563, Catholics began a Jesuit-led counteroffensive against Protestants. At the time of John Calvin's death in 1564, Geneva had become both a refuge for Europe's persecuted Protestants and an international school for Protestant resistance, producing leaders fully equal to the new Catholic challenge. Genevan Calvinism and the reformed Catholicism of the Council of Trent were two equally dogmatic, aggressive, and irreconcilable church systems.

WHY DID religious divisions lead to war?

Calvinism adopted a presbyterian form of church government, in which elders representing individual congregations determined church policy. By contrast, the Counter-Reformation affirmed Catholicism's dedication to a centralized episcopal system, governed by a clerical hierarchy and owing absolute obedience to the pope. Calvinism attracted proponents of political decentralization who opposed totalitarian rulers, whereas Catholicism was congenial to proponents of absolute monarchy who believed that order required "one king, one church, one law."

Wars of religion were both national conflicts and international wars. Catholics and Protestants struggled for control of France, the Netherlands, and England. The Catholic governments of France and Spain fought the Protestant regimes in England and the Netherlands. The Thirty Years' War, which began in 1618, drew in every major European nation before it ended.

FRENCH WARS OF RELIGION (1562–1598)

When Henry II (r. 1547–1559) died in 1559, his sickly 15-year-old son, Francis II (d. 1560), came to the throne under the regency of the queen mother, Catherine de Médicis (1519–1589). With the monarchy weakened, three powerful families competed for control. The Guises were by far the strongest, and they were militant Catholics. The Bourbon and Montmorency-Châtillon families, in contrast, developed strong Huguenot sympathies, largely for political reasons. (French Protestants were called **Huguenots**.)

Huguenots
French Calvinists.

Ambitious aristocrats and discontented townspeople joined Calvinist churches in opposition to the Guise-dominated French monarchy. Many apparently hoped to establish within France a principle of territorial sovereignty akin to that secured within the Holy Roman Empire by the Peace of Augsburg.

After Francis II died, Catherine de Médicis continued as regent for her second son, Charles IX (r. 1560–1574). Wanting a Catholic France but not a Guise-dominated monarchy, Catherine sought allies among the Protestants. Early in 1562 she granted Protestants limited freedoms—though even limited royal toleration ended when the Duke of Guise surprised a Protestant congregation worshiping illegally at Vassy in Champagne and proceeded to massacre several score of them, marking the beginning of the French wars of religion.

In 1572, apparently to cover up her role in an attempt to assassinate a Huguenot leader, Catherine convinced Charles that a Huguenot coup was afoot. On the eve of Saint Bartholomew's Day, August 24, 1572, 3,000 Huguenots were butchered in Paris. Within three days an estimated 20,000 Huguenots were executed throughout France.

The St. Bartholemew's Day Massacre. In this notorious event, here depicted by the contemporary Protestant painter François Dubois, 3,000 Protestants were slaughtered in Paris, and an estimated 20,000 others died throughout France. The massacre transformed the religious struggle in France from a contest for political power into an all-out war between Protestants and Catholics.

Do you think these events would be portrayed differently by a Catholic artist?

Read the Document
Account: Massacre
St. Bartholomew 1572
at **myhistorylab.com**

This event changed the nature of Protestant–Catholic conflict both within France and beyond. In Protestant eyes, it became an international struggle for survival against an adversary whose cruelty justified any means of resistance.

Henry III (r. 1574–1589) sought to steer a middle course, and in this effort he received support from a growing body of neutral Catholics and Huguenots who put the political survival of France above its religious unity. Such *politiques*, as they were called, were prepared to compromise religious creeds to save the nation. Henry III allied with his Protestant cousin and heir, Henry of Navarre, against the Catholic League, supported by the Spanish, which dominated Paris in the mid-1580s. When a fanatical Dominican friar murdered Henry III, the Bourbon Henry of Navarre became Henry IV of France (r. 1589–1610).

Henry IV believed that a royal policy of tolerant Catholicism would be the best way to achieve peace. On July 25, 1593, he publicly abjured the Protestant faith and embraced the traditional religion of his country. "Paris is worth a Mass," he is reported to have said. Henry IV's famous Edict of Nantes (1598) recognized and sanctioned minority religious rights within what was to remain an officially Catholic country. This religious truce granted the Huguenots, who by this time numbered well over a million, freedom of public worship, the right of assembly, admission to public offices and universities, and permission to maintain fortified towns.

Read the Document
The Edict of Nantes 1598
at **myhistorylab.com**

Henry IV was assassinated in 1610. Although he is best remembered for the Edict of Nantes, the political and economic policies he put in place laid the foundations for the transformation of France into the absolutist state it would become in the seventeenth century.

IMPERIAL SPAIN AND THE REIGN OF PHILIP II (1556–1598)

Until the English defeated his mighty Armada in 1588, Philip II of Spain was the late-sixteenth century's greatest ruler. He focused first on Turkish expansion. On October 7, 1571, a Holy League of Spain, Venice, and the pope defeated the

Turks at Lepanto. Before the engagement ended, 30,000 Turks had died and over one-third of the Turkish fleet had been sunk or captured. But Philip failed when he attempted to impose his will within the Netherlands and on England and France.

The Netherlands was the richest area in Europe. Its merchant towns were Europe's most independent, and many were Calvinist strongholds. A stubborn opposition to the Spanish overlords formed when Philip II insisted on enforcing the decrees of the Council of Trent in the Netherlands. William of Nassau, the Prince of Orange (r. 1533–1584), emerged as the leader of a broad movement for the Netherlands' independence from Spain. Like other successful rulers in this period, William of Orange was a *politique* who placed the Netherlands' political autonomy and well-being above religious creeds.

The ten largely Catholic southern provinces (roughly modern Belgium) came together in 1576 with the seven largely Protestant northern provinces (roughly the modern Netherlands) in unified opposition to Spain. This union, known as the Pacification of Ghent, declared internal regional sovereignty in matters of religion. In January 1579 the southern provinces made peace with Spain. The northern provinces continued the struggle. Spain was preoccupied with France and England, and the northern provinces drove out all Spanish soldiers by 1593.

ENGLAND AND SPAIN (1558–1603)

Elizabeth I (r. 1558–1603), the daughter of Henry VIII and Anne Boleyn, may have been the most astute politician of the sixteenth century. She repealed the anti-Protestant legislation of her predecessor Mary Tudor and guided a religious settlement through Parliament that prevented England from being torn asunder by religious differences in the sixteenth century.

Catholic extremists hoped to replace Elizabeth with the Catholic Mary Stuart, Queen of Scots (1542–1587), but Elizabeth acted swiftly against assassination plots and rarely let emotion override her political instincts.

Elizabeth dealt cautiously with the Puritans, Protestants who sought to "purify" the national church. The Puritans had two special grievances: (1) the retention of Catholic ceremony and vestments within the Church of England, and (2) the continuation of the episcopal system of church governance. Sixteenth-century Puritans were not separatists, however. They worked through Parliament to create an alternative national church of semiautonomous congregations governed by representative presbyteries (hence, Presbyterians). More extreme Puritans wanted every congregation to be autonomous. Elizabeth refused to tolerate these Congregationalists, whose views she considered subversive.

Despite religious differences, both Elizabeth and Spain's Philip II hoped to maintain a peaceful coexistence between their nations. Nonetheless, a series of events—culminating in Elizabeth's execution of Mary, Queen of Scots, on February 18, 1587—led inexorably to war between England and Spain. On May 30, 1588, a mighty fleet of 130 Spanish ships bearing 25,000 sailors and soldiers set sail for England. But the day belonged completely to the English. English and Dutch ships, assisted by an "English wind," dispersed the waiting Spanish fleet, over a third of which never returned to Spain.

The Milch Cow. This sixteenth-century satirical painting depicts the Netherlands as a land all the great powers of Europe wish to exploit. Elizabeth of England is feeding her (England had long-standing commercial ties with Flanders); Philip II of Spain is attempting to ride her (Spain was trying to reassert its control over the entire region); William of Orange is trying to milk her (he was the leader of the anti-Spanish rebellion); and the king of France holds her by the tail (France hoped to profit from the rebellion at Spain's expense).

The "Milch Cow." Rijksmuseum, Amsterdam.

Which character shown here could be considered most successful in the way history actually played out?

⊙ See the **Map**
The Netherlands during the Dutch Revolt, ca. 1580
at **myhistorylab.com**

Elizabeth I (1558–1603), Standing on a Map of England in 1592. An astute, if sometimes erratic, politician in foreign and domestic policy, Elizabeth was one of the most successful rulers of the sixteenth century.

National Portrait Gallery, London/SuperStock.

What qualities of kingship are conveyed in this portrait of Elizabeth I?

The Armada's defeat gave heart to Protestant resistance everywhere. Spain never fully recovered. By the time of Philip's death on September 13, 1598, his forces had been rebuffed by the French and the Dutch. His seventeenth-century successors were all inferior leaders. The French soon dominated the Continent, while the Dutch and the English whittled away Spain's overseas empire. Elizabeth died on March 23, 1603, leaving behind her a strong nation poised to expand into a global empire.

THE THIRTY YEARS' WAR (1618–1648)

The Thirty Years' War in the Holy Roman Empire was the last and most destructive of the wars of religion. Religious and political hatreds had become entrenched, and various groups were determined to sacrifice all for their territorial sovereignty and religious beliefs. As the conflicts multiplied, it became the worst European catastrophe since the Black Death of the fourteenth century. When the hostilities ended in 1648, the peace terms shaped much of the map of northern Europe as we know it today.

During the second half of the sixteenth century, Germany was an almost ungovernable land of 360 autonomous political entities. In 1555, the Peace of Augsburg had given each a significant degree of sovereignty within its own borders. Political decentralization and fragmentation characterized Germany as the seventeenth century opened; it was not a unified nation like Spain, England, or even strife-torn France. (See Map 16–4.)

The Holy Roman Empire was about equally divided between Catholics and Protestants, the latter having perhaps a slight numerical edge by 1600. After the Peace of Augsburg, Lutherans had gained political control in many Catholic areas, as had the Catholics in a few previously Lutheran areas. There was also religious strife between liberal and conservative Lutherans and between Lutherans and the growing numbers of Calvinists. Calvinism had not been recognized as a legal religion by the Peace of Augsburg, but it established a strong foothold within the empire when the devoutly Calvinist Elector Frederick III (r. 1559–1576) made it the official religion within the Palatinate in 1559. By 1609 Palatine Calvinists headed a Protestant defensive alliance supported by Spain's sixteenth-century enemies: England, France, and the Netherlands.

Jesuits were also active within the Holy Roman Empire. From staunchly Catholic Bavaria, supported by Spain, Jesuits launched successful missions throughout the empire. In 1609 Maximilian, Duke of Bavaria (1573–1651), organized a Catholic League to counter the Palatine-based Protestant alliance. When the Catholic League fielded a great army, it launched the Thirty Years' War.

In 1648 all hostilities within the Holy Roman Empire were brought to an end by the Treaty of Westphalia. It firmly reasserted the major feature of the Peace of Augsburg: Rulers were again permitted to determine the religion of their lands. The treaty also gave the Calvinists their long-sought legal recognition, while denying it to sectarians. The independence of the Swiss Confederacy and the United Provinces of Holland, long recognized in fact, now became law.

The Treaty of Westphalia perpetuated German division and political weakness into the modern period, although Austria and Brandenburg-Prussia attained international significance during the seventeenth century. In Europe at large, distinctive nation-states, each with its own political, cultural, and religious identity, reached maturity in the seventeenth century and firmly established the competitive nationalism of the modern world.

MAP 16–4.   Religious Division ca. 1600. By 1600 few could expect Christians to return to a uniform religious allegiance. In Spain and southern Italy Catholicism remained relatively unchallenged, but note the existence elsewhere of large religious minorities, both Catholic and Protestant.

Why did the wars of religion fail to reestablish religious uniformity in the Holy Roman Empire?

SUPERSTITION AND ENLIGHTENMENT: THE BATTLE WITHIN

Religious reform and warfare moved intellectuals to rethink human nature and society. One side of that reconsideration was dark and cynical, perhaps because the peak years of religious warfare had also been those of the great European witch hunts. Another side was brilliantly skeptical and constructive, reflecting the growing scientific movement of the years between 1500 and 1700.

WHO WERE some of the most significant writers and thinkers between 1500 and 1700?

Two Witches by Hans Baldung Grien (1523). German artist Hans Baldung Grien presents the powers and temptations of two enchanted, monumental witches as they sow the wind.

What types of people were most vulnerable to accusations of witchcraft?

•••••Read the **Document**
Malleus Maleficarum 1486
at **myhistorylab.com**

QUICK REVIEW

Witch Hunts

- "Cunning folk" traditionally helped villagers
- Christian clergy monopolized "magic"
- Older, single women were most vulnerable to accusations of witchcraft
- Witch trials could be destabilizing

Watch the Video
at **myhistorylab.com**

WITCH HUNTS AND PANIC

The witch hunts and panics that erupted in almost every Western land reveal the dark side of early modern thought and culture. Between 1400 and 1700, courts sentenced an estimated 70,000 to 100,000 people to death for harmful magic (*maleficium*) and diabolical witchcraft. In addition to harming their neighbors, witches were said to fly to mass meetings known as *sabbats*. They were accused of indulging in sexual orgies with the devil, practicing cannibalism (especially the devouring of small Christian children), and engaging in a variety of rituals that denied or perverted Christian beliefs.

Many factors contributed to the great witch panics of the second half of the sixteenth and the early seventeenth centuries. Religious division and warfare were major influences. The church had traditionally provided defenses against the devil and demons; the Reformation forced people to find alternative ways to handle their anxieties. The growing strength of governments intent on weeding out nonconformists also played a part.

In village societies, feared and respected "cunning folk" had long helped people cope with natural disasters and disabilities by magical means. For local people, these were important services, and possession of magical powers made one an important person in the village. Vulnerable people, such as old, single women, often claimed power. Witch beliefs may also have been a way for villagers to defy urban Christian society's attempts to impose its beliefs, laws, and institutions on the countryside.

The Christian clergy also practiced magic, transforming bread and wine into the body and blood of Christ, and converting eternal punishments for sins into temporal ones. Clergy exorcised demons, too. In the late thirteenth century the church declared its magic the only legitimate magic. Since such power was not human, the theologians reasoned, anyone who practiced magic outside the church did so on behalf of the devil. Attacking accused witches became a way for the church to extend its spiritual hegemony. To accuse, try, and execute witches was a declaration of moral and political authority.

Roughly 80 percent of the victims of witch hunts were women, most single and between 45 and 60 years of age. Older single women were particularly vulnerable for many reasons. More women than men laid claim to supernatural powers, so they were at disproportionate risk. Many of these women were midwives, so they were associated with deaths during childbirth. Both the church and their neighbors were prepared to think and say the worst about them.

Many factors helped end the witch hunts. A more scientific worldview made it difficult to believe in the powers of witches. Witch hunts also tended to get out of hand. Tortured witches sometimes alleged having seen leading townspeople at sabbats, at which point the trials threatened anarchy.

WRITERS AND PHILOSOPHERS

By the end of the sixteenth century, many could no longer embrace either the old Catholic or new Protestant absolutes. Intellectually as well as politically, the seventeenth century would be a period of transition. Some writers and philosophers of the late sixteenth and seventeenth centuries tried to straddle the two ages (Cervantes and Shakespeare), others ignored or opposed new developments that seemed to threaten traditional values (Pascal), and still others embraced emerging ideas and social structures (Spinoza, Hobbes, and Locke).

In Spain, the intertwining of Catholic piety and Spanish political power fostered a literature preoccupied with medieval chivalric virtues, especially honor and loyalty.

Generally acknowledged to be the greatest Spanish writer of all time, Miguel de Cervantes Saavedra (1547–1616) educated himself by insatiable reading in vernacular literature and immersion in the school of life. In 1570 he became a soldier and was decorated for gallantry at Lepanto (1571). He began his most famous work, *Don Quixote*, in prison in 1603, after conviction for theft.

Many believe the intent of *Don Quixote* was to satirize the chivalric romances so popular in Spain, but Cervantes shows deep affection for his characters. Don Quixote, a none-too-stable middle-aged man, is driven mad by reading too many chivalric romances. He comes to believe that he is an aspirant to knighthood and must prove his worthiness. He acquires a rusty suit of armor, mounts an aged horse, and chooses for his inspiration a peasant girl whom he fancies to be a noble lady. Sancho Panza, a wise peasant who serves as Don Quixote's squire, watches with skepticism and sympathy as his lord repeatedly makes a fool of himself. The story ends tragically with Don Quixote's humiliating defeat by a well-meaning friend who forces him to renounce his quest for knighthood. Throughout *Don Quixote*, Cervantes juxtaposed the down-to-earth realism of Sancho Panza with the old-fashioned religious idealism of Don Quixote. Cervantes admired the one as much as the other and demonstrated that to be truly happy, men and women need dreams—even impossible ones—just as much as a sense of reality.

Surprisingly little is known about William Shakespeare (1564–1616), the greatest playwright in the English language. He apparently worked as a schoolteacher, acquiring broad knowledge of Renaissance learning and literature. He took the new commercialism and the bawdy pleasures of the Elizabethan Age in stride and with amusement. References to contemporary political events fill his plays. By modern standards he was a political conservative, accepting the social rankings and the power structure of his day and demonstrating unquestioned patriotism.

Shakespeare was a playwright, actor, and part owner of a theater. His work brought together the best past and current achievements in the dramatic arts. He particularly mastered the psychology of human motivation and passion. Shakespeare wrote histories, comedies, and tragedies. Four of his best tragedies were written within a three-year period: *Hamlet* (1603), *Othello* (1604), *King Lear* (1605), and *Macbeth* (1606). In his lifetime and ever since, Shakespeare has been immensely popular with both audiences and readers. As Ben Jonson (1572–1637), a contemporary classical dramatist who created his own school of poets, put it in 1623: "He was not of an age, but for all time."

Blaise Pascal (1623–1662) was a French mathematician and a physical scientist widely acclaimed by his contemporaries. He was torn between the continuing dogmatism and the new skepticism of the seventeenth century. Pascal believed that reason and science, though attesting to human dignity, remained of no avail in religion. Here only the reasons of the heart and a "leap of faith" could prevail. Pascal saw two essential truths in the Christian religion: A loving God, worthy of human attainment, exists; and human beings, because they are corrupted in nature, are utterly unworthy of God.

Pascal made a famous wager with the skeptics. It is a better bet, he argued, to believe that God exists and to stake everything on his promised mercy than not to do so; if God does exist, everything will be gained by the believer, whereas the loss incurred by having believed in a nonexistent God is minimal. Pascal urged his contemporaries to seek self-understanding by "learned ignorance" and to discover humankind's greatness by recognizing its misery, thereby countering what he saw as the false optimism of the new rationalism and science.

Leviathan. Thomas Hobbes's political treatise, *Leviathan*, portrayed rulers as absolute lords over their lands, incorporating in their persons the individual wills of all their people.

Look closely at this picture: What does it show?

┄┄╋╴Read the **Document**
Leviathan at **myhistorylab.com**

The most controversial thinker of the seventeenth century was Baruch Spinoza (1632–1677), the son of a Jewish merchant of Amsterdam. He criticized the dogmatism of Dutch Calvinists and championed freedom of thought. Spinoza's most influential writing, *Ethics*, appeared after his death in 1677. Religious leaders universally condemned it for its apparent espousal of pantheism. According to Spinoza there is only one substance, which is self-caused, free, and infinite, and God is that substance. Everything that exists is in God and cannot even be conceived of apart from him. Such a doctrine is not literally pantheistic, but in Spinoza's view, statements about the natural world are also statements about divine nature. Mind and matter are seen to be extensions of the infinite substance of God; what transpires in the world of humankind and nature is a necessary outpouring of the Divine.

Thomas Hobbes (1588–1679) was the most original political philosopher of the seventeenth century. Although he never broke with the Church of England, he came to share basic Calvinist beliefs, especially the low view of human nature and the ideal of a commonwealth based on a covenant, both of which find eloquent expression in his political philosophy. Hobbes was an enthusiastic supporter of the new scientific movement. During the 1630s he visited Paris, where he came to know Descartes; after the outbreak of the Puritan Revolution (see Chapter 19) in 1640, he lived as an exile in Paris until 1651. Hobbes also spent time with Galileo (see Chapter 21) in Italy and took a special interest in the works of William Harvey, the physiologist famed for the discovery of how blood circulates through the body.

Hobbes was driven to political philosophy by the English Civil War (see Chapter 19). In 1651 his *Leviathan* appeared. Its subject was the political consequences of human passions, and its originality lay in (1) its making natural law, rather than common law (i.e., custom or precedent), the basis of all positive law, and (2) its defense of a representative theory of absolute authority against the theory of the divine right of kings. Hobbes maintained that statute law found its justification only as an expression of the law of nature and that rulers derived their authority from the consent of the people.

The key to Hobbes's political philosophy is a brilliant myth of the original state of humankind. According to this myth, human beings in the natural state are generally inclined to a "perpetual and restless desire of power after power that ceases only in death."[3] Whereas earlier and later philosophers saw the original human state as a paradise from which humankind had fallen, Hobbes saw it as a corruption from which only society had delivered people. According to Hobbes, people escape the impossible state of nature only by entering a social contract that creates a commonwealth tightly ruled by law and order. The social contract obliges every person, for the sake of peace and self-defense, to agree to set aside personal rights. The social contract also establishes the coercive force necessary to compel compliance. Hobbes conceived of the ruler's power as absolute and unlimited. There is no room in Hobbes's political philosophy for political protest in the name of individual conscience or for resistance to legitimate authority by private individuals—features of *Leviathan* criticized by Catholics and Puritans alike.

John Locke (1632–1704) has proved to be the most influential political thinker of the seventeenth century.[4] His political philosophy was embodied in the so-called Glorious Revolution of 1688 to 1689 (Chapter 19). Although he was not as original as Hobbes, his political writings were a major source of the later Enlightenment criticism of absolutism, and they gave inspiration to both the American and French Revolutions.

---

[3]*Leviathan*, Parts I and II, ed. by H. W. Schneider (Indianapolis, IN: Bobbs-Merrill, 1958), p. 86.

[4]Locke's scientific writings are discussed in Chapter 23.

Locke's two most famous works are the *Essay Concerning Human Understanding* (1690) (discussed in Chapter 21) and *Two Treatises of Government* (1690), in which he argued that rulers are not absolute in their power. Rulers remain bound to the law of nature, which is the voice of reason, teaching that "all mankind [are] equal and independent, [and] no one ought to harm another in his life, health, liberty, or possessions,"[5] since all human beings are the images and property of God. People enter social contracts, empowering legislatures and monarchs to arbitrate their disputes, precisely to preserve their natural rights, not to give rulers an absolute power over them. From Locke's point of view, absolute monarchy was "inconsistent" with civil society and could be "no form of civil government at all."[6]

SUMMARY

 WHY DID western Europeans start exploring, trading, and settling around the world in the fifteenth century?

The Discovery of a New World. In the late fifteenth century, Europe began to expand around the globe. Driven by both commercial and religious motives, the Portuguese pioneered a sea route around Africa to India and the Far East, and the Spanish discovered the Americas. The social, political, and biological consequences were immense. *page 386*

 WHO WERE the early Protestant leaders?

The Reformation. The Reformation began in Germany with Martin Luther's attack on indulgences in 1517. The Reformation shattered the religious unity of Europe. In Switzerland, Zwingli and Calvin launched their own versions of Protestantism. In England, Henry VIII repudiated papal authority when the pope refused to grant him a divorce. The different Protestant sects were often as hostile to each other as they were to Catholicism. The Roman Catholic Church also acted to reform itself. The Council of Trent tightened church discipline and reaffirmed traditional doctrine. The Jesuits converted many Protestants back to Catholicism. *page 389*

 HOW DID family life change during the Reformation era?

The Reformation and Daily Life. The Reformation led to far-reaching changes in religious beliefs, practices, and institutions. Family life changed in this period, as couples married later in life. *page 398*

WHY DID religious divisions lead to war?

The Wars of Religion. The religious divisions of Europe led to more than a century of warfare from the 1520s to 1648. The chief battlegrounds were in France, the Netherlands, and Germany. When the Thirty Years' War ended in 1648, Europe was permanently divided into Catholic and Protestant areas. *page 401*

WHO WERE some of the most significant writers and thinkers between 1500 and 1700?

Superstition and Enlightenment: The Battle Within. The Reformation led to both dark and constructive views of human nature. Witch crazes erupted across Europe. Thousands of innocent people, mostly women, were persecuted and executed as witches between 1400 and 1700. In literature and philosophy, these years witnessed an outpouring of creative thinking. Among the greatest thinkers of the age were Cervantes, Shakespeare, Pascal, Spinoza, Hobbes, and Locke. *page 405*

KEY TERMS

consubstantiation (p. 394)

Counter-Reformation (p. 397)

Diet of Worms (p. 392)

Huguenots (HYEW-guh-nahts) (p. 401)

indulgence (p. 392)

ninety-five theses (p. 392)

Reformation (p. 389)

transubstantiation (p. 394)

---

[5]*The Second Treatise of Government*, ed. by T. P. Peardon (Indianapolis, IN: Bobbs-Merrill, 1952), chap. 2, sects. 4–6, pp. 4–6.

[6]Ibid.

REVIEW QUESTIONS

1. What impact did expansion have on European economies?

2. What were the main problems of the church that contributed to the Protestant Reformation? Why was the church unable to suppress dissent as it had earlier?

3. How did the theologies of Luther, Zwingli, and Calvin differ? Were their differences only religious, or did they have political consequences for the Reformation as well?

4. Why did the Reformation begin in Germany and not in France, Italy, England, or Spain?

5. What was the Catholic Reformation? Did the Council of Trent alter the character of traditional Catholicism?

6. Why did Henry VIII break with the Catholic Church? Was the "new" religion he established really Protestant?

7. Were the wars of religion really over religion? Explain.

8. Henry of Navarre (later Henry IV of France), Elizabeth I, and William of Orange have been called *politiques*. What does that term mean, and how might it apply to each?

9. Why was England more successful than other lands in resolving its internal political and religious divisions peacefully during the sixteenth and seventeenth centuries?

10. Consider some of the leading intellectuals of this period: Cervantes, Shakespeare, Pascal, Spinoza, Hobbes, and Locke. Whose ideas do you find most challenging, and why? Which one would you most like to meet?

Note: To learn more about the topics in this chapter, please turn to the Suggested Reading s at the end of the book. For additional sources related to this chapter please see www.myhistorylab.com

PEARSON myhistorylab Connections

Reinforce what you learned in this chapter by studying the many documents, images, maps, review tools, and videos available at **www.myhistorylab.com**

Read and Review

Research and Explore

((●─[Hear the Audio

Hear the audio file for Chapter 16
at **www.myhistorylab.com**

CHRISTIANITY

RELIGIONS OF THE WORLD

Christianity is based on the teachings of Jesus of Nazareth, a Jew who lived in Palestine during the Roman occupation. His simple message of faith in God and self-sacrificial love of one's neighbor attracted many people. The Roman authorities, perceiving his large following as a threat, crucified him. After Jesus' crucifixion, his followers proclaimed that he had been resurrected from the dead and that he would return in glory to defeat sin, death, and the devil, and take all true believers with him to heaven—a radical vision of judgment and immortality that has driven Christianity's appeal since its inception. In the teachings of the early church, Jesus became the Christ, the son of God, the long-awaited Messiah of Jewish prophecy. His followers called themselves Christians.

Christianity proclaimed the very incarnation of God in a man, the visible presence of eternity in time. According to early Christian teaching, the power of God's incarnation in Jesus lived on in the preaching and sacraments of the church under the guidance of the Holy Spirit. According to the Christian message, in Jesus, eternity has made itself accessible to every person here and now and forevermore.

The new religion attracted both the poor and powerless and the socially rising and well-to-do. For some, the gospel of Jesus promised a better material life. For others, it imparted a sense of spiritual self-worth regardless of one's place or prospects in society.

In the late second century the Romans began persecuting Christians as "heretics" (because of their rejection of the traditional Roman gods) and as social revolutionaries (for their loyalty to a lord higher than the emperor of Rome). At the same time dissenting Christians, particularly sects claiming direct spiritual knowledge of God apart from Scripture, internally divided the young church. To meet these challenges the church established effective weapons against state terrorism and Christian heresy: an ordained clergy, a hierarchical church organization, orthodox creeds, and a biblical canon (the New Testament). Christianity not only gained legal status within the Roman Empire, but also, by the fourth century, most favored religious status thanks to Emperor Constantine's embrace of it.

Pentecost. This exquisite enamel plaque, from the Mosan school that flourished in France in the eleventh and twelfth centuries, shows the descent of the Holy Spirit upon the apostles, fifty days after the resurrection of Jesus, on the ancient Jewish festival called the "feast of weeks," or Pentecost.

Mosan, The Pentecost, ca. 1150—1175. Champleve enamel on copper gilt; 4 1/16 x 4 1/6 in. (10.3 x 10.3cm). The Metropolitan Museum of Art, The Cloisters Collection, 1965 (65.105). Photograph 1989 The Metropolitan Museum of Art.

How did the church gain power in Europe?

After the fall of the Western Roman Empire in the fifth century C.E., Christianity became one of history's great success stories. Aided by the enterprise of its popes and the example of its monks, the church cultivated an appealing lay piety centered on the Lord's Prayer, the Apostles' Creed, veneration of the Virgin, and the sacrament of the Eucharist. Clergy became both royal teachers and bureaucrats within the kingdom of the Franks. Despite a growing schism between the Eastern (Byzantine) and Western churches, and a final split in 1054, by 1000 the church held real economic and political power. In the eleventh century reform-minded prelates put an end to presumptuous secular interference in its most intimate spiritual affairs by ending the lay investiture of clergy in their spiritual offices. For several centuries thereafter the church remained a formidable international force, able to challenge kings and emperors and inspire Crusades to the Holy Land.

By the fifteenth century the new states of Europe had stripped the church of much of its political power. It was thereafter progressively confined to spiritual and moral authority. Christianity's greatest struggles ever since have been not with kings and emperors over political power, but with materialistic philosophies and worldly ideologies, matters of spiritual and moral hegemony within an increasingly pluralistic and secular world. Since the sixteenth century a succession of humanists, skeptics, Deists, Rationalists, Marxists, Freudians, Darwinians, and atheists have attempted to explain away some of traditional Christianity's most basic teachings. In addition, the church has endured major internal upheavals. After the Protestant Reformation (1517–1555) made the Bible widely available to the laity, the possibilities for internal criticism of Christianity multiplied geometrically. Beginning with the split between Lutherans and Zwinglians in the 1520s, Protestant Christianity has fragmented into hundreds of sects, each claiming to have the true interpretation of Scripture. The Roman Catholic Church, by contrast, has maintained its unity and ministry throughout perilous times, although present-day discontent with papal authority threatens the modern Catholic Church almost as seriously as the Protestant Reformation once did.

Christianity has remained remarkably resilient. It possesses a simple, almost magically appealing gospel of faith and love in and through Jesus. In a present-day world whose religious needs and passions still run deep, evangelical Christianity has experienced a remarkable revival. The Roman Catholic Church, still troubled by challenges to papal authority, has become more pluralistic than in earlier periods. The pope has become a world figure, traveling to all continents to represent the church and advance its position on issues of public and private morality. A major ecumenical movement emerging in the 1960s has promoted unprecedented cooperation among evangelical Christian denominations. Everywhere Christians of all stripes are politically active, spreading their divine, moral, and social messages. Meanwhile, old hot-button issues, such as the ordination of women, are being overtaken by new ones, particularly the marriage of gay men and women and the removal of clergy who do not maintain the moral discipline of their holy orders.

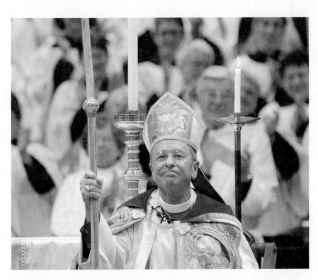

Gay bishop. V. Gene Robinson is applauded after his investiture as the Episcopal Church's bishop of New Hampshire in March 2004. Robinson is the Episcopal Church's first openly gay bishop. The issue of homosexuality has divided Christian churches across the world.

What other controversies have divided Christians?

- Over the centuries what have been some of the chief factors attracting people to Christianity?

- What forces have led to disunity among Christians in the past? What factors cause tensions among modern Christians?

17

Conquest and Exploitation: The Development of the Transatlantic Economy

((•─[Hear the Audio for Chapter 17 at www.myhistorylab.com

Negroes for Sale.

A Cargo of very fine stout Men and Women, in good order and fit for immediate service, just imported from the Windward Coast of Africa, in the Ship Two Brothers.——

Conditions are one half Cash or Produce, the other half payable the first of January next, giving Bond and Security if required.

The Sale to be opened at 10 o'Clock each Day, in Mr. Bourdeaux's Yard, at No. 48, on the Bay.

May 19, 1784.   JOHN MITCHELL.

Thirty Seasoned Negroes

To be Sold for Credit, at Private Sale.

AMONGST which is a Carpenter, none of whom are known to be dishonest.

Also, to be sold for Cash, a regular bred young Negroe Man-Cook, born in this Country, who served several Years under an exceeding good French Cook abroad, and his Wife a middle aged Washer-Woman, (both very honest) and their two Children. Likewise, a young Man a Carpenter.

For Terms apply to the Printer.

Slave Auction Notice. Africans who survived the voyage across the Atlantic were immediately sold into slavery in the Americas. This eighteenth-century advertisement relates to a group of slaves whose ship had stopped at Charleston, South Carolina, and then landed elsewhere in the region to auction its human cargo. Notice the concern to assure potential buyers that the slaves were healthy, as a small-pox epidemic was then raging on the mainland.

Why were Africans treated as commodities during the era of the transatlantic slave trade?

T he fifteenth-century encounter between the European and American continents changed the entire world. Centuries of European domination and government made the Americas a region where European languages, legal and political institutions, trade patterns, and religion prevail. African populations, economies, and political structures were altered by the slave trade into the Americas. Europe gained more influence over other world cultures than it could otherwise have achieved.

GLOBAL PERSPECTIVE

THE ATLANTIC WORLD

The exchanges of people, goods, ideas, and plants, animals, and microorganisms between the American, European, and African continents in the fifteenth and sixteenth centuries transformed world history. In the Americas, the native peoples—whose ancestors had migrated from Asia millennia before—had established a wide variety of civilizations. Some of their most remarkable architectural monuments and cities were constructed during the very centuries when European civilizations were reeling from the collapse of Roman power. (See Chapter 13.) While trade and culture had long linked parts of Africa and regions in Eurasia (see Chapter 14) the civilizations of the Americas and the civilizations of Eurasia and Africa had had no significant contact with each other prior to the era of European exploration.

Within half a century of the landing of Columbus, millions of America's native peoples in Florida, the Caribbean islands, Mesoamerica, and South America had experienced the impact of Europeans intent on conquest, exploitation, and religious conversion. The Europeans' rapid conquest was the result of several factors—their advanced weapons and navies; the new diseases they brought with them; and internal divisions among the Native Americans. Thereafter, Spain and Portugal dominated Central and South America (what we now, as a result of this history, call Latin America), and England, France, and Holland set out to settle North America. The Europeans imported their own food crops, such as wheat and apples, while also taking advantage of American plants, such as potatoes, corn, tomatoes, and tobacco.

Throughout the Americas and the Caribbean basin, Europeans established economies of exploitation. In Latin America, they developed various institutions to extract native labor. Plantation owners from the Mid-Atlantic English colonies through the

El Morro, Puerto Rico. This fortress was built by the Spanish in the sixteenth century to protect Spain's valuable trading rights against British, Dutch, and pirate ships.

Why did Spain strive to control sea lanes?

((•—[Hear the Audio
at **myhistorylab.com**

Within decades of the European voyages of discovery, Native Americans, Europeans, and Africans began to interact in a manner unprecedented in human history. The Native Americans of North and South America encountered bands of European conquerors and missionaries. Technological and military superiority as well as political divisions among the Native Americans allowed the Europeans to realize their material and religious ambitions. By the middle of the sixteenth century Europeans had begun to import Africans into the American continents as chattel slaves, converting them to Christianity in the process. By the close of the sixteenth century Europe, the Americas, and Africa had become linked in a vast transatlantic economy that extracted material and agricultural wealth from the American continents largely on the basis of the nonfree labor of impressed Native Americans and imported African slaves.

The next century would see English and French colonists settling in North America and the Caribbean, introducing both Protestantism and different political values. As they exploited the North American wilderness, the colonists interacted with Native Americans, sometimes destroying indigenous cultures and whole peoples, sometimes converting Native Americans to Christianity; Native Americans, too, were drawn into the transatlantic economy.

Beginning in the sixteenth century, the importation of African slaves and the use of slave labor were fundamental to the plantation economy that eventually extended from Maryland to Brazil. Slaveholding and economic entanglement in the slave trade also extended into the British colonies north of Maryland. The slave trade intimately connected portions of Africa to the transatlantic economy. The slave trade had a devastating effect on the African people and cultures involved in it, but it also enriched the Americas with African culture and religion. ■

Caribbean and into Brazil preferred slaves forcibly imported from Africa. African slaves were hardier than indigenous laborers, who lacked immunity to European diseases, and they could be better controlled than indentured servants from Europe. With the exception of tobacco, plantation crops derived largely from the Old World; some Africans were already familiar with the cultivation of, for example, rice. The emergent Atlantic world drew the economies and peoples of Europe, Africa, and the Americas into a vast worldwide web of production based on slave labor.

Slavery had its most striking impact on the lives of the millions of humans who over the centuries were torn from their birthplaces, their families, and their cultures. The slave trade corroded the political and social structures of African societies. African slaves suffered from high mortality and sharply reduced birthrates; they were subjected to harsh working conditions and brutally dehumanizing treatment.

Focus Questions

◆ How did the encounter of Europe and Africa with the Americas change the global ecological balance?

◆ Why was the Spanish Empire based on economies of exploitation? How was the labor of non-European peoples drawn into the economy of this empire?

◆ How and why did the plantation economy develop? Why did it rely on African slaves for its labor? What were the consequences of the slave trade for individuals and institutions in each of the three continents constituting the Atlantic world?

◆ Why do we think of the plantation economy as a global, rather than regional, system of production? Why was it the "engine" of Atlantic basin trade?

PERIODS OF EUROPEAN OVERSEAS EXPANSION

Since the late fifteenth century, European contacts with the rest of the world have gone through four distinct stages. The first was the European discovery, exploration, initial conquest, and settlement of the Americas and commercial expansion elsewhere. The second was an era of trade rivalry among Spain, France, and Great Britain. During this period (to 1820), the British colonies of North America and the Spanish colonies of Mexico and Central and South America broke free from European control. The third period spanned the nineteenth century and was characterized by the development of European empires in Africa and Asia. Imperial ideology at this time involved theories of trade, national honor, race, religion, and military strength. The last period of European experience with empire occupied the mid-twentieth century and was a time of decolonization—a retreat from empire.

Technological advantages—naval power and gunpowder, not innate cultural superiority—enabled Europeans to exercise global dominance disproportionate to Europe's size and population for four and a half centuries. The legacy of European imperialism continues to influence contemporary events.

WHAT WERE the four periods of European contact with the world?

MERCANTILIST THEORY OF ECONOMIC EXPLOITATION

The early modern European empires of the sixteenth through the eighteenth centuries were based on commerce. Extensive trade rivalries sprang up around the world, and competitors developed navies to protect their interests. Spain, with the largest empire, constructed elaborate naval, commercial, and political structures to exploit and govern it.

WHAT WAS mercantilism?

Mercantilism. As this painting of the Custom House Quay in London suggests, trade from European empires and the tariffs imposed on it were expected to generate revenue for the home country. But behind many of the goods carried in the great sailing ships in the harbor and landed on these docks lay the labor of African slaves working on the plantations of North and South America.

Samuel Scott, "Old Custom House Quay" Collection. V&A Images, the Victoria and Albert Museum, London.

What kinds of trade goods are visible in this painting?

These empires depended largely on slave labor. The Atlantic slave trade forcibly brought together the lives and cultures of peoples in Africa and the New World. It also enriched many European merchants.

To the extent that any formal economic theory lay behind the conduct of these empires, it was **mercantilism**, a system in which governments heavily regulate trade and commerce to increase national wealth. From beginning to end, the economic well-being of the home country was the primary concern. Mercantilists believed that a nation had to gain more gold and silver bullion than its rivals and that one nation's economy could grow only at the expense of others. Nations grew by establishing colonies overseas to provide markets and natural resources for the home country, which furnished military security and political administration for the colonies. The home country and its colonies were to trade exclusively with each other. The colonies were assumed to be inferior partners in a monopolistic relationship.

By the early eighteenth century, it was clear that mercantilist assumptions did not correspond with reality. Colonial and home markets did not mesh. Spain, for instance, could not produce enough goods for South America, while manufacturing in the British North American colonies challenged production in England and led to British attempts to limit certain colonial industries. Colonists of different countries wished to trade with each other. English colonists could buy sugar more cheaply from the French West Indies than from English suppliers. The eighteenth century became the "golden age of smugglers."[1] Governments could be dragged into war by clashes among their colonies. Problems associated with the mercantile empires led to conflicts around the world.

ESTABLISHMENT OF THE SPANISH EMPIRE IN AMERICA

WHAT ROLES did the Roman Catholic Church play in Spanish America?

mercantilism
Term used to describe close government control of the economy that sought to maximize exports and accumulate as much precious metal as possible to enable the state to defend its economic and political interests.

•◄•┤Read the Document
2nd Letter, Hernan Cortez
to King Charles V
at **myhistorylab.com**

•◄•┤Read the Document
del Castillo, History of Conquest
at **myhistorylab.com**

CONQUEST OF THE AZTECS AND THE INCAS

Within twenty years of the arrival of Columbus (1451–1506), Spanish explorers in search of gold had claimed the major islands of the Caribbean and brutally suppressed the native peoples. These actions presaged what was to occur on the continent.

In 1519 Hernán Cortés (1485–1547) landed in Mexico with about 500 men and a few horses. He opened communication with Moctezuma II (1466–1520), the Aztec emperor. Moctezuma may initially have believed Cortés to be the god Quetzalcoatl, who, according to legend, had been driven away centuries earlier but had promised to return. Whatever the reason, Moctezuma hesitated to confront Cortés, attempting at first to appease him with gifts of gold. Cortés forged alliances, most importantly with Tlaxcala, a traditional enemy of the Aztecs. His forces then marched on the Aztec capital of Tenochtitlán (modern Mexico City), where Moctezuma welcomed him. Cortés soon made Moctezuma a prisoner. When Moctezuma died in unexplained circumstances, the Spaniards were driven from Tenochtitlán and nearly wiped out. But they returned, and the Aztecs were defeated in late 1521. Cortés proclaimed the Aztec Empire to be New Spain.

---

[1]Walter Dorn, *Competition for Empire, 1740–1763* (New York: Harper, 1940), p. 266.

In 1532, Francisco Pizarro (ca. 1478–1541) landed on the western coast of South America to take over the Inca Empire. His force included about 200 men armed with guns, swords, and horses. Pizarro lured the Inca ruler, Atahualpa (ca. 1500–1533), into a conference, then seized him and had him garroted in 1533. The Spaniards then captured Cuzco, the Inca capital, ending the Inca Empire. The Spanish faced insurrections, however, and fought among themselves for decades. Effective royal control was not established until the late 1560s.

The conquests of Mexico and Peru are among the most dramatic and brutal events in modern world history. Small military forces armed with advanced weapons and in alliance with indigenous enemies of the rulers subdued two advanced, powerful peoples. European diseases, especially smallpox, aided the conquest, since much of the native population succumbed to diseases against which they had no immunity. But beyond the drama and bloodshed, these conquests marked a turning point. Whole civilizations with long histories and a record of enormous social, architectural, and technological achievement were effectively destroyed. Native American cultures endured, but European culture had the upper hand.

THE ROMAN CATHOLIC CHURCH IN SPANISH AMERICA

The Spanish conquest of the West Indies, Mexico, and South America opened a vast region to the Roman Catholic faith. Religion played a central role; as in the reconquest of the Iberian Peninsula from the Moors, the obligation Christians felt to spread their faith was used to justify military conquest and political control. As a consequence, the Roman Catholic Church in the New World was a conservative force working to protect the power and prestige of the Spanish authorities. Indeed, the papacy turned over much of the control of the church in the New World to the Spanish monarchy. In the sixteenth century, as the papacy and the Habsburg monarchy fought Protestantism, the Roman Catholicism that spread throughout the Spanish domains of America was the zealous faith of the Counter-Reformation.

The Roman Catholic Church, with the aid first of the Franciscans and the Dominicans and later the Jesuits, sought to convert the Native Americans and eradicate Indian religious practices. Converts, however, did not enjoy equality with Europeans. Real tension existed between the early Spanish conquerors and the mendicant friars. Without conquest the church could not convert the Native Americans, but the priests often deplored the harsh conditions imposed on indigenous peoples. By far the most effective and outspoken critic was Bartolomé de Las Casas (1474–1566), a Dominican. He contended that conquest was not necessary for conversion. One result of his campaign was new royal regulations after 1550.

Las Casas's writings inspired the "**Black Legend**," according to which all Spanish treatment of Native Americans was inhumane. Although substantially true, the Black Legend exaggerated the case against Spain. Certainly the rulers of the native empires had often themselves been cruel to their subject peoples.

By the end of the sixteenth century, the church in Spanish America largely upheld the colonial status quo. Although individual priests defended the communal rights of Native American tribes, the colonial church prospered through its

QUICK REVIEW

Francisco Pizarro (ca. 1478–1541)

- ◆ Invasion force landed in South America in 1532
- ◆ Forces included 200 men, horses, guns, and swords
- ◆ Executed the Inca ruler and captured Cuzco in 1533

Spanish Conquest of Mexico. A sixteenth-century drawing depicts a battle during the Spanish conquest of Mexico. The Aztecs are on the right. Note how the Spaniards bring up the rear, behind their native allies, the Tlaxcalteca.

How does the position of the Tlaxcalteca leading the attack on the Aztecs offer a different perspective on the conquest of the Americas?

•••┤Read the Document
New Laws Indies for Good Treatment 2
at **myhistorylab.com**

Black Legend
The argument that Spanish treatment of Native Americans was uniquely inhumane.

•••┤Read the Document
Account of Devastation of Indies
at **myhistorylab.com**

exploitation of the resources of the New World. By the late eighteenth century, the Roman Catholic Church had become one of the most conservative forces in Latin American society.

ECONOMIES OF EXPLOITATION IN THE SPANISH EMPIRE

 HOW DID Spaniards attempt to control labor in the Americas?

Colonial Spanish America had an economy of exploitation in two senses. First, its organization of labor involved dependent servitude or slavery. Second, America's resources were exploited for the economic advantage of Spain.

VARIETIES OF ECONOMIC ACTIVITY

conquistadores
A term meaning "conquerors"; the Spanish conquerors of the New World.

The early **conquistadores** ("conquerors") had been interested primarily in gold, but by the middle of the sixteenth century silver mining provided the chief source of metallic wealth. The great silver mining centers were in northern Mexico and Potosí, in present-day Bolivia. The Spanish crown received one-fifth (the *quinto*) of all mining revenues. Overall, silver was a great source of wealth, and its production for the benefit of Spaniards and the Spanish crown epitomized the extractive economy on which Latin American colonial life was based.

The Silver Mines of Potosí. Worked by conscripted Indian laborers under extremely harsh conditions, these mines provided Spain with a vast treasure in silver.

What does the puny size of the Indians in this painting suggest about their status in the Spanish American society?

This extractive economy required labor, but there were too few Spanish colonists to provide it, and most of the colonists who came to the Americas did not want to work for wages. So, the Spaniards turned first to the native population for workers and then to African slaves. Indian labor dominated on the continent and African labor in the Caribbean.

The Spanish devised a series of institutions to exploit Native American labor. The first was the **encomienda**, a formal grant by the crown of the right to the labor of a specific number of Native Americans for a particular time. But the Spanish monarchy was distressed by reports from clergy that the Native Americans were being mistreated and feared that *encomienda* holders were becoming a powerful noble class in the New World. *Encomienda* as an institution declined by the middle of the sixteenth century.

The *encomienda* was followed by another arrangement of labor servitude, the **repartimiento**, which was largely copied from the *mita* labor practices of the Incas. *Repartimiento* required adult male Native Americans to devote a set number of days of labor annually to Spanish economic enterprises. The time limitation on *repartimiento* led some Spanish managers to work teams of men to exhaustion—sometimes to death—before replacing them with the next rotation.

encomienda
The grant by the Spanish crown to a colonist of the labor of a specific number of Native Americans for a set period of time.

repartimiento
A labor tax in Spanish America that required adult male Native Americans to devote a set number of days a year to Spanish economic enterprises.

Outside the mines, the **hacienda** dominated rural and agricultural life in Spanish colonies on the continent. Royal land grants led to the establishment of large landed estates owned by **peninsulares** (whites born in Spain) or Creoles (whites born in America). The core activity of the haciendas, livestock grazing, required less labor than did the mines. But laborers on the hacienda were usually in formal servitude to the owner and had to buy goods for everyday living on credit from him. They were rarely able to repay their debts and thus could not leave. This system was known as **debt peonage**. The hacienda economy produced foodstuffs for mining areas and urban centers, and haciendas became one of the most important features of Latin American life.

COMMERCIAL REGULATION AND THE FLOTA SYSTEM

Because Queen Isabella of Castile (r. 1474–1504) had commissioned Columbus, the legal link between the New World and Spain was the crown of Castile. Its powers were subject to few limitations. Government of America was assigned to the Council of the Indies, which, in conjunction with the monarch, nominated the viceroys of New Spain and Peru. These viceroys were the chief executives in the New World. Each of the viceroyalties included subordinate judicial councils known as *audiencias*. Local officers included the *corregidores*, who presided over municipal councils. These offices provided the monarchy with a vast array of opportunities for patronage. Political power flowed from the top of this political structure downward; there was little or no local initiative or self-government (see Map 17–1).

hacienda
A large landed estate in Spanish America.

peninsulares
Native-born Spaniards who emigrated from Spain to settle in the Spanish colonies.

debt peonage
A system that forces agricultural laborers (peons) to work and live on large estates (*haciendas*) until they have repaid their debts to the estate's owner.

MAP EXPLORATION

To explore this map further, go to **http://www.myhistorylab.com**

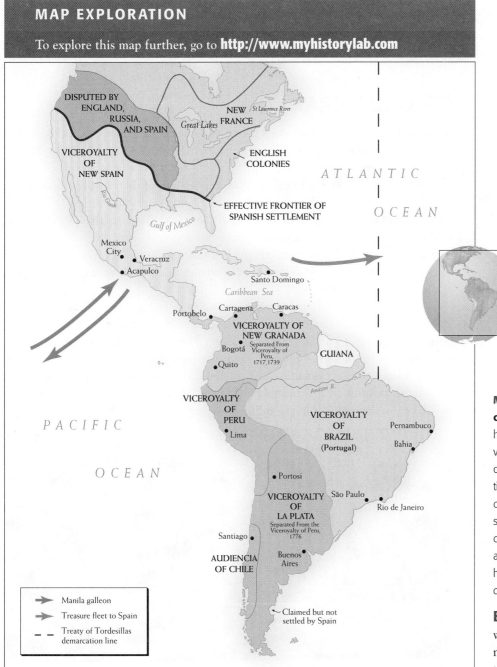

MAP 17–1.   The Americas, ca. 1750. Spain organized its vast holdings in the New World into viceroyalties, each of which had its own governor and other administrative officials. The English colonies clung to the North American seaboard. French possessions centered on the St. Lawrence River and the Great Lakes. Portuguese holdings in Brazil were mostly confined to the coast.

Based on this map, what were the strengths and weaknesses of the Spanish Empire in the Americas?

Colonial political structures supported the commercial goals of Spain. Spanish control of its American empire involved a system of monopolistic trade regulation, although Spain's trade monopoly was often breached. The Casa de Contratación (House of Trade) in Seville regulated all trade with the New World; it was the single most influential institution of the Spanish Empire. Each year a fleet of commercial vessels (the *flota*) controlled by Seville merchants, escorted by warships, carried merchandise from Spain to a few specified ports in America. These included Portobello, Veracruz, and Cartagena; there were no authorized ports on the Pacific coast. Buenos Aires and other areas received goods only after the shipments had been unloaded at an authorized port. After selling their wares, the ships were loaded with silver and gold bullion. They usually wintered in heavily fortified Caribbean ports and then sailed back to Spain. Each year a Spanish ship also crossed the Pacific from Spanish Manila to Acapulco, bringing Chinese silk and porcelain. It returned to Manila laden with Mexican silver. The *flota* system worked imperfectly, but trade outside it was illegal. Spanish colonists were prohibited from trading directly with each other, and foreign merchants were forbidden to breach the Spanish monopoly.

COLONIAL BRAZIL

HOW WERE sugar and slavery entwined in colonial Brazil?

◉ See the **Map**
Spanish and Portuguese Exploration
at **myhistorylab.com**

Spain and Portugal originally had rival claims to the Americas. In 1494, by the Treaty of Tordesillas, the pope divided the seaborne empires of Spain and Portugal by drawing a line west of the Cape Verde Islands. In 1500 a Portuguese explorer landed on the coast of present-day Brazil, which extended east of the papal line of division, and thus Portugal gained a major hold on the South American continent. Portugal, however, had fewer resources to devote to its New World empire than did Spain. Its rulers left exploitation of the region to private entrepreneurs. Because the native peoples in the lands that Portugal claimed were nomadic, the Portuguese, unlike the Spanish, imported Africans as slaves rather than using the native Indian population as their workforce.

By the mid-sixteenth century, sugar production had gained preeminence in the Brazilian economy. Because sugarcane was grown on large estates (*fazendas*) with African slave labor, the dominance of sugar also meant the dominance of slavery. Slavery became even more important when, in the early eighteenth century, significant gold deposits were discovered in southern Brazil. The expansion of gold mining increased the importation of African slaves. Nowhere, except perhaps in the West Indies, was slavery as important as it was in Brazil, where it persisted until 1888.

QUICK REVIEW

Brazil's Colonial Economy

◆ Indigenous peoples were nomads, so Portuguese entrepreneurs imported African slaves for labor

◆ Sugar production and gold mining were most significant elements of economy

◆ Portuguese crown was less involved in colonial administration than Spanish crown

Sugar plantations of Brazil and the West Indies were a major source of the demand for slave labor. Slaves are here shown grinding sugarcane and refining sugar, which was then exported to the consumer markets in Europe.

How did the labor requirements for sugar production differ from those for other colonial economic activities?

The taxation and administration associated with gold mining brought new, unexpected wealth to the Portuguese monarchy, allowing it to rule without recourse to the Cortés or traditional parliament for taxation. Through transatlantic trade the new wealth generated from Brazilian gold also filtered into all the major trading nations, which could sell their goods to Portugal as well as profit from the slave trade.

In Brazil, the basic unit of production was the plantation, which did not require a vast colonial administration; agricultural products were much easier to keep track of than the precious metals of Spanish American mines. The Portuguese were willing to allow more local autonomy than was Spain. In Spanish America the use of Native American labor was supervised by the government. Brazil, less dependent on Native American labor, felt no such constraints. Indeed, the Portuguese government condoned policies whereby indigenous tribes were driven into the back country or exterminated. Throughout the eighteenth century the Portuguese government favored the continued importation of slaves.

FRENCH AND BRITISH COLONIES IN NORTH AMERICA

Both England and France had important sugar islands in the Caribbean with plantations worked by African slaves. The trade and commerce of the northern British colonies were closely related to meeting the needs of these islands. The major presence of both nations, however, spread across different parts of the North American continent.

French explorers had pressed down the St. Lawrence River valley in Canada during the seventeenth century. French fur traders and Roman Catholic Jesuit missionaries had followed, with the French government supporting the missionary effort. By the end of the seventeenth century, a significant but sparsely populated French presence existed in Canada (see Map 17–1). The largest settlement was Quebec, founded in 1608. Since trade rather than settlement generally characterized the French effort, there was little conflict between the French and the Native Americans; some Frenchmen married Native American women. It was primarily through the fur trade that French Canada participated in the early transatlantic economy.

From the first successful settlement in Jamestown, Virginia, in 1607, through the establishment of Georgia in 1733, English colonies spread along the eastern seaboard of the future United States. The Dutch, Swedes, and others founded settlements too, but all of them were taken over during the seventeenth century by the English. Settlements were founded for a variety of reasons. Virginia and New Amsterdam (after 1664, New York) aimed for profits through farming and trade. Others, such as the Carolinas, were developed by royal favorites who were given vast land tracts. James Oglethorpe founded Georgia as a refuge for English debtors. The pursuit of religious liberty was the driving force of the Pilgrim and Puritan founders of Massachusetts, the Baptist Roger Williams in Rhode Island, the Quaker William Penn in Pennsylvania, and the Roman Catholic Lord Baltimore in Maryland.

With the exception of Maryland, these colonies were Protestant. The Church of England dominated the southern colonies. In New England, varieties of Protestantism associated with or derived from Calvinism were in the ascendancy. In their religious affiliations, the English-speaking colonies manifested two important traits derived from the English experience. First, much of their religious life was organized around self-governing congregations. Second, their religious outlook derived from those forms of Protestantism that were suspicious of central political authority. In this regard, their

HOW WERE the economies of the French and British North American colonies integrated into the transatlantic economy?

Read the **Document**
Albanel from Jesuit Relation
at **myhistorylab.com**

See the **Map**
European Empires ca. 1600
at **myhistorylab.com**

Fur Trade. A Native American hands a pelt to a European buyer while two spectators—one European, one Indian—nonchalantly observe the transaction. By 1700 the fur trade had decimated the beaver population in southern Canada and New England.

1777 engraving. © The Granger Collection, New York.

How did the relationships between French traders and Native Americans tend to differ from the relationships between English settlers and Native Americans?

((•●[Hear the Audio
at **myhistorylab.com**

QUICK REVIEW

British North America

- ◆ Jamestown, Virginia: Became first successful British settlement in 1607
- ◆ Religion shaped the organization of British colonies
- ◆ English colonies had a complex relationship with Native Americans

Columbian Exchange
Biological exchange of plants, animals, and diseases between the Americas and the rest of the world.

cultural and political outlook differed sharply from that of the Roman Catholics of the Spanish Empire. In a sense, the ideologies of the extreme Reformation and Counter-Reformation confronted each other in the Americas.

The English colonists had complex interactions with the Native American populations. They had only modest interest in missionary enterprise. New diseases imported from Europe took a high death toll among the native population. North America had no large Native American cities; indigenous populations were dispersed, and intertribal animosity was intense. The English often encountered well-organized resistance, as from the Powhatan conspiracy in Virginia and the Pequots in New England. The most powerful of the Native American groups was the Iroquois Nation, organized in the early eighteenth century in New York. The Iroquois battled successfully against other tribes and long negotiated successfully with both the Dutch and the English. The English often used one tribe against another, and the Native Americans also tried to use the English or the French in their own conflicts. Struggles between the English settlers and the Native Americans rarely resulted in full victory for either side. From the late seventeenth century through the American Revolution, Native American alliances became important for the Anglo-French conflict on the Continent, which was intimately related to their rivalry over transatlantic trade (see Chapter 19).

The economies of the English-speaking colonies were primarily agricultural. From New England through the Middle Atlantic, small farms were mostly tilled by free white labor; from Virginia southward a plantation economy dependent on slavery predominated. The principal ports of Boston, Newport, New York, Philadelphia, Baltimore, and Charleston were the chief centers through which goods moved back and forth between the colonies and England and the West Indies. The commercial economies of these cities were all related to the transatlantic slave trade.

Until the 1760s the political values of the Americans resembled those of their English counterparts. The colonials were thoroughly familiar with events in England and sent many of their children there to be educated. They were monarchists but suspicious of monarchical power. Their politics involved vast amounts of patronage and individual favors. Their society was clearly hierarchical, with an elite that functioned like a colonial aristocracy and many ordinary people who were dependent on that aristocracy. Throughout the colonies during the eighteenth century, the Anglican Church grew in influence and membership. The prosperity of the colonies might eventually have led them to separate from England, but in 1750 few people thought that would occur.

THE COLUMBIAN EXCHANGE: DISEASE, ANIMALS, AND AGRICULTURE

WHAT WAS the "Columbian Exchange"?

The European encounter with the Americas produced remarkable ecological transformations that have shaped the world to the present time (see Map 17–2). Alfred Crosby, the leading historian of the process, has named this cross-continental flow the **Columbian Exchange**.

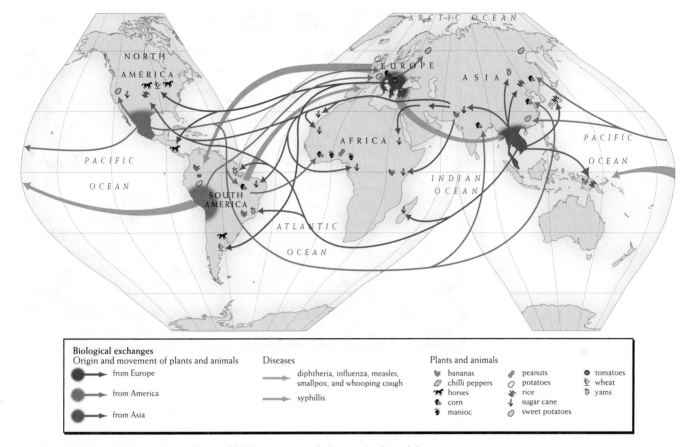

Biological exchanges
Origin and movement of plants and animals

➤ from Europe	
➤ from America	
➤ from Asia	

Diseases

➤ diphtheria, influenza, measles,
  smallpox, and whooping cough

➤ syphillis

Plants and animals

bananas	peanuts	tomatoes
chilli peppers	potatoes	wheat
horses	rice	yams
corn	sugar cane	
manioc	sweet potatoes	

MAP 17–2   Biological Exchanges.   The worldwide movement of plants, animals, and diseases.

How did the Columbian Exchange alter environments around the world?

DISEASES ENTER THE AMERICAS

The American continents had been biologically separated from Europe, Africa, and Asia for tens of thousands of years. The only animal native to the Americas that could serve as a beast of burden was the llama, which could transport only about a hundred pounds. The American continents included vast grassland that lacked grazing animals to transform plants into animal protein. It appears that native peoples had not experienced major epidemics.

By the second voyage of Columbus (1493), that picture began to change in remarkable ways. Columbus brought a number of animals and plants to Hispaniola and other islands of the Caribbean that were previously unknown to the New World. His sailors and the men on subsequent European voyages also carried diseases new to the Americas.

European diseases ultimately played at least as big a role in defeating indigenous Americans as advanced European weaponry did. Much controversy surrounds the question of the actual size of the populations of Native Americans in the Caribbean islands, Mexico, Peru, and the North Atlantic coast. Those populations were significant, with those of Mexico numbering many millions. In the first two centuries after the encounter, wherever Europeans went, extremely large numbers of Native Americans died from diseases they had never before encountered. Smallpox, the most deadly, destroyed millions of people. Bubonic plague, typhoid, typhus, influenza, measles, chicken pox, whooping cough, malaria, and diphtheria produced localized epidemics. An unknown

•●•┤Read the **Document**

Smallpox epidemic in Mexico 1520 and
Smallpox epidemic in New England
at **myhistorylab.com**

Smallpox. Introduced by Europeans to the Americas, smallpox had a devastating effect on Native American populations. It swept through the Aztec capital of Tenochtitlán soon after the Spaniards arrived, contributing to the fall of the city. This illustration of the effect of the plague in the Aztec capital is from a postconquest history known as the Florentine Codex compiled for Spanish church authorities by Aztec survivors.

What other diseases did Europeans bring to the Americas?

disease, possibly typhus, caused major losses among the Native Americans of New England between approximately 1616 and 1619.

On the reverse side of the equation it seems likely that syphilis originated in the New World. Until the discovery of penicillin in the 1940s, this rampant sexually transmitted disease remained a major public health concern throughout the world.

ANIMALS AND AGRICULTURE

The introduction of European livestock revolutionized American agriculture. The most important new animals were pigs, cattle, horses, goats, and sheep. The horse became first

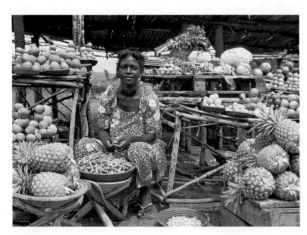

Global Foods. A woman in the African country of Uganda offers beans and pineapples for sale, both of which originated in the Americas.

What other American plants were introduced to Africa?

the animal of conquest and then the animal of colonial Latin American culture. Native Americans had no prior experience with such large animals that would obey the will of a human rider; they were initially fearful of the mounted Spanish horsemen. After the conquest, however, the Americas from Mexico southward became the largest horse-breeding region of the world. By the nineteenth century, the possession of horses allowed the Plains Indians of North America to resist European encroachment. Pigs, cattle, and sheep produced enormous quantities of hides and wool. The Americas from the sixteenth century through the present supported a diet more plentiful in animal protein than anywhere else in the world.

Europeans also brought plants to the New World, including peaches, oranges, grapes, melons, bananas, rice, onions, radishes, and various green vegetables. Sugarcane cultivation created the major demand for slavery. European wheat, over time, allowed the Americas not only to feed themselves but also to export large amounts of grain throughout the world.

The only American animal that came to be raised in Europe was the turkey. The Americas, however, were the source of plants that eventually changed the

OVERVIEW   The Columbian Exchange

To the Americas

Diseases	smallpox, influenza, bubonic plague, typhoid, typhus, measles, chicken pox, malaria, and diphtheria
Animals	pigs, cattle, horses, goats, sheep, chickens
Plants	apples, peaches, pears, apricots, plums, oranges, mangos, lemons, olives, melons, almonds, grapes, bananas, cherries, sugarcane, rice, wheat, oats, barley, onions, radishes, okra, dandelions, cabbages, and other green vegetables

From the Americas

Diseases	syphilis (?)
Animals	turkeys
Plants	maize, tomatoes, sweet peppers, chilis, potatoes, sweet potatoes, squash, pumpkins, manioc (tapioca), beans, cocoa, peanuts, cans, pineapples, guavas, avocados, blueberries, and tobacco

Watch the Video
at **myhistorylab.com**

European diet. Maize and potatoes had the greatest impact. Both crops grow rapidly, supplying food quickly and steadily if not attacked by disease. There is good reason to believe the cultivation of the potato was a major cause of the population increase in eighteenth- and nineteenth-century Europe. Africa received many of these same foodstuffs as well. Maize became a staple in Africa. Tobacco also originated in the Americas.

SLAVERY IN THE AMERICAS

Slavery was the final mode of forced or subservient labor in the New World. Unlike the labor exploitation of Native Americans, enslavement of Africans and their descendants extended throughout the Spanish Empire, Portuguese Brazil, and the English-speaking colonies of North America. The heartland of transatlantic slavery lay in the Caribbean islands.

WHY WAS the transatlantic slave trade so economically important?

THE BACKGROUND OF SLAVERY

Virtually every premodern state around the globe depended on slavery to some extent (see Map 17–3 on page 428). Slave institutions in sub-Saharan Africa were ancient. The Islamic states of southwestern Asia and North Africa imported slaves from both the Sudan and Horn of Africa as well as the East African coast, although they took even more slaves from eastern Europe and Central Asia. Both Mediterranean Christian and Islamic peoples were using slaves—mostly Greeks, Bulgarians, Turkish prisoners of war, and Black Sea Tartars, but also Africans—well before the voyages of discovery opened sub-Saharan sources of slaves for the new European colonies overseas.

Read the Document
Slavery in Africa late 1700s, Mungo Park
at **myhistorylab.com**

Not all forms of slavery were as dehumanizing as the chattel slavery that came to predominate—with the sanction of Christian authorities—in the Americas. Chattel slaves were outright possessions of their masters, indistinguishable from any material possession; they were not recognized as persons under the law, so they had no legal rights; they could not claim any control over their bodies, their time, their labor, or even their own children.

MAP EXPLORATION

To explore this map further, go to **www.myhistorylab.com**

MAP 17–3.   The Slave Trade, 1400–1860.   Slavery is an ancient institution, and complex slave-trading routes were in existence in Africa, the Middle East, and Asia for centuries, but it was the need to supply labor for the plantations of the Americas that led to the greatest movement of peoples across the face of the earth.

How does this map show the global nature of the slave trade?

African societies suffered immense political, economic, and social devastation when they were the chief supplier of slaves to the world. The New World societies that were built to a great extent on the exploitation of African slavery also suffered enduring consequences, including racism.

ESTABLISHMENT OF SLAVERY

As the numbers of Native Americans in South America declined due to disease and exploitation, the Spanish and the Portuguese turned to the labor of imported African slaves. By the late 1500s, in the West Indies and many cities of South America, black slaves surpassed the white population.

On much of the South American continent dominated by Spain, slavery declined during the late seventeenth century, but it continued to thrive in Brazil and in the Caribbean. In British North America, beginning with the importation of slaves to Jamestown in 1619, it quickly became a fundamental institution.

One of the forces that led to the spread of slavery in Brazil and the West Indies was the cultivation of sugar. Sugarcane required a large investment in land and equipment, and only slave labor could provide enough low-cost workers to make the plantations profitable. As the European appetite for sugar grew, so did the slave population. By 1725, black slaves may have constituted almost 90 percent of the population of the West Indies. There and in Brazil and the British colonies in the South, prosperity and slavery went hand in hand. The wealthiest colonies were those that raised consumer staples, such as sugar, rice, tobacco, or cotton, by slave labor.

THE PLANTATION ECONOMY AND TRANSATLANTIC TRADE

The **plantation economy** encompassed plantations that stretched from Maryland through the West Indies and into Brazil. They formed a vast corridor of slave societies in which social and economic subordination was based on both involuntary servitude and race. This kind of society, in its total dependence on slave labor and racial differences, had never existed before. The social and economic influence of plantation slavery persisted through the British effort to outlaw the slave trade during the first half of the nineteenth century, the Latin American wars of independence, the Emancipation Proclamation issued in 1863 in the United States, and the Brazilian emancipation of 1888. Every society in which it existed still contends with its effects.

The slave trade was part of the larger system of transatlantic trade that linked Europe, Africa, and the European colonies in South America, the Caribbean, and North America. The Americas supplied labor-intensive raw materials such as tobacco, sugar, coffee, precious metals, cotton, and indigo. Europe supplied manufactured goods such as textiles, liquor, guns, metal wares, and beads, and cash in various forms. Africa supplied gold, ivory, wood, palm oil, gum, and other products, as well as the slaves whose labor created the American products. By the eighteenth century slaves were Africa's predominant export.

plantation economy
The economic system stretching between the Chesapeake Bay and Brazil that produced crops, especially sugar, cotton, and tobacco, using slave labor on large estates.

SLAVERY ON THE PLANTATIONS

The American plantations to which African slaves arrived were located in rural isolation. The plantation might raise food for its owners and their slaves, but the main production was intended for export. Plantation owners imported virtually all the finished or manufactured goods they used.

The living conditions of plantation slaves varied. Most owners possessed few slaves. Black slaves living in Portuguese areas had the fewest legal protections. In the Spanish colonies the church attempted to provide some protection for black slaves but devoted much more effort to protecting Native Americans. Slave codes were developed in the British and the French colonies during the seventeenth century, but they provided only the most limited protection. Virtually all slave owners feared a slave revolt; slave laws favored the master rather than the slave. Masters were permitted to

⊙ See the **Map**
Atlantic Slave Trade
at **myhistorylab.com**

•••• Read the **Document**
Overseer in Cotton Plantation
at **myhistorylab.com**

African American Culture. This eighteenth-century painting depicts a celebration in the slave quarters on a South Carolina plantation. One planter's description of a slave dance seems to fit this scene: the men leading the women in "a slow shuffling gait, edging along by some unseen exertion of the feet, from one side to the other—sometimes curtseying down and remaining in that posture while the edging motion from one side to the other continued." The women, he wrote, "always carried a handkerchief held at arm's length, which was waved in a graceful motion to and fro as she moved."

Abby Aldrich Rockefeller Folk Art Museum, Colonial Williamsburg Foundation, VA.

Why did slave owners suppress traditional African religious practices?

punish slaves by whipping and other harsh corporal punishment, and slaves were often forbidden to gather in groups lest they plan a revolt. Slave marriages generally had no legal standing. The child of an enslaved woman was born a slave, the property of the mother's owner. Owners could separate slave families.

The daily life of most slaves was one of hard agricultural labor, poor diet and clothing, and inadequate housing. The death rate among slaves was high. Their welfare and their lives were sacrificed to make their owners wealthy and to produce the goods demanded by consumers in Europe.

The African slaves who were transported to the Americas were, like the Native Americans, converted to Christianity: in the Spanish domains to Roman Catholicism, and in the English colonies to Protestantism. They were forbidden to practice their traditional faiths: Activities that were not directly related to economic production, or that suggested links to African culture, were suppressed. Some African practices survived in muted forms, however, and slaves managed to mix African religion with Christianity.

European settlers and slave traders were prejudiced against black Africans. Many Europeans thought Africans were savage, and many European languages attached negative connotations to blackness. In virtually all plantation societies, race was an important element in keeping black slaves subservient. Although racial thinking in regard to slavery became more important in the nineteenth century, the fact that slaves were differentiated from the rest of the population by race as well as by their status as chattel property was fundamental to the system.

AFRICA AND THE TRANSATLANTIC SLAVE TRADE

HOW DID the slave trade impact Africa?

The establishment of plantations reliant on slave labor drew Africa and its peoples into the heart of the transatlantic economy. The Portuguese were the principal carriers early in the African slave trade. Their virtual monopoly was broken by the Dutch in the 1640s. The French and the English came into the trade later, yet during the eighteenth century, which saw the greatest number of slaves shipped, they carried almost half the total traffic. Americans, too, were avid slavers who managed to make considerable profits, even after Britain and the United States outlawed the transatlantic slave trade in 1807 and 1808, respectively.

Slaving was an important part of the massive new overseas trade that financed much European and American economic development during the nineteenth century. The success and considerable profits of this trade, bought at the price of immense human suffering, helped propel Europe and some of its colonial offshoots in the Americas into world dominance.

SLAVERY AND SLAVING IN AFRICA

The trade that supplied African slaves to the Mediterranean and Asia long before the fifteenth century has conventionally been termed the "Oriental" slave trade. The Sudan and the Horn of Africa were the main sources of slaves for this trade. The Afro-European trade, conventionally called the **"Occidental" slave trade**, can be traced at

"Occidental" slave trade
The trade in slaves from Africa to the Islamic Mediterranean and Asia that predated the transatlantic slave trade.

least to the thirteenth century, when Europeans established sugarcane plantations on Cyprus. This industry subsequently spread westward to Crete and Sicily and, in the fifteenth century, to the Portuguese Atlantic islands of Madeira and São Tomé. The Portuguese developed the plantation system of slave labor as they began their expansion into the Atlantic. Voyages beginning in the fifteenth century by the Portuguese and other Europeans made the western coasts of Africa as far south as Angola the prime slaving areas. A less important source region for both Occidental and Oriental trades was the eastern coast of Africa below the Horn.

Prior to the full development of the transatlantic slave trade, slavery and slave trading had been no more significant in Africa than anywhere else in the world.[2] Indigenous African slavery resembled that of other premodern societies. Probably about 10,000 slaves per year, most of them female, were taken from sub-Saharan Africa through the Oriental slave trade.

By about 1650 the Occidental slave trade had become as large as the Oriental trade and for the ensuing two centuries far surpassed it. It affected all of Africa, disrupting especially western and central African societies. As a result of the demand for young male slaves on the plantations of the Americas, West Africa experienced a sharp drain on its productive male population. Moreover, as the external trade destroyed the regional male–female population balance, an internal market for female slaves arose. Internal warfare in western and central Africa increased. These developments accelerated during the eighteenth century. Slave prices increased. Owing to population depletion and regional migrations, however, the actual number of slaves sold declined in some areas.

As European and American nations slowly began to outlaw first the slave trade and then slavery itself in the nineteenth century, the Oriental and internal trades increased. Slave exports from East Africa and the Sudan and Horn increased significantly after about 1780, and indigenous African slavery, predominantly of women, also expanded. By about 1850 the internal African trade surpassed the combined Oriental and (outlawed) Occidental trade. This traffic was dominated by the same figures— merchants, warlords, and rulers—who had previously profited from external trade.

African slavery began a real decline only at the end of the nineteenth century, in part because of the dominance of European colonial regimes and in part because of internal changes. The formal end of African indigenous slavery occurred only in 1928 in Sierra Leone. Late in the twentieth century, however, in various locations around the world—mostly places with endemic, severe poverty and weak civil authority, including the Sudan—patterns of involuntary servitude and human trafficking emerged that constitute modern-day slavery.

CHRONOLOGY

CONQUEST OF THE AMERICAS AND THE TRANSATLANTIC SLAVE TRADE

1494	Treaty of Tordesillas divides the seaborne empires of Spain and Portugal
1500	The Portuguese arrive in Brazil
1519–1521	Hernán Cortés conquers the Aztec Empire
1531–1533	Francisco Pizarro conquers the Inca Empire
1607	Jamestown, Virginia, first permanent English settlement in North America
1608	The French found Quebec
1619	First African slaves brought to British North America
1700s	Over 6 million slaves imported from Africa to the Americas
1794	Slavery abolished throughout the French Empire
1807	The importation of slaves abolished in British domains
1808	The importation of slaves abolished in the United States
1817–1820	Spain abolishes the slave trade
1833	Slavery abolished throughout the British Empire
1850	Importation of slaves abolished in Brazil
1874–1928	Indigenous African slavery abolished
1888	Slavery abolished in Brazil

View the Image
West African Slave Market
at **myhistorylab.com**

---

[2]The summary follows closely that of P. Manning, *Slavery and African Life: Occidental, Oriental, and African Slave Trades* (Cambridge: Cambridge University Press, 1990), pp. 127–140.

King Affonso I of the Kongo holds an audience with European ambassadors who kneel before him.

What roles did Africans play in the transatlantic slave trade?

THE AFRICAN SIDE OF THE TRANSATLANTIC TRADE

Africans were actively involved in the transatlantic slave trade. Except for the Portuguese in central Africa, European slave traders generally obtained their human cargoes from Africans at coastal forts or simply at anchorages along the coast. Africans were motivated to control the inland trade, and Europeans were vulnerable to tropical disease. Thus it was largely African middlemen who undertook the actual capture or procurement of slaves and the difficult, dangerous task of marching them to the coast. These middlemen were generally either wealthy merchants who could mount slaving expeditions inland or the agents of African kingdoms who sought to profit from the trade.

The media of exchange for slaves varied. At first they usually involved mixed barter for goods that ranged from gold dust or firearms to beads and alcohol. As time went on they came increasingly to involve monetary payment. This exchange drained productive resources (human beings) from Africa in return for nonproductive wealth.

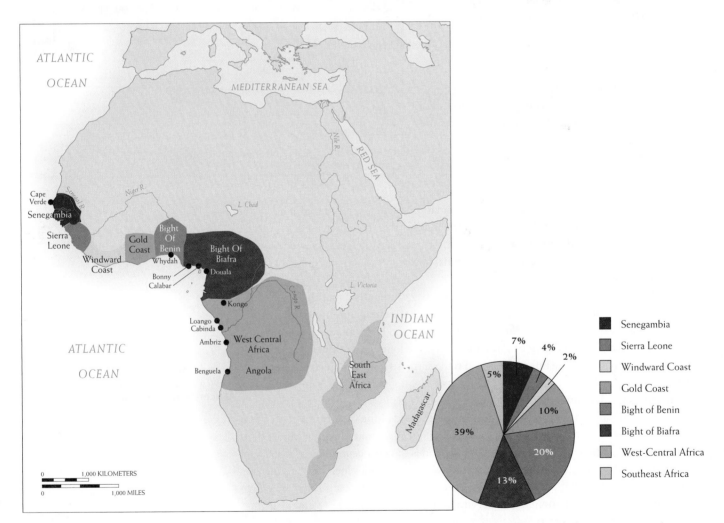

MAP 17–4   Origins of African Slaves Sent to the Americas.   Captive Africans came from eight regions. West Central Africa sent more captives to the Americas than any other region.

What factors influenced the origins of enslaved Africans?

The chief western and central African slaving regions provided different numbers of slaves at different times, and the total number of exported slaves varied sharply between periods (see Map 17–4). When one area was unable to produce sufficient numbers to meet demand, the European traders shifted their buying to other points. Between 1526 and 1550 the major sources of slaves for the transatlantic trade were the Kongo-Angola region (34 percent), the Guinea coast of Cape Verde (25.6 percent), and Senegambia (23.5 percent).[3] By contrast, between 1761 and 1810 the French drew some 52 percent of their slaves from Angola and 24 percent from the Bight of Benin, but only 4.8 percent from Senegambia, whereas the British relied most heavily on the Bight of Biafra and central Africa.[4] Traders naturally went where population density and the presence of active African suppliers promised the most slaves and the lowest prices, although prices do not seem to have varied radically in a given period.

THE EXTENT OF THE SLAVE TRADE

The overall number of African slaves exported during the Occidental trade—effectively between 1451 and 1870—is still debated. A major unknown for both the Occidental and the Oriental trades is the number of slaves who died under the brutal conditions to which they were subjected when captured and transported overland and by sea. The **Middle Passage**, the portion of the journey in which Africans were packed onto dangerous and unhealthy boats for the voyage across the Atlantic Ocean, claimed untold numbers; others were lost to other forms of brutality associated with the trade. (See Document, "A Slave Trader Describes the Atlantic Passage" on page 434.)

Historians now estimate that from the sixteenth through the nineteenth century over 35,000 transatlantic slave ship voyages forcibly transported more than 11 million Africans to America. The slave trade varied sharply in extent from period to period (see Figure 17–1). The period of greatest activity, from 1701 to 1810, accounted for over 60 percent of the total. Despite Great Britain's abolition of the slave trade in its colonies in 1807 and the United States' abolition of the slave trade in 1808, the Portuguese still transported more than a million slaves to Brazil between 1811 and 1870. Other nations also continued to trade in slaves in the nineteenth century. In fact, more slaves landed in the Americas in the final years of the trade than during the entire seventeenth century.[5]

Estimates for the older, smaller, and more dispersed Oriental trade are even more problematic, but a figure of million or more is probably realistic. According to one expert's estimate, an additional 15 million people were enslaved within African societies themselves.[6]

Middle Passage

The transatlantic crossing of ships carrying slaves from Africa to the Americas and Caribbean.

View the Image

Diagram: Slave Ship Filled for Middle Passage at **myhistorylab.com**

FIGURE 17–1. The Atlantic Slave Trade, 1400–1800. From Caizares-Esguerra, Jorge; Seeman, Eric, The Atlantic in Global History; 1500–2000, © 2007. Electronically reproduced by permission of Pearson Education, Inc., Upper Saddle River, New Jersey.

Why did the slave trade increase so dramatically in the eighteenth century?

---

[3]Scholars have spent decades attempting to assemble trustworthy statistics on the slave trade; the database by Eltis et al., *The Trans-Atlantic Slave Trade: A Database on CD-ROM* (Cambridge and New York: Cambridge University Press, revised 2008), has marshaled a great deal of information in one spot, but new data continue to emerge. Philip Curtin, *The Atlantic Slave Trade: A Census* (Madison: University of Wisconsin Press, 1969), provided the first detailed analysis of the various proposed figures for the slave trade; see especially p. 101.

[4]Curtin, *The Atlantic Slave Trade*, pp. 101, 129; James A. Rawley, *The Trans-Atlantic Slave Trade: A History* (New York: W. W. Norton, 1981), p. 129. Note that precise statistics are subject to revision in light of more recent scholarship; see, for example, Eltis et al., *The Trans-Atlantic Slave Trade: A Database on CD-ROM*.

[5]Rawley, *The Transatlantic Slave Trade*, p. 429; Curtin, *Atlantic Slave Trade*, p. 268.

[6]Manning, *Slavery and African Life*, pp. 37, 170–171.

DOCUMENT

A Slave Trader Describes the Atlantic Passage

During 1693 and 1694, Captain Thomas Phillips carried slaves from Africa to Barbados on the ship Hannibal. The financial backer of the voyage was the Royal African Company of London, which held an English crown monopoly on slave trading. Phillips sailed to the west coast of Africa, where he purchased the Africans who were sold into slavery by an African king. Then he set sail westward.

- **Who** are the various people described in this document who in one way or another were involved in or profited from the slave trade? What dangers did the Africans face on the voyage? What contemporary attitudes could have led this captain to treat and think of his human cargo simply as goods to be transported? What are the grounds of his self-pity for the difficulties he met?

Having bought my complement of 700 slaves, 480 men and 220 women, and finish'd all my business at Whidaw [on the Gold Coast of Africa], I took my leave of the old king and his *cappasheirs* [attendants], and parted, with many affectionate expressions on both sides, being forced to promise him that I would return again the next year, with several things he desired me to bring from England. . . . I set sail the 27th of July in the morning, accompany'd with the East-India Merchant, who had bought 650 slaves, for the Island of St. Thomas. . . . from which we took our departure on August 25th and set sail for Barbadoes.

We spent in our passage from St. Thomas to Barbadoes two months eleven days, from the 25th of August to the 4th of November following: in which time there happened such sickness and mortality among my poor men and Negroes. Of the first we buried 14, and of the last 320, which was a great detriment to our voyage, the Royal African Company losing ten pounds by every slave that died, and the owners of the ship ten pounds ten shillings, being

the freight agreed on to be paid by the charter-party for every Negro delivered alive ashore to the African Company's agents at Barbadoes. . . . The loss in all amounted to near 6500 pounds sterling.

The distemper which my men as well as the blacks mostly died of was the white flux, which was so violent and inveterate that no medicine would in the least check it, so that when any of our men were seized with it, we esteemed him a dead man, as he generally proved. . . .

The Negroes are so incident to [subject to] the small-pox that few ships that carry them escape without it, and sometimes it makes vast havoc and destruction among them. But tho' we had 100 at a time sick of it, and that it went thro' the ship, yet we lost not above a dozen by it. All the assistance we gave the diseased was only as much water as they desir'd to drink, and some palm-oil to annoint their sores, and they would generally recover without any other helps but what kind nature gave them. . . .

But what the smallpox spar'd, the flux swept off, to our great regret, after all our pains and care to give them their messes in due order and season, keeping their lodgings as clean and sweet as possible, and enduring so much misery and stench so long among a parcel of creatures nastier than swine, and after all our expectations to be defeated by their mortality. . . .

No gold-finders can endure so much noisome slavery as they do who carry Negroes; for those have some respite and satisfaction, but we endure twice the misery; and yet by their mortality our voyages are ruin'd, and we pine and fret ourselves to death, and take so much pains to so little purpose.

Source: From Thomas Phillips, "Journal," *A Collection of Voyages and Travels*, Vol. 6, ed. by Awnsham and John Churchill (London, 1746), as quoted in Thomas Howard, ed., *Black Voyage: Eyewitness Accounts of the Atlantic Slave Trade* (Boston: Little, Brown, and Company, 1971), pp. 85–87.

A Closer Look

The Slave Ship *Brookes*

This print, published in 1788 in England by the Plymouth Chapter of the Society for Effecting the Abolition of the Slave Trade, became the single most important and widely circulated abolitionist image of the horrific conditions of the Middle Passage. It records the main decks of the 320-ton slave ship *Brookes*, which measured 25 feet wide and 100 feet long.

The average space for each African destined for slavery in the Americas was 78 inches by 16 inches. The Africans were normally shackled to assure discipline and to prevent their injuring the crew. Iron shackles also prevented Africans from committing suicide on the voyage.

Through the most inhumane use of space efficiency, 609 slaves could be crammed onboard for the nightmarish passage to America. A Parliamentary inquiry in 1788 found that the ship had been designed to carry no more than approximately 450 persons.

(See Document *"A Slave Trader Describes the Atlantic Passage."***)**

Questions

1. What response is this image, showing the crowded conditions on the slave ship *Brookes*, expected to arouse in the viewer? How do you think the response of viewers in the early twenty-first century might differ from those in the late-eighteenth and early-nineteenth centuries?

2. In recent years some commentators have criticized this image as indicating passivity on the part of the enslaved Africans and activity only on the part of the abolitionists. Why might this interpretation be directed toward the image?

3. Do you think that British viewers of this image of the *Brookes* would necessarily have associated their own nation with the slave trade? Why or why not?

Job ben Solomon. Captured by Mandingo enemies and sold to a Maryland tobacco planter, Job ben Solomon accomplished the nearly impossible feat of returning to Africa as a freeman. By demonstrating his talents as a Muslim scholar, including his ability to write the entire Qur'an from memory, he astonished his owners and eventually convinced them to let him go home.

"The Fortunate Slave," An Illustration of African Slavery in the early eighteenth century by Douglas Grant (1968). From "Some Memoirs of the Life of Job," by Thomas Bluett 1734. Photo by Robert D. Rubic/Precision Chromes, Inc., Rare Books Division, the New York Public Library, Lenox and Tilden Foundations/Art Resource, New York.

What was a more typical fate for a slave in the Americas?

QUICK REVIEW

Difficulties in Determining Consequences of the Slave Trade

- Do not know how the slave trade affected specific West African regions
- Cannot determine number of slaves captured during wars and captured during slave raiding
- Do not know how slave trading affected commerce in African products

CONSEQUENCES OF THE SLAVE TRADE FOR AFRICA

These statistics hint at the massive impact slave trading had on African life and history. The question of specific effects remains difficult.

We cannot be certain whether the transatlantic trade brought net population loss or gain to specific areas of West Africa. The wide and rapid spread of maize and cassava cultivation after these plants had been imported from the Americas may have fueled African population increases that offset slave-trade losses. We know, however, that slaving took away many of the strongest young men in various areas and, in the Oriental trade zones, most of the young women.

Similarly, we do not know if more slaves were captured as by-products of local wars or from targeted slave raiding. Nor do we know if slaving always inhibited development of trade or perhaps sometimes stimulated it because commerce in a range of African products—from ivory to wood and hides—often accompanied that in slaves. We do know that the exchange of productive human beings for money or goods that were generally not used to build a productive economy was a great loss for African society as a whole.

Finally, because we do not yet have accurate estimates of the total population of Africa at different times over the four centuries of the transatlantic slave trade, we cannot determine with certainty its demographic impact. We can, however, make some educated guesses. If, for example, tropical Africa had possibly 50 million inhabitants in 1600, it would then have had 30 percent of the combined population of the Americas, the Middle East, Europe, and North Africa. If in 1900, after the depredations of the slave trade, it had 70 million inhabitants, its population would have dropped to only slightly more than 10 percent of the combined population of the same world regions. Accordingly, current best estimates indicate that overall African population growth suffered significantly as a result of the devastating numbers of people lost to enslavement or to the increased warfare and decreased birthrate tied to the slave trade. Figures like these also give some idea of slavery's probable impact on Africa's ability to engage with developments that, elsewhere in the world, led to the emergence of the modern industrializing world.[7]

It is important to remember that even in West and central Africa, which bore the brunt of the transatlantic trade, its impact and the response to it were varied. In a few cases, kingdoms such as Dahomey (the present Republic of Benin) seem to have sought and derived immense economic profit by making slaving a state monopoly. Other kingdoms, such as Benin, sought to stay almost completely out of slaving. In instances including the rise of Asante power or the fall of the Yoruba Oyo Empire, it appears that increased slaving was a result as well as a cause of regional instability and change. Increased warfare meant increased prisoners to be enslaved and a surplus to be sold off. Whether slaving was a motive for war is still an unanswered question.

Similarly, the consequences of the major increase in indigenous slavery are unknown, and they varied with the specifics of regional situations. For example, in West Africa relatively more men were taken as slaves than women, whereas in the Sahelian Sudanic regions relatively more women than men were taken. In the west the loss of so many men increased the pressures for polygamy, whereas in the Sahelian Sudanic regions the loss of women may have stimulated polyandry and reduced the birthrate significantly.

---

[7]On all of the preceding points regarding the probable impact of the trade, see Manning, *Slavery and African Life*, pp. 126–148, 168–176. Also consult Eltis et al., *The Trans-Atlantic Slave Trade: A Database on CD-ROM.*

Even though slavery existed previously in Africa, the scale of the transatlantic trade was unprecedented and, hence, had an unprecedented impact on indigenous social, political, and economic realities. The slave trade measurably changed patterns of life and balances of power, whether by stimulating trade or warfare, by disrupting previous market and political structures, by substantially increasing slavery inside Africa, or by disturbing the male–female ratio and, consequently, the workforce balance and birthrate patterns. The overseas slave trade siphoned indigenous energy into ultimately counterproductive or destructive directions. True economic development was inhibited, especially in central and coastal West Africa. The transatlantic slave trade must by any standard be described as one of the most tragic aspects of European involvement in Africa.

Watch the Video
at **myhistorylab.com**

SUMMARY

 WHAT WERE the four periods of European contact with the world?

Periods of European Overseas Expansion. Europe's disproportionate influence on world history has gone through four phases: conquest and commercial exploitation (roughly 1500–1700); trade rivalry, especially among Spain, France, and Great Britain (roughly 1700–1820); European colonization in Africa and Asia (nineteenth century and first half of twentieth century); and decolonization (mid-twentieth century). *page 417*

WHAT WAS mercantilism?

Mercantilist Theory of Economic Exploitation. Early European empires were based on mercantilism, the idea that the nation could be enriched by controlling trade with colonial markets. *page 417*

 WHAT ROLES did the Roman Catholic Church play in Spanish America?

Establishment of the Spanish Empire in America. Within half a century of the landing of Columbus, millions of America's native peoples had encountered Europeans intent on conquest, exploitation, and religious conversion. Because of their advanced weapons, navies, and the new diseases they brought with them, as well as internal divisions among the Native Americans, the Europeans achieved a rapid conquest. The Roman Catholic Church was generally aligned with the conquerers, but some priests became advocates for Native Americans. *page 418*

 HOW DID Spaniards attempt to control labor in the Americas?

Economies of Exploitation in the Spanish Empire. In Spanish America, various institutions were developed to extract native labor. The *flota*, controlled by administrators in Seville, sought to monopolize trade. *page 420*

 HOW WERE sugar and slavery entwined in colonial Brazil?

Colonial Brazil. Brazil was Portugal's largest American holding. The Brazilian economy was dominated by sugarcane, which depended on African slave labor. *page 422*

 HOW WERE the economies of the French and British North American colonies integrated into the transatlantic economy?

French and British Colonies in North America. Early French colonists were few in number. They were more interested in commerce (especially transatlantic fur-trading) and Christianity than in settlement, so their relationships with Native Americans were relatively nonconfrontational. English colonists were mostly agriculturalists who had varied and complicated interactions with Native American populations. The economies of North America's port cities were intertwined with the transatlantic slave trade. *page 423*

WHAT WAS the "Columbian Exchange"?

The Columbian Exchange: Disease, Animals, and Agriculture. Until the European explorations, the civilizations of the Americas, Eurasia, and Africa had had no significant contact with each other. Native Americans had no immunity to several significant European diseases, so many died. Exchanges of plants and animals transformed agriculture in the Americas, Europe, and Africa. *page 424*

 WHY WAS the transatlantic slave trade so economically important?

Slavery in the Americas. From the Mid-Atlantic English colonies through the Caribbean and into Brazil, slave-labor plantation systems were established. The economies and peoples of Europe, Africa, and the Americas were thus drawn into a vast worldwide web of production based on slave labor. *page 427*

HOW DID the slave trade impact Africa?

Africa and the Transatlantic Slave Trade. On the African continent, the impact of the slave trade was immense, though difficult to document specifically. The social, economic, and personal effects were enormous, given the extent and duration of the trade. The loss of population and productive resources helped set the stage for European colonization. The Atlantic slave trade's impact continues to be felt at both ends of the original "trade." *page 430*

KEY TERMS

Black Legend (p. 419)
Columbian Exchange (p. 424)
conquistadores (kon-KEES-tuh-DOR-ays) (p. 420)
debt peonage (p. 420)
encomienda **(EN-koh-MYEN-dah)** (p. 420)
hacienda (HAH-see-EN-dah) (p. 420)

mercantilism (MUR-kuhn-tihl-izm) (p. 418)
Middle Passage (p. 433)
"Occidental" slave trade (p. 430)
peninsulares (p. 420)
plantation economy (p. 429)
repartimiento **(ray-PAHR-tih-MYEN-toh)** (p. 420)

REVIEW QUESTIONS

1. How were small groups of Spaniards able to conquer the Aztec and Inca Empires?

2. What was the basis of the mercantilist theory of economics? What was the relationship between the colonial economies and those of the homelands?

3. What was the relationship between conquistadores and missionaries in Spain's American colonies?

4. Describe the economies of Spanish America and Brazil. What were the similarities and differences between them and the British and French colonies in the Caribbean and North America? What role did the various colonies play in the transatlantic economy?

5. Explain the chief factors involved in the Columbian Exchange. Which animals from Europe flourished in the Americas? Why? Which American plants produced broad impact in Europe and elsewhere in the world?

6. Why did forced labor and slavery develop in tropical colonies? How was slavery in the Americas different from slavery in earlier societies?

7. What historical patterns emerged in the slave trade(s) within and out of Africa? Consider the gender and age distribution of slaves, their places of origin, and their destinations.

8. Compare and contrast the Oriental and Occidental slave trades. What was the effect of the transatlantic slave trade on West African societies? On East Africa? What role did Africans themselves play in the slave trade?

Note: To learn more about the topics in this chapter, please turn to the Suggested Readings at the end of the book. For additional sources related to this chapter please see www.myhistorylab.com

PEARSON
myhistorylab Connections

Reinforce what you learned in this chapter by studying the many documents,
images, maps, review tools, and videos available at **www.myhistorylab.com**

Read and Review

✓—[Study and Review   Chapter 17

•◦•—[Read the Document   *2nd Letter, Hernan Cortez to King Charles V, p. 418*

del Castillo, History of Conquest, p. 418

New Laws Indies for Good Treatment 2, p. 419

Account of Devastation of Indies, p. 419

Albanel from Jesuit Relation, p. 423

Smallpox epidemic in Mexico 1520 and Smallpox epidemic in New England, p. 425

Slavery in Africa late 1700s, Mungo Park, p. 427

Overseer in Cotton Plantation, p. 429

👁—[See the Map   *Spanish and Portuguese Exploration, p. 422*

European Empires ca. 1600, p. 423

Atlantic Slave Trade, p. 429

◉—[View the Image   *West African Slave Market, p. 431*

Diagram: Slave Ship Filled for Middle Passage, p. 433

Research and Explore

◉—[Watch the Video   *Columbian Exchange, p. 427*

◉—[Watch the Video   *Triangle Trade Routes, p. 437*

((•—[Hear the Audio

Hear the audio file for Chapter 17
at **www.myhistorylab.com**

18

East Asia in the Late Traditional Era

((•─[Hear the Audio for Chapter 18 at www.myhistorylab.com

Seventeenth-century screen painting of a Shintō river festival in Tsushima (a town near Nagoya city) held annually in July to ward off epidemics in the heat of the summer. Among the throng of spectators at the river's edge are shopkeepers, other townspeople, Buddhist priests, and palanquin bearers (at the left). Of the five boats on the river (which are not shown), each with 550 lanterns, only one mast with five red lanterns can be seen at the center of the panel.

Tosa (attributed to): people along the river. Detail from screen representing the River Festival. 17th century. Painting on paper. Photo: Arnaudet. Musee des Arts Asiatiques-Guimet, Paris, France. Reunion des Musees Nationaux/Art Resource, New York.

What overall impression of Japanese society is conveyed by this painting?

LATE IMPERIAL CHINA

MING (1368–1644) AND QING (1644–1911) DYNASTIES *page 442*

WHERE DID China expand under the Qing?

JAPAN

WARRING STATES ERA (1467–1600) *page 453*

WHAT IMPACT did military technology have on Japanese society in this period?

TOKUGAWA ERA (1600–1868) *page 456*

HOW WAS Japanese culture transformed during the Tokugawa era?

KOREA AND VIETNAM

KOREA *page 466*

WHAT WAS Korea's relationship to China?

VIETNAM *page 469*

HOW DID Vietnam expand southward during this time?

E*ast Asian countries shared cultural traits. A range of social values was shared, at least by the elites. To the extent that it was based on Confucianism, the similarity may have been greatest in the mid-nineteenth century, when China, Japan, Korea, and Vietnam had become more Confucian than ever before.*

But when we examine histories and institutions, the similarities are fewer. China and Japan were furthest apart. Korea and Vietnam, even while forging an identity in reaction to their borrowings from China, were more directly influenced by China. Tang Dynasty China (618–907) had forged a pattern of government so efficient and closely geared to the deeper familial and educational constitution of the society that it was rebuilt after each dynastic breakdown. The histories of the Ming (1368–1644) and the Qing (1644–1911) dynasties have a recognizable cyclical cast, though they also demonstrate historical trends that cut across dynastic lines. Japanese political history, in contrast, is not cyclical. The Nara, early Heian, Kamakura bakufu, Ashikaga, Warring States, and "feudal" periods of Japanese history each reflect a new and different configuration. Like Europe, Japan never found a pattern of rule that worked so well and was so deeply embedded in the institutions of the society that it was re-created over and over again.

This chapter underlines the dynamism of both China and Japan during these late centuries. In both countries society became more integrated, and the apparatus of government more sophisticated than ever before. Korea and Vietnam did not lack dynamism, though they

EAST ASIA IN THE LATE TRADITIONAL ERA

Why did the West, and not East Asia or any other region, open the door to modernity? Why did an industrial revolution not develop within the sophisticated commercial economies of Japan and China? The answer, obviously, must be found within Western history. Still, a few comparisons with the West may illuminate aspects of premodern East Asia.

1. The sociologist Max Weber saw Western capitalism as inspired by the Protestant ethic—which he found lacking in India, China, and Catholic Europe. But is the East Asian family-centered ethic of frugality, savings, and hard work not a "Protestant ethic" of sorts? And if a deeper Calvinist anxiety about salvation is required, as Weber theorized, then why has East Asia achieved such explosive growth since World War II?

2. Was the Scientific Revolution of the seventeenth century critical to the industrial revolution? Some historians say that industry was well under way before science began to make a substantial contribution from the late nineteenth century.

3. The self-educated technicians of England who invented the water loom and steam engine reaped enormous honors and rewards. In China and Japan no patents protected inventors, and no economists wrote of inventors as the benefactors of society. Wealth and honors were reserved for officials and gentry, who were literary and political in orientation and despised those who worked with their hands. (Of course, in earlier dynasties, Chinese had been brilliantly inventive without patent protection.)

4. Bureaucracy is sometimes viewed as a key component of modernity. Bureaucracy does for administration what the assembly line does for production: It breaks complex tasks into simple ones, to achieve huge gains in efficiency. In the West bureaucracies appeared only in recent centuries. They strengthened monarchies and nation-states against landed aristocrats; they represented the triumph of ability over hereditary privilege. Chinese bureaucrats shared many of the same virtues. They were an elite of talent educated in the Confucian classics as British officials were educated in those of Greece and Rome. But they were somehow different. They had wielded power for at least a millennium

also had problems aplenty. But we must note that, in the West, the Renaissance, the Reformation, the Scientific Revolution, the formation of nation-states, the industrial revolution, the Enlightenment, and the democratic revolution happened while the Ming and the Qing dynasties were reigning in China. All these developments, in the East and in the West, shaped East Asian responses to the West during the nineteenth century. ■

LATE IMPERIAL CHINA

MING (1368–1644) AND QING (1644–1911) DYNASTIES

WHERE DID China expand under the Qing?

The Ming and the Qing were China's last dynasties. The Ming was Chinese, whereas the Qing was a foreign dynasty (Manchus) established by conquest. The two were nevertheless remarkably similar in their institutions and pattern of rule; historians sometimes speak of "Ming–Qing despotism" as if it were a single system. Certain demographic and economic trends also exhibited striking continuities through the Ming and Qing dynasties.

LAND AND PEOPLE

China's population reached about 410 million people in the mid-nineteenth century, from a level of 60 to 90 million at the start of the Ming Dynasty (1368). This population density stimulated commerce and gave new prominence to the scholar-gentry class.

An increase in the food supply paralleled population growth. During the Ming, the spread of Song agricultural technology and new strains of rice accounted and were a segment of the landed gentry class in a country from which hereditary aristocrats had long since disappeared. Despite their talent, in the nineteenth century they would constitute a major obstacle to modernity. Were samurai bureaucrats of the Tokugawa era closer to their Western counterparts?

Putting aside comparisons with Europe, we also note the difference between Chinese and Japanese attitudes toward outside civilizations. When the Jesuits tried to introduce science, the Chinese response was occasional curiosity and general indifference. A few Jesuits were appointed as interpreters or court astronomers or were used to cast cannons for China's armies. The Chinese lack of interest in foreign cultures can be explained by the coherence of China's core institutions: the emperor, bureaucracy, examination system, Confucian schools, and gentry. These were so deeply rooted and highly appreciated as to constitute a closed system. In contrast, despite a national policy of seclusion, the Japanese reached out for Dutch medicine and science—as they had earlier reached out for Chinese Neo-Confucianism.

In the middle of the nineteenth century, this openness helps explain Japan's rapid advance.

That Vietnam and Korea did not achieve industrial revolutions requires less explanation. They were smaller and less commercially developed than China or Japan. Vietnam was preoccupied with wars and its expansion to the south. In Korea—sometimes called the "hermit Kingdom"—the elites were open only to Chinese culture and engaged in endless factional struggles.

Focus Questions

◆ What features of Japan or China, other than those mentioned above, bear on their lack of progress from commerce to industry? What other factors presented in the chapters on Europe are relevant?

◆ Why was Tokugawa Japan more open to Western learning than Qing China? Was population a positive, a negative, or a neutral factor?

for 40 percent of the higher yields, and newly cultivated lands accounted for the rest. During the Qing, half the increased food supply was due to new lands and the other half to better seeds, fertilizers, and irrigation. New crops introduced from the Americas during the late Ming, such as maize, sweet potatoes, and peanuts, also bolstered the food supply.

In north China the population had declined from 32 million to 11 million during the Mongol conquests. The Ming government repopulated its open lands; the movement of people to the north continued until the nineteenth century. In the north, most farmers owned the land they worked and at times used hired labor. The land consisted mainly of irrigated dry fields, and the chief crops were millet, sorghum, and wheat.

South and southwest China also saw an influx of migrants from the densely populated lower Yangzi region, many settling in agriculturally marginal foothills. Other Chinese crossed over to Taiwan or emigrated overseas. During the Qing Dynasty, large Chinese mercantile communities became established in Southeast Asia.

The Yangzi basin, meanwhile, became even more densely populated. The lower Yangzi region and the delta, well supplied with waterways, had long been the rice basket of China, but from the late Ming agricultural cash crops, such as silk and cotton, predominated. Absentee landlords owned almost half of the land. South China also had extensive absentee landlordism, but far more land was owned collectively by clans.

There are many unanswered questions regarding the population growth during these centuries. Was there a decline in the death rate? Or did the development of new lands and technology enable more mouths to be fed? Certainly, the Ming–Qing era was the longest continuous period of good government in Chinese history. How much did good governance contribute to population growth? The growth of China's population more than overcame losses to plagues and epidemics in 1586–1589, 1639–1644, 1756, and 1820–1822. Because of the growth in agriculture and population, most accounts view the eighteenth century as the most prosperous in Chinese history. But by the early

◉ See the Map
Ming and Qing China
at **myhistorylab.com**

nineteenth century the Chinese standard of living may have begun to decline. An ever-increasing population was no blessing.

CHINA'S THIRD COMMERCIAL REVOLUTION

Commerce in China expanded and contracted cyclically. Early Ming emperors were isolationists with an agrarian orientation. They established government monopolies that stifled enterprise and depressed the southeastern coastal region by restricting maritime trade and shipping. In the mid-sixteenth century, commerce started to grow again, buoyed by the surge of population and agriculture and a relaxation of government controls. If the growth during the Han and Song dynasties may be called China's first and second commercial revolutions, then the expansion between 1500 and 1800 was its third. By the early nineteenth century, China was the most highly commercialized nonindustrial society in the world.

One stimulus to commerce was imported silver. The Chinese balance of trade was favorable. Beginning in the mid-sixteenth century, silver from Japan entered China, and from the 1570s, Spanish galleons brought in Mexican and Peruvian silver. In the eighteenth century, private **Shanxi banks** opened branches throughout China to facilitate the transfer of funds and extend credit for trade.

The influx of silver and the overall increase in liquidity led to inflation in China, as it did in Europe. The price of land rose steadily. During the sixteenth century the

Shanxi banks
Private financial institutions specializing in long-distance funds transfers for business and trade; they appeared first in Shanxi province.

A porcelain enameled plate, from the Ming Dynasty, late sixteenth century.

Plate, Ming Dynasty, late 16th–early 17th century, "Kraakporselein," probably from the Ching-te Chen kilns. Porcelain, painted in underglaze blue. Diameter 14 1/4 in. The Metropolitan Museum of Art, Rogers Fund, 1916 (16.13). Photograph (c)1980 The Metropolitan Museum of Art. Art Resource, New York.

What was China's role in world trade during the Ming Dynasty?

thirty or forty early Ming taxes on land that were payable in grain, labor service, and cash were consolidated into one tax payable in silver, the so-called Single Whip Reform. To obtain the silver, some farmers switched from grain to cash crops.

Urban growth between 1500 and 1800 was mainly at the level of market towns, which provided the link between the local markets and the larger provincial capitals and cities. Interregional trade also gained, but China did not develop a national economy. Seven or eight regional economies, each the size of a large European nation, were the focus for most economic activity. But a new level of trade developed among them, especially where water transport made such trade economical. A final feature of eighteenth-century Chinese economic life was the so-called putting out system in textiles, under which merchant capitalists organized and financed each stage of production from fiber to dyed cloth.

The Confucian family ideal changed little. A woman was expected to obey her parents, then her husband, and finally her son. Physically, women were more restricted as footbinding spread through the upper classes and to some commoners (see Figure 18–1). Most girls were subjected to this cruel and deformative procedure. One exception to the rule was the Hakka people of south China. Hakka women with unbound feet worked in the fields alongside their male kinsmen. Another exception was the Manchus. One Manchu (Qing) emperor issued an edict banning footbinding, but the Chinese ignored it.

As population grew and the size of the average landholding shrank, more women worked at home, making textiles and other products for commercial markets. And as their contribution to the household income grew, their voice in household decisions became larger. But at the same time, women's property rights—to inheritance and control of dowries—became more limited. Furthermore, the commercial revolution increased the number of rich townsmen who could afford concubines and patronized tea houses, restaurants, and brothels. (See Document, "The Thin Horse Market" on page 446.)

POLITICAL SYSTEM

Despite these massive demographic and economic changes, political structures in China changed little. Government during the Ming and Qing was much like that of the Song or Yuan, only stronger. Sources of strength included the spread of education, the use of Confucianism as an ideology, stronger emperors, better government finances, more competent officials, and a larger gentry class with an expanded role in local society.

Confucian teachings were more widespread than ever before. There were more schools in villages and towns. Academies preparing candidates for the civil service examinations multiplied. Publishing flourished, and literacy outpaced population growth. The Confucian view of society was patriarchal. The family, headed by the father, was the basic unit. The emperor, the son of heaven and the ruler-father of the empire, stood at its apex. In between were the district magistrates, the "father–mother officials." The idea of the state as the family writ large was not just a matter of metaphor but also carried with it duties and obligations at every level.

In comparison to Europe, where religious philosophies were less involved with the state and where a revolution in science was reshaping religious and political doctrines, Neo-Confucian metaphysics gave China greater unity and a more integrated worldview.

FIGURE 18–1. A Bound Foot. This diagram shows the twisted and cramped bone structure of a bound ("lily") foot, as compared with that of a normal foot. Bound tightly with cloth from the age of 5, a little girl's foot grew painfully into this deformed but erotically admired shape.

From East Asia, The Great Tradition, E.O. Reischauer, JK FairBank, Houghton Mifflin 1960.

What were the roles of women in late imperial China?

QUICK REVIEW

Women under Qing and Ming

- Confucian family ideals changed little during the Ming and Qing eras
- Footbinding spread among the upper classes and some commoners
- As population grew, more women worked at home

DOCUMENT

The Thin Horse Market

In China, ancestors without descendants to perform the rites ran the danger of becoming hungry ghosts or wandering spirits. Consequently, having a son who would continue the family line was an act of filial piety. If a wife failed to produce an heir, an official, merchant, or wealthy landowner might take a concubine and try again. Or he might do so simply because he was able to, because it gave him pleasure and because it was socially acceptable. For a poor peasant household, after a bad harvest and faced with high taxes, the sale of a comely daughter often seemed preferable to the sale of ancestral land.

- **CONCUBINES** usually had no choice in the matter, but neither did many brides in premodern China. Was a woman better off as the wife of a poor peasant, experiencing hardship, hunger, and want, or as the concubine in a wealthy household with servants, good food, and the likelihood that her children would receive an education? What does the following passage tell us about attitudes toward women in premodern China?

Upwards of a hundred people in Yangzhou earn a living in the "thin horse" business.[*] If someone shows an interest in taking a concubine, a team of a broker, a drudge, and a scout stick to him like flies. Early in the morning, the teams gather to wait outside the doors of potential customers, who usually give their business to the first team to arrive. Any teams coming late have to wait for the next opportunity. The winning team then leads their customer to the broker's house. The customer is then served tea and seated to wait for the women. The broker leads out each of them, who do what the matchmaker tells them to do. After each of her short commands, the woman bows to the customer, walks forward, turns toward the light so the customer can see her face clearly, draws back her sleeves to show him her hands, glances shyly at him to show her eyes, says her age so he can hear her voice, and finally lifts her skirt to reveal whether her feet are bound. An experienced customer could figure out the size of her feet by listening to the noise she made as she entered the room. If her skirt made noise when she walked in, she had to have a pair of big feet under her skirt. As one woman finishes, another comes out, each house having at least five or six. If the customer finds a woman to his liking, he puts a gold hairpin in her hair at the temple, a procedure called "inserting the ornament." If no one satisfies him, he gives a few hundred cash to the broker or the servants.

If the first broker gets tired, others will willingly take his place. Even if a customer has the stamina to keep looking for four or five days, he cannot finish visiting all the houses. Nevertheless, after seeing fifty to sixty white-faced, red-dressed women, they all begin to look alike and he cannot decide which are pretty or ugly. It is like the difficulty of recognizing a character after writing it hundreds or thousands of times. Therefore, the customer usually chooses someone once his mind and eyes can no longer discriminate. The owner of the woman brings out a piece of red paper on which are listed the "betrothal presents," including gold jewelry and cloth. Once he agrees to the deal, he is sent home. Before he even arrives back at his lodgings, a band and a load of food and wine are already waiting there. Before long, presents he was to send are prepared and sent back with the band. Then a sedan chair and all the trimmings—colorful lanterns, happy candles, attendants, sacrificial foods—wait outside for the customer's arrangement. The cooks and the entertainer for the wedding celebration also arrive together with foods, wine, candy, tables, chairs, and tableware. Without the customer's order, the colorful sedan chair for the girl and the small sedan chair for her companion are dispatched to get the girl. The new concubine performs the bowing ceremony with music and singing and considerable clamor. The next morning before noon the laborers ask for rewards from the man, then leave to prepare another wedding for another customer in the same manner.

Source: Reprinted with the permission of The Free Press, a division of Simon & Schuster Adult Publishing Group, from *Chinese Civilization: A Sourcebook,* Second Edition by Patricia Buckley Ebrey. Copyright © 1993 by Patricia Buckley Ebrey. All rights reserved.

[*]A horse market is for the sale of horses. A "thin horse" market is the market for concubines. The name implies a measure of criticism.

Ming–Qing emperors made all important decisions. They wielded despotic powers at their courts. They had secret police and prisons where those who committed even minor offenses might be tortured. The dedication and loyalty even of officials who were cruelly mistreated attest to the depth of their Confucian ethical training. During the Qing the life-and-death authority of emperors did not diminish, but officials were generally better treated. As foreign rulers, the Manchu emperors took care not to alienate Chinese officials.

The Forbidden Palace in Beijing was an icon of the emperor's majesty. The entire palace complex focused on the ruler. Its massive walls and vast courtyards progressed to the audience hall where the emperor sat on an elevated dais above the officials, who knelt before him. Behind the audience hall were the emperor's private chambers and his harem. By the seventeenth century, there were 9,000 palace ladies and perhaps as many as 70,000 eunuchs.

Government was better financed than during earlier dynasties. As late as the 1580s, huge surpluses were accumulated at both the central and the provincial levels. Only during the last fifty years of the Ming did soaring military expenses bankrupt the government. When, in the second half of the seventeenth century, the Manchus reestablished a strong central government, they restored the flow of taxes to levels close to those of the Ming.

The good government of the Ming–Qing system in China was largely a product of the ethical commitment and ability of its officials. No officials in the world today approach in power or prestige those of the Ming and the Qing. When the Portuguese arrived early in the sixteenth century, they called these officials "mandarins." The rewards of an official career were so great that the competition to enter it became ever fiercer. After being screened at the district office, a candidate took the county examination. If he passed, he became a member of the gentry and was exempted from state labor service. This examination required years of study. About half a million passed each year. The second hurdle was the provincial examination held every third year. Only one in a hundred was successful. The final hurdle was the metropolitan examination, passed by fewer than ninety each year.

The **gentry** class was an intermediate layer between the elite bureaucracy above and the village below. The Chinese gentry was largely urban, living in market towns or district seats. Socially and educationally, its members were of the same class as the bureaucracy's district magistrates—a world apart from clerks, runners, or village headmen. As absentee landlords whose lands were worked by sharecroppers, they were often exploitative, but they were also local leaders, representing community interests to the bureaucracy. They performed quasi-official functions on behalf of their communities: maintaining schools and Confucian temples; repairing roads, bridges, canals, and dikes; and writing local histories. The gentry class was the local upholder of Confucian values.

gentry
In China, a largely urban, landowning class that represented local interests and functioned as quasi-bureaucrats under the magistrates.

The collapse of the Ming Dynasty in 1644 and the establishment of Manchu rule was less of a break than might be imagined. First, the transition was short. Second, the Manchus, unlike the Mongols, were already partially Sinicized. Even before entering China, they had ruled over the Chinese settled in Manchuria.

In the late sixteenth century an able leader unified the Manchurian tribes and proclaimed a new dynasty, establishing a Confucian government with Chinese institutions. When the Ming collapsed and rebel forces took over China, the Manchus presented themselves as the conservative upholders of the Confucian order. The Chinese gentry preferred the Manchus to Chinese rebel leaders. Most Chinese scholars and officials served the new dynasty. The Qing as a Chinese dynasty dates from 1644, when the capital was moved to Beijing.

Examination Stalls. The dilapidated remains of the examination stalls at Nanjing. Doors to individual cubicles can be seen to the right and left of the three-story gate. Thousands of such cubicles made up the old examination stalls. Those who passed the exams governed China.

Why was the examination system so central to Chinese government?

As a tiny minority, the Manchus adopted institutions to maintain themselves as an elite group. One was their military organization. Manchu garrison forces were segregated and not put under the jurisdiction of Chinese officials. They were given stipends and lands to cultivate. They were forbidden to marry Chinese, their children had to study Manchu, and they were not permitted to bind the feet of their daughters. In 1668, northern and central Manchuria was cordoned off by a willow palisade to keep Chinese immigrants out.

CHRONOLOGY

LATE IMPERIAL CHINA

MING DYNASTY 1368–1644

1368–1398	Reign of first Ming emperor; Chinese armies invade Manchuria, Mongolia, and eastern Central Asia
1402–1424	Reign of third Ming emperor; Chinese armies invade Vietnam and Mongolia
1405–1433	Voyages of Zheng He to India and Africa
1415	Grand Canal reopened
1472–1529	Wang Yangming, philosopher
1592–1598	Chinese army battles Japanese army in Korea

QING (MANCHU) DYNASTY 1644–1911

1668	Manchuria closed to Chinese immigrants (by Willow Palisade)
1661–1722	Reign of Kangxi
1681	Suppression of revolts by Chinese generals
1683	Taiwan captured
1689	China and Russia sign Treaty of Nerchinsk
1736–1795	Reign of Qianlong
1793	Macartney mission

The second institutional feature was the appointment of one Chinese and one Manchu to each key post in the central government. At the provincial level, Chinese governors were overseen by Manchu governor-generals. Most officials and all district magistrates beneath the governors were Chinese.

An important strength of the Manchu Dynasty was the long reigns of two extremely able emperors, Kangxi (1661–1722) and Qianlong (1736–1795). Kangxi was a model emperor. A man of great vigor, he rose at dawn to read official documents before meeting with officials. He presided over palace examinations. Well versed in the Confucian classics, he won the support of scholars. Kangxi studied European science with Jesuit court astronomers; he opened four ports to foreign trade; he carried out public works; and he made six tours of China's southern provinces.

Qianlong, Kangxi's grandson, began his reign in 1736. Under his rule the Qing Dynasty attained its highest level of prosperity and power. But in his last years Qianlong permitted a court favorite to practice corruption on an almost unprecedented scale. In 1796, the White Lotus Rebellion broke out. Qianlong's successor put down the rebellion, but the ample financial reserves that had existed throughout the eighteenth century were never reestablished. China nevertheless entered the nineteenth century with its government intact and with a peaceful and stable society.

MING–QING FOREIGN RELATIONS

Some scholars have contended that post-Song China was not an aggressive or imperialist state. The early Ming convincingly disproves this contention. The first Ming emperor (r. 1368–1398) oversaw the vigorous expansion of China's borders. At his death, China controlled the northern steppe from Hami at the gateway of Central Asia to the Sungari River in Manchuria and had regained control of the southern tier of Chinese provinces as well. The Mongols were expelled from Yunnan in 1382 (see Map 18–1 on page 450).

During the reign of the third Ming emperor (1402–1424), China became even more aggressive. The emperor sent troops into northern Vietnam, which became a Chinese province for two decades. He also personally led five expeditions into the Gobi Desert in pursuit of Mongol troops.

Whenever possible, the third emperor and his successors "managed" China's frontiers with the tribute system. Ambassadors of vassal kings acted out their subordination to the universal ruler of the celestial kingdom by approaching the emperor, performing the kowtow (kneeling three times and each time bowing his head to the floor three times), and presenting gifts. In return, the vassal kings were sent seals confirming their status, given permission to use the Chinese calendar and year-period names, and appointed to the Ming nobility.

The most far-ranging ventures of the third Ming emperor were the maritime expeditions that sailed to Southeast Asia, India, the Arabian Gulf, and East Africa between 1405 and 1433. They were commanded by the eunuch Zheng He, a Muslim from Yunnan (see Map 18–1). The first of these armadas had sixty-two major ships and carried 28,000 sailors, soldiers, and merchants. The expeditions were intended to make China's glory known to distant kingdoms and to enroll them in the tribute system. They ended abruptly: They were costly and offered little return at a time when the dynasty was fighting in Mongolia and building Beijing. What was remarkable about these expeditions was not that they came half a century earlier than the Portuguese voyages of discovery, but that China had the necessary maritime technology and yet decided not to use it. China lacked the combination of restlessness, greed, religious faith, and curiosity that would motivate the Portuguese.

Emperor Qianlong. The great Manchu emperor Qianlong (r. 1736–1795).

Unidentified Artist, 16th century. Qing Dynasty (1644–1911). Hanging scroll; ink and color on silk; Overall: 63 1/2 x 30 1/2in. (161.3 x 77.5cm). The Metropolitan Museum of Art, Rogers Fund, 1942. (42.141.8). Photograph © 1980 The Metropolitan Museum of Art. Art Resource, New York.

How did the Manchus maintain control over a much larger Chinese population?

Read the **Document**
A Ming Naval Expedition 15th century
at **myhistorylab.com**

MAP 18–1.   The Ming Empire and the Voyages of Zheng He.   The inset map shows the voyages of Zheng He to Southeast Asia and India. Some ships of his fleet even reached East Africa. (Zheng himself did not.)

What was the purpose of Zheng He's voyages?

Giraffe with Attendant. Some emperors had private zoos and gladly received exotic animals as gifts from tribute states.

A painting by Shen Du (1357–1438), "The Tribute: Giraffe with Attendant." Philadelphia Museum of Art: Gift of John T. Dorrance, 1977.

Besides keeping exotic animals, what were some other ways Chinese emperors made their power visible?

The chief threat to the Ming Dynasty was the Mongols. In disarray after the collapse of their rule in China, the Mongols had broken up into eastern, western, and southern tribes. The Chinese, "using the barbarian to control the barbarian," made allies of the southern tribes (those settled just north of the Great Wall) against the more fearsome grassland Mongols. This policy worked most of the time, but twice the Mongols formed confederations—pale imitations of the war machine of Genghis—strong enough to defeat Chinese armies: In the 1430s they captured the emperor, and in 1550 they overran Beijing. The Mongol forces involved in the latter attack were defeated by a Chinese army in the 1560s and signed a peace treaty in 1571.

A second threat came from Japan, whose pirates raided the Chinese coast in the fifteenth and sixteenth centuries. After Hideyoshi unified Japan, he twice invaded and occupied Korea in 1592 and between 1597 and 1598. China sent troops, and the Japanese withdrew after the death of Hideyoshi. But the strain on Ming finances had severely weakened the dynasty.

The final foreign threat to the Ming was the Manchus. After coming to power in 1644, the Manchu court spent decades consolidating its rule within China. The emperor Kangxi took Taiwan in 1683, making it part of China for the first time.

As always, the principal foreign threats to Qing China came from the north and northwest. By the 1660s, Russian traders, trappers, and adventurers had reached northern Manchuria, where they built forts and traded with the eastern Mongols. During the 1680s, Kangxi drove the Russians from the lower Amur River. This victory during the early years of the reign of Peter the Great (1682–1725) led to the 1689 Treaty of Nerchinsk, which excluded Russia from northern Manchuria while permitting its caravans to visit Beijing.

In the west there was a complex, three-sided relationship among Russia, the western Mongols, and Tibet. Kangxi, and then Qianlong, campaigned against the Mongols, invaded Tibet, and in 1727 signed a new treaty with Russia. During the campaigns, the Chinese temporarily came to control millions of square miles of new territories. Ever since, even after China's borders contracted, the Chinese have insisted that the Manchu conquests define their legitimate borders. The roots of present-day border contentions, and the Chinese claim to Tibet, go back to these events during the eighteenth century.

Europeans had reached China during the Tang and the Yuan dynasties. But only with Europe's oceanic expansion in the sixteenth century did they arrive in large numbers. Some came as missionaries, of whom the most successful were the Jesuits. The Jesuits studied Chinese and the Confucian classics and conversed with scholars. They used their knowledge of astronomy, geography, engraving, and firearms to win entry to the court at Beijing and appointments in the bureau of astronomy. When the Manchus came to power, the Jesuits kept their position. They tried to propagate Christianity, attacking Daoism and Buddhism, but arguing that Confucianism as a rational philosophy complemented Christianity. They interpreted the Confucian rites of ancestor worship as secular and compatible with Christianity. A few high court officials were converted. But the Jesuits' rivals, the Franciscans and Dominicans, reported to Rome that the Jesuits condoned Confucian rites. Papal bulls in 1715 and 1742 forbade Chinese Christians to participate in ancestor worship, and the emperor banned Christianity in China.

Other Europeans came to China to trade. The Portuguese came first in the early sixteenth century but behaved badly and were expelled. They returned in midcentury and were permitted to trade on a tiny peninsula at Macao that was walled off from China. They were followed by Dutch from the East Indies (Indonesia), by the British East India Company in 1699, and by Americans in 1784. By the early eighteenth century, Westerners could trade only at Canton. They could not bring their wives to China. They were subject to Chinese law and were controlled by official merchant guilds. Nevertheless, the trade was profitable to both sides.

The British East India Company developed a triangular commerce among China, India, and Britain. For China, this trade produced an influx of specie, and the Chinese officials in charge grew immensely wealthy. Chafing under the restrictions, in 1793 the British government sent negotiators. The emperor Qianlong permitted Lord Macartney (1736–1806) to present his gifts, which the Chinese described as tribute, but he turned down Macartney's requests. Western trade remained encapsulated at Canton.

MING–QING CULTURE

One thing that can be said of Ming–Qing culture, like population or agricultural productivity, is that there was more of it. Whether considering gentry, scholar officials, or a professionalized class of literati, their numbers and works were far greater than in previous dynasties. Even local literary figures or philosophers were likely to publish their collected works or have them published by admiring disciples. Bookstores came of age

QUICK REVIEW

Chinese Contacts with the West

◆ Europeans arrived in China in large numbers after the sixteenth century

◆ The most successful missionaries were the Jesuits

◆ By the eighteenth century, Europeans could trade only at Canton

Le Pere Adam Schaal.

Jesuit Missionary. A late seventeenth-century color engraving of the Jesuit missionary Johann Adam Schall depicts him in traditional Confucian dress holding a sextant and a compass. A globe is behind him on the left.

Why were the Manchus interested in Western science?

in the Ming, selling not only books but also colored prints, novels, erotica, and model answers for the civil service examinations.

Chinese culture had begun to turn inward during the Song in reaction to Buddhism. This tendency was accelerated by the Chinese antipathy to Mongol rule and continued into the Ming and Qing, when Chinese culture became virtually impervious to outside influences. Even works on mathematics and science translated into Chinese by the Jesuits left few traces in Chinese scholarly writings. Chinese cultural self-sufficiency reflected a tradition and a social order that had stood the test of time, but it also indicated a closed system of ideas with weaknesses that would become apparent in the nineteenth century. Orthodox thought during these five centuries was Zhu Xi Neo-Confucianism. From the mid- to the late Ming, some perturbations were caused by the Zen-like teachings of the philosopher Wang Yangming (1472–1529), whose activism caused him to be jailed, beaten, and exiled at one point in an otherwise illustrious official career.

Several other original thinkers had only a limited influence on their own times. The most interesting was Gu Yanwu, who wrote on both philology and statecraft. He used philology and historical phonetics to get at the original meanings of the classics and contrasted their practical ethics with the "empty words" of Wang Yangming. Gu's successors extended his philological studies, developing empirical methods for textual studies, but lost sight of their implications for politics. The Manchus clamped down on unorthodox thought, and the seventeenth-century burst of creativity narrowed into a bookish, conservative scholasticism. Not until the end of the nineteenth century did thinkers draw from these studies the kind of radical inferences that philological studies of the Bible had produced in Europe.

Ming and Qing Chinese esteemed most highly the traditional categories of high culture: painting, calligraphy, poetry, and philosophy. Porcelains of great beauty were also produced. In the early Ming the blue-on-white glazes predominated. During the later Ming and Qing more decorative wares with enamel painted over the glaze became widespread. The pottery industry of Europe was begun during the sixteenth century to imitate these wares, and Chinese and Japanese influences have dominated Western ceramics ever since.

Chinese today, however, look back and see the novel as the characteristic cultural achievement of the Ming and Qing. The Chinese novel grew out of plot-books used by earlier storytellers. Most authors were scholars who had failed the examinations, which may account for their caustic comments on officials. They generally used pseudonyms and wrote in colloquial Chinese.

Two collections of lively short stories from this period have been translated into English: *Stories from a Ming Collection* and *The Courtesan's Jewel Box*. Many other stories were pornographic. In fact, the Ming may have invented the humorous pornographic novel. One example available in English is *The Carnal Prayer Mat*. This genre was suppressed in China during the Qing and rediscovered in Japanese collections in the twentieth century.

JAPAN

The two segments of "late traditional" Japan could not be more different. The Warring States era (1467–1600), which was really the last phase of Japan's medieval history, saw the unleashing of internal wars and anarchy that scourged the old society from the bottom up. Within a century all vestiges of the old manorial or estate system had been scrapped, and virtually all of the Ashikaga lords had been overthrown. The Tokugawa era (1600–1868) that followed saw Japan reunited and stable, with a more competent government than ever. The culture was also brilliantly transformed, preparing it for the challenge it would face during the mid-nineteenth century.

WARRING STATES ERA (1467–1600)

War is the universal solvent of old institutions. Nowhere in history was this clearer than in Japan between 1467 and 1600. In 1467 a dispute arose over who would be the next Ashikaga shōgun. The dispute led to war between territorial lords who supported the respective contenders. Conflicts raged throughout Japan for eleven years. Most of Kyoto was destroyed in the fighting, and the authority of the Ashikaga *bakufu* came to an end. This first war ended in 1477, but the fighting resumed and continued for more than a century.

WHAT IMPACT did military technology have on Japanese society in this period?

WAR OF ALL AGAINST ALL

Even before 1467, the Ashikaga equilibrium had been precarious. The regional **daimyo** lords had relied on their relationship to the bakufu to hold their stronger vassals in check, while relying on these vassals to preserve their independence against strong neighbors. The collapse of bakufu authority after 1467 left the regional lords standing alone, removing the last barrier to internecine wars. The regional lords became prey to the stronger among their vassals as well as to powerful neighboring states.

By the end of the sixteenth century virtually all Ashikaga daimyo had fallen. In their place emerged hundreds of little "Warring States daimyo," each with his own warrior band. In one prefecture along the Inland Sea, the remains of 200 hillside castles of such daimyo have been identified. The constant wars among these men were not unlike those of the early feudal era in Europe. A Japanese term for "survival of the fittest"—"the strong eat and the weak become the meat"—is often applied to this century of warfare. Of the daimyo bands, the most efficient in revamping their domain for military ends survived.

As fighting continued, hundreds of local states gave way to tens of regional states. The castles of such regional states were often located on plains, and as castle

daimyo
A term meaning "great name"; these men were the most powerful feudal leaders in Japan from the tenth to the nineteenth century.

Daimyo Castle. Construction of the "White Heron" castle in Himeji was begun during the Warring States era and was completed shortly after 1600. During the Tokugawa peace, it remained as a monument to the glory of the daimyo. Today it can be seen from the "bullet train."

Morris Simoncelli, Japan Airlines Photo.

How was central authority reasserted over the daimyo?

towns grew up around them, merchants flocked to supply the needs of their growing soldiery. Eventually, alliances of these regional states fought it out, until in the late sixteenth century all of Japan was brought under the hegemony of a single lord. Oda Nobunaga (1534–1582) completed the initial unification of central Honshu and would have finished the job had a treacherous vassal not assassinated him in 1582. Toyotomi Hideyoshi (1536–1598), who had begun life as a lowly foot soldier, completed the unification in 1590. After his death his vassal generals once again went to war, and it was only with the victory of Tokugawa Ieyasu (1542–1616) at the battle of Sekigahara in 1600 that true unification was finally achieved. Ieyasu's unification of 1600 superficially resembled that of the Minamoto in 1185 but was in fact based on a sweeping transformation of Japan's society.

FOOT SOLDIER REVOLUTION

During the Warring States period, the foot soldier replaced the aristocratic mounted warrior as the backbone of the military. Soldiers were still called samurai and were still vassals of a lord, but their numbers, social status, and techniques of warfare changed dramatically. All public lands and estates, including the emperor's, were seized and converted into fiefs, which were privately governed by the fief holder. A fief was not divided among heirs but passed intact to the ablest son.

With larger revenues, Warring States daimyo built bigger armies. They recruited mainly from the peasantry. By the late sixteenth century hundreds of thousands of troops were deployed in major campaigns. In the mid-fourteenth century a new weapon was developed: a thrusting spear with a thick shaft and a heavy chisel-like blade. Held in both hands, it could penetrate medieval armor; it could also be swung about like a quarterstaff. It was used by soldiers positioned at intervals of three feet in a pincushion tactic to impale charging cavalry. The weapon spelled the end of the aristocratic warrior in Japan. Its use coincided with the recruitment of peasant soldiers, for it required only short training. A second change in military technology was the introduction of the musket by the Portuguese in the mid-sixteenth century. Warring States generals quickly adopted it. As individual combat gave way to mass armies, warfare became pitiless, cruel, and bloody.

The society that emerged from the Warring States period was, in some senses, feudal. By the late sixteenth century, all warriors in Japan were part of a pyramid of vassals and lords headed by a single overlord, and warriors of rank held fiefs and vassals of their own. But in other respects, Japan was more like post-feudal Europe. First, most of the military class was made up of soldiers, not aristocrats. Even though they were called samurai and were vassals, they were something new. They were not given fiefs but were paid stipends of rice bales. Second, in mid-sixteenth-century Japan the military class may have reached 7 or 8 percent of the population (in feudal England, for example, it was about one quarter of 1 percent). It was more of a size with the mercenary armies of Europe during the fifteenth or sixteenth century. Third, the recruitment of village warriors

CHRONOLOGY

WARRING STATES JAPAN AND THE ERA OF UNIFICATION (1467–1600)

1467–1568	Battles throughout Japan
1543	Portuguese arrive in Japan
1568	Oda Nobunaga takes Kyoto and partially unifies Japan
1575	Battle of Nagashino
1582	Nobunaga assassinated
1588	Hideyoshi starts sword hunt
1590	Hideyoshi completes unification
1592, 1597–1598	Hideyoshi sends armies to Korea
1597	Hideyoshi bans Christianity
1598	Hideyoshi dies, his generals battle for succession
1600	Battle of Sekigahara; Tokugawa Ieyasu reunifies Japan

added significantly to the power of Warring States daimyo but gave rise to problems as well. Taxes became harder to collect. Local samurai were often involved in uprisings. When organized by Pure Land Buddhist congregations, these uprisings sometimes involved whole provinces. Again, the parallels with post-feudal Europe seem closer. Fourth, even in a feudal society, not everything is feudal. The commercial growth of the Kamakura and Ashikaga periods continued through the dark decades of the Warring States era.

FOREIGN RELATIONS AND TRADE

Japanese pirate-traders plied the seas of East Asia during the fifteenth and sixteenth centuries. To halt their depredations, the Ming emperor invited the third Ashikaga shōgun to trade with China. An agreement was reached in 1404. However, piracy stopped only after Japan was reunified at the close of the sixteenth century.

Early Japanese exports to China were raw materials, but by the sixteenth century, manufactured goods were rising in importance. In exchange, Japan received copper cash, porcelains, paintings, books, and medicines. After establishing his hegemony over Japan, Hideyoshi permitted only ships with his vermilion seal to trade with China, a policy the Tokugawa continued. Between 1604 and 1635 over 350 ships went to China in this "vermilion-seal trade." Then, in 1635, the policy of national seclusion ended Japan's foreign trade. No Japanese were permitted to leave Japan, and the construction of large ships was prohibited.

Overlapping Japan's maritime expansion in the seas of East Asia was the arrival of European ships. Portuguese pirate-traders made their way to Goa in India, to Malacca, to Macao in China, and arrived in Japan in 1543. Spanish galleons came in 1587 via Mexico and the Philippines. The Iberians were followed by the Dutch and the English after the turn of the century.

The Portuguese, from a tiny country with a population of 1.5 million, were motivated by a desire for booty and profits, and by religious zeal. Their ships were superior. Taking advantage of the Chinese ban on maritime commerce, they became important as shippers. They carried Southeast Asian goods and Japanese silver to China and Chinese silk to Japan and then used their profits to buy Southeast Asian spices for the European market.

Traders brought with them Jesuit missionaries, who concentrated their efforts on the samurai. Christian converts numbered about 300,000 in 1600—a higher percentage of Japanese than are Christian today. It is difficult to explain why Christianity met with greater success in Japan than in other Asian lands. There seemed little difference to the Japanese between the cosmic Buddha of Shingon and the Christian God, between the paradise of Amida and the Christian heaven, or between prayers to Kannon—the female *bodhisattva* of mercy—and to the Virgin Mary. The Japanese also noted the theological similarity between the pietism of the Pure Land sect and that of Christianity. To Japanese ears, the passage in Romans 10:13, "whosoever shall call upon the name of the Lord shall be saved," was reminiscent of the Pure Land practice of invoking the name of Amida. The Jesuits, too, noted these parallels and felt that the devil had established these sects in Japan to test their faith. Although Jesuit intolerance gave rise to certain tensions and animosities, the personal example of the Jesuits—their asceticism, devoutness, and learning—was also important in facilitating the spread of Christianity.

Arrival of the Portuguese in Japan.
Portuguese merchants arrived in Japan in 1543 from India and the East Indies. Their crews were multiethnic, and they brought Jesuit priests as well.

"Arrival of the Portuguese in Japan" Detail—central section of the boat, 1594–1618. Screen. Paint, gold, paper. Museo, Soares Dos Reis, Porto, Portugal. Bridgeman-Giraudon/Art Resource, New York.

How are the Portuguese depicted in this painting?

The fortunes of Christianity began to decline in 1597, when six Spanish Franciscans and twenty Japanese converts were crucified in Nagasaki, apparently because a Spanish pilot had boasted that merchants and priests were preparing Japan for conquest. Sporadic persecutions continued until 1614, when Tokugawa Ieyasu formally banned the foreign religion. The last resistance was an uprising in 1637 to 1638 in which 37,000 Christians died. After that, Christianity survived in Japan only as a hidden religion with secret rites and devotions to "Maria-Kannon," the mother of Jesus represented or disguised as the Buddhist goddess of mercy holding a child in her arms.

A few of these "hidden Christians" reemerged in the later nineteenth century. Otherwise, apart from muskets and techniques of castle building, all that remained of the Portuguese influence were certain loan words that became a permanent part of the Japanese language: *pan* for bread, *birōdo* for velvet, *kasutera* for sponge cake, *karuta* for playing cards, and *tempura* for that familiar Japanese dish.

TOKUGAWA ERA (1600–1868)

HOW WAS Japanese culture transformed during the Tokugawa era?

POLITICAL ENGINEERING AND ECONOMIC GROWTH DURING THE SEVENTEENTH CENTURY

From 1467 to 1590 Japan's energies were absorbed in wars. But after the unifications of 1590 and 1600 Japan's leaders sought to create a peaceful, stable, orderly society. The transition was slow. By the middle or late seventeenth century, however, Japan's society and political system had been radically reengineered. Vigorous economic and demographic growth had also occurred. This combination of political and economic change made the seventeenth century a period of great dynamism.

One pressing problem faced by Japan's unifiers was how to cope with an armed peasantry. In war, village warriors fought for their lord: The benefit they offered the lord was greater than their cost. In peace, only the cost remained: their resistance to taxation and the threat of local uprisings. Accordingly, in the summer of 1588 Hideyoshi ordered a "sword hunt" to disarm the peasants. Once the hunt was completed, the 5 percent of the population who remained samurai used their monopoly on weapons to control the other 95 percent.

Hideyoshi next froze the social classes. Samurai were prohibited from quitting the service of their lord. Peasants were barred from abandoning their fields to become townspeople. Samurai, farmers, and townspeople tended to marry within their respective classes. Each class developed a unique cultural character—though we must note the vast range of social gradations within each class. A farmer who was a landlord and a district official, for example, was a more important figure than most lower samurai and lived in a different social world from a landless "water-drinking" peasant too poor to buy tea.

Having disarmed the peasantry, Hideyoshi ordered land surveys, which defined each parcel of land by location, size, soil quality, product, and cultivator's name. Hideyoshi's survey laid the foundations for a systematic land tax. Based on these surveys, domains and fiefs were henceforth ranked in terms of their assessed yield.

Despite all the evidence of Warring States political behavior, Hideyoshi assumed that his vassals would honor their oaths of loyalty to his heir. He was especially trustful of his great ally Tokugawa Ieyasu. His trust was misplaced. After his death in 1598, Hideyoshi's former vassals, paying little attention to his heir, broke apart into two opposing camps. In 1600, they fought a great battle from which Ieyasu emerged victorious.

"Picture-treading" Plaque. Fumi-e, or "picture-treading" plaques are bronze images representing Christ or the Virgin, used by the Tokugawa with increasing intensity from 1614 onward to extirpate the foreign religion. In the fumi-e ceremony suspected converts were obliged to tread on the plaques to show that they rejected Christianity.

DNP Archives.Com Company, Ltd./Tokyo National Museum.

Why was Christianity banned in Japan?

Like the Minamoto of twelfth-century Kamakura, Ieyasu spurned the Kyoto court and established his headquarters in Edo (today's Tokyo), in the center of his military holdings in eastern Japan (see Map 18–2 on page 459). He took the title of shōgun in 1603 and called his government the *bakufu*. In Edo he built a great castle, surrounded by massive fortifications of stone and concentric moats (the inner portions remain today as the Imperial Palace). Ieyasu then used his military power to reorganize Japan.

Ieyasu's first move was to confiscate the lands of his defeated enemies and to reward his vassals and allies. During the first quarter of the seventeenth century the *bakufu* confiscated the domains of 150 daimyo, some of former enemies and some for infractions of the Tokugawa legal code, and transferred 229 daimyo from one domain to another. The transfers completed the work of Hideyoshi's sword hunt by severing long-standing ties between daimyo and their disarmed former village retainers. When a daimyo was transferred to a new fief, he took his samurai retainers with him. During the second quarter of the seventeenth century transfers and confiscations ended and the system settled down. The rearrangement created a defensive system, with the staunchest Tokugawa supporters nearest to the center of power.

The Tokugawa also established other systemic controls. Legal codes regulated the imperial court, temples and shrines, and daimyo. Military houses were enjoined to use men of ability and to practice frugality. They were prohibited from engaging in drinking parties, wanton revelry, sexual indulgence, habitual gambling, or the ostentatious display of wealth. Only with *bakufu* consent could daimyo marry or repair their castles.

A second control was a hostage system, firmly established by 1642, that required the wives and children of daimyo to reside permanently in Edo and the daimyo themselves to spend every second year in Edo. Like the policy of French king Louis XIV (r. 1643–1715) at Versailles, this requirement transformed feudal lords into courtiers. The palatial Edo compounds of the daimyo contained hundreds or thousands of retainers and servants and occupied much of the city.

A third key control, established during the 1630s, was the national policy of seclusion. Seclusion was no barrier to cultural imports from China and Korea. But except for small Chinese and Dutch trading contingents at Nagasaki, no foreigners were permitted to enter Japan, and on pain of death, no Japanese were allowed to go abroad. Nor could oceangoing ships be built. This policy was strictly enforced until 1854. Seclusion enclosed the system of Tokugawa rule, cutting off outside political contacts.

Edo Castle. Edo first became a castle town in the mid-fifteenth century. Tokugawa Ieyasu made the castle his residence and headquarters in 1590, and, after his great victory in 1600, rebuilt and extended it. This early Edo period screen painting shows (upper right) the keep or inner citadel, which was not rebuilt after a fire in 1657. Korean envoys (bottom center) enter the castle grounds. They have brought tiger skins and other gifts. Onlookers gawk at their unfamiliar garb. Warriors (top, far right) practice archery. The inner castle compounds shown in the painting were only the central part of an elaborate system of moats, stone-block ramparts, and gates. In 1868, after the Meiji Restoration, Edo was renamed Tokyo (Eastern Capital) and became the residence of the emperor.
How does Edo castle symbolize the power of Tokugawa Ieyasu?

Forces of political centralization and decentralization were delicately balanced. Representing the forces of centralization was the *bakufu*, which governed its own domain and also administered the controls over the whole system. Representing decentralization were the domains of the 260 or so daimyo. Their domain governments, like miniature *bakufu*, were staffed by their samurai vassals. Each domain had its own autonomous military, finances, judiciary, schools, paper money, and so on. Some Japanese scholars label the Tokugawa polity the "*bakufu*-domain system."

The political dynamism of the period from Hideyoshi through the first century of Tokugawa rule was matched by economic growth. The spread of improved agricultural techniques had been impeded by regionalism and wars. During the seventeenth century methods of water control and irrigation that made double-cropping easier, better tools, new seed strains, the use of bony fish or of night soil from cities as fertilizers, and other techniques were widely applied. Resources no longer needed for war were allocated to land reclamation. This doubled food production, which led to a doubling of population from about 12 million in 1600 to 24 million in 1700. The production of agricultural by-products, including cotton, silk, indigo, lumber, dyes, and *sake*, also grew.

On coming to power, Nobunaga and Hideyoshi knew that political unification alone was not enough. They recognized that prosperity would make their rule easier, and, acknowledging the enterprise of merchants, they abolished the medieval guilds and freed Japan's central markets from monopolistic restrictions. The result was a burgeoning of trade and the formation of a national market network atop the domain economies. As this network expanded during the seventeenth century, economic functions became more differentiated and efficient.

The sharp decline in foreign trade caused by seclusion did not dampen Japan's domestic economy because of the tax system and consumption patterns. Tokugawa tax policy was based on land, not commerce. Taxes took about one-third of the peasant's production. It was a heavier tax rate than that in neighboring China and bespeaks the effective grasp that the military class had on Japanese society. The 87 percent of the population who lived in the countryside paid almost one-third of the country's agricultural wealth to the 5 percent in the military class. The remaining 8 percent of townspeople also lived off the tax flow by providing goods and services for samurai. This distribution of benefits was mirrored in the three-area city planning common to all castle towns: a large parklike area with castle, trees, stone walls, and moats for the daimyo and his government; an extensive samurai quarter; and a meaner townspeople's quarter. Just as the castle towns were the consumption centers of the regional tax economies, so was Edo the national consumption center and a super-castle town. It had the same three-area layout on a grander scale. By 1700 Edo had a population of about 1 million.

To support their Edo establishments, the daimyo sold tax rice in Osaka. The "kitchen of Japan," Osaka became the redistribution center from which competing fleets of coastal shippers brought food, clothing, lumber, oil, and other supplies to Edo. By 1700 Osaka's population was about 400,000. Kyoto, rebuilt after its destruction in the early Warring States period, was almost as big. It continued as a center of handicraft production. It also was the location of the "captive" imperial court, which, after suffering penury during the Warring States era, was given support lands equivalent in revenues to those of a small daimyo.

The system of alternate-year attendance at Edo contributed to the development of overland transportation. The most traveled grand trunk road was the Tōkaidō Road between Edo and Kyoto (see Map 18–2). The artist Hiroshige (1797–1858) made a series of woodblock prints that depicted the scenery at its fifty-three post stations.

MAP EXPLORATION

To explore this map further, go to **http://www.myhistorylab.com**

MAP 18–2. Tokugawa Japan and the Korean Peninsula. The area between Edo and Osaka in central Honshu was both the political base of the Tokugawa *bakufu* and its rice basket. The domains that would overthrow the Tokugawa *bakufu* in the late nineteenth century were mostly in outlying areas of southwestern Japan.

What controls did the Tokugawa impose to restrain the daimyo?

The growth of a national economy led to a richness and diversity in urban life. Townsmen governed their districts. Samurai city managers watched over the city as a whole. Public schools, police, and companies of firefighters provided public services. There were also servants, cooks, messengers, restaurant owners, priests, doctors, teachers, sword sharpeners, book lenders, instructors in the martial arts, prostitutes, and bathhouse attendants. In the world of popular arts there were woodblock printers and artists, book publishers, puppeteers, acrobatic troupes, storytellers, and **Kabuki** and **Nō** actors. Merchant establishments included money changers, pawnbrokers, peddlers, small shops, single-price retail establishments like the House of Mitsui, and great

Kabuki

A realistic form of Japanese theater similar to English Elizabethan drama.

Nō

A highly stylized form of Japanese theater performed on a simple stage.

The Commercial District of Osaka, the "kitchen" of Tokugawa Japan. Warehouses bear the crests of their merchant houses. Ships (upper right) loaded with rice, cotton goods, sake, and other goods are about to depart for Edo (Tokyo). Their captains vied with one another to arrive first and get the best price.

How did commerce develop in the Tokugawa period?

QUICK REVIEW

The Japanese Economy

◆ Agricultural production doubled from 1600 to 1700

◆ Peace sustained economic growth

◆ Economic growth and national integration led to a rich and diverse urban society

---

wholesale merchants. Merchant households furnished the raw materials for the personae of Edo fiction: the skinflint merchant who pinches every penny, the profligate son who runs through an inheritance to an inevitable bankruptcy, an erring wife, or the clerk involved in a hopeless affair with a prostitute.

EIGHTEENTH AND EARLY NINETEENTH CENTURIES

By the late seventeenth century, the political engineering of the Tokugawa state was complete. In the economy, too, dynamic growth gave way to slower growth within a high-level equilibrium. Yet changes of a different kind were under way.

The eighteenth century began with high drama. In 1701, a daimyo at Edo Castle drew his sword and wounded an official who had insulted him. It was a capital crime to unsheath a sword within the castle, and the daimyo was ordered to commit *harakiri* (that is, to disembowel himself), which he promptly did. This made his retainers *rōnin*, masterless samurai.

Twenty-one months later, on a snowy night in January, forty-seven of the retainers attacked the residence of the *bakufu* official, took his head, and then surrendered to the authorities. Their act struck the imagination of the citizenry of Edo and was widely acclaimed. But the *bakufu* council ordered all forty-seven to commit *harakiri*. The incident embodied the perennial theme of duty versus human feelings. Writers of Kabuki drama and puppet theater quickly took up the incident. To this day, there have been many characterizations of Ōishi Kuranosuke, the leader of the band of forty-seven, as the story has been reworked into novels, movies, and television scripts.

Viewed historically, three points may be noted about the incident. First, in a similar situation the more practical samurai of the Warring States period would have forgotten their former lord and rushed to find a new one. But in the Tokugawa era, with the authority of the daimyo backed by that of the shōgun, there was no room for disloyalty. So loyalty became deeply internalized and was viewed almost as a religious obligation. Second, the incident tells something of the state in Tokugawa Japan. The 1615 "Laws for the Military Houses" contains the passage: "Law is the basis of the social order. Reason may be violated in the name of law, but law may not be violated in the name of reason."[1] One Tokugawa law forbade private vendettas. So, despite the moral purity of their act, the forty-seven "virtuous warriors" had to die. Third, loyalty and idealism were not the monopoly of males. In the drama, at least, samurai wives and daughters displayed the same heroic spirit of self-sacrifice.

---

[1] R. Tsunoda, W. T. de Bary, and D. Keene, eds., *Sources of the Japanese Tradition* (New York: Columbia University Press, 1958), p. 336.

A Closer Look

Bridal Procession

Yohime, the twenty-first daughter of the eleventh shogun, approaches the main Edo estate of the Kaga daimyo.

An array of samurai precedes the bride's palanquin. Among them are men bearing gifts for the daimyo, which are covered by a cloth with the Tokugawa crest.

A red gate built in 1827 in celebration of the wedding. Extending from the gate is the wall that circled the huge Edo estate of the Kaga daimyo. In modern times his estate became the main campus of Tokyo University. The gate still stands today and is routinely used by students.

Yohime rides in a palanquin decorated with the hollyhock crest of the Tokugawa House. She is on her way to marry the Kaga daimyo, lord of the largest domain in Japan. The eleventh shogun had 28 sons and 27 daughters by more than 40 concubines.

Behind the palanquin are Yohime's ladies in waiting. They are of a number befitting her status.

Questions

1. What was the political meaning of such a marriage?

2. What does this print say of the steeply hierarchical nature of the Tokugawa warrior class?

Most political history of late Tokugawa Japan is written in terms of alternating cycles of laxity and reform. Even during the mid-seventeenth century, the expenses of the bakufu and daimyo states were often greater than their income. Taxes were based on agriculture in an economy that was becoming commercial. It was simple mathematics: After the samurai were paid their stipends, not enough was left for the expenses of domain government and the costs of the Edo establishments. Meanwhile, daimyo and retainers of rank had developed a taste for luxury.

Over the years a pattern emerged. To make ends meet, domains would borrow from merchants. Then, as finances became even more straitened, a reformist clique of officials would appear, take power, and return the domain to a more frugal and austere way of life. Debts would be repaid or repudiated. A side effect of reform was the depression of the local merchant economy. Since no one likes to practice frugality forever, after some of the goals of the reform had been achieved, a new clique would take over the government and a new round of spending would begin. The *bakufu* carried out three great reforms on Tokugawa lands:

1716–1733	Tokugawa Yoshimune	17 years
1787–1793	Matsudaira Sadanobu	6 years
1841–1843	Mizuno Tadakuni	2 years

The first two were long and successful; the third was not. Its failure set the stage for the ineffective response of the *bakufu* to the West in the mid-nineteenth century. Daimyo domains also carried out reforms. Some were successful, enabling them to respond more effectively to the political crisis of the mid-nineteenth century.

The balance between centralization and decentralization lasted until the end of the Tokugawa era. Not a single domain ever tried to overthrow the bakufu hegemony. Nor did the bakufu ever try to extend its control over the domains. But bureaucracy grew steadily. Public authority extended into areas that had been private. In 1600 most samurai fiefs were run by their samurai fief holders. By 1850, however, district officials administered all but the largest of samurai fiefs. They collected the standard domain taxes and forwarded their income to the samurai. In periods of retrenchment, samurai were often paid only half the amount due. Paperwork proliferated: records of births, adoptions, name changes, samurai ranks, fief registers, court proceedings, and so on.

Of course, there were limits to bureaucratization. Only samurai could aspire to official posts, and decision-making posts were limited to upper-ranking samurai. But in periods of financial crises a demand arose for men of ability, and middle- or lower-middle-ranking samurai became staff assistants to bureaucrats of rank.

By 1700, the economy approached the limit of expansion within the available technology. The population reached 26 million early in the eighteenth century and remained at that level into the mid-nineteenth century, a period during which the population of China more than doubled. After 1700, taxes were stabilized and land surveys were few. Evidence suggests little increase in grain production and only slow growth in agricultural by-products. Some families made conscious efforts to limit their size to raise their standard of living. Contraception and abortion were commonplace, and infanticide was practiced in hard times. But periodic disease, shortages of food, and late marriages among the poor were more important factors in limiting population growth.

Some farmers remained independent cultivators, but by the mid-nineteenth century, about a quarter of all cultivated lands were worked by tenants. Most landlords had small holdings. The misery of the lower stratum of rural society contributed to an increase in peasant uprisings during the late eighteenth and early nineteenth centuries. Authorities had no difficulty quelling them, and no uprising in Japan approached those that erupted in late Manchu China.

Commerce grew slowly during the late Tokugawa. In the early eighteenth century, it was again subjected to regulation by guilds. Merchants paid set fees in return for monopoly privileges in central marketplaces. Guilds were also reestablished in the domains, and some domains created domain-run monopolies on products such as wax, paper, indigo, or sugar. The problem facing domain leaders was how to share in the profits without injuring the competitive standing of domain exports. Most late Tokugawa commercial growth was in rural industries—*sake*, soy sauce, dyes, silks, or cotton. Some were organized and financed by city merchants. Others competed with city merchants, shipping directly to the end markets to circumvent monopoly controls. The expansion of labor in rural industries may explain why the population of late Tokugawa cities declined.

The largest question about the Tokugawa economy concerns its relation to Japan's rapid industrialization in the late nineteenth century. Some scholars have suggested that Japan had a "running start." Others have stressed Japan's backwardness in comparison with European developers. The question remains unresolved.

TOKUGAWA CULTURE

Two hundred and fifty years of peace and prosperity provided a base for an ever more complex culture and a broader popular participation in cultural life. A satire by Saikaku (1642–1693), a drama by Chikamatsu (1653–1724), or a woodblock print of a beauty by Utamaro (1753–1806) may be taken to represent the new urban culture of the Tokugawa era. In such works, one discerns a new secular consciousness, an exquisite taste put to plebeian ends, occasional vulgarities, and a sense of humor only occasionally encountered in the earlier Japanese tradition.

In the villages, Buddhism became more deeply rooted, and new folk religions proliferated. By the early nineteenth century, most well-to-do farmers could read and write. The aristocratic culture of the ranking samurai houses also remained vigorous. Nō plays continued to be staged. The medieval tradition of black ink painting was continued by the Kanō school and other artists. The Ashikaga tradition of restraint, simplicity, and naturalness in architecture was extended. The gilded and colored screen paintings that had surged in popularity during Hideyoshi's rule developed further, culminating in the powerful works of Ogata Kōrin (1658–1716). Zen Buddhism, having declined during the Warring States period, was revitalized by the monk Hakuin (1686–1769), who was also a writer, a painter, a calligrapher, and a sculptor.

Some scholars have described Tokugawa urban culture as having two divisions. One was the work of serious, high-minded samurai, who produced a vast body of Chinese-style paintings, poetry, and philosophical treatises. The other was the product of the townspeople: low-brow, irreverent, secular, satirical, and often scatological. The samurai esteemed Song-style paintings of mountains and waterfalls, often adorned with quotations from the Confucian classics or Tang poetry. The townspeople collected prints of people and scenes from everyday life. Samurai moralists saw money as the root of evil; merchants saw it as their goal in life. (In Osaka, merchants even held an "abacus festival," at which their adding machines were consecrated to the gods of wealth and commerce.)

In poetry, too, a double structure appeared. Bashō (1644–1694) was born a samurai but gave up his status to live as a wandering poet. He is famous for his travel journal, *The Narrow Road of Oku*, and especially for his haiku, exquisitely crafted and elevated word-picture poems. The haiku of a townsman would be more likely to exemplify worldly humor.

The greatest works of literature and philosophy of Tokugawa Japan were produced between 1650 and 1725, just as the initial political transformation was being completed, but the economy was still growing and the society was not yet set in its

Mother Bathing Her Son. Woodblock print by Kitagawa Utamaro (1753–1806). Utamaro was so popular a master of his genre that publishers hired unknown artists to produce fakes in his name. This led him to sign some works "the genuine Utamaro." He boasted of his high fees, comparing himself to a great courtesan and his imitators to streetwalkers. Note the tub's skillful design, the mother's wooden clog, and her simple yet elegant kimono. A second kimono hangs to dry at the upper-right corner.

The Nelson-Atkins Museum of Art, Kansas City, Missouri (Purchase: Nelson Trust). © The Nelson Gallery Foundation. All Reproduction Rights Reserved.

What commentary on women's roles does this woodblock print provide?

ways. One of the major literary figures and certainly the most entertaining was Ihara Saikaku (1642–1693), who is generally credited with having recreated the Japanese novel with works including *The Life of an Amorous Man* and its sequel, *The Life of an Amorous Woman*. Saikaku wrote more than twenty other works, including *The Japanese Family Storehouse*, which humorously chronicles the contradictions between the pursuit of wealth and the pursuit of pleasure.

Another major figure was the dramatist Chikamatsu Monzaemon (1653–1724). Born a samurai, Chikamatsu wrote for both the Kabuki and the puppet theater. In contrast to Saikaku's protagonists, the men and women in Chikamatsu's dramas struggle to fulfill the duties and obligations of their stations in life. Only when their passions become uncontrollable, which is generally the case, do the plays end in tragedy.

Kabuki had begun early in the seventeenth century as suggestive skits and erotic dances performed by actresses. In 1629, the *bakufu* forbade women to perform on the stage. By the 1660s, Kabuki had evolved into a more serious drama with male actors playing both male and female roles. In the early eighteenth century Kabuki was displaced in popularity by the puppet theater (Bunraku). The word *puppet* does not do justice to the half-life-sized human figures. Manipulated by a team of three, they rival Nō masks in their artistry. In the late eighteenth century the puppet theater, in turn, declined, and Kabuki again blossomed as Japan's premier form of drama.

The most important change in Tokugawa intellectual life was that the ruling elite abandoned the religious worldview of Buddhism in favor of the more secular values of Confucianism. The great figures of Tokugawa Confucianism adapted Chinese Confucianism to fit Japanese society in the late seventeenth and early eighteenth centuries. For example, in Chinese Confucianism there was no place for a shōgun, whereas in the Japanese tradition of sun-line emperors, there was no room for the Mandate of Heaven. Most Tokugawa thinkers handled this discrepancy by saying that heaven gave the emperor its mandate and that the emperor then entrusted political authority to the shōgun. (This solution was not very realistic, since the emperor was just a figurehead.) Another problem was the difference between China's centralized bureaucratic government and Japan's system of lord–vassal relationships. Samurai loyalty was clearly not that of a scholar-official to the Chinese emperor. Some Japanese Confucianists solved this problem by saying that it was China that had deviated from the feudal society of the Zhou sages, whereas in Japan, Tokugawa Ieyasu had re-created that society. A third problem concerned the "central flowery kingdom" and the barbarians around it. No philosopher could bring himself to say that Japan was the real middle kingdom, but some argued that centrality was relative, whereas others suggested that China under barbarian Manchu rule had lost its claim to universality.

Japanese thought retained its intellectual vitality into the mid-nineteenth century. Thinkers were stimulated in part by disputes among different schools of Confucianism and, perhaps, by Japan's lack of an examination system. The best energies of its samurai youth were not channeled into writing sterile essays. Official preferment—within the constraints of Japan's hereditary system—was more likely to be obtained by writing a proposal for domain reforms.

Schools expanded rapidly, beginning in the early eighteenth century. By the mid-nineteenth century, about 40 to 50 percent of the male population and 15 to 20 percent of the female population was literate—a far higher rate than in most of the world and on a par with late developers in Europe.

For Tokugawa scholars, the emotional problem of how to deal with China was vexing. Their response was usually ambivalent. They praised China as the teacher country and respected its creative tradition. They studied its history, philosophy, and literature, and began a tradition of scholarship on China that has remained powerful to this day. But they also sought to retain a separate Japanese identity.

Most scholars dealt with this problem by adapting Confucianism to fit Japan. But two schools—never in the mainstream of Tokugawa thought, but growing in importance during the eighteenth and early nineteenth centuries—arrived at more radical positions.

Two important schools of scholarship—National Studies and Dutch Studies—were diametrically opposed in most respects but alike in criticizing the Chinese influence on Japanese life and culture. **National Studies** began as a philological examination of ancient Japanese texts. Scholars in the National Studies tradition tried to find in the Japanese classics the original true character of Japan before it had been influenced by Chinese ideas. They concluded that the early Japanese spirit was spontaneous, lofty, and honest, in contrast to the Chinese spirit, which they characterized as rigid, cramped, and artificial. National Studies also reaffirmed Japan's imperial institution. National Studies became influential during the late Tokugawa era and influenced the Meiji Restoration. Its doctrines continued thereafter as one strain of Japanese ultranationalism.

A second development was **Dutch Studies**. After Christianity had been proscribed and the policy of seclusion adopted, all Western books were banned in Japan. The ban on Western books (except for those propagating Christianity) was ended in 1720 by the shōgun Tokugawa Yoshimune (r. 1716–1745). Japanese pioneers recognized early that Western anatomy texts were superior to Chinese. By the mid-nineteenth century, there were schools of Dutch Studies in the main cities of Japan. Those who studied Dutch focused on medicine, but some knowledge of other Western sciences and arts also entered Japan.

Starting in the late eighteenth century, the Japanese began to think of the West, and especially of Russia, as a threat to Japan. A sudden expansion in Dutch Studies occurred after Commodore Matthew Perry's visits to Japan in 1853 and 1854. During the 1860s, Dutch Studies became Western Studies, as English, French, German, and Russian were added to the languages studied at the *bakufu* Institute for the Investigation of Barbarian Books. Dutch Studies was not a major influence on Tokugawa thought, but it laid a foundation on which the Japanese built quickly when the need for knowledge of the West arose.

CHRONOLOGY

TOKUGAWA ERA (1600–1868)

1600	Tokugawa Ieyasu reunifies Japan
1615	"Laws of Military Houses" issued
1639	Seclusion policy adopted
1642	Edo hostage system in place
1644–1694	Bashō, poet
1653–1724	Chikamatsu Monzaemon, dramatist
1701	The forty-seven rōnin avenge their lord
1853, 1854	Commodore Matthew Perry visits Japan

National Studies

A Japanese intellectual tradition that emphasized native Japanese culture and institutions and rejected the influence of Chinese Confucianism.

Dutch Studies

Scholarship based on books imported by Dutch traders, particularly medical and scientific texts.

KOREA AND VIETNAM

Korea and Vietnam are an unlikely duo. Korea is a northern land; Vietnam is tropical. Yet both countries, like Japan, took in Tang civilization and adapted it to their own purposes. Chinese civilization in the sixth and seventh centuries was the only high civilization in the area. Chinese laws, philosophies, and political institutions may be thought of as a technology of a kind. That other countries would borrow them was little different from Third World countries today that borrow the science, technology, and political ideas of the recent West.

But Koreans and Vietnamese also gained identities separate from China. In time, they took pride in their independence. Germany might be a parallel case in Europe: It borrowed the heartland Greco-Christian culture of the Mediterranean area, but it kept its original tongue and elements from its earlier culture.

KOREA

WHAT WAS Korea's relationship to China?

Geography shaped Korean history. A range of mountains along its northern rim divides the Korean peninsula from Manchuria, making it a distinct geographical unit. Mountains continue south through the eastern third of Korea, while in the west and south are coastal plains and broad river valleys. Two further geographical factors affected Korean history. One was that the northwestern corner of Korea was only 300 miles from the northeastern corner of historical China: close enough for Korea to be vulnerable to invasions by its powerful neighbor but far enough away so that most of the time China found it easier to treat Korea as a tributary than to control it directly. The second factor was that the southern rim of Korea was just 100 miles distant from the Japanese southern island of Kyushu across the Tsushima Straits (see Map 18–3).

EARLY HISTORY

During its old and new stone ages, Tungusic tribes moving south from northeast Asia peopled Korea. They spoke an Altaic tongue—related to Japanese and to Manchurian, Mongolian, and Turkic. They lived by hunting, gathering, and fishing, and, like other

MAP 18–3. Early Korean States.

How is early Korean history shaped by geography?

early peoples of northeast Asia, they made comb-patterned pottery and practiced an animistic religion. They worshiped the sun, moon, sea, and other forces of nature, and they communicated with the spirits of the dead through shamans. Important leaders were buried in megalithic tomb mounds. The early society was transformed by the introduction of bronze in 1300 B.C.E., agriculture in 1000 B.C.E., and iron in 400–300 B.C.E. Most of the population originally lived in small coastal or riverside villages and only gradually spread inland. Koreans were still ruled by tribal chiefdoms in 108 B.C.E. when the Han emperor Wudi sent an army into North Korea to menace the flank of the Hunnish Xiongnu Empire that spread across the steppe to the north of China. Wudi built a Chinese city—near Pyongyong, the present-day capital of North Korea—which survived into the fourth century C.E., and established commanderies and prefectures to administer the land.

Between the fourth and seventh centuries C.E., as Chinese control collapsed, three archaic states emerged from earlier tribal confederations. One of them, Silla, conquered the other two in the seventh century, with help from Tang armies. The Chinese armies wanted to stay and rule Korea, but they withdrew after battles with Silla troops, and Silla was recognized by China in 675 as an autonomous tribute state. The period of Silla rule may be likened to eighth-century Nara Japan. The capital was laid out, like China's Chang'an, on a checkerboard pattern. Korea borrowed Chinese writing, established government offices on the Chinese model, sent annual embassies to the Tang court, and sent thousands of students to study at the Tang capital. It embraced Chinese Buddhism, arts, and philosophies. Yet within the Silla government, birth mattered more than scholarship and rule by aristocrats continued, while in village Korea, the worship of nature deities was only lightly touched by the Buddhism that spread among the ruling elites.

Silla underwent a normal end-of-dynasty decline, with coups, wars, and barbarian attacks across the frontier. Rebel kingdoms fought until 918, when a warlord general founded a new dynasty, the Koryo. The English word "Korea" is derived from this dynastic name. This was a creative period. Korean scholars advanced in their mastery of Chinese principles of government. New genres of poetry and literature appeared. Korean potters made celadon vases rivaling those of China. The craft of history advanced: The earliest surviving history of Korea was compiled in 1145. Printing using movable metallic type was invented during the thirteenth century. Most important of all was the growth of Buddhism. Temples, monasteries, and nunneries were built throughout the land, and Buddhist arts flourished. During the thirteenth century, Buddhist scholars produced in classical Chinese a printed edition of the Tripitaka, a huge compendium of sutras and other sacred writings.

The Koryo was more "Chinese" than the Silla: Government offices resembled those in China and Chinese-type laws were enacted. But even then, the aristocracy monopolized posts in the central government, and only a third of the 300 district magistates were sent out from the capital; the rest were appointed from local nobles or dignitaries. Apart from nobles, Koryo society was made up of commoners (the "good people") and slaves. Commoners were burdened by heavy taxes of rice, labor, and military service. Hereditary slaves made up almost one-third of the population.

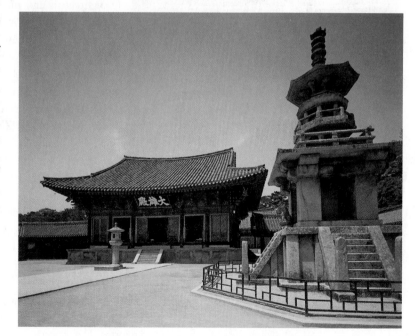

Pulguksa temple, built in 751 (and recently restored) near the ancient Silla capital of Kyongju. At right is a stupa containing a *sutra*, or relic of the Buddha.

What role did Silla play in early Korean history?

Despite cultural advances, the Koryo state was weak. For one thing, the Koryo economy was undeveloped: Trade was by barter, money did not circulate, and Chinese missions commented on the extravagance of officials in the capital and the squalor of commoners and slaves in Korea's villages. For another, the dynasty was aristocratic from the start, and as centuries passed, private estates and armies arose, and civil officials were replaced by military figures. Furthermore, frequent Mongol incursions from across the northern border weakened state finances. The Koryo court survived as long as it did by becoming in succession the tributary of the Song, Liao, Jin, and Mongol dynasties.

CHOSON DYNASTY

In 1392, a Koryo general, Yi Songgye, was sent to fight invading Ming (Chinese) armies. He decided that assuming power in Korea was more advantageous; he made peace with the Chinese and founded the Choson Dynasty. It lasted until 1910. Its amazing longevity was directly related to the stability of Ming–Qing China; it served China's interest to prop up an obliging Korean state.

In the fifteenth century 10 to 15 percent of Korea's population was composed of noble families—**yangban**—who were the ruling class. Most had possessed *yangban* status during the previous dynasty; only families that had opposed the Yi's coming to power lost their position. A little over 30 percent of the population were slaves. Early Choson Korea was the only "slave society" in the history of East Asia. Korean scholars argue that Korean slaves were not like slaves in other lands: There were no slave auctions, and, in line with Confucian teachings, wives and husbands were not separated. But slaves were nonetheless property. They were often attached to land, they could be given as gifts, and their children were slaves to be used as their owners willed. During the eighteenth and nineteenth centuries, the number declined sharply, possibly because it was easier to tax agricultural slaves than to own them. By the nineteenth century, only household slaves remained. A majority of the Korean population were commoner farmers, who were heavily taxed and usually bore their lot stoically.

yangban
Elite Korean families of the Choson period.

A Badge of Rank. In Choson Korea—as in China—the rank of an official was indicated by the embroidered square affixed to his gown. Some squares showed ducks, pheasants, egrets, leopards, or tigers. Here we see a crane flying among the clouds and rainbows below.

How did badges of rank reflect Confucian values in Korean society?

If the preceding Koryo period was Korea's age of Buddhist faith, the Choson was its Neo-Confucian age. Confucian teachings as interpreted by Zhu Xi became firmly established as the state orthodoxy. Civil and military examinations, for which only the *yangban* had the time and means to prepare, became the primary route to official promotion. Schools and academies increased in number. By the late fifteenth century, Korean philosophers were making original contributions to Zhu Xi philosophy. The shift from Buddhism to Neo-Confucianism as the ideology of the ruling elite may be seen as "East Asian" in that it paralleled changes that had occurred in China during the Song Dynasty and would occur in Japan during the Tokugawa era.

The history of Choson kings and their courts is filled with colorful drama. There were good ministers and bad, usurpations, assassinations, purges, and reforms. The *yangban* domination of the bureaucracy enabled them to resist any reform by the throne that would have injured their propertied interests. But they were united only in defense of their prerogatives, and more often were divided into factions that waged bitter struggles. The struggles can be explained, in part, by the fact that exam-passers outnumbered the official posts available. Contention between bureaucratic cliques for control of the government in Seoul was almost constant, losers often being executed or imprisoned. As the struggles continued, the effectiveness of government declined, except for a brief recovery during the early eighteenth century. High officials in Seoul used their power to garner private agricultural estates and establish schools to prepare their kinsmen for examinations.

Wise rulers and periods of good government should also be noted. An early ruler, King Sejong (r. 1418–1450), reformed land taxes, made loans of grain to farmers during spring planting, and encouraged the spread of better agricultural technology. He also reformed the army and navy, attacked pirate strongholds on Tsushima Island, and expanded Korea's borders north of the Yalu River. In 1420, he established a Hall of Worthies to encourage scholarship. Scholars at his court made sundials, water clocks, and astronomical instruments. But even Sejong suffered setbacks. The outstanding achievement of the Hall of Worthies was the creation of an alphabetic script known as *hangu*. But the script was never widely used and then only for informal purposes. Chinese remained the language of scholarship and official communications: it had prestige, authority, and the support of the educated *yangban* class. Sejong also promoted the use of coins and paper money to stimulate commerce, but they never caught on. Artisans for the most part were attached to noble households, and barter remained the rule. King Sejong was also unable to provide for an orderly succession: he had twenty sons and fourteen daughters, but after his death, his uncle usurped the Korean throne.

At mid-dynasty, invasions dealt a severe blow to Choson society. Having brought all of Japan under his control, Hideyoshi decided to conquer China by invading through Korea. His samurai armies devastated Korea in 1592 and 1596. The invasions ended with his death in 1598. On both occasions the Ming court sent troops to aid its tributary, but the Chinese armies devastated the land almost as badly as the Japanese. A third disaster occurred in 1627 and 1637 when Manchu troops invaded pro-Ming Korea. The result of these multiple incursions was a roughly 75 percent drop in taxable land. Behind this statistic lay famine, death, and misery.

Had the Choson government been stronger, it might have recovered. Instead, from the mid-seventeenth century on, Korea offers a mixed picture. Literacy rose, and a new popular fiction of fables, romances, and novels appeared. Women writers became important for the first time. Among some *yangban* there was a call for "practical learning" to renew Korean society, and scholars outlined plans for administrative reforms and the encouragement of commerce. Their recommendations were not adopted, and society continued its decline. More Koreans died in the famine of 1671 than during Hideyoshi's invasions. Overtaxation, drought, floods, pestilence, famine, and crime became commonplace. Disgruntled officials led peasants in revolts in 1811 and 1862. Because of the concentration of officials, wealth, and military power at Seoul and because of Manchu support for the ruling house, neither revolt toppled the dynasty, but Korea was weak. It had neither the will nor the means to meet the challenges it would soon face.

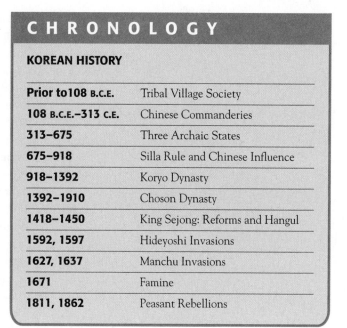

CHRONOLOGY

KOREAN HISTORY

Prior to 108 B.C.E.	Tribal Village Society
108 B.C.E.–313 C.E.	Chinese Commanderies
313–675	Three Archaic States
675–918	Silla Rule and Chinese Influence
918–1392	Koryo Dynasty
1392–1910	Choson Dynasty
1418–1450	King Sejong: Reforms and Hangul
1592, 1597	Hideyoshi Invasions
1627, 1637	Manchu Invasions
1671	Famine
1811, 1862	Peasant Rebellions

VIETNAM

VIETNAM IN SOUTHEAST ASIA

HOW DID Vietnam expand southward during this time?

Four movements shaped the historical civilizations of Southeast Asia. Vietnam was touched by each and by a fifth, as well. The first was the movement of peoples and languages from north to south. Ranges of mountains rising in Tibet and South China extend southward, dividing Southeast Asia into river valleys. The Mon and Burmese peoples had moved from the southeast slopes of the Tibetan plateau into the Upper Irrawaddy by 500 B.C.E. and continued south along the Irrawaddy and Salween rivers, founding the kingdom of Pagan in 847 C.E. Thai tribes moved south from China down the valley of the Chao Phraya River somewhat later, founding the kingdoms of Sukhothai (1238–1419) and Ayutthaya (1350–1767). Even today Thai-speaking peoples are found in several southern provinces of China. The origins of the Vietnamese are less clear, but they, too, first inhabited the north and moved into present-day central and southern Vietnam only in recent historical times.

A second movement was the Indianization of Southeast Asia. Between the first and fifteenth centuries Indian traders and missionaries crossed the Bay of Bengal and established outposts throughout Southeast Asia. As Hinduism and Buddhism spread throughout the region, Indian-type states with god-kings were established, and Indian scripts, legal codes, literature, drama, art, and music were adopted by the indigenous peoples. Today, Burma, Thailand, and Cambodia retain an Indian-type Buddhism; Bangkok temple walls are painted with scenes from the great Hindu epic, the *Mahabharata*. This early wave of Buddhism reached Vietnam but was later supplanted by Chinese Buddhism.

A third movement was of Arab and Indian traders who sailed across the Indian Ocean to trade with the Spice Islands (the Moluccas of present-day Indonesia) between the thirteenth and fifteenth centuries. Settling on the coasts and islands of Southeast Asia, they married into local ruling families and spread the teachings of Islam. Local rulers who converted became sultans. Today Malaysia and Indonesia are predominantly Muslim. The Cham state (located in what today is central Vietnam) also became Muslim. Islam did not directly affect Vietnam, although Arab and Indian traders en route to China would visit Vietnamese coastal harbors or travel up the Red River to Hanoi.

A fourth movement, much later, was the Chinese diaspora. The emigration of Chinese throughout the world but especially to Southeast Asia gathered momentum after 1842 and the post–Opium War treaties. Most Chinese went, initially, as indentured labor to work on plantations. But in time many moved to cities and opened shops. The mercantile ethos of the Chinese was more developed than that of peoples to the south. Even today the casual visitor to Bangkok sees shopkeepers sitting in front of their shops reading Chinese newspapers. Their children became educated; some entered banking or law. In most of Southeast Asia the urban economies were largely developed and controlled by Chinese. Assimilation occurred but at a generational pace. The greatest concentrations of Chinese, apart from Singapore (three quarters of the population), were in Malaysia, Indonesia, and Thailand. But many of the "boat people" who fled Vietnam after the Vietnam War were Chinese Vietnamese.

A fifth movement or event, which affected only Vietnam and made it a part of East Asia, was conquest by China.

VIETNAMESE ORIGINS

Another perspective on Vietnam begins with geography. Vietnam has been likened to two baskets on a carrying pole. One basket is the Red River basin, centering on Hanoi in the north, the other the delta of the Mekong River, centering on Saigon (Ho Chi Minh City) in the south. The carrying pole is the narrow mountainous strip of central Vietnam, with little river valleys opening to the South China Sea (see Map 18-4).

Until the late fifteenth century, the Vietnamese people inhabited only the basin of the Red River, which flows from west to east and empties into the Gulf of Tongking. The Chams, a wholly different people, occupied central Vietnam and part of the southeastern coast. The seafaring Chams became Hindu-Buddhist and later Muslim. They were united in the kingdom of Champa and waged intermittent wars against the Vietnamese to their north. A third people, the Khmers or Cambodians, inhabited the Mekong River Delta. They were a part of the Hindu-Buddhist Cambodian (Khmer) Empire that had its capital at Angkor in present-day Cambodia.

The early history of the Vietnamese in the Red River valley is known only through archaeology. Agriculture began early; slash-and-burn techniques were practiced in the highlands and crude paddy fields in the lowlands. Bronze entered, probably from China, during the first millennium B.C.E. and iron during the first or second century B.C.E. Pots made on potting wheels and bronze arrowheads and fishhooks are found in excavations, but plows were still tipped with stone. The people lived in villages under tribal leaders and worshiped the spirits of nature; men tattooed their bodies.

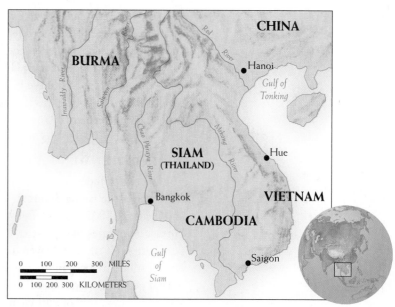

MAP 18–4. **Vietnam and Neighboring Southeast Asia**

How did China's proximity influence Vietnamese history?

A MILLENNIUM OF CHINESE RULE: 111 B.C.E.–939 C.E.

Vietnamese political history began in 208 B.C.E. when a renegade Han Dynasty general formed the state of Nan Yueh. Its capital was near the present-day Chinese city of Guangzhou. It ruled over peoples in both southeastern China and the Red River basin. The Chinese ideograph for Yueh is read *Viet* in Vietnamese. The name Vietnam, literally, "Viet to the south," is derived from the name of this early state. Nan Yueh lasted for a century until Han armies conquered it and brought it under Chinese control in 111 B.C.E. After that, the Red River basin was ruled by China for more than 1,000 years.

For the first seven centuries, Vietnam was governed by a Chinese military commandery like those established in Korea. The Chinese governor ruled indirectly through local Vietnamese chiefs or magnates. Refugees fleeing China after the fall of the Former Han Dynasty were appointed as officials in Vietnam. In a famous incident of 39 C.E., the Trung sisters led a revolt against Chinese rule. But in that age there was little sense of "country," and the only consequence of the revolt was a further strengthening of Chinese controls.

Vietnamese society changed during the centuries of Chinese rule. New agricultural techniques and metal plows, introduced from China, allowed permanent settlements and denser populations. Tribal organization gave way to village society and matrilineal to patrilineal descent—though women continued to enjoy a higher status than in China. Buddhism mingled with earlier animistic beliefs. Chinese officials sometimes married Vietnamese women, and a Sino-Vietnamese social elite arose in the capital.

During the Tang Dynasty (618–907), Vietnam was still treated as a border region, but Chinese administration became stronger. The Red River basin was divided into provinces, which the Chinese referred to collectively as **Annam**, the "pacified south." When the French came to Vietnam in the nineteenth century, they picked up the term and called the north Vietnamese *Annamese*.

There are parallels between the introduction of Tang culture in Vietnam and in Japan and Korea: In all three societies Buddhism entered, flourished in the capitals, and gradually percolated into local areas, where it absorbed elements from earlier indigenous religions. In all three, other aspects of China's higher culture affected mainly

Bronze drum engraved with intricate geometric designs from circa 800 B.C.E. Vietnam. An artifact of the early Bronze Age, it was made for ceremonial purposes. Whether early Vietnamese bronze technology was indigenous or whether it came from China is an open question.

What role did China play in the development of early Vietnamese culture?

Annam

The name given by the Chinese to modern-day Vietnam, meaning "peaceful" or "pacified South."

the elites, while an older way of life continued in villages with only small changes. But where Japanese and Korean rulers reached out for Chinese learning and technology and used it for their own ends, the Vietnamese had it thrust upon them.

Ten major revolts occurred during the thousand years of Chinese rule—not an unusual number for a Chinese border region with a non-Chinese population. The last revolt, which took place in 939, when China was weak, led to the establishment of an independent Vietnamese government. Vietnam never again became a part of China.

AN INDEPENDENT VIETNAM

The history of independent Vietnam is conventionally divided into dynastic blocks named after the ruling family: Ly (1009–1225), Tran (1225–1400), Le (1428–1787), and Nguyen (1802–1880s). But Vietnamese "dynasties" were not strong, centralized, bureaucratic states like those of China. There were tensions between the center and peripheries. At the center were the social elites who ruled the population of the Red River Delta. At the periphery were magnates, powerful local figures, who controlled upland peoples and possessed armies of their own. Thanh Hoa, a province 100 miles south of Hanoi, was of particular importance with magnates who often opposed the "dynasty." Often, several independent states coexisted during the timespan of a single "dynasty."

Chinese invasions also affected Vietnamese history. Some Chinese dynasties, as they expanded, attempted to reconquer the "south" that had once been a part of China. Ming armies occupied Vietnam for twenty years beginning in 1407. But Vietnam was distant and hard to control. Rather than engaging in wars, Chinese rulers found it easier to enroll Vietnam as a tributary: Vietnamese dynasties sent ambassadors who professed the Vietnamese ruler's submission to the Chinese emperor. In official communications to China the Vietnamese rulers styled themselves as "kings," indicating a subordinate status.

Their submission, however, was purely formal. Within Vietnam, Vietnamese rulers styled themselves as "emperors" and claimed that their mandate to rule came directly from Heaven. It was separate but equal to the mandate received by the Chinese emperor. They also denied the universality of the Chinese imperium by referring to China not as the Middle Kingdom but as the Northern Court—their own government being the Southern Court.

THE MARCH SOUTH

After twenty years of exploitative Ming rule, Le Loi, a landowner from Thanh Hoa, drove out the occupying Chinese armies in 1427. He used war-elephants in his attack against the Chinese forces. After his victory, he established the Le Dynasty (1428–1787).

Two momentous developments began in Vietnam during the fifteenth century and continued during the centuries that followed. One was a more extensive adoption of Chinese institutions. For Vietnam's rulers, Chinese institutions and culture were not so much "Chinese" as they were an advanced technology that could be used for their own purposes. The reforms of Le Thanh Tong (1442–1497), an immensely talented early ruler, were especially notable. He divided his realm into thirteen provinces and then into prefectures, counties, and departments. He weakened the nobility by holding civil service examinations for the selection of officials, and he set up nine ranks of civil and military officials. He established schools, introduced Neo-Confucian learning, and promoted public works. He registered the population and reinstituted a Chinese-type land tax. After his death, some of these reforms broke down, but in time other reformers appeared and continued his work. Chinese institutions and culture proved far more powerful than Chinese armies.

The second development, also begun by Le Thanh Tong, was what Vietnamese historians call "the march to the south." The "march" took more than two centuries. In the first leg of the march, in 1471, Le armies moved south to conquer the Muslim state of Champa. To secure the Champa lands, Le established self-supporting colonies of Vietnamese soldier-peasants along the coast of the former kingdom. These gradually merged with the local population. To rule the Muslim Chams, in 1483 he promulgated a Confucian-tinged legal code that remained in effect for a century or more. It appealed to "universal" values that both Vietnamese and Chams could accept. Successors to the Le throne, however, were unable to maintain control over the central coast, and autonomous Vietnamese states arose. These impeded the passage of settlers from the densely populated Red River basin to the south during the sixteenth and early seventeenth centuries.

The second leg of the march south was the conquest of the Mekong Delta. Within Vietnam there had emerged a balance between the Trinh (the Le had become figure-heads), who held power in Hanoi, and the Nguyen who ruled the central coast from their capital at Hue. The Nguyen gradually extended their power to the sparsely settled Mekong Delta in the south: They seized control of Saigon in 1698 and by 1757 ruled the south as far west as the Gulf of Siam. Political control facilitated the flow of people from the north and the central coast to the south, though Vietnamese remained a minority in southern Vietnam throughout the eighteenth century.

The last phase of premodern Vietnamese history was the Nguyen conquest of the north in 1802. This led to the founding of the Nguyen Dynasty with its capital at Hue. Several French advisers and adventurers who had aided the first Nguyen emperor were rewarded with high posts in the new government. But from the time of the second emperor, the Nguyen Dynasty turned against the French and began a new wave of borrowing from China. It adopted the law codes of Qing China, recruited civil and military officials by examination, and established in Hue Chinese institutions such as the Six Boards, the Hanlin Academy, and a Censorate. These moves were designed to placate Confucian scholars in the north, strengthen the authority of the court, and weaken the generals who had helped the dynasty's rise.

During the first half of the nineteenth century, Vietnam was governed better than in any previous era and better than any other Southeast Asian state. By any traditional standard, it was competent. But it had weaknesses as well. There were tensions between the north, which was overpopulated, well schooled, and furnished most of the official class, and the south, which was ethnically diverse, educationally backward, and poorly represented in government. Commerce and artisanal skills were less developed than in China and Japan, only small amounts of specie circulated, and periodic markets were more common than market towns. The government rested on a society composed largely of self-sufficient villages. In sum, Vietnam entered the second half of the nineteenth century less prepared than China or Japan for the challenges it would soon face.

CHRONOLOGY

VIETNAMESE HISTORY

111 B.C.E.–939 C.E.	Vietnam as a part of China
First 7 centuries	Rule by Chinese commanderies
7th and 8th centuries	Sinification during Tang rule
939–1880s	An independent Vietnam
Ly Dynasty 1009–1225	
Tran Dynasty 1225–1400	
Occupation by Ming troops 1407–1426	
Le Dynasty 1428-1787	
1442–1487	Reforms by Le Thanh Tong
1471	Conquest of Champa
1698	Rule over Saigon
1757	Control of Mekong Delta
Nguyen Dynasty	1802–1880s
1802	Nguyen unites Vietnam with Hue as its capital

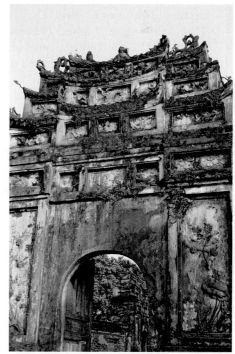

Hue. A gate from the imperial citadel.
Where is Hue?

SUMMARY

 WHERE DID China expand under the Qing?

China: Ming and Qing Dynasties. China's last two imperial dynasties were the Ming (1368–1644) and the Qing or Manchus (1644–1911). Chinese society became more integrated and its government more sophisticated. The population reached 410 million, cities grew, and commerce expanded. Chinese government rested on a bureaucracy educated in Confucian teachings and the gentry class. Under the Qing, China expanded to the west and east, establishing claims to Tibet, Central Asia, and Taiwan. Trade with the West grew under the control of Chinese officials. *page 442*

 WHAT IMPACT did military technology have on Japanese society in this period?

Japan: Warring States Era. With the collapse of the Ashikaga *bakufu*, daimyo lords fought among themselves. The military was transformed by new weapons and tactics, and Europeans arrived as traders and missionaries. *page 453*

 HOW WAS Japanese culture transformed during the Tokugawa era?

Japan: Tokugawa Era. The Tokugawa shōgun (1600–1868) restored order. The government, based at Edo, controlled the military houses and encouraged economic growth. Japan became closed to the outside world except for a small Dutch presence at Nagasaki. Japanese drama, literature, and art flourished, as did commercial life. *page 456*

 WHAT WAS Korea's relationship to China?

Korea. Korea was a tributary of China but developed according to its own internal dynamics. Korea was notable for its Confucian culture and *yangban* aristocracy. *page 466*

 HOW DID Vietnam expand southward during this time?

Vietnam. Vietnamese history during this period was notable for its conquest and peopling of the Mekong Delta. Fifteenth-century ruler Le Thanh Tong took an early lead in introducing administrative reforms based on Chinese government, and in expanding to the south. *page 469*

KEY TERMS

Annam (p. 471)
daimyo (dye-myoh) (p. 453)
Dutch Studies (p. 465)
gentry (p. 447)
Kabuki (p. 459)

Nō (p. 459)
National Studies (p. 465)
Shanxi banks (p. 444)
yangban (yahng-bahn) (p. 468)

REVIEW QUESTIONS

1. What factors led to economic and population growth in late traditional China? Was the pattern the same in Japan during those centuries?

2. How was Manchu rule like Mongol rule during the Yuan Dynasty? How was it like the rule by Chinese emperors during the Ming?

3. What were the social and administrative foundations of the absolute power of Ming–Qing emperors?

4. Compare and contrast the bureaucracies of China and Japan in this period. What influences might you expect their differences to have on the later histories of these countries?

5. How did advances in military technology change warfare in sixteenth-century Japan? How was the strategic balance of power reflected in the government created by Tokugawa Ieyasu?

6. Did literacy change the samurai? How did literate samurai "fit" the changed society of the late eighteenth century?

7. What was Dutch Studies? With what ideas did Dutch Studies compete, and why is it important?

8. Who were the yangban, and how did they influence Korean history?

9. How and why did Vietnam expand to the south?

10. Summarize the relationship between Vietnam and China and between Korea and China. Was either relationship stronger or more significant? Explain.

Note: To learn more about the topics in this chapter, please turn to the Suggested Readings at the end of the book. For additional sources related to this chapter please see www.myhistorylab.com

PEARSON
myhistorylab Connections

Reinforce what you learned in this chapter by studying the many documents, images, maps, review tools, and videos available at **www.myhistorylab.com**

Read and Review

✓●⎯Study and Review   Chapter 18

•●⎯Read the Document   Mitamura, p. 447
A Ming Naval Expedition 15th c., p. 449
Injunctions, Tokugawa Shogunate, p. 457
Shohatto, p. 457

👁⎯See the Map   Ming and Qing China, p. 443

Research and Explore

👁⎯See the Map   Trade Routes in Southeast Asia, 1300–1650

👁⎯See the Map   Voyages of Zheng-He

((●⎯Hear the Audio

Hear the audio file for Chapter 18
at **www.myhistorylab.com**

19

State Building and Society in Early Modern Europe

((●─[Hear the Audio for Chapter 19 at www.myhistorylab.com

Schonbrunn Palace, Vienna.
Between 1743 and 1763 the Austrian Empress Maria Theresa carried out the construction of the Schonbrunn Palace on the outskirts of Vienna to symbolize Habsburg authority. Like other European monarchs, she was influenced by Louis XIV of France. In the seventeenth century, to symbolize his vast royal authority, Louis XIV had constructed a vast new palace at Versailles outside Paris as the center of his government.

Compare this photograph of Schonbrunn Palace with the painting of Versailles on page 482 [A Closer Look]. How are the two buildings similar?

From the early seventeenth to mid-twentieth centuries, Europe dominated the world politically, militarily, and economically, as no region had before. Two broad factors accounted for this situation. First, by the mid-eighteenth century, five major states—Great Britain, France, Austria, Prussia, and Russia—had come to dominate European politics and would continue to do so until at least World War I. These states began to fight among themselves, first in Europe and then also in their colonial empires, in the late seventeenth century. These conflicts had major consequences for the non-European world.

GLOBAL PERSPECTIVE

EARLY MODERN EUROPE

During the seventeenth and eighteenth centuries political and economic developments occurred in Europe that set the continent on a path that by the nineteenth century resulted in a period of European world domination that ultimately proved temporary. The major states of northwestern Europe consolidated themselves politically and militarily in strong, often aggressive political units. The economy of this region of Europe would take the first steps toward industrialization and the capacity to produce vast quantities of both consumer and capital goods. The Netherlands, France, and Great Britain developed sophisticated financial structures that fueled overseas commercial empires, protected by strong navies.

These world-transforming developments occurred slowly. At the beginning of this era of political and economic consolidation, much of Europe resembled other major world civilizations. European states displayed certain problems that also characterized the governments of China and Japan during the same epochs. In particular, as in Japan, the problem of a balance between centralization and decentralization arose in virtually all the European states. In France, Russia, and Prussia, the forces of centralization proved quite strong. In Austria

the forces of decentralization were powerful. England achieved a rather delicate balance. Furthermore, as in Tokugawa Japan, European states of the eighteenth century generally saw an increase in legal codification and in the growth of bureaucracy. Only in Prussia did the military influence on society resemble that in Japan.

The role of the personality of the monarch in Europe bore some resemblance to that of certain Manchu emperors in China, such as Kangxi (1662–1722) and Qianlong (r. 1736–1795). Louis XIV and Peter the Great had no less influence on their nations than did these great Manchu emperors. All of them built up military strength and fostered innovation. However, although European rulers developed state bureaucracies, none of them put together so brilliant a group of trained civil servants as those who administered China. The roots of the Chinese civil service went back centuries, and Chinese civil servants, unlike those in Europe, tended to resist modernization of the Chinese government and economy for both practical and ideological reasons. Civil servants in Europe tended to foster rather than obstruct modernization, which posed no threat to their power or worldview.

The second factor was a series of economic advances, primarily in northwestern Europe, that laid the foundation for the social and economic transformation of the world. For the first time in their history, Europeans began to achieve a more or less stable food supply. The population of Europe commenced a major period of growth. New inventions and institutions, known collectively as the industrial revolution, gave Europe a productive capacity previously unknown in human history. Economic advances provided Europeans the tools to dominate much of the world. ■

EUROPEAN POLITICAL CONSOLIDATION

HOW DID England and France provide models for governance in early modern Europe?

TWO MODELS OF EUROPEAN POLITICAL DEVELOPMENT

In the second half of the sixteenth century, changes in European military organization, weapons, and tactics sharply increased the cost of warfare and forced monarchs to seek new revenues. Rulers like the king of France, who established secure financial bases without the support of nobles or assemblies, exercised absolute rule. The English monarch, by contrast, could govern only with Parliament by the end of the seventeenth century. These two governmental systems—**absolutism** in France and **parliamentary monarchy** in England—shaped Europe's political evolution.

TOWARD PARLIAMENTARY GOVERNMENT IN ENGLAND

When Elizabeth I died childless in 1603, the English crown passed to James VI of Scotland, the son of Mary, Queen of Scots. He became James I of England (r. 1603–1625), founder of the Stuart Dynasty. The Stuart kings aspired to absolute power, and their pursuit of an income to support it threatened the economic well-being

absolutism

Term applied to strong centralized continental monarchies that attempted to make royal power dominant over aristocracies and other regional authorities.

parliamentary monarchy

A state headed by a monarch but whose power is shared with a national representative body.

The global commercial empires of the Netherlands, France, Spain, and England gave rise to fierce commercial rivalries. The drive for empire and commercial supremacy propelled these states into contact with Africa, Latin America, India, China, and Japan. Spain and Portugal had long exploited Latin America as their own monopoly, an arrangement that England challenged in the eighteenth century. China's lack of interest in dominating the Indian Ocean opened the way for European adventurers and traders in India. France and England fought for commercial supremacy in India, and by the 1760s England had, in effect, conquered the subcontinent. The slave trade between Africa and the New World flourished throughout the seventeenth and the eighteenth centuries. European merchants and navies also sought to penetrate East Asia, although their success was limited until the advent of nineteenth-century "gunboat diplomacy." As this term implies, European success in Africa, Asia, and the Indian Ocean was always closely linked to its sophisticated military technology, and especially the construction of sturdy ships able to carry heavy cannons. As a result of these developments, European commerce dominated the world for the next two centuries. Moreover, beginning in the early eighteenth century with the slow but later steady growth of industrialism, the political power of the European states became linked to a qualitatively different economic base than any seen elsewhere in the world. That political and economic combination allowed Europe to dominate the world from the 1750s to the Second World War II.

Focus Questions

- How did European states resemble those in other parts of the world in the mid-eighteenth century? How did they differ?
- What was the relationship between military technology, especially naval power, and the growth of European colonial empires?
- What factors led to the political and economic transformation of western Europe and its emergence as a region that would eventually (for a time) dominate much of the world?

of the nobility and elites represented in Parliament. These groups invoked traditional English liberties and effectively resisted the Stuarts. **Puritans** (Calvinists), who wanted a more radical reformation of the Anglican Church, also opposed the kings. Both James I and his son Charles I (r. 1625–1649) had Catholic sympathies and favored peaceful relations with the Roman Catholic powers Spain and France. Consequently, the first two Stuarts confronted a combined political and religious opposition to their absolutist policies.

In 1642, the conflict between Charles I and Parliament erupted into civil war, which the parliamentary and Puritan forces won in 1645. In 1649, a "rump" Parliament (one from which the opposition had been removed) beheaded Charles I and abolished the monarchy, the House of Lords, and the established church. England became a Puritan republic led by the victorious general Oliver Cromwell (1599–1658). After Cromwell died, disillusionment with Puritan strictness and republican mismanagement prompted restoration of the Stuart monarchy under Charles II (r. 1660–1685). His Parliament was dominated by conservative members of the Church of England, and the policies it pursued severely restricted both Protestant Non-Conformists and Roman Catholics. Parliament's Test Act established as a qualification for office an oath that no Roman Catholic could take in good conscience.

James II (r. 1685–1688), the brother who succeeded Charles in 1685, was a Roman Catholic. He decreed toleration for both Roman Catholics and Protestant Non-Conformists and imprisoned seven Anglican bishops who refused to publicize his suspension of laws against Catholics. James's policy of toleration had as its goal the extension of royal authority over all English institutions.

The English political classes had hoped that James would be succeeded by Mary (r. 1689–1694), his Protestant eldest daughter. She was married to William of Orange (1650–1702), stadtholder of the Netherlands and the leader of European opposition to Louis XIV. But on June 20, 1688, James II's Catholic second wife gave birth to a son.

Puritans
English Protestants who sought to "purify" the Church of England of any vestiges of Catholicism.

Read the Document
The Divine Right of Kings, 1598, James I at **myhistorylab.com**

View the Image
Allegorical View: Cromwell as Savior England at **myhistorylab.com**

Read the Document
Cromwell Abolishes English Monarchy 1651 at **myhistorylab.com**

QUICK REVIEW

Charles II (r. 1660–1685)
- England returned to the 1642 status quo when Charles assumed the throne
- Charles favored religious toleration
- Issued Declaration of Indulgence in 1672 suspending all laws against non-Anglicans

Charles I ruled for several years without calling Parliament, but once he began a war with Scotland, he needed revenues that only Parliament could supply.

Anthony van Dyck, "Portrait of Charles I. Hunting." c. 1635. Oil on Canvas. 8'11" x 6'11 1/2" (2.72 x 2.12 m). Musee du Louvre, Paris. RMN Reunion des Musees Nationaux/Art Resource, New York.

Compare this image of Charles I with the portraits of Louis XIV on page 481 and the Qianlong emperor on page 449. How are the three portraits similar? How are they different?

Glorious Revolution

The largely peaceful (at least within England) replacement of James II by William and Mary as English monarchs in 1688-1689. It marked the beginning of constitutional monarchy in Britain.

•••Read the Document
The English Bill of Rights, 1689
at **myhistorylab.com**

There was now a Catholic male heir to the throne. The parliamentary opposition invited William to invade England to preserve its "traditional liberties," that is, the Protestant Church of England and parliamentary government.

THE "GLORIOUS REVOLUTION"

William of Orange arrived with his army in November 1688. James fled to France. Parliament in 1689 proclaimed William III and Mary II the new monarchs, thus completing the so-called **Glorious Revolution** (its glory lay in its supposed bloodlessness). William and Mary, in turn, recognized a Bill of Rights that limited the powers of the monarchy and guaranteed the civil liberties of the English privileged classes. Henceforth, England's monarchs would be subject to law and would rule by the consent of Parliament, which was to be called into session every three years. The Bill of Rights also prohibited Roman Catholics from occupying the English throne. The Toleration Act of 1689 permitted worship by all Protestants but outlawed Roman Catholics and those who denied the Christian doctrine of the Trinity.

The Glorious Revolution has traditionally been seen as a relatively peaceful event. Recent scholarship, however, has disclosed considerable resistance in both Scotland and Ireland, which resulted in significant loss of life. Conversely, events in England itself now appear to have been driven not only by the long-recognized actions of the political elite but also by a genuinely popular resistance to James II. Furthermore, the political results of the revolution went well beyond the assertion of parliamentary authority. William and Mary introduced many new policies, including those favoring more modern economic activity, and a foreign policy shift toward direct opposition to France.

The Act of Settlement in 1701 ended a century of strife by bequeathing the English crown to Germany's Protestant House of Hanover if Anne (r. 1702–1714), the second daughter of James II and the heir to the childless William and Mary, died childless. At Queen Anne's death in 1714, the Elector of Hanover became George I of England (r. 1714–1727), the third foreigner to occupy its throne in just more than a century.

Under the Hanoverians, Britain achieved political stability and economic prosperity during the first quarter of the eighteenth century. Robert Walpole (1676–1745), George I's chief minister from 1721 to 1742, was adept at handling the House of Commons and exercising influence through patronage. He maintained peace abroad and promoted the status quo at home. Because the dominant economic groups were represented in Parliament, they were willing to pay the taxes to support a powerful military force, particularly a strong navy. As a result, Great Britain became not only a European power of the first order, but also eventually a world power.

The power of the British monarchs and their ministers was limited, and Parliament could not ignore popular pressure. Many members of Parliament held independent views. Newspapers and public debate flourished. Free speech could be exercised, as could freedom of association. No standing army intimidated the populace. The English state showed how military power could coexist with political liberty, and Britain became the model for European progressives who opposed the absolutist

CHRONOLOGY

ENGLAND

1603	James VI of Scotland becomes James I of England
1625	Charles I becomes king of England
1629	Charles I dissolves Parliament and embarks on eleven years of personal rule
1642	Outbreak of the Civil War
1649	Charles I executed
1649–1660	Various attempts at a Puritan Commonwealth
1660	Charles II restored to the English throne
1672	Parliament passes the Test Act
1685	James II becomes king of England
1688–1689	Glorious Revolution; William III and Mary II become king and queen of England
1701	Act of Settlement provides for Hanoverian Succession
1702–1714	Queen Anne, the last of the Stuarts
1714	George I of Hanover becomes king of England
1721–1742	Ascendancy of Sir Robert Walpole

regimes on the Continent. The political ideas that emerged in the British Isles during the seventeenth century also took root in Britain's North American colonies.

RISE OF ABSOLUTE MONARCHY IN FRANCE: THE WORLD OF LOUIS XIV

The French monarchy trod a very different political path. Louis XIV (r. 1643–1715) came to the throne at the age of 5. During his childhood his chief minister, Cardinal Mazarin (1602–1661), tried to impose direct royal administration on France. These efforts aroused a series of widespread rebellions among French nobles between 1649 and 1652 known as the Fronde (after the French word for the slingshot used by street boys).

YEARS OF PERSONAL RULE

After Mazarin's death in 1661, Louis XIV assumed personal control of the government. Louis concentrated unprecedented authority in the monarchy but, with the Fronde in mind, respected local social and political institutions. Because he governed directly, rebels could not defend themselves from a charge of treason by claiming that they opposed only bad ministers and not the king.

Louis XIV was innovative in the use of the physical setting of his court to enhance his political power. The palace at Versailles, which was built between 1676 and 1708, was a temple to royalty. Its splendor proclaimed the majesty of the Sun King, as Louis was known. It housed thousands of the more important nobles, royal officials, and servants, and preoccupation with elaborate court ceremonies kept nobles from the real business of government.

Louis XIV of France (r. 1643–1715) was the dominant European monarch in the second half of the seventeenth century. The powerful centralized monarchy he created established the prototype for the mode of government later termed absolutism.

What do you notice about Louis XIV's body, his clothes, and his surroundings?

A Closer Look

Versailles

Louis XIV constructed his great palace at Versailles, as painted here in 1668 by Pierre Patel the Elder (1605–1676), to demonstrate the new centralized power he sought to embody in the French monarchy.

The outer wings, extending from the front of the central structure, housed governmental offices.

The central building is the hunting lodge his father Louis XIII had built earlier in the century. Its interior and that of the wings added to it were decorated with themes from mythology presenting Louis XIV as the "Sun King," around whom all his kingdom revolved.

The gardens and ponds behind the main structure were the sites of elaborate entertainments, concerts, and fireworks.

Pierre Patel, "Perspective View of Versailles." Châteaux de Versailles et de Trianon, Versailles, France. Photo copyright Bridgeman-Giraudon/Art Resource, New York.

Questions

1. How might the size alone of Versailles, as experienced by visitors and by viewers of paintings and prints of the structure, have served to overawe Louis's subjects? What other buildings of the day might have approached Versailles in size? In particular, how might French nobility have reacted to the setting?

2. Do you think some people who saw Versailles or images of it might have wondered how this extraordinary royal community was financed and might have drawn critical conclusions about the structure of French taxes?

3. By the end of his life Louis rarely ventured outside Versailles, and neither did his eighteenth-century royal successors. How might the limitation of so much royal experience to the region of Versailles have distorted the monarchs' view of their kingdom?

4. How might the images of Louis in mythological scenes have created a sense that his character and his power were vaster than those of ordinary mortals?

Louis owed his concept of royal authority to his devout tutor, the political theorist Bishop Jacques-Bénigne Bossuet (1627–1704). Bossuet defended what he called the **"divine right of kings."** He cited examples of Old Testament rulers divinely appointed by and answerable only to God. Medieval popes had insisted that only God could judge a pope; so Bossuet argued that only God could judge the king. As God's regents on Earth, kings could not be bound by nobles and parliaments, for as Louis XIV allegedly explained: "*L'état, c'est moi*" ("I am the state").

Louis was determined to unify France religiously, and in October 1685 he revoked the Edict of Nantes (1598), which had protected France's Huguenots. Protestant churches and schools were closed, Protestant ministers exiled, nonconverting laity condemned as galley slaves, and Protestant children taken to be baptized by Catholic priests. More than a quarter million people fled and joined France's opponents in England, Germany, the Netherlands, and the New World.

As will be seen later in the chapter, Louis used most of the wealth and authority he had amassed to lead France into a long series of wars that ultimately weakened the nation by the time of his death in 1715. Yet despite those failures he had established a model of strong centralized monarchy that other monarchs in central and eastern Europe would copy.

RUSSIA ENTERS THE EUROPEAN POLITICAL ARENA

The emergence of Russia as an active European power was a new development. Previously, Russia had hardly been considered part of Europe, and prior to 1673 it maintained no permanent ambassadors in western Europe. Hemmed in by Sweden on the Baltic and by the Ottoman Empire on the Black Sea, Russia had no warm-water ports. Its chief outlet for trade to the west was Archangel on the White Sea, which was icebound part of the year.

BIRTH OF THE ROMANOV DYNASTY

The last half of the reign of Ivan IV (r. 1533–1584), or Ivan the Terrible, was a time of enormous political turmoil in Russia. An era called the Time of Troubles followed, and in 1613, an assembly of nobles tried to stabilize the situation by electing as tsar a 17-year-old boy, Michael Romanov (r. 1613–1645). He began the dynasty that ruled Russia until 1917, but his country remained weak and impoverished. The *boyars*, the old nobility, controlled its bureaucracy, and the *streltsy*, or guards of the Moscow garrison, constantly threatened mutiny.

PETER THE GREAT

In 1682, a 10-year-old boy named Peter (r. 1682–1725) ascended the throne with the help of the *streltsy*, who expected to exploit him. Like Louis XIV, the turmoil of his youth convinced Peter that the power of the tsar had to be made supreme over the *boyars* and the *streltsy* and that the tsar needed a strong military.

Northwestern Europe, particularly the military resources of the maritime powers, fascinated Peter I, who eventually became known as Peter the Great. In 1697, Peter toured western Europe incognito (allowing him to avoid the ceremony that would have attended an official royal visit). He spent his happiest moments inspecting shipyards, docks, and shops that produced military hardware, and he returned to Moscow determined to copy the technology he had seen abroad. He also understood that his plans for making Russia into a great nation would require him to oppose the long-standing power and traditions of the Russian nobles.

Peter the Great (r. 1682–1725), seeking to make Russia a military power, reorganized the country's political and economic structures. His reign saw Russia enter fully into European power politics. Here he is depicted as a latter-day St. George, slaying a dragon.

The Apotheosis of Tsar Peter I the Great 1672–1725 by unknown artist 1710. Historical Museum Moscow Russia. E.T. Archive. Art Archive/Picture Desk Inc./Kobal Collection.

What forces might the dragon symbolize?

☀━View the Image
Battle of Poltava, 1709
at **myhistorylab.com**

◖•━Hear the Audio
at **myhistorylab.com**

•••━Read the Document
Peter the Great with Alexis Russia
at **myhistorylab.com**

While Peter was abroad, the *streltsy* had rebelled. On his return, Peter suppressed the revolt. Approximately a thousand rebels were put to death, and their corpses remained on public display to discourage future disloyalty. Peter then built a new military that would serve him, not itself. He employed ruthless methods of conscription and over the course of his reign drafted about 300,000 men. He adopted policies for the officer corps and general military discipline patterned on those of west European armies.

Peter attacked the *boyars* and their attachment to tradition. He personally shaved the long beards of the court *boyars* and sheared off the customary long hand-covering sleeves of their shirts and coats, which had made them the butt of jokes among other European courts. Peter skillfully balanced one group against another as he rebuilt Russian government and military forces along the lines of the more powerful European states.

Peter built a navy to compete with the Ottoman Empire in the Black Sea, and in 1695 he began a war with the Ottomans. He also constructed a Baltic fleet to fight the Great Northern War with Sweden (1700–1721). In 1721, the Peace of Nystad confirmed Russia's conquest of Estonia, Livonia, and part of Finland. Peter had acquired the ice-free ports that were to give Russia influence in European affairs.

Peter's domestic and foreign policies intersected on the Gulf of Finland where he founded his new capital city, St. Petersburg, in 1703. He built government structures and compelled the *boyars* to construct town houses. St. Petersburg symbolized a new Western orientation for Russia and Peter's determination to hold his position on the Baltic coast.

Peter was jealous of his son Aleksei, who had never demonstrated much intelligence or ambition. Late in 1717, Peter suspected that Aleksei had become the focal point for a seditious plot. He personally interrogated Aleksei, who was eventually condemned to death and died under mysterious circumstances on June 26, 1718.

The interrogations surrounding Aleksei had revealed greater degrees of court opposition than Peter had suspected. Recognizing he could not eliminate his numerous opponents the way he had attacked the *streltsy* in 1698, Peter undertook radical administrative reforms designed to bring the nobility and the Russian Orthodox Church more closely under the authority of persons loyal to the tsar.

In 1717 Peter reorganized his domestic administration, using the model of Swedish institutions called *colleges*—bureaus of several persons operating according to written instructions rather than departments headed by a single minister. He established eight colleges to handle matters such as the collection of taxes, foreign relations, war, and economic affairs. Each college had a foreign adviser, and by making careful appointments Peter balanced influence within these colleges between nobles and people he trusted.

He also curtailed the independence of the Russian Orthodox Church, some of whose clergy sympathized with the tsar's son. In 1721, Peter abolished the post of patriarch and submitted the church to a government department called the Holy Synod, consisting of several bishops headed by a layman. The Holy Synod made sure that the church supported the tsar's secular agenda.

St. Petersburg. Peter the Great built St. Petersburg on the Gulf of Finland to provide Russia with better contact with western Europe. He moved Russia's capital there from Moscow in 1703. This is an eighteenth-century view of the city.

Why would an image of St. Petersburg emphasize its position on the sea?

Vûe des bords de la Neva en descendant la rivière entre le Palais d'hyver de Sa Majesté Impériale & les batimens de l'Académie des Sciences

In 1722 Peter published a **Table of Ranks** intended to draw the nobility into state service. That table equated a person's social position and privileges with his rank in the bureaucracy or the military rather than with his lineage among the traditional landed nobility. Peter thus made the social standing of individual *boyars* a function of their willingness to serve the state.

For all the decisive actions Peter had taken since 1717, he still had not settled on a successor. Consequently, when he died in 1725, there was no clear line of succession to the throne. For more than thirty years, soldiers and nobles again determined who ruled Russia. Peter had laid the foundations of a modern Russia, but not the foundations of a stable state.

THE HABSBURG EMPIRE AND THE PRAGMATIC SANCTION

After 1648 the Habsburg family retained a firm hold on the title of Holy Roman Emperor, but the emperor's power rested on the allegiance of various political bodies in the empire. These included German states, cities, bishoprics, and other territories. The Habsburgs also began to consolidate their power within their hereditary possessions outside the Holy Roman Empire, including the kingdom of Bohemia (in modern Czechoslovakia), the duchies of Moravia and Silesia, Hungary, Croatia, and Transylvania. In each of their many territories, the Habsburgs ruled by virtue of a different title and needed the cooperation of the local nobility. They often had to bargain with nobles in one part of Europe to maintain their position in another.

Table of Ranks

An official hierarchy established by Peter the Great in imperial Russia that equated a person's social position and privileges with his rank in the state bureaucracy or army.

CHRONOLOGY	
RISE OF RUSSIAN POWER	
1533–1584	Reign of Ivan the Terrible
1584–1613	Time of Troubles
1613	Michael Romanov becomes tsar
1682	Peter the Great becomes tsar as a boy
1689	Peter assumes personal rule
1697	European tour of Peter the Great
1698	Peter suppresses the *streltsy*
1700	The Great Northern War opens between Russia and Sweden; Russia defeated at Narva by Charles XII
1703	Saint Petersburg founded
1709	Russia defeats Sweden at Poltava
1718	Death of Aleksei, son of Peter the Great
1721	Peace of Nystad ends the Great Northern War
1721	Peter establishes control over the Russian church
1722	The Table of Ranks
1725	Peter dies, leaving an uncertain succession

See the Map

Expansion of Russia under Peter Great at **myhistorylab.com**

Pragmatic Sanction

The legal basis negotiated by the Emperor Charles VI (r. 1711–1740) for the Habsburg succession through his daughter Maria Theresa (r. 1740–1780).

Despite these internal weaknesses, Leopold I (r. 1658–1705) blocked the advances of the Turks into central Europe and thwarted aggression by Louis XIV. The Ottomans recognized his sovereignty over Hungary in 1699, and he extended his territorial holdings over much of the Balkan Peninsula and present-day western Romania (see Map 19-1).

In the early eighteenth century the Habsburg emperor Charles VI (r. 1711–1740) had no male heir, and there was only a weak precedent for a female ruler of the Habsburg domains. Charles feared that on his death the Austrian Habsburg lands might fall prey to the surrounding powers. Determined to prevent that disaster and to provide his domains with the semblance of legal unity, he devoted most of his reign to seeking the approval of his family, the estates of his realms, and the major foreign powers for a document called the **Pragmatic Sanction**.

This instrument provided the legal basis for a single line of inheritance within the Habsburg dynasty through Charles VI's daughter Maria Theresa (r. 1740–1780). When Charles VI died, he believed that he had secured legal recognition of the unity of the Habsburg Empire and the succession of his daughter. However, his failure to provide Maria Theresa with a strong army or a full treasury left her lands vulnerable to foreign aggression. Less than two months after his death in December 1740, Frederick II of Prussia invaded the Habsburg province of Silesia, and Maria Theresa had to fight for her inheritance.

MAP 19–1.   The Austrian Habsburg Empire, 1521–1772.   The empire had three main units— Austria, Bohemia, and Hungary. Expansion was mainly eastward: eastern Hungary from the Ottomans (seventeenth century) and Galicia from Poland (1772). Silesia was lost after 1740, but the Habsburgs remained Holy Roman Emperors.

How did Europe's ruling families try to minimize the risks associated with succession?

THE RISE OF PRUSSIA

The rise of Prussia occurred within the German power vacuum created by the Peace of Westphalia. It is the story of the extraordinary Hohenzollern family, which had ruled Brandenburg since 1417. Through inheritance the family had acquired a series of territories, most of which were not contiguous with Brandenburg. By the late seventeenth century, however, their scattered holdings constituted a block of territory within the Holy Roman Empire second only to that of the Habsburgs. Beginning in the mid-seventeenth century, Hohenzollern rulers forged their geographically separated holdings into a powerful state and built an army that empowered them to rule without the approval of the local nobility.

There was, however, a political and social trade-off between the Hohenzollerns and their nobles, the **Junkers**. In exchange for obedience to the Hohenzollerns, the Junkers received the right to total authority over the serfs on their estates. Furthermore, the heaviest taxes were imposed on the peasants and the urban classes. Junkers increasingly dominated the army officer corps, and all officials and army officers took an oath of loyalty to the Hohenzollern rulers. The army provided the state with a semblance of unity and made Prussia a desirable ally. As thanks for aiding the Habsburg emperor in 1701, the Hohenzollerns were permitted the title of "King" in Prussia, one of their parcels of territory that lay inside Poland and outside the authority of the Holy Roman Emperor.

Under Frederick William I (r. 1713–1740) the Prussian military grew from about 39,000 in 1713 to over 80,000 in 1740, making it the third- or fourth-largest army in Europe. Prussia's population, in contrast, ranked thirteenth in size. Separate laws applied to the army and to civilians. Laws, customs, and royal attention made the officer corps the highest social class of the state.

⊙ See the **Map**
Growth of Brandenburg-Prussia, 1618–1786
at **myhistorylab.com**

Junkers
The noble landlords of Prussia.

Vue du Camp de l'Irmé Prussienne dessinée sur le naturel dans la pleine de Lowenburg en Pomeranie . Par le Sieur Vale le jeune .   à Paris chez mondhare rue St Jaques à l'Oeil de chains

A Prussian Military Camp.
This print shows a Prussian encampment in the Pomerania, on the south coast of the Baltic Sea. By 1800 this entire region had come under Prussian control.

What role did the military play in the Prussian rise to power?

Although Frederick William I built the best army in Europe, he avoided conflict. His army was a symbol of Prussian power and unity, not an instrument of aggression. At his death in 1740 he passed to his son Frederick II (Frederick the Great, r. 1740–1786) this superb military machine, but not the wisdom to refrain from using it. Almost immediately, Frederick II upset the Pragmatic Sanction and invaded Silesia. He thus crystallized the Austrian-Prussian rivalry for the control of Germany that would dominate central European affairs for over a century.

EUROPEAN WARFARE: FROM CONTINENTAL TO WORLD CONFLICT

WHY WERE the European wars of the eighteenth century global in scope?

Whereas religious zeal had largely fueled the European wars of the Reformation era, dynastic and commercial rivalry drove wars from the reign of Louis XIV through the conclusion of the Seven Years' War in 1763. Each round of warfare was geographically more widespread. Through these conflicts the European powers extended their military and political presence to match their expanding commercial presence in the Americas and in Asia.

THE WARS OF LOUIS XIV

By the late 1660s France had become superior to any other European nation in administrative bureaucracy, armed forces, and national unity. Louis XIV could afford to raise and maintain a large and powerful army and was in a position to dominate Europe.

In 1667, Louis XIV led France into the first of four major wars designed to expand his territory, and he was soon regarded as a menace to the whole of western Europe, Catholic and Protestant alike. In 1681, Louis's forces occupied the free city of Strasbourg, prompting defensive coalitions to form against him. One of these, the League of Augsburg, grew to include England, Spain, Sweden, the United Provinces, and the major German states, including the Habsburg Empire. Between 1689 and 1697, the League of Augsburg and France battled each other on European fronts in the Nine Years' War, while England and France also warred in North America. In 1697, the Peace of Ryswick secured Holland's borders and thwarted Louis's expansion into Germany.

Then on November 1, 1700, Charles II of Spain (r. 1665–1700) died and bequeathed his estate to Louis's grandson, Philip of Anjou, or Philip V of Spain (r. 1700–1746). This tipped the balance of power in Europe in France's favor, and England, Holland, and the Holy Roman Empire formed the Grand Alliance as a countermeasure. The War of the Spanish Succession (1701–1714) soon enveloped western Europe. France finally made peace with England at Utrecht in July 1713 and with Holland and the emperor at Rastadt in March 1714. Philip V retained Spain, but England got Gibraltar, a base for action in the Mediterranean. The long war left France economically and politically exhausted. (See Map 19-2.)

THE EIGHTEENTH-CENTURY COLONIAL ARENA

The Treaty of Utrecht in 1713 established boundaries for the colonial empires of the first half of the eighteenth century. Except for Portugal's Brazil, Spain claimed all of mainland South America, Mexico, Cuba, half of Hispaniola, Florida, and California. Britain held the North Atlantic seaboard, Nova Scotia, Newfoundland, Jamaica, and Barbados as well as a few trading stations on the Indian subcontinent. The Dutch controlled Surinam (Dutch Guiana) and various trading stations in Ceylon, Bengal, and Java (modern-day Indonesia). The French claimed the St. Lawrence River val-

◉ See the Map
Europe after the Treaty of Utrecht, 1714
at **myhistorylab.com**

MAP EXPLORATION

To explore this map further, go to **http://www.myhistorylab.com**

MAP 19–2. Europe in 1714. The War of the Spanish Succession ended a year before the death of Louis XIV. The Bourbons had secured the Spanish throne, but Spain had forfeited its possessions in Flanders and Italy.

Which regions of Europe seem to have experienced political consolidation, and which seem most splintered?

ley; the Ohio and Mississippi River valleys; Saint Domingue (Haiti), Guadeloupe, and Martinique in the West Indies; and trading stations in India and West Africa. French and English settlers in North America clashed throughout the eighteenth century (see Map 19-3 on page 490).

Each of the powers sought to make its imperial holdings into impenetrable trading areas, but the Spanish government in particular lacked the capacity to

MAP 19–3. The Colonial Arena.   The acquisition of overseas colonies by European powers led to intense rivalries on a global scale. Territories frequently changed hands during the eighteenth century.

Why were colonies central to European conflicts in the eighteenth century?

maintain a commercial monopoly over its sprawling territory. The Treaty of Utrecht gave the British a thirty-year *asiento*, or contract, to furnish slaves to the Spanish Empire and the right to send one ship each year to the trading fair at Portobello (in present-day Panama). The British cheated, and when the Spanish decided to enforce its restrictions, the stage was set for conflict.

A Dutch Merchant and His Wife in Batavia (Java). Attributed to Jacob Cuyp (1594–1651), this painting from 1650 shows the Dutch merchant Jacob Mathieusen and his wife in front of Batavia's harbor, on the island of Java in the East Indies. The merchant points to his ships while a slave shelters the couple from the tropical sun with a parasol.

How is the relation between the merchant and his wife depicted? Between the Europeans and the non-European?

WAR OF JENKINS'S EAR

In 1731, when a Spanish patrol boarded a British vessel to search for contraband, a fight ensued and an English captain, Robert Jenkins, had his ear cut off. He preserved it in a jar of brandy and in 1738 displayed it to the British Parliament as evidence of alleged Spanish atrocities inflicted on British merchants. Late in 1739, Great Britain went to war with Spain and, in conjunction with Prussia's aggression on the continent, began a series of worldwide European wars.

THE WAR OF THE AUSTRIAN SUCCESSION (1740–1748)

In December 1740, as noted earlier in the chapter, Frederick II of Prussia seized the Austrian province of Silesia. Maria Theresa of Austria preserved the Habsburg Empire by sacrificing some of the power of its crown. She ensured the loyalty of the Magyars of Hungary, the most important of her domains, by granting them considerable local autonomy. The link between her war with Prussia, the War of the Austrian Succession, and the British–Spanish commercial conflict was made by France. French aristocrats pushed their government to support Prussia against Austria, France's long-standing enemy. French aid to Prussia helped consolidate a new and powerful German state, a threat that brought Great Britain into the continental war against France and Prussia. In 1744, the conflict expanded beyond the continent when France decided to support Spain against Britain in the New World. The war ended in stalemate in 1748. By the Treaty of Aix-la-Chapelle, Prussia retained Silesia. This was a truce, not a permanent peace.

THE SEVEN YEARS' WAR (1756–1763)

Before the rivalries again erupted into war, a dramatic shift of alliances took place. In 1756 Prussia and Great Britain signed the Convention of Westminster. The Prussians and the British hoped that their alliance

CHRONOLOGY	
EUROPEAN CONFLICTS OF THE MID–EIGHTEENTH CENTURY	
1739	Outbreak of War of Jenkins's Ear between England and Spain
1740	War of the Austrian Succession commences
1748	Treaty of Aix-la-Chapelle
1756	Convention of Westminster between England and Prussia
1756	Seven Years' War opens
1759	British forces capture Quebec
1763	Treaty of Hubertusburg
1763	Treaty of Paris

The Taking of Quebec. The capture of Quebec in September 1759 by British forces, followed by the seizure of Montreal a year later, signaled the demise of French power in Canada.

How did the French lose control in Canada?

View of the Taking of QUEBECK by the English Forces Commanded by Gen.ˡ Wolfe Sep: 13.ᵗʰ 1759.

QUICK REVIEW

The Seven Years' War (1756–1763)

◆ Prussian invasion of Saxony sparked war

◆ War spread into North America

◆ Treaty of Paris ended war in 1763

would dissuade Russia and France from invading Germany. When Austria countered the loss of its British ally by turning to France, the European alliances of the previous century were reversed.

In August 1756, Prussia invaded Saxony to head off what Frederick II thought was a conspiracy by Saxony, Austria, and France. This began the Seven Years' War. In the spring of 1757, France and Austria formed a new alliance targeted at Prussia, and Sweden, Russia, and the smaller German states joined them. Two factors in addition to Frederick's strong leadership saved Prussia: British financial aid and the death in 1762 of Empress Elizabeth of Russia (r. 1741–1762). Her successor, Tsar Peter III (d. 1762), fervently admired Frederick and immediately made peace with Prussia. The Treaty of Hubertusburg of 1763 ended the Seven Years' War with no changes in borders.

More impressive than Prussia's survival were Great Britain's victories in every theater of conflict. These were the work of William Pitt the Elder (1708–1778), who was named secretary of state in charge of the war in 1757. North America, however, was Pitt's real concern. He won control of all of North America east of the Mississippi for Great Britain in what American historians call the French and Indian War. Pitt's aspirations were global. He took Quebec from the French in 1759 and Montreal a year later. The French West Indies fell to the British fleet. British forces on the Indian subcontinent, under Robert Clive (1725–1774), defeated the French in 1757 and cleared the way for the conquest of all India by the British East India Company. Never had a European power experienced such a complete worldwide military victory.

The Treaty of Paris of 1763 was somewhat less triumphant. George III (r. 1760–1820) had succeeded to the British throne, and Pitt was no longer in office. Britain received all of Canada, the Ohio River valley, and the eastern half of the Mississippi River valley. France retained footholds in India at Pondicherry and Chandernagore and regained the West Indies sugar islands of Guadeloupe and Martinique.

The midcentury wars among European powers resulted in a new balance of power on the European continent and the high seas. Great Britain gained a world empire, and Prussia was recognized as a great continental power. With the surrender of Canada,

France retreated from North America and thus opened the way for a continent largely dominated by the English language and Protestantism. By contrast, Latin America remained dominated by the Spanish and Portuguese languages and Roman Catholicism. For many years, West Africa would continue to furnish slaves to the economies of both Americas. On the subcontinent of India the foundations were laid for almost two centuries of British dominance.

THE OLD REGIME

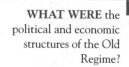

During the turmoil of the French Revolution and its aftermath, it became customary to refer to the patterns of social, political, and economic relationships that had existed in France before 1789 as the *ancien régime*, or the **Old Regime**. The term has come to be applied generally to the social life and institutions of all prerevolutionary Continental Europe. Politically, it meant the rule of theoretically absolute monarchies with growing bureaucracies and aristocratically led armies. Economically, the Old Regime was characterized by food shortages, the predominance of agriculture, slow transport, a low level of iron production, comparatively unsophisticated financial institutions, and, in some cases, competitive commercial overseas empires. Socially, men and women saw themselves less as individuals than as members of distinct corporate bodies that possessed certain privileges or rights as a group. Few persons outside the political, commercial, and intellectual elite actually wanted change or innovation. As yet, only Britain had experienced early industrial development.

HIERARCHY AND PRIVILEGE

The medieval sense of hierarchy became more rigid during the eighteenth century. Eighteenth-century Europeans did not enjoy what Americans regard as individual rights. Instead, persons enjoyed such rights and privileges as were guaranteed to the communities or groups of which they were a part. The "community" might include the village, the nobility, the guild, a university, or the parish. Each of these bodies enjoyed certain privileges, ranging from exemption from taxation or degrading punishment, to the right of one's children to pursue a particular occupation, or for the church, the right to collect the tithe.

ARISTOCRACY

The eighteenth century was the great age of the aristocracy. Nobles constituted about 1 to 5 percent of the population of any given country. They were the single wealthiest group, and land was the chief source of their income. They possessed the widest range of powers and dominated polite society. Aristocracy everywhere was a matter of birth and legal privilege, but in other respects, aristocrats differed markedly from country to country. Great Britain boasted the smallest, wealthiest, and most socially responsible aristocracy. Moving eastward across Europe, aristocrats became more numerous, not always wealthy, but possessing increasing degrees of arbitrary, repressive authority.

An **aristocratic resurgence** marked the eighteenth century as various nobilities sought to defend their privileges against the expanding power of monarchies and the growing wealth of commercial classes. The nobles restricted entry into their ranks and institutions. They tried to curtail royal authority by using institutions they already controlled: the British Parliament, the French *parlements*, their local estates, and provincial diets. Nobles also pressed the peasantry for higher rents or long-forgotten feudal dues as a way to shore up their position and reassert traditional privileges. To contemporaries, this aristocratic resurgence was one of the most fundamental political facts of the day and one to which monarchs had to pay attention.

WHAT WERE the political and economic structures of the Old Regime?

Old Regime
Term applied to the pattern of social, political, and economic relationships and institutions that existed in Europe before the French Revolution.

QUICK REVIEW

Servants under the Old Regime
- Worked in exchange for room, board, and wages
- Usually young and not socially inferior to the employer
- Work as servants allowed young people to save toward independence

aristocratic resurgence
Eighteenth-century aristocratic efforts to resist the expanding power of European monarchies.

An Aristocratic Couple. Portraits such as this one of the English landowner Robert Andrews and his wife, by Thomas Gainsborough (1728–1788), contain many clues to the aristocratic dominance of landed society: Andrews's gun and dog indicate his exclusive right to hunt game on his land. His wife's sitting against the expanse of his landed estate suggests the character of their legal relationship, whereby he could have controlled her property, which would have thus become an extension of his. The market price of the wheat raised on his estate (known in England as corn) would have been protected by various import laws enacted by the English Parliament, whose membership was dominated by landowners such as Andrews himself.

© National Gallery, London/Art Resource.

What seems to be the relationship between husband and wife? Between the humans and the land?

◆◆◆─[Read the **Document**
Domat: Social Order, Monarchy
at **myhistorylab.com**

◆◆◆─[Read the **Document**
Voltaire: Condition, 18th Century France
at **myhistorylab.com**

PEASANTS AND SERFS

Land was the economic basis of eighteenth-century life in Europe as it was throughout the rest of the world. Well over three-fourths of Europe's population lived on the land. Most spent their entire lives within a few miles of their birthplaces; they were poor, and their lives were hard.

Those who worked the land were subject to domination by landowners. This was true to different degrees for free peasants, such as English tenants and most French cultivators, and for the serfs of Germany, Austria, and Russia, who were bound to individual plots of land and particular lords. Generally, the power of landlords increased the farther east one traveled, but nearly all peasants were subject to feudal dues and to forced labor on a lord's estate for a certain number of days each year.

Throughout continental Europe the burden of state taxation fell on the tillers of the soil. Through various legal privileges and the ability to demand concessions from their monarchs, the landlords escaped the payment of numerous taxes. In Prussia and Austria, despite attempts by the monarchies to improve the lot of serfs, landlords exercised almost complete control over them. The serf's condition was worst in Russia, where they were regarded merely as economic commodities. Landlords could demand up to six days a week of labor from them, and like Prussian and Austrian landlords, they could punish their serfs. Although serfs had little recourse against their lords, custom, tradition, and law provided a few protections. For example, the marriages of serfs, unlike those of most slaves, were legally recognized. The landlord could not disband the family of a serf.

Peter the Great gave whole villages of serfs to favored nobles, and Catherine the Great (r. 1762–1796) confirmed the authority of the nobles over their serfs in exchange for the nobility's political cooperation. More than fifty peasant revolts between 1762 and 1769 culminated between 1773 and 1774 in Pugachev's Rebellion, the largest peasant uprising of the eighteenth century. When it was brutally suppressed, any discussion of liberalizing the condition of Russia's serfs was postponed for a generation. Smaller peasant revolts or disturbances occurred in Bohemia in 1775, in Transylvania in 1784, in Moravia in 1786, and in Austria in 1789. Peasants and serfs normally directed their wrath against property rather than persons, and they sought to reassert traditional or customary rights against practices they perceived as innovations. In this respect, the peasant revolts were conservative.

FAMILY STRUCTURES AND THE FAMILY ECONOMY

In preindustrial Europe, the household was the basic unit of production and consumption. Very few productive establishments employed more than a handful of people not belonging to the owner's family. The household mode of organization predominated on farms, in artisans' workshops, and in small merchants' shops. With that mode of economic organization, there developed what is known as the **family economy**.

THE FAMILY ECONOMY

Throughout Europe, family members saw themselves as working together in an interdependent rather than an independent or individualistic manner. The goal of the family household was to produce or secure through wages enough food to support its members. In the countryside, they usually farmed. In cities and towns, artisan production or working for another person was the usual pattern. Almost everyone lived within a household. Except for members of religious orders, people living outside a household were viewed as potentially criminal, disruptive, or a drain on the charity of others.

Within the family economy, all of the goods and income produced benefited the household, not individual family members. The need to survive poor harvests or economic slumps meant no one could be idle. Few peasant households in western Europe had enough land to support themselves by farming alone. One or more family members had to work elsewhere and send wages home. It was not uncommon for a father to become a migrant worker and shift the burden of farm work to his wife and children.

In the urban version of the family economy, the father was usually a chief craftsman who employed one or more servants. But he also expected his children to work in his shop. His eldest child was usually trained in the trade, and his wife might sell the wares he produced or pursue another trade. The wife of a merchant also often ran her husband's business, especially when he traveled to purchase new goods. When business was poor, family members looked for other employment to help the family unit survive.

WOMEN AND THE FAMILY ECONOMY

The family economy shaped the lives of women in preindustrial western Europe. A woman's life experience was largely a function of her ability to establish and maintain a household. Marriage was an economic necessity, since a woman outside a household was highly vulnerable. Unless she was an aristocrat or a member of a religious order, she probably could not support herself. Consequently, much of a woman's

WHAT WAS the role of women in the family economy?

family economy
The basic structure of production and consumption in preindustrial Europe. Interdependent family members functioned as an economic unit.

Farm Family. Painted by the English artist Francis Wheatley (1747–1801) near the close of the eighteenth century, this scene is part of a series illustrating a day in the life of an idealized farm family. Note the artist's assumptions about the division of labor by gender. Men work in the fields, while women work in the home or look after the needs of men and children. As other illustrations in this chapter show, many eighteenth-century women in fact worked outside the home, but considerable social pressure was developing at this time to restrict them to domestic roles. This painting and the others in the series are thus more prescriptive than descriptive, intended in part to persuade their viewers that women belonged in their separate family sphere. Many, perhaps most, families living in the countryside could not maintain the closeness that these paintings extol. To survive, many had to send members to work on other farms or even to other regions.

Francis Wheatley (RA) (1747–1801), "Evening," signed and dated 1799, oil on canvas, 17 1/2 × 21 1/2 in. (44.5 × 54.5 cm), Yale Center for British Art, Paul Mellon Collection, Bridgman Art Library (B1977.14.118).

How have images such as this one influenced the way we view preindustrial society?

life was devoted first to serving her parents' household and then to establishing one of her own. In most cases, bearing and rearing children were subordinate to these goals.

By the age of 7, a girl was expected to begin to do household work. On a farm, she might look after chickens or water animals or carry food to adults working the land. In an urban artisan's household, she would do some form of light work, such as cleaning, carrying, sewing, or weaving. She remained in her parents' home until they found more remunerative work for her elsewhere. An artisan's daughter might not leave home until marriage because she was learning valuable skills from her parents. Girls who grew up on farms usually left home by the age of 12 or 14. They were likely to migrate to a nearby town or city to become household servants but would rarely travel more than 30 miles from their parents' home. (See Document, "Priscilla Wakefield Demands More Occupations Be Opened to Women.")

Marriage within the family economy was a joint economic undertaking. A young woman's chief goal was to accumulate a dowry, capital she could contribute to setting up a household. It might take ten years or more to accumulate a dowry, so marriage was usually postponed until a woman's mid- to late twenties. Within marriage, domestic duties, childbearing, and child rearing were subordinate to economic survival. Consequently, couples often practiced birth control, usually through the imperfect method of *coitus interruptus*, or male withdrawal before ejaculation.

Women held active, often decisive roles in the family economy. If economic disaster struck, more often than not it was the wife who took the lead in sending off family members to find work elsewhere or even to beg in the streets.

QUICK REVIEW

Women in Preindustrial Society

◆ By age 7 girls contributed to household work

◆ Most girls left home between the ages of 12 and 14

◆ A young woman's chief goal was to accumulate a dowry

THE REVOLUTION IN AGRICULTURE

 WHAT WAS the connection between population increase and agricultural improvements in the eighteenth century?

The main goal of traditional European peasant society was to ensure the stability of the local food supply. That supply was never certain and became more uncertain the farther east one traveled. A failed harvest could mean death from either outright starvation or protracted debility. Food was often harder to find in the country than in cities because city governments usually stored reserve supplies of grain.

French Peasants. During the seventeenth century the French Le Nain brothers painted scenes of French peasant life. Although the images softened many of the harsh realities of peasant existence, the clothing and the interiors were based on actual models and convey the character of the life of better off French peasants whose lives would have continued very much the same into the eighteenth century.

What evidence here suggests that these were among the "better off" French peasants of their time?

DOCUMENT

Priscilla Wakefield Demands More Occupations Be Opened to Women

At the end of the eighteenth century, several English women writers began to demand a wider life for women. Priscilla Wakefield was among such authors. She was concerned that women found themselves able to pursue only occupations that paid poorly or excluded from work on the grounds of their alleged physical weakness. She also believed that women should receive equal wages for equal work. Many of the issues she raised have yet to be adequately addressed on behalf of women.

- **FROM** reading this passage, what do you understand to have been the arguments at the end of the eighteenth century to limit the kinds of employment that women might enter? Why did women receive lower wages for work similar to or the same as that done by men? What occupations traditionally filled by men does Wakefield believe women might also pursue?

Another heavy discouragement to the industry of women, is the inequality of the reward of their labor, compared with that of men; an injustice which pervades every species of employment performed by both sexes.

In employments which depend on bodily strength, the distinction is just; for it cannot be pretended that the generality of women can earn as much as men, when the produce of their labor is the result of corporeal exertion; but it is a subject of great regret, that this inequality should prevail even where an equal share of skill and application is exerted. Male stay-makers, mantua-makers, and hair-dressers, are better paid than female artists of the same professions; but surely it will never be urged as an apology for this disproportion, that women are not as capable of making stays, gowns, dressing hair, and similar arts, as men; if they are not superior to them, it can only be accounted for upon this principle, that the prices they receive for their labor are not sufficient to repay

them for the expense of qualifying themselves for their business; and that they sink under the mortification of being regarded as artisans of inferior estimation. . . .

Besides these employments which are commonly performed by women, and those already shown to be suitable for such persons as are above the condition of hard labor, there are some professions and trades customarily in the hands of men, which might be conveniently exercised by either sex.–Watchmaking requiring more ingenuity than strength, seems peculiarly adapted to women; as do many parts of the business of stationer, particularly, ruling account books or making pens. The compounding of medicines in an apothecary's shop, requires no other talents than care and exactness; and if opening a vein occasionally be a indispensable requisite, a woman may acquire the capacity of doing it, for those of her own sex at least, without any reasonable objection. . . . Pastry and confectionery appear particularly consonant to the habits of women, though generally performed by men; perhaps the heat of the ovens, and the strength requisite to fill and empty them, may render male assistants necessary; but certain women are most eligible to mix up the ingredients, and prepare the various kinds of cakes for baking.–Light turnery and toymaking depend more upon dexterity and invention than force, and are therefore suitable work for women and children. . . .

Farming, as far as respects the theory, is commensurate with the powers of the female mind: nor is the practice of inspecting agricultural processes incompatible with the delicacy of their frames if their constitution be good.

Source: From Priscilla Wakefield, *Reflections on the Present Condition of the Female Sex* (1798), (London, 1817), pp. 125–127, as quoted in Bridget Hill, ed., *Eighteenth-Century Women: An Anthology*. Copyright © 1984 George Allen & Unwin, pp. 227–228.

During the eighteenth century, bread prices rose slowly but steadily, spurred by demand from a growing population. Prices rose faster than urban wages and brought no advantage to the small peasant producer. The beneficiaries were landlords and the wealthier peasants who had surplus grain to sell. The increasing price of grain encouraged innovation in farm production and began an **agricultural revolution**.

agricultural revolution

The innovations in farm production that began in the eighteenth century and led to a scientific and mechanized agriculture.

●●●●|Read the Document
Gluckel of Hameln: Memoirs
at **myhistorylab.com**

◉|See the Map
English Common Lands Enclosed by Acts
at **myhistorylab.com**

enclosure
The consolidation or fencing in of common lands by British landlords to increase production and achieve greater commercial profits. It also involved the reclamation of waste land and the consolidation of strips into block fields.

New Crops and New Methods

The agricultural revolution began during the sixteenth and seventeenth centuries in the Low Countries, where Dutch landlords and farmers devised better ways to build dikes and to drain land so that they could farm more extensive areas. They also experimented with new crops, such as clover and turnips, that increased the supply of animal fodder and replenish the soil.

These methods spread to England during the early eighteenth century. Agricultural innovations were adopted slowly; many were incompatible with the existing organization of land in Britain. In 1700 approximately half the arable land in Britain was farmed by the "open-field method." Small cultivators in village communities usually tilled unconnected strips, and their traditional two- or three-field systems of rotation left much land fallow and unproductive each year. Decisions about planting were made communally. The system discouraged innovation and aimed to produce a steady, but not a growing, supply of food. By the second half of the century, the rising price of wheat encouraged landlords to consolidate or enclose their lands to increase production. **Enclosure** involved fencing common lands, reclaiming previously untilled waste, and transforming cultivated strips into block fields. These procedures disrupted the economic and social life of the countryside and incited riots. The larger landlords resorted to parliamentary acts for help in enclosing lands. Between 1761 and 1792, almost 500,000 acres were enclosed through parliamentary acts. In 1801, a general enclosure act streamlined the process.

The enclosures have remained controversial. They increased food production but disrupted small traditional communities. They forced off the land some independent farmers, who had needed the common pasturage, and very poor cottagers, who had lived on the reclaimed waste land. In some counties where the enclosures took place, however, the population increased. New soil had come into production, and

The Lincolnshire Ox (1790) by George Stubbs. The "Lincolnshire Ox" was a prize Hereford that grew to an enormous size by being fed solely on grass. The fascination with the Lincolnshire Ox, which was displayed for over a year in London, was characteristic of the general interest in agricultural improvements.

How did agricultural improvements alter traditional peasant lives?

services subsidiary to farming also expanded. This advance in food production was necessary for an industrial society to develop. It ensured adequate food for the cities and freed surplus agricultural labor for industrial production.

POPULATION EXPANSION

Agricultural improvement was both a cause and a result of an immense growth in the population of Europe. Exact figures are lacking, but the best estimates suggest that in 1700 Europe's population was between 100 million and 120 million people. By 1800, the figure had risen to almost 190 million, and by 1850, to 260 million (see Figure 19–1). Such extraordinary growth put new demands on all resources and considerable pressure on existing social organization. The causes of this growth are unclear. The death rate declined, thanks to fewer wars and epidemics in the eighteenth century. But changes in the food supply itself may have been the chief reason for sustained population growth. One contributing factor was the widespread cultivation of a New World tuber, the potato. Enough potatoes could be raised on a single acre to feed one peasant's family for an entire year. With this more certain food supply, more children could be reared, and more could survive.

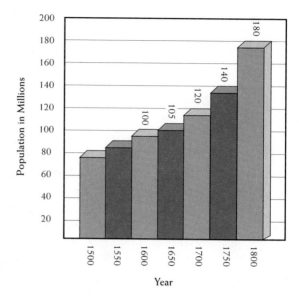

FIGURE 19-1.   Population of Europe, 1500–1800.
What caused population growth to accelerate in the eighteenth century?

THE EIGHTEENTH-CENTURY INDUSTRIAL REVOLUTION: AN EVENT IN WORLD HISTORY

In the second half of the eighteenth century the European economy began very slowly to industrialize. This development, more than any other, distinguished the West from the rest of the world for the next two centuries. While this economic development was occurring, people did not call it a *revolution*. That term was applied to technology-based advances in productivity only after the French Revolution, when writers contended that what had taken place in Britain was the economic equivalent of the political events in France. From this comparison arose the concept of an *industrial* revolution.

The European **industrial revolution** of the eighteenth century permitted sustained economic growth, despite subsequent downturns and depressions. At considerable social cost and dislocation, industrialism produced more goods and services than ever before in human history and eventually overcame the economy of scarcity. The new means of production demanded new kinds of skills, new discipline in work, and a large labor force. In the long run, industrialism raised living standards; the poverty in which most Europeans had always lived was overcome.

Over time the wealth produced by industrialism upset the political and social structures of the Old Regime and led to political and social reforms. The economic elite of the emerging industrial society eventually challenged the political dominance of the aristocracy. Industrialization also undermined traditional communities and, along with the growth of cities, displaced many people. These processes repeated themselves virtually everywhere that industrialization occurred during the next two centuries.

The consumer products of industrialization encouraged more international trade in which Western nations supplied finished goods in exchange for raw materials. Other areas of the globe became economically dependent on European and American demand. The wealth achieved through this uneven commerce allowed Europeans to

WHY DID the industrial revolution begin in England?

Read the Document
Friend of Men: Treatise on Population
at **myhistorylab.com**

industrial revolution
Mechanization of the European economy that began in Britain in the second half of the eighteenth century.

Hear the Audio
at **myhistorylab.com**

dominate world markets for almost two centuries. Furthermore, by the early nineteenth century iron and steel production and the new technologies of manufacture allowed European states and later the United States to build more powerful military forces, especially navies, than those of Africa, Latin America, or Asia. Both the economic and the military dominance of the West arose directly from industrialization.

Much of the history of the non-Western world from the middle of the eighteenth century to the present can be understood in terms of how the nonindustrialized nations initially reacted to exposure to Europeans and Americans made wealthy and powerful through industrialized economies. Africa and Latin America became generally dependent economies. Japan, by the middle of the nineteenth century, decided it must imitate the European pattern and did so successfully. China did not make that decision and became indirectly ruled by Europeans. The Chinese revolutions of the twentieth century largely represented efforts to achieve real self-direction. Southeast Asia and the Middle East became drawn into the network of resource supply to the West; they could achieve movement toward economic independence only through imitation or, like Arab nations in the early 1970s, by refusing to supply oil to the West. The process of industrialization that commenced in small factories in eighteenth-century Europe has changed the world more than any other single development in the last two centuries.

INDUSTRIAL LEADERSHIP OF GREAT BRITAIN

Great Britain remained the industrial leader of Europe and the world until the late nineteenth century (see Map 19–4). Several factors contributed to the early start of industrialization in Britain. Britain was the single largest free-trade area in Europe, with good roads and waterways and no internal trade barriers. There were rich deposits of coal and iron ore. The political structure was stable, and property rights were secure. Banking and public credit systems created a good investment climate. Taxation was heavy, but fair. There was both domestic consumer demand and demand from the North American colonies. Finally, British society was relatively open and allowed people who earned money to rise socially.

Textile production inaugurated the industrial revolution. The peasant family living in a one- or two-room cottage, not the factory, was the basic unit of production in the eighteenth century. The same peasants who tilled the land in spring and summer often spun thread or wove textiles in winter. Under the **domestic** or **putting-out system**, agents of urban textile merchants distributed wool or other fibers to the homes of peasants, who spun it into thread. The agent then transported the thread to other peasants, who wove it into cloth, and the merchant sold the final product. Sometimes the spinners or weavers owned their own equipment, but more often than not the merchant capitalist owned the machinery as well as the raw material.

By midcentury, production bottlenecks had developed within the domestic system. Thanks to population growth, especially in Great Britain, demand for cotton textiles was growing more rapidly than production. The most famous inventions of the industrial revolution were devised in response to consumer demand for cotton textiles. John Kay's invention of the flying shuttle in the 1730s gave weavers the technical capacity to produce enough fabric to satisfy demand, but spinners could not make enough thread for the weavers. Manufacturers offered prizes for the invention of a machine to correct this imbalance, and in about 1765 James Hargreaves (d. 1778) invented the **spinning jenny**.

The spinning jenny was a piece of machinery for cottage use. The invention that moved cotton textile manufacture into the factory was Richard Arkwright's (1732–1792) **water frame**, patented in 1769. When Arkwright lost his patent rights, other manufacturers used his invention, and numerous factories sprang up in the

domestic or putting-out system
Method of production in which agents furnished raw materials to households, whose members created finished products, which the agents then sold.

spinning jenny
A machine invented in England by James Hargreaves around 1765 to mass-produce thread.

water frame
A water-powered device invented by Richard Arkwright to produce a more durable cotton fabric. It led to the shift in the production of cotton textiles from households to factories.

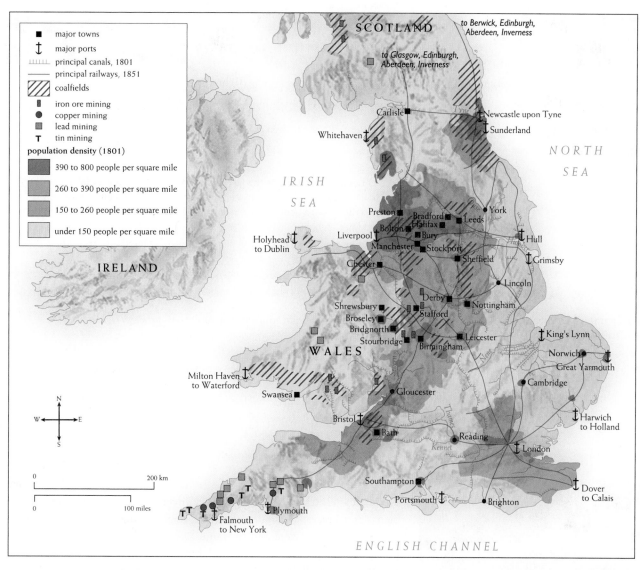

MAP 19–4.   The Industrial Revolution in Britain.   Richly endowed with coal and iron ore and possessing many natural ports and a network of navigable waterways, Britain exploited these advantages to become the world's first industrial nation.

How does this map show the connections between industry and urbanization?

countryside near streams that provided water power. By 1815, cotton composed 40 percent of the value of British domestic exports, and by 1830 just over 50 percent.

The critical invention that enabled industrialization to spread from one industry to another was the steam engine. For the first time in history, human beings were able to tap an unlimited source of inanimate power. Unlike engines powered by water or wind, the steam engine, fueled by coal, provided a portable, steady source of power that could be applied to many industrial and transportation uses.

CHRONOLOGY

MAJOR INVENTIONS IN THE TEXTILE-MANUFACTURING REVOLUTION

1733	John Kay's flying shuttle
1765	James Hargreaves's spinning jenny (patent 1770)
1769	James Watt's steam engine patent
1769	Richard Arkwright's water frame patent
1787	Edmund Cartwright's power loom

OVERVIEW Why the Industrial Revolution Began in Britain

Great Britain was the home of the industrial revolution, and until the middle of the nineteenth century, it maintained the industrial leadership of Europe. Several factors contributed to the early industrialization of Britain.

Natural Resources

Britain had extensive deposits of coal and iron ore.

Infrastructure

Britain had an extensive network of roads and canals that facilitated the shipment of raw materials and goods.

Society

1. The predominance of London: London was the largest city in Europe and the social, commercial, financial, and political center of Britain. It was thus both an enormous market for consumer goods itself and created a demand for these goods in the rest of Britain, which sought to emulate London fashions.
2. The prevalence of newspapers: Newspapers thrived in Britain, and advertisements in them increased consumer demand for goods.
3. Wealth in Britain brought status: British society was relatively mobile. Wealthy merchants and entrepreneurs could rise socially, enter the aristocracy, and enjoy political influence.

Government, Financial Institutions, and Empire

1. The rule of law: Britain had a stable government that guaranteed property rights.
2. Britain was a free-trade area. No internal tolls inhibited the shipment of goods and raw materials within Britain.
3. Britain had a sound system of banking and public credit that created a stable climate for investing in commerce and industry.
4. Taxes were collected efficiently and fairly. No class was exempt from paying taxes.
5. The colonial empire: British colonies were both a market for British goods and sources of raw materials for British manufacturers.

Blacksmith Shop. During the eighteenth century, most goods were produced in small workshops, such as this English blacksmith shop shown in a painting by Joseph Wright of Derby (1734–1797), or in the homes of artisans. Not until very late in the century, with the early stages of industrialization, did a few factories appear.

How does this painting reveal the artist's attitude toward what is going on here?

The first practical engine using steam power was invented by Thomas Newcomen (1663–1729) in the early eighteenth century. It was large, inefficient, and practically immovable, but English mine operators used it to pump water out of coal and tin mines. In 1769, James Watt (1736–1819) patented an improved design, but it required precise metalwork. Watt's partner Matthew Boulton (1728–1809), a toy manufacturer, worked with John Wilkinson (1728–1808), a cannon manufacturer, to find ways to drill the precise metal cylinders required by Watt's engines. Boulton then persuaded Watt to adapt the engine for use in running cotton mills. By the early nineteenth century the steam engine had become the prime mover in every industry. Applied to ships and then to wagons on iron rails, it also revolutionized transportation.

The manufacture of high-quality iron was essential for industrial development. In the course of the eighteenth century, British ironmakers began to use coke (derived from coal) instead of charcoal to smelt ores, and the steam engine provided power for high-temperature blast furnaces. Britain had large coal deposits, and the steam engine improved iron production while increasing demand for iron. In 1784, Henry Cort (1740–1800) introduced a new method for melting and stirring molten ore that yielded a purer iron. He also developed a rolling mill that shaped molten metal into bars, rails, or other forms. (Previously, metal had been pounded into shape.) All of these innovations achieved a better, more versatile, and cheaper product, and by the early nineteenth century, annual British iron production amounted to more than a million tons. The lower cost of iron in turn lowered the cost of steam engines and allowed them to be used more widely.

EUROPEAN CITIES

PATTERNS OF PREINDUSTRIAL URBANIZATION

Remarkable changes occurred in the pattern of city growth between 1500 and 1800. In 1500 there were approximately 156 cities within Europe (excluding Hungary and Russia) with a population greater than 10,000. Only Paris, Milan, Venice, and Naples had more than 100,000 inhabitants. By 1800 approximately 363 cities had 10,000 or more inhabitants, and 17 of those had populations larger than 100,000. The percentage of the European population living in urban areas had risen from just over 5 percent to just over 9 percent. The urban concentration had also shifted from southern Mediterranean Europe to the north.

HOW DID population growth lead to changes in urban social structures?

URBAN CLASSES

At the top of the urban social structure stood a generally small group of nobles, major merchants, bankers, financiers, clergy, and government officials. These men usually constituted a self-appointed and self-electing oligarchy who governed the city through its corporation or city council. In a few cities, artisan guilds also participated in government.

The middle class, or *bourgeoisie*—merchants, tradesmen, bankers, and professional people—were the most dynamic element of the urban population. The middle class had less wealth than most nobles but more than urban artisans. They lived in the cities and towns, and their sources of income had little or nothing to do with the land. They normally supported reform, change, and economic growth. Resenting aristocratic privilege and social exclusiveness, they wanted rational regulations for trade and commerce.

As the century passed, the bourgeoisie increasingly begrudged the aristocracy, and as the middle class grew in size and wealth and aristocratic control of political and ecclesiastical power tightened, tension increased. The middle class tended to fear the lower urban classes as much as they resented the nobility. The lower orders constituted

Dress Shop. Consumption of all forms of consumer goods increased greatly in the eighteenth century. This engraving illustrates a shop, probably in Paris. Here women, working apparently for a woman manager, are making dresses and hats to meet the demands of the fashion trade.

What spurred the growing demand for consumer goods?

QUICK REVIEW

Urban Classes

- Upper classes: nobles, large merchants, bankers, financiers, clergy, government officials
- Middle class: prosperous merchants, tradesmen, bankers, professionals
- Lower orders: shopkeepers, wage earners, artisans

a potentially violent element in society; a potential threat to property; and, in their poverty, a drain on national resources. The lower orders, however, were much more varied than either the city aristocracy or the middle class cared to admit.

Shopkeepers, artisans, and wage earners constituted the single largest group in any city, and they suffered from the grasping of both the middle class and the local nobility. They had their own culture, values, and institutions and, like the rural peasants, were conservative. Their economic position was highly vulnerable, and their lives centered on their work. They usually lived near or at their place of employment and worked in shops with fewer than a half dozen other people. They formed guilds to protect their interests, particularly in central Europe, but by the eighteenth century these had declining influence and reinforced conservative values.

THE JEWISH POPULATION: AGE OF THE GHETTO

 HOW WERE European Jews segregated from European society?

Although the small Jewish communities of Amsterdam and other western European cities became famous for their intellectual life and financial institutions, most European Jews lived in eastern Europe. In the eighteenth century, at least 3 million Jews dwelled in Poland, Lithuania, and Ukraine. There were perhaps 150,000 in the Habsburg lands, primarily in Bohemia, around 1760. Fewer than 100,000 lived in Germany and approximately 40,000 in France. England and Holland had Jewish populations of fewer than 10,000. There were even smaller groups of Jews in Italy.

In 1762, Catherine the Great of Russia specifically excluded Jews from a manifesto that welcomed foreigners to settle in Russia, although she eased this restriction a few years later. The first partition of Poland in 1772 (see Chapter 22) gave Russia a large Jewish population and created larger Jewish communities in Prussia and Austria.

Jews did not have the same rights as Christians, unless such rights were specifically granted to them by a sympathetic monarch. They were resident aliens whose status could change at the whim of a government. Under the Old Regime, they lived apart from non-Jews, in separate villages in the countryside or in urban districts called **ghettos**. Thus this period in Jewish history, which may be said to have begun with the expulsion of the Jews from Spain in 1492, is known as the age of the ghetto.

During the seventeenth century a few Jews helped finance the wars of major rulers. These financiers often grew close to the rulers and came to be known as "court Jews." They tended to marry among themselves. Perhaps the most famous was Samuel Oppenheimer (1630–1703), who helped the Habsburgs finance their struggle against the Turks, including the defense of Vienna. Their position at court and their financial abilities may have brought them privilege and fame, but court Jews, including Oppenheimer, often failed to have their loans repaid.

Most European Jews lived in poverty. A few were moneylenders, but most worked at the lowest occupations. Their religious beliefs, rituals, and community set them apart. A wall of laws and social institutions—as well as the physical walls of the ghetto—kept them in positions of social inferiority. They were not free to pursue the professions; they could be expelled from the cities where they dwelled, and their property could be

Ghetto in Cracow. During the Old Regime, European Jews were separated from non-Jews, typically in districts known as ghettos. Relegated to the least desirable section of a city or to rural villages, most lived in poverty. This watercolor painting depicts a street in Kazimlesz, the Jewish quarter of Cracow, Poland.

Judaica Collection. Max Berger, Vienna Austria/©Erich Lessing/Art Resource, New York.

Even though this painting shows an outwardly peaceful scene, how does it also show segregation?

ghettos
Separate communities in which Jews were required by law to live.

confiscated. Jews could be required to listen to sermons that insulted them and their religion; their children could be taken away and given Christian instruction. And they knew their non-Jewish neighbors might suddenly turn violently against them.

Under the Old Regime, it is important to emphasize, this discrimination was based on religious separateness. Jews who converted to Christianity could participate in the political and social institutions of European society. As will be seen in subsequent chapters, the end of the Old Regime brought major changes in the lives of Jews and in their relationship to the larger culture.

SUMMARY

HOW DID England and France provide models for governance in early modern Europe?

European Political Consolidation. In the seventeenth and eighteenth centuries, Britain, France, Russia, Austria, and Prussia emerged as great powers in Europe. Through their military strength, economic development, and in some cases colonial empires, they would affect virtually every other world civilization. In the seventeenth century, conflict between the Stuart kings and Parliament led to civil war, the execution of Charles I, a short-lived English republic under Oliver Cromwell, and the Glorious Revolution (1688–1689) that finally established the supremacy of Parliament. Under Louis XIV (r. 1643–1715), France became the model of an absolute monarchy. Russia became a great power under Peter the Great (r. 1682–1725), who opened Russia to Western influence. The Habsburgs remained Holy Roman Emperors, but the rise of Prussia under the Hohenzollerns challenged Habsburg dominance in central Europe. The Hohenzollern rulers built Prussia into a great power by developing a powerful army. *page 478*

WHY WERE the European wars of the eighteenth century global in scope?

European Warfare: From Continental to World Conflict. In a series of worldwide colonial struggles with France, Britain profited from France's entanglements in Europe and emerged supreme in North America and India. Louis pursued an aggressive foreign policy that expanded France's borders but cost France dearly in wealth and resources and provoked strong opposition from the other European powers. In the War of the Spanish Succession, he succeeded in placing his grandson on the throne of Spain, but the war left France

exhausted. Prussia emerged as one of the strongest European states and the rival to Habsburg power in central Europe. *page 488*

WHAT WERE the political and economic structures of the Old Regime?

The Old Regime. Eighteenth-century European society was traditional, hierarchical, corporate, and privileged—features that had characterized Europe and the world for centuries. All societies also confronted scarce food supplies. For the eighteenth century, however, an improved food supply helped support a larger population. New agricultural techniques and the expanding population created pressures on social structures. *page 493*

WHAT WAS the role of women in the family economy?

Family Structures and the Family Economy. Production and consumption in preindustrial Europe were organized around the household. The family, not the individual, was the basic economic unit. Women's dowries helped establish households, and marriages were economic partnerships. *page 495*

WHAT WAS the connection between population increase and agricultural improvements in the eighteenth century?

The Revolution in Agriculture. Traditional agriculture focused on avoiding famine; it discouraged innovation. Growing population and new techniques transformed food production. Agriculture became more commercialized, and increased food production contributed to population growth. *page 496*

WHY DID the industrial revolution begin in England?

The Eighteenth-Century Industrial Revolution: An Event in World History. The eighteenth century witnessed the beginning of industrial production. New inventions greatly increasing productive capacity first appeared in the English textile industry. The steam engine provided a portable source of energy. Industrialization affected Europe's relations with the rest of the world. *page 499*

 HOW DID population growth lead to changes in urban social structures?

European Cities. Cities expanded and commerce grew during the eighteenth century. The expansion of the European population stimulated change and challenges to tradition and hierarchy. New wealth meant that birth would cease to determine social relationships. *page 503*

 HOW WERE European Jews segregated from European Society?

The Jewish Population: Age of the Ghetto. Europe's Jews were segregated from non-Jews in separate villages or, within cities, in ghettoes. They did not have the same rights and privileges as their compatriots, unless those rights had been specifically granted by their monarch. *page 504*

KEY TERMS

absolutism (p. 478)
agricultural revolution (p. 497)
aristocratic resurgence (p. 493)
boyars (p. 483)
divine right of kings (p. 483)
domestic or putting-out system (p. 500)
enclosures (p. 498)
family economy (p. 495)
ghettos (p. 504)
Glorious Revolution (p. 480)

industrial revolution (p. 499)
Junkers (YOONG-kurs) (p. 487)
Old Regime (p. 493)
parliamentary monarchy (p. 478)
Pragmatic Sanction (p. 486)
Puritans (p. 479)
spinning jenny (p. 500)
streltsy (p. 483)
Table of Ranks (p. 485)
water frame (p. 500)

REVIEW QUESTIONS

1. By the end of the seventeenth century, England and France had different systems of government with different religious policies. What were the main similarities and differences? Why did each nation develop as it did?

2. How and why did Russia emerge as a great power? Discuss the character of Peter the Great. How were his domestic reforms related to his military ambitions?

3. What were the main points of conflict between Britain and France in North America, the West Indies, and India? What were the results of these conflicts by 1763? Which countries emerged stronger from the Seven Years' War and why?

4. Why were Europe's wars during this period so significant for the rest of the world?

5. In what ways could aristocrats and peasants be described as conservative? Was conservatism a wise choice for nobles? For peasants? Why or why not?

6. How would you define the term *family economy*? In what ways were the lives of women constrained by the family economy in preindustrial Europe?

7. What caused the agricultural revolution? How did technological innovations help change European agriculture? What were some of the reasons for peasant revolts in Europe in the eighteenth century?

8. What factors led to the industrial revolution of the eighteenth century? What were some of the technological innovations, and why were they important? Why did Great Britain take the lead in the industrial revolution?

9. Describe city life during the eighteenth century. What changes took place in the distribution of population in cities and towns?

10. What was the status of European Jews in the Old Regime? How were they made to live as a people apart from the rest of the European population?

Note: To learn more about the topics in this chapter, please turn to the Suggested Readings at the end of the book. For additional sources related to this chapter please see www.myhistorylab.com

PEARSON
myhistorylab Connections

Reinforce what you learned in this chapter by studying the many documents, images, maps, review tools, and videos available at **www.myhistorylab.com**

Read and Review

✓● Study and Review Chapter 19

●●●● Read the Document *The Divine Right of Kings, 1598, James I, p. 479*

Cromwell Abolishes English Monarchy, 1651, p. 479

The English Bill of Rights, 1689, p. 480

Peter the Great with Alexis Russia, p. 484

Domat: Social Order, Monarchy, p. 494

Voltaire: Condition, 18th Century France, p. 494

Gluckel of Hameln: Memoirs, p. 498

Friend of Men: Treatise on Population, p. 499

👁● See the Map *Growth of Brandenburg-Prussia, 1618–1786, p. 487*

Europe After the Treaty of Utrecht, 1714, p. 488

English Common Lands Enclosed by Acts, p. 498

●● View the Image *Allegorical View: Cromwell as Savior England, p. 479*

Ivan the Terrible, p. 483

Michael Romanov, p. 483

Peter the Great, p. 483

Battle of Poltava, 1709, p. 484

Research and Explore

👁● See the Map *Russia under Peter the Great, p. 486*

👁● See the Map *Rise of Prussia, 1440–1795*

─── ((●● Hear the Audio ───

Hear the audio file for Chapter 19
at **www.myhistorylab.com**

20

The Last Great Islamic Empires, 1500–1800

((•●─[Hear the Audio for Chapter 20 at www.myhistorylab.com

Akbar Inspecting the Construction of Fatehpur-Sikri, ca. 1590. Sometime around 1570, construction began on a new Mughal capital, Fatehpur-Sikri ("City of Victory"), a few miles southwest of Agra. Akbar (r. 1556–1605), the emperor who ordered the building of Fatehpur-Sikri, had a keen interest in architecture. Here he stands at the construction site, gesturing to a mason as the imperial entourage looks on. In every sense, he lived up to his epithet as the "architect of the spiritual and material world."

Why was cultural patronage important to a ruler like Akbar?

Between 1450 and 1650 Islamic culture, society, and statecraft blossomed. The creation of three powerful empires and several strong regional states was the culmination of long processes in the Islamic eastern Mediterranean and West Asia. During this time the ideal of a universal Islamic caliphate yielded to the reality of multiple secular, albeit distinctively "Islamic," sultanates.

The simultaneous growth of the Ottoman, Safavid, and Mughal empires, sometimes called the "gunpowder empires," marked the global apogee of Islamic society, culture, and economic power. By 1600 the Ottoman Turks controlled Asia Minor, the Fertile Crescent, the Balkans, Crimean Europe, the eastern Mediterranean, and Arabia; the Safavids ruled all of greater Iran; and descendants of Timur—the Mughals—governed Afghanistan and most of South Asia. Around these empires were arrayed Islamic khanates of Central Asia and Russia, sultanates of Southeast Asia, savannah empires of West Africa, the port cities of East Africa, the Sharifian state of Morocco, and regional empires of the Sudan in which Islam was significant (see Map 20–1, p. 512).

In 1600 Islamic civilization seemed as strong as that of Europe, China, or Japan. But military, economic, and political strength were partially deceptive. By the late seventeenth century, Islamic power was in retreat before the rising tide of western European military and economic imperialism, even though Islamic cultural life and Muslim religion flourished.

In this chapter we turn first to the period's three major Islamic empires and then briefly to the smaller Islamic political-cultural centers of Central, South, and Southeast Asia, where European power was encroaching on what had been a virtual Muslim monopoly on maritime trade. ■

THE LAST GREAT ISLAMIC EMPIRES

The Islamic region's vitality between 1450 and 1800 was exemplified by the three great, prosperous imperial states of the Ottomans, Safavids, and Mughals. Each built extensive civilian and military bureaucracies, enjoyed inspired military and civilian leaders, revived Islamic social and cultural life, and improved on its predecessors.

Islamic ideology, society, and culture were important to the success of the Ottomans, Safavids, and Mughals; military, social, and commercial innovations were key to each dynasty's rise to global importance. Their rulers built arguably the greatest cities of their time in Istanbul, Isfahan, and Delhi. They patronized the arts, stimulating new traditions of Islamic literature, calligraphy, painting, and architecture. Yet all were essentially conservative societies. Economically they remained closely tied to agricultural production, long-distance trade, and taxation based on land. Perhaps because they were so successful, these societies did not undergo the kind of social or religiopolitical revolutions that rocked Europe after 1500. Thus, much like the societies of China and Japan in the same period, they did not experience the sort of generative changes in material and intellectual life that the

comparatively underdeveloped western European societies, for all their diversity, saw in the sixteenth, seventeenth, and eighteenth centuries. There was no compelling challenge to traditional Islamic ideals of societal organization and human responsibility, even though many Islamic movements in the eighteenth century did call for communal and personal reform.

As one historian has put it, the striking growth of Islamic societies and cultures in this age was "not one of *origination*, but rather one of *culmination* in a culture long already mature." In their heydays, these empires produced much scientific work, but no scientific revolution; much art, architecture, and literature of high quality, but none that departed radically from previous traditions; political consolidation and also expansion, but no conquest of significant new markets or territories; prosperous long-distance trade, but no beginnings of a commercial or industrial revolution. By the mid-nineteenth century, all three empires were at various stages of economic, political, social, and military disarray in comparison to Europe. By contrast, western Europe, having lagged behind the Islamic world in economic, social, and cultural development as well as political and military might since

THE OTTOMAN EMPIRE AND THE EAST MEDITERRANEAN WORLD

WHY DID the Ottoman Empire find it increasingly difficult to compete with European powers?

ORIGINS AND DEVELOPMENT OF THE OTTOMAN STATE BEFORE 1600

The Ottomans were a Turkish dynasty that originated in the groups of western Oghuz Turks from the steppes of Central Asia who came to Anatolia as settlers and Muslim frontier warriors.[1] The Ottomans reached Anatolia (Asia Minor) in the time of the Seljuks of Rum (1098–1308), the first western Turks to have founded a lasting state there (see Chapter 12). By about 1300, the newcomers ruled one of several small military states along the Byzantine-Seljuk frontier in western Anatolia. In the ensuing century several vigorous leaders expanded their territory east into central Anatolia and (in 1356) west across the Dardanelles into the European Byzantine lands of Macedonia and modern Bulgaria. Exchanging grants of revenue-producing, conquered land (*timars*) for military service, the Ottomans built both a formidable fighting force and a loyal military aristocracy.

By 1402 the center of Ottoman rule had shifted northwest to Edirne on the Balkan Peninsula itself. Ottoman control then extended northwest to the Danube and east across central Anatolia. Constantinople formed an alien pocket in these dominions, and it finally fell in 1453 to Sultan Mehmed II, "the Conqueror" (r. 1451–1481). Renamed "Istanbul," it became the Ottoman capital. After centuries of power, Byzantium, the center of Eastern Christendom, had vanished, although the Ottomans allowed the

---

[1]The Ottomans, sometimes called *Osmanlis*, are named after Osman (1259–1326), also rendered *Othman* or *Uthman*, a *ghazi* said to have founded the dynasty when he set up a border state about 1288 on the Byzantine frontier in northwestern Anatolia.

the Early Middle Ages, was by the nineteenth century in the midst of industrial, financial, social, and military revolutions and poised to challenge the Islamic empires from the Mediterranean to South Asia.

Thus it is not entirely surprising that European global expansionism gradually dominated Africa, India, Indonesia, and the heartland culture of the Islamic world, rather than the reverse. Neither the great imperial Islamic states, the smaller Islamic sultanates and emirates, the diverse Hindu kingdoms, nor the varied African states (let alone the smaller societies of Africa, the Americas, and the South Pacific) fared well in their eventual clashes with European expansion during this age. The growing European domination of the seas, of the flow of gold and silver, and of global consumable products allowed Europeans to contain as well as to bypass the major Islamic lands in their quest for commercial empires. Ironically, the Islamic states' hold on the Silk Road from the East may have been one factor in Europe's turn to the Atlantic.

Industrial development and military technology joined economic wealth, social prosperity, and political stability by the early 1800s to give western Europe global military supremacy for the first time. Before 1800 the Europeans were able to bring only minor Islamic states under colonial administrations. The footholds they gained in Africa, India, and Southeast Asia laid the groundwork for rapid colonial expansion by the 1850s. The age of the last great Islamic empires was the beginning of the first great modern European empires. The colonialism of the nineteenth century accompanied the aggressive advance of west European industrial, commercial, and military power that held sway into the mid-twentieth century.

Focus Questions

◆ How did the trajectory of development between the Islamic empires and Europe differ in the period 1500–1850?

◆ Why, after centuries as the "underdog," was Europe by the early nineteenth century finally able to challenge the power of the Islamic empires?

◆ Why was the Islamic world, more than China and Japan, increasingly subject to European intrusion during the early modern period?

Christian patriarch to remain in Istanbul to preside over the Eastern church. The conquest of Constantinople was both the culmination of previous war efforts and a springboard for Ottoman European ambitions. As the Ottomans' extraordinary, expansionist conquests continued, often justified in the name of Islam, they became in Christian European eyes the feared scourge of God.

By 1512 Ottoman rule was secure in virtually all of southeastern Europe and north of the Black Sea in most of the Ukraine. Under Selim I (r. 1512–1520) and Süleyman, "the Lawgiver" (known in the West as "the Magnificent," r. 1520–1566), Ottoman sovereignty expanded. Selim subjugated the Egyptian Mamluks (1517) and annexed Syria-Palestine, most of North Africa, the Yemen, and Mecca and Medina. He also nullified the Shi'ite threat from Iran in the east (see below). Süleyman took control of Kurdistan, Georgia (in the Caucasus), Mesopotamia, and Iraq, and advanced Ottoman borders in eastern Europe. Having won much of Hungary and nearly taken Vienna by siege in 1526–1529, he was able by battle and treaty to bring virtually all of Hungary under direct rule in the 1540s.

The Ottoman ruler could now claim to be the Abbasid heir and caliph for all Muslims. This was symbolized by the addition (by Selim I, after the Mamluk conquest in 1517) of the title "Protector of the Sacred Places [Mecca and Medina]" to that of emperor, **padishah**. At this point, Ottoman military might was unmatched globally, except possibly by China. Its vast territories—home to numerous linguistic and ethnic groups—made it truly an empire (see Map 20–2, p. 513).

THE "CLASSICAL" OTTOMAN ORDER

Mehmed II was the true founder of the Ottoman Empire. He replaced tribal chieftains with loyal servants of the ruler, initiated a tradition of formal governmental legislation with his **Qanun-name** ("Lawbook"), and organized the *ulama* hierarchically under a

Read the **Document**
Mehmed II (15th century)
at **myhistorylab.com**

Read the **Document**
Ogier Ghiselin de Busbecq, "Süleyman the Lawgiver," at **myhistorylab.com**

See the **Map**
The Ottoman Empire to 1566,
at **myhistorylab.com**

padishah
Persian for "master-king"; the title is comparable to emperor.

Qanun-name
A book of laws promulgated by Ottoman sultans.

MAP EXPLORATION

To explore this map further, go to **http://www.myhistorylab.com**

MAP 20–1. The Islamic Heartlands, ca. 1700. The three rival "gunpowder" empires—the Safavid, Mughal, and Ottoman empires—dominated the Islamic heartlands.

Does this map suggest that the Islamic world was in decline by 1700?

Shari'a
Islamic religious law.

harem
The wives, concubines, female relatives, and servants in a Muslim household; they were usually confined to a section of a house or palace.

single "Sheikh of Islam." In the next century Süleyman earned his title "Lawgiver" by his legislation touching all aspects of life and all social ranks, his reconciliation of customary law and **Shari'a** (religious law), and his regularization of both law and bureaucracy.

The entire Ottoman state was organized as one vast military institution. All members, whatever their function, held military ranks as the standing "army" of the state under the hereditary leadership of the sultan. This centralized state was supported by the productivity of its Muslim and non-Muslim subjects, such as Jewish and Armenian merchants. The ruling class was Muslim, shared the common Ottoman culture, and had to give utter allegiance to the sultan. The state organization included the palace, the administrative or ruling institution, the military institution, and the religious or learned institution. The palace included the sultan, his **harem**, his ministers, and the servants. The privy council, headed by the grand vizier, together with the chancery, the imperial treasury, and the remaining civil bureaucracy, formed the backbone of the

MAP 20–2. The Ottoman Empire at Its Zenith. This large and multiethnic empire spanned three continents and lasted more than 400 years. It is shown here at its largest extent around 1600.

What were the strengths and weaknesses of the Ottoman Empire's geographical position?

ruling or administrative institution. Although men held the keys to power, women also had important roles, generally concealed from the public eye. Traditional Turkish customs assumed that power was vested collectively in the family. Women had some ceremonial functions, but also played vital roles in court politics, especially in selecting officers and negotiating economic policy.

Several measures helped ensure the strength of the sultan. Young Ottoman princes received administrative and leadership training in the provinces, which kept them from being sheltered in the palace and gave them experience of life outside the capital. Stability of succession was traditionally guaranteed by the practice of fratricide in the ruling family: While theoretically left to God, succession to the sultanate went to the aspirant who could assert himself and seize power, after which he was expected to execute his brothers to eliminate competing claims to the throne. Legalized in Mehmed II's *Qanun-name*, this practice continued until the late sixteenth century.

··▶ Read the **Document**
Women in Ottoman society
at **myhistorylab.com**

Istanbul, from a 1537 Turkish map. Its strategic location on the Bosphorus straits enabled it to dominate trade in the eastern Mediterranean.

What features of Istanbul does this map draw attention to?

Grand Mufti
The chief religious authority of the Ottoman Empire. Also called "the Shaykh of Islam."

Qanun
Ottoman administrative law.

devshirme
The system under the Ottoman Empire that required each province to furnish a levy of Christian boys who were raised as Muslims and became soldiers in the Ottoman army.

Janissaries
Elite Ottoman troops who were recruited through the devshirme.

The Ottomans co-opted the legal-religious and educational-intellectual roles of the religious scholars, or *ulama*, for the service of the state. They were an arm of the government under a single religious authority, the **Grand Mufti** or "Sheikh of Islam." This highly organized branch of state was open only to Muslim men and included the entire system of courts and judges. It was based on a comprehensive network ranging from local mosque schools to the four elite madrasas built around the Süleymaniye Mosque in Istanbul during Süleyman's reign. Scholars' ranks within the graded *ulama* hierarchy reflected the level of schooling and teaching they had attained.

The state itself was formally committed to maintaining the divinely ordained *Shari'a*, and the *ulama* enjoyed great esteem. This helps explain why the Ottoman *ulama* usually functioned tamely as part of the state apparatus, whereas the *ulama* in both Safavid Iran and Mughal India often differed with their rulers.

Although the religious establishment upheld the supremacy of the *Shari'a* and the sultan recognized its authority, the functional law of the land was the highly organized state administrative law—the practical code, or **Qanun**, established by the ruler. Still, the *Shari'a* as interpreted by the *ulama* theoretically governed the *Qanun*. The conformity of these regulations to the *Shari'a* sometimes reflected the genuine piety of a particular administrator or ruler, and sometimes was only a pious fiction—something also true for Safavid Iran and Mughal India.

The key ingredient of Ottoman power, however, was the military. The Ottoman rulers kept the military's loyalty by two means. First, the state checked the power of the cavalry-gentry through careful registry and control of revenue-bearing lands. Second, the sultan employed slave soldiers whose allegiance was only to him. The state held all conquered agricultural land as its direct property, granting peasants hereditary land use but not ownership. Under the *timar* system, the tax revenues from parcels of conquered lands were granted for specified periods to cavalry officers, in lieu of cash wages. Careful records were kept of the revenue due on all lands, and as long as the state was strong, so too was its control over productive land and the aristocracy whom *timar* revenues supported. But even as early as 1400 the Ottoman rulers tried to reduce the cavalry-gentry's preeminence by employing specialized infantry troops of well-trained and well-paid slave soldiers (equipped, unlike the cavalry, with firearms) whose loyalty was to the sultan alone.

To sustain the quality of these slave troops, the Ottomans developed a unique institution: the provincial slave levy, or **devshirme**. This institution selected young Christian boys from the provincial peasantry to be raised as Muslims; most came from the Balkans. They were trained to serve in both army and bureaucracy at all levels. The most famous slave corps was the *yeni cheri* (young troops), or **Janissaries**, the elite infantry troops of the empire. Muslim boys were not allowed into the slave corps, although some parents tried to buy them a place in what offered the most promising careers in the empire. Until 1572 marriage was forbidden to the slave soldiers, which further ensured loyalty and prevented hereditary claims on office.

AFTER SÜLEYMAN: CHALLENGES AND CHANGE

The reign of Süleyman marked the peak of Ottoman prestige and power. Further territorial gains were made in the seventeenth century, and the Ottoman state long remained a major force in European and Asian politics. But beginning with the reign of Süleyman's weak son, Selim II (1566–1574), the empire was plagued by military corruption, governmental decentralization, and maritime setbacks. Economically there were agricultural failures, commercial imbalances, and inflation. Yet culturally and intellectually, the seventeenth and eighteenth centuries were periods of impressive activity and accomplishments. For these two centuries, the state alternated between decline and vitality.

The post-Süleyman era began badly, with the loss of territory in the Caucasus and Mesopotamia to the Safavids of Iran (1603). The Ottoman military apparatus was already weakened, partly from fighting two-front wars with the Safavids and the Habsburgs and partly by European advances in military and naval technology. The Janissaries became increasingly disruptive. By 1600 they had largely replaced the provincial cavalry as new warfare styles made cavalry obsolete. By 1600 Muslims were allowed into the Janissary corps, marriage was possible, and the *devshirme* was declining in use. During the seventeenth century, the Janissaries became increasingly corrupt as they tampered with politics and tried to influence dynastic succession. Finally, the increasing employment of mercenaries resulted in the peacetime release of masses of armed men into the countryside, leading to the sacking of provincial towns, banditry, and revolts.

Murad IV (r. 1623–1640) introduced reforms and ruled with an iron hand, but his death left a weak central authority. Two capable viziers, the Köprülüs, father and son (r. 1656–1676), briefly renewed strong administrative control and military success, but thereafter the central institutions decayed.

Financing the Ottoman state became ever more difficult. The increase in the Janissary corps from 12,000 to 36,000 men during the sixteenth century drained state coffers. Inflation grew as the coinage was debased. In contrast to mercantilist and protectionist policies of European powers, the Ottomans discouraged exports and encouraged imports to keep domestic prices low. This damaged the economy in the long run. The population doubled in the sixteenth century, and unemployment grew after 1600. Increased decentralization paved the way for the rise of provincial notables—**ayan**—who became virtually independent in the eighteenth century. Tax farming went hand-in-glove with the rise of large private estates. New taxes were imposed, old emergency levies regularized, and taxes demanded in cash rather than in kind—and increasingly on a communal rather than individual basis.

The seventeenth and eighteenth centuries were an era of genuine vitality in poetry, prose, music, painting, cartography, historiography, astronomy, and other fields. The Ottomans' patronage of the arts and sciences was one way to assert their claim to Islamic and universal authority. The seventeenth century saw especially lively intellectual exchange, both religious and secular. But it was also a time when the *ulama* became an aristocratic, increasingly corrupt elite. Major religious posts became hereditary sinecures for members of a handful of families who had produced prominent *ulama*, and the posts were often sold or leased. (See Document, "The Distinctiveness of Ottoman Identity and Culture" on page 516.)

Of many learned individuals in the seventeenth and eighteenth centuries, Katib Chelebi (d. 1657) was the most illustrious; he wrote histories, social commentary, geographies, and encyclopedic works. Other important writers were the great historian of the Ottomans, Na'ima (d. 1716), the tireless traveler and travel writer Evliya Chelebi (d. ca. 1685), and probably the greatest Ottoman poet, Nedim (d. 1730). Ottoman art had been highly eclectic in the first century after Mehmed II, but in the later sixteenth century a more conservative turn produced distinctively Ottoman artistic and architectural forms. The greatest name here is that of the imperial master architect Sinan (d. 1578). The first half of the eighteenth century was the golden age of Ottoman poetry and art; it also saw the first Ottoman printing press and the beginning of strong European influence in the arts, architecture, and manners. In the popular sphere, the now classical form of Turkish theater (in which two men play male and female parts) began as early as the sixteenth century, perhaps under Jewish immigrant influence.

Socially, the period saw the consolidation of Ottoman society as a multiethnic, multireligious state. The empire encompassed a dizzying array of languages, religions, and ethnic identities. All subjects, Muslim and non-Muslim, were organized into communities called **millets** that were responsible for their members from the cradle to

Süleyman the Lawgiver. Süleyman giving advice to the Crown Prince, Mehmed Khan. From a contemporaneous Ottoman miniature.

Suleyman I (Kanuni); Shehzade by Talikizade Suphi. Folio 79a of the Talikizade Shehnamesi, Library at the Topkapi Palace Museum, A3592, Photograph courtesy of Talat Halman.

What regions did Süleyman bring under Ottoman control?

✓•—**Study** and **Review**
at **myhistorylab.com**

◉—**See** the **Map**
The Decline of the Ottoman Empire
at **myhistorylab.com**

ayan
Ottoman notables.

QUICK REVIEW

Ottoman Culture
- Katib Chelebi (d. 1657): most illustrious figure in Ottoman literature
- Distinctly Ottoman artistic forms emerged in the late sixteenth century
- Sinan (d. 1578) was the leading Ottoman architect of his day

millets
Within the Ottoman Empire, religious communities that administered their own educational, charitable, and judicial affairs.

DOCUMENT

The Distinctiveness of Ottoman Identity and Culture

Presiding over a pluralistic culture, the Ottoman Turks, themselves a people from the periphery of the central Islamic lands, developed an "Ottoman" identity and culture that was especially evident in their ruling elite. The following selections from members of that elite describe some of the values and qualities they saw as important to Ottoman identity. In the first, Mustafa Ali (d. 1600), a major historian, intellectual, and state official, lists the special divine favors granted the Ottoman rulers. In the second, another historian, Kinalizade Ali, adopts an ancient political saying attributed to Aristotle and others to describe the prerequisites for an ordered polity under the Shari'a.

- **COMPARE** the two passages. What common themes emerge?

1 THE GIFTS OF DIVINE FAVOR GIVEN THE OTTOMAN DYNASTY

The first gift: They reside all by themselves in a palace like unique jewels in the depth of the oyster-shell, and totally sever all relations with relatives and dependents. The slave girls and slave pages that have access to their honored private quarters (harem), who are evidently at least three to four thousand individuals, are all strangers and the person of the monarch is like a single gem in their midst . . . .

The second gift: Their religious convictions being immaculate and their character like a shining mirror, it has never happened that a single member of that noble family ever swerved from the road of orthodoxy or that one valiant sultan befriended himself with an unseemly doctrine.

The third gift: The Lord, the Creator and Protector, has always hidden that great race under His protection and it has never been heard that the plague would have entered their flourishing palace or that an individual belonging to that blemishless progeny would have been struck by the horror of the pestilence and would have died of it.

The fourth gift: Whenever they conquered a province and, destroying and eradicating its castles and estates, were confronted with the necessity of appointing a magistrate and assigning a substantial force on their own authority they considered it a sign of weakness, like Alexander the Great, to appoint again one of the great of that province and to assign him certain revenues; may [that province] be as far away as can be, they would opt to send one of the attendants of their Gate of Happiness [there] as san-jaq begi, and to Yemen and Ethiopia and to very remote places like Algeria a begler-begi. No such absolute power was given to the earlier sovereigns.

The fifth gift: The various special troops in their victory-oriented army and the various tools of war and battle use that are given to them were not available to the brawny fists of anyone of the countless armies [of previous times]. To their attacks going downward and going upward are the same, to their victory-imprinted military music low and high notes are of the same level and equal. In their eyes, as it were, the conquest of a castle is like destroying a spider's web, and in their God-assisted hands to beat the enemies is clearly like pulling out a hair from the beard of a decrepit old man.

The sixth gift: The coherence of the figures in the registers of their revenues and the order of the recordings in the ledgers of their expenses are so strict that they and their salaried classes are free of worries. Consequently, their income exceeds their necessary expenses, their gain is larger than [the expenses for] the important affairs of state.

2 THE NEED OF AUTHORITY TO UPHOLD THE SHARI'A

There can be no royal authority without the military
There can be no military without wealth
The subjects produce the wealth
Justice preserves the subjects' loyalty to the sovereign
Justice requires harmony in the world
The world is a garden, its walls are the state
The Holy Law [Shari'a] orders the state
There is no support for the Holy Law except through royal authority.

Source: Selection 1 from Andreas Tietze, *Mustafa Ali's Counsel for Sultans of 1581*, Verlag Der Osterreichischen Akademie Der Wissenshaften, Vienna, 1979, pp. 38–39. Selection 2 from Cornell H. Fleischer, *Bureaucrat and Intellectual in the Ottoman Empire: The Historian Mustafa Ali (1541–1600)*, Princeton University Press, 1986, p. 262.

the grave. The millets administered educational, charitable, and judicial affairs and assisted the central government in collecting taxes. Typically the millets were headed by a religious leader and enjoyed some degree of internal autonomy. Thus early on the Ottoman Empire became a haven for numerous minority groups, especially Jews. Considerable immigration of Jews into Ottoman societies following their expulsion from Spain during the Spanish Inquisition (1492) had brought new craftsmen, physicians, bankers, scholars, and even entertainers. The large Christian population of the empire was generally well treated, but in the eighteenth and nineteenth centuries they began to suffer from increasing taxes and other discrimination. As a result Ottoman Christians began to look to Christian Europe and Russia for liberation.

State policy encouraged just treatment of all subjects. In the eighteenth century, however, relations between Muslims and non-Muslims deteriorated, in part because of the remarkable rise in the economic and social status of non-Muslims—in particular the mercantile middle class. Non-Muslims virtually monopolized foreign trade, and in the eighteenth century European countries gave many of them citizenship. This qualified them for the trade privileges that the sultan granted to foreign governments.

One of the major social institutions of later Ottoman society, the coffeehouse, flourished from the mid–1500s on. It probably originated as a Sufi institution that accompanied coffee to the Mediterranean from the Yemen. The Ottoman coffeehouse rapidly became a major common space for socializing. People gathered to drink coffee, play games, watch puppet shows, read books, discuss public affairs, and even engage in political agitation. The sheikh of Islam banned coffee because of its stimulant qualities, but it could not be suppressed. (Neither could another imported habit, cigarette smoking.) The coffeehouse fostered a common Ottoman urban culture among lower and middle classes.

THE DECLINE OF OTTOMAN MILITARY AND POLITICAL POWER

After their failure in 1683 to take Vienna, the Ottomans were driven out of Hungary and Belgrade and never again threatened Europe. In 1774 Russia took the Crimea and formally became protector of Orthodox Christians in the Ottoman Empire. Whereas in the seventeenth century the Empire was relatively self-contained and self-sufficient, by the late 1700s it was increasingly dependent on international market systems, particularly those of western Europe. Previously the empire's economic growth had been based on conquest and control of

Devshirme. An Ottoman portrayal of the *devshirme*. This miniature painting (c. 1558) depicts the recruiting of Christian youths for the sultan's elite Janissary corps. The boys, dressed in red, are at the bottom, while their parents, who look pleased, congregate on the right.

Arifi, "Suleymanname," Topkapi Palace Museum, II 1517, fol. 31b, photograph courtesy of Talat Halman.

Why would parents be pleased at their children's recruitment as Janissaries?

◆◆◆ Read the **Document**
Portrait of an Ottoman Gentleman
at **myhistorylab.com**

CHRONOLOGY

THE OTTOMAN EMPIRE

1301	Foundation of early Ottoman principality in Bursa by Osman
1356	Ottomans cross Dardanelles into Europe
1451–1481	Rule of Sultan Mehmed II, "the Conqueror"
1453	Fall of Constantinople to Mehmed the Conqueror
1512–1520	Rule of Selim I
1517	Ottoman conquest of Egypt, assumption of claim to Abbasid caliphal succession from Mamluks
1520–1566	Rule of Süleyman, "the Lawgiver"
1526–1529	First Ottoman siege of Vienna
1578	Death of Ottoman master architect, Sinan
1656–1676	Governance of Köprülüs as viziers
1683	Second Ottoman siege of Vienna
1699	Treaty of Karlowitz, loss of Hungarian and other European territory
1774	Loss of Crimea to Russia; Tsar becomes formal protector of Ottoman Orthodox Christians
1918	End of empire at the end of World War I

A Turkish Coffeehouse. This early nineteenth-century rendering of a coffeehouse in Istanbul reflects the exoticism that Europeans cultivated in their portrayals of things Islamic.

What role did coffeehouses play in Ottoman society?

WHAT ROLE did Shi'ite ideology play in the Safavid Empire?

Sufi

Sufism is a mystic tradition within Islam that encompasses a diverse range of beliefs and practices dedicated to Divine love and the cultivation of the elements of the Divine within the individual human being. The chief aim of all Sufis is to let go of all notions of duality, including a conception of an individual self, and to realize the Divine unity.

pirs

Shi'ite holy men.

⊙ See the Map
Atlas Map: Iran Under the Safavids, ca. 1252–1524, at **myhistorylab.com**

land as a source of wealth. But as its expansion was stopped, the Sultanate was unprepared for an increasingly Europe-dominated world economy geared toward capitalist accumulation and industrialization. Henceforth, the Ottomans were prey to the West, never regaining their earlier power and influence before their collapse in 1918.

Outflanked by Russia to the north and European sea power south and west, the Ottomans were blocked in the east by their Safavid foes in Iran. They could not sustain sufficient external trade to support their expensive wars, especially when, in the eighteenth century, Italian, French, British, and Dutch traders obtained special concessions for their trade in the Fertile Crescent, Persian Gulf, and Red Sea regions, which Ottoman merchants did not receive. Ultimately, Ottoman dependence on a decentralized agrarian-age, local-market economy proved insufficient to face the rising commercial and industrial powers of Europe.

THE SAFAVID EMPIRE AND THE WEST ASIAN WORLD

ORIGINS

As noted in Chapter 12, Iranian history changed after 1500 under the Safavid Dynasty. The Safavids had begun in the fourteenth century as hereditary Turkish spiritual leaders of a Sunni **Sufi** order in Azerbaijan, in northwestern Iran. In the 1400s the Safavid order evolved a new, militant Shi'ite Sufi ideology. By claiming descent from the imams of Twelver Shi'ism (see Chapter 12), Safavid spiritual masters (*sheikhs* or **pirs**) became the focus of Shi'ite religious allegiance. Many adherents were won to the *tariqa*, or Sufi brotherhood, and eventually to Shi'ism from among the Turkoman tribesmen of eastern Anatolia, northern Syria, and northwestern Iran. These mounted warriors were called *Qizilbash* ("Red Heads") after their distinctive crimson uniform hats that signaled allegiance to the twelve Shi'ite imams and their Safavid Sufi master.

The growing strength of the Safavid brotherhood engendered conflicts with the dominant Sunni Turkoman groups around Tabriz. The Safavids emerged victorious in 1501 under the leadership of the young Safavid Sufi-master-designate Isma'il. Recognized as a divinely appointed representative of the "hidden" imam (see Chapter 10), Isma'il gained sovereignty over the southern Caucasus, Azerbaijan, the Tigris-Euphrates valley, and all of western Iran by 1506. By 1512, unified under a common religious identity and in league with Babur, the Timurid ruler of Kabul, the Safavids took from the Uzbek Turks all of eastern Iran from the Oxus south to the Arabian Sea. Because of the loss of these territories, the largely pastoralist Uzbeks became implacable foes of the Safavids. Throughout the ensuing century the Safavids were often forced to fight a debilitating two-front war against Uzbeks in the east and Ottomans in the west.

Strong central rule now united traditional Iranian lands for the first time since the heyday of the Abbasid caliphate. It was a regime based on existing Persian bureaucratic institutions, which in turn stemmed from Seljuk institutions. Shah Isma'il ruthlessly enforced Shi'ite conformity, which slowly took root across the realm—perhaps bolstered by a rising Iranian self-consciousness in the face of the Sunni Ottomans, Arabs, Uzbeks, and Mughals who surrounded Iran. In the latter part of his reign, Shah Isma'il took steps to rule, both culturally and politically, through a reconstruction of the historic Iranian monarchy, rather than as leader of a Sufi brotherhood. Although Isma'il had loyal tribal and religious support internally, he had tenuous ties with his neighbors. The Ottoman sultans vigorously fought the spread of his Sufi-inspired Shi'ite monarchy into eastern Anatolian lands widely populated by other Sufi orders.

◆◆◆ **Read** the **Document**
Shah Isma'il Describes Himself to His Followers, at **myhistorylab.com**

In 1514 the better-armed Ottoman army of Selim I defeated the Safavid forces at Chaldiran in Iranian Azerbaijan, initiating an extended series of Ottoman-Safavid border wars over the next two centuries. Chaldiran marked the beginning of Qizilbash disaffection with Shah Isma'il and fueled subsequent efforts to seize power from the Safavids. This defeat brought Ottoman control to the Fertile Crescent, forcing the Safavids to move their capital and their focus eastward to Qazwin and subsequently Isfahan.

SHAH ABBAS I

Isma'il's successor, Tahmasp I (r. 1524–1576), survived repeated attacks by both Ottomans and Uzbeks, thanks to the strength of Shi'ite religious feeling and the allegiance of the Iranian bureaucracy. Twelve years later, the most able Safavid ruler, Shah Abbas I (r. 1588–1629) brought real leadership to Safavid Iran. He regained provincial land for the state and used the revenue to support new troops from his Caucasian territories as a counterweight to the unruly Qizilbash. They, like the Ottoman cavalry, were supported by land-revenue assignments. Abbas not only pushed the Ottomans out of Azerbaijan and Iraq but also repelled new Uzbek invasions in Khorasan. He sought alliances with the Ottomans' European enemies. This tactic, used by several Safavid rulers, reflected one of several military and economic divisions in the often-assumed unity of the Islamic world.

Dancing Sufis, their arms raised in ecstasy, congregate at the tomb of the great Persian medieval poet, Sa'adi.
What were some highlights of Persian culture under the Safavids?

Empires, Islamic or not, were essentially divided from each other by self-interested desire for absolute control of their territories and resources. Abbas also broke the century-long Portuguese monopoly on trade along Persian shores and opened trade relations with the English and Dutch East India commercial companies. His reign brought considerable prosperity to Iran. The magnificent capital he built at Isfahan epitomized Safavid grandeur and vision, most vividly in its regal central square, the Maydan-i Shah.

◆◆◆ **Read** the **Document**
Fathers Simon and Vincent Report on Shah Abbas I, the Safavid Ruler of Persia, at **myhistorylab.com**

The enduring element of Safavid consolidation of power was the replacement in Iran of Sunni with Shi'ite Islam as the majority faith. Because Twelver Shi'ism was not as strongly grounded in Iranian religious tradition as Sufi traditions were, the Safavids imported religious scholars (*ulama*), primarily from today's Lebanon and Syria, to lend legitimacy to the government. They discouraged pilgrimage to Mecca and instead emphasized visits to Karbala and the shrine of Husayn, the Prophet Muhammad's grandson. Eventually, however, the government–*ulama* relations became strained. By the 1600s, the *ulama* withdrew from political participation, refusing to confer direct legitimacy on the shah.

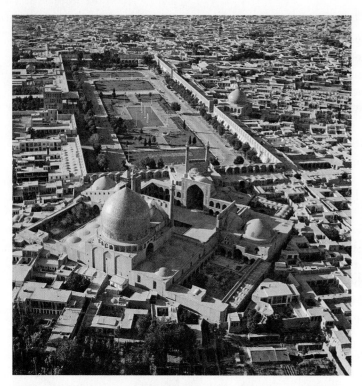

Maydan-i-Shah. The enormous rectangular-shaped plaza at the top of this aerial photo connects with the equally impressive Masjid-i-Shah Mosque, constructed between 1611 and 1638.

How does this photo show the close connection between spiritual and temporal power in Safavid society?

Safavid Art. *Woman with a Veil,* by Riza Abbasi, ca. 1595. In Safavid times, artists began to depict everyday life and people, such as this graceful, sinuous young woman.

What were the roots of the Safavid artistic tradition?

SAFAVID DECLINE

After Shah Abbas, the empire rarely again enjoyed able leadership. The chief causes of eventual decline and collapse were (1) continued two-front pressure from Ottoman and Uzbek forces, (2) economic decline, (3) social unrest among the provincial elites, and (4) the increasing landholding power of the Shi'ite *ulama*. The conservative *ulama* introduced a form of Islamic legalism and emphasized their own authority as interpreters of the law over that of the monarch. They persecuted religious minorities and encouraged anti-Sunni hatred. Some of the Iranian *ulama* and merchant class sought closer ties with European commercial communities. Local administrators were content to maintain the traditional decentralized Safavid system in their own interests, which only increased dependency on the increasingly corrupt Safavid family.

In the end, an Afghan leader captured Isfahan and forced Husayn I (1694–1722) to abdicate. A few Safavid princes managed to retake control of western Iran, but the empire's greatness was gone. A revived, formally Safavid monarchy under the talented Qizilbash tribal leader Nadir Shah (r. 1736–1747) and several successors restored much of Iran's lost territories, but military ventures sapped the empire's finances. After Nadir's brutal, autocratic reign ended in 1747, Iran's provincial elites, *ulama*, and merchants struggled to regain some political and economic stability. Only by the early nineteenth century was some success achieved under the Qajar kings (see Chapter 26).

CULTURE AND LEARNING

The Safavid age also saw a distinctively Shi'ite and Sufi piety develop to give a firmly Shi'ite character to Iranian culture and traditions. It focused on commemorating the suffering of the imams, life as a struggle for social justice, and loyalty to the Shi'ite *ulama*, who alone provided guidance in the absence of the hidden imam (see Chapter 10).

Safavid patronage of scholarship and the arts was funded by fortunes from trade in silk, silver, and other long-distance commodities. The Safavids supported an impressive cultural and intellectual renaissance in the sixteenth and seventeenth centuries. Traditions of painting, with their origins in the powerful miniatures of the preceding century, were cultivated and modified in Safavid times. Portraiture and scenes from everyday life became popular. High-quality craft-works included ceramic tiles, porcelains, shawls, and carpets. The magnificent city of Isfahan, especially the exquisite gardens and grand arches and domes constructed under Shah Abbas, gives breathtaking evidence of the Safavid sense of proportion, color, and design as well as the superb architectural technology and urban planning. Isfahan was said to be "half the world," a lofty epithet suggesting it to be the quintessence of Iranian global preeminence. It marks a high point in the sophisticated use of space and lavish deployment of ceramic tiles.

In intellectual life, the *Ishraqi* or "Illuminationist" school was a form of Shi'ite religious speculation about the nature of divine truth and its accessibility to human reason and imagination. It drew on both the mystical, Sufi bent of Iranian Islamic thought and the long Islamic traditions of Aristotelianism and Platonism. Transcendence and a "realm of images" were key concepts for the Illuminationists. They conceived of transcendence in terms of a divine light, the Light of Truth, expressed most fully in Muhammad and the Shi'ite imams. The realm of images was a sphere in which the attuned spirit could experience true visions. These ideas reconceived human experience of the Divine in a way that transcended logic, requiring individual experience. At stake were basic notions of the human psyche and the larger cosmos. The most prominent Iranian exponent of the *Ishraqi school* was Mulla Sadra (d. 1640).

THE MUGHALS

ORIGINS

In a recurring pattern of Indian history, invaders from beyond the Oxus River to the northwest began a new era in the subcontinent in the early sixteenth century. These invaders were Chaghatay Turks descended from Timur (Tamerlane) and known to history as the **Mughals** (a Persianate form of *Mongol*). They ended the political fragmentation that by 1500 had reduced the Delhi sultanate to only one among many Indian states. In 1525 to 1527 the founder of the Mughal Dynasty, Babur, marched on India, replaced the last sultan of Delhi, and then defeated a Rajput confederacy. Before his death in 1530, he ruled an empire stretching from the Oxus to Bihar and the Himalayas to the Deccan. But the real founder of the Mughal Empire and the greatest Indian ruler since Ashoka (ca. 264–223 B.C.E.) was Akbar "the Great" (r. 1556–1605). He was at least as great a ruler as his famous contemporaries, Elizabeth I of England (r. 1558–1603), the Holy Roman Emperor Charles V (r. 1519–1556), and Shah Abbas I (r. 1587–1629).

AKBAR'S REIGN

Akbar began his reign with impressive military successes. He added North India and the northern Deccan to the Mughal dominions. Even more significant were his governmental reforms, cultural patronage, and religious toleration. He completely reorganized central and provincial government and rationalized the tax system. His marriages with Rajput princesses and his appointment of Hindus to positions of power eased Muslim-Hindu tensions. So did his cancellation of the poll tax on non-Muslims (1564) and his efforts to reduce the power of the more literalist, "hard-line" *ulama*. Under his leadership the Mughal Empire became a truly Indian Empire.

Akbar was a religious eclectic who showed not only tolerance but also unusual interest in different religious traditions. He frequently brought together representatives of all faiths—Jain and Buddhist monks, Brahmans, *ulama*, Parsis (Zoroastrians), and Jesuits—to discuss religion. These debates took place in a special hall in Akbar's magnificent palace complex at Fatehpur-Sikri outside the Mughal capital, Agra.

THE LAST GREAT MUGHALS

Akbar's three immediate successors were Jahangir (r. 1605–1627), Shah Jahan (r. 1628–1658), and Awrangzeb (r. 1658–1707). They left behind significant achievements, but the problems of sustaining an Indian empire gradually undercut Mughal strength. The reigns of Jahangir and Shah Jahan were arguably the golden age of Mughal culture, notably in architecture and painting, when a distinctive Mughal style based on traditional Hindi and Persian styles solidified. But the costs of new building, military campaigns, and the erosion of Akbar's administrative and tax reforms brought economic decline. Jahangir set a fateful precedent in permitting English merchants to establish a trading post, or "factory," at Surat on the western coast in Gujarat. Shah

WHAT ROLE did religious intolerance play in the decline of the Mughal Empire?

Mughals
Descendants of the Mongols who established an Islamic Empire in India in the sixteenth century with its capital at Delhi.

Hear the Audio at **myhistorylab.com**

Study and Review at **myhistorylab.com**

View the Image Akbar, Emperor of India, at **myhistorylab.com**

QUICK REVIEW

Akbar (r. 1556–1605)
- Added North India and the northern Deccan to Mughal Empire
- Carried out extensive governmental reforms
- Interested in a variety of religious faiths

QUICK REVIEW

Awrangzeb (r. 1658–1707)

◆ Reversed policy of religious toleration

◆ Persecuted non-Muslims

◆ Policies coincided with spread of militant Sikh movement and rise of Hindu Maratha nationalism

◉ See the **Map**

Mughal Empire
at **myhistorylab.com**

◉ See the **Map**

The Maratha Kingdoms 1
at **myhistorylab.com**

Jahan brought the Deccan wholly under Mughal control but lost Kandahar to Safavid forces in 1648. His wars further strained the Mughal economy. Other financial burdens were his elaborate building projects, the most magnificent of which was the white-stoned Taj Mahal (built 1632–1653), the unparalleled tomb with its Persian-style dome that he built for his beloved consort, Mumtaz.

With Shah Jahan, internal disorder and instability hastened the decline of Mughal power. Religious toleration retreated; the narrow religious conservatism of his son, Awrangzeb, all but reversed Akbar's earlier policies. He persecuted non-Muslims, destroying Hindu temples, reimposing the poll tax (1679), and alienating the Rajput leaders, whose forebears Akbar had so carefully cultivated. His intransigent policies coincided with and likely contributed to the rise of the Sikh movement's militant reformism throughout the Punjab, and Hindu Maratha nationalism in western India.

SIKHS AND MARATHAS

In the late sixteenth and early seventeenth centuries the Sikhs, who trace their origins to the irenic teachings of Guru Nanak (d. 1538), became a distinctive religious movement. Neither Muslim nor Hindu, they had their own scripture, ritual, and moralistic, reformist ideals. Awrangzeb earned their opposition by persecution culminating in the martyrdom of their ninth leader, or *guru*, Teg Bahadur, in 1675. Thereafter, the tenth and last Sikh guru, Gobind Singh (d. 1708), developed the Sikhs into a formidable military force whose repeated uprisings plagued Awrangzeb and his successors.

The Hindu Marathas, led by the charismatic Shivaji (d. 1680), rose in religious and nationalistic fervor to found their own regional empire in about 1646. At Shivaji's death, the Maratha state controlled the mountainous Western coast, and its army was the most disciplined force in India. Despite Awrangzeb's subsequent defeat of the Marathas and his conquest of the entire south of India, the Marathas continued to fight. After his death they built a confederation of almost all the Deccan states under their leadership. After about 1740, while formally acknowledging Mughal sovereignty, the Marathas actually controlled far more of India than did the Mughals.

POLITICAL DECLINE

In addition to the Rajput, Sikh, and Maratha wars, other factors sealed the fate of the once-great Mughal Empire after Awrangzeb's death in 1707: the rise in the Deccan of the powerful Islamic state of Hyderabad in 1724; the Persian invasion of North India by Nadir Shah in 1739; invasions (1748–1761) by the Afghan tribal leader Ahmad Shah Durrani (r. 1747–1773), "founder of modern Afghanistan"; and British victories over Bengali forces at Plassey in Bengal (1757) and over the French on the southeastern coast (1740–1763). By 1819 the dominance of the British East India Company had eclipsed Mughal as it did Maratha and almost all regional Indian power, even though the Mughal line did not officially end until 1858.

RELIGIOUS DEVELOPMENTS

The period from about 1500 to 1650 was of major importance for Indian religious life. Akbar's eclecticism mirrored the atmosphere of the sixteenth century in India. A number of religious figures preached a spiritually or mystically oriented piety that transcended the legalism of both the *ulama* and the Brahmans and rejected caste distinctions.

Fatehpur-Sikri. The Diwan-i-Khas, one of the many pavilions in the enormous imperial palace complex.

How does this building reflect the grandeur of Mughal imperial architecture?

A Closer Look

The Mughal Emperor Jahangir Honoring a Muslim Saint over Kings and Emperors

BICHITR (d. late 1650s), Mughal miniaturist master who painted from ca. 1620, depicts the Emperor Jahangir (r. 1605-27) seated on an hourglass throne with sands running through it, showing preference to the Sufi saint and shaykh of the Chishti Sufi order, Husayn, over three temporal rulers: the Ottoman emperor, the king of England, and a Hindu prince. One of the inscriptions reads, "although to all appearances kings stand before him, Jahangir looks inwardly towards the [Sufi] dervishes."

Jahangir presents a book to Shaykh Husayn, descendant of the great saint Mu'inuddin Chishti, apparently ignoring the three great temporal rulers ranked beneath Husayn on the left side of the painting (along with the lowest figure, representing the artist himself wearing a red turban). This presumably points to Jahangir's piety and preference of spirituality over temporal power(s).

The portrait of King James I of England was copied by Bichitr from an English portrait by John de Critz (d. 1642) given to Jahangir by Sir Thomas Roe, British ambassador to the Mughal court from 1615 to 1619. The realistic style of the original is faithfully reproduced here to scale.

The naked cupid figures also are clearly copied from a European painting, as are the two clothed cupids writing on the hourglass at the bottom of the throne.

Janangir is seated on the hourglass throne and hence above time itself, just as his elevated seat puts him high above the earthly potentates depicted and even above Shaykh Husayn. The two clothed cupid figures are inscribing the throne with the wish that Jahangir might live a thousand years. The stool below the throne carries Bichitr's name, on which Jahangir would have to step to mount the throne.

Bichitr, *Jahangir Preferring a Sufi Shaikh to Kings*, ca. 1660–70, Album Page; Opaque watercolor, gold and ink on paper, 25.3 × 18.1 cm. Courtesy of the Freer Gallery of Art, Smithsonian Institution, Washington, DC.

Questions

1. What allegorical meaning might Jahangir's elevated seat above the hour-glass, the royal rulers, and even the Muslim saint suggest here?

2. The radiant Sun disk combined with the crescent moon is clearly symbolic or allegorical as well, and one of the inscriptions speaks of Jahangir as "light of the faith." What might Bichitr be saying with these symbols and texts about Jahangir's exalted status?

3. What do the disparate elements of the painting tell us about the relative international awareness of the Indian court in the early 1600s?

CHRONOLOGY

INDIA: THE MUGHALS AND CONTEMPORARY INDIAN POWERS

1525–1527	Rule of Babur, founder of Indian Timurid state
1538	Death of Guru Nanak, founder of Sikh religious tradition
1556–1605	Rule of Akbar "the Great"
1605–1627	Rule of Jahangir
1628–1658	Rule of Shah Jahan, builder of the Taj Mahal
1646	Founding of Maratha Empire
1658–1707	Rule of Awrangzeb
1680	Death of Maratha leader, Shivaji
1708	Death of tenth and last Sikh guru, Gobind Singh
1724	Rise of Hyderabad state
1739	Iranian invasion of North India under Nadir Shah
1757	British East India Company victory over Bengali and French forces at Plassey
1857–1858	Indian Uprising and the death of the last Mughal ruler, Bahadur Shah II

◆◆◆ Read the Document
A Sikh Guru's Testimony of Faith
at **myhistorylab.com**

In these ideas, we can see both Muslim Sufi and Hindu *bhakti* influences at work. Ramananda and Kabir were two forerunners of such reformers (see Chapter 12). Guru Nanak took up Kabir's ideas and preached faith and devotion to one loving, merciful God. He opposed narrow allegiance to particular creeds and excessive pride in external religious observance. Nanak's hymns of praise contain both Hindu and Muslim ideas and imagery. Dadu (d. 1603) preached a similar message. He was born a Muslim but, like Kabir and Nanak, preached that one must transcend either Muslim or Hindu allegiance in love and service of God.

There was also an upsurge of *bhakti* devotionalism that amounted to a Hindu revival. It was epitomized by the Bengali Krishna devotee Chaitanya (d. ca. 1533), who stressed total devotion to Lord Krishna. The forebears of present-day Hare Krishna devotees, his followers spread widely his ecstatic public praise of God and his message that all are equal in God's sight. The other major Hindu devotional figure in this era was Tulasidas (d. 1623), whose Hindi retelling of the Sanskrit *Ramayana* epic remains among the most popular works of Indian literature. Tulasidas used the story of Rama's adventures to present *bhakti* ideas that remain as alive in everyday Hindu life as do his verses.

Muslim eclectic tendencies came primarily from Sufis. By 1500 many Sufi retreat centers had been established in India. Sufis' enthusiastic forms of worship and inclination to play down the externals of religion meshed well with Indian sensibilities. Sufis were, however, often opposed by more puritanical *ulama*, many of whom held powerful positions as royal advisers and judges. To check *ulama* puritan bigotry, Akbar named himself the supreme spiritual authority in the empire, ordering that toleration be the law of the land.

After Akbar's death the inevitable reaction set in. The Indian leader of the central Asian Sufi order of the Naqshbandiya, Ahmad Sirhindi (d. 1624), sought to purge Sufism of popular practices not sanctioned by the schools of law, for example. He especially condemned practices reflecting Hindu influence and rejected toleration of Hindus themselves. Among Akbar's successors, Awrangzeb, as noted above, was known for strictures against non-Muslims. While his persecutions are often exaggerated, his narrowness of spirit did finally win out. The possibilities for Hindu–Muslim rapprochement in Akbar's time gradually waned, presaging the communal strife that has marred South Asian history in recent times.

CENTRAL ASIA: ISLAMIZATION IN THE POST-TIMUR ERA

WHAT WERE the most important Islamic states in Central and southern Asia?

Islam established a solid footing in Central Asia in the post-Timur era of the fifteenth century. In the preceding century, as the peoples of western Central Asia had begun to shift from a nomadic to a settled existence, the familiar pattern of Islamic diffusion from trading and urban centers to the countryside had set in. Islamization by Sunni and

Shi'ite Sufis, traders, and tribal rulers went on apace thereafter, even as far as western China and Mongolia. It was slowed only in the late 1500s by the conversion of the tribes of Mongolia proper to the Buddhism of the Tibetan lamas. Thus, after 1500 the Safavid Shi'ite Empire was bounded by Islamic Sunni states in India, Afghanistan, Anatolia, Mesopotamia, Transoxiana, and western Turkistan (Khwarizm, between the Aral and Caspian seas). In these last two areas, the most important states were ruled by Uzbek and Chaghatay Turks.

UZBEKS AND CHAGHATAYS

During the fifteenth century Timur's heirs had ruled Transoxiana and most of Iran (see Chapter 12). To the north, above the Jaxartes River (Syr Darya) and the Aral Sea, a new steppe khanate had been formed by the unification in 1428 of assorted clans of Turks and Mongols known as the Uzbeks. Muhammad Shaybani (d. 1510), an Uzbek leader who was descended from Genghis Khan, invaded Transoxiana (1495–1500). There he founded a new Uzbek Islamic empire that replaced Timurid rule, which shifted south to Kabul and eventually India, as described earlier. Muhammad's line continued Uzbek rule in Transoxiana at Bukhara into the eighteenth century, while another Uzbek line ruled the independent khanate of Khiva in western Turkestan from 1512 to 1872.

Of the other Central Asian Islamic states after 1500, the most significant was that of the Chaghatay Turks. The Chaghatays had been the successors of Genghis Khan in the whole region from the Aral Sea and the Oxus River to China (see Map 20–1). After 1350, Timur's invasion broke up their khanate. From about 1514 a revived Chaghatay state flourished in eastern Turkestan. Although the Chaghatay rulers lasted until 1678 in one part of the Tarim basin, their real power was lost after about 1555 to various Khoja princes, Sunni zealots who claimed to be *Sharifs* (descendants of the Prophet).

CONSEQUENCES OF THE SHI'ITE RIFT

On the face of it, the Ottoman, Mughal, Safavid, and Central Asian Islamic states had much in common: Muslim faith and culture, similar systems of taxation and law, the Persian language, and Turkish rulers. Yet the deep religious division between the Shi'ite Safavids and all their Sunni neighbors proved stronger than their common bonds. The result was a serious geographic division that isolated Central Asian Muslims.

Shi'ite-Sunni political competition was sharpened by Safavid militancy, to which the Sunni states responded in kind. Attempts to form alliances with non-Muslim states, previously unheard of in the Islamic world, became a commonplace of Shi'ite political strategy. The Sunnis also resorted to such tactics: The Ottomans, for example, made common cause with Protestants against their Catholic Habsburg enemies. Although trade continued, the presence of a militant Shi'ite state astride the major overland trade routes of the larger Islamic world hurt the international flow of Islamic commerce.

The Safavid Shi'ite schism also changed the shared cultural traditions of the "Abode of Islam." This change was especially reflected in the fate of Persian literary culture. As a result of its association with Shi'ism after the rise of the Safavids, Persian made little further progress as a potential common language alongside Arabic in Sunni lands. Outside Iran it was destined to remain a language of high culture, the court, and bureaucracy, where it was the mark of the educated person: Mastery of the Persian language and

The Great Central Square of the Registan, in Samarkand, with the seventeenth-century Shir Dar Madrasa on the right and the fifteenth-century Ulugh Beg Madrasa on the left. Samarkand and other major Central Asian cities were centers of Islamic culture and learning as well as political power.

What are the similarities between this square and the Maydan-i-Shah (see page 520) and Fatehpur-Sikir (see page 522)? What does this suggest?

Persian classic texts largely defined what it meant to be an Ottoman or Mughal "gentleman." In India, Urdu became the shared Muslim idiom (see Chapter 12), and in Ottoman and Central Asian lands, various Turkic tongues were spoken in everyday life. The Persian classics inspired Persian learning among educated Sunnis, but Safavid Persian literature was largely ignored.

Central Asia was ultimately the Islamic region most decisively affected by the Shi'ite presence in Iran. Combined with the growing pressure of Christian Russian power, Iran's militant Shi'ism isolated Central Asia from the rest of the Muslim world. Political, economic, cultural, and religious interchange with other Islamic lands became increasingly difficult after 1500. However healthy Islam remained in this region, its contact with the original Islamic heartlands and India shrank. Contact came primarily through a few pilgrims, members of Sufi orders, *ulama*, and students. Central Asian Islam mostly developed in isolation, peripheral to the Islamic mainstream communities.

POWER SHIFTS IN THE SOUTHERN OCEANS

HOW DID the arrival of Europeans affect maritime trade in Southeast Asia?

SOUTHERN-OCEANS TRADE

The period from 1000 to 1500 witnessed the gradual spread of Islamic religion and culture along the southern rim of Asia, from the Red Sea and East Africa to Indonesia and the South China Sea. In ports of Java, Sumatra, the Malay Peninsula, South India, Gujarat, East Africa, Madagascar, and Zanzibar, Islamic traders established thriving communities. Their enclaves often became centers of local life. Initially the Muslims' economic stature attracted especially the socially mobile groups in these cosmopolitan ports; many also found Muslim ideas and practices compelling. Typically these first conversions were followed by Islam's transmission to surrounding areas and finally to inland centers. In this, Sufi orders and their preachers and holy men played the main roles. However, conquest by Muslim coastal states accelerated the process in Indonesia and East Africa.

Afro-Indian merchant. This superb painting of an Indian of African origin shows the many connections linking the Indian Ocean world together. The man in this image is a merchant, probably a member of the Janjeera people, originally from Ethiopia. Janjeera merchants immigrated to India in the Middle Ages. Some remained there, and from the fifteenth century they and their descendants obtained positions of power and authority in local governments. The sumptuous dress and dignified bearing of this man suggest wealth and influence.

How did European traders in the Indian Ocean and South Seas differ from traders who had come before?

The international trade network Muslims inherited from the Indian Ocean to the South China sea was ancient. Before 1200, much of the trade in these waters had been dominated by Hindu or Buddhist kingdoms of the Malay Peninsula or Sumatra (see Chapter 12). Arab traders had also been active in the Indian Ocean. Hindu culture had been carried, along with an Indonesian language, as far west as Madagascar in the first millennium C.E. Hindus were the chief religious community the Muslims displaced. In the East, Islam never ousted the Indian Buddhist cultures of Burma, Thailand, and Indochina, although Muslim traders thrived in their ports. Islam did, however, gradually win most of Malaysia, Sumatra, Java, and the "Spice Islands" of the Moluccas—first the coastal areas, then inland regions.

CONTROL OF THE SOUTHERN SEAS

The Portuguese reached the East African coast in 1498. In the ensuing three centuries, the history of the lands along the sea trade routes of Asia, from East Africa to Indonesia, was intertwined not only with Islamic religious, cultural, and commercial networks, but also with the rising power of Christian western Europe. The key attractions of these diverse lands were their commercial and strategic possibilities (see Map 20–3).

MAP 20–3. **European Commercial Penetration of Southeast Asia.**   Beginning with the Portuguese and Spanish in the sixteenth century, and then the Dutch and British in the seventeenth, West European powers established commercial bases throughout Southeast Asia, often cooperating with local Islamic, Hindi, or Buddhist rulers.

What were the motives for European maritime imperialism in Southeast Asia?

OVERVIEW   The Religions of Southeast Asia

Predominately Buddhist	Burma
	Thailand, with a significant Muslim minority
	Cambodia
	Laos
	Vietnam, with a large Roman Catholic minority
	Singapore, with Muslim, Christian, and Hindu minorities
Predominately Muslim	Indonesia, with a large Christian minority and the Hindu island of Bali
	Malaysia, with Hindu, Buddhist, Chinese, and Christian minorities
	Brunei
Predominately Christian	The Philippines, with a sizable Muslim minority
	East Timor

In the sixteenth century the Europeans began to forcibly displace the Muslims who, by 1500, dominated the maritime southern rim of Asia. European success was based on two key factors: the national support systems that backed their naval and commercial ventures, and their superior warships. In the early sixteenth century, this combination enabled the Portuguese to carve out a major power base along the west coast of India at the expense of the Muslims who dominated Indian maritime trade. They did so through superior naval power and by exploiting indigenous rivalries and terrorizing all who opposed them.

However, in the southern-seas trade centers, Islamization continued, even in the face of Christian proselytizing and growing European political and commercial presence. The Muslims, unlike most European Christians, were everywhere largely assimilated with the local populations. They rarely abandoned their faith, which proved generally attractive to new peoples they encountered. The result was typically an Islamized, racially mixed population.

As a result, while European gunboat imperialism had considerable military and economic success, often at the expense of Islamic states, European culture and Christianity made little headway against Islam. From East Africa to the Pacific, only in the northern Philippines did a substantial population become largely Christian.

THE EAST INDIES: ACHEH

The Indonesian archipelago's history has always been heavily influenced by international demand for its spices, peppers, and other produce. By the fifteenth century its coastal Islamic states were centered on the trading ports of the Malay Peninsula, the north shores of Sumatra and Java, and the Moluccas, or "Spice Islands." The last great Hindu kingdom of inland Java was defeated by an Islamic coalition of states in the early 1500s. Several substantial Islamic sultanates arose in the sixteenth and seventeenth centuries, even as Europeans were carving out economic empires in the region. The most powerful Islamic state was Acheh, in northwestern Sumatra (ca. 1524–1910).

CHRONOLOGY

THE SOUTHERN SEAS: ARRIVAL OF THE EUROPEANS

1498	Portuguese reach the East African coast and west coast of India
1500–1512	Portuguese establish bases on west Indian coast, replace Muslims as Indian Ocean power
early 1500s	Muslim sultanates replace Hindu states in Java, Sumatra
1524–1910	State of Acheh in northwestern Sumatra
1600s	Islamization spreads widely; connected spread of Malay language in the archipelago
1641	Dutch conquest of Malacca
ca. 1800	Dutch replace Muslim states as main archipelago power
1873–1910	War between Holland and Acheh

In its early years Acheh provided the only counterpoise to Portuguese presence across the straits in Malacca (Malaysia). Although the Acheh sultans were unable to defeat the better-armed invaders, neither could the Portuguese subdue them. Despite Portuguese control of Indies commerce, Acheh continued to thrive and dominated the Sumatran pepper trade until nearly 1600. In the first half of the seventeenth century the sultanate controlled both coasts of Sumatra and parts of the Malay Peninsula. Meanwhile, the Dutch replaced the Portuguese in milking the Indies of their wealth, and by the 1700s they were doing so just as ruthlessly and more efficiently. The Dutch finally won full control in the region, but only after nearly forty years of intermittent war with Acheh (1873–1910).

SUMMARY

 WHY DID the Ottoman Empire find it increasingly difficult to compete with European powers?

The Ottoman Empire and the East Mediterranean World. The period from 1500 to 1800 marks the cultural and political blossoming of the last Islamic empires and their gradual decline. The Ottoman Empire built up from a small principality in the fourteenth century to a great empire under rulers including Mehmet II and Süleyman in the fifteenth and sixteenth centuries. The empire was well organized and had one of the strongest militaries in the world. In the seventeenth century, it still posed a threat to Europe, but in the eighteenth century it declined, particularly in relation to the industrializing West. *page 510*

 WHAT ROLE did Shi'ite ideology play in the Safavid Empire?

The Safavid Empire and the West Asian World. Shi'ite Sufi Safavids unified the traditional Iranian heartland under Shah Isma'il early in the sixteenth century. Shah Abbas I, whose rule straddled the turn of the seventeenth century, was a masterful ruler who consolidated Shi'te power in Iran. Safavid artists and intellectuals left a rich legacy, and the capital city of Isfahan was renowned as "half the world." *page 518*

WHAT ROLE did religious intolerance play in the decline of the Mughal Empire?

The Mughals. India was reunified under the Mughals in the sixteenth century. The great ruler Akbar (1558–1603) expanded Mughal territory and modeled religious tolerance. But Hindu–Muslim tensions increased after Akbar's reign, and both Sikhs and Hindu Marathas resisted Mughal authority. In the nineteenth century, the British East India Company gained power. *page 521*

 WHAT WERE the most important Islamic states in Central and southern Asia?

Central Asia: Islamization in the Post-Timur Era. The Uzbeks and Chaghatays of Central Asia were Sunni Muslims, geographically isolated from the mainstream Islamic community by the militant Shi'ism of the Safavids. *page 524*

 HOW DID the arrival of Europeans affect maritime trade in Southeast Asia?

Power Shifts in the Southern Oceans. Islamic traders attracted converts and established vibrant, multiethnic seaport communities around the rim of East Africa and southern Asia. Europe's growing economic and naval dominance allowed it to control many southern sea trade centers, but Islamization continued. *page 526*

KEY TERMS

ayan (p. 515)
***devshirme* (dev-sheer-MEH)** (p. 514)
Grand Mufti (grand MOOF-tee) (p. 514)
harem (p. 512)
Janissaries (JANN-ihss-AYR-ees) (p. 514)
millets (p. 515)
Mughals (MOO-gahlz) (p. 521)
padishah (p. 511)
pirs (p. 518)
Qanun (p. 514)
Qanun-name (p. 511)
Shari'a (sha-REE-ah) (p. 512)
Sufi (SOO-fee) (p. 518)

REVIEW QUESTIONS

1. Why did the Ottoman Empire expand so rapidly? Why did the empire fail to hold certain areas in Europe?

2. Why did the Safavid Empire succeed in Iran? What roles did Islamic religion and favorable geography have in this development? Who were the major foes of this empire?

3. What were the most important elements that united all Islamic states? Why was there a lack of unity between these states from 1500 to 1850? How and why were the European powers able to promote division among these various states?

4. What were Akbar's main policies toward the Hindu population? Why did he succeed and his followers fail in this area? What were his main governmental reforms?

5. How and why did the Sikhs develop into a formidable military power? Why did they become separatists in their orientation to the larger Indian world?

6. Akbar, Abbas, and Süleyman are considered some of the most successful world leaders in history. Compare and contrast their strengths, weaknesses, and long-term influence.

7. Compare the Sunni–Shi'ite differences and similarities within the Islamic world (1500–1800) with that of the Protestant–Catholic split within the Christian world during that same period. For example, can we compare relations between England and Spain in the sixteenth century to those between the Ottomans and the Safavids? Explain.

8. Why were outside powers attracted to the lands of the southern seas? Why did the European powers triumph in the struggle to control this area?

9. Which of the cultures described in this chapter seems most appealing to you? Which would you most like to live in, and why?

Note: To learn more about the topics in this chapter, please turn to the Suggested Readings at the end of the book. For additional sources related to this chapter please see www.myhistorylab.com

Connections

Reinforce what you learned in this chapter by studying the many documents, images, maps, review tools, and videos available at **www.myhistorylab.com**

Read and Review

✓ Study and Review **Chapter 20**

Read the Document *Mehmed II (15th century), p. 511*
Ogier Ghiselin de Busbecq, "Süleyman the Lawgiver,"
  p. 511
Women in Ottoman society, p. 513
Portrait of an Ottoman Gentleman, p. 517
Shah Isma'il Describes Himself to His Followers, p. 519
Fathers Simon and Vincent Report on Shah Abbas I, the
  Safavid Ruler of Persia, p. 519
A Sikh Guru's Testimony of Faith, p. 524

See the Map *The Ottoman Empire to 1566, p. 511*
Atlas Map: Iran under the Safavids, ca. 1252–1524,
  p. 518
Mughal Empire, p. 522
The Maratha Kingdoms 1, p. 522

View the Image *Akbar, Emperor of India, p. 521*

Research and Explore

Watch the Video *Why Does It Matter How We Use The Term "Empire"?*

See the Map *The Decline of the Ottoman Empire, p. 515*

((•— Hear the Audio

Hear the audio file for Chapter 20
at **www.myhistorylab.com**

21

The Age of European Enlightenment

((•—Hear the Audio for Chapter 21 at www.myhistorylab.com

Enlightenment Salon. The salon of Madame Marie-Thérèse Geoffrin (1699–1777) was one of the most important gathering spots for Enlightenment writers during the middle of the eighteenth century. Well-connected women such as Madame Geoffrin were instrumental in helping the *philosophes* they patronized to bring their ideas to the attention of influential people in French society and politics.

Châteaux de Malmaison et Bois-Preau, Rueil-Malmaison. Bridgeman-Giraudon/Art Resource, New York.

What kinds of people are depicted here?

estern science, and the technology that flows from a scientific understanding of nature, have transformed every region of the world during the past three centuries. The impact of scientific thinking was felt first in Europe and then elsewhere only when the conviction spread that change and reform were possible and desirable. This attitude came into its own in Europe after 1700. The movement that fostered it is called the **Enlightenment**. *It was an expression of confidence in the power of rational criticism to challenge the intellectual authority of tradition and revealed religion. Enlightenment thinkers believed human beings could comprehend the operation of physical nature and mold it to the ends of material and moral improvement. The rationality of the material world became a standard against which the customs and traditions of society could be measured and criticized. The spirit of innovation and improvement came to characterize modern Western society and became perhaps the most important European cultural export to the rest of the world.* ■

Enlightenment
The eighteenth-century movement led by the *philosophes* that held that change and reform were both possible and desirable through the application of reason and science.

THE SCIENTIFIC REVOLUTION

WHY IS the Scientific Revolution important to world history?

The sixteenth and seventeenth centuries witnessed a sweeping change in the scientific view of the universe. From being considered the center of the universe, the earth was now seen as only another planet orbiting the sun. The sun itself became one of millions of stars. This transformation led to a vast rethinking of moral and religious matters as well as of scientific theory. Science and the scientific method became so impressive and so influential that they set a new standard for evaluating knowledge in the Western world.

GLOBAL PERSPECTIVE

THE EUROPEAN ENLIGHTENMENT

Of all the movements of modern European thought, the most influential are the Scientific Revolution and the Enlightenment. A direct line of intellectual descent exists from those movements to the science and social criticism of the present day. From the eighteenth century to the present, the writers of the Enlightenment provided a pattern for intellectuals who wished to make their societies more rational, scientific, economically productive, reform-minded, and religiously tolerant. The Enlightenment model of society in the West (and via the West, in the rest of the world) became synonymous with "modern."

This particular view of modernization tended to frame the European and later North American experience as the necessary pattern for all advanced societies. This outlook originated with the majority of Enlightenment writers themselves. A minority of those writers of the eighteenth century, as with many present-day commentators, questioned whether even a rational, critical, and economically productive Europe should be the pattern for all human societies. Thus the Enlightenment also fostered its own internal self-criticism.

In terms of political thought, the heritage of the Enlightenment was complex with different strands of political thought often in tension or outright conflict with each other. Virtually all Enlightenment writers believed in some form of religious toleration or recognition of religious pluralism. Beyond that viewpoint there was much disagreement. Some Enlightenment thinkers drawing upon the English political experience championed constitutionalism and other modes of government that circumscribed the authority of the central government. Montesquieu, for example, influenced the Constitution of the United States and the numerous constitutions which that document, in turn, influenced. Another strand of Enlightenment political thought, found in Voltaire, contributed to the growth of strong monarchical governments, associated with enlightened absolutism. Such writers believed that a monarch and a strong central bureaucracy could formulate and impose rational solutions to political and social problems and hence overcome competing social and political interests. Still another variety of Enlightenment political thought, arising from

---

Scientific Revolution

The sweeping change in the scientific view of the universe that occurred in the West in the sixteenth and seventeenth centuries.

◉—See the **Map**
Science and the Enlightenment, ca. 1450,
at **myhistorylab.com**

◆◆◆—Read the **Document**
Nicolaus Copernicus: On the Revolution of
the Heavenly Spheres (1500s)
at **myhistorylab.com**

The process that established the new view of the universe is normally termed the *Scientific Revolution*. The revolution-in-science metaphor must be used carefully, however. Not everything associated with the "new" science was necessarily new. Sixteenth- and seventeenth-century natural philosophers were often reexamining and rethinking theories and data from the ancient world and the Late Middle Ages. Moreover, the word *revolution* normally denotes rapid, collective political change involving large numbers of people. The Scientific Revolution was *not* rapid. It was a complex movement with many false starts and many brilliant people suggesting wrong as well as useful ideas. It involved only a few hundred people who labored in widely separated studies and crude laboratories located in Poland, Italy, Bohemia, France, and Great Britain. The achievements of the new science were not simply the function of isolated brilliant scientific minds: The leading figures of the Scientific Revolution drew upon the aid of artisans and craftspeople to help them construct new instruments for experimentation and to carry out their experiments. Thus, the Scientific Revolution involved a reappropriation of older knowledge as well as new discoveries. In addition, because the practice of science involves social activity as well as knowledge, the revolution also saw the establishment of new social institutions to support the emerging scientific enterprise.

NICOLAUS COPERNICUS REJECTS AN EARTH-CENTERED UNIVERSE

Nicolaus Copernicus (1473–1543) was a Polish astronomer who had a good reputation, though he was not considered an original thinker. In 1543, the year of his death, Copernicus published *On the Revolutions of the Heavenly Spheres*, which provided an intellectual springboard for a complete criticism of the then-dominant view of the position of the earth in the universe.

Rousseau, led to the socialist concern with inequality of wealth and a desire for radical democratic government. Because of the complexity of Enlightenment political thought, modern governments displaying liberalism, socialism, and bureaucratic centralism may find roots in eighteenth-century thinkers.

Present-day political movements finding themselves essentially at odds with the Enlightenment heritage are those attached to radical Islamic groups who define themselves in opposition to most Western values. Those values tend to be derived from the Enlightenment. Most particularly these groups oppose the religious pluralism, cultural relativism, and expansion of traditional social roles for women that have flowed over time from the expansion of Enlightenment values.

As we observed in Chapter 17, the seventeenth and eighteenth centuries, whose ideas fostered the Enlightenment, also saw the rise of European colonial empires and the establishment of plantation economies based on slavery. Europeans' treatment of non-Europeans, as well as their warfare against each other in this era, often belied the principles of the Enlightenment. Certain Enlightenment writers, a minority, sharply criticized those empires. In this respect, contemporary critics of Western influence throughout the world can find roots in this eighteenth-century critique of empire.

Focus Questions

◆ How did Enlightenment values, including Enlightenment admiration of science, become one of the chief defining qualities of societies regarded as advanced, progressive, and modern?

◆ How has the political thought of the Enlightenment influenced the development of modern political philosophies and modern governments?

◆ How could modes of thought developed to criticize various aspects of eighteenth-century European society be transferred to other traditions of world civilizations?

At the time, the standard explanation of the place of the earth in the heavens was the **Ptolemaic system**. It combined the mathematical astronomy of Ptolemy, contained in the *Almagest* (150 C.E.), with the physical cosmology of Aristotle. Over the centuries, most writers commenting on Ptolemy's system had assumed that the earth was the center of the universe, an outlook known as *geocentricism*. Drawing on Aristotle, these commentators assumed that above the earth lay a series of concentric spheres, one of which contained the moon, another the sun, and still others the planets and the stars. At the outer regions of these spheres lay the realm of God and the angels. The earth had to be the center because of its heaviness. The stars and the other heavenly bodies had to be enclosed in the spheres so that they could move, since nothing could move unless something was actually moving it. The state of rest was presumed natural; motion required explanation. This was the astronomy found in such works as Dante's *Divine Comedy*.

Numerous problems with the Ptolemaic model had long been recognized. The most important was the observed motions of the planets, which at times appeared to

Ptolemaic system
The pre-Copernican explanation of the universe, which placed the earth at the center of the universe.

The Ptolemaic System. The "Emperor's Astronomy" (dedicated to the Holy Roman emperor Charles V) elegantly depicts the cosmos and heavens according to the 1,400-year-old Ptolemaic system, which maintained that the sun revolved around the earth. By means of hand-colored maps, Petrus Apianus (1495–1552) laid out the mechanics of a universe that was earth- and human-centered. Within three years of Apianus's book, this view was challenged by Copernicus's assertion that the earth revolved around the sun.

Why was the question of the earth's position in the universe of such importance?

go backwards. The Ptolemaic system explained these strange motions by proposing the *epicycle*: a second revolution by a planet in an orbit tangent to its primary orbit around the earth. The Ptolemaic explanations were effective as long as one accepted Aristotelian physics and the Christian belief that the earth rested at the center of the created universe.

Copernicus challenged this picture in the most conservative way possible. He suggested that if the earth were assumed to move around the sun in a circle, there were fewer difficulties with the Ptolemaic system. With the sun at the center of the universe, mathematical astronomy would make more sense. The epicycles became smaller, and the retrograde motion of the planets could be explained as an optical illusion arising from an observer viewing the planets from a moving earth. Except for the modification in the position of the earth, most of Copernicus's book was Ptolemaic. It prompted others who were discontented with the Ptolemaic system to think in new ways, however. Copernicus's combination of mathematics, empirical data, and observation established the model for scientific thinking.

((•─[Hear the **Audio**
at **myhistorylab.com**

TYCHO BRAHE AND JOHANNES KEPLER

Danish astronomer Tycho Brahe (1546–1601) spent most of his life opposing Copernicus and advocating a different kind of earth-centered system. He suggested that the moon and the sun revolved around the earth and that the other planets revolved around the sun. His major weapon against Copernican astronomy was a series of new astronomical observations made with the naked eye. Brahe constructed the most accurate tables of observations that had been drawn up for centuries. Brahe's data ended up disproving both his own and Copernicus's hypotheses.

When Brahe died, his tables came into the possession of Johannes Kepler (1571–1630), a German astronomer. Kepler was a convinced Copernican for philosophical, not scientific, reasons. Kepler was deeply influenced by Renaissance Neo-Platonists who, following Plato's (ca. 428–ca. 328 B.C.E.) association of knowledge with light, honored the sun. These Neo-Platonists searched for mathematical harmonies that would support a sun-centered universe. After much work, Kepler discovered that to keep the sun at the center of things, he must abandon the Copernican concept of circular orbits. The mathematical relationships that emerged from Brahe's observations suggested that the orbits of the planets were elliptical. Kepler published his findings in 1609 in a book entitled *On the Motion of Mars*. He had solved the problems of planetary orbits by using Copernicus's sun-centered universe and Brahe's empirical data.

None of the available theories could explain why the planetary orbits were elliptical. That solution awaited the work of Sir Isaac Newton.

Tycho Brahe in the Uranienburg Observatory on the Danish island of Hven (1587). Brahe made the most important observations of the stars since antiquity. Kepler used his data to solve the problem of planetary motion in a way that supported Copernicus's sun-centered view of the universe. Ironically, Brahe himself had opposed Copernicus's view.

How was empiricism at the center of the Scientific Revolution?

GALILEO GALILEI

In 1609 an Italian scientist named Galileo Galilei (1564–1642) first turned a telescope on the heavens. He saw stars where none had been known to exist, mountains on the moon, spots moving across the sun, and moons orbiting Jupiter. The heavens were far more complex than anyone had formerly suspected. None of these discoveries proved that the earth orbited the sun, but they did reveal the inadequacy of the Ptolemaic system. Some of Galileo's colleagues at the University of Padua were so unnerved that they refused to look through the telescope because it revealed the heavens to be different from the teachings of the church and from Ptolemaic theories.

Galileo publicized his findings in his *Dialogues on the Two Chief Systems of the World* (1632). It was condemned by the Roman Catholic Church, which compelled him to recant his opinions. He did so, but reputedly muttered, "It [the earth] still moves."

Galileo's most important achievement was to articulate the concept of a universe totally subject to mathematical laws. Copernicus had proposed that the heavens exhibited mathematical regularity; Galileo saw this regularity throughout all physical nature. He believed that the smallest atom behaved with the same mathematical precision as the largest heavenly sphere.

FRANCIS BACON: THE EMPIRICAL METHOD

In the course of the seventeenth century, both mathematical analysis and empirical induction proved fundamental to scientific investigation.

Francis Bacon (1561–1626) was a multitasking Englishman: He was a lawyer, a high royal official, and the author of histories, moral essays, and philosophical discourses. Traditionally, he has been regarded as the father of **empiricism** and of experimentation in science. Much of this reputation was unearned, but he did help set an intellectual tone and create a climate conducive to scientific work.

In books including *The Advancement of Learning* (1605), the *Novum Organum* (1620), and the *New Atlantis* (1627), Bacon attacked the scholastic belief that most truth had already been discovered. He urged contemporaries to strike out on their own in search of a new understanding of nature, based on an examination of empirical evidence. Bacon was one of the first major European writers to champion the desirability of innovation and change. He believed that human knowledge should produce useful results. In particular, knowledge of nature should be brought to the aid of the human condition.

Bacon directed investigators of nature to a new method and a new purpose. Bacon's own theory of induction from empirical evidence was unsystematic, but his insistence on appealing to experience influenced others whose methods were more productive. Bacon's linkage of science and material progress, though not fully accurate, has continued to influence Western civilization up to the present. It has made science and those who can appeal to the authority of science major forces for change and innovation. As a person actively associated with politics, Bacon believed that the pursuit of new knowledge would increase the power of governments and monarchies. Here, his thought opened the way for the eventual strong linkage between governments and the scientific enterprise.

ISAAC NEWTON DISCOVERS THE LAWS OF GRAVITATION

The question that continued to perplex seventeenth-century scientists who accepted the theories of Copernicus, Kepler, and Galileo was how the planets and other heavenly bodies moved in an orderly fashion. When the Englishman Isaac Newton (1642–1727) successfully addressed this issue, he established a basis for physics that endured for more than two centuries.

In 1687 Newton published *The Mathematical Principles of Natural Philosophy*, better known by its Latin title of *Principia Mathematica*. Galileo's mathematical bias permeated Newton's thought, as did Galileo's view that inertia applied to bodies both at rest and in motion. Newton reasoned that the planets and all other physical objects in the universe moved through mutual attraction, or gravity. Every object in the universe affected every other object through gravity. Newton proved the gravitational relationship between the planets mathematically; he made no attempt to explain the nature of gravity itself.

empiricism
The use of experiment and observation derived from sensory evidence to construct scientific theory or philosophy of knowledge.

•••—[Read the Document
Francis Bacon, from *Novum Organum* at **myhistorylab.com**

QUICK REVIEW

Francis Bacon (1561–1626)
- Attacked belief that most truth had already been discovered
- One of the first Europeans to champion innovation and change
- Persuaded others that scientific thought must proceed by means of empirical observation

Newton's Telescope. Behind it is a copy of *Principia Mathematica*, his most famous work.

What was the significance of Newton's work on gravity?

•••┤Read the Document

Isaac Newton, from Opticks
at **myhistorylab.com**

Newton was a great mathematical genius, but he also upheld the importance of empirical data and observation. Like Bacon, he believed that one must observe phenomena before attempting to explain them. The final test of any theory or hypothesis for him was whether it described what was actually observed. Consequently, as Newton's own theory of universal gravitation became increasingly accepted, so, too, was Baconian empiricism.

WOMEN IN THE WORLD OF THE SCIENTIFIC REVOLUTION

The same factors that had long excluded women from participating in most European intellectual life continued to exclude them from working in the emerging natural philosophy. The institutions of European intellectual life—monasteries and universities— were associated with celibate male clerical culture. With a few exceptions in Italy, women were not admitted to European universities until the end of the nineteenth century. Women influenced princely courts where natural philosophers, such as Galileo, sought patronage, but they usually did not determine those patronage decisions or benefit from them. Queen Christina of Sweden was an exception by engaging René Descartes, the major French philosopher of science, to provide the regulations for a new science academy. When scientific societies were founded, women were not admitted to membership.

Yet a few isolated women from two very different social settings— noblewomen and women from the artisan class—managed to engage in the new scientific activity. In both cases, they did so through their husbands or other men in their families.

The social standing of certain noblewomen allowed them to command the attention of ambitious natural philosophers who were part of their husbands' social circles. Margaret Cavendish (1623–1673), whose marriage to the duke of Newcastle introduced her into a circle of natural philosophers, made significant contributions with scientific works including *Observations upon Experimental Philosophy* (1666) and *Grounds of Natural Philosophy* (1668). She was the only woman in the seventeenth century to be allowed to visit a meeting of the Royal Society of London.

Women and Learning. René Descartes, the French philosopher, is on the right, tutoring Queen Christina (1626–1689) of Sweden, seated on the left.

Pierre-Louis the Younger Dumesnil (1698–1781), "Christina of Sweden (1626-89) and her Court: detail of the Queen and Rene Descartes (1596-1650) at the Table." Oil on canvas. Chateau de Versailles, France/Bridgeman Art Library.

What roles did women play in the Scientific Revolution?

Women associated with artisan crafts achieved greater freedom in pursuing the new sciences than did noblewomen. Traditionally, women had worked in artisan workshops, often with their husbands, and they sometimes took over the business when their spouse died. Much German astronomy, for example, occurred with women assisting their fathers or husbands. German astronomer Maria Cunitz published a book on astronomy that many people thought her husband had written until he added a preface supporting her sole authorship. Elisabetha and Johannes Hevelius constituted a wife-and-husband astronomical team, as did Maria Winkelmann and her husband Gottfried Kirch. Although Winkelmann discovered a comet in 1702, not until 1930 was the discovery ascribed to her rather than to her husband.

Some women were able to use books or personal friendships to get around exlusionary policies. Cavendish wrote a *Description of a New World, Called the Blazing World* (1666) to introduce women to the new science. Other scientific writings for a female audience were Bernard de Fontenelle's *Conversations on the Plurality of Worlds* and Francesco Algarotti's *Newtonianism for Ladies* (1737). During the 1730s, Emilie du Châtelet aided Voltaire in his composition of an important French popularization of Newton's science. Her knowledge of mathematics was more extensive than his and crucial to completing the book.

•••┤Read the Document

Galileo Galilei, Letter to the Grand
Duchess Christina (1630s)
at **myhistorylab.com**

Still, with only a few exceptions, women were barred from science and medicine until the late nineteenth century, and not until the twentieth century did they enter these fields in any significant numbers. Not only did the institutions of science exclude them, but also the ideas associated with medical practice, philosophy, and biology suggested that women and their minds were essentially different from, and inferior to, men and theirs. By the early eighteenth century, it had become a fundamental assumption of European intellectual life that the pursuit of natural knowledge was a male vocation.

JOHN LOCKE

John Locke (1632–1704) attempted to discover laws governing the human mind similar to those that Newton had discovered as explanations for natural phenomena. No other philosopher had so profound an impact on European and American thought during the eighteenth century.

Locke's *Essay Concerning Human Understanding* (1690) postulated that the human mind is blank at the time of birth. People have no innate ideas. All their knowledge derives from information that comes through their physical senses. Given that people's intellects are shaped by the interaction between their minds and the world, Locke argued that human nature could be modified by changing the environment. Locke's thinking thus represented an early form of behaviorism. Locke in effect rejected the Christian view that human beings were flawed by original sin. Human beings do not need to wait for divine aid; they can take charge of their own destinies.

In his *Two Treatises of Government*, written during the reign of Charles II (r. 1660–1685), Locke made a case against absolute monarchy. The law of nature, he argued, teaches that human beings are equal and independent; they should not harm one another or disturb one another's property because all persons are the images and property of God. People voluntarily relinquish some of their freedom and contract with their rulers for the protection and preservation of their natural rights. Rulers are, therefore, not absolute but bound by natural laws. A monarch who does not comply with natural law can legitimately be overthrown. In his *Letter Concerning Toleration*, Locke argued that governments existed to protect property and civil order. They should not legislate on religion, for the pursuit of salvation is the responsibility of the individual. Locke himself drew the line in England against toleration of Roman Catholics and Unitarians. During the eighteenth century, however, the logic of his argument was extended to advocate toleration for those faiths as well.

●●●─Read the **Document**
John Locke, Essay Concerning Human Understanding at **myhistorylab.com**

((●●─Hear the **Audio**
at **myhistorylab.com**

OVERVIEW   Major Figures in the Scientific Revolution

Nicolaus Copernicus (1473–1543)	On the basis of mathematical analysis argued that the earth moved around the sun.
Tycho Brahe (1546–1601)	Compiled accurate tables of astronomical observations.
Johannes Kepler (1571–1601)	Used Brahe's data to argue that the orbits of the planets were elliptical.
Galileo Galilei (1564–1642)	First astronomer to use a telescope. Argued that mathematical laws governed the universe.
Francis Bacon (1561–1626)	Argued that scientific thought must conform to empirical evidence. Championed innovation and change.
Isaac Newton (1642–1727)	Described the effect of gravity mathematically and established a theoretical basis for physics that endured until the late nineteenth century.
John Locke (1632–1704)	Argued that the human mind is a blank slate that may be molded by modifying the environment. Human beings could thus take charge of their own destiny without divine aid.

THE ENLIGHTENMENT

HOW DID
Enlightenment thinkers argue for the reform of society?

philosophes
The eighteenth-century writers and critics who forged the new attitudes favorable to change. They sought to apply reason and common sense to the institutions and societies of their day.

(((•◦ Hear the Audio
at **myhistorylab.com**

◉ See the Map
Science and the Enlightenment, ca.1450, at **myhistorylab.com**

•◦•◦ Read the Document
Voltaire, Letters on England
at **myhistorylab.com**

The movement known as the Enlightenment included writers living at different times in various countries. Its early exponents, the **philosophes**, popularized the rationalism and scientific ideas of the seventeenth century. They exposed contemporary social and political abuses and argued that reform was necessary and possible. They confronted oppression and religious condemnation and by midcentury had brought enlightened ideas to the European public in a variety of formats.

VOLTAIRE

The most influential of the *philosophes* was the French writer François Marie Arouet, called Voltaire (1694–1778). In 1733, after visiting England, he published *Letters on the English*, which praised the intellectual and political freedom found in England and indirectly criticized French society. In 1738, he published *Elements of the Philosophy of Newton*, which popularized the thought of the great scientist. Voltaire's essays, history, plays, stories, and letters made him the literary dictator of Europe. He turned the bitter venom of his satire and sarcasm against one evil after another in French and European life. His most famous satire is *Candide* (1759), in which he attacked war, religious persecution, and what he regarded as unwarranted optimism about the human condition. Like most *philosophes*, Voltaire believed that human society could and should be improved. But he was never certain that reform, if achieved, would be permanent. The optimism of the Enlightenment constituted a tempered hopefulness rather than a glib certainty. Pessimism was an undercurrent in most of the works of the period.

THE *ENCYCLOPEDIA*

One of the greatest monuments of the Enlightenment was the *Encyclopedia*. Under the heroic leadership of Denis Diderot (1713–1784) and Jean le Rond d'Alembert (1717–1783), the first volume appeared in 1751. When completed in 1772, it numbered seventeen volumes of text and eleven of plates. The *Encyclopedia* was a collective effort of more than 100 authors, and its editors had solicited articles from all the major French *philosophes*. Attempts were made to censor it and halt its publication, but it was ultimately completed. The *Encyclopedia* made a plea for freedom of expression and set forth the most advanced critical ideas in religion, government, and philosophy. It also provided practical information in areas such as manufacturing, canal building, and agriculture. (See Document: "The *Encyclopedia* Praises Mechanical Arts and Artisans.")

Between 14,000 and 16,000 copies of various editions of the *Encyclopedia* were sold before 1789. The project had been designed to secularize learning, and the articles concentrated on humanity and its well-being. The encyclopedists looked to antiquity rather than

Denis Diderot was the heroic editor of the *Encyclopedia*, which was published in seventeen volumes of text and eleven volumes of prints between 1751 and 1772. Through its pages many of the chief ideas of the Enlightenment reached a broad audience of readers.

Jean-Simon Berthelemy (1743–1811), "Denis Diderot" (1713–1784). Writer and Encyelopaedist. Oil on canvas, 55 × 46 cm. Inv.: P 2082. Photo: Bulloz. Musee de la Ville de Paris, Musee Carnavalet, Paris, France/ Art Resource, New York.

Which has more influence on society, the dissemination of information or the creation of new knowledge?

DOCUMENT

The *Encyclopedia* Praises Mechanical Arts and Artisans

One of the most remarkable features of the Encyclopedia *is the vast quantity of information it included about the mechanical arts of the day. Not only are there many articles on such work, but a large number of engravings portrayed eighteenth-century French artisans in their workplace. In the "Preliminary Discourse," which served as a general introduction to the* Encyclopedia, *D'Alembert explained the importance of the mechanical arts as well as the manner whereby the authors had explored these arts and the workshops where they were carried out.*

- **HOW** does D'Alembert defend the importance of the mechanical arts? Why does he think they have not always received proper attention and appreciation? How did the authors of the *Encyclopedia* familiarize themselves with such work? What kind of conversation might have occurred between one of those authors and a skilled artisan operating his machinery?

The mechanical arts, which are dependent upon manual operation and are subjugated (. . .) to a sort of routine, have been left to those among men whom prejudices have placed in the lowest class. . . . However, the advantage that the liberal arts have over the mechanical arts . . . is sufficiently counterbalanced by the quite superior usefulness which the latter for the most part have for us. It is this very usefulness which reduced them perforce to purely mechanical operations in order to make them accessible to a larger number of men. But while justly respecting great geniuses for their enlightenment, society ought not to degrade the hands by which it is saved. . . .

* * * * * * * *

Too much has been written on the sciences; not enough has been written well on the mechanical arts . . . . Thus everything impelled us to go directly to the workers.

We approached the most capable of them . . . We took the trouble of going into their shops, of questioning them, of writing at their dictation, of developing their thoughts and of drawing therefrom the terms peculiar to their professions, of setting up tables of these terms and of working out definitions for them, of conversing with those from whom we obtained memoranda, and (an almost indispensable precaution) of correcting through long and frequent conversations with others what some of them imperfectly, obscurely, and sometimes unreliably had explained. There are some artisans who are also men of letters, and we would be able to cite them here; but their numbers are very small. Most of those who engage in the mechanical arts have embraced them only by necessity and work only by instinct . . . .

But there are some trades so unusual and some operations so subtle that unless one does the work oneself, unless one operates a machine with one's own hands, and sees the work being created under one's own eyes, it is difficult to speak of it with precision. Thus several times we had to get possession of the machines, to construct them, and to put a hand to the work. It was necessary to become apprentices, so to speak, and to manufacture some poor object ourselves in order to learn how to teach others the way good specimens are made.

Source: Jean Le Rond d'Alembert, *Preliminary Discourse to the Encylopedia of Diderot*, Richard N. Schwab, trans. (Indianapolis, IN: ITT Bobbs-Merrill Educational Publishing Company, 1985), pp. 41–42, 122–123.

to the Christian centuries for their inspiration, and they believed that the welfare of humankind lay not in the pursuit of revelation but in the application of reason to human relationships. The *Encyclopedia* diffused enlightened thought throughout the continent and drew German and Russian thinkers into the movement (see Map 21–1 on page 542).

Read the **Document**
Diderot's Encyclopedia—Plate Illustrating Agricultural Techniques
at **myhistorylab.com**

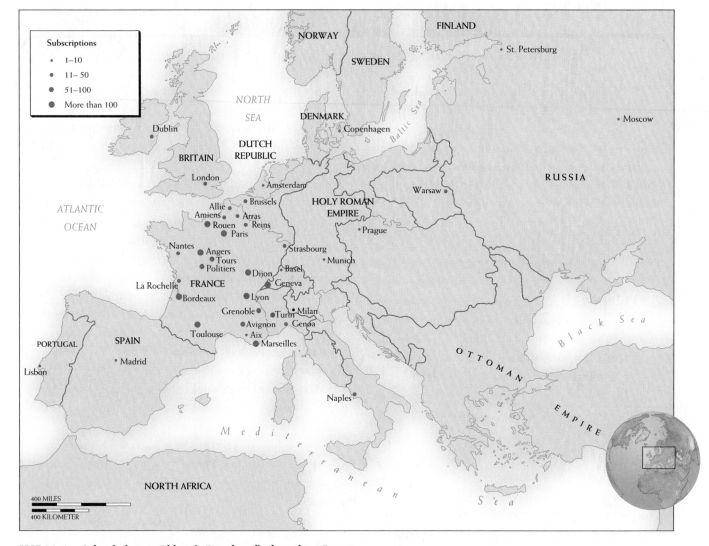

MAP 21–1. **Subscriptions to Diderot's *Encyclopedia* throughout Europe.**

Why are the greatest number of subscriptions to the *Encyclopedia* concentrated in western Europe?

THE ENLIGHTENMENT AND RELIGION

WHY DID the *philosophes* regard the church as the chief enemy of reform and human happiness?

In the eyes of the *philosophes*, the chief enemy of the improvement and happiness of humankind was the church. They were especially critical of Roman Catholicism. But all the Christian churches advocated a religious rather than a scientific view of humankind and taught that human beings were sinful and in need of divine grace. Religion turned attention away from this world and the solution to its problems to the world to come. The *philosophes* also indicted the churches for fostering intolerance and bigotry.

DEISM

The *philosophes* believed that religion should be reasonable and lead to moral behavior. Newton argued that nature was a rational system; many believed that the God who had created it must also be rational. Locke argued that all human knowledge derived from empirical experience, casting doubt on the possibility of divine revelation.

The rational religion of the Enlightenment is called **deism**. The deists regarded God as resembling a divine watchmaker who had set the mechanism of nature to work and then let it operate without intervention.

There were two major points in the deists' creed. The first was a belief in the existence of God, which they thought could be empirically deduced from the contemplation of nature. Because nature provided evidence of a rational God, that Deity must also favor rational morality. The second point in the deists' creed was a belief in life after death, when rewards and punishments would be meted out according to the virtue of the life a person led on this earth.

Deism was empirical, tolerant, reasonable, and capable of encouraging virtuous living. It was the major positive religious component of the Enlightenment.

TOLERATION

The centuries immediately preceding the Enlightenment had been characterized by bloody religious wars, and *philosophes* hoped that the triumph of reason and science would end denominational hatred and establish religious toleration.

Voltaire championed this cause. In 1762, the French authorities tortured and executed a Huguenot named Jean Calas (1698–1762) for having allegedly murdered his son to prevent him from converting to Roman Catholicism. In 1763, Voltaire published the *Treatise on Toleration,* and he continued to hound the authorities until the decision against Calas was reversed in 1765. For Voltaire, the case illustrated the dangers of religious fanaticism and the need for rational judicial reform. In 1779, Gotthold Lessing's (1729–1781) play about a Jew, *Nathan the Wise,* broadened the plea for toleration beyond Christian sects to include all religious faiths. These calls for toleration argued that secular values were more important than religious ones.

ISLAM IN ENLIGHTENMENT THOUGHT

Except in the Balkan Peninsula, Islam had few adherents in eighteenth-century Europe. Although European merchants traded with the Ottoman Empire and other Islamic regions, most Europeans learned what little they knew about Islam through books that were generally hostile to Islam and deeply misleading.

Islam continued to be seen as a rival to Christianity. European writers portrayed Islam as a false religion and Muhammad as an impostor because he had not performed miracles. They also attacked Islam as a sexually promiscuous religion because of its teaching that heaven was a place of sensuous delights, its permission for a man to have more than one wife, and the presence of harems in the Islamic world. Christian authors ignored the Islamic understanding of the life and mission of Muhammad. They referred to Islam as Muhammadanism, implying that Muhammad was divine rather than a human being with whom God had chosen to communicate.

Enlightenment *philosophes* had conflicting views regarding Islam. Voltaire indicated his opinion in the title of his 1742 tragedy, *Fanaticism, or Mohammed the Prophet.* Islam in general represented one more example of the religious fanaticism he so often criticized among Christians. Some *philosophes* criticized Islam on cultural and political grounds. In *The Persian Letters* (1721), the political philosopher Montesquieu (1689–1755) used Islamic culture as a foil to criticize his own European society. But by the time he wrote his more influential *Spirit of the Laws* (1748), discussed later in this chapter, Montesquieu associated Islamic society with the passivity of people subject to political despotism. Like other Europeans, Montesquieu believed the excessive influence of Islamic religious leaders prevented the Ottoman Empire from adapting itself to new advances in technology.

deism

A belief in a rational God who had created the universe, but then allowed it to function without his interference according to the mechanisms of nature and a belief in rewards and punishments after death for human action.

Illustration from the *Encyclopedia*. The *Encyclopedia* included illustrations of machinery and working people from across the globe. *Encyclopedia* editor Denis Diderot was deeply hostile to slavery. This engraving illustrated a sugar mill and sugar boiling house run with slave labor in the New World. The sugar produced in such mills was used in the European coffee houses where the ideas of the *philosophes* were often discussed.

How does this illustration demonstrate the *Encyclopedia's* emphasis on practical learning?

••─Read the **Document**
Voltaire, "On Universal Toleration"
at **myhistorylab.com**

Map of Turkey and View of Constantinople (Istanbul). Few Europeans visited the Ottoman Empire. What little they knew about it came from reports of travelers and from illustrations such as this view of Istanbul, the empire's capital.

Why did the Ottoman Empire arouse so much interest among Enlightenment thinkers?

QUICK REVIEW

Enlightenment and Islam: Cross-Cultural Views

- ◆ European popular view of Islam biased
- ◆ European scholarship on Islam hostile
- ◆ Lady Montagu provided sympathetic view of Islam
- ◆ Islam dismissive of Christianity, disinterested in European writers

CHRONOLOGY

MAJOR PUBLICATION DATES OF THE ENLIGHTENMENT

1687	Newton's *Principia Mathematica*
1690	Locke's *Essay Concerning Human Understanding*
1733	Voltaire's *Letters on the English*
1738	Voltaire's *Elements of the Philosophy of Newton*
1748	Montesquieu's *Spirit of the Laws*
1750	Rousseau's *Discourse on the Moral Effects of the Arts and Sciences*
1751	First volume of the *Encyclopedia* edited by Diderot and d'Alembert
1755	Rousseau's *Discourse on the Origin of Inequality*
1762	Rousseau's *Social Contract*
1763	Voltaire's *Treatise on Tolerance*
1776	Smith's *Wealth of Nations*
1779	Lessing's *Nathan the Wise*
1792	Wollstonecraft's *A Vindication of the Rights of Woman*

Some Enlightenment writers, however, spoke well of the Islamic faith. The deist John Toland, who opposed prejudice against both Jews and Muslims, contended that Islam derived from early Christian writings and was thus a form of Christianity (thus offending both Christians and Muslims). Edward Gibbon (1737–1794), who blamed Christianity for contributing to the fall of the Roman Empire, wrote with respect of Muhammed's leadership and Islam's success in conquering so vast a territory in the first century of its existence. Other commentators approved of Islam's tolerance and the charitable work of Muslims.

One of the most positive commentators on eighteenth-century Islam was Lady Mary Wortley Montagu (1689–1762). Between 1716 and 1718, she lived in Constantinople with her husband, the British ambassador to Turkey. In her *Turkish Embassy Letters* (1763), she praised much about Ottoman society and urged the English to copy the Turkish practice of vaccination against smallpox. Unlike European males, Montagu had access to the private quarters of women in Istanbul, and she thought upper-class Turkish women were remarkably free and well treated by their husbands. Montagu declared that many of the hostile comments about Islam and Islamic morality were simply wrong.

Yet the European voices demanding fairness for Islam were rare. Nor were Muslims very curious about the Christian West. Only a handful of people from the Ottoman or Safavid empires visited western Europe in the eighteenth century. The ulama, the Islamic religious establishment, taught that God's revelations to Muhammed meant Islam had superseded Christianity; therefore, there was little to be learned from the Christian culture of Europe.

●●►⌐Read the **Document**
Lady Mary Wortley Montagu, Letters:
(a) on Constantinople; (b) on Smallpox;
(c) on Vaccination in Turkey
at **myhistorylab.com**

THE ENLIGHTENMENT AND SOCIETY

Humanity was the center of the *philosophes'* interest. The *philosophes* believed that the application of human reason to society would reveal laws in human relationships similar to those found in physical nature. Although the term did not appear until later, the idea of social science originated with the Enlightenment. The purpose of discovering social laws was to remove the inhumanity that was a by-product of ignorance.

HOW DID the *philosophes* hope that reason would change society?

MONTESQUIEU AND *THE SPIRIT OF THE LAWS*

Charles Louis de Secondat, Baron de Montesquieu's (1689–1755) *The Spirit of the Laws* (1748) was perhaps the most influential book of the century. Montesquieu took an empirical approach to the study of law, evaluating legal texts from ancient as well as modern nations. He concluded that no single set of laws could apply to all peoples at all times and in all places. Only a careful analysis of many variables could reveal what mode of government would prove most beneficial for a given people.

The French, Montesquieu believed, would be served best by a monarchy whose power was limited by intermediary institutions: the aristocracy, the towns, the *parlements*, and other corporate bodies whose liberties the monarch had to respect. Their role was to preserve the liberty of subjects by restraining the power of their ruler. Montesquieu was a political conservative, but he believed that France's oppressive and inefficient monarchy was degrading life in France and that it needed reform.

One of Montesquieu's most influential ideas was the division of power. He thought that Great Britain's government provided an excellent example. It vested executive power in its monarch, legislative power in its Parliament, and judicial power in its courts, and any two of these branches of government could check the power of the other. His perception of the eighteenth-century British constitution was incorrect, but his analysis made a strong case for limiting the power of rulers by constitutional means and relying on legislatures, not monarchs, to make laws. Montesquieu's ideas had a profound and enduring effect on the liberal democracies of the next two centuries.

◉⌐View the **Image**
The Spirit of the Laws, Montesquieu: Frontispiece, at **myhistorylab.com**

●●►⌐Read the **Document**
Baron de Montesquieu, Excerpt from The Spirit of the Laws
at **myhistorylab.com**

Printing Shops. Shops such as this were the productive centers for the book trade and newspaper publishing, which spread the ideas of the Enlightenment.

How did tradespeople, craftsmen, and artisans contribute to the Scientific Revolution and the Enlightenment?

Read the Document
Adam Smith, Intro. to the Wealth of
Nations (1776) and Wealth of Nations,
Adam Smith (1776) at **myhistorylab.com**

laissez-faire
French phrase meaning "allow to do."
In economics, the doctrine of minimal
government interference in the working of the economy.

QUICK REVIEW

Adam Smith (1723–1790)

◆ Advocated abolition of mercantile
system

◆ Saw nature as a set of physical resources
to be exploited by human beings

◆ Was in favor of limited government
activity in the economy

ADAM SMITH ON ECONOMIC GROWTH AND SOCIAL PROGRESS

The most important Enlightenment exposition of economics was Adam Smith's (1723–1790) *An Inquiry into the Nature and Causes of the Wealth of Nations* (1776). Smith urged abolition of England's mercantile system. It was a basic assumption of mercantilism that the earth's resources are limited and scarce, so that one nation can acquire wealth only at the expense of others. Smith saw the resources of nature—water, air, soil, and minerals—as boundless. He believed that if individuals were unleashed to pursue their self-interest, the result would be economic expansion, for the rational demands of the marketplace would guide their productive activities. In effect, Smith was saying that the nations and peoples of Europe need not be poor.

Smith is usually regarded as the founder of *laissez-faire* economic thought and policy, which favors a limited role for the government in economic life. *The Wealth of Nations* was, however, a complex book. For example, he did not oppose all government activity touching the economy. The state, he argued, should provide schools, armies, navies, and roads. It should also undertake certain commercial ventures, such as the opening of dangerous new trade routes that were economically desirable but too expensive or risky for private enterprise. Smith, like most of the *philosophes*, was less doctrinaire than any brief summary of their thought suggests.

Smith's theories helped to justify Western imperialism. Smith endorsed a model popular with other social theorists of his day: the *four-stage theory*. It divided human societies into four categories according to their economic basis: hunting and gathering, pastoral or herding, agricultural, and commercial. Movement through these stages was assumed to be progress. This meant that economic development was the indicator of where a group fell on the continuum between barbarism and civilization. Smith's theory allowed Europeans to view their society as the pinnacle of human achievement and to justify their pursuit of imperial domination of the world as a civilizing mission.

ROUSSEAU

Jean-Jacques Rousseau (1712–1778) held a different view of political power. Rousseau was a strange, isolated genius who never felt comfortable with the other *philosophes*. More than any other writer of the mid-eighteenth century, he transcended the thought and values of his own time. His *Discourse on the Moral Effects of the Arts and Sciences* (1750) contended that civilization and enlightenment had corrupted, not elevated, human nature. In a *Discourse on the Origin of Inequality* (1755), he argued that maldistribution of property, not lack of production, was the world's greatest economic problem. Rousseau felt that the purpose of society should be to nurture better, not wealthier, people.

His vision of reform was much more radical than that of other philosophers. Most eighteenth-century political thinkers regarded society as a collection of independent individuals pursuing selfish goals, and they advocated liberating these individuals from the undue bonds of government. Rousseau, by contrast, opens *The Social Contract* (1762) with the declaration, "All men are born free, but everywhere they are in chains."[1] The rest of the volume constitutes a defense of the chains of a properly organized society over its members. Rousseau claimed that society was more important than the individual because individuals become moral creatures only through their relationship to the larger community. Rousseau, drawing on

---

[1]Jean-Jacques Rousseau, *The Social Contract and Discourses*, trans. by G. D. H. Cole (New York: Dutton, 1950), p. 3.

Plato and Calvin, claimed that true freedom was obedience to law—that is, rules determined by the general will. The opinion of the majority of voting citizens, acting with adequate information and under the influence of virtuous customs and morals, was always right.

Rousseau's assault on the eighteenth-century cult of the individual and selfishness and was at odds with the commercial spirit that was transforming his world.

ENLIGHTENED CRITICS OF EUROPEAN EMPIRE

Most European thinkers associated with the Enlightenment favored the extension of European empires across the world, believing that this amounted to the spread of progress and civilization. There were, however, a few Enlightenment voices who criticized the European empires. They were troubled by the European conquest of the Americas, the treatment of Native Americans, and the enslavement of Africans on the two American continents. The most important of these critics were Denis Diderot and two German philosophers, Immanuel Kant (1724–1804) and Johann Gottfried Herder (1744–1803).

Rousseau. The writings of Jean-Jacques Rousseau (1712–1778) raised some of the most profound social and ethical questions of the Enlightenment. This portrait by Maurice Quentin was made in about 1740.

What did Rousseau believe should be the goal of Enlightened reform?

These critics shared important ideas. As Sankar Muthu has recently written, "The first and most basic idea is that human beings deserve some modicum of moral and political respect simply because of the fact that they are human."[2] In other words, the Enlightenment critics of empire argued for the existence of a form of shared humanity that the sixteenth-century European conquerors in the Americas and other imperialists had ignored. Diderot, Kant, and Herder rejected this dismissive outlook and the harsh policies that flowed from it. They believed no single definition of human nature could be made the standard throughout the world and then used to dehumanize people whose appearance or culture differed from that standard.

A second essential idea was the conviction that the people whom Europeans had encountered in the Americas possessed cultures that should have been respected and understood, rather than being destroyed. They embraced an outlook later known as cultural relativism.

A third, closely related idea was that human beings may develop distinct cultures possessing intrinsic values that cannot be directly compared. Each culture possesses deep inner social and linguistic complexities that make any simple comparison impossible. Indeed, Diderot, Kant, and Herder argued that one fundamental aspect of humanity is the ability to develop a variety of distinctly different cultures.

These arguments critical of empire often involved criticism of New World slavery and were part of the antislavery movement (see Chapter 22). Whereas the antislavery arguments took strong hold in both Europe and America from the late eighteenth century onward, the arguments critical of empire did not. They stand generally isolated from the rest of Enlightenment political thought and were not widely deployed until new anticolonial voices were raised at the close of the nineteenth century.

WOMEN IN THE THOUGHT AND PRACTICE OF THE ENLIGHTENMENT

Women, especially in France, helped promote the careers of the *philosophes*. In Paris the salons of women such as Marie-Thérèse Geoffrin (1699–1777), Julie de Lespinasse (1733–1776), and Claudine de Tencin (1689–1749) gave the *philosophes* access to useful social and political contacts and a receptive environment for their ideas. The marquise de Pompadour (1721–1764), the mistress of Louis XV, for example, played a key role in overcoming efforts to censor the *Encyclopedia*.

---

[2]Sankar Muthu, *Enlightenment against Empire* (Princeton, NJ: Princeton University Press, 2003), p. 268. This section draws primarily from this excellent recent book.

Despite their reliance on female patrons, their general enthusiasm for reform, and their tendency to reject ascetic views of sexual relations, the *philosophes* advocated no radical changes in the social condition of women. Montesquieu, for example, believed that women were not naturally inferior to men and that they should play a greater role in society, but he also believed that men should dominate marriage and family. Although he opposed laws that oppressed women, he exalted chastity as the primary female virtue.

The views about women expressed in the *Encyclopedia* were less generous. Diderot and d'Alembert saw little need to include articles by women. Most of the articles that dealt with women emphasized their physical weakness and inferiority, usually attributed to menstruation or childbearing. Contributors disagreed on the social equality of women. The encyclopedists discussed women primarily in a family context and considered motherhood their most important occupation. On sexual behavior, the encyclopedists upheld a double standard. In contrast to the articles, however, illustrations in the *Encyclopedia* showed women deeply involved in the economic activities of the day. The illustrations also showed the activities of lower- and working-class women, about whom the articles have little to say.

Rousseau urged women to embrace their traditional roles. In his novel *Émile* (1762), he declared that women should be educated to be subordinate to men and to center their lives on bearing and rearing children. He portrayed women as weaker and inferior to men, except perhaps for their capacity for feeling and giving love. He excluded them from public affairs and confined them to the domestic sphere. Many of these attitudes were not new—some have roots in Roman law—but Rousseau's powerful presentation and the influence of his other writings gave them new life, including in the legislation of the French Revolution.

Paradoxically, despite these views (and his own ill treatment of the many women he impregnated), Rousseau achieved a vast following among women. They may have responded to the stress he put on women's emotions and subjective feelings. By portraying domestic life and the roles of wife and mother as noble vocations, he gave middle- and upper-class women confidence that their lives had purpose.

In 1792 in *A Vindication of the Rights of Woman*, Mary Wollstonecraft (1759–1797) brought Rousseau before the judgment of the rational Enlightenment ideal of progressive knowledge. Wollstonecraft (who, like many women of her day, died shortly after childbirth of puerperal fever) argued that to confine women to the separate domestic sphere was to make them the sensual slaves of men. As victims of male tyranny, women could never achieve their own moral or intellectual identity. Denying good education to women impeded the progress of all humanity. Wollstonecraft was demanding for women the kind of intellectual liberty that male writers of the Enlightenment had been championing for men for more than a century.

ENLIGHTENED ABSOLUTISM

WHAT WERE the goals of enlightened absolute rulers?

During the last third of the century it seemed that several European rulers had embraced many of the reforms set forth by the *philosophes*. *Enlightened absolutism* indicates monarchical government dedicated to the rational strengthening of the central absolutist administration at the cost of lesser centers of political power. The monarchs most closely associated with it—Frederick II of Prussia, Joseph II of Austria, and Catherine II of Russia—often found that the political and social realities of their realms caused them to moderate both their enlightenment and their absolutism. Frederick II corresponded with the *philosophes*, invited Voltaire to his court, and even wrote history and political tracts. Catherine II consciously cultivated the image of being enlightened, to make her nation seem more modern and Western. She read the works of the *philosophes*, befriended Diderot and Voltaire, and made frequent references to their ideas. Joseph II continued numerous initiatives begun by his mother, Maria Theresa, and imposed a series of religious, legal, and social reforms that contemporaries believed he had derived from suggestions of the *philosophes*.

((•—{Hear the Audio
 at **myhistorylab.com**

The relationship between these monarchs and the writers of the Enlightenment was complicated. The rulers did wish to see their subjects enjoy better health, more accessible education, a more rational political administration, and economic prosperity. But they also sought the rational economic and social integration of their realms so they could achieve military strength. After the Seven Years' War all the states of Europe understood that they required stronger armed forces, which meant they needed new revenues. The search for more political support for their rule led these monarchs to make "enlightened" reforms. Consequently, they and their advisers used rationality to pursue many goals admired by the *philosophes* but also to further what the *philosophes* considered irrational militarism.

JOSEPH II OF AUSTRIA

No eighteenth-century ruler embodied rational, impersonal authority more than Emperor Joseph II of Austria. He prided himself on his narrow, passionless rationality, but he genuinely wanted to improve the lot of his people. Paradoxically, his well-intentioned efforts prompted rebellions by both aristocrats and peasants from Hungary to the Austrian Netherlands.

The Habsburgs' empire was Europe's most diverse political entity. Its rulers never succeeded in creating a unified government or enlisting the loyalties of its various groups of aristocrats. Maria Theresa preserved the monarchy during the War of the Austrian Succession (1740–1748) by guaranteeing independence for aristocrats, especially the Hungarians. She also improved her position in Austria and Bohemia by imposing a more comprehensive and efficient system of tax collection. She expanded primary schooling and redirected educational institutions to training officials for royal service. Concern for peasants and serfs (from whom she recruited her military manpower) led her to limit the services that landowners could demand from them.

Joseph II's reforms were more wide ranging than his mother's. He aspired to expand at the expense of Poland, Bavaria, and the Ottoman Empire. But his greatest ambition was to overcome the pluralism of the Habsburg holdings by increasing the power of the central monarchy in areas of political and social life that Maria Theresa had wisely not disturbed. In particular, Joseph sought to lessen Hungarian autonomy. He refused to have himself crowned king of Hungary and even had the Crown of Saint Stephen sent to Vienna. He thus avoided having to guarantee existing or new Hungarian privileges in a coronation oath. He reorganized local government in Hungary to increase the authority of his own officials, and he required the use of the German language in all governmental matters. But the Magyar nobility resisted, and in 1790 Joseph had to rescind most of his centralizing measures.

Another target of Joseph's absolutism was religion. In October 1781 Joseph extended freedom of worship to Lutherans, Calvinists, and the Greek Orthodox. They were permitted to have their own churches, sponsor schools, enter skilled trades, and hold academic appointments and public service positions. From 1781 through 1789 Joseph relieved the Jews of certain taxes and signs of personal degradation and gave

A Closer Look

An Eighteenth-Century Artist Appeals to the Ancient World

Jacques Louis David completed *The Oath of the Horatii* in 1784. Like many of his other works, it used themes from the supposedly morally austere ancient Roman Republic to criticize the political life of his own day. David intended the painting to contrast ancient civic virtue with the luxurious aristocratic culture of contemporary France.

The Horatii take an oath their father administers to protect the Roman Republic against enemies even if it means sacrificing their own lives. One of these enemies is romantically involved with one of their sisters in the right of the painting. Patriotism must be upheld over other relationships.

The sharp division of the painting with a male world on the left and a female world on the right illustrates how eighteenth-century republican thinkers, such as Rousseau, excluded women from civic life and political participation.

The sisters and mother of the Horatii weep in a separate part of the scene. The emotion of the women and their uncertain policital loyalty suggests that civic virtue pertains only to men.

Jacques Louis David (1748–1825) "The Oath of the Horatii," c. 1784, oil on canvas, 330 x 425 cm Inv: 3692. Photo: G. Blot / C. Jean. (c) Reunion des Musees Nationaux/Art Resource, New York/Louvre, Paris, France.

Questions

1. The Enlightenment is usually associated with modern or progressive ideas. How and why did enlightened writers and readers still find the ancient world important to their reformist agendas?

2. How does the portrayal of women in this painting enter into the contemporary debate over the role of women in public life?

3. Do you think this painting and similar images of ancient virtue would have effectively undermined social respect and confidence in the eighteenth-century French aristocracy or was the audience for such paintings too small?

myhistorylab To examine this image in an interactive fashion, please go to **www.myhistorylab.com**

them the right of private worship. (Jews still did not enjoy general legal rights equal to those of other Habsburg subjects.) Above all, Joseph sought to bring the various institutions of the Roman Catholic Church directly under his control. He forbade direct communication between the bishops of his realms and the pope, dissolved over 600 monasteries, and replaced the traditional Roman Catholic seminaries with eight general seminaries that emphasized parish duties. Joseph's policies ended the influence of the church as an independent institution in Habsburg lands. In many respects his policies, known as *Josephinism*, prefigured those of the French Revolution.

Regarding serfdom and the land, Joseph II expanded policies initiated by Maria Theresa. He introduced reforms that touched the heart of rural society. He abolished the legal status of serfdom defined in terms of servitude to another person. He gave peasants much more personal freedom: They could marry, engage in skilled work, or have their children trained without permission of the landlord. The procedures of the manorial courts were reformed, and avenues of appeal to royal officials were opened. Joseph also encouraged landlords to change land leases, so that it would be easier for peasants to inherit them or to transfer them to another peasant without bringing into doubt the landlord's title of ownership. Joseph believed that reducing traditional burdens would make the peasant tillers of the land more productive and industrious.

In 1789 Joseph proposed a new and daring system of land taxation. All proprietors were to be taxed, regardless of social status. He commuted peasants' compulsory service into a monetary tax, split between the landlord and the state. The decree was drawn up, but resistance from the nobles delayed its implementation. Joseph died in 1790, and the decree never went into effect. However, his measures had stirred up turmoil throughout the Habsburg realms. Peasants revolted, and nobles protested.

On Joseph's death, the crown went to his brother Leopold II (r. 1790–1792). Although sympathetic to Joseph's goals, Leopold repealed many of the most controversial decrees, including land tax reform.

CATHERINE THE GREAT OF RUSSIA

After the death of Peter the Great in 1725, the court nobles and the army determined the Russian succession. As a result, the crown fell into the hands of people with little talent until 1741, when Peter's daughter Elizabeth came to the throne. At her death in 1762 Elizabeth was succeeded by Peter III, one of her nephews. He was a weak and possibly insane ruler who had been married in 1745 to a young German princess, the future Catherine the Great (r. 1762–1796). Catherine had neither love nor loyalty for her demented husband. When Peter III was deposed and murdered (with Catherine's approval, if not aid), she was immediately proclaimed empress.

Catherine's familiarity with the Enlightenment and the general culture of western Europe convinced her that Russia needed to make major reforms if it were to remain a great power. In 1767 Catherine summoned over 500 delegates drawn from all sectors of Russian life to advise her on revising law and government. Before this Legislative Commission convened, Catherine wrote a set of *Instructions*, containing ideas drawn from the political writings of the *philosophes*. The revision of Russian law, however, did not occur for more than half a century. In 1768 Catherine dismissed the

Catherine the Great ascended to the Russian throne after the murder of her husband. She tried initially to enact major reforms, but she never intended to abandon absolutism. She assured the nobility of their rights and by the end of her reign had imposed press censorship. **Did Catherine the Great achieve her goals for Russia?**

commission before several of its key committees had reported. Yet the commission had gathered a vast amount of information about the conditions of local administration and economic life throughout Russia. The inconclusive debates and the absence of programs from the delegates themselves suggested that most Russians saw no alternative to an autocratic monarchy. Catherine herself had no intention of departing from absolutism.

Catherine proceeded to carry out limited reforms on her own authority while supporting the rights and local power of the nobility. In 1775 she reorganized local government to solve problems brought to light by the Legislative Commission. She put most local offices into the hands of nobles rather than creating a royal bureaucracy. In 1785 Catherine issued the Charter of the Nobility, which guaranteed many noble rights and privileges. She issued a similar charter to the towns of her realms. In part, the empress had to favor the nobles. There were too few educated subjects in her realm to establish an independent bureaucracy, and the treasury could not afford an army strictly loyal to the crown. So Catherine wisely made a virtue of necessity: She strengthened the stability of her crown by a convenient alliance with her nobles and urban leaders.

Catherine continued the Russian drive for warm-water ports (see Map 21–2). This led to warfare with the Turks between 1768 and 1774, when the Treaty of Kuchuk-Kainardji gave Russia a direct outlet on the Black Sea, free navigation rights in its waters, and free access through the Bosphorus. Moreover, the Crimea became an independent state, which Catherine painlessly annexed in 1783.

MAP 21–2. **Expansion of Russia, 1689–1796.** The overriding territorial aim of the two most powerful Russian monarchs of the eighteenth century, Peter the Great (in the first quarter of the century) and Catherine the Great (in the last half of the century) was to secure navigable outlets to the sea in both the north and the south for Russia's vast empire; hence Peter's push to the Baltic Sea and Catherine's to the Black Sea. Russia also expanded into Central Asia and Siberia during this time period.

Which empire came into direct conflict with Russian expansion?

THE PARTITION OF POLAND

These Russian military successes made the other states of eastern Europe uneasy. Their anxieties were allayed by the First Partition of Poland. The Russian victories along the Danube River in what is today Romania were most unwelcome to Austria, which had its own ambitions there. At the same time, the Ottoman Empire was pressing Prussia for aid against Russia. Frederick the Great made a proposal to Russia and Austria that would give each something it wanted, prevent conflict among them, and save appearances. After long, complicated, secret negotiations, the three powers agreed that Russia would abandon the Danubian provinces in return for a large chunk of Polish territory with almost 2 million inhabitants. As a reward for remaining neutral, Prussia annexed most of the Polish territory between East Prussia and Prussia proper, which allowed Frederick to unite two previously separate sections of his realm. Finally, Austria took Galicia, with its important salt mines, and other Polish territory with over 2.5 million inhabitants. The Polish state had lost approximately one-third of its territory.

There were two additional partitions of Poland by Russia and Prussia, and one more by Austria. They occurred in 1793 and 1795 and removed Poland from the map of Europe until 1919. The great powers contended that they were saving themselves, and by implication the rest of Europe, from Polish anarchy. The argument was plausible to some contemporaries because of fears spurred by the French Revolution (see Chapter 22). However, the truth was that Poland's political weakness made the country and its resources a rich field for plunderous aggression.

Charter of Nobility. Granted by Empress Catherine II in 1785, this charter concluded the legal consolidation of Russian nobility as a class and provided for its political and corporate rights, privileges, and principles of self-organization. In this printing, the imperial title is hand written in gold and is surrounded by engraved coats of arms of the provinces of the Russian Empire.

Zhalovannaia Gramota Dvorianstvu (Charter Granted to the Nobility), *1785.*

How does this charter illustrate the principles of enlightened absolutism?

SUMMARY

 WHY IS the Scientific Revolution important to world history?

The Scientific Revolution. The scientific ideas of the sixteenth and seventeenth centuries changed the way Western intellectuals thought about the world and humankind. Western thinkers came to rely on mathematical laws, empirical data, and experimentation. Copernicus, Kepler, and Galileo overturned the ancient idea that the earth was the center of the universe. Galileo and Descartes maintained that the world was governed by mathematical laws. Francis Bacon encouraged observation and experimentation. Newton hypothesized gravity and established an enduring basis for physics. Locke argued that

 Read the **Document**
Immanuel Kant defines the Enlightenment, 1784, at **myhistorylab.com**

human beings are shaped by their sense experiences and are hence creatures of their environment subject to reform and possible progress. Women were largely excluded from scientific practice. *page 533*

HOW DID Enlightenment thinkers argue for the reform of society?

The Enlightenment. The Enlightenment *philosophes* used reason as a basis for reform and to advocate progressive social, economic, and political movements. Voltaire's prodigious literary output outlined major issues in Enlightenment thought, and Diderot's *Encyclopedia* helped Enlightenment ideas diffuse throughout Europe. *page 540*

WHY DID the *philosophes* regard the church as the chief enemy of reform and human happiness?

The Enlightenment and Religion. The *philosophes* believed that the Christian church distracted people from finding rational solutions to their problems. They particularly attacked religious intolerance. Many were followers of deism, a belief in a rational, "divine watchmaker" God. Like most Europeans of their age, many *philosophes* had a distorted view of Islam, but some admired aspects of Islamic culture. *page 542*

 HOW DID the *philosophes* hope that reason would change society?

The Enlightenment and Society. Montesquieu and other *philosophes* argued for limited, constitutional government. Adam Smith linked economics and social progress. Rousseau wished to reform society in the name of virtue rather than material happiness. He maintained that in the pursuit of virtue the needs of society were more important than those of the individual. Enlightenment thinkers criticized imperial conquest as dehumanizing, but they generally failed to support improvements in women's social standing. The competing strands of the Enlightenment continue to pervade Western society. *page 545*

 WHAT WERE the goals of enlightened absolute rulers?

Enlightened Absolutism. Enlightened absolutism was a form of monarchical government dedicated to the rational strengthening of the central government. Many of the reforms enlightened monarchs imposed were influenced by the ideas of the *philosophes*, but the chief goal of these rulers was to increase their own authority and military strength, as witnessed by the partitions of Poland among Russia, Prussia, and Austria at the end of the eighteenth century. The most important enlightened monarchs were Frederick II of Prussia, Joseph II of Austria, and Catherine the Great of Russia. *page 548*

KEY TERMS

deism (DEE-izm) (p. 543)

empiricism (p. 537)

Enlightenment (p. 533)

laissez-faire (leh-say-FAYR)
    (p. 546)

philosophes (FILL-uh-SOHFS)
    (p. 540)

Ptolemaic system
    (TAHL-uh-MAY-ik) (p. 535)

Scientific Revolution (p. 534)

REVIEW QUESTIONS

1. What was the Scientific Revolution? What were the major contributions of Copernicus, Brahe, Kepler, Galileo, Bacon, and Newton? Do you think they regarded themselves as revolutionaries?

2. How and to what extent did women participate in the Scientific Revolution?

3. Define the Enlightenment. Is it best seen as a single movement or as a series of related movements? What was the relationship of the Enlightenment to the new science? How did the Enlightenment further the idea of progress and the superiority of European civilization?

4. Why did the *philosophes* believe they must comment so extensively on religion? Why did they criticize Christianity? Why did some of them champion deism?

5. What were the differing views of the *philosophes* toward Islam?

6. Was there a single Enlightenment view of politics? Why could writers so dedicated to reform have so many different political paths to achieve reform?

7. How has the political thought of the Enlightenment influenced the development of modern political philosophies and modern governments?

8. Summarize the Enlightenment critique of European empires. Do you see any flaws in this line of reasoning? Why do you think it was not more influential?

9. What were the prevailing attitudes of the *philosophes* toward women and women's roles? Do these attitudes present any contradiction to other Enlightenment positions? Explain.

10. Define *enlightened absolutism*. What were the similarities in the policies of Frederick the Great, Joseph II, and Catherine the Great? To what extent do their policies actually seem to stem from the ideas of the Enlightenment *philosophes*?

Note: To learn more about the topics in this chapter, please turn to the Suggested Readings at the end of the book. For additional sources related to this chapter please see www.myhistorylab.com

myhistorylab Connections

Reinforce what you learned in this chapter by studying the many documents, images, maps, review tools, and videos available at **www.myhistorylab.com**

Read and Review

✓●─Study and Review Chapter 21

●●●─Read the Document *Nicolaus Copernicus: On the Revolution of the Heavenly Spheres (1500s), p. 534 and p. 540*

Francis Bacon, from Novum Organum, p. 537

Isaac Newton, from Opticks, p. 538

Galileo Galilei, Letter to the Grand Duchess Christina (1630s), p. 538

John Locke, Essay Concerning Human Understanding, p. 539

Voltaire, Letters on England, p. 540

Diderot's Encyclopedia—Plate Illustrating Agricultural Techniques, p. 541

Voltaire, "On Universal Toleration," p. 543

Lady Mary Wortley Montagu, Letters:
  (a) on Constantinople;
  (b) on Smallpox;
  (c) on Vaccination in Turkey, p. 545

Baron de Montesquieu, Excerpt from The Spirit of the Laws, p. 545

Adam Smith, Intro. to the Wealth of Nations (1776) and Wealth of Nations, Adam Smith (1776), p. 546

Catherine the Great's Constitution (1767), p. 552

Immanuel Kant defines the Enlightenment, 1784, p. 553

●●●─View the Image *The Spirit of the Laws, Montesquieu: Frontispiece, p. 545*

Catherine the Great, p. 552

Research and Explore

◉─See the Map *Science and the Enlightenment, p. 534 and p. 540*

◉─See the Map *Expansion of Russia, 1689–1796, p. 552*

(((•─Hear the Audio

Hear the audio file for Chapter 21
at **www.myhistorylab.com**

22

Revolutions in the Transatlantic World

Guerrilla Warfare. Haitian slaves ambush French forces during their successful revolt led by Toussaint L'Ouverture and Jean-Jacques Dessalines in 1794. The Haitian Revolution included the largest emancipation of slaves to occur in the eighteenth century.

Why was the Haitian Revolution the great exception in the American Wars of Independence in the late eighteenth and early nineteenth centuries?

B etween 1776 and 1824 a world-transforming series of revolutions occurred in France and the Americas. Within half a century the peoples of the two American continents established their independence. The French monarchy collapsed from the forces of aristocratic resistance and popular revolution. All the revolutionary leaders sought to establish new governments based largely, though never entirely, on Enlightenment principles.

From start to finish these revolutions were connected. The financial pressures from the Seven Years' War (1756–1763) had led Britain, Spain, and France to seek revenues in ways that destabilized the Americas and France itself. Once the American Revolution began, France aided the colonists, exacerbating its own financial problem. The French Revolution and the ensuing Napoleonic Wars created situations in Spain and Portugal to which the colonial elites in Latin America responded by seeking independence.

The era also witnessed the beginning of a vast international crusade, first to abolish the slave trade and then to abolish slavery in the transatlantic world. Opponents of slavery were inspired by the same Enlightenment ideas that inspired many of the revolutionaries, as well as by religious convictions. The political and economic dislocations of the revolutionary era helped the antislavery forces achieve their goals. The political, social, and economic life of the transatlantic world would never be the same. ■

REVOLUTION IN THE BRITISH COLONIES IN NORTH AMERICA

RESISTANCE TO THE IMPERIAL SEARCH FOR REVENUE

After the Treaty of Paris in 1763 ended the Seven Years' War (see Chapter 19), the British government faced two problems. The first was the cost of defending the empire it had acquired. The second was the need to organize a vast new territory: all of North America east of the Mississippi.

WHAT WAS radical about the American Revolution?

THE TRANSATLANTIC REVOLUTIONS

The revolutions and the crusade against slavery that occurred throughout the transatlantic world between 1776 and the 1830s transformed the political, social, and economic life of three continents. First in North America, then in France and other parts of Europe, and finally in South America bold political experiments challenged colonial government, monarchies, and aristocratic governments and laid the foundations for modern liberal democracy. These revolutions and the effort to abolish slavery owed much to the philosophical inspiration of the Enlightenment and bear witness to its immense influence in world history.

As a result of the events of this age of transatlantic revolution, the largest republic since ancient times was established in North America. In Europe the absolutist governments were overthrown across the continent by the impact of the French Revolution and the armies of Napoleon. Slaves on Haiti overthrew the French colonial regime and established the first black republic. By the close of the first quarter of the nineteenth century wars of independence across Latin America had closed the era of European empire with the establishment of republics everywhere except Brazil.

No less important, this era witnessed the beginning of an international effort to bring about the abolition of the slave economies that had long dominated the transatlantic economy.

The expanding forms of political liberty found their counterparts in an economic life freed from the constraints of the old colonial empires and eventually from the economies based on plantation slave labor. The new American republic constituted a vast free-trade zone, with its commerce and ports open to the entire world.

For the first time since the encounter with Europe, all of Latin America could trade freely with its own peoples and those of the rest of the world.

In Europe the reforms of the French Revolution and the new Napoleonic Code of law removed many regional economic barriers and led to more standard weights and measures.

National law formed the framework for economic activity. The movement to abolish slavery fostered a wage economy of free laborers. That kind of economy generated its own set of problems and social dislocation, including a sort of sharecropping serfdom for many former slaves, but it was nonetheless an

The British drive for revenue began in 1764 with the Sugar Act. Britain hoped to enhance revenue from imports of sugar into the colonies by the rigorous collection of what was actually a reduced tax. Smugglers were to be tried in admiralty courts without juries. A year later, Parliament passed the Stamp Act, a tax on legal documents and other items. The British considered these taxes just because they had been approved by Parliament and because the revenue was to be spent in the colonies that paid them. The Americans, however, objected that they were not represented in Parliament and insisted that they alone had the right to tax themselves. Furthermore, the Americans feared that if colonial government were financed from Britain, they would cease to control it. Following disorder in its American lands (particularly in Massachusetts), Parliament repealed the Stamp Act in 1766 but asserted its right to legislate for the colonies.

AMERICAN POLITICAL IDEAS

The political ideas of the American colonists had largely arisen from the struggle of seventeenth-century English aristocrats and gentry against the absolutism of the Stuart monarchs. The American colonists believed that the English Revolution of 1688 had established liberties that belonged to them as well as to the British. They claimed that George III (r. 1760–1820) and the British Parliament were dissolving the bonds of allegiance that united the two peoples by attacking those liberties. These Whig political ideas, derived largely from John Locke (1632–1704), were only a part of the English ideological heritage that affected the Americans. Colonists also had become familiar with a series of British political writers called the *Commonwealthmen*. These authors held republican political ideas that stemmed from the radical branches of the Puritan revolution. They dismissed much parliamentary taxation as nothing more than a economy of free human beings who were the chattel of no other human being.

Finally, the age of transatlantic revolutions saw the emergence of nationalism as a political force. All of the revolutions, because of their popular political base, had given power to the idea of nations defined by their own character and historical past rather than by dynastic rulers. Americans saw themselves as forming a new kind of nation. The French had demonstrated the power of a nation fully mobilized for military purposes. In turn France's aggression had aroused national sentiment, especially in Great Britain, Spain, and Germany. The new nations of Latin America also sought to define themselves by their heritage and historical experience rather than by their past in the Spanish and Portuguese empires.

These various revolutions, their political doctrines, and their social and economic departures provided examples to peoples elsewhere in the world. But even more important, the transformations of the transatlantic revolutions and eventual abolition of slavery meant that new political classes and newly organized independent nations would become actors on the world scene. Europeans would have to deal with a score of new nations in the Americas. The rest of the world confronted new nations freed from the direction and authority of European powers. In turn, the political changes in Europe meant that those nations and their relationships with the rest of the world would be directed by a broader range of political groups and forces than in the past. Ironically, however, by the close of the nineteenth century several of the European nations as well as the United States that had become liberal democratic states would commence a new wave of colonialism throughout Africa and Asia and would impose new economic dominance on the republics of Latin America.

Focus Questions

◆ What is the relationship between the Enlightenment and the transatlantic revolutions? Between the Enlightenment and the crusade against slavery?

◆ How did the transatlantic revolutions fundamentally alter the relationship between Europe and the Americas?

◆ What is the relationship between the transatlantic revolutions and nationalism? Why did such a relationship exist?

means of financing political corruption, and they feared standing armies as instruments of tyranny. The policy of Great Britain toward America after the Treaty of Paris made many colonists believe that the suspicions of the Commonwealthmen were correct.

CRISIS AND INDEPENDENCE

In May 1773, Parliament allowed the East India Company to import tea directly into the American colonies. Although the law lowered the price of tea, it levied a tea tax that was imposed without the colonists' consent. Protestors in Boston reacted by throwing a shipload of tea into the harbor, an event that became known as the Boston Tea Party.

The British ministry of Lord North (1732–1792) was determined to assert the authority of Parliament over the colonies. In 1774, Parliament closed the port of Boston, reorganized the government of Massachusetts, quartered troops in private homes, and transferred the trials of royal customs officials to England. Parliament also extended the boundaries of Quebec to include the Ohio River valley, an act that the Americans regarded as an attempt to prevent them—and their political ideas—from spreading westward beyond the Appalachian Mountains.

Committees of correspondence, composed of citizens critical of Britain, had been established throughout the colonies, and in September 1774, these committees organized the First Continental Congress in Philadelphia. This body failed to persuade Parliament to abandon its attempt at direct supervision of colonial affairs. In 1775, the battles of Lexington, Concord, and Bunker Hill were fought, and the Second Continental Congress undertook to govern the colonies. In August 1775, George III

Boston Massacre. This view of the Boston Massacre of March 5, 1770, by Paul Revere owes more to propaganda than to fact. There was no order to fire, and the innocent citizens portrayed here were really an angry, violent mob.

What were the purposes of propaganda such as this painting?

CHRONOLOGY

THE AMERICAN REVOLUTION

1760	George III becomes king
1763	Treaty of Paris concludes the Seven Years' War
1764	Sugar Act
1765	Stamp Act
1766	Sugar Act repealed and Declaratory Act passed
1770	Boston Massacre
1773	Boston Tea Party
1774	Intolerable Acts
1774	First Continental Congress
1775	Second Continental Congress
1776	Declaration of Independence
1778	France enters the war on the side of America
1781	British forces surrender at Yorktown
1783	Treaty of Paris concludes War of the American Revolution

((•─Hear the Audio
at **myhistorylab.com**

declared the colonies in rebellion. During the winter, Thomas Paine's (1737–1809) pamphlet *Common Sense* galvanized public opinion in favor of separation from Great Britain. A colonial army and navy were organized, and on July 4, 1776, the Continental Congress adopted the Declaration of Independence. The War of the American Revolution continued until 1781, when the forces of George Washington (1732–1799) defeated those of Lord Cornwallis (1738–1805) at Yorktown. Meanwhile, the war had widened into a European conflict. In 1778, the French government supported the rebellion in the hope of weakening its traditional enemy, Great Britain. In 1779, Spain also came to the aid of the colonies. The 1783 Treaty of Paris concluded the conflict and recognized the independence of the thirteen American colonies.

As the crisis with Britain unfolded, the American colonists at first saw themselves as preserving traditional English liberties. As the war went on, however, they developed a different understanding of what liberty meant. By the mid-1770s, they had rejected monarchy and embraced republicanism. After the Constitution was adopted in 1788, a bill of rights was added to protect civil liberties. The colonists rejected the aristocratic social hierarchy that had existed in the colonies in favor of democratic ideals. Although they limited the right to vote, they asserted the equality of white male citizens before the law and in social relations. They rejected social ranking based on birth and inheritance and asserted that all citizens must have the opportunity to improve their social standing and economic lot by engaging in free commercial activity. Although the American Revolution did not free slaves or address the rights of women and Native Americans, it produced a society freer than any the world had yet seen—one in which political and social liberties would continue to increase. The American Revolution was a genuinely radical movement, the influence of which increased as Americans moved across the continent and as other peoples began to question traditional European government. The political and social values of the American Revolution would inspire the wars of independence in Latin America and, to a lesser extent, political movements in Europe.

REVOLUTION IN FRANCE

HOW DID the French Revolution and Napoleon transform France's government and society?

The French monarchy emerged from the Seven Years' War defeated and deeply in debt. Then French support for the American Revolution exacerbated their financial difficulties. Given France's economic vitality, the government debt was not overly large, but the government was unable to collect sufficient taxes to stay solvent.

Between 1786 and 1788, Louis XVI (r. 1774–1792) appointed several different ministers to deal with the financial crisis. All failed to persuade the aristocracy and the church to pay more taxes. As these negotiations dragged on, the *parlement* of Paris declared that only the Estates General could institute new taxes. The Estates General had not met since 1614, but in 1788, Louis XVI agreed to convene it the following year.

REVOLUTIONS OF 1789

Third Estate
The branch of the French Estates General representing all of the kingdom outside the nobility and the clergy.

The Estates General had three divisions: the First Estate of the clergy, the Second Estate of the nobility, and the **Third Estate**, representing everyone else. Before the Estates General met at Versailles in May 1789, there had been much public debate over how its votes should be conducted. The nobility wanted all votes to be taken by estate, which would have allowed the nobles and clergy to outvote the Third Estate. The Third Estate wanted each member to vote individually so that, with its larger membership, it would dominate.

The Third Estate invited the clergy and the nobles to join it in organizing a new legislative body. A few of the lower clergy did so. On June 17 that body declared itself the National Assembly.

Three days later, finding themselves accidentally locked out of their usual meeting place, the National Assembly moved to an indoor tennis court. There, its members took the famous Tennis Court Oath, pledging to continue to sit until they had given France a constitution. Louis XVI ordered the National Assembly to desist, but shortly afterward most of the clergy and many nobles joined the assembly. On June 27 the king capitulated, and the National Assembly reorganized as the National Constituent Assembly, where voting would occur by head rather than by order.

Two new factors soon intruded. First, Louis XVI tried to regain the initiative by mustering troops near Versailles and Paris. The National Constituent Assembly was beginning to demand a constitutional monarchy. Louis refused to consider this proposal and hoped that a show of military force would head off revolution.

The second new factor was the populace of Paris. The mustering of royal troops created anxiety in the city, where already there had been several bread riots. Parisians began organizing a citizen militia. On July 14 a crowd marched to the Bastille, a great fortress that had once held political prisoners, in search of weapons for the militia. Troops in the Bastille fired into the crowd, killing ninety-eight. The crowd then stormed the fortress, released its seven prisoners (none of whom was there for political reasons), and killed several soldiers and the governor. They found no weapons, but the fall of the Bastille signaled that the political future of the nation would not be decided solely by the National Constituent Assembly. Similar disturbances took place in the provincial cities. Soon Louis XVI came to Paris and recognized both the newly elected government of the city and its National Guard.

As disturbances erupted in various cities, the *Great Fear* swept across the French countryside. Peasants rose up to vent their anger at injustices and reclaim rights and property that they had lost during the aristocratic resurgence of the previous quarter century. Châteaux were burned, documents were destroyed, and peasants refused to pay feudal dues. On August 4, 1789, liberal nobles and churchmen in the assembly surrendered their special rights and exemptions, formally relinquishing what they had already lost. Now France's laws applied equally to all citizens.

On August 27, 1789, the assembly issued the *Declaration of the Rights of Man and Citizen*, drawing on the political language of the Enlightenment. It proclaimed that all men were born free and equal with natural rights to liberty, property, and personal safety. Governments existed to protect those rights. All political sovereignty resided in the nation and its representatives. All citizens were equal before the law and equally eligible for public offices. There was to be due process of law, and innocence was to be presumed until proof of guilt. Freedom of religion was affirmed. Taxation was to be apportioned equitably according to capacity to pay. Property rights were declared sacred.

Louis XVI stalled before ratifying either the declaration or the aristocratic renunciation of feudalism. Meanwhile, bread shortages continued. On October 5 several thousand Parisian women marched to Versailles, demanding more bread. This was one of several occasions when women played a major role in the actions of the Parisian

View the **Image**

Oath of the Tennis Court
at **myhistorylab.com**

QUICK REVIEW

National Assembly

♦ June 17, 1789: Third Estate declares itself National Assembly

♦ Tennis Court Oath: Pledge to sit until France had a constitution

♦ June 27, 1789: King capitulates to National Assembly

Women's March. The women of Paris marched to Versailles on October 7, 1789. The following day the royal family was forced to return to Paris with them. Henceforth, the French government would function under the constant threat of mob violence.

Anonymous, eighteenth century, "To Versailles, to Versailles." The Women of Paris going to Versailles, October 7, 1789. French, Musée de la Ville de Paris, Musée Carnavalet, Paris, France. Photograph copyright Bridgeman-Giraudon/Art Resource, New York.

Looking at the individual faces and dresses, what kinds of women seem to be participating in this demonstration?

A Closer Look

Challenging the French Political Order

This late eighteenth-century cartoon satirizes the French social and political structure as the events and tensions leading up to the outbreak of the French Revolution unfolded. This image embodies the highly radical critique of the French political structure that erupted from about 1787, when the nobility and church refused to aid the monarchy in overcoming a financial crisis.

Behind the king ride a Roman Catholic bishop and a noble magistrate. The bishop holds a document associating the clergy with religious persecution and protection of church property. The noble holds a statement championing the powers of the aristocratic *parlements*.

Louis XVI is portrayed as the chief rider of the poor citizen holding a whip and declaring that feudal dues and the rights of the landowners should prevail. This positioning of the king suggests that the cartoon was drawn after the calling of the Estates General when, until the representation of the Third Estate was doubled, Louis was seen as siding with the church and nobility against the people. Prior to then, he had been seen as a paternal protector of the French people.

At the bottom of the heap is a poor, blinded ordinary French citizen in the chains of taxation and feudal obligations. The image suggests that the chains of obligation and the orders of privilege maintaining the chains need to be removed.

Questions

1. This image points to the monarchy, the aristocracy, and established French Roman Catholic Church as political units in conflict with each other. How did they come into conflict? How did their conflicts allow the poor French citizens shown here at the bottom of the heap to come to the fore as agents of social and political change?

2. Does this cartoon illustrate all of the political and social tensions ready to erupt in France at the time of the Revolution? What others emerged? Why did all of

these conflicts then lead to the intervention of foreign powers against the revolution? Why are no foreign powers portrayed in this cartoon?

3. If leaders of the American Revolution had viewed this cartoon and then wanted to draw one of their own, how might theirs have appeared? How might one drawn by the leaders of the Haitian Revolution have appeared? What common forces did all of the revolutions of the day seek to overturn—or were there no common forces?

    To examine this image in an interactive fashion, please go to **www.myhistorylab.com**

crowd. The king agreed to sanction the decrees of the assembly. Then the crowd insisted that Louis and his family return to Paris. On October 6, 1789, the king and his family followed the women back to Paris and settled in the palace of the Tuileries. The assembly joined them. Things then remained relatively quiet until the summer of 1792.

RECONSTRUCTION OF FRANCE

The National Constituent Assembly set about reorganizing France. The assembly was determined to protect property, but limit the political influence of small property owners and those who did not own property. While championing equality before the law, the assembly spurned social equality and extensive democracy. In this it charted a course that nineteenth-century liberals across Europe and in other areas of the world were to follow.

The Constitution of 1791 established a constitutional monarchy. There was a unicameral Legislative Assembly. The monarch could delay, but not halt, legislation. Only about 50,000 male citizens in the French nation of 26 million could actually elect or serve in the Legislative Assembly.

Olympe de Gouges (d. 1793), a butcher's daughter who became a leading radical in Paris, quickly composed a *Declaration of the Rights of Woman* (1793), which she ironically addressed to Queen Marie Antoinette (1755–1793). The document was based on the *Declaration of the Rights of Man and Citizen* with the word "woman" strategically inserted; it called for women to be regarded as citizens and not merely as daughters, sisters, wives, and mothers of citizens. de Gouges further outlined property, marriage, and educational rights for women. These demands illustrated how the public listing of rights in the *Declaration of the Rights of Man and Citizen* created universal civic expectations. (See Document: "Olympe de Gouges Issues a Declaration of the Rights of Woman" on page 564.)

The National Constituent Assembly reorganized provincial administration, instituted uniform courts, simplified legal procedures, and abolished the most degrading punishments. It also suppressed the guilds, removed regulations on the grain trade, and established the metric system of uniform weights and measures. In 1790, it placed the burden of proof and the obligation to pay compensation on peasants who tried to rid themselves of residual feudal dues. In 1791, it forbade worker associations, crushing efforts by urban workers to protect their wages. Peasants and laborers were left to the mercy of the free market.

The National Constituent Assembly decided to pay the troublesome royal debt by confiscating and selling the lands of the Roman Catholic Church in France. The Assembly issued **assignats**, or government bonds, guaranteed by the revenue to be generated from the sale of church property. When the *assignats* began to circulate as currency, the Assembly issued increasing quantities of them, causing their value to fall. Inflation put new stress on the lives of the urban poor.

In July 1790 the Assembly issued the Civil Constitution of the Clergy, transforming the Roman Catholic Church in France into a branch of the state. The measure aroused immense opposition within the French church. The Assembly unwisely demanded that all clergy take an oath to support the Civil Constitution; few did. In reprisal, the Assembly removed those who refused from their clerical functions.

In February 1791 the pope condemned not only the Civil Constitution of the Clergy but also the *Declaration of the Rights of Man and Citizen*. This marked the opening of a Roman Catholic offensive against liberalism in Europe and revolution throughout the world that continued for over a century. Within France itself, many were torn between religious devotion and revolutionary loyalty.

Read the **Document**

Declaration of the Rights of Man and Citizen, 1789 at **myhistorylab.com**

assignats
Government bonds based on the value of confiscated church lands issued during the early French Revolution.

QUICK REVIEW

Constitution of 1791
- Established constitutional monarchy
- Monarch could delay, but not halt, acts of unicameral Legislative Assembly
- Voting limited to 50,000 elite men

DOCUMENT

Olympe de Gouges Issues a Declaration of the Rights of Woman

On August 26, 1789, the National Assembly passed the Declaration of the Rights of Man and Citizen. Its very broad principles could readily be extended beyond the domestic male French citizens to whom it applied. Within months various civically disadvantaged groups stepped forward to demand inclusion within the newly proclaimed realm of civic rights.

In September 1791 Olympe de Gouges published a Declaration of the Rights of Woman, which paralleled in many respects the Declaration of the Rights of Man and Citizen. A self-educated butcher's daughter, she had written widely on a number of reform topics. Radical as she was, she remained loyal to the monarchy and was eventually executed by the revolutionary government in 1793.

- **WHAT** are the specific parallels that de Gouges drew between the rights of man and the rights of woman? How does her declaration suggest civic responsibilities for women as well as rights? How does the language suggest her familiarity with Enlightenment writers?

Mothers, daughters, sisters [and] representatives of the nation demand to be constituted into a national assembly. . . . Consequently, the sex that is as superior in beauty as it is in courage during the sufferings of maternity recognizes and declares in the presence and Woman and of Female Citizens.

ARTICLE I

Woman is born free and lives equal to man in her rights. Social distinctions can be based only on the common utility.

ARTICLE IV

Liberty and justice consist of restoring all that belongs to others; thus, the only limits on the exercise of the natural rights of woman are perpetual male tyranny; these limits are to be reformed by the laws of nature and reason. . . .

ARTICLE VI

The law must be the expression of the general will; all female and male citizens must contribute either personally or through their representatives to its formation; it must be the same for all: male and female citizens, being equal in the eyes of the law, must be equally admitted to all honors, positions, and public employment according to their capacity and without other distinctions besides those of their virtues and talents. . . .

ARTICLE XVII

Property belongs to both sexes whether united or separate; for each it is an inviolable and sacred right; no one can be deprived of it, since it is the true patrimony of nature, unless the legally determined public need obviously dictates it, and then only with a just and prior indemnity.

POSTSCRIPT

Woman, wake up; the tocsin of reason is being heard throughout the whole universe; discover your rights.

Source: As quoted in Darline Gay Levy, Harriet Branson Applewhite, and Mary Durham Johnson, eds., *Women in Revolutionary Paris, 1789–1795* (Urbana: University of Illinois Press, 1980), pp. 87–96.

In the summer of 1791, the queen and some nobles persuaded Louis XVI to flee, but the royal family was caught and returned to Paris. Assembly leaders now saw the king as a counterrevolutionary. On August 27, 1791, Leopold II of Austria (r. 1790–1792), brother of Marie Antoinette, and Frederick William II (r. 1786–1797) of Prussia promised to intervene in France to protect the royal family if the other major European powers agreed that they could do so. The latter provision rendered the declaration meaningless, since Great Britain would not consent. France's revolutionaries, however, became convinced that they were surrounded by monarchical foes.

DOCUMENT

A Free Person of Color from Saint Domingue Demands Recognition of His Status

In the spring of 1791 Julian Raymond, a free person of color from the French Caribbean colony of Saint Domingue (Haiti), petitioned the French National Assembly invoking the Declaration of the rights of Man and Citizen to recognize persons such as himself as free citizens. The National Assembly did so in May 1791, but later rescinded the decree. Only in March 1792 did the Assembly firmly recognize the civic equality of such persons. The background for the request and for the confusion of the French National Assembly over the matter was the eruption of the slave revolution in Haiti.

- **HOW** does Raymond portray himself as free but still victimized by the Assembly in Saint Domingue being composed exclusively of white members? In a slave society such as that on Saint Domingue, how might a person such as Raymond be legally free but still subject to various modes of discrimination? How can he invoke the principles of the Declaration of the Rights of Man and Citizen to apply pressure on the French National Assembly?

Remaining to this day under the oppression of the white colonists, we dare hope that we do not ask the National Assembly in vain for the rights, which it has declared, belong to every man.

In our just protests, if the troubles, the calumnies that you have witnessed until today under the legislation of white colonists, and finally, if the truths which we had the honor of presenting yesterday to the bar of the Assembly do not overcome the unjust pretensions of the white colonial legislators who want to [proceed] without our participation, we beg the Assembly not to jeopardize the little remaining liberty we have, that of being able to abandon the ground soaked with the blood of our brothers and of permitting us to flee the sharp knife of the laws they will prepare against us.

If the Assembly has decided to pass a law which lets our fate depend on twenty-nine whites [in the colonial Assembly], our decided enemies, we demand to add an amendment to the decree which would be rendered in this situation, that free men of color can emigrate with their fortunes so that they can be neither disturbed nor hindered by the whites.

Mr. President, this is the last recourse which remains for us to escape the vengeance of the white colonists who menace us for not having given up our claims to the rights which the National Assembly has declared belong to every man.

Source: As quoted in Laura Mason and Tracey Rizzo, *The French Revolution: A Document Collection* (Boston: Houghton Mifflin Company, 1999), p. 109.

Near its close in September 1791 the National Constituent Assembly forbade any of its own members to sit in the Legislative Assembly then being elected. This new body met on October 1 to confront immense problems.

A SECOND REVOLUTION

Since the earliest days of the revolution, clubs of politically like-minded persons had sprung up in Paris. The best organized were the **Jacobins**, who had links with similar groups in the provinces. On April 20, 1792, the Legislative Assembly, led by a group of Jacobins known as the Girondists (because many came from the department of the Gironde), voted to declare war on Austria, which was allied to Prussia. The war with Austria led to what is usually called the second revolution, which overthrew the constitutional monarchy and established a republic.

The war went badly, and the looming threat radicalized French politics. Late in July, under radical working-class pressure, the government of Paris passed from the elected council to a committee, or commune, of representatives from the municipal wards. On August 10, 1792, a large crowd invaded the Tuileries, forcing Louis XVI and Marie Antoinette to take refuge in the Legislative Assembly. Several hundred

Jacobins
The radical republican party during the French Revolution.

Execution of Louis XVI. On January 21, 1793, the Convention executed Louis XVI.

Execution of Louis XVI. Aquatint. French, eighteenth century. Musée de la Ville de Paris, Musée Carnavalet, Paris, France. Giraudon/Art Resource, New York.

Why would the execution of Louis XVI be held in public?

Convention

French radical legislative body from 1792 to 1794.

sans-culottes

Meaning "without breeches." The lower middle classes and artisans of Paris during the French Revolution.

See the **Map**
Revolutionary France
at **myhistorylab.com**

Reign of Terror

The period between the summer of 1793 and the end of July 1794 when the French revolutionary state used extensive executions and violence to defend the Revolution and suppress its alleged internal enemies.

levée en masse

The French revolutionary conscription (1793) of all males into the army and the harnessing of the economy for war production.

of the royal guards and many Parisians were killed, the royal family was imprisoned, and the king's political functions were suspended.

The Paris Commune compelled the Legislative Assembly to call for the election, by universal manhood suffrage, of a new assembly to write a democratic constitution. That body, called the **Convention** after its American counterpart of 1787, met on September 21, 1792. The Convention declared France a republic.

The second revolution had been the work of Jacobins more radical than the Girondists, and of the people of Paris known as the *sans-culottes*, meaning "without breeches." (Working men wore long trousers instead of the knee breeches favored by aristocratic courtiers.) The *sans-culottes* were shopkeepers, artisans, wage earners, and a few factory workers. The politics of the Old Regime had ignored them, and the policies of the National Constituent Assembly had not protected them from an unregulated free-market economy.

The *sans-culottes*, whose labor and military service were needed for the war effort, generally knew what they wanted, beginning with price controls for food. They resented most forms of social inequality and were hostile to the aristocracy and the original leaders of the revolution. They advocated a community of small property owners. They were antimonarchical, republican, and suspicious of government. The Jacobins, by contrast, were republicans who favored representative government and an unregulated economy. However, once the Convention began its deliberations, the more extreme Jacobins, known as the Mountain because of their seats high in the assembly hall, worked with the *sans-culottes* to pass revolutionary reforms and win the war.

In December 1792, Louis XVI was put on trial and convicted of conspiring against the state. He was beheaded on January 21, 1793. The killing of a king shocked Europe, and France found itself isolated and at war with virtually everyone. Civil war broke out as well. In March 1793, aristocratic officers and priests raised a royalist revolt in western France and won local popular support.

THE REIGN OF TERROR AND ITS AFTERMATH

The **Reign of Terror** is the name given to the months of quasi-judicial executions and murders stretching from the autumn of 1793 to the midsummer of 1794. The Terror can be understood only in the context of the internal and external wars, on the one hand, and the revolutionary expectations of the Convention and the *sans-culottes*, on the other.

In April 1793, the Convention established a Committee of Public Safety charged with saving the revolution from enemies at home and abroad. It eventually assumed quasi-dictatorial power and generally enjoyed a working political relationship with the *sans-culottes* of Paris.

In June 1793, the Parisian *sans-culottes* invaded the Convention, drove out the Girondists, and gave the Mountain complete control. On August 23 the Convention decreed a **levée en masse**, or general military requisition of population. It conscripted males into the army and mobilized economic production for military purposes. On September 29, price controls were imposed in accordance with the *sans-culottes*' demands. During these same months, the armies of the revolution crushed many of the counterrevolutionary disturbances in the provinces.

Revolutionary women established their own institutions. In May 1793 Pauline Léon and Claire Lacombe founded the Society of Revolutionary Republican Women. Its members sought stricter price controls and worked to ferret out food hoarders. The women demanded the right to wear the revolutionary cap that male citizens had adopted. By October 1793, the Jacobins in the Convention had begun to fear the turmoil the increasingly radical society was causing, and it banned all women's clubs and societies. Other women's political activities were repressed, too. When Olympe de Gouges spoke out against the Terror, she was tried and guillotined in November 1793. Women were excluded from the French army and from entering the galleries to watch the debates of the Convention.

The pressures of war made it relatively easy to dispense with legal due process. But the Convention and the Committee of Public Safety felt morally justified, for they saw themselves as creating something new in history: a republic devoted to eradicating aristocratic and monarchical corruption and promoting civic virtue. Marie Antoinette, other members of the royal family, and many aristocrats were executed in October 1793. They were followed by Girondist politicians. By early 1794, the Terror had moved to the provinces, where thousands were executed.

The "republic of virtue" attempted to dechristianize France. In the autumn of 1793 the Convention proclaimed a new calendar dating from the first day of the French Republic. There were twelve months of thirty days with names associated with the seasons and climate. The Cathedral of Notre Dame was renamed the Temple of Reason. The legislature enforced dechristianization in the provinces by closing churches and persecuting clergy and believers. Dechristianization roused much opposition and alienated the provinces from the revolutionary government in Paris.

During late 1793 and early 1794, Maximilien Robespierre (1758–1794) emerged as the chief figure on the Committee of Public Safety. The Jacobin Club provided his base of power, and he had the support of the *sans-culottes* of Paris. He considered dechristianization a political blunder and concluded that the worship of reason was too abstract for most citizens. In May 1794, at the height of his power, he inaugurated the Cult of the Supreme Being. But he did not preside over this new religion for long: On July 27 his opponents staged a coup, and Robespierre was executed the next day.

The Reign of Terror soon ended, having claimed as many as 40,000 victims. Most were peasants and *sans-culottes*. The tempering of the revolution, a phase called the **Thermidorian Reaction**, began in July 1794 with the establishment of a new constitutional regime. Wealthy middle-class and professional people gained influence. By late summer, provincial uprisings had been crushed, and the war against foreign enemies was going well. Many of the people responsible for the Terror were removed from public life, and the Jacobin Club of Paris was closed.

The Thermidorian Constitution of the Year III was a conservative document that provided for bicameral legislative government dedicated to protecting the rights of property owners. Its executive branch was a five-person Directory elected by the upper legislative house.

By the Treaty of Basel of March 1795, the Convention concluded peace with Prussia and Spain. With the war effort succeeding, the Convention severed its ties with the *san-sculottes*. Price ceilings were repealed. Rising prices led to food riots during

QUICK REVIEW

The Terror

◆ Began with creation of revolutionary tribunals in summer of 1793

◆ Executions spread from Paris to the provinces

◆ Reign of Terror claimed about 40,000 victims

Revolutionary Calendar. To symbolize the beginning of a new era in human history, French revolutionary legislators established a new calendar. This calendar for Year Two (1794) proclaims the indivisible unity of the revolution and the goals of Liberty, Equality, and Fraternity.

How would the creation of a new calendar further the aims of a revolutionary regime?

Thermidorian Reaction
The reaction against the radicalism of the French Revolution that began in July 1794. Associated with the end of Terror and establishment of the Directory.

••◆–⌐Read the Document
Maximilien Robespierre "Speech to National Convention: The Terror Justified" at **myhistorylab.com**

CHRONOLOGY

THE FRENCH REVOLUTION

1789	May 5	Estates General opens at Versailles
	June 17	Third Estate declares itself the National Assembly
	June 20	National Assembly takes the Tennis Court Oath
	July 14	Fall of the Bastille
	August 4	Nobles surrender their feudal rights in a meeting of the National Constituent Assembly
	August 26	*Declaration of the Rights of Man and Citizen*
	October 5–6	Parisian women march to Versailles and force Louis XVI and his family to return to Paris
1790	July 12–14	Civil Constitution of the Clergy adopted and accepted by the king
1791	June 20–24	Louis XVI and his family attempt to flee France and are stopped
1792	April 20	France declares war on Austria
	August 10	Tuileries palace stormed, and Louis XVI takes refuge in the Legislative Assembly
	September	September Massacres; monarchy abolished
1793	January 21	Louis XVI executed
	February 1	France declares war on Great Britain
	March	Counterrevolution breaks out in the Vendée
	April 6	Committee of Public Safety formed
	July	Robespierre enters Committee of Public Safety
	August 23	*Levée en masse* proclaimed
	November 10	Cult of Reason proclaimed; revolutionary calendar beginning in September
1794	May 7	Cult of the Supreme Being proclaimed
	June 8	Robespierre leads the celebration of Festival of the Supreme Being
	July 28	Robespierre executed
1795	August 22	Constitution of the Year III adopted, establishing the Directory

the winter of 1794–1795, but the Convention suppressed them. On October 5, 1795, when a Paris mob rioted, a general named Napoleon Bonaparte (1769–1821) commanded the cannon and with what he termed a "whiff of grapeshot" dispersed the crowd.

THE NAPOLEONIC ERA

Napoleon Bonaparte was born in 1769 to a poor noble family in Corsica. Because France had annexed Corsica in 1768, he was able to obtain a commission as a French artillery officer. At the start of his career, he was a fiery Jacobin. In 1793, he played a leading role in recovering the port of Toulon from the British. This won him promotion to the rank of brigadier general, and his defense of the Directory in 1794 won him a command in Italy. By October 1797, he had crushed the Austrians and concluded the Treaty of Campo Formio, which took Austria out of the war and left France dominant over Italy and Switzerland.

((•—[Hear the Audio
Napoleon 1
at **myhistorylab.com**

In November 1797, the triumphant Bonaparte returned to Paris to confront France's only remaining enemy, Britain. Judging it impossible to invade England, he decided to try to capture Egypt from the Ottoman Empire and cut off Britain's communication with India. However, Admiral Horatio Nelson (1758–1805) destroyed the French fleet and stranded the French army in Egypt. The Russians, Austrians, and Ottomans then joined Britain to form the Second Coalition, and in 1799, the Russian and Austrian armies defeated the French in Italy and Switzerland and threatened to invade France.

Bonaparte abandoned his men in Egypt and returned to France. On November 10, 1799, he overthrew the Directory, and in December 1799, he issued the Constitution of the Year VII and gave himself the title First Consul. The constitution was approved in a rigged election, and a government called the **Consulate** brought the revolution to an end.

Bonaparte quickly won peace for France. Russia had already left the Second Coalition, and in 1800, a French victory at Marengo in Italy took Austria out of the war. In 1802, Britain concluded the Treaty of Amiens, and all of Europe was at peace—at least temporarily.

Bonaparte also restored peace and order at home. He used generosity, flattery, and bribery to win over some of his enemies, issued a general amnesty, and employed persons from all political factions. Bonaparte was also ruthless and efficient in suppressing political opposition. He established a highly centralized administration, employed secret police, and stamped out royalist rebellion.

Napoleon placated French Catholics who had been angered by revolutionary attacks on religion. In 1801, he concluded a concordat with Pope Pius VII (r. 1800–1823). All clergy were forced to resign. Their replacements received spiritual investiture from the pope, but the state named the bishops and paid their salaries and the salary of one priest in each parish. In return, the church gave up claims to its confiscated property, the clergy swore oaths of loyalty to the state, and the Organic Articles of 1802 established the supremacy of the state over the church. Similar laws applied to Protestant and Jewish religious organizations, reducing still further the privileged position of the Catholic Church.

An 1802 plebiscite ratified Bonaparte's appointment as consul for life. He set about transforming the basic laws and institutions of France on the basis of both liberal principles derived from the Enlightenment and the revolution, and conservative principles going back to the Old Regime and the spirit that had triumphed at Thermidor. This was especially true of the Civil Code of 1804, usually called the Napoleonic Code. It stopped far short of the full equality advocated by liberal rationalists. Fathers were granted extensive control over their children and men over their wives. Labor unions were forbidden, and the rights of workers were subordinated to those of employers.

In 1804, Bonaparte used the fear created by a failed assassination attempt to strengthen his hold on power. A plebiscite ratified another new constitution, which designated Napoleon Emperor of the French. Napoleon summoned the pope to Notre Dame to take part in the coronation, though Napoleon crowned himself; the emperor did not want anyone to think that his authority depended on the approval of the church. Henceforth he was called Napoleon I.

Between his coronation as emperor and his final defeat at Waterloo (1815), Napoleon conquered most of Europe in military campaigns that astonished the world (see Map 22-1 on page 571). France's victories changed the map of Europe, ended the Old Regime and its feudal trappings in western Europe, and forced the eastern European states to reorganize. Everywhere, Napoleon's advance unleashed the passions of nationalism.

Read the **Document**

Madame de Remusat on the Rise of Napoleon at **myhistorylab.com**

Consulate
French government dominated by Napoleon from 1799 to 1804.

Napoleon. In December 1799 Napoleon seized power and established himself as First Consul. The title of "Consul" came from the ancient Roman Republic; by 1894 Napoleon would assume the title of "Emperor" as the French Republic gave way to the Napoleonic Empire. The simplicity of this modest military dress as First Consul also gave way to flowing imperial robes.

What was the significance of a title derived from ancient Rome?

See the **Map**
Napoleon's Empire in 1812 at **myhistorylab.com**

William Pitt and Napoleon. In this early nineteenth-century cartoon, England, personified by a caricature of Prime Minister William Pitt, and France, personified by a caricature of Napoleon, are carving out their areas of interest around the globe.

How did Napoleon achieve such great military success in Europe?

Napoleon's military interventions led Britain to issue an ultimatum to him and finally, in May 1803, to declare war. Britain persuaded Russia and Austria once again to try to block France's expansion. On October 21, 1805, Britain scored a major victory. Lord Nelson destroyed the French and Spanish fleets at the battle of Trafalgar just off the Spanish coast. Nelson was killed, but his victory guaranteed Britain control of the sea.

On land, between October 1805 and July 1807, Napoleon defeated the armies of Austria, Prussia, and Russia. He forced Austria to withdraw from northern Italy. He replaced the Holy Roman Empire with the Confederation of the Rhine. Prussia and Russia were compelled to become his allies.

Napoleon could not be secure, however, until he had defeated Britain. He tried to cut off British trade with Europe, hoping to cripple British commercial and financial power and drive the British from the war. This strategy, called the Continental System, harmed the European economies and roused opposition to Napoleon. The British economy survived because of its access to the Americas and the eastern Mediterranean.

In 1807, a French army invaded the Iberian Peninsula to force Portugal to abandon its alliance with Britain. When a revolt broke out in Madrid in 1808, Napoleon deposed the Spanish Bourbons and placed his brother Joseph (1768–1844) on the Spanish throne. Attacks on the privileges of the church increased public outrage. Napoleon's Spanish opponents launched a guerrilla war, and the British supported them by sending an army under Sir Arthur Wellesley (1769–1852), later the Duke of Wellington. This began a long campaign that played a critical role in Napoleon's ultimate defeat.

Encouraged by the French troubles in Spain, the Austrians renewed the war in 1809. They were swiftly defeated, and Austria lost much territory and 3.5 million subjects. Napoleon married the Archduchess Marie Louise (1791–1847), Francis I's 18-year-old daughter, after divorcing his wife Josephine de Beauharnais (1763–1814), with whom he had not produced children.

The Franco-Russian alliance began to falter. The Continental System had harmed the Russian economy, and Napoleon's establishment of a Polish state, the Grand Duchy of Warsaw, on Russia's doorstep angered Tsar Alexander I (r. 1800–1825). Napoleon's annexation of Holland and his marriage to an Austrian princess further disturbed the tsar. In 1810 Russia withdrew from the Continental System and began to prepare for war.

Francisco de Goya, *The Third of May, 1808*, 1814–1815. Napoleon sent troops into Spain in 1807 after the king of Spain had agreed to aid France against Portugal, which was assisting Britain. By early 1808 Spain had essentially become an occupied nation. On May 2 riots took place in Madrid between French troops and Spanish civilians. In response to the riots, the French marshall Joachim Murat ordered numerous executions, especially of artisans and clergy, during the night of May 2 and 3.

Francisco de Goya, "Los fusilamientos del 3 de Mayo, 1808," 1814. Oil on canvas, 8′6″ × 11′4″. © Museo Nacional Del Prado, Madrid.

What is the mood of this painting, and with whom does Goya seem to sympathize?

To stifle the Russian military threat, Napoleon amassed a so-called Grand Army of more than 600,000 men and invaded the country. Russia's generals decided to oppose him by retreating before his advance and stripping the countryside of supplies. Russia was too vast for Napoleon to maintain supply lines, and his men could not live off the devastated land. Terrible rains, fierce heat, shortages of food and water, and the courage of the Russian rear guard eroded the morale of Napoleon's army.

MAP 22–1. Napoleonic Europe in late 1812. By mid-1812 the areas shown in peach were incorporated into France, and most of the rest of Europe was directly controlled by or allied with Napoleon. But Russia had withdrawn from the failing Continental System, and the decline of Napoleon was about to begin.

Why did certain regions mount more concentrated resistance to Napoleon's troops?

In September 1812 at Borodino, west of Moscow, the bloodiest battle of the Napoleonic era cost the French 30,000 casualties and the Russians almost twice as many. Yet the Russian army was not destroyed, and Napoleon had won nothing substantial. By October, after occupying Moscow, the Grand Army was forced to retreat. By December Napoleon realized that the Russian fiasco would encourage plots against him at home, so he returned to Paris, leaving the remnants of his army to struggle westward. Perhaps only 100,000 lived to tell the tale. Even as the news of the disaster reached the West, the total defeat of Napoleon was far from certain. He was able to suppress his opponents in Paris and raise another 350,000 men.

In 1813, patriotic pressure and national ambition brought together the last and most powerful coalition against Napoleon. With British financing, the Russians drove westward to be joined by Prussia and Austria. From the west, Wellington marched his peninsular army into France. Napoleon waged a skillful campaign but met decisive defeat in October at Leipzig. At the end of March 1814, the allied army marched into Paris. Napoleon abdicated and went into exile on the island of Elba off the coast of Italy.

⟐ Read the Document

Napoleon's Exile to Saint Helena (1815)
at **myhistorylab.com**

THE CONGRESS OF VIENNA AND THE EUROPEAN SETTLEMENT

Once Napoleon was gone, the allies began to pursue their separate ambitions. Even before the victorious allied armies entered Paris, Britain had negotiated the Treaty of Chaumont (March 9, 1814). It restored the Bourbons to the French throne and returned France to its 1792 frontiers. Remaining problems were left for a conference at Vienna.

The Congress of Vienna met from September 1814 until November 1815. The victors agreed that no single state should be allowed to dominate Europe. They constructed a series of states to prevent French expansion (see Map 22–2). They established the kingdom of the Netherlands in the north and added Genoa to Piedmont in the south. Prussia was given new territories in the west; Austria obtained control of

MAP EXPLORATION

To explore this map further, go to **http://www.myhistorylab.com**

MAP 22–2. **Europe 1815, after the Congress of Vienna.** The Congress of Vienna achieved the post-Napoleonic territorial adjustments shown on the map. The most notable arrangements dealt with areas along France's borders (the Netherlands, Prussia, Switzerland, and Piedmont) and in Poland and northern Italy.

Why did the Congress of Vienna seek to place strong states on the borders of France?

CHRONOLOGY

NAPOLEONIC EUROPE

1797	Napoleon concludes Treaty of Campo Formio
1798	Nelson defeats French navy at Aboukir
1799	Consulate established
1801	Concordat between France and papacy
1802	Treaty of Amiens
1803	War renewed between France and Britain
1804	Execution of Duke of Enghien; Napoleonic Civil Code issued; Napoleon crowned emperor
1805	Nelson defeats French fleet at Trafalgar (October 21); Austerlitz (December 2)
1806	Continental System established by Berlin Decrees
1807	Treaty of Tilsit
1808	Beginning of Spanish resistance to Napoleonic domination
1809	Wagram; Napoleon marries Archduchess Marie Louise of Austria
1812	Invasion of Russia
1813	Leipzig (Battle of the Nations)
1814	Treaty of Chaumont (March) establishes Quadruple Alliance; Congress of Vienna convenes (September)
1815	Napoleon returns from Elba (March 1); Waterloo (June 18); Holy Alliance formed (September 26); Quadruple Alliance renewed (November 20)
1821	Napoleon dies on Saint Helena

northern Italy. Most of Napoleon's arrangements in the rest of Germany were left untouched, and the Holy Roman Empire was not revived. The Congress established the rule of legitimate monarchs and rejected any compromise with the republican and democratic politics that had flowed from the French Revolution.

However, the settlement of eastern Europe sharply divided the victors. Alexander I wanted Russia to govern all of Poland. Prussia wanted all of Saxony. Austria, however, refused to allow Prussia's power to grow or Russia to expand. The Polish-Saxon question gave France a chance to regain influence in international affairs. French Foreign Minister Talleyrand (1754–1838) negotiated a secret treaty with Britain and Austria. When the news leaked out, the tsar agreed to accept jurisdiction over a smaller Poland, and Frederick William III of Prussia (r. 1797–1840) agreed to settle for part of Saxony. Thereafter, France was included as a fifth great power in the deliberations.

Napoleon's escape from Elba on March 1, 1815, unified the victors. Although Napoleon promised a liberal constitution and a peaceful foreign policy, the allies declared him an outlaw (a new device under international law). Wellington and the Prussians defeated Napoleon at Waterloo in Belgium on June 18, 1815. Napoleon was exiled to Saint Helena, a tiny island off the coast of Africa, where he died in 1821.

The Hundred Days, as the period of Napoleon's return is called, made the peace settlement somewhat harsher for France, but the main outlines of the Vienna Settlement remained in place. The Quadruple Alliance between England, Austria, Prussia, and Russia was renewed on November 20, 1815. Its operation represented an important departure in European affairs. The statesmen at Vienna had seen the armies of the French Revolution change borders and overturn the political and social order of the continent. They were determined to prevent a recurrence of those upheavals. Their purpose was not to punish France but to establish a framework for future stability. The great powers, through the Vienna settlement, agreed to work together to defend the status quo.

See the **Map**

Europe after the Congress of Vienna, 1815
at **myhistorylab.com**

The Congress of Vienna produced a long-lasting peace. Its work has been criticized for failing to recognize and provide for the great movements that would stir the nineteenth century—nationalism and democracy—but such criticism is unrealistic. The settlement, like all such agreements, was aimed at solving past ills, and in that it succeeded. It spared Europe a general war until 1914.

WARS OF INDEPENDENCE IN LATIN AMERICA

WHY WAS the Haitian Revolution significant to world history?

The French Revolution and the Napoleonic Wars inspired movements for independence throughout Latin America. France was driven from Haiti, Portugal from Brazil, and Spain from all its American empire except Cuba and Puerto Rico.

REVOLUTION IN HAITI

Between 1791 and 1804, the French colony of Haiti (Saint Domingue) achieved independence. This event was of key importance for two reasons. First, it was sparked by policies of the French Revolution overflowing into its New World Empire. Second, the Haitian Revolution demonstrated that slaves of African origins could lead a successful revolt against white masters and mulatto freemen. For years thereafter, the example of the Haitian Revolution terrified slaveholders throughout the Americas.

The slave–master relationship had been particularly violent in eighteenth-century Haiti. French colonists had exploited racial divisions between black slaves and mulatto freemen to their own political advantage. Once the French Revolution had broken out in France, the French National Assembly decreed in the spring of 1791 that free property owners of all races were entitled to the same rights as white plantation owners. Haiti's Colonial Assembly resisted. (See Document: "A Free Person of Color from Saint Domingue Demands Recognition of His Status," on page 565.)

In August 1791, a slave conspiracy erupted into a full-fledged slave rebellion. François-Dominique Toussaint L'Ouverture (1743?–1803), himself a former slave, quickly emerged as its leader. The rebellion involved enormous violence and loss of life on both sides. When this rebellion collapsed, mulattos and free blacks took up arms against

Toussaint L'Ouverture. L'Ouverture (1744–1803) began the revolt that led to Haitian independence in 1804.

Why did the Haitian Revolution have such repercussions throughout the Atlantic world?

MAP 22–3. The Haitian Revolution.

What does the expansion of Haitian territory during and after the revolution suggest about the revolutionaries' power?

the white colonial masters to gain the rights the French National Assembly had promised. The revolutionary government in Paris sent officials to support the rebels, and slaves soon came to the aid of an invading French force. In early 1793, the French abolished slavery in Haiti.

Spain and Great Britain each separately attempted to intervene in Haiti. Both were opposed to the end of slavery, and both coveted Haiti's rich sugar-producing lands. Toussaint L'Ouverture and his force of ex-slaves again supported the French against the Spanish and the British. By 1800, his army had achieved dominance throughout the island of Hispaniola. He imposed an authoritarian constitution on Haiti and made himself governor-general for life, but he preserved formal ties with France.

The French government under Napoleon distrusted L'Ouverture and feared his example would undermine French authority elsewhere. In 1802, Napoleon sent an army to Haiti to capture L'Ouverture, who spent the remainder of his life imprisoned in France. Other Haitian military leaders of slave origin, the most important of whom was Jean-Jacques Dessalines (1758–1806), continued to resist. When Napoleon found himself again at war with Britain in 1803, he abandoned his American empire, selling Louisiana to the United States and withdrawing his forces from Haiti. Haiti declared independence in 1804.

Thus, the Haitian slave-led rebellion became the first successful assault on colonial government in Latin America. Haiti's experience also foreshadowed a less fortunate trend in decolonization: The break with the colonial power was not clean. In Haiti's case, France required exorbitant reparations payments before formally recognizing Haitian independence in 1825. The reparations were later reduced, but they crippled Haiti's economy for decades and are cited as factors in laying the groundwork for the once-wealthy nation's current poverty.

EIGHTEENTH-CENTURY DEVELOPMENTS IN THE SPANISH EMPIRE

After Spain's defeat in the Seven Years' War in 1763, its king, Charles III (r. 1759–1788), decided that the American colonial system had to be changed. He abolished the monopolies of Seville and Cádiz, opened more South American and Caribbean ports to trade, and authorized direct trade between American ports. In 1776, he organized a fourth viceroyalty that encompassed much of present-day Argentina, Uruguay, Paraguay, and Bolivia. Charles III also tried to make tax collection more efficient and to eliminate bureaucratic corruption by appointing *intendents*, bureaucrats loyal only to the crown.

These reforms returned the empire to direct Spanish control. Many *peninsulares* (whites born in Spain) went to the New World to fill newly created posts, depriving **Creoles** (whites born in America) of opportunity. Expanding trade brought more Spanish merchants to Latin America, where economic activity continued to be organized for the benefit of Spain.

FIRST MOVEMENTS TOWARD INDEPENDENCE ON THE SOUTH AMERICAN CONTINENT

Generally speaking, on the South American continent it was the Creole elite—merchants, landowners, and professional people—who led the movements against Spain and Portugal. Few Indians, blacks, mestizos, mulattos, or slaves were involved or benefited from the end of Iberian rule. Indeed, the Haitian slave revolt haunted the Creoles, as did an Indian revolt in the Andes in 1780–1781. The Creoles were

View the **Image**
Slave Revolt in Saint Domingue, 1791 at **myhistorylab.com**

peninsulares
Native-born Spaniards who emigrated from Spain to settle in the Spanish colonies.

Creoles
Persons of European descent who were born in the Spanish colonies.

determined that political independence from Spain and Portugal should not result in the loss of their social and economic privileges. Creole complaints resembled those of the American colonists against Great Britain: Latin American merchants wanted to trade more freely, and they wanted commercial regulations that would benefit them rather than Spain. They deeply resented Spanish policies favoring *peninsulares*, and believed the royal patronage system was another device by which Spain extracted wealth and income from America for its own people rather than its colonial subjects.

From the 1790s onward, Spain suffered military reverses in the wars associated with the French Revolution and Napoleon, and the commercial situation turned sharply against the inhabitants of the Spanish Empire. The military pressures led the Spanish monarchy into a desperate search for new revenues, including increased taxation and the confiscation of property in the American empire. The policies harmed the economic life of the Creole elite.

Creole leaders had read the Enlightenment *philosophes* and believed that the political reforms the *philosophes* championed would benefit their region. They were also well aware of the political arguments that had justified the American Revolution. The event that crystallized Creole discontent into revolt against Spain was Napoleon's overthow of the Portuguese monarchy in 1807 and the Spanish government in 1808. The Portuguese royal family fled to Brazil, but the Bourbon monarchy of Spain seemed vanquished. The Creole elite feared that a monarchy headed by Napoleon's brother in Spain would harm their economic and social interests and would drain the region of resources for Napoleon's wars. Creole juntas, or political committees, formed between 1808 and 1810 and claimed the right to govern regions of Latin America. Ten years of warfare ensued before Spain conceded Latin American independence.

View the Image

The Great Liberator, Independence Leader, Caudillo, and Future President Simón Bolívar at **myhistorylab.com**

SAN MARTÍN IN RÍO DE LA PLATA

The first region to assert its independence was the Río de la Plata (modern Argentina). In 1810, the junta in Buenos Aires thrust off Spanish authority and sent soldiers to liberate Paraguay and Uruguay. They were defeated, but Paraguay asserted its own independence, and Brazil absorbed Uruguay.

The Buenos Aires government then attempted to liberate Peru, the greatest remaining stronghold of royalist power on the continent (see Map 22–4). In 1814, José de San Martin (1778–1850) led an army over the Andes Mountains. By early 1817, he had occupied Santiago in Chile and established Bernardo O'Higgins (1778–1842) as supreme dictator. In 1821, he drove royalist forces from Lima and assumed the title of Protector of Peru.

SIMÓN BOLÍVAR'S LIBERATION OF VENEZUELA

While San Martín liberated the southern portion of the continent, Simón Bolívar (1783–1830) pursued a similar task in the north. A firm advocate of independence and republicanism, Bolívar had helped organize a liberating junta in Caracas, Venezuela, in 1810. Between 1811 and 1814, civil war broke out as royalists, slaves, and cowboys challenged his republican government and drove him into exile. In 1819, with help from Haiti, he captured Bogotá, capital of New Granada (modern Colombia, Bolivia, and Ecuador) and established a base for attacking Venezuela. In 1821, his forces captured Caracas, and he was named president.

Simón Bolívar. Bolívar was the liberator of much of Latin America. He inclined toward a policy of political liberalism.

What were the policy differences between Bolívar and San Martin?

MAP 22-4.   The Independence Campaigns of San Martín and Bolívar. José de San Martín and Simón Bolívar fought for independence in different parts of South America in the early 1800s. In 1822 they collaborated to liberate Quito, but they disagreed over post-independence political structures: San Martín was a monarchist, while Bolívar was a republican.

How do the wars for independence in Latin America compare with the colonists' revolt against British rule in North America?

In July 1822, the armies of Bolívar and San Martín liberated the city of Quito, but the two leaders disagreed about the future political structure of Latin America. San Martín believed in monarchies; Bolívar favored republics. Shortly thereafter, San Martín retired from public life and moved to Europe. In 1823, Bolívar sent troops into Peru and on December 9, 1824, at the battle of Ayacucho, defeated the Spanish royalist forces. The battle marked the conclusion of Spain's effort to retain its American empire.

Read the **Document**

Simon de Bolívar, "Address to Second National Congress" (Venezuela), 1819 at **myhistorylab.com**

INDEPENDENCE IN NEW SPAIN

The drive for independence in New Spain (modern Mexico, Texas, California, and the rest of the southwestern United States) illustrates how socially conservative the Latin American colonial revolutions were. As elsewhere, a local governing junta was organized. But before it had time to act, a Creole priest, Miguel Hidalgo y Costilla (1753–1811), incited the Indians of his parish to rebel. They and other repressed groups responded to Father Hidalgo's call for social reform, and he soon had 80,000 followers. But in July 1811, he was captured and executed. Leadership of his movement then passed to José María Morelos y Pavón (1765–1815), a more radical mestizo priest. In 1815, he too was captured and executed.

In 1820, a revolution in Spain forced Ferdinand VII (r. 1813–1833) to accept a liberal constitution, and conservative Mexicans feared that a liberal Spanish monarchy

Read the **Document**

Jose Morelos, Sentiments of the Nation (Mexico), 1813, at **myhistorylab.com** would try to impose liberal reforms on Mexico. Therefore, for the most conservative of reasons, they declared Mexico independent under a government determined to resist social reform.

Great Britain was highly sympathetic to the Latin American independence movements, since they opened the markets of the continent to British trade and investment. In 1823, Great Britain supported the American Monroe Doctrine that prohibited further colonization and intervention by European powers in America, and Britain quickly recognized the Spanish colonies as independent states. Through the rest of the century, British commercial interests dominated Latin America.

BRAZILIAN INDEPENDENCE

Brazilian independence came relatively peacefully. The arrival of the Portuguese royal family and several thousand officials in 1807 (as noted previously) transformed Rio de Janeiro into a court city. The prince regent Joao (r. 1816–1826) in 1815 declared Brazil a kingdom and no longer merely a colony of Portugal. In 1820, a revolution took place

CHRONOLOGY

THE WARS OF LATIN AMERICAN INDEPENDENCE

1759–1788		Charles III of Spain carries out imperial reforms
1776		Organization of Viceroyalty of Río de la Plata
1780–1781		Revolt of Indians in the Andes
1794		Toussaint L'Ouverture leads slave revolt in Haiti
1804		Independence of Haiti
1807		Portuguese royal family flees to Brazil
1808		Spanish monarchy falls to Napoleon
1808–1810		Creole Committees organized to govern much of Latin America
1810		Buenos Aires junta sends forces to liberate Paraguay and Uruguay
1811		Miguel Hidalgo y Costilla leads rebellion in New Spain and is executed
1811–1815		José María Morelos y Pavón leads rebellion in New Spain and is executed
1814		San Martín organizes army
1815		Brazil declared a kingdom
1816		Bolívar invades Venezuela
1817		San Martín occupies Santiago, Chile
1820		Revolution in Spain
1821	February 24	New Spain declares independence
	June 29	Bolívar captures Caracas, Venezuela
	July 28	San Martín liberates Peru
1822	July 26–27	San Martín and Bolívar quarrel at Guayaquil; San Martín goes into exile in Europe
	September 7	Dom Pedro declares Brazilian independence
1824		Battle of Ayacucho—final Spanish defeat

in Portugal, and its leaders offered the throne to Joao and demanded the return of Brazil to colonial status. Joao, who had become Joao VI in 1816, returned to Portugal and left his son Pedro (r. 1822–1831) as regent in Brazil. In 1822, Pedro asserted Brazil's independence and became emperor of Brazil. The country remained a monarchy until 1889.

The determination of Brazil's political and social elite to preserve slavery aided the peaceful transition. The wars of independence elsewhere had led to the abolition of slavery or moved the independent states closer to abolition. Any attempt to gain independence from Portugal through warfare might have caused social as well as political turmoil that would open the slavery question.

TOWARD THE ABOLITION OF SLAVERY IN THE TRANSATLANTIC ECONOMY

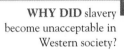

WHY DID slavery become unacceptable in Western society?

In 1750, few questioned the institution of slavery; by 1888 slavery no longer existed in the transatlantic economy. This vast transformation of economic and social life occurred as the result of an international effort, first to abolish the slave trade and then to abolish slavery itself. No previous society in world history had attempted to abolish slavery. Its elimination in the transatlantic world is one of the most significant achievements of the eighteenth-century Enlightenment and revolutions.

The eighteenth-century crusade against slavery originated among writers of the Enlightenment and religious critics. Although some *philosophes*, including John Locke, were reluctant to question slavery and even defended it, the general Enlightenment rhetoric of equality stood in sharp contrast to the radical inequality of slavery. Montesquieu satirized slavery in *The Spirit of the Laws*. Adam Smith's emphasis in *The Wealth of Nations* on free labor and the efficiency of free markets undermined economic defenses of slavery. Much eighteenth-century literature idealized primitive peoples as embodying a lost human virtue. Slavery, once considered the natural and deserved result of some deficiency in slaves themselves, grew to be regarded as an unmitigated evil. Other Enlightenment ethical thinking led reformers to believe that by working against slavery, they would realize their own highest moral character.

Religious protest against slavery originated among English Quakers, a radical Protestant group founded by George Fox in the seventeenth century. Some early Quakers owned slaves in the West Indies and participated in the transatlantic slave trade. During the Seven Years' War (1756–1763), however, many Quakers experienced economic hardship and other difficulties. Certain Quakers decided that the presence of the evil of slavery explained these troubles. They took action against the whole system of slavery that characterized the transatlantic economy.

Just as the slave system was a transatlantic affair, so was the crusade against it. During the American Revolution small groups of reformers, usually spearheaded by Quakers in Philadelphia and elsewhere, had established an antislavery network. Emancipation gradually spread among the northern states. In 1787 the Continental Congress forbade slavery in the newly organized Northwest Territory north of the Ohio River.

Despite these American developments, Great Britain was the center for the antislavery movement. During the early 1780s, reformers there decided to work toward ending the slave trade rather than the institution of slavery itself. The horrors of the slave trade caught the public's attention in 1783 when the captain of the slave ship *Zong* threw more than 130 slaves overboard in order to collect insurance. Soon after, groups from the Church of England and the English Quakers formed the Society for the Abolition of the Slave Trade. The most famous of the new leaders was William Wilberforce, who, each year for the rest of his life, introduced a bill to end the slave

Spanish Slave Ship. After 1807 the British Royal Navy patrolled the West African coast attempting to intercept slave-trading ships. In 1846 the British ship HMS *Albatross* captured a Spanish slave ship, the *Albanoz*, and freed the slaves. A British officer depicted the appalling conditions in the slavehold in this watercolor.

Why did British reformers focus first on abolishing the slave trade, not slavery itself?

trade. For many, the slave trade seemed worse than the holding of slaves, and attacking slavery raised complicating issues of property rights. If the trade were ended, it seemed likely that planters would treat their remaining slaves more humanely.

While the British reformers worked for the abolition of the slave trade, slaves in some areas took matters into their own hands. Indeed, the largest emancipation of slaves to occur in the eighteenth century came in the course of the Haitian Revolution (discussed earlier in this chapter). The slave revolt that launched Haiti's revolution stood as a warning to slave owners throughout the West Indies. Other slave revolts occurred, including those in Virginia led by Gabriel Prosser in 1800 and by Nat Turner in 1831, in South Carolina led by Denmark Vesey in 1822, in British-controlled Demarra in 1823 and 1824, and in Jamaica in 1831. Each of these was brutally suppressed.

For reasons that had nothing to do with religion or enlightened humanitarianism, some British West Indies planters decided that abolition of the slave trade might be in their best interest. They were experiencing soil exhaustion and increased competition from French planters. There was a glut of sugar on the market, and the price was falling. Without new slaves, the French would lack the labor they needed to exploit their islands. During the Napoleonic Wars, the British captured a number of the French islands. To protect the planters of the older British West Indies islands from economic competition, the British Cabinet in 1805 forbade the importation of slaves into the newly acquired islands, and in 1807 Parliament finally passed Wilberforce's prohibition on slave trading from any British port. Thereafter, suppression of the slave trade became a major goal of nineteenth-century British foreign policy. The British navy maintained a squadron off West Africa to halt slave traders. The French and Americans also patrolled the West African coast, although neither was deeply committed to ending the slave trade.

Leaders of the Latin American wars of independence were disposed by Enlightenment ideas to disapprove of slavery, and they sought the support of slaves by promises of emancipation. The newly independent nations slowly freed their slaves to maintain good relations with Britain, from which they needed economic support. Slavery had disappeared from Latin America by the middle of the century, with the important exception of Brazil.

Having slowly recognized that the abolition of the slave trade had not actually improved the lot of slaves, British reformers in 1823 adopted as a new goal the gradual emancipation of slaves and founded the Abolition Society. The savagery with which West Indian planters put down slave revolts in 1823 and 1824 and again in 1831 strengthened the resolve of the antislavery reformers. By 1830 the reformers demanded immediate and complete abolition of slavery. In 1833, following the passage of the Reform Bill in Great Britain, they achieved that goal when Parliament abolished the right of British subjects to hold slaves. In the British West Indies, 750,000 slaves were freed within a few years.

The other old colonial powers in the New World were slower to abolish slavery. Portugal ended slavery elsewhere in its American possessions in 1836, but Brazil's independent government continued slavery. The Swedes abolished slavery in their possessions in 1847; the Danes in 1848; but the Dutch not until 1863. France, despite a significant antislavery movement, did not abolish slavery in the West Indies until the revolutions of 1848.

Despite opposition, slavery actually expanded in some parts of the transatlantic world in the early nineteenth century: the lower south of the United States, Brazil, and Cuba. World demand for the products of these regions—cotton, coffee, and sugar, respectively—made the slave system economically viable. Slavery ended in the United States only after the Civil War. In Cuba it persisted until 1886, and full emancipation did not occur in Brazil until 1888 (see Chapters 24, 25, and 26).

The emancipation crusade, like slave trading, drew Europeans into African affairs, including efforts to move former slaves back to Africa, Christian missionary endeavors, and commercial ventures. When the American Civil War finally halted large-scale demand for transatlantic slaves, reformers concentrated on ending the slave trade in East Africa and the Indian Ocean, contributing to the establishment of the late-nineteenth-century European colonial empires (see Chapters 17 and 26).

QUICK REVIEW

Impact on Africa of Opposition to Slavery

- British navy blockades West Africa
- Sierra Leone, Libreville, and Liberia established in West Africa
- Reformers spread Christianity and free trade in Africa
- Antislavery campaign within Africa facilitates colonization

SUMMARY

 WHAT WAS radical about the American Revolution?

Revolution in the British Colonies in North America. North Americans rejected British attempts to raise revenue through colonial taxes. The ideas of John Locke, the Commonwealthmen, and others pushed the colonists to the American Revolution. As the crisis continued, Americans became increasingly radicalized, rejecting monarchy and aristocratic social structures in favor of democracy and republicanism. The colonies gained independence in 1783 and adopted a constitution in 1788. Though women, slaves, Native Americans and others still lacked rights, American society was the freest yet in the world and helped inspire political movements throughout the Americas and in Europe. *page 557*

HOW DID the French Revolution and Napoleon transform France's government and society?

Revolution in France. The French monarchy, too, was troubled by finances. The need to appease taxpayers led to the 1789 calling of the Estates General. In conjunction with mass action by Parisian women, *sans-culottes*, and others, politics and protest turned, within four years, to two revolutions followed by the Reign of Terror. Some stability returned with Napoleon, whose rule began in 1799 and whose wars remade the map of Europe. In the post-Napoleonic settlement at the Congress of Vienna (1814–1815), European leaders tried to institutionalize peaceful relations throughout the continent. French society had experienced multiple disruptions, perhaps most notably the changes in the role of the church. *page 560*

 WHY WAS the Haitian Revolution significant to world history?

Wars of Independence in Latin America. The American, French, and Haitian (1794–1804) revolutions, as well as the resentment Creole elites felt toward Iberian exploitation, helped spur independence movements in Latin America. These revolutions were socially conservative, particularly in Mexico. Brazil achieved independence peacefully, in part because slaveholders there wanted to minimize the risk of social disruption that might lead to calls for abolition. *page 574*

 WHY DID slavery become unacceptable in Western society?

Toward the Abolition of Slavery in the Transatlantic Economy. English Quakers were in the forefront of the fight against first slave trading and then slavery itself. Enlightenment ideas and slave revolts throughout the Americas were also significant factors. Abolition proceeded slowly, however, and early in the nineteenth century it coexisted with an expansion of slaveholding in regions where plantation-grown cash crops were highly profitable (cotton in the southern United States, sugar in the Caribbean, and coffee in Brazil). *page 579*

KEY TERMS

assignats (ASS-ihn-YAHTS) (p. 563)
Consulate (p. 569)
Convention (p. 566)
Creoles (p. 575)
Jacobins (p. 565)
levée en masse (le-VAY ahn MAHS) (p. 566)
peninsulares (pen-IN-soo-LAHR-ayes) (p. 575)
Reign of Terror (p. 566)
sans-culottes (SANZ-koo-LAHTZ) (p. 566)
Thermidorian Reaction (p. 567)
Third Estate (p. 560)

REVIEW QUESTIONS

1. Discuss the American Revolution in the context of transatlantic history. To what extent were the colonists influenced by their position in the transatlantic economy? To what extent were they influenced by European ideas and political developments? How did their demands for liberty compare and contrast with the ideas of liberty championed during the French Revolution?

2. How was the Estates General transformed into the National Assembly? How does the *Declaration of the Rights of Man and Citizen* reflect the social and political values of the eighteenth-century Enlightenment? What were the chief ways in which France and its government were reorganized in the early years of the revolution?

3. What was the revolution of 1792, and why did it occur? What were the causes of the Reign of Terror, and what political coalitions made it possible?

4. How did Napoleon rise to power? What were his major domestic achievements? Did his rule more nearly fulfill or betray the ideals of the French Revolution?

5. What were the results of the Napoleonic Wars? Why did Napoleon decide to invade Russia? Why did he fail? What were the major outlines of the peace settlement achieved by the Congress of Vienna?

6. How was the Haitian Revolution influenced by the French Revolution? How did the Haitian Revolution influence other revolutionary movements in the Americas? How did it influence conservative movements in the Americas?

7. What political changes took place in Latin America in the twenty years between 1804 and 1824? What were the main reasons for Creole discontent with Spanish rule?

8. A motto of the French Revolution was "liberty, equality, and fraternity." How might one compare the American Revolution, the French Revolution, the Haitian Revolution, and the Latin American wars of independence in regard to the achievement of these goals?

9. What intellectual and religious factors contributed to the rise of the antislavery movement? What was the impact of slave revolts? To what extent did nonhumanitarian forces contribute to it? What opposition did it meet? Why did slavery receive a new lease on life during the same years that the antislavery movement emerged?

10. What, if any, advances did women make as a result of these revolutions in the transatlantic world? Which groups tended to benefit most, and which least, from the events discussed in this chapter?

Note: To learn more about the topics in this chapter, please turn to the Suggested Readings at the end of the book. For additional sources related to this chapter please see www.myhistorylab.com

myhistorylab Connections

Reinforce what you learned in this chapter by studying the many documents, images, maps, review tools, and videos available at **www.myhistorylab.com**

Read and Review

✓•─[**Study** and **Review** Chapter 22

•••─[Read the Document *Declaration of the Rights of Man and Citizen, 1789, p. 563*
Maximilien Robespierre, "Speech to National Convention: The Terror Justified," p. 567
Madame de Remusat on the Rise of Napoleon, p. 569
Napoleon's Exile to Saint Helena (1815), p. 572
Simon de Bolívar, "Address to Second National Congress" (Venezuela), 1819, p. 577
Jose Morelos, Sentiments of the Nation (Mexico), 1813, p. 577

⊙─[See the Map *Revolutionary France, p. 566*
Napoleon's Empire in 1812, p. 569

⊙─[View the Image *Oath of the Tennis Court, p. 561*
Slave Revolt in Saint Domingue, 1791, p. 575
The Great Liberator, Independence Leader, Caudillo, and Future President Simón Bolívar, p. 576

((•─[Hear the Audio *Napoleon 1, p. 568*

Research and Explore

(◦)─[Watch the Video *Revolution in the Atlantic World*

⊙─[See the Map *Europe after the Congress of Vienna, 1815, p. 573*

((•─[**Hear** the **Audio**

Hear the audio file for Chapter 22
at **www.myhistorylab.com**

23

Political Consolidation in Nineteenth-Century Europe and North America

((•—|Hear the Audio for Chapter 23 at www.myhistorylab.com

Garibaldi at Naples, by Antonio Licata. One of the extraordinary figures of the nineteenth century, Giuseppe Garibaldi (1807–1882) was the forceful and spiritual leader of the movement for Italian unification, which was achieved, after many conflicts, in 1861.

Why is it significant that Garibaldi is portrayed in southern Italy?

D uring the nineteenth century two fundamental long-term developments occurred in the northern transatlantic world. First, a process of political consolidation took place in both Europe and North America that made these regions' nation-states the strongest of the period. Second, and directly contributing to that political strength, powerful new industrial economies emerged in Europe and North America, accompanied by a new kind of society, no longer based primarily on the land. As a direct result of this political consolidation and industrialization, the nations of the northern transatlantic became the world's major military powers. By the close of the nineteenth

EUROPEAN AND NORTH AMERICAN POLITICAL CONSOLIDATION

During the first three quarters of the nineteenth century the nations of Europe and North America underwent major political consolidation. Great Britain emerged from the Napoleonic Wars as the strongest power on the globe and maintained that position for more than a century. France experienced decades of changing political regimes but remained a major political and military force. The third quarter of the century saw Germany and Italy transformed from relatively soft regions of small principalities into major unified nation-states. Similarly the Austrian Empire reorganized itself. As will be seen in Chapter 24, Russia also undertook major political and social reforms to consolidate the strength of the tsarist government. On the other side of the Atlantic the United States became a major nation aspiring to stretch across the North American continent, as did Canada. These developments laid the foundation for the major transatlantic state system of the late nineteenth and early twentieth centuries.

The movement toward strong, centralized national states in Europe and North America during the nineteenth century had counterparts elsewhere in the world. In Asia during this same period, Japan sought to imitate the military and economic power of the European states. Late nineteenth-century Latin America enjoyed one of its most successful and stable periods. The governments of that region established centralized regimes on the basis of relatively prosperous economies. In the United States the

Civil War established the power of the central federal government over that of the individual states. The role of the war in forging a single American nation was similar to the role that military force played in the unifications of Italy and Germany and the suppression of the Paris Commune.

In the cases of Italy and Germany many people regarded the triumph of nationalism as a positive achievement. However, the last half of the century also saw various national and ethnic groups use the power of the national state to repress or dominate other minority groups. Examples include the Hungarian treatment of smaller subject nationalities and the British treatment of the Irish. To some extent, this phenomenon can be explained by the geographical borders of the new nations that were carved out of former European monarchies and empires, such as the Austro-Hungarian Empire. In many cases, the new national boundaries ignored the reality that many, perhaps most, regions were home to more than one ethnic group, with religions, languages, and ethnicities different from those of their rulers and the governing class. In the premodern world, loyalty to a ruling dynasty, rather than shared history, language, or ethnicity, was the primary determinant of group identity or membership in a polity above the local level. People saw themselves first as members of a tribe, clan, village, or town, and second as the subjects of a ruler who might not even speak their language and whose

century and well into the twentieth, this political and military power allowed the nations of Europe and the United States to exert unprecedented political, military, and economic influence around the globe.

The present chapter will examine the process of political consolidation in the northern transatlantic world, while Chapter 24 will explore the social changes that occurred there in the nineteenth century. Although we will consider the two processes separately, each contributed to the other. ∎

THE EMERGENCE OF NATIONALISM IN EUROPE

WHAT IS nationalism?

nationalism

The belief that one is part of a nation, defined as a community with its own language, traditions, customs, and history that distinguish it from other nations and make it the primary focus of a person's loyalty and sense of identity.

Nationalism proved to be the single most powerful European political ideology of the nineteenth and early twentieth centuries. Politically, **nationalism** is based on the relatively modern concept that a nation is composed of people who are joined together by the bonds of common language, customs, culture, and history, and who, because of those bonds, should share the same government. The idea that political and ethnic boundaries should coincide came into its own in Europe during the late eighteenth and early nineteenth centuries. Nationalists opposed the principle upheld at the Congress of Vienna that legitimate monarchies or dynasties should provide the basis for political unity. Nationalists rejected the concept of multinational states such as the Austrian or Russian Empires. They also objected to peoples of the same ethnic group, such as authority often impinged very little on their daily lives. Thus ethnic or linguistic minorities posed less of an obstacle to monarchical rulers than to governments of nation-states, where national identity is often based on shared language and ethnicity. This problem has continued to bedevil national states in Europe and elsewhere in the world into the modern era and is an important cause for many recent conflicts in regions as diverse as eastern Europe, Asia, and Africa.

Elsewhere around the globe during the nineteenth century strong central governments often simply repressed minority populations, especially indigenous peoples, or allowed them fewer rights of civic participation and protection. In almost all cases the repression of minority groups generated social and political problems that haunted the twentieth century. Native Americans failed to gain rights in Latin America. In the United States the westward movement brought warfare against Native Americans, and legislation facilitated the segregation of American black citizens. In Canada, English speakers fared better than French speakers. In Australia, Aborigines were killed or forcibly relocated in many regions before and after that country's government gained sovereignty from England.

Finally, the emergence of strong European nation-states set the stage for the extension of their rivalries from Europe to other areas of the globe. The militarily and economically strong states of Europe soon turned to foreign adventures that subjugated vast areas of Africa and Asia. This imperialism led many colonized peoples to become aware that only strong nationalistic movements of their own could eventually end subjugation by the militarily stronger Europeans. Consequently, during the first quarter of the twentieth century, the nationalistic principle that less than fifty years earlier had dominated European politics began to influence the politics of the peoples on whom Europeans had imposed their government and administration. As these former colonies achieved independence and established their own nation-states, however, their governments experienced problems similar to those of the European nations in balancing the demands for unity of the majority with the rights of the diverse ethnic and religious minorities inhabiting their territory.

Focus Questions

◆ What role has military and economic power played in strengthening nation-states?

◆ Why do most nation-states have ethnic minorities? Why have these minorities tended to be oppressed?

◆ How did the rivalry among the European nation-states affect other regions of the world? What impact did it have on the development of nationalism outside of Europe?

Germans and Italians, dwelling in political units smaller than the ethnic nation. Consequently, nationalists challenged both the domestic and the international order of the Vienna settlement.

CREATING NATIONS

Nationalists actually created nations in the nineteenth century. Early nineteenth-century writers spread nationalistic concepts. Many of these writers were historians who chronicled a people's past, or literary scholars who established a national literature by collecting and publishing earlier writings in the people's language. In effect, they gave a people a sense of their past and a literature of their own, which schoolteachers then spread. The language to be used in schools and government was a point of contention for nationalists. A uniform language helped to persuade people who had not thought of themselves as constituting a nation to believe that they were a nation. Yet even in 1850, less than half of the inhabitants of France, for example, spoke official French (see Map 23–1 on page 588).

MEANING OF NATIONHOOD

Nationalists used a variety of arguments and metaphors to express what they meant by nationhood. Some claimed that gathering Italians, for example, into a unified Italy would promote economic and administrative efficiency. Others insisted that nations, like biological species, were distinct creations of God. Throughout the nineteenth

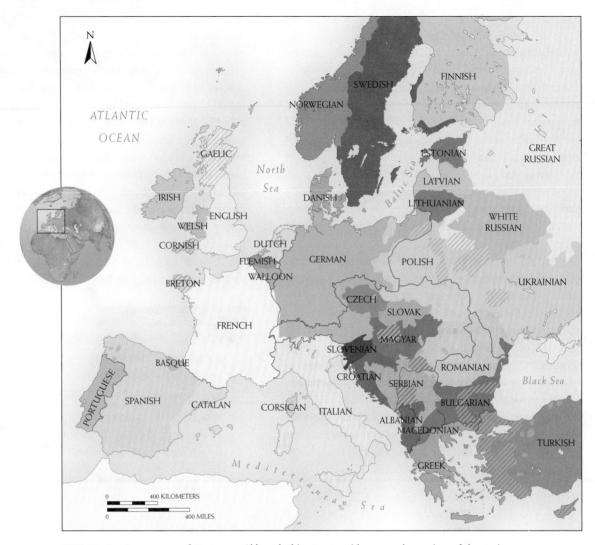

MAP 23–1. **Languages of Europe.** Although this map provides a good overview of the main languages of nineteenth-century Europe, it does not show the vast number of dialects that were the primary tongue of most speakers. A speaker of the Piedmont dialect from northwestern Italy, for example, would not understand a speaker from Sicily.

Why was language significant for nationalists?

century, for example, Polish nationalists portrayed Poland as the suffering Christ among nations, implicitly suggesting that Poland, like Christ, would experience resurrection and a new life.

A significant difficulty for nationalism has been determining which ethnic groups could be considered nations, with claims to territory and political autonomy. In theory, any of them could, but in reality nationhood came to be associated with groups that were large enough to support a viable economy, that had a history of significant cultural association, that possessed a cultural elite that could nourish and spread the national language, and that could conquer other peoples to establish and protect their own independence. Many smaller ethnic groups claimed to fulfill these criteria but could not effectively achieve independence or recognition. They could and did, however, create domestic unrest within the political units they inhabited.

REGIONS OF NATIONALISTIC PRESSURE IN EUROPE

During the nineteenth century nationalists challenged the political status quo in six major areas of Europe. Irish nationalists wanted independence from Britain, or at least self-government. German nationalists sought political unity for all German-speaking peoples, challenging the multinational Austrian Empire and pitting Prussia and Austria against each other. Italian nationalists sought to unify the peninsula and drive out the Austrians. Polish nationalists struggled to restore Poland as an independent nation. In eastern Europe, Hungarians, Czechs, Slovenes, and others sought either autonomy or formal recognition within the Austrian Empire. Finally, in the Balkans national groups sought independence from Ottoman and Russian control. In each area, nationalist activity ebbed and flowed. During the century, however, nationalists changed the political map and political culture of Europe.

EARLY NINETEENTH-CENTURY POLITICAL LIBERALISM

The term *liberal* as used in present-day American political rhetoric has virtually no relationship to the kinds of ideologies that were described as liberal in the nineteenth century.

WHAT WERE the basic goals of European liberals?

POLITICS

European **liberalism** derived from the Enlightenment, the example of English liberties, and the French *Declaration of the Rights of Man and Citizen*. Liberals favored legal equality, religious toleration, and freedom of the press. They believed that the legitimacy of government emanated from the freely given consent of the governed expressed through elected parliaments. Most important, free government required that state or crown ministers be responsible to the representatives of the nation rather than to the monarch.

However limited these goals seem, none of the major European countries in 1815 met them all. The people who espoused these changes in government tended to be those who were excluded from the existing political processes, but whose wealth and education made them believe such exclusion was unjustified. Liberals were often products of career fields that admitted and rewarded people on the basis of talent (academics, members of the learned professions, and people involved in commerce and manufacturing).

European liberals were not democrats. They despised the lower classes. Liberals transformed the eighteenth-century concept of aristocratic liberty into a new concept of privilege based on wealth and property. By midcentury, throughout Europe, liberals had separated themselves from the working class. In the first half of the nineteenth century, political liberals generally did not support political rights for women, but liberal political principles provided women with strong arguments, as seen for example in the *Declaration of Female Independence* issued by the Seneca Falls convention in the United States in 1848.

liberalism
In the nineteenth century, support for representative government dominated by the propertied classes and minimal government interference in the economy.

Read the Document
The Seneca Falls Convention (1848)
at **myhistorylab.com**

ECONOMICS

The economic goals of the liberals furthered their separation from the working class. European economic liberals opposed the old paternalistic legislation that established wages and labor practices by government regulation or by guild privileges. Labor was simply one more commodity to be bought and sold freely. Liberals sought what they regarded as structures of economic liberty in which people were free to use their talents and property to enrich themselves. The liberals contended that this would lead to more goods and services for everyone at lower prices, providing the basis for material progress.

The manufacturers of Great Britain, the landed and manufacturing middle class of France, and the commercial interests of Germany and Italy favored the removal of international tariffs as well as internal barriers to trade. To that end, liberals favored the rapid construction of railways from the 1830s onward.

The economic goals of European liberals found many followers outside Europe among groups that favored the expansion of free trade, new transport systems, and a free market in labor. In the United States people of this outlook often attacked slavery as an inefficient, paternalistic institution. In Latin America political liberals sought to remove paternalistic legislation that had protected Native Americans under the Spanish Empire.

RELATIONSHIP OF NATIONALISM AND LIBERALISM

Nationalism was not necessarily or logically linked to liberalism, but the two were often complementary. Behind the concept of a people joined naturally by the bonds of common language, customs, culture, and history lurked the idea of popular sovereignty. The idea of the career open to talent could be applied to suppressed national groups that were not permitted to realize their cultural or political potential. The efficient government and administration required by commerce and industry would mean joining small German and Italian states into larger political units. Nationalist groups in one country could gain the sympathy of liberals in other nations by espousing representative government and political liberty.

LIBERALISM AND NATIONALISM IN MODERN WORLD HISTORY

A CONVENTION OF HEMMERS AND STIT HERS HELD AT LYNN, FEB. 28, FOR ADOPTING A LIST OF PRICES; MRS. E. HALL, PRESIDING.—See page 284.)

Female Liberal Political Activism. The ideas of political liberalism spoke deeply to the situation of women throughout the transatlantic world. Women demanded entrance into the political forum as demonstrated by the first women's rights convention in Seneca Falls, New York in 1848, and this meeting of women strikers in Lynn, Massachusetts in 1860.

How successful were women in gaining rights during this period?

The French Revolution had demonstrated that the ideals of political liberalism could easily cross dynastic borders. In time those liberal ideals as well as those of nationalism would spread around the globe. Thus, what began as a European development is also important for global history. The concept of the "rights of man and citizen" was used during the wars of independence in Latin America to challenge Spanish government; by the close of the twentieth century, those same ideals had been turned against European colonial governments in Africa and Asia (see Chapters 25 and 26). The belief that people should have the right to govern themselves inspired the settlers who spread across both the United States and Canada as well as those who settled in Australia and New Zealand. Similarly, the belief that individual ethnic groups should constitute independent nations became a major political conviction that led peoples living under European colonial government during the late nineteenth and twentieth centuries to challenge the right of Europeans and later Americans to govern them or dominate their lives through economic power. Thus, political developments in Europe during the early nineteenth century profoundly affected global politics during the twentieth century.

EFFORTS TO LIBERALIZE EARLY NINETEENTH-CENTURY EUROPEAN POLITICAL STRUCTURES

European nations moved toward liberal political structures haltingly and in the face of conflict. Most conservatives hoped the Congress of Vienna had established walls against liberal advances. Three examples indicate the different experiences that European liberals confronted early in the nineteenth century.

WHY WERE efforts to achieve political liberalism more successful in France and Britain than in Russia?

RUSSIA: THE DECEMBRIST REVOLT OF 1825 AND THE AUTOCRACY OF NICHOLAS I

In the process of driving Napoleon's army across Europe and then occupying defeated France, many officers in the Russian army were introduced to the ideas of the French Revolution and the Enlightenment. They realized how economically backward and politically stifled Russia was, and groups within the officer corps began to form secret societies. In 1825, they decided to stage a coup d'état the following year.

Events intervened. In November 1825, Tsar Alexander I died unexpectedly, creating two crises. The first was a dynastic one: Alexander had no direct heir. His brother Constantine, who commanded Russian forces in Poland, had renounced any claim to the throne. Secret instructions left by Alexander and made public only after his death named the tsar's younger brother, Nicholas (r. 1825–1855), his successor, but the legality of Alexander's orders was uncertain. Constantine acknowledged Nicholas as tsar, and Nicholas acknowledged Constantine. For about three weeks, Russia had no ruler. Then, in early December, the army command reported to Nicholas the existence of a conspiracy among officers, and Nicholas had himself declared tsar.

The second crisis now unfolded—a plot by junior officers to rally their troops to compel reform. On December 26, 1825, the army was to take the oath of allegiance to Nicholas, who was less popular than Constantine and regarded as more conservative. Nearly all of the regiments did so, but the Moscow regiment refused. Its chief officers, surprisingly, were not secret society members, but they marched into the Senate Square in Saint Petersburg calling for Constantine and a constitution. Nicholas ordered cavalry and artillery to attack the insurgents. Five of the plotters were executed, and more than one hundred other officers were exiled to Siberia.

Liberalism was crushed in Russia. Nicholas I manifested extreme conservatism in foreign affairs, too, providing troops to suppress liberal and nationalist movements throughout Europe. Except for a modest experiment early in the twentieth century, tsarist Russia never experienced liberal political structures.

Decembrist Revolt. When the Moscow regiment refused to swear allegiance to Nicholas, he ordered the cavalry and artillery to attack them. Though a total failure, the Decembrist Revolt came to symbolize the yearnings of all Russian liberals in the nineteenth century for a constitutional government.

The Insurrection of the Decembrists at Senate Square, Saint Petersburg on 14th December, 1825 (w/c on paper) by Russian School (19th century). Private Collection/Bridgeman Art Library.

Why did liberalism fail in Russia?

Liberty Leading the People by Eugene Delacroix is a famous evocation of the Revolution of 1830.

Giraudon/Art Resource, New York.

How does Delacroix mythologize the events of 1830?

July Monarchy

The French regime set up after the overthrow of the Bourbons in July 1830.

REVOLUTION IN FRANCE (1830)

In 1824 Louis XVIII (r. 1814–1824), the Bourbon king restored to the French throne by the Congress of Vienna, died and was succeeded by his brother, Charles X (r. 1824–1830). The new king considered himself a monarch by divine right. He wanted to restore lands that the French aristocrats had lost during the revolution and pressed other conservative measures through the Chamber of Deputies. Opposition soon developed. After elections in 1827, Charles moderated his conservatism, but French liberals pressed for a constitutional regime. In 1829, Charles appointed an ultraroyalist ministry. This move backfired.

In 1830 Charles X called for new elections, and the liberals scored a stunning victory. The king and his ministers decided to undertake a royalist seizure of power. In June and July 1830 the ministry had sent a naval expedition against Algeria. On July 9 reports of its victory, and the consequent foundation of a French empire in North Africa, reached Paris. On July 25, 1830, acting under the euphoria of this foreign diversion, Charles X issued the Four Ordinances, which restricted freedom of the press, dissolved the recently elected Chamber of Deputies, and called for new elections under a franchise restricted to the wealthiest people in the country.

Liberal newspapers immediately called on the nation to reject the monarch's actions. Parisian laborers, burdened by an economic downturn, took to the streets and erected barricades. The king called out troops, and more than 1,800 people died during the ensuing battles. On August 2 Charles X abdicated and left for exile in England. The liberals in the Chamber of Deputies named a new ministry composed of constitutional monarchists. They proclaimed Louis Philippe (r. 1830–1848), head of the liberal branch of the royal family, the new monarch. Under the **July Monarchy**, Louis Philippe was called the king of the French rather than of France. The king had to cooperate with the Chamber of Deputies; he could not dispense with laws on his own authority. The revolutionary tricolor replaced the white flag of the Bourbons. The Charter, or constitution, was regarded as embodying the rights of the people rather than as a concession granted by the monarch. Catholicism was recognized only as the religion of the majority of the people, not as the official religion. Censorship was abolished. The franchise, though still restricted, was extended.

Socially, however, the Revolution of 1830 proved quite conservative. The landed oligarchy retained its economic, political, and social influence. Money became the path to power and influence in the government. There was much corruption. Most important, the liberal monarchy displayed scant sympathy for the lower and working classes.

Great Reform Bill (1832)

A limited reform of the British House of Commons and an expansion of the electorate to include a wider variety of the propertied classes. It laid the groundwork for further orderly reforms within the British constitutional system.

THE GREAT REFORM BILL IN BRITAIN (1832)

The passage of Britain's **Great Reform Bill**, which became law in 1832, was the result of events different from those that occurred on the Continent. In Britain the forces of conservatism and reform compromised with each other. Great Britain came to be regarded as the exemplary liberal state not only of Europe but of the world.

English determination to maintain union with Ireland began the reform process. The Act of Union in 1800 between England and Ireland had suppressed the separate Irish Parliament and seated Irish representatives in the British Parliament at Westminster. Only Protestant Irishmen, however, could be elected to represent what was an overwhelmingly Catholic country. Irish nationalists agitated for **Catholic emancipation**, as the movement for legal rights for Roman Catholics was known. In 1828 Daniel O'Connell (1775–1847) was elected to Parliament but could not legally take his seat until the Duke of Wellington (1769–1852) steered the Catholic Emancipation Act through Parliament. This, together with the repeal in 1828 of restrictions against Protestant nonconformists, ended the monopoly held by members of the Church of England on British political life.

Catholic emancipation alienated many of Wellington's Tory supporters, who believed that Catholic emancipation had passed only because of corruption in the House of Commons. After the 1830 elections, King William IV (r. 1830–1837) turned to the Whigs to form a government. The Whigs soon presented a major reform bill that had two broad goals. The first was to replace "rotten" boroughs, which had few voters, with representatives for the previously unrepresented manufacturing districts and cities. The second was to increase the number of voters in England and Wales. Parliament rejected the bill twice, leading to mass meetings throughout the country and riots in several cities. Finally, William IV agreed to create enough new peers to give a third reform bill a majority in the House of Lords. The measure became law in 1832.

The Great Reform Act expanded the size of the English electorate, but it was not a democratic measure. The electorate was increased by more than 200,000 persons (almost 50 percent), but the basis of voting remained a property qualification. New urban boroughs gave the growing cities a voice in the House of Commons, but each new urban electoral district was balanced by a new rural district. Nonetheless, the Great Reform Act established the foundations for long-term political stability in Britain. New groups and interests were absorbed into existing political processes. A large body of ideas emphasizing competition and individualism was accepted by members of all classes. Even the leaders of trade unions asked only to receive some of the fruits of prosperity and to prove their own social respectability. During the 1840s a major working-class political movement known as **Chartism** brought the demands of industrial workers into the political process. Great Britain continued to symbolize the confident liberal state.

Benjamin Disraeli (1804–1881), leader of the Conservatives in the House of Commons, hoped to appeal to portions of the working class and the growing suburban middle class by passing social reform legislation. Disraeli supported the Second Reform Act (1867), which increased the number of voters from approximately 1,430,000 to 2,470,000. The election of 1868 dashed Disraeli's hopes: the Liberal Party's William Gladstone (1809–1898) became the new prime minister. Gladstone's ministry from 1868 to 1874 witnessed the culmination of classical British liberalism. Gladstone introduced the secret ballot, brought competitive examinations into the civil service, and abolished the purchase of officers' commissions. The British government took responsibility for all primary education.

The liberal policy of creating popular support by extending political liberty and

Catholic emancipation
The grant of full political rights to Roman Catholics in Britain in 1829.

◉ View the Image
Reform Bill of 1832–Cartoon
at **myhistorylab.com**

Chartism
The first large-scale European working-class political movement. It sought political reforms that would favor the interests of skilled British workers in the 1830s and 1840s.

A House of Commons Debate. William Ewart Gladstone, standing on the right, is attacking Benjamin Disraeli, who sits with legs crossed and arms folded. Gladstone served in the British Parliament from the 1830s through the 1890s. Four times the Liberal Party prime minister, he was responsible for guiding major reforms through Parliament. Disraeli, regarded as the founder of modern British conservatism, served as prime minister from 1874 to 1880.

What were the significant differences between the policies of Gladstone and Disraeli?

◉—View the Image
Gladstone and Disraeli–Punch Cartoon
at **myhistorylab.com**

reforming abuses had its conservative counterpart in concern about social reform. Disraeli succeeded Gladstone as prime minister in 1874. Whereas Gladstone looked to individualism, free trade, and competition to solve social problems, Disraeli believed the state should protect weaker citizens. In his view, paternalistic legislation would alleviate class antagonism. His most important measures were the Public Health Act of 1875 and the Artisans Dwelling Act of 1875, through which the government became involved in providing housing for the working class.

Ireland proved a profoundly disruptive force in British politics. From the late 1860s onward, Irish nationalists had sought **home rule**, or more Irish control of local government. In the election of 1885 the Irish Party, led by Charles Stewart Parnell (1846–1891), emerged holding the balance of power between the English Liberals and Conservatives. (See Document, "Parnell Calls for Home Rule for Ireland.") Gladstone supported home rule for Ireland, so Parnell supported him. This split the Liberal Party, however, and a group known as the Liberal Unionists joined with the Conservatives to defeat Gladstone's Home Rule Bill in 1886. Conservatives formed a ministry under Lord Salisbury (1830–1903) and attempted to placate the Irish through public works and administrative reform, with only marginal success. In 1892 Gladstone returned to power and sponsored a second Home Rule Bill that was defeated in the House of Lords. Finally, a Liberal ministry passed the third Home Rule Bill in the summer of 1914. However, implementation of home rule was suspended for the duration of World War I.

1848: YEAR OF REVOLUTIONS IN EUROPE

In 1848 a series of liberal and nationalistic revolutions and revolts spread across Europe (see Map 23–2 on page 596). No single factor caused this revolutionary groundswell, but similar conditions existed in several countries. Severe food shortages had prevailed since 1846 due to poor harvests. The commercial and industrial economy was in recession, causing widespread unemployment. However, the dynamic for change in 1848 originated not with the working classes but with middle-class political liberals, who pushed for more representative governments, civil liberty, and unregulated economic life.

To put additional pressure on their governments, the liberals began to appeal for the support of the urban working classes, even though their goals were different. The working classes sought improved employment and better working conditions. The liberals refused to follow political revolution with social reform and thus isolated themselves from their temporary working-class allies. Once separated from potential mass support, the liberal revolutions were easily suppressed by the armies of reactionary governments. As a result, the revolutions of 1848 failed to establish genuinely liberal or national states.

Revolutionary. In 1848, Ana Ipatescu helped to lead Transylvanian revolutionaries against Russian rule. (Transylvania is part of present-day Romania.) The revolutions of 1848 in eastern Europe were primarily the risings of nationalist groups. Although generally repressed in the revolutions of that year, subject nationalities would prove a source of political upheaval and unrest in the region throughout the rest of the century, ultimately providing the spark for the outbreak of World War I.

Where was nationalist unrest most prevalent?

The results of the continental revolutions of 1848 were important for the individual nation-states. In France the monarchy of Louis Philippe was overthrown and briefly replaced by a republic, overthrown in turn by a nephew of Napoleon Bonaparte. Thereafter Louis Napoleon cre-

DOCUMENT

Parnell Calls for Home Rule for Ireland

Since 1800, Ireland had been governed as part of Great Britain, sending representatives to the British Parliament in Westminster. Throughout the century, there had been tension and violent conflict between the Irish and their English governors. Agitation for home rule, whereby the Irish would directly control many of their own affairs, reached a peak in the 1880s. Charles Stewart Parnell was the chief leader for the cause of Irish nationalism during that decade. His program at the time was home rule for Ireland, by which he meant Irish administration of Irish domestic affairs while preserving an ill-defined union with England. In 1885, he made a speech outlining the resentments the Irish had felt toward the English since the Act of Union of 1800. He also drew direct parallels between the relationship of Ireland to England and that of Hungary to Austria. The efforts to achieve home rule failed during the nineteenth century.

- **HOW** does Parnell say the Act of Union affected Irish sentiment toward England? What parallel does he draw with Hungary and Austria? Why might Parnell be regarded as a moderate nationalist?

It is not possible for human intelligence to forecast the future in the matter; but we can point to this—we can point to the fact that under 85 years of parliamentary connection with England, Ireland has become intensely disloyal and intensely disaffected; that notwithstanding the Whig policy of so-called conciliation, alternative conciliation and coercion . . . that disaffection has broadened, deepened, and intensified from day to day. Am I not, then, entitled to assume that one of the roots of this disaffection and feeling of disloyalty is the assumption by England of the management of our affairs. It is admitted that the present system can't go on, and

what are you going to put in its place? My advice to English statesmen considering this question would be this— trust the Irish people altogether or trust them not at all. . . . Whatever chance the English rulers may have of drawing to themselves the affection of the Irish people lies in destroying the abominable system of legislative union between the two countries by conceding fully and freely to Ireland their right to manage her own affairs. It is impossible for us to give guarantees, but we can point to the past; we can show that the record of English rule is a constant series of steps from bad to worse, that the condition of English power is more insecure and more unstable at the present moment than it has ever been. We can point to the example of other countries; of Austria and of Hungary—to the fact that Hungary having been conceded self-government became one of the strongest factors in the Austrian empire. We can show the powers that have been freely conceded in the colonies [such as Canada and Australia have led to loyalty] . . . I am confident that the English statesman who is great enough . . . to carry out these teachings . . . to give Ireland full legislative liberty, full power to manage her own domestic concerns will be regarded in the future by his countrymen as one who has removed the greatest peril to the English empire—a peril, I firmly believe, which if not removed will find some day . . . an opportunity of revenging itself to the destruction of the British empire for the misfortunes, the oppressions, and the misgovernment of our country.

Source: From Charles Stewart Parnell, "Speech at Wicklow," October 5, 1885, as quoted in Raymond Phineas Stearns, *Pageant of Europe: Sources and Selections from the Renaissance to the Present Day* (New York: Harcourt, Brace and Company, 1948), pp. 634–635.

ated the Second Empire and took the title of Napoleon III. In Prussia and the Austrian Empire short-lived revolutions brought political liberals and nationalists to the fore, but in each case those revolutions were put down by the military. The same was true of efforts by Italian nationalists to thrust off Austrian rule of Italy.

From the standpoint of world history, the chief importance of the failed revolutions of 1848 was the emergence of strongly conservative governments that would dominate Europe for the next quarter century. The turmoil of 1848 through 1850

See the Map
European Centers of Rebellion and Revolution, 1820–1848
at **myhistorylab.com**

MAP 23–2. **Centers of Revolution in 1848–1849.** The revolution that toppled the July Monarchy in Paris in 1848 soon spread to Austria and many of the German and Italian states. Yet by the end of 1849, most of these uprisings had been suppressed.

Which regions were most affected by the uprisings of 1848 and 1849?

•◊•⌐ Read the Document

Metternich on the Revolutions of 1848
at **myhistorylab.com**

ended the era of liberal revolution that had begun in 1789; political initiative passed for a time to the conservatives. Liberals and nationalists had discovered that rational argument and local insurrections would not help them to achieve their goals. The working class also adopted new tactics and organization. In the future, workers would turn to trade unions and political parties, rather than riot and urban insurrection, to achieve their political and social goals.

The defeat of liberal political forces in 1848 also influenced the modernization of Japan. Within a few years Japan would emerge from its long self-imposed isolation and look to European examples of successful modern nations. The nation Japan would most clearly copy was the conservative, militaristic Germany that emerged after the defeat of the liberals of 1848.

TESTING THE NEW AMERICAN REPUBLIC

TOWARD SECTIONAL CONFLICT

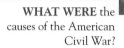

WHAT WERE the causes of the American Civil War?

While the nations of western Europe very slowly embraced political liberalism, the United States of America was continuing its bold republican political experiment. By the first quarter of the century, however, serious sectional tensions had arisen, the most important of which related to the presence of black slavery in the southern states.

The Constitutional Convention of 1788 had debated several aspects of slavery. A compromise allowed the slaveholding states to count three-fifths of their slaves when calculating their population for representation in Congress. The Constitution also forbade any federal attempt to prevent the importation of slaves before 1808.

Westward expansion raised new questions about slavery. The Ordinance of 1787, passed by Congress under the Articles of Confederation, had prohibited slavery in the Northwest Territory. Territory south of the Ohio River and beyond the Mississippi River was, however, open to slavery. By 1820, when Missouri was admitted as a slave state and Maine as a free one, the number of slave and free states was evenly divided. Congress decided that in the future no slave states would be carved out of land north of the southern border of Missouri. For the time being, this Missouri Compromise ended congressional debate over slavery (see Map 23-3 on page 598).

Meanwhile, the economies of the North and the South were rapidly diverging. In the North, family farms, free labor, commerce, and early industrialization in textiles characterized the economy. Northern farms were relatively small and worked by families, producing mostly foodstuffs for the local community. Slavery was abolished in the North by the early nineteenth century. The political spokesmen for the North tended to favor tariffs to protect their young industries from cheaper foreign competition. (In this, American liberals differed from their European counterparts.) Northern textile factories used cotton that was produced in the South, though most southern cotton was sold overseas.

Nineteenth-century innovations in transportation led to the fuller integration of different parts of the northern economy. Canals were built to link the major rivers with manufacturing and agricultural markets. The Ohio, Mississippi, and Missouri rivers were made navigable for steamboats. By the late 1840s, in America as in Europe, the major transportation innovation was the railroad. Most railways linked the Northeast and the West and fostered the commercial agriculture of the Midwest, making much of the northern economy just as rural and agricultural as the southern. Railway construction aided the

●◆━┤Read the **Document**
"A Defense of the Slave Trade," July 1740 at **myhistorylab.com**

((●●━┤Hear the **Audio**
Slavery 1 at **myhistorylab.com**

The Excelsior Iron Works, located in New York City. This print from the 1840s shows the works as a beehive of activity. Iron mills produced the material for railroads, ships, and machinery.

How did the economy of the North differ from that of the South?

MAP EXPLORATION

To explore this map further, go to **http://www.myhistorylab.com**

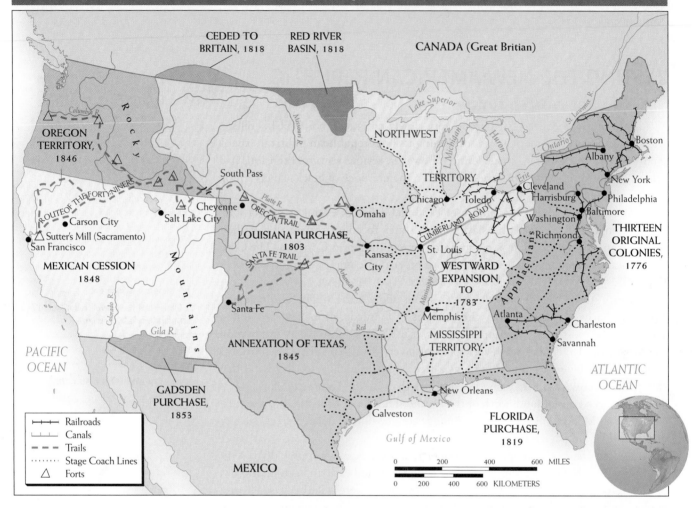

MAP 23–3. The United States, 1776–1850. During the nineteenth century the United States expanded across the entire North American continent. The revolutionary settlement had provided most of the land east of the Mississippi. The single largest addition thereafter was the Louisiana Purchase of 1803. The annexation of Texas, and later the Mexican Cession following the Mexican War, added the major Southwestern territories. The borders of the Oregon Territory were settled through long, difficult negotiations with Great Britain.

What is the connection between the westward expansion of the United States and the Civil War?

development of the northern coal and iron industries. The midcentury expansion of railways caused new sectional tensions, as it became clear the railways could open vast territories for settlement and could thus also open a national debate over slavery.

What most distinguished North from South was free versus slave labor. In the South, cotton was king, and cotton cultivation was organized around slavery. The invention of the cotton gin by Eli Whitney (1765–1825) in 1793 made cotton cultivation much more profitable. The industrial revolution in textiles kept cotton prices high, and the expansion in world population kept the demand for cotton cloth steady. The expansion of the cotton empire in the Mississippi Delta in the early nineteenth century gave slavery a new lease on life.

Read the Document

The History of Mary Prince (1830s)
at **myhistorylab.com**

SLAVERY

Although most Southern families never owned slaves, and most slave owners possessed only a few slaves, the institution of slavery survived for many reasons. For one, it was economically viable, and no one could devise a way to abolish it that was politically or socially acceptable to white Southerners. Throughout American society, North and South, there was a strong commitment to the protection of private property, including slaves. Perhaps most basic, however, was the racist thinking—in the North and in the South—that saw blacks as fundamentally inferior to whites.

All American slaves were nonwhite, the descendants of Africans who had been forcibly captured and shipped in wretched conditions to the United States (see Chapter 17). Despite racial mixing among Africans and their white slave owners and Native Americans, slave codes defined as black virtually anyone who had any African ancestors. Slaves were regarded as chattel property: They could be sold, given away, or even gambled away like any other piece of property. They had no recourse to law or constitutional protections, and they could be whipped or beaten. Slaves suffered from overwork and from diseases associated with poor nutrition, substandard sanitation, and inferior housing.

Slaves worked primarily in the fields, where they plowed, hoed, and harvested cotton, rice, sugar, tobacco, or corn. They were usually organized into work gangs supervised by white overseers. This work, like all farming, was seasonal, but during planting or harvest seasons, labor lasted from sunrise to sunset. Children would help in the fields. Older or more privileged slaves might work in the house.

Slave communities helped preserve the family life and inner personalities of slaves. Some elements of African culture persisted: African legends were passed on orally. Religion proved extraordinarily important. Slaves adopted for their own cultural needs the Old Testament stories of the Jews' liberation from Egypt. They also often combined elements of African religion with evangelical Protestantism. Yet the marriages and family lives of slaves had no legal recognition, and the integrity of the slave family could be violated at any time. White masters and their sons often sexually exploited black slave women. In a world of white dominance, the institutions, customs, and religions of the slave community were the only refuge available to black slaves.

Scars of Slavery. This Louisiana slave named Gordon was photographed in 1863 after he had escaped to Union lines during the Civil War. He bears the permanent scars of the violence that lay at the heart of the slave system. Few slaves were so brutally marked, but all lived with the threat of beatings if they failed to obey.

Do you believe evidence of the cruelty of slavery, such as this photograph, influenced Lincoln's decision to issue the Emancipation Proclamation?

THE ABOLITIONIST MOVEMENT

During the 1830s a militant antislavery movement emerged in the North. Its members refused to accept what they regarded as the moral compromise of living in a nation that tolerated slavery. Abolitionists such as William Lloyd Garrison, editor of the *Liberator*, condemned the Union and the Constitution as structures that perpetuated slavery. Former slaves who had escaped slavery, such as Frederick Douglass and Sojourner Truth, and freeborn black Americans, such as Daniel A. Payne, were prominent in the cause.

The antislavery movement gained new adherents during the 1840s as the question of extending slavery into new territories came to the fore. Texas was annexed in 1845, the vast Oregon Territory was acquired in 1846, and victory in the Mexican War (1846–1848) added significant new territory in the Southwest and California (see Map 23–3).

Southerners feared that changing attitudes and the opening of territories where slavery was prohibited would give the South a minority status. Northerners believed that a slave-power conspiracy controlled the federal government. The Kansas-Nebraska Bill, introduced by Stephen A. Douglas (1813–1861) in 1845, proposed that the people of each new territory decide whether to permit slavery.

See the **Map**
The Americas, 1800–1836
at **myhistorylab.com**

The Compromise of 1850, a group of laws that balanced slave and free interests, briefly restored political calm. But then the Republican Party was organized in 1854 largely in opposition to the Kansas-Nebraska Bill. Kansas, where abolitionist John Brown and his sons mounted guerilla attacks against slaveholding settlers, earned the nickname "Bleeding Kansas." In the 1857 *Dred Scott* decision, the Supreme Court effectively repealed the Missouri Compromise by declaring that Congress could not prohibit slavery in the territories, that slaves did not become free by living in free states, and that slaves did not have basic rights. Thereafter, slavery dominated national political debate.

In 1859 Brown seized the federal arsenal at Harpers Ferry, Virginia, as part of an effort to foment a slave rebellion. He was captured, tried, and hanged, further increasing sectional polarization.

The Republican Party opposed slavery, although most Republicans did not favor outright abolition. In 1860, the Republican candidate Abraham Lincoln (1809–1865) was elected president, which Southerners perceived as a threat. In December 1860 southern states began to secede, forming the Confederate States of America. When Confederate forces fired on Fort Sumter in Charleston harbor in April 1861, the most destructive war in U.S. history began.

THE CIVIL WAR

The Civil War lasted almost exactly four years, and a different nation emerged from the violence. In 1863 Lincoln emancipated the slaves in the rebelling states. The Emancipation Proclamation transformed the northern cause from that of suppressing a southern rebellion into that of extending liberty. By the time the Confederacy was defeated in 1865, the South was occupied by northern armies, its farms often fallow, its transportation network disrupted, and many of its cities in ruins. Southern political leaders had virtually no impact on immediate postwar policy. The Thirteenth, Fourteenth, and Fifteenth Amendments to the Constitution recast the character of the Union. The Thirteenth abolished slavery, the Fourteenth granted citizenship to the former slaves, and the Fifteenth allowed them to vote. The Fourteenth Amendment also prohibited much political activity by people who had taken up arms against the Union. These amendments resolved the issues of slavery and the relative roles of the state and federal governments.

The Civil War and the Reconstruction era that followed it overturned the social and political order of the South. For a time, freed slaves participated broadly and actively in politics. For more than ten years federal troops occupied parts of the South. Many of the antebellum southern leaders left political life. Economically, the South remained generally rural and still dependent on cotton. For the first time since the earliest colonial days, it became an area of free labor. Many of the freed slaves and poor whites who tilled the land remained hopelessly in debt to wealthier landowners. Attempts to bring manufacturing into the South met with limited success. Rampant racism blocked free economic development. For the rest of the century the South remained in a semicolonial relationship to the North, and rural poverty was the norm.

Within the context of world history, the American Civil War is important for several reasons. It was the second-largest war (after the Taiping Rebellion in China from 1851 to 1864) between the defeat of Napoleon in 1815 and the onset of World War I in 1914. It resulted in the establishment of a continentwide free labor market, even though freed blacks lived in great poverty and an economic dependence not unlike that of the rural classes of Latin America. This free labor market helped open the entire North American continent to economic development. The war also allowed American political and economic interests to develop without the distraction of the debates over states' rights and the morality of slavery.

THE CANADIAN EXPERIENCE

HOW DID Canada achieve united self-government?

Under the Treaty of Paris of 1763, all of Canada came under the control of Great Britain. Canada then, as now, included both an English-speaking and a French-speaking population, the latter concentrated in Quebec. The Quebec Act of 1774 made the Roman Catholic Church the established church in Quebec. During the American Revolution approximately 30,000 English loyalists fled the colonies and settled in Canada, strengthening English influences.

Tension between the French and English populations contributed to the Constitutional Act of 1791, which divided the colony into Upper Canada (primarily English in ethnic composition) and Lower Canada (primarily French). Each section had its own legislature, and a governor-general presided over the two provinces on behalf of the British Crown. Newfoundland, Nova Scotia, New Brunswick, Cape Breton Island, and Prince Edward Island remained separate colonies.

In the early nineteenth century relations with the United States were often tense. There were local disputes over the fur trade and fear that the United States would dominate Canada. That apprehension and the Anglo-French ethnic divisions became two of the major themes of Canadian history.

By the late 1830s, tension arose between long-established families with powerful economic interests in both Upper and Lower Canada and new settlers seeking their own prosperity. There were quarrels over the influence of the British Crown in local affairs. In 1837 rebellions occurred in both Upper and Lower Canada. There were relatively few casualties, but the British took action.

Canadian rail passengers board a train of the Great Western Railway at Clifton Depot in southern Ontario, sometime in the late 1850s. As in the United States, the growth of railroads transformed Canada in the nineteenth century.

Were there significant regional differences within Canada?

ROAD TO SELF-GOVERNMENT

The British government was determined to avoid another North American revolution. Consequently, it sent the Earl of Durham (1792–1840) to Canada with extensive powers to make reforms. His 1839 *Report on the Affairs of British North America* advocated uniting both Canadian provinces into one political unit. He believed that only foreign policy and defense should remain under British control. In effect, Durham wanted Canadians to govern themselves, so that English culture would dominate. His policy was carried out in the Canada Act of 1840, which gave the nation a single legislature composed of two houses.

The Durham *Report* established the broad political pattern that the British government followed with its other English-speaking colonies during the nineteenth century. Britain sought to foster responsible self-government in Australia, New Zealand, and South Africa. But until well into the twentieth century, the British and other Western imperial powers generally believed that nonwhite peoples, such as those of India, required direct colonial administration.

KEEPING A DISTINCTIVE CULTURE

Canadians exercised self-government, but distinct English and French cultures continued to exist. Within the legislature there were frequent trade-offs between the eastern and western sections of the nation. During the American Civil War, fears that the American republic might seek to invade or dominate Canada led to an attempt to unite the Maritime Provinces in 1862 and to consideration of a stronger federation among all the parts of Canada.

The British North America Act of 1867 created a Canadian federation. Canadians hoped to avoid what they regarded as flaws in the Constitution of the United States. The Canadian system of government was federal but placed much less emphasis on states' rights than did the United States. Canadians established a parliamentary mode of government but also chose to retain the presence of the British monarchy in the person of the governor-general as head of state. John A. MacDonald (1815–1891) was the person most responsible for establishing this new government, and he led it for most of the period between 1867 and 1891.

MIDCENTURY POLITICAL CONSOLIDATION IN EUROPE

WHAT WERE the steps that led to Italian and German unification?

While the United States and Canada were establishing themselves as strong, unified political entities in North America, major political consolidation occurred in Europe as well. War made change possible, by disrupting the international balance that had prevailed since 1815 and unleashing forces that upset the internal political situation in several states.

THE CRIMEAN WAR

The Crimean War (1854–1856), named after the Black Sea peninsula on which it was largely fought, originated from a long-standing rivalry between Russia and the Ottoman Empire over Ottoman provinces in the Balkans. In 1853 Russia went to war against the Ottomans on a pretext. The next year France and Great Britain supported the Ottoman Empire to protect their interests in the eastern Mediterranean, but the war bogged down after the French and the British invaded the Crimea. In March 1856 a peace conference in Paris concluded a treaty highly unfavorable to Russia.

The Crimean War shattered the image of Russian invincibility that had prevailed since the close of the Napoleonic Wars. It also shattered the power of the Concert of Europe to settle international disputes on the Continent. The major European powers were no longer willing to cooperate to maintain the existing borders between themselves and their neighbors. For the next twenty-five years instability prevailed, allowing adventurism in foreign policy.

ITALIAN UNIFICATION

See the Map
The Unification of Italy, 1859–1870
at **myhistorylab.com**

View the Image
Garibaldi Surrendering Power—British
Cartoon, 1860 at **myhistorylab.com**

Italian nationalists had long wanted to unite the small absolutist principalities of the peninsula into a single state but could not agree on how to do it. Romantic republicans such as Giuseppe Mazzini (1805–1872) and Giuseppe Garibaldi (1807–1882) sought to drive out the Austrians by popular military force and then to establish a republic. They not only failed but also frightened more moderate Italians. The person who eventually achieved unification was Count Camillo Cavour (1810–1861), the prime minister of Piedmont.

A Closer Look

The Crimean War Recalled

Although the nineteenth century is often regarded as a relatively peaceful century because of its contrast with the twentieth, the third quarter of the century saw major armed conflicts in both Europe and North America. The wars of the third quarter of the nineteenth century brought European armies once again to the foreground in European culture and art. Beginning with the Crimean War (1853–1856) and ending the wars of German unification (1870), the armed forces of the various nation-states re-forged European political life. In the United States, the Civil War resulted in unprecedented American casualties as the North firmly unified the nation under the federal government and ended slavery.

Over time these conflicts became the subject of historical paintings. Artists might record even the most difficult moments of warfare. Here, the English artist Elizabeth Thompson, Lady Butler, portrayed *Roll Call after an Engagement, Crimea.* A pioneering woman artist, she completed the work in 1874 two decades after the war, and Queen Victoria purchased it.

The abilities of the aristocratic officers leading the British army had been discredited, so Butler here portrays ordinary troops who had suffered grievously during the Crimean war.

A certain nostalgia for the comradeship of soldiers even under the most difficult circumstances penetrates this scene at a time when Britain had not engaged in a major war for many years.

Royal Collection Enterprises Ltd./Lady Elizabeth Thompson Butler (1846–1933), "The Roll Call: Calling the Roll after an Engagement, Crimea (unframed)." The Royal Collection (c) 2005, Her Majesty Queen Elizabeth II. Photo by SC.

The poor equipment of the troops during the war had been a public scandal, and the evident suffering of these troops recalls that.

Questions

1. Lady Butler had herself never witnessed war. How do you think she was able to portray this and other war scenes?

2. Do you view this painting as a realistic image of the experience of soldiers, or do you think it represents Lady Butler's interpretation?

3. How might one conclude that this painting represents warfare during an era of growing democratization?

4. Why do you think that paintings such as *Roll Call after an Engagement, Crimea,* fell from favor by the early twentieth century?

Piedmont (officially the "Kingdom of Sardinia"), in northwestern Italy, was the most independent state on the peninsula. It had fought unsuccessfully against Austria in 1848 and 1849. In 1852 the new monarch Victor Emmanuel II (r. 1849–1878) chose Cavour—an economic liberal and a strong monarchist who rejected republicanism—as his prime minister.

Cavour believed that if Italians proved themselves to be efficient and economically progressive, the great powers might let Italy govern itself. He worked for free trade, railway construction, credit expansion, and agricultural improvement. He also fostered the Nationalist Society, which established chapters in other Italian states to press for unification under Piedmontese leadership. Cavour joined the French and British in the Crimean War because he wanted French help with unification. France's Napoleon III (r. 1852–1870) was sympathetic, and in 1858 Cavour and the French emperor plotted to start a war with Austria.

In April 1859 war erupted between Piedmont and Austria. France came to Piedmont's aid, but soon concluded a separate peace with Austria. Cavour felt betrayed by France, but nonetheless the war had driven Austria from most of northern Italy. Within months other Italian states voted to unite with Piedmont.

Soon thereafter, Garibaldi began a successful unification campaign in Sicily. To forestall a republican victory Cavour rushed troops south to confront Garibaldi. On the way Cavour's troops conquered most of the Papal States. Garibaldi's nationalism won out over his republicanism, and he unhappily accepted the Piedmontese domination. In late 1860 Naples and Sicily voted to join the northern union. In March 1861 Victor Emmanuel II was proclaimed king of Italy. Three months later Cavour died. The new state was governed by Piedmont's conservative constitution. Italy gained Veneto (the region surrounding Venice) in 1866 as a result of the war between Austria and Prussia, and Rome in 1870 as a result of the Franco-Prussian War.

kleindeutsch

Meaning "small German." The argument that the German-speaking portions of the Habsburg Empire should be excluded from a united Germany.

Creating Nations. The proclamation of the German Empire in the Hall of Mirrors at Versailles, January 18, 1871, after the defeat of France in the Franco-Prussian War. Kaiser Wilhelm I is standing at the top of the steps under the flags; Otto von Bismarck is in the center in a white uniform. The new nation possessed enormous economic resources and nationalistic ambitions.

What was the significance of German unification?

GERMAN UNIFICATION

The unification of Germany was the single most important political development in Europe between 1848 and 1914. It was spearheaded by Prussia's conservative army, monarch, and prime minister, who outflanked the kingdom's liberals.

William I's (r. 1861–1888) primary concern was the Prussian army. In 1860, his war minister and chief of staff proposed enlarging the army and increasing the service of conscripts from two to three years, but the liberal-dominated parliament refused to approve the necessary taxes. A two-year deadlock ensued.

In 1862 William I turned for help to Otto von Bismarck (1815–1898), the person who did more than anyone else to shape the next thirty years of European history. Bismarck held traditional Prussian values: admiration for the monarchy, the nobility, and the army. After being appointed prime minister and foreign minister, Bismarck sought a cause that would draw popular support away from the liberals, who formed the majority in Parliament, and toward the monarchy and the army. He used foreign affairs to divert public attention from domestic matters by having Prussia assume leadership of the effort to unify Germany.

Bismarck favored what was known as the **kleindeutsch** ("small German") solution to unification. It excluded Austria. To promote his plan, he fought two brief wars. In 1864, he went to war with Denmark

CHRONOLOGY

GERMAN AND ITALIAN UNIFICATION

1854		Crimean War opens
1855		Cavour leads Piedmont into war on side of France and England
1856	July 20	Treaty of Paris concludes Crimean War
1858		Secret conference between Louis Napoleon and Cavour
1859		War of Piedmont and France against Austria
1860		Garibaldi lands his forces in Sicily and conquers southern Italy
1861	March 17	Proclamation of the Kingdom of Italy
	June 6	Death of Cavour
1862		Bismarck becomes prime minister of Prussia
1864		Danish War
1866		Austro-Prussian War; Veneto ceded to Italy
1867		North German Confederation formed
1870	June 6–July 12	Crisis over Hohenzollern candidacy for the Spanish throne
	July 13	Bismarck publishes edited press dispatch
	July 19	France declares war on Prussia
	September 1	France defeated at Sedan and Napoleon III captured
	September 4	French Republic proclaimed
	October 2	Italian state annexes Rome
1871	January 18	Proclamation of the German Empire at Versailles
	March 18–May 28	Paris Commune
	May 10	Treaty of Frankfurt between France and Germany

over the status of the duchies of Schleswig and Holstein, German-speaking areas that had long been administered by the Danish monarchy. The Austrians helped defeat Denmark and joined Prussia in jointly administering the two duchies. Bismarck then made alliances with France and Italy against Austria, and in the summer of 1866, decisively defeated Austria in the Seven Weeks' War. The consequent Treaty of Prague excluded the Habsburgs from German affairs and left Prussia the only major power among the German states.

In 1867 Hanover, Hesse, Nassau, and the city of Frankfurt, all of which had supported Austria during the war, were annexed by Prussia and their rulers deposed. Prussia and these newly incorporated territories, plus Schleswig and Holstein and the rest of the German states north of the Main River, constituted the North German Confederation. Prussia was its undisputed leader.

THE FRANCO-PRUSSIAN WAR AND THE GERMAN EMPIRE

Bismarck looked for an opportunity to bring the states of southern Germany into the confederation. It appeared as a result of complex diplomacy surrounding the possibility of a cousin of William I of Prussia becoming king of Spain. France opposed this.

•●•─Read the **Document**

A Letter from Bismarck (1866)
at **myhistorylab.com**

Bismarck goaded the French into war by tricking them into believing that William I had insulted the French ambassador. Once the war began, the states of southern Germany supported Prussia. On September 1, 1870, the Germans defeated the French army and captured Napoleon III. Paris capitulated on January 28, 1871. Ten days earlier, in the Hall of Mirrors at the Palace of Versailles, the German Empire had been proclaimed. The rulers of the states of southern Germany had requested that William I accept the imperial title—allowing them to retain their kingly titles and thrones.

The unification of Germany established a strong, coherent state in the middle of Europe. It had been forged by the Prussian army and monarchy and would be dominated by Prussian institutions. It possessed enormous economic resources and nationalistic ambitions. For some, the unification of Italy and Germany showed that nationalistic aspirations could only be fulfilled by armed force. France, in the wake of its defeat by Prussia, again became a republic—the Third Republic—governed by a chamber of deputies, a senate, and a president.

See the Map
The Unification of Germany, 1866–1871
at **myhistorylab.com**

UNREST OF NATIONALITIES IN EASTERN EUROPE

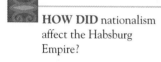

HOW DID nationalism affect the Habsburg Empire?

In an age increasingly characterized by national states, liberal institutions, and industrialism, the Habsburg domains remained dynastic, absolutist, and agrarian. Following the revolutions of 1848, Emperor Francis Joseph (r. 1848–1916) and his ministers attempted to impose a centralized administration on the multinational empire. The system amounted to a military and bureaucratic government dominated by German-speaking Austrians. This particularly annoyed the Hungarians. Austria's shrinking power compelled Francis Joseph to come to terms with the Hungarian nobility. The **Ausgleich** (Compromise) of 1867 transformed the Habsburg Empire into a dual monarchy. Francis Joseph was crowned king of Hungary in Budapest. Except for the common monarch, foreign policy, and army, Austria and Hungary functioned largely as separate states (see Map 23–4).

Ausgleich

Meaning "compromise." The agreement between the Habsburg emperor and the Hungarians to give Hungary considerable administrative autonomy in 1867. It created the Dual Monarchy, or Austria-Hungary.

Other national groups within the empire opposed the compromise because it permitted the German-speaking Austrians and the Hungarian Magyars to dominate all other nationalities. The Czechs of Bohemia were the most vocal group. By the turn of the century, they and German-speaking groups in the Austrian Reichsrat disrupted the Parliament rather than permit a compromise on language issues. The emperor ruled thereafter by imperial decree. Constitutionalism survived in Hungary only because the Magyars used it to dominate competing national groups.

QUICK REVIEW

Nationalist Unrest

- Significant impact on German, Russian, and Austrian empires
- Hungarian Magyars won significant rights
- Many Slavic groups oriented toward Russia
- Destabilizing influence; led to World War I

Nationalist unrest within the Habsburg Empire constituted one of the major sources of political instability for all of central and eastern Europe. Virtually all the nationality problems had a foreign policy as well as a domestic political dimension. Both the Serbo-Croatians and the Poles believed they deserved a wholly independent state in union with their fellow nationals who lived outside the empire. Ukrainians, Romanians, and Bosnians saw themselves as potentially linked to Russia, Romania, Serbia, or some larger Slavic state. Many nationalities looked to Russia for protection, contributing to the tensions that would spark World War I. The dominant German population of Austria proper was generally loyal to the emperor. However, a significant segment was strongly nationalistic and yearned to be part of Bismarck's German state. These nationalistic Germans in the Austrian Empire often hated the non-German national groups, particularly the Jews. These attitudes influenced Adolf Hitler (1889–1945) in his youth, shaping his political opinions.

See the Map
The Nationalities of Austria-Hungary, 1867
at **myhistorylab.com**

MAP 23–4.   Nationalities within the Habsburg Empire.   The patchwork appearance reflects the unusual problem of the numerous ethnic groups that the Habsburgs could not, of course, meld into a modern national state. Only the Magyars were recognized in 1867, leaving nationalist Czechs, Slovaks, and the others chronically dissatisfied.

How did the Compromise of 1867 affect the Habsburg Empire?

Each of the three great central and eastern European empires—German, Russian, and Austrian—was touched by nationality problems from the 1860s through the outbreak of World War I. All had Polish populations. Each shared at least two other major national groups. Each nationality regarded its own aspirations and discontents as being more important than the larger good. The government of each empire would be overturned during the war, and the Austrian Empire would disappear. The same unresolved problems of central and eastern European nationalism would then lead directly to World War II. More recently, they led to civil war in what was Yugoslavia and to the breakup of Czechoslovakia.

RACIAL THEORY AND ANTI-SEMITISM

Racial thinking, or **racism**, had long existed in Europe, but articulated racial theory constituted a new component of late-century nationalistic unrest. Late eighteenth-century linguistic scholars had observed similarities between many European languages

HOW DID racial theory influence anti-Semitism?

racism
The pseudoscientific theory that biological features of race determine human character and worth.

and Sanskrit, and postulated the existence of an ancient race called the Aryans, who spoke the original language from which the rest derived. During the Romantic period, writers had called the different cultures of Europe *races*. The debates over slavery in the European colonies and the United States had spurred the development of racial theory. In the late nineteenth century the concept of race emerged as the dominant explanation of the history and the character of large groups of people.

Arthur de Gobineau (1816–1882), a reactionary French diplomat, theorized that race was the major determinant of human history. In his four-volume *Essay on the Inequality of the Human Races* (1853–1854), Gobineau portrayed the troubles of Western civilization as being the result of degeneration of the original white Aryan race through intermarriage with inferior races. Gobineau saw no way to reverse this degeneration.

Houston Stewart Chamberlain (1855–1927), an Englishman who settled in Germany, put racial theory on an alleged scientific basis in his widely read two-volume work, *Foundations of the Nineteenth Century* (1899). Chamberlain argued in opposition to Gobineau that the human race could be improved and that a superior race could be developed. He pointed to the Jews as the major obstacle to European racial regeneration. Chamberlain's book and others claiming that Jews threatened traditional German national life aided the spread of **anti-Semitism**.

anti-Semitism
Prejudice, hostility, or legal discrimination against Jews.

ANTI-SEMITISM AND THE BIRTH OF ZIONISM

Political and racial anti-Semitism, which cast such dark shadows across the twentieth century, emerged in part from this atmosphere of racial thought. Religious anti-Semitism dated from at least the Middle Ages, but following the French Revolution, western European Jews had gradually gained entry into civil society in Austria, Britain, France, and Germany. Popular anti-Semitism, which identified the Jewish community with money and banking interests, persisted. Racial thought added a new strand to anti-Semitism, the belief that no matter how well Jews assimilated, the problem of race was in their blood. In Austria, France, and Germany various political leaders and parties used their anti-Semitism to considerable political advantage.

Zionism
The movement to create a Jewish state in Palestine (the biblical Zion).

An important Jewish response to this new, rabid anti-Semitism was the launching in 1896 of the Zionist movement to found a separate Jewish state. Its founder was the Austro-Hungarian Theodor Herzl (1860–1904), whose experiences and observations of discrimination convinced him that the institutions of the liberal state could not protect the Jews in Europe. In 1896 Herzl published *The Jewish State*, calling for a separate state in which the Jews of the world might be assured of their rights and liberties. Herzl followed the tactics of late-century mass democratic politics by directing his appeal to the economically poor Jews who lived in the ghettos of eastern Europe and the slums of western Europe. The original call to **Zionism** combined a rejection of the anti-Semitism of Europe with a desire to establish some of the ideals of both liberalism and socialism in a state outside Europe.

Theodor Herzl. Herzl's visions of a Jewish state would eventually lead to the creation of Israel in 1948.

Why did anti-Semitism become more virulent in the nineteenth century?

Racial thinking and revived anti-Semitism were part of a wider late-century nationalism. Previously, nationalism had been a literary and liberal movement. From the 1870s onward, however, nationalism became a movement with mass support, well-financed organizations, and political parties. Nationality was redefined in terms of race and blood. The new nationalism opposed the internationalism of both liberalism and socialism; it was used to overcome the pluralism of class, religion, and geography. The nation and its duties could become a secular religion, for example, in the hands of state schoolteachers who were replacing the clergy as the instructors of youth. This aggressive, racist nationalism would prove to be the most powerful ideology of the early twentieth century.

SUMMARY

 WHAT IS nationalism?

The Emergence of Nationalism in Europe. Nationalism is the modern concept that people who share the same customs, culture, language, and history should also share the same government. It became the most powerful European political ideology of the nineteenth and early twentieth centuries. Nationalists challenged both the domestic and the international order of the Vienna settlement in the decades after 1815. *page 586*

WHAT WERE the basic goals of European liberals?

Early Nineteenth-Century Political Liberalism. Politically, nineteenth-century liberals sought to establish constitutional governments that recognized civil liberties and made the executive responsible to a legislature elected by property-owning men. Economically, liberals wanted a laissez-faire economy with minimal government involvement. Liberals often supported nationalists' efforts to create a single national state that could function as a more efficient economic unit. *page 589*

 WHY WERE efforts to achieve political liberalism more successful in France and Britain than in Russia?

Efforts to Liberalize Early Nineteenth-Century European Political Structures. Efforts to liberalize tsarist Russia failed, particularly after the ultraconservative Tsar Nicholas fired on his own officers during the 1825 Decembrist Revolt. Liberalism largely triumphed in France after the Revolution of 1830 and in Britain after the passage of the Great Reform Bill. The British were, however, unable to resolve the problem of Irish nationalism in the nineteenth century. *page 591*

 WHAT WERE the causes of the American Civil War?

Testing the New American Republic. In the United States, westward expansion and war against Mexico brought vast new territories into the republic from the Mississippi River to the Pacific, but sectional conflict between North and South over economic issues and slavery led to the outbreak of the Civil War in 1861. Northern victory led to the abolition of slavery, the creation of a continent-wide free labor market, and enormous economic development. *page 597*

 HOW DID Canada achieve united self-government?

The Canadian Experience. Canada achieved self-government with the Canada Act of 1840 and created a united Canadian federation in 1867. However, Canada remained part of the British Empire and retained its connection with the British monarchy. Anglo-French tension is a recurring theme in Canadian history, but legislative trade-offs and the federation's de-emphasis on states' rights have maintained Canadian unity. *page 601*

 WHAT WERE the steps that led to Italian and German unification?

Midcentury Political Consolidation in Europe. With French assistance, Piedmont under Count Camillo Cavour managed to unite most of the peninsula in the kingdom of Italy by 1860. German unification was achieved by Prussia under the leadership of Otto von Bismarck between 1864 and 1871. In three victorious wars against Denmark, Austria, and France, Bismarck forged the German states into a German Empire dominated by Prussia. *page 602*

 HOW DID nationalism affect the Habsburg Empire?

Unrest of Nationalities in Eastern Europe. Nationalism created problems for the three eastern European empires—Germany, Russia, and Austria—but Habsburg Austria faced the greatest challenge from nationalism because it was a dynastic, not a national, state. In 1867 Hungary became an autonomous kingdom under the Habsburg emperor. Czechs, Croats, and other nationalities in the empire became increasingly dissatisfied. *page 606*

 HOW DID racial theory influence anti-Semitism?

Racial Theory and Anti-Semitism. In the late nineteenth century, biological determinism, the concept that some peoples or races were inherently superior to others, took root in Western thought. In Germany, Austria, and France, some nationalists used the concept of race to blame the Jews for their countries' economic and political problems. Part of the Jewish response was the launching of the Zionist movement to found a separate Jewish state. *page 607*

KEY TERMS

anti-Semitism (p. 608)

Ausgleich (OWS-gleyek) (p. 606)

Catholic emancipation (p. 593)

Chartism (p. 593)

Great Reform Bill (p. 592)

home rule (p. 594)

July Monarchy (p. 592)

kleindeutsch **(KLEYEN-doytch)** (p. 604)

liberalism (p. 589)

nationalism (p. 586)

racism (p. 607)

Zionism (ZEYE-ahn-izm) (p. 608)

REVIEW QUESTIONS

1. Define *nationalism*. What were the goals of nationalists? What were the difficulties they confronted in realizing those goals? Why was nationalism a special threat to the Austrian Empire? What areas saw significant nationalist movements between 1815 and 1830? Which were successful and which were unsuccessful?

2. What were the tenets of liberalism? Who were the liberals, and how did liberalism affect the political developments of the early nineteenth century? What relationship does liberalism have to nationalism?

3. Compare and contrast the movement toward political liberalism between 1815 and 1830 in Russia, France, and Great Britain.

4. What economic differences between the American North and South gave rise to sectional conflict? Why was slavery the core issue in that conflict? How did westward expansion contribute to making slavery such an important issue?

5. How did Canada unify and become self-governing?

6. What is the significance of the Crimean War? How did it impact Russia? Why did the Crimean War have a destabilizing effect on Europe?

7. Why was it so difficult to unify Italy? What were the contributions of Cavour and Garibaldi to Italian unification?

8. Who was Otto von Bismarck, and why did he try to unify Germany? What was Bismarck's method of unification, and why did he succeed? What effect did the unification of Germany have on the rest of Europe?

9. How did British politicians handle the Irish Question? What were the parallels between England's relationship with Ireland and the nationality problem of the Austrian Empire?

10. What were the origins of the modern idea of racial theory? Who were its major proponents? How did the rise of such a theory change European anti-Semitism?

Note: To learn more about the topics in this chapter, please turn to the Suggested Readings at the end of the book. For additional sources related to this chapter please see www.myhistorylab.com

PEARSON myhistorylab™ Connections

Reinforce what you learned in this chapter by studying the many documents, images, maps, review tools, and videos available at **www.myhistorylab.com**

Read and Review

✓•⌐**Study** and **Review**   Chapter 23

•‡•⌐**Read** the Document   *The Seneca Falls Convention (1848), p. 589*
Metternich on the Revolutions of 1848, p. 596
"A Defense of the Slave Trade," July 1740, p. 597
The History of Mary Prince (1830s), p. 598
A Letter from Bismarck (1866), p. 605

👁⌐**See** the Map   *The Americas, 1800–1836, p. 599*
The Unification of Germany, 1866–1871, p. 606
The Nationalities of Austria-Hungary, 1867, p. 606

•👁⌐**View** the Image   *Reform Bill of 1832–Cartoon, p. 593*
Gladstone and Disraeli—Punch Cartoon, p. 594
Garibaldi Surrendering Power—British Cartoon, 1860, p. 602

((•●⌐**Hear** the Audio   *Slavery 1, p. 597*

Research and Explore

👁⌐**See** the Map   *European Centers of Rebellion and Revolution, 1820–1848, p. 595*

👁⌐**See** the Map   *The Unification of Italy, 1859–1870, p. 602*

((•●⌐Hear the **Audio**

Hear the audio file for Chapter 23
at **www.myhistorylab.com**

24

Northern Transatlantic Economy and Society, 1815–1914

((•●—Hear the Audio for Chapter 24 at www.myhistorylab.com

Russian society. A detail from the "Parade on Tsarina's Meadow" by G. G. Chernetson, 1831. Tsarina's Meadow was a vast space outside Saint Petersburg that often held military parades and reviews in nineteenth-century Russia. The different classes and ethnic groups of the Russian Empire can be seen mingling about.

How do the different clothing styles worn by the people in this painting comment on Russian society during this time?

EUROPEAN FACTORY WORKERS AND URBAN ARTISANS *page 614*

WHAT IS *proletarianization?*

NINETEENTH-CENTURY EUROPEAN WOMEN *page 616*

WHAT SOCIAL and legal disabilities did European women confront in the nineteenth century?

JEWISH EMANCIPATION *page 621*

HOW DID emancipation affect Jewish life in Europe outside of Russia?

EUROPEAN LABOR, SOCIALISM, AND POLITICS TO WORLD WAR I *page 622*

WHY DID Marxism become so influential among European Socialists?

NORTH AMERICA AND THE NEW INDUSTRIAL ECONOMY *page 629*

HOW DID industrialization in the United States differ from industrialization in Europe?

THE EMERGENCE OF MODERN EUROPEAN THOUGHT *page 635*

WHO WERE some of the intellectuals at the forefront of modern European thought?

ISLAM AND LATE NINETEENTH-CENTURY EUROPEAN THOUGHT *page 638*

WHAT WERE some influential views on the relationship between Islam and the West?

*D*uring the eighteenth century, northwestern Europe and the United States developed major industrial economies, which produced unprecedented levels of goods and services. This economic achievement undergirded the enormous international political power exerted by the industrial nations of the West from that time to the present.

In the first half of the nineteenth century, a new kind of industrial labor force emerged, especially in Europe. These laborers worked in factories and generally lived in cities. The presence and growth of this new labor force were the most important social developments of the century. It was out of the experiences of this workforce that the political movement known as socialism arose.

In the second half of the nineteenth century European and American political, economic, and social life assumed many characteristics of our present-day world. In Europe nation-states with large electorates, political parties, centralized bureaucracies, and universal military service emerged. In the United States the politics associated with the Progressive movement brought the

613

GLOBAL PERSPECTIVE

THE BUILDING OF NORTHERN TRANSATLANTIC SUPREMACY

Between 1850 and 1914 Europe had more influence throughout the world than it had before or has had since. Although Europe and North America together were the most industrially advanced regions of the world, the preponderance of economic power lay with Europe. Its industrial base was more advanced than that of any other region, including the still-developing United States. European banks exercised vast influence across the globe. Europeans financed the building of railways in Africa, Asia, and the Americas. Financial power brought political influence. The armaments industry gave European armies and navies predominant power over the peoples of Africa and Asia, whereas the United States began to exercise such power only as a result of the Spanish-American War. These economic developments established a pattern that still persists. First European, and later American, banks, companies, and corporations penetrated the economies and societies of Asia, Africa, and Latin America. These nonpolitical groups often expected their own governments to protect their interests. Thus, what started as commercial

contact often evolved into the exercise of direct political influence, even over nations that had never been European colonies.

During these years European culture was probably also enjoying its greatest influence. Capital cities in Latin America, especially Buenos Aires and Montevideo, adopted European-style architecture. Paris became synonymous with high fashion. Paris, London, and Vienna were world intellectual centers. The rest of the world regarded the advanced industrial and urban civilization of Europe as a model, in part because more non-Europeans were visiting and studying in Europe than ever before. During this period many American artists and writers flocked to Europe to absorb its culture. Another cultural feature of western Europe and the United States that affected the rest of the world during the era was the emerging role of women. In particular, the demand for the entrance of women into the political process and the professions became a hallmark of the twentieth century. On both sides of the Atlantic, women assumed leadership roles in social reform movements.

presidency to the center of American political life. On both sides of the North Atlantic, business adopted large-scale corporate structures, and the labor force organized itself into trade unions. The number of white-collar laborers grew, and urban life became predominant throughout western Europe. But even as new vast cities arose in the United States, farming continued to spread across the central Midwest and upper Southwest. During this period, too, women began to assert new political awareness and to become politically active in both Europe and America.

Europe grew dependent on the resources and markets of the rest of the world. Farms in the United States, Canada, Latin America, Australia, and New Zealand supplied food to much of the world. Before World War I this dependence was concealed by Europe's industrial, military, and financial supremacy. Europeans assumed their supremacy to be natural, but the twentieth century would reveal it to have been temporary. While it prevailed, Europeans dominated most of the other peoples of the earth and displayed extreme self-confidence. The United States, having achieved the status of a major industrial power as well as an agricultural supplier, entered the world stage as a military power, defeating Spain in the Spanish-American War in 1898. With that victory, the United States also acquired its first colonial territories.

At the same time, major new sets of ideas arose. Theories of evolution in biology, relativity in physics, the irrational in philosophy, and psychoanalysis in psychology shaped much of the intellectual outlook for the next century. ■

proletarianization

The process whereby independent artisans and factory workers lose control of the means of production and of the conduct of their own trades to the owners of capital.

WHAT IS *proletarianization?*

((•─ **Hear** the **Audio**
Industrial Revolution
at **myhistorylab.com**

EUROPEAN FACTORY WORKERS AND URBAN ARTISANS

Industrial production had begun in the eighteenth century, and in the nineteenth century much of Europe headed toward a more fully industrial society. By 1830 only Great Britain had attained that status, but new factories and railways were being constructed elsewhere. What characterized the second quarter of the century, though, was less the triumph of industrialism than the final gasps of those economic groups that opposed it

The nation that most clearly understood the nature of European power and sought to imitate it was Japan. After the Meiji Restoration (1868), Japanese administrators came to Europe to study the new technology, political structures, and military organizations. The Japanese political and military reorganization that resulted proved sufficiently successful to allow them to defeat Russia in 1905, providing the first example of a non-European nation using Western weapons, organizations, and economic power to defeat a European nation. In the twentieth century other non-European nations found ways to import or manufacture technology that permitted them to challenge European and later American hegemony. Indeed, today the proliferation of weaponry usually developed in the United States or Europe has allowed regional powers to challenge Western dominance. This destabilizing arms trade began in the second half of the nineteenth century.

In contrast to Japan, China, India, the countries of the Middle East, and Africa were overwhelmed by the economic and military power of Europe. In time, however, the peoples of those lands under European domination embraced the ideologies of revolutionary protest, most particularly those of nationalism and socialism. As people from the colonial world came to work or study in Europe, they encountered ideas and criticisms that were most effective against European and Western culture. They adapted those ideas to their own cultural contexts and then turned them against their colonial governors.

Focus Questions

◆ What was the relationship between nineteenth-century Europe's economic power and its political hegemony around the globe?

◆ How did European colonies use ideologies fostered in Europe against their colonial rulers?

and were displaced by it. Intellectually, the period saw the formulation of the major creeds supporting and criticizing the new society.

The specter of poor harvests still haunted Europe. The worst was the failure of potato crops that produced the Irish famine from 1845 to 1847. Half a million Irish peasants starved to death; hundreds of thousands emigrated. All over Europe there was a vast uprooting of people from the countryside as the revolution in landholding led to greater agricultural production.

In northern Europe both artisans and factory workers underwent a process of **proletarianization**, meaning they entered into a wage economy and lost significant ownership of the means of production, such as tools and equipment, and control over the conduct of their own trades. The process occurred rapidly wherever the factory system arose. The factory owner provided the financial capital to construct the factory, purchase the machinery, and secure the raw materials. The factory workers contributed their labor for a wage. Those workers submitted to factory discipline, which meant that work conditions became largely determined by the demands for smooth operation of the machines. Factory workers had no direct say over the quality of the product or its price. (It should be noted that factory conditions were often better than those of textile workers who resisted the factory mode of production.)

Urban artisans in the nineteenth century experienced proletarianization more slowly than factory workers, and

Il Quarto Stato (The Fourth Estate), 1901. Giuseppe Pellizza da Volpedo (1868–1907) was a powerfully committed Italian socialist artist. The title of his painting is taken from the French socialist Jean Jaurès, who believed that workers would soon displace the traditional three estates of the clergy, aristocracy, and commoners. Pellizza and other artists embracing social realism moved painting away from nostalgic, sentimental depictions of peasants to images of industrial or farm laborers experiencing hunger, poverty, and awakening political consciousness.

Oil on canvas, 283 cm × 550 cm. Civica Galleria d'Arte Moderna-Milano. Photo by Marcello Saporetti.

What is the significance of the woman carrying the baby?

OVERVIEW   Major European Cities, 1850–1914

	1850	1880	1914
Berlin	419,000	1,122,000	2,071,000
Birmingham	233,000	437,000	840,000
Frankfurt	65,000	137,000	415,000
London	2,685,000	4,470,000	7,256,000
Madrid	281,000	398,000	600,000
Paris	1,053,000	2,269,000	2,888,000
Vienna	444,000	1,104,000	2,031,000

QUICK REVIEW

Factory Work

- Proletarianization: loss of ownership of the means of production
- Factory work demanded submission to a new kind of work discipline
- Factory workers were better off than the hand-loom workers who competed with them

✓● Study and Review
Industrial Side Effects
at **myhistorylab.com**

machinery had little to do with the process. The emergence of factories in itself did not harm urban artisans. Many even prospered. Metal workers and craftsmen in the building trades, for example, saw increased demand for their work. The lower prices for machine-made textiles aided artisans involved in the making of clothing by reducing the costs of their raw materials. Where the urban artisans encountered difficulty and found their skills and livelihood threatened was in the organization of production.

In the eighteenth century a European town or city workplace had usually consisted of a few artisans laboring for a master, first as apprentices and then as journeymen, according to established guild practices. The master owned the workshop and the larger equipment, and the others owned their tools. The journeyman could expect to become a master. This guild system had allowed considerable worker control over labor recruitment and training, production pace, product quality, and price. In the nineteenth century, political and economic liberals disapproved of labor and guild organizations and attempted to make them illegal.

There were other changes in the organization of artisan production. Masters often found themselves under increased competitive pressure from larger establishments. Many masters began to follow a practice, known in France as *confection*, whereby goods such as shoes, clothing, and furniture were produced in standard sizes and styles rather than by individual order. This practice increased the division of labor in the workshop, so less skill was required of each artisan and the particular skills possessed by a worker became less valuable. Migrants from the countryside sometimes created a surplus of relatively unskilled workers. The dilution of skills and lower wages made it more difficult for urban journeymen to become masters with their own workshops. Increasingly, artisans became lifetime wage laborers.

NINETEENTH-CENTURY EUROPEAN WOMEN

WHAT SOCIAL and legal disabilities did European women confront in the nineteenth century?

WOMEN IN THE EARLY INDUSTRIAL REVOLUTION

The industrial economy had an immense impact on the home and the family life of women. First, it took virtually all productive work out of the home and allowed many families to live on the wages of the male spouse alone. This allowed a new concept of gender-determined roles. Women came to be associated with domestic duties and men almost exclusively with breadwinning. Children were reared to match these gender patterns. Previously, this domestic division of labor had prevailed only among the relatively small middle and gentry classes. Second, industrialization created new modes of employment that allowed many young women to earn enough money to marry or support themselves independently. Third, industrialism, though fostering more employment for women, lowered the skills required of them.

The early Industrial Revolution began in textile production, so women and their labor were deeply involved from the start. When spinning and weaving had been domestic industries, women worked in all stages of production. When these activities moved into factories and involved large machines, however, men displaced women. With the next generation of machines in the 1820s, unmarried women rapidly became employed in the factories, in jobs that tended to require few skills. There was thus a certain paradox in the impact of the factory on women: New jobs opened to them, but those jobs were less skilled than those that had been available to them before. Women in the factories were almost always young and single or widows. Factory owners disliked employing married women because of the likelihood of pregnancy, the influence of husbands, and the duties of child rearing.

At midcentury, industrial factory work accounted for less than half of all employment for women. The largest group of employed women in France continued to work on the land. In England they were domestic servants. Domestic industries, such as garment making, employed many women. The charwoman was a common sight across the Continent. Women's conditions of labor were almost always harsh, wherever they worked, and they were vulnerable to exploitation.

SOCIAL DISABILITIES CONFRONTED BY ALL WOMEN

During the early nineteenth century, virtually all European women faced social and legal disabilities in property rights, family law, and education. By the close of the century each area had shown improvement. All Europeans led lives that reflected their social rank, yet within each rank, women remained economically dependent and legally inferior to men.

Until late in the nineteenth century in most European countries, married women could not own property in their own names. Women's legal identities were subsumed into their husbands', and they had no independent standing before the law. Reform of women's property rights came slowly. By 1882 Great Britain allowed married women to own property. In France, however, a married woman could not even open a savings account in her own name until 1895, and not until 1907 were married women granted possession of their own wages. In 1900 Germany allowed women to take jobs without their husbands' permission, but a German husband retained control of most of his wife's other property. Similar laws prevailed elsewhere in Europe.

European family law also worked to the disadvantage of women. Legal codes required wives to obey their husbands. The Napoleonic Code and the remnants of Roman law made women legal minors throughout Europe. Divorce was difficult. Extramarital sexual relations of husbands were more tolerated than those of wives. The authority of husbands also extended to children. A husband could take children away from their mother and give them to someone else to rear. Contraception and abortion were illegal. The law on rape normally worked against women. Wherever they turned—whether to physicians or lawyers—women confronted an official world populated and controlled by men.

Throughout the nineteenth century women had less access to education than did men, and what was available to them was inferior. Most women were educated only enough for the domestic careers they were expected to follow. The percentage of illiterate women exceeded that of men.

Women in Textile Factories. As textile production became increasingly automated in the nineteenth century, textile factories required fewer skilled workers and more unskilled attendants. To fill these unskilled positions, factory owners turned increasingly to unmarried women and widows, who worked for lower wages than men and were less likely to form labor organizations. The two women shown here, holding "shuttles" used in textile factories, worked in the Lowell Mills, in Massachusetts, around 1860. **What do you notice about these women's clothes, hair, shoes, and bodies?**

◆●●—[Read the Document

Industrial Society and Factory Conditions (early 1800s) at **myhistorylab.com**

QUICK REVIEW

Women's Work

- ◆ Women involved in preindustrial textile production
- ◆ In the 1820s, unmarried women found employment in textile factories
- ◆ In mid-nineteenth-century England the largest group of employed women was domestic servants

◆●●—[Read the Document

Ellen Key, from The Century of the Child at **myhistorylab.com**

Middle-Class Family. Family was central to the middle-class conception of a stable and respectable social life. This portrait of the Bellelli family is by Edgar Degas. Notice that the husband and father sits at his desk, suggesting his association with business and the world outside the home, whereas the wife and mother stands with their children, suggesting her domestic role.

Edgar Degas (1834–1917), The Bellelli Family, c. 1858–60. Musée d'Orsay, Paris, France. Photograph Copyright Bridgeman-Giraudon/Art Resource, New York.

How were gender roles established in the nineteenth century?

CHRONOLOGY

MAJOR DATES IN LATE NINETEENTH-CENTURY AND EARLY TWENTIETH-CENTURY EUROPEAN WOMEN'S HISTORY

1857	Revised English divorce law
1865	University of Zurich admits women for degrees
1869	John Stuart Mill's *The Subjection of Women*
1878	University of London admits women as candidates for degrees
1882	English Married Woman's Property Act
1894	Union of German Women's Organizations founded
1901	National Council of French Women founded
1903	British Women's Social and Political Union founded
1907	Norway permits women to vote on national issues
1910	British suffragettes adopt radical tactics
1918	Vote extended to some British women
1918	Weimar constitution allows German women to vote
1920–1921	Oxford and Cambridge Universities award degrees to women
1922	French Senate defeats bill extending vote to women
1928	Britain extends vote to women on same basis as men

University and professional education remained reserved for men until at least the third quarter of the century. Italian universities were more open to both women students and women instructors than similar institutions elsewhere in Europe. Restricting women's access to secondary and university education helped bar women from social and economic advancement. Women benefited only marginally from the expansion of professional employment during the late nineteenth and early twentieth centuries.

Schoolteaching at the elementary level became a professional haven for women. The few women who pioneered in the professions were seen as challenging the clear separation of male and female spheres that had emerged during the nineteenth century. Women themselves often hesitated to support feminist causes because they had been so thoroughly acculturated into the recently stereotyped roles. Many women saw a real conflict between family responsibilities and feminism.

NEW EMPLOYMENT PATTERNS FOR WOMEN

During the late nineteenth century, two major developments affected the economic lives of women. The first was an expansion in the variety of jobs available outside the better-paying learned professions. The second was a withdrawal of married women from the workforce. These two seemingly contradictory developments require explanation.

The expansion of governmental bureaucracies, the emergence of large-scale businesses, and the expansion of retail stores opened many new employment opportunities for women. The need for elementary schoolteachers grew with compulsory education laws. Innovations such as the typewriter and eventually the telephone exchange fostered female employment. Women by the thousands became secretaries and clerks for governments and private businesses, while others became shop assistants.

Although these jobs did open new and often better employment opportunities for women, they nonetheless required low-level skills and involved minimal training. They were occupied primarily by unmarried women or widows. Employers continued to pay women low wages because they assumed that a woman did not need to support herself independently.

The industrial occupations that women had filled in the mid-nineteenth century, especially textile and garment making, were shrinking. The decline in the number of births also meant that fewer married women were needed to look after other women's children. The real wages paid to male workers increased during this period, reducing families' need for a second income. Thanks to improving health, men lived longer, so wives were less likely to be thrust into the workforce by an emergency. Smaller families also reduced the need for supplementary wages. Working children stayed at home longer and continued to contribute to the family's wage pool.

Finally, the cultural dominance of the middle class established a pattern of social expectations. The more prosperous a working-class family became, the less involved in employment its women were supposed to be.

Yet behind these generalities stands the enormous variety of social and economic experience late nineteenth-century women actually encountered. Social class largely determined individual experiences.

Women Working at a Telephone Exchange. The invention of the telephone opened new employment opportunities for women.

What made telephone exchanges suitable workplaces for women?

LATE NINETEENTH-CENTURY WORKING-CLASS WOMEN

Though less dominant than earlier in the century, the textile industry and garment making continued to employ many women. The German clothing-making trades illustrate women's vulnerable economic situations. The manufacture of mass-made clothes in Germany was designed to require minimal capital investment. A major manufacturer would arrange to produce clothing through a putting-out system: He would purchase the material and then put it out for tailoring. The clothing was made in independently owned, small sweatshops or by workers in their homes.

In Berlin in 1896 there were more than 80,000 garment workers, mostly women. When business was good, employment for these women was high. If business became poor, however, women were idled. In effect, the workers carried much of the risk of the enterprise. Even women in factories were subject to layoffs. Women were nearly always treated as casual workers.

THE RISE OF POLITICAL FEMINISM

Liberal society and its values did not automatically improve the lot of women. In particular, it did not give them the vote or access to political activity. Male liberals feared that granting the vote to women would benefit political conservatives because women

Women Laundry Workers. Although new opportunities opened to them in the late nineteenth century, many working-class women, like these women ironing in a laundry, remained in traditional occupations. As the wine bottle suggests, alcoholism was a problem for women as well as men engaged in tedious work. The painting is by Edgar Degas (1834–1917).

Réunion des Musées Nationaux/Art Resource, New York.

Compare this painting with the photograph on page 617. What is similar? What is different?

were thought to be unduly controlled by the clergy. Consequently, anticlerical liberals often had difficulty working with feminists.

Women were often reluctant to support feminist causes. Some women considered their class and economic interests higher political priorities. Others subordinated feminist political issues to national unity and nationalistic patriotism. Still others would not support particular feminist organizations because of differences over tactics or religious beliefs. Except in England, it was often difficult for working-class and middle-class women to cooperate.

Liberal society and law presented women with many obstacles but also provided feminists with many intellectual and political tools. As early as 1792 in Britain, Mary Wollstonecraft (1759–1797) had applied the revolutionary doctrines of the rights of man to the predicament of women in *The Vindication of the Rights of Women*. John Stuart Mill (1806–1873) and his wife Harriet Taylor (1804–1858) had applied the logic of liberal freedom to the position of women in *The Subjection of Women* (1869). The arguments for utility and efficiency so dear to middle-class liberals could be used to expose the human and social waste implicit in the inferior role assigned to women. Furthermore, the socialist criticism of capitalist society often included a harsh indictment of women's social and economic positions.

The earliest statements of feminism arose from critics of the existing order and were often associated with people who had unorthodox opinions about sexuality, family life, and property. This hardened resistance to the feminist message. These difficulties prevented Continental feminists from raising the kind of massive public support or mounting the large demonstrations that feminists in Great Britain and the United States could.

Europe's most advanced women's movement was in Great Britain. Millicent Fawcett (1847–1929) led the moderate National Union of Women's Suffrage Societies. She believed Parliament would grant women the vote only when convinced that women would be responsible in their political activity. In 1908 this organization could rally almost half a million women in London, using liberal tactics.

Emmeline Pankhurst (1858–1928) led a radical branch of British feminists. She was familiar with the disruptive political tactics used in both labor and Irish nationalist politics. In 1903 Pankhurst and her daughters founded the Women's Social and Political Union. For several years they and their followers, known derisively as **suffragettes**, lobbied for women's suffrage. By 1910 they turned to the violent tactics of arson, window breaking, and sabotage of postal boxes. They marched en masse on Parliament. The Liberal government of Herbert Asquith (1852–1928) imprisoned many of the demonstrators and force-fed those who went on hunger strikes in jail. Only in 1918, and then as a result of their contribution to the war effort, did some British women receive the vote.

The cases of France and Germany show how advanced the British women's movement was. In France, when Hubertine Auclert (1848–1914) began campaigning for the vote in the 1880s, she stood virtually alone. Most leaders of French feminism believed that the vote could be achieved through careful legalism. French women did not receive the right to vote until 1944 at the end of World War II. German law actually forbade German women from political activity.

suffragettes
British women who lobbied and agitated for the right to vote in the early twentieth century.

Women's Suffrage. The creator of this poster cleverly reveals the hypocrisy and foolishness of denying the vote to women.

How does this poster show the obstacles that stood in the path of women's suffrage?

By 1902 the Union of German Women's Organizations (BDFK) was calling for the right to vote. The German Social Democratic Party also supported women's suffrage, but the party was so disdained by the German authorities and German Roman Catholics that this support only made suffrage more suspect in their eyes. Women received the vote in Germany only in 1918 under the constitution of the Weimar Republic. Before World War I, only in Norway (1907) could women vote on national issues.

•••┌Read the **Document**
John Stuart Mill on Enfranchisement of
Women (1869) at **myhistorylab.com**

JEWISH EMANCIPATION

One of the most important social changes to occur throughout Europe during the nineteenth century was the emancipation of European Jews from the narrow life of the ghetto into a world of nearly equal citizenship and social status.

HOW DID emancipation affect Jewish life in Europe outside of Russia?

EARLY STEPS TO EQUAL CITIZENSHIP

Emancipation began in the late eighteenth century and continued throughout the nineteenth. It moved at different paces in different countries. In 1782 Joseph II (r. 1765–1790), the Habsburg emperor, issued a decree that placed the Jews of his empire under more or less the same laws as Christians. In France the National Assembly recognized Jews as French citizens in 1789. During the Napoleonic Wars, Jewish communities in Italy and Germany were allowed to mix on a generally equal footing with the Christian population.

pogroms
Organized riots against Jews in the Russian Empire.

These various steps toward political emancipation were vulnerable to changes in rulers or governments. Even in countries that granted them political rights, Jews could not own land and could be subject to discriminatory taxes. Nonetheless, by the first half of the nineteenth century Jews in western Europe and to a much lesser extent in central and eastern Europe had begun to acquire equal or nearly equal citizenship.

In Russia, however, the traditional modes of prejudice and discrimination continued unabated until World War I. Jews were treated as aliens under Russian rule. The government undermined Jewish community life, limited publication of Jewish books, restricted areas where Jews might live, required internal passports from Jews, and banned them from many forms of state service and from many institutions of higher education. The police and others were allowed to conduct **pogroms**—organized riots—against Jewish neighborhoods and villages.

Dedication of a New Synagogue. The social life of Europe became transformed in numerous ways during the nineteenth century. Beyond the expansion of cities and the rise of industrial society, there also occurred numerous changes in religious life. One of the most important of these changes was the gradual emancipation of European Jews from sharply restricted lives in urban ghettos to fuller political participation and social assimilation. This painting by G. E. Opitz portrays the dedication of a new synagogue in Alsace in 1820.

How does this painting show the assimilation of Jews into nineteenth-century European society?

BROADENED OPPORTUNITIES

After the revolutions of 1848, especially in western Europe, the situation of European Jews improved for several decades. Throughout Germany, Italy, the Low Countries, and Scandinavia, Jews were allowed full rights of citizenship. After 1858 Jews in Great Britain could sit in Parliament. In Austria-Hungary full legal rights were extended to Jews in 1867. From approximately 1850 to 1880 there was relatively little organized or overt prejudice toward Jews. Legal prohibitions against marriages between Jews and non-Jews were repealed.

Outside of Russia, Jewish political figures served in the highest offices of the state. Politically they tended to be aligned with liberal parties because such groups had championed equal rights. Especially in eastern Europe, many Jews became associated with the Socialist parties.

Jews still encountered personal prejudice throughout Europe, but in western Europe the Jewish populations seem to have felt relatively secure. Religious prejudice persisted in rural Russia and eastern Europe, and hundreds of thousands of European Jews immigrated to the United States from these regions.

Attitudes changed again during the last two decades of the nineteenth century. In the 1870s, some attributed the economic stagnation of that decade to Jewish bankers and financial interests. In the 1880s organized anti-Semitism erupted in Germany, as it did in France in the 1890s. As we saw in the previous chapter, those developments gave birth to Zionism, the movement to establish a Jewish state in Palestine. Most Jewish leaders, however, believed their communities would remain safe under the nineteenth century's legal protections, an analysis that would be proved disastrously wrong during the 1930s and 1940s.

EUROPEAN LABOR, SOCIALISM, AND POLITICS TO WORLD WAR I

WHY DID Marxism become so influential among European Socialists?

THE WORKING CLASSES IN THE LATE NINETEENTH CENTURY

After 1848 European workers ceased to riot over their grievances and stopped trying to revive the guilds. After midcentury the labor force accepted the fact of modern industrial production and attempted to receive more benefits from that system. Workers turned to new institutions and ideologies to defend their interests: trade unions, democratic political parties, and socialism.

Legal protections were extended to unions throughout the second half of the century. Unions became fully legal in Great Britain in 1871 and were allowed to picket in 1875. In France the Third Republic fully legalized unions in 1884. After 1890 they could function in Germany. Most trade unions were slow to enter the political process directly, as long as the traditional governing classes looked after labor interests.

Midcentury union efforts aimed to improve the wages and working conditions of skilled workers. By the close of the century large industrial unions for unskilled workers were also being organized. They confronted extensive opposition from employers. In the decade before 1914 strikes were common throughout Europe as the unions attempted to raise wages to keep up with inflation. Unions represented a new collective way for workers to confront the economic difficulties of their lives. Union membership grew in 1910 to approximately 3 million in Britain, 2 million in Germany, and 977,000 in France, but they never included a majority of the industrial labor force.

The democratic franchise gave workers direct political influence. Except for Russia, all the major European states adopted broad-based, if not perfectly democratic, electoral systems. The expansion of the electorate brought into the political processes many people who had to be organized and taught the nature of power and influence in the liberal democratic state. The mass political party—with its workers, newspapers, offices, social life, and discipline—was the vehicle that mobilized the new voters. The largest single group in these expanded electorates was the working class. The democratization of politics presented the Socialists with opportunities and required the traditional ruling class to vie with them for the support of the new voters.

MARXIST CRITIQUE OF THE INDUSTRIAL ORDER

During the 1840s, Karl Marx (1818–1883) produced a powerful critique of the industrial order. Later in the century his analysis was adopted by the leading Socialist political party in Germany, which in turn influenced most other European Socialist parties.

((•—[Hear the Audio
Industrial Side Effects
at **myhistorylab.com**

Marx's Jewish middle-class parents sent him to the University of Berlin, where he became deeply involved in radical politics. German authorities drove him into exile, first in Paris, then in Brussels, and finally in London.

In 1844 Marx met another young German, Friedrich Engels (1820–1895), whose father owned a textile factory in Manchester, England. The next year, Engels published *The Condition of the Working Class in England*, which presented a devastating picture of industrial life. The two men became fast friends. Late in 1847 they were asked to write a pamphlet for a short-lived secret Communist league. *The Communist Manifesto*, published in German, appeared early in 1848. Marx, Engels, and the league had adopted the name *Communist* because it implied the outright abolition of private property, making it more radical than *Socialist*. The *Manifesto* was a work of fewer than fifty pages. It would become the most influential political document of modern European history, though its initial impact was minimal, and it did not have any effect on the revolutionary events of 1848.

In *The Communist Manifesto* Marx and Engels contended that human history must be understood rationally. History is the record of humankind's coming to grips with physical nature to produce the goods necessary for survival. That basic productive process determines the structures, values, and ideas of a society. The organization of the means of production has always involved conflict between the classes who owned and controlled the means of production and the classes who worked for them. (See Document: "Karl Marx and Friedrich Engels Describe the Class Struggle" on page 624.) That necessary conflict has provided the engine for historical development; it is not an accidental by-product of mismanagement or bad intentions. Consequently, only a radical social transformation, not piecemeal reforms, can eliminate the social and economic evils inherent in the very structures of production. Such a revolution will occur as the inevitable outcome of the development of capitalism.

In Marx's and Engels's eyes, during the nineteenth century the class conflict that had characterized previous Western history had become a struggle between the bourgeoisie and the proletariat or between the middle class and the workers. The character of capitalism ensured the sharpening of the struggle. Capitalist production and competition would steadily increase the size of the unpropertied proletariat. As business structures grew larger, smaller middle-class units would be squeezed out. Competition would intensify the suffering of the proletariat, and as workers' suffering increased, they would foment revolution and finally overthrow the few remaining owners of the means of production. For a time the workers would organize the means of production through a dictatorship of the proletariat, which would eventually give way to a propertyless and classless communist society.

This proletarian revolution was inevitable, according to Marx and Engels. Although the class conflict involved in the contemporary process resembled that of the past, it differed in that the struggle between the capitalistic bourgeoisie and the industrial proletariat would culminate in a wholly new society, free of class conflict. The victorious proletariat, by its very nature, could not be a new oppressor class. The victory

Trade Union Membership Certificate.
Trade unions continued to grow in late nineteenth-century Great Britain. The effort to curb the unions eventually led to the formation of the Labour Party. The British unions often had quite elaborate membership certificates, such as this one for the National Union of Gas Workers and General Labourers of Great Britain and Ireland.

How are labor and work depicted here?

Read the **Document**
The Communist Manifesto, Karl Marx (1848) at **myhistorylab.com**

DOCUMENT

Karl Marx and Friedrich Engels Describe the Class Struggle

The Communist Manifesto (1848) is arguably the most influential political pamphlet of modern European history. In that relatively brief document, Karl Marx and Friedrich Engels portrayed human history as developing from ancient times to the present through a series of economic class struggles. In the contemporary world, they saw the complex struggles of the past reduced to a head-on economic, political, and social clash between the bourgeoisie, or capital-owning class, and the proletariat, or workers. Both groups had emerged in the course of history. The bourgeoisie had arisen from medieval townsmen asserting their liberty against feudal landowners and then against other groups of aristocrats. In turn, as the bourgeoisie came to dominate the economy and invest their capital in modern industry, they produced the contemporary wage-labor force. Over time this labor force came to see that its interests opposed that of its economic masters. The result was to be the final class conflict of history because, as Marx and Engels argued, the proletariat, unlike any previous group seeking to establish its liberty, was so large that its victory was also the victory of humanity itself.

- **Whom** do Marx and Engels portray as the previous enemies of the bourgeoisie? How did bourgeois economic development and dominance lead to a society based on the "cash nexus"? Why is the bourgeoisie responsible for the emergence of the proletariat? Why is the victory of the proletariat inevitable?

The history of all hitherto existing society is the history of class struggles....

Our epoch, the epoch of the bourgeoisie, possesses, however, this distinctive feature: it has simplified the class antagonisms. Society as a whole is more and more splitting up into two great hostile camps, into two great classes directly facing each other: Bourgeoisie and Proletariat....

Each step in the development of the bourgeoisie was accompanied by a corresponding political advance of that class....

The bourgeoisie, wherever it has gotten the upper hand, has put an end to all feudal, patriarchal, idyllic relations. It has pitilessly torn asunder the motley feudal ties that bound man to his "natural superiors," and has left remaining no other nexus between man and man than naked self-interest, than callous "cash payment."...

The proletariat goes through various stages of development. With its birth begins its struggle with the bourgeoisie....

But with the development of industry the proletariat not only increases in number; it becomes concentrated in greater masses, its strength grows, and it feels that strength more. The various interests and conditions of life within the ranks of the proletariat are more and more equalized, in proportion as machinery obliterates all distinctions of labour, and nearly everywhere reduces wages to the same low level....

The bourgeoisie finds itself involved in a constant battle....

Of all the classes that stand face to face with the bourgeoisie today, the proletariat alone is a really revolutionary class....

All previous historical movements were movements of minorities, or in the interest of minorities. The proletarian movement is the self-conscious, independent movement of the immense majority, in the interest of the immense majority....

The advance of industry, whose involuntary promoter is the bourgeoisie, replaces the isolation of the labourers, due to competition, by their revolutionary combination, due to association. The development of Modern Industry, therefore, cuts from under its feet the very foundation on which the bourgeoisie produces and appropriates products. What the bourgeoisie, therefore, produces, above all, is its own grave-diggers. Its fall and the victory of the proletariat are equally inevitable....

The proletarians have nothing to lose but their chains. They have a world to win.

Source: Karl Marx and Friedrich Engels, *The Communist Manifesto*, in Lawrence H. Simon, ed., Karl Marx, *Selected Writings* (Indianapolis, IN: Hackett Publishing Company, Inc., 1994), pp. 158, 159, 160, 161, 165, 166–167, 168, 169, 186. © 1994 International Publishers Co. Reprinted by permission of International Publishers Co., Inc./New York.

of the proletariat over the bourgeoisie represented the culmination of human history and would result in "an association, in which the free development of each is the condition for the free development of all." [1] Marx's analysis was conditioned by the unemployment and deprivation of the 1840s. Capitalism, however, did not collapse as he predicted, nor did the middle class become proletarianized.

In reality, more people came to benefit from the industrial system. Nonetheless, within a generation **Marxism** had captured the imagination of many Socialists and large segments of the working class. Its doctrines were allegedly based on the empirical evidence of hard economic fact, which helped legitimize Marxism as science became more influential. Marx had made the ultimate victory of socialism seem certain. His works also proclaimed that the path to socialism lay with revolution rather than reform. As Marxist thought permeated the international socialist movement during the next seventy-five years, it would provide the ideological basis for some of the most momentous and ultimately repressive political movements in the modern world.

GERMANY: SOCIAL DEMOCRATS AND REVISIONISM

Marxism was adopted by the German Social Democratic Party (SPD). Founded in 1875, the SPD was vehemently opposed by Otto von Bismarck (1815–1898). Following an 1878 attempt to assassinate Emperor William I (r. 1861–1888), Bismarck unfairly blamed the Socialists. He steered antisocialist laws through the Reichstag, the German Parliament, to little avail. When repression failed, Bismarck enacted social welfare legislation to wean German workers from Socialist loyalties. These measures provided health insurance, accident insurance, and old age and disability pensions. The German state thus organized a system of social security that did not change the system of property holding or politics.

In 1891, after forcing Bismarck's resignation, Emperor William II (r. 1888–1918) legalized the SPD. Party leaders declared the imminent doom of capitalism and the necessity of socialist ownership of the means of production; these goals were to be achieved by legal political participation rather than by revolutionary activity. Since the revolution was inevitable, they argued, the immediate task of Socialists was to improve workers' lives. The SPD was prepared to function within the institutions of the German Empire.

This situation generated an important internal challenge to the orthodox Marxist analysis of capitalism and the socialist revolution. Eduard Bernstein (1850–1932) wrote what was regarded as socialist heresy. Bernstein, who was familiar with the British **Fabians**, questioned whether Marx and his later orthodox followers had been correct in their pessimistic appraisal of capitalism and the necessity of revolution. In *Evolutionary Socialism* (1899), Bernstein pointed to the rising standard of living in Europe, the power of the middle class, and the opening of the franchise to the working class. He argued that a humane socialist society required not revolution, but more democracy and social reform. Bernstein's doctrines, known as **revisionism**, were widely debated among German Socialists. Bernstein's critics argued that evolution toward social democracy might be possible in liberal, parliamentary Britain but not in authoritarian, militaristic Germany. While in practice the German SPD continued to pursue a peaceful, reformist program, the party condemned Bernstein's theory and officially advocated revolution.

The German debate over revisionism became important for the later history of Marxist socialism. All Socialists noted the rejection of reform, in favor of revolution,

Marxism
The theory of Karl Marx (1818–1883) and Friedrich Engels (1820–1895) that history is the result of class conflict, which will end in the inevitable triumph of the industrial proletariat over the bourgeoisie and the abolition of private property and social class.

Fabians
British Socialists in the late nineteenth and early twentieth centuries who sought to achieve socialism through gradual, peaceful, and democratic means.

revisionism
The advocacy among nineteenth-century German Socialists of achieving a humane socialist society through the evolution of democratic institutions, not revolution.

---

[1] Robert C. Tucker, ed., *The Marx-Engels Reader* (New York: W. W. Norton, 1972), p. 353.

Beatrice and Sidney Webb. These most influential British Fabian Socialists, shown in a photograph from the late 1920s, wrote many books on governmental and economic matters, served on special parliamentary commissions, and agitated for the enactment of socialist policies.

What were the beliefs of the Fabians?

by the most successful prewar Socialist Party. Most significant, Lenin adopted this position, as did the other leaders of the Russian Revolution. Thereafter, wherever Soviet Marxism was influential, the goal of its efforts would be revolution rather than reform.

GREAT BRITAIN: THE LABOUR PARTY AND FABIANISM

No form of socialism made significant progress in Great Britain, the most advanced industrial society of the day. The members of the growing trade unions normally supported Liberal Party candidates. The "new unionism" of the late 1880s and the 1890s organized dock workers, gas workers, and similar unskilled groups. Employer resistance to unions heightened class antagonism. In 1893 the Socialist Independent Labour Party was founded, but it remained ineffective.

In 1901, however, a court decision removed the legal protection previously accorded union funds. The Trades Union Congress responded by launching the Labour Party, which sent twenty-nine members to Parliament in the election of 1906. Their goals did not yet encompass socialism. The British labor movement also became more militant, staging scores of strikes for wages to meet the rising cost of living. The government intervened to mediate.

British socialism itself remained primarily the preserve of intellectuals. The Socialists who exerted the most influence were from the Fabian Society, founded in 1884. The society took its name from a Roman general who defeated Hannibal by waiting before attacking, indicating the society's gradualist approach to social reform. Its leading members were Sydney Webb (1859–1947) and Beatrice Webb (1858–1943), H. G. Wells (1866–1946), and George Bernard Shaw (1856–1950). Many Fabians were civil servants who believed that the problems of industry, the expansion of ownership, and the state direction of production could be handled gradually, peacefully, and democratically. They sought to educate the country to the rational wisdom of socialism. They were particularly interested in collective ownership on the municipal level, or so-called gas-and-water socialism.

RUSSIA: INDUSTRIAL DEVELOPMENT AND THE BIRTH OF BOLSHEVISM

Following its defeat in the Crimean War, Russia's tsarist government had undertaken major reforms. The most important reform was the emancipation of the serfs in 1861, through a complicated process that in effect required serfs to pay for their land. The poverty of the emancipated serfs became a political cause for groups of urban revolutionaries. One such group, the People's Will, assassinated Tsar Alexander II (r. 1855–1881) in 1881. Thereafter, the government pursued a policy of political repression.

The late nineteenth-century tsarist government was determined to make Russia an industrial power. It favored the growth of heavy industries, such as railways, iron, and steel. A small but significant industrial proletariat arose. By 1900 Russia had approximately 3 million factory workers, whose working and living conditions were bad by any standard.

New political organizations emerged. The Social Revolutionary Party, founded in 1901, opposed industrialism and looked to the communal life of rural Russia as a model for the economic future. In 1903 the Constitutional Democratic Party, or Cadets, was formed. The Cadets were drawn from people who participated in the *zemstvos* (local governments), and they modeled themselves on the Liberal parties of western Europe. They wanted a parliamentary regime with responsible ministries, civil liberties, and economic progress.

The situation for Russian Socialists differed radically from that in other major European countries. Russia had no representative political institutions and only a small working class. The Russian Social Democratic Party had been established in 1898. It was Marxist and its members greatly admired the German SPD, but tsarist repression meant that it had to function in exile. The leading late nineteenth-century Russian Marxist was Georgii Plekhanov (1857–1918), based in Switzerland. His chief disciple was Vladimir Illich Ulyanov (1870–1924), who took the name of Lenin. After briefly practicing law in Saint Petersburg, Lenin was exiled to Siberia from 1895 to 1900 and spent most of the following seventeen years in Switzerland.

Russian Social Democrats quarreled about the proper nature of a Marxist revolution in primarily rural Russia. They were modernizers who favored further industrial development. Most believed that Russia must develop a large proletariat before the revolution could come, and they hoped to mold a mass political party like the German SPD.

Lenin dissented from both positions. In *What Is to Be Done?* (1902), he condemned trade unionism that settled for short-term gains rather than true revolutionary change for the working class. Lenin rejected the concept of a mass party composed of workers, claiming that an elite party of professional revolutionaries had to bring revolutionary consciousness to the working class.

In 1903, at the London Congress of the Russian Social Democratic Party, Lenin's faction assumed the name **Bolsheviks**, meaning "majority" (despite having lost most votes at the Congress), and the more moderate, democratic revolutionary faction became known as the **Mensheviks**, or "minority." In 1905 Lenin published a program for revolution in Russia, urging that the socialist revolution unite the proletariat and the peasants. He grasped the profound discontent in the Russian countryside and knew that an alliance of workers and peasants in rebellion could not be suppressed. Lenin's two principles—an elite party and a dual social revolution—allowed the Bolsheviks to capture the leadership of the Russian Revolution in late 1917.

The Russian Socialists had no immediate influence within Russia. In 1904 Russia went to war with Japan and lost. On January 22, 1905, a priest led thousands of workers to petition the tsar for improvements in industrial conditions. As the petitioners approached the Winter Palace in Saint Petersburg, troops opened fire, killing about a hundred people.

Revolutionary disturbances spread throughout Russia. In early October 1905 strikes broke out in Saint Petersburg, and worker groups, called *soviets*, virtually controlled the city. Tsar Nicholas II (r. 1894–1917) promised constitutional government. Early in 1906 the tsar announced the election of a bicameral parliament, the **Duma**, but he reserved important appointments for himself and named as his chief minister P. A. Stolypin (1862–1911). The government's sole conciliatory gesture was to forgive any payments still owed by peasants from the emancipation of the serfs in 1861. Thereafter Stolypin repressed rural discontent.

Stolypin was assassinated in 1911. At this time the imperial family was surrounded by scandal over the influence of Grigori Rasputin (1871?–1916), who seemed able to heal the tsar's hemophilic son. Ongoing social discontent and the conservative resistance to liberal reforms rendered the position of the tsar uncertain after 1911.

CHRONOLOGY

MAJOR DATES IN THE DEVELOPMENT OF SOCIALISM

1864	International Working Men's Association (the First International) founded
1875	German Social Democratic Party founded
1876	First International dissolved
1878	German antisocialist laws passed
1884	British Fabian Society founded
1889	Second International founded
1891	German antisocialist laws permitted to expire
1895	French *Confédération Générale du Travail* founded
1899	Eduard Bernstein's *Evolutionary Socialism*
1902	Formation of the British Labour Party
1902	Lenin's *What Is to Be Done?*
1903	Bolshevik-Menshevik split

Read the Document
Socialism at **myhistorylab.com**

Bolsheviks
Meaning the "majority." Term Lenin applied to his faction of the Russian Social Democratic Party. It became the Communist Party of the Soviet Union after the Russian Revolution.

Mensheviks
Meaning the "minority." Term Lenin applied to the majority moderate faction of the Russian Social Democratic Party opposed to him and the Bolsheviks.

soviets
Workers' and soldiers' councils formed in Russia during the Revolution.

Duma
The Russian Parliament, after the Revolution of 1905.

See the Map
The Growth of Russia to 1914
at **myhistorylab.com**

A Closer Look

Bloody Sunday, Saint Petersburg, 1905

On Bloody Sunday, January 22, 1905, troops of Tsar Nicholas II fired on a peaceful procession of workers at the Winter Palace who sought to present a petition for better working and living conditions. The scene in a Saint Petersburg square portrayed here, that can still be visited today, depicts one of the enduring images of events leading to the subsequent Russian Revolutions of 1905 and 1917. It figured in at least two movies: the 1925 anti-tsarist Soviet silent film called *The Ninth of January* and *Nicholas and Alexandra*, the lavish 1971 movie that was sympathetic to the tsar and blamed Bloody Sunday on frightened and incompetent officials. While Nicholas had not ordered the troops to fire and was not even in Saint Petersburg on Bloody Sunday, the event all but destroyed any chance of reconciliation between the tsarist government and the Russian working class.

The workers are visibly defenseless in the face of the rifles being fired at them.

Although the square before the Winter Palace toward the right of the troops is large and might have allowed an escape route of sorts for the workers' procession, the troops forced the crowd into an area of narrow escape.

The view is the one that officials in the Winter Palace, which lay behind the row of troops with rifles, would have seen.

Questions

1. How did the invention of photography and the making of movies transform the recording and interpretation of the past?

2. Do you think the firing on the crowd in 1905 was as orderly an affair as this picture from a later Bolshevik film made it appear?

3. How did the ongoing recollection and reenactment of this dramatic, violent moment in the Revolution of 1905 serve to continue to discredit the tsarist government and to champion the later Bolshevik Revolution?

myhistorylab To examine this image in an interactive fashion, please go to **www.myhistorylab.com**

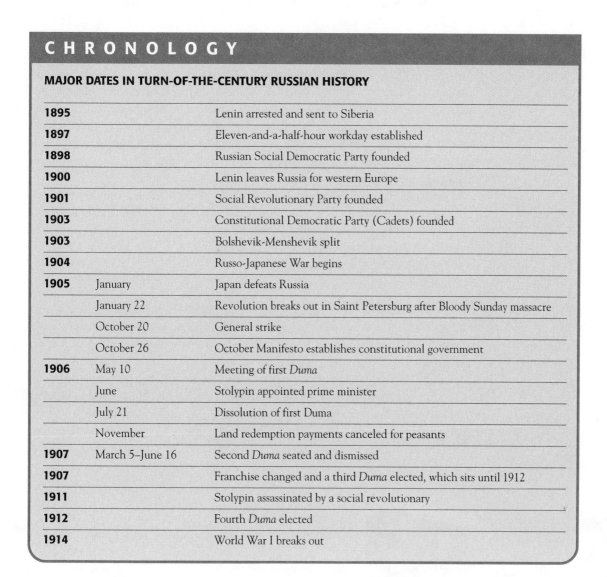

CHRONOLOGY

MAJOR DATES IN TURN-OF-THE-CENTURY RUSSIAN HISTORY

1895		Lenin arrested and sent to Siberia
1897		Eleven-and-a-half-hour workday established
1898		Russian Social Democratic Party founded
1900		Lenin leaves Russia for western Europe
1901		Social Revolutionary Party founded
1903		Constitutional Democratic Party (Cadets) founded
1903		Bolshevik-Menshevik split
1904		Russo-Japanese War begins
1905	January	Japan defeats Russia
	January 22	Revolution breaks out in Saint Petersburg after Bloody Sunday massacre
	October 20	General strike
	October 26	October Manifesto establishes constitutional government
1906	May 10	Meeting of first *Duma*
	June	Stolypin appointed prime minister
	July 21	Dissolution of first Duma
	November	Land redemption payments canceled for peasants
1907	March 5–June 16	Second *Duma* seated and dismissed
1907		Franchise changed and a third *Duma* elected, which sits until 1912
1911		Stolypin assassinated by a social revolutionary
1912		Fourth *Duma* elected
1914		World War I breaks out

EUROPEAN SOCIALISM IN WORLD HISTORY

The debates among late nineteenth- and early twentieth-century European Socialists were significant to world history for two reasons. First, Europeans who immigrated to North and South America carried many of these socialist ideas and quarrels with them. Second, by the end of the nineteenth century numerous students from the European empires in Africa and Asia traveled to Europe for education, where they, too, were immersed in these debates. Many of those students later became leaders of their own political movements.

NORTH AMERICA AND THE NEW INDUSTRIAL ECONOMY

Industrialization in the United States largely followed the European pattern: The first industry to become thoroughly mechanized was textile manufacture, followed by growth in the iron and steel industries. There were significant differences, however. The United States industrialized considerably later than Great Britain. Its major expansion in iron

HOW DID industrialization in the United States differ from industrialization in Europe?

and steel took place after the Civil War, approximately contemporary to the economic rise of the newly united Germany. American manufacturers and commercial developers encountered little of the prejudice against trade and commerce that existed among the European aristocracy. Wealthy American businessmen had considerable political influence. The United States possessed an immense internal market free of trade restraints. British bankers saw the United States as an area of secure investment, so they provided much of the necessary capital. Finally, the United States had a relative shortage of labor and consequently relatively high wages, factors that attracted many immigrants to the industrial sector during the second half of the nineteenth century.

In America as in Europe, railways spurred the most intense industrial growth. The number of railway miles increased from approximately 50,000 in the mid-1860s to almost 200,000 by 1900. The railways created enormous demand for iron, steel, coal, and lumber. They also stimulated settlement, vastly expanded markets, and helped to knit the country together.

EUROPEAN IMMIGRATION TO THE UNITED STATES

The same conditions that made life difficult for black people and Native Americans (see Chapter 22) turned the United States into a land of vast opportunity for white European immigrants. These immigrants faced religious and ethnic discrimination as well as frequent poverty in the United States, but the social and economic structures of the United States allowed for assimilation and remarkable upward social mobility. This was especially true of those immigrants who arrived between approximately 1840 and 1890—the great period of German, English, Welsh, Scottish, and Irish immigration (see Map 24–1). Among this group, the Irish encountered the most difficulties and resistance.

Toward the end of the nineteenth century and well into the twentieth—in what is sometimes known as the New Immigration—millions of people arrived from economically depressed areas of the Mediterranean, eastern Europe, and the Balkans. These new immigrants, who generally came to work in the growing industrial cities, were perceived as fundamentally different from those who had come before them. Racial theory held that they were from less desirable stocks. Predominately Roman Catholic, Orthodox, and Jewish, they encountered much intolerance. They often settled into communities of people from their own ethnic background, held together by various private organizations including churches and synagogues.

Although none of these immigrants faced the same legal discrimination as did American blacks, Jews encountered restricted covenants on real estate and other obstacles. Asian immigrants to the West Coast of the United States faced harsher prejudice.

Immigrant Labor. Chinese laborers, known as "coolies," performed most of the backbreaking work on the construction of the railroads in the American West. The workers depicted here are laying down track near Promontory, Utah.

What role did railroads play in the industrialization of the United States?

UNIONS: ORGANIZATION OF LABOR

As in Europe, American workers attempting to organize labor unions faced resistance from employers and those who feared that unions would lead to socialism. Other difficulties were peculiar to the United States: White laborers would not organize alongside black workers, and different ethnic minorities would not cooperate. The ongoing flood of immigration ensured a supply of workers willing to work for low wages. The owners of businesses could divide and conquer the sprawling, ethnically mixed labor force.

MAP EXPLORATION

To explore this map further, go to **http://www.myhistorylab.com**

Legend:
— Emigration from Europe
— Emigration from Japan
— Emigration from China
— Emigration from India
— Migration from European Russia

Number of Immigrants		
From Asia		700,000
Main groups		
Chinese	370,000	
Japanese	275,000	
From Canada		2,200,000
From Europe		30,000,000
Main groups		
Germans	5,000,000	
Irish	4,500,000	
Italians	4,500,000	
Poles	2,600,000	
English	2,600,000	
Jews	2,000,000	
From Latin America		900,000

MAP 24–1. **Patterns of Global Migration, 1840–1900.** Emigration was a global process by the late nineteenth century. But more immigrants went to the United States than to every other nation combined.

HOW DID global migration alter societies of the late nineteenth century?

Ellis Island. In 1892 the federal government opened the immigration station on Ellis Island, located in New York City's harbor, where about 80 percent of the immigrants to the United States landed. As many as 5,000 passengers per day reported to federal immigration officers for questions about their background and for physical examinations, such as this eye exam. Only about 1 percent were quarantined or turned away for health problems.

How did immigration patterns change over time?

The National Labor Union attempted to organize railroad unions in the 1870s. In 1881 the American Federation of Labor (AFL) was founded, focusing on higher wages and better working conditions for skilled workers. Among its most effective leaders was Samuel Gompers (1850–1924). Other unions, such as the United Mine Workers and the Railway Brotherhoods, organized workers by industry.

Serious depressions occurred in both the 1870s and the 1890s. What little relief there was came from local authorities and private charities, a pattern that would continue until the Great Depression of the 1930s. Economic turmoil during the 1880s and 1890s spawned violent strikes and the notorious breaking of the Pullman strike in Chicago in 1894 by federal troops. The major goal of labor thereafter was to achieve the full legal right to organize, achieved only through the legislation of Franklin Roosevelt's (1882–1945) New Deal in the 1930s.

Socialism was a path closed to American labor. The leaders of conservative unions worked against the Socialists, and businesses blocked socialist influence. The federal and state governments repressed socialist activities. Virtually all American Socialists were persecuted as Bolshevists during the 1920s and beyond. Thus, in the United States, many social issues were addressed by trade unions rather than by Socialist parties. Although many conservative American political and business leaders disliked them, unions were not legally attacked in the United States.

In many European countries, Socialist parties (or leaders attempting to outflank the Socialists) passed legislation providing social security and other social services. No significant legislation of this kind was passed in the United States, at any level, until the New Deal.

THE PROGRESSIVES

Political bosses held much of the power in American politics in the decades after the Civil War. This system depended on patronage: In return for jobs, contracts, licenses, favors, and sometimes actual services, the boss received political support. Government was a vehicle for distributing spoils. Boss politics was a crude way of organizing the disorderly social and economic forces of growing cities with diverse populations.

Deeply disturbed by corruption, reform-minded political figures ushered in what has been called the Progressive era, which lasted from approximately 1890 through 1914. Usually upper-middle-class whites who feared a loss of political and social influence, these reformers saw unacceptable disorder in urban slums. They wanted more efficient government to act as a direct agent of reform.

The Progressives began in the cities, where in place of patronage they demanded social and municipal services. Progressive mayors called for lower utility rates and streetcar fares and also attacked police corruption. Progressives then launched into national politics.

QUICK REVIEW

American Progressives

- Reformers, particularly opposed to boss politics
- Mostly upper-middle-class whites
- In the South, often disenfranchised blacks and poor
- Linked to "Social Gospel"

SOCIAL REFORM

Churches joined the Progressive crusade. The "Social Gospel" preached that Christianity involved civic action. Young men and women began to work in settlement houses in the slums. The most famous was Chicago's Hull House, led by Jane Addams (1860–1935). Others became active in housing and health reform, education, and charities. They believed that social order, as envisioned by the white middle class, could be made to prevail.

On the state government level, Progressives attempted to protect groups of people perceived as unable to protect themselves against exploitation. Virtually all of these reformers partook of the cult of science that was so influential in the late nineteenth century. They believed that the problems of society were susceptible to scientific, rational management. The general public interest should replace special interests.

Child Labor in the United States. A young girl works at a loom in a cotton mill in the Carolinas. At the dawn of the twentieth century, children worked in textile mills, particularly in the South, which was in the process of moving toward a less agriculturally-based economy. It wasn't until the 1930s that state legislation effectively brought an end to child labor in textile mills.

In what regions or industries is child labor still a problem today?

One area of concern for the Progressive movement was child labor. In the United States and Europe children had labored in both rural and industrial settings throughout the nineteenth century. Various reform efforts had attempted to limit the employment of children. Factory laws had been passed in England as early as the 1830s. In the United States at the close of the nineteenth century children worked in textile mills, especially in the South as that region attempted to move toward a less agriculturally based economy. Child labor was relatively cheap, and children often worked in mills along with their parents. In addition to working long hours around dangerous equipment in unhealthy conditions, these children rarely received significant education.

In the late nineteenth century labor organizations criticized the employment of children in the textile mills but to little effect. In 1894 the National Child Labor Committee was organized to work for reform. It published pamphlets and photographs of the harsh conditions endured by children. Federal legislation was passed during Woodrow Wilson's administration but was declared unconstitutional. During the 1920s the use of child labor in textile mills declined through changes in factory technology. In the next decade state legislation effectively brought an end to textile mill child labor. The federal Fair Labor Standards Act of 1938 established new standards for the employment of children.

The problem of child labor, especially in migrant agricultural work, has continued, however. Child labor exploitation remains an issue in many parts of the world today. American firms subcontracting to factories in South America and Asia have been accused of exploiting the labor of children in order to bring American consumers cheap clothing and other products.

●◆●─┤Read the **Document**
The Sadler Report: Child Labor in the United Kingdom, 1832
at **myhistorylab.com**

THE PROGRESSIVE PRESIDENCY

Theodore Roosevelt became president in 1901 after the assassination of William McKinley (1843–1901). By force of personality and intelligence, Roosevelt created the modern American presidency, making it the most important and powerful branch of government. He set the agenda for national affairs, surrounded himself with strong advisers, and used his own knowledge of party patronage to beat the bosses at their game.

In domestic policy, Roosevelt believed no economic power should be stronger than the federal government. He successfully moved against some of the country's most powerful business trusts and financiers, including J. P. Morgan and John D. Rockefeller. Through "Square Deal" legislation, Roosevelt attempted to assert the public interest. He was not opposed to big business in itself, but he wanted it to operate according to rules established by the government for the public good.

Roosevelt sought to make the presidency and the federal government the guarantor of fairness in economic relations. In 1902 Roosevelt brought the moral power of the presidency to the aid of striking mine workers, appointing a commission to arbitrate the dispute. He fostered the passage of the Pure Food and Drug Act and the Meat Packing Act in 1906, to protect the public against adulterated foodstuffs. His conservation policies ensured that millions of acres of national forests came under the care of the federal government.

Roosevelt's foreign policy was vigorous and imperialistic. In 1898 McKinley had led the nation into the Spanish-American War, and the United States had emerged as an imperial power with control of Cuba, Puerto Rico, Guam, and the Philippines. Roosevelt believed that the United States should be a major world power, and he sent a war fleet around the world. In Latin America naval intervention assured a new government in Panama, and a treaty allowed the United States to construct and control a canal across the Isthmus of Panama. In these actions, the United States was following the model of the European great powers, which had been intervening in Africa and Asia. In both Europe and the United States, a conviction of racial superiority helped drive these imperialist policies (see Chapter 28).

Roosevelt was succeeded in 1909 by William Howard Taft (1857–1930), and the 1912 election was a three-way contest among Taft, Roosevelt (running as a third-party candidate), and Woodrow Wilson. The Democrat Wilson won and brought a different concept of progressivism to the White House.

Woodrow Wilson (1856–1924) was a former president of Princeton University and a reforming governor of New Jersey. Like Roosevelt, Wilson accepted a modern industrialized nation. Wilson intrinsically disliked big business, however, and believed the government should protect the weak. Wilson termed his policy the New Freedom, although in office he followed a policy of moderate regulation of business. Wilson saw the presidency as responsible for leading Congress to legislative decisions. He presented Congress with a vast agenda of legislation and then worked carefully with the Democratic leadership to see that it was passed.

•••─[Read the **Document**
Speech before Congress
at **myhistorylab.com**

Wilson retained many beliefs that have disappointed later admirers. For example, he reinstated racial segregation in the federal civil service and opposed female suffrage.

War broke out in Europe in August 1914. Although Wilson was reelected in 1916 on the slogan "He Kept Us Out of War!" in April 1917 he led the nation into the European conflict. The expertise Progressives had brought to efficient domestic government was turned to making the nation an effective military force. These two impulses—the first toward domestic reform, the second toward a strong international role—had long marked the Progressive movement and would shape American history in the years after the war.

The American Progressives resembled political leaders of their generation in Great Britain, France, and Germany, who had supported various social reforms to forestall the advance of socialism and to address the problems of industrialization and urbanization. All had favored unprecedented use of central government authority.

THE EMERGENCE OF MODERN EUROPEAN THOUGHT

The last quarter of the nineteenth century and the first decade of the twentieth century were the crucible of modern Western thought. Philosophers, scientists, psychologists, and artists began to portray physical reality, human nature, and society in ways different from their counterparts of the past. The vast change in thinking commenced in the realm of biology.

WHO WERE some of the intellectuals at the forefront of modern European thought?

••◆—[Read the **Document**
On Darwin's 1860s
at **myhistorylab.com**

DARWIN'S THEORY OF NATURAL SELECTION

Charles Darwin's (1809–1882) *On the Origin of Species*, published in 1859, carried the mechanical interpretation of physical nature into the world of living things. The concept of evolution had already been widely discussed, but Darwin and, working independently, Alfred Russel Wallace (1823–1913) formulated the principle of natural selection, which explains *how* species evolve over time.

Darwin and Wallace contended that more living organisms come into existence than can survive in their environment. Organisms with any advantage in the struggle for existence produce more surviving offspring and repopulate their species. Darwin called this principle of survival of the fittest, **natural selection**. What could not be explained in the nineteenth century was the origin of the variations that gave some living things new traits. Only after 1900, when Gregor Mendel's (1822–1884) work on heredity received public attention, did the mystery of those variations begin to be unraveled.

Darwin's and Wallace's mechanistic theory removed the idea of preconceived divine purpose from organic nature. It contradicted the biblical narrative of the Creation. It also undermined both the deistic argument for the existence of God from the design of the universe, and the belief that the universe was a fixed, stable system. If the world of nature was in flux, it implied that society, values, customs, and beliefs might also be changeable.

In 1871, in *The Descent of Man*, Darwin applied the principle of evolution by natural selection to human beings. Darwin contended that humankind's moral nature and religious sentiments, as well as its physical frame, had evolved in response to the requirements of survival. Neither the origin nor the character of humankind required postulating a deity to explain their existence. The blow to human pride was comparable to Copernicus removing the earth from the center of the universe.

The theory of evolution by natural selection was criticized by both the religious and the scientific communities. The broad scientific community accepted Darwin's mechanism of natural selection only after it was combined with modern genetics in the 1920s and 1930s.

natural selection
According to Darwin, the process in nature by which only the organisms best adapted to their environment tend to survive and transmit their genes, while those less adapted tend to be eliminated.

Darwin's theories about the evolution of humankind from the higher primates aroused enormous controversy. This caricature shows him with a monkey's body holding a mirror to an apelike creature.

Why are Darwin's theories still controversial?

THE REVOLUTION IN PHYSICS

By the late 1870s, many physical scientists were questioning whether mechanistic models, solid atoms, and absolute time and space truly described the universe. In 1883, Ernst Mach (1838–1916) published *The Science of Mechanics*, in which he urged that scientists consider their concepts descriptive not of the physical world but of the sensations of the scientific observer. Similarly, the French scientist Henri Poincaré (1854–1912) urged that the theories of scientists be regarded as hypothetical constructs of the human mind rather than as true descriptions of nature. By World War I, few scientists believed they could portray the "truth" about physical reality.

Marie Curie (1869–1934) and Pierre Curie (1859–1906) were two of the most important figures in the advance of physics and chemistry. Marie was born in Poland but worked in France for most of her life. She is credited with the discovery of radium, for which she was awarded the Nobel Prize in Chemistry in 1911.

How did the discovery of radiation contribute to a revolution in physics?

((•●—Hear the **Audio**
Reform of Thought
at **myhistorylab.com**

relativity
Theory of physics, first expounded by Albert Einstein in 1905, in which time and space exist not separately, but rather as a combined continuum.

•●◆—Read the **Document**
Werner Heisenberg, "Uncertainty"
(Germany) at **myhistorylab.com**

Discoveries in the laboratory supported the view that nature was more complex than Newton had imagined. In December 1895, Wilhelm Roentgen (1845–1923) published a paper on his discovery of X rays, a form of energy that penetrated opaque materials. Major steps in the exploration of radioactivity followed within months. In 1896, Henri Becquerel (1852–1908) discovered that uranium emitted a similar form of energy. The next year, J. J. Thomson (1856–1940), at Cambridge University, formulated the theory of the electron, and the interior world of the atom became a realm for human exploration. In 1902, Ernest Rutherford (1871–1937) explained radiation as the disintegration of atoms of radioactive materials. He also speculated on the immense store of energy in the atom.

The discovery of radioactivity contributed to revolutionary theories in physics. In 1900, Max Planck (1858–1947) pioneered the quantum theory of energy, according to which energy is a series of discrete quantities, or packets, rather than a continuous stream. In 1905, Albert Einstein (1879–1955) published his first papers on **relativity** in which he contended that time and space form a continuum, and that measurement of time and space depends on the observer as well as on the entities being observed. In 1927, Werner Heisenberg's (1901–1976) uncertainty principle stated that the behavior of subatomic particles could only be inferred by statistical probability. The physical universe had become ambiguous.

FRIEDRICH NIETZSCHE AND THE REVOLT AGAINST REASON

During the second half of the century, philosophers such as the German Friedrich Nietzsche (1844–1900) began to question the adequacy of rational thinking. Nietzsche attacked Christianity, democracy, nationalism, rationality, science, and progress. He sought less to change values than to probe their sources in the human character. He wanted to tear away the masks of respectable life and explore how human beings made such masks.

His first important work was *The Birth of Tragedy* (1872) in which he urged that the nonrational aspects of human nature are as important and noble as reason itself. He insisted that instinct and ecstasy had important functions and that the strength to live heroically derived from sources beyond rationality.

In later works including *Thus Spake Zarathustra* (1883) Nietzsche criticized democracy and Christianity, claiming that they promoted mediocrity. He announced the death of God and proclaimed the coming of the *Overman* (*Übermensch*). The term was frequently interpreted as referring to a superman or super race, but Nietzsche had in mind the kind of heroism that had motivated the ancient Greeks. He thought humans were hobbled by the values of Christianity and bourgeois morality.

In two of Nietzsche's most profound (and difficult) works, *Beyond Good and Evil* (1886) and *The Genealogy of Morals* (1887), he sought to uncover the social and psychological sources of judgments of good and evil. He claimed that morality was only a human convention and that people could create new life-affirming values, glorifying pride, assertiveness, and strength.

THE BIRTH OF PSYCHOANALYSIS

The major figures of late nineteenth-century science, art, and philosophy shared a determination to probe beneath surface appearances. They sought to discern the undercurrents, tensions, and complexities within atoms, families, rationality, and social relationships. This was particularly true of Sigmund Freud (1856–1939).

In 1886, Freud, an Austrian Jew, opened a medical practice in Vienna, where he lived until driven out by the Nazis in 1938. His earliest medical interests were psychic disorders; he had studied the use of hypnosis to treat cases of hysteria.

In the mid-1890s, Freud abandoned hypnosis and began urging patients to talk spontaneously about themselves. He found that they associated their particular neurotic symptoms with a chain of experiences going back to childhood and that sex was significant in his patients' problems. By 1897, he had developed a theory of infantile sexuality, suggesting that human beings are sexual creatures from birth. He thus questioned the concept of childhood innocence and made sexuality one of the bases of mental order and disorder.

Freud also examined dreams, believing there must be a reasonable, scientific explanation for their seemingly irrational content. He concluded that dreams give free play to unconscious wishes and drives that have been excluded from everyday conscious life. During waking hours, the mind represses or censors certain wishes, which are as important to the individual's psychological makeup as conscious thought is. In fact, Freud argued, unconscious drives and desires contribute to conscious behavior. Freud developed these ideas in his most important book, *The Interpretation of Dreams*, published in 1900.

In later books and essays, Freud developed a new model of the mind as an arena in which three entities struggle: the id, the superego, and the ego. The **id** consists of amoral, irrational instincts for sexual gratification, aggression, and general physical and sensual pleasure. The **superego** embodies the external moral imperatives and expectations imposed on the personality by society and culture. The **ego**, by mediating between the impulses of the id and the standards of the superego, helps the personality cope with the inner and outer demands of its existence.

Freud was a realist who wanted human beings to live free of fear and illusion by rationally understanding themselves and their world. He understood the immense sac-

⊷⊷[Read the Document

Friedrich Nietzsche, Beyond Good and Evil at **myhistorylab.com**

QUICK REVIEW

Sigmund Freud

- ◆ Founder of psychoanalysis
- ◆ Worked in Vienna until he was driven out by the Nazis in 1938
- ◆ Focused attention on infantile sexuality
- ◆ Emphasized the importance of what happens in the mind below the level of consciousness

id
According to Freudian theory, the part of the mind that consists of amoral, irrational, driving instincts for sexual gratification, aggression, and physical and sensual pleasure.

superego
According to Freudian theory, the part of the mind that embodies the external moral imperatives and expectations imposed on the personality by society and culture.

ego
According to Freudian theory, the part of the mind that mediates between the impulses of the id and the asceticism of the superego and allows the personality to cope with the inner and outer demands of its existence.

Read the **Document**
Richard Freiherr von Krafft-Ebing,
Psychopathia Sexualia (Germany), 1886
at **myhistorylab.com**

rifice of instinctual drives required for rational civilized behavior. He believed that excessive repression could lead to mental disorder, but he also believed that civilization and the survival of humankind required some repression of sexuality and aggression. Freud thought the sacrifice and struggle were worthwhile, but he was pessimistic about the future of civilization in the West.

ISLAM AND LATE NINETEENTH-CENTURY EUROPEAN THOUGHT

WHAT WERE some influential views on the relationship between Islam and the West?

Al-Afghani. One of the most influential thinkers in the Muslim world in the nineteenth century, al-Afghani tried to reconcile modern science with Islam.

What kind of future did al-Afghani foresee for Islam?

QUICK REVIEW

Islam and the West

◆ European thinkers applied the same scientific critique to Islam as they did to Christianity

◆ European racism shaped attitudes toward Arabs

◆ Response to Western ideas and technology varied in the Islamic world

The few late nineteenth-century European thinkers who wrote about Islam interpreted it as a historical phenomenon that, like the other great world religions, was merely a product of a particular culture. The influential French writer Ernest Renan (1823–1892) and sociologists such as the German Max Weber saw Muslim religion and cultures as incapable of developing science and as closed to new ideas. Their views were opposed by one of the rare Islamic writers who directly contested a European thinker, Jamal al-din Al-Afghani (1839–1897). Al-Afghani, an Egyptian intellectual, argued that given time (since Islam was 600 years younger than Christianity), Islam would produce cultures as modern as those in Europe.

European racial and cultural outlooks framed concepts of the Arab world. Christian missionaries reinforced this by blaming Islam for Arab economic backwardness, for mistreating women, and for condoning slavery. Because the penalty for abjuring Islam is death, missionaries made few converts among Muslims. So they turned their efforts to establishing schools and hospitals. These institutions taught young Arabs Western science and medicine, and many of their students became leaders in the Middle East. As missionary families lived for long periods among Arabs, they became more sympathetic to Arab political aspirations.

Within the Islamic world, political leaders who championed Western scientific education and technology confronted a variety of responses from religious thinkers. Some of these thinkers (the Salafi or the salafiyya movement, for example) believed there was no inherent contradiction between science and Islam. They believed that Muhammad had addressed the issues of his day and that a reformed Islamic faith could modernize itself without imitating the West. The Arab world should cease direct imitation of the West and modernize itself on the basis of a pure, restored Islamic faith. The Salafi emphasized a rational reading of the Qur'an and saw Ottoman decline as the result of Muslim religious error. This outlook, which had originally sought to reconcile Islam with the modern world, in the twentieth century led many Muslims to oppose Western influence.

Other Islamic religious leaders simply rejected the West and modern thought. They included the Mahdist movement in Sudan, the Sanussiya movement in Libya, and the Wahhabi movement in the Arabian Peninsula (see Chapter 26). Such religious-based opposition was strongest in portions of the Middle East where the European presence was least direct. It had little influence in Morocco, Algeria, Egypt, and Tunisia, which were effectively under the control of Western powers by 1900, and Turkey, where Ottoman leaders had long been deeply involved with the West.

SUMMARY

 WHAT IS *proletarianization*?

European Factory Workers and Urban Artisans. During the course of the nineteenth century, European workers underwent a process of proletarianization as the process of industrialization spread across the Continent. Workers labored for wages; they lost ownership of their tools and equipment, and they lost control over the conduct of their trades. *page 614*

WHAT SOCIAL and legal disabilities did European women confront in the nineteenth century?

Nineteenth-Century European Women. Nineteenth-century women were divided along class lines. Unlike working-class women, most women of the upper and middle classes did not work outside the home. Most jobs available to women were low paying and insecure. Women of all classes faced social, political, and legal disabilities that were only gradually improved in the late nineteenth and early twentieth centuries. Before World War I, only Norway allowed women to vote, and few women could earn university degrees or enter the professions. *page 616*

HOW DID emancipation affect Jewish life in Europe outside of Russia?

Jewish Emancipation. With the exception of Russia, European countries had abolished their legal restrictions on Jews by the mid-nineteenth century. Jews became more fully integrated into European political and economic life. After 1880, however, anti-Semitism increased as Jews were blamed for economic and social problems. *page 621*

 WHY DID Marxism become so influential among European Socialists?

European Labor, Socialism, and Politics to World War I. To protect their interests, European workers joined trade unions and Socialist parties, such as the Labour Party in Britain. The Marxist critique of modern capitalism strongly influenced European socialism when the German Social Democratic Party adopted the thought

of Karl Marx. Lenin founded the Bolsheviks as an elite Marxist party that advocated the overthrow of Russia's tsarist regime through a revolution of workers and peasants. *page 622*

 HOW DID industrialization in the United States differ from industrialization in Europe?

North America and the New Industrial Economy. Despite the creation of a mass industrial workforce, socialism did not take root in the United States. Under presidents Theodore Roosevelt and Woodrow Wilson, the Progressive movement enacted social and political reforms. The United States also embarked on a more aggressive foreign policy with the acquisition of a colonial empire and, under Wilson, participation in World War I. *page 629*

 WHO WERE some of the intellectuals at the forefront of modern European thought?

Modern European Thought. In 1850, learned Europeans regarded the physical world as rational, mechanical, and dependable. By the early twentieth century intellectuals began to portray physical reality, human nature, and society in ways that seem familiar to us today. Leaders in this intellectual transformation included the biologist Charles Darwin, Albert Einstein and other physicists, philosopher Friedrich Nietzsche, and pioneering psychoanalyst Sigmund Freud. *page 635*

 WHAT WERE some influential views on the relationship between Islam and the West?

Islam and Late Nineteenth-Century European Thought. Within the Islamic world, modern European thought produced a variety of often conflicting responses. Egyptian intellectual Jamal al-din Al-Afghani wrote that Islamic culture was simply younger than Christian Europe's, but would in time become modern. Leaders of the Salafi movement held that Islam could modernize without imitating the West. The Sudanese Mahdist movement and others rejected Western modernism. *page 638*

KEY TERMS

Bolsheviks (BOHL-shuh-vihks) (p. 627)

Duma (DOO-muh) (p. 627)

ego (p. 637)

Fabians (FAY-bee-uhns) (p. 625)

id (p. 637)

Marxism (p. 625)

Mensheviks (MEN-shuh-vihks) (p. 627)

natural selection (p. 635)

pogroms (poh-GRAHMZ) (p. 621)

proletarianization (p. 615)

relativity (p. 636)

revisionism (p. 625)

soviets (p. 627)

suffragettes (p. 620)

superego (p. 637)

REVIEW QUESTIONS

1. What were the chief factors accounting for the proletarianization of the European labor force? How much of the change in the situation of workers was a result of technology, and how much was the result of alterations in how workers were organized?

2. How did the class position of a European woman determine much of her experience? How did industrialization change women's experiences? What factors limited all women's opportunities? How had women's positions improved by 1914?

3. What were the major characteristics of Jewish emancipation in the nineteenth century? How did late-century economic developments contribute to increasing prejudice against Jews?

4. What were the essential ideas of Karl Marx? How did his ideas come to dominate late nineteenth-century European socialism?

5. What was the status of working-class groups in the United States and Europe in 1860? What improvements if any had been achieved by 1914?

6. What caused the emergence of trade unions and organized mass political parties in Europe?

7. How did the American Progressives, as reformers, differ from the various European Socialists?

8. How did Lenin's view of socialism differ from that of Socialists in western Europe? Why did socialism not emerge as a major political force in the United States?

9. What were the major changes in science in the late nineteenth century? How did both Darwin and turn-of-the-century physicists challenge assumptions of earlier science? How did Nietzsche and Freud undermine confidence in human rationality?

10. What were the chief characteristics of Western attitudes toward Islam in the nineteenth century? How did Islamic thinkers respond to modern Western thought?

Note: To learn more about the topics in this chapter, please turn to the Suggested Readings at the end of the book. For additional sources related to this chapter please see www.myhistorylab.com

myhistorylab Connections

Reinforce what you learned in this chapter by studying the many documents,
images, maps, review tools, and videos available at **www.myhistorylab.com**

Read and Review

✔•⎯Study and Review   Chapter 24

•⎔•⎯Read the Document   *Industrial Society and Factory
Conditions (early 1800s), p. 617*
Ellen Key, from the Century of the Child, p. 617
*John Stuart Mill on Enfranchisement of Women (1869),
p. 621*
The Communist Manifesto, Karl Marx (1848), p. 623
Socialism, p. 627
*The Sadler Report: Child Labor in the United Kingdom,
1832, p. 633*
Speech before Congress, p. 634
On Darwin's 1860s, p. 635
Werner Heisenberg, "Uncertainty" (Germany), p. 636
Friedrich Nietzsche, Beyond Good and Evil, p. 637
*Richard Freiherr von Krafft-Ebing, Psychopathia Sexualia
(Germany), 1886, p. 638*

((•⎯Hear the Audio   *Industrial Revolution, p. 614*
Industrial Side Effects, p. 622
Reform of Thought, p. 636

✔•⎯Study and Review   *Industrial Side Effects, p. 616*

Research and Explore

⊙⎯See the Map
The Growth of Russia to 1914, p. 627

⎯⎯ ((•⎯Hear the Audio ⎯⎯

Hear the audio file for Chapter 24
at **www.myhistorylab.com**

Latin America from Independence to the 1940s

((•—[Hear the Audio for Chapter 25 at www.myhistorylab.com

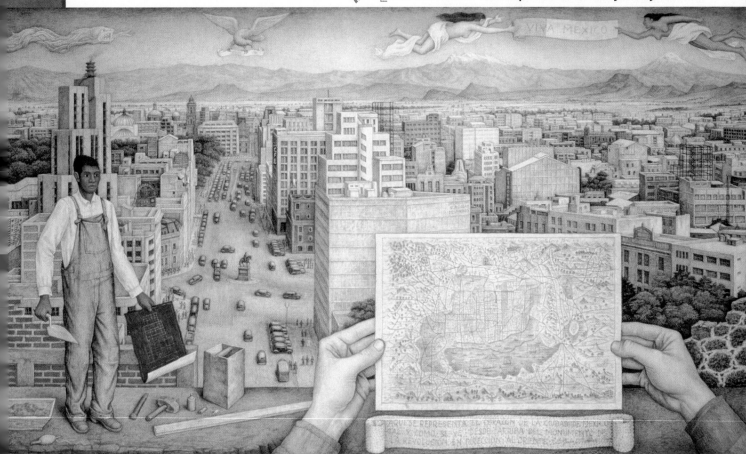

Mexico City. Juan O'Gorman (1905–1982) was best known as an architect whose most famous work is the library at the Universidad Nacional Autónima de Mexico. In 1932, he took the helm of Mexico City's department of building and construction. His interests in architecture, art (he became a renowned muralist), and the development of Mexico City are all on display in his 1949 painting, "El Ciudad de Mexico." The painting, complete with angels heralding "Viva Mexico," shows the city and the country as a work in progress.

What elements make this painting of Mexico City distinctly Latin American?

B y the mid-1820s, Latin Americans had driven out their colonial rulers and broken the colonial trade monopolies. Though rich in natural resources, the region did not achieve widespread prosperity and long-lasting political stability after independence. The wars of independence had not been popular grass-roots movements. They had originated with the creole elite, who were seeking to resist the imposition of European liberalism by Napoleon or, later, the Spanish liberals. In effect, the wars had been fought to break the colonial trade monopolies and to preserve the existing social structure. The military leaders of the wars held much of the political power in the new nations the wars had created.

The wars had destroyed much of the economic infrastructure of the region. Mines had been flooded, livestock depleted, and the workforce disrupted. Whereas previously colonial Latin America had been dependent on Spain for its exports and financial credits, it now became dependent on Great Britain and later on the United States.

Postindependence Latin America had much in common with Africa and Asia during the nineteenth and early twentieth centuries. In all three regions, nations or areas would specialize in a particular niche, providing, for example, sugar or coffee to the world economy. Huge mining industries, meanwhile, extracted resources such as copper, phosphates, gold, and diamonds. Virtually all such enterprises were dominated by Europeans or North Americans. Supplying raw products might bring initial prosperity, but it provided too narrow an economic base for sustained economic well-being. In contrast, the economic advance of the United States and Europe was largely due to their ability to exploit niche economies around the globe. ∎

INDEPENDENCE WITHOUT REVOLUTION

IMMEDIATE CONSEQUENCES OF LATIN AMERICAN INDEPENDENCE

The wars of independence liberated Latin America from direct European control but left it economically exhausted and politically unstable (see Map 25–1 on page 646).

HOW DID the absence of a social revolution affect Latin America after independence?

GLOBAL PERSPECTIVE

LATIN AMERICAN HISTORY

Since the early nineteenth century, Spanish- and Portuguese-speaking America stretching from the Rio Grande to Cape Horn has posed a paradox. Languages, religion, economic ties, and many political institutions render the area part of the Western world. Yet the economics, politics, and social life of Latin America have developed differently from other parts of the West. Exceedingly rich in natural resources, possessing gold, silver, nitrates, and oil, the region has been plagued with extreme poverty. As other Western nations have moved toward liberal democracy and social equality, the states of Latin America have had millions of citizens living in situations of marked inequality and social dependence. For almost two centuries, authoritarian regimes, uncertain democracy, and a general tendency toward instability have characterized Latin American political life.

Latin America shares many cultural features with Europe and North America. Its languages are primarily European, although much of its population speaks Native American languages. Its primary religion is Roman Catholicism. Its nations have often adopted the constitutional traditions of Europe and the United States. Many of its elite have studied abroad. Despite these important similarities, the economic and political development of Latin America has been different from that of much of Europe or the United States.

Three major explanations have been set forth to account for these difficulties that have led to so much tragedy and human suffering.

The first and most widely accepted view contends that after the wars of independence the new states of Latin America remained economically and culturally dependent on Europe and, later, the United States. In effect, proponents of this view—called **dependency theory**—argue that the colonial framework was never abolished. Under Spanish and Portuguese rule, Latin America's wealth was extracted and exported for the benefit of those powers. After independence, the **creole** elite turned toward foreign investors, first British and then American, to finance economic development and to provide the technology for mining, transport, and industry. As a result, Latin America again became dependent on wealthy foreign powers for investment and for markets. These foreign powers, interested in strong governments that would protect their interests, threw their support behind dictators whose policies impoverished their people and suppressed democratic dissent.

A second explanation emphasizes the Iberian heritage. Its advocates contend that Latin America should be viewed as a region on the periphery of the Western world in the same manner that Spain, Portugal, and Italy lie on the Mediterranean periphery of Europe. All of these Latin nations, dominated by Roman

dependency theory
Theory that contends that after the states of Latin America achieved independence in the early to mid-nineteenth century, they remained economically and culturally dependent on Europe and later the United States.

creoles
Persons of European descent who were born in the Spanish colonies.

((•—[Hear the Audio
Latin America
at **myhistorylab.com**

Only Brazil prospered. The new republics of the former Spanish Empire felt themselves vulnerable. Since the wars of independence had been civil wars, much of the population did not support the new governments. Economic life contracted: In 1830, overall production was lower than in 1800. Rugged terrain over vast distances made interregional trade difficult, and few institutions fostered it. The old patterns of overseas trade had been disrupted. There was an absence of domestic funds for investment. Many wealthy *peninsulares* departed. Consequently, Latin American governments and businesses looked to Britain for protection, markets, and investment.

Independence also created new sources of discontent. There was much disagreement about the character of the future government. Institutions such as the Roman Catholic Church sought to maintain their privileges. Indian communities found themselves subject to new exploitation. Quarrels arose between the creole elites of different regions of the new nations. The agricultural hinterlands resented the predominance of the port cities. Investors or merchants from one Latin American nation found themselves in conflict with those of others over tariffs or mining regulations. Civilians became rivals of the military for political authority.

ABSENCE OF SOCIAL CHANGE

All the elites opposed substantial social reform. The creole victors in the wars of independence granted equal rights to all persons and, except in Brazil, had abolished slavery by 1855. However, the right to vote depended on property qualification, and peasants remained subservient to their landlords. Colonial racial codes disappeared,

Catholicism, have had similar unstable and often authoritarian governments. They have frequently tended toward some version of dictatorship, uneven development, anticlericalism, and social cleavage between urban and rural areas and between wealthy middle-class or landed elites and poor peasant populations. Viewed in this Iberian-Mediterranean context, Latin America seems less puzzling than when it is viewed in the context of northern Europe.

A third explanation emphasizes conscious political, economic, and cultural decisions the Latin American creole elite took after independence. This explanation contends that the elite, including the army officers who won the wars, sought to enrich themselves and to maintain their positions at the cost of all other segments of the population, who in many of these countries differed ethnically and racially from the elite. These officers, landowners, and urban middle-class leaders aligned their national economies with the industrializing regions of Europe and North America, and aligned themselves culturally as well, thus differentiating themselves from the lower classes and indigenous peoples and culture. They also adopted European liberal political and economic ideologies to justify unlimited exploitation of economic resources on the basis of individualist enterprise. They then used the wealth generated by this exploitation to maintain their power. They embraced European concepts of progress to dismiss the legitimacy of the culture and communal values of the Indians or the peasants.

In addition to these views, it helps to consider Latin America within a global perspective. Beginning in the nineteenth century much of the region, like much of Asia and Africa, was drawn into an integrated worldwide economic system dominated by Europe and North America. Many nations in Latin America and elsewhere, having developed narrow economies based on the export of one or a few raw materials or semifinished products, became vulnerable to fluctuations in worldwide demand for these products and to political and economic interference from Europe and North America.

Focus Questions

◆ What is dependency theory? How can it help to understand the history of Latin America since independence?

◆ Is Latin America's Iberian heritage a likely explanation of why Latin America has developed along such different lines from North America?

◆ What role did the creole elite play in the economic and political instability that has characterized Latin America in the modern era?

but not racial prejudice. Although **mestizos**, **mulattos**, and even Indians who achieved economic success were assimilated into the higher ranks of the social structure, whites or light-complexioned people tended to constitute the elite of Latin America. Most important, there were no major changes in landholding; the ruling classes protected the interests of landholders.

Except for Mexico in 1910, no Latin American nation until the 1950s experienced a revolution that overthrew the social and economic structures dating from the colonial period. The absence of such social revolution is perhaps the most important factor in Latin American history during the first century of independence. The rise and fall of political regimes represented quarrels among the elites. Everyday life for most of the population did not change. Throughout the social structure, there was no mutual trust or allegiance to the political system.

CONTROL OF THE LAND

Most Latin Americans during the nineteenth century lived in the countryside. Agriculture was dominated by large *haciendas*, or plantations. The landowners ruled these estates as small domains. The *latifundia* (large rural estates) grew larger during the nineteenth century from confiscated church lands and conquered Indian territories. Work was labor intensive because little machinery was available. For some products—salted meats, for example—there was a limited manufacturing stage in Latin America. Most crops, including grains, tobacco, sugar, coffee, and cacao, were exported.

mestizos
Persons of mixed Native American and European descent.

mulattos
Persons of mixed African and European descent.

QUICK REVIEW

Landowners

- *Haciendas*: large plantations that dominated Latin American agriculture
- Landowners controlled the institutions of the government
- Rural workforce was dependent on the landowners

MAP EXPLORATION

To explore this map further, go to **http://www.myhistorylab.com**

MAP 25–1. Latin America in 1830. By 1830 most of Latin America had been liberated from Europe. This map shows the initial borders of the states of the region with the dates of their independence. The United Provinces of La Plata formed the nucleus of what later become Argentina.

Which countries' borders differ significantly from what they are today?

Landowners constituted a society of their own. They sometimes formed family alliances with the wealthy urban classes who were involved in export commerce or the law. Younger sons might enter the army or the church. Landowners served in the national parliaments. Their wealth, literacy, and social connections made them the rulers of the countryside, and the army would protect them from any social uprising. The landowners lived well and comfortably, though often on isolated estates.

The rural workforce was socially and economically dependent on the landowners. In Brazil, slavery persisted until 1888. In other rural areas, many people lived as virtual slaves. **Debt peonage** was widespread and often tied a peasant to the land like a serf. Later in the nineteenth century, the new lands that were opened were generally organized as large holdings with tenants rather than as small landholdings with independent farmers. This was different from both the United States and Canada. Poor transportation made internal travel difficult and kept many people on the land. Little effort was made to provide education, leaving Latin American peasants ignorant, lacking technological skills, and incapable of improving their condition.

debt peonage

A system that forces agricultural laborers (peons) to work and live on large estates (*haciendas*) until they have repaid their debts to the estate's owner.

The second half of the nineteenth century witnessed a remarkable growth in Latin American urban life (see Figure 25–1). There was some movement from the countryside to the city, and an influx of European immigrants as well as some from Asia took place. The creole elite favored European immigration, which increased the size of the white population; Asian immigration was a source of inexpensive labor. Throughout this period there arose a political and social trade-off between the urban and rural elites. Each permitted the other to pursue its economic self-interest and repress discontent. Nonetheless, the growth of the urban centers shifted political influence to the cities and gave rise to an urban working class. Urban growth in Latin America created difficulties not unlike those that arose in Europe and the United States at about the same time.

	1870	1914
Rio de Janiero	275,000	1,000,000
São Paulo	31,000	450,000
Buenos Aires	178,000	1,200,000
Lima	90,000	200,000
Guayaquil, Ecuador	12,000	75,000
Mexico City	200,000	700,000

FIGURE 25-1. Population of Latin American Cities, 1870–1914 Source: United Nations.

SUBMISSIVE POLITICAL PHILOSOPHIES

Economic liberalism and the need for British investment led to free trade. After independence, Latin America exported less than it had under colonial rule and achieved a trade balance only by exporting precious metals. Because these metals often came from stocks mined years earlier, this amounted to a flight of capital. The general economic view was that Latin America would produce raw materials for export in exchange for manufactured goods imported from Europe, especially from Britain.

For most of the nineteenth century, the landed sector of the economy dominated because cheap imports and a shortage of local capital discouraged indigenous industrialism. Latin American liberals championed the extension of great landed estates and the social dependence associated with them. The produce of the new land could contribute export goods to pay for the import of finished goods. Liberals favored confiscating land owned by the church and the Indians because they did not exploit their lands in what liberals considered a progressive manner.

During the second half of the century, **positivism**—the political ideas stemming from the French positivist philosopher Auguste Comte (1798–1857)—swept across Latin America. Comte and his followers had advocated the cult of science and technological progress. This highly undemocratic outlook suggested that either technocrats or dictatorial governments could best achieve modernization. It was especially popular among military officers and influenced the ongoing Latin American struggle between

positivism

The philosophy of Auguste Comte that science is the final, or positive, stage of human intellectual development because it involves exact descriptions of phenomena, without recourse to unobservable operative principles, such as gods or spirits.

Peonage. This 1845 lithograph by Carlos Morel (1813–1894) shows a night watch by a group of peons or laborers in the Pampas, Argentina. The great landowners of Latin America ruled their huge estates as small domains.

Picture Desk, Inc./Kobal Collection.

What impact did landowners have on Latin American society?

civilian and military elites. The great slogan of Latin American positivism, emblazoned on the flag of the Brazilian republic, was "Order and Progress." Social or political groups that created disorder or challenged the existing social order were by definition unprogressive.

Toward the close of the century the military forces in various countries—following Germany's model—became more professionalized. Their training often made the officer corps the most important educated elite in a country. Their education and loyalty gave them considerable influence, generally of a conservative character.

Finally, the late nineteenth-century European theories of "scientific" racism were used to preserve the social status quo. Racial theory could attribute the economic backwardness of the region to its vast nonwhite or mixed-blood population. This explanation shifted responsibility for the economic difficulties of Latin America away from the mostly white governing elites toward Indians, blacks, mestizos, and mulattos, who had long been exploited or repressed. (See Document, "A Peruvian Commentator Decries Racial Thinking.")

This conservative intellectual heritage affected twentieth-century political thought. It can be seen in the ongoing tendency of military groups in Latin America to view themselves as the guarantors of order, ready to protect the status quo or thwart social change. It is also reflected in the way the political elites of Latin America opposed communism after the Russian Revolution. Although many Latin American nations had small organized communist parties, governments used the fear of communism to resist virtually all political movements that advocated social reform or questioned property arrangements. From the 1920s onward, the fear of communism brought support to conservative governments, whether civilian or military. Communism would become an even more powerful regional issue after the successful Cuban Revolution of 1957 installed a communist state in Latin America.

DOCUMENT

A Peruvian Commentator Decries Racial Thinking

Manuel Gonzalez Prada (1848–1918) was a Peruvian social and political critic. He had spent much time in France, where he became acquainted with European scientific thought and contemporary theories of race. (See Chapters 23 and 24.) He personally embraced much European idealism and strongly opposed social Darwinism and racism. In an essay of 1904, entitled "Our Indians," Prada decried the treatment of the Native Americans in Peru by the republican government and the racial ideas that supported such treatment. He saw the case of Peruvian Indians as only one among many contemporary examples of peoples suffering serious discrimination and maltreatment on the basis of race. He contended that the republic of Peru, because of racial theory and cultural assumptions of white superiority, put modern Peruvian Indians in a situation worse than their Inca forebears had experienced with the various forced labor practices of the Spanish Empire. The racial outlooks that Prada condemns were widespread across Latin America and were one of several factors that held back social and political progress.

- **HOW** does Prada present the situation of Peruvian Indians as one of numerous cases of the impact of racial thinking globally? How does he connect the degradation of Peruvian Indians with greed? Why does he see the treatment of Peruvian Indians as contradicting republican political ideals?

How convenient an invention ethnology is in the hands of some men! If one grants the division of humanity into superior and inferior races and recognizes the superiority of the whites and their consequent right to govern the planet, nothing is more natural than the suppression of the Negro in Africa, the redskin in the United States, the Tagalog in the Philippines, or the Indian in Peru. . . .

[A]s a general rule, the dominant [group in Peru] approach the Indian only to deceive him, oppress him or corrupt him. And we should remember that not only the national half-caste acts with inhumanity and bad faith. When Europeans become wool traders, mine owners, or hacienda proprietors, they show themselves fine exactors, extortionists, rivaling the old *encomenderos* and the present day *hacendados*. The white skinned animal, wherever he is born, is afflicted with the disease of gold. In the final analysis he yields to the instinct of rapacity. . . .

Does the Indian suffer less under the republic than under Spanish rule? While neither *corregimientos* nor *encomiendas* exist, forced labor and its recruitment remain. What we make him suffer is enough to call down upon us the execration of humanity. We hold him in ignorance and servitude, we debate him in the garrisons, we brutalize him with alcohol, we set him to destroying himself in civil war, and from time to time we organize hunting parties and massacres. . . .

It is an unwritten axiom that the Indian has no rights, only obligations. In his case a personal complaint is considered insubordination, a collective claim a plot of rebellion. The Spanish royalists killed the Indian when he tried to escape the yoke of his conquerors; we republicans exterminate him when he protests against onerous taxes or tires of enduring in silence the inequities of some satrap.

Our form of government is in essence a great lie, because a state in which two or three million individuals live outside the law does not deserve to be called a democratic republic. . . .

The political and social organization of the ancient Inca empire astonishes revolutionary reformers today. . . . Morally speaking, the native of the republic is inferior to the native encountered by the conquerors; but moral depression because of political servitude is not the same as an absolute incapacity by organic constitution to achieve civilization.

Source: Manuel Gonzalez Prada, from *Horas de lucha* (first published 1908) as quoted in Harold Eugene Davis, *Latin American Social Thought: The History of Its Development Since Independence, with Selected Readings* (Washington, DC: University Press of Washington, DC, 1961) pp. 202, 203, 205.

ECONOMY OF DEPENDENCE

WHAT WAS the economy of dependence?

The wars of independence destroyed the Spanish and Portuguese colonial trade monopolies. Where previously only a few dozen ships called annually at any port, hundreds laden with goods from all over the world could now drop anchor. Consequently, Latin America had many new trading partners. Trade was free and the nations were politically independent, but economic life was still fundamentally shaped by the demand of other nations for Latin American commodities.

One of the chief reasons for this dependence was the absence of large internal markets. Trade after independence flowed in the same direction that it had flowed before independence because Europe remained the source of finished goods. Geographical barriers hindered internal trade. The jungles of the Amazon and the Andes Mountains made east–west trade difficult. A lack of road systems prevented goods from moving between countries or even easily within them, and there was little domestic investment in transport. European and American investments in railways during the nineteenth century generally facilitated exports rather than internal trade.

NEW EXPLOITATION OF RESOURCES

The wars of independence disrupted the Latin American economy. To restore old industries such as mining and gain access to steamships and railroads, Latin Americans had to turn to European and North American investors. For decades, Britain dominated Latin America economically. The desire to pour manufactured goods into Latin America led Britain and other nations to discourage the development of manufacturing industries there. Foreign investment did help revive the mining industry in Mexico, Peru, and Chile, but mining produces raw materials, not manufactured goods.

To pay for imports and foreign services, Latin American nations turned to the production of agricultural commodities for which there was great European demand. Rural areas and the commercial centers serving agriculture became politically and economically more important than many of the old colonial urban centers. The production of wheat, beef, hides, hemp, coffee, cocoa, and other foodstuffs for the export market also raised the value of land. Because so much land was available, agricultural production was increased by extending areas of cultivation rather than by finding more efficient ways to farm. So much wealth could be accumulated through land speculation and land development that little incentive existed for alternative investments in manufacturing. It would also have been difficult for new Latin American industries to compete with the cheap goods imported from more established industrial economies.

After 1850, the Latin American republics became relatively more prosperous. Chile exported copper and nitrates as well as wheat. Peru exported guano for fertilizer. Coffee was becoming king in Venezuela, Brazil, Colombia, and Central America. Sugar continued to be produced in the West Indies and Cuba, which remained under Spanish control. Argentina supplied hides and tallow. But this limited prosperity was based on the export of agricultural commodities or raw materials and the importation of finished goods.

Nevertheless, the period from approximately 1870 through 1930 came to be seen as a kind of golden age for the Latin American economy. There was more prosperity than ever before, especially in Chile, Argentina, Brazil, and Mexico. The economies of the Latin American nations grew because industrial production in Europe and the United States created a demand for three broad varieties of exports. First were foodstuffs raised in Latin America that were more or less like those that could be raised in Europe, chiefly wheat and beef products, for which Argentina became the great exporter. Second were distinctly tropical products, such as bananas, sugar, and coffee. Third were natural resources, including metals, of which copper was the most important; minerals, such as nitrates; and later, oil.

Both the trading patterns for these goods and the internal improvements in Latin American production deeply and inextricably linked the economy of the region to Europe and, after 1900, to the United States. The region could not control its own economic destiny. Europeans and North Americans provided capital and the technological and managerial skills to build bridges, roads, railroads, steam lines, and new mines. Whenever the economy of Europe or the United States floundered, Latin America was hurt.

INCREASED FOREIGN OWNERSHIP AND INFLUENCE

During the late nineteenth century, the growing European demand gave Latin Americans a false sense of security. The vast profits to be made through mining and agricultural exports discouraged investment in local industry. Foreigners saw no reason to capitalize local industry that might replace imported goods. By late in the century, the wealthy in Latin America had, in effect, lost control of valuable sectors of their economy. For example, in 1901 British and other foreign investors owned approximately 80 percent of the Chilean nitrate industry. Foreigners also owned and operated most of the steamship lines and railroads.

The European and U.S. economic penetration of Latin America was more subtle than that experienced by India or China, but it was no less real. Foreign powers also used their political and military influence to protect their economic interests. Britain, as the dominant power until the turn of the century, was frequently involved in the political affairs of the Latin American nations. From the Spanish-American War of 1898 onward, the United States began to exercise more direct influence in the region. In 1903, to facilitate its plans to build a canal across Panama, the United States participated in the rebellion that allowed Panama to separate from Colombia. The U.S. military intervened in the Caribbean and Central America. By the 1920s, the United States had replaced Britain as Latin America's dominant trading partner.

U.S. interventions were one cost of Latin America's dependent economy. More significant costs, however, arose from fundamental shifts in world trade that were brought on by World War I and continued through the 1920s. First, the amount of trade carried on by European countries decreased. Second, during the 1920s, world prices of agricultural commodities dropped. Latin American nations had to produce more goods to pay for their imports. Third, synthetic products manufactured in Europe or North America replaced the natural products supplied by Latin America. Finally, petroleum began to replace other natural products as an absolute percentage of world trade. Petroleum-exporting countries, such as Mexico, gained a greater share of export income.

ECONOMIC CRISES AND NEW DIRECTIONS

The Great Depression produced a crisis in this **neocolonial economy**. Commodity prices collapsed. The republics of Latin America could not repay their debts to foreign banks. A new economic era began in Latin America after the conclusion of

Brazilian Coffee being loaded onto a British ship. Most Latin American countries developed an export economy based on the exchange of agricultural products, raw materials, and semifinished goods for finished goods and services from abroad. Until recently, the coffee industry dominated both the political and economic life of Brazil.

Compare this photograph with the one on page 652. Both photos are from the same time period. How are they similar?

neocolonial economy
An economic relationship between a former colonial state and countries with more developed economies in which the former colony exports raw materials to and imports manufactured goods from the more developed nations.

Banana Republic. For most of the twentieth century the United Fruit Company, an American conglomerate, exerted tremendous economic influence throughout Central America, with extensive coffee and banana plantations throughout the region. The company also wielded significant political power, especially in Guatemala, where workers in this photograph are harvesting bananas.

Why were foreign entities able to exert so much power in Latin America?

import substitution
The replacement of imported goods with goods manufactured domestically.

World War II. It was marked by economic nationalism and a determination to create national economies that were not wholly dependent on foreign events and wealth.

With the Depression, it became necessary to substitute domestic manufactured goods for those imported from abroad. Various nations pursued **import substitution** policies, and by the mid-1940s there were three varieties of manufacturing in Latin America. First, there were industries that, as in the past, transformed raw materials for export, such as food processing, mining, and petroleum refining. Second, there were industries addressing local demands, such as power plants and machine shops. Third, there were industries, basically assembly plants, that transformed imported materials to take advantage of cheap labor. None of this manufacturing was particularly sophisticated, and none of it involved heavy industry. Not until the 1950s would significant steel production, for example, occur in the region.

SEARCH FOR POLITICAL STABILITY

WHO WERE the *caudillos*?

caudillos
Latin American strongmen, or dictators, usually with strong ties to the military.

The new states of independent Latin America had little or no experience in self-government. The Spanish Empire had been ruled directly by the monarchy and by Spanish-born royal bureaucrats. This monarchical or paternalistic heritage survived in two forms. First, many traditionalists and conservatives favored the establishment of monarchies in Latin America, including José de San Martín (1778–1850). Monarchy was briefly established in Mexico. In Brazil, an emperor from the Portuguese royal family governed until 1889.

The second heritage of the colonial monarchy was the proclivity of the Latin American political elites to tolerate or support strong executives. The constitutions of the early republics were frequently suspended or rewritten, so that a strong leader could consolidate his power. Such figures were called **caudillos**. They usually came from the officer corps or enjoyed strong ties to the army. The real basis of their rule was force. *Caudillos* might support conservative causes, such as protection of the church or strong central government, or they might pursue liberal policies, such as the confiscation of church land, the extension of landed estates, and the development of education.

These strongmen encountered little opposition because of their repressive policies. Later in the century the new relative prosperity of expanding economies quieted potential discontent. The dictators became more skilled at both repression and patronage. The political and social elites also rallied to their support when, around the turn of the century, the young labor movement called strikes.

Even when *caudillos* were forced from office and parliamentary government was more or less restored, the regimes that replaced them were neither genuinely liberal nor democratic. Parliamentary governments usually ruled by courtesy of the military and in the economic interest of the existing elites. No matter who ruled, the life of the over-whelming mass of the population changed little. Except for the Mexican Revolution of 1910, Latin American politics was run by and for the elite.

THREE NATIONAL HISTORIES

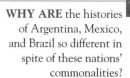

Argentina, Mexico, and Brazil encompass more than 50 percent of the land, people, and wealth of the region. Their histories illustrate the general themes of Latin American history.

WHY ARE the histories of Argentina, Mexico, and Brazil so different in spite of these nations' commonalities?

ARGENTINA

Argentine history from independence to World War II can be divided into three eras. From the rebellion against Spain in 1810 until the mid-nineteenth century, the question of which region of the nation would be dominant was foremost. From 1853 until 1916, Argentina experienced economic expansion and large-scale immigration from Europe, which transformed its society and its world position. From 1916 to 1943, Argentines failed to establish a democratic state and struggled with an economy they did not control.

In 1810, the junta in Buenos Aires overturned Spanish rule. However, the other regions of the viceroyalty of Río de la Plata refused to accept its leadership. Paraguay, Uruguay, and Bolivia went their separate ways. Conflicts between Buenos Aires and the remaining provinces dominated the first seventy years of Argentine history. Eventually, Buenos Aires established its primacy because it dominated trade on the Río de la Plata and controlled the international customhouse, which assured revenue.

Between 1821 and 1827 Bernardino Rivadavia (1780–1845) worked to create a liberal political state, but he could not overcome the forces of regionalism. His major accomplishment was a commercial treaty in 1823 that established Great Britain as a dominant trading partner. Thus began a deep intermeshing of trade and finance between the two nations that would continue for over a century. After Rivadavia's resignation in 1827 came the classical period of *caudillo* rule in Argentina. The strongman of the province of Buenos Aires, Juan Manuel de Rosas (1793–1877), controlled foreign relations, trade, and the customhouse, while the other provinces were left to run their own internal affairs. His major policies were expansion of trade and agriculture, suppression of the Indians, and nationalism.

Rosas was overthrown in 1852, and the next year a federal constitution was promulgated for the Argentine republic. Buenos Aires remained aloof until the republic conquered the province in 1859. The economic prosperity of the late nineteenth century gave the capital new prominence.

The Argentine economy was overwhelmingly agricultural, the chief exports at midcentury being animal products. Internal transportation was poor and the country was sparsely populated. Technological advances changed this situation. In 1876 the first refrigerator ship, *La Frigiorique*, steamed into Buenos Aires. Henceforth, it would be possible to transport large quantities of Argentine beef to Europe. At about the same time it became clear that wheat could be farmed throughout the pampas. The Argentine government carried out a major campaign against the Indian population known as the Conquest of the Desert. The British built railways to carry wheat from the interior to the coast, where it was loaded on British and other foreign steamships. Government policy made the purchase of land by wealthy Argentines simple and cheap.

Juan Manuel de Rosas (1793–1877), a *caudillo* **of Buenos Aires from 1827 to 1852.** Rosas was the archetypal *caudillo*, waging relentless war on the natives of Patagonia.

How do the *caudillos* **compare with modern dictators?**

•••—Read the **Document**

Domingo F. Sarmiento, "Civilization and Barbarism," 1845 at **myhistorylab.com**

Immigrant Hotel, Buenos Aires, ca. 1900.
More than 8 million people from Europe and Asia immigrated to South America and the Caribbean between 1860 and 1920. In this photograph, European immigrants dine in a communal hall at a hotel set aside specifically for them.

Look closely at this photo. Why are there no women present?

pampas
The fertile South American lowlands that include the Argentine provinces of Buenos Aires, La Pampa, Santa Fe, and Córdoba, most of Uruguay, and the southernmost end of Brazil, Rio Grande do Sul, covering more than 750,000 km² (289,577 sq mi).

The development of the **pampas** and the vastly increased production of beef and wheat made Argentina one of the wealthiest nations of Latin America and a major agricultural rival of the United States. The opening of land, even if only for tenant farming and not ownership, encouraged hundreds of thousands of Europeans, particularly from Spain and Italy, to immigrate to Argentina. The immigrants also provided workers for the food-processing, service, and transportation industries in Buenos Aires. By 1900 Argentina was much more urbanized and industrialized. The predominance of both large landowners and foreign business interests continued, however.

Prosperity quieted political opposition for a time. The conservative landed oligarchy governed under presidents who perpetuated a strong export economy. Like similar groups elsewhere, they ignored the social questions raised by urbanization and industrialization.

In 1890 members of the urban middle and professional classes founded the Radical Party. It achieved little until 1912, when the conservative government expanded the franchise and provided for the secret ballot. Four years later, Radical Party leader Hipólito Irigoyen (1850–1933) was elected president (first term 1916–1922). Argentina remained neutral in World War I, in order to trade with both

CHRONOLOGY

ARGENTINA

1810	Junta in Buenos Aires overthrows Spanish government
1827–1852	Era of Rosas's dictatorial government
1876	Ship refrigeration makes possible export of beef around the world
1879–1880	General Roca carries out *Conquest of the Desert* against the Indian population
1914–1918	Argentina remains neutral in World War I
1930s	Period of strong influence of nationalist military
1943–1956	Era of Juan and Eva Perón

sides. The war put great pressure on the economy, resulting in labor agitation. Though previously sympathetic toward labor, Irigoyen as president used troops against strikers.

By the end of the 1920s, the Radical Party had become corrupt and directionless. The worldwide commodity depression hurt exports. In 1930, the military staged a coup. The officers returned power to conservative civilians, and Argentina remained dependent on the British export market. U.S. interests also began to establish plants in Argentina, removing still more economic activity from Argentine control.

In the 1930s, a right-wing nationalistic movement, **nacionalismo**, arose among writers, journalists, and a few politicians. It resembled the fascist political movements then active in Europe. Its supporters equated British and American domination of the economy with imperialism. In effect, they were anti-imperialistic, socially concerned, authoritarian, and sympathetic to the rule of a modern *caudillo*. World War II gave these attitudes new influence.

nacionalismo
A right-wing Argentine nationalist movement that arose in the 1930s and resembled European fascism.

World War II closed almost all of Europe to Argentine exports, creating a sudden economic crisis. The country's leadership seemed incapable of responding, and in 1943 the military again seized control. Many military officers were children of immigrants and were fiercely nationalistic; some had become deeply impressed by the Fascist and Nazi movements and their rejection of European liberal politics. The officers also shared the Fascist and Nazi hostility to Britain. They contended that the government must address social questions, industrialize the country, and liberate it from foreign economic control. In all these respects, they echoed the *nacionalistas*.

Between 1943 and 1946 Juan Perón (1895–1974), one of the colonels involved in the 1943 coup, forged social discontent and authoritarian political attitudes into a remarkable political movement known as **Peronism**. It was initially militaristic, anticommunist, and socially progressive. In 1946 he made himself the voice of working-class democracy, even though after his election to the presidency he created an authoritarian regime that only marginally addressed industrial problems. He was greatly aided by his wife, the former actress Eva Duarte (1919–1952). A charismatic figure, she enjoyed fervent support among trade-union members and the working class.

Argentine president Juan Domingo Perón and his wife Eva address a throng of supporters from a balcony in Buenos Aires.

What were the bases of Perón's support?

Perón became the most famous of the postwar Latin American dictators, but his power and appeal were rooted in the antiliberal attitudes that had been fostered by the corruption and aimlessness of Argentine politics during the Depression. He was the supreme twentieth-century embodiment of the *caudillo*. He was ousted in 1956, but long-term stability would elude Argentine politics after his departure.

Peronism
An authoritarian, nationalist movement founded in Argentina in the 1940s by the dictator Juan Perón.

MEXICO

The heritage of Mexican independence was a combination of the thwarted social revolution led by Father Hidalgo and José María Morelos between 1811 and 1815, and the conservative political coup carried out in 1820 by the creole elite against a potentially liberal Spanish crown. For the first century of independence conservative forces held sway, but in 1910 the Mexican people launched the most far-reaching revolution in Latin American history.

A Closer Look

Benito Juarez

Benito Juarez (1806–1872) was one of the most remarkable figures to lead Mexico or any other Latin American nation during the nineteenth century. In 1861 he became the first and only Amerindian to hold the office of president in Mexico. Dedicated to bringing liberal reforms and economic advancement to Mexico, Juarez's political movement was known as *La Reforma* to indicate that it stood in favor of constitutional government in opposition to the autocracy of Santa Anna and conservative political groups in Mexico. He worked to defend and protect the rights of Native Americans in Mexico and opposed the political authority still often exercised by the Roman Catholic Church in Mexico. He also favored economic development in his nation. In all these respects he stood in agreement with most political liberals throughout the nineteenth-century transatlantic world. His most heroic moment came in his firm resistance during the 1860s to any kind of compromise with the effort of the Austrian Prince Maximilian to establish a conservative European empire over Mexico. The Mexican victory over Maximilian was the single most important example of an American nation rejecting and overcoming European efforts to impose direct political control.

This portrait was painted in 1948 by the famous Mexican painter Diego Rivera (1886–1957). Rivera was himself a communist and a radical anticlerical. Note his emphasis in the portrait on Juarez as a civilian.

In the upper left is a portrayal of the execution of the Emperor Maximilian before a firing squad.

In the upper right Rivera pictures the construction of what appears to be a railroad bridge symbolizing Juarez's dedication to economic development, as do the tools for engineering drawings in the foreground.

Questions

1. How does Rivera's portrayal of Juarez present Juarez as a particular kind of Mexican patriot?

2. Looking at the portrait, could one discern that it had been painted after the violence of the Mexican Revolution and that it might be idealizing a Mexican leader of the third quarter of the nineteenth century?

3. Why might Rivera have wanted to trace the ideal of national and economic independence of Mexico to the middle of the previous century?

myhistörylab   To examine this image in an interactive fashion, please go to **www.myhistorylab.com**

The years from 1820 to 1876 were a time of turmoil, economic floundering, and humiliation. Independent Mexico attempted no liberal political experiments. Its first ruler was Agustín de Iturbide (1783–1824), who ruled until 1823 as an emperor. Thereafter, Mexico was governed by a succession of *caudillo* presidents, who depended on the army for support. The strongest of these figures was Antonio López de Santa Anna (1795–1863), a general and a political opportunist who usually supported conservative political and social interests. He ruled in a thoroughly dictatorial manner. More than once he was driven from office, but he inevitably returned until finally exiled in 1855.

The midcentury movement against Santa Anna's autocracy was called **La Reforma**. In theory, its supporters were liberal, but Mexican liberalism was associated primarily with anticlericalism, confiscation of church lands, and opposition to military influence on politics. *La Reforma* aimed to produce political stability, civilian rule, and an economic policy that would attract foreign capital and immigrants. Having deposed Santa Anna, the leaders of the reform movement passed legislation to break up large landed estates, particularly those owned by the church, and to promote the establishment of small farms. However, the actual content of the laws permitted existing landowners to purchase additional land cheaply. The legislative attack on the privileges of the church led to further civil war between 1857 and 1860. In January 1861 Benito Juárez (1806–1872) entered Mexico City as the temporary victor.

Political instability was matched by economic stagnation. After 1820 many Spanish officials and merchants fled, taking with them large quantities of gold and silver. The mines that had produced Mexico's colonial wealth were in poor condition, and the country could not repair them. The hacienda system left farming in a backward condition. Cheap imports of manufactured goods stifled domestic industries. Transportation was primitive. The government's remedy was massive foreign borrowing, and soon interest payments consumed the national budget.

Political weakness and economic disarray invited foreign intervention. In 1823 the Mexican government allowed Stephen F. Austin (1793–1836) to begin the colonization of Texas. During the next decade, the policies of Santa Anna stirred resentment among the Texas settlers, and in 1835 they rebelled. The next year Santa Anna destroyed the defenders of the Alamo but was decisively defeated at the battle of San Jacinto. Texas became an independent republic that was annexed by the United States in 1845. Border clashes between Mexican and U.S. forces enabled President James Polk to launch a war against Mexico in 1846 that saw the United States army occupy Mexico City. Through the treaty of Guadalupe Hidalgo (1848), the United States gained a vast portion of Mexican territory, including what is now New Mexico, Arizona, and California.

As a result of Juárez's liberal victory in 1861, Mexican conservatives and clerics invited the Austrian Archduke Maximilian (1832–1867) to become the emperor of Mexico. Napoleon III (r. 1852–1870) of France supported this venture. Maximilian became emperor but was unable to build political support. In 1867, Juarez captured the unhappy emperor and executed him.

Once restored to office, the liberal leaders continued their measures against the church but failed to rally significant popular support. In 1876 Porfirio Díaz (1830–1915) seized power and retained it until 1911. He maintained one of the most successful dictatorships in Latin American history by giving almost every political sector something it wanted. He allowed landowners to purchase public land cheaply; he cultivated the army; and he made peace with the church. He used

La Reforma
The nineteenth-century Mexican liberal reform movement that opposed Santa Anna's dictatorship and sought to foster economic progress, civilian rule, and political stability. It was strongly anticlerical.

The Execution of Maximilian of Mexico, June 19, 1867, by the French Impressionist painter Edouard Manet. Between 1867 and 1869 Manet completed a series of compositions depicting the execution of the Mexican emperor. This is the final and largest work.

Edouard Manet (1832-1883), "The Execution of Emperor Maximilian of Mexico, June 19, 1867," Oil on canvas. Location: Staedtische Kunsthalle, Mannheim, Germany. Art Resource, New York.

Does this painting glorify or belittle the execution of the emperor?

repression against opponents and bribery to cement the loyalty of his supporters. Foreign companies, especially from the United States, invested heavily in what, by 1900, appeared to be a thoroughly stable country.

Yet problems remained. The peasants wanted land and resented the power of the landlords. Food production declined during the Díaz regime, so many Mexicans were malnourished. Labor unrest and strikes afflicted the textile and mining industries. The Panic of 1907 in the United States disrupted the Mexican economy. By 1910 the so-called *Pax Porfiriana* was unraveling.

In 1911, Francisco Madero (d. 1913), a wealthy landowner and moderate liberal, led an insurrection that drove Díaz into exile. Shortly thereafter, Madero was elected president. He recognized the rights of trade unions to organize and to strike, but he was unwilling to change the pattern of landholding. Radical leaders emerged, calling for social change. Pancho Villa (1874–1923) in the north and Emiliano Zapata (1879–1919) in the south rallied mass followings of peasants who demanded fundamental structural changes in rural landholding. In late 1911 Zapata proclaimed his Plan of Ayala, which in effect set forth a program of large-scale peasant confiscation of land.

Madero found himself squeezed between the conservative supporters of the deposed Díaz and the radical peasant revolutionaries. No one trusted him, and in early 1913 he was overthrown by General Victoriano Huerta (1854–1916), who had the help of the United States. Huerta, who was basically a dictator, failed to quash the peasant rebellion. Meanwhile, Venustiano Carranza (1859–1920), a wealthy landowner, put himself at the head of a large Constitutionalist Army—so called because it advocated the restoration of constitutional government in opposition to the political dictatorship of Huerta—that initially received the support of both Zapata and Villa. Huerta's government collapsed on August 15, 1914, when Constitutionalist forces entered Mexico City. Thereafter disputes erupted between Carranza and Villa and then between Carranza and Zapata. These conflicts arose both from simple political rivalry and from Carranza's refusal to embrace the kind of radical agrarian reform the two peasant leaders sought. Carranza eventually won out, thanks to his political skills and the effectiveness of his army.

Carranza's political skills helped him build a broad base. He addressed himself to the concerns of urban industrial workers as well as the land hunger of rural peasants, successfully separating the two groups. This division ultimately doomed the effort to implement an agrarian revolution. Carranza made many promises, especially about agrarian reform, that he had little or no intention of carrying out. Beginning in early 1915 Carranza's military forces began an ultimately successful campaign against Villa and Zapata. The peasant leaders still commanded regional support but could not win control of the nation. During 1916 Carranza confronted U.S. military intervention along the border that continued until early 1917, when the United States became involved in World

CHRONOLOGY

MEXICO

1820–1823	Agustín de Iturbide rules unsuccessfully as emperor
1833–1855	Santa Anna dominates Mexican political scene
1846–1848	Mexico defeated by United States and loses considerable territory
1861	Victory of liberal forces under Juárez
1862–1867	French troops led by Archduke Maximilian of Austria unsuccessfully invade Mexico
1876–1911	Era of Porfirio Díaz
1911	Beginning of Mexican Revolution
1911	Zapata proclaims Plan of Ayala
1917	Forces of Carranza proclaim constitution
1929	Institutional Revolutionary Party organized

War I in Europe. After years of deadly and destructive civil war, Carranza's forces wrote the constitution of 1917, setting forth a program for ongoing social revolution—never pursued with any vigor—and political reform.

Carranza and his immediate subordinates recognized the agrarian problem but were cautious about changing existing property arrangements. They were determined to modernize Mexican political life and attract capital investment; Mexican leaders would share these goals from that time onward. Thus, despite radical rhetoric and the peasant upheaval, the Mexican Revolution saw the victory of a middle-class elite who would attempt to govern through enlightened paternalism. With Carranza's victory the general direction of Mexican political life had been established.

In 1929 Plutarco Elías Calles (1877–1945) organized the **PRI**, the Institutional Revolutionary Party, which quickly became the most important political force in the nation. The Mexican political system became dominated by a single party within which most political debate occurred, rather than a system dominated by a single strong leader. Despite external criticism and internal tensions, the PRI would oversee the longest period of political stability experienced by any Latin American nation in the twentieth century.

In 1934 Lázaro Cárdenas (1895–1970) was elected president and moved directly to fulfill the promises and programs of 1917. He turned tens of millions of acres of land over to peasant villages. In 1938, when Mexico was the third largest producer of petroleum, he expropriated the oil industry. His nationalization policy established PeMex, the Mexican national oil company. Cárdenas left other mineral industries in private and generally foreign hands. His extensive reforms went through smoothly because he worked through bureaucratic and administrative means.

With the election of Manuel Ávila Camacho (1897–1955) in 1940, the era of revolutionary politics ended. Thereafter, the major issues in Mexico were those generally associated with postwar economic development. But unlike other Latin American nations, Mexico, because of its revolution, could confront those issues with a democratic perspective and a sense of collective social responsibility, no matter how imperfectly those goals might be realized.

QUICK REVIEW

Venustiano Carranza (1859–1920)

- Wealthy landowner who initially joined Villa and Zapata in opposition to Huerta's dictatorship
- Led Constitutionalist Army
- Broke with Villa and Zapata over agrarian reforms; defeated them in civil war
- Constitution of 1917 promised reform; Carranza instead led middle-class elite in imposing enlightened paternalism

PRI

The Institutional Revolutionary Party, which emerged from the Mexican Revolution of 1911 and governed Mexico until the end of the twentieth century.

The Mexican Revolution. The forces of Emiliano Zapata march on Xochimilco in 1914. Women fought alongside men and played other prominent roles during the Mexican Revolution.

What impressions of the fighters do you get from this photograph?

BRAZIL

Postcolonial Brazil, the largest Latin American country, differed in several important respects from other newly independent nations in the region. Its language and colonial heritage were Portuguese rather than Spanish. For the first sixty-seven years of its independence it had a relatively stable monarchical government. And it retained slavery until 1888.

Brazil had moved directly from being part of the Portuguese monarchy to becoming an independent empire in 1822. The first emperor, Pedro I (r. 1822–1831), while serving as regent for his father, the king of Portugal, had put himself at the head of the independence movement. Although he granted Brazil a constitution in 1823, Pedro's high-handed rule led to his abdication in 1831. Brazilians then took hold of their own destinies.

After a decade of political uncertainty under a regency, Pedro II (r. 1831–1889), the 15-year-old son of Pedro I, assumed direct power in 1840 and governed Brazil until 1889. Pedro II made wise and shrewd use of patronage. He asked leaders of both the conservative and the liberal political parties to form ministries. Consequently, Brazil enjoyed remarkable political stability. However, the government took few initiatives to develop the economy.

The great divisive issue in Brazil was slavery. Sugar production remained the mainstay of the economy until the 1850s. Soil exhaustion and inefficient farming methods made profits impossible without the cheap labor of slaves. From about 1850 coffee cultivation began to spread in the southern provinces, and soon coffee cultivation dominated Brazilian agriculture. Coffee producers also used slave labor, but their profits were much larger than those of the sugar producers. Coffee planters tended to see themselves as economic progressives, so they were more open to emancipation.

The Brazilian government had made a treaty with Great Britain in 1826, agreeing to suppress the slave trade. By 1850 Brazil had virtually ceased importing slaves, freeing the capital once spent on slaves for investments in coffee. The end of slave imports effectively doomed the institution of slavery because the birthrate among slaves was too low for the slave population to reproduce itself, but abolition was still a difficult step. The emperor favored gradual emancipation. A law in 1871 freed slaves owned by the crown and decreed legal freedom for future children of slaves, but it required them to work on plantations until the age of 21. The abolition movement grew in Brazil throughout the 1870s and 1880s. In 1888 Pedro II was in Europe for medical treatment, and his daughter was regent. She favored abolition rather than gradual emancipation. When Parliament passed a law abolishing slavery without any compensation to the slave owners, she signed it.

The abolition of slavery brought other issues to a head. Planters who received no financial compensation for their slaves were resentful. Roman Catholic clerics were disaffected by disputes with the emperor over education. Pedro II was unwell; his daughter was unpopular and distrusted. The officer corps of the army wanted more political influence. In November 1889 the army exiled Pedro II, and the monarchy collapsed.

The Brazilian republic lasted from 1891 to 1930. Like the monarchy, it was dominated by a small group of the

Read the Document
Friederich Hassaurek, How to Conduct a Latin American Revolution, 1865
at **myhistorylab.com**

Antislavery Print. Slavery lasted longer in Brazil than in any other nation in North or South America. Antislavery groups circulated prints such as this one published in France to illustrate the brutality of slave life in Brazil.

Why did slavery last so long in Brazil?

wealthy, mostly coffee planters. Fixed elections and patronage kept the system in operation. Literacy replaced property as the qualification for voting, leaving few people qualified to vote. There was consequently little organized opposition and, for that matter, little political life at all.

Around 1900 Brazil was producing over three-fourths of the world's coffee. The crop's success led to overproduction. To meet this problem, the government subsidized prices with loans from foreign banks and taxes on the rest of the economy, which felt exploited by the coffee interests. High world coffee prices encouraged competition from other Latin American producers, which in turn required more price supports in Brazil. Throughout the life of the republic, Brazil remained essentially a country producing a single product for export and few goods for internal consumption.

The end of slavery, the expansion of coffee production, and the beginning of a slow growth of urban industry attracted foreign immigrants to Brazil. They tended to settle in the cities and constituted the core of the early industrial labor force. World War I caused major economic disruption accompanied by urban labor discontent and a general strike in São Paulo in 1917. The failure to address urban and industrial social problems and the political corruption of the republic led to attempted military coups in 1922 and 1924. Both revolts failed, but they indicated profound discontent.

In 1929 coffee prices hit record lows; currency exchange rates fell; and foreign loans were unavailable. Millions of bags of coffee lay in warehouses. Government reserves were depleted in an unsuccessful attempt to hold up the price of coffee and to pay for imports no longer being funded by coffee exports. The collapse of the coffee market brought the republic down with it. In October 1930 a military coup installed Getulio Vargas (1883–1954) in the presidency. Vargas governed Brazil until 1945.

The Vargas years were a major turning point. Vargas was initially supported by the reform elements in the military, by professional middle-class groups, and by urban workers. He recognized the new social and economic groups shaping Brazilian political life. First with constitutionalism and then with dictatorship, he attempted to allow the government to act on behalf of those groups without allowing them to influence or direct the government in a genuinely democratic manner. Vargas was an experimentalist and pragmatist who primarily wanted to hold on to power and to make Brazil a modern nation. He did not form his own political party or movement as Perón would

OVERVIEW   Latin American Products for Export 1820–1930

Argentina	animal products (meat, leather, wool), grain
Bolivia	tin, silver, wool
Brazil	coffee, sugar, rubber
Chile	copper
Colombia	coffee, cattle
Ecuador	bananas
Mexico	silver, cattle, oil
Peru	nitrates, silver
Uruguay	animal products (meat, leather)
Venezuela	coffee, cattle

Vargas and the Military. Getulio Vargas became ruler of Brazil in 1930 through a military coup. Here he stands with his military supporters. One of the purposes of such pictures was to remind the public that any serious opposition might be put down by the military.

Who seems to hold more power here, Vargas or the military officers?

Estado Novo

The "new state" based on political stability and economic and social progress supposedly established by the dictator Getulio Vargas after 1937.

CHRONOLOGY

BRAZIL

1822	Brazil becomes an independent empire
1840	Pedro II assumes personal rule
1840s and 1850s	Spread of coffee cultivation
1865–1870	Paraguayan War
1871	First law curbing slavery
1888	Slavery abolished
1889	Fall of the monarchy
1917	General strike in São Paulo
1929	Collapse of coffee prices
1930–1945	Vargas era
1957	Construction of Brasília begins
1964	Military takes control of the government

later do in Argentina or as the Mexican revolutionaries had done. Rather, Vargas attempted to function as a ringmaster directing the various forces in Brazilian life. His failure to establish a stable institutional framework for including multiple political interest groups has influenced Brazil to the present day.

Vargas and his supporters sought to lessen dependence on coffee by fostering industries to produce goods that had been imported from abroad. The policy succeeded, and by the mid-1930s domestic manufacturing was increasing. In the constitution of 1934 Vargas established a legal framework for labor relations. The structures were paternalistic but included an eight-hour day and a minimum wage.

In the late 1930s, however, Vargas confronted opposition from both the Brazilian Communist Party (founded in 1922) and a new right-wing movement called *Integralism*, and in 1937 he assumed personal dictatorial power. His regime thereafter was repressive. Like the European dictators of the same era, Vargas used censorship, secret police, and torture against his political opponents. He claimed to have established an ***Estado Novo*** ("new state"). He used his newly assumed power to diversify and modernize the economy. Siding with the Allies in World War II, Brazil built up large reserves of foreign currency through the export of foodstuffs. By the end of the war Brazil was becoming the major Latin American industrial power.

Participation in World War II had led many in Brazil to believe that they should not remain subject to a dictatorship. This attitude was widespread in the military, which had fought in Europe and established close contact with the United States. In 1945 the military carried out a coup, and Vargas retired temporarily from political life.

The new regime, which was democratic, continued the general policy of economic development through foreign-financed industrialization. The state, however, assumed a much smaller role. Vargas was elected president in 1950;

his actions and appointments soon became controversial. The military demanded that Vargas resign. Instead he took his own life in 1954, leaving a public testament in which he presented himself as the protector of the poor and of the broad national interest.

In the decade after Vargas's death, Brazil remained a democracy, though a highly unstable one. The government itself began to undertake vast projects, including the enormously costly construction of the new capital of Brasília, begun in 1957. The rapid growth of cities and the expansion of a working class radicalized political life. Widespread poverty and illiteracy continued to plague both the cities and the countryside. In a structural problem created by the constitution of 1946, the presidency was controlled by urban voters, whereas the congress was controlled by rural voters.

By the early 1960s, when President João Goulert (1918–1977) took office, Brazilian political life was in turmoil. Goulert's predecessors had attempted to balance interests or to move among various political forces without firmly favoring a single sector. Goulert committed himself to a policy favored by the left and announced his support for land reform. Goulert also questioned the authority of the military hierarchy. Moreover, Brazil faced economic problems: Both industrial and farm production had fallen from the levels achieved in 1960, fostering discontent. In March 1964 the military, claiming to protect Brazil from communism, seized control of the government, ending its post–World War II experiment with democracy.

SUMMARY

 HOW DID the absence of a social revolution affect Latin America after independence?

Independence without Revolution. In the 1820s, Latin America threw off Spanish and Portuguese rule, but the traditional elites—landowners, military officers, and the church—remained in control. The creole elite discriminated against nonwhites. The predominant philosophies were conservative. *page 643*

◆●◆ Read the Document
Francisco Bilbao, America in Danger, 1862
at **myhistorylab.com**

WHAT WAS the economy of dependence?

Economy of Dependence. Because Latin American economies remained dependent on producing agricultural commodities for export, foreign nations, particularly Britain, dominated Latin American economic life. When commodity prices collapsed during the Great Depression, Latin American economies were devastated. The crisis led to the beginnings of manufacturing in many Latin American countries in an effort to avoid dependence on imports. *page 650*

 WHO WERE the *caudillos*?

Search for Political Stability. A series of strongmen called *caudillos* dominated most Latin American republics. They were generally repressive and conservative. *page 652*

WHY ARE the histories of Argentina, Mexico, and Brazil so different in spite of these nations' commonalities?

Three National Histories. Argentina was dominated by Buenos Aires. Agricultural exports contributed to a strong economy. However, urban social discontent and the growth of nationalism in the 1930s led to military intervention in politics and the corporatist dictatorship of Juan Perón from 1946 to 1956. Mexico was unstable after independence. It lost half its territory to the United States and was invaded by France in the 1860s. The long-lasting dictatorship of Porfirio Díaz brought political stability but increasing discontent. The Mexican Revolution that began in 1911 produced cautious reform under the one-party rule of the PRI, the Institutional Revolutionary Party, which remained in power until the end of the century. Brazil was a stable constitutional monarchy after independence until 1889. It retained slavery until 1888. The establishment of a republic did not change Brazil's dependence on coffee exports, and the collapse of coffee prices in 1929 led to dictatorship. Though politically repressive, Getulio Vargas instituted social reforms and promoted industrial development, which continued to expand in the decade after his death in 1954. *page 653*

KEY TERMS

caudillos (kauw-DEE-lyohs) (p. 652)

creole (p. 644)

debt peonage (p. 647)

dependency theory (p. 644)

Estado Novo (p. 662)

import substitution (p. 652)

La Reforma (p. 657)

mestizos (mess-TEE-zohs) (p. 645)

mulattos (muh-LAHT-ohs) (p. 645)

nacionalismo (p. 655)

neocolonial economy (p. 651)

pampas (PAHM-puhs) (p. 654)

Peronism (p. 655)

positivism (p. 647)

PRI (p. 659)

REVIEW QUESTIONS

1. What was the condition of the Latin American economies after independence? What was their relation to Britain? Why were most Latin American states slow to develop an industrial base? What role did their economies play in the worldwide economy that developed in the nineteenth century?

2. Did the structure of Latin American societies change after independence? What role did the traditional elites play in the economic and political life of their nations? What was the condition of the mass of the population?

3. How did European and U.S. investment in Latin America affect the region economically? Politically?

4. Why did so many Latin American nations find it difficult to develop stable political regimes? What role did the military play?

5. What was the effect of increased European immigration on Argentina? How did the Argentine elite cope with growing urbanization and industrialization?

6. Why was Juan Perón able to seize and hold power? What was the role of "Evita"?

7. Did Mexico experience a real revolution in the early twentieth century? How does this experience distinguish Mexico from other Latin American countries? What caused the turmoil?

8. During the period covered in this chapter, what influence did the shared border with the United States have on Mexican history?

9. Why was the Brazilian experience of independence and early nationhood different from that of Spanish-speaking Latin America? What was the role of slavery in Brazil's history? How are abolition and coffee connected?

10. How did the Vargas regime change the Brazilian economy? Why did Brazilian democracy end in a military coup in 1964?

Note: To learn more about the topics in this chapter, please turn to the Suggested Readings at the end of the book. For additional sources related to this chapter please see www.myhistorylab.com

PEARSON myhistorylab Connections

Reinforce what you learned in this chapter by studying the many documents, images, maps, review tools, and videos available at **www.myhistorylab.com**

Read and Review

✓● Study and Review Chapter 25

●●● Read the Document Domingo F. Sarmiento, "Civilization and Barbarism," 1845, p. 653
Friederich Hassaurek, "How to Conduct a Latin American Revolution," 1865, p. 660
Francisco Bilbao, "America in Danger," 1862, p. 663

((●● Hear the Audio Latin America, p. 644

Research and Explore

◉● See the Map The Americas, ca. 1900

((●● Hear the Audio

Hear the audio file for Chapter 25
at **www.myhistorylab.com**

26

India, the Islamic Heartlands, and Africa, 1800–1945

((•─[Hear the Audio for Chapter 26 at www.myhistorylab.com

The Indian Mutiny of 1857. The mutinous Sepoy cavalry attacking British infantry at the battle of Cawnpore. Although the uprising was suppressed, it was not easily forgotten. In its aftermath the British reorganized the government of India.

What impression does this image give you of the Sepoys' chances of success against the British?

THE INDIAN EXPERIENCE

BRITISH DOMINANCE AND COLONIAL RULE *page 668*

HOW DID British rule affect India?

FROM BRITISH CROWN RAJ TO INDEPENDENCE *page 671*

WHAT ROLE did Gandhi play in ending British rule in India?

THE ISLAMIC EXPERIENCE

DECLINING ISLAMIC POWER AND INDEPENDENCE *page 674*

WHY IS the invasion of Egypt by Napoleon's army in 1798 symbolically important?

ISLAMIC RESPONSES TO FOREIGN ENCROACHMENT *page 676*

WHAT WERE three typical Islamic reactions to Western encroachment?

THE AFRICAN EXPERIENCE

NEW POWER CENTERS AND ISLAMIC REFORM MOVEMENTS *page 680*

WHAT WAS the *mfecane?*

PATTERNS IN EUROPEAN COLONIZATION AND AFRICAN RESISTANCE *page 682*

HOW DID Africans resist European colonialism?

THE RISE OF AFRICAN NATIONALISM *page 688*

WHAT WERE the goals of African nationalists?

T he European encroachment on the rest of the world from the late fifteenth century onward brought radical, often devastating changes. In the West itself, spiritual and material disruption accompanied the Renaissance, Reformation, Enlightenment, and industrial and scientific revolutions. When Western expansion brought the ideas and innovations of these watershed European developments to Asia and Africa, the challenges and changes that ensued were accelerated. Furthermore, they were accompanied by the intrusion of European military and economic power. Consequently, they were received typically with virulent resistance or cautious adaptation.

To speak of these complex processes under the rubric of "modernization" does not reflect the acute differences between events in western Europe and the more disruptive changes that European imperialism and colonialism brought to other parts of the world. Nor does it do

THE CHALLENGE OF MODERNITY: INDIA, ISLAM, AND AFRICA

The period from 1800 to World War II was hard on the fortunes of South Asia, Africa, and the Islamic heartlands. For centuries there had been a rough, long-term balance in advances and setbacks in material and intellectual culture, commercial development, and political stability among the major cultural regions of the world. Suddenly, over a period of 150 years, Europe, long a relative backwater in world history, came to dominate.

The Middle East, Africa, Iran, Central Asia, India, and Southeast Asia, along with Central and Latin America—later the so-called Third World of "developing nations"—were most drastically affected by European imperialism and colonialism. Notwithstanding indigenous developments in these regions, this era's decisive development was new and unprecedented domination of the world's economy, intellectual life, and political and military history by a single segment of the global community. Certainly the histories of the less "developed" (in the sense of evolving toward European-style "modernity") nations of the world in this age had their own internal dynamics; in fact, many smaller African or Latin American societies were not even directly affected by Western dominance until recently. Still, the effects of Western military, economic, and cultural power were considerable. While not synonymous with "progress" as Westerners and modernization theorists often think, these effects have been a hallmark of "modernity" in most of Asia, Africa, and Latin America. Whether by rejection, adaptation, or imitation, peoples worldwide have had to contend with the immense power of the West.

The vitality of many of the cultures and traditions that bore the brunt of the Western onslaught has been striking. Arab, Iranian, Indian, African, and other encounters with Western material and intellectual domination produced differing, often very creative responses. These have produced significant instances of political, economic, and intellectual independence only since

justice to the degree to which the West appropriated the very concept of "modernity." Modernity is now identified with a novel set of ideas and institutions that evolved in Europe between the Renaissance and the early twentieth century and was then gradually exported to, or imposed upon, other societies around the globe. The expression "the impact of modernity" refers to how "modern" Western civilization affected traditional cultures.

The spread of Western culture has had such massive consequences that today non-Western peoples are often seen as merely its passive recipients. A simplistic dualism tends to contrast the "modern" West with the "backward" "Orient," as though all of the world outside Europe, North America, and their most Westernized offshoots were a monolithic, archaic "Other."

As parochial as such chauvinistic generalizations are, the impingement of the West has been a major element in the recent history of African, Asian, Indian, and other civilizations. Here, Western modernity encountered cultures that had flourishing social, religious, and political traditions of their own. Through processes of profound transformation, peoples have sought to delicately balance the unforeseen challenges of modernity with the familiarity of tradition. That transformation took place throughout Asia and Africa as these continents became sites in a fierce European competition for raw materials and influence. The "great game" and the "scramble for colonies" would permanently alter the cultural, economic, and political landscapes in Asia and Africa as well as in Europe. ■

THE INDIAN EXPERIENCE

BRITISH DOMINANCE AND COLONIAL RULE

HOW DID British rule affect India?

In the eighteenth century Britain became the dominant power in the southern seas (see Chapter 20). In India by the early nineteenth century the British had built the largest European colonial empire in the Afro-Asian world. India, the greatest traditional civilization to come under direct European colonial rule, was the "jewel in the crown" of that empire.

1945. However, they began much earlier. Modern Islamic reform began in the eighteenth century, although it has only recently become a major global factor. Indian national, as opposed to regional, consciousness developed from the late 1800s in response to British imperial domination, even though it brought union and independence only after World War II. Ironically, exposure of indigenous elites to European political and social philosophies gave future colonial-independence leaders intellectual resources for ideologies of self-rule framed in "modern" terms. Creative thinkers like M. K. Gandhi (1869–1948) merged European thought with ideas from their own cultures to create new ideologies that could inspire Western sympathizers as well as their indigenous followers to oppose European oppression. African nationalist leaders such as Julius Nyerere (1922–1999) and Jomo Kenyatta (1889–1978) similarly found creative ways to merge European nationalist and indigenous cultural models.

Certainly one widespread result of the imperial-colonial experience has been to sharpen the cultural self-consciousness and self-confidence of those peoples most adversely affected by Western dominance. The experiences of Third World nations with outside domination may well prove to have been sources of not only misery and reversal, but also necessary preparation for positive development and resurgence, despite the problems plaguing many of these nations.

View the Image
Mahatma Gandhi at
myhistorylab.com

Focus Questions

◆ How did Western domination affect South Asia, the Islamic heartlands, and Africa in the nineteenth century?

◆ How did these societies develop ideologies of resistance that helped them achieve independence?

BUILDING THE EMPIRE: THE FIRST HALF OF THE NINETEENTH CENTURY

It was no simple undertaking for Britain to penetrate multiethnic, multilingual, multiconfessional India. The British used a multipronged approach to convince various strata of Indian society and various ethnic groups that cooperation with Britain's imperial enterprise was in their best interests.

A half century before the British Crown asserted direct rule over India in 1858, the British wielded effective imperial control through the East India Company. As the company's pressure on smaller states to pay "subsidies" for military "protection" brought them to either collapse or rebellion, the British annexed more territory. Areas not annexed were recognized as independent princely states. These independent states retained their status only as long as they remained faithfully allied to Britain and contributed money to their common "defense." Members of Indian elites often colluded with the British against local rulers. The India that resulted was a mixture of small and large tributary states and provinces that the British administered directly.

The economic impact of company rule was extensive. To pay the debts incurred by their military actions, the company's administrators organized and exploited Indian land revenues. Squeezed by these demands, many peasants deserted their land; by the 1830s land revenues were in sharp decline. In addition, demand for Indian indigo, cotton, and opium declined, and famines brought widespread suffering despite economic and social reforms.

Company rule affected the physical face of India. Company policies encouraged settled agriculture and small commodity production at the expense of nomadic and pastoralist cultures. British "pacification" involved land clearing to deny cover to military enemies and forced settlement of peasants in new regions. Early in the nineteenth century European entrepreneurs undertook massive commercial logging operations, causing extensive deforestation. Ecological destruction was a major by-product of the transformation of India into a more homogeneous peasant farming society that provided a better base for colonial administration. Indians resisted this exploitation. The first half of

Hear the Audio
India's Imperialism
at **myhistorylab.com**

Read the Document
Dadabhai Naoroji, The Benefits of British Rule in India, 1871 at **myhistorylab.com**

•❖•⌐Read the Document
The Indian Revolt (1857) at
myhistorylab.com

QUICK REVIEW

Causes of the Indian Uprising
of 1857

◆ Addition of Sikhs, Gurkhas, and lower-caste soldiers to army

◆ Deteriorating economic conditions

◆ Excessive tax rates

◆ British annexation of Awadh

raj
The years from 1858 to 1947 during which India was governed directly by the British Crown.

•❖•⌐Read the Document
Lord William Bentinck, on the Suppression of Sati, 1829
at **myhistorylab.com**

Portrait of Ram Mohan Roy, the most influential Indian thinker in the early nineteenth century.

What does Roy's clothing suggest about his views toward the West?

the nineteenth century saw almost constant revolt in one place or another, culminating in the watershed Indian Uprising of 1857 (the so-called Sepoy Mutiny or Rebellion).

The immediate cause of this revolt was concern among Bengal troops that animal grease on newly issued rifles exposed them to ritual pollution, a violation of the rules of their religion. Behind this issue lay a variety of grievances, together with a desire to recover and rebuild a pre-British political order in North India. The revolt was not an all-India affair. It centered on Delhi, where the last Mughal emperor joined in the rebel cause, and involved other cities, towns, and in some cases the rural peasantry.

The British eventually won the day. With their forces augmented by Sikhs from the Panjab and Gurkhas from Bengal, they overcame the divided Indian opposition. By the end of 1857, the revolt was broken, often with great brutality. In 1858, the East India Company was dissolved, and India came under direct rule of the British Crown. The "Mutiny" of 1857 had highlighted resentment of the burdens of foreign domination that were to grow increasingly oppressive for Indians of all regions and religions during the ensuing ninety years of crown rule, known as the **raj.**

BRITISH-INDIAN RELATIONS

The overall impact of the British presence on the Indian masses was brutal but impersonal and largely economic. India was effectively integrated into Britain's economy, becoming a market for British goods and providing Britain with raw materials and other products. Britain's involvement in India's internal affairs included politics, education, the civil service infrastructure, communications, and transportation, but the consequences of its domination and exploitation of India's labor and resources were especially far-reaching.

British cultural imperialism was never a policy of the East India Company. Many Britons expressed interest in and some openness to Indians and their culture. The company itself required many of its officers to learn Persian and Sanskrit. It opposed Christian missionary activity in India until the 1830s and 1840s, partly because the caste system facilitated imperial policy. Nonetheless the British–Indian relationship had a paternalistic and patronizing dimension, both before and after the events of 1857. The ethos of the British rulers included the understanding that they had the task of governing an inferior "race" that could not handle the job by itself. Even Indians whose university degrees or army training gave them impeccable British qualifications were never accepted as true equals. From army to civil service ranks, the upper echelon of command was British; the middle and lower echelons of administration were Indian.

Despite this unequal relationship, British ideas and ways of doing things influenced a small but powerful Indian elite. Ram Mohan Roy (1772–1833), for example, a Bengali Hindu, rose to the top of the native ranks of East India Company service and became a strong voice for reform, both of Hindu life and practice and of British colonial policy where it deviated from European and Christian ideals. Roy was an avowed modernist who wanted to meld the best of European-Christian morality and thought with the best of Hindu piety and thought. His wide-ranging writings and public campaigns for education, political involvement, and social progress and against the "backward" practices and ideas of many of his Hindu compatriots alienated most of the leading Hindu thinkers and activists of his age, but twentieth-century Indians have often seen him as a visionary.

Britons at home became increasingly aware of India and Indians after 1858. The information that reached them, however, was filtered by interpreters who were often neither sympathetic nor objective. After the implementation of direct crown rule, a stricter social segregation of white rulers from Indian subjects set in. Overall the British, much more than their Central Asian Mughal predecessors, treated Indians as backward heathens in need of the "civilizing" influences of their own "enlightened" culture, law, political system, education, and religion.

Most Indians resented their subordinate status. The nationalist movement at the end of the nineteenth century extended to the grassroots level among tribal groups, peasant farmers, and home or small-industry workers. Whatever their status, the distrust and animosity most Indians felt toward their foreign rulers continued to grow.

FROM BRITISH CROWN RAJ TO INDEPENDENCE

THE BURDEN OF CROWN RULE

The Revolt of 1857 had numerous consequences beyond the transfer of administration to the British Crown. Before the revolt, the British had maintained a largely native army under British officers. After the revolt, they tried to maintain a ratio of at least one British to three Indian soldiers. The army was financed by Indian, not British, revenues. This imposed a huge economic burden on India, diverting one-third of its annual revenues to pay for its own occupation.

British economic policies and accelerating population growth put great strains on India's poor. Cheap British machine-produced goods were exchanged for Indian raw materials and the products of its home industries, harming or destroying Indian craft industries. Industrialization, which might have provided work for India's unemployed masses, was avoided. The Civil War in the United States (1861–1865) interrupted Britain's source of cotton from the American South, causing a shift from food to cotton farming in India. This shift, combined with a drought in the 1870s, led to widespread famine. Many peasants were forced to immigrate to Britain's dominions in South Africa, where they worked as indentured servants.

The Revolt of 1857 also created a poisonous distrust of Indians within the British colonial administration. **Cantonments** segregated white masters from natives in Indian towns and cities. One exception to this trend was the tenure of the Marquess of Ripon (1827–1909) as viceroy of India from 1880 to 1884. Ripon fought to erase legal racial discrimination, earning him the hatred of most of his British compatriots in India. Although his foes agitated successfully to dilute his measures, they unwittingly gave Indians a model for political agitation of their own.

INDIAN RESISTANCE

Indians soon took up political activism. Late in the nineteenth century they founded the institutions that would help overcome traditional regionalism, build national feeling, and ultimately end colonial rule. In 1885 Indian modernists formed the Indian National Congress to reform traditional Hindu and Muslim practices that were out of line with their liberal ideals and to change British Indian policies that were equally out of line with British democratic ideals. Other Indians agitated for the rejection of British rule altogether. The Muslim League developed as a counterbalance to the Hindu-dominated Congress and ultimately gained a separate independent Muslim state, Pakistan. Heavy-handed British policies in legal administration, political representation, and taxation strengthened the growing desire for independence.

Internal divisions were a major obstacle to Indian independence. These divisions included the many language groups and princely states of the subcontinent. Furthermore, the Indian elite had little in common with the masses. Conflict among Hindus, Muslims, Sikhs, and Jains also impeded concerted political action. Nonetheless, a nationalist movement took root. Three principal elements within the independence movement led to the creation of India and Pakistan in 1947.

WHAT ROLE did Gandhi play in ending British rule in India?

Read the Document
Karl Marx, "The British Rule in India," 1853 at **myhistorylab.com**

cantonments
The segregation of areas in which Europeans lived in British-ruled India from those areas inhabited by native Indians.

British Officer Reclining. This photograph of a British officer reclining while being fanned and served by two Indian attendants provides a glimpse into the colonial lifestyle in British India. It also gives insight into race, class, and labor divides.

What factors discouraged peer-to-peer interactions between Indians and Britons?

Read the Document
Amrita Lal Roy, English Rule in India, 1886 at **myhistorylab.com**

Watch the Video
Gandhi in India
at **myhistorylab.com**

The first element consisted of those in the National Congress organization who sought gradual reform and progress toward Indian self-governance, or *svarāj*. This position did not preclude outright opposition to the British, but it did mean trying to change the system from within. Among the proponents of this approach were G. K. Gokhale (1866–1915), the champion of moderate, deliberate, peaceful work toward self-determination; the spiritual and political genius Mohandas K. Gandhi (1869–1948); and his follower Jawaharlal Nehru (1889–1964), who would become the first prime minister of India. Gandhi directed the all-India drive that finally forced the British out. An English-trained lawyer, Gandhi drew on not only his own native Hindu (and Jain and Buddhist) heritage but also on the ideas of Western liberal and Christian thinkers like Henry David Thoreau (1817–1862) and Leo Tolstoy (1828–1910). In the end, Gandhi became a world figure as well as an Indian leader.

The second element consisted of the militant Hindu nationalists, whose leader, the extremist B. G. Tilak (1856–1920), stressed the use of Indian languages and a revival of Hindu culture and learning. Tilak subscribed to an anti-Muslim, Hindu communalist vision of Indian self-governance. The Hindu extremists looked to a return to traditional Indian values and self-sufficiency. Their ideas still influence Indian political life, as witnessed by the resurgence of Hindu extremist groups and communal strife.

Muslims made up the third element, but there were many divergent Muslim constituencies. Generally their leaders made common cause only because they feared they would lose power in a Hindu-majority state. Muslims had been slower than the Hindus to take up British ideas and education and thus lagged behind the Hindu intelligentsia in numbers and influence. Because of their prominence in the 1857 revolt, the British were at first less inclined to foster Muslim advancement than that of Hindus. Nonetheless, Muslims sought rapprochement with the British, rather than risk being submerged in Hindu-led movements of opposition. Sayyid Ahmad Khan (1817–1898) was a longtime supporter of modernist ideas and of cooperation with the British, though he could also be sharply critical of British mistakes. His opposition to Muslim participation in the National Congress foreshadowed later Hindu–Muslim tensions and conflict.

HINDU-MUSLIM FRICTION ON THE ROAD TO INDEPENDENCE

In the twentieth century the rift between Indian Muslims and Hindus grew wider, despite periods of cooperation against the British. Muslim arguments for coexistence with Hindus floundered while fears of loss of communal identity and rights grew. In the end the great Indo-Muslim poet and "spiritual father of Pakistan," Muhammad Iqbal (1873–1938), and the "founder of Pakistan," Muhammad Ali Jinnah (1876–1949), helped move Muslims to separatism.

India and Pakistan achieved independence only with violence and suffering. Much blood was spilled in the long battle with the British and in the communal violence among Indians themselves—especially between Hindus and Muslims during partition in 1947, and the still festering dispute over Kashmir. Still, the victory of 1947 gave all peoples of the subcontinent a sense of agency and of political participation on their own terms. The British legacy was not all bad, as it also consisted of administrative and political unity and egalitarian and democratic ideals that Indian nationalists turned to their own uses.

CHRONOLOGY	
INDIA	
1772–1833	Ram Mohan Roy, Hindu reformer
1857–1858	Sepoy Revolt, or "Mutiny," followed by direct Crown rule as a British colony
1869–1948	Mohandas K. Gandhi
1873–1938	Muhammad Iqbal
1876–1949	Muhammad Ali Jinnah
1885	Indian National Congress formed
1889–1964	Jawaharlal Nehru
1947	Independence and partition

Read the Document
Gandhi Speaks against the Partition of
India (pre-1947) at **myhistorylab.com**

A Closer Look

Gandhi and His Spinning Wheel

Gandhi premised his civil disobedience and resistance movement against the British colonial hegemony over India on a return to basics of Indian life: attaining *swadeshi*, self-sufficiency (e.g., rejecting machine-made European clothing for home-industry spinning of simple khadi cloth), moral independence and superiority (nonviolent civil disobedience in the face of British armed control), and *swaraj*, self-governance or home rule (replacing the British Raj). The spinning wheel (Hindi *charkha*, etymologically related to Sanskrit *chakra*) became the tangible symbol of these fundamentals in Gandhi's message and his practice, and was later taken onto the national flag of India in identity with the wheel, or *chakra*, from early Buddhist teaching, as noted in Chapter 4.

The simple wooden, 16-spoke spinning wheel, or *charkha*, became the major symbol of the independence movement that Gandhi led, referring both to making one's own clothing and also to the nobility of physical work.

Note the simple loincloth, or *dhoti*, which Gandhi took up, along with a shoulder shawl, both made of simple khadi cotton, after he abandoned the European dress of his earlier life as a London-trained lawyer in South Africa.

Questions

1. Why do you think the emphasis, by the educated Gandhi and other members of the independence-movement elite, on the importance of simple work, such as spinning for one's own clothing, had such resonance for millions of Indians under British rule in the Subcontinent?

2. What elements might have made the identification of the *charkha* with the Ashokan and Buddhist *chakra* so compelling as a conjoined symbol for India as a nation?

3. How might spinning one's own cloth relate to nonviolence (*ahimsa*) as well as to economic resistance to the British?

myhistorylab To examine this image in an interactive fashion, please go to **www.myhistorylab.com**

THE ISLAMIC EXPERIENCE
DECLINING ISLAMIC POWER AND INDEPENDENCE

WHY IS the invasion of Egypt by Napoleon's army in 1798 symbolically important?

The eighteenth century saw the great Muslim empires weaken as the West became ascendant in international trade, military-political power, imperialist expansion, industrial productivity, and technological progress. Diverse Islamic peoples and states plunged from positions of global power into a struggle for survival. As with India, the decline of Islamic preeminence was due both to the rise of the modern West and to internal problems.

By the nineteenth century all of the largest Muslim empires—Mughal, Ottoman, Safavid/Qajar, Moroccan, and Central Asian—had declined politically, militarily, and economically in relation to western European empires (see Map 26–1). They had grown decentralized and destabilized, and they were increasingly dominated by entrenched hereditary elites. Furthermore, new sea routes meant that it was no longer necessary to cross through the Middle East to get from Europe to Asia and back. Middle Eastern and Mediterranean economies became peripheral to the world economy. The Middle East, especially, became enmeshed in the European imperial competition for industrial resources, and most of the area came under Western political and economic domination.

MAP 26–1.   West Asia, Central Asia, and the Mediterranean, ca. 1850.   Compare this map with Map 20–2 on p. 513. Though the Ottoman Empire still technically ruled a large area, in actuality it had lost much control over regions on the periphery.

Why did the Ottoman Empire lose control of so much territory?

Western powers—including Britain, Russia, Germany, and France—extracted capitulations favorable to their own interests from Islamic governments. These capitulations took the form of treaty clauses granting commercial concessions, special protection, and "extraterritorial" legal status to European merchant enclaves. Such concessions had originally been reciprocal and had also served the commercial purposes of Muslim rulers and some merchants. However, they eventually provided Western powers with pretexts for direct intervention in Ottoman, Iranian, Indian, and African affairs. The Ottoman Empire suffered from internal disunity; its provincial rulers, or *pashas*, were virtually independent. This disunity, combined with the economic problems facing all the agrarian societies of Asia and Africa, made it easy for the Western powers to take control. Repeated Ottoman defeats made that once great imperial power "the sick man of Europe" after 1800; similar weaknesses allowed Westerners to control Indian and Iranian states.

The beginning of European domination of the Islamic heartlands was marked symbolically by Napoleon Bonaparte's (1769–1821) invasion of Egypt in 1798 (see Chapter 22). The invasion highlighted Muslim military weakness and heralded a new era of European imperialism in the Middle East. The French continued to contest British ascendancy in the Middle Eastern area, but Russia presented the most serious nineteenth-century challenge to Britain's colonial empire. Russia, having won control of the Black Sea from the Ottomans, sought to gain territory and influence in Iran, the Caucasus, and Central Asian regions. Afghanistan, an independent kingdom established by Ahmad Shah Durrani (r. 1737–1773), prevented Russia from penetrating into British India. In the Iranian and Ottoman regions, however, Russia and Britain struggled for supremacy. The Crimean War of 1854 to 1856 (see Chapter 23) was one result.

THE CASE OF IRAN

Beyond the overt political and commercial impact of the West, Western political ideology, culture, and technology contributed to change in Islamic societies. Outside of India, this effect was felt most strongly in Egypt, Lebanon, North Africa, and Anatolia (modern Turkey). The Islamic states least and last affected by Western "modernity" were Iran, Afghanistan, and the Central Asian khanates. The Iranian case deserves brief attention.

The rulers of Iran from 1794 to 1925 were the absolutist Qajar shahs. This period saw the emergence of a traditionalist doctrine that encouraged all Shi'ites to choose a *mujtahid*—a qualified scholarly guide—from among the *ulama* and follow his religious and legal interpretations. As a result, the *ulama* were often the chief critics of the government (especially governmental attempts to admit Western influences) and exponents of the people's grievances.

A prime demonstration of *ulama* power occurred when the Qajar shah granted a fifty-year monopoly on tobacco sales to a British corporation in 1890. In 1891 the leading authority in the *ulama* spearheaded a tobacco boycott in protest. This popular action was also supported by modernist-nationalist opponents of the Qajar regime who had strong connections to Iran's commercial, or *bazaari*, middle classes. The shah had to rescind the concession in a symbolic triumph over Western commercial interests. Yet ironically this action made Iran more dependent on Western capital. The Iranian government was forced to compensate the British corporation, necessitating a foreign loan from a British bank and making Iran more reliant on Western institutions thereafter.

Younger Iranian intellectuals began to warm to Western liberalism, especially in the latter half of the century. As in other Islamic countries, the seeds of a new, secular

•••—Read the **Document**
Religious Minorities in the Middle East (late 19th–early 20th century) at **myhistorylab.com**

mujtahid
A Shi'ite religious-legal scholar.

bazaari
The Iranian commercial middle class.

QUICK REVIEW

The Qajar Shahs

- Rulers of Iran from 1794 to 1925
- Under Qajar rule, the *ulama* of the Shi'ite community was less strongly connected to the state
- The *ulama* were often chief critics of Qajar rule

nationalism were sown, coinciding with a growing desire for a voice in government. An uneasy alliance of Iranian radical nationalists, liberal *bazaaris*, and conservative *ulama* proved a sometimes effective counterforce to Qajar absolutism, as in the tobacco boycott and in the early stages of the effort to force the Qajars to accept a constitution in 1906 to 1911. Yet such alliances did not last.

ISLAMIC RESPONSES TO FOREIGN ENCROACHMENT

WHAT WERE three typical Islamic reactions to Western encroachment?

•◆•⌐Read the Document
Ottoman at **myhistorylab.com**

Each Islamic people or state had a different experience with Western impingement. The shared objective of Muslim reformers, politicians, and intellectuals was to ascertain the basis of European ascendancy. Could European secular learning and technological superiority be transferred to the Middle East or other regions? Could the once dominant Islamic word regain vitality by importing European values, education, and technology? Could Islamic values be adapted or reformed to foster the kind of societal progress Europe seemed to have managed, without succumbing entirely to secularization?

There were at least three typical styles of reaction to the West: (1) a traditionalist rejection of things Western; (2) an attempt to join Western innovations with traditional Islamic institutions; and (3) a tendency to emulate Western ideas and institutions. Of course, none of these styles was uniform within a country or across political, ethnic, and cultural boundaries.

Wahhabis
Followers of Ibn Abd al-Wahhab (1703–1792), who sought to combat the excesses of popular and sufi piety in Islam and looked to the Qur'an and the traditions of the Prophet as the sole authoritative guidance in religion.

PURIFICATION AND REVIVAL OF ISLAM

One kind of Muslim reaction to Western dominance has emphasized Islamic values and ideals to the exclusion of "outside" forces. This approach has involved either the kind of purist or reformist revivalism seen in Wahhabism or the kind of conservatism often associated with Sunni or Shi'ite "establishment" *ulama*, as in Iran since 1979. Both conservative and revivalist Muslim thinkers share the conviction that answers to the questions facing Muslims in the modern world are to be found within the Islamic tradition.

In the eighteenth century in rural areas, where neither urban Muslim ideas nor European power had penetrated significantly, reformers emphasized a strict construction of what "true" Islam entails. For example, **Wahhabis**, the followers of Ibn Abd al-Wahhab (1703–1792) in Arabia, sought to combat excesses of piety and conformity, favoring instead the exercise of independent judgment. The only authorities were to be the Qur'an and the traditions of the Prophet. Allied with a local Arab prince, Sa'ud, the Wahhabi movement swept much of the Arabian Peninsula. It was crushed in the early nineteenth century by the Ottoman regime but was resuscitated at the onset of the twentieth century and is the guiding ideology of present-day Saudi Arabia.

Linking Asia and Europe. The opening of the Suez Canal in 1869 was a major engineering achievement. It also became a major international waterway, reducing the distance from London to Bombay by half.

What roles did trade and technology play in Western dominance over Islamic lands?

Other Muslim reform movements reflected similar revivalist, even militantly pietist responses to Islamic decadence and decline. Examples include those of Usman Dan Fodio in Africa in the late eighteenth century and the Muslim Brotherhood in modern Egypt (see Chapter 33). Such groups called for a pristine Islam divested of the authoritarianism of the medieval legal schools, *ulama* theological conformity, and degenerate sufi orders. These movements inspired an uncritical nostalgia for a time when Islamic societies were ascendant, even dominant. This vision still rallies movements from Africa to Indonesia and has provided a response to the challenge of Western-style "modernity."

Traditionalist conservatism is much harder to pin down as the ethos of particular movement. Whereas reformist revivalism (today commonly called Islamism) usually focuses on the Qur'an and the Prophetic example as the sole authorities for Islamic life, Muslim conservatism commonly champions those forms of Islamic life and thought embodied in traditional law, theology, and even Sufism. It is seen in the legalistic tendencies that have often resurfaced when Islamic norms have been threatened by the breakdown of traditional society and the rise of secularism. Although such conservatism has been associated with the most reactionary forces in Islamic society, it has also served to preserve basic Muslim values while allowing for gradual change in a way that reformist revivalism could not accept. Where conservatives have formed alliances with governments or simply been co-opted by them, the credibility of the establishment *ulama* has often been destroyed. This is because the masses of Muslims have been increasingly attracted to Islamist agendas for rapid change.

INTEGRATION OF WESTERN AND ISLAMIC IDEAS

During the eighteenth and nineteenth centuries in major urban areas, influential reformers proposed adaptionist reform that sought to reengineer the armies, institutions, and societies of the Middle East to conform to the political reality of European domination. The attempt to join modernization with traditional Islamic institutions and ideas is exemplified in the thought of famous Muslim intellectuals such as Jamal al-Din al-Afghani (1839–1897), Muhammad Abduh (1845–1905), and Muhammad Iqbal (1873–1938). These thinkers argued for a progressive Islam rather than a materialist Western secularism as the best answer to life in the modern world. Other intellectuals sought to redefine what it meant to be Muslim in a modern age by emphasizing the malleability of the religion.

Al-Afghani is best known for his emphasis on the unity of the Islamic world, or **pan-Islamism**, and on a populist, constitutionalist approach to political order. His ideas and his charismatic personality influenced political activist movements in Egypt, Iran, Ottoman Turkey, and elsewhere. His Egyptian disciple, Muhammad Abduh, sought to modernize Muslim education. He argued that a Qur'anic base could be combined harmoniously with modern science and its open questioning of reality. His modernist reforms affected even the curriculum of the most venerable traditionalist institution of higher learning in the Islamic world, the great al-Azhar in Cairo.

Poet and essayist Muhammad Iqbal, the most celebrated Indian Muslim thinker of the twentieth century, argued for a modernist revival of the Muslim faith focused on purifying and uplifting the individual self above enslavement either to reason or to traditionalist conformity. Often credited with the original idea of a separate Muslim state in the Indian subcontinent (today's Pakistan), Iqbal still felt that Islam was essentially nonexclusivist and supranationalist.

EMULATION OF THE WEST

The career of Ottoman viceroy Muhammad Ali (ca. 1769–1849), the virtually independent pasha of Egypt from 1805 to 1849, exemplifies a strategy of emulation. Ali set out to rejuvenate Egypt's failing agriculture, introduce modern mechanized industry, modernize the army, and introduce European education. He set his country on

Frontispiece from the Arab Literary-Scientific Journal *al-Muqtataf*, founded by Yaqub Sarruf in the 1860s. A group of such periodicals provided a public arena for political debate despite Ottoman, Egyptian, and British censors. They were a way for the burgeoning educated middle class of the Arab world (especially in Egypt) to develop national identities and debate social, economic, and political issues and policies. The crossed pen and hammer suggest a call to action, while the floral border is reminiscent of traditional Islamic manuscripts.

What other institutions or movements helped create national identities in the Middle East?

pan-Islamism
The movement that advocates that the entire Muslim world should form a unified political and cultural entity.

Muhammad Ali (1769–1849), the famous viceroy of Egypt.
What were some of Muhammad Ali's attempted reforms?

protectorate

Form of rule in which a local ruler keeps his title but cedes real power, especially over foreign affairs, defense, and finances, to colonial advisers or officials. The arrangement is purported to be temporary.

Tanzimat

Reform movement that started in 1839 in an attempt to bring the Ottoman Empire into the modern era and to help integrate non-Muslims and non-Ottomans into the Empire.

▶ **Watch the Video**
The Ottoman Tanzimat Period
(1839–1876): The Middle East Confronts
Modernity at **myhistorylab.com**

the path to becoming a nation-state. A later Egyptian statesman and patriot, Sa'd Zaghlul Pasha (1857–1927), led a *Wafd* or delegation to Paris in 1919 to protest the 1914 British **protectorate** imposed on Egypt. Zaghlul Pasha and his companions did not defeat the British occupation, but the *Wafd* Party survived well beyond the last occupying British troop.

Efforts to appropriate Western experience and success were made by several Ottoman sultans and viziers after the defeat of the Turks by Russia in 1774. Most notable were the reforms of Selim III (r. 1762–1808), Mahmud II (r. 1808–1839), and the so-called **Tanzimat**, or beneficial "legislation" era, from about 1839 to 1880. Selim attempted economic, administrative, and military reform, whereas Mahmud dismantled the Janissary corps and encouraged Western military and educational methods among the Ottoman elites. Like Selim and Muhammad Ali, Mahmud was less interested in promoting European Enlightenment ideas about citizen rights and equity than in building a stronger, more modern centralized government, which often resulted in the consolidation of political power among a select few. The Tanzimat reforms were intended to bring the Ottoman state in line with ideals espoused by the European states, to give European powers less cause to intervene in Ottoman affairs, and to regenerate confidence in the state. Although they failed to save the empire, they paved the way for the rise of Turkish nationalism, the "Young Turk" revolution of 1908, and the nationalist revolution of the 1920s that produced modern Turkey. (This development simultaneously frustrated similar nationalist aspirations among old Ottoman minorities including Greeks, Armenians, and Kurds.)

The creation of the Turkish republic out of the ashes of the Ottoman state after World War I is probably the most extreme example of an effort to modernize and nationalize an Islamic state on a Western model. (It could alternatively be the most successful case of integration.) This state was largely the child of Mustafa Kemal (1881–1938), known as "Atatürk" ("father of the Turks"), its founder and first president (1922–1938). Atatürk's major reforms ranged from the introduction of a

Tanzimat. A sitting of the new (1909) Turkish Parliament following the abolition of the 1876 Constitution in 1878 by the Sultan Abdul Hamid II. Sessions were held in a lavish chamber with the delegates from the Balkans, Anatolia, and Fertile Crescent (Syria, Lebanon, Iraq, Jordan, and Palestine) seated facing a high podium at the front of the chamber.
Why type of reform did the Tanzimat exemplify?

European-style code of civil law to the abolition of the caliphate, sufi orders, Arabic script, and the Arabic call to prayer. These changes constituted a radical attempt to secularize an Islamic state and to separate religious from political and social institutions. Nothing quite like it has ever been repeated. Despite some adjustments and even reversals of Atatürk's measures, Turkey has maintained its independence, reaffirmed its commitment to democratic government, and emerged with a unique but still distinctly Islamic identity.

Read the Document
The Young Turk Revolution, 1908
at **myhistorylab.com**

WOMEN AND REFORM IN THE MIDDLE EAST

Some Middle Eastern women raised the issue of women's roles in modern society. Most notably, women demanded political rights: Iranian women, who confronted the Iranian Parliament to oppose capitulation to Russian-British demands in December 1911; Egyptian women, who threw off their veils and declared themselves the new Egyptian women after having accompanied their husbands to Paris where the men had been humiliated by the Versailles powers in 1919; Palestinian women, who convened a Women's Congress of Palestine to address the political issues that followed the Wailing Wall riots in 1929. It is also noteworthy that a number of journals and magazines devoted to women's concerns emerged in the late nineteenth and early twentieth centuries. Most of them focused on traditional women's topics such as cooking, parenting, and fashion, but some stressed that women were an essential part of society and should not be excluded from commerce and politics. The Egyptian Feminist Union was founded in 1923 by Huda Sha'rawi (1879–1947) to fight for women's suffrage, reform of marriage laws, and equal access to education. In a well-publicized gesture, Sha'rawi and her colleague Saize Nabrawi removed their veils in the midst of the crowd at Cairo's train station. For them the veil symbolized the inadequate public status of women in Middle Eastern countries. Many Middle Eastern feminists today, however, stress that women's inequality is rooted in wide-ranging cultural, political, and economic structures that are more important than the veil issue.

CHRONOLOGY

ISLAMIC HEARTLANDS, 1700–1938

1703–1792	Ibn Abd al-Wahhab
1737–1773	Rule of Ahmad Shah Durrani, founder of modern Afghanistan
1794–1925	Qajar shahs of Iran
1798	Napoleon Bonaparte invades Egypt
1805–1849	Muhammad Ali rules Egypt
ca. 1839–1880	Ottoman Tanzimat reforms
1839–1897	Jamal al-Din al-Afghani
1845–1905	Muhammad Abduh
1891-92	Iranian Tobacco Boycott
1908	"Young Turk" revolution
1922–1938	Mustafa Kemal, "Atatürk," in power

NATIONALISM

Nationalism is a product of modern European history (see Chapter 23). Although not merely a response to Western encroachment, nationalist movements in the Islamic world have been either stimulated by Western models or produced in reaction to Western imperialist exploitation and colonial occupation. During the late nineteenth century, many intellectuals in Asia and Africa grappled with questions of identity, debating whether their ethnic or linguistic group constituted a distinct nation or whether they were part of a larger whole. The answer was not always self-evident, given the mosaics of ethnicities, religions, and language groups across Africa and Asia. Yet the division of the colonial world by European administrators demanded an answer. In the European capitals new "nations" were created that reflected the interests of imperialism rather than actual facts on the ground. In due time, these borders have taken on an aura of legitimacy. However, forging nations within artificial parameters has proven to be a difficult process. As in India, nationalism has been an important aspect of the response to Western domination in the Islamic heartlands. In Turkey in the 1920s it took a secularist form; in Libya, Iran, and elsewhere since the 1970s it has taken an Islamic-revivalist form. As an Afro-Asian phenomenon, it is discussed in the next section and in Chapter 33.

mfecane
A period of widespread warfare and chaos among Bantu peoples in east-central Africa during the early nineteenth century.

THE AFRICAN EXPERIENCE

WHAT WAS the
mfecane?

The period between 1800 and 1945 saw striking change throughout Africa, especially in sub-Saharan Africa. North Africa and Egypt were more closely implicated in the politics of the Ottoman Empire and Europe throughout this period. Except for South Africa below the Transvaal, tropical and southern Africa did not come under colonial control until after 1880. Before then, internal developments—first, demographic and power shifts, and then the rise of Islamic reform movements—overshadowed the increasing European presence in the continent.

NEW POWER CENTERS AND ISLAMIC REFORM MOVEMENTS

SOUTHERN AFRICA

In Africa south of the Limpopo River, the first quarter of the nineteenth century saw devastating internal warfare, depopulation, and forced migrations of many Bantu peoples in what is known as the *mfecane*, or "crushing" era. Likely brought on by exploding population and fueled by increasing economic competition, the *mfecane*

Moshoeshwe, king and founder of Lesotho. Not all of the Bantu peoples followed the militaristic example of Shaka. Moshoeshwe, a Sotho prince, fought off Zulu attacks and led his people to a mountain stronghold in southern Africa, where through diplomacy and determination he founded a small nation that has endured to the present. The kingdom became the British protectorate of Basutoland in 1868. In 1966 it achieved independence as the kingdom of Lesotho under Moshoeshwe's great-grandson, King Moshoeshwe II.
Why were most African states formed during this period short-lived?

was marked by the rapid rise of sizable military states among the northern Nguni-speaking Bantu. Its result was warfare and chaos; widespread depopulation by death and emigration; and the creation of new, multiethnic states in the territory of modern Zimbabwe, Mozambique, Malawi, Zambia, and Tanzania.

The Nguni warrior-king Dingiswayo formed the first of the new military states between about 1800 and 1818. The most important state was formed by his successor, Shaka, leader of the Nguni-speaking Zulu nation and kingdom (ca. 1818–1828). Shaka's brutal military tactics led to Zulu conquest of a vast dominion in southeastern Africa and the virtual depopulation of some 15,000 square miles. Refugees from Shaka's "total war" zone fled north into Sotho-speaking Bantu territory, or south where they put pressure on the southern Nguni peoples.

The net result, beyond widespread suffering and death, was the creation of diverse new states. Some groups tried to imitate the unique military state of Shaka; others fled to mountainous areas and built new defensive states; still others went west into the Kalahari. The most famous new state was Lesotho, the Sotho kingdom of King Moshoeshwe, which survived as long as he lived (from the 1820s until 1870). Moshoeshwe defended his people from the Zulu and held off Afrikaners, missionaries, and the British until his death.

The new state-building spawned by the *mfecane* was nullified by Boer expansion and British annexation of Natal province (1843). These developments stemmed from the **Great Trek** of Boer *voortrekers* between 1835 and 1841. This migration brought about 6,000 Afrikaners from the Cape Colony northeastward into more fertile regions. It resulted in the creation after 1850 of the Afrikaner republics of the Orange Free State between the Orange and Vaal rivers, and the South African Republic north of the Vaal.

CHRONOLOGY

SOUTHERN AFRICA

ca. 1800–1818	Dingiswayo, Nguni Zulu king, forms new military state
ca. 1800–1825	The *mfecane* among the Bantu of southeastern Africa
1806	British take Cape Colony from the Dutch
ca. 1818–1828	Shaka's reign as head of the Nguni state; major warfare, destruction, and expansion
ca. 1825–1870	Sotho kingdom of King Moshoeshwe in Lesotho region
1835–1841	Great Trek of Boers into Natal and north onto the high veld beyond the Orange
1843	British annexation of Natal province
1852–1860	Creation of the Orange Free State and South African Republic

Great Trek
The migration between 1835 and 1841 of Boer pioneers (called *voortrekkers*) north from British-ruled Cape Colony to establish their own independent republics.

EAST AND CENTRAL AFRICA

In East and east-central Africa, increasing external trade led to the formation of several strong regional states. In the Lakes region, peoples such as the Nyamwezi to the east of Lake Tanganyika and the Baganda west of Lake Victoria gained regional power starting in the late 1700s through trade with the Arab-Swahili eastern coast and the eastern Congo states to the west. The chief traffic in this east–west commerce involved slaves, ivory, copper, and, from the outside, Indian cloth, firearms, and other manufactured goods.

WEST AFRICA

In West Africa the slave trade was only slowly curtailed. European demand for other products—notably palm oil and gum arabic—gained importance by the 1820s. In the first half of the century *jihad* movements of the Fulbe (or Fulani) and others shattered the stability of the western savannah and forest-lands from modern Senegal and Ghana through southern Nigeria. Protracted wars and dislocation gave rise to regional kingdoms, such as those of Asante and Dahomey (modern Benin), which flourished before succumbing to internal dissension and British and French colonial ambitions.

Elephant Tusks, Congo. Ivory was a prized possession used for decorative purposes and jewelry.

How did the ivory and slave trades interact with European colonization in Africa?

ISLAMIC REFORM MOVEMENTS

The expansive vitality of Islam has been a significant agent of change throughout Africa. In 1800 Islam was long-established from West Africa across the Sudan to the Red Sea and along the East African coast, as well as over all of Arabic-speaking North Africa. It had long been widespread in the southern Sahara and northern Sahel and was common among merchant classes in parts of West Africa. Islam was the law of the land in states such as the sultanate of Zanzibar on the eastern coast and the waning Funj sultanate in the eastern Sudan. Even so, the rural populace was often pagan, and even the ruling and urban elites were frequently only nominally Muslim.

A series of strong militant Islamic revivalist and reform movements of *jihad* in the nineteenth century aimed at a wider allegiance to Muslim values. The West African movements originated in the seventeenth century with reformist sufi brotherhoods from the north. These movements eventually spread to other regions and flourished, especially in the eighteenth century.

The most important *jihad* movement came at the beginning of the nineteenth century and was led by a Fulbe Muslim scholar from Hausa territory in the central Sahel. Usman Dan Fodio (1754–1817) was influenced by the reformist ideas that spread throughout the Muslim world in the eighteenth century. Shortly after 1804 he gathered an immense army of fervent supporters and conquered most of the Hausa lands of modern Nigeria, bringing an explicitly Islamic order to the area. Dan Fodio left behind an impressive sultanate centered on the new capital of Sokoto and governed by one of his sons, Muhammad Bello, until 1837. The Fulbe became the ruling class in the Hausa regions, and Islam spread into the countryside, where it still predominates.

Other nineteenth-century reform movements gained political power and spread a reformist Islamic message. Most notable outside West Africa were the Sanusi movement of Libya and the eastern Sahara (after about 1840) and the Mahdist uprising of the eastern Sudan (1880s and 1890s). The Libyan movement provided the focus for resistance to the Italian invasion of 1911. The Sudanese Muhammad Ahmad (1848–1885) condemned the widespread corruption of Islamic ideals and declared himself the awaited deliverer, or **Mahdi**, in 1881. He led the northern Sudan in rebellion against Ottoman-Egyptian control, defeating the British forces under Gordon at Khartoum. His successor governed the Sudan until the British finally destroyed the young Islamic state in 1899 (see Map 26–2).

Mahdi
A redeemer who will appear on earth and establish a just society prior to the final judgment. The Mahdi is central to Shi'ite belief, but controversial in other branches of Islam.

PATTERNS IN EUROPEAN COLONIZATION AND AFRICAN RESISTANCE

EUROPEAN EXPLORERS AND CHRISTIAN MISSIONARIES

HOW DID Africans resist European colonialism?

During the nineteenth century, Europe came to dominate Africa's politics and economy. Before the mid-1800s, Europeans had rarely ventured beyond coastal areas, although the transatlantic slave trade had affected inland areas. This changed drastically as, first, trading companies and explorers, then missionaries and, finally, colonial troops and governments moved into Africa. Ironically, the gradual elimination of the slave trade (see Chapter 22) was accompanied by increased European exploration and increased Western Christian missionary activity in Africa, which ushered in imperial and colonial ventures that had devastating consequences.

Nineteenth-century European explorers—mostly English, French, and German—gradually uncovered for Westerners the great "secrets" of Africa: the sources of the Niger, Nile, Zambezi, and Congo rivers; natural wonders, such as Mount Kilimanjaro and Lake

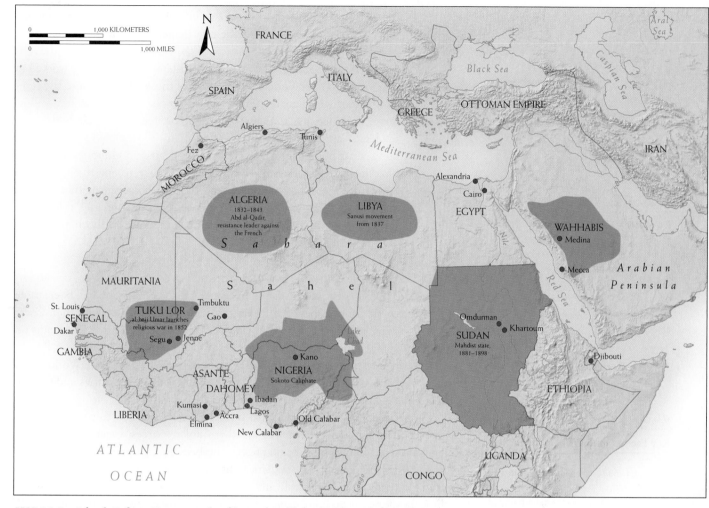

MAP 26–2.   **Islamic Reform Movements in Africa and Arabia in the Nineteenth Century.**

How did reform movements influence African culture and history?

Tanganyika; and fabled places like Timbuktu. The history of European exploration is one of fortune hunting, self-promotion, and violence as well as perseverance, bravery, and dedication. Many of the explorers were accomplished authors and lecturers; tales of their adventures stimulated European interest in Africa and opened the way for traders, missionaries, and finally soldiers and governors from the Christian West. One of the greatest explorers was Dr. David Livingstone (1813–1873), a Scottish Presbyterian missionary, physician, and abolitionist.

The latter nineteenth century saw a mounting influx of Christian missionaries, both Protestant and Catholic—some 10,000 by 1900. Part of their motivation for coming to Africa was to eradicate the remaining slave trade. Their accounts of Africa contained chauvinistic and misleading descriptions, but they also brought real knowledge of Africa to Europe. Their

Henry Morton Stanley and His Servant Kalula. Stanley was a journalist-turned-explorer who generated a great deal of publicity for his efforts to "find" abolitionist-turned-explorer David Livingstone. Livingstone (who had not, in fact, been lost) was joined by Stanley near Lake Tanganyika in 1871. Stanley claimed to have greeted him with, "Dr. Livingstone, I presume."

What influence did explorers have on European colonization efforts in Africa?

A Missionary Visit to a Zulu Kraal. The nineteenth-century European and American enthusiasm for working toward "the evangelization of the world in our time" found one of its major outlets in missionary efforts in Africa.

Were missionaries "agents of colonization"?

QUICK REVIEW

Key Factors in the "Scramble for Africa"

◆ Popular and commercial interests in Africa spurred by exploration

◆ Intra-European competition for power and prestige

◆ Technological and material superiority of Europe

scramble for Africa
The late-nineteenth-century takeover of most of Africa by European powers.

translation work and mission schools brought alphabetic culture and literacy to Africans. Although their settlements, often in remote areas, provided European governments with convenient pretexts for intervention in African affairs, the missionaries themselves frequently worked in opposition to the colonial officers. Half of those who went into the tropical regions succumbed to indigenous diseases, such as malaria, yellow fever, and sleeping sickness. Through the ideals of their faith, they modeled—intentionally or not—a weapon of principle for Africans to use against European exploiters. African Christian churches, for example, later played a leading role in the resistance to apartheid in South Africa, despite white Christian collusion with racism in that country and elsewhere in Africa (see Chapter 33). Thus missionaries' roles in the European domination of Africa cannot be monolithically characterized.

THE COLONIAL "SCRAMBLE FOR AFRICA"

Before 1850 the only significant European-African armed conflicts over African territory were in South Africa and Algeria. In South Africa, as noted above, Boers came into conflict with Bantu tribes after leaving the British Cape Colony on their Great Trek to find new lands. The French invaded Algeria in 1830, settled Europeans on choice farmlands, and battled indigenous resistance fighters. Over most of Africa, the European presence was felt with real force only from the 1880s. By World War I virtually the whole continent was divided into a patchwork of territories under European colonial administrations (see Map 26–3).

European popular and commercial interest in Africa fueled this takeover. The European desire for industrial markets and natural resources, together with intra-European competition for power and prestige, pushed one European state after another to claim whatever segments of Africa they could (see Chapter 28). The West's superior economic, technological, and military power made the takeover possible. Technical expertise gave Europeans access to the interior of the continent in the late nineteenth century. Except for the Nile and the Niger, the great African rivers have impassable waterfalls only a short way inland from the sea, where the coastal plains rise sharply. European-built steamboats above the falls and railroads around them permitted new levels of commercial and colonial exploitation.

Great Britain and France were the vanguard of the European nations that sought to include African lands in their imperial domains. Beginning in the mid-1880s the major European powers sought mutual agreement to their claims on particular segments of Africa. Leopold II of Belgium (r. 1865–1909) and Otto von Bismarck (1815–1898) in Germany established their own claims to parts of Africa. France and England set about consolidating their African interests. Italy took African colonial territory in Eritrea, Somaliland, and Libya, but Ethiopia used its newly modernized army to defeat an Italian invasion in 1896. Italy finally conquered Ethiopia in 1935. The **scramble for Africa** was largely over by the outbreak of World War I. After the war Germany lost its African possessions. Europe's colonies in Africa did not gain independence until the worldwide balance of power and attitudes toward colonial rule changed following World War II (see Chapter 33).

EUROPEAN COLONIAL RULE

European colonial rule in Africa is one of the uglier chapters of modern history. German, French, Belgian, Portuguese, and Boer rule was notoriously brutal, but Britain too had its share of misrule. The regions with large-scale white settlements produced the worst exploitation. Colonies with relatively high settler populations tended to be

MAP EXPLORATION

To explore this map further, go to **http://www.myhistorylab.com**

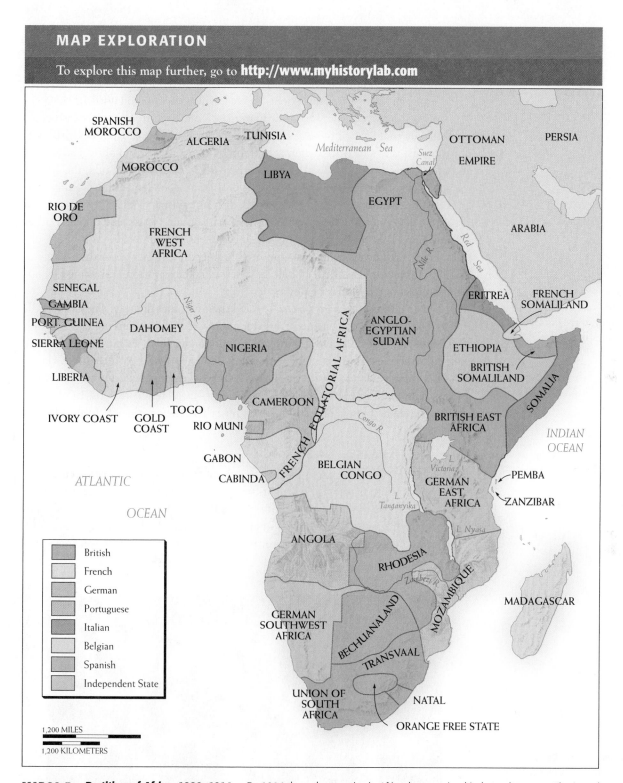

MAP 26–3. Partition of Africa, 1880–1914.   By 1914 the only countries in Africa that remained independent were Liberia and Ethiopia. The occupying powers included most large European states

Why did Britain and France control so much territory in Africa?

places where the environment could support plantation-style, export-oriented agriculture and where the diseases to which Europeans were most susceptible were less prevalent. Settler colonies included Algeria, Kenya, Mozambique, Rhodesia (Zimbabwe), and South Africa. Among the worst legacies of the European presence was the apartheid government of South Africa, which did not end until 1994.

British taxpayers were reluctant to fund colonial ventures. Since British colonial officials could afford to pay the salaries of only a tiny contingent of British administrators, they put British men at the top of existing African political structures and ruled through local leaders. Often, in the early days of colonial rule, the British would make a show of removing a few high-profile, independent-minded indigenous leaders. The remaining leaders and their British supervisors would then engage in a delicate balancing act: The chiefs and the colonists came to depend on each other for power and legitimacy, but neither could command perfect loyalty from their subjects. Frederick Lugard, who was appointed high commissioner of northern Nigeria in 1900, formalized this British style of colonial administration and named it, appropriately enough, **indirect rule**.

Other European powers generally ruled their colonies directly: They were willing to bankroll the placement of greater numbers of Europeans in the colonies themselves, and they hired local Africans to work under them within European-style political structures. The French were the most explicit about their intentions, claiming that their goal was for Africans to "evolve"—through education, imitation, assimilation, and the course of many generations—into French citizens. In practice, however, French colonial officials were loath to share the prestige of citizenship.

indirect rule
The British practice of administering African colonies through indigenous political structures and leaders.

AFRICAN RESISTANCE

African states were not simply passive objects of European manipulation and conquest. Many astute native rulers sought, by diplomacy, trade, and warfare, to use the European presence to their own advantage. The Baganda king Mutesa in the 1870s, in what is today Uganda, is an example of an African ruler who benefited, at least for a while, from European interest in his territory. Direct armed resistance was inevitably

Mutesa of Buganda and His Court. Noted for his cunning and diplomatic skill and for his autocratic and often cruel conduct, Mutesa was one of the few African rulers able to maintain a powerful, successful army and court, which enabled him to deal effectively with Egyptian and British efforts to encroach on his sphere of influence.

Why did direct armed resistance by Africans to European encroachment generally fail?

DOCUMENT

Oginga Odinga on European Influences

Oginga Odinga (ca. 1911–1994) was an early Kenyan nationalist leader. Born into a leading family of the Luo tribe, he grew up in western Kenya, near Lake Victoria. After Kenyan independence in 1963, he opposed many of President Jomo Kenyatta's policies. He published his biography, Not Yet Uhuru, in 1967; "Uhuru" in Swahili means "freedom" or "independence." In the book, Odinga argues that Kenya's post-colonial leaders worked at creating a new African elite (themselves) rather than serving the masses of Africans who worked for independence.

These are Odinga's recollections of his first experiences with Europeans.

- **WHAT** made the strongest impression on Odinga? What overall attitude does he evidence toward Europeans? What can you infer here about Luo culture?

We connected Whites and Government with five main things. There were the inoculations against the plague from which the children ran in fear. There were the tax collections. There was the order to the villagers to work on the roads. There were clothes, kanzu, the long robes copied from Arab garb at the coast, given free to the chiefs and elders to wear to encourage others in the tribe to clothe themselves in modern dress. There were the schools, which came later, and to which, in the beginning, only orphans, foster children, poor nieces and nephews and never the favourite sons were sent, for the villagers distrusted the pressure on them to send their children out of the home and away from herding the animals; and the more alert objected to the way the Christian missions taught 'This custom (yours) is bad, and this (ours) is good', for they could see that the children at the missions would grow up to despise Luo ways. . . .

Oginga Odinga, Not Yet Uhuru: An Autobiography (Nairobi, Kenya: Heinemann, 1967), pp. 2-3.

---

doomed because of European technological superiority. Nevertheless, such resistance was widespread and continued into the twentieth century. In the end, colonial rule was the product of ongoing conflict and negotiation between European desires, backed up by technological superiority, and the enduring power of African individuals and institutions.

Africans resisted European domination throughout the continent. Often the most efficient way for Africans to resist was to disengage, attempting to avoid payment of colonial taxes or participation in forced labor schemes. Riots, marches, and rebellions were more frequent and forceful than colonial administrators wanted to admit, and accounts of such events were sometimes suppressed during the colonial era. Resistance tended to be more overt and sustained in settler colonies, where Africans and Europeans were most likely to come into direct contact. In places where Europeans had seized large swaths of fertile land—the highlands of Kenya, for example—resistance could become violent and chronic, as in the **Mau Mau** uprising that began as a protest against land alienation among Kenya's Kikuyu people. Through the course of the 1950s, tens of thousands of Kenyans were killed, and the British imprisoned many more suspected insurgents and sympathizers in detention camps, while the Mau Mau revolt became a nationalist insurgency.[1]

Mau Mau

An uprising that began among the Kikuyu of the Kenya highlands and lasted through the 1950s. The British referred to it as the "Kenya Emergency."

---

[1] The history of Mau Mau is still contested. British administrators deliberately destroyed much of the documentary evidence. For recent attempts to reconstruct events and their meanings, see D. Anderson, *Histories of the Hanged: The Dirty War in Kenya and the End of Empire* (New York: W.W. Norton & Co., 2005), and C. Elkins, *Imperial Reckoning: The Untold Story of Britain's Gulag in Kenya* (New York: Henry Holt & Co., 2004).

Mau Mau freedom fighters in a Kenyan hideout, around 1950.

Why is the history of Mau Mau still contested?

THE RISE OF AFRICAN NATIONALISM

WHAT WERE the goals of African nationalists?

The key factor in European colonialism's demise was the rise of nationalism across Africa, especially after World War I. However little the colonial partition of Africa reflected native linguistic, racial, or cultural divisions, it still influenced both nationalist movements and the eventual shape of African states. The "national" consciousness of the diverse peoples of a given colonial unit was fueled by common opposition to foreign rule. It was also fed by the use of a common European tongue and through the assimilation of European thought and culture. The ranks of indigenous, educated elites gradually increased in the early twentieth century. From them came the leaders of Africa's nationalist movements between the two world wars and of Africa's new independent nations after World War II (see Chapter 33).

Mass political parties emerged in the postwar period. These include the Convention People's Party in the Gold Coast (Ghana) under Kwame Nkrumah (1909–1972) and the African Democratic Assembly, which drew members from a number of French West African colonies under the leadership of Félix Houphouët-Boigny (1905–1993), who became the first president of the Ivory Coast.

An important countervailing trend was the emergence of movements seeking to transcend both

Champion of Negritude,
Leopold Senghor.

colonial boundaries and ethnic or "tribal" divisions and foster an inclusive African identity. One example is **Negritude**, a literary and intellectual movement to celebrate all aspects of African civilization that was exemplified by the writings of Leopold Senghor (1906–2001). Senghor later became the first president of Senegal.

The most severe indigenous critiques of the Western treatment of Africa often drew on Western religious and political ideals. Twentieth-century African leaders learned well from the West and used their learning to help end Western domination. African independence movements were based on modern nationalist models from Europe and America rather than ancient ones derived from native tradition. The national independence movements typically ejected the colonial intruders, without trying to return to an earlier status quo. Their aim was to take over and to run the Western institutions introduced by colonialism. This legacy from the West is still visible today.

Negritude
A movement begun among African students in 1930s Paris to celebrate African culture and thought.

SUMMARY

 HOW DID British rule affect India?

British Dominance and Colonial Rule. The East India Company brought increasing areas of India under British control throughout the early nineteenth century. After the Indian Uprising of 1857, Crown rule was instituted. India became part of Britain's economy. Indian labor and resources were exploited. Indian elites were influenced by British culture. Indians of all classes resented their subordination. *page 668*

WHAT ROLE did Gandhi play in ending British rule in India?

From British Crown Raj to Independence. Relations between Indians and Britons were increasingly distrustful. Many strands of Indian nationalism developed, and Gandhi's thought was exceptionally influential. Gandhi's philosophies of passive resistance and self-reliance laid the groundwork for the political movement that brought Indian independence. *page 671*

 WHY IS the invasion of Egypt by Napoleon's army in 1798 symbolically important?

Declining Islamic Power and Independence. Muslim empires were in decline, as Western economic, political, military, and technological power was increasing. European imperialism in the Middle East and Central Asia was encapsulated in Napoleon's invasion of Egypt in 1798.

Iran under the Qajar shahs (1794–1925) saw the rise of Shi'ite *ulama* power to oppose Qajar absolutism. *page 674*

 WHAT WERE three typical Islamic reactions to Western encroachment?

Islamic Responses to Foreign Encroachment. Reform movements proposed various relationships between Islam and the West. Islamic revivalism, integration of Islamic and Western ideas, emulation of the West, and nationalism were among the cultural responses to Western domination in Islamic regions. Women proposed new roles for themselves. *page 676*

 WHAT WAS the *mfecane*?

New Power Centers and Islamic Reform Movements. In southern Africa, Bantu migrations caused the disruptions of *mfecane*—literally, "crushing"—as states and individuals were squeezed by population growth and warfare. This was followed by large-scale displacements of Africans as Boers moved inland in the Great Trek. Elsewhere, trade was generally a precursor to more direct European involvement. A series of Islamic revival and reform movements spread across northern Africa and Arabia in the nineteenth century. Usman Dan Fodio Islamicized Hausa lands, while the Sanusi movement opposed Italians in Libya, and the Mahdist uprising defeated the British at Khartoum. *page 680*

HOW DID Africans resist European colonialism?

Patterns in European Colonization and African Resistance. Different European powers had different strategies and mechanisms for administering African territories, and areas with heavy white settlement generally experienced more exploitation than those with a thinner European presence. A few African rulers were able to use the presence of Europeans to their own advantage, but in general Africans opposed and resisted Europeans. *page 682*

 WHAT WHERE the goals of African nationalists?

The Rise of African Nationalism. Although colonial boundaries were artificial, they gained cultural meaning as Africans within particular colonies forged nationalist independence movements. There were also pan-African movements, such as Negritude. *page 688*

KEY TERMS

bazaari (p. 675)

cantonments (p. 671)

Great Trek (p. 681)

indirect rule (p. 686)

Mau Mau (MOW MOW) (p. 687)

Mahdi (MAH-dee)(p. 682)

mfecane **(mm-fuh-KAHN-ay)** (p. 680)

mujtahid (p. 675)

Negritude (p. 689)

pan-Islamism (p. 677)

protectorate (p. 678)

raj (p. 670)

scramble for Africa (p. 684)

Tanzimat (TAHNZ-ee-MAT) (p. 678)

Wahhabis (wah-HAH-bees) (p. 676)

REVIEW QUESTIONS

1. What does the "impact of modernity" mean to traditional Afro-Asian-Indian cultures? What patterns of reaction can you discern? Why was the West able to impose itself on these cultures?

2. Why was India called the "jewel in the crown" of the British Empire? How did the British gain control of India? What policies did they follow in government and economics?

3. What kinds of political activism against British rule can you cite from Indian history after 1800? What kinds of success or failure did they have?

4. How was the Islamic world internally divided after 1800? How did those divisions influence the coming of European powers?

5. What roles did women play in critiquing Muslim culture during this period?

6. How did nationalism affect European control in South Asia, Africa, and the Middle East? How and when did its various manifestations arise? Were there any successful "national states" from these regions before 1945?

7. Discuss the new African states and power centers of sub-Saharan Africa before 1870. Why did no modern nation-state develop in the area? How did Islam affect the development of new entities? What role did trade play?

8. What were Europeans' main interests in Africa? Why were Africans unable to stop the "scramble for Africa"?

9. What factors influenced Africans' experience of colonial rule in different regions?

10. What was the role of African nationalism in resisting foreign control?

Note: To learn more about the topics in this chapter, please turn to the Suggested Readings at the end of the book. For additional sources related to this chapter please see www.myhistorylab.com

PEARSON
myhistorylab Connections

Reinforce what you learned in this chapter by studying the many documents, images, maps, review tools, and videos available at **www.myhistorylab.com**

Read and Review

✓● Study and Review Chapter 26

●●● Read the Document *Dadabhai Naoroji, The Benefits of British Rule in India, 1871, p. 669*
The Indian Revolt (1857), p. 670
Lord William Bentinck, on the Suppression of Sati, 1829, p. 670
Karl Marx, "The British Rule in India," 1853, p. 671
Amrita Lal Roy, English Rule in India, 1886, p. 671
Gandhi Speaks against the Partition of India (pre-1947), p. 672
Religious Minorities in the Middle East (late 19th-early 20th century), p. 675
Ottoman, p. 676
The Young Turk Revolution, 1908, p. 679

●● View the Image *Mahatma Gandhi, p. 669*

((●● Hear the Audio *India's Imperialism, p. 669*

●● Watch the Video *Gandhi in India, p. 672*
The Ottoman Tanzimat Period (1839–1876): The Middle East Confronts Modernity, p. 678

Research and Explore

●● Watch the Video *Imperialism and Colonialism: Empires in Africa*

●● Watch the Video *The Three M's*

((●● Hear the Audio

Hear the audio file for Chapter 26
at **www.myhistorylab.com**

ISLAM

Islam is one of the youngest major world religions. Since its inception during the lifetime of the Prophet Muhammad (632 B.C.E.), it has grown, like the Christian and Buddhist traditions, into a worldwide community not limited by national boundaries or defined in racial or ethnic terms. It began among the Arabs but spread widely. Islam's historical heartlands are those Arabic-, Turkic-, and Persian-speaking lands of the Near East between Egypt and Afghanistan. However, today more than half of its faithful live in Asia east of Karachi, Pakistan; and more Muslims live in sub-Saharan Africa than in all of the Arab lands. There are also growing Muslim minorities in the United States and Europe.

The central vision of Islam is a just and peaceful society where people can freely worship God. It focuses on a human community of worshipers who recognize the absolute sovereignty and oneness of God and strive to do God's will. Muslims believe that the Divine will is found first in God's revealed word, the Qur'an; then as elaborated and specified in the actions and words of his final prophet, Muhammad; and finally as interpreted and extended in the scriptural exegesis and legal traditions of the Muslim community over the past thirteen and a half centuries.

The Muslim vision thus centers on one God who has guided humankind throughout history by means of prophets or apostles and repeated revelations. God is the Creator of all, and in the end all will return to God. God's majesty would seem to make him a distant, threatening deity of absolute justice; there is such an element in the Muslim understanding of the wide chasm between the human and the Divine. Still, there is an immanent as well as a transcendent side to the Divine in the Muslim view. Indeed, Muslims have given us some of the greatest images of God's closeness to his faithful worshiper, images that have a special place in the thought of the Muslim mystics, who are known as *sufis* (taken originally from *suf*, "wool," because of the early Muslim ascetics' use of simple wool dress).

Muslims understand God's word in the Qur'an and the elaboration of that word by tradition to be a complete prescription for human life. Thus Islamic law is not law in the Western sense of civil, criminal, or international systems. Rather, it is a comprehensive set of standards for the moral, ritual, social, political, economic, aesthetic, and even hygienic and dietary dimensions of life. By being faithful to God's law, the Muslim hopes to gain salvation on the Last Day, when human history shall end and all of God's creatures who have ever lived will be resurrected and called to account for their thoughts and actions during their lives on earth. Some will be saved, but others will be eternally damned.

Thus *Islam*, which means "submission [to God]," has been given as a name to the religiously defined system of life that Muslims have sought to institute wherever they have lived. Muslims have striven to organize their societies and political realities around the ideals represented in the traditional picture of the Prophet's community in Medina and Mecca. This approach necessitated compromise in which power was given to temporal rulers and accepted by Muslim religious leaders as long as those rulers protected God's Law, the *Shari'a*. The ideal of a single international Muslim community, or *Umma*, has never fully been realized politically, but it remains an ideal.

Many reform movements over the centuries have called for greater adherence to rigorist interpretations of Islamic law and greater dominance of piety and religious values in sociopolitical as well as individual life. The most famous of these movements— the Wahhabis in eighteenth-century Arabia—remains influential in much of the Muslim world, including Saudi Arabia. The Wahhabis' puritanical zeal in fighting what they consider "innovations" in many regional Islamic contexts, such as Shi'ism, sufi traditions, and more liberal forms of Islamic practice, continues to the present day. Wahhabism has had considerable success in the past half century and was apparently the spawning ground of the extremist views of Osama bin Laden's al-Qa'ida terrorist movement, which is largely Arab in its ethnic makeup and which has turned from fighting Muslim states it regards as un-Islamic to opposing what it

Muhammad and Ali. This sixteenth-century Persian miniature shows the prophet Muhammad and his kinsman Ali purifying the Ka'ba in Mecca of pagan idols. The Ka'ba is the geographical point toward which all Muslims face when performing ritual prayer.

Art Resource/Bildarchiv Preussischer Kulturbesitz.

What might be the purpose of miniature illustrations such as this?

The Qur'an's First Chapter. This nineteenth-century hand-copied Qur'an in Arabic is open to the *Fatiha*, the opening chapter of Islam's holy book. In seven very short verses, the Fatiha sums up man's relation to God in prayer. Muslims repeat the invocation of verse one, "In the name of God, the Merciful Compassionate One," before eating, drinking, or performing any other significant act.

Koran. Hand-copied in Arabic by Kohazadeh Ahmad Rashid Safi. Decorated by Adham Gharbaldesh at Balawi, probably Persian, nineteenth century. African and Middle Eastern Division, Library of Congress.

How is God portrayed in these opening lines of the Qur'an?

Muslim School Children in Malaysia, 1997. Although most non-Muslims associate Islam with the Middle East, Islam has deep roots in Southeast Asia. About 212 million Muslims live in Indonesia, making it the most populous Muslim country in the world.

Does this photograph conflict with any commonly held perceptions about Islam and the veil?

considers the U.S. intrusion into the Arab Islamic world and its unpopular foreign policy in the region. While mainstream Muslims everywhere reject bin Laden's extremism, Wahhabi zealotry has adherents on the fringes of Islamic communities around the world. In this respect, Islam is not unlike Christianity, Judaism, Hinduism, or other major religions, each of which has over its history spawned literalists, zealots, and extremists, who have urged violence in the name of their version of their parent faith.

The major sectarian, or minority, groups among Muslims are those of the Shi'ites, who have held out for an ideal of a temporal ruler who is also the spiritual heir of Muhammad and God's designated deputy on earth. Most Shi'ites, notably those of Iran, hold that after eleven designated blood descendants of the prophets had each failed to be recognized by the majority of Muslims as the rightful leader, or *Imam*, the twelfth disappeared and remains to this day physically absent from the world, although not dead. He will come again at the end of time to vindicate his faithful followers.

Muslim piety takes many forms. The common duties of Muslims are central for Muslims everywhere: showing faith in God and trust in his Prophet; regularly performing ritual worship (*Salat*); fasting during daylight hours every day in Ramadan (the ninth month of the lunar year); giving one's wealth to the needy (*zakat*); and at least once in a lifetime, if able, making the pilgrimage to Mecca and its environs (*Hajj*). Other regional or popular practices are also important. Celebration of the Prophet's birthday indicates the exalted popular status of Muhammad, even though any divine status for him is strongly rejected theologically. Recitation of the Qur'an permeates all Muslim practice, from daily worship to celebrations of all kinds. Visitation of saints' tombs is a prominent form of popular devotion. Sufi chanting or even ecstatic dancing are also practiced by Muslims around the world.

Muslims vary enormously in their physical environment, language, ethnic background, and cultural allegiances. What binds them now as in the past are not political allegiances but religious affinities and a shared heritage of religious faith and culture. How these allegiances and sensibilities will fare in the face of global challenges will be an important factor in shaping the world of the twenty-first century.

◆ How has the ideal of a single, international Muslim community influenced Islamic history? World history?

◆ What impact have reform movements had on Islam since its inception? What impact do they have today?

27
Modern East Asia

((•●─[Hear the Audio for Chapter 27 at www.myhistorylab.com

Woodblock, Munakata Shikō, 1945. In modern Japan, woodblock prints are divided between modernists who, initially at least, took their inspiration from the West, and those who went through a "Western phase" and then built on the native folk art tradition. Among the latter, the greatest was Munakata Shikō (1903–1975). Munakata was born in Aomori Prefecture, a sparsely populated area in northernmost Honshu known for its long bitter winters, rocky soil, and strong folk religion tradition. At age 24 Munakata went to Tokyo, where for two years he experimented with oils, but then he switched to print-making. In 1937, at age 34, he took up the Buddhist subjects for which he is best known. His most famous prints are sensuous Buddhist deities and Bodhisattvas such as the one depicted here.

What is "modern" about this woodblock print? What elements make it traditional?

MODERN JAPAN (1853–1945)

WHAT ROLE did Chōshū and Satsu-ma play in the overthrow of Tokugawa rule?

WHAT POWERS did the Meiji Constitution give to the emperor?

WHY DID Japan set out to build a modern economy?

HOW DID political parties develop in Japan?

HOW WAS Japan similar to and different from Germany during this period?

MODERN CHINA (1839–1949)

WHAT WERE the most serious threats to Manchu rule in the nineteenth century?

WHO WERE the key figures in the revolution of 1911?

WHY WAS Marxism-Leninism so appealing to Chinese intellectuals?

WHO WAS Jiang Jieshi?

F*rom the mid-nineteenth century, the West was expanding, aggressive, and imperialistic. Its industrial goods and gunboats reached every part of the globe. It believed in free trade and had the military might to impose it on others. It was a trigger for change throughout the world. But the response to the Western impact depended on the internal array of forces in each country. In fact, the "response to the West" was only one small, though vital, part of the history of each country in*

MODERN EAST ASIA

From the late nineteenth century most countries wanted to become modern. They coveted the wealth and power of the West. But what does it mean to be modern?

Three stages may be noted in Japan's development as the world's first and most advanced non-Western modernizer: preconditions, Westernization, and assimilation.

Even before contact with the modern West, Japan had some of the preconditions needed for industrialization: a fairly literate people, an ethic of duty and hard work, a market economy, secular thought, some bureaucracy, and a protonationalism. In sum, there was an adequate base for an "external modernization."

Building on these preconditions, Japan Westernized after 1868, adopting a range of new institutions: post offices, banks, customhouses, hospitals, police forces, joint stock companies, universities with faculties of science and engineering, and so on. Japanese thinkers brought in modern ideas and values: Spencer and Guizot, Turgenev and Tolstoy, Adam Smith and Marx. Japanese writers began experimenting with new forms.

Little by little Japan *assimilated* what it had borrowed. The *zaibatsu* combines were modern, with the most recent technologies, yet their business organizations were unlike those of the West. The spare beauty of traditional architecture was transferred to the glass, steel, concrete, and stone of the modern. A new literature, completely Japanese yet also completely modern, appeared.

Japan may serve as a useful model in that its modernization—as analyzed in terms of the above three stages—has gone further than that in any other non-Western country. We note the absence in India or the Islamic world of comparable preconditions. After the end of colonialism, countries in these areas had to create the necessary preconditions even as they borrowed the new technologies. The difficulty explains their limited success. In Africa the dearth of preconditions was even more pronounced.

China, like Japan but unlike countries of South Asia, the Middle East, or Africa, had many of the necessary preconditions—they might be called East Asian preconditions—in place. But when it came to Westernization, the government by Confucian literati that had long been China's outstanding asset became its greatest liability. It took decades to topple the dynasty and to advance beyond Confucian ideas.

View the Image
Japanese Woodcut on Perry's Arrival
at **myhistorylab.com**

this period. Japan and China were both relatively successful in their responses, for neither became a colony.

The two countries' governing elites were educated in Confucianism, which receded when faced with the powerful secularism of nineteenth-century science and the doctrines associated with it. In both Japan and China, however, core values of the Confucian sociopolitical identity endured, and some of those values transmuted into a strong new nationalism.

In most other respects, modern Japan and China could hardly be more different. Perhaps the difference was only to be expected, given the pattern of recurrent dynasties in China's premodern history and of feudal evolution in Japan's.

The coming of Commodore Matthew Perry (1794–1858) in 1853–1854 precipitated rapid change in Japan. The old Tokugawa regime collapsed, and the Japanese built a modern state. Economic growth followed. By 1900, Japan had defeated China and was about to defeat Russia. After the Great Depression, Japan, like Italy and Germany, became an aggressive and militarized state and was defeated in World War II. But after the war, Japan reemerged more stable and productive with a strong parliamentary government.

The Chinese polity, in contrast, easily weathered the Opium War (1839–1842), an event of considerably greater magnitude than Perry's visit to Japan. The hold of tradition in China was remarkable, as was the effectiveness of traditional remedies in dealing with political ills. In one sense the strength of tradition was China's weakness, for only after the overthrow of the Manchu Dynasty in 1911 were the Chinese able to begin the modernization that Japan had started in 1868. Even then they were unsuccessful. Along with warlordism and other typical end-of-dynasty disruptions, new trauma resulted from the rending of the dynastic pattern itself and the unprecedented experience of being confronted by more powerful nations. That China in some sense "failed" during this modern century is the view the Chinese themselves hold. ∎

Then, in the maelstrom of the May Fourth Movement, intellectual change occurred at a furious pace, but new doctrines alone could not provide a stable polity. Nationalism emerged as the common denominator of Chinese thought. The Nationalists (Guomindang) drew on it at the Huangpu Academy, during the march north, and in the Nanjing government. But other groups could also appeal to it. The Chinese communists won out by 1949.

It is beguiling to view the Chinese Communist Party (CCP) cadres as a new class of literati operating the machinery of a monolithic, centralized state, with the teachings of Marx and Lenin replacing those of Confucius, and local party organization replacing the Confucian gentry. But this interpretation is too simple. Communism stressed science, materialism, and class conflict. It broke with the Chinese past.

Communism itself was also modified in China. Marx had predicted that socialist revolutions would break out in advanced economies where the contradictions of capitalism were sharpest. Lenin had shifted the emphasis from spontaneous revolutions by workers to the small but disciplined revolutionary party, the vanguard of the proletariat. He thereby changed communism into what it has been ever since: a movement capable of seizing power only in backward nations. At the level of doctrine, Mao Zedong modified Lenin's ideas only slightly—by theorizing that "progressive" peasants were a part of the proletariat. But he went beyond this theory in practice, virtually ignoring city workers while relying on China's villages for recruits for his armies, who were then indoctrinated using Leninist techniques.

Yet, the organizational techniques that were so effective in creating a party and army would prove less so for economic development. It soon became clear that mass mobilization was no substitute for individual incentives.

Focus Questions

◆ What are the preconditions for modernization along Western lines? Why are they so important?

◆ Compare and contrast the process of modernization in Japan and China in the twentieth century. Which country was more successful? Why?

MODERN JAPAN (1853–1945)
OVERTHROW OF THE TOKUGAWA *BAKUFU* (1853–1868)

From the seventeenth century into the nineteenth, the natural isolation of the islands of Japan was augmented by its policy of seclusion. Then at midcentury, the American ships of Commodore Perry came and forced Japan to sign a treaty opening it to foreign intercourse. Fourteen years later, the entire *bakufu*-domain system collapsed, and a group of talented leaders seized power.

Little changed during the first four years after Perry. The break came in 1858 when the *bakufu*, ignoring the imperial court's disapproval, was persuaded to sign a commercial treaty with the United States. Some daimyo, who wanted a voice in national policy, criticized the treaty as contravening the hallowed policy of seclusion. Younger samurai, frustrated by their exclusion from office, started a movement to "honor the emperor." The *bakufu*, in turn, responded with a purge. But in 1860, the head of the *bakufu* council was assassinated by extremist samurai. His successors lacked the nerve to continue his tough policies.

In 1861, two domains, Chōshū and Satsu-ma, emerged to heal the breach between the *bakufu* and the court. First, Chōshū officials proposed a policy that favored the *bakufu* but made concessions to the court. Next, Satsu-ma advocated a policy that made further concessions and ousted Chōshū as "the friend of the court." In response, the moderate reformist government of Chōshū adopted the anti-*bakufu* policy of its extremist faction and, in turn, ousted Satsu-ma. Satsu-ma then seized the court in 1863 in a military coup.

WHAT ROLE did Chōshū and Satsu-ma play in the overthrow of Tokugawa rule?

•••—Read the **Document**
President Millard Fillmore, Letter to the Emperor of Japan, 1852
at **myhistorylab.com**

•••—Read the **Document**
The Views of Ii Naosuke, 1853
at **myhistorylab.com**

A Closer Look

East Meets the West

Commodore Perry presents a letter from President Fillmore to Japanese representatives.

Perry came in 1853 with only four ships.

Commodore Matthew C. Perry (commodore is a rank equivalent to admiral) had fought against Barbary Pirates, had taken Key West, and had been active in the Spanish-American War. He entered Edo Bay in 1853 and threatened to shell Japanese installations on the shore if he were not given a treaty. He got the Treaty of Friendship in 1854 and retired from the navy in 1855.

Two-sworded *bakufu* officials face Perry. Perry did not know the difference between emperor and shogun and thought he was meeting officials of the emperor.

Americans and Japanese could not communicate. Perry used as an interpreter a Hong Kong Chinese, who spoke English and could write in Chinese, which the Japanese representatives could read. The interpreter wears his hair in a queue, the token of Chinese submission to their Manchu rulers.

Questions

1. What did Perry have in mind during this meeting? What did the *bakufu* representatives want?

2. How did so innocuous a meeting lead 15 years later to the overthrow of Tokugawa rule?

myhistorylab To examine this image in an interactive fashion, please go to **www.myhistorylab.com**

Four points may be noted about the 1861–1863 diplomatic phase of domain action: (1) Even after 250 years of *bakufu* rule, several domains were still able to act autonomously when the opportunity arose; (2) the two domains that acted first and most of those that followed were large domains with many samurai and substantial financial resources; (3) both Satsu-ma and Chōshū had fought against the Tokugawa in 1600 and remembered an earlier independence; (4) by 1861 to 1863, new politics had opened decision making to middle-ranking samurai officials in a way that would have been impossible before 1853.

The 1863 Satsu-ma coup at the Kyoto court initiated a military phase of politics. As long as Satsu-ma and Chōshū remained enemies, politics stalemated and the *bakufu* continued as hegemon. But when the two domains became allies in 1866, the *bakufu* was overthrown in less than two years.

Factors contributing to this process included the movement for a "union of court and camp": Daimyo campaigned for a new conciliar rule in which they would participate together with the emperor and withdrew support from the *bakufu*. A second feature of this period was antiforeignism. A third was the formation of new rifle units, commanded mostly by lower samurai. These units transformed political power in Japan. A fourth development was a cultural shift in Japanese self-perception. During the Tokugawa era, the Japanese had seen themselves as civilized Confucians and much of the rest of the world as barbarians. But in 1868 Fukuzawa Yukichi (1835–1901) proposed that the West, with its technology, science, and humane laws, was "civilized and enlightened"; China, Japan, and countries like Turkey were half civilized; and other areas were dismissed as barbarian. Technology grew out of the Western legal, political, economic, and educational systems. Fukuzawa argued that Western systems required political freedoms and a citizenry with a spirit of independence. Fukuzawa's writings became immensely influential after the Restoration, eventually sparking the "Civilization and Enlightenment Movement" of the 1870s.

BUILDING THE MEIJI STATE (1868–1890)

The idea of a "developing nation" did not exist in the mid-nineteenth century. Yet Japan after the 1868 **Meiji Restoration** was just such a nation. (The years from 1868 to 1912 are referred to as the "Meiji period," after the era name that accompanied the accession of the new emperor.) It was committed to wealth and power of the kind Western industrial nations possessed. The government faced tough decisions as it advanced by trial and error. It also demanded that the Japanese people make sacrifices for the sake of the future.

The announcement of the restoration of rule by an emperor was made on January 3, 1868. In the battles that followed, Chōshū and Satsu-ma troops defeated those of the *bakufu*. Edo surrendered and was renamed Tokyo, the "eastern capital." Edo castle became the imperial palace. At the start the Meiji government was made up of a small group of samurai leaders from Chōshū, Satsu-ma, and a few other domains. They have been described, only half humorously, as twelve bureaucrats in search of a bureaucracy. But their vision defined the goals of the new government.

CENTRALIZATION OF POWER

Their immediate goal was to centralize political power. By 1871, the young leaders had replaced the domains with prefectures controlled from Tokyo. To ensure a break with the past, each new prefectural governor was chosen from samurai of other regions.

Having centralized political authority, in 1871 about half of the most important Meiji leaders went abroad for a year and a half to study the West. (See Document, "On Wives and Concubines" on page 700.) They traveled in the United States and Europe visiting parliaments, schools, and factories.

WHAT POWERS did the Meiji Constitution give to the emperor?

Meiji Restoration
The overthrow of the Tokugawa *bakufu* in Japan in 1868 and the transfer, or "restoration," of power to the imperial government under the Emperor Meiji.

Read the **Document**
Japanese Impressions of American Culture (1860) at **myhistorylab.com**

DOCUMENT

On Wives and Concubines

During the 1870s and 1880s leading Japanese thinkers introduced a wide range of Western ideas into their country. Among them were freedom and equality as rights inherent in human nature. Debating the questions of equality in marriage and the rights of wives, intellectuals voiced a radical criticism of concubinage and prostitution. As a consequence of these debates, laws were passed during the 1880s and 1890s that strengthened the legal status of wives. Mori Arinori (1847–1889), who had studied in the United States and England, wrote the following passage in 1874. He later became a diplomat and, between 1885 and 1889, the minister of education.

- **THINK** of comparable instances in American or European history where new ideas led to dramatic social change. How long did the changes last, and how deeply rooted did they become?

The relation between man and wife is the fundamental of human morals. The moral path will be achieved by establishing this fundamental, and the country will only be firmly based if the moral path is realized. When people marry, rights and obligations emerge between them so that neither can take advantage of the other.

There have hitherto been a variety of marriage practices [in our country]. . . . Sometimes there may be one or even several concubines in addition to the wife, and sometimes a concubine may become the wife. Sometimes the wife and the concubines live in the same establishment.

Sometimes they are separated, and the concubine is the favored one while the wife is neglected. . . .

Taking a concubine is by arbitrary decision of the man and with acquiescence of the concubine's family. The arrangement, known as *ukedashi*, is made by paying money to the family of the concubine. This means, in other words, that concubines are bought with money. Since concubines are generally geisha and prostitutes patronized by rich men and nobles, many descendants in the rich and noble houses are the children of bought women. Even though the wife is superior to the concubine in households where they live together, there is commonly jealousy and hatred between them because the husband generally favors the concubine. Therefore, there are numerous instances when, the wife and the concubines being scattered in separate establishments, the husband repairs to the abode of the one with whom he is infatuated and willfully resorts to scandalous conduct. . . .

Thus, I have here explained that our country has not yet established the fundamental of human morality, and I hope later to discuss how this situation injures our customs and obstructs enlightenment.

Source: From Meiroku Zasshi, *Journal of the Japanese Enlightenment*, trans. and with introduction by William Reynolds Braisted, assisted by Adachi Yasushi and Kikuchi Yūji (Cambridge, MA: Harvard University Press, 1976), pp. 104–105. © 1976 by the President and Fellows of Harvard College. Reprinted by permission of Harvard University Press.

The second task of the Meiji leaders was to stabilize government revenues. The government converted the grain tax to a money tax. But a third of the revenues still went to pay for samurai stipends, so in 1873 the government raised a conscript army and abolished the samurai class. The samurai were paid off in government bonds, but as the bonds fell during the inflation of the 1870s, most former samurai became impoverished. What had begun as a reform of government finance ended as a social revolution. Some samurai rebelled. The last and greatest uprising was in 1877. When it was suppressed in 1878, the Meiji government became militarily secure.

POLITICAL PARTIES

Other samurai opposed the government by forming political parties and campaigning for popular rights, elections, and a constitution. They drew heavily on liberal Western models and proposed that parties in a national assembly would unite the emperor and the people, curbing the Satsu-ma-Chōshū clique. Samurai were the mainstay of the early party movement, despite its doctrines proclaiming all classes to be equal. With the government's formation of prefectural assemblies in 1878, more political parties emerged. Many farmers joined, wanting their taxes cut; the poor joined too, hoping to improve their condition. In 1881, the government promised a constitution and a national assembly within ten years. As the date for national elections approached, the parties gained strength, and the ties between party notables and local men of influence grew closer.

THE CONSTITUTION

The government viewed the party movement with distaste but was not sure how to counter it. Under Itō Hirobumi (1841–1909), the conservative Prussian constitution of 1850 was adapted to Japanese uses. As promulgated in 1889, the Meiji Constitution granted extensive powers to the emperor and severely limited the powers of the lower house in the **Diet** (the English term for Japan's bicameral national assembly).

The emperor was sovereign. According to the constitution, he was "sacred and inviolable," and in Itō's commentaries this was defined in Shinto terms. The emperor was given direct command of the armed forces. The emperor had the right to name the prime minister and to appoint the cabinet. He could dissolve the lower house of the Diet and issue imperial ordinances when the Diet was not in session. The Imperial Household Ministry, which was outside the cabinet, administered the great wealth given to the imperial family during the 1880s. The constitution itself was presented as a gift from the emperor to his subjects. The lower house of the Diet was given the authority only to approve budgets and pass laws, and even these powers were hedged. Itō's intention was not to create a parliamentary system but to devise a constitutional system that included a parliament.

The government also created institutions designed to limit the future influence of the political parties. In 1884, it created a new nobility with which to stock the future House of Peers. Itō, born a lowly foot soldier, ended as a prince. In 1885, he established a cabinet system and became the first prime minister. In 1887, Itō established a Privy Council, with himself as its head, to approve the constitution he had written. Civil service examinations were instituted in 1888. The bureaucracy became highly systematized. In 1890 there were 24,000 officials; by 1908 there were 72,000.

Japan's first foreign mission, headed by Prince Iwakura, ambassador extraordinary and plenipotentiary, leaving Yokohama for the United States and Europe on December 23, 1871.

What was Japan's attitude toward the West at this time?

Read the **Document**
Emperor Meiji, The Constitution of the Empire of Japan at **myhistorylab.com**

Read the **Document**
Japan: The Imperial Rescript on Education, 1890 at **myhistorylab.com**

Diet
The bicameral Japanese Parliament.

The Promulgation of the Meiji Constitution in 1889. The emperor, standing under the canopy, was declared "sacred and inviolable." Seated on the throne, at the left, is the empress.

Shosai Ginko (Japanese, act. 1874–1897), View of the Issuance of the State Constitution in the State Chamber of the New Imperial Palace, March 2, 1889 (Meiji 22), Ink and color on paper, 14 1/8 x 28 3/8 in. The Metropolitan Museum of Art, Gift of Lincoln Kirstein, 1959 (JP3233-3235) Photograph © The Metropolitan Museum of Art. Art Resource, New York.

What was the basis of the Meiji Constitution?

GROWTH OF A MODERN ECONOMY

WHY DID Japan set out to build a modern economy?

The late Tokugawa economy was similar to the economies of other East Asian countries. Almost 80 percent of the population lived in the countryside at close to a subsistence level. Taxes were high, and two thirds of the land tax was paid in kind. Money had only partially penetrated the rural economy. Japan had not developed factory production with machinery, steam power, or large accumulations of capital.

Early Meiji reforms unshackled the economy. Occupations were freed, which meant that farmers could trade and samurai could farm. The abolition of domains threw open regional economies and a groundswell of new commercial ventures and traditional, agriculturally based industries followed. Silk was Japan's wonder crop. The government introduced mechanical reeling, enabling Japan to win markets previously held by China's hand-reeled silk. Silk production rose from 2.3 million pounds in the post-Restoration era to 93 million pounds in 1929.

A parallel unshackling occurred on the land. The land tax reform of the 1870s created a powerful incentive for growth. Progressive landlords bought fertilizer and farm equipment. Rice production rose from 149 million bushels a year during 1880 to 1884 to 316 million during 1935 to 1937. Population grew from about 30 million in 1868 to 45 million in 1900 to 73 million in 1940. Because the farm population remained constant, the extra hands were available for factory and other urban jobs.

FIRST PHASE: MODEL INDUSTRIES

The modern sector of the economy was the government's greatest concern. It developed in four phases, beginning with the era of model industries, which lasted until 1881. With military strength as a major goal, the Meiji government expanded arsenals and shipyards, built telegraph lines, started railroads, developed mines, and established factories. The quantitative output of these early industries was insignificant; they were pilot-plant operations that doubled as "schools" for technologists and labor.

Just as important to economic development were a variety of other new institutions—banks, post offices, ports, roads, commercial laws, a system of primary and secondary schools, and a government university. They were patterned after European and American examples, although the pattern was often altered to fit Japan's needs. For example, Tokyo Imperial University had a faculty of agriculture earlier than any university in Europe.

zaibatsu
Large industrial combines that came to dominate Japanese industry in the late nineteenth century.

SECOND PHASE: 1880s–1890s

Substantial growth in the modern sector took place during the 1880s and 1890s. It was marked by the appearance of what would later become the great industrial combines known as *zaibatsu*. Accumulating capital was the greatest problem. Iwasaki Yatarō (1834–1885) used political connections. After the Restoration he gained control of the ships that he had managed as a samurai official for the Tosa domain. He next acquired government ships that had been used to transport troops in 1874 and during the 1877 Satsu-ma Rebellion. From these beginnings he built a shipping line to compete with foreign companies, started a bank, and invested in the enterprises that later became the Mitsubishi combine.

One of the first industries to benefit was cotton textiles. By 1896, the production of yarn had reached 17 million pounds, and by 1913 it was more than ten times that amount. Production of cotton cloth rose as well. Another area of growth was railroads, which gave Japan an internal circulatory system, opening up hitherto isolated regions. In 1872, Japan had 18 miles of track; in 1894, 2,100 miles; and by 1934, 14,500 miles.

Cotton textiles and railroads were followed during the 1890s by cement, bricks, matches, glass, beer, chemicals, and other private industries. The government created a

Silk-Weaving Mill in Japan, late nineteenth century. Note the division of labor: the women do the manual labor, while the man, dressed in formal attire, supervises.

How did the silk industry develop in Japan?

favorable climate for growth: The society and the polity were stable, the yen was sound, capital was safe, and taxes on industry were low. The conditions enjoyed by Japan's budding entrepreneurs differed in every respect from those of China.

THIRD PHASE: 1905–1929

The economy continued to grow after the 1905 Russo-Japanese War (see "The Politics of Imperial Japan" in this chapter) and spurted ahead during World War I. The economy grew slowly during the 1920s because of factors including renewed competition from Europe and the great earthquake that destroyed Tokyo in 1923. Agricultural productivity leveled off during the twenties: It became cheaper to import foodstuffs than to invest in new agricultural technology at home.

By the 1920s, Japanese society, especially in the cities, was becoming modern. The Japanese were healthier and lived longer. Personal savings rose with the standard of living. Even factory workers drank beer, went to movies, and read newspapers. By 1925, primary school education was universal. Japan had done what no other non-Western nation had even attempted: It had achieved universal literacy. Nevertheless, an immense cultural and social gap remained between the majority who had only a primary school education and the 3 percent who attended university. This gap emerged as a basic weakness in the 1920s.

It should also be noted that despite overall improvements in the condition of the Japanese, the human costs of growth were high. Well into the twentieth century women made up more than half of the industrial labor force. They went to the textile mills after leaving primary school and returned to their villages before marrying. Their working hours were long, their dormitories crowded, and their movements restricted. Some contracted tuberculosis, the plague of late nineteenth- and early twentieth-century Japan, and were sent back to their villages to die.

FOURTH PHASE: DEPRESSION AND RECOVERY

A Japanese bank crisis in 1927, followed by the worldwide Great Depression in 1929, plunged Japan into unemployment and suffering. The political consequences were enormous. Yet most of Japan recovered by 1933, more rapidly than any other industrial nation.

The recovery was fueled by an export boom and military procurements. During the 1930s, the production of pig iron, raw steel, and chemicals doubled. By 1937, Japan had a merchant fleet of 4.5 million tons, the third largest and the newest in the world. The quality of Japan's manufacturers rose. The outcry in the West against Japanese exports at this time was not because of volume—a modest 3.6 percent of world exports in 1936—but because Japanese products for the first time were competitive in terms of quality.

QUICK REVIEW

Development of the Japanese Economy

- First Phase (up to 1881): Development of model industries
- Second Phase (1880s–1890s): Emergence of the *zaibatsu* and growth of the railroads
- Third Phase (1905–1929): Slow economic growth and modernization of Japanese society
- Fourth Phase (1929–1937): Depression and recovery

THE POLITICS OF IMPERIAL JAPAN (1890–1945)

HOW DID political parties develop in Japan?

Parliaments began in the West and have functioned better there than in the rest of the world. For Japan to establish a constitution during the nineteenth century was a bold experiment. Even a constitution as cautious as that of Meiji had no precedent outside the West. How are we to view the Japanese political experience after 1890? One view is that the Japanese were not ready for constitutional government, so the militarism of the 1930s was inevitable. Japanese society certainly had weaknesses, but the Diet was growing in importance, and power was being transferred from the bureaucratic Meiji leaders to political party leaders. The transfer fell short of full parliamentary government, but the advance toward parliamentary government might well have continued if not for the Great Depression and other events.

FROM CONFRONTATION TO THE FOUNDING OF THE SEIYŪKAI (1890–1900)

In 1890 the Meiji leaders—sometimes called *oligarchs*, the few who rule—were concerned with nation building, not politics. They saw the cabinet as "transcendental," serving the emperor and nation, not partisan interests. They saw the lower house of the Diet as a place to let off steam without interfering in the government's serious work of building a new Japan. But the oligarchs had miscalculated, and they were drawn into political struggles.

The first act of the parties in the new 1890 Diet was to slash the government's budget. Prime Minister Yamagata had to make concessions to get some funds restored. This pattern continued for ten years. The government tried to intimidate and bribe the parties but failed. Political parties had the support of the voters, mostly well-to-do landowners, who opposed the government's heavy land tax.

In 1900, Itō Hirobumi formed a new party, called the Rikken Seiyūkai, or "Friends of Constitutional Government." For most of the next twenty years, it was the most important party in Japan, providing parliamentary support for successive governments through its control of the lower house. This arrangement was satisfactory to both sides: Prime ministers got the support necessary for the government to function smoothly, and party politicians got cabinet posts and pork barrel legislation with which to reward their supporters. Itō had made the constitution work, but at the cost of relinquishing transcendental cabinets.

THE GOLDEN YEARS OF MEIJI

The years around turn of the century represented the culmination of what the government had striven for since 1868. Economic development was under way, and the "unequal treaties" were revised. However, it was events abroad that won Japan recognition as a world power.

The first event was a war with China in 1894 to 1895 over Korea. From its victory, Japan secured Taiwan and other territory, an indemnity, and a treaty giving it the same privileges in China as those enjoyed by the Western powers (see Map 27–1). The second event was Japan's participation in the international force that relieved the Boxers' siege in Beijing in 1900. A third development was the Anglo-Japanese Alliance of 1902.

Russo-Japanese War. Japanese soldiers with flag and bayonets charge across a smoky field to engage Russian troops in the 1904–1905 Russo-Japanese War. Victory over Russia gave Japan Korea and a new international standing. The popularity of postcards, such as this one, reflected the new nationalism of Japan.

What were some of the roots of Japanese nationalism?

MAP 27–1.   Formation of the Japanese Empire.   The Japanese Empire grew in three stages: the Sino-Japanese War of 1894–1895, the Russo-Japanese War of 1904–1905, and Japanese conquests in Manchuria and northern China after 1931.

Why did Japan want an empire on the Asian mainland?

For Britain, this alliance ensured Japanese support for its East Asian interests. For Japan, the alliance meant it could fight Russia without fear of intervention by a third party.

The fourth event was the war with Russia that began in 1904. Japanese armies drove the Russians from their railway zones in Manchuria and seized Mukden in March 1905. The Russians sent their Baltic fleet to join the battle, but it was annihilated by Admiral Tōgō (1847–1934). The peace treaty gave Japan the Russian lease in the Liaotung Peninsula, the Russian railway in south Manchuria, the southern half of Sakhalin, and a recognition of Japan's interest in Korea, which was annexed in 1910.

Japan joined the imperialist scramble for colonies because it wanted equality with the great Western powers, and military power and colonies were the best credentials. Enthusiasm for empire was shared by political party leaders, most liberal thinkers, and conservative leaders.

See the **Map**

Japanese Colonial Expansion to 1914
at **myhistorylab.com**

RISE OF THE PARTIES TO POWER

The founding of the Seiyūkai by Itō in 1900 ended a decade of confrontation between the Diet and government. The aging oligarch Itō soon found intolerable the day-to-day experience of dealing with party politicians. Hara Takashi (1856–1921) assumed the presidency of the party in 1914. Born a generation after the founding fathers of the Meiji state, he helped Itō to found the Seiyūkai and was the most able politician in Japan. His goals, like those of Itō or Yamagata, centered on the expansion of national wealth and power. But he felt that they should be achieved by party government, not oligarchic rule, and he worked to expand the power of his party. The years between 1905 and 1921 were marked by the struggle between these two conceptions of government.

Party strength increased through a buildup of the Seiyūkai party machine and through strengthening of the Diet vis-à-vis other elites within the government in Tokyo. For the former, Hara obtained campaign funds from moneyed interests. Constituencies that supported Seiyūkai candidates got new schools, bridges, dams, roads, or even railroad lines.

In co-opting other governmental elites, the Seiyūkai had mixed success. The party increased its representation in the cabinet and gained some patronage appointments in the bureaucracy, although most bureaucrats remained professionals and resisted the intrusion of political appointees. The House of Peers and the Privy Council, which ratified treaties, remained independent. The Seiyūkai had no success in penetrating the military services.

The weakening of oligarchic control reflected the aging of the "men of Meiji." In 1900, Itō was the last oligarch to become prime minister. From 1901 to 1912, Katsura Tarō (1847–1913), a Chōshū general and Yamagata's protégé, and Saionji, Itō's protégé, took turns in the post. Both had Seiyūkai support. The oligarchs were also weakened by changes within the elites. A younger generation of officers in the military services chafed at the continuing domination by the old cliques. In the civil bureaucracy, younger officials who saw the bureaucracy as an independent service were achieving positions of responsibility. The oligarchs maintained their power to act for the emperor in appointing prime ministers until the deaths of Itō in 1909 and Yamagata in 1922.

A wave of liberalism began during World War I and culminated in the period of party governments from 1924 to 1932. Joining the Allies in World War I, Japan had been influenced by democratic thought. Scholars discussed revising the Meiji Constitution. Labor unions were organized. A social movement was launched to improve conditions in Japan's industrial slums and to pass social and labor legislation. Japan's second political party, the Kenseikai, which had been out of power since 1916, grew more liberal and adopted several of the new social causes as its own, such as universal manhood suffrage. When Hara cut the tax qualification for voting from 10 to 3 yen—a considerable extension of the franchise—the Kenseikai criticized the change as insufficient.

In 1924, the Kenseikai and the Seiyūkai formed a coalition government. For the next eight years, the presidents of one or the other of the two major parties were appointed as prime ministers.

The cabinets (1924–1926) of Katō Kōmei are considered the peak of parliamentarianism in prewar Japan. Katō advocated a British model of government. His ministry passed universal manhood suffrage, cut the military budget, and enacted social and labor legislation. Katō's cabinet brought Japan close to a true parliamentary government.

MILITARISM AND WAR (1927–1945)

The future of Japan's parliamentary government seemed assured during the mid-1920s. The economy was growing, society was stable, and party leaders were experienced. Japan's international position was secure. But by 1945 Japan had been defeated in a devastating war and was occupied by foreign troops for the first time in its history.

A small shift in the balance of power among the governmental elites established by the Meiji constitution had produced a major change in Japan's foreign policy. The parties had forced the other elites to compromise between 1890 and 1926. Beginning in 1932 military men replaced party presidents as prime ministers. In 1937 Japan went to war with China; by the end of 1941 Japan was allied with Germany and Italy, had clashed with the Soviet Union, and had gone to war with the United States.

From their inception, the military services in Japan had been constructed on different principles from Japan's civilian society. The armed services had their own schools, which inculcated discipline, bravery, and loyalty. Soldiers saw themselves as the true heirs of the founders of the modern Japanese state and the guardians of Japanese tradition. They contrasted their loyalty to the emperor and their concern for all Japanese with the special-interest pandering by the political parties.

The military resented its diminished national stature during the 1920s, when military budgets were cut and the prestige of a military career declined. But there had been no change in the constitutional position of the services. The general staffs remained directly responsible to the emperor. With the passing of the Meiji oligarchs, this meant they were responsible to no one but themselves.

New multilateral treaties (the 1921–1922 Washington Conference and the 1930 London Conference) recognized the existing colonies of the victors in World War I but opposed new colonial ventures. Japan's position in Manchuria was ambiguous. Because Japan maintained its interests through a tame Chinese warlord, Manchuria was not, strictly speaking, a colony. But Japan saw its claim to Manchuria as similar to that of Western nations and their colonies. The Guomindang unification of China and the blossoming of Chinese nationalism threatened Japan's special position. Japanese army units murdered the Manchurian warlord when he showed signs of independence. In 1931, while the party government in Tokyo equivocated, the army provoked a crisis, took over Manchuria, and proclaimed it an independent state in 1932. When the League of Nations condemned this action, Japan withdrew from the league.

Yearning for Military Heroes. Japanese patriotic society members dressed as samurai around 1925.

What had happened to the real samurai?

The Great Depression cast doubts on the international economic order and on the *zaibatsu*, which were seen as rich capitalist profiteers in a country full of suffering and want. While Japan's government acted effectively to counter the Great Depression, the recovery came too late to help the political parties. By 1936, political trends that had begun during the worst years of the Depression had become irreversible.

The Depression galvanized the political left and right. The political left was composed mainly of socialist moderates. Supported by unionists and white-collar workers, they would reemerge as a stronger force after World War II. There was also a radical left, consisting of many little Marxist parties and of the Japanese Communist Party, founded in 1922. Though small, the radical parties became influential in intellectual circles during the 1920s and 1930s.

During the 1930s, an array of right-wing organizations went beyond the emperor-centered nationalism in which all Japanese were steeped to challenge the status quo. Civilian ultranationalists used Shinto myths and Confucian values to attack Western liberalism. Some bureaucrats looked to the example of Nazi Germany and argued for the exclusion of party politicians from government. Military officers envisioned a "defense state"; they urged military expansion and an autarchic colonial empire insulated from the uncertainties of the world economy. Young officers of the revolutionary right advocated "direct action" against the elites of the parliamentary coalition and called for a second restoration of imperial power.

The last group precipitated political change. On May 15, 1932, junior army and navy officers attacked key civilian offices and murdered Prime Minister Inukai. This attack occurred at the peak of right-wing agitation and the pit of the Depression. Saionji decided it would be unwise to appoint another party president as prime minister, choosing instead a moderate admiral. For the next four years cabinets were led by moderate military men but with continuing party participation. These cabinets satisfied neither the parties nor the radical young officers. Japanese politics continued to drift to the right. In 1936, young officers attempted a coup in Tokyo. They killed cabinet ministers and occupied the Diet and other government buildings. They wanted their army superiors to form a new government. Saionji and other men around the emperor stood firm; the navy opposed the rebellion, and within three days it was suppressed. The ringleaders were tried and executed. It was the last "direct action" by the radical right in prewar Japan.

The military continued interfering in the formation of cabinets. From 1936 on, moderate prime ministers gave way to more outspokenly militaristic figures. Opposition to militarism remained substantial nonetheless. In the 1937 election, the two major centrist parties won 354 Diet seats. The Japanese people were more level-headed than their leaders. But the Diet could not oppose a government in wartime, and by summer, Japan was at war in China.

There were three critical junctures between the outbreak of war with China and the World War II campaign in the Pacific. The first was the decision in January 1938 to strike a knockout blow at the Nationalist Party (GMD) government. The war had begun as an unplanned skirmish between Chinese and Japanese troops in the Beijing area but had spread quickly. The general staff argued that the only way to end the war was to convince the Chinese nationalists that fighting was hopeless. The Japanese army occupied most of the cities and railroads of eastern China, but Jiang Jieshi refused to give in. A stalemate ensued that lasted until 1945. China was never a major theater of the war in the Pacific.

The second critical decision was the signing of the **Tripartite Pact** with Germany and Italy in September 1940. In 1936, Japan had joined Germany in the Anti-Comintern Pact directed against international communism. It also wanted an alliance with Germany against the Soviet Union, but Germany insisted that any alliance would also have to be directed against the United States and Britain. The Japanese

Tripartite Pact
The alliance between Japan and Nazi Germany and Fascist Italy that was signed in 1940.

CHRONOLOGY

MODERN JAPAN

Overthrow of Tokugawa *Bakufu*

1853–1854	Perry obtains Treaty of Friendship
1858	*Bakufu* sign commercial treaty
1861–1863	Chōshū and Satsu-ma emerge
1866	Chōshū defeats *bakufu* army
1868	Meiji Restoration

Nation Building

1868–1871	Shaping a new state
1871–1873	Iwakura mission
1873–1878	Social revolution from above
1877	Satsu-ma Rebellion
1881	Promise of constitution
1889	Meiji Constitution promulgated
1890	First Diet session

Imperial Japan

1894–1895	Sino-Japanese War
1900	Seiyūkai formed
1904–1905	Russo-Japanese War
1910	Korea annexed

Era of Party Government

1918	Hara becomes prime minister
1924	Katō becomes prime minister
1925	Universal manhood suffrage passed

Militarism

1931	Japan takes Manchuria
1937	War with China
1941	Japan attacks Pearl Harbor
1945	Japan surrenders

disagreed. When Japanese troops skirmished with Russian troops on the Mongolian border in the summer of 1939, sentiment rose in favor of an alliance with Germany, but then Germany "betrayed" Japan by signing a nonaggression pact with the Soviet Union. Japan tried to improve its relations with the United States, but America insisted that Japan get out of China. By the late spring of 1940, German victories in Europe again led military leaders in Japan to favor an alliance with Germany.

Japan signed the Tripartite Pact with three objectives in mind: to isolate the United States, to take over the Southeast Asian colonies of the countries defeated by Germany in Europe, and to improve its relations with the Soviet Union. The last objective was reached when Japan signed a neutrality pact with the Soviet Union in April 1941. Two months later, Germany attacked the Soviet Union without consulting Japan and then asked Japan to attack the Soviet Union in the east. Japan waited and, when the German advance was stopped short of Moscow, decided to honor its neutrality pact with the Soviet Union and turn south. This effectively ended Japan's participation in the Axis. Yet instead of deflecting American criticism as intended, the pact, by linking Japan to Germany, led to a hardening of America's position on China.

The third fateful decision was to go to war with the United States. In June 1940, following Germany's defeat of France, Japanese troops had moved into northern French Indochina. When Japanese troops took southern Indochina in July 1941, the United States embargoed all exports to Japan; this cut Japanese oil imports by 90 percent. Japan's military argued that oil reserves would last only two years and pressed for the capture of the oil-rich Dutch East Indies. But it was too dangerous to move against Dutch and British colonies in Southeast Asia with the United States in the Philippines. The navy, therefore, planned a preemptive strike against the United States, and on December 7, 1941, it bombed Pearl Harbor. The Japanese decision for war wagered Japan's land-based airpower, shorter supply lines, and what it saw as greater willpower against American productivity. At the Imperial Conference where the all-or-nothing decision was taken, the navy's chief of staff compared the war with the United States to a dangerous operation that might save the life of a critically ill patient.

JAPANESE MILITARISM AND GERMAN NAZISM

HOW WAS Japan similar to and different from Germany during this period?

Some features of Japanese militarism afford an interesting comparison with Nazi Germany. Both countries were late developers with elitist, academic bureaucracies and strong military traditions. Both had patriarchal family systems and relatively new parliamentary systems. Both tried to solve the economic problems created by the Great Depression with territorial expansion. Both had modernized their military services, schools, governments, and communications to support authoritarian regimes, but their values were not sufficiently modern or democratic to resist antiparliamentary forces.

The differences between the two countries are also striking. Japan was more homogeneous than Germany. It had no Catholic–Protestant split, no Junker class, and no significant socialist movement. Japan did not suffer from inflation and the Depression did not decimate its middle class. In Germany, parliament ruled, and the Nazis had to win an election to come to power. Japan's Diet was weaker. Control of the government was taken away from the Seiyūkai and Minseitō even while they continued to win elections.

Tōjō Hideki (1884–1948), prime minister at the time of the attack on Pearl Harbor in 1941 and one of the chief figures in the rise of Japanese militarism.

What happened to Tōjō Hideki after Pearl Harbor?

The process by which the two countries went to war was also different. The Nazis created a mass party and a totalitarian state and then declared war. In Japan, there was neither a mass party nor a single group of leaders in continuous control of the government. It was not the totalitarian state that made war as much as it was war that made the state totalitarian—creating a nationalism so intense that university students became suicide (*kamikaze*) pilots after the outbreak of hostilities.

The Allies compared General Tōjō Hideki (1884–1948), Japan's prime minister, with Hitler. However, although Nazi authority survived until Hitler died in a Berlin bunker, General Tōjō was removed from office when American planes began to bomb Japan in 1944. The military continued to prosecute the war, but when the Imperial Conference on August 14, 1945, divided three to three over the Allied ultimatum demanding unconditional surrender, the emperor broke the deadlock, saying that the unendurable must be endured. It was the only important decision that he had ever been allowed to make.

MODERN CHINA (1839–1949)

China's modern century was not the century in which it became modern but the one in which it encountered the modern West. Its first phase, from the Opium War to the fall of the Qing or Manchu Dynasty (1911), was little affected by Western impact. Only during the decade before 1911 did the Confucian tradition begin to be discarded in favor of new ideas from the West. The second phase, from 1911 to the establishment of a communist state in 1949, was a time of turmoil: decades of warlord rule, war with Japan, and then four years of civil war.

CLOSE OF MANCHU RULE

WHAT WERE the most serious threats to Manchu rule in the nineteenth century?

THE OPIUM WAR

The eighteenth-century three-country trade—British goods to India, Indian cotton to China, and Chinese tea to Britain—was in China's favor. The silver flowing into China spurred the monetization of Chinese markets. Then the British replaced cotton with Indian opium, and by the 1820s the balance of trade was reversed.

To check the evil of opium and the outflow of silver, the Chinese government banned opium in 1836. In 1839, the government sent Lin Zexu (1785–1850) to Guangzhou (Canton) to superintend the ban. He destroyed a six-month supply of opium belonging to foreign merchants, leading to a confrontation with the British.

War broke out in November 1839. Chinese troops, with their antiquated weapons, were ineffective. The war ended in August 1842 with the Treaty of Nanjing, the first of the "unequal treaties." The treaty gave Britain the island of Hong Kong and a huge indemnity. It also opened five ports: Fuzhou, Guangzhou, Ningpo, Shanghai, and Xiamen (Amoy). British merchants and their families could reside in the ports and engage in trade; Britain could appoint a consul for each city; and British residents within China were subject to British, not Chinese, law. In 1844, similar treaties followed with the United States and France.

After the treaty, Chinese imports of opium increased, but other kinds of trade did not grow rapidly. Western merchants blamed Chinese officials; Chinese authorities were incensed by the export of coolies to work in Cuba and Peru. A second war broke out in 1856, and the British captured Beijing in 1860. New treaties provided for indemnities,

◆◆─[Read the Document

William Hunter, "Description of European Factories in Guangzhou," 1824
at **myhistorylab.com**

◆◆─[Read the Document

The Treaty of Nanjing, 1842
at **myhistorylab.com**

The Opium War, 1840. Armed Chinese junks were no match for British warships. The war ended in 1842 with the Treaty of Nanjing.

How did the Opium War demonstrate Western military superiority?

the opening of eleven new ports, the stationing of foreign diplomats in Beijing, the propagation of Christianity anywhere in China, and the legalization of the opium trade.

Meanwhile, the Russians were encroaching on China's northern frontier. In 1858, China ceded the north bank of the Amur to Russia, and in 1860, China gave Russia the Maritime Province between the Ussuri River and the Pacific.

REBELLIONS AGAINST THE MANCHU

A more immediate threat to Manchu rule than foreign gunboats were the Taiping, Nian, and Muslim Rebellions that convulsed China between 1850 and 1873 (see Map 27–2 on page 712). The torment and suffering they caused were unparalleled. Estimates of those killed during the twenty years of the **Taiping Rebellion** range from 20 to 30 million. Adding in losses due to other rebellions, droughts, and floods, China's population dropped by 60 million and did not recover to pre-rebellion levels until almost the end of the dynasty in 1912.

The Taipings were begun by Hong Xiuquan (1814–1864). Influenced by Protestant tracts, Hong announced that he was the younger brother of Jesus and that God had told him to rid China of Manchus, Confucians, Daoists, and Buddhists. Like earlier rebels, the Taipings combined moral reform, religious fervor, and a vision of egalitarian society. The Taipings were soon joined by peasants, miners, and workers. Fighting spread until the Taipings controlled most of the Yangzi basin and had entered sixteen of the eighteen Chinese provinces. Their army numbered close to a million.

The movement had several weaknesses, most notably poor education among the leadership that prevented them from governing effectively. Many Taiping ideals remained unfulfilled; for example, land was not redistributed.

Other rebellions were of lesser note but longer duration. The Nian, north of the Taipings along the Huai River, were organized in secret societies and raided the countryside. Eventually they built an army, collected taxes, and ruled 100,000 square miles. Muslims revolted in the southwest and the northwest; one rebel set up an Islamic kingdom with himself as sultan. All these rebellions took advantage of the weakened state of the dynasty and occurred in areas that had few officials and no Qing military units.

Against the rebellions, the imperial forces proved helpless, so in 1852 the court sent Zeng Guofan (1811–1872) to south-central China to organize a local army. Zeng saw the Manchu government, of which he was an elite member, as the upholder of morality and the social order. He recruited members of the gentry as officers. They were

Taiping Rebellion
A nineteenth-century revolt against China's Manchu Dynasty that was inspired by quasi-Christian ideas and that led to enormous suffering and destruction before its collapse in 1868.

((•—[**Hear** the **Audio**
China at **myhistorylab.com**

QUICK REVIEW

Rebellions
- Taiping: Led by Hong Xiuquan (1814–1864), the Taiping assembled an army of close to a million men
- Nian: Located along the Huai River, the Nian came to control a 100,000-square-mile area
- Muslim rebellions: Occurred in the southwest and northwest, areas where China had few officials and little military presence

MAP 27–2.   The Taiping, Nian, and Muslim Rebellions.   Between 1850 and 1873 China was wracked by rebellions that almost ended the Manchu Dynasty. The dynasty was saved by Chinese "gentry armies."

How did these rebellions influence Chinese history?

self-strengthening

A movement attempting to restore dynastic power by adopting Western technological innovations while retaining traditional Confucian power structures.

Between 1850 and 1864, China was wracked by a great civil war between the Taiping rebels and the gentry-led militia of the Qing government. The victory of the latter delayed the collapse of the Qing Dynasty until 1912. The scene above shows troops arrayed in battle formation.

How did rebellions help the Manchus to survive?

Confucian and, as landlords, had the most to lose from rebel rule. They recruited soldiers from their local areas and stopped the Taipings' advance.

In 1860, when the British and French occupied Beijing, a reform government began internal changes, adopted a policy of cooperation with Western powers, and put Zeng in charge of suppressing all the rebellions. The Taipings collapsed when Nanjing was captured in 1864. The Nian were suppressed by 1868 and the Muslim rebellion was put down five years later. Scholar-officials, relying on local gentry, had saved the dynasty.

SELF-STRENGTHENING AND DECLINE (1874–1895)

Chinese resiliency in the two decades after the suppression of the rebellions was impressive. But if we compare China's progress with that of Japan, then China during the same decades looks almost moribund. China was relatively weaker at the end of the period of **self-strengthening** than at the start.

China's inability to act effectively is explained partly by the situation at the court. Prince Gong (1833–1898) and the empress dowager Cixi (1835–1908) were coregents for the young emperor. Prince Gong was eager to exchange ideas with foreigners, but he was outmaneuvered by the empress dowager and was ousted in 1884. The empress dowager had produced the only male child of the former emperor, and her single goal was power. She forged a court just able to survive but too weak to govern effectively.

The most vital figures during these decades were a handful of able governors-general. Each had an army and was in charge of two or three provinces. They were loyal to the dynasty that they had restored and were allowed great autonomy. The governors-general mobilized the gentry again, this time for rebuilding. They set up refugee centers, reduced taxes in the devastated Yangzi valley, reclaimed lands gone to waste, began water-control projects, and built granaries. By the early 1890s, well-being had been restored. Their second task was self-strengthening—the adoption of Western arms and technology. The Chinese built arsenals and shipyards, a telegraph company, railways, and cotton mills. The formula applied in running these enterprises was "official supervision and merchant operation." Major decisions were made by scholar-officials, but day-to-day operations were left to merchants.

The **treaty ports**, of which there were fourteen by the 1860s, were little islands of privilege and security under the rule of foreign consuls, where capital was safe from confiscation, trade was free, and "squeeze" (extortion by officials) was minimal. Foreign companies naturally located in these ports, as well as some Chinese merchants. Well into the twentieth century, the foreign concessions (treaty-port lands leased in perpetuity by foreigners) remained the vital sector of China's modern economy.

Under the low tariffs mandated by the treaties, Chinese industries had little protection from imports. Native cotton spinning was almost destroyed by imports of yarn. Chinese tea lost ground to Indian tea and Chinese silk to Japanese silk. China found few products to export. The level of foreign trade stayed low, and China's interior markets were affected only slightly.

By the 1870s, foreign powers had reached an accommodation with China. They counted on the court to uphold the treaties; in return, they became a prop for the dynasty. By 1900, for example, the court's revenues from customs fees were larger than those from any other source. The fees were collected by the Maritime Customs Service, an efficient and honest treaty-port institution.

THE BORDERLANDS: THE NORTHWEST, VIETNAM, AND KOREA

China's other foreign relations were with fringe lands that China claimed by right of past conquest or as tributaries. During the late nineteenth century, China's self-image as a universal empire was strengthened in the northwest but was dealt a fatal blow in Vietnam and Korea.

In the northwest, China confronted tsarist Russia. Conservatives at the Manchu court ordered Zuo Zongtang, who had suppressed Muslim rebels within

The Empress Dowager Cixi (1835–1908) sits upon a throne. The empress dowager manipulated the levers of power at the Manchu court in Beijing. Historians have long criticized the empress dowager as despotic, greedy, and power-hungry, though some believe this criticism is unfair.

Do you think a male leader in an equivalent position would be subject to the same criticisms as Cixi?

treaty ports
Chinese ports ruled by foreign consuls where foreigners enjoyed commercial privileges and immunity from Chinese laws.

The Bund. After the Opium War, Shanghai became a treaty port in 1842 and foreign settlements arose along the Huangpu River, north of the old walled city. British and other companies built offices along the river's muddy waterfront, which they called the "Bund"—an Anglo-Indian term derived from "band," the Urdu word for embankment. Before World War II, oceangoing ships docked along the Bund in the heart of commercial Shanghai. Today, this stretch of the river is fronted by the Zhongshan Road. On one side are banks, insurance companies, and hotels; on the other, a park. Ships no longer dock.

What kinds of people and activities can you identify in this photograph?

The French in Vietnam. Arrival in Saigon of Paul Beau (1857–1927), governor general of Indochina, 1902–1907, from "Le Petit Journal," November 1902.

How are the Vietnamese depicted in this illustration? How do they compare with the way the French are depicted?

View the Image

American Cartoon on Western Powers Carving up China at **myhistorylab.com**

QUICK REVIEW

Korea in the Late Nineteenth Century

◆ Tributary of China

◆ The Korean state was weak in the last decades of the nineteenth century

◆ After 1876, Japan contended with China for influence in Korea

China, to suppress a Muslim leader who had founded an independent state in the Tarim basin. By 1878 Zuo's army had regained the area, which was subsequently renamed Xinjiang, or the "New Territories." A treaty signed with Russia in 1881 also restored most of the Ili region in western Mongolia to Chinese control. These victories strengthened court conservatives who wished to take a stronger stance toward the West.

To the south, Vietnam had retained its independence from China since 935 and saw itself as an independent state. China simply saw Vietnam as a tributary. During the 1840s, the Vietnamese emperor moved to reduce French influences and suppress Christianity. The French responded by seizing Saigon and Cochin China in 1859, establishing a protectorate over Cambodia in 1864, and taking Hanoi in 1882. China in 1883 sent troops to aid its tributary, but after a two-year war with France, China was forced to abandon its claims to Vietnam. By 1893, France had brought together Vietnam, Cambodia, and Laos to form the Federation of Indochina, which remained a French colony until 1940.

Unlike Vietnam, Korea saw itself as a tributary of China on Chinese terms. During the last decades of the Choson Dynasty (1392–1910), the Korean state was weak. It hung on to power in part by enforcing a policy of seclusion. Its only foreign ties were with China and Japan. In 1876, Japan "opened" Korea to international relations, using much the same tactics that Perry had used against Japan. Japan then contended with China for influence in Korea.

In 1893 a popular religious sect unleashed a rebellion against the Seoul government. China sent troops to help suppress the rebellion, but Japan sent more, and in 1894 war broke out between China and Japan. Japan won handily thanks to the discipline and the superior tactics of the Japanese units. Defeat by Japan convinced many in China that basic changes were inevitable.

FROM DYNASTY TO WARLORDISM (1895–1926)

WHO WERE the key figures in the revolution of 1911?

Confucian officials ruled China. Their intellectual formation was highly resistant to change. For most, the foreign crises of the nineteenth century were "coastal phenomena" that, like bee stings, were painful for a time but then forgotten. Few officials realized the magnitude of the foreign threat.

China's defeat by Japan, a nation for which China had little regard, came as a shock. China responded with a new wave of reform proposals. The most influential thinker was Kang Youwei (1858–1927), who described China as "enfeebled" and "soundly asleep atop a pile of kindling." For this state of affairs, Kang blamed the "conservatives." They did not understand that Confucius himself had been a reformer who had invented the idea of a past golden age to persuade the rulers of his own age to adopt his ideas. All of history, Kang continued, was evolutionary, an advance from absolute monarchy to constitutional monarchy to democracy. Kang's reinterpretation of the essentials of Confucianism removed a major barrier to the entry of Western ideas into China.

In 1898 the emperor himself became sympathetic to Kang's ideas and launched "one hundred days of reform." He took as his models Peter the Great (r. 1682–1725) and the Japanese Meiji emperor (r. 1867–1912). Edicts were issued to reform China's schools, railroads, police, laws, military, bureaucracy, post offices, and examination system. But conservative resistance was nationwide. At court, the empress dowager regained control and ended the reforms. Kang and most of his associates fled to Japan.

The response of the Western powers to China's 1895 defeat has been described as "carving up the melon." Each nation defined a sphere of interest—usually a leasehold with railway rights and special commercial privileges. Russia took Port Arthur; Germany, Shandong; Britain, the New Territories at Hong Kong. New ports and cities were opened to foreign trade. The United States, busy acquiring the Philippines and Guam, was in a weaker position in China, so it enunciated an "open-door" policy: equal commercial opportunities for all nations and the preservation of China's territorial integrity.

There was in China at this time a religious society called the **Boxers**. The Chinese name translates more literally as "Righteous and Harmonious Fists." The Boxers had rituals, spells, and amulets that they believed made them impervious to bullets. They rebelled first in Shandung in 1898, and, gaining court support, entered Beijing in 1900. The court declared war on the treaty powers, and there followed a two-month siege of the foreign legation quarter. Pent-up resentments against decades of foreign encroachments fueled support for the rebellion. Eventually an international force captured Beijing, won a huge indemnity, and obtained the right to maintain permanent military forces in the capital. The Russians occupied Manchuria.

The defeat of the Boxers convinced even conservative Chinese leaders of the futility of clinging to old ways. A more powerful reform movement began with the empress dowager in its vanguard. But the dynasty could not control the movement.

Educational reforms began in 1901. Women were admitted to newly formed schools. In place of Confucianism, instructors taught science, mathematics, geography, and an anti-imperialist version of Chinese history. Western doctrines, such as classical economics, liberalism, socialism, anarchism, and social Darwinism, were introduced. By 1906, there were 8,000 Chinese students in Japan, which became a hotbed of Chinese reformist and revolutionary societies.

Military reforms were begun by Yuan Shikai (1859–1916), whose New Army drew on Japanese and Western models. Young men from gentry families, spurred by patriotism, joined the New Army as officers. Their loyalty was to their commanders and their country, not to the dynasty.

Political reforms began with a modification of the examination system to accommodate Western learning. Then in 1905 the examination system was abolished altogether. Henceforth, officials would be directly recruited from the graduates of Western-model schools and those who had studied abroad. Provincial assemblies were formed in 1909, and a consultative assembly with some elected members was established in Beijing in 1910. These representative bodies became forums for the expression of interests at odds with those of the dynasty.

In sum, during the first decade of the twentieth century the three vital components of the imperial system—Confucian education, the bureaucracy, and the gentry—were changed in ways that a few decades earlier would have been unimaginable. These

Boxers

A nationalistic Chinese religious society that attacked foreigners and their encroachments on China in the late nineteenth century.

QUICK REVIEW

Post-Boxer Rebellion Reforms

- Education: women schooled, new subjects introduced, study in Japan
- Military: New Army modeled on Japan and West, young gentry officers
- Politics: provincial assemblies, consultative assembly

changes sparked the 1911–1912 revolution, which began with an uprising against a government plan to nationalize railways. The players were:

1. Gentry who stood to lose their investments in the railways.

2. Qing military commanders, who broke with Beijing, declaring their provinces independent.

3. Sun Zhongshan (or Sun Yat-sen) (1866–1925), a republican revolutionary. Born a peasant, he had learned English and become a Christian in Hawaii, studied medicine in Guangzhou and Hong Kong, organized the Revolutionary Alliance in Tokyo in 1905, and was also associated with the 1912 Nationalist Party.

4. Yuan Shikai, who was made a commander to preserve the dynasty. Instead, he arranged for the last child emperor to abdicate, for Sun to step aside, and declared himself president of the new Republic of China.

•••[**Read** the **Document**

Long Yu, The Abdication Decree, 1912
at **myhistorylab.com**

The Nationalist Party won the election called in 1913. Yuan thereupon had its leader assassinated, crushed military governors who supported them, and forced Sun Zhongshan and other revolutionaries to flee again to Japan. Yuan proclaimed a new dynasty with himself as emperor. The idea of another dynasty, however, met opposition from all quarters. Yuan died in June 1916. China then fell into the hands of warlord armies. The years until the late 1920s were a time of agony for the Chinese people. Yet they were also a time of intense intellectual ferment.

CULTURAL AND IDEOLOGICAL FERMENT: THE MAY FOURTH MOVEMENT

WHY WAS Marxism-Leninism so appealing to Chinese intellectuals?

A period of freedom and vigorous experimentation with new doctrines began in 1914 and extended into the 1920s. It is called the May Fourth Movement because on that date in 1919, thousands of students in Beijing protested the settlement at Versailles that awarded former German possessions in Shandung to Japan. This kind of nationalist fervor also caused leading thinkers to judge ideas in terms of their value in solving China's problems. This era of intellectual excitement corresponded almost exactly with the period of warlord rule—which afforded a breathing space between the ideological constraints of the old dynasty and those of the Nationalist and Communist eras that would follow.

Beijing was the center of May Fourth era thought. Cai Yuanpei (1868–1940), the chancellor of Beijing University, and Chen Duxiu (1879–1942), dean of letters, made Beijing University a haven for scholars who had returned from study in Japan or the West. In his magazine *New Youth*, Chen Duxiu called for a generation of progressive, cosmopolitan, and scientific youth who would uphold the values of liberty, equality, and fraternity. China's greatest modern writer, Lu Xun (1881–1936), published *A Madman's Diary* in *New Youth* in 1918. Lu Xun's message was that only the vision of a madman could truly comprehend an abnormal and inhumane society.

May Fourth Movement ideas quickly spread to the rest of China, especially its urban centers. Protest demonstrations against imperialist privilege broke out. Nationalism and anti-imperialist sentiment were stronger than liberalism, although most leaders spoke of democracy. Only members of an older generation of reformers, appalled by the slaughter of World War I and what they saw as Western materialism, advocated a return to traditional philosophies.

At the onset of China's intellectual revolution, Marx's critique of capitalist society did not fit Chinese conditions. More persuasive was the anarchism of Peter

Kropotkin (1842–1921), who taught that mutual aid was as much a part of evolution as the struggle for survival. But after the Russian Revolution of 1917, Marxism-Leninism entered China. The Leninist definition of imperialism as the last crisis stage of capitalism put the blame for China's ills on the West and offered "feudal" China the possibility of leapfrogging over capitalism to socialism. Marxist study groups formed in Beijing and other cities. In 1919, a student from Hunan, Mao Zedong, who had worked in the Beijing University library, returned to Changsha to form a study group. The Chinese Communist Party (CCP) was formed in Shanghai in 1921; Zhou Enlai (1898–1976) formed a similar group in Paris the same year. The numbers involved were small but grew steadily.

NATIONALIST CHINA

GUOMINDANG UNIFICATION OF CHINA AND THE NANJING DECADE (1927–1937)

Sun Zhongshan had fled to Japan during the 1913–1916 rule by Yuan Shikai. He returned to Guangzhou in 1916, but he was a poor organizer, and his **Guomindang (GMD)**—or Nationalist Party—made little headway. Sun began to receive Soviet support in 1923. He reorganized his party on the Leninist model with an executive committee on top of a national party congress, provincial and county organizations, and local party cells.

Sun enunciated "three principles of the people": nationality, livelihood, and rights. Sun's nationalism was directed against Western imperialism. Livelihood was defined in terms of equalizing landholdings and nationalizing major industries. By "people's rights" Sun meant democracy, although he argued that it must be preceded by a preparatory period of single-party dictatorship. Sun sent his loyal lieutenant Jiang Jieshi (Chiang Kai-shek) (1887–1975) to the Soviet Union for study. Jiang returned with a cadre of Russian advisers and established a military academy at Huangpu south of Guangzhou in 1924. Sun died in 1925. By 1926, the Huangpu Academy had graduated several thousand officers, and the GMD army numbered almost a hundred thousand. The GMD had become the major political force in China; its leadership was divided between a left wing and a right wing.

The growth of the party was spurred by changes within Chinese society. Industries arose in the cities. Labor unions were organized. New ventures were begun outside the treaty ports. A politically conscious middle class developed. Another important sociopolitical element was China's several million students. In May 1925, students demonstrated in Shanghai. Police in the international settlement fired on the demonstrators. The incident inflamed national and anti-imperialist feelings. Strikes and boycotts of foreign goods were called throughout China.

Under these conditions the CCP also grew and was influential in student organizations, labor unions, and even within the GMD, which Sun had permitted CCP members to join as individuals.

WHO WAS Jiang Jieshi?

Guomindang (GMD)
China's Nationalist Party, founded by Sun Zhongshan.

Jiang Jieshi (or Chiang Kai-shek, 1887–1975), as a young revolutionary officer, stands behind Sun Zhongshan (or Sun Yat-sen, 1866–1925), father of China's 1911–1912 Republican Revolution, taken around 1925.
What were Sun Zhongshan's core beliefs?

By 1926, Jiang Jieshi felt ready to march against the warlords. He worried about the growing communist strength, however, and before setting off he ousted the Soviet advisers and CCP members from the GMD offices in Guangzhou. The march north began in July. By the spring of 1927, Jiang's army had reached the Yangzi, defeating warlord armies as it advanced (see Map 27–3). After entering Shanghai in April 1927, Jiang carried out a sweeping purge of the CCP, killing many. Surviving CCP members fled to the mountainous border region of Hunan and Jiangxi to the southwest and established the "Jiangxi Soviet." Jiang's army took Beijing and gained the nominal submission of most northern Chinese warlords during 1928. Most foreign powers recognized the GMD regime in Nanjing as the government of China.

Jiang believed in military force. He was unimaginative, strict, and incorruptible. Jiang venerated Sun Zhongshan and his three "people's principles." But where Sun was a revolutionary, Jiang was conservative and, though a Methodist, often appealed to Confucian values. The New Life Movement begun by Jiang in 1934 was an attempt

MAP 27–3. The Northern Expeditions of the Guomindang. These expeditions, from 1926 to 1928, unified most of China under the Nationalist (Guomindang) government of Jiang Jieshi, inaugurating the Nanjing decade. Warlord armies continued to hold power on the periphery.

What were the key weaknesses of the Guomindang?

to revitalize these values. Jiang's power rested on the army, the party, and the bureaucracy. The army was dominated by the Huangpu clique, which was loyal to Jiang, and by officers trained in Japan. After 1927, German advisers reorganized Jiang's army along German lines with a general staff system. The larger part of GMD revenues went to the military, which was expanded into a modernized force of three hundred thousand. Huangpu graduates also controlled the secret military police and used it against communists and any others who opposed the government. The GMD was a dictatorship under a central committee. Jiang became president of the party in 1938.

The densely populated central and lower Yangzi provinces were the area of GMD strength. The party, however, was unable to control outlying areas occupied by warlords, communists, and the Japanese. Warlords ruled some areas until 1949. In 1931, Jiang attacked the Jiangxi Soviet. In 1934, the communists were forced to flee to the southwest and then to Shaanxi province in northwestern China in the epic **Long March**. During this march, Mao Zedong wrested control of the CCP from the Moscow-trained, urban-oriented leaders and established his unorthodox view that a Leninist party could base itself on the peasantry. (See Map 27–4.)

Long March
The flight of the Chinese communists from their Nationalist foes to northwest China in 1934.

MAP 27–4. The Long March, 1934–1935. Arrows trace the Chinese communists' "Long March," from Jiangxi Soviet to Yan'an in northwestern China.

How did the Communists gain power?

The Japanese had held special rights in Manchuria since the Russo-Japanese War of 1905. When Jiang's march north and the rise of Chinese nationalism threatened the Japanese position, Japan's forces in Manchuria engineered a military coup and established a puppet state in 1932. In the years that followed, Japanese army units moved south as far as the Great Wall. Chinese national sentiment demanded that Jiang resist, but Jiang, well aware of the disparity between his armies and those of Japan, felt that the internal unification of China should take precedence. On a visit to Xian in 1936 Jiang was captured by a northern warlord and held until he agreed to join with the CCP in a united front against Japan. In the following year, however, a full-scale war with Japan broke out, and China's situation again changed.

WAR AND REVOLUTION (1937–1949)

In 1937 the GMD controlled most of China and was recognized as its government, whereas the CCP survivors of the Long March had just begun to rebuild their strength in arid Shaanxi, a remote area beyond the reach of Jiang's army. But by 1949 CCP forces had conquered China, including border areas never under GMD rule, and Jiang and the GMD had fled to Taiwan. What had happened?

The war with Japan began in July 1937 as an unplanned clash at Beijing and then quickly spread. Beijing and Tianjin fell to Japan within a month, Shanghai was attacked in August, and Nanjing fell in December. During the following year, the Japanese took Guangzhou and set up puppet regimes in Beijing and Nanjing. In 1940, the leader of the left wing of the GMD and many of his associates joined the Japanese puppet government. Japan proclaimed its "New Order in East Asia." It expected Jiang to submit. Instead, in 1938 he relocated his capital to Chongqing, far to the west, and was joined by thousands of Chinese students and professors.

Jiang's stubborn resistance won admiration from all sides. But the withdrawal to Chongqing cut the GMD off from most of the Chinese population, programs for modernization ended, and the GMD's former tax revenues were lost. Crippling inflation exacerbated corruption and destroyed morale. The United States sent advisers and military equipment to strengthen Jiang's forces after the start of the Pacific War. Jiang, however, did not want to fight the Japanese but wanted instead to husband his forces for a postwar confrontation with the communists. The surge of anti-Japanese patriotism was not converted to popular support for the GMD.

For the communists headquartered at Yan'an, the Japanese occupation was an opportunity. While compromising with other political and social groups, the party strengthened itself internally. Party membership expanded from 40,000 in 1937 to 1.2 million in 1945. Schools were established in Yan'an to train party cadres. Orthodoxy was maintained by a rectification campaign. Those tainted by impure tendencies were made to repent at public meetings. Mao's thought was supreme. To the Chinese at large, Mao represented himself as the successor to Sun Zhongshan, but within the Communist Party he presented himself as a theoretician in the line of Marx (1818–1883), Engels (1820–1895), Lenin (1870–1924), and Stalin (1879–1953).

Mao Zedong (1893–1976) at his cave headquarters in Shaanxi province during World War II. He wears a padded winter jacket and writes with a Chinese brush. On his desk are the *Collected Works of Lu Hsun*.

What innovation did Mao introduce to Marxist-Leninist thought?

Whereas the GMD ruled through officials and often in cooperation with local landlords, the communists learned to operate at the grassroots level. They infiltrated Japanese-controlled areas and also penetrated some GMD organizations and military units. CCP armies were built up from 90,000 in 1937 to 900,000 in 1945. These armies were supplemented by a rural people's militia and by guerrilla forces.

The Yan'an leadership and its party, army, and mass organizations possessed a cohesion, determination, and high morale that were lacking in Chongqing. But the strength of the Chinese communists as of 1945 should not be overstated. When the war in the Pacific ended in 1945, China's future was unclear. Even the Soviet Union recognized the GMD as the government of China and expected it to win the postwar struggle. The Allies directed Japanese armies to surrender to the GMD forces in 1945. The United States flew Jiang's troops to key eastern cities. His armies were by then three times the size of the communists' forces and far better equipped.

A civil war broke out immediately. Efforts by U.S. General George Marshall (1880–1959) to mediate were futile. Until the summer of 1947, GMD armies were victorious, even capturing Yan'an. But the tide turned in July as CCP armies went on the offensive in north China. In January 1949, Beijing and Tianjin fell. A few months later all of China was in communist hands. Many Chinese fled with Jiang to Taiwan or escaped to Hong Kong. In China apprehension was mixed with anticipation. The disciplined, well-behaved soldiers of the People's Liberation Army were certainly a contrast to those of the GMD. As villages were liberated, lands were taken from landlords and given to the landless. In the cities crowds welcomed the CCP troops as liberators. The feeling was widespread that the future of China was once again in the hands of the Chinese.

CHRONOLOGY

MODERN CHINA

Close of Manchu Rule

1839–1842	Opium War
1850–1873	Taiping and other rebellions
1870s–1880s	Self-strengthening movement
1894–1895	Sino-Japanese War
1898	One hundred days of reform
1898–1900	Boxer Rebellion
1911-1912	Republican revolution overthrows Qing Dynasty

Warlordism

1912–1916	Yuan Shikai president of Republic of China
1916–1928	Warlord era
1919	May Fourth incident

Nationalist China

1924	Founding of Huangpu Military Academy
1926–1928	Jiang's march north and Nationalist reunification of China
1928–1937	Nanjing decade
1934–1935	Chinese communists' Long March to Yan'an
1937–1945	War with Japan
1945–1949	Civil war and the establishment of the People's Republic of China

SUMMARY

 WHAT ROLE did Chōshū and Satsu-ma play in the overthrow of Tokugawa rule?

Overthrow of the Tokugawa *Bakufu* (1853–1868). The Tokugawa regime collapsed only fifteen years after Perry's arrival in 1853. Chōshū and Satsu-ma led diplomatic efforts to unify the *bakufu* and the court between 1861 and 1863; the two domains fought against each other until 1866. Then they united and led the overthrow of the *bakufu*. *page 697*

 WHAT POWERS did the Meiji Constitution give to the emperor?

Building the Meiji State (1868–1890). The new Meiji government began sweeping Westernizing reforms in every field. Power was centralized, land taxes were reformed, political parties were created, and the Meiji Constitution was promulgated. *page 699*

 WHY DID Japan set out to build a modern economy?

Growth of a Modern Economy. The Japanese government hoped a modern economy would help it build military strength. Reforms spurred economic growth. *page 702*

 HOW DID political parties develop in Japan?

The Politics of Imperial Japan (1890–1945). The emperor became the unifying symbol for traditional and conservative thinkers. The Diet (Japan's Parliament)

became the focus for progressives and liberals. A shifting balance between conservatives and liberals ensued, with parliamentary democracy making gains into the 1920s. But then the Great Depression and a crisis in Manchuria opened the way for the rise of militarism in the 1930s. *page 704*

 HOW WAS Japan similar to and different from Germany during this period?

Japanese Militarism and German Nazism. There were notable similarities between Japan and Germany, particularly after the Great Depression as each expanded its territory. But there were also differences, beginning with Japan's greater homogeneity. *page 709*

 WHAT WERE the most serious threats to Manchu rule in the nineteenth century?

Close of Manchu Rule. The Opium War (1839–1842) posed little threat to the Qing heartland. Far more serious were the Taiping and other rebellions. Gentry armies succeeded in suppressing these rebellions. Not until the very end of the century did the Chinese begin substantial Westernizing reforms—and by then it was too late for the dynasty. *page 710*

 WHO WERE the key figures in the revolution of 1911?

From Dynasty to Warlordism (1895–1926). The Boxer Rebellion convinced even conservatives that fundamental reforms were needed. The gentry and military commanders were early leaders in rebellion. After the Qing fell in 1912, China was ruled by regional warlords. *page 714*

 WHY WAS Marxism-Leninism so appealing to Chinese intellectuals?

Cultural and Ideological Ferment: The May Fourth Movement. The newly entering flood of Western ideas fed a growing nationalism. The Marxist critique of capitalism did not apply to China, but Marxism-Leninism gained adherents. *page 716*

WHO WAS Jiang Jieshi?

Nationalist China. Nationalism permeated the Guomindang (or Nationalist) army under Jiang Jieshi; it lent legitimacy to the army's march north and to the establishment of the Nanjing government. Then Japan invaded and occupied areas on which the Guomindang had depended. The communists built up their army, extended their influence, and won the civil war that ended in 1949. *page 717*

KEY TERMS

Boxers (p. 715)
Diet (p. 701)
Guomindang (GMD)
(GWO-MIHN-DONG)
(p. 717)
Long March (p. 719)
Meiji Restoration (MAY-JEE)
(p. 699)

self-strengthening (p. 712)
Taiping Rebellion
(TEYE-PIHNG) (p. 711)
treaty ports (p. 713)
Tripartite Pact (p. 708)
zaibatsu **(zeye-BAHT-soo)**
(p. 702)

REVIEW QUESTIONS

1. How did the Chōshū and Satsu-ma domains become instrumental in the development of Japan's government?

2. How did political parties develop in Japan?

3. After the Meiji Restoration, what steps did Japan's leaders take to achieve their goal of "wealth and power"?

4. What were some social costs of economic development in Japan?

5. What were the strengths and weaknesses of Japan's prewar parliamentary institutions? What led to the sudden rise of militarism during the 1930s?

6. Which had the greater impact on China, the Opium War or the Taiping Rebellion?

7. How did the Qing (Manchu) Dynasty recover from the Taiping Rebellion? Why was the recovery inadequate to prevent the overthrow of the dynasty in 1912?

8. Did the May Fourth Movement prepare the way for the Nationalist revolution? The Communist revolution? Or was it incidental to both?

9. How did Marxism gain adherents in China?

10. What were Jiang Jieshi's strengths and weaknesses as a leader?

11. Compare and contrast the process of modernization in Japan and China in the twentieth century. Which country was more successful? Why?

Note: To learn more about the topics in this chapter, please turn to the Suggested Readings at the end of the book. For additional sources related to this chapter please see www.myhistorylab.com

myhistorylab Connections

Reinforce what you learned in this chapter by studying the many documents, images, maps, review tools, and videos available at **www.myhistorylab.com**

Read and Review

✓●⎯Study and Review Chapter 27

●●●⎯Read the Document *President Millard Fillmore, Letter to the Emperor of Japan, 1852, p. 697*
The Views of Ii Naosuke, 1853, p. 697
Japanese Impressions of American Culture (1860), p. 699
Emperor Meiji, The Constitution of the Empire of Japan, p. 701
Japan: The Imperial Rescript on Education, 1890, p. 701
William Hunter, "Description of European Factories in Guangzhou," 1824, p. 710
The Treaty of Nanjing, 1842, p. 710
Long Yu, The Abdication Decree, 1912, p. 716

●●●⎯View the Image *Japanese Woodcut on Perry's Arrival, p. 696*
American Cartoon on Western Powers Carving up China, p. 714

((●●⎯Hear the Audio *China, p. 711*

Research and Explore

◉⎯See the Map *Japanese Colonial Expansion to 1914, p. 705*

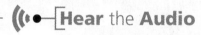

((●●⎯Hear the Audio

Hear the audio file for Chapter 27
at **www.myhistorylab.com**

28

Imperialism and World War I

((●─Hear the Audio for Chapter 28 at www.myhistorylab.com

The British Dominions Beyond the Seas:
Natives of the Greatest Empire the World
has ever known.

SPECIALLY PAINTED FOR "THE ILLUSTRATED LONDON NEWS."

(For Details, see the Key on the Opposite Page and the Appendix.)

The global British Empire dominated the nineteenth-century European imperial experience. The empire was popularized in newspapers, books, and novels, as well as in thousands of illustrations and photographs. This illustration seeks to portray the worldwide reach of the British Empire and the varied peoples whom it governed abroad and, at the same time, as seen in the caption, sought to build domestic pride in the imperial achievement. Similar illustrations could be found portraying the empires of France, Germany, the Netherlands, Belgium, and Russia.

Why did empires become attractive to European powers in the late nineteenth century?

*D*uring the second half of the nineteenth century, and especially after 1870, Europe exercised unprecedented influence and control over the rest of the world. The Americas, Australia, and New Zealand became in some ways part of the European world as great streams of European immigrants populated them. Almost all of Africa was divided among a number of European nations (see Chapter 26). Europe also imposed its economic and political power across Asia (see Map 28–1 on page 728 and Chapter 27). By the next century, European dominance had brought every part of the globe into a single world economy. Events in any corner of the world had significant effects thousands of miles away.

These developments helped foster competition and hostility among the great powers of Europe and to bring on a terrible war. The frenzy for imperial expansion that seized Europeans in the late nineteenth century did much to destroy Europe's peace and prosperity and its dominant place in the world. ■

EXPANSION OF EUROPEAN POWER AND THE "NEW IMPERIALISM"

Explosive developments in nineteenth-century science, technology, industry, agriculture, transportation, communication, and weaponry enabled a few Europeans (and Americans) to impose their will on other peoples many times their number. Westerners had institutional as well as material advantages—particularly the mobilizing power of national states and a belief in the superiority of their civilization.

WHAT WAS the New Imperialism?

725

GLOBAL PERSPECTIVE

IMPERIALISM AND THE GREAT WAR

European imperialism in the last part of the nineteenth century brought Western countries into contact with almost all the inhabited areas of the world and intensified their activity in places where they had already been interested. By the time World War I broke out, European nations had divided Africa among themselves for exploitation. The vast subcontinent of India had long been a British colony, producing primary products such as raw cotton that fed British industry. Much of China had fallen under European control, and Indochina was under French rule. The islands of the Pacific had been divided among Western powers. Much of the Middle East was under the nominal control of the Ottoman Empire, which was in its death throes and under European influence. The Monroe Doctrine made Latin America a protectorate of the United States. Japan, pushed out of its isolation, had itself become an imperial power at the expense of China and Korea. What all of the Western imperial powers, as well as Japan, had in common was a need to extract raw materials from their colonies to feed their industries. Their colonies in turn were to serve as markets for Western manufactured goods, even at the expense of indigenous manufactures, as in the case of India's ancient cloth weaving industry. This, as well as the prestige that colonies afforded, helps explain why nations were so determined to obtain and retain colonies.

The emergence of a new, powerful German state at the center of Europe upset the old balance of power and threatened the peace established in 1815. Germany's Chancellor Bismarck created a new system of alliances that preserved the peace for as long as he remained in power, but the new German emperor, William II, abandoned this policy of restraint and sought greater power and influence for his country. The result was a new system of alliances that divided Europe into two armed camps and greatly increased the chances of a general war. What began as yet another Balkan War involving the European powers became a world war. As the terrible war of 1914–1918 dragged on, the real motives that

Watch the Video
The Origins of Modern Imperialism and Colonialism at **myhistorylab.com**

New Imperialism
The extension in the late nineteenth and early twentieth centuries of Western political and economic dominance to Asia, the Middle East, and Africa.

The expansion of European influence was not new. Spain, Portugal, France, Holland, and Britain had controlled overseas territories for centuries. By the midnineteenth century, only Great Britain retained extensive overseas holdings, and there was general hostility to territorial expansion. The dominant doctrine of free trade opposed political interference in other lands. But after 1870, European states swiftly exerted control over about a fifth of the world's land area and a tenth of its population in a movement called the **New Imperialism**.

THE NEW IMPERIALISM

Imperialism can be defined as extending a nation's influence by some form of power over foreign peoples. The usual pattern of the New Imperialism was for the European nation to invest capital in a "less developed" country and thereby to transform its economy and culture. To guarantee their investments, European states would establish different degrees of political control ranging from full annexation as a colony, to protectorate status (whereby the local ruler was controlled by the dominant European state), to "spheres-of-influence" status (whereby the European state received special privileges without direct political involvement).

MOTIVES FOR THE NEW IMPERIALISM

A predominant interpretation of the motives for the New Imperialism has been economic, in the form given by the English radical economist J. A. Hobson (1858–1928) and later adapted by Lenin. Lenin saw imperialism as the final stage in capitalism's development—the pursuit of monopoly. Competition inevitably eliminates inefficient capitalists and therefore leads to monopoly. Powerful industrial and financial capitalists soon run out of profitable areas of investment in their own countries and persuade their governments to gain colonies in "less developed" countries. Here they can find higher profits from their investments, new markets for their products, and safe sources of raw materials.

QUICK REVIEW

Interpreting the New Imperialism
◆ Economic: Capitalists profit more in less developed countries
◆ Cultural: Bring civilization to backward peoples
◆ Demographic: Provide land for surplus European population
◆ Prestige: Control more territory and resources than other European nations

had driven the European powers to fight gave way to public affirmations of the principles of nationalism and self-determination. Peoples under colonial rule took seriously the public statements, and sometimes the private promises, made to secure their cooperation in supplying the war effort and sought to win their independence and nationhood. For the most part they were disappointed by the peace settlement. The establishment of the League of Nations and the system of mandates in place of open colonial rule did not change much. The British Empire inherited vast territories from the defeated German and the defunct Ottoman empires and was larger than ever. The French retained and expanded their holdings in Africa, the Pacific, and the Middle East. The Americans added to the islands they controlled in the Pacific. Japanese imperial ambitions were rewarded at the expense of China.

A glance at the new map of the world might suggest that the old imperial nations, especially Britain and France, were more powerful than ever. However, that impression would be superficial and misleading. The great western European powers paid an enormous price in lives and money for their victory in the war. Colonial peoples pressed for the rights that Western nations proclaimed as universal but denied to their colonies; influential minorities in the countries that ruled them sympathized with colonial aspirations for independence. Tension between colonies and their ruling nations was one cause of the instability in the world created by the Paris treaties of 1919.

Focus Questions

◆ Why were Western powers eager to obtain colonies?

◆ Why is World War I a turning point in history?

◆ How did World War I alter the relationship between imperial powers and colonized peoples?

The facts, however, do not support this viewpoint. Only a small part of European investments overseas went to the colonies acquired by the New Imperialism. Most of it went to older, established areas like the United States, Canada, and Australia. Colonies were not usually important markets for the great imperial nations, and it is not even clear that control of the new colonies was particularly profitable. A full understanding of the New Imperialism requires a search for other motives.

At the time, advocates of imperialism gave various justifications for it. Some argued that the advanced European nations had a duty to bring the benefits of their higher culture and superior civilization to so-called backward peoples. Religious groups demanded that Western governments support Christian missionaries politically and even militarily. Some politicians and diplomats supported imperialism as a tool of social policy. In Germany, for instance, some people suggested that imperial expansion would deflect public interest away from domestic politics and social reform. Yet Germany acquired few colonies, and such considerations played little, if any, role in its colonial policy. In Britain, Joseph Chamberlain (1836–1914), the colonial secretary from 1895 to 1903, argued for the empire as a source of profit and economic security that would finance a great program of domestic reform and welfare, but these arguments were made well after Britain had acquired most of its empire. Another apparently plausible justification for imperialism was that colonies would attract a European country's surplus population. In fact, most European emigrants went to areas their countries did not control, chiefly the Americas and Australia.

Knitting the World. The New Imperialism was not restricted to Europe. An advertisement for the Singer Sewing Machine Company, based in New York, shows a seamstress sewing together the two halves of the Western Hemisphere. By the late nineteenth century, U.S. firms like Singer created a global demand for their goods. Singer sewing machines came with instruction booklets printed in 54 languages. Of the fifteen factories making the machines, only seven were in the United States.

What was the role of the United States in the New Imperialism?

THE "SCRAMBLE FOR AFRICA"

Multiple motives were on display in the late nineteenth century, when European imperial powers expanded their economic and political control of Africa. During this so-called scramble for Africa, which occurred between the late 1870s and about 1900, the European powers sought to maximize their control of African territory and raw

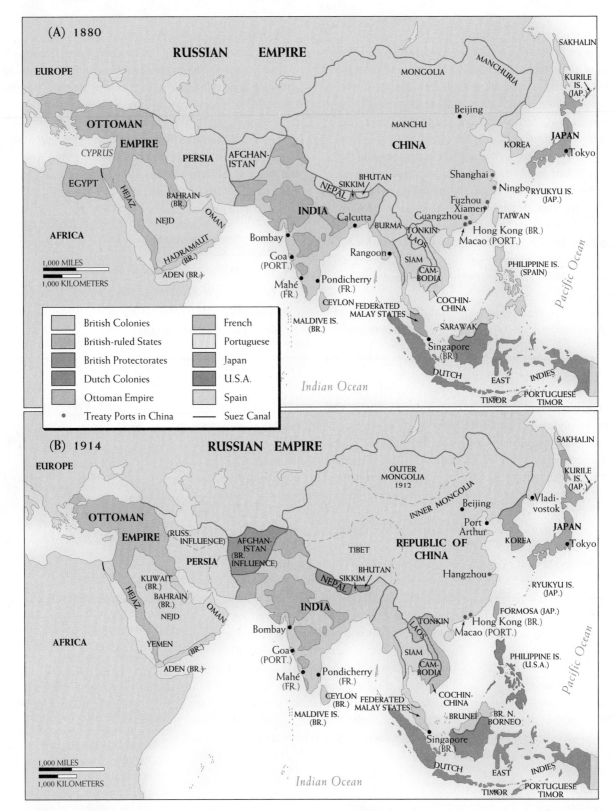

MAP 28–1. Asia, 1880–1914.   As in Africa (see Map 26–3 on page 685), the late nineteenth century saw imperialism spread widely and rapidly in Asia. Two new powers, Japan and the United States, joined the British, French, and Dutch in extending control both to islands and to the mainland and in exploiting an enfeebled China.

How did the new Japanese empire affect the balance of power in Asia?

DOCUMENT

Social Darwinism and Imperialism

One of the intellectual foundations of the New Imperialism was the doctrine of social Darwinism, a pseudoscientific application of Darwin's ideas about biology to nations and races. The impact of social Darwinism was substantial. In the selection that follows, an Englishman, Karl Pearson (1857–1936), attempts to connect concepts from evolutionary theory—the struggle for survival and the survival of the fittest—to the development of human societies.

- **HOW** does the author connect Darwin's ideas to the concept of human progress? Is it reasonable to equate biological species with human societies, races, or nations? How do the author's ideas justify imperial expansion? What arguments can you make against the author's assertions?

History shows me one way, and one way only, in which a state of civilisation has been produced, namely, the struggle of race with race, and the survival of the physically and mentally fitter race. This dependence of progress on the survival of the fitter race, terribly black as it may seem to some of you, gives the struggle for existence its redeeming features; it is the fiery crucible out of which comes the finer metal. You may hope for a time when the sword shall be turned into the ploughshare, when American and German and English traders shall no longer compete in the markets of the world for raw materials, for their food supply, when the white man and the dark shall share the soil between them, and each till it as he lists. But, believe me, when that day comes mankind will no longer progress, there will be nothing to check the fertility of inferior stock; the relentless law of heredity will not be controlled and guided by natural selection. Man will stagnate.... The path of progress is strewn with the wreck of nations; traces are everywhere to be seen of the hecatombs of inferior races, and of victims who found not the narrow way to the greater perfection. Yet these dead peoples are, in very truth, the stepping stones on which mankind has arisen to the higher intellectual and deeper emotional life of today.

Source: From Karl Pearson, *National Life from the Standpoint of Science*, 2d ed. (Cambridge, UK: Cambridge University Press, 1907), pp. 21, 26–27, 64.

materials. Motivated by intense economic and political competition, they rationalized their expansionary policies on both religious and cultural grounds. The imperial powers eventually divided almost all the continent among themselves.

For centuries, European slave-trading bases had dotted the African coastline, but few Europeans had penetrated the interior. This changed in the late 1870s. (See Chapter 26.) The Congress of Vienna had prohibited the Atlantic slave trade in 1815, a ban that Western—primarily British—naval patrols enforced. Those patrols and the abolition of slavery in the Americas during the nineteenth century meant that Africa was no longer a source for slave labor except in central and East Africa, where Arab slave traders continued to export slaves to the Muslim world until at least the 1890s. Instead, Africa became an important supplier of raw materials, such as ivory, rubber, and, notably, diamonds and gold to the West. The British, French, Belgians, Germans, Italians, and Portuguese sought to maximize their access to these resources. The competition was so fierce and the scramble for African territories so frantic and volatile that the imperial powers were constantly negotiating with each other about how to parcel Africa among them without the contest leading to war. To set the rules, the German chancellor Otto von Bismarck called a conference in Berlin in 1884–1885 that mapped out a European-controlled Africa. African colonies had become both trophies for European powers and possible bargaining chips in their economic and political competition with each other.

See the **Map**
Africa before the Scramble
at **myhistorylab.com**

In North Africa, the experience of European imperialism was slightly different from that in sub-Saharan Africa. Because much of North Africa was still technically part of the Ottoman Empire, the European powers secured their interests primarily in two ways: through economic penetration (investments and loans) and diplomatic pressure. Force, however, was always an option. By 1914, European powers controlled all of North Africa. France had begun the conquest of Algeria in 1830 (see Chapter 19). The French also took control of Tunisia in the early 1880s and of Morocco between 1901 and 1912. Italy seized Libya from Turkey in 1911–1912. Egypt, the richest North African country, fell under the control of Britain.

Egypt was an unusual case. For most of the nineteenth century, it had been a semi-independent province of the Ottoman Empire under the hereditary rule of a Muslim dynasty. The Khedives, as these rulers were titled, had tried to modernize the country by building new harbors, roads, and a European-style army. To pay for these projects, the Egyptian government borrowed money from European creditors. To earn the money to repay these loans, it forced farmers to plant cash crops. Ultimately, the Egyptian government became utterly dependent on European creditors. The construction of the Suez Canal, which opened in 1869, was the final blow to Egypt's finances. Built by French engineers with European capital, the canal connected the Mediterranean to the Red Sea, which meant that ships from Europe no longer had to sail around Africa to reach Asia. Yet Egypt did not benefit. By 1876, the Khedive was bankrupt; most of his shares in the company that ran the canal were sold to Britain. Egypt's European creditors took more than 50 percent of Egyptian revenue each year to repay their loans and forced the Egyptian government to increase taxes. This provoked a rebellion, and in 1881 the Egyptian army took over the government to defend Egypt from foreign exploitation. Then Britain easily defeated the Egyptians.

Egypt never became an official part of the British Empire, but for seventy years the British exercised control through a relatively small number of British administrators and soldiers. Their primary goal was stability and control of the Suez Canal, which the British regarded as their "lifeline" to their empire in India and the Far East. They also prevented the Egyptians from establishing a textile industry that would compete with Britain's own textile mills. While the Egyptian economy grew and tax revenues increased, per capita income actually declined among Egyptians, most of whom were peasant farmers. This led to the growth of Egyptian nationalism and to increasing demands that the British leave Egypt.

Perhaps the most remarkable story in the European scramble for Africa was the acquisition of the Belgian Congo. In the 1880s, the lands drained by the vast Congo River became the personal property of King Leopold II of Belgium (r. 1865–1909). As a young monarch, he had become determined that Belgium, despite its small territory, must acquire colonies. No doubt he was inspired by the great commercial wealth that the neighboring Netherlands had accumulated from its long history of colonial trade. The Belgian government, however, had no interest in acquiring colonies. So despite being a constitutional monarch, Leopold used his own wealth and political guile to realize his colonial ambitions under the guise of humanitarian concern for Africans. He recruited the English-born journalist and explorer Henry Morton Stanley (1841–1904) to undertake a major expedition into the Congo. Between 1879 and 1884, Stanley made "treaties" on Leopold's behalf with local rulers who had no idea what they were signing. Leopold became the personal ruler of an African domain that was over seventy times the size of Belgium itself. Leopold's administration used slave labor, intimidation, torture, mutilation, and mass murder to extract rubber and ivory from what became known as the Congo Free State. Eventually Leopold's crimes were exposed, and he formally turned the Congo over to Belgium in 1908.

•••—Read the Document
A British View of Egyptian Agriculture, 1840 at **myhistorylab.com**

•••—Read the Document
Edward D. Morel, The Black Man's Burden at **myhistorylab.com**

The cruelties in the Congo, which became the basis for Joseph Conrad's classic novel *Heart of Darkness* (1902), were recorded for posterity in photographs, eyewitness accounts, and newspaper articles, and by an official Belgian commission. The most responsible historical estimates suggest that the exploitation Leopold's administration carried out halved the population of the Congo in about thirty years.

South Africa's fertile pastures and farmland and its vast deposits of coal, iron ore, gold, diamonds, and copper made it appealing to a host of people. The Afrikaners or Boers, descendants of seventeenth- and eighteenth-century Dutch settlers, had long inhabited the area around the Cape of Good Hope, and the British started to settle there after Britain took over from the Dutch during the Napoleonic Wars. Although the British met with considerable native resistance from the Zulu, Shona, and Ndebele peoples, they eventually established colonies in what is now South Africa, Botswana, Zambia, and Zimbabwe. In 1910, after a series of bloody wars with the white Afrikaners, who consistently resented and opposed British rule, the British formed a pact with them that guaranteed the rule of the European minority over the majority black and nonwhite population. Africans and people of mixed race whom the British referred to as "colored" were forbidden to own land, denied the right to vote, and excluded from positions of power. To preserve their political power and economic privileges, the white elite of South Africa eventually enforced a policy of racial apartheid—"separateness"—that turned the country into a totally segregated land. The result was decades of oppression, racial tensions, and economic exploitation.

Cruelty in the Belgian Congo. A naked slave, tied to the ground, is whipped by an overseer.

Why were there so many atrocities in the Belgian Congo?

THE NEW IMPERIALISM IN ASIA AND THE PACIFIC

The emergence of Japan as a great power frightened the other powers that were interested in China (see Chapter 27). The Russians were building a railroad across Siberia to Vladivostok and were afraid of any threat to Manchuria. Together with France and Germany, they applied diplomatic pressure that forced Japan out of the Liaotung Peninsula in northern China and its harbor, Port Arthur. All pressed feverishly for concessions in China. Fearing that China, its markets, and its investment opportunities would soon be closed to U.S. citizens, the United States proposed the open-door policy in 1899. This policy opposed foreign annexations in China and allowed entrepreneurs of all nations to trade there on equal terms. British support helped win acceptance of the policy by all the powers except Russia.

The United States had only recently emerged as a force in international affairs. The Monroe Doctrine of 1823 had, in effect, made the entire Western Hemisphere an American protectorate. Cuba's attempt to gain independence from Spain was the spark for the new U.S. involvement in international affairs. Sympathy for the Cuban cause, U.S. investments on the island, the desire for Cuban sugar, and concern over the island's strategic importance in the Caribbean all helped persuade the United States to fight Spain.

Victory in the Spanish-American War of 1898 brought the United States an informal protectorate over Cuba and the annexation of Puerto Rico. The United States forced Spain to sell the Philippine Islands and Guam, and Germany bought the other Spanish islands in the Pacific. The United States and Germany also divided Samoa between them. France and Britain took Spain's remaining Pacific islands. The United

States had dominated Hawaii for some time and annexed it in 1898, five years after an American-backed coup had overthrown the native Hawaiian monarchy. This burst of activity after the Spanish-American War made the United States an imperial and Pacific power.

Thus, by the turn of the century, most of the world had come under the control of the industrialized West. The one remaining area of great vulnerability was the Ottoman Empire. Its fate, however, was closely tied up with European developments.

EMERGENCE OF THE GERMAN EMPIRE

WHAT WERE
Bismarck's goals for Germany?

FORMATION OF THE TRIPLE ALLIANCE (1873–1890)

Prussia's victories over Austria and France and its creation of a large, powerful German Empire in 1871 revolutionized European diplomacy. The sudden appearance of a vast, wealthy, industrialized, and militarized state that brought together most of the German people posed new problems.

The balance of power created at the Congress of Vienna was altered radically. Britain and Russia retained their positions. Austria, however, had lost ground and was threatened by nationalism within the Austro-Hungarian Empire. French power and prestige were badly damaged by the Franco-Prussian War and the German annexation of Alsace-Lorraine. The French were both afraid of Germany and resentful of their loss of territory and traditional dominance in western Europe.

BISMARCK'S LEADERSHIP (1873–1890)

Until 1890 Otto von Bismarck (1815–1898) continued to guide German policy. He insisted after 1871 that Germany wanted no further territorial gains, and he meant it. He wanted to avoid a war that might lead to Germany's disintegration. He tried to assuage French resentment by cultivating friendly relations and by supporting French colonial aspirations. He also prepared for the worst. If France could not be conciliated, it must be isolated. Bismarck sought to prevent an alliance between France and any other European power—especially Austria or Russia—that would threaten Germany with a war on two fronts.

Bismarck's first move was to establish the Three Emperors' League in 1873. The league brought together the three great conservative empires of Germany, Austria, and Russia. It collapsed when Russia went to war with Turkey in 1877. The tottering Ottoman Empire was preserved chiefly by the competing aims of those powers that awaited its demise. Ottoman weakness encouraged its Slavic subjects in the Balkans to rebel.

When Russia entered the fray, it created an international crisis. The Russians hoped to gain control of Constantinople. Russian intervention also reflected the influence of the **pan-Slavic movement**, which sought to bring all the Slavs, even those under Austrian or Ottoman rule, under the protection of Holy Mother Russia.

The Ottoman Empire was forced to sue for peace. The Treaty of San Stefano of March 1878 was a Russian triumph. The Slavic states in the Balkans were freed of Ottoman rule, and Russia obtained territory and an indemnity. But the terms of the Russian victory alarmed the other great powers. Austria feared that the new Slav states and the increase in Russian influence would threaten its own Balkan provinces. The British were alarmed by the possible Russian control of Constantinople. Disraeli (1804–1881) was determined to resist, and British public opinion supported him.

QUICK REVIEW

Bismarck's Goals

- No additional territorial expansion
- Tried to cultivate friendship with France
- Sought to prevent alliance between France and any other European power that would threaten Germany on two fronts

---

pan-Slavic movement
The movement to create a nation or federation that would embrace all the Slavic peoples of eastern Europe.

Disraeli sent a fleet to Constantinople, and Britain and Austria forced Russia to agree to an international conference at which the provisions of San Stefano would be reviewed by the other great powers. The resulting Congress of Berlin met in June and July of 1878 under Bismarck's leadership. The Congress's decisions were a blow to Russian ambitions. Bulgaria lost two-thirds of its territory. Austria-Hungary was given Bosnia and Herzegovina to "occupy and administer" under formal Ottoman rule. Britain received Cyprus, and France gained permission to occupy Tunisia. These were compensations for the gains that Russia was permitted to keep. Germany asked for nothing, but the Russians were angry. The Three Emperors' League was dead.

The major trouble spot now was in the south Slavic states of Serbia and Montenegro. They deeply resented the Austrian occupation of Bosnia and Herzegovina, as did many of the natives of those provinces. The south Slavic question, as well as the estrangement between Russia and Germany, was a threat to the peace of Europe.

Bismarck could ignore the Balkans but not the breach in his eastern alliance system. With Russia alienated, he concluded a secret treaty with Austria in 1879. The resulting Dual Alliance provided that if either Germany or Austria was attacked by Russia, the ally would help the attacked party. If either was attacked by someone else, each promised at least to maintain neutrality. The treaty was renewed every five years until 1918. As the central point in German policy, it was criticized at the time; some have judged it mistaken in retrospect. It appeared to tie the German fortunes to those of the troubled Austro-Hungarian Empire and thus to borrow trouble. It also isolated the Russians and pushed them to alliances in the West.

Bismarck was aware of these dangers but discounted them. He never allowed the alliance to drag Germany into Austria's Balkan quarrels. He made it clear to the Austrians that Germany would never attack Russia. Bismarck expected the Austro-German negotiations to frighten Russia into seeking closer relations with Germany, and he was right. By 1881, he had renewed the Three Emperors' League on a firmer basis.

In 1882, Italy, annoyed by the French preemption of Tunisia, asked to join the Dual Alliance. Bismarck was now allied with three of the great powers and was friendly with Great Britain, which held aloof from all alliances. France was isolated. Although the Three Emperors' League was allowed to lapse, the Triple Alliance (Germany, Austria, and Italy) was renewed for another five years in 1887. To restore German relations with Russia, Bismarck negotiated the Reinsurance Treaty that same year, in which both powers promised to remain neutral if either was attacked. However, a change in the German monarchy overturned Bismarck's system.

In 1888, William II (r. 1888–1918) came to the German throne. Like many Germans of his generation, he was filled with a sense of Germany's destiny as the leading power of Europe. To achieve a "place in the sun," he wanted a navy and colonies like Britain's. These aims, of course, ran counter to Bismarck's policy. In 1890, William dismissed Bismarck. During Bismarck's time, Germany was a force for European peace. This position would not have been possible without its great military power. But it also required a statesman who could exercise restraint and understand what his country needed and what was possible.

Read the **Document**
Serbian Society of National Defense, Program for Nationalism
at **myhistorylab.com**

See the **Map**
Congress of Berlin at **myhistorylab.com**

Bismarck and the Kaiser. Bismarck and the young Kaiser William II meet in 1888. The two disagreed over many issues, and in 1890 William dismissed the aged chancellor.

Why did Kaiser William II disagree with Bismarck?

FORGING THE TRIPLE ENTENTE (1890–1907)

Almost immediately after Bismarck's retirement, his system of alliances collapsed. His successor, General Leo von Caprivi (1831–1899), refused the Russian request to renew the Reinsurance Treaty, which he considered incompatible with the Austrian alliance. Political isolation and the need for foreign capital drove the Russians toward France. The French, who were even more isolated, were glad to pour capital into Russia if it would help produce security against Germany. In 1894 the Franco-Russian alliance was signed.

Britain now became the key to the international situation. Colonial rivalries pitted the British against the Russians in central Asia and against the French in Africa. Traditionally, Britain had also opposed Russian control of Constantinople and French control of the Low Countries. There was no reason to think that Britain would soon become friendly to its traditional rivals or abandon its friendliness toward the Germans. Yet within a decade of William II's accession, Germany had become the enemy in the minds of the British because of Germany's foreign and naval policies.

At first Germany tried to win over the British to the Triple Alliance, but when Britain clung to "splendid isolation," Germany sought to demonstrate its worth as an ally by making trouble for Britain. The Germans began to exert pressure against Britain in Africa by barring British attempts to build a railroad from Cape Town to Cairo. They also openly sympathized with the Boers of South Africa in their resistance to British expansion.

In 1898, William's dream of a German navy began to achieve reality with the passage of a naval law providing for nineteen battleships. In 1900, a second law doubled that figure. The architect of the new navy, Admiral Alfred von Tirpitz (1849–1930), proclaimed that Germany's naval policy was aimed at Britain. As the German navy grew and German policies seemed more threatening, the British abandoned their traditional policies (see Figure 28–1).

The first breach in Britain's isolation came in 1902 when an alliance was concluded with Japan to help defend British interests in the Far East against Russia. In 1904, Britain concluded a series of agreements with the French, collectively called the Entente Cordiale. It was not a formal treaty and had no military provisions, but it settled all outstanding colonial differences between the two nations. The Entente Cordiale was a big step toward aligning the British with Germany's great potential enemy.

FIGURE 28–1.   Warship Tonnage of the World's Navies, 1880–1910.   Naval strength was the primary index of power before World War I.

Paul Kennedy, *Rise and Fall of the Great Powers* (New York: Random House, 1987), p. 203.

Which countries experienced dramatic change in warship tonnage?

In March 1905, William II landed at Tangier and challenged the French predominance there in a speech in favor of Moroccan independence. Germany's chancellor, Prince Bernhard von Bülow (1849–1929), intended to show France how weak it was and how little it could expect from Britain; he also hoped to gain colonial concessions. The Germans might have achieved their aims, but they demanded an international conference to exhibit their power. The conference met in 1906 at Algeciras in Spain. Austria sided with its German ally, but Spain, Italy, and the United States voted with Britain and France. The French were confirmed in their position in Morocco, and German bullying had driven Britain and France closer together. Sir Edward Grey (1862–1933), the British foreign secretary, authorized conversations between the British and French general staffs. By 1914, French and British military and naval plans were so mutually dependent that the two countries were effectively allies.

Britain's new relationship with France was surprising enough. Hardly anyone believed that Britain and Russia could ever be allies. The 1904–1905 Russo-Japanese War made such a development seem even less likely because Britain was allied with Russia's enemy. But defeat and the Russian Revolution of 1905 left Russia weak and reduced British apprehensions. The British were also concerned that Russia might drift into the German orbit. With French support, in 1907 an agreement settled Russo-British quarrels in central Asia and Persia and opened the door for wider cooperation. The Triple Entente, an informal but powerful association of Britain, France, and Russia, was now ranged against the Triple Alliance. Because Italy was unreliable, Germany and Austria-Hungary stood surrounded by two great land powers and Great Britain.

William II and his ministers had turned Bismarck's nightmare of the prospect of a two-front war with France and Russia into a reality and had added Britain to the hostile coalition. Bismarck's alliance system had been intended to maintain peace, but the new one increased the risk of war and made the Balkans, where Austrian and Russian ambitions clashed, a likely spot for it. Bismarck's diplomacy had left France isolated and impotent; the new arrangement found France associated with the two greatest powers in Europe, apart from Germany. The Germans could rely only on Austria, whose troubles made it more likely to need aid than to provide it.

WORLD WAR I

THE ROAD TO WAR (1908–1914)

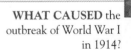

WHAT CAUSED the outbreak of World War I in 1914?

The situation in the Balkans was exceedingly complicated. The weak Ottoman Empire controlled the central strip running west from Constantinople to the Adriatic. North and south of it were the independent states of Romania, Montenegro, Serbia, and Greece; Bulgaria, while technically still part of the empire, was legally autonomous and practically independent. The Austro-Hungarian Empire included Croatia and Slovenia and since 1878 had "occupied and administered" Bosnia and Herzegovina.

Except for the Greeks and the Romanians, most of the inhabitants of the Balkans were Slavs and felt a kinship with one another and with Russia. For centuries they had been ruled by Austrians, Hungarians, or Turks, and the nationalism that characterized late nineteenth-century Europe made many Slavs eager for liberty or at least autonomy. The more radical among them longed for a union of the south Slavic, or Yugoslav, peoples in a single nation led by independent Serbia. They hoped to detach all the Slavic provinces (especially Bosnia, which bordered on Serbia) from Austria. Serbia was to unite the Slavs at the expense of Austria, as Piedmont had united the Italians and Prussia the Germans.

In 1908, modernizing reformers called the Young Turks overthrew the Ottoman government. This threatened to revive the empire and precipitated a series of Balkan crises that would lead to world war. Austria and Russia decided to act before Turkey became stronger. They agreed to call an international conference in which each of them would support the other's demands. Russia would agree to the Austrian annexation of Bosnia and Herzegovina, and Austria would support Russia's request to open the Dardanelles to Russian warships.

See the **Map**
Diplomatic Crises, 1905–1914
at **myhistorylab.com**

Austria, however, declared the annexation unilaterally before any conference was called. The British, concerned about their own position in the Mediterranean, rejected the Russian demand. The Russians were furious. The Serbs were enraged by the annexation of Bosnia. The Russians were too weak to do anything but accept the new situation. The Germans were unhappy because Austria's action threatened their relations with Russia. But Germany felt so dependent on the Dual Alliance that it assured Austria of its support. To an extent, German policy was being made in Vienna. It was a dangerous precedent. At the same time, the failure of Britain and France to support Russia strained the Triple Entente and made it harder for them to oppose Russian interests again if they wanted to retain Russian friendship.

The second Moroccan crisis, in 1911, emphasized the French and British need for mutual support. When France sent an army to Morocco to put down a rebellion, Germany took the opportunity to extort colonial concessions in the French Congo by sending the gunboat *Panther* to the port of Agadir in Morocco, allegedly to protect German citizens there. As in 1905, the Germans went too far.

Anglo-German relations had already been deteriorating, chiefly because of the naval race. The British now mistakenly believed that the Germans meant to turn Agadir into a naval base on the Atlantic. The crisis passed when France yielded bits of the Congo and Germany withdrew from Morocco. The main result was to draw Britain closer to France. Plans were formulated for a British expeditionary force to help defend France against German attack, and the British and French navies agreed to cooperate.

After the second Moroccan crisis, Italy feared that France would move into Ottoman Libya. Consequently, in 1911 Italy attacked the Ottoman Empire to forestall the French and obtained Libya and the Dodecanese Islands in the Aegean. The Italian victory encouraged the Balkan states to try their luck. In 1912, Bulgaria, Greece, Montenegro, and Serbia attacked the Ottoman Empire and won easily. The Serbs and the Bulgarians then quarreled about the division of Macedonia, and in 1913, Turkey and Romania joined Greece and Serbia against Bulgaria, which lost much of what it had gained since 1878.

The Austrians were determined to limit Serbian gains and prevent the Serbs from obtaining a port in Albania on the Adriatic. An international conference sponsored by Britain in early 1913 resolved the matter in Austria's favor and called for an independent kingdom of Albania. But Austria felt humiliated by the public airing of Serbian demands and in October unilaterally forced Serbia to withdraw from Albania. Russia again let Austria have its way.

The lessons learned from this affair influenced behavior in the final crisis of 1914. The Russians had, as in 1908, been embarrassed by their passivity, and their allies were now more reluctant to restrain them. The Austrians were determined not to accept an international conference again. They and their German allies had seen that better results might be obtained from a threat of force.

QUICK REVIEW

Second Moroccan Crisis

◆ 1911: France sends an army to Morocco and Germany sends gunboat to Moroccan port of Agadir

◆ British overreaction leads to naval arms race between Germany and Britain

◆ Chief effects of the crisis were to increase suspicion between Germany and Britain and to draw France and Britain closer together

SARAJEVO AND THE OUTBREAK OF WAR (JUNE–AUGUST 1914)

On June 28, 1914, a Bosnian nationalist killed the Austrian Archduke Francis Ferdinand (1863–1914), heir to the Austro-Hungarian throne, and his wife in the Bosnian capital of Sarajevo. The assassin was a member of a political terrorist society. It was generally (and correctly) believed that Serbian officials were implicated. The assassination was condemned throughout Europe. To those Austrians who had long favored an attack on Serbia as a solution to the empire's Slavic problem, the opportunity seemed irresistible. But Count Stefan Tisza (1861–1918), speaking for Hungary, resisted. Count Leopold Berchtold (1863–1942), the Austro-Hungarian foreign minister, knew that German support would be required if Russia should decide to protect Serbia and to persuade the Hungarians to go to war. The question of peace or war, therefore, had to be answered in Berlin.

William II and Chancellor Theobald von Bethmann-Hollweg (1856–1921) readily promised German support for an attack on Serbia. It has often been said that they gave the Austrians a "blank check," but their message was firmer than that. They urged the Austrians to move swiftly while the other powers were still angry at Serbia. They also indicated that a failure to act would be evidence of Austria-Hungary's uselessness as an ally. The Austrians hoped, with the protection of Germany, to avoid a general European conflict but were prepared to risk one. The Germans also knew that they risked a general war but hoped to "localize" the fight between Austria and Serbia. Bethmann-Hollweg hoped that German support would deter Russian involvement. Failing that, he believed that rapid victory over France would allow a full-scale attack on the Russians, who were slow to bring their strength into action. This policy depended on British neutrality, and the German chancellor convinced himself that the British could be persuaded to stand aloof. But all these hopes were futile.

The Austrians were slow to act. They did not even deliver their deliberately unacceptable ultimatum to Serbia until July 24, when the general hostility toward Serbia had begun to subside. Serbia returned an embarrassingly conciliatory answer, but the Austrians were determined to fight. On July 28, they declared war on Serbia, even though they could not field an army until mid-August.

The Russians responded angrily. Nationalists, pan-Slavs, and most of the politically conscious classes demanded action. The government ordered partial **mobilization** against Austria only. This policy was militarily impossible, but its purpose was diplomatic: to pressure Austria to hold back its attack on Serbia.

Mobilization of any kind, however, was generally understood to be equivalent to an act of war. It was especially alarming to German General Helmuth von Moltke (1848–1916). Russian mobilization could upset the delicate timing of Germany's battle plan—the **Schlieffen Plan**, which required an attack on France first—and would endanger Germany. From this point on, Moltke pressed for war. The pressure of military necessity became irresistible (see Map 28–2 on page 739).

Assassination of the Archduke. Above: The Austrian Archduke Franz Ferdinand and his wife in Sarajevo on June 28, 1914. Later in the day the royal couple were assassinated by young revolutionaries trained and supplied in Serbia, igniting the crisis that led to World War I. Below: Moments after the assassination the Austrian police captured one of the assassins.

Why did this assassination trigger World War I?

●●●―Read the Document
Borijove Jevtic: The Murder of Archduke Franz Ferdinand at Sarajevo
(28 June 1914) at **myhistorylab.com**

((●―Hear the Audio
World War 1 at **myhistorylab.com**

mobilization
The placing of a country's military forces on a war footing.

Schlieffen Plan
Germany's plan for achieving a quick victory in the West at the outbreak of World War I by invading France through Belgium and Luxembourg.

CHRONOLOGY

COMING OF WORLD WAR I

1871	End of the Franco-Prussian War; creation of the German Empire; German annexation of Alsace-Lorraine
1873	Three Emperors' League (Germany, Russia, and Austria-Hungary)
1875	Russo-Turkish War
1878	Congress of Berlin
1879	Dual Alliance between Germany and Austria
1881	Three Emperors' League is renewed
1882	Italy joins Germany and Austria in Triple Alliance
1888	William II becomes German emperor
1890	Bismarck dismissed
1894	Franco-Russian alliance
1898	Germany begins to build battleship navy
1902	British alliance with Japan
1904	Entente Cordiale between Britain and France
1904–1905	Russo-Japanese War
1905	First Moroccan crisis
1907	British agreement with Russia
1908–1909	Bosnian crisis
1911	Second Moroccan crisis; Italy attacks Turkey
1912–1913	First and Second Balkan Wars
1914	Outbreak of World War I

The western European powers were not eager for war. The French gave the Russians the same assurances that Germany had given its ally. The British worked hard for another conference of the powers, but Austria would not hear of it. The Germans privately supported the Austrians but were publicly conciliatory in the hope of keeping the British neutral.

Bethmann-Hollweg soon realized what he should have known all along: If Germany attacked France, Britain must fight. While Bethmann-Hollweg was urging restraint on the Austrians, Moltke was pressing them to act. In any case, it was too late for the Austrians to back down.

On July 30, Austria ordered mobilization against Russia. Russia and Germany then ordered general mobilization. The Schlieffen Plan went into effect. The Germans invaded Belgium on August 3. The British had guaranteed Belgian neutrality, so Britain was now united against Germany. Germany then invaded France. On August 4, Britain declared war on Germany. The Great War had begun; Europe would never be the same.

STRATEGIES AND STALEMATE (1914–1917)

Jubilation greeted the outbreak of war throughout Europe. No general war had been fought since Napoleon, and the horrors of modern warfare were not yet understood. The dominant memory was of Bismarck's swift and decisive campaigns in which costs and casualties were light and the rewards great. Both sides expected quick victory. The Triple Entente powers—or the Allies, as they came to be called—had superior numbers and financial resources as well as command of the sea. Germany and Austria, the Central Powers, had the advantages of internal lines of communication and of having launched their attack first.

After 1905 Germany's only war plan was the one developed by Count Alfred von Schlieffen (1833–1913), chief of the German general staff from 1891 to 1906 (see Map 28–2). It aimed to outflank the French defenses by sweeping through Belgium to the Channel, then wheeling to the south and east to envelop the French and crush them against the German fortresses in Lorraine. In the East the Germans planned to stand on the defensive against Russia until France had been beaten, a task they thought would take only six weeks.

The execution of his plan, however, was left to Helmuth von Moltke, a gloomy and nervous man, who made enough tactical mistakes to cause it to fail by a narrow margin. As a result, the French and British were able to stop the Germans at the battle of the Marne in September 1914. Thereafter, the war in the West became one of position. Both sides dug in behind a wall of trenches protected by barbed wire that stretched from the North Sea to Switzerland. Machine-gun nests made assaults dangerous. Both sides, nonetheless, attempted massive attacks initiated by artillery bombardments of unprecedented force and duration. The defense always prevented a breakthrough.

In the East, the Russians advanced into Austrian territory and inflicted heavy casualties, but Russian incompetence and German energy soon reversed the situation. General Erich Ludendorff (1865–1937), under the command of the elderly Paul von Hindenburg (1847–1934), destroyed or captured an entire Russian army at the battle of Tannenberg. In 1915, the Central Powers drove into the Baltic States and western Russia, inflicting more than 2 million casualties. Russian confidence was shaken (see Map 28–3 on page 740).

Both sides sought new allies. Turkey and Bulgaria joined the Central Powers. Italy joined the Allies in 1915, after they agreed to give Italy **Italia Irredenta** (i.e., the Trentino, the South Tyrol, Trieste, and some of the Dalmatian Islands) from Austria after victory.

MAP 28–2. The Schlieffen Plan of 1905. Germany's grand strategy for quickly winning the war against France in 1914 is shown by the wheeling arrows on the map. The crushing blows at France were, in the original plan, to be followed by the release of troops for use against Russia on Germany's Eastern Front. But the plan was not adequately implemented, and the war on the Western Front became a long contest instead.

Why did the Schlieffen Plan fail?

Trench Warfare. French infantry soldiers approach German soldiers during a battle near Champagne, France in 1917. This scene of trench warfare characterizes the twentieth century's first great international conflict.

How did military tactics change in World War I?

Italia Irredenta
Meaning "unredeemed Italy." Italian-speaking areas that had been left under Austrian rule at the time of the unification of Italy.

See the **Map**
The Actual German Advance, 1914
at **myhistorylab.com**

Read the **Document**
British Soldiers on the battle of the Somme
at **myhistorylab.com**

See the **Map**
The Western Front, 1914–1918
at **myhistorylab.com**

Romania joined the Allies in 1916 but was quickly defeated and driven from the war. In the Far East, Japan honored its alliance with Britain and overran the German colonies in China and the Pacific.

In 1915, the Allies undertook to break the deadlock in the fighting by going around it. The idea came chiefly from Winston Churchill (1874–1965), first lord of the British Admiralty. He proposed to attack the Dardanelles and capture Constantinople. This policy would knock Turkey out of the war and ease communication with Russia. Success depended on daring leadership, which was lacking. Before the campaign was abandoned, the Allies lost almost 150,000 men.

Both sides turned back to the west in 1916. Erich von Falkenhayn (1861–1922), who had succeeded Moltke in September 1914, sought success by an attack on the French stronghold of Verdun. It failed. The Allies, in turn, launched a major offensive along the River Somme in July, resulting in enormous casualties on both sides. The land war dragged on with no end in sight.

MAP 28–3. World War I in Europe.   Despite the importance of military action in the Far East, in the Middle East, and at sea, the main theaters of activity in World War I were in the European areas shown here.

Which regions were most affected by military action?

A Closer Look

The Development of the Armored Tank

Warfare frequently proves a source of technological innovation. Such was true of World War I, which witnessed the development of numerous new weapons. Among the most important of these was the tank—an armored vehicle using a caterpillar track rather than wheels for transport. The caterpillar track had been invented in Great Britain but was then purchased by the American Holt tractor company, which devised a caterpillar tractor in the first decade of the century to cultivate areas with either wet or loose earth where a wheeled vehicle would sink into the ground. During World War I the British modified the caterpillar tractor by introducing a heavily armored closed compartment for a crew armed with machine guns. These early slow-moving tanks could drive over trenches, small hills, and rough terrain and through mud and thus bring mobility to the combat zones where trench warfare had made any kind of effective assault on troops difficult. The tank was used primarily by France and the United States in relatively small numbers in World War I, but later rapidly moving tanks became the major weapons of subsequent twentieth-century warfare.

In the first illustration notice how the design of the driver's area of the tractor was intended to allow the driver a wide area of vision and also was fully exposed.

Notice also how the caterpillar track on the tractor would allow it to move over difficult or wet ground without sinking.

In this illustration of a British World War I tank captured by the Germans, notice how the armament of the tank was intended to protect the crew from small-arms fire while the opening on the top permitted the mounting of a machine gun.

Observe how the interior of the tank allowed for a small crew. The crew worked in an extremely hot environment and had little chance of escape if the tank was hit by artillery fire or became bogged down on difficult ground.

Questions

1. What technological developments prior to World War I made tank warfare possible? What military developments made it desirable?

2. What advantages does tank warfare offer?

3. How do tanks interact with other military units to achieve success?

4. What devices and tactics have modern armies developed to combat the tank?

A German U-Boat at Its Mooring, 1917. By this date German submarine warfare had been severely curtailed.

How did submarines transform naval warfare?

Control of the sea gained importance. In spite of international law, the British imposed a strict blockade to starve out the enemy. The Germans responded with submarine warfare to destroy British shipping. They declared the waters around the British Isles a war zone, where even neutral ships would not be safe. Both policies were unwelcome to neutrals, especially the United States, but the sinking of neutral ships by German submarines was both more dramatic and offensive than Britain's blockade.

In 1915, the British *Lusitania* was torpedoed by a German submarine. Among the 1,200 drowned were 118 Americans. President Woodrow Wilson (1856–1924) protested, and the Germans desisted rather than further anger the United States. This development gave the Allies a considerable advantage. The German fleet that had cost so much played no significant part in the war.

In December 1916, President Wilson attempted to bring about a negotiated peace. But neither side would give up its hopes for total victory. The war seemed likely to continue until one or both sides reached exhaustion.

Two events early in 1917 changed the situation. One was the February 1 announcement by the Germans of the resumption of unrestricted submarine warfare. Another was the overthrow of Russia's tsarist government in March 1917. Since Wilson conceived of the war as an idealistic crusade "to make the world safe for democracy," the presence of autocratic tsarist Russia among the Allies had been a deterrent to American intervention. The United States declared war on Germany on April 6.

THE RUSSIAN REVOLUTION

WHY WERE the Bolsheviks able to seize power in Russia?

👁 **See** the **Map**
Russian Armies in the Eastern Front
at **myhistorylab.com**

soviets
Workers' and soldiers' councils formed in Russia during the Revolution.

◆◆◆ **Read** the **Document**
Bolshevik Seizure of Power, 1917
at **myhistorylab.com**

The March revolution in Russia was neither planned nor led by any political faction. It was the result of the collapse of the monarchy's ability to govern. Military and domestic failures produced massive casualties, widespread hunger, worker strikes, and disorganization. All political factions were discontented.

In early March 1917, strikes and demonstrations erupted in Petrograd, as Saint Petersburg had been renamed. The ill-disciplined troops in the city refused to fire on the demonstrators, and the tsar abdicated on March 15. The Duma formed a provisional government composed chiefly of Constitutional Democrats with Western sympathies. Various Socialists also began to organize the workers into councils called **soviets**. Initially, they allowed the provisional government to function without actually supporting it. But they became estranged as the Constitutional Democrats failed to control the army or purge "reactionaries" from the government.

The provisional government decided to continue the war against Germany, but a new offensive in the summer of 1917 collapsed. Disillusionment with the war, shortages of food and other necessities, and the demand for land reform undermined the government, even after its leadership had been taken over by the moderate Socialist Alexander Kerensky (1881–1970).

The Bolsheviks had been working against the provisional government since April. The Germans had rushed V. I. Lenin (1870–1924) in a sealed train from his exile in Switzerland to Petrograd in the hope that he would cause trouble for the revolutionary government. The Bolsheviks demanded that all political power go to the soviets, which they controlled. They attempted a coup, but it failed. Lenin fled to Finland, and his chief collaborator, Leon Trotsky (1877–1940), was imprisoned. An abortive right-wing counter-coup gave the Bolsheviks another chance. Trotsky, released from prison, led the powerful Petrograd Soviet. Lenin returned in October, and by the extraordinary force of his personality persuaded his colleagues to act. Trotsky organized the November 6 coup that concluded with an armed assault on the provisional government. The Bolsheviks seized power.

The victors moved to fulfill their promises and to assure their own security. The provisional government had decreed an election for late November to select a Constituent Assembly. The Social Revolutionaries won a large majority over the Bolsheviks. When the assembly gathered in January, the Red Army, controlled by the Bolsheviks, dispersed it. All other political parties ceased to function in any meaningful fashion. The Bolshevik government nationalized the land and turned it over to its peasant proprietors. Factory workers were put in charge of their plants. Banks were seized for the state, and the debt of the tsarist government was repudiated. The property of the church was also seized.

The Bolsheviks believed the war benefited only capitalism. They signed an armistice with Germany in December 1917. On March 3, 1918, they accepted the Treaty of Brest-Litovsk, by which Russia yielded Finland, Poland, the Baltic States, the Ukraine, and Georgian territory in the Transcaucasus. The Bolsheviks also agreed to pay an indemnity. These terms were a high price to pay for peace, but the Bolsheviks needed time to impose their rule on a devastated and chaotic Russia.

The Bolsheviks confronted massive domestic resistance. A civil war erupted between the "Red" Russians supporting the revolution and the **"White" Russians**, who opposed the Bolsheviks and received aid from the Allies. In the summer of 1918, the tsar and his family were murdered. Led by Trotsky, the Red Army overcame the opposition. By 1921, Lenin and his supporters were in firm control.

QUICK REVIEW

The Russian Revolution

◆ March 1917: tsar abdicates, formation of provisional government

◆ November 1917: Bolsheviks seize power

◆ Bolsheviks withdraw from World War I

◆ Bolsheviks defeat "White" Russians in civil war

((◦•─Hear the Audio
World War 1 at **myhistorylab.com**

"White" Russians
Those Russians who opposed the Bolsheviks (the "Reds") in the Russian Civil War of 1918–1921.

Petrograd Munitions Workers Demonstrating in 1917. The barely legible slogan at the top of the banner reads, "Victory to the Petrograd Workers!"

Who benefited from the Russian Revolution?

OVERVIEW　Casualties of the Major Belligerents in World War I

COUNTRY	KILLED	WOUNDED
Austria-Hungary	1.1 million	3.62 million
Belgium	38,000	44,000
Britain	723,000	1.16 million
Bulgaria	88,000	152,000
France	1.4 million	2 million
Germany	2 million	4.2 million
Italy	578,000	947,000
Ottoman Empire	804,000	400,000
Romania	250,000	120,000
Russia	1.8 million	1.45 million
Serbia	278,000	138,000
United States	114,000	205,000
Total:	**9,173,000**	**14,436,000**

END OF WORLD WAR I

WHY DID the Versailles settlement leave Germany bitter?

◆◆◆ Read the Document

Woodrow Wilson, The Fourteen Points (1918) at **myhistorylab.com**

Fourteen Points

President Woodrow Wilson's (1856–1924) idealistic war aims.

MILITARY RESOLUTION

The Treaty of Brest-Litovsk brought Germany to the peak of its success. In 1918, it decided to gamble everything on a last offensive. But the German army could not get beyond the Marne. Germany was exhausted. The Allies, on the other hand, bolstered by the arrival of American troops in ever-increasing numbers, launched a counteroffensive that was irresistible. As the Austrian fronts in the Balkans and Italy collapsed, the German high command knew that the end was imminent but wanted peace to be made before the army could be thoroughly defeated in the field, so that responsibility would fall on civilians. The army allowed a new government to be established on democratic principles to seek peace. The new government, under Prince Max of Baden (1867–1928), asked for peace on the basis of the **Fourteen Points** that President Wilson had declared as the American war aims. These were idealistic principles, but Wilson insisted that he would deal only with a democratic German government that spoke for the German people.

The disintegration of the German army forced William II to abdicate on November 9, 1918. The Social Democratic Party proclaimed a republic to prevent the establishment of a soviet government. Two days later this republican, socialist-led government signed an armistice and accepted German defeat. The German people were, in general, unaware that their army had been defeated. No foreign soldier stood on German soil. Many Germans expected a mild settlement. The real peace embittered the German people, many of whom came to believe that Germany had been betrayed by republicans and socialists at home.

Casualties on all sides came to about 10 million dead and twice as many wounded. The financial resources of the European states were badly strained. The victorious Allies, formerly creditors to the world, became debtors to the new American colossus.

The old international order was dead. Russia was ruled by a Bolshevik dictatorship that preached world revolution. Germany was in chaos. Austria-Hungary had

John Singer Sargent, *Gassed*, **1918–1919.** Many new weapons were used extensively for the first time in the Great War of 1914–1918, including machine guns, barbed wire, tanks, airplanes, and several kinds of poison gas. The Germans were the first to employ gas as a weapon, firing a nonlethal kind of tear gas at the Russians on the Eastern Front in January 1915. By April, they had learned how to use the poison gas chlorine against the Allies on the Western Front. *Gassed*, by the American painter John Singer Sargent, can be compared to ancient Greek friezes depicting mythical battles. There is, however, an important difference in treatment: While Greek sculptures always portray an element of heroism along with death and suffering, Sargent's painting reveals only the horror of battle.

John Singer Sargent (1856–1925), "Gassed, an Oil Study." 1918–19 Oil on Canvas. Private Collection. Photo © Christie's Images. The Bridgeman Art Library International.

Why did World War I alter European attitudes toward warfare?

disintegrated. These changes also stirred the colonial empires ruled by the European powers. Europe was no longer the center of the world, free to interfere when it wished or to ignore the outer regions if it chose. Its easy confidence in progress was shattered. The memory of war shook the nerve of the victorious Western powers in the postwar world.

SETTLEMENT AT PARIS

Representatives of the victorious states gathered at Versailles and other Parisian suburbs in the first half of 1919. Wilson speaking for the United States, David Lloyd George (1863–1945) for Britain, Georges Clemenceau (1841–1929) for France, and Vittorio Emanuele Orlando (1860–1952) for Italy made up the Big Four. Japan, recognized for the first time as a great power, also had an important part in the discussions.

Wilson's idealism came into conflict with the war aims of the victorious powers and with the secret treaties that had been made before and during the war. The British and French people had been told that Germany would be made to pay for the war. Romania had been promised Transylvania at the expense of Hungary. Italy and Serbia had competing claims in the Adriatic. During the war, the British had encouraged Arab hopes of an independent Arab state carved out of the Ottoman Empire; those plans conflicted with the Balfour Declaration (1917), in which the British seemed to accept Zionism and to promise the Jews a national home in Palestine. Both of these plans conflicted with an Anglo-French agreement to divide the Near East between themselves.

The national goals of the victors presented further obstacles to an idealistic "peace without victors." France was eager to achieve a settlement that would permanently weaken Germany and preserve French political and military superiority. Italy sought to acquire *Italia Irredenta*; Britain looked to its imperial interests; Japan pursued its own advantage in Asia; and the United States insisted on freedom of the seas, which favored American commerce, and on its right to maintain the Monroe Doctrine.

QUICK REVIEW

The Big Four at Versailles

♦ Woodrow Wilson, United States

♦ David Lloyd George, Britain

♦ Georges Clemenceau, France

♦ Vittorio Emanuele Orlando, Italy

♦ Significant role for Japan

♦ The Soviet Union and Germany excluded

••◆—[Read the **Document**
The Balfour Declaration, 1917
at **myhistorylab.com**

Finally, the peacemakers of 1919 faced a world in turmoil. The greatest immediate threat appeared to be Bolshevism. While Lenin and his colleagues were distracted by civil war, the Allies landed small armies in Russia to help overthrow the Bolshevik regime. Communist governments were established in Bavaria and Hungary. Berlin also experienced an abortive communist uprising. The Allies were so worried that they supported the suppression of these communist movements by right-wing forces. They even permitted an army of German volunteers to fight the Bolsheviks in the Baltic States. But, contrary to Marxist-Leninist theory, there was little affinity and less coordination between these communist movements, and all except Russia's were quickly suppressed. Russia's civil war continued into the early 1920s, but the White Russians were politically fragmented and militarily undersupplied, so they were eventually defeated. Meanwhile, fear of Germany remained the chief concern for France, and traditional interests governed the policies of the other Allies.

The Paris settlement consisted of five separate treaties between the victors and the defeated powers. Formal sessions began on January 18, 1919, and the last treaty was signed on August 10, 1920. The notion of "a peace without victors" became a mockery when the Soviet Union (as Russia was now called) and Germany were excluded from the peace conference. The Germans were simply presented with a treaty and compelled to accept it, which fully justified their complaint that the treaty had not been negotiated but dictated. The principle of national self-determination was, unavoidably, violated many times. The diplomats of the small nations were angered by their exclusion from decision making. The undeserved adulation accorded Wilson on his arrival gradually turned into equally undeserved scorn. He had not abandoned his ideals lightly but had merely given way to the irresistible force of reality.

Wilson put great faith in the new **League of Nations**. Its covenant was an essential part of the peace treaty. The league was not intended as an international government but as a body of sovereign states that agreed to pursue common policies. If war threatened, the members promised to submit the matter to an international court or the League Council. Refusal to abide by this agreement would justify league intervention in the form of economic or military sanctions. But the league was to have no armed forces. Action would require the unanimous consent of its council, which was to consist of Britain, France, Italy, the United States, Japan, and four other states with temporary seats. The league was generally seen as a device to ensure the security of the victorious powers, and the exclusion of Germany and the Soviet Union undermined the league's claim to evenhandedness.

Provisions of the covenant that dealt with colonial areas and disarmament were ineffective. Members of the league remained fully sovereign and continued to pursue their national interests. In the West, the main territorial issue was the fate of Germany (see Map 28-4). The French would have liked to set up the Rhineland as a buffer state, but Lloyd George and Wilson would not permit that. France did receive Alsace-Lorraine and the right to work the coal mines of the Saar for fifteen years. Germany west of the Rhine, and 50 kilometers east of it, was to be a demilitarized zone; Allied troops could stay on the west bank for fifteen years. The treaty also provided that Britain and the United States would guarantee to aid France if it were attacked by Germany. Such an attack was made more unlikely by the permanent disarmament of Germany. Its army was limited to 100,000 men; its fleet was all but eliminated; and it was forbidden to have war planes, submarines, tanks, heavy artillery, or poison gas. As long as these provisions were observed, France would be safe.

The settlement in the East ratified the collapse of the empires that had ruled it for centuries. Germany lost part of Silesia, and East Prussia was cut off from the rest of Germany by a corridor carved out to give the revived state of Poland access to the sea.

League of Nations

The association of sovereign states set up after World War I to pursue common policies and avert international aggression.

Read the Document

The Covenant of the League of Nations
at **myhistorylab.com**

MAP 28–4.   World War I Peace Settlement in Europe and the Middle East.   The map of central and eastern Europe, as well as that of the Middle East, underwent drastic revision after World War I. The enormous territorial losses suffered by Germany, Austria-Hungary, the Ottoman Empire, Bulgaria, and Russia were the other side of the coin represented by gains for France, Italy, Greece, and Romania and by the appearance, or reappearance, of at least eight new independent states from Finland in the north to Yugoslavia in the south. The mandate system for former Ottoman territories outside Turkey proper laid foundations for several new, mostly Arab, states in the Middle East.

How did the creation of new countries in central and eastern Europe set the stage for future conflicts?

Peacemakers. The Allies promoted Arab efforts to secure independence from Turkey in an effort to remove Turkey from the war. Delegates to the peace conference of 1919 in Paris included British Colonel T. E. Lawrence, who helped lead the rebellion against Turkey, and representatives from the Middle East. Prince Feisal, the third son of King Hussein, stands in the foreground of this picture; Lawrence is in the middle row, second from the right; and Brigadier General Nuri Pasha Said of Baghdad is second from the left.

What happened to the Ottoman Empire?

👁 **See the Map**
Southeastern Europe, 1914
at **myhistorylab.com**

▶ **Watch the Video**
The Continuing Legacy of World War I
in the Middle East
at **myhistorylab.com**

war guilt clause
Clause of the Versailles Treaty that assigned responsibility for World War I solely to Germany.

The Austro-Hungarian Empire disappeared. Most of its German-speaking people in the small Republic of Austria were forbidden to unite with Germany. The Magyars occupied the much-reduced kingdom of Hungary.

The Czechs of Bohemia and Moravia joined with the Slovaks and Ruthenians to form Czechoslovakia, which also included several million dissatisfied Germans. The southern Slavs were united in the kingdom of Serbs, Croats, and Slovenes, or Yugoslavia. Italy gained the Trentino and Trieste. Romania gained Transylvania from Hungary and Bessarabia from Russia. Bulgaria lost territory to Greece and Yugoslavia. Finland, Estonia, Latvia, and Lithuania became independent states, and much of Poland was carved out of formerly Russian soil. In the Caucasus, the new nations of Georgia, Armenia, and Azerbaijan took advantage of the turmoil following the Russian Revolution to enjoy a period of independence (1918–1921). Ukraine and Russia were also briefly autonomous.

The old Ottoman Empire disappeared. The new republic of Turkey was limited to little more than Constantinople and Asia Minor. Palestine and Iraq came under British control and Syria and Lebanon under French control as mandates under the purely theoretical authority of the League of Nations. Germany's former colonies in Africa and the Pacific were divided among the victors. In practice, mandated territories were treated as colonies, and colonialism remained a problem.

Perhaps the most debated part of the peace settlement dealt with reparations. Before the armistice, the Germans promised to pay compensation "for all damages done to the civilian population of the Allies and their property." France and Britain, however, wanted Germany to pay the full cost of the war. No sum was fixed at the conference; Germany was to pay $5 billion annually until 1921, when a final figure would be set, which Germany would have to pay within thirty years. The French calculated that either Germany would be bled into impotence or refuse to pay and justify French intervention.

To justify these huge reparation payments, the Allies inserted the notorious **war guilt clause** into the treaty, which placed the responsibility for the war solely on Germany. The Germans bitterly resented the charges but were given no opportunity to negotiate. The German government led by the Social Democrats and the Catholic Center Party signed the treaty. These parties formed the backbone of the German Republic, but they never overcame the stigma of accepting the Treaty of Versailles.

EVALUATION OF THE PEACE

Few peace settlements have been more attacked than the Treaty of Versailles, but many of the attacks on it are unjustified. Germany was neither dismembered nor ruined. Reparations were scaled down, and until the Great Depression of the 1930s, the German economy recovered. The attempt at achieving self-determination for nationalities was less than perfect, but it was the best Europe had ever accomplished.

The peace, nevertheless, was unsatisfactory. The elimination of the Austro-Hungarian Empire, however inevitable, created serious problems. Economically it was disastrous, for it separated raw materials from manufacturing areas and producers from their markets. Poland and especially Czechoslovakia contained unhappy German minorities. Disputes over territories in eastern Europe promoted further tension. The peace also rested on a defeat that Germany did not admit. Germans believed they had been cheated.

Finally, the peace failed to accept reality. Germany and Russia must inevitably play an important part in European affairs, yet they were excluded from the settlement and from the League of Nations. Given the many discontented parties, the peace was not self-enforcing; yet no satisfactory machinery for enforcing it was established. The League of Nations was never a serious force for this purpose, particularly after Wilson's political mistakes helped prevent American ratification of the treaty. It was left to France, with no guarantee of support from Britain and no hope of help from the United States, to defend the new arrangements. France was simply not strong enough for the task if Germany were to rearm. The Treaty of Versailles was neither conciliatory enough to remove the desire for change nor harsh enough to make another war impossible. A lasting peace required enforcing German disarmament while the more obnoxious clauses of the peace treaty were revised. Such a policy demanded continued attention to the problem, unity among the victors, and far-sighted leadership; none of these was present in adequate supply during the next two decades.

SUMMARY

WHAT WAS the New Imperialism?

Expansion of European Power and the "New Imperialism." Economic and social factors—especially the pursuit of prestige—were significant drivers of the New Imperialism. By 1914, European nations had divided Africa among themselves and controlled large parts of Asia and the islands of the Pacific. Much of the Middle East was under the nominal control of the Ottoman Empire, which was itself under European influence. The Monroe Doctrine made Latin America a protectorate of the United States. Japan had become an imperial power at the expense of China and Korea. *page 725*

WHAT WERE Bismarck's goals for Germany?

Emergence of the German Empire. Bismarck masterminded the creation of the German Empire and created a system of treaties and alliances to ensure that Germany would not be threatened on two fronts simultaneously. In 1890, the young Kaiser William II dismissed Bismarck, and soon Russia and France were allied against Germany. By 1914, Britain too was enmeshed in military partnership with France against Germany. *page 732*

WHAT CAUSED the outbreak of World War I in 1914?

World War I. The alliance system divided Europe into two armed camps. What began as yet another Balkan war

involving the European powers became a world war that influenced the rest of the world. As the terrible war of 1914 to 1918 dragged on, the motives that had driven the European powers to fight gave way to public affirmations of the principles of nationalism and self-determination. *page 735*

 ### WHY WERE the Bolsheviks able to seize power in Russia?

The Russian Revolution. Russia suffered during the war, and many groups blamed the government. In March 1917, the tsar was overthrown. The provisional government was overturned by the Bolsheviks in November, largely thanks to Lenin's persuasive powers. Russia withdrew from the war soon thereafter. *page 742*

 ### WHY DID the Versailles settlement leave Germany bitter?

End of World War I. Europe's imperial nations, especially Britain and France, paid an enormous price in lives, money, and will for their victory in the war. The peace settlement at Versailles has been criticized for many reasons, both fair and unfair. Certainly it left many tensions unresolved. Germany was given many obligations to fulfill, without being given any opportunity to negotiate. Tension between colonies and their ruling nations was a cause of instability in the world created by the Paris treaties of 1919. *page 744*

KEY TERMS

Fourteen Points (p. 744)

Italia Irredenta (ih-TAL-ee-yuh IHR-ih-DENT-ah) (p. 739)

League of Nations (p. 746)

mobilization (p. 737)

New Imperialism (p. 726)

pan-Slavic movement (p. 732)

Schlieffen Plan (SHLEE-fehn) (p. 737)

soviets (p. 742)

war guilt clause (p. 748)

"White" Russians (p. 743)

REVIEW QUESTIONS

1. Which explanation or combination of explanations for the New Imperialism seem most plausible and why?

2. Summarize the experiences of three regions in Africa with the New Imperialism.

3. What role did Bismarck envisage for the new Germany after 1871? How successful was he in carrying out his vision? Was he wise to tie Germany to Austria-Hungary?

4. Why and in what stages did Britain abandon "splendid isolation" at the turn of the century? Were the policies it pursued instead wise ones, or should Britain have followed a different course?

5. How did developments in the Balkans lead to the outbreak of World War I? What was the role of Serbia? of Austria? of Russia? What was the aim of German policy in July 1914? Did Germany want a general war?

6. Why did the United States enter World War I? Were there good reasons for it to enter the war when it did, or would it have been better for the United States to enter earlier, later, or not at all?

7. Why did Germany lose World War I? Could Germany have won, or was victory never a possibility?

8. Why was Lenin successful in establishing Bolshevik rule in Russia? What role did Trotsky play? Was it wise policy for Lenin to take Russia out of the war?

9. Assess the settlement of Versailles. What were its benefits to Europe, and what were its drawbacks? Was the settlement too harsh or too conciliatory? Could it have secured lasting peace in Europe? How might it have been improved?

10. How did World War I alter the relationship between imperial powers and colonized peoples?

Note: To learn more about the topics in this chapter, please turn to the Suggested Readings at the end of the book. For additional sources related to this chapter please see www.myhistorylab.com

myhistorylab Connections

Reinforce what you learned in this chapter by studying the many documents, images, maps, review tools, and videos available at **www.myhistorylab.com**

Read and Review

✓•─Study and Review Chapter 28

•••─Read the Document *A British View of Egyptian Agriculture, 1840, p. 730*
Edward D. Morel, The Black Man's Burden, p. 730
Serbian Society of National Defense, Program for Nationalism, p. 733
Borijove Jevtic: The Murder of Archduke Franz Ferdinand at Sarajevo (28 June 1914), p. 737
British Soldiers on the Battle of the Somme, p. 740
Bolshevik Seizure of Power, 1917, p. 742
Woodrow Wilson, The Fourteen Points (1918), p. 744
The Balfour Declaration, 1917, p. 745
The Covenant of the League of Nations, p. 746

👁─See the Map *Africa before the Scramble, p. 729*
Congress of Berlin, p. 733
Diplomatic Crises, 1905–1914, p. 736
The Actual German Advance, 1914, p. 740
The Western Front, 1914–1918, p. 740
Russian Armies in the Eastern Front, p. 742
Southeastern Europe, 1914, p. 748

((•─Hear the Audio *World War 1, p. 737*
World War 1, p. 743

Watch the Video *The Origins of Modern Imperialism and Colonialism, p. 726*
The Continuing Legacy of World War I in the Middle East, p. 748

Research and Explore

Watch the Video *New Imperialism*

Watch the Video *World War I*

((•─Hear the Audio

Hear the audio file for Chapter 28
at **www.myhistorylab.com**

29

Depression, European Dictators, and the American New Deal

((●●─[Hear the **Audio** for Chapter 29 at www.myhistorylab.com

Weimar Germany. In this painting, which reflects the mood of social and political disillusionment that prevailed in much of Europe in the 1920s, George Grosz satirized conservative and right-wing groups in Weimar Germany, including the army, the courts, the newspapers, and the Nazi Party.

Grosz, George (1893–1959) © VAGA, NY, Stuetzen der Gesellschaft (pillars of Society), 1926. Oil on canvas, 2000,0 108,0 cm. Photo: Joerg P. Anders. Nationalgalerie, Staatliche Museen zu Berlin, Berlin, Germany.

What references to violence can you find in this painting?

I n the two decades that followed the conclusion of the Paris settlement, the Western world saw a number of experiments in politics and economic life. Two broad factors accounted for these experiments. First, the war, the Russian Revolution, and the peace treaty had transformed the political face of Europe. The new regimes that emerged in the wake of the collapse of the monarchies of Germany, Austria-Hungary, and Russia faced economic dislocation, nationalistic resentments, and in some cases doubts about their legitimacy.

Second, the Great Depression caused political instability and economic crisis. In Europe, government responses often produced authoritarian regimes. In the United States the response led to an increased role for the federal government. ■

AFTER VERSAILLES: DEMANDS FOR REVISION AND ENFORCEMENT

The Paris settlement fostered resentments that sullied European politics for the next two decades. The arrangements for reparations led to endless haggling. National groups in eastern Europe felt that injustice had been done to them and demanded border

WHICH GROUPS were dissatisfied with the Versailles settlement?

753

GLOBAL PERSPECTIVE

THE INTERWAR PERIOD IN EUROPE AND THE UNITED STATES

The two decades between the great wars marked a period of immense political and economic transition around the globe. Many regions endured political turmoil and economic instability, followed by the establishment of militaristic authoritarian regimes. In Italy, it was the Fascists; in Germany, the Nazis; in the Soviet Union, Stalin's regime. Spain too came under the rule of a military dictator who rose to power with the assistance of the Nazis. Many Europeans, battered by the global economic crisis of the 1930s and, in the case of Germany, the harsh terms of the Treaty of Versailles, believed that only strong leaders could bring prosperity to their countries again in the global competition for resources and territory. In East Asia, Japan came into the grip of a right-wing militaristic government. China saw more than twenty years of civil war and revolution that would culminate with the communists' rise to power under Mao. Most of Latin America came under the sway of dictators or governments heavily influenced by the military.

With the exception of Russia (and later China), all of these governments were right-wing. In fact, the Russian Revolution was a pivotal factor in the rise of right-wing and Fascist dictators, who often justified their power on the basis of their firm opposition to the "Red Menace" and the growing popularity enjoyed by socialism and communism in many European countries during the economic crisis of the 1930s.

To many observers in the late 1930s, the day of liberal parliamentary democracy appeared to be ending. The disruptions arising from World War I and the social and economic turmoil of the Depression seemed to pose problems that liberal governments could not address. Only the radical medicine of socialism, communism, or right-wing dictatorships seemed capable of resolving the crisis. Deep political divisions between the right and left brought some nations, such as France in the mid-1930s, to the brink of civil war. Spain became engulfed in the civil war that brought General Francisco Franco (1892–1975) to power in 1939.

The interwar period also departed from the nineteenth-century ideal of *laissez-faire* economics, in which central governments assumed little responsibility for guiding the economies of their countries. The German inflation of the early 1920s, the worldwide financial collapse of the late 1920s, the vast unemployment of the early 1930s, and the agricultural crisis of both decades roused demands for government action as millions of people experienced

adjustments. The victorious powers, especially France, often believed that the treaty was being inadequately enforced. Voters' demands to either revise or enforce the Paris treaties contributed to domestic political turmoil across the Continent.

WHAT FACTORS made the Great Depression so severe and long lasting?

TOWARD THE GREAT DEPRESSION IN EUROPE

Three factors combined to bring about the severity and the extended length of the **Great Depression**. First, a financial crisis stemmed directly from the war and the peace settlement. In addition, a crisis erupted in the production and distribution of goods in the world market. Finally, these difficulties were exacerbated because no major western European country or the United States provided responsible economic leadership.

Great Depression
A prolonged worldwide economic downturn that began in 1929 with the collapse of the New York Stock Exchange.

FINANCIAL TAILSPIN

France was determined to collect reparations from Germany. The United States was no less determined that its allies repay the wartime loans it had extended to them. German reparations were to provide the means of repaying these debts.

((•—⌐Hear the Audio
Depression at **myhistorylab.com**

The quest for payment of German reparations caused a major diplomatic crisis, which resulted in further economic upheaval. In early 1923, the Allies—France in particular—declared Germany to be in default of its reparation payments. On January 11, French troops occupied Germany's Ruhr mining and manufacturing district. The **Weimar Republic** ordered passive resistance. Confronted with this tactic, the French ran the German mines and railroads. The Germans paid, but Britain became more sympathetic to Germany. The cost of the Ruhr occupation, moreover, damaged the French economy.

Weimar Republic
The German democratic regime that existed between the end of World War I and Hitler's coming to power in 1933.

very real, and often sudden, economic hardship and suffering. One reason for these demands was simply that more governments throughout the world were responsible to mass democratic electorates. Governments that failed to adequately address the problems were put out of office. This happened to the Republicans in the United States, the Socialist and Liberal parties in Germany, the left-wing parties in Japan, and various political parties in Latin America that failed to deal with the Depression. Paradoxically, many democratic electorates actually turned themselves over to politically authoritarian regimes as they searched for social and economic stability.

Extreme forms of nationalism in both Europe and Japan also spawned authoritarianism. The authoritarian governments of Germany, Italy, and Japan all had agendas of nationalistic aggression. They shared the nineteenth-century conviction that territorial expansion was essential to national prestige and economic security. As a result, they were prepared to move wherever they saw fellow nationals living outside their borders (a legacy of the creation of nation-states in the eighteenth and nineteenth centuries) or where they could establish dominance over other peoples and thus become imperial powers. Japan moved against Manchuria and later other parts of Asia. Italy invaded Ethiopia. Germany sought union with German-speaking peoples in Austria and Czechoslovakia and then sought to expand throughout eastern Europe. In turn, those actions challenged the dominance of Great Britain and the vital security interests of the United States. By the end of the 1930s the authoritarian regimes and the liberal democracies stood on the brink of a major confrontation.

Focus Questions

◆ Why did many people in the 1930s lose faith in liberal democracy and *laissez-faire* economics?

◆ What led many countries to adopt authoritarian regimes during this period? Why did authoritarian governments seem to offer a solution to economic hardship and social instabililty?

◆ What was the relationship between extreme nationalism and the outbreak of World War II?

The political and economic turmoil of the Ruhr invasion led to international attempts to ease German payment of reparations. The most famous such attempts were the Dawes Plan of 1924 and the Young Plan of 1929, both devised by Americans. At the time, American investment capital was pouring into Europe. However, the crash of Wall Street in October 1929—the result of unregulated speculation—saw the loss of large amounts of money. Thereafter, little American capital was available for investment in Europe.

In May 1931, the Kreditanstalt—a primary lending institution for much of central and eastern Europe—collapsed. The German banking system then came under severe pressure. As German difficulties increased, U.S. President Herbert Hoover (1874–1964) announced in June 1931 a one-year moratorium on all payments of international debts. The Hoover moratorium was a prelude to the end of reparations. In the summer of 1932, the Lausanne Conference, in effect, ended the era of reparations.

PROBLEMS IN AGRICULTURAL COMMODITIES

The 1920s witnessed a contraction in the market demand for European goods. The difficulty arose from agriculture. Better methods of farming and more extensive transport facilities all over the globe vastly increased the quantity of grain. Wheat prices fell to record lows, decreasing the income of

Jarrow Crusade. In what was known as the "Jarrow Crusade" during the autumn of 1936, a group of approximately 200 protesters marched from the town of Jarrow in northeastern England to London to demonstrate their need for employment and the plight of their town, where the previous year the shipyard had been closed.

Why was unemployment so widespread in Europe in the 1930s?

European farmers while increasing the cost of the industrial goods they used. Consequently, farmers had great difficulty paying off their debts. These problems were especially acute in central and eastern Europe and abetted farmers' disillusionment with liberal politics. German farmers, for example, would become prime supporters of the National Socialist Workers Party (Nazis).

Outside Europe similar problems affected wheat, sugar, coffee, rubber, wool, and lard producers. The people who produced these goods in underdeveloped nations could no longer make enough money to buy finished goods from industrial Europe. Commodity production had outstripped world demand.

The result was stagnation and depression for European industry. Coal, iron, and textiles had depended largely on international markets. Unemployment spread from these industries to those producing consumer goods. Unemployment in Britain and Germany during the 1920s had created "soft" domestic markets. Governments reduced spending, which further weakened domestic demand. By the early 1930s, the Depression was feeding on itself.

DEPRESSION AND GOVERNMENT POLICY

The governments of the late 1920s and the early 1930s were not well suited to confront the unemployment and social insecurity caused by the Depression. The electorates demanded action. Government response depended largely on the severity of the Depression in a particular country and on the self-confidence of its political system.

Great Britain and France undertook moderate political experiments. In 1924, Britain's Labour Party governed for the first time, under Prime Minister Ramsay MacDonald (1866–1937). Under the pressure of the Depression, MacDonald organized a National Government, a coalition of the Labour, Conservative, and Liberal parties that remained in power from 1929 until 1935, when the Conservatives regained power.

The most important French political experiment was the **Popular Front** Ministry, which came to office in 1936. This government was composed of socialists, radicals, and communists—the first time that socialists and communists had cooperated in a ministry. The Popular Front addressed major labor problems in the French economy, but by 1938 it came to an end.

The political experiments of the 1920s and 1930s that reshaped world history involved a Soviet government in Russia, a Fascist regime in Italy, and a Nazi dictatorship in Germany.

THE SOVIET EXPERIMENT

 HOW DID Stalin gain and keep power in the Soviet Union?

The Bolshevik Revolution in Russia led to the most durable of all twentieth-century authoritarian governments. The Communist Party of the Soviet Union retained power from 1917 until the end of 1991, and it influenced the history of much of the world. Unlike the Italian Fascists or the German National Socialists, the Bolsheviks seized power. Their leaders long felt insecure about their hold on the country. The Communist Party was neither a mass party nor a nationalistic one. The Bolsheviks confronted a much less industrialized economy than that of Italy or Germany. They believed in and practiced the collectivization of economic life attacked by right-wing dictatorships. The Marxist-Leninist ideology was broader than the nationalism of the Fascists and the racism of the Nazis. Communists regarded their government and their revolution as epoch-making events in the development of humanity. Fear of communism and determination to stop its spread were leading political forces in western Europe and the United States for most of the rest of the century.

WAR COMMUNISM

Within the Soviet Union, the Red Army had suppressed opposition. A new secret police, known as *Cheka*, appeared. Throughout the Russian civil war Lenin had declared that the Bolshevik Party, as the vanguard of the revolution, was imposing the dictatorship of the proletariat. Under the economic policy of **War Communism**, the revolutionary government confiscated banks, transport facilities, and heavy industry. The state also requisitioned grain and shipped it from the countryside to feed the army and the cities.

War Communism helped the Red Army defeat its opponents, but it generated domestic opposition. Many Russians were no longer willing to make the sacrifices demanded by central party bureaucrats. In 1920 and 1921, strikes occurred. Peasants resisted the requisition of grain. In March 1921, the navy mutinied. The proletariat itself was opposing the dictatorship of the proletariat. Also, by late 1920, it had become clear that revolution would not sweep across the rest of Europe. The Soviet Union was a vast island of revolutionary socialism in a sea of worldwide capitalism.

THE NEW ECONOMIC POLICY

Lenin made a strategic retreat. In March 1921, he outlined the **New Economic Policy**, or **NEP**. Apart from "the commanding heights" of banking, heavy industry, transportation, and international commerce, private economic enterprise was allowed and peasants could farm for a profit. The countryside became more stable, and a secure food supply seemed assured for the cities. Similar free enterprise flourished within light industry and retail trade. The revolution seemed to have transformed Russia into a land of small farms and private shops and businesses.

STALIN VERSUS TROTSKY

The NEP had caused sharp disputes within the Politburo, the highest governing committee of the Communist Party. These frictions increased when Lenin suffered a stroke in 1922 and died in 1924. Two factions emerged from an intense struggle for leadership of the party. One was led by Lenin's long-time colleague, Leon Trotsky (1879–1940), the other by Joseph Stalin (1879–1953), who had become general secretary of the party in 1922.

The power struggle was fought over the question of Russia's path toward industrialization and the future of the communist revolutionary movement. Trotsky, speaking for what became known as the left wing, urged rapid industrialization and looked to voluntary collectivization of farming by poor peasants as a means of increasing agricultural production. Trotsky further argued that the revolution in Russia could succeed only if new revolutions took place elsewhere. A right-wing faction manipulated by Stalin pressed for the continuation of Lenin's NEP and a policy of relatively slow industrialization. Stalin was the ultimate victor. He was much less an intellectual and internationalist than the other early Bolshevik leaders. He was also much more brutal. His power lay in his command of bureaucratic and administrative methods. He mastered the crucial details of party structure, including admission and promotion. He had the support of the lower levels of the party.

In 1924, Stalin enunciated the doctrine of "socialism in one country." Russian success did not depend on the fate of the revolution elsewhere. Stalin thus nationalized

Lenin. Anxiety over the spread of the Bolshevik Revolution was a fundamental factor of European politics during the 1920s and 1930s. Images like this Soviet portrait of Lenin as a heroic revolutionary conjured fears among people in the rest of Europe of a political force determined to overturn their social, political, and economic institutions.

Gemalde von A. M. Gerassimow, "Lenin as Agitator"/Bildarchiv Preussischer Kulturbesitz.

Compare this painting of Lenin with the image of Stalin on page 760. What are the similarities and differences in how the two men are portrayed?

War Communism
The economic policy adopted by the Bolsheviks during the Russian Civil War to seize the banks, heavy industry, railroads, and grain.

New Economic Policy (NEP)
A limited revival of capitalism, especially in light industry and agriculture, introduced by Lenin in 1921 to repair the damage inflicted on the Russian economy by the civil war and War Communism.

((•—[Hear the Audio
Communism at **myhistorylab.com**

the previously international scope of the Marxist revolution. By 1927, Trotsky had been ousted from the party. In 1929, he was expelled from Russia and was eventually murdered in 1940 in Mexico by one of Stalin's agents. Stalin was firmly in control of the Soviet state.

DECISION FOR RAPID INDUSTRIALIZATION

During the Depression, the Soviet Union registered tremendous industrial advance. As usual in Russia, the direction and impetus came from the top. Stalin far exceeded the tsars in the coercion and terror he brought to the task. Russia achieved its economic growth during the 1930s only at the cost of millions of human lives. Stalin's economic policy clearly proved that his earlier rivalry with Trotsky had been a matter of political power, not ideological difference.

Through 1928, Lenin's NEP steered Soviet economic development. A few farmers, the *kulaks*, became prosperous. During 1928 and 1929, the kulaks and other farmers withheld grain from the market because prices were too low. Food shortages in the cities caused unrest. Stalin came to a momentous decision. Russia must industrialize rapidly to match the power of the West. Agriculture must be collectivized to produce sufficient grain for food and export and to free peasant labor for the factories. This program unleashed a second Russian revolution.

In 1929, Stalin ordered party agents to confiscate hoarded wheat. As part of the general plan to collectivize farming, the government undertook to eliminate the kulaks as a class. (See Document: "Stalin Calls for the Liquidation of the *Kulaks* as a Class.") A kulak, however, soon came to mean any peasant who opposed Stalin's policy. In the countryside, peasants at all levels of wealth resisted stubbornly. They wreaked their vengeance on the policy of **collectivization** by slaughtering more than 100 million horses and cattle between 1929 and 1933. The situation in the countryside amounted to open warfare. As many as 10 million peasants were killed, and millions of others were sent to labor camps. Because of the turmoil, famine persisted in 1932 and 1933. Yet Stalin persevered. Peasants had their lands incorporated into large collective farms. The state controlled the machinery for these units.

The government now had primary direction over the food supply. Peasants could no longer determine whether there would be stability or unrest in the cities. Stalin and the Communist Party had won the battle of the wheat fields, but the problem of producing enough grain still plagues the former Soviet Union.

The revolution in agriculture had been undertaken for the sake of industrialization. The increased grain supply was to feed the labor force and provide exports to finance the imports required for industrial development. The Soviet Union's industrial achievement between 1928 and World War II was one of the most striking accomplishments of the twentieth century. Soviet industrial production rose approximately 400 percent between 1928 and 1940. Few consumer goods were produced. Labor for this development was supplied internally. Capital was raised from the export of grain, even at the cost of internal shortage. Technology was borrowed from industrialized nations.

The organizational vehicle for industrialization was a series of five-year plans that began in 1928. The State Planning Commission, or Gosplan, set the production

Kulaks. During Stalin's drive to collectivize agriculture, wealthy peasants known as kulaks become the object of his wrath. Here a group of mostly peasant women demonstrate against the kulaks.

What happened to the kulaks?

DOCUMENT

Stalin Calls for the Liquidation of the *Kulaks* as a Class

The core of Stalin's agricultural policy undertaken in the late 1920s and early 1930s was the replacement of private farms with large collective farms run by the state. The greatest obstacle to this policy was the kulaks—prosperous, productive peasants. In this speech of 1929, Stalin first explains why collective farms must replace small peasant farming to achieve an adequate food supply for the cities and the industrial workers. He then calls for the liquidation of the kulaks as a class. As might be expected, the kulaks resisted collectivization by destroying crops and farm animals. In turn, Communist Party agents killed millions of peasants to achieve collectivization.

- **WHAT** were the goals of the collectivization of farms in the Soviet Union? How did the kulaks stand in the way of collectivization? How does Stalin dehumanize the kulaks by discussing them entirely as a class and as part of the capitalistic system?

Can we advance our socialized industry at an accelerated rate as long as we have an agricultural base, such as is provided by small-peasant farming, which is incapable of expanded reproduction, and which, in addition, is the predominant force in our national economy? No, we cannot. . . .

What, then, is the solution? The solution lies in enlarging the agricultural units, in making agriculture capable of accumulation, of expanded reproduction, and in thus transforming the agricultural bases of our national economy.

[T]he socialist way [to enlarge farming units], which is to introduce collective farms and state farms in agriculture, the way which leads to the amalgamation of the small-peasant farms into large collective farms, employing machinery and scientific methods of farming, and capable of developing further, for such agricultural enterprises can achieve expanded reproduction. . . .

The characteristic feature in the work of our Party during the past year is that we, as a Party, as the Soviet power,

(a) have developed an offensive along the whole front against the capitalist elements in the countryside;

(b) that this offensive, as you know, has brought about and is bringing about very palpable, positive results.

What does this mean? It means that we have passed from the policy of restricting the exploiting proclivities of the *kulaks* to the policy of eliminating the *kulaks* as a class. . . .

Until recently the Party adhered to the policy of restricting the exploiting proclivities of the *kulaks*. . . .

Could we have undertaken such an offensive against the *kulaks* five years or three years ago? Could we then have counted on success in such an offensive? No, we could not. That would have been the most dangerous adventurism. It would have been playing a very dangerous game at offensive. We would certainly have failed, and our failure would have strengthened the position of the *kulaks*. Why? Because we still lacked a wide network of state and collective farms in the rural districts which could be used as strongholds in a determined offensive against the *kulaks*. Because at that time we were not yet able to substitute for the capitalist production of the *kulaks* the socialist production of the collective farms and state farms. . . .

Now we are able to carry on a determined offensive against the *kulaks*, to break their resistance, to eliminate them as a class and substitute for their output the output of the collective farms and state farms. Now, the *kulaks* are being expropriated by the masses of poor and middle peasants themselves, by the masses who are putting solid collectivization into practice. Now, the expropriation of the *kulaks* in the regions of solid collectivization is no longer just an administrative measure. Now, the expropriation of the *kulaks* is an integral part of the formation and development of the collective farms. Consequently it is now ridiculous and foolish to discourse on the expropriation of the *kulaks*. You do not lament the loss of the hair of one who has been beheaded.

Source: From Stalin, "Problems of Agrarian Policy in the USSR," Speech at a conference of Marxist students of the Agrarian question, December 27, 1929, in *Problems of Leninism*, pp. 391–393, 408–409, 411–412, as quoted in Robert V. Daniels, *A Documentary History of Communism*, rev. ed. (Hanover, NH: University Press of New England, 1984), pp. 224–227. Reprinted by permission.

Propaganda. Stalin used intimidation and propaganda to support his drive to collectivize Soviet agriculture. The poster shows an idealized Soviet collective farm on which tractors owned by the state have replaced peasant labor. In reality, collectivization provoked fierce resistance and caused famines in which millions of peasants died.

1932 (colour litho) by Klutchis (fl.1932). Deutsches Plakat Museum, Essen, Germany/Archives Charmet/The Bridgeman Art Library.

Why might collages such as this, which mixed printed slogans with portions of multiple photographs, have been effective propaganda?

goals and organized the economy to meet them. Coordinating all facets of production was difficult and complicated. A vast program of propaganda was undertaken to sell the five-year plans to the Russian people. The industrial labor force became subject to regimentation similar to that being imposed on the peasants. The accomplishment of the three five-year plans probably allowed the Soviet Union to survive the German invasion. Industries that had never existed in Russia now challenged or surpassed their counterparts in the rest of the world. Large new industrial cities had been built and populated by hundreds of thousands of people.

Great Purges

The imprisonment and execution of millions of Soviet citizens by Stalin between 1934 and 1939.

THE PURGES

Stalin's decisions to industrialize rapidly and to move against the peasants aroused internal political opposition because they were departures from Lenin's policies. In 1933, Stalin began to fear that he would lose control over the party apparatus. These fears were probably paranoid. Nevertheless, they resulted in the **Great Purges**, which were among the most mysterious and horrendous political events of the twentieth century.

On December 1, 1934, Sergei Kirov (1888–1934), the popular party chief of Leningrad (formerly Saint Petersburg), was assassinated. In the wake of the shooting, thousands of people were arrested, and still more were expelled from the party and sent to labor camps. It now seems certain that Stalin himself authorized Kirov's assassination to forestall any threat from him.

The purges after Kirov's death were just the beginning. Between 1936 and 1938, spectacular show trials were held in Moscow. Soviet leaders publicly confessed political crimes and were executed. Their confessions were palpably false. Other leaders and party members were tried in private and shot. Thousands received no trial at all. After the civilian party members had been purged, important officers, including heroes of the civil war, were killed. The exact numbers of executions and imprisonments are unknown but ran into the millions. The scale of the political turmoil was unprecedented. The Russians themselves did not comprehend what was occurring. The only rational explanation is found in Stalin's concern for his own power. The purges created a new party structure absolutely loyal to him.

Party Congress, 1936. By the mid-1930s Stalin's purges had eliminated many leaders and other members from the Soviet Communist Party. This photograph of a meeting of a party congress in 1936 shows a number of the surviving leaders with Stalin, who sits fourth from the right in the front row. To his left is Vyacheslav Molotov, longtime foreign minister. The first person on the left in the front row is Nikita Khrushchev, who headed the Soviet Union in the late 1950s and early 1960s.

Why did the Soviet experiment attract political admirers around the world for much of the twentieth century?

Despite the violence and repression, the Soviet experiment found many sympathizers. The Soviet Union had fostered Communist parties subservient to Moscow throughout the world. Even non-party members sympathized with what they believed to be the Soviet Union's goals. For decades, the Soviet Union managed to capture the imagination of some intellectuals around the globe who hoped for a utopian egalitarian transformation of society. During much of the 1930s, the Soviet Union also appeared as an enemy to the Fascist experiments in Italy and Germany. Marxist ideology appealed to many people living in the European colonial empires as a vehicle for freedom. The Soviet Union welcomed and trained many anticolonial leaders. With what is now known about Soviet repression, it is difficult to understand the power the nation exercised over many people's political imaginations, but that attraction was a factor in world politics from the 1920s through at least the early 1970s.

Read the Document

John Scott, excerpt from Behind the Urals: An American Worker in Russia's City of Steel at **myhistorylab.com**

THE FASCIST EXPERIMENT IN ITALY

The first authoritarian political experiment in western Europe that arose in part from fears of the spread of bolshevism occurred in Italy. The general term *fascist*, which has been used to describe the various right-wing dictatorships that arose between the wars, was derived from the Italian Fascist movement of Benito Mussolini (1883–1945).

WHY DID the Fascists achieve power in Italy?

Governments regarded as Fascist were antidemocratic, anti-Marxist, antiparliamentary, and frequently anti-Semitic. They hoped to hold back the spread of bolshevism, which seemed a real threat at the time. They sought a world that would be safe for the middle class and small farmers. **Fascism** rejected the political ideas of the French Revolution and of liberalism. Facists believed that parliamentary politics sacrificed national greatness to petty party disputes. They wanted to overcome the class conflict of Marxism and the party conflict of liberalism by consolidating all classes within the nation for great national purposes. Fascist governments were usually single-party dictatorships rooted in mass political parties and characterized by terrorism and police surveillance. (See Document: "Mussolini Heaps Contempt on Political Liberalism" on page 763.)

Read the Document

Filippo Tommaso Marinetti, "Futuristic Manifesto" at **myhistorylab.com**

fascism

Nationalist, antidemocratic, anti-Marxist, antiparliamentary, and often anti-Semitic political movement. Benito Mussolini (1883–1945) founded the first Fascist regime in Italy in the 1920s.

RISE OF MUSSOLINI

The Italian *Fasci di Combattimento* ("Band of Combat") was founded in 1919 in Milan. Most of its members were war veterans who felt that the sacrifices of World War I had been in vain. They feared socialism, inflation, and labor unrest.

Hear the Audio

Fascism at **myhistorylab.com**

Their leader or **Duce**, Benito Mussolini, had been active in Italian socialist politics but broke with the socialists in 1914 and supported Italian entry into the war. He then established his own newspaper, *Il Popolo d'Italia*, and was wounded in the army. In 1919 Mussolini was just another politician, his organization one of many small political groups in Italy.

Duce

Meaning "leader." Mussolini's title as head of the Fascist Party.

Postwar Italian politics was a muddle. Many Italians were dissatisfied with the parliamentary system. They felt that Italy had not been treated as a great power at the peace conference and had not received the territories it deserved. Between 1919 and 1921, Italy was also wracked by social turmoil. Numerous strikes occurred, and workers occupied factories. Peasants seized land. Parliamentary government seemed incapable of dealing with this unrest. Many Italians believed that a communist revolution might break out.

Read the Document

Benito Mussolini, "The Political and Social Doctrine of Fascism" at **myhistorylab.com**

Mussolini first supported the factory occupations and land seizures but soon reversed himself. He had discovered that many upper- and middle-class Italians who were pressured by inflation and feared property loss had no sympathy for the workers or peasants. They wanted order. Consequently, Mussolini and his Fascists took direct action. They terrorized

Benito Mussolini became famous for bombastic public speeches delivered in settings surrounded by his Fascist followers and military supporters.

Compare this photograph with the one of Hitler on page 769. Do you see any similarities? What are the differences?

socialists, attacked strikers and farm workers, and protected strikebreakers. Conservative land and factory owners were grateful. The government ignored these crimes. By early 1922, the Fascists controlled the local government in much of northern Italy.

In 1921, Mussolini and thirty-four of his followers had been elected to the Chamber of Deputies. The Fascist movement now had hundreds of thousands of supporters. In October 1922, the Fascists, dressed in their characteristic black shirts, began a march on Rome. King Victor Emmanuel III (r. 1900–1946) refused to use the army against them, ensuring a Fascist seizure of power. The cabinet resigned. On October 29, the king telegraphed Mussolini in Milan and asked him to become prime minister. The next day Mussolini arrived in Rome by train, as head of the government.

Technically, Mussolini had come into office by legal means. The monarch had the power to appoint the prime minister. Mussolini, however, had no majority in the Chamber of Deputies. Behind the legal facade lay the months of terrorist intimidation and the threat of the Fascists' October march.

THE FASCISTS IN POWER

Mussolini, who had not expected to be appointed prime minister, succeeded because of the impotence of his rivals, his use of his office, his power over the masses, and his ruthlessness. On November 23, 1922, the king and Parliament granted Mussolini dictatorial authority for one year to restore order. Wherever possible, Mussolini appointed Fascists to office. In 1924, Parliament changed the election law so that the party that gained the largest popular vote (with at least 25 percent) received two-thirds of the seats in the chamber. Coalition government, with all its compromises and hesitations, would no longer be necessary. In the election of 1924, the Fascists won complete control of the Chamber of Deputies. They used that majority to end legitimate parliamentary life. Laws permitted Mussolini to rule by decree. In 1926, Italy was transformed into a single-party, dictatorial state.

One domestic initiative brought Mussolini significant political dividends and respectability. Through the Lateran Accord of February 1929, the Roman Catholic

QUICK REVIEW

Mussolini's Rise to Power

- Broke with socialists to support Italian entry in World War I
- Built political base in northern Italy
- Terrorized opponents
- Appointed prime minister by king

DOCUMENT

Mussolini Heaps Contempt on Political Liberalism

- **WHO** would be some nineteenth-century liberal political leaders included in Mussolini's attack? Why might Mussolini's audience have been receptive to these views? What events or developments within liberal states allowed Mussolini to portray liberalism as so corrupt and powerless?

Liberalism is not the last word, nor does it represent the definitive formula on the subject of the art of government.... Liberalism is the product and the technique of the nineteenth century.... It does not follow that the Liberal scheme of government, good for the nineteenth century, for a century, that is, dominated by two such phenomena as the growth of capitalism and the strengthening of the sentiment of nationalism, should be adapted to the twentieth century, which announces itself already with characteristics sufficiently different from those that marked the preceding century....

I challenge Liberal gentlemen to tell if ever in history there has been a government that was based solely on popular consent and that renounced all use of force whatsoever. A government so constructed there has never been and never will be. Consent is an ever-changing thing like the shifting sand on the sea coast, it can never be permanent: It can never be complete.... If it be accepted as an axiom that any system of government whatever creates malcontents, how are you going to prevent this discontent from overflowing and

constituting a menace to the stability of the State? You will prevent it by force. By the assembling of the greatest force possible. By the inexorable use of this force whenever it is necessary. Take away from any government whatsoever force—and by force is meant physical, armed force—and leave it only its immortal principles, and that government will be at the mercy of the first organized group that decides to overthrow it. Fascism now throws these lifeless theories out to rot.... The truth evident now to all who are not warped by [liberal] dogmatism is that men have tired of liberty. They have made an orgy of it. Liberty is today no longer the chaste and austere virgin for whom the generations of the first half of the last century fought and died. For the gallant, restless and bitter youth who face the dawn of a new history there are other words that exercise a far greater fascination, and those words are: order, hierarchy, discipline....

Know then, once and for all, that Fascism knows no idols and worships no fetishes. It has already stepped over, and if it be necessary it will turn tranquilly and step again over, the more or less putrescent corpse of the Goddess of Liberty.

Source: From Benito Mussolini, "Force and Consent" (1923), as trans. in Jonathan F. Scott and Alexander Baltzly, eds., *Readings in European History Since 1814* (New York: F. S. Crofts, 1931), pp. 680–682.

Church and the Italian state made peace with each other. The agreement recognized the pope as the temporal ruler of Vatican City. The Italian government agreed to pay an indemnity to the papacy for confiscated land. The state also recognized Catholicism as the religion of the nation, exempted church property from taxes, and allowed church law to govern marriage.

GERMAN DEMOCRACY AND DICTATORSHIP

THE WEIMAR REPUBLIC

WHAT ROLE did terror play in Nazi Germany?

The German Weimar Republic was born from the defeat of the imperial army, the revolution of 1918, and the hopes of German Liberals and Social Democrats. Its name derived from the city of Weimar, where its constitution was written in August 1919. While the constitution was being debated, the republic, headed by the Social Democrats,

((•·┤Hear the **Audio**
Nazis 1 at **myhistorylab.com**

Reichstag

The German Parliament, which existed in various forms until 1945.

Inflation in Germany. During the German inflation of 1923, currency literally was not worth the paper on which it was printed.
What led to such extreme inflation in postwar Germany?

accepted the humiliating Versailles Treaty. Although its officials had signed only under duress, the republic was permanently associated with the national disgrace. Throughout the 1920s, nationalists and military figures whose policies had brought on the tragedy and defeat of the war blamed the young republic and the socialists for its results. In Germany, the desire to revise the treaty was related to a desire to change the form of government.

The Weimar Constitution was an enlightened document. It guaranteed civil liberties and provided for direct election, by universal suffrage, of the **Reichstag** and the president. It also, however, contained structural flaws that eventually allowed it to be overthrown. A complicated system of proportional representation made it relatively easy for small political parties to gain seats in the Reichstag, creating instability. The president appointed and removed the chancellor, the head of the cabinet. Article 48 allowed the president, in an emergency, to rule by decree. This permitted a possible presidential dictatorship.

Violence was the hallmark of the first five years of the republic. In March 1920, a right-wing Kapp, or armed insurrection, erupted in Berlin. It failed, but only after government officials had fled the city. In the same month, strikes took place in the Ruhr, and the government sent in troops. Such extremism from both the left and the right haunted the republic. In May 1921, the Allies presented a reparations bill for 132 billion gold marks. The German government accepted this preposterous demand only after new Allied threats. Throughout the early 1920s, there were assassinations or attempted assassinations of republican leaders.

Inflation brought on the major crisis of this period. The value of German currency fell due to the war and postwar deficit spending. By early 1921, the German mark traded against the American dollar at a ratio of 64 to 1, compared with a ratio of 4.2 to 1 in 1914. The German financial community contended that the mark could not be stabilized until the reparations issue had been solved. Meanwhile, the government kept issuing paper money, which it used to redeem government bonds. The French invasion of the Ruhr in January 1923 and the German response of passive economic resistance produced cataclysmic inflation. Unemployment spread, creating a drain on the treasury and reducing tax revenues. The printing presses had difficulty providing enough paper currency to keep up with the daily rise in prices. Money was literally not worth the paper it was printed on. Stores were unwilling to exchange goods for the worthless currency, and farmers hoarded produce.

The values of thrift and prudence were undermined. Middle-class savings, pensions, insurance policies, and investments in government bonds were wiped out. Debts and mortgages could not be paid off. Speculators made fortunes, but to the middle and lower-middle classes, inflation was another trauma coming hard on the heels of military defeat and the peace treaty. This social and economic upheaval laid the groundwork for the later German desire for order and security at almost any cost.

In 1923, Adolf Hitler (1889–1945) made his first significant appearance on the German political scene. The son of a minor Austrian customs official, Hitler absorbed the rabid German nationalism and extreme anti-Semitism that flourished in Vienna.

He came to hate Marxism, which he associated with Jews. During World War I, Hitler fought in the German army, was wounded, rose to the rank of corporal, and won the Iron Cross for bravery.

After the war, Hitler settled in Munich and became associated with a small nationalistic, anti-Semitic party that in 1920 adopted the name the National Socialist German Workers Party, better known as the **Nazis**. The group paraded under a red banner with a black swastika. Its program called for repudiation of the Versailles Treaty, unification of Austria and Germany, exclusion of Jews from German citizenship, agrarian reform, prohibition of land speculation, confiscation of war profits, state administration of the giant cartels, and replacement of department stores with small retail shops.

The "socialism" of Hitler and the Nazis had nothing to do with traditional German socialism. It meant not state ownership of the means of production but instead the subordination of all economic enterprise to the welfare of the nation. It often implied protection for small economic enterprises. The party appealed to economic groups that were at risk and under pressure. Nazis often tailored their messages to the particular local problems these groups confronted in different parts of Germany. The Nazis also found considerable support among war veterans, who faced economic and social displacement in Weimar society. The ongoing Nazi demand for revision of the Versailles Treaty appealed to a broad spectrum of economic groups as well as the disaffected war veterans.

Nazi stormtroopers, or **SA** (*Sturm Abteilung*), were organized under the leadership of Captain Ernst Roehm (1887–1934). The stormtroopers were the chief Nazi instrument for terror and intimidation before the party controlled the government. The organization constituted a means of preserving military discipline and values outside the small army permitted by the Paris settlement. The existence of such a private party army was a sign of the potential for violence in the Weimar Republic and of contempt for the republic.

The social and economic turmoil following the French occupation of the Ruhr and the German inflation gave the Nazis an opportunity for direct action against the Weimar Republic. By this time, Hitler dominated the Nazi Party. On November 9, 1923, Hitler and a band of followers, accompanied by General Erich Ludendorff (1865–1937), attempted an unsuccessful putsch (an attempt to overthrow the government) at a beer hall in Munich. Local authorities crushed the rising, and sixteen Nazis were killed. Hitler and Ludendorff were tried for treason. The general was acquitted. Hitler made himself into a national figure. In his defense, he condemned the republic, the Versailles Treaty, and the Jews. He was sentenced to five years in prison but spent only a few months in jail before being paroled. During this time, he dictated *Mein Kampf* (*My Struggle*). Another result of the brief imprisonment was his decision to seize political power by legal methods.

Gustav Stresemann (1878–1929) was primarily responsible for reconstruction of the republic and its achievement of a sense of self-confidence. Stresemann abandoned the policy of passive resistance in the Ruhr. With the aid of banker Hjalmar Schacht (1877–1970), he introduced a new German currency. The rate of exchange was 1 trillion of the old German marks for one new Rentenmark. Stresemann also moved against challenges from both the left and the right. He supported the crushing of both Hitler's abortive putsch and smaller communist disturbances. In late November 1923, after four months as chancellor, he became foreign minister, a post he held until his death in 1929.

In 1924 the Weimar Republic and the Allies renegotiated the reparation payments. The Dawes Plan lowered the annual payments and allowed them to fluctuate

Nazis
The German Nationalist Socialist Party.

QUICK REVIEW

National Socialism
- Hitler became associated with the National Socialist German Workers Party (Nazis) in 1920
- Party goals included repudiation of Treaty of Versailles, unification of Austria and Germany, and exclusion of Jews from German citizenship
- Nazi "socialism" meant the subordination of economic enterprises to the welfare of the nation

SA
Sturm Abteilung, or Nazi stormtroopers.

Read the Document
Adolf Hitler, excerpt from *Mein Kampf*
at **myhistorylab.com**

Mein Kampf
Meaning "My Struggle." Hitler's statement of his political program, published in 1924.

according to the fortunes of the German economy. The last French troops left the Ruhr in 1925. That same year, Field Marshal Paul von Hindenburg (1847–1934), a military hero and a conservative monarchist, was elected president of the republic. He governed in strict accordance with the constitution, and conservative Germans seemed reconciled to the republic. The latter 1920s were prosperous, and prosperity helped to establish broader acceptance and appreciation of the republic.

In foreign affairs, Stresemann pursued a conciliatory course. He fulfilled the provisions of the Versailles Treaty but attempted to revise it by diplomacy. He accepted the settlement in the west but aimed to recover German-speaking territories lost to Poland and Czechoslovakia and possibly to unite with Austria, chiefly by diplomatic means.

These developments gave rise to the Locarno Agreements of October 1925. Foreign ministers Austen Chamberlain (1863–1937) for Britain and Aristide Briand (1862–1932) for France accepted Stresemann's proposal for a fresh start. France and Germany accepted the western frontier established at Versailles. Britain and Italy agreed to intervene if either side violated the frontier or if Germany sent troops into the demilitarized Rhineland. No such agreement was made about Germany's eastern frontier, but the Germans made treaties with Poland and Czechoslovakia, and France strengthened its alliances with those countries. France supported German membership in the League of Nations and agreed to withdraw its occupation troops from the Rhineland in 1930, five years earlier than specified at Versailles.

Germany was pleased to have achieved respectability and a guarantee against another Ruhr occupation, as well as the possibility of revision in the East. Britain enjoyed playing a more evenhanded role. Italy was glad to be recognized as a great power. The French were happy, too, because the Germans voluntarily accepted the permanence of their western frontier, which was also guaranteed by Britain and Italy, and France maintained its allies in the East.

The Locarno Agreements brought new hope to Europe. Chamberlain, Briand, and Stresemann received the Nobel Peace Prize. The spirit of Locarno was carried even further when the leading European states, Japan, and the United States signed the Kellogg-Briand Pact in 1928, renouncing "war as an instrument of national policy." The joy and optimism were not justified. France had merely recognized its inability to coerce Germany without help. Britain had shown its unwillingness to uphold the settlement in the East. Germany was not reconciled to the eastern settlement.

In both France and Germany, moreover, the conciliatory politicians represented only a part of the populace. In Germany especially, most people continued to reject Versailles and regarded Locarno as an extension of it. Despite these problems, war was by no means inevitable. Europe, aided by American loans, was returning to prosperity. German leaders like Stresemann would certainly have continued to press for change but not through warfare. Continued prosperity and diplomatic success might have won the loyalty of the German people for the Weimar Republic and moderate revisionism, but the Great Depression of the 1930s brought new forces to power.

DEPRESSION AND POLITICAL DEADLOCK

The outflow of foreign, and especially American, capital from Germany that began in 1928 undermined the prosperity of the Weimar Republic. The resulting economic crisis brought parliamentary government to a halt. In 1928, a coalition of center parties and the Social Democrats governed. When the Depression struck, the coalition partners differed sharply on economic policy, and the coalition dissolved in March

QUICK REVIEW

Locarno Agreements

- October 1925: Britain and France accepted revision of the Treaty of Versailles
- Agreements brought new hope to Europe
- Many people in both Germany and France were unhappy with Locarno

MAJOR POLITICAL EVENTS OF THE 1920s AND 1930s

1919	August	Constitution of the Weimar Republic promulgated
1920		Kapp insurrection in Berlin
1921	March	Lenin initiates New Economic Policy
1922	October	Fascist march on Rome leads to Mussolini's assumption of power
1923	January	France invades the Ruhr
	November	Hitler's Beer Hall Putsch
1924		Death of Lenin
1925		Locarno Agreements
1928		Kellogg-Briand Pact; first Five-Year Plan launched in USSR
1929	January	Trotsky expelled from USSR
	February	Lateran Accord between the Vatican and the Italian state
	October	New York stock market crash
	November	Stalin's central position in the USSR affirmed
1930	March	Brüning government begins in Germany
		Stalin calls for moderation in his policy of agricultural collectivization because of "dizziness from success"
	September	Nazis capture 107 seats in German Reichstag
1931	August	National Government formed in Britain
1932	March 13	Hindenburg defeats Hitler for German presidency
	May 31	Franz von Papen forms German Cabinet
	July 31	German Reichstag election
	November 6	German Reichstag election
	December 2	Kurt von Schleicher forms German cabinet
1933	January 30	Hitler made German chancellor
	February 27	Reichstag fire
	March 5	Reichstag election
	March 23	Enabling Act consolidates Nazi power
1934	June 30	Purge of the Nazi Party
	August 2	Death of Hindenburg
	December 1	Assassination of Kirov leads to the beginning of Stalin's purges
1936	May	Popular Front government in France
	July–August	Most famous of public purge trials in Russia

1930. President von Hindenburg appointed Heinrich Brüning (1885–1970) as chancellor. Lacking a majority in the Reichstag, the new chancellor governed through emergency presidential decrees. The Weimar Republic had become a presidential dictatorship.

German unemployment rose from 2,258,000 in March 1930 to more than 6,000,000 in March 1932. The economic downturn and the parliamentary deadlock worked to the advantage of extremists. In the election of 1928, the Nazis had won only 12 seats in the Reichstag and the communists won 54. In the election of 1930, the Nazis won 107 seats and the communists won 77.

The power of the Nazis in the streets also rose. Unemployment brought thousands of men into the stormtroopers, which had almost 1 million members in 1933. The SA attacked communists and Social Democrats. For the Nazis, politics meant the capture of power through terror and intimidation as well as through elections. Decency and civility in political life vanished. Nazi rallies resembled religious revivals. They paraded through the streets and the countryside. They gained powerful supporters in the business, military, and newspaper communities. Some intellectuals were also sympathetic. The Nazis transformed the discipline and enthusiasm born of economic despair and nationalistic frustration into electoral results.

HITLER COMES TO POWER

Brüning governed for two years. The economy did not improve, and the political situation deteriorated. In 1932, the 83-year-old president stood for reelection. Hitler ran against him and Hindenburg won. But Hitler got 36.8 percent of the final vote, convincing Hindenburg that Brüning had lost the confidence of conservative Germans. In May 1932, he appointed Franz von Papen (1878–1969) chancellor. Papen was one of a small group of extremely conservative advisers on whom Hindenburg had become dependent. With the continued paralysis in the Reichstag, the advisers' influence over the president amounted to control of the government.

View the Image
Nazis 2 at **myhistorylab.com**

Papen and the circle around the president wanted to draw the Nazis into cooperation with them without giving Hitler effective power. The government needed the popular support on the right that only the Nazis seemed able to generate. The Hindenburg circle decided to convince Hitler that the Nazis could not come to power on their own. Papen removed the ban on Nazi meetings that Brüning had imposed and called a Reichstag election for July 1932. The Nazis won 230 seats and polled 37.2 percent of the vote. Hitler would enter the cabinet only if he were made chancellor. Hindenburg refused. Another election was called in November. The Nazis gained only 196 seats, and their percentage of the popular vote dipped to 33.1 percent. Hindenberg's advisers still refused to appoint Hitler to office.

In early December 1932, Papen resigned and General Kurt von Schleicher (1882–1934) became chancellor. People were now afraid of civil war between the extreme left and the far right. Schleicher tried to fashion a coalition of conservatives and trade unionists. The Hindenburg circle did not trust Schleicher's motives, which have never been clear. They persuaded Hindenburg to appoint Hitler chancellor. To control him, Papen was named vice chancellor, and other traditional conservatives were appointed to the cabinet. On January 30, 1933, Adolf Hitler became the chancellor of Germany.

Hitler had come into office by legal means. The proper procedures had been observed, so the civil service, courts, and other government agencies were able to support him in good conscience. He had forged a rigidly disciplined party structure and had mastered the techniques of mass politics and propaganda. His support appears to have come from across the social spectrum. Pockets of resistance appeared among Roman Catholic voters in the country and small towns. Support for Hitler was strong among farmers, veterans, and the young, who had suffered from the insecurity of the 1920s and the Depression. Hitler promised them security, effective government in place of petty politics, and a strong, restored Germany.

There is little evidence that business contributions made any crucial difference to the Nazis' success. Hitler's supporters were frequently suspicious of business and giant capitalism. They wanted a simpler world in which small property would be safe from both socialism and large-scale capitalist consolidation. These people looked to Hitler and the Nazis rather than to the Social Democrats because the Social Democrats never appeared sufficiently nationalistic. The Nazis won out over other conservative nationalistic parties because only the Nazis addressed the problem of social insecurities.

Hitler. Hitler's mastery of the techniques of mass politics and propaganda—including huge staged rallies like this one in 1938—was an important factor in his rise to power.

Why do you think people participated in mass events such as this rally?

HITLER'S CONSOLIDATION OF POWER

Once in office, Hitler moved swiftly to consolidate his control. This process had three facets: the capture of full legal authority, the crushing of alternative political groups, and the purging of rivals within the Nazi Party itself. On February 27, 1933, a mentally ill Dutch communist set fire to the Reichstag building in Berlin. The Nazis claimed that the fire proved the existence of a communist threat to the government. To the public, this seemed plausible. Hitler suspended civil liberties and arrested communists or alleged communists under a decree that was not revoked for as long as Hitler ruled Germany.

In early March another Reichstag election took place. The Nazis received only 43.9 percent of the vote, but the arrest of the newly elected communist deputies and the political fear aroused by the fire meant that Hitler could control the Reichstag. On March 23, 1933, the Reichstag passed an Enabling Act that permitted Hitler to rule by decree. Thereafter, there were no legal limits on his power. The Weimar Constitution was never formally repealed—it was simply supplanted.

Hitler understood that he and his party had come to power because his potential opponents had stood divided between 1929 and 1933. To prevent them from regrouping, Hitler outlawed or undermined any German institutions that might have served as rallying points for opposition. By the close of 1933, all major institutions of potential opposition—trade unions, other political parties, the federal state governments—had been eliminated.

The final element in Hitler's personal consolidation of power involved the Nazi Party itself. Ernst Roehm, the commander of the SA, was a possible rival to Hitler. The German officer corps, whom Hitler needed to rebuild the army, were jealous of the SA. To protect his own position and to shore up support with the army, Hitler ordered the murder of key SA officers, including Roehm. Between June 30 and July 2, 1934, more than 800 people were killed, including the former chancellor Kurt von Schleicher and his wife. The German army, which might have prevented the murders, did nothing. On August 2, 1934, President Hindenburg died, and the offices of chancellor and president were combined. Hitler was now the sole ruler, or **Führer**, of Germany and of the Nazi Party.

THE POLICE STATE

As Hitler consolidated his power, he oversaw the organization of a police state. The chief vehicle of police surveillance was the **SS** (*Schutzstaffel*), or security units, commanded by Heinrich Himmler (1900–1945). This group was a more elite paramilitary

Führer
Meaning "leader." The title taken by Hitler when he became dictator of Germany.

SS
Schutzstaffel, elite paramilitary police surveillance unit under the Nazis.

Anti-Jewish Policies. Soon after seizing power, the Nazi government began harassing German Jewish businesses. Non-Jewish German citizens were urged not to buy merchandise from shops owned by Jews.

Why did the Nazis target Jews?

Kristallnacht

Meaning "crystal night" because of the broken glass that littered German streets after the looting and destruction of Jewish homes, businesses, and synagogues across Germany on the orders of the Nazi Party in November 1938.

organization than the larger SA. In 1933, the SS had approximately 52,000 members. It was the instrument that carried out the blood purges of the party in 1934. By 1936, Himmler had become head of all police matters in Germany.

The police character of the Nazi regime permeated society, but the people who most consistently experienced its terror were the Jews. Anti-Semitism had been a key plank of the Nazi program, an anti-Semitism based on biological racial theories stemming from late nineteenth-century thought rather than from religious discrimination. Before World War II, the Nazi attack on the Jews went through three stages. In 1933, the Nazis excluded Jews from the civil service and attempted to enforce boycotts of Jewish businesses. The boycotts won little public support. In 1935, the Nuremberg Laws robbed German Jews of their citizenship. All persons with at least one Jewish grandparent were defined as Jews. The professions and major occupations were closed to Jews. Marriage and sexual intercourse between Jews and non-Jews were prohibited. Legal exclusion and humiliation of the Jews became the norm.

The persecution of the Jews increased again in 1938. In November, under orders from the Nazi Party, thousands of Jewish stores and synagogues were destroyed. The Jewish community itself had to pay for the damage that occurred on this **Kristallnacht** because the government confiscated the insurance money. In both large and petty ways, the German Jews were harassed. This persecution allowed the Nazis to inculcate the rest of the population with the concept of a master race of pure German "Aryans" and also to display their own contempt for civil liberties.

After the war broke out, Hitler decided in 1942 to destroy the Jews in Europe. It is thought that over 6 million Jews, mostly from eastern European nations, died as a result of that decision, unprecedented in its scope and implementation.

WOMEN IN NAZI GERMANY

The Nazis believed in separate social spheres for men and women. Men belonged in the world of action, women in the home. Women who sought to liberate themselves and to adopt roles traditionally followed by men in public life were considered symptoms of cultural decline. Respect for women should arise from their function as wives and mothers.

These attitudes conflicted with the social changes that German women, like women elsewhere in Europe, had experienced during the first three decades of the twentieth century. German women had become much more active and assertive. They worked in factories or were independently employed and had begun to enter the professions. Under the Weimar Constitution, they voted. Throughout the Weimar period, there was also a lively discussion of women's emancipation. For the Nazis, these developments were signs of cultural weakness.

The Nazis' point of view was supported by women of a conservative outlook and women who followed traditional roles as housewives. In a period of high unemployment, the Nazi attitude also appealed to many men because it discouraged women from competing with them in the workplace. Such competition had begun during World War I, and many Nazis considered it symptomatic of the social confusion that had followed the German defeat.

The Nazi discussion of the role of women was also rooted in Nazi racism. It was the special task of German mothers to preserve racial purity. Hitler championed the

A Closer Look

The Nazi Party Rally

Nazi rallies were a centerpiece of the party effort to generate mass support and to embody its broad appeal. These rallies were also often associated with raising money to support the party. Furthermore, the Nazis intended their rallies to generate fervent nationalistic group solidarity that would demonstrate that whatever other divisions might exist in the nation, loyalty to the Nazi Party and to the nation would be more important than any other group loyalty.

The Nazi Party had used what later became the ever-present swastika (or hooked cross) symbol since 1920. Hitler himself claimed to have chosen the symbol, which he and other Nazis associated with an allegedly racially pure Aryan past. In fact, many cultures had used the swastika as a symbol, which dated to ancient times in Asia. Rediscovery of the symbol during nineteenth-century archaeological excavations led to its revived use by various groups prior to the Nazis, often, though not excusively, in relation to ideas of racial purity. By the 1920s it had become almost exclusively associated with the Nazis in the public mind and has remained so to the present. The Nazis adopted the swastika as the German national flag in 1935.

It should be noted that young women were enthusiastic supporters among the crowd at this 1938 Nazi rally, extending the Nazi salute. The image in the photo illustrates the gender divisions Nazi ideology fostered. Men were portrayed as defenders of the homeland. Women were to pursue traditional domestic roles and to bear children for the nation.

Questions

1. How might the holding of rallies serve to give the sense that loyalty to the Nazi Party and the nation overrode all other social and political loyalties?

2. How could the experience of attending Nazi rallies or viewing them through movies or news reels convey to the German and non-German public throughout Europe a sense of inevitable Nazi success and widespread support?

OVERVIEW   **Characteristics Shared by Fascist, Nazi, and Soviet Communist Regimes of the 1920s and 1930s**

1. Well-organized, highly disciplined political parties
2. Intense nationalism (often denied while realized in practice in the Soviet Union)
3. Programs that promised to cure social, political, and economic malaise
4. A monopoly over mass communications and propaganda
5. Highly effective instruments of terror and police power
6. Real or imagined national, class, or racial enemies who could be demonized to whip up mass support
7. Command over modern technology and its capacity for immense destruction

view that women were to breed strong sons and daughters for the German nation. Nazi journalists often compared the role of women in childbirth to that of men in battle. Each served the state in particular gender roles. In both cases, the good of the nation was superior to that of the individual. The Nazis attacked feminist outlooks. Women were encouraged to bear many children because the Nazis believed the declining German birthrate was the result of emancipated women who had spurned their natural roles as mothers. The Nazis sponsored schools that taught women how to rear children. The Nazis saw women as educators of the young and thus the protectors of German cultural values. Through cooking, dress, music, and stories, mothers were to instill a love for the nation. As consumers for the home, women were to buy German goods and avoid Jewish merchants.

The Nazis realized that in the midst of the Depression many women would need to work, but the party urged them to pursue employment that the Nazis considered natural to their character. These tasks included agriculture, teaching, nursing, social work, and domestic service. Nonetheless, the percentage of women employed in Germany changed little from the Weimar to the Hitler years: 37 percent in 1928 and the same again in 1939. Thereafter, because of the war, many more women were recruited into the German workforce.

THE GREAT DEPRESSION AND THE NEW DEAL IN THE UNITED STATES

HOW DID FDR's policies affect the role of the federal government?

The United States emerged from World War I as a world power. It retreated from that role when the Senate refused to ratify the Versailles Treaty and failed to join the League of Nations. In 1920, Warren Harding (1865–1923) became president and urged a return to what he termed "normalcy," which meant minimal involvement abroad and conservative economic policies at home. Business interests remained in the ascendant, and the federal government took a relatively inactive role in national life, especially under Harding's successor, Calvin Coolidge (1872–1933).

The first seven or eight years of the decade witnessed remarkable American prosperity. New electrical appliances such as the radio, phonograph, washing machine, and vacuum cleaner appeared on the market. Real wages rose for many workers. Industry grew at a robust rate. Automobile manufacturers assumed a major role in national economic life. Factories became mechanized. Engineers and efficiency experts were the heroes of the business world. The stock market boomed. This activity stood in marked contrast to the economic dislocations of Europe.

This material prosperity emerged in a divided society. Segregation remained a basic fact of life for black Americans. The Ku Klux Klan, which sought to terrorize blacks, Roman Catholics, and Jews, enjoyed a resurgence. Lynchings of African Americans continued, especially in the South. The Prohibition Amendment of 1919 (repealed in 1933) forbade the manufacture and transport of alcoholic beverages. In the wake of this divisive national policy, major criminal operations arose to supply liquor and disrupt civic life. Many immigrants came from Mexico and Puerto Rico, settling in cities where their labor was desired but where they were often not welcomed or assimilated. Finally, the wealth of the nation was concentrated in few hands.

Women Members of the Ku Klux Klan in New Castle, Indiana, August 1, 1923. The revived Klan was a powerful presence in scores of American communities during the early 1920s, especially among native-born white Protestants, who feared cultural and political change. In addition to preaching "100 percent Americanism," local Klan chapters also served a social function for members and their families.

Does the fact that these Klu Klux Klan members are from Indiana complicate commonly held notions about racial tolerance in the United States?

ECONOMIC COLLAPSE

In March 1929 Herbert Hoover became president, the third Republican in as many elections. On October 29, 1929, the New York stock market crashed. The other financial markets also went into a tailspin. During the next year the stock market continued to fall. The banks that had loaned people money with which to speculate in the market suffered great losses.

The financial collapse of 1929 triggered the Great Depression in America, although there were other underlying domestic causes. Manufacturing firms had not made sufficient capital investment. The disproportionate amount of profits going to about 5 percent of the U.S. population had begun to undermine the purchasing power of other consumers. Agriculture had been in trouble for years. Finally, the economic difficulties in Europe and Latin America, which predated those in the United States, meant foreigners were less able to purchase U.S.-made products.

The most pervasive problem of the Great Depression was unemployment. Joblessness hit unskilled workers first, then moved to factory and white-collar workers. As unemployment spread, small retail businesses suffered. In the major American manufacturing cities, hundreds of thousands of workers could not find jobs. The price of corn fell so low in some areas that it was not profitable to harvest it. By the early 1930s, banks began to fail, and people lost their savings.

The federal government was not equipped to address the emergency. There was no tradition of federal action to alleviate economic distress. President Hoover organized economic conferences and encouraged the Federal Reserve to make borrowing easier. He supported the ill-advised Hawley-Smoot Tariff Act of 1930, which was intended to protect American industry by erecting a high tariff barrier. Hoover believed relief was a matter for local government and voluntary organizations; however, many local relief agencies had run out of money by 1931. By 1932 U.S. unemployment had risen to over 23 percent, and thousands of banks had failed. The gross national product had slipped, with international trade falling by approximately two-thirds since 1929.

●●●─|**Read** the **Document**
The Great Depression:
An Oral Account (1932)
at **myhistorylab.com**

NEW ROLE FOR GOVERNMENT

The election of 1932 was one of the most crucial in American history. The Democratic Party's candidate, Franklin Delano Roosevelt (1882–1945), promised "a new deal for the American people." He overwhelmingly defeated Hoover and quickly redirected federal policy toward the Depression.

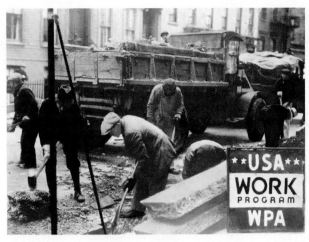

The Works Progress Administration. This group of men repairing a street worked for the Works Progress Administration, one of the chief New Deal agencies designed to create public works projects that would generate employment.

What was the New Deal?

Works Progress Administration (WPA)

New Deal program created by the Roosevelt administration in 1935 that provided relief for the unemployed in the industrial sector during the Great Depression in the United States.

QUICK REVIEW

New Deal

◆ Legislated extensive government involvement in economy

◆ Did not end unemployment

◆ Demonstrated flexibility and strength of democracy and capitalism

Roosevelt had been born into a moderately wealthy New York family and was a distant cousin of Theodore Roosevelt (1858–1919). After serving in World War I as assistant secretary of the navy, in 1920 he ran as the Democratic vice presidential candidate. The next year he was struck with polio and his legs became paralyzed, but he went on to be elected governor of New York in 1928. As president, he attempted to convey to the nation the same kind of optimistic spirit that had informed his personal recovery.

Roosevelt's first goal was to give the nation a sense that the federal government was meeting the economic challenge. The first hundred days of his administration became legendary. He immediately closed all the banks and permitted only sound institutions to reopen. Congress rapidly passed a new banking act and then enacted the Agricultural Adjustment Act and the Farm Credit Act to aid farmers. To provide jobs, Roosevelt sponsored the Civilian Conservation Corps. The Federal Emergency Relief Act funded state and local relief agencies. To restore confidence, Roosevelt began making speeches, known as "fireside chats," to the American people.

Roosevelt's most ambitious program was the National Industrial Recovery Act (NIRA), which established the National Recovery Administration (NRA). This agency attempted to foster codes written by various industries to regulate wages and prices, in hopes that regulated competition might protect jobs and assure production.

The NIRA and other New Deal legislation, such as the Wagner Act of 1935, which established the National Labor Relations Board and the Fair Labor Standards Act of 1938, provided a larger role in the American economy for organized labor. It became easier for unions to organize. Union membership grew steadily, and American unionism took on a new character. Previously, most unions had organized by craft and had been affiliated with the American Federation of Labor (AFL). In the 1930s, however, whole industries composed of workers in various crafts were organized in a single union. The most important of these organizations were the United Mine Workers and United Automobile Workers. These new unions organized themselves into the Congress of Industrial Organizations (CIO). The CIO and the AFL were rivals until they merged in the 1950s. These organizations introduced a powerful new force into the American economic scene.

In 1935 the U.S. Supreme Court declared the NRA unconstitutional. Thereafter, Roosevelt deemphasized centralized economic planning. The number of federal agencies increased, but they operated in general independence from each other.

Through New Deal legislation, the federal government was far more active in the economy than it had ever been. The government itself attempted to provide industrial employment. The major institution of the relief effort was the **Works Progress Administration (WPA)**. Created in 1935, the WPA began a massive program of public works.

New Deal programs involved the federal government directly in economic development rather than turning such development over to private enterprise. Through the Tennessee Valley Authority (TVA), the government became directly and extensively involved in the economy of the four states of the Tennessee River Valley. The TVA built dams and then produced and sold hydroelectricity. Another major new function for the government was providing security for the elderly through the establishment of the Social Security Administration in 1935.

In one area of American life after another, government was now expected to provide personal economic security. These actions established a mixed economy in the United States, in which the federal government would play an active, ongoing role alongside the private sector. The New Deal changed much of American life, but it did not solve the unemployment problem. In the late 1930s, the economy began to falter again. Only the nation's entry into World War II brought the U.S. economy to full employment.

There were limitations to the liberalism of the New Deal, the most significant of which related to race. Southern Democratic senators, who provided Roosevelt with necessary votes to pass his economic legislation, opposed federal legislation to prohibit lynchings. Roosevelt played pragmatist and so did not support anti-lynching legislation.

At the same time, many businesspeople found Roosevelt too liberal and his policies too activist.

Despite shortcomings, the New Deal preserved capitalism in a democratic setting of free political debate—much of it critical of the administration. The experience of the United States under the New Deal stood in marked contrast to the economic and political experiments in Europe. The United States had demonstrated that a nation with a vast industrial economy could confront its gravest economic crisis and still preserve democracy.

SUMMARY

 WHICH GROUPS were dissatisfied with the Versailles settlement?

After Versailles: Demands for Revision and Enforcement. The Versailles settlement bred political discontent and resentment throughout Europe among both victors and the defeated. Wrangles over reparations between Germany and the Allied powers persisted through the 1920s. *page 753*

 WHAT FACTORS made the Great Depression so severe and long lasting?

Toward the Great Depression in Europe. After World War I, Europe never recovered its prewar prosperity or stability. The Great Depression was triggered by a financial crisis relating to German reparations and a commodity crisis caused by overproduction. It caused severe economic, social, and political problems throughout Europe, and no government offered responsible financial leadership. *page 754*

 HOW DID Stalin gain and keep power in the Soviet Union?

The Soviet Experiment. The Bolsheviks were forced to consolidate their regime within Russia.

Lenin's New Economic Policy gave the state control over heavy industry, transportation, and international commerce but allowed for small-scale private enterprise and peasant farms. Stalin abandoned this policy to push for rapid industrialization. He abolished private enterprise, collectivized agriculture, and eliminated his opponents in a series of purges in which millions were imprisoned or killed. Despite the violence and oppression, Marxists and others around the world were attracted to the Soviet Union as the world's only communist state and the enemy of fascism. *page 756*

 WHY DID the Fascists achieve power in Italy?

The Fascist Experiment in Italy. Many Italians were dissatisfied with the terms of the Versailles Treaty and frightened by the social unrest that followed World War I. Benito Mussolini promised order and a strong state. Although he achieved power by legal means, he soon transformed Italy into a single-party dictatorship. In 1929 he came to terms with the Catholic Church by negotiating the Lateran Accord, which recognized the pope as the independent ruler of Vatican City. *page 761*

WHAT ROLE did terror play in Nazi Germany?

German Democracy and Dictatorship. The Weimar Republic was buffeted by social, political, and financial instability. Many Germans refused to accept Germany's defeat in World War I or the terms of the Versailles Treaty. Rampant inflation destroyed middle-class savings, and the Great Depression brought financial collapse and massive unemployment. Once Adolf Hitler came to power in 1933, he established a one-party dictatorship based on police terror, propaganda, racial anti-Semitism, and the cult of Hitler as supreme leader. Jews, in particular, were persecuted. *page 763*

HOW DID FDR's policies affect the role of the federal government?

The Great Depression and the New Deal in the United States. The United States emerged from World War I as a world power but retreated into isolation during the 1920s. The prosperity of the 1920s ended in the Great Depression. Franklin Delano Roosevelt's New Deal greatly expanded the power of the federal government in social and economic affairs and preserved capitalism in a democratic setting. *page 772*

KEY TERMS

collectivization (p. 758)
Duce (DOO-chay) (p. 761)
fascism (p. 761)
Führer (p. 769)
Great Depression (p. 754)
Great Purges (p. 760)
Kristallnacht (p. 770)
Mein Kampf (p. 765)
Nazis (p. 765)
New Economic Policy (NEP) (p. 757)

Popular Front (p. 756)
Reichstag (REYEKS-tahg) (p. 764)
SA (p. 765)
SS (p. 769)
War Communism (p. 757)
Weimar Republic (p. 754)
Works Progress Administration (WPA) (p. 774)

REVIEW QUESTIONS

1. Were there any groups that supported the Versailles settlement?

2. Explain the causes of the Great Depression. Why was it more severe, and why did it last longer, than previous economic downturns? Could it have been avoided?

3. What was the cause of disagreement between Trotsky and Stalin? What was the outcome of their disagreement?

4. How did Stalin achieve supreme power in the Soviet Union? Why did he decide that Russia had to industrialize rapidly? Why did this require the collectivization of agriculture? Was the policy a success? How did it affect the Russian people? What were the causes of the Great Purges?

5. What influence did the Soviet Union exert on other parts of Europe during this period?

6. Why was Italy dissatisfied and unstable after World War I? How did Mussolini achieve power?

7. What were the characteristics of the Fascist state?

8. Why did the Weimar Republic collapse in Germany? Discuss Hitler's rise to power. Which groups in Germany supported Hitler, and why were they pro-Nazi? How did he consolidate his power?

9. Compare the authoritarian regimes in the Soviet Union, Italy, and Germany. What characteristics did they have in common? What role did terror play in each?

10. Why did the U.S. economy collapse in 1929? What policies did Roosevelt use to combat the Depression? How did his policies affect the role of the federal government in national life?

Note: To learn more about the topics in this chapter, please turn to the Suggested Readings at the end of the book. For additional sources related to this chapter please see www.myhistorylab.com

Reinforce what you learned in this chapter by studying the many documents, images, maps, review tools, and videos available at **www.myhistorylab.com**

Read and Review

✓● Study and Review Chapter 29

⊶● Read the Document *Stalin Demands Rapid Industrialization of the USSR (1931), p. 758*
Irina Ivanovna Kniazeva, A Life in a Peasant Village (USSR) 1917–1930s, p. 758
John Scott, excerpt from Behind the Urals: An American Worker in Russia's City of Steel, p. 761
Filippo Tommaso Marinetti, "Futuristic Manifesto," p. 761
Benito Mussolini, "The Political and Social Doctrine of Fascism," p. 761
Adolf Hitler, excerpt from Mein Kampf, p. 765
The Great Depression: An Oral Account (1932), p. 773

(((●● Hear the Audio *Depression, p. 754*
Communism, p. 757
Fascism, p. 761
Nazis 1, p. 764

●● View the Image *Nazis 2, p. 768*

✓● Study and Review *Lenin, 1920, vs. Stalin, 1931, p. 758*

Research and Explore

●● View the Image *Bread Line during the "Great Depression"*

●● View the Image *Works Project Administration (WPA)*

(((●● **Hear** the **Audio**

Hear the audio file for Chapter 29
at **www.myhistorylab.com**

30
World War II

((•—Hear the Audio for Chapter 30 at www.myhistorylab.com

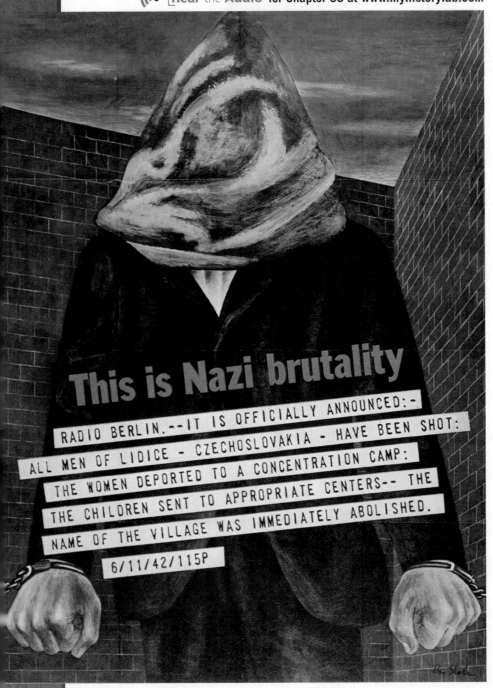

This is Nazi brutality

RADIO BERLIN.--IT IS OFFICIALLY ANNOUNCED:-
ALL MEN OF LIDICE - CZECHOSLOVAKIA - HAVE BEEN SHOT:
THE WOMEN DEPORTED TO A CONCENTRATION CAMP:
THE CHILDREN SENT TO APPROPRIATE CENTERS-- THE
NAME OF THE VILLAGE WAS IMMEDIATELY ABOLISHED.
6/11/42/115P

Nazi Terror. In this vivid poster, the artist Ben Shahn (1898–1969) memorialized the destruction of Lidice. The Czechoslovakian town was obliterated by the Nazis on June 11, 1942, in retaliation for Czech resistance against their Nazi rulers.

How did the Nazis gain control of Czechoslovakia?

T*he more idealistic survivors of the first World War, especially in the United States and Great Britain, thought of it as "the war to end all wars" and "a war to make the world safe for democracy." Only thus could they justify the awful slaughter, expense, and upheaval. How appalled they would have been had they known that only twenty years after the peace treaties, a second great war would break out that would be more truly global than the first. In this war the democracies would be fighting for their lives against militaristic, nationalistic, authoritarian, and totalitarian states in Europe and Asia. Great Britain and the United States would be allied with the communist Soviet Union. The defeat of the militarists and dictators would not bring the longed-for peace, but rather a Cold War in which the European states became second-class powers, subordinate to the two new great powers, partially or fully non-European: the Soviet Union and the United States.* ■

AGAIN THE ROAD TO WAR (1933–1939)

World War I and the Versailles Treaty had only a marginal relationship to the world Depression of the 1930s. But in Germany, where the reparations settlement had contributed to the vast inflation of 1923, economic and social discontent focused on the Versailles settlement as the cause of all ills. Throughout the late 1920s, Adolf Hitler and the Nazi Party denounced Versailles as the source of Germany's troubles; the economic woes of the early 1930s seemed to bear them out. This, coupled with Nazi Party discipline and a message of fervent nationalism, helped Hitler overthrow the Weimar Republic and take control of Germany.

WHAT WERE the main events between 1933 and 1939 that led to World War II?

See the **Map**
Expansion of Germany in the 1930s
at **myhistorylab.com**

HITLER'S GOALS

Hitler's racial theories and goals were central to his thought. He meant to go far beyond Germany's 1914 borders to bring the entire German people (*Volk*), understood as a racial group, into a single nation. The new Germany would include all the Germanic

WORLD WAR II

The second great war of the twentieth century (1939–1945) grew out of the unsatisfactory resolution of the first. In retrospect, the two wars appear to some people to be one continuous conflict—a kind of twentieth-century Thirty Years' War—with the two main periods of fighting separated by an uneasy truce. To others, that point of view distorts the situation by implying that the second war was the inevitable result of the first and its inadequate peace treaties.

The latter opinion seems more sound. Whatever the flaws of the treaties of Paris, the world suffered an even more terrible war than the first as a result of failures of judgment and will on the part of the victorious democratic powers. The United States, which had become the wealthiest and potentially the strongest nation in the world, disarmed almost entirely and withdrew into a shortsighted and foolish isolation; it could play no important part in restraining the angry and ambitious dictators who brought on the war. Britain and France refused to face the reality

of the threat the Axis powers posed until the most deadly war in history was required to put it down. If the victorious democracies had remained strong, responsible, and realistic, they could have remedied whatever injustices or mistakes arose from the treaties without endangering the peace.

Equally important, however, was the unwillingness of the victorious powers to adjust the peace treaties from World War I, or to compel compliance even in the face of Germany's obvious unwillingness or inability to pay the war reparations the victors demanded. Here too, the isolationism of the United States played a pivotal role, as the government insisted that its allies in World War I, France and Britain, whose economies were also struggling after the war, repay their debts to the United States. France and Britain, in turn, sought to fund their war debts using reparations extracted primarily from Germany. The inability of the democratic German government of the Weimar Republic to negotiate a better deal from the victors of

---

Lebensraum

German for "living space," the term refers to the Nazi plan to colonize and exploit eastern Europe.

•••[Read the Document
Adolf Hitler, "The Obersalzberg Speech"
at **myhistorylab.com**

parts of the old Habsburg Empire, including Austria. This virile nation would need more space to live (***Lebensraum***), which would be taken from the Slavs, a lesser race. The new Germany would be purified by the removal of the Jews, the most inferior race in Nazi theory. The plan required the conquest of Poland and the Ukraine as the primary areas for the settlement of Germans and for the provision of food. However, neither *Mein Kampf* nor later statements of policy were blueprints for action. Hitler was a brilliant improviser who exploited opportunities as they arose. But he never lost sight of his goal, which would almost certainly require a major war. (See Document: "Hitler States His Plans for Russia" on page 782.)

WEAKNESS OF THE VERSAILLES TREATY AND THE LEAGUE OF NATIONS

When Hitler came to power, Germany was weak. Germany withdrew from the League of Nations, and, in March 1935, Hitler violated the Versailles Treaty with the formation of an air force. Soon Hitler reinstated conscription, aiming at an army of half a million men. His path was made easier because the League of Nations was ineffective. In September 1931, Japan occupied Manchuria. China appealed to the league, which condemned the Japanese action. Japan withdrew from the league and kept Manchuria.

The league formally condemned Hitler's decision to rearm Germany but took no steps to prevent it. France and Britain met with Italian leader Benito Mussolini (1883–1945) in June 1935 to form the so-called Stresa Front and agreed to maintain the status quo in Europe by force if necessary. But Britain soon made a separate naval agreement with Hitler, allowing him to rebuild the German fleet to 35 percent of the British navy.

QUICK REVIEW

Discrediting the League of Nations

◆ Germany withdrew from league to pursue rearmament

◆ Japan withdrew from league to keep Manchuria

◆ League sanctions against Italy for invading Ethiopia were ineffective

ITALY ATTACKS ETHIOPIA

Using a border incident as an excuse, Mussolini attacked Ethiopia in October 1935, in part to avenge a humiliating Italian defeat there in 1896. The League of Nations voted economic sanctions and imposed an arms embargo. But Britain and France were afraid of alienating Mussolini, so they refused to place an embargo on oil, the one sanction

World War I added to the perception of ordinary Germans that it was weak and inept and thus contributed to its downfall.

The second war itself was plainly a global war. The Japanese occupation of Manchuria in 1931, though not technically a part of that war, was a significant precursor. Italy attacked Ethiopia in 1935. Italy, Germany, and the Soviet Union intervened in the Spanish Civil War (1936–1939). Japan attacked China in 1937. European colonies or former colonies, such as Australia and other South Pacific islands, the Philippines, and regions of the Middle East and North Africa became theaters of war or, like India, were drawn into the conflict by helping to supply the combatants. Men and women from all the inhabited continents thus took part. The use of atomic weapons brought the frightful struggle to a close, but what are called conventional weapons did almost all the damage while state-sponsored genocide, such as Hitler's Holocaust, killed millions of civilians. The world reached a level of destructiveness that threatened the very survival of civilization, even without the use of atomic or nuclear devices.

The aftermath of World War II, and the victors' analysis of the causes of the conflict, led to the creation of the United Nations, an international organization designed to forestall future conflict through improved international diplomacy.

Focus Questions

◆ What was the relationship between World War I and World War II? Why was the United States' isolationism after World War I such an important factor in the advent of World War II?

◆ Why was World War II truly a global war?

◆ What lessons did the world learn from the experiences of World War I and World War II?

that could have prevented Italian victory. The British also permitted Italian troops and munitions to move through the Suez Canal. The League of Nations and collective security were discredited, and Mussolini turned to Germany. By November 1, 1936, he could speak publicly of a Rome-Berlin "Axis."

REMILITARIZATION OF THE RHINELAND

Hitler noted the Western powers' lack of determination and, on March 7, 1936, sent a small armed force into the demilitarized Rhineland. This was a breach of both the Versailles Treaty and the Locarno Agreements, and it removed an important element of French security. Yet Britain and France, weakened by growing pacifism, made only feeble protests.

A Germany that was rapidly rearming and had a defensible western frontier presented a new problem to the Western powers. Their response was the policy of **appeasement**. It was based on the assumption that Germany had real grievances, that Hitler's goals were limited, and that the wise thing to do was to make concessions before a crisis could lead to war. Behind this approach was the horror of another war. As Germany armed, the French huddled behind the defensive Maginot Line, and the British hoped for the best.

THE SPANISH CIVIL WAR

The new European alignment was made clearer by the Spanish Civil War, which broke out in July 1936. In 1931, the Spaniards had established a republic. The left won elections in February 1936, but the Falangists (Spanish Fascists) and other groups would not accept defeat at the polls. In July, General Francisco Franco (1892–1975) led an army against the republic.

The ensuing civil war lasted almost three years, killed hundreds of thousands, and provided a training ground for World War II. The Soviet Union sent equipment and advisers to the Republicans. Liberals and leftists from Europe and America volunteered to fight in the Republican ranks against fascism. Germany and Italy aided

appeasement
The Anglo-French policy of making concessions to Germany in the 1930s to avoid a crisis that would lead to war. It assumed that Germany had real grievances and that Hitler's aims were limited and ultimately acceptable.

•◆•▪[Read the Document
Constancia de la Mora from "In Place of Splendor" at **myhistorylab.com**

DOCUMENT

Hitler States His Plans for Russia

As was revealed in detail only after World War II, Hitler had definite, if vainglorious, views on Russians and positive plans for Germany's exploitation of Russia in the event of Germany's victory.

- **WHAT** were Hitler's plans for Russia under German rule? How did they fit his racial theories? How would he justify his plans for Russia and the Russians?

The German colonists ought to live on handsome, spacious farms. The German services will be lodged in marvelous buildings, the governors in palaces. Beneath the shelter of the administrative services, we shall gradually organize all that is indispensable to the maintenance of a certain standard of living. Around the city, to a depth of thirty to forty kilometers, we shall have a belt of handsome villages connected by the best roads. What exists beyond that will be another world, in which we mean to let the Russians live as they like. It is merely necessary that we should rule them. In the event of a revolution, we shall only have to drop a few bombs on their cities, and the affair will be liquidated. Once a year we shall lead a troop of Kirghizes through the capital of the Reich, in order to strike their imaginations with the size of our monuments.

What India was for England, the territories of Russia will be for us.

When one contemplates this primitive world, one is convinced that nothing will drag it out of its indolence unless one compels the people to work. The Slavs are a mass of born slaves, who feel the need of a master. . . . It's better not to teach them to read. They won't love us for tormenting them with schools. Even to give them a locomotive to drive would be a mistake. . . .

The Germans—this is essential—will have to constitute amongst themselves a closed society, like a fortress. The least of our stable-lads must be superior to any native.

For German youth, this will be a magnificent field of experiment. We'll attract to the Ukraine Danes, Dutch, Norwegians, Swedes. The army will find areas for maneuvers there, and our aviation will have the space it needs.

Source: Hitler's Secret Conversations, 1941–1944, trans. by Norman Cameron and R. H. Stevens (New York: Farrar, Straus and Young, 1953), pp. 20, 28-29.

Pablo Picasso, *Guernica*, 1937. The Spanish Civil War divided Europe, with Fascist Italy and Nazi Germany assisting Franco, and Soviet Russia aiding the republic. Before its end in 1939, the war in Spain took some 500,000 lives. On April 26, 1937, planes from the German Condor Legion bombed the Basque town of Guernica, killing some 1,000 men, women, and children and destroying about 70 percent of the buildings. It was the most effective aerial bombardment of a city up to that time, and its purpose was simply to create terror.

Pablo Picasso, "Guernica" 1937, Oil on canvas. 11'5 1/2 × 25'5 3/4. Museo Nacional Centro de Arte Reina Sofia/(c)2007 Estate of Pablo Picasso/Artists Rights Society (ARS), New York.

Why is the Spanish Civil War sometimes described as a rehearsal for World War II?

Franco with troops and supplies. This brought them closer together and led to the Rome-Berlin **Axis** Pact. Japan joined the Axis powers in the Anti-Comintern Pact, ostensibly against communism but really as part of a powerful new diplomatic alliance. By early 1939 the Fascists effectively controlled Spain.

AUSTRIA AND CZECHOSLOVAKIA

In 1938 the new diplomatic situation encouraged Hitler to attempt a Nazi coup in Austria. The resulting *Anschluss*, or union of Germany and Austria, had great strategic significance. Czechoslovakia was now surrounded by Germany on three sides. It was allied both to France and the Soviet Union but contained about 3.5 million ethnic Germans who lived in the Sudetenland, a portion of Czechoslovakia near the German border (see Map 30–1). Supported by Hitler, they agitated for privileges and autonomy within the Czech state. In September 1938, German intervention seemed imminent. British prime minister Neville Chamberlain (1869–1940) sought to appease Hitler by compelling the Czechs to grant the Sudetenland separate status. But Hitler then

Axis
The alliance between Nazi Germany and Fascist Italy. Also called the Pact of Steel.

Anschluss
Meaning "union." The annexation of Austria by Germany in March 1938.

QUICK REVIEW

The Occupation of the Sudetenland

- May 1938: Czechs mobilize their army in response to rumors of German invasion
- September 1938: Neville Chamberlain forces Czechs to separate the Sudetenland from Czechoslovakia
- September 29, 1938: Sudetenland is given to Germany at Munich conference

MAP EXPLORATION

To explore this map further go to **http://www.myhistorylab.com**

MAP 30–1. Partitions of Czechoslovakia and Poland, 1938–1939. The immediate background of World War II is found in the complex international drama unfolding on Germany's eastern frontier in 1938 and 1939. Germany's expansion inevitably meant the victimization of Austria, Czechoslovakia, and Poland. With the failure of the Western powers' appeasement policy and the signing of a German-Soviet pact, the stage for the war was set.

How did the failure of appeasement lead to war?

Agreement at Munich. On September 29–30, 1938, Hitler met with the leaders of Britain and France at Munich to decide the fate of Czechoslovakia. The Allied leaders abandoned the small democratic nation in a vain attempt to appease Hitler and avoid war. Hitler sits in the center of the picture. To his right is British Prime Minister Neville Chamberlain.

What is appeasement?

Hear the **Audio**
World War II 1 at **myhistorylab.com**

See the **Map**
Partitions of Czechoslovakia and Poland, 1938–1939 at **myhistorylab.com**

increased his demands and insisted on immediate German military occupation of the Sudetenland.

FAILURE OF APPEASEMENT

France and Britain prepared for war. At the last moment, Mussolini proposed a conference of Germany, Italy, France, and Britain, which met on September 29 at Munich. Hitler received almost everything he had demanded. The Sudetenland became part of Germany, thus depriving the Czechs of any chance of self-defense. In return, the rest of Czechoslovakia was spared. Hitler promised, "I have no more territorial demands to make in Europe." Chamberlain told a cheering crowd, "I believe it is peace for our time."

Appeasement was a failure. On March 15, 1939, Hitler broke his promise and occupied Prague, putting an end to Czech independence and to illusions that his only goal was to restore Germans to the Reich. Munich remains an example of short-sighted policy that helped bring on a war in disadvantageous circumstances, as a result of the fear of war and the failure to prepare for it.

Poland was the next target of German expansion. In the spring of 1939, the Germans pressured Poland to restore the formerly German city of Danzig and allow a railroad and a highway through the Polish corridor to connect East Prussia with the rest of Germany. On March 31, Chamberlain announced a Franco-British guarantee of Polish independence. Hitler did not take the guarantee seriously, knowing that both countries were unprepared for war. Furthermore, neither France nor Britain could physically get help to the Poles. The only way to defend Poland was to bring Russia into the alliance against Hitler, but the French and British were hostile to communism and distrusted Stalin. Besides, both Poland and Romania were suspicious of Russian intentions—with good reason. As a result, Western negotiations with Russia were slow and cautious.

THE NAZI-SOVIET PACT

The Russians resented being left out of the Munich agreement and were annoyed by the low priority that the West seemed to give to negotiations with Russia. They rightly feared that the Western powers meant for them to bear the burden of the war against Germany. As a result, they opened negotiations with Hitler, and on August 23, 1939, the world was shocked to learn of a Nazi-Soviet nonaggression pact. Its secret provisions divided Poland between them and allowed Russia to annex the Baltic States and take Bessarabia from Romania.

The Nazi-Soviet Pact sealed the fate of Poland. On September 1, 1939, the Germans invaded Poland. Two days later, Britain and France declared war on Germany. World War II had begun.

WORLD WAR II (1939–1945)

WHY WAS 1942 the turning point in World War II?

World War II was truly global. Fighting took place in Europe and Asia, the Atlantic and the Pacific oceans, the Northern and Southern hemispheres. The demand for the fullest exploitation of material and human resources for increased production, the use of blockades, and the intensive bombing of civilian targets made the war of 1939 even more "total"—that is, comprehensive and intense—than that of 1914.

CHRONOLOGY

EVENTS LEADING TO WORLD WAR II

1919	June	Versailles Treaty
1923	January	France occupies the Ruhr
1925	October	Locarno Agreements
1931	Spring	Onset of Great Depression in Europe
1933	January	Hitler comes to power
	October	Germany withdraws from League of Nations
1935	March	Hitler renounces disarmament, starts an air force, and begins conscription
	October	Mussolini attacks Ethiopia
1936	March	Germany reoccupies and remilitarizes the Rhineland
	July	Outbreak of Spanish Civil War
	October	Formation of the Rome-Berlin Axis
1938	March	Anschluss with Austria
	September	Munich Conference and partition of Czechoslovakia
1939	March	Hitler occupies Prague; France and Great Britain guarantee Polish independence
	August	Nazi-Soviet pact
	September 1	Germany invades Poland
	September 3	Britain and France declare war on Germany

GERMAN CONQUEST OF EUROPE

The speed of the German victory over Poland astonished the world, and the Russians hastened to collect their share of the booty. On September 17, Russia invaded Poland from the East, dividing the country with the Germans. The Russians then absorbed Estonia, Latvia, and Lithuania. In November 1940, the Russians invaded Finland, but the Finns fought back and retained their independence.

The Western Front was quiet until April 1940, when the Germans invaded Denmark and Norway. A month later, a combined land and air attack struck the Low Countries. The Dutch surrendered in a few days, and the Belgians soon thereafter. British and French armies in Belgium were forced to flee to the English Channel to evacuate the beaches of Dunkirk. More than 200,000 British and 100,000 French soldiers were saved, but valuable equipment was abandoned.

The Maginot Line ran from Switzerland to the Belgian frontier. Hitler's swift advance through Belgium therefore circumvented France's main line of defense. The French army, poorly led, collapsed. Mussolini attacked France on June 10, though without success. Less than a week later, the French government asked for an armistice. The terms of the June 22 armistice allowed the Germans to occupy more than half of France, including the Atlantic and English Channel coasts. To prevent the French from fleeing to North Africa to continue the fight, Hitler left southern France unoccupied. A collaborationist regime was established at the resort city of Vichy. Most of the French were too stunned to resist. A few, notably General Charles de Gaulle (1890–1969), fled to Britain and organized the French National Committee of Liberation, or "Free French." As expectations of a quick German victory faded, French resistance arose.

Battle of Britain. A rubble-strewn street in London after the city had experienced a night of German bombing. Despite many casualties and widespread devastation, the German bombing of London did not break British morale or prevent the city from functioning.

What did Hitler hope to accomplish by the aerial bombing of Britain?

QUICK REVIEW

Operation Barbarossa

◆ Surprise invasion of Soviet Union by Germany launched June 22, 1941

◆ Germany advanced rapidly in the early stages of the campaign

◆ German failure to deliver a decisive blow delayed victory until winter set in, turning the tide in Soviet favor

⬤ See the Map
The Nazi Empire in 1942
at **myhistorylab.com**

Luftwaffe
The German air force in World War II.

blitzkrieg
Meaning "lightning war." The German tactic early in World War II of employing fast-moving, massed armored columns supported by airpower to overwhelm the enemy.

BATTLE OF BRITAIN

Hitler expected to make a deal with the British. He was prepared to allow Britain to retain its empire in return for a free hand in Europe. Any chance of such terms disappeared when Winston Churchill (1874–1965) replaced Chamberlain as prime minister in May 1940.

One of Churchill's greatest achievements was establishing a close relationship with the American president Franklin D. Roosevelt (1882–1945). In 1940 and 1941, before the United States was at war, America sent military supplies, traded destroyers for leases on British naval bases, and even convoyed ships across the Atlantic to help the British survive. As Britain remained defiant, Hitler was forced to contemplate an invasion, which required control of the air. The German air force (**Luftwaffe**) destroyed much of London. About 15,000 people were killed. But theories of victory through airpower alone proved vain; casualties were much less than expected, and the bombings made the British people more resolute. Moreover, the Royal Air Force (RAF), aided by the newly developed technology of radar, inflicted heavy losses on the *Luftwaffe*. Hitler lost the Battle of Britain in the air and was forced to abandon his plans for invasion.

GERMAN ATTACK ON RUSSIA

Operation Barbarossa, the code name for the German invasion of Russia, was aimed at knocking Russia out of the war before winter could set in. Success required an early start. Here Hitler's Italian alliance proved costly. Mussolini had launched an attack against the British in Egypt and also invaded Greece. (See Map 30-2.) The British counterattacked successfully in North Africa, and the Greeks repulsed the Italians. In March 1941, the British sent help to the Greeks, and Hitler was forced to divert his attention to the Balkans and North Africa. General Erwin Rommel (1891–1944) soon drove the British back into Egypt. In the Balkans, the German army occupied Yugoslavia and crushed Greek resistance. All this cost Hitler six weeks. Operation Barbarossa was launched against Russia on June 22, 1941, and it almost succeeded. Stalin panicked. By November, the German army stood at the gates of Leningrad, on the outskirts of Moscow, and on the Don River. Of the 4.5 million troops with which the Russians had begun the fighting, they had lost 2.5 million; of their 15,000 tanks, only 700 were left.

A German victory seemed imminent, but then Hitler diverted significant forces to the south. By the time he marched on Moscow, winter was setting in. The German army lacked appropriate equipment, and Stalin had reorganized, fortified the city, and brought in troops from Siberia. In November and December, the Russians counterattacked. Hitler's **blitzkrieg** ("war by lightning strokes") turned into a war of attrition.

HITLER'S EUROPE

The demands of war and Hitler's defeat prevented him from fully carrying out his plans. But the measures he took before his death suggest a regime unmatched in history for planned terror and inhumanity. Hitler regarded most conquered lands merely as a source of plunder, slave labor, and ultimately *Lebensraum* for Germans. He stripped them of entire industries and their peoples of basic necessities. Regions inhabited by people Hitler considered racially akin to the Germans (Scandinavia, the Low Countries, Switzerland) were to be absorbed into Germany.

RACISM AND THE HOLOCAUST

The most horrific aspect of Nazi rule in Europe arose from the inhumanity inherent in Hitler's racial doctrines. He considered the Slavs *Untermenschen*, subhuman creatures like beasts. In Poland the upper and professional classes were jailed, deported, or killed; harsh living conditions were imposed on everyone else. Russia was worse: Hitler spoke of his Russian campaign as a war of extermination. Some 6 million Russian prisoners of war and deported civilian workers may have died under Nazi rule.

■ **Read** the **Document**
Wannsee Protocol at **myhistorylab.com**

MAP 30–2. Axis Europe 1941. On the eve of the German invasion of the Soviet Union, the Germany–Italy Axis bestrode most of western Europe by annexation, occupation, or alliance—from Norway and Finland in the north to Greece in the south and from Poland to France. Britain, the Soviets, a number of insurgent groups, and, finally, the United States had before them the long struggle of conquering this Axis "fortress Europe."

What were the strengths and weaknesses of Germany's territorial position in 1941?

Roundup of Hungarian Jewish Women.
World War II resulted in the near-total destruction of the Jews of Europe, victims of the Holocaust spawned by Hitler's racial theories of the superiority and inferiority of particular ethnic groups. Hitler placed special emphasis on the need to exterminate the Jews, to whom he attributed particular wickedness. This picture shows Hungarian Jewish women, after "disinfection" and head shaving, marching to the concentration or death camp at Auschwitz-Birkenau.

Photo by Bernhard Walter; source: National Archives and Records Administration.

How did the Holocaust fundamentally transform European society?

MAP 30–3. The Holocaust. The Nazi policy of ethnic cleansing—targeting Jews, Gypsies, political dissidents, and "social deviants"—began with imprisoning them in concentration camps, but by 1943 the *Endlösung*, or Final Solution, called for the systematic extermination of "undesirables."

Which countries were most severely affected by the Holocaust?

Hitler had special plans for the Jews. He meant to make all Europe *Judenrein* ("free of Jews"). For a time he thought of deporting Jews but later decided on the "final solution of the Jewish problem": genocide. The Nazis built extermination camps in Germany and Poland and used the latest technology to kill millions of men, women, and children just because they were Jews. Before the war was over, 6 million Jews had died in what has come to be called the **Holocaust**. Only about a million remained alive, mostly in pitiable condition (see Map 30–3).

⏺ View the Image
Emaciated Woman at Bergen-Belsen at
myhistorylab.com

Holocaust
The Nazi extermination of millions of European Jews between 1940 and 1945. Nazis called it the "final solution to the Jewish problem."

THE ROAD TO PEARL HARBOR AND AMERICA'S ENTRY INTO THE WAR

The war took on truly global proportions in December 1941. The Japanese were already at war with China, and between the outbreak of that war in 1937 and the opening of the World War II campaign in the Pacific, there were three critical junctures. The first was Japan's January 1938 invasion of China to overthrow the Chinese Nationalist Party government in Nanjing. The Japanese army occupied most of the cities and railroads of eastern China, killing more than 300,000 people and brutally raping 7,000 women. Chinese Nationalist leader Jiang Jieshi (Chiang Kai-shek), however, refused to surrender. The ensuing stalemate lasted until 1945.

The second critical decision was the Tripartite Pact that Japan signed with Germany and Italy in September 1940. Germany's European victories in late spring 1940 seemed a prelude to German victory, and Japan hoped that the pact would help it achieve three objectives: to isolate the United States (which was demanding that Japan withdraw from China); to take over the Southeast Asian colonies of Britain, France, and the Netherlands; and to improve its relations with the Soviet Union through Germany's help. This last objective was reached when Japan signed a neutrality pact with the Soviet Union in April 1941. Japan remained neutral when Germany attacked the Soviet Union and ceased at that point to work with the Axis powers.

The third and fateful decision was to go to war with the United States. In June 1941, following Germany's defeat of France, Japanese troops had occupied northern French Indochina. The United States retaliated by limiting strategic exports to Japan. In July 1941 Japanese troops took southern Indochina, and the United States embargoed all exports to Japan, cutting Japanese oil imports by 90 percent. The Japanese navy urged seizure of the oil-rich Dutch East Indies, but this was dangerous as long as the United States held the Philippines. Japan's navy, therefore, planned a preemptive strike against the United States. On December 7, 1941, Japan launched an air attack on Pearl Harbor, Hawaii, the chief American naval base in the Pacific. The next day, the United States and Britain declared war on Japan. Three days later, Germany and Italy declared war on the United States.

Pearl Harbor. The successful Japanese attack on the American base at Pearl Harbor in Hawaii on December 7, 1941, together with simultaneous attacks on other Pacific bases, brought the United States into war against the Axis powers. For Japan, it was the opening phase of a campaign to capture European and American colonies in Southeast Asia. This picture shows the battleships USS *West Virginia* and USS *Tennessee* in flames as a small boat rescues a man from the water.

How was Japan's attack on Pearl Harbor the beginning of its ultimate demise?

THE TIDE TURNS

The potential power of the United States was enormous, but America was ill prepared for war. The army was tiny, inexperienced, and poorly supplied; American industry was not ready for war. The Japanese swiftly captured Guam, Wake Island, and the

MAP 30–4. **The War in the Pacific.** As in Europe, the Allies initially had trouble recapturing areas that the Japanese had seized quickly early in the war. The map shows the initial expansion of the Japanese and the long struggle of the Allies to push them back to their homeland and defeat them.

What was the American strategy for defeating Japan in World War II?

✦✦✦ Read the Document

Japanese Total War Research Institute; Plan for the Greater East Asia Co-Prosperity Sphere, 1942 at **myhistorylab.com**

Watch the Video

FDR on Winning the War at **myhistorylab.com**

Philippines (see Map 30–4). They also attacked Hong Kong, Malaya, Burma, and Indonesia. By the summer of 1942, the Japanese Empire stretched from the western Aleutian Islands south almost to Australia, and from Burma east to the Gilbert Islands in the mid-Pacific.

In the same year, the Germans almost reached the Caspian Sea in their drive for Russia's oil fields. In Africa, Rommel drove the British back toward the Suez Canal and was finally stopped at El Alamein, only 70 miles from Alexandria. Relations between the democracies and their Soviet ally were not close; German submarines were threatening British supplies; the Allies were being thrown back on every front, and the future looked bleak.

The tide turned at the battle of Midway in June 1942. A month earlier, both sides had suffered massive losses in the battle of the Coral Sea, but greater U.S. ship production made such sacrifices more costly for Japan. At Midway, American planes destroyed four Japanese aircraft carriers. Soon American Marines landed on

Guadalcanal in the Solomon Islands. The war in the Pacific was far from over, but Japan was checked sufficiently to allow the Allies to concentrate first on the West.

In the spring of 1943, the German army was trapped by British and American forces in Tunisia and crushed. The Mediterranean was now under Allied control, and southern Europe was exposed. In July and August 1943 the Allies took Sicily. Mussolini was driven from power, the Allies landed in Italy, and Marshal Pietro Badoglio (1871–1956), the leader of the new Italian government, declared war on Germany. German resistance was tough; the need to defend Italy left the Germans vulnerable on other fronts.

The Russian campaign became especially demanding. In the summer of 1942 the Germans had resumed the offensive on all fronts. In the south, their goal was the oil fields near the Caspian Sea, and they got as far as Stalingrad on the Volga. The battle of Stalingrad raged for months with unexampled ferocity. The Russians lost more men there than the Americans lost in combat during the entire war, but their heroic defenses prevailed. Stalingrad marked the turning point of the Russian campaign. Thereafter, as the German military and material resources dwindled, the Russians advanced inexorably westward.

In 1943 the Allies also gained ground in production and logistics. The industrial might of the United States neared full force. New technology and tactics reduced the submarine menace. The American and British air forces began a series of massive bombardments of Germany. This bombing did not have much effect on the war until 1944, when the Americans introduced long-range fighters that could protect the bombers. By 1945 the Allies could bomb at will.

⊙ View the Image
Operation Overlord, Normandy, 1944
at **myhistorylab.com**

DEFEAT OF NAZI GERMANY

On June 6, 1944 (D-Day), in one of the greatest amphibious assaults ever attempted, Allied troops landed in force on the coast of Normandy (see Map 30–5 on page 792). By the beginning of September France had been liberated.

D-Day. American soldiers land at Omaha Beach in Normandy on D-Day, June 6, 1944.

The Allied invasion of Normandy was the greatest amphibian assault in history. Does this photo capture the scale and size of the invasion?

MAP 30–5.   Defeat of the Axis in Europe, 1942–1945. Here we see some major steps in the progress toward Allied victory against Axis Europe. From the south through Italy, the west through France, and the east through Russia, the Allies gradually conquered the continent to bring the war in Europe to a close.

Why was it important for the Allies to force the Germans to fight on more than one front?

⊙ See the Map
World War II in Europe, 1939–1945
at **myhistorylab.com**

All went smoothly until December, when the Germans launched a counterattack called the battle of the Bulge through the Forest of Ardennes. It was their last gasp. The Allies recovered the momentum and pushed eastward. They crossed the Rhine in March 1945, and German resistance crumbled. This time there could be no doubt that the Germans had lost the war on the battlefield.

In the East, the Russians were within reach of Berlin by March 1945. Because the Allies insisted on unconditional surrender, the Germans fought on. Hitler committed suicide in an underground hideaway in Berlin on May 1, 1945, and the Russians occupied the city. The Third Reich had lasted a dozen years instead of the millennium predicted by Hitler.

FALL OF THE JAPANESE EMPIRE

The war in Europe ended on May 8, 1945, and by then victory over Japan was in sight (see also Chapter 27). The original Japanese attack on the United States had been a calculated risk against the odds. The longer the war lasted, the greater the impact of American superiority in industrial production and human resources. Beginning in 1943 American forces began a campaign of "island hopping," selecting strategic locations along the enemy supply line. Starting from the Solomons, they moved northeast toward the Japanese homeland. American bombers launched a terrible wave of bombings that destroyed Japanese industry and disabled the Japanese navy. But still the Japanese government, dominated by a military clique, refused to surrender. Confronted with Japan's determination, the Americans made plans for a frontal assault on the Japanese homeland, which, they calculated, would cost unacceptable American casualties and even greater losses for the Japanese.

At this point, science and technology presented the Americans with another choice. Since early in the war a secret program had been working to use atomic energy for military purposes. On August 6, 1945, an American plane dropped an atomic bomb on the city of Hiroshima. More than 70,000 of its 200,000 residents were killed. Two days later the Soviet Union declared war on Japan and invaded Manchuria. The next day a second atomic bomb fell, this time on Nagasaki. Even then it was only the unprecedented intervention of Emperor Hirohito (r. 1926–1989) that forced the Japanese government to surrender on August 14. President Harry Truman (1884–1972), who had come to office on April 12, 1945, on the death of Franklin D. Roosevelt, accepted one condition: Japan could keep its emperor. Peace was formally signed on September 2, 1945.

THE COST OF WAR

World War II was the most terrible war in history. Military deaths are estimated at 15 million, and at least as many civilians were killed. If deaths linked indirectly to the war are included, as many as 40 million may have died. Most of Europe and significant parts of Asia were devastated. The dawn of the Atomic Age that brought a dramatic end to the war made people conscious that another major war might destroy humanity. Everything depended on the conclusion of a stable peace. Yet even as the fighting ended, the victors began to quarrel.

Hiroshima. This photo, taken a few days after an atomic bomb was dropped, poignantly captures the total devastation wreaked on the city.

Why did the United States use nuclear weapons against Japan?

THE DOMESTIC FRONTS

World War II represented an effort of total war by all the belligerents. Never before had so many men and women and so many resources been devoted to military effort. One result was the carnage that occurred on the battlefields and at sea. Another was an unprecedented organization of civilians on the various home fronts. Each domestic effort and experience was different, but almost no one escaped the impact of the conflict. Shortages, propaganda campaigns, and new political developments were ubiquitous. In this section we look at the home fronts of the principal European belligerents.

HOW DID war affect civilians in Germany, France, Britain, the United States, and the Soviet Union?

GERMANY: FROM APPARENT VICTORY TO DEFEAT

Hitler had expected to defeat all his enemies by *blitzkrieg*. Such campaigns would scarcely have affected Germany's society and economy. During the first two years of the war, Hitler demanded few important sacrifices from the German people. The failure to

Youth Rally. Members of the Nazi German Women's Youth Movement perform calisthenics.

What roles did the Nazis encourage for women?

knock out the Soviet Union changed everything. Because sufficient food could no longer be imported from the East, Germany had to mobilize for total war, and the government demanded major sacrifices.

A great expansion of the army and military production began in 1942. Major German business enterprises aided the growth of wartime production. Germany met its military needs instead of making consumer goods. Between 1942 and late 1944 the output of military products tripled, but as the war went on the army absorbed more men from industry, hurting the production of even military goods. Beginning in 1942 everyday products became scarce. Prices and wages were controlled, but the standard of living of German workers fell. Burdensome food rationing began in April 1942.

By 1943 there were also serious labor shortages. The Nazis required German teenagers and retirees to work in the factories, and increasing numbers of women joined them. To achieve total mobilization the Germans closed retail businesses, raised the maximum age of women eligible for compulsory service, shifted non-German domestic workers to wartime industry, moved artists and entertainers into military service, closed theaters, and reduced basic services such as mail. Finally, the Nazis forced thousands of people from conquered lands to labor in Germany.

Hitler assigned women a special place in the war effort. The celebration of motherhood continued, with an emphasis on women who were the mothers of important military figures. Films portrayed ordinary women who became especially brave and patriotic during the war and remained faithful to their husbands who were at the front. The government portrayed other wartime activities of women as the natural fulfillment of their maternal roles. As air raid wardens they protected their families;

Bombing of Cologne. The Allied campaign of aerial bombardment did terrible damage to German cities. This photograph shows the devastation it delivered to the city of Cologne on the Rhine.

What was the overall effect of Allied aerial bombing?

as factory workers in munitions plants they aided their sons on the front lines. Women working on farms were providing for their soldier sons and husbands; as housewives they were helping to win the war by conserving food and managing their households frugally. Finally, by their faithful chastity, German women were protecting racial purity.

There was an intensification of political propaganda beyond what occurred in other countries. Hitler and other Nazis believed that weak domestic support had led to Germany's defeat in World War I, and they were determined that this would not happen again. Nazi propaganda blamed the outbreak of the war on the British. It stressed the might of Germany and the inferiority of its foes. Later in the war government broadcasts exaggerated claims of Nazi victories. As the German armies were checked on the battlefield, propaganda became a substitute for victory. To stiffen German resolve, propaganda also aimed to frighten the German population about the consequences of defeat.

After May 1943, when the Allies began their major bombing offensive over Germany, the German people had much to fear. Cities endured heavy bombing, fires, and destruction. But the bombing did not undermine German morale—on the contrary, it may have confirmed the general fear of defeat at the hands of such savage opponents and increased German resistance.

Every area of the economy and society came under the direct influence or control of the Nazi Party. The Nazis were determined that they, rather than the traditionally honored German officer corps, would profit from the new authority flowing to the central government because of the war effort. Throughout the war years there was minimal opposition to Hitler or his ministers. In 1944 a small group of army officers made an attempt to assassinate Hitler, but the effort failed, and it had no significant popular support.

The war brought great changes to Germany, but what transformed the country afterward was the experience of defeat accompanied by vast physical destruction, invasion, and occupation. Hitler and the Nazis had brought the nation to such a complete and disastrous end that only a new kind of state with new political structures could emerge.

FRANCE: DEFEAT, COLLABORATION, AND RESISTANCE

In France the Vichy government cooperated closely with the Germans for a variety of reasons. Some of the collaborators believed that the Germans were sure to win and wanted to be on the victorious side. A few sympathized with the ideas and plans of the Nazis. Many conservatives regarded the French defeat as a judgment on what they saw as the corrupt, secularized, liberal Third Republic; conservatives and extreme rightists saw the Vichy government as a device to reshape the French national character.

The Vichy regime embraced an intense, chauvinistic nationalism. It encouraged the long-standing prejudice against foreigners working in France and persecuted those who were not regarded as genuinely French. The chief victims were French Jews. Anti-Semitism was not new in France. Even before Germany undertook Hitler's "final solution," the French had begun to remove Jews from government, education, and publishing. In 1941 the Germans began to intern Jews living in occupied France; soon they carried out killings and imposed large fines collectively on the Jews of the occupied zone. In the spring of 1942 the Germans began deporting Jews, ultimately over 60,000, to the extermination camps of eastern Europe. The Vichy government made no protest.

Most of the French were not active collaborators and remained demoralized by defeat. Resistance seemed imprudent and futile. A few Frenchmen had fled to join de Gaulle's Free French forces soon after the defeat of 1940. Serious internal resistance to the German occupiers and to the Vichy government developed only late in 1942. The total number of resisters was small: Less than 5 percent of the adult French population appear to have been involved.

By early 1944 the tide of battle had shifted. An Allied victory appeared inevitable, and the Vichy government was clearly doomed. Only then did an active Resistance assert itself. From Algiers on August 9, 1944, the Committee of National Liberation declared the authority of Vichy illegitimate. Soon French soldiers joined in the liberation of Paris and established a government for Free France. On October 21, 1945, France voted to adopt a new constitution as the basis of the Fourth Republic. Bitter quarrels over who had done what during the occupation and the Vichy period divided the French for decades to come.

GREAT BRITAIN: ORGANIZATION FOR VICTORY

•••[Read the Document

Winston Churchill, "Their Finest Hour" (Great Britain), 1940 at **myhistorylab.com**

On May 22, 1940, the British Parliament gave the government emergency powers. Churchill and the British war cabinet quickly mobilized the nation. By the end of 1941 British production had surpassed Germany's. To meet the heavy demands on the labor force, factory hours were extended, and great numbers of women joined the workforce. Unemployment disappeared, and the working classes had more money than they had had for many years. To avoid inflation, savings were encouraged and taxes were raised.

The bombing "blitz" conducted by the German *Luftwaffe* in the winter and spring of 1940 to 1941 was the most immediate experience of the war for most British people. The German air raids killed thousands and destroyed the homes of many more. Many families removed their children to the countryside. Gas masks were issued to thousands of city dwellers, who were frequently compelled to take shelter from the bombs in the London subways. In England as in Germany, however, bombing did not break the people's spirit but seems to have made them more determined.

During the worst months of the "blitz" the remarkable speeches of Winston Churchill cheered and encouraged the British people. He united them with a sense of common suffering and purpose. They were called on to make many sacrifices: Transportation facilities were strained, food and clothing for civilians were in short supply, and the government adopted strict rationing to achieve a fair distribution.

The British established their own propaganda machine. The British Broadcasting Company (BBC) sent programs to every country in Europe in the local language to encourage resistance against the Nazis. At home the government used the radio to unify the nation. Soldiers at the front heard the same programs as their families at home.

For most of the population the standard of living actually improved over the course of the war, as did the general health of the nation. These gains should not be exaggerated, but many connected them with the active involvement of the government in the economy and the lives of the citizens. This wartime experience may have contributed to the Labour Party's victory in 1945.

THE UNITED STATES: AMERICAN WOMEN AND AFRICAN AMERICANS IN THE WAR EFFORT

In the United States, the induction of millions of men into the armed forces created a demand for new workers, especially in the burgeoning defense industries. It was filled in part by women. Economic pressures caused by the Great Depression of the 1930s

A Closer Look

Rosie the Riveter

The United States' entry into the Second World War called for rapid and vast increases in American industrial production to meet the needs of the nation and its allies. At the same time the removal of millions of American men from the workforce by the requirements of military service created unprecedented demands for workers to fill the gaps. To encourage women to go into war work, the U.S. government conducted a publicity campaign to celebrate a new role for women as patriotic citizens fully capable of supporting the war effort by taking jobs even in heavy industry. The best known symbol created was "Rosie the Riveter"—feminine but strong and able, the ideal woman worker: loyal, efficient, and patriotic. A hit song, "Rosie the Riveter," first used the name in 1942 and made it very popular. Soon, the government commissioned posters that featured Rosie over the caption "We Can Do It." Rosie became the most famous representation of a new and important role for women in winning the war.

Norman Rockwell painted her on the cover of the *Saturday Evening Post* on May 29, 1943 showing her eating a sandwich.

Her riveting gun lies in her lap.

Her feet rest on a copy of Hitler's *Mein Kampf*

Questions

1. Why was it necessary to lure great numbers of women into industrial jobs?

2. What is the significance of Rosie's footrest?

3. Based on what you have read about the years prior to U.S. involvement in World War II, how much of a departure is this image from the "traditional" role of women at the time? Was this the precursor to a new direction for women in U.S. society, or did things return to the way they had been once the war ended?

 To examine this image in an interactive fashion, please go to **www.myhistorylab.com**

had already brought many more women into the workforce than had been common before. Even so, the heavy burden of housework and the widespread hostility to the idea of women working outside the home kept the vast majority of women at home.

America's entry into the war changed things quickly. The need for vast amounts of equipment to wage the war called for and attracted new groups to seek work in the many enlarged and newly created factories. African Americans from the South came to northern and western cities to seek well-paying jobs, and women, too, came forward in greater numbers than ever before. In October 1942, President Roosevelt made the new situation clear: "In some communities employers dislike to hire women. In others they are reluctant to hire Negroes. We can no longer afford to indulge such prejudice."

Many women already working moved over to jobs in the defense industries; others entered the workforce for the first time, lured less by wages than by patriotism. A popular song, "Rosie the Riveter," told of a young woman working in an aircraft factory to provide protection for her boyfriend in the Marines. Rosie came to be one of the best-known symbols of the war effort when she appeared on the cover of the *Saturday Evening Post*. (See "A Closer Look" on page 797.)

THE SOVIET UNION: "THE GREAT PATRIOTIC WAR"

No nation suffered greater loss of life or more extensive physical destruction during World War II than the Soviet Union. Perhaps as many as 16 million people were killed, and vast numbers of Soviet troops were taken prisoner. Hundreds of cities and towns and well over half the industrial and transportation facilities of the country were devastated. The Germans sent thousands of Soviet prisoners to work in factories in Germany as forced labor. The Germans also confiscated grain supplies and drew mineral resources and oil from the Soviet Union to serve their own war effort.

Stalin conducted the war as virtual chief of the armed forces, and the State Committee for Defense provided strong central coordination. In the decade before the war, Stalin had already made the Soviet Union a highly centralized nation; he had attempted to manage the entire economy centrally through the Five-Year Plans, the collectivization of agriculture, and the purges. The country was thus on what amounted to a wartime footing long before the conflict erupted. When the war began, millions of citizens entered the army, but the army's influence did not grow at the expense of the state and the Communist Party—that is, Stalin.

Soviet propaganda differed from that of other nations. Because the Soviet government distrusted the loyalty of its citizens, it confiscated radios to prevent the people from listening to German propaganda. In major cities the government erected large loudspeakers to broadcast to the people in place of radios.

Soviet propaganda emphasized Russian patriotism, not Marxist class conflict. The struggle was called "The Great Patriotic War." As in other countries, writers and playwrights helped sustain public support for the war. Sometimes they drew on communist themes, but they also portrayed the common Soviet citizen as contributing to a patriotic struggle. Some wrote straightforward propaganda fostering hatred of the Germans. Great Russian novels of the past reappeared; more than half a million copies of Tolstoy's *War and Peace* were published during the siege of Leningrad. The great filmmaker Sergei Eisenstein (1898–1948) produced a vast epic entitled *Ivan the*

Home front. Russian women apply grease to howitzer shells at a munitions plant during World War II.

How was the entire Russian society mobilized for war during World War II?

Terrible, which glorified one of the most brutal tsars of Russia's past. Musicians, such as Dimitri Shostakovich (1906–1975), wrote scores that sought to evoke heroic emotions, including his Seventh Symphony—also known as the "Leningrad Symphony."

Stalin even made peace with the Russian Orthodox Church. Stalin hoped that this new policy would give him more support at home and improve the Soviet Union's image in those parts of eastern Europe where the Orthodox Church predominated.

Within occupied portions of the western Soviet Union, an active resistance movement arose against the Germans. The swiftness of the German invasion had stranded thousands of Soviet troops, some of whom escaped and carried on irregular resistance warfare behind enemy lines. Stalin supported partisan forces in lands held by the enemy for two reasons: He wanted to cause as much difficulty as possible for the Germans; and the Soviet-sponsored resistance reminded the peasants in the conquered regions that the Soviet government had not disappeared. Stalin feared that the peasants' hatred of the communist government might lead them to collaborate with the invaders.

As the Soviet armies reclaimed the occupied areas and then moved across eastern and central Europe, the Soviet Union established itself as a world power second only to the United States. Stalin had been a reluctant belligerent, but he emerged a major victor. The war and the extraordinary patriotic effort and sacrifice it generated consolidated the power of Stalin and the party more effectively than had the political and social policies of the previous decade.

QUICK REVIEW

The Soviet Union in World War II
- High casualties, extensive damage
- Patriotism and propaganda both surged
- Stalin's power consolidated
- Soviet Union's global standing elevated

PREPARATIONS FOR PEACE

The split between the Soviet Union and its wartime allies that followed the war should cause no surprise. As the self-proclaimed center of world communism, the Soviet Union was openly dedicated to the overthrow of the capitalist nations, although this message was muted when the occasion demanded. The Western allies were equally open about their hostility to communism and its chief purveyor, the Soviet Union.

Although cooperation against a common enemy and strenuous propaganda efforts in the West helped improve Western feeling toward the Soviet ally, Stalin remained suspicious and critical of the Western war effort. Likewise, Churchill never ceased planning to contain the Soviet advance into Europe. Roosevelt seems to have hoped that the Allies could continue to work together after the war, but even he was losing faith by 1945. Differences in historical development and ideology, as well as traditional conflicts over political power and influence, soon dashed hopes of a mutually satisfactory peace settlement and continued cooperation.

WHY DID cooperation between the Soviet Union and the Western powers break down in 1945?

THE ATLANTIC CHARTER

In August 1941, even before America entered the war, Roosevelt and Churchill had agreed to the Atlantic Charter. A broad set of principles in the spirit of Wilson's Fourteen Points, it provided a theoretical basis for the peace they sought. When Russia and the United States joined Britain in the war, the three powers entered a purely military alliance in January 1942, leaving all political questions aside. The first political conference was the meeting of foreign ministers in Moscow in October 1943. The ministers reaffirmed earlier agreements to fight on until the enemy surrendered unconditionally and to continue cooperating after the war in a united nations organization.

●◆● **Read** the **Document**

Roosevelt and Churchill: The Atlantic Charter, 1941 at **myhistorylab.com**

TEHRAN

The first meeting of the three leaders took place at Tehran, the capital of Iran, in 1943. Western promises to open a second front in France the next summer (1944) and Stalin's agreement to join in the war against Japan (when Germany was defeated) created an atmosphere of goodwill in which to discuss a postwar settlement. Stalin wanted to retain what he had gained in his pact with Hitler and to dismember Germany. Roosevelt and Churchill made no firm commitments.

The most important decision was for the Western Allies to attack Germany from Europe's west coast instead of from southern Europe by way of the Mediterranean. This decision meant, in retrospect, that Soviet forces would occupy eastern Europe and control its destiny. At Tehran in 1943 the Western Allies did not foresee this clearly, for the Russians were still fighting deep within their own frontiers. Among other important concessions Roosevelt and Churchill made to Stalin was to move Poland's western border to the Oder and Neisse rivers.

By 1944 the situation was different. In August, Soviet armies were in sight of Warsaw, which had risen in expectation of liberation. But the Russians turned south into the Balkans, allowing the Polish rebels to be annihilated. The Russians gained control of Romania and Hungary. Alarmed by these developments, Churchill went to Moscow and met with Stalin in October. They agreed to share power in the Balkans, though these agreements were not enforceable without American approval, and the Americans frowned on such un-Wilsonian devices as "spheres of influence."

The three powers easily agreed on Germany's disarmament and denazification and on its division into four zones of occupation by France and the Big Three (the USSR, Britain, and the United States). Churchill, however, began to balk at Stalin's plan to dismember Germany and objected to his demand for reparations in the amount of $20 billion as well as for forced labor from all the zones, with Russia to get half of everything. These matters were left to fester and cause dissension in the future.

The settlement of eastern Europe remained a problem. Everyone agreed that the Soviet Union deserved neighboring governments that were friendly, but the West insisted that they also be independent, autonomous, and democratic. Stalin knew that independent, freely elected governments in Poland and Romania might not be friendly to Russia. Under pressure from the Western leaders, Stalin signed a Declaration on Liberated Europe, promising self-determination and free democratic elections. Stalin feared that the Allies might still make an arrangement with Germany and betray him. He was eager to avoid conflict before the war with Germany was over, and he probably thought it worth endorsing some meaningless principles as the price of continued harmony. In any case, he wasted little time violating these agreements.

YALTA

The next meeting of the Big Three was at Yalta in the Crimea in February 1945. The Western armies had not yet crossed the Rhine, and the Soviet army was within 100 miles of Berlin. The war with Japan continued, and no atomic explosion had yet taken place. Roosevelt, faced with an invasion of Japan and prospective heavy losses, was eager to bring the Russians into the Pacific war as soon as possible.

As a true Wilsonian, Roosevelt also suspected Churchill's determination to maintain the British Empire and Britain's colonial advantages. The Americans thought that Churchill's plan to set up British spheres of influence in Europe would encourage the Russians to do the same and lead to friction and war. To encourage Russian

View the **Image**
The Big Three at Yalta,
at **myhistorylab.com**

participation in the war against Japan, Roosevelt and Churchill made extensive concessions to Russia in Asia. Again in the tradition of Wilson, Roosevelt stressed a united nations organization. Soviet participation in this venture seemed well worth concessions elsewhere.

POTSDAM

The Big Three met for the last time in the Berlin suburb of Potsdam in July 1945. Much had changed by then. Germany was defeated, and news of the successful experimental explosion of an atomic weapon reached the American president during the meetings. The cast of characters was also different: President Truman had replaced Roosevelt; Clement Attlee (1883–1967), leader of the Labour Party, replaced Churchill during the conference. Previous agreements were reaffirmed, but progress on undecided questions was slow.

Russia's western frontier was moved far into what had been Poland and included part of German East Prussia. In compensation, Poland was allowed "temporary administration" over the rest of East Prussia and parts of eastern Germany. In effect, Poland was moved about 100 miles west, at the expense of Germany, to accommodate the Soviet Union. The Allies agreed that Germany would be divided into occupation zones until the final peace treaty was signed. The country remained divided until the end of the Cold War more than forty years later.

A Council of Foreign Ministers was established to draft peace treaties for Germany's allies. Growing disagreements made the job difficult, and it was not until February 1947 that Italy, Romania, Hungary, Bulgaria, and Finland signed treaties. The Russians signed their own agreements with the Japanese in 1956.

Big Three at Potsdam. This photograph shows the "Big Three" at Potsdam. By the summer of 1945 only Stalin remained of the original leaders of the major Allies. Roosevelt and Churchill had been replaced by Harry Truman and Clement Attlee.

What agreements did the Allied leaders reach at the end of the war?

SUMMARY

 WHAT WERE the main events between 1933 and 1939 that led to World War II?

Again the Road to War (1933–1939). The second great war of the twentieth century (1939–1945) grew out of the unsatisfactory resolution of the first. But whatever the flaws of the treaties of Paris, the world suffered an even more terrible war than the first as a result of failures of judgment and will on the part of the victorious democratic powers. Italy attacked Ethiopia in 1935. Italy, Germany, and the Soviet Union intervened in the Spanish Civil War (1936–1939). Japan attacked China in 1937. Aggressive forces were on the march around the globe, and the defenders of the world order lacked the will to

stop them. Britain and France refused to face the threat posed by the Axis powers until the deadliest war in history was required to put it down. *page 779*

 WHY WAS 1942 the turning point in World War II?

World War II (1939–1945). The formation of the Axis among Germany, Italy, and Japan guaranteed that a second war would be fought around the world with battles in Asia, Africa, the islands of the Pacific, and Europe. Hitler's demented racial theories combined with preexisting anti-Semitism to create the concentration camps where millions of Jews and other "undesirables" were killed. In 1942, the United States won the battle of Midway, Allied forces controlled North Africa, and the Russians went on the offensive. The use of atomic weapons brought the struggle to a close. *page 784*

 HOW DID war affect civilians in Germany, France, Britain, the United States, and the Soviet Union?

The Domestic Fronts. All the belligerents strove for total war. Economic mobilization and propaganda campaigns were noteworthy features of involvement on the home front. Other experiences varied: Hitler restructured German society, but these changes largely disappeared with the Reich; France was largely passive, until the Resistance became a significant force near the end of the conflict; the British government was more involved in citizens' lives than ever; the United States relied on the labor of women, African Americans, and others who previously had been discouraged from seeking high-paying jobs; and the Soviet Union united around Russian nationalism. *page 793*

 WHY DID cooperation between the Soviet Union and the Western powers break down in 1945?

Preparations for Peace. A series of conferences and meetings among the victors brought the war to a close without a formal peace treaty in Europe. The world quickly split into two unfriendly camps, led by the United States and the Soviet Union, as the ideological opposition between communism and capitalism reemerged. *page 799*

KEY TERMS

Anschluss (AHN-shloos) (p. 783)

appeasement (p. 781)

Axis (p. 783)

blitzkrieg (BLIHTZ-kreeg) (p. 786)

Holocaust (p. 789)

Lebensraum (LAY-behnz-ROWM) (p. 780)

Luftwaffe (LOOFT-vah-fah) (p. 786)

REVIEW QUESTIONS

1. What was the relationship between World War I and World War II? Why was the isolationism of the United States after World War I such an important factor in the advent of World War II?

2. Why was World War II truly a global war?

3. What were Hitler's foreign policy aims? Was he bent on conquest in the East and dominance in the West, or did he simply want to return Germany to its 1914 boundaries?

4. What was Hitler's "final solution" to the "Jewish problem"? Why did Hitler want to eliminate Slavs as well?

5. Why did Britain and France adopt a policy of appeasement in the 1930s? What were its main features? Did the appeasers buy the West valuable time to prepare for war by their actions at Munich in 1938?

6. How was Hitler able to defeat France so easily in 1940? Why was the air war against Britain a failure? Why did Hitler invade Russia? Why did the invasion ultimately fail? Could it have succeeded?

7. Why did Japan attack the United States at Pearl Harbor? What was the significance of American intervention in the war?

8. Why did the United States drop atomic bombs on Japan? Did President Truman make the right decision when he ordered the bombs used?

9. What impact did World War II have on the civilian population of Europe? How did experiences on the domestic front of Great Britain differ from those of Germany and France? What impact did "The Great Patriotic War" have on the people of the Soviet Union? Did participation in World War II solidify Stalin's hold on power?

10. Some historians have looked at the twentieth century and have seen a period of great destruction as well as of great progress. Can the twentieth century be described as a "century of Holocaust"? Discuss.

Note: To learn more about the topics in this chapter, please turn to the Suggested Readings at the end of the book. For additional sources related to this chapter please see www.myhistorylab.com

PEARSON myhistorylab Connections

Reinforce what you learned in this chapter by studying the many documents, images, maps, review tools, and videos available at **www.myhistorylab.com**

Read and Review

✓●—Study and Review Chapter 30

●●●—Read the Document Adolf Hitler, "The Obersalzberg Speech," p. 780
Constancia de la Mora from "In Place of Splendor," p. 781
Wannsee Protocol, p. 787
Japanese Total War Research Institute; Plan for the Greater East Asia Co-Prosperity Sphere, 1942, p. 790
The Franck Report, p. 793
An Eyewitness to Hiroshima (1945), p. 793
Gertrud Scholtz-Klink, "Speech to the Nazi Women's Organization" (Germany), 1935, p. 794
Winston Churchill, "Their Finest Hour" (Great Britain), 1940, p. 796
Roosevelt and Churchill: The Atlantic Charter, 1941, p. 799

●—See the Map Partitions of Czechoslovakia and Poland, 1938–1939, p. 784
The Nazi Empire in 1942, p. 786
World War II in Europe, 1939–1945, p. 792
World War II in the Pacific, 1939-1945, p. 793

●—View the Image Emaciated Woman at Bergen-Belsen, p. 789
Operation Overlord, Normandy, 1944, p. 791
Nagasaki Atomic Bomb Attack–August 1945, p. 793

((●●—Hear the Audio World War II 1, p. 784

●—Watch the Video FDR on Winning the War, p. 790

Research and Explore

●—See the Map The Expansion of Germany in the 1930s, p. 779

●—View the Image The Big Three at Yalta, p. 800

((●●—Hear the Audio

Hear the audio file for Chapter 30
at **www.myhistorylab.com**

31

The West since World War II

The "beautiful game," by way of Europe. In the twentieth century the sport of soccer became the most popular game in the world. The World Cup, which takes place every four years, is a truly global event. The 2006 Cup attracted over 28 billion television viewers—the most watched event in history. Here Florent Malouda from France is taken down by two Italian players in the final in Berlin on July 10, 2006. Like several other players from the French squad, Malouda was an emigré. Indeed, the captain of the French team, Zinedine Zidane, who was ejected in a controversial call late in the game, has been quoted as saying, "First I am an Algerian from Marseille, and then a Frenchman." Italy went on to win the match 5–3 in penalty kicks.

Why has immigration changed European society?

S ince the conclusion of World War II, Europe's influence on the world scene has been transformed. The destruction of the war itself left Europe incapable of exercising the kind of power it had formerly exerted. The Cold War between the United States and the Soviet Union made Europe, along with other parts of the world, a divided and contested territory. The European powers themselves

THE WEST SINCE 1945

Immediately after 1945 the nations of the West entered the Cold War. That ideological, economic, and military rivalry between the United States and the Soviet Union dominated political struggles throughout the world for more than half a century. It divided Europe between NATO and Warsaw Pact military forces and forced nations outside of Europe—in Asia, Africa, and Latin America—to side with one or the other of the superpowers. Hence the Cold War too became a world war that had an important impact on non-Western nations. At times these other nations became theaters of conflict in which indigenous civil wars melded into the struggle between the United States and the Soviet Union, as in the case of Cuba, Angola, Korea, and Vietnam. A neutral stance in this conflict became extremely difficult for any nation to sustain.

In the later 1980s, however, the Cold War unexpectedly ended as the Soviet Union and the nations of Eastern Europe, their economies exhausted from failed experiments in central planning and repression, experienced enormous internal political changes and began the difficult transition to democracy and capitalism.

These changes have clearly opened a new epoch of Western history. The United States has emerged from the Cold War as the single remaining superpower. Western Europe has achieved a new level of economic and political unity under the auspices of the European Union, although its peoples and governments are hesitant to press the process too far too rapidly. The economic success of the European Union has inspired other regional global treaties to promote free markets, including NAFTA (North Atlantic Free Trade Association), as well as the global WTO (World Trade Organization). Europe has also been more ambitious than the United States in promoting international organizations such as the World Court designed to discipline countries that oppress their neighbors or threaten world peace. Eastern Europe and the former Soviet Union are experiencing economic turmoil and political uncertainty. Although some Eastern European countries such as Poland, the Czech Republic, and Hungary were better prepared than others to join the European Union, the fact that all Eastern European nations aspire to become EU members bodes well for the future of this

could not determine the outcome of the superpowers' struggle for world dominance. Furthermore, less than five years after the war Europeans began to lose control of their overseas empires.

The greatest change that took place after 1945 was the emergence of the United States as a fully active great power. The American retreat from leadership that occurred in 1919 was not repeated. The United States' decision to take an activist role in world affairs touched virtually every aspect of the postwar world. American domestic politics and foreign policy became intertwined as never before.

European society continued to develop in new directions. Yet for forty-five years after World War II, Europe remained divided between a Western region generally characterized by democracies and an Eastern region characterized by Communist Party authoritarian states dominated by the Soviet Union. From the late 1970s onward there were political stirrings and economic stagnation in Eastern Europe and the Soviet Union. These culminated in 1989 with revolutions throughout Eastern Europe and in 1991 with the collapse of communist government in the Soviet Union itself.

Since then, Europeans have sought new political direction. The movement toward unification, particularly of the currency, continues in Western Europe. Political confusion and economic stagnation afflict some of the nations that emerged from the Soviet Union, and the attacks of September 11, 2001, on the United States led to events that have challenged the post–World War II Western alliance. The world financial crisis originating in 2008 has brought serious challenges to European economic life. ■

THE COLD WAR ERA

WHAT WERE the causes of the Cold War?

AREAS OF EARLY COLD WAR CONFLICT

The tense relationship between the United States and the Soviet Union that dominated world history during the second half of the twentieth century originated in the closing months of World War II. In part, the coldness arose from the mutual feeling that each region. Except for Latvia, Estonia, and Lithuania, newly independent former regions of the Soviet Union such as Ukraine, Georgia, and Belarus have an even more difficult path ahead of them in developing their economies and societies. Together with the Islamic countries, such as Uzbekistan, Turkmenistan, and Kazakhstan, these states face added difficulties from the legacy of repressive authoritarian government and centrally planned economies. The security of Europe's eastern borders will depend on the success of these Eastern European nations and former Soviet republics in making the transition to democracy.

Another important factor in the history of both the United States and Europe since World War II has been the rising immigration from the rest of the world. Germany has seen the influx of significant numbers of Islamic *gastarbeiters* (guest workers) from Turkey, while France, Italy, and Spain receive more Islamic immigrants from North Africa and the Middle East, many from their former colonies. The United States, with its long history as an immigrant nation, has been more comfortable dealing with the influx of non-European

immigrants, but struggles persist over language, cultural identity, and assimilation. Europe, less accustomed to non-European immigration, has found it even more difficult to accommodate immigrants whose religions, languages, and appearance differ from those of Europeans and who may not seek to assimilate to the cultures of the nations where they have come to reside.

Focus Questions

◆ What was the Cold War, and why can we rightly call it a world war?

◆ How has the relationship between the United States and Europe changed since World War II? How might it develop in the future?

◆ What immediate and long-term factors accounted for the collapse of the Soviet Union?

◆ How has immigration changed the face of Europe since 1945? What is the religious dimension of that immigration?

---

had violated previous agreements. The Russians were plainly asserting permanent control of Poland and Romania under puppet communist governments. The United States, meanwhile, was taking a harder line on the extent of German reparations to the Soviet Union.

Hostility among the former allies emerged quickly. In February 1946 both Stalin and his foreign minister, Vyacheslav Molotov (1890–1986), gave public speeches in which they spoke of the Western democracies as enemies. A month later Churchill (1874–1965) delivered a speech in which he spoke of an Iron Curtain that had descended on Europe, dividing a free and democratic West from an East under totalitarian rule. He warned against communist subversion and urged Western unity and strength to counter the new menace. In this atmosphere, difficulties grew.

◉ See the **Map**
Cold War 1 at **myhistorylab.com**

Read the **Document**
Josef Stalin, excerpts from the "Soviet Victory" Speech, 1946
at **myhistorylab.com**

Read the **Document**
Iron Curtain Speech, Winston Churchill
at **myhistorylab.com**

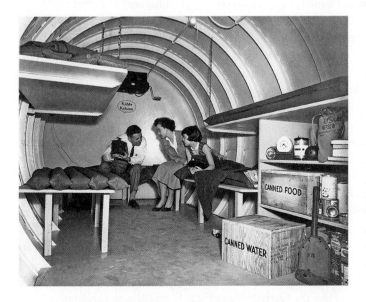

H-bomb Shelter. In 1950 Albert Einstein wrote that "Radioactive poisoning of the atmosphere and hence annihilation of any life on earth has been brought within the range of technical possibilities. . . . In the end, there beckons more and more clearly general annihilation." The U.S. government, however, fostered belief in manageable atomic warfare in spite of the evidence from Japan, and backyard bomb shelters were a 1950s fad. This one could house a small family for up to five days. Standard features included canned food and water, sterno stove, battery-powered radio, chemical toilet, flashlight, blankets, and first-aid kit. During peacetime, the shelter could be used as a spare bedroom, for storage space, or even to cultivate mushrooms.
Why does this family appear to be at ease even though it is sitting inside a bomb shelter?

Cold War
The ideological and geographical struggle between the United States and its allies, and the USSR and its allies that began after World War II and lasted until the dissolution of the USSR in 1989.

•••—Read the Document
The Truman Doctrine (1947) Harry S. Truman at **myhistorylab.com**

Marshall Plan
The U.S. program, named after Secretary of State George C. Marshall, that provided economic aid to Europe after World War II.

•••—Read the Document
George C. Marshall, The Marshall Plan, 1947 at **myhistorylab.com**

Berlin Airlift. The Allied airlift in action during the Berlin Blockade. Every day for almost a year Western planes supplied the city until Stalin lifted the blockade in May 1949.

Why was the lifting of the Berlin blockade a major victory for the West?

The attempt to deal cooperatively with the problem of atomic energy was an early victim of the **Cold War**. The Americans proposed a plan to place the manufacture and control of atomic weapons under international control, but when the Russians balked at certain requirements the plan fell through. The United States continued to develop its own atomic weapons in secrecy, and the Russians did the same. By 1949, the Soviet Union had exploded its own atomic bomb, and the race for nuclear weapons was on.

The resistance of Westerners to what they perceived as Soviet intransigence and communist subversion took clearer form in 1947. Since 1944, civil war had been raging in Greece between the royalist government restored by Britain and insurgents supported by the communist countries. In 1947, Britain informed the United States that it was financially no longer able to support the Greeks. On March 12, President Truman (1884–1972) asked Congress to provide funds to support Greece and Turkey, which was also under Soviet pressure. Congress complied. In what became known as the Truman Doctrine, the American president advocated a policy of supporting "free people who are resisting attempted subjugation by armed minorities or by outside pressures," by implication anywhere in the world.

American aid to Greece and Turkey took the form of military equipment and advisers. For Western Europe, where the menacing growth of Communist parties was fueled by postwar poverty and hunger, the Americans devised the European Recovery Program. Named the **Marshall Plan** after George C. Marshall (1880–1959), the secretary of state who introduced it, this program provided broad economic aid to European states only on condition that they work together. The Soviet Union forbade its satellites to take part. The Marshall Plan helped restore prosperity to Western Europe, setting the stage for its unprecedented economic growth, and led to the establishment of solid democratic regimes in this region of the world.

From the Western viewpoint, this policy of "containment" was a new and successful response to the Soviet and communist challenge. Stalin may have considered it a renewal of the old Western attempt to isolate and encircle the USSR. Stalin's answer was to replace all multiparty governments behind the Iron Curtain with thoroughly communist regimes under his control. In 1947, he organized the Communist Information Bureau (Cominform), dedicated to spreading revolutionary communism throughout the world. In February 1948 a brutal display of Stalin's new policy took place in Prague. The communists expelled the democratic members of what had been a coalition government, murdered the foreign minister, and forced the president to resign. Czechoslovakia was brought fully under Soviet rule.

These Soviet actions increased America's determination to make its own arrangements in Germany. The Russians dismantled German industry in the eastern zone, but the Americans tried to make Germany self-sufficient, which meant restoring its industrial capacity. To the Soviets restoration of a powerful industrial Germany was unacceptable.

Disagreement over Germany produced the most heated postwar debate. When the Western powers agreed to go forward with a separate constitution for the western sectors of Germany in February 1948, the Soviets walked out of the joint Allied Control Commission. Berlin, though well within the Soviet zone, was governed by all four powers. The Soviets sealed off the city by closing all railroads and highways to West Germany. Their purpose was to drive the Western powers out of Berlin. The Western allies responded to the Berlin Blockade with an airlift of supplies that lasted almost a year. In May 1949, the Russians were forced to reopen access to Berlin. The incident greatly increased tensions and suspicions between the two powers and hastened the separation of Germany into two states, which prevailed for forty years. West Germany became the German Federal Republic in September 1949, and the eastern region became the German Democratic Republic a month later.

NATO AND THE WARSAW PACT

Meanwhile, the nations of Western Europe were coming closer together. The Marshall Plan encouraged international cooperation. In April 1949, Belgium, Britain, Denmark, France, Iceland, Italy, Luxembourg, the Netherlands, Norway, and Portugal signed a treaty with Canada and the United States that formed the North Atlantic Treaty Organization (NATO) for mutual assistance in case of attack. NATO formed the West into a bloc. A few years later Greece, Turkey, and West Germany joined the alliance. The formation of NATO was the culmination of the United States' containment policy, which had originated with the Truman Doctrine and Marshall Plans. This policy assumed that the Soviet Union by its fundamental political character sought to be an expansionist power, which must be resisted or contained. (See Document: "The United States National Security Council Proposes to Contain the Soviet Union" on page 810.)

The states of Eastern Europe were under direct Soviet domination through local Communist parties controlled from Moscow and overawed by the Red Army. The Warsaw Pact of May 1955, which included Albania, Bulgaria, Czechoslovakia, East Germany, Hungary, Poland, Romania, and the Soviet Union, merely gave formal recognition to the existing system: Europe stood divided into two unfriendly blocs.

Stalin died in 1953; later that year an armistice was concluded in Korea (see Chapter 32). Both events produced hope that international tensions might lessen, but the rivalry of power and polemics soon resumed.

Hear the Audio
Cold War 1, Slide 2
at **myhistorylab.com**

CRISES OF 1956

The events of 1956 had considerable significance both for the Cold War and for what they implied about the realities of European power in the postwar era.

In July 1956, President Gamal Abdel Nasser (1918–1970) of Egypt nationalized the Suez Canal. Britain and France feared that this action would imperil their supplies of oil in the Persian Gulf. In October 1956, war broke out between Egypt and Israel. The British and French intervened. The United States, however, refused to support them, and the Soviet Union protested vehemently. The Anglo-French forces had to be withdrawn, and control of the canal remained with Egypt. The Suez intervention proved that without the support of the United States, the nations of Western Europe could no longer impose their will on the rest of the world.

Read the Document
Gamal Abdel Nasser, Speech on the Suez Canal (Egypt), 1956
at **myhistorylab.com**

Developments in Eastern Europe demonstrated similar limitations on independent action among the Soviet bloc nations. When the prime minister of Poland died, the Polish Communist Party refused to ratify the successor selected by Moscow. Considerable tension developed. In the end, Wladyslaw Gomulka (1905–1982) emerged as the new communist leader of Poland. He proved acceptable to the Soviets because he promised to keep Poland in the Warsaw Pact. However, he halted the collectivization of Polish agriculture and improved relations with the Polish Roman Catholic Church.

Hungary provided the second trouble spot for the Soviet Union. In late October, fighting erupted in Budapest. A new ministry headed by Imre Nagy (1896–1958) was installed. Nagy was a communist who sought an independent position for Hungary. Unlike Gomulka, he called for Hungarian withdrawal from the Warsaw Pact, a position unacceptable to the Soviet Union. Soviet troops deposed Nagy, who was later executed, and imposed Janos Kadar (1912–1989) as premier.

Watch the Video
Escaping the Berlin Wall at
myhistorylab.com

QUICK REVIEW

Polish-Soviet Relations
- 1956: Wladyslaw Gomulka comes to power in Poland
- Gomulka confirmed Poland's membership in Warsaw Pact, promised an end to collectivization, and improved relations with the Catholic Church
- Compromise prompted Hungary to seek greater autonomy

THE COLD WAR INTENSIFIED

The events of 1956 ended the era of fully autonomous action by the European nation-states. The two superpowers had demonstrated the new political realities. After 1956 the Soviet Union began to talk about "peaceful coexistence" with the United

DOCUMENT

The United States National Security Council Proposes to Contain the Soviet Union

In response to the domination of Eastern Europe by Communist parties beholden to the Soviet Union and the occupation of these nations by Soviet troops, the United States government in 1950 adopted a policy of "containment" of the Soviet Union. This policy had been debated for many months and had for all practical purposes been in effect since the declaration of the Truman Doctrine in 1947. It was formally set forth after a period of implementation in what became known as the National Security Council Paper 68, arguably the most important statement of American foreign policy of the mid-twentieth century. The paper presented the Soviet Union as a nation determined to pursue an expansionist foreign policy and ideological struggle. As a long-term solution to that challenge, it proposed a policy of containing the influence of the Soviet Union diplomatically and militarily.

- **HOW** did the National Security Council characterize Soviet policy? How did the Council actively encourage U.S. engagement with the rest of the world? What were the goals of containment? Why did the Council urge that the Soviet Union always be given opportunity to save face and to back down with dignity?

The fundamental design of those who control the Soviet Union and the international communist movement is to retain and solidify their absolute power, first in the Soviet Union and second in the areas now under their control. . . .

The design, therefore, calls for the complete subversion or forcible destruction of the machinery of government and structure of society in the countries of the non-Soviet world and their replacement by an apparatus and structure subservient to and controlled from the Kremlin. . . .

Our overall policy at the present time may be described as one designed to foster a world environment in which the American system can survive and flourish. It therefore rejects the concept of isolation and affirms the necessity of our positive participation in the world community.

This broad intention embraces two subsidiary policies. One is a policy which we would probably pursue even if there were no Soviet threat. It is a policy of attempting to develop a healthy international community. The other is the policy of "containing" the Soviet system. . . .

As for the policy of "containment," it is one which seeks by all means short of war to (1) block further expansion of Soviet power, (2) expose the falsities of Soviet pretensions, (3) induce a retraction of the Kremlin's control and influence, and (4) in general, so foster the seeds of destruction within the Soviet system that the Kremlin is brought at least to the point of modifying its behavior to conform to generally accepted international standards. . . .

One of the most important ingredients of power is military strength. . . . Without superior aggregate military strength . . . a policy of "containment"—which is in effect a policy of calculated and gradual coercion—is no more than a policy of bluff.

At the same time, it is essential to the successful conduct of a policy of "containment" that we always leave open the possibility of negotiation with the USSR. . . .

In "containment" it is desirable to exert pressure in a fashion which will avoid so far as possible directly challenging Soviet prestige, to keep open the possibility for the USSR to retreat before pressure with a minimum loss of face and to secure political advantage from the failure of the Kremlin to yield or take advantage of the openings we leave it.

Source: National Security Council, Paper Number 68, Foreign Relations of the United States (Washington, DC: U. S. Government Printing Office, 1977), Sections: III, IV, VI, as cited on http://www.seattleu.edu/artsci/history/us1945/docs/nsc68-1.htm.

Read the Document
The Kitchen Debate at
myhistorylab.com

States. In 1959 tensions relaxed sufficiently for Soviet Premier Nikita Khrushchev (1894–1971) to tour the United States. A summit meeting was scheduled for May 1960 in Paris, and American President Dwight D. Eisenhower (1890–1969) was to go to Moscow.

Just before the gathering, however, the Soviet Union shot down an American U-2 aircraft that was flying reconnaissance over Soviet territory. As a result, Khrushchev refused to take part in the summit conference, and Eisenhower's trip was canceled. In fact, the Soviets had long been aware of the American flights. They chose to protest at this time for two reasons. Khrushchev had hoped that the leaders of Britain, France, and the United States would be so divided over the future of Germany that a united Allied front would be impossible. These divisions did not arise. Second, by 1960 the communist world had become split between the Soviets and the Chinese, who accused the Russians of lacking revolutionary zeal. Khrushchev's action was an attempt to prove the Soviet Union's hard-line credentials.

The abortive Paris conference opened the most difficult period of the Cold War. Throughout 1961, thousands of refugees from East Germany had fled to West Berlin. To stop this outflow, in August 1961 the East Germans erected a barrier—the Berlin Wall—completely surrounding the Western sectors that would remain until November 1989. A year later the Cuban Missile Crisis brought the most dangerous days of the Cold War. The Soviet Union placed missiles in Cuba, a nation friendly to Soviet aims lying less than 100 miles from the United States. The United States blockaded Cuba, halted the shipment of new missiles, and demanded the removal of existing installations. After a tense week the Soviets backed down.

CHRONOLOGY

MAJOR DATES IN THE COLD WAR ERA

1948		Berlin Blockade
1949		Formation of the North Atlantic Treaty Organization (NATO)
1950		Outbreak of the Korean War
1953		Death of Stalin
1956	July	Egypt seizes the Suez Canal
	October	Anglo-French attack on the Suez Canal; Hungarian Revolution
1957		Treaty of Rome establishes the European Economic Community (EEC)
1960		Paris Summit Conference collapses
1961		Berlin Wall erected
1962		Cuban Missile Crisis
1963		Russian-American Test Ban Treaty
1968		Russian invasion of Czechoslovakia
1975		Helsinki Accords
1979		Russian invasion of Afghanistan
1981		Military crackdown on Solidarity Movement in Poland
1985		Reagan-Gorbachev summit
1987		Major American-Soviet Arms Limitation Treaty
1989		Berlin Wall comes down
1991		Soviet Union dissolves

Watch the **Video**
Cold War Connections: Russia, America, Berlin, and Cuba at **myhistorylab.com**

QUICK REVIEW

The Cuban Missile Crisis

♦ 1959: Fidel Castro comes to power as a result of the Cuban revolution

♦ 1962: Khrushchev orders construction of missile bases in Cuba

♦ Tense negotiations resulted in the Soviets backing down and removing the missiles

MISSILE EQUIPMENT
MARIEL PORT FACILITY
4 NOVEMBER 1962
4 MISSILE TRANSPORTERS
OXIDIZER TRAILERS
OXIDIZER TRAILERS
FUEL TRAILERS

Cuban Missile Crisis of 1962. The American ambassador to the United Nations displayed photographs to persuade the world of the threat to the United States less than 100 miles from its own shores.

Does a photograph such as this one directly demonstrate the presence of a threat, or does the photograph need to be interpreted and explained?

President Ronald Reagan and Premier Mikhail Gorbachev confer at a summit meeting in December 1989.

Why are the missile agreements signed by Gorbachev and Reagan among their most important accomplishments?

DÉTENTE AND AFTERWARD

In 1963 the two powers concluded a Nuclear Test Ban Treaty. This agreement marked the start of a détente, or lessening in tensions, between the United States and the Soviet Union that intensified during the presidency of Richard Nixon (1913–1994). This policy involved trade agreements and mutual reduction of strategic armaments. But the Soviet invasion of Afghanistan in 1979 hardened relations between Washington and Moscow, and the U.S. Senate refused to ratify the Strategic Arms Limitation Treaty of 1979.

President Ronald Reagan (1911–2004) and Soviet leader Mikhail S. Gorbachev (b. 1931) held a friendly summit meeting in 1985, the first East–West summit in six years. Other meetings followed. In December 1987, the United States and the Soviet Union agreed to dismantle more than 2,000 medium- and shorter-range missiles. The treaty provided for mutual inspection. This action represented the most significant agreement since World War II between the two superpowers.

The political upheavals in Eastern Europe and the Soviet Union soon overwhelmed the issues of the Cold War. The Soviet Union abandoned its support for communist governments in Eastern Europe. By the close of 1991, the Soviet Union itself had collapsed. The Cold War concluded in a manner that virtually no one had predicted.

TOWARD WESTERN EUROPEAN UNIFICATION

WHY HAVE European nations chosen to unify their economies?

Since 1945, the nations of Western Europe have taken unprecedented steps toward economic cooperation. The process is not complete and has been complicated by the collapse of the Soviet Union and the emergence of new free governments in Eastern Europe.

The Marshall Plan and NATO gave the involved countries new experience in working with each other and demonstrated the productivity, efficiency, and simple possibility of cooperative action. In 1950 France, West Germany, Italy, and the "Benelux" countries (Belgium, the Netherlands, and Luxembourg) organized the European Coal and Steel Community. Its success reduced the suspicions of government and business groups about the concept of coordination and economic integration.

European Economic Community (EEC)
The economic association formed by France, Germany, Italy, Belgium, the Netherlands, and Luxembourg in 1957. Also known as the Common Market.

It took more, however, to draw European leaders toward further unity. The unsuccessful Suez intervention and the resulting diplomatic isolation of France and Britain persuaded many Europeans that only through unified action could they significantly influence the two superpowers or control their own destinies. In 1957, through the Treaty of Rome, the six members of the Coal and Steel Community agreed to form a new organization: the **European Economic Community (EEC)**, or Common Market. The members sought to achieve the eventual elimination of tariffs, a free flow of capital and labor, and similar wage and social benefits in all the participating countries. The Common Market was a stunning success. By 1968, all tariffs among the six members had been abolished. Trade and labor migration among the members grew steadily. Moreover, nonmember states began to seek membership. In 1973, Denmark, Great Britain, and Ireland became members, and Austria, Finland, Greece, Portugal, Spain, and Sweden were eventually admitted.

The Euro. Some thousand people stand around a huge euro symbol in a park in Frankfurt's banking district in Germany, January, 1, 1997.

How has the euro given Europeans a new identity?

In 1988, the leaders of the EEC decided to create a virtual free-trade zone throughout the member community. In 1991, the Treaty of Maastricht called for a unified currency and a strong central bank. The European Community was renamed the **European Union (EU)**. The most striking instance of expanding economic cooperation was the adoption of a common currency, the **euro**. In January 2002 the national currencies of twelve nations—mostly in western Europe—were replaced by new coins and notes denominated in the euro. Such a widespread common currency is unprecedented in European history. In 2004, the EU accepted ten new members (see Map 31–1). Expansion has posed enormous challenges, because the economies of the newer members (mostly former states from the Eastern Soviet bloc) are much less developed than those of the original members. Newer members will be permitted to adopt the euro only when their economies have become sufficiently strong.

In 2007 the heads of state of the European Union signed the Lisbon Treaty. The purpose of this agreement was to create new institutions within the Union, which would allow it to function more nearly as a unitary body on the world scene. The treaty established a presidency and also created vehicles for unified policy on matters such as climate change. It strengthened the enforcement of rights for citizens of the Union. The treaty stirred considerable debate in the various countries of the Union, but it went into effect in late 2009.

Read the Document

A Common Market and European Integration (1960) at **myhistorylab.com**

European Union (EU)

The new name given to the EEC in 1993. It included most of the states of western Europe.

euro

The common currency created by the EEC in the late 1990s.

Read the Document

Treaty on European Union at **myhistorylab.com**

View the Image

European Union Flag at **myhistorylab.com**

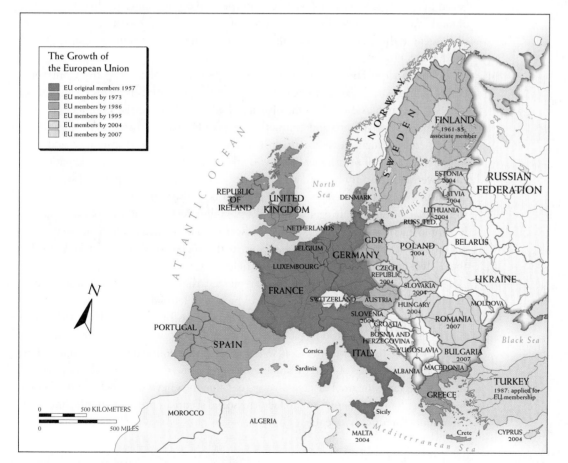

MAP 31–1.   The Growth of the European Union.   This map traces the growth of membership in the European Union from its founding in 1957 through 2007. Note that Turkey has applied for membership, but it has not yet been admitted.

What are the advantages and disadvantages of European Union membership?

See the Map
Contemporary Europe
at **myhistorylab.com**

Ongoing debate over the possible admission of Turkey serves as a proxy for debate over the cultural and religious character of the EU itself. Religion has not been a major topic of discussion within the EU, but the possible admission of a nation with an overwhelmingly Islamic population has brought the issue to the fore. Similarly the determination of France to assert the secular character of its state by attempting to forbid Muslim women students from wearing headscarves has raised much controversy. The Italian government has moved to remove crucifixes from classrooms in public schools. All of these factors and others have begun to stir more public discussion about the character of religious freedom and the relationship of church and state in the European Union. The Roman Catholic Church has vigorously asserted the role of Christianity in the formation of European identity and has urged the recognition of religious freedom as a human right.

EUROPEAN SOCIETY IN THE SECOND HALF OF THE TWENTIETH CENTURY AND BEYOND

WHAT MAJOR trends have marked European society since World War II?

TOWARD A WELFARE STATE SOCIETY

The Great Depression, the rise of authoritarian states, and the experiences of World War II changed how many Europeans thought about social welfare. Governments began to spend more on social welfare than they did on the military. This reallocation of funds was a reaction to the state violence of the first half of the century and was possible because the NATO defense umbrella, which the United States primarily staffed and funded, protected Western Europe.

The modern European welfare state was broadly similar across the Continent. Before World War II, except in Scandinavia, the two basic models for social legislation were the German and the British. Bismarck had introduced social insurance in Germany during the 1880s to undermine the German Social Democratic Party. In effect, the imperial German government provided workers with social insurance and thus some sense of social security while denying them significant political participation. In early twentieth-century Britain, where all classes had access to the political system, social insurance was targeted toward the poor. In both the German and British systems, workers were insured only against the risks from disease, injury on the job, and old age. Unemployment was assumed to be only a short-term problem and often one that workers brought on themselves. People higher in the social structure could look out for themselves and did not need government help.

After World War II, the concept emerged that social insurance against predictable risks was a social right and should be available to all citizens. The first major European nation to begin to create a welfare state was Britain in 1945 to 1951. The spread of welfare legislation (including unemployment insurance) within Western Europe was related to both the Cold War and domestic political and economic policy. The communist states of Eastern Europe were promising their people social security as well as full employment. The capitalist states came to believe they had to provide similar security for their people, but, in fact, the social security of the communist states was often more rhetoric than reality.

RESISTANCE TO THE EXPANSION OF THE WELFARE STATE

Western European attitudes toward the welfare state have reflected three periods that have marked economic life since the end of the war. The first period was one of reconstruction from 1945 through the early 1950s. It was followed by twenty-five years of generally steady and expanding economic growth. The third period brought first an era of inflation in the late 1970s and then one of relatively low growth and high unemployment from the 1990s to the present. During each of the first two periods, a general conviction existed that the foundation of economic policy was government involvement in a mixed economy. From the late 1970s, more people came to believe the market should be allowed to regulate itself and that government should be less involved in the economy.

The most influential political figure in reasserting the importance of markets was Margaret Thatcher (b. 1925) of the British Conservative Party who served as prime minister from 1979 to 1990. Her goal was to make the British economy more efficient and competitive. Although her administration aroused enormous controversy, over time the British Labour Party itself largely came to accept what was at the time known as the Thatcher Revolution.

While Thatcher redirected the British economy, continental Europe's government-furnished welfare services began to encounter resistance. The leveling off of population growth in Europe has imperiled the benefits of the welfare state. The next generation will have fewer workers to support the retired elderly population. Confidence in the ability of market forces rather than government intervention to sustain social cohesion has also spread in the past twenty-five years. Governments across the Continent, including those normally associated with left-of-center politics, such as the British Labour Party and the German Social Democratic Party, have limited further growth of the welfare state and have reduced benefits. In that respect, Europeans in the next few decades may look at the second half of the twentieth century as the Golden Age of welfare states and may find their own societies dealing with social welfare differently.

THE MOVEMENT OF PEOPLES

Many people migrated from, to, and within Europe during the half century following World War II. In the decade and a half after 1945, approximately a half million Europeans each year settled elsewhere in the world. Many of these migrants were educated city dwellers. Decolonization in the postwar period contributed to an inward flow of European colonials and non-European inhabitants of the former colonies to Europe. This influx has caused social tension and conflict. In Great Britain, for example, during the 1980s clashes arose between the police and non-European immigrants. France has had similar difficulties. Moreover, large Islamic populations now exist in several European nations and have become political factors in France and Germany.

World War II and its aftermath created millions of refugees (see Map 31-2 on page 816). Once the Cold War set in, Soviet domination made it impossible for Eastern Europeans to migrate to other parts of Europe. The major motivation for internal migration from the late 1950s onward has been economic opportunity. The prosperous nations of northern and Western Europe offered jobs that paid good wages and provided excellent benefits. There was a flow of workers from the poorer countries of Greece, Italy, Portugal, Spain, Turkey, and Yugoslavia into the wealthier countries of the Benelux nations, France, Switzerland, and West Germany. The establishment of the EEC in 1957 facilitated this movement.

In the late 1980s politics again became a major factor in European migration. With the collapse of the communist governments, people from all over Eastern Europe migrated to the West. Civil war in the former Yugoslavia also created many refugees. Europe has been in recession, however, and the new migrants are generating tension, resentment, and strife. Several nations have taken legal and administrative steps to

QUICK REVIEW

Western Europe's Consumer Society

- Western Europe's economy emphasized consumer goods in the second half of the twentieth century
- Soviet bloc economies focused on capital investments and the military
- Discrepancy between Western and Eastern European standards of living caused resentment in the East

MAP 31–2. Displaced Peoples in East and Central Europe, 1945–1950. World War II left millions of Europeans displaced. In an attempt to reestablish ethnic and linguistic uniformity within political boundaries, more than 31 million people were resettled between 1945 and 1952.

What influence has human migration had on European history since World War II?

restrict migration. The financial collapse that commenced in 2008 has led many people who had moved from eastern to western Europe in pursuit of employment to move back to their original countries of residence.

THE NEW MUSLIM POPULATION

Well into the twentieth century Europeans encountered Muslims, if at all, as subjects in their colonies. With the exception of a few minority communities in the Balkans and the former Soviet Empire, Europeans saw themselves and their national cultures as Christian or secular.

European indifference toward Islam had dissolved by the end of the twentieth century as a sizable Muslim population settled in Europe. This highly diverse immigrant community had become an issue in Europe even before the events of September 11, 2001, discussed later in this chapter.

The immigration of Muslims into Europe and particularly Western Europe arose from two chief sources: European economic growth and decolonization. As Western economies recovered in the wake of World War II, a labor shortage developed in Europe, and laborers ("guest workers"), many of whom came from Muslim nations, were imported to fill it. For example, Turkish "guest workers" were invited to move to West Germany—on a temporary basis, it was presumed—in the 1960s, and Britain welcomed Pakistanis. The aftermath of decolonization and the quest for a better life led Muslims from East Africa and the Indian subcontinent to settle in Great Britain. The Algerian war brought many Muslims from North Africa into France. Today there are approximately 1.3 million Muslims in Great Britain, 3.2 million in Germany, and 4.2 million in France. Smaller but still significant numbers have settled in Italy, Spain, Sweden, Denmark, and the Netherlands, nations that had previously had generally homogeneous populations.

These Muslim immigrant communities share certain social and religious characteristics. Many Muslims came to Europe expecting eventually to return to their homelands, an expectation their host countries shared. Unlike the United States, few European countries had any experience in dealing with large-scale immigration, and many Muslim communities have remained unassimilated. This apartness has provided internal community support for Muslim immigrants but prevented them from fully engaging with the societies in which they live. Many of their children have not learned European languages well, and Muslim women tend to remain strictly confined to their homes.

The world around these communities has changed. Many of the largely unskilled jobs that the immigrants originally filled have disappeared. Most of the Muslim immigrants to Europe were neither highly skilled nor professionally educated, and many of the unskilled jobs that they originally filled have disappeared. As European economic growth has slowed, Muslims have been blamed for a host of problems, from crime to unemployment.

The radicalization of parts of the Islamic world has also touched the Muslim communities in Europe. Although Turkish Muslims living in Germany come from a nation that has been secularized since the 1920s and thus tend to be less religiously observant than Pakistani Muslims dwelling in Great Britain, Muslims from both countries have been involved in radical Islamic groups; some belonged to organizations involved in the September 11, 2001, attack on the United States. By contrast, the French government has exerted more control over its Muslim community.

Despite the fact that Europe's Muslims are not a homogeneous group—they come from different countries, have different class backgrounds, and espouse different Islamic traditions—their communities are often plagued by poverty and unemployment.

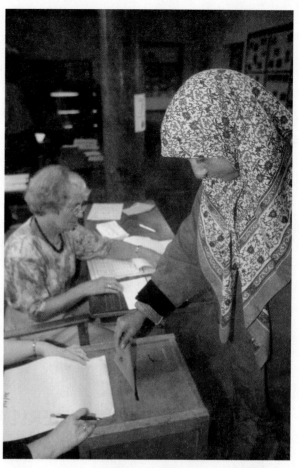

A Muslim woman wearing a traditional headscarf in Hamburg, Germany votes in the Bundestag elections. The presence of foreign-born Muslims whose labor is necessary for the prosperity of the European economy is an important issue in contemporary Europe. Many of these Muslims live in self-contained communities.

Why do some non-Muslim Europeans find headscarves threatening?

QUICK REVIEW

Muslims in Europe

◆ Many Muslims immigrated to Europe as "guest workers"

◆ Assimilation rates are low

◆ Unemployment rates are high

◆ Islamic radicalization affects Muslim immigrant communities

NEW PATTERNS IN THE WORK AND EXPECTATIONS OF WOMEN

The work patterns and social expectations of women have changed markedly since World War II. In all social ranks, women have begun to assume larger economic and political roles. They have entered the professions and are filling major managerial positions.

Simone de Beauvoir, here with her companion, the philosopher Jean-Paul Sartre, was the major feminist writer in postwar Europe.

How have women's roles changed in postwar Europe?

Despite enormous gains, gender inequality remained a major characteristic of European societies at the opening of the twenty-first century. After World War II, Simone de Beauvoir's (1908–1986) book, *The Second Sex* (1949), was a major influence on European feminism. She and other feminists documented the social, legal, and economic disadvantages of their gender, challenged discrimination against women in family law, and called attention to social problems such as spousal abuse.

The number of married women in the work force has risen sharply in both middle and working classes. In the twentieth century children were no longer expected to make substantial contributions to family income. They spent much of their time in compulsory schools. When families needed more income than one worker could provide, both parents worked. Even without financial necessity, both parents were now likely to work when both were motivated to pursue careers.

Within Europe women's childbearing age has risen. Women have tended to bear children in their early twenties in eastern Europe and in their late twenties in western Europe. In urban areas, childbearing occurs later and the birthrate is lower than elsewhere. Many women have begun to limit sharply the number of children they bear or to forgo childbearing and child rearing altogether. Both men and women continue to expect to marry, but the new careers open to women and the desire of couples to maintain as high a standard of living as possible have contributed to a declining birthrate.

AMERICAN DOMESTIC SCENE SINCE WORLD WAR II

 WHAT ARE the main themes that have characterized postwar America?

Three major themes have characterized the postwar American experience—an opposition to the spread of communism, an expansion of civil rights to blacks and other minorities at home, and a determination to achieve ongoing economic growth. Virtually all of the major postwar political debates and social divisions have arisen from these issues.

TRUMAN AND EISENHOWER ADMINISTRATIONS

The foreign policy of President Harry Truman was directed against communist expansion in Europe and East Asia. He enunciated the Truman Doctrine in regard to Greece and Turkey and initiated the Marshall Plan for European reconstruction. As will be discussed in Chapter 32 he led the United States to support the UN intervention against aggression in Korea. Domestically, the Truman administration tried to continue the New Deal. However, Truman encountered opposition from conservative Republicans, who in 1947 passed the Taft-Hartley Act limiting labor union activity. Truman won the 1948 election against great odds. Through policies he called the Fair Deal, he sought to extend economic security. Those efforts were frustrated by fears of a domestic communist menace fanned by Senator Joseph McCarthy (1909–1957) of Wisconsin.

War hero Dwight D. Eisenhower (1890–1969) was elected in 1952. In retrospect, his presidency seems a period of calm. Eisenhower ended the Korean War. The country was generally prosperous. Home building increased dramatically, and the vast interstate highway system was initiated. The president was less activist than either Roosevelt or Truman had been. Beneath the apparent quiet, however, stirred forces that would lead to the disruptions of the 1960s.

CIVIL RIGHTS

In 1954, the U.S. Supreme Court, in *Brown v. Board of Education of Topeka,* declared racial segregation unconstitutional. Shortly thereafter, the Court ordered the desegregation of schools. In 1957, President Eisenhower had to send troops into Little Rock, Arkansas, to integrate the schools, but resistance continued in other Southern states.

American blacks began to protest segregation in other areas. In 1955 the Reverend Martin Luther King Jr. (1929–1968) organized a boycott in Montgomery, Alabama, against segregated buses. The Montgomery bus boycott marked the beginning of the use of civil disobedience to fight racial discrimination in the United States. Drawing on the ideas of Henry David Thoreau (1817–1862) and the experience of Mohandas Gandhi (1869–1948) in India, the leaders of the civil rights movement went to jail rather than obey laws they considered unjust. The civil rights struggle continued well into the 1960s. One of its most dramatic moments was the 1963 march on Washington by tens of thousands of supporters of civil rights legislation. The greatest achievements of the movement were the Civil Rights Act of 1964, which desegregated public accommodations, and the Voting Rights Act of 1965, which cleared the way for black Americans to vote. Black citizens came closer to the mainstream of American life than they had ever been.

Much, however, remained undone. In 1967 major race riots occurred in several American cities, resulting in significant loss of life. Those riots, followed by the assassination of Martin Luther King Jr., in 1968, weakened the civil rights movement. Although African Americans had more access to education and public office, especially in urban areas, they continued to lag behind other Americans economically and in their prospects for good health.

Martin Luther King Jr., pictured here with his wife Coretta, was the most prominent civil rights leader in the United States. Here he leads a protest march in 1965.

What did the civil rights movement accomplish in the United States? Is its work complete?

NEW SOCIAL PROGRAMS

The advance of the civil rights movement in the late 1950s and early 1960s represented the cutting edge of a new advance of political liberalism, which proved to be relatively short-lived. In 1960, John F. Kennedy (1917–1963) narrowly won the presidential election. He attempted unsuccessfully to expand medical care under the Social Security program, but the reaction to his assassination in 1963 allowed his successor, Lyndon Johnson (1908–1973), to press for activist legislation. Johnson's domestic program, known as the War on Poverty, established major federal programs to create jobs and provide job training. It also added new entitlements to the Social Security program, including Medicare, which provides medical services for the elderly and disabled. Johnson's drive for what he called the Great Society ended the era of major federal initiatives that had begun under Franklin Roosevelt. By the late 1960s the electorate had begun to become much more conservative.

THE VIETNAM WAR, DOMESTIC TURMOIL, AND WATERGATE

Johnson's activist domestic vision was overshadowed by the U.S. involvement in Vietnam (see Chapter 32). By 1965, Johnson had decided to send American troops to Vietnam. This policy led to the longest of American wars. At home, the war and the

Read the Document
Martin Luther King Jr., Letter from Birmingham City Jail, 1963
at **myhistorylab.com**

QUICK REVIEW

Desegregation Landmarks
- *Brown v. Board of Education of Topeka,* 1954
- Montgomery bus boycott, 1955
- Little Rock schools integrated, 1957
- Civil Rights Act, 1964

See the Map
The Vietnam War
at **myhistorylab.com**

military draft provoked large-scale protests; the Vietnam War divided the nation as had no conflict since the Civil War.

Johnson decided not to seek reelection in 1968. Richard Nixon led the Republicans to victory. His election marked the beginning of an era of American politics dominated by conservative policies. Perhaps the most important act of his administration was to establish diplomatic relations with the People's Republic of China. Although half of the casualties in the Vietnam War occurred under Nixon's administration, he concluded the war in 1972. That same year he was reelected, but the Watergate scandal began to erode his administration.

On the surface, the Watergate scandal involved only the burglary of the Democratic Party national headquarters by White House operatives in 1972. The deeper issues related to presidential authority and the right of the government to intrude into the lives of citizens. In 1974, audiotapes revealed that Nixon had ordered federal agencies to try to cover up White House participation in the burglary. Nixon became the first American president to resign from office.

Watergate shook public confidence in the government. It was also a distraction from the major problems facing the country, especially inflation, which had resulted from fighting the war in Vietnam while expanding domestic expenditures. The administrations of Gerald Ford (1974–1977; 1913–2006) and Jimmy Carter (1977–1981; b. 1924) battled inflation and high interest rates without success.

Kent State Protest. The clash between protesting students and the Ohio National Guard at Kent State University was the most violent moment in the protests against the U.S. involvement in Vietnam.

What makes a photograph such as this one disturbing to so many people?

THE TRIUMPH OF POLITICAL CONSERVATISM

In 1980 Ronald Reagan was elected president by a large majority and reelected four years later. Reagan was the first fully ideological conservative to be elected in the postwar era. Reagan sought to reduce the role of the federal government in American life. The chief vehicle to this end was a major tax cut and reform of the taxation system. Thereafter the American economy experienced its longest peacetime expansion.

The straightforward conservatism of the Reagan administration proved offensive to many Americans who had traditionally supported a liberal political and social agenda. His policies were regarded as hostile to blacks and women. High officials were involved in scandals, particularly the sale of arms to Iran in exchange for the promised release of American hostages in Lebanon. Despite these difficulties, Reagan left office as probably the most popular and successful of the post–World War II American presidents.

In 1988, Reagan's vice president George H. W. Bush (b. 1924) was elected to the presidency. In the summer of 1990, in response to Iraq's invasion of Kuwait, he forged a worldwide coalition that forced Iraq out of Kuwait in 1991. But Bush stumbled in the face of serious economic problems. In 1992, the Democratic nominee, Governor William (Bill) Clinton (b. 1946) of Arkansas, won the election. In 1994, the Republican Party won majorities in both houses of Congress in an election that marked a major conservative departure in American political life. This Congress continued the conservative redirection of federal policy that had begun under Reagan. President Clinton and a Republican-dominated Congress were reelected in 1996, but scandals plagued both parties. Because of a personal sexual scandal and allegations of perjury, President Clinton was impeached in 1998 but acquitted. In terms of policy, Clinton moved the Democratic Party to a centrist stance.

•◦•─[Read the Document
Republican Party Nomination Acceptance
at **myhistorylab.com**

The presidential election of 2000 between Texas governor George W. Bush (the son of the former president) and Vice President Al Gore was the closest in modern American history. Gore won a majority of the popular vote but failed to win a majority in the electoral college. The pivotal electoral votes depended on which candidate carried Florida, where the final vote count was disputed for more than a month. After complicated legal proceedings, the U.S. Supreme Court voted 5 to 4 to halt a ballot recount, which resulted in Bush being declared the winner.

On September 11, 2001, a surprise terrorist attack on New York City and Washington, D.C., transformed the political life of the United States. The nation rallied to respond, with remarkable bipartisan cooperation. In October 2001, the United States began a war against terrorism with air attacks against terrorist positions in Afghanistan. U.S. forces also attacked the forces of the extremist Islamic Taliban regime in Afghanistan, which had tolerated the presence of Islamic terrorists. In 2003 the United States invaded Iraq (an event discussed further in the last section of this chapter and in Chapter 33).

Read the **Document**
Addresses by George W. Bush, 2001
at **myhistorylab.com**

In 2004 President Bush overcame Democratic challenger John Kerry, this time being elected with a popular and electoral college majority vote. In the congressional elections of 2006 the Democratic Party regained control of both houses of Congress in an election fought largely over the American intervention in Iraq. In 2008 in the wake of criticism of the Bush foreign policy and the growing worldwide financial meltdown, Senator Barack Obama of Illinois was elected as the first African American president of the United States. The Democratic Party expanded its control of both houses of Congress. The new administration faced the most challenging economic crisis since the Great Depression. Its initial moves involved extensive government spending in support of the financial system and the creation of new jobs.

THE SOVIET UNION TO 1989

The Soviet Union emerged from World War II as a major world power, but Stalin did little or nothing to modify the repressive regime he had fostered. Stalin's personal authority over the party and the nation remained unchallenged. In foreign policy he solidified Soviet control over Eastern Europe for the purposes of both communist expansion and Soviet national security. The Soviet army assured subservience to the goals of the Soviet Union. This continued until Stalin died on March 6, 1953.

HOW DID leaders after Stalin attempt to reform Soviet government?

THE KHRUSHCHEV AND BREZHNEV YEARS

No single leader immediately replaced Stalin. By 1956 Nikita Khrushchev became premier, but without the extraordinary powers of Stalin.

In 1956, at the Twentieth Congress of the Communist Party, Khrushchev denounced Stalin and his crimes. This "Secret Speech" shocked party circles and opened the way for limited internal criticism of the Soviet government. Under Khrushchev, intellectuals were somewhat freer to express their opinions. In economic policy, Khrushchev made moderate efforts to decentralize economic planning, but the consumer sector improved only marginally. The ever-growing defense budget and the space program that successfully

The Kitchen Debate. One of the most famous incidents of the Cold War was a spontaneous debate between Nikita Khrushchev and Vice President Richard Nixon at a trade fair in Moscow. Because it took place at a display of kitchen appliances, it is sometimes called the Kitchen Debate.
Did either Nixon or Khrushchev "win" the Kitchen Debate?

launched the first human-engineered earth satellite, *Sputnik*, in 1957 made major demands on the nation's productive resources. Khrushchev redirected Stalin's agricultural policy, removing the most restrictive regulations on private cultivation, but the agricultural problem continued to grow. The Soviet Union could not feed its own people; by the 1970s the Soviet Union imported vast quantities of grain from the United States and other countries.

By 1964 Communist Party leaders had concluded that Khrushchev had tried to do too much too soon and had done it too poorly. His foreign policy, culminating in the backdown over the Cuban Missile Crisis, appeared a failure. On October 16, 1964, Khrushchev was forced to resign. Leonid Brezhnev (1906–1982) emerged as his successor.

The Soviet government became more repressive after 1964. Intellectuals enjoyed less freedom, and Jewish citizens were harassed. The internal repression gave rise to a dissident movement. A few Soviet citizens dared to criticize the regime for violating the human rights provisions of the 1975 Helsinki Accords. The Soviet government responded with further repression.

In foreign policy the Brezhnev years witnessed attempts both to reach accommodation with the United States and to continue to expand Soviet influence and maintain Soviet leadership of the communist movement. Growing spending on defense squeezed the consumer side of the economy.

In December 1979, the Soviet Union invaded Afghanistan for reasons that remain unclear. The Afghanistan invasion exacerbated tensions with the United States and tied the hands of the Soviet government in Eastern Europe. Soviet hesitation to react to events in Poland during the 1980s stemmed in part from the military commitment in Afghanistan and from the condemnation the invasion provoked from many governments. The Soviet government also lost support at home as its army became bogged down and suffered steady losses.

COMMUNISM AND SOLIDARITY IN POLAND

In July 1980 the Polish government raised meat prices, causing strikes across the country. In August, a strike at the Lenin shipyard at Gdansk spread to other shipyards, transport facilities, and factories. The Gdansk strike, led by Lech Walesa (b. 1944), ended on August 31 after the government promised the workers the right to organize an independent union, called Solidarity. Less than a week later the Polish communist head of state was replaced; later that year the state-controlled radio—for the first time in thirty years—broadcast a Roman Catholic Mass.

In the summer of 1981, for the first time in any European communist state, secret elections for the Polish party congress permitted choices among the candidates. Poland remained a communist state, but real debate was temporarily permitted within the party congress. This experiment ended in December 1981, when General Wojciech Jaruzelski (b. 1923) became head of the party. Martial law was declared and continued until late in the 1980s.

GORBACHEV ATTEMPTS TO REDIRECT THE SOVIET UNION

Both of Brezhnev's immediate successors, Yuri Andropov (1914–1984) and Constantin Chernenko (1911–1985), died after holding office for short periods. In 1985, Mikhail S. Gorbachev (b. 1931) came to power and immediately set about making the most remarkable changes that the Soviet Union

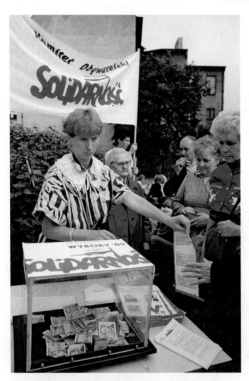

•••◦[Read the **Document**
Nikita Khrushchev, Speech to the Twenty-Second Congress of the Communist Party, 1962 at **myhistorylab.com**

The Polish Trade Union "Solidarity" in 1989 successfully forced the Polish communist government to hold free elections. In June of that year Solidarity, whose members here are collecting funds for their campaign, won overwhelmingly.

Which members of Polish society belonged to Solidarity?

had witnessed since the 1920s. His reforms unleashed forces that within seven years would force him to retire and end both communist rule and the Soviet Union itself.

Initially, Gorbachev and his supporters challenged the way the party and bureaucracy managed the Soviet government and economy. Under the policy of *perestroika*, or "restructuring," they proposed major economic and political reforms. The centralized economic ministries were streamlined. By early 1990, Gorbachev had even begun to advocate private ownership of property. He and his advisers considered policies to move the economy rapidly toward a free market. However, the Soviet economy, instead of growing, stagnated and even declined. Shortages of food, consumer goods, and housing became chronic. Old-fashioned communists blamed these results on the abandonment of centralized planning, while democratic critics blamed them on overly slow reform.

Gorbachev also allowed public criticism of Soviet history and Soviet Communist Party policy. This development was termed *glasnost*, or "openness." In factories, workers were permitted to criticize party officials and the economic plans of the party and the government. Censorship was relaxed and free expression encouraged. Dissidents were released from prison. In 1988, a new constitution permitted contested elections. After real political campaigning, the Congress of People's Deputies was elected in 1989 and then formally elected Gorbachev as president.

perestroika
Meaning "restructuring." The attempt in the 1980s to reform the Soviet government and economy.

Read the **Document**
Mikhail Gorbachev on the Need for Economic Reform (1987)
at **myhistorylab.com**

glasnost
Meaning "openness." The policy initiated by Mikhail Gorbachev in the 1980s of permitting open criticism of the policies of the Soviet Communist Party.

1989: YEAR OF REVOLUTIONS IN EASTERN EUROPE

In 1989 Soviet domination and communist rule in Eastern Europe came to an abrupt end. None of these revolutions could have taken place without the Soviet Union's refusal to intervene militarily as it had done in 1956 and 1968. For the first time since the end of World War II, the peoples of Eastern Europe could shape their own political destiny. Once they realized the Soviets would stand back, thousands of citizens denounced Communist Party domination and asserted their desire for democracy.

The generally peaceful character of most of these revolutions may have resulted in part from the shock with which the world responded to the violent repression of prodemocracy protesters in Beijing's Tiananmen Square in May 1989. The Communist Party officials of Eastern Europe and the Soviet Union clearly decided that they could not offend world opinion with a similar attack.

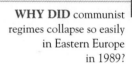

WHY DID communist regimes collapse so easily in Eastern Europe in 1989?

View the **Image**
Statue of Lenin Toppled during Soviet Collapse at **myhistorylab.com**

SOLIDARITY REEMERGES IN POLAND

During the mid-1980s, Poland's government relaxed martial law. By 1984, the leaders of Solidarity began again to work for free trade unions and democratic government. New dissenting organizations emerged. Poland's economy continued to deteriorate. In 1988, new strikes occurred. This time the communist government failed to reimpose control. Solidarity was legalized.

Jaruzelski, with the tacit consent of the Soviet Union, promised free elections to Parliament. When elections were held in 1989, the communists lost overwhelmingly to Solidarity candidates. On August 24, 1989, after negotiating with Lech Walesa and getting Gorbachev's approval, Jaruzelski named Tadeusz Mazowiecki (b. 1927) the first noncommunist prime minister of Poland since 1945.

Statue of Lenin. The collapse of Communist Party governments in Eastern Europe and the Soviet Union was the most important political event of the closing years of the twentieth century. It was accompanied by the destruction of the public symbols of those governments. Throughout the region gigantic statues of Communist Party leaders were torn down. Here, Hungarians explore a toppled statue of Lenin.

Why were most Eastern European revolutions peaceful?

HUNGARY MOVES TOWARD INDEPENDENCE

Hungary had for some time shown the greatest economic independence from the Soviet Union in Eastern Europe. The Hungarian government had emphasized the production of food and consumer goods. In early 1989, the Hungarian communist government permitted independent political parties and free travel between Hungary and Austria, opening the first breach in the Iron Curtain. Thousands of East Germans then moved through Hungary and Austria to West Germany.

In May 1989, Premier Janos Kadar (1912–1989) was voted from office by the Parliament. In October, Hungary promised free elections. By 1990, a coalition of democratic parties governed the country.

THE BREACH OF THE BERLIN WALL AND GERMAN REUNIFICATION

In the autumn of 1989 demonstrations erupted in East German cities. The streets filled with people demanding an end to Communist Party rule.

Gorbachev told the leaders of the East German Communist Party that the Soviet Union would no longer support them. They resigned, making way for a younger generation of Communist Party leaders who promised reforms. Few East Germans were convinced, however. In November 1989, the government of East Germany ordered the opening of the Berlin Wall, and thousands of East Berliners crossed into West Berlin. By early 1990, the communist government of East Germany had been swept away.

The citizens of the two Germanys were determined to reunify. By February 1990, reunification had become a foregone conclusion, accepted by the United States, the Soviet Union, Great Britain, and France.

THE VELVET REVOLUTION IN CZECHOSLOVAKIA

Late in 1989, in "the velvet revolution," communist rule in Czechoslovakia unraveled. In November, under popular pressure from street demonstrations and well-organized political opposition, the Communist Party began to retreat from office. The patterns were similar to those occurring elsewhere: Old leadership resigned, and younger communists replaced them, but the changes they offered were inadequate.

The popular new Czech leader was Václav Havel (b. 1936), a renowned playwright whom the government had imprisoned. Havel and his group, called Civic Forum, negotiated changes with the government that included an end to the political dominance of the Communist Party and the inclusion of noncommunists in the government. In late December 1989, Havel was elected president.

VIOLENT REVOLUTION IN ROMANIA

The most violent upheaval of 1989 occurred in Romania, where President Nicolae Ceausescu (1918–1989) had governed without opposition for almost a quarter century. Romania was a corrupt, one-party state with total centralized economic planning. Ceausescu, who had long been at odds with the Soviet government, maintained his Stalinist regime in the face of Gorbachev's reforms. He was supported by a loyal security force.

A Closer Look

Collapse of the Berlin Wall

No single structure so illustrated the divisions of the Cold War as the Berlin Wall, which was erected in 1961. The most symbolic moment in the collapse of communism across Eastern Europe came in November 1989 when that wall was breached.

English graffiti had been placed on the wall to ensure that an international television audience, which was largely English-speaking, would understand the aspirations of those people who wanted the wall to come down.

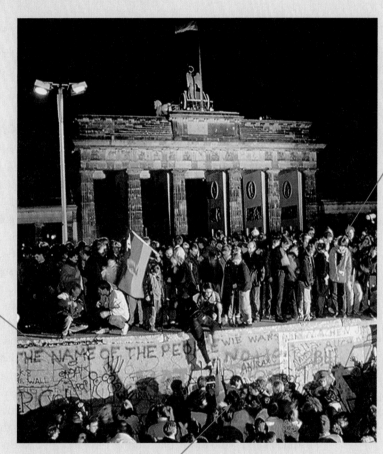

The sight of hundreds of Germans standing on top of the wall would have been unthinkable just days before. Armed East German and Soviet guards had for over a quarter-century prevented Germans from crossing the wall except at a few heavily guarded checkpoints.

The overwhelmingly youthful crowd indicates the repudiation of the Cold War divisions by the new generation of Germans and Europeans.

Questions

1. How did the vast numbers of photographs of this event, as well as amateur movies and videos, illustrate that governments could no longer control the manner in which information was dispersed?

2. In June 1989, the Chinese government had violently suppressed a vast rally in Tiananmen Square in Beijing. How does this picture from Berlin about six months later illustrate the decision of the Soviet and East German governments to behave differently in the face of popular opposition?

3. What does this picture both reveal and fail to reveal about the motives of the East Germans who crossed the Berlin Wall in November 1989?

On December 15, troubles erupted in the city of Timisoara in western Romania. The security forces fired on demonstrators, and casualties ran into the hundreds. By December 22, Bucharest was in full revolt. Fighting broke out between the army, which supported the revolution, and the security forces. Ceausescu and his wife attempted to flee the country but were captured and executed on December 25. His death ended the fighting. The provisional government in Bucharest announced the first free elections since the end of World War II.

THE COLLAPSE OF THE SOVIET UNION

WHO WERE the leaders in the period surrounding the collapse of the Soviet Union?

Gorbachev believed that the Soviet Union could no longer afford to support communist governments in Eastern Europe. He also saw that the Communist Party within the Soviet Union was losing power.

RENUNCIATION OF COMMUNIST POLITICAL MONOPOLY

In early 1990, Gorbachev formally proposed that the Soviet Communist Party relinquish its monopoly of power. After intense debate, the Central Committee abandoned the Leninist position that only a single elite party could act as the vanguard of the revolution and forge a new Soviet society.

Gorbachev confronted challenges from three major political forces by 1990. One group—considered conservative in the Soviet context—wanted to maintain the influence of the Communist Party and the Soviet army. They were distressed by the country's economic stagnation and disorder. They appeared to have significant support. During late 1990 and early 1991, Gorbachev, who himself seems to have been disturbed by the nation's turmoil, began to appoint members of this group to government posts. In other words, Gorbachev seemed to be making a strategic retreat. He apparently believed that these more conservative forces could give him the support he needed against opposition from a second group, led by Boris Yeltsin (b. 1931), who wanted to move quickly to a market economy and a more democratic government. In 1990, Yeltsin was elected president of the Russian Republic, the most important of the Soviet Union's constituent republics. That position gave him a firm political base from which to challenge Gorbachev's authority and increase his own.

The third force was regional unrest, especially from the three Baltic republics of Estonia, Latvia, and Lithuania. During 1989 and 1990, the parliaments of the Baltic republics tried to increase their independence, and Lithuania actually declared itself independent. Discontent also arose in the Soviet Islamic republics in Central Asia. Gorbachev sought to negotiate new constitutional arrangements between the republics and the central government but failed. This may have been the most important reason for the rapid collapse of the Soviet Union.

THE AUGUST 1991 COUP AND THE YELTSIN YEARS

The turning point came in August 1991 when the conservative forces that Gorbachev had brought into the government attempted a coup. Armed forces occupied Moscow, and Gorbachev himself was placed under house arrest in the Crimea. Yeltsin denounced the coup and asked the world for help.

Within two days the coup collapsed. Gorbachev returned to Moscow, but in humiliation, having been victimized by the groups he had turned to for support. From that point on, Yeltsin steadily became the dominant political figure in the nation. The Communist Party, compromised by its participation in the coup, collapsed. On December 25, 1991, the Soviet Union ceased to exist, Gorbachev left office, and the Commonwealth of Independent States came into being (see Map 31–3).

MAP 31–3. The Commonwealth of Independent States. In December 1991 the Soviet Union broke up into its fifteen constituent republics. Eleven of these were loosely joined in the Commonwealth of Independent States. Also shown is the autonomous region of Chechnya, which has waged two bloody wars with Russia in the past two decades.

What does the breakup of the Soviet Union say about the importance of nationalism in the modern world?

As president of Russia, Yeltsin was head of the largest and most powerful of the new states, but by 1993 he faced serious problems. Opposition to Yeltsin personally and to his economic and political reforms grew in the Russian Parliament, whose members were mostly former communists. In September 1993, Yeltsin suspended Parliament, which responded by deposing him. The military, however, backed Yeltsin and surrounded the Parliament building. On October 4, 1993, after pro-Parliament rioters rampaged through Moscow, Yeltsin ordered tanks to attack the Parliament building, crushing the revolt.

These actions temporarily consolidated Yeltsin's position and authority. The major Western powers supported him. But the crushing of Parliament left Yeltsin highly dependent on the military, and the country's continuing economic problems bred unrest. In the December 1993 parlimentary elections, radical nationalists made an uncomfortably strong showing. In 1994 and again after 1999, the central government faced war in the province of Chechnya. In December 1999, Yeltsin, who suffered from poor health, resigned and was succeeded as president by Vladimir Putin (b. 1952), who promised strong leadership.

PUTIN TESTS RUSSIAN POWER

Putin was elected president in his own right in March 2001. He renewed the war against the rebels in Chechnya, which resulted in heavy casualties and enormous destruction there, but strengthened Putin's political support within Russia.

The Chechen war spawned an appalling terrorist act. In September 2004, a group of Chechens captured an elementary school in Beslan, in the north Caucasus. Approximately 1,200 students, teachers, and parents were held hostage for several days. When government troops stormed the school, approximately 330 of the hostages were killed. By the middle of the decade, however, Russian forces had clearly established the upper hand over the Chechen rebels and the drive toward independence was firmly checked—at a very high cost in lives on both sides.

Putin sought to diminish local autonomy and centralize power in his own hands. He won broad Russian public support for imprisoning some leading oligarchs and other businessmen. These enormously wealthy and economically powerful figures were viewed as one of the causes of the economic hardship of the 1990s. Putin also imprisoned political critics and moved against independent newspapers and television stations.

Under Putin a clear trade-off occurred between political freedom and economic and political stability. The Russian economy improved: Foreign debts were paid, the Russian ruble was accepted as a serious currency, and many more consumer goods were available. Much of this relative prosperity was the result of the oil resources available to the Russian Federation and the rising price of oil on the world market. In 2008 Putin left the elected presidency, turning the office over to his handpicked successor Dmitri Medvedev (b. 1965). At the same time, Putin assumed the office of prime minister and clearly remained the chief political figure in the country. (See Document, "Vladimir Putin Outlines a Vision of the Russian Future.")

Putin has been determined to use the nation's economic recovery and new wealth to allow Russia to reassert its position as a major power. After the 2001 terrorist attacks on the United States, Putin supported the American assault on Afghanistan, largely because the Russian government feared the spread of Islamic extremism within Russia and neighboring states. This period of cooperation was brief, however, and Putin became one of the leading critics of American policy.

Putin has also been sharply critical of the ongoing expansion of NATO which has embraced nations directly bordering the Russian Federation. His government continued to attempt to exert influence in various of the new nations, such as the former Soviet republics of Ukraine and Georgia, that came into existence with the collapse of the former Soviet Union. For nearly twenty years both the European Union and NATO had been expanding into regions previously dominated by or part of the former Soviet Union. The Russian Federation found itself unable to stop or significantly influence these expansions. The United States had indicated support for bringing both Ukraine and Georgia into NATO. Putin and other leaders of the Russian Federation had witnessed the manner in which various regions of the former Yugoslavia, most recently Kosovo in February 2008, had broken away from Serbia and established their own independence. The Russian Federation feared that Kosovo might serve as an example for potential breakaway regions in the Russian Federation. It also feared encirclement by NATO member nations where the United States might locate military bases.

Russia's determination to dominate nations that were once part of the Soviet Union dramatically displayed itself in August 2008, when Russian Federation troops invaded the Republic of Georgia. Shortly before, Georgia had sent troops into South

DOCUMENT

Vladimir Putin Outlines a Vision of the Russian Future

Vladimir Putin served as president of the Russian Federation from 1998 to 2008 when he moved to the office of prime minister. In one of his last presidential speeches he outlined his view of a democratic Russian future as well as his concerns about the relationship of the Russian Federation to NATO. His speech embraced a strong rhetoric of democracy, but at the same time placed considerable limits on the kind of activity and criticism that democratic parties might exercise. Note that he made no provision about who might decide if parties were behaving in a fashion dangerous to the national interest. In his own time in office he imprisoned numerous political opponents. Also note his concerns about the Russian Federation's future place in the world and his strong commitment to expansion of its military defense capacities.

- **HOW** does Putin seem to embrace democratic reform? What are the limits that he places on democratic activity? How might those limits lead to government interference with the activity of political parties? What are Putin's concerns regarding NATO and the place of the Russian Federation in world affairs?

The desire of millions of our citizens for individual freedom and social justice is what defines the future of Russia's political system. The democratic state should become an effective instrument for civil society's self-organization. . . .

Russia's future political system will be centered on several large political parties that will have to work hard to maintain or affirm their leading positions, be open to change and broaden their dialogue with the voters.

Political parties must not forget their immense responsibility for Russia's future, for the nation's unity and for our country's stable development.

No matter how fierce the political battles and no matter how irreconcilable the differences between parties might be, they are never worth so much as to bring the country to the brink of chaos.

Irresponsible demagogy and attempts to divide society and use foreign help or intervention in domestic political struggles are not only immoral but are illegal. They belittle our people's dignity and undermine our democratic state. . . .

No matter what their differences, all of the different public forces in the country should act in accordance with one simple but essential principle: do nothing that would damage the interests of Russia and its citizens and act only for Russia's good, act in its national interests and in the interest of the prosperity and security of all its people. . . .

It is now clear that the world has entered a new spiral in the arms race. This does not depend on us and it is not we who began it. . . .

NATO itself is expanding and is bringing its military infrastructure ever closer to our borders. We have closed our bases in Cuba and Vietnam, but what have we got in return? New American bases in Romania and Bulgaria, and a new missile defense system with plans to install components of this system in Poland and the Czech Republic soon it seems. . . .

We are effectively being forced into a situation where we have to take measures in response, where we have no choice but to make the necessary decisions. . . .

Russia has a response to these new challenges and it always will. Russia will begin production of new types of weapons over these coming years, the quality of which is just as good and in some cases even surpasses those of other countries.

Source: Validmir Putin, Speech at Expanded Meeting of the State Council on Russia's Development Strategy through to 2020, February 8, 2008, President of Russia, Official Web Portal, *http://www.kremlin.ru/eng/text/speeches/2008/02/08/1137_type82912typ e82913_159643.shtml*

Ossetia, itself a part of the former Soviet Union that had been divided into regions dominated by Russia and Georgia. Georgia sought greater influence there. Russian troops first drove the Georgians out of South Ossetia and then continued into Georgia itself. Russia withdrew after a ceasefire, but had succeeded in demonstrating its power

Russian Invasion of Georgia. The aftermath of an attack by a Russian warplane on an apartment block in Gori, Georgia during the conflict in South Ossetia in August 2008. Here a Georgian man cradles the body of a relative killed during the bombing, which killed at least five people.

What were Russia's objectives in this conflict?

See the **Map**

Successor Republics of the Soviet Union

at **myhistorylab.com**

in the region. The absence of any effective resistance to Russian actions in Georgia from either the United States or the European Union nations raised doubts about the capacity of either to influence events in the Black Sea region. Therefore, though the Russian incursion into Georgia was relatively brief, it demonstrated that the classic issues of European great power politics remain alive in the new Europe. It also demonstrated Russian willingness to take advantage of American involvement in Iraq and Afghanistan to reassert its potential authority in those regions it has dominated since the wars of Catherine the Great in the eighteenth century.

In late 2008 another question suddenly confronted Russia. As one element in the worldwide financial crisis, commodity prices dropped sharply, including the price of oil. It remains to be seen whether Russia will be able to maintain its economic growth and political resurgence in the face of declining income.

THE COLLAPSE OF YUGOSLAVIA AND CIVIL WAR

HOW DID the West respond to the collapse of Yugoslavia?

Yugoslavia was created after World War I. It included six major national groups—Serbs, Croats, Slovenes, Montenegrins, Macedonians, and Bosnians (Muslims)—among whom there have been ethnic disputes for centuries (see Map 31–4). The Croats and Slovenes are Roman Catholic and use the Latin alphabet. The Serbs, Montenegrins, and Macedonians are Eastern Orthodox and use the Cyrillic alphabet. The Bosnians are Islamic. Most members of each group reside in a region with which they are associated historically, and these regions constituted individual republics within Yugoslavia. Many Serbs, however, lived outside Serbia proper.

Yugoslavia's first communist leader, Marshal Tito (1892–1980) held Yugoslavia together largely through a cult of personality. After his death, ethnic differences came to the fore. Nationalist leaders—most notably Slobodan Milošević (b. 1941) in Serbia and Franjo Tudjman (b. 1922) in Croatia—gained increasing authority. Ethnic tension and violence soon resulted.

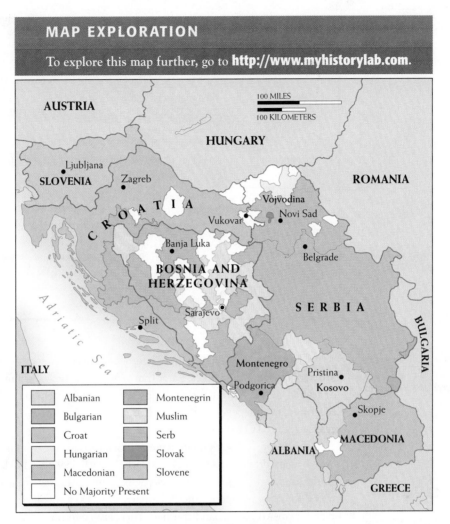

MAP EXPLORATION

To explore this map further, go to **http://www.myhistorylab.com**.

MAP 31–4. Ethnic Composition in the Former Yugoslavia.

The rapid changes in Eastern Europe during the close of the 1980s intensified longstanding ethnic tensions in the former Yugoslavia. This map shows where Yugoslavia's ethnic population lived in 1991, before internal conflicts escalated.

How does the Balkans conflict illustrate the importance of ethnic identity in the modern world?

During the summer of 1990, in the wake of the changes in the former Soviet bloc nations, Slovenia and Croatia declared independence from the central Yugoslav government. By June 1991, full-fledged war had erupted between Serbia and Croatia. In 1992, Croatian and Serbian forces divided Bosnia-Herzegovina. The Muslims in Bosnia—who had lived alongside Serbs and Croats for generations—were soon crushed between the opposing forces. The Serbs in particular, pursuing a policy called ethnic cleansing, killed or forcibly moved many Bosnian Muslims.

Destruction of Sarajevo.
An elderly parishioner walks through the ruins of St. Mary's Roman Catholic Church in Sarajevo. The church was destroyed by Serb shelling in May 1992.

Which other regions of the world have experienced "ethnic cleansing" in recent years?

CHRONOLOGY

THE BREAKUP OF YUGOSLAVIA

1991 June		Slovenia declares independence
		Croatia declares independence
1992 January		Macedonia declares independence
	April	Serbia and Montenegro proclaim a new Federal Republic of Yugoslavia
	April	War erupts in Bosnia and Herzegovina after Muslims and Croats vote for independence
1995 November		Peace agreement reached in Dayton, Ohio
1998 March		War breaks out in Kosovo, a province of Serbia
1999 March		NATO bombing of Serbia begins
2000		Milošević regime overthrown

Read the **Document**

Zlata Filipovi, from Zlata's Diary: A Child's Life in Sarajevo at **myhistorylab.com**

The United Nations attempted unsuccessfully to intervene. In 1995, NATO forces carried out strategic air strikes. Later that year, under the leadership of the United States, the leaders of the warring forces completed a peace agreement in Dayton, Ohio, which recognized an independent Bosnia. The terms of the agreement were enforced by the presence of NATO troops.

In the late 1990s Serbian aggression against ethnic Albanians in the province of Kosovo again provoked a NATO response. In early 1999 NATO launched an air attack against the Serbian forces. The Serbian army withdrew from Kosovo, and NATO ground forces protected ethnic Albanians. In 2000 a revolution overthrew the regime of Slobodan Milošević, and the new Yugoslav government handed him over in June 2001 to the International War Crimes Tribunal at the Hague for trial as a war criminal. (Milošević died in prison in 2006 of natural causes.)

See the **Map**

The Former Yugoslavia after 1991 at **myhistorylab.com**

CHALLENGES TO THE ATLANTIC ALLIANCE

IS NATO still a viable alliance in the post–Cold War era?

CHALLENGES ON THE INTERNATIONAL SECURITY FRONT

Since the collapse of the Soviet Union, NATO has expanded its membership to include Poland, the Czech Republic, Hungary, and nine other formerly Eastern-bloc nations. Yet the present purpose of NATO remains ill defined. NATO attempted to assume the role of internal peacekeeper in the new Europe, but some members and European publics disapproved.

NATO's uncertain mission and continental Europe's inward-looking tendency shaped reactions to the September 11, 2001, attack by al-Qa'ida on the United States. Initially, Europeans sympathized deeply with Americans, but a significant split soon developed over President George W. Bush's response to the terrorist assault. In what Bush termed "a war on terrorism," the United States overthrew the Taliban government of Afghanistan in late 2001. This destroyed some of al-Qa'ida's bases but not its leadership.

The Bush administration then set forth a new policy of preemptive strikes and intervention against potential enemies of the United States, which marked a major departure from previous United States foreign policy and aroused controversy both at home

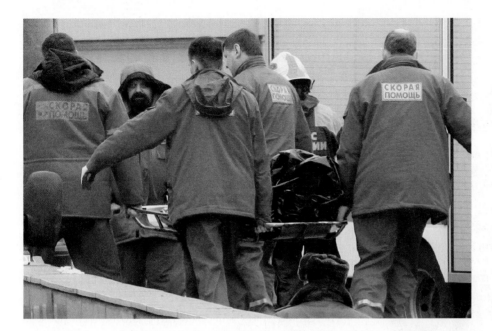

and abroad. The American invasion of Iraq in 2003 received the support of numerous
European governments, but some traditional European allies of the United States—particularly France and Germany—sharply criticized American decision making and actions. Popular political opinon across Europe dissented vocally from American policy.

Terrorists have struck in Europe and have shown how al-Qa'ida–sponsored attacks can influence European politics. On March 11, 2004, at least 190 people were
killed in commuter train bombings in Madrid, Spain, and on July 7, 2005, more than
50 were killed by a similar attack in London. The Spanish attack occurred just before
an election, and the Spanish government that had supported the American invasion
of Iraq was voted from office.

Profound divisions have arisen between the United States and many of its historic
postwar allies. Many Europeans see their values and their emerging political community
as different from those of Americans. Over time, external events and the wider conflict
between the West and radical political Islam will most likely determine the character of
the Atlantic alliance, just as the division between a democratic West and a communist
East did in the past.

Read the **Document**
Statement from Chancellor Schröder on
the Iraq Crisis (2003)
at **myhistorylab.com**

STRAINS OVER ENVIRONMENTAL POLICY

The impact of economic development on the environment has been a growing concern. This concern has involved issues of pollution of water from industrial and urban
waste and the pollution of the atmosphere from the emissions of hydrocarbons set
loose in the air by industrial plants and the ever-growing number of automobiles and
other vehicles using internal combustion engines as well as coal-burning utility plants
and other industrial sites. One result of this new interest in the environment has been
the rise of politically active environmental movements around the world. Some of
these movements have worked within the existing political system; others have taken
more radical courses of action, including ecological terrorism, sabotage, and confrontation with police at major meetings of world leaders, particularly at the G-8
Summit meetings.

Environmental issues have proved divisive within the industrial democracies. During the past decade the political tensions arising from environmentalism have begun to
impinge upon international relations, too. The chief issue has been the emission of what

Read the **Document**
European Criticism of American
Environmental Policies, 2007
at **myhistorylab.com**

Watch the **Video**
The Role of the Environment in History
at **myhistorylab.com**

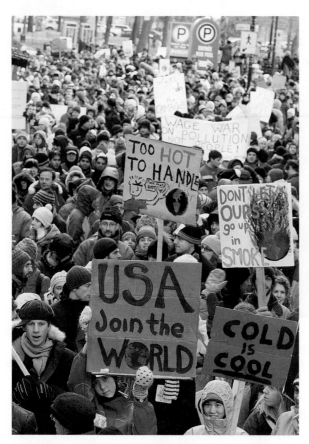

Protesters at the UN Climate Change Conference, Montreal.
Thousands of people march through the streets of Montreal on
December 3, 2005, as part of a worldwide day of protest
against global warming. The demonstration coincided with a
United Nations Climate Change Conference.

**Why are most of the demonstrators in this photograph young
people?**

◆●◆⎯Read the Document
The Kyoto Protocol to the United Nations
Framework Convention on Climate
Change, Article Two
at **myhistorylab.com**

are termed *greenhouse gases*, which the scientific community has concluded is raising the temperature of the planet.

In 1997 various members of the United Nations signed the Kyoto Protocol on Climate Change. This treaty set specific mandatory goals for reducing the emission of greenhouse gases in the most developed industrial countries against 1990 benchmarks. Those gases include carbon dioxide, methane, hydrofluorocarbons, and sulphur hexafluoride, among others. The Kyoto Protocol received the support of numerous major nations including Japan, Russia, and the European Union and became binding on its signatories in 2005. But the United States has not ratified the protocol. The Bush administration indicated that it feared implementation would harm economic growth in the United States. The administration also criticized those parts of the treaty that permit developing nations such as China and India not to reduce their emissions, contending this would disadvantage the United States in world trade.

The United States' stance on the Kyoto Protocol put it at odds with traditional European allies as well as Japan. Moreover, as the United States pursued its intervention in Iraq, numerous European governments criticized the American government for pressing unilateral policies on a number of fronts. In the spring of 2007 the United States sought to modify its position, offering to enter into negotiations with all nations that are major contributors to greenhouse emissions including India and China, and to negotiate specific targets for elimination of emissions. Germany and other nations, meanwhile, have proposed ambitious goals for the reduction of greenhouse emissions. The exact position of the Obama administration on international environmental issues remains to be determined, but it will probably pursue a less unilateral policy than the Bush administration.

Numerous factors account for the recent shifts in U.S. environmental policy statements. The American National Academy of Sciences has determined that the rate of worldwide greenhouse emissions is growing faster than anyone has predicted. Many industrial and commercial companies have found it to their advantage to embrace the environmental cause. Several companies and industries have even come to believe they can prosper by addressing climatic issues. Across the globe, advocates for a more rapid response to the growing environmental challenge appear to have been making great strides in persuading public opinion that their case is both valid and urgent, a development reflected by changes in the stances of various governments— even of those that have not embraced the Kyoto Protocol.

Two developments lie ahead in the immediate future. First, environmental pollution will continue to grow. Second, a period of protracted negotiations will ensue. Those negotiations will contribute to ongoing tension between the United States and its traditional Atlantic partners.

SUMMARY

 WHAT WERE the causes of the Cold War?

The Cold War Era. U.S.–Soviet cooperation did not survive World War II. After 1945 Europe was divided into a Soviet-dominated zone in the East (the Warsaw Pact) and a U.S.-led zone in the West (NATO). U.S.–Soviet rivalry played itself out around the world from the 1950s to the 1980s, although gradually a spirit of détente arose between the two powers, especially under President Ronald Reagan and Soviet leader Mikhail Gorbachev. The Cold War ended with the dissolution of the Soviet Union in 1991. *page 806*

 WHY HAVE European nations chosen to unify their economies?

Toward Western European Unification. Participation in the Marshall Plan and NATO gave some Western European nations a taste of the benefits of cooperation. Since then, the region has moved slowly but seemingly inexorably toward political and economic unification symbolized by the adoption of a common currency, the euro, in 2002. *page 812*

 WHAT MAJOR trends have marked European society since World War II?

European Society in the Second Half of the Twentieth Century and Beyond. Since World War II, European society has been reshaped by migration. Debates about the proper roles of the welfare state and of religion in the secular state have recurred, while women have gained more rights and opportunities. *page 814*

WHAT ARE the main themes that have characterized postwar America?

American Domestic Scene since World War II. The major themes in postwar American history were opposition to communism at home and abroad, the expansion of civil rights to African Americans, and economic prosperity. Politically, the relatively liberal years from the late 1950s through the 1970s were succeeded by a growing conservatism, especially under the presidencies of Ronald Reagan, George Bush, and George W. Bush. Even the democratic President Bill Clinton was more centrist than liberal. After the terrorist attacks of September 11, 2001, the United States embarked on a war on terrorism that led to wars in Afghanistan and Iraq. *page 818*

 HOW DID leaders after Stalin attempt to reform Soviet government?

The Soviet Union to 1989. Khrushchev loosened the grip of the Stalinist state, but his foreign policy failures—notably the Cuban Missile Crisis—led to his resignation in 1964. The Brezhnev era saw both increased repression at home and attempts to reach accommodations with the West. Poland's Solidarity movement was temporarily suppressed. Gorbachev's reformist policies were built around the concepts of *perestroika* (restructuring) and *glasnost* (openness). *page 821*

 WHY DID communist regimes collapse so easily in Eastern Europe in 1989?

1989: Year of Revolutions in Eastern Europe. Solidarity reemerged in Poland, and in 1989 Gorbachev approved Poland's first postwar noncommunist prime minister. In Hungary in 1990, open elections displaced communist rule. East Germany opened the Berlin Wall in late 1989, and soon Germany reunified. Vaclev Havel, a playwright, led the "velvet revolution" in Czechoslovakia. In Romania, however, the overturn of communist rule was violent, ending with the execution of dictatorial president Ceausescu. *page 823*

 WHO WERE the leaders in the period surrounding the collapse of the Soviet Union?

The Collapse of the Soviet Union. The failure of the communist regimes in Eastern Europe and the Soviet Union to produce economic prosperity or political liberalization led to their growing unpopularity. Soviet economic difficulties led Mikhail Gorbachev to institute liberal reforms that led to the collapse of communist rule first in Eastern Europe, then in the Soviet Union itself. The disappearance of the Soviet Union led to independence for much of the former Soviet Empire. Russia experienced social, economic, and political turmoil under Boris Yeltsin. Vladimir Putin has used a firm hand and oil wealth to project Russian power. *page 826*

 HOW DID the West respond to the collapse of Yugoslavia?

The Collapse of Yugoslavia and Civil War. In the former Yugoslavia, the end of communist rule led to dismemberment and civil war. In the 1990s the NATO powers, led by the United States, intervened to halt the fighting and end a pattern of ethnic atrocities. *page 830*

 IS NATO still a viable alliance in the post–Cold War era?

Challenges to the Atlantic Alliance. NATO has endured and grown, but its mission is unclear. The Bush administration's unilateralism alienated traditional American allies. Environmental policy is another area of disagreement between Europe and the United States. *page 832*

KEY TERMS

Cold War (p. 808)

euro (p. 813)

European Economic Community (EEC) (p. 812)

European Union (EU) (p. 813)

glasnost (GLAZ-nohst) (p. 823)

Marshall Plan (p. 808)

perestroika (PAYR-uhs-TROY-kuh) (p. 823)

REVIEW QUESTIONS

1. What were the causes of the Cold War? What was the effect of the Cold War on Europe?

2. How did the outcome of World War II affect Europe's position in the world? What prompted European unification? How successful has it been?

3. What were the chief characteristics of Western European society in the decades after 1945? What was the experience of Eastern Europe during the same period, and why was it different? Be sure to discuss women's roles.

4. How has immigration changed the face of Europe since 1945?

5. What were the most important developments in the domestic history of the United States between 1945 and 1968? How did the Vietnam War affect American society? When did the shift to political conservatism occur in the United States? What did it mean for the role of the federal government?

6. Describe the Soviet economy between 1945 and 1990. Did it meet the needs of the Soviet people? What were the causes of the collapse of the Soviet Union? What role did Gorbachev play in that process?

7. Describe the collapse of communist rule in Eastern Europe. Why was it a relatively bloodless revolution? What problems have ensued?

8. Why did Yugoslavia break apart and slide into civil war? How did the West respond to this crisis?

9. How did the American response to the attacks of September 11, 2001, cause significant rifts in the NATO alliance? Why do some European nations dissent from U.S. policy?

10. What aspects of environmental policy have divided the United States and Europe?

Note: To learn more about the topics in this chapter, please turn to the Suggested Readings at the end of the book. For additional sources related to this chapter please see www.myhistorylab.com

myhistorylab Connections

Reinforce what you learned in this chapter by studying the many documents, images, maps, review tools, and videos available at **www.myhistorylab.com**

Read and Review

✓●-[**Study** and **Review** Chapter 31

●●●-[Read the Document   *Josef Stalin, excerpts from the "Soviet Victory" Speech, p. 807*
Iron Curtain Speech, Winston Churchill, p. 807
The Truman Doctrine (1947), Harry S. Truman, p. 808
George C. Marshall, The Marshall Plan, 1947, p. 808
Gamal Abdel Nasser, Speech on the Suez Canal (Egypt), 1956, p. 809
The Kitchen Debate, 810
A Common Market and European Integration (1960), p. 813
Treaty on European Union, p. 813
Martin Luther King Jr., Letter from Birmingham City Jail, 1963, p. 819
Republican Party Nomination Acceptance, p. 820
Addresses by George W. Bush. 2001, p. 821
Nikita Khrushchev, Speech to the Twenty-Second Congress of the Communist Party, 1962, p. 822
Mikhail Gorbachev on the Need for Economic Reform (1987), p. 823
Zlata Filipovi, from Zlata's Diary: A Child's Life in Sarajevo, p. 832
Statement from Chancellor Schröder on the Iraq Crisis (2003), p. 833
European Criticism of American Environmental Policies, 2007, p. 833
The Kyoto Protocol to the United Nations Framework Convention on Climate Change, Article Two, p. 834

👁-[See the Map   *Cold War 1, p. 807*
Contemporary Europe, p. 814
The Vietnam War, p. 819
Successor Republics of the Soviet Union, p. 830
The Former Yugoslavia after 1991, p. 832

👁-[View the Image   *European Union Flag, p. 813*
Statue of Lenin Toppled during Soviet Collapse, p. 823

((●-[Hear the Audio   *Cold War 1, Slide 2, p. 809*

▶-[Watch the Video   *Escaping the Berlin Wall, p. 809*
Cold War Connections: Russia, America, Berlin, and Cuba, p. 811
The Role of the Environment in History, p. 833

Research and Explore

▶-[Watch the Video   *Is the USA an Imperial Power? Is this an Imperial Age?*

▶-[Watch the Video *BP Environmental Disaster*

((●-[Hear the Audio

Hear the audio file for Chapter 31
at **www.myhistorylab.com**

32

East Asia: The Recent Decades

((•—|Hear the Audio for Chapter 32 at www.myhistorylab.com

The Price of Growth. A coal-powered plant in Hebei province, northern China, February 2006. According to the Worldwatch Institute, sixteen of the world's twenty most polluted cities are in China. On average, China builds one coal-fired plant a week.

What are the costs of China's economic expansion?

T*he history of East Asia since World War II may be divided into two phases. In the first, from 1945 to 1980, Japan, and then South Korea and Taiwan (along with Singapore and Hong Kong), demonstrated amazing economic growth. The values of the East Asian heritage seemed, if given half a chance, to lead to economic growth. In stark contrast, those East Asian nations that became communist—China, Vietnam, and North Korea—did poorly. Vietnam was wracked by wars. North Korea was impossibly totalitarian. The government of China proved incapable of tapping the talents and energies of its people, despite having gained undisputed authority over a territory comparable to the Qing Empire.*

After 1980, the situation changed (see Map 32–1 on page 842). Those nations that had prospered during the first phase continued to do so. Japan was free and democratic, and despite new problems, enjoyed a European level of economic well-being, as well as social stability and a rich cultural life. South Korea and Taiwan transformed themselves into democracies and continued to prosper. But the most striking change was in China, which in 1978 launched a semi-capitalist market economy. Long suppressed entrepreneurial abilities surfaced, production grew, and exports boomed. Within a few decades, China became an important player in global markets. Chinese society, too, was slowly transformed. Vietnam adopted a weaker version of the Chinese policy, encouraging private enterprise and opening its markets to foreign capital. Only North Korea resisted the changes sweeping the rest of the communist world. The rigidities of its singular brand of communism inflicted hunger and misery on its people and led its government to pursue desperate policies. ■

GLOBAL PERSPECTIVE

MODERN EAST ASIA

Before World War II, only Europe, the United States, and Japan had successfully combined the ingredients needed for modern economic growth. It was as though these countries had a magic potion that the rest of the world lacked. Industrialization in East Asia during the second half of the twentieth century made clear that there was no magic potion: The West and Japan just got there first. The industrialization of East Asia raises issues that powerfully affect relations among nations.

One question is whether high-wage nations will be able to compete with those low-wage nations that have found the formula for growth. Until recently, advanced nations were satisfied with their share of world trade. They sold the products of their heavy industries and advanced technologies and bought raw materials and labor-intensive products. They assumed that their technological edge was permanent—that they would always be sufficiently ahead of the less developed nations to maintain high wages for their workers. This assumption is now challenged. Since the 1960s, Taiwan, South Korea, Hong Kong, and Singapore have achieved

modern growth in high technological fields well before their wages reached Western levels. This has made them formidable competitors in precisely those areas the West saw as its own. Since the late 1980s, China has done the same. The United States kept its market open and regained a measure of competitiveness during the 1990s, but at the cost of holding down wages, corporate restructuring, relocating jobs abroad, and huge trade deficits. Can it continue to pay this price? Will the new competition, combined with runaway immigration, create a permanent two-tier system of wages? China, the most recent East Asian industrializer, will have fairly cheap labor for decades. As it advances, the impact on high-wage nations will be massive.

A second issue is natural resources. An oil crisis occurred in the early 1970s when demand outran supply. There were shortages at the pumps, a steep rise in the price of oil, and a transfer of wealth from industrial to oil-rich nations. Market forces, however, uncovered new sources of supply and the crisis faded. Yet oil reserves are still dwindling. At some point demand, including new demand from

JAPAN

HOW DID the postwar occupation change Japan politically?

See the Map
Japan in 1945 at **myhistorylab.com**

By early 1945, most Japanese were poor, hungry, and ill-clothed. Cities were burnt out, factories scarred by bombings; ships had been sunk, railways were dilapidated, and trucks and cars were scarce. On August 15, 1945, the emperor broadcast Japan's surrender to the Japanese people. They expected a harsh and vindictive occupation, but when they found it constructive, their receptivity to new democratic ideas and their repudiation of militarism led one Japanese writer to label the era "the second opening of Japan."

THE OCCUPATION

General Douglas MacArthur was the supreme commander for the Allied powers in Japan, and the occupation forces were mostly American. The chief concern of the first phase of the occupation was demilitarization and democratization. Civilians and soldiers abroad were returned to Japan, and the military was demobilized. Wartime leaders were brought to trial for "crimes against humanity." Shinto was disestablished as the state religion, labor unions were encouraged, and the holding companies of *zaibatsu* combines were dissolved. Land reform expropriated landlord holdings and sold them to landless tenants at a fractional cost.

The new constitution, written by MacArthur's headquarters in 1947 and passed into law by the Japanese Diet, fundamentally changed Japan's polity in five respects:

1. A British-style parliamentary state was established along with an American-style independent judiciary and a federal system of prefectures with elected governors.

2. Women were given the right to vote.

3. The rights to life, liberty, the pursuit of happiness, a free press, and free assembly were guaranteed. These were joined by newer rights, such as academic freedom, collective bargaining, sexual equality in marriage, and minimal standards of wholesome and cultural living.

Article 9 of the No-War Constitution
Article 9 of the Japanese constitution forbids not only the use of force as a means to settling international disputes but also the maintenance of an army, navy, or air force.

China, India, and Brazil, will outstrip supply. Will struggles over scarce resources shape future international relations?

A third issue is population. Japan's population quadrupled in the course of industrialization and then leveled off. Its pattern resembled that of western Europe. China, in contrast, had a huge population when it began industrialization. Since it could ill afford a further quadrupling, it adopted tough policies to limit births. Its population may peak at 1.6 billion in 2030. Whether other less developed nations in the world follow the Japanese or Chinese pattern will depend on their particular circumstances, but for many, the Chinese model may be unavoidable. More people are no blessing.

A fourth issue is politics. The recent history of Taiwan and South Korea suggests that East Asian dictatorships may evolve toward democracy as standards of living rise. Will this happen in China? China is prospering; its people are caught up in consumerism; but the Chinese Communist Party shows no signs of relaxing its monopoly on government. Also, postwar Taiwan and South Korea were less thoroughly authoritarian to begin with

and were strongly influenced by the United States. It is too early to make predictions.

A final issue is pollution, the dark companion of industrial and demographic growth. When the world was underdeveloped, industrial wastes seemed to vanish harmlessly into the vast reaches of surrounding lands and seas. But as the world industrializes, pollution threatens. It is particularly severe in China. And even apart from disasters such as Minamata and Chernobyl, automobile fumes, industrial effluents, chimney gases, pesticides, garbage, and sewage cause lakes to die, forests to wither, and levels of toxins to rise.

Focus Questions

◆ What is the impact of East Asian economic growth on the world's natural resources? On international relations?

◆ Does recent history suggest that the Chinese government will become more democratic as its citizens become more prosperous?

4. **Article 9**, the no-war clause, stipulated: "The Japanese people forever renounce war as a sovereign right of the nation" and will never maintain "land, sea, and air forces" or "other war potential." This article, though never strictly observed, made Japan into something unique in the world: a major power without commensurate military strength.

5. The constitution defined the emperor as "the symbol of the state, deriving his position from the will of the people with whom resides sovereign power."

The Japanese people accepted the new constitution and embraced democracy with uncritical enthusiasm. (See Document, "Two Views of the 'Symbol Emperor'" on page 843.)

To create a climate in which the new democracy could flourish, the occupation in its second phase turned to Japan's economic recovery. It dropped plans to deconcentrate big business further, encouraged the Japanese government to curb inflation, and cracked down on communist unions. The United States also gave Japan $2 billion in economic aid.

The outbreak of the Korean War in 1950 marked the start of the third and final phase of the occupation. The American military had little time for Japan, and the Japanese cabinet and Diet began to assume more responsibility for the country. When Japan regained its sovereignty in April 1952, the changeover was hardly noticeable in the daily life of the Japanese people. On the same day as the peace treaty, Japan signed a security treaty with the United States, which became the cornerstone of Japan's minimalist defense policy.

Emperor Hirohito and General MacArthur. The two men met at the U.S. Embassy in Tokyo in 1945. MacArthur felt the emperor contributed to the stability of Japan and made the work of the occupation easier. The emperor was glad to be of use and relieved that he was not hanged as a war criminal.

What was the occupation?

MAP 32–1.   Contemporary East Asia.

Which nations in East Asia are communist today?

PARLIAMENTARY POLITICS

In 1945, Japan had a parliamentary potential that harked back to the rise of party power in the Diet between 1890 and 1932. It also had an authoritarian potential compounded of those factors that had led to the rise of militarism. Had the country been occupied by the Soviet Union, the efficiency of its bureaucracy, its wartime economic planning organs, its educated and disciplined work force, and its receptivity to change after defeat would doubtless have made Japan a model communist state. Occupied by the United States, the parliamentary potential emerged.

Japan's postwar politics can be divided into three periods. In the first, from 1945 to 1955, prewar politics continued, with modifications to fit the new environment.

●●● Read the Document

The Constitution of Japan (1947) at
myhistorylab.com

DOCUMENT

Two Views of the "Symbol Emperor"

The murkiest aspect of Japan's prewar emperor-centered ideology was the juxtaposition of the emperor as a modern monarch and the emperor as a living deity, ultimately descended from the sun goddess. In the first selection, former Prime Minister Yoshida Shigeru, a product of Meiji Japan, basically accepts the prewar ideology but argues that because in fact the emperor exercised little power before World War II, nothing was changed by the postwar constitution. In the second selection, Nobel Prize winner Ōe Kenzaburō, a humanistic and slightly leftist novelist, recognizes that the emperor has been stripped of his former authority but worries about a revival of his Shinto identity.

- **WHAT** does Yoshida mean by "as naturally," and why does Ōe call the prewar emperor an "absolute ruler"?

1. In regard to the question of the Imperial structure of government, as it existed in Japan, I pointed out that the Meiji Constitution had originated in the promises made to the Japanese people by the Emperor Meiji at the beginning of his reign, and there was little need to dwell on the fact that democracy, if we were to use the word, had always formed part of the traditions of our country, and was not—as some mistakenly imagined—something that was about to be introduced with the revision of the Constitution. As for the Imperial House, the idea and reality of the Throne had come into being among the Japanese people as naturally as the idea of the country itself; no question of antagonism between Throne and people could possibly arise; and nothing contained in the new Constitution could change that fact. The word "symbol" had been employed in the definition of the Emperor because we Japanese had always regarded the Emperor as the symbol of the country itself—a statement which any Japanese considering the issue dispassionately would be ready to recognize as an irrefutable fact.

2. Japan's emperor system, which had apparently lost its social and political influence after the defeat in the Pacific War, is beginning to flex its muscles again, and in some respects it has already recouped much of its lost power—with two differences: first, the Japanese today will not accept the prewar ideology-cum-theology that held the emperor to be both absolute ruler and living deity. Nevertheless, imperial rites performed quite recently were done in such a manner as to impress upon us that the emperor's lineage can be traced to a deity; I am referring here to the rituals associated with the present emperor's enthronement and the so-called Great Thanksgiving Service that followed it. These ceremonies provoked little objection from either the government or the people, indeed most Japanese seemed to take it all very much for granted.

1. Yoshida Shigeru, *The Yoshida Memoirs.* Copyright © 1961 Heineman Books, p. 139. 2. From "Speaking on Japanese Culture Before a Scandinavian Audience," *Japan, The Ambiguous and Myself: The Nobel Prize Speech and Other Lectures by Kenzaburō Ōe.* Published by Kodansha International, Ltd., 1995. Copyright © 1992 by Kenzaburō Ōe. All rights reserved. Reprinted by permission.

Two conservative parties, the Liberals and the Democrats, and the Japanese Socialist Party emerged. For most of this decade, the Liberals held power.

In the long second period from 1955 to 1993, the Liberal Democratic Party (**LDP**), which was formed by a merger of the two conservative parties, held power and the Japanese Socialist Party was the permanent opposition. The LDP became identified as the party that was rebuilding Japan and maintaining Japan's security through close ties with the United States. Despite the cozy relationships that developed between the LDP and business, periodic scandals, and a widespread distrust of politicians, the Japanese people voted to keep it in power. Rule by a single party for such a long period provided an unusual continuity in government policies.

A third era of politics began with the 1993 election. The notable feature of this era was the decline and fall of the left. The end of the Cold War and the worldwide

LDP

The Liberal Democratic Party. A conservative party that has dominated postwar Japanese politics.

CHRONOLOGY

JAPAN SINCE 1945

1948–1954	Yoshida ministries
1950–1953	Korean War
1952	Peace and security treaties
1955	Liberal and Democratic parties merge to form the LDP
1955–1973	Double-digit economic growth
1972	Japan recognizes the People's Republic of China
1973–1989	Economic growth continues at slower pace
1990	Bubble bursts and recession begins
1993	Socialists lose half of their Diet seats
1994–1996	Non-LDP coalitions govern; LDP-led coalitions reestablished
2001–2006	Koizumi Junichirō of the LDP as prime minister
2003	Japan sends troops to Iraq
2009	Hatoyama Ichirō becomes prime minister
2009	Hatoyama Yukio becomes prime minister
2010	Kan Naoto becomes prime minister

rejection of Marxism contributed to the demise of socialism in Japan, and the Communist Party also slumped.

The collapse of the left inaugurated an era of multiparty conservative politics. The players were the LDP, still the largest party, a shifting number of smaller conservative parties, and the Clean Government Party. Japanese electoral politics during the 1990s was punctuated by scandals and factional strife, but the overriding issue was the economy. In 1993 the LDP lost 52 of its 275 seats, a punishment for failing to end the recession. In its place, a non-LDP Conservative coalition held power between 1994 and 1996. Political scientists hailed this development as the beginning of the two-party conservative government. The possibility was not absent. But as the economic crisis continued, voters again turned to the LDP in the hope that its more seasoned politicians would be better able to cope with the lagging economy. To some extent it did, and the LDP stayed in power until 2009. Most LDP prime ministers were easily forgettable. The quirky but charismatic Koizumi Junichirō held office from 2001 to 2006. But all LDP prime ministers offered Japan more of the same: dependency on the bureaucracy, pork barrel projects for LDP voters, and public works to keep employment up.

But the electorate had tired of programs that led Japan deeper into debt. Also, the number of voters who saw themselves as "independents" increased. In the election of 2009, the LDP dropped from 293 seats in the Lower House to 119. The winner with 305 of the 480 Diet seats was the Democratic Party of Japan, a new party cobbled together 11 years earlier from a variety of small opposition parties. The new prime minister was Hatoyama Ichirō, who was a grandson of a prime minister, a graduate of Tokyo University, and a Ph.D recipient in engineering from Stanford. His platform included stricter control of the bureaucracy, better relations with China, and equality with the United States.

ECONOMIC GROWTH

The extraordinary story of the postwar East Asian economy started with Japan. Japanese growth continued at a double-digit pace for almost two decades. By the late 1970s, Sony, Toyota, Honda, Panasonic, Toshiba, Seiko, and Canon were known throughout the world for the quality of their products. Several factors explain this growth. An infrastructure of banking, marketing, and manufacturing skills had carried over from prewar Japan. The international situation was also favorable: Oil was cheap, access to raw materials and export markets was easy, and American sponsorship gained Japan early entry into international financing organizations. A tradition of frugality created a rate of savings close to 20 percent, which helped reinvestment.

A revolution in education contributed as well. By the early 1980s, almost all middle school graduates went on to high school, and a rising percentage went on to higher education. By the early 1980s, Japan was graduating more engineers than the United States. (The annual output of law schools in the United States equals the total number of lawyers in Japan.) This upgrading of human capital and channeling of its best minds into productive careers let Japan tap the huge backlog of technology that had developed in the United States during and after the war years. After "improvement engineering," Japan sold its products to the world.

High-quality, cheap labor was abundant. The population in 1950 was 83 million; by 2010 it approached 128 million. It is expected to stabilize and then decline in the twenty-first century. Workers quickly moved from agriculture to industry, and labor organizations proved no bar to economic growth. The government also aided manufacturers with tariff protection, foreign exchange, and special depreciation allowances. Industries engaged in advanced technologies benefited from cheap loans, subsidies, and research products of government laboratories. Critics who spoke of "Japan Inc." as though Japan were a single gigantic corporation overstated the case, but government was more supportive of business than it was regulative.

By 1973, the Japanese economy had become "mature." Double-digit growth gave way to 4 percent growth. Smokestack industries declined while service industries, pharmaceuticals, specialty chemicals, scientific equipment, computers, and robotics grew. Japan's trade began to generate huge surpluses. The surpluses were generated mainly by the appetite of world markets for Japanese products, but they were also a result of protectionist policies that the United States and Europe insisted be abolished.

Convinced that their boom would never end, Japanese bid up the price of corporate shares and land to unrealistic levels—several times those of Europe and America. In 1991 the "bubble" burst: The price of land and stocks plummeted. Japanese who had bought shares of stock or real estate at exaggerated prices were hard hit; banks that had made housing or margin loans incurred huge losses. As banks and individuals retrenched, the economy slowed. Incremental growth characterized the next two decades. Thousands of small companies went bankrupt; large companies restructured and cut research budgets; some workers were laid off or retired early; fewer new graduates were hired and unemployment rose.

Mixed trends appeared during the first decade of the twenty-first century. (1) As in the United States and Europe, some industrial production moved abroad in search of cheap, skilled labor. Sony television sets were no longer

Nissan Motors. An almost completely automated assembly line at the company's Zama factory. The high cost of labor in Japan makes such robot-intensive production economical.

Why are labor costs high in Japan?

View the Image
Japanese Technician Testing Equipment at **myhistorylab.com**

QUICK REVIEW

Factors in Japan's Postwar Growth

- Survival of prewar service and skills infrastructure
- High savings rate facilitated reinvestment
- Growing, well-educated labor force
- Pro-business government policies

manufactured in Japan. (2) Chinese demand for Japanese high-tech products rose, helping Japan to recover from the world recessions in 2000 and 2007; Japanese economists began to speak of the "complementarity" of Japanese and Chinese markets. (3) The government had no program in place to address its national debt—relative to GDP, it was the largest of all industrial nations. Most working Japanese, still protected by the cocoon of lifetime employment, were unwilling to accept higher taxes. (Large personal savings and foreign currency reserves partially offset the national debt.)

A Comparison of Japan with Germany and France Combined, 2009 Estimates		
GDP (in trillions)	Population (in millions)	Per Capita GDP
Germany $3.34	82	$40,731
France $2.65	65	$40,769
Total $5.99	147	$40,748 (average)
Japan $5.09	127	$39,921

FIGURE 32–1. The above GDP figures represent purchasing power. Japanese economy is almost the equal of the two leading European nations.

What is remarkable about Japan's economic growth?

But Japanese strengths remained formidable: Industry was restructured during the 1990s, with greater rewards for those who displayed talent. Japanese automobiles were coveted throughout the world, and the Japanese export surplus grew. Even Japan's management skills seemed exportable: Nissan's Tennessee plant took 17.37 hours to assemble an automobile, while at General Motors the average was 26.75. Equally notable was Japan's determination to maintain its lead in flat screens, fermentation chemistry, robotics, and materials research and to become a world force in biotechnology, medical instruments, and airplanes. Today, new science and engineering buildings on the Tokyo University campus dwarf the dreary prewar brick buildings of the faculties of law, letters, economics, and education.

At the dawn of the third millennium Japan's economy loomed large. It was second only to that of the United States, and almost as large as the economies of Germany and France combined. (See the comparative data in Figure 32–1.) Japan had achieved affluence through the peaceful development of human resources in a free society.

SOCIETY AND CULTURE

The triple engines of change—occupation reforms, economic growth, and rapid expansion of higher education—transformed Japanese society. In 1945, almost half of the population lived in villages; sixty years later most Japanese lived in cities, more than a quarter in the Tokyo–Osaka industrial corridor. A tiny percentage of the population produced the food for the rest. Families changed, too. In 1945 the three-generation extended family of grandparents, parents, and children was held up as the ideal, and most marriages were arranged. Fifty years later the nuclear family of parents and children was the norm, and most marriages were "love matches." In the 1950s and 1960s, companies and government offices built huge apartment blocks for their employees on the edges of cities. In the 1960s and 1970s, larger apartments, called "mansions" in Japanese, were built in cities and purchased by middle- and higher-income families; only the rich could afford city houses. As incomes rose, people bought rice cookers, washing machines, dryers, televisions, computers, and other electronic equipment. Consumerism was constrained only by the small size of living units.

Reforms imposed during the American occupation gave women the right to vote, legal equality, and equal inheritance rights. As women were admitted to prestigious universities and embarked on careers, the average age of marriage rose and more

Middle School Students in a Japanese Literature Class. Girls and boys wear school uniforms and study together. Desks are pushed together to accommodate large classes. The teacher is dressed like a businessman.

What role has education played in Japan's development?

wives worked outside the home. A working wife had a greater say in household matters. Greater economic leeway also made divorce an option: The number tripled to European levels between 1970 and 2010.

Prospering in the new Japan depended on education, and a rigorous system of examinations determined admission at every level. A few students rebelled against the rigid system, but most realized that the pressure to excel was for their own good and limited their rebellion to reading violent and sadistic *manga* [stylized mature-content comic books].

The enormous prewar gap between a tiny educated elite and those with only a middle school education disappeared. More than 90 percent of Japanese saw themselves as middle class—though the percentage below the poverty line was about the same as that of the United States. This consciousness was the social base for the new democracy. More education also explains Japan's tremendous consumption of newspapers, magazines, and books. Bookstores stock every variety of books imaginable: serious fiction, mysteries, histories, poetry, science fiction, romances, cookbooks, and translations, as well as books on investing, self-improvement, and home repairs.

A new respect for personal autonomy helped diminish some traditional ethnic prejudices toward the approximately 2 percent of the population that are minorities.

As the new millennium began, a serious social problem facing Japan was the aging of its population. In 1980, there were five workers for every retired person; in 2010 there were fewer than two. A recurring question is how the old will be supported and how they will vote. This problem, of course, is not unique to Japan. All developed nations have experienced a shift from high to lower fertility and mortality, but the imbalance was exaggerated by wartime population losses and postwar baby booms in Japan, Italy, and Germany. Urban Japan is crowded, and some see its current low birthrate as an opportunity to reduce population. The problem of too few workers, some argue, can be solved by raising the retirement age and tapping the reservoir of nonworking, middle-aged women. Others advocate incentives to encourage marriage and larger families. The average Japanese family today has 1.23 children, one of the lowest figures in the world. During the past two decades, people of Japanese descent from Brazil and Peru and illegal immigrants from other parts of Asia have taken the lowly jobs that Japanese shun. In the recession of 2008–2009, some illegal immigrants were deported, and some Brazilian Japanese were given one-way tickets home. The barriers to immigration are still high.

The cultural strains produced by Japan's rapid transformation have dislocated some people and created followings for new religions. One aberrant apocalyptic cult released nerve gas in a Tokyo subway in 1995. White-collar workers, or "salary men," spent hours commuting to work in crowded buses and trains. In Japan's corporate world *karōshi*, or death from overwork, became a recognized phenomenon.

Yet the ability of the society—family, school, office, and workshop—to absorb strains and lend support to the individual was impressive. Lifetime employment gave both workers and salaried employees a sense of security. Even during the long recession of the 1990s, layoffs were exceptional. Japanese wives, if public opinion polls are to be believed, felt better off than their American counterparts. By most comparative measures Japanese society was stable and orderly.

Japanese culture also remained vital. The traditional arts were maintained. The awareness of nature, so evident in films like Kurosawa Akira's *Rashomon* or *The Seven Samurai*, carried over to television dramas. Japanese films, music, literature, and even clothing design are admired around the world. Postwar Japan amply supports an argument for parallelism between economic and cultural dynamics.

Comic Book. Raised from childhood in the arts of *ninja*, the young heroine Azumi slays evil men. The popularity of this *Bigu Komikku* (Big Comic) led to a movie (*anime*, or animated) version. Was this the Japanese model for the American movie *Kill Bill*? Japan has specialized comics for every demographic group—children, teenage boys, teenage girls, and adults.

Why might the escapism of comic books be particularly appealing for the Japanese?

Body Language. Japanese businessmen exchange business cards in Tokyo. A businesswoman stands to one side and observes. An almost diplomatic formality governs such occasions.

What social changes have resulted from economic growth?

JAPAN AND THE WORLD

At the start of the new millennium, Japan had three sets of critical international relationships: with the world, East Asia, and the United States. With the world, Japan was a trading partner and, as it described itself, a "UN nation." It gave generous foreign aid to developing countries and was a member of major international economic organizations. A second set was with its East Asian neighbors. For reasons of history and proximity, Japan was extraordinarily alert to developments in Korea, Taiwan, China, and the Russian Far East. China's growing military strength was a concern. The third critical relationship was with the United States. The two countries were political allies, major trading partners, and linked by mutual security concerns. The 1952 security treaty remained the cornerstone of Japanese defense planning. In recent decades Japan has moved toward more positive military cooperation—within the limits of its constantly reinterpreted and elastic "peace constitution." When terrorists struck at the United States in September 2001, Prime Minister Koizumi spoke out in support of the United States and against terrorism. The Diet passed legislation that allowed Japanese Self-Defense Force to participate in non-combat roles in international military actions, and in 2003 Japan sent troops to Iraq. In 2006 the Self-Defense Agency became a cabinet ministry. In an East Asia in which China, Russia, and the United States have atomic arsenals, and even North Korea has A-bombs, Japanese feel increasingly vulnerable. If its trust in the U.S. "nuclear umbrella" should ever waver, Japan would become a nuclear power overnight.

CHINA

WHY DID Mao launch the Cultural Revolution?

•••─[Read the **Document**
China's One-Child Family Policy (1970s)
at **myhistorylab.com**

The story of China after 1949 is rooted in theories about economics and population. Marx rejected the Malthusian hypothesis that population growth tends to outstrip food production as a myth of capitalist societies, and Mao Zedong agreed. From 1949 until 1981, China's population increased from 550 million to nearly 1 billion. Growth in the Chinese economy was eaten up by all the new mouths, and in 1981 China adopted a policy of one child per family. This policy runs contrary to the deep-rooted Chinese sense of family, but the government argued that without it, China's future would be bleak. Thereafter population growth slowed dramatically, but the population still crossed the 1.3 billion mark in 2005. Since the median age in China is low, the birthrate is high—despite the one-child policy. Population will peak, it is predicted, in 2030, and then very slowly decline.

SOVIET PERIOD (1950–1960)

Civil war in China ended in 1949 as the last of Jiang Jieshi's troops fled to Taiwan. The People's Republic of China was proclaimed in October. The following year, China entered into an alliance with the Soviet Union. The decade that followed is often called the Soviet period because the Soviet model was adopted for the government, the army, the economy, and higher education.

The first step taken by the communist government was military consolidation. Areas inhabited by Tibetans, Uighur Turks, Mongols, and other minorities were occupied by the Chinese army and settled by Chinese immigrants.

A Closer Look

Trial of a Landlord

During the early 1950s, land redistribution followed the communist victory in China. Former landlords were put on trial for their crimes against the people.

Villagers who gather to watch the proceedings.

The village.

A soldier of the People's Liberation Army. He grasps his weapon and wears a regulation cap, but on his back, to protect him from the south China sun when not on duty, he carries a peasant hat.

The landlord, bound and barefoot, kneels on stones and awaits his sentence.

The judges are Communist Party members, former tenants, or members of the Peoples' Liberation Army. They sit at tables, their hats underneath.

Questions

1. How would you distinguish between a judicial procedure and political theater?

2. Why are army representatives present at the trial?

To examine this image in an interactive fashion, please go to **www.myhistorylab.com**

Hear the **Audio**
Communist China 3 at
myhistorylab.com

QUICK REVIEW

Sino-Soviet Relations

◆ 1958: Mao abandons Soviet economic model in favor of Great Leap Forward

◆ Disputes over borders and Chinese dissatisfaction with Soviet aid leads to deteriorating relations

◆ 1960: Soviet Union halts economic aid and withdraws engineers

brainwashing

Attempting to "reeducate" or alter a person's thoughts and beliefs to create behavior desired by the state, regardless of the individual's wishes.

Great Leap Forward

Mao's disastrous attempt to modernize the Chinese economy in 1958.

Performance during Cultural Revolution. Members of the Xiangyang Commune in Jiangsu province take part in the campaign to "Criticize Lin Biao and Confucius," one of the last large "campaigns" directed by members of the government in charge of the Cultural Revolution. Here, the commune's amateur troupe performs a ballad criticizing Confucius. The campaign began after the death of Lin Biao, who for a time was Mao Zedong's chosen successor but later was accused of attempting to seize power.

What was the Cultural Revolution?

Political consolidation followed. The Communist Party held the key levers of power in the government, army, and security forces. Mao was chairman of the party and head of state. He ruled through the Politboro and a system of regional, provincial, and district committees with party cells in every village, factory, school, and government office. Party members were exhorted to enforce the local enactment of government policies. Economic reconstruction was attempted on a massive scale, with the help of the Soviet Union, which sent financial aid as well as engineers and planners.

Rural society underwent two fundamental changes: land redistribution and collectivization. In the early 1950s, party cadres visited villages and held meetings at which landlords were denounced and forced to confess their crimes. Some were rehabilitated, others were sent to labor camps, and hundreds of thousands—perhaps several million—were killed. Their holdings were redistributed to the landless, and local responsibilities formerly borne by landlord gentry were shifted to associations dominated by former tenant farmers. Then in 1955–1956, before the new landowners had time to put down roots as private landowners, all lands were seized by the state and collectivized. The timing was important: In the Soviet Union, collectivization had come six years after redistribution; it was resisted by the *kulaks*, who had had time to put down roots.

During the early 1950s, intellectuals and universities also became a target for thought reform; the Chinese slang term was **brainwashing**. This involved study and indoctrination in Marxism, group pressures to produce an atmosphere of insecurity and fear, followed by confession, repentance, and reacceptance by society. The indoctrination was intended to strengthen party control and mobilize human energies on behalf of the state. By the late 1950s, Mao was disappointed with the results of collectivization, and in 1958, he resorted to mass mobilization to unleash the productive energies of the people, a policy called the **Great Leap Forward**. Campaigns were organized to accomplish vast projects, and village-based collective farms gave way to communes of 30,000 persons or more. The results were disastrous. Between 1958 and 1962, 20 to 30 million Chinese reportedly starved to death. Policies were modified, but agricultural production continued to fall through the 1970s, plagued by the ills of low incentives and collective responsibility.

Sino-Soviet relations also deteriorated. Disputes arose over borders. China was dissatisfied with Soviet aid. The Soviet Union condemned the Great Leap Forward as "leftist fanaticism" and resented Mao's view of himself, after Stalin's death, as the foremost exponent of world communism. In 1960, the Soviet Union halted economic aid and withdrew its engineers from China. Each country deployed about a million troops along their mutual border. The Sino-Soviet split was arguably the single most important development in postwar international politics.

The years between 1960 and 1965 saw conflicting trends. The failure of the Great Leap Forward led some Chinese leaders to turn away from Mao's reckless radicalism toward more moderate policies. Mao remained head of the party but had to give up his post as head of state. Yet, even as the government moved toward realistic goals and stable bureaucratic management, ideological indoctrination was revived. A new mass movement was also begun to transform education.

THE GREAT PROLETARIAN CULTURAL REVOLUTION (1965–1976)

In 1965, Mao once again emerged to dominate Chinese politics. He feared that the Chinese revolution—his revolution—would end up as a Soviet-style bureaucratic communism run for the benefit of officials. So he called for a new revolution to create a truly egalitarian culture.

Obtaining army support, Mao urged students and teenagers to form bands of Red Guards to carry out a new **Cultural Revolution**. Mao's sayings, the "Little Red Book," assumed the status of scripture. Universities were shut down as student factions fought. Teachers were beaten, imprisoned, and humiliated. Books were burned and art was destroyed. Homes were ransacked for foreign books, and Chinese who had studied abroad were persecuted. Red Guards beat to death those viewed as reactionaries. High officials were purged. Chinese today recall these events as a species of mass hysteria that defies understanding.

Eventually Mao tired of the violence and near anarchy. In 1968 and 1969 he called in the army to take over the revolutionary committees. In 1969, a new Central Committee, composed largely of military men, was established, and Lin Biao was named as Mao's successor. As violence ended, millions of students and intellectuals were sent to the countryside to work on farms. In 1970 and 1971 revolutionary committees were reconstituted as party committees. Worsening relations with the Soviet Union also made China's leaders desire greater stability at home. In 1969, a pitched battle had broken out between Chinese and Russian troops over an island in the Ussuri River. It was just at this time that President Nixon began to withdraw U.S. troops from Vietnam. When he proposed a renewal of ties, China quickly responded. Nixon visited Beijing in 1972, opening a new era of diplomatic relations.

The second phase of the Cultural Revolution between 1969 and 1976 was moderate only in comparison with what had gone before. On farms and in factories, ideology was still substituted for economic incentives. Universities reopened, but students were admitted by class background, not examination. In 1971, the so-called Gang of Four, which included Mao's wife and was abetted by the aging Mao, came to power. Class struggle was revived, and an official campaign was launched attacking the rightist "political swindlers" Lin Biao and Confucius.

POLITICS AND SOCIETY AFTER MAO

Mao's death in 1976 brought immediate changes. The Gang of Four and their radical supporters were arrested. In their place, Deng Xiaoping (1904–1997) emerged as the dominant figure in Chinese politics. Deng ousted his enemies, rehabilitated those purged during the Cultural Revolution, and put his supporters in power. After the lunacy of the Cultural Revolution, a "normal" Communist Party dictatorship was a relief. The people could now enjoy a measure of security and material improvement. There continued, however, a tension between the determination of the

Read the **Document**
Decision Concerning the Great Proletarian Cultural Revolution at
myhistorylab.com

Cultural Revolution

A movement launched by Mao between 1965 and 1976 against the Soviet-style bureaucracy that had taken hold in China. It involved widespread disorder and violence.

See the **Map**
China in the Era of Revolution and Civil War at **myhistorylab.com**

Hear the **Audio**
Communist China 4 at **myhistorylab.com**

CHRONOLOGY

CHINA SINCE 1949

1949	Communist victory; People's Republic of China established
1950	Sino-Soviet alliance; China occupies Tibet
1953	First Five-Year Plan
1958	Great Leap Forward
1960	Sino-Soviet split
1965–1976	Cultural Revolution
1972	Nixon visits Beijing
1976	Mao Zedong dies
1978–1997	Deng Xiaoping in power
1980–2007	China's economy grows at double-digit rate
1989	Tiananmen Square incident
2003	Hu Jintao becomes premier
2008	Beijing hosts Olympic games
2010	Chinese economy becomes second largest in the world

Goddess of Democracy and Freedom.
Student activists construct a "Goddess of Democracy and Freedom," taking the Statue of Liberty as their model. The goddess was in place in Tiananmen Square shortly before tanks drove students from the square in June 1989.

What happened in Tiananmen Square?

•••┤Read the Document
Deng Xiaoping, on Introducing
Capitalist Principles to China
at **myhistorylab.com**

ruling party to maintain its grip on power and its desire to obtain the benefits of liberalization.

The tension was most visible in China's intellectual life. The government's repudiation of the Cultural Revolution had led to an outpouring of stories, plays, and reports. But criticism of Deng's rule was not allowed. In 1983, 1985, and 1987, the government organized campaigns against "spiritual pollution," "capitalist thinking," and "bourgeois democracy," respectively.

Universities returned to normal in 1977. Entrance examinations were reinstituted, purged teachers returned to their classrooms, and scholars were sent to study in Japan and the West. Students began to demand still greater freedoms and even political democracy. During the late 1980s, the ferment that marked Eastern Europe and the Soviet Union under Gorbachev also appeared in China: it was as if a new virus had entered the communist world.

Student demands came to a head in April and May of 1989, when hundreds of thousands of students, workers, and people from all walks of life demonstrated for democracy in Tiananmen Square in Beijing and in dozens of other cities. The government sent in tanks and troops. Hundreds of students were killed, and leaders who did not escape abroad were jailed. The event defined the political climate in China for the decades that followed: Freedom was allowed in most areas of life, but no challenge to Communist Party rule was tolerated.

Deng officially stepped down in 1992, though he continued to exert strong "backroom power" until his death in 1997. Meanwhile Jiang Zemin, a generation younger, served as a figurehead. He argued, among other things, that the CCP must represent "the most advanced economic forces in society." One Chinese newspaper responded, not wholly inaccurately, with the headline "China's Communists Recruit Capitalist." Jiang stepped down in 2002 and Hu Jintao became president of China. His policies are not unlike those of Deng and Jiang, but the China he governs has changed immensely.

CHINA'S ECONOMY AFTER MAO

In the economic sphere, China's leaders repudiated the policies of Mao. Deng's great achievement in the years after 1978 was to demonstrate in China the superiority of market incentives to central planning. In China's villages, as the family farm once again became the basic unit of production, grain production rose.

The state sector, the glory of the Maoist command economy, underwent radical surgery. The role of the state continued to be larger than in Japan, South Korea, and Taiwan—nations in which the state played a greater role than in the West. But most Chinese government enterprises were sold to private concerns. The new owners fired excess workers and turned to production for national and international markets. During the 1990s, joint ventures with foreign firms became increasingly prominent.

The surge in new enterprises began in "special economic zones" along the border with Hong Kong and up the coast, but soon spread. Shanghai, with a population of more than 20 million (in 2010), became a city of skyscrapers and industrialists and the site of China's first stock exchange. Shandong and Manchuria, in the northeast, attracted huge foreign investments and achieved stunning growth. Wuhan, a large city on the Yangzi that manufactured automobiles, averaged growth of 17 percent during the 1990s. In 2010 China became the largest automobile manufacturer in the world.

In 2010, China passed Japan to become the second largest economy in the world. Per capita income has risen to a level that is ahead of India, Vietnam, and Indonesia, but still behind Thailand and Malaysia. In Japan, South Korea and Taiwan, rapid growth ended when per capita incomes reached the $14,000 level. If that figure applies to China, growth may continue for several decades more.

FOREIGN RELATIONS AFTER MAO

The Cold War largely defined the first phase of China's foreign relations. The United States, Japan, South Korea, and U.S.-protected Taiwan were enemies. Other communist nations—the Soviet Union, North Korea, and North Vietnam—were allies. But then China broke with the Soviet Union in 1960 and remained hostile thereafter. Overall, China's foreign relations until after Mao's death in 1976 reflected the revolutionary tumult within.

A second phase of international relations, China as an "emerging nation," began in 1980. Its new market capitalism was coupled with an emphasis on export-led economic growth, which necessitated improved relations with the world's nations. The opening broadened as the Cold War drew to an end after 1989. China reestablished relations with Russia and Vietnam, and more importantly, improved relations with the United States, Japan, Korea, Taiwan, and Europe.

Ties to the United States were complicated, despite the U.S. recognition of China in 1979. American military alliances with Japan and South Korea, its support of Taiwan, and its ties to the noncommunist nations of Southeast Asia continued to act as the main countervailing force to Chinese hegemony in the region. China resented this U.S. support for the independence of other East Asian nations within what it considered—in Middle Kingdom fashion—its own proper sphere of influence. Americans appreciated Chinese goods but criticized the extreme imbalance in trade: China's exports to the United States had increased from $5 billion to $296 billion between 1986 and 2009; but its imports from the United States measured only from $5 billion to $69 billion. The United States also protested the continuing Chinese piracy of hundreds of millions of dollars' worth of U.S. movies, computer software, and CDs each year, and was critical of Chinese human rights abuses. Despite disagreements, Chinese and American presidents regularly exchanged visits. In the World Trade Organization, the United Nations, and elsewhere, China slowly began to adapt to the standards of the larger international community.

The third phase of foreign relations was China's emergence as a power to be reckoned with in the world. This phase began soon after the beginning of the twenty-first century, though it is difficult to give an exact date. Was it when China's per capita income doubled, or was it when its national product became greater than that of leading European states? Was it in 2003 when China began to cooperate with South Korea, Japan, Russia, and the United States to negotiate an end to North Korean nuclear endeavors? Was it during the first decade of the new century when China began buying up natural resource companies in Africa, Australia, and elsewhere? Or should it be defined by China's purchase of submarines from Russia and the continued modernization

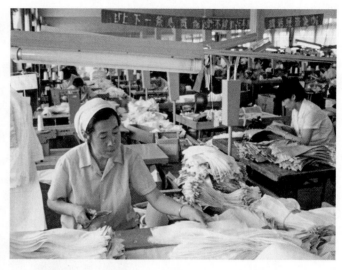

Cheap Labor. Wages at this Beijing shirt factory are low by Western standards but high by Chinese standards. This is not a sweatshop but a modern factory.

Should Western nations leave the production of textiles to low-wage nations? What about steel or microelectronics?

View the Image
Modern Hong Kong
at **myhistorylab.com**

QUICK REVIEW

Sino-American Relations

♦ 1979: United States recognizes China

♦ China resents U.S. military alliances in region

♦ United States criticizes China's human rights record, nuclear testing, and arms sales

♦ Immense imbalance in U.S.-China trade

Olympics. Performers pass National Stadium, also known as the "Bird's Nest," during rehearsals for the opening ceremonies for the 2008 Olympic Games in Beijing. China's hosting of the Olympics was yet another confirmation of its status as a major player on the world stage.

Can China be described as a "superpower"?

◉ See the **Map**
The Emergence of Modern China, 1919 to the Present
at **myhistorylab.com**

of its military and nuclear weapons? Was it inaugurated by the extravagent 2008 Beijing Olympics? Or was it in 2009 when China's foreign currency reserves passed the $2 trillion mark and reached 2.6 trillion and China produced more automobiles than any other nation? Taken together, these developments mark China's advance to a new level.

TAIWAN

HOW DO U.S. and Chinese policies toward Taiwan differ?

Taiwan is a mountainous island less than 100 miles off the coast of central China. A little larger than Massachusetts, it has a population of 22.9 million. It was part of the Qing Empire before becoming a Japanese colony in 1895. The Japanese colonial government suppressed opium and bandits, eradicated epidemic diseases, built roads and railroads, reformed the land system, and improved agriculture. It also introduced mass education and light industries.

Anticolonial feelings rose slowly, but the Taiwanese were happy to see the Japanese leave in 1945. Kuomintang (Guomindang, or GMD) officials, however, looted the economy and ruled harshly. By the time Jiang Jieshi and 2 million other military and civilian mainlanders fled to the island in 1949, its economy and society were in disarray. Taiwanese hated their new rulers and even compared them unfavorably to the Japanese.

From the 1950s onward three interdependent developments occurred: the economy grew, politics became democratic, and the relation to the Chinese mainland changed.

In managing the economy, the GMD, which had failed in China, succeeded in Taiwan. Its control of the island was complete, and the times were peaceful. By the mid-1950s it had restored order, and rapid growth followed. Heavy industries were put under state control; other former Japanese industries were sold to private parties. With the outbreak of the Korean War in 1950, U.S. aid became substantial. Foreign investment was welcomed. Light industries were followed by consumer electronics, steel, and petrochemicals and then by computers and semiconductors. Private industries led the way. By the late 1990s, Taiwan was the world's largest producer of monitors, keyboards, motherboards, and computer mice; it was second in notebook PCs and fourth in integrated circuits. Many of these goods were actually manufactured in Taiwanese-owned plants in mainland China. By 2009, Taiwanese investments in China rose to $150 billion, and Chinese investments in Taiwan were permitted for the first time. Estimated Taiwanese GDP in 2009 was $360 billion (or as measured in purchasing power, $700 billion and a per capita income of $30,000).

The transition to democratic government in Taiwan was not unlike that in South Korea. For the first twenty years, the GMD government was a dictatorship, ruling as it had on the mainland. It maintained that it was the legitimate government of all of China. Social changes began during the 1960s. Education advanced, with rising numbers entering universities. Taiwanese and mainlanders began to intermarry. As the economy advanced, a new middle class emerged. Jiang Jieshi died in 1975. His son Jiang Jingguo was president from 1978 to 1988; in 1987, he ended martial law and permitted opposition parties to form.

After that, changes came quickly. In 1988 a native-born Taiwanese, who had risen to the top of the GMD, became president. In 1996, he was reelected in what he billed as "the first free election in 5,000 years of Chinese history." In

The World's Tallest Building. Evening traffic swirls around the Taipei 101, a building with 101 floors. At 1,671 feet, it was the only building in the world in 2004 to be over a half kilometer in height. The design was inspired by traditional Chinese architecture. **What regions of China have benefited most from economic growth?**

2000, another Taiwanese, the leader of an opposition party, became president in an election hailed by one scholar as "the first peaceful transition of power from one political party to another in Taiwanese history, and probably in all of Chinese history." He was reelected in 2004. A GMD candidate, Ma Jing-jeou, won the 2008 election. Ma was born in Hong Kong and educated at National Taiwan University, New York University, and Harvard. He campaigned on a platform of economic revitalization and better relations with China. Possibly his victory signaled the beginning of a two-party system in Taiwan.

Since 1949, Beijing has maintained that Taiwan is a province of China and has spoken of reclaiming the island by force. It refused ties with any nation maintaining diplomatic ties with Taiwan. From the outbreak of the Korean War in 1950 until 1979, Taiwan was a protégé of the United States, which provided for the island's defense. But in 1979 the United States formally broke off relations with Taipei and recognized Beijing as the legitimate government of a China that included Taiwan. The United States stressed, nevertheless, that any reunion of China and Taiwan should be peaceful. It continued to trade with Taiwan and sell it arms. Curiously, it was during the years of diplomatic limbo after the 1979 break that Taiwan's economy grew and its society became democratic.

At the onset of the twenty-first century, the status of Taiwan was still an issue. China was concerned that a democratically elected government gave Taiwan a claim to legitimacy and that Taiwan's prosperity would make its peoples less willing to rejoin the mainland. Occasionally it spoke of taking the island by force.

But China was keenly aware that doing so would enormously disrupt China's world trade. China also knew that economic ties between Taiwan and China, and China's rising prosperity, might eventually make an invasion unnecessary. China is Taiwan's number one trading partner, and almost a million Taiwanese live in China. The United States watched, with some unease, the steady rise of Chinese military power. But as of 2010, all sides seemed content to leave the status of Taiwan to an indefinite future.

KOREA

HOW DID South Korean and North Korean postwar developments differ?

Korea and Vietnam both became colonies: Korea, annexed by Japan in 1910; Vietnam, a part of French Indochina in 1883. In both countries, the imposition of colonialism on peoples with strong indigenous cultures and national identities engendered powerful anticolonial nationalisms. After World War II, both countries were divided into a communist north and a noncommunist south, Korea immediately and Vietnam years later. Both experienced civil war. In each case, the United States entered the conflicts to stem the spread of communism. Never before had the United States fought in countries about which it knew so little.

KOREA AS A JAPANESE COLONY

The political, economic, and social ills of Choson Korea increased during the nineteenth century. As the century drew to a close, a three-cornered, imperialist rivalry arose among China, Japan, and Russia, with Korea as the prize. Japan won by defeating China in the Sino-Japanese War (1894–1895) and Russia in the Russo-Japanese War (1904–1905). Japan made Korea a protectorate in 1905 and annexed it in 1910.

Japan strove to make Korea a model colony. A land survey and land tax reform clarified land ownership. Public hygiene was enforced, infectious diseases dropped sharply, and the population grew from 14 million in 1910 to 24 million in 1940. School attendance increased. Banks were established. As in Taiwan, huge investments were made in transportation and communications. The 1920s saw more diversified investments. Most large-scale industries were Japanese-owned, but Korean entrepreneurs began textile mills, shipping lines, and small industries.

The colonial transformation was not limited to economics. By the 1930s a modern culture was forming in Korea's cities. In sum, Korea became vastly different from what it had been in 1910.

Being a Japanese colony was nonetheless a hard road to modernity. The colonial government was authoritarian. Its goal was to make Korea into a subordinate part of Imperial Japan, and benefits to Koreans were incidental. The Japanese in Korea received better salaries, medical care, education, and jobs than their Korean counterparts. After 1937, the Japanese policy of "assimilation" grew even harsher: Koreans were pressured to adopt Japanese names, drafted to fight in Japan's wars, and sent to labor in factories in Japan. "Comfort women" were recruited, occasionally by force, to service Japanese troops. This bitter colonial legacy has only begun to subside in recent decades.

Comfort Women. South Korean women, who were forced by the Japanese military to serve in brothels during World War II, protest near the Japanese Embassy in Seoul, January 2003.

What is the relationship between Japan and South Korea today?

NORTH AND SOUTH

On Japan's defeat in 1945, Soviet troops entered the North; a month later U.S. forces occupied Korea south of the thirty-eighth parallel. Despite a promise of unification, two separate states developed. In the South, the United States initially aimed at the formation of a democratic, self-governing nation but settled for the anticommunist and authoritarian government of Syngman Rhee (1875–1965), a longtime nationalist leader whose party won the 1948 election. His government was strongly supported by conservative Koreans and by the million or so Koreans who fled from the North.

In the North, the Russians established a communist government under Kim Il Sung (1912–1994). Kim had worked with the Chinese communists during the 1930s and subsequently with the Soviet Union. When the South held elections in 1948, the North hurriedly followed suit, and the Democratic People's Republic of Korea was established. At the end of 1948 the Soviet Union withdrew its troops from North Korea. During 1949 and early 1950 the United States withdrew most of its troops from the South, as part of a larger American disengagement from continental Asia after the communist victory in China.

THE KOREAN WAR AND U.S. INVOLVEMENT

In June 1950, North Korea invaded the South in an attempt to reunify Korea. Kim Il Sung, the North Korean leader, had received Stalin's permission for the invasion and a promise from Mao to send Chinese troops if the United States entered the war. He planned for a quick victory before the United States had time to react. But the Cold War had already begun in Europe, and the invasion, coming four months after the signing of the Sino-Soviet Alliance, was seen by the United States as an act of aggression by world communism. The United States rushed troops from Japan to South Korea and obtained United Nations backing. It also sent naval forces to protect Taiwan, and over the next several years, entered into military alliances with the noncommunist states of Southeast Asia. The Korean War was the catalyst for a major turn in postwar American foreign policy.

During the first months of the war, the unprepared American and South Korean forces were driven southward to Korea's southeastern rim (see Map 32–2). But then, amphibious units led by the United Nations commander General Douglas MacArthur landed at Inchon in the middle of Korea's western coast and drove back the North Korean armies beyond the thirty-eighth parallel deep into North Korea. American policy shifted from the containment of communism to a rollback.

The UN forces in Korea were half American and two-fifths Korean; the rest were contingents from Britain, Australia, Turkey, and twelve other nations. In the final phase of the war, China sent in "volunteers" to rescue the beleaguered North Korean forces. Chinese troops pushed the overextended UN forces back to a line close to the thirty-eighth parallel. The war became stalemated in 1951 and ended with an armistice in July 1953. Thereafter the two Koreas maintained a hostile peace. The 142,000 American casualties made the war the fourth largest in U.S. history.

QUICK REVIEW

Two Koreas

* After defeat of Japan in 1945, U.S. troops occupied the South and Soviet troops occupied the North
* United States supported government of Syngman Rhee in the South
* Soviets supported government of Kim Il-Sung in the North

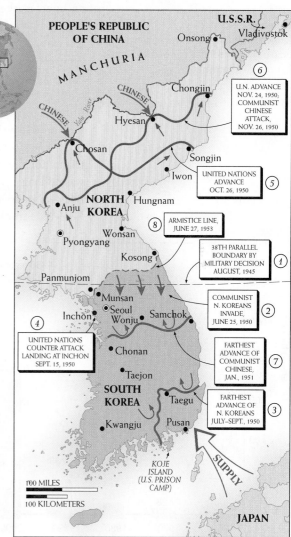

MAP 32–2. The Korean War, 1950–1953.

Why did the Korean War end in stalemate?

SOUTH KOREA: GROWTH AND DEMOCRACY

After the armistice, two intertwined stories unfolded in South Korea: stunning economic growth and the rise of a democratic polity. Massive student demonstrations forced Rhee to retire in 1960. There followed twenty-seven years of rule by two generals. Park Chung-Hee seized power in a military *coup d'état* in 1961, then won a rigged election and became a civilian president. His rule was semiauthoritarian: Opposition parties were legal and active, but their leaders were often jailed. In time, even Koreans who approved of Park's economic policies came to resent his police tactics. But when Park was assassinated by his intelligence chief in 1979, another general seized power, transformed himself into a civilian president, and ruled until 1987 in the pattern established by his predecessor.

At the inception of Park's rule, unemployment had been rife and poverty widespread. Emphasizing science and technology, both Park and his successor supported business and expanded higher education. Labor was disciplined, hardworking, and cheap. The United States gave large amounts of aid and provided an open market for Korean exports. The result was several decades of double-digit growth. Especially notable was the growth of **chaebol** such as Hyundai or Daewoo, which resembled the Mitsui or Mitsubishi *zaibatsu* of prewar Japan. South Korea's economic growth policies were hugely successful. Korea's gross national product rose dramatically (see Figure 32–2). With an average income in 2009 of $16,500 (with a purchasing power of $28,000), South Korea became a prosperous nation with one the world's largest economies. Its voice in world affairs grew accordingly.

The second development since 1987 was the rise of democracy. Ironically, industrialization and urbanization had created an affluent and educated middle class that was no longer willing to tolerate authoritarian rule. The presidential elections held at five-year intervals between 1987 and 2007 reflect a new consciousness within Korea. In 1987, a third ex-general was elected, but the election was free and fair. In 1992, a conservative politician with no ties to the military became president. He purged the generals who had supported the two previous presidents, replacing them with officers willing to work with party governments. He also launched investigations of his predecessors' finances, uncovering hundreds of millions of dollars in secret bank accounts.

In 1997 and 2002, a deeper break with the past occurred when liberal leaders of opposition parties were elected as presidents. Both Kim Dae-Jung and Roh Moo-Hyun continued to emphasize economic growth. Unlike their predecessors, they also attempted a rapprochement with North Korea. This was known as the "sunshine policy," which for a time had popular support. Koreans were patriotic and wanted to see their country reunited. The sunshine policy ultimately failed, when South Korean initiatives were spurned by the North. In 2007, in reaction to the failure, the conservative Lee Myung-Bak was elected as president. Since then, tensions with the North have increased. But the principle that conservatives and liberals—both committed to the electoral process—may alternate in power appears to have been established within the South Korean polity.

View the Image
South Korea Enters the
U.S. Auto Market
at **myhistorylab.com**

chaebol
Large family-owned business conglomerates with strong ties to the South Korean government.

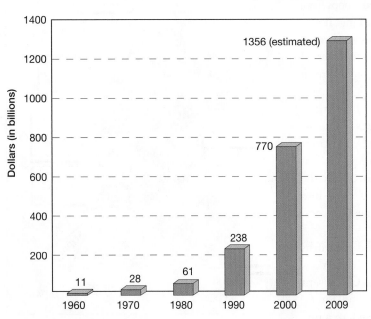

FIGURE 32–2. Growth of South Korean Gross Domestic Product, as Measured in Purchasing Power.

What enabled South Korea's economy to grow so dramatically?

North Korea

Japanese industries in colonial Korea were mainly in the North, which gave its postwar industrialization an early edge. North Korea's planned economy, however, was enclosed within a tightly sealed, authoritarian state, which stressed heavy industry, collectivized farms, and totally controlled education and the media. By the 1970s, its economy stagnated, and shortages of food, clothing, and necessities were chronic. During the 1990s and after the turn of the century, periods of famine were not uncommon.

The misery of the North Korean people was highlighted by the lavish lifestyle of its leaders. The cult of personality surrounding "the great leader" Kim Il Sung went beyond that of even Stalin or Mao. The Korean Communist Party was Marxist-Leninist, but the kinship terminology used to describe the fatherly leader, the mother party, and the familial North Korean state gave the official state philosophy a Confucian tinge. Kim designated his son, "the beloved leader" Kim Jong-Il (b. 1942), as his successor, and when the father died in 1994, the son became the leader of North Korea—the only instance of hereditary succession in a communist state.

The North Korean record was poor in every respect: It ran prison camps, threatened Japan, and engaged in counterfeiting and drug smuggling to obtain hard currency. With a garrison state mentality, it used a Pakistani connection to import nuclear technology and develop its own atomic weapons. When charged with this in 2003, it first denied and then boasted of the development.

Early on, North Korea was backed by the Soviet Union and China. After the collapse of the Soviet Union, however, Russia had little interest in its former ally. China continued to offer aid and trade, but it was put off by the North's poverty and radical eccentricity. China was more attracted by the economically vibrant South Korea, with which it established diplomatic relations in 1992. Since then, South Koreans have invested billions in China and trade between the two nations has flourished—in 2010 South Korea was China's third most important export market.

Since 2003, the United States, China, Russia, South Korea, and Japan have tried to persuade North Korea to abandon its nuclear weapons. Even China did not want a nuclear North Korea on its doorstep. But both China and South Korea were reluctant to apply pressure, fearing a North Korean collapse and a flood of refugees. In October 2006 North Korea detonated its first atomic bomb. This led China to toughen its stance. The failure of the "sunshine policy" and the election of a conservative president made South Korea more willing to apply sanctions. As of early 2010, the future was unclear. All that can be said with certainty is that a small, isolated, bankrupt dictatorship has kept the attention of its larger neighbors for more than a decade.

The Two Kims. South Korean President Kim Dae-Jung traveled to Pyongyang in June 2000 to promote his "sunshine policy." As he departed he gave Kim Jong-Il, the North Korean leader, a hug. When the North Korean leader failed to return his visit or to ease tensions, sunshine turned to rain and Kim Dae-jung's popularity sagged.

Why is North Korea such a closed society?

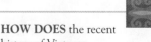

●●●—Read the **Document**
Famine in North Korea, 2002
at **myhistorylab.com**

VIETNAM

The Colonial Backdrop

The Nguyen Dynasty that reunited Vietnam in 1802 was still vigorous in 1858, but was no match for France. France completed its conquest of Vietnam and Cambodia in 1883, formed the Indochinese Union in 1887, and added Laos to the Union in 1893.

Indochina was a classic example of colonial rule: a people of one race and culture, for the sake of economic benefits and national glory, controlling and exploiting a people of another race and culture in a far-off land. To obtain access to the country's natural resources, the French built harbors, roads, and a railway linking Saigon, Hanoi, and southern China. They established rubber and tea plantations, introduced modern mining technology, and built factories. Large industries were dominated by the French,

HOW DOES the recent history of Vietnam illustrate the legacies of both colonialism and the Cold War?

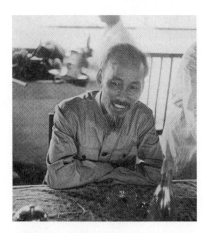

Ho Chi Minh (1892–1969). Ho became a communist in France in 1920, studied in Moscow, and founded the Indochinese Communist Party in 1930. He fought, in succession, against the Japanese, French, Americans, and South Vietnamese. He did not live to see the communist victory in 1975.

How did Ho Chi Minh use Western ideas in his fight against Western imperialism?

smaller enterprises by Vietnamese-Chinese. Workers were paid poorly. Vietnamese were mainly laborers, except for the few who became landlords. Although new irrigation works in the Mekong Delta quadrupled the area of rice fields, peasant consumption of rice declined. The skewed distribution of wealth meant that no indigenous middle class developed, apart from landlords. The French did little to educate the Vietnamese: in 1939, over 80 percent of the population was illiterate.

In the early twentieth century, Vietnamese nationalists in exile in China, Japan, and France formed political parties. Within Vietnam, only clandestine parties survived. The most skilled party organizer was Ho Chi Minh (1892–1969), who had participated in the founding of the French Communist Party in 1920, studied in Moscow in 1923, and worked under the Comintern agent Mikhail Borodin in Canton in 1925. Ho founded the Revolutionary Youth League of Vietnam in 1925 and sent its cadres to China and the Soviet Union for training. He then founded the Indochinese Communist Party in 1930. When the Popular Front gained power in France (1936–1938), opposition parties were briefly tolerated in Vietnam and Ho's party was the strongest. After 1938 the French again suppressed all opposition groups. Shortly before the outbreak of the Pacific War, the Japanese occupied Vietnam. For their own convenience, until March 1945, they ruled through Vichy French puppets. Ho, who in 1941 had formed the **Viet Minh** (League for the Independence of Vietnam) as a popular front organization to resist the Japanese, proclaimed the Democratic Republic of Vietnam after Japan's defeat in 1945 and became the preeminent nationalist leader in his country. There followed three cycles of war and three decades of peace.

THE ANTICOLONIAL WAR

The first war lasted from 1946 to 1954. On one side was the Viet Minh, led by Ho. It was controlled by communists but included representatives of nationalist parties. On the other side were the French, who had reoccupied Vietnam immediately after the war, and their conservative Vietnamese allies. Starting in 1950, the French received American aid. But the French lost a major battle at Dien Bien Phu in 1954 and departed in defeat.

The country was divided into a communist North and a noncommunist South. In the South, Ngo Dinh Diem, a nationalist leader who had not collaborated with the French, came to power and established the Republic of Vietnam. Much of his political support came from the 900,000 Vietnamese who fled from the North.

THE VIETNAM WAR

The second cycle of war, from 1959 to 1975, began with guerrilla attacks against Southern troops in the late 1950s. Local incidents eventually turned into a full-scale war between the North and the South (see Map 32–3). The North received material aid but no "volunteers" from the Soviet Union and China. The United States sent troops to aid the South: 600 military advisers in 1961, 16,000 troops in 1963, 70,000 in 1965, and over half a million in 1969. Despite this massive support, South Vietnam—and the United States—lost the war. The reasons were several.

1. The South was difficult to govern. In comparison to the North, the region had been less deeply influenced by Chinese culture. It was ethnically diverse and religiously divided. The inability of successive Southern governments to unify their fragmented society was a basic weakness in their struggles with the communist North.

2. All too often corrupt, the South Vietnamese government inspired little loyalty in its citizens.

3. Ho Chi Minh was a national hero to many South Vietnamese as well as to Northerners. Even noncommunists sometimes viewed the United States as the successor to the French and the communist guerrillas as fighting an anticolonial war.

4. Both communist guerrillas in the South and North Vietnamese troops fought better than the soldiers of the South Vietnamese government.

5. In the jungle terrain of Vietnam, the technological edge of the United States was blunted. A greater tonnage of bombs was dropped on supply trails in Cambodia than on Japan in World War II, yet supplies continued to flow south.

At the beginning, the U.S. government saw the war as part of its struggle against world communism. After the Sino-Soviet split, they saw it as a war to halt the spread of Chinese communism. Few in the United States understood the depth of Vietnamese ambivalence toward China. As the war dragged on and casualties mounted, Americans turned against the war. When Richard Nixon became president, he called for the "Vietnamization" of the war and began to withdraw American troops. In January 1973, a ceasefire was arranged in Paris, and two months later the last U.S. troops left. Fighting broke out anew between North and South; South Vietnamese forces collapsed in 1975; the country was reunited under the Hanoi government in the North; Saigon was renamed Ho Chi Minh City.

After the war, few areas of the world were as devastated as Vietnam and its neighbors. After unifying the country, Hanoi sent thousands of those associated with the former South Vietnamese government to labor camps, collectivized agricultural lands, and in 1976 began a five-year plan for the economy. Several hundred thousand Vietnamese and ethnic Chinese fled by boat or across the Chinese border.

WAR WITH CAMBODIA

Pol Pot (1926–1998) and his radical **Khmer Rouge** (Red Cambodia) came to power in Cambodia in 1975. During the next three years, he evacuated cities and towns, abolished money and trade, banned Buddhism, and executed or caused to die of starvation an estimated 1 million persons, roughly 15 percent of the Cambodian population. Schoolteachers and the educated were singled out as special targets. Vietnam was Cambodia's historical enemy, as China was Vietnam's. When Pol Pot purged the Khmer Rouge of pro-Vietnamese elements in 1978, Vietnam invaded and occupied most of Cambodia, setting up a puppet government. Cambodians accepted the government because they feared Pol Pot more than they hated Vietnam. But Vietnamese troops were unable to suppress Pol Pot's guerrilla forces completely.

The unified Vietnam of 1975 became an ally of the Soviet Union and gave the Soviets a naval base in return for economic, military, and diplomatic support. But relations with China soured. Vietnam feared Chinese domination and resented Nixon's

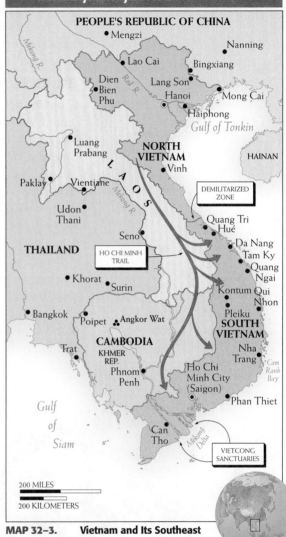

MAP EXPLORATION

To explore this map further, go to
www.myhistorylab.com

MAP 32–3.   Vietnam and Its Southeast Asian Neighbors.

The map identifies important places during the war in Vietnam.

Which neighboring countries were most affected by the Vietnam War?

Khmer Rouge
Meaning "Red Cambodia." The radical communist movement that ruled Cambodia from 1975 to 1978.

See the **Map**
The Vietnam War
at **myhistorylab.com**

visit to China in 1972, when American troops were still fighting on its soil. China, for its part, felt Vietnam had not duly appreciated its wartime aid, resented Vietnam's treatment of its ethnic Chinese, and feared Vietnam's close ties to the Soviet Union. In 1979, China decided to "teach Vietnam a lesson" and invaded four northern provinces. Seasoned Vietnamese troops repelled the invaders, but losses were heavy on both sides. For years thereafter China supported Pol Pot's guerrillas and occasionally shelled Vietnam's northern border.

RECENT DEVELOPMENTS

The situation changed abruptly in the late 1980s. The collapse of the Soviet Union ended Vietnam's primary foreign relation. In 1989 Vietnam withdrew from its costly occupation of Cambodia in favor of a UN-sponsored government. Eight years later one faction, led by a pro-Vietnamese leader, took over the Cambodian government in a coup. His role was strengthened in 1998 when Pol Pot died and the Khmer Rouge collapsed. Vietnam-Chinese relations improved, and China's landlocked province of Yunnan began using the Vietnamese port of Haiphong as an outlet for its products. In 1995, Vietnam joined the Association of Southeast Asian Nations (ASEAN), and also reestablished diplomatic relations with the United States. As it moved toward "normal" relations with the rest of the world, Europeans and Americans began to take package tours to Vietnam, visiting scenic locales that only two decades earlier had been battle zones.

By the late 1990s, a "Chinese pattern" emerged in Vietnam. On the one hand, the communist government in Hanoi monopolized political power and controlled the army, police, and media. On the other, the leaders, aware that victories in wars were hollow as long as their people remained destitute, embraced capitalism as the road to growth. In place of collective agriculture, farmers were allowed to keep the rice they grew: Vietnam went from near starvation to become the world's second largest exporter of rice. Stock markets were established in Hanoi and Ho Chi Minh City. Taxes were kept low and a premium was put on education. Garment manufacturing, food processing, and the production of other consumer goods grew apace. Between 1991 and 2007, the economy averaged over 8 percent growth and received more offers of foreign investment than it could absorb. Taiwan and Singapore were the largest investors, but Intel, Nike, and other American companies were not far behind. Vietnam's exports to the United States in 2006 were nine times greater than its imports, a pattern not unlike that of China and the United States. By the turn of the millennium, shops in Vietnam were full of food and goods, when only a decade or so earlier there had been regional famines. During the first decade of the millennium, Vietnam experienced the second fastest economic growth in the world. South Vietnam was the engine of this economy. Even northern Vietnamese saw its openness, pluralism, and cosmopolitanism as attractive.

With a population of 87 million, Vietnam is one of the world's most densely populated nations. The government limits families to two children. Hanoi had a population of 130,000 in the 1930s and has 7 million today; Ho Chi Minh

Skulls. A worker cleans a skull excavated from a mass grave in Cambodia. The Khmer Rouge, under Pol Pot, murdered about one-sixth of the Cambodian population. Doctors, teachers, and other educated people were targeted.

Who were the Khmer Rouge?

City (Saigon) rose from less than a million at the war's end in 1975 to 8 million today. As the economy grew, the gap between rural and urban widened. More than half of the population was born after 1975, and labor is still cheap. But conditions have improved immensely: in 1990, the national product was less than $10 billion; in 2010 it will reach $92 billion (or $258 billion in purchasing power), and per capita income has risen to $1057, with a purchasing power of about $3,000. In short, Vietnam illustrates the trajectory common to all East Asian nations, except North Korea.

SUMMARY

 ### HOW DID the postwar occupation change Japan politically?

Japan. The U.S.-led occupation after World War II established a democratic government and set Japan on the way to its remarkable postwar prosperity. By the twenty-first century, Japan had the second largest economy in the world. Politically, the conservative Liberal Democratic Party has remained dominant, despite occasional electoral losses. Socially, Japan has remained stable with the world's highest longevity rate. *page 840*

 ### WHY DID Mao launch the Cultural Revolution?

China. Communist rule was established in 1949. Until his death in 1976, Mao Zedong controlled China. Mao broke with the Soviet Union in the 1960s and launched the disastrous Cultural Revolution in 1965 in an ill-conceived effort to avoid Soviet-style bureaucratization. After Mao's death, China opened its economy to free-market reforms. The result has been surging economic growth and rising prosperity. Politically, the Communist Party has blocked democratic reform, even using force in 1989 to crush a pro-democracy movement. *page 848*

 ### HOW DO U.S. and Chinese policies toward Taiwan differ?

Taiwan. The Nationalist Party set up a separate state in Taiwan under U.S. protection after its defeat in the Chinese civil war in 1949. Since then Taiwan has moved from poverty to prosperity, from dictatorship to democracy. The Chinese government insists that Taiwan is a province of China. The status of Taiwan is an outstanding issue between the United States and China. *page 854*

 ### HOW DID South Korean and North Korean postwar developments differ?

Korea. The postwar occupation of Korea by the Soviet Union and the United States led to its division into the communist state of North Korea and pro-Western South Korea. This division survived the Korean War of 1950 to 1953. The prosperity of democratic South Korea contrasts with the poverty and hunger of North Korea. North Korea remains a closed society and now has nuclear capabilities. *page 856*

 ### HOW DOES the recent history of Vietnam illustrate the legacies of both colonialism and the Cold War?

Vietnam. From the end of World War II until the 1970s, Vietnam was almost continuously involved in war, first against the reimposition of French colonial rule, then against the United States and its South Vietnamese allies. North Vietnam's victory over South Vietnam in 1975 reunified the country. Vietnam has recently embraced free-market principles. *page 859*

KEY TERMS

Article 9 of the No-War Constitution (p. 840)
brainwashing (p. 850)
chaebol (JHE-buhl) (p. 858)
Cultural Revolution (p. 851)

Great Leap Forward (p. 850)
Khmer Rouge (p. 861)
LDP (p. 843)
Viet Minh (p. 860)

REVIEW QUESTIONS

1. Is postwar Japan better understood as a return to the relative liberalism of the 1920s or as a fresh start based on occupation reforms? Why did the occupation of Japan go so smoothly, in contrast to the American occupation of Iraq?

2. How has Japanese society changed since 1945? In what ways does it seem to be a more fair and open society? Is there a downside to the changes?

3. Compare present-day Chinese and Japanese income levels and standards of living. In Japan, what factors led double-digit growth to turn into single-digit growth? Will the same factors come into play in China?

4. Is China from 1949 until the death of Mao better understood as an outgrowth of its earlier history or as a communist state comparable to the old Soviet Union? And to what country would you compare post–Deng China?

5. Does recent history suggest that the Chinese government will become more democratic as its citizens become more prosperous?

6. How did the precolonial and colonial eras of Korea and Vietnam shape their history after World War II? How did the Cold War shape their history?

7. What factor or factors were most important in the defeat of South Vietnam (and the United States) in the Vietnam War?

8. Given the failure of South Korea's "sunshine policy" toward North Korea, can you see any way to improve relations between the two Koreas or to improve relations between other countries and North Korea?

9. If you were the U.S. secretary of state, what long-term China policy would you propose to the president? Where would Japan fit into your policy?

10. What has been the impact of East Asian economic growth on international relations?

Note: To learn more about the topics in this chapter, please turn to the Suggested Readings at the end of the book. For additional sources related to this chapter please see www.myhistorylab.com

PEARSON myhistorylab™ Connections

Reinforce what you learned in this chapter by studying the many documents, images, maps, review tools, and videos available at **www.myhistorylab.com**

Read and Review

✓● Study and Review Chapter 32

●●● Read the Document *The Constitution of Japan (1947)*, p. 842
China's One-Child Family Policy (1970s), p. 848
Decision Concerning the Great Proletarian Cultural Revolution, p. 851
Deng Xiaoping, on Introducing Capitalist Principles to China, p. 852
James F. Schnabel, from United States Army in the Korean War, p. 857
Famine in North Korea, 2002, p. 859
Ho Chi Minh, "Equality!", p. 860
Resolution Establishing the Viet Minh, 1941, p. 860
Ho Chi Minh on Self-Determination (1954), p. 860

●— See the Map *Japan in 1945*, p. 840
The Emergence of Modern China, 1919 to the Present, p. 854

● View the Image *Japanese Technician Testing Equipment*, p. 845
Modern Hong Kong, p. 853
South Korea Enters the U.S. Auto Market, p. 858

((●— Hear the Audio *Communist China 3*, p. 850
Communist China 4, p. 851

✓● Study and Review *Frantz Fanon and Ho Chi Minh Speak Out against Imperialism*, p. 860

Research and Explore

●— See the Map *China in the Era of Revolution and Civil War*, p. 851

●— See the Map *The Vietnam War*, p. 862

((●— **Hear** the **Audio**

Hear the audio file for Chapter 32
at **www.myhistorylab.com**

33

Postcolonialism and Beyond: Latin America, Africa, Asia, and the Middle East

((●—[**Hear** the **Audio** for Chapter 33 at **www.myhistorylab.com**

Darfur, Western Sudan. Distraught Sudanese refugees wait at a food and clothing aid distribution point. The conflict, which began in February 2003, has killed as many as 400,000 people through violence, hunger, and disease. Some 2.5 million people have been displaced by the fighting.

Why do you think this photograph shows mostly women and children?

he decades after World War II saw Europe eclipsed by the rise of two superpowers—the United States and the Soviet Union—and then the collapse of the Soviet Union. Elsewhere in the world, the postwar decades witnessed the end of Western colonialism and challenges to imperialism. New nations emerged in Africa and Asia.

Two developments in non-Western regions have major implications for the future. First, as explored in the previous chapter, Japan, and more recently China, have emerged as major political and economic powers. Second, the rise of militant, politicized Islam as a result of developments in the postcolonial Middle East now presents a challenge to the global status quo. The waning of imperial and colonial dominance of the many by the few and the emergence of powerful new forces from the formerly colonized world must, however, be set within a larger historical perspective. Since the 1500s, many regions of the globe had been drawn into the European sphere of economic and political influence. Those areas to be treated here— Latin America, Africa, Central Asia, South and Southeast Asia, and the Middle East—were often conquered, exploited, and colonized by European powers. The period of colonialism that began in earnest in the seventeenth century was a fateful, but relatively brief, episode in world history. The last significant colonial territories gained their independence in the 1970s. ■

BEYOND THE POSTCOLONIAL ERA

With the collapse of apartheid in South Africa, the fall of the Berlin Wall, and economic growth in India and China, it may be argued that the postcolonial era has ended. Remnants of pre-1950s colonialism persist in many global regions today, however. Even with the global recession of 2009–2010, industrial nations have in

WHAT ARE the two main developments that have occurred in the postcolonial world?

GLOBAL PERSPECTIVE

DEMOCRATIZATION, GLOBALIZATION, AND TERRORISM

Two remarkable political and economic developments have shaped our era: democratization and globalization.

Since 1970, on one continent or another, democratic political rights have expanded. Authoritarian regimes of both the right and the left have been reformed or collapsed. Dictatorships, military juntas, or one-party autocracies have begun to yield to more representative governments. Progress has not been uniform, but more and more people everywhere aspire to have a voice in how they are governed. This process of political change, usually termed democratization, involves expanding participation in political processes, as well as both orderly selection and succession of executive and legislative leaders through elections and establishment of viable civil societies. Many autocracies and authoritarian states still flourish, but more nations than ever before have seen democratic or semidemocratic forms of government instituted.

An unprecedented series of economic linkages, generally termed *globalization*, has paralleled the spread of more democratic institutions. This process has included the forging of new trade and manufacturing agreements, such as NAFTA, among leading industrial nations. Globalization has reduced trade barriers, including tariffs and other regulations hindering circulation of goods, services, and labor among nations. The emergence of worldwide trading and investment networks has led to consolidation of economic enterprises as owners of capital seek to locate their centers of production in the most advantageous labor and resource markets. The giant corporations of the United States, Europe, and Asia now operate in a multinational setting.

Globalization's supporters contend that it will produce more goods and services at lower consumer cost than a highly regulated economy. Critics argue that globalization concentrates power in the hands of unregulated corporations and that governments have surrendered too much of their authority to regulate the economy, preserve the environment, and protect workers. Critics also believe that the new economic structures mean that poor nations, many of them the emerging nations discussed in this chapter, become poorer as rich nations become richer. Globalization rode the wave of prosperity that seems to have crested in the

((•─┤Hear the Audio
Decolonization 1
at **myhistorylab.com**

decolonization
The achievement of political self-determination for former colonies, usually through national independence.

globalization
Term used to describe the increasing economic and cultural interdependence of societies around the world.

the past decade experienced strong economic growth, much as in the early 1990s in East Asia. We have also seen new regional and transregional political alignments emerge; internal struggles to build political systems that encourage civil society and limit oligarchic or dictatorial power; and, most dramatically, the determination of radical Islamists to contest European and American political and economic global power.

After 1945 two distinct developments occurred in the world. The first—in a process generally termed **decolonization**—was the emergence of the various parts of Africa and Asia from the direct administration of foreign powers (see Map 33–1 on page 870). The second was the organization of those previous colonial dependencies into independent states with greater or lesser degrees of stability.

The End of Empire. A statue of Queen Victoria is removed from the front of the Supreme Court building in Georgetown, former capital of the British colony of Guyana, in February 1970, in preparation for the transition to independence.

Why was there a wave of decolonization in the mid-twentieth century?

Postcolonial societies have experienced four stages in their relationship to the industrial European and Europeanized nations: the influence of Cold War rivalries on the new states, the economic effects of **globalization**, progress in the spread of the ideals of civil society and participatory government, and finally a resurgence of cultural and religious traditions.

A central question for the present era is whether to see the global variety of social, cultural, and religious traditions as a creative late 1990s. It remains to be seen what will occur in today's more difficult times.

The debate over globalization has made its admirers and detractors more aware of the vast, persistent areas of deep poverty around the world, especially in South and Central America, the Caribbean, Africa, and much of Asia—regions still struggling with the legacy of European colonialism. Most of these regions were impoverished even in the late nineteenth century by globalization when it was just beginning, but today's enormous prosperity in much of the Northern Hemisphere has made poorer regions more conscious of their poverty and, especially in Africa and the Middle East, ripe for political extremism. Among Muslims, such extremism has often been associated with political Islamism. The United States and Europe have become particular targets of those suffering from and opposed to globalization.

The economic, military, and diplomatic involvement of the United States and its European allies in other regions has led some to view them as imperial powers and even to use terrorist tactics against them. The overwhelming American support for the state of Israel, the festering Israeli-Palestinian conflict, and, most recently, the U.S. invasion of Iraq have also convinced many peoples, especially those in the Muslim world, that the United States especially is inimical to Islam. Within the United States and also around the world, debate continues over the future role of the United States and whether it can best protect its citizens' interests and world peace and prosperity through unilateral, preemptive invasions such as that of Iraq or through greater cooperation with international bodies such as the United Nations.

Focus Questions

◆ What are the arguments of the proponents and opponents of globalization?

◆ How has the legacy of European colonialism affected the Middle East, Asia, and Africa?

◆ Why has the United States become a prime target for terrorists?

or divisive force in the twenty-first century and beyond. One model for understanding the complex international scene today is that of the "West versus the Rest," in which the European and Europeanized world and its ethos are seen as the hope of the future, while all other social, religious, and cultural traditions are depicted as rallying points for opposition to the spread of European-style "modernity." This analysis pits Islamic, European and Eastern Orthodox Christian, Buddhist, Hindu, Confucian, and other religious, social, and cultural traditions against one another in a **clash of civilizations**. This concept became popular following the terrorist attack of September 11, 2001, on the United States.

Other observers urge that studying the world's varied cultural traditions leads to an understanding of the modern world as a domain in which many cultural, religious, and political traditions interact and compete but in which people of all kinds can get along. Our common need for solutions to transnational, planetwide problems must take precedence over vague "civilizational" differences.

In any case, we must recognize the persistent influence of the great religious and moral traditions of humankind. In particular, Buddhist, Christian, and Islamic faith and values continue to claim the allegiance of major sectors of our globe. No longer can we assume that secular rationalism will monopolize ideology during the process of material modernization. Rather, we can expect a pluralistic global community in which diverse traditions best coexist and learn from one another.

clash of civilizations
Political theory, most often identified with Harvard political scientist Samuel P. Huntington, that contends that conflict between the world's religiocultural traditions or "civilizations" increasingly dominates world affairs.

LATIN AMERICA SINCE 1945

Starting in the second half of the twentieth century, the nations of Latin America experienced divergent paths of political and economic change. Leaders tried repeatedly to alleviate their people's dependence on the more developed portions of the globe. These efforts produced mixed results, at best.

WHERE IN Latin America did the major attempts to establish revolutionary governments occur?

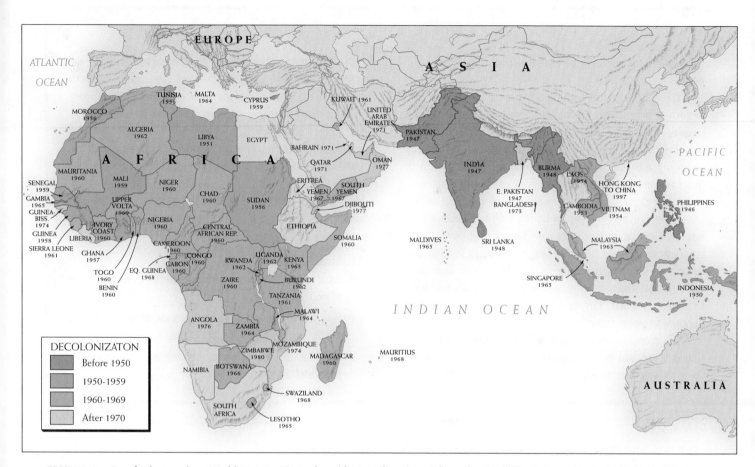

MAP 33–1. Decolonizaton since World War II. Europe's rapid retreat from imperialism after World War II is graphically depicted on this map, showing half the globe—from Africa to the Pacific.

How are the effects of colonialism still present in Africa and Asia today?

Before World War II, the states of Latin America had been economically dependent on the United States and western Europe. Beginning in the 1950s, Latin America became an arena for confrontations between the United States and the Soviet Union. Attempts were made to expand the industrial base and agricultural production of the various national economies. Financing came from U.S. and western European banks or from Soviet subsidies. Enormous debts were contracted that made Latin American economies virtual prisoners to fluctuations in interest rates or Soviet preferences. These new relationships did not alter the underlying character of most Latin American economies, which remain exporters of agricultural commodities and mineral resources. Since the 1970s, Latin America has also shipped massive amounts of cocaine to the United States and Europe. This has led to political turmoil and civil war in Colombia. In recent years the problem of drug cartels has erupted in Mexico. The desire to halt drug trafficking has led to formal and informal interventions by the United States. These efforts have involved incentives to diversify local economies away from drug cultivation as well as providing arms to governments seeking to disrupt drug lords. The real question in Colombia, parts of Mexico, and other regions of the Andes is whether governments or drug cartels actually hold authority.

The social structures of the Latin American nations have become more complicated since World War II. A culture of poverty remains the dominant social characteristic of the area. (See Document, "Lourdes Arizpe Discusses the Silence of Peasant Women" on page 872.) Even periods of economic boom, such as that fostered in Mexico by oil production in the late 1970s, proved brief and were almost inevitably followed by decline. Migration into the cities from the countryside has created tremendous urban over-crowding and slums inhabited by the desperately poor (see Figure 33–1). In many countries standards of health and nutrition have fallen. The growth of service industries in the cities has fostered the emergence of a professional, educated middle class. This new middle class has displayed little taste for radical politics, major social reform, or revolution.

FIGURE 33–1. Population of Major South American Cities, 1930–2006. **What trend is clearly visible?**

Political events in Latin America led to the establishment of authoritarian governments of both the left and the right and to a retreat from the model of parliamentary democracy. Only Mexico, Colombia, Venezuela, and Costa Rica remained parliamentary states throughout this period. Elsewhere, two paths of political development were followed. In Cuba and Nicaragua, and briefly in Chile, revolutionary socialist governments with close ties to the Soviet Union were established. Elsewhere, often in response to the fear of revolution or communism, military governments held power, sometimes punctuated with brief interludes of civilian rule. Such were the situations in Argentina, Bolivia, Brazil, Chile, Peru, and Uruguay. Governments of both the left and the right engaged in political repression.

These political changes fostered new roles for the military and the Roman Catholic Church. Latin American armies have played key political roles since the wars of independence. But since World War II, they have frequently assumed the direct government of nations. Many Roman Catholic priests and bishops have protested inequalities and attacked political repression. Certain Roman Catholic theologians have combined traditional Christian concern for the poor with Marxist ideology to formulate what is called **liberation theology**, which has been attacked by the Vatican; as a result its impact has diminished.

During the last decade and a half, Latin America has changed significantly. Several nations have moved toward democratization and free-market economies. Yet in most nations, the military keeps a watchful eye on possible disorder. The end of the Cold War brought to a close one source of external political challenge, but internal social problems continue to raise difficulties.

•**⊷ Read** the Document
Liberation Theology (1950s)
at **myhistorylab.com**

•**⊷ Read** the Document
Address before the
Puebla Conference (1979)
at **myhistorylab.com**

liberation theology
The effort by certain Roman Catholic theologians to combine Marxism with traditional Christian concern for the poor.

REVOLUTIONARY CHALLENGES: CUBA, CHILE, AND NICARAGUA

Several Latin American nations experienced major attempts to establish revolutionary governments pursuing profound social and economic change, including Cuba in 1959, Chile in 1970, and Nicaragua in 1979. Each of these initiatives involved some form of Marxist political organization, each pursued a close relationship with the Soviet Union, and each had immense symbolic importance in and beyond Latin America. The establishment of these governments provoked active resistance by the United States. In recent years leftist governments led by Hugo Chavez in Venezuela and Evo Morales in Bolivia have embraced policies reminiscent of those regimes including strong populist criticism of the United States, but they have not produced the regional impact of the earlier revolutionary governments.

DOCUMENT

Lourdes Arizpe Discusses the Silence of Peasant Women

Lourdes Arizpe, a Mexican anthropologist, wrote extensively on the plight of peasant women in the 1970s. In this passage she discusses how the lives and history of Mexican peasant women are shrouded in silence. Although her remarks are directed toward the situation in Mexico, they may well apply to peasant women in other cultures as well.

- **WHAT** are the factors that Arizpe cites as leading to the historical silence of peasant women? Why does she believe it is important for such women to learn to speak with their own voices? How do the stereotypes of Mexican peasant women both contribute to and arise from the silence? Why does she believe peasant women to be the most marginalized of all women?

History has imposed a greater silence on peasant women than on any other social group. Perhaps it is the solitude of the plains or the obligatory circumspection of their gender or merely political repression, but circumstances combine to force them to live in a secret world. Doubtless there are those who would assert that their tie to nature leads them to express themselves with actions rather than words. But the male peasant lives in the natural world without being silenced.

Silence, when not deliberate (although, how can we be sure it isn't?) could be anger or wisdom or, simply, a gesture of dignity. When there is no one worth talking to, I stay silent. If someone doesn't want to recognize my existence, I stay silent. In the spectrum of invisibility that history has imposed on women, perhaps the most invisible of the invisibles have been the peasants.

When direct expression is not permitted, the possibility of knowledge is lost and we fill that disturbing vacuum with phantoms. It is therefore not surprising that the Mexican mentality is filled with myths and stereotypes about peasant women. There is the submissive Indian woman who is a product of condescending maternalism; the wild woman both fantasized about and feared by men; the brazen hussy of melodramatic soap operas; the faint-hearted but treacherous small-town woman invented by the urban mind. Silence is also created by everyone's desire to hear what they want to hear rather than listen to what women are trying to say.

Today it seems that everyone mouths concerns about peasant women without any sincere interest. . . . What is important today is to create opportunities for peasant women to speak.

It is not that they have never spoken, only that their words have never been recognized. Because their words are discomforting when they denounce exploitation; disturbing when they display a deep understanding of the natural world not shared by their city sisters; strange when they describe an integrating vision of the universe; and because, being women's words, they are not important to androcentric [male-centered] history. Of all the marginalized peoples, peasant women are the most marginalized.

Source: Lourdes Arizpe, "Peasant Women and Silence," trans. by Laura Beard Milroy in *Women's Writing in Latin America: An Anthology*, by Sara Castro-Klarén, Sylvia Malloy, and Beatriz Sarlo. Copyright © 1992 by Westview Press. Reprinted by permission of Westview Press.

Cuba Cuba remained a colony of Spain until the Spanish-American War of 1898. It achieved independence within a sphere of U.S. influence that took the form of economic domination and military intervention. The governments of the island were ineffective and corrupt. During the 1950s, Fulgencio Batista (1901–1973), a dictator supported by the United States, ruled Cuba. On July 26, 1953, Fidel Castro Ruz (b. 1926), his close associate Ernesto Che Guevara, and others attacked a government army barracks. The revolutionary movement that Castro thereafter came to lead in exile took its name from that date: the Twenty-Sixth of July Movement. In 1956, Castro and a handful of followers landed in Cuba and attacked Batista's forces. Batista fled Cuba on New Year's Day in 1959.

Castro undertook the most extensive political, economic, and social reconstruction seen in recent Latin American history. Castro aligned himself with the Cuban Communist Party and with the Soviet bloc. He rejected parliamentary democracy. The revolutionary government concentrated on the agricultural sector and carried out major land redistribution. Sugar preserved its leading role, fostering dependence on large Soviet subsidies and Soviet-bloc markets.

The United States was hostile toward Castro and toward the presence of a communist state less than 100 miles from Florida. Throughout the Cold War, Cuba assumed an importance far greater than its size might suggest. After 1959, Cuba served as a center for the export of communist revolution; it sent troops to Angola in the late 1970s. The U.S. government, seeking to prevent a second Cuban Revolution in Latin America, intervened in other revolutionary situations and supported authoritarian governments in the hemisphere. In 1961, the United States and Cuban exiles launched the unsuccessful Bay of Pigs invasion. The close Cuban relationship to the Soviet Union led to the missile crisis of 1962, the most dangerous incident of the Cold War.

Despite the collapse of the Soviet Union—and the resulting loss of economic subsidies—the Castro government continues firmly in charge. Cuba remains the only state closely associated with the former Soviet bloc that has not experienced substantial political or economic reform. In 2006 Castro experienced serious problems with his health and disappeared from public sight. His brother Raul assumed the daily oversight of the government. Some observers believe Castro's death will cause a collapse of the government; others believe that the bureaucracy Castro created may endure.

Chile Until the 1970s, Chile was Latin America's exemplar of parliamentary democracy. During the 1960s, however, Chilean politics had become polarized. There was high unemployment, labor unrest, and popular resentment of Chile's economic domination by large U.S. corporations. The situation came to a head in 1970 when Salvador Allende (1908–1973), a Marxist, was elected president. His coalition did not control the Chilean congress, nor did it have the support of the military. Allende nationalized some businesses. Other policies were blocked in the congress, so Allende governed by decree. He began to expropriate foreign property, frightening Chilean business owners without satisfying workers. Inflation ballooned. Harvests were poor. By 1973, Allende had little domestic political support and many foreign enemies. The army became hostile, and the Nixon administration supported the discontent. In mid-September 1973, an army coup overthrew Allende, who was killed.

For the next fifteen years Chile was governed by a military junta under General Augusto Pinochet (1915–2006). The military government pursued a close relationship with the United States and resisted Marxism in the region. It established a state-directed free-market economy and reversed the expropriations of the Allende years. There was also harsh political repression. In a referendum held in late 1988, Chileans rejected Pinochet's bid for another term as president. Democratization was relatively smooth, and during the past two decades Chile has moved toward a more liberal constitutional government. Civilian governments, moving slowly to avoid provoking the military, investigated the political repression of the Pinochet years and uncovered thousands of cases of torture and murder. During the first decade of the present century politics in Chile were vigorously contested, with peaceful changes between governments of the left and the right.

Nicaragua In the summer of 1979, a Marxist guerrilla force, the **Sandinistas**, overthrew the corrupt dictatorship of the Somoza family in Nicaragua. The Sandinistas established a collective government that pursued social and economic reform and reconstruction. The movement, with Roman Catholic priests on its

QUICK REVIEW

Salvador Allende
- Elected president of Chile in 1970
- Lacked support in congress and military
- Marxist policies led to economic crisis
- Assassinated in 1973 army coup

Pariah. A 1977 poster from a New York protest highlights the enormous international opposition to the policies of General Pinochet.

Which other political leaders have been accused of "crimes against humanity" in recent times?

Sandinistas
The Marxist guerrilla force that overthrew the Somoza dictatorship in Nicaragua in 1979.

leadership council, epitomized the new political and social forces in Latin America. The Sandinistas also had close ties to the Soviet Union. The revolutionary government confronted significant domestic political opposition and military challenge from the Contra guerrilla movement.

The government of the United States, particularly under the Reagan administration (1981–1989), was hostile to the Sandinistas, fearing the spread of Marxist revolutionary activity in Central America. It provided both direct and indirect aid to the Contras.

Sandinista rule came to a relatively quick end. In early 1990, after a negotiated peace settlement with the Contras, they lost the presidential election to an opposition coalition and relinquished power peacefully. A democratic government supported by the United States has remained in control despite persistent economic weaknesses.

PURSUIT OF STABILITY UNDER THE THREAT OF REVOLUTION: ARGENTINA, BRAZIL, AND MEXICO

Argentina In 1955, the Argentine army revolted against the Perón dictatorship and Juan Perón (1895–1974) went into exile. Two decades of economic stagnation and social unrest followed. By 1976, the army had undertaken direct rule. There was widespread repression; thousands of citizens disappeared, never to be heard of again. In April 1982, General Leopoldo Galtieri (b. 1926) launched a disastrous invasion of the Islas Malvinas (Falkland Islands). Argentina was defeated by Britain, and the military junta was thoroughly discredited.

In 1983 civilian rule was restored, and Argentina set out on the road to democratization. Under President Raúl Alfonsín (b. 1927), many of the figures responsible for repression received prison sentences. Argentina has provided the most extensive example in Latin America of the restoration of democracy after military rule. Peaceful elections and transitions of governments have occurred for over two decades. During the same era, however, the Argentine economy has endured ongoing turmoil; no government has been able to stabilize production and prices.

Brazil In 1964 the military assumed the direct government of Brazil and held it until 1985, stressing order and using repression to maintain it. Non-Brazilian corporations were invited to spearhead the drive toward industrialization. One result was a massive foreign debt, the servicing and repayment of which have lingered as a national problem. Brazil became the major industrialized nation in Latin America, which has had a huge impact on the Brazilian rain forest. By 1998, large landowners, encouraged by subsidies and tax incentives, had cleared 12 percent of Brazil's rain forest.

Brazil's critical question is how growing urbanization and other social changes wrought by industrialism will receive political accommodation. In 2003, in the wake of economic turmoil, Luiz Inácio Lula da Silva became the first person from a working-class background to be elected president of Brazil. He was reelected in 2006. His administration has combined socialist concern for social services with an austere economic policy. Those policies set Brazil on a path of sustained economic growth. Furthermore, those workers at the bottom of the income scale achieved greater improvement than anywhere else in Latin America. Like the rest of the world, Brazil encountered difficulties in the recent economic slump, but it appears to be regaining its footing.

◆•◆ Read the Document

Juan Perón, excerpt from The Voice of Perón
at **myhistorylab.com**

◆•◆ Read the Document

Brazil's Constitution of 1988
at **myhistorylab.com**

Deforestation in the Amazon. A cut and burned section of trees on federal land in Brazil's Amazonian state of Para. The problems of deforestation, wood trafficking, habitat destruction, slave labor, land grabbing, and violence are all intertwined as colonization of the region accelerates.

What is the global impact of deforestation in the Amazon?

Mexico Institutionally, Mexico has undergone relatively few political changes since World War II. In theory, the government continued to pursue the goals of the revolution. The Partido Revolucionario Institucional (PRI) held power for decades. Yet shifts had occurred. In the early 1950s, certain large landowners were exempted from the expropriation and redistribution of land. The Mexican government maintained relations with Cuba and the other revolutionary regimes of Latin America, but resisted Marxist doctrines within Mexico.

Mexico experienced an oil boom from 1977 to 1983, but did not achieve stable growth. Like other states in the region, Mexico amassed large foreign debts and thus surrendered real economic independence.

After the hotly contested 1988 election, the PRI leadership began to decentralize the party. President Carlos Salinas moved to privatize economic enterprise. He also favored free-trade agreements. The most important of these was the North American Free Trade Agreement (NAFTA), which created a vast free-trade area including Mexico, Canada, and the United States. In 1991, Salinas made new accommodations with the Roman Catholic Church, thus moving away from the traditional anticlericalism of Mexican politics. By 1991, the PRI appeared to have regained its political ascendancy.

In 1994, however, Mexico underwent a number of political shocks. Troops had to quell armed rebellion in Chiapas. The leading candidate in that year's election was assassinated and party members were charged with complicity. Early in 1995, Mexico suffered a major economic downturn, and only loans from the United States saved the economy. Ernesto Zedillo, elected president in 1994, blamed Salinas and his family for the situation, and the corruption of the Salinas government became public. The government faced further unrest in Chiapas, growing power among drug lords, and turmoil within the governing party itself. In 2000 the PRI candidate for president lost to Vicente Fox of the National Action Party (PAN). Fox's term ended in late 2006 with an election narrowly won by another PAN candidate, Felipe Calderón. Calderón pursued policies of social conservatism tied to liberal economic policies. His administration has also been marked by expanding conflict between the state and the drug cartels.

CONTINUITY AND CHANGE IN RECENT LATIN AMERICAN HISTORY

The most striking aspect of the past six decades in Latin America is its tragic continuity with the region's previous history. Revolution has brought moderate social change, but at the price of authoritarian government, economic stagnation, and dependence on foreign powers. Real independence has not been achieved.

The recent trends toward democratization and market economics may mark a break in that pattern. The region could enjoy healthy economic growth if inflation were contained and investment fostered. The challenge will be to see that the fruits of any new prosperity are shared in a way that prevents new political resentment and turmoil. Furthermore, as in the past, economic turmoil far from Latin America may have an adverse impact on its destiny. Each time such turmoil has occurred, the governments of Latin America have found themselves economically dependent on either the United States or European governments and bankers.

Read the **Document**
Chico Mendes on the Rainforest (1980s) at **myhistorylab.com**

See the **Map**
Latin America, 2004
at **myhistorylab.com**

The Turn to the Left in Latin American politics is represented by Venezuelan president Hugo Chávez, who has oil wealth to fund his ambitions, and Evo Morales, the first indigenous president of Bolivia. Chávez assumed power in 1999, Morales in 2006.

Why have Latin American politics generally been dominated by conservative leaders?

A Closer Look

Mexican Farmers Protest the North American Free Trade Agreement

The North American Free Trade Agreement (1994), or NAFTA, was actually a series of agreements involving the United States, Canada, and Mexico. Its purpose was to remove trade barriers among these nations. In this respect it represented one of the early moves toward economic globalization, though it was restricted to North America. The free flow of agricultural commodities represented one of the chief goals of NAFTA. By 2008, agreements eliminated or phased out all agricultural tariffs between the United States and Mexico. The value of U.S. agricultural exports to Mexico rose significantly, having declined prior to the agreement. Farmers in Mexico often felt that the elimination of these tariffs worked to their disadvantage, with cheaper U.S. products replacing their products in the market. In January 2008, Mexican farmers riding their tractors protested the recent trade liberalization, which they argued opened Mexican markets to the importation of less expensive maize (corn) produced in the United States. Jobs had been lost in the Mexican agricultural sector because of the cheaper U.S. products—products made cheaper because of U.S. government subsidies to agriculture. Mexican government subsidies to agriculture had fallen in the same period. The farmers saw themselves as caught in a downward economic spiral.

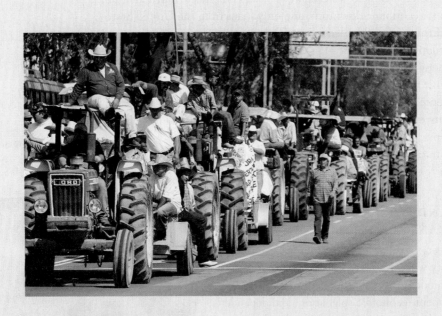

Questions

1. Even when tariffs and other trade barriers are lowered, how can other government policies place different economic sectors at a disadvantage? Why is agriculture especially vulnerable to such arrangements?

2. Why are Mexican farmers at a greater disadvantage in protesting policies that work to their detriment than unionized workers in manufacturing industries?

3. This picture illustrates the challenges faced by Mexican farmers. During the same period many U.S. manufacturers moved factories to Mexico, where wages are lower. How did this economic shift work to the disadvantage of U.S. wage earners in previously highly industrialized regions of the United States, such as Michigan and other parts of the Midwest?

4. What are the pros and cons of economic globalization?

POSTCOLONIAL AFRICA

Most of Africa's modern nations follow colonial boundaries; colonial capitals have typically become national capitals. Africa provides striking examples of how attractive nationalism can be as a motive for supratribal and transregional state formation. In World War II the important roles that Africa was called on to play with its natural and human resources, as well as the experience of thousands of Africans who were conscripted or volunteered to fight or labor abroad, proved a catalyst for African nationalism. After the war, Europe was largely disposed to give up its colonial empires.

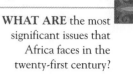

WHAT ARE the most significant issues that Africa faces in the twenty-first century?

THE TRANSITION TO INDEPENDENCE

Europe's colonization of Africa had occurred in the historical blink of an eye (see Chapters 26 and 28). Independence came almost as quickly. In 1950, only Egypt, Liberia, Ethiopia, and white-controlled South Africa were sovereign states. By 1980 no sizeable African territory was ruled by a European state, although South Africa and Namibia continued to be white-dominated. African leaders, such as Kwame Nkrumah (1909–1972) in the Gold Coast (modern Ghana), Jomo Kenyatta (1893–1978) in Kenya, Julius Nyerere (1922–1999) in Tanganyika (later Tanzania), and Patrice Lumumba (1925–1961) in the Congo became symbols of African self-determination and independence.

The actual transition from colonial administrative territories to independent national states was generally peaceful. Violence was more likely in colonies with large populations of European settlers (such as Algeria) or lucrative exports of minerals or other resources (Congo, for example). The internal conflicts that arose in some newly independent states, however, were intense.

Much of the instability in African states has been a legacy of both the colonial powers' minimal efforts to prepare their colonial subjects for self-government and the haphazard nineteenth-century division of the continent into arbitrary colonial units. Before World War II, colonial powers largely assumed they would govern their African colonies indefinitely. Few African states had the numbers of educated and experienced native citizens needed to staff the apparatuses of a sovereign country.

After independence, corruption and military coups were rife; the attempt to implement planned economies on a socialist model often brought economic catastrophe; and tribal and regional revolts at times led to civil war. The separatist struggles, civil wars, and border clashes that grew out of the independence struggles tended to ratify the postcolonial state divisions (instead of regional or tribal/linguistic divisions).

Prime Minister Kwame Nkrumah (center) waves to crowds of supporters on March 6, 1957 in celebration of Ghana's independence from Great Britain. Ghana was the first sub-Saharan country to gain independence.

Why were most African transitions to independence initially peaceful?

QUICK REVIEW

African Independence

◆ By 1980, no African state was ruled by a European state

◆ Transition to independent states was more peaceful than expected

◆ Internal conflicts since independence have led to instability and violence

STRIVING FOR STABILITY AND CIVIL SOCIETY: NIGERIA, SOUTH AFRICA, CONGO, AND RWANDA

Nigeria The modern Republic of Nigeria is the most populous state in Africa, with about 150 million inhabitants in 2009. Nigeria achieved independence from Britain in 1960 as arguably the most powerful and potentially successful state in independent Africa. The republican constitution of 1964 federated three provincial regions—the Eastern, Western, and Northern—under a national government based in Lagos, the

See the **Map**
Africa, 2004
at **myhistorylab.com**

QUICK REVIEW

Nigeria

◆ Achieved independence in 1960

◆ Collapse of three-province federation led to dictatorship and civil war

◆ Brutality, instability, and corruption have marked Nigerian government since 1975

Watch the **Video**
Creating Apartheid
in South Africa
at **myhistorylab.com**

apartheid
"Apartness," the term referring to racist policies enforced by the white-dominated regime that existed in South Africa from 1948 to 1992.

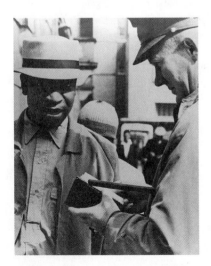

Apartheid. A police officer checks a black African's identification card, under the *apartheid* system's hated pass laws.

Can apartheid be compared to segregation in the United States? How were they similar? How were they different?

former British administrative capital. Nigeria's largest ethnic and linguistic groups are the major ones of the same three regions: Igbo in the Eastern, Yoruba in the Western, and Hausa and Fulani in the Northern province.

A 1966 *coup d'état* brought a military government into power. Its leader was soon assassinated, and Lieutenant Colonel Yakubu Gawon (b. 1934) took over amid ethnic unrest. In May 1967, the Eastern Province's assembly empowered its leader to form a new, independent state of Biafra. Biafra secured arms and support from France, South Africa, and Portugal, and developed successful worldwide propaganda depicting itself as a small, brave, Christian country fighting for its survival against a hostile, oppressive, Muslim central government. The ensuing two and a half years saw a tragic civil war. The larger federal forces slowly chipped away at the Biafran state. The estimated death toll soared above a million—the overwhelming majority of whom were Igbo civilians, mostly refugees who died of starvation—before the Biafrans surrendered in January 1970.

Gawon was overthrown by another military commander in 1975. In the ensuing years Nigeria was plagued by political instability at the top, with its leadership passing usually from one military ruler to another.

Nobel laureate author Wole Soyinka (b. 1934) led protest demonstrations against the military government in 1994. Novelist and environmental activist Kenule "Ken" Saro-Wiwa (1941–1995) was executed by the military in 1995. Military rule was replaced in 1999 by civilian government under an elected president, Olusegun Obasanjo, and a new constitution was implemented. Umaru Musa Yar'Adua succeeded Obasanjo as president after a flawed election in April 2007. Problems of religious animosities and ethnic divisions remain. Despite the nation's wealth, Nigeria's development has been hampered by corruption, lack of infrastructure, and mismanagement.

South Africa The Union of South Africa was governed under the racist policy of **apartheid** ("apartness") from the time the Afrikaner-led National Party (NP) came to power in 1948 until 1991. The white minority (in 1991, 5.4 million persons) ran the country, maintaining economic and political control and privilege. Its 31 million blacks, 3.7 million "coloreds" (people with dual ancestry), and 1 million Indians [all figures from 1991] were kept strictly segregated—treated, at best, as second-class citizens. This system was maintained chiefly by repression.

In part as a result of worldwide opposition to apartheid, South Africa was increasingly isolated. In the 1960s and 1970s the government created three tiny "independent homelands" for blacks, so that they could be treated as immigrant "foreigners" in the parts of South Africa where most had to work. The international community refused to recognize the homelands, or "Bantustans." Zulu chief Albert Luthuli (1898?–1967) and Anglican bishop Desmond Tutu (b. 1931) were awarded Nobel Prizes in 1969 and 1984, respectively, for their work against apartheid.

By 1978, as Pieter Botha (1916–2006) came to power, apartheid was failing: The homelands were economic and political catastrophes; the country was in an inflationary recession; skilled whites were emigrating; and South Africa was becoming a pariah state. Beginning in 1986, many nations responded to Tutu's call and imposed economic sanctions against the government. Strikes by black workers in 1987 led the government to declare a state of emergency: Western nations embargoed trade. In 1988 more than 2 million black workers went on strike to protest new repressive labor laws and political bans. Botha resigned in 1989.

In 1990 president F. W. de Klerk (b. 1936) began a series of landmark actions: lifting the ban on the African National Congress (ANC), the main anti-apartheid organization; releasing ANC leader Nelson Mandela after twenty-seven years of imprisonment; and repealing the Separate Amenities Act, the legal basis for segregation in public places. In early 1991 de Klerk announced plans to end all apartheid laws. De Klerk and Mandela led the endorsement of a new interim constitution, for which they shared the Nobel Peace Prize for 1993.

Multiracial elections were held in April 1994. The ANC won 63 percent of the vote. Nelson Mandela was elected president of what Tutu called the Rainbow Nation, in honor of South Africa's racial and political diversity. The **Truth and Reconciliation Commission (TRC)**, established in 1995, offered an unprecedented way to come to terms with the country's past: Rather than attempting to bring to justice the many perpetrators of human rights abuses during the apartheid era, the TRC offered amnesty in exchange for testimony and provided victims a platform for detailing their losses. The TRC's premises were controversial—some victims of apartheid atrocities protested that their persecutors were evading punishment—but it is unlikely that any other mechanism could have generated a more comprehensive account of apartheid's abuses.

The governments of Thabo Mbeki (b. 1942), who succeeded Mandela in 1999, then Kgalema Motlanthe (b. 1949), who completed Mbeki's unfinished term in 2008–2009, and Jacob Zuma (b. 1942), the current president, have striven to deal with the major challenges that the country's 49 million citizens face. Despite substantial mineral resources and the highest GNP in Africa, South Africa's problems are immense: one of the world's highest rates of HIV/AIDS infection (18.1 percent); high unemployment, poverty, and crime rates; extreme income inequality; inadequate public services and infrastructure; and water shortages. Only time will tell how well the new democracy can handle these serious issues and whether it can meet the nation's hopes for a new era of socioeconomic progress.

Congo European rule in Africa may have reached its nadir in the Congo Free State. In this personal fiefdom of Belgium's King Leopold II between 1885 and 1908, Africans were routinely mutilated or killed for offenses such as failing to meet local officials' quotas for rubber collection. As a Belgian colony, Congo fared only slightly better, and since independence in 1960 Congo's history has been infamous for ongoing atrocities.

The Republic of Congo gained independence on June 30, 1960, with Patrice Lumumba (1925–1961) as prime minister and Joseph Kasavubu (1910–1969) as president. Lumumba and Kasavubu belonged to different parties. Kasavubu dismissed Lumumba from office; Lumumba resisted. In the ensuing crisis the Congolese Army's chief of staff, Joseph-Désiré Mobutu (1930–1997), overthrew them both. Lumumba was assassinated in 1961. Various presidents served brief terms until 1965, when Mobutu again seized power. This time he had the backing of the U.S. Central Intelligence Agency, and he kept power for more than thirty years. Mobutu outlawed all political parties except his own, the Popular Movement of the Revolution, from 1967 to 1990. He launched the Authenticité campaign to celebrate African culture, and he renamed the country Zaire. Mobutu developed a powerful cult of personality. Corruption made his rule a kleptocracy.

The combination of the end of the Cold War and Mobutu's failing health created an opening for opposition leaders. Refugees from Rwanda's genocide (see below) further destabilized the country, and, starting in 1996, insurgents supported by Rwanda, Uganda, Zambia, and Angola captured much of eastern Zaire. Most of these outsiders backed Laurent Kabila (1939–2001) when he was sworn in as president on

Nelson Mandela campaigning for the presidency of post-apartheid South Africa.

Why is Mandela so widely admired?

Truth and Reconciliation Commission (TRC)
A quasi-judicial body that investigated apartheid-era human rights abuses. The TRC emphasized disclosure over punishment and generally offered amnesty in exchange for testimony.

Read the Document

Nelson Mandela, from Freedom, Justice and Dignity for All South Africa
at **myhistorylab.com**

View the Image

Voters Waiting to Vote in South Africa's First Open Election, 1994
at **myhistorylab.com**

Rwandan Refugees carry their belongings as they stream out of the Mugunga refugee camp in Zaire (Congo) back toward Rwanda, in the aftermath of the 1994 genocide.

How did events in Zaire and Rwanda become interconnected?

◆◆◆⌐Read the Document

Alain Destexhe, excerpt from Rwanda and Genocide in the Twentieth Century at **myhistorylab.com**

May 29, 1997. The country was again renamed, this time as the Democratic Republic of the Congo (DRC). Since then, what has been called the Second Congo War (the revolt against Mobutu being the first) or even the African World War has roiled the DRC. In 2001, Kabila was assassinated; his son, Joseph Kabila, took office. In 2006, in disputed elections, he defeated other candidates for the presidency.

The DRC is immense and possesses vast natural resources, especially valuable minerals. Nonetheless its future is uncertain; fighting continues, much infrastructure has been destroyed, and most citizens understandably mistrust their government.

Rwanda Rwanda is roughly one one-hundredth the size of the Democratic Republic of the Congo, but during and after the Rwandan genocide of 1994 the two countries' histories became intertwined. Under Belgian administration, ethnicity in Ruanda-Urundi (now, Rwanda and Burundi) was determined by wealth: Since the minority Tutsi tribe already constituted the elite, anyone deemed wealthy by the Belgians became a "Tutsi," and most others were designated as belonging to the largest preexisting ethnic group, the "Hutu." (Rwanda also has a significant minority population of Twa forest people, or "pygmies.") At independence in 1961, Rwanda and Burundi separated, and Rwanda became a republic with Hutu leadership.

Over the following decades, many crossborder clashes took place between Rwanda, Burundi, and Uganda. This violence was usually labeled as Tutsi versus Hutu, regardless of its actual roots. On April 6, 1994, when a helicopter carrying the (Hutu) presidents of Rwanda and Burundi was shot down over Rwanda's capital, killing both presidents, Tutsis were blamed. The groundwork had been laid for interethnic civil war. Over the following months, approximately 800,000 Tutsis and moderate Hutus were killed in a massive genocide. The Uganda-based, Tutsi-led Rwandan Patriotic Front (RPF) under Paul Kagame (b. 1957) gradually took control of the country, and millions of Hutu refugees fled to Zaire. RPF and Ugandan forces pursued them into Zaire, creating one of the triggers for Mobutu's overthrow in 1997.

United Nations peacekeepers were on the ground in Rwanda when the genocide began, but under the terms of their deployment they were unable to intervene. United States President Bill Clinton was harshly criticized for failing to take action.

Following a period of transitional government, a new constitution was approved, and Kagame was elected president in 2003. Although Kagame has been criticized for stifling dissent, his administration has been marked by some democratic and economic progress; average income tripled from 1999 to 2009. In 2008 Rwanda became the first country with a majority of women elected to its legislature.

THE AFRICAN FUTURE

Most African states have not achieved peace and prosperity. Some conflicts—most notably in eastern Congo and the Darfur region of Sudan—are still ongoing, their human consequences catastrophic and ultimate resolution unclear. However, the last half-century has seen radical change and development. Overall, prospects for future governmental stability have never been stronger. Economic problems remain extremely threatening, but progress is being made after decades of failures. Some burdens of the past have been overcome, but problems of public health, environmental degradation, social instability, and development still pose formidable hurdles.

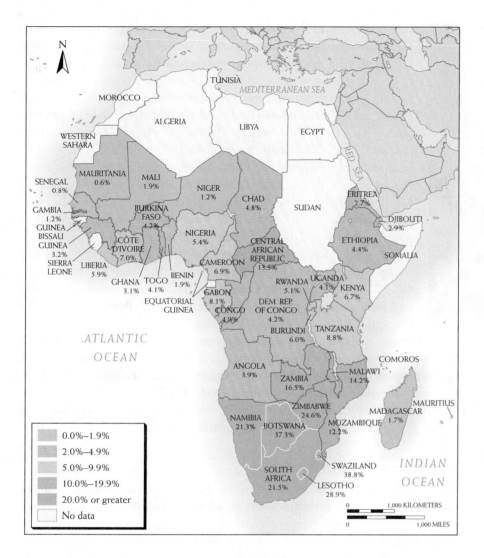

MAP 33–2.   Distribution of HIV Infection Rates in Africa.

What general trends do you notice in HIV infection rates in Africa?

Health and Environment A variety of health and environmental challenges face Africa, the most notorious of which is **HIV/AIDS**. In late 2008, an estimated 22.4 million people in sub-Saharan Africa were living with HIV. There are significant regional variations in HIV infection rates: In general, rates are highest in southern Africa and lowest in West Africa (see Map 33–2). Governments have varied tremendously in their responses to HIV/AIDS. Uganda, for example, embarked on an aggressive public education campaign in the 1990s, which seems to have helped reduce infection rates there. In contrast, in early 2000, South African President Mbeki publicly questioned whether HIV causes AIDS and made statements that contributed to an atmosphere of denial and shame surrounding HIV/AIDS in South Africa.

Other diseases, while less likely to capture headlines in the West, sicken or kill millions of Africans every year. The World Health Organization declared the prevalence of tuberculosis an emergency in Africa in 2005. Malaria and other tropical diseases reduce life expectancy, increase school and job absenteeism, and reduce economic productivity almost everywhere in Africa. Only very recently have significant global health initiatives, such as the Global Network for Neglected Tropical Diseases (established in 2006), begun to target Africa's interrelated health challenges.

African environmental challenges run the gamut from wildlife poaching to soil erosion to improper disposal of hazardous waste. Africans have been in the forefront of

HIV/AIDS

Collection of symptoms and infections resulting from the specific damage to the immune system caused by the human immunodeficiency virus (HIV). The late stage of the condition leaves individuals susceptible to opportunistic infections and tumors. Although treatments for AIDS and HIV exist to decelerate the virus's progression, there is currently no known cure.

Read the **Document**

Nelson Mandela, Closing Address at the 13th International AIDS Conference, July 2000
at **myhistorylab.com**

Ellen Sirleaf-Johnson was elected president of Liberia in 2005. She is the first woman elected to lead an African nation.

What are some significant issues facing African nations today?

─[**See** the **Map**
HIV Prevalence in Africa
at **myhistorylab.com**

the environmental justice movement, with activists including Ken Saro-Wiwa and Nobel laureate Wangari Maathai, leader of Kenya's Green Belt Movement, building grass-roots environmental campaigns.

Social Change   African society has changed rapidly during the postcolonial period, though many traditions endure. Rapid urbanization began in colonial times and continues to the present. The explosive growth of urban centers at the expense of rural areas has disrupted the continent's traditionally agrarian-based societies, family and community allegiances, religious values, and sociopolitical systems. Migrants flock to cities in search of wage labor, but African urban economies have never grown as quickly as their populations; many cities harbor large slums where masses of people live in severely inadequate housing, lacking plumbing and other essential infrastructure. Men have been more likely to migrate to urban areas than women, so there are often gender imbalances in both rural and urban areas.

Women were active in anticolonial and anti-apartheid movements and took leadership roles in some post-independence rebellions (for example, in Uganda). Only since the mid-1990s, however, have women been elected in growing numbers to parliaments and other national offices. Ellen Sirleaf-Johnson, the first woman elected to lead an African nation, won the presidency of Liberia in 2005.

Demography and religion help shape African societies. Population growth has been rapid throughout Africa, while deaths from HIV/AIDS have created new population trends, such as the large numbers of "AIDS orphans." Christianity and Islam both continue to gain converts. Evangelical Christianity, in particular, is growing rapidly.

TRADE AND DEVELOPMENT

During the Cold War, one of the areas in which the West and the Soviet bloc competed was dispensing development aid in Africa. Starting in the 1990s, trade has been emphasized as the best mechanism for improving African economies and standards of living. Under President Clinton, for example, the United States encouraged private-sector trade and investment through the Partnership for Economic Growth and Opportunity in Africa. President George W. Bush supported the African Global Competitiveness Initiative (AGCI) to build sub-Saharan Africa's capacity for trade and competitiveness. A factor of rapidly growing importance is trade with, and direct investment by, China. African economies still need to grow tremendously to meet their populations' needs.

THE ISLAMIC HEARTLANDS FROM NORTH AFRICA TO INDONESIA

HOW HAS Islam affected politics in the developing world?

The lands today marked by Islamic culture and Muslim-majority populations or major Muslim minorities are found in the Arab world from Morocco to Iraq and the Gulf; in West and East Africa; in the Balkans, the Turkish-speaking world of Turkey and the former Soviet Central Asian republics; in Persian-speaking Iran and Central Asia, in western China, and in South and Southeast Asia. The Muslims of the entire Arab world number only about 275 million. Indonesia, Pakistan, India, and Bangladesh have the four largest Muslim populations in the world, with about 207, 171, 156, and 130 million Muslims, respectively. These varied nations illustrate the many different ways in which Islamic allegiances manifest themselves and affect political life.

TURKEY

Turkey is the product of a modernist republican experiment that has attempted to create a democratic government and civil society despite struggles over the roles of the military, ethnicity, culture, and religion. The Turkish military has repeatedly deposed elected governments and supervised selection of new leadership. Economically, Turkey has had difficulties, but it and Israel are still the most economically advanced Middle Eastern countries. It may be the most progressive Muslim nation in its range of tolerated interpretations of Islam. With the creation of new Turkic-language states in post-Soviet Central Asia, Turkey is seeking to play a major role in this underdeveloped region.

Geographically and culturally Turkey belongs to both Europe and Asia. Turkey is a member of NATO and is a candidate country for admission into the European Union. Many Europeans, however, are skeptical about admitting an overwhelmingly Muslim nation into the Union. Persecution of Turkey's Kurdish minority and other human rights violations, ongoing denial of the Armenian genocide nearly a century ago, as well as indebtedness to the International Money Fund, have worked against Turkey's case for EU admission. The emergence of Islamist parties in Turkey has only complicated the political landscape. It remains to be seen whether Turkey will align itself more with Europe, the Middle East, or Central Asia in the years ahead; currently, it is making a strong effort to join Europe while reaching out to Central Asia.

✓●─[**Study** and **Review**
Soviet and Turkish Plans for
Industrialization at **myhistorylab.com**

IRAN AND ITS ISLAMIC REVOLUTION

Iran was ruled as a monarchy from 1925 to 1941 by a former army commander, Reza Khan. He came to power through a British-supported military takeover and governed as Reza Shah with the ancient Persian name Pahlavi. Much like his Turkish contemporary, Atatürk (1881–1938), he attempted to introduce modernist economic, educational, and governmental reforms. He tried to create a rich landlord and industrial class with few benefits for the pastoral, peasant, and urban classes. Reza Shah built a highly centralized autocracy, not a parliamentary state. His reforms differed from Atatürk's in that he did not have to deal with a battle-tested, well-armed military or an experienced and eager middle class, both of whom Atatürk had to placate to realize his social and industrialization projects.

By the time Russian and British forces deposed Reza Shah in 1941 and installed his son, Muhammad Reza, as shah, the activism of radical trade unionists and the socialist-leaning intelligentsia had been crushed, and the power of Shi'ite religious leaders, or *ulama*, had been muted through the consolidation of a strong, centralized state. The son sought legitimacy through linkage with the imperial dynasties of pre-Islamic Persia and continued his father's secular and industrial state building from after World War II until 1978, with one interruption from 1951 to 1953. Those three years saw Muhammad Mosaddeq (1881–1967) become prime minister by successfully drawing together a broad coalition of workers, *bazari* merchants, religious leaders, intelligentsia, and government workers. They formed a political force, the National Front, which won the minds and hearts of Iranians with the nationalization of the British-owned Anglo-Iranian Oil Company in Abadan in 1951. Mosaddeq was ousted by the U.S. Central Intelligence Agency and British Military Intelligence in a 1953 *coup d'etat*, earning the United States and Britain generations of distrust.

Having clamped down on opponents after the 1953 coup, in the 1960s Muhammad Reza Shah still faced two opposition groups, one led by educated secularists and the other by the *ulama*. Land reform and other Pahlavi initiatives were opposed by

Khomeini. The bearded ayatollah waves to a cheering throng in Tehran, Iran, in February 1979.

Who supported the Iranian Revolution that brought Khomeini to power?

Iranian Nobel Prize Winner Shirin Ebadi at the Street Children's Home That She Founded in Tehran. Ebadi was awarded the prestigious prize for her work in defending human rights. She was the first Muslim woman to be awarded a Nobel.

Does Ebadi's accomplishment contradict widely held views in the West on the status of women in the Muslim world?

◉ View the Image
Ayatollah Khomeini
at **myhistorylab.com**

QUICK REVIEW

Islamic Revolution in Iran

- 1978: Shi'ites and secularists joined to overthrow shah
- 1979: Republican constitution is Islamic, not secular
- Shi'ite leader Ayatollah Ruhollah Khomeini takes power

✓ ◉ Study and Review
The Political Vision of Atatürk and Khomeini at **myhistorylab.com**

both groups for different reasons. The shah's heavy-handed, often brutal repression of any protest backfired. While the *ulama* preferred continuing nonviolent opposition through the 1970s, the middle- and upper-class professionals opted for tactical, violent clashes with the regime and its U.S. ally. For all the modernizing military and economic buildup that the United States and the shah initiated, the gap between the extremely wealthy few and the extremely poor masses never narrowed. That fully half of Iran's 60-odd million inhabitants are Turkish, Kurdish, Arabic, and other minorities did little to help Reza consolidate and strengthen his centralized monarchy.

Finally, in 1978 religious leaders and secularist revolutionaries joined forces to end the shah's long regime through a revolution engaging a wide spectrum of emotion, ideology, and secular as well as religious symbolism. What had begun as an "Iranian Revolution" ended up as an "Islamic Revolution," so that in 1979 the new post-shah republic that emerged was not a secular but an Islamic one crafted under the guidance of the Shi'ite religious leader, Ayatollah Ruhollah Khomeini (1902–1989).

A protracted war with Iraq (1980–1988) and new repression followed. Still, the new state—with religious leaders exercising a degree of influence over politics not seen since early Safavid times in the sixteenth century—has survived. Khomeini and his successors have continued to struggle to find a new formula for combining Muslim values and norms with contemporary *Realpolitik*.

Mohammad Khatami was elected president in 1997 in the first real national leadership election since the 1979 revolution. Khatami tried to steer Iran on a more moderate, liberal course. Wide-ranging reforms failed to materialize, however. In 2003, Iranian lawyer Shirin Ebadi won the Nobel Peace Prize for her work to improve the status of women and children in Iran; Iran's leadership paid no attention. In 2005, Mahmud Ahmadinejad (b. 1956), a veteran of the Iraq–Iran War, won the presidential election. The United States and its allies (particularly Israel) oppose his policies on nuclear energy and military involvement in Iraq. The Obama administration's policies toward Iran are still evolving, and the future of Iran's international relations remains uncertain.

AFGHANISTAN AND THE FORMER SOVIET REPUBLICS

North of Iran, 40 million Central Asian Muslims predominate in the broad region that stretches across the south-central reaches of the former Soviet Union between the Crimea and China, in addition to at least 20 million Chinese Muslims, concentrated in adjacent southwestern China. In the 1980s both Soviet and Chinese Muslims appeared to be asserting themselves. The 1979 Soviet occupation of Afghanistan, whose people had close ties to Soviet Muslims, reflected the potential importance of this movement.

The Soviet invasion of Afghanistan had unexpected results. Thousands of Muslims, mostly fundamentalists, had arrived in Afghanistan to oust the Soviets and their Afghan puppets. Conservative Arab states and the United States supported this effort. The conservative Arab states saw the Afghan War as an opportunity both to resist the expansion of Soviet influence and to divert the energies of their own religious extremists. The United States saw the Afghan War as another round in the Cold War. The militant Muslim fundamentalists saw it as a religious struggle against an impious non-Muslim power.

The Soviets withdrew in 1988, leaving a power vacuum. By 1998, extreme rigorist Muslims known as the *Taliban* seized control. They imposed their own literalist version of Islamic law, involving strict regimentation of women and public executions or mutilations for criminal offenses. The Taliban allowed Muslim terrorist groups such as *al-Qa'ida* ("the base") to establish training camps in Afghanistan. The terrorists who attacked U.S. targets on September 11, 2001, came from these camps. As will be seen later, one American response to those attacks was a military campaign against the Afghani Taliban government.

INDIA

India, a largely Hindu state, and Pakistan, a largely Muslim state, gained independence in 1947 after the British agreed to a partition of the subcontinent. Much of their subsequent history has been one of mutual antagonism. About 8 million Muslims were displaced from the new India, and another 8 million Hindus and Sikhs were displaced from the new Pakistan. The two states still have not resolved their major differences, including their conflicting claims to Kashmir. Their rivalry has been exacerbated by Indian underground nuclear tests in 1998, which were closely followed by similar Pakistani tests.

Since the assassination of Mohandas Gandhi (1869–1948) by a Hindu fanatic, India has been directed for most of its existence by the leaders of Gandhi's Congress Party. Jawaharlal Nehru (1889–1964) developed India's famous theory of political neutrality vis-à-vis world alignments. His secularist, reconciliatory policies reduced communal hatreds, religious zealotry, and regional tensions, and he also made progress in the huge task of economic development of the overpopulated, underdeveloped new nation. Nehru's resolute opposition to caste privilege helped improve equality of citizenship.

Indira Gandhi (1917–1984; no familial relation to Mohandas Gandhi) similarly managed to steer a tricky course of neutralism during the Cold War. India's 1971 victory over Pakistan and the subsequent creation of Bangladesh to replace East Pakistan strengthened her political control, but the failure of her efforts to reduce national poverty overcame her postwar popularity. Her resolute efforts to quell Sikh separatism brought about her assassination in 1984 by two Sikhs from her own palace guard.

Indira Gandhi's son, Rajiv Gandhi (1944–1991), was elected prime minister after her, and his handling of the thorny Sikh issue was generally applauded. Indications that he and Pakistan's prime minister Benazir Bhutto (1953–2007) might work together to resolve some Indian–Pakistani hostilities were also promising. But he was assassinated by a Sri Lankan Tamil suicide bomber in 1991.

Because no party won the subsequent national vote, the leader of the Congress Party, P. V. Narasimha Rao, was asked to form a government. He and the Congress managed to make substantial economic progress. In 1997, Vice President K. R. Narayanan, a former academic and foreign service officer, assumed the presidency. He and his party were displaced in 2004 by an unexpected Congress Party victory that brought Manmohan Singh, formerly finance minister (1991–1996) in as prime minister, a post he retained in the 2009 general elections.

India's problems continue to loom large. Poverty and disease remain serious. Separatist movements have pulled at the unity of the Indian state. Industrialization and agricultural modernization have recently made great strides, yet India's population is now at about 1 billion and growing at nearly 2 percent per year. New outbreaks of communal violence between Hindus and India's large Muslim minority threaten political stability. As the world's largest functioning democracy, India will be an important model of representative government and pluralistic society if it succeeds in staying together and reducing its harshest problems: overpopulation and mass poverty.

Hindu Militants. Hindu militants attack a Muslim mosque in Ayodhya, India, December 6, 1992. The razing of this mosque at the hands of a mob led by Hindu communalist extremists touched off a wave of Hindu–Muslim violence in India. The Hindus claimed the mosque, built some 500 years ago, occupied the site of what had originally been a Hindu temple and sought to have a new temple built once the mosque was cleared away.

Why have Hindus and Muslims been in conflict in India?

•••[Read the Document

Jawaharlal Nehru, "Why India Is Non-Aligned" (India), 1956 at **myhistorylab.com**

QUICK REVIEW

Nehru Dynasty

- Jawaharal Nehru (1889–1964): First prime minister of India
- Indira Gandhi (1917–1984): Daughter of Nehru, prime minister of India (1966–1977)
- Rajiv Gandhi (1944–1991): Son of Indira Gandhi, prime minister of India (1984–1989)

PAKISTAN AND BANGLADESH

The first president of Pakistan, Muhammad Ali Jinnah (1876–1948), oversaw the creation of a Muslim state comprising the widely separated East and West Pakistan in the two predominantly Muslim areas of northwest India and East Bengal. In 1971 East Pakistan seceded and became the new Islamic nation of Bangladesh.

Read the Document

Jinnah, the "Father" of Pakistan
at **myhistorylab.com**

Pakistan's groping efforts to create a fully Islamic society and to solve its massive economic problems have been hampered by periodic lapses into dictatorship. A military coup brought the military leader Zia ul-Haqq (1924–1988) to power in 1977. The elections of November 1988, following his death in a suspicious air crash, opened the door again to parliamentary rule, but Pakistan has not stabilized. Benazir Bhutto (1953–2007), the daughter of the man whom Zia ul-Haqq had overthrown and executed, was elected prime minister following Zia's death, becoming the first female leader of a major Islamic state in the twentieth century. But her time in office was cut short by the president's dismissal of her government in August 1990; she was elected again in 1993, only to be deposed on charges of corruption in 1996. The successor government did not last long; in 1999, General Parviz Musharraf took over as president until his resignation under increasing protest in 2008. Bhutto had tried the previous year to win back her post as prime minister, only to be assassinated in December 2007. Upon Musharraf's resignation the following summer, her husband, Asif Ali Zardari was elected president in September 2008.

Of all Central Asian governments, that of Pakistan has confronted the most direct challenge from radical Islam, and the presence of armed groups of Taliban or their sympathizers in west and northwest Pakistan continues to be a source of instability and threat for the governments of both Pakistan and Afghanistan. Whether Pakistan can achieve real stability remains an open question.

INDONESIA AND MALAYSIA

Indonesia was created in 1949 as a republic, succeeding the long Dutch and brief Japanese colonial dominions in the East Indies. As the largest Muslim country in the world (over 200 million of its people, or an estimated 88% of its population, are Muslim), Indonesia must determine how the Muslim religious faith is to be reconciled with secularist government.

The much smaller territory of Malaya received its independence from British colonial rule in 1957 as a federation under a rotating monarch; it was later joined by the states of Sarawak and Sabah in northern Borneo, forming the federation of Malaysia. The overriding problem for Malaysia (population 26 million) has been the cleft between the largely Chinese (24 percent) and partly Indian (7 percent) non-Muslim minority on the one hand, and the largely Muslim majority of Malay and other indigenous peoples (60 percent) on the other.

Both Indonesia and Malaysa have rich cultural traditions and natural resources; it remains to be seen how each will preserve them while meeting the demands of modern global politics and participation in the global economy. Not just the future of these two Asian states, but an important part of Islam's future as a global religiocultural tradition is at stake.

THE POSTCOLONIAL MIDDLE EAST

HOW DID the creation of the state of Israel affect the history of the modern Middle East?

POSTCOLONIAL ARAB NATIONS IN THE MIDDLE EAST

The modern Middle East arose from the fall of the Ottoman Empire and the intervention in the region by Western powers, which carved out new nations and protectorates. Egypt, Iraq, and Saudi Arabia became sovereign states after World War I; Lebanon and Syria were given independence by France during World War II. Subsequently, other

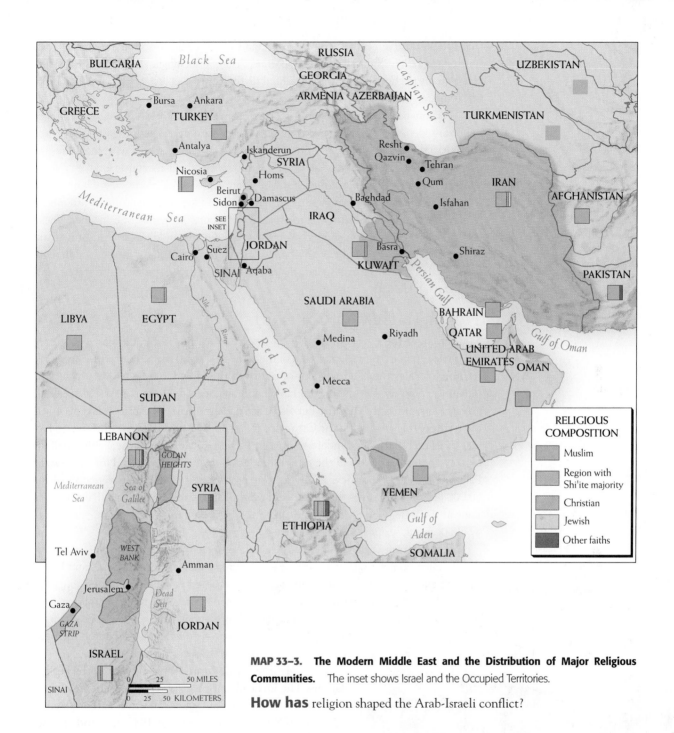

MAP 33–3. **The Modern Middle East and the Distribution of Major Religious Communities.** The inset shows Israel and the Occupied Territories.

How has religion shaped the Arab-Israeli conflict?

Arab states gained independence: Jordan, 1946; Libya, 1951; Morocco and Tunisia, 1956; Algeria, 1962; and, by 1971, Yemen, Oman, and the small Arabian/Persian Gulf sheikhdoms. (Palestine/Israel is a special case; see below.) (See Map 33–3.)

As elsewhere in the industrializing world, these states have sought political self-determination amidst political instability and autocratic rule. All share the classical Arabic written language, but the spoken colloquial language varies. Attempts to create pan-Arab alliances or federations have failed primarily because of regional differences and political interests, but appeals to Arab nationalism remain powerful.

In the wake of World War II, many of the leaders of Arab nationalism, such as Gamal Abdel Nasser of Egypt (1918–1970), were sympathetic to socialism or to the Soviet Union. Soviet-style communism, however, was so overtly secular and antireligious that it held little appeal to Arab, Turkish, and Iranian Muslims. Popular among both secular and religious middle-class supporters, "Islamic socialism" had gained considerable support in the 1980s until discredited by the contradictory actions of Arab, Turkish, Iranian, and Kurdish leaders.

Nationalism in the basic sense of "patriotism to the homeland" remains the most important ideology from Morocco to India. Arab governments, defining themselves according to the values of nationalism, have worked out arrangements with local Muslim authorities. For example, the Saudi royal family turned over its educational system to adherents of a rigorist, puritanical form of Islam called *Wahhabism* (see Chapter 26) while modernizing the country's infrastructure. The Egyptian government attempted to play different Islamic militant and professional groups off against one another. These governments retained the support of prosperous, devout middle-class Muslims while doing little about the plight of the poor. Consequently, for many in the Middle East today Arab nationalism and socialism are associated with deceptions, self-interest, and a failed Arab identity.

THE ARAB-ISRAELI CONFLICT

Nowhere have the effects of the West's interventions in the Middle East been more sharply felt than in the 1948 creation of the state of Israel in the former British mandate territory of Palestine. The concept of return to the Holy Land had a long history in Judaism. Under the Ottomans, the Holy Land had been the home of Arabic-speaking Palestinians, primarily Muslims, but also Christians and Jews. The British had occupied the territory since defeating the Ottomans in World War I; in 1923 they received a formal League of Nations Mandate to govern Palestine. Meanwhile the British Balfour Declaration of 1917 favored the establishment of a national homeland for the Jews in Palestine as long as "non-Jewish" rights were preserved. By 1920 there were only about 60,000 Jews and ten times that number of Muslim and Christian Arabs in Palestine. As some at the time, such as the American King-Crane Commission, foresaw, and events would bear out, serious trouble lay ahead.

⊙ ⊙ See the Map
The Partition of Palestine after World War II, 1948
at **myhistorylab.com**

The interwar years saw increasing Jewish settlement and growing communal conflict. Immigration of Jews, largely from eastern Europe, increased in the 1920s and 1930s. Britain's efforts to restrict it in 1936 tragically prevented many Jews from escaping the Nazi Holocaust. After the war, the Zionist movement received a tremendous boost from Jews worldwide who felt a desperate need for a homeland where they might be safe from future persecutions, and from Allied nations that felt the need to atone for the Holocaust by securing such a refuge.

In 1947, the British turned the issue over to the United Nations. The UN called for partition of the mandate territory into a Jewish and an Arab state. The Arab states refused to accept the UN resolution, but in May 1948, Jews in Palestine proclaimed the independent state of Israel. Egypt, Iraq, Jordan, Lebanon, Saudi Arabia, and Syria promptly attacked Israel but lost to the better-armed, better-trained, and more resolute Israelis. The Israeli-Arab war of 1948 to 1949 won the Jews not only the UN-proposed territory but also a substantial portion of that proposed for a Palestinian state.

Since 1948, nearly 75 percent of the Palestinians in the world have been refugees from their homeland. The United Nations has established 60 UN Relief and Works Agency (UNRWA) Palestinian refugee camps in Gaza, the West Bank, Jordan, Lebanon, Syria, and Egypt. Seven regional

Israeli Invasion of Gaza. Palestinian students view the ruins of the Islamic University in Gaza City, destroyed on December 29, 2008 during the 22-day offensive by Israel in Gaza.

Why has the peace process broken down?

wars and two Palestinian *Intifadahs* (uprisings: literally, "shaking off") have further swelled the ranks of refugees. Today, 4 million Palestinians live in diaspora from Turkey to Texas. The Palestinians understandably do not see why they should be displaced, either because of another people's historic religious attachment to the land or as reparation for Europe's sins against the Jews.

Since 1948 there has been, at best, an armed truce between Israel and its neighbors. Israel (with the support of the United States) has taken aggressive measures, often in defiance of world opinion and international law regarding **occupied territories**. The most serious military confrontations have been the Suez Crisis of 1956, when Israel (and briefly France and England) invaded the Sinai; the 1967 June war (the "Six Day War"), when Israel occupied the Sinai, the Golan Heights, and the West Bank (of the Jordan River); the October (Yom Kippur) war of 1973, when the Egyptians and Syrians staged a surprise attack on Israel; the Israeli invasions of Lebanon in 1978, 1982, and 2006 to extirpate anti-Israeli terrorist havens; and the 2009 Israeli invasion of Gaza.

Arab and some non-Arab states have been equally intransigent in refusing to recognize Israel's right to exist. Egypt was the first notable exception to this policy. Egypt's President Anwar Sadat (1918–1981) and Israel's prime minister Menachem Begin (1913–1994), with the mediation of U.S. President Jimmy Carter (b. 1924), reached an agreement—the Camp David Accords—in 1978 and in 1979 signed a formal peace treaty. Sadat was assassinated in 1981 by Egyptian Muslim extremists, but the treaty has held up.

In 1991, in the wake of the Gulf War that followed Iraq's invasion of Kuwait, the parties to the Arab-Israeli conflict began peace negotiations. The resulting 1993 Middle East Peace Agreement, also known as the Oslo Agreement, raised hopes for a negotiated settlement and the creation of an independent Palestinian state alongside the Jewish state of Israel. But there has been little substantive progress since then, as extremists on both sides have put up obstacles to peace.

Jordan and Egypt did agree in 1994 to a peace treaty with Israel, but many other Arab states—Syria foremost—have not been willing to negotiate with Israel, and Israel has continued to develop settlements and roads in ways that minimize the availability of contiguous territory with which to form a viable Palestinian state.

The Palestinian Authority created by the 1993 peace agreement, under the leadership of Yasser Arafat (1929–2004), grew steadily more corrupt, ineffective, and out of touch with its constituencies. Despite the efforts of the Palestinian and Israeli security forces, Palestinian guerrillas of the extremist wing of the resistance organization Hamas found ways to kill Israelis in a sustained effort to torpedo the already shaky **peace process**. These terrorist attacks led Israel to seal its borders, resulting in the additional loss of 11 percent of West Bank Palestinian farmlands, a source of livelihood for thousands of Arabs in the occupied territories who normally work in Israel proper. This has exacerbated Gaza's plight, in turn feeding the extremist resistance groups.

In March 2000, Ariel Sharon became Israel's prime minister. His administration was marked by an escalation of violence on both sides. Sharon proposed that Israel withdraw from Gaza and close Israeli settlements in that region, a proposal that proved controversial on both sides. His government erected a massive fence separating Israeli and Palestinian territory.

Arafat died in late 2004. His passing presented a new opportunity for negotiations with the Palestinians, now led

Intifadah
Literally, "shaking." Uprisings by the Palestinians against Israeli occupation.

occupied territories
Land occupied by Israel as a result of wars with its Arab neighbors in 1948–1949, 1967, and 1973.

Read the **Document**
Israel-PLO Declaration of Principles on Interim Self-Government Arrangements (1993) at **myhistorylab.com**

View the **Image**
Rabin and Arafat Shake Hands at the White House, 1993 at **myhistorylab.com**

peace process
Efforts, chiefly by the United States, to broker a peace between the State of Israel and the PLO.

Palestinian Rocket Attack. An Israeli surveys the damage in a school classroom caused by a Palestinian rocket on December 31, 2008, in Beer Sheva, Israel.

What new developments in world history can you imagine that might help facilitate peaceful coexistence between the Palestinians and the Israelis?

by Mahmoud Abbas, who was elected to the Palestinian presidency in January 2005. However, the virtual pullback of the United States in the later Bush administration from serious effort at bringing either Israelis or Palestinians back into negotiations meant that this opportunity was lost. With a new American administration since 2009, some increased efforts at a return to negotiation have been made, but in early 2010, the hardline Israeli leader, Binyamin Natanyahu, approved a new settlement in East Jerusalem, despite the opposition of the United States and world opinion. Meanwhile, neither Abbas nor anyone from any Palestinian faction seems able or willing to come seriously to the negotiating table even if Netanyahu were to change his antagonistic position.

Added to this bleak history and current struggle is the ugly legacy of hate instilled in many on both sides for decades. Arabs and even many Muslims outside the Arab world have come to label non-Israeli Jews, Israelis, and both religious and political Zionists as oppressors and enemies, making no distinctions among them. Many Israelis and many Jews around the world have similarly vilified all Arabs and Muslims. In some ways Arab-Israeli and Muslim-Jewish relations are at an all-time low, and it may require one or several generations to displace the prejudice, stereotyping, and hatred so long accumulated. The human crisis is far from over, even if peace were to arrive tomorrow.

MIDDLE EASTERN OIL

The oil wealth of the Arab and Iranian world has been both a blessing and a curse for the people and countries of the Middle East. World demand for oil has surged since the 1908 discovery of oil in Iran. In the mid-1970s, oil became a major bargaining chip in international diplomacy, one the Arab and other oil-rich Third World states—such as Venezuela, Nigeria, Iran, and Indonesia—have used to their advantage. In the Arab countries of North Africa and especially of Arabia and the Gulf, oil production and wealth have changed every aspect of life. Oil has propelled formerly peripheral countries into major roles in the world of international banking and finance. Oil has also boosted the self-confidence of the Arab world, damaged by a century and a half of European domination. Testimony to the global importance of Middle Eastern oil was the willingness of the United States and European nations to form a coalition with some Arab countries and commit massive forces to expel Iraq from Kuwait after Iraq's invasion of its neighbor in 1990.

⊙ See the Map
The Modern Middle East
at **myhistorylab.com**

Though the economic benefits of oil are obvious, this resource, as already noted, has not necessarily had political benefits for people in the Middle East. Oil has been the motivator for considerable foreign involvement in the Middle East. George W. Bush's invasion of Iraq in 2003 was arguably once again motivated in part by interest in Iraqi and Central Asian oil outlets.

THE RISE OF MILITANT ISLAMISM

The increase in the global importance of the oil-producing states of the Middle East has coincided with a surging movement there and elsewhere for the revival of pristine Muslim values and reformation of Muslim societies. Many Muslims have sought to return to the "fundamentals" of Islam, which they see as a means for rejuvenating societies corrupted by Western secularist and materialist values. A major new element in Muslim revivalism is a consciousness of being a viable response to the destructive influence of Western-style "modernity."

Such Muslim fundamentalism—or more correctly, "Islamist reformism"—motivated the overthrow of the shah of Iran in 1978, the Muslim Brethren movement in Egypt and elsewhere, and many other groups, from Morocco to the Persian Gulf and beyond the Middle East.

Much of the appeal of Islamist groups everywhere is their willingness and ability to address the needs of the underclasses. Where governments of Muslim-majority countries have failed to provide social services such as housing, medical care, education, and jobs, the Islamist groups have succeeded. Although the world press reports only on the relatively small fringe groups of Islamist extremists, Muslims at the grass-roots level have watched while the major Islamist groups in the dictatorships or military regimes under which most of them live provide services for which the state has long abdicated responsibility. Whether these movements will bring lasting change to Islamic societies is an open issue, but there is no question about their current attraction and influence.

THE MODERN MIDDLE EASTERN BACKGROUND

The background to modern Islamist reform lies in the European expansion over much of the globe in just a few centuries. This expansion brought far more social and political change than religious or cultural change to the Islamic world. It saw the emergence globally of European-style nationalism and the idea of the nation-state; of post-Enlightenment ideals of individual liberties, rights, and representative government; and of the concept of one's religious faith and affiliation as a strictly private, "religious" matter and one's citizenship as a public, "secular" matter. Such ideas proved disruptive in the Islamic world, especially in this century.

Parts of the Islamic world today have a checkered history of autocratic governments that are as far removed from their citizenries as any medieval or premodern dynasty. Experiments with European-style parliamentary government have only rarely taken hold; nor have either liberal democratic or Marxist-socialist ideals proven viable for the long term. Until recently, however, political discourse in Islamic lands has given little serious thought to *Islamic* alternatives.

The postcolonial independence of many national states divorced politics from Islamic religious traditions and norms. In the late twentieth and early twenty-first centuries, Islamic religious allegiance has commonly been invoked to bolster a ruler's claim to legitimacy and to cloak mundane objectives and programs in pious garb. The recent past has seen no realization of an "ideal" Islamic state in which religious authority and political authority are conjoined. Even in the postrevolutionary Islamic Republic of Iran a clear division exists between political realities and religious standards. Calls for a congruence of religion and politics trace less to some ideal model of a religious state or so-called **theocracy** than to a sorely felt need for simple social and political justice. The cries for a *jihad* of Muslims are aimed less often outward than inward, less at foreign "devils" and more at domestic tyrants, corruption, and social and economic injustice. The most international and widely influential of all contemporary Islamic revivalist or reform movements, the Tabligh-i Jama'at, is explicitly apolitical. It aims to convert the individual to true submission (*islam*), not lip service, on the principle that reform of the world begins with oneself.

As for those reform movements that are avowedly political, be they activist but nonviolent (the majority) or extremist and violent, they feed on the deep sense of socioeconomic and political injustice that citizens of most Islamic countries rightfully feel. When such feelings go over the edge, the result is extremism and terrorism. Osama bin Laden, the disposessed Saudi millionaire who founded and has led al-Qa'ida from the 1990s to the present, stunned the world by using U.S. civilian airliners to destroy the World Trade Center towers and part of the Pentagon building on September 11, 2001. His motive was revenge for the American military presence in Saudi Arabia, the American-led blockade of Iraq, and the American support of Israel against the Palestinians.

theocracy
A state ruled by religious leaders who claim to govern by divine authority.

These carefully executed and massively destructive attacks have involved the U.S. military ever more deeply in the Middle East and Central Asia. In October 2001, the United States attacked the Taliban government of Afghanistan, rapidly overthrew it, and dispersed—but did not destroy—al-Qa'ida's organization. Whether this military response to the threat of terrorism will be successful remains to be seen. Certainly the ongoing war on terrorism is radically changing the security needs of the United States. The U.S. military is transferring many of its troops and bases, previously located in western Europe and East Asia, closer to the Middle East. American troops will not soon leave this part of the world. Further United States intervention followed in 2003 with the invasion of Iraq.

IRAQ: INTERVENTION AND OCCUPATION

The modern nation of Iraq was established after World War I. Iraq as such had never been a distinct political unit and until 1921 was primarily a geographic term, referring to today's southern Iraq. Postwar imperial concern and the potential of oil under Iraqi soil motivated the British government to oversee the creation of an Iraq that they felt would best protect their interests in the region. Given the disparate ethnic and religious groups in the country, the British could not find a suitable native leader. They imported a politician from Arabia, Faysal ibn Husayn, and crowned him first king of the Hashemite monarchy. The dynasty ruled with British help until 1958.

Iraqis developed a sense of national identity that led them to resent the foreign presence in their country, and in 1958 a bloody coup, led by Abd al-Karim Qasem, terminated the monarchy. By 1979, the Ba'ath Party had become the dominant force in Iraq politics, bringing Saddam Hussein to the start of his tyrannical reign. Following a long, bloody, and unsuccessful war with Iran (1980–1988), Saddam Hussein invaded and occupied Kuwait (1990). After an international military coalition under the leadership of the United States expelled the Iraqi army from Kuwait in Operation Desert Storm, Iraq became an international pariah. It was subject to economic sanctions monitored by the United Nations until 1998, when the Iraqi government expelled the UN inspectors; the United Nations was unable to reinsert them for almost five years.

In the wake of the September 11, 2001, terrorist attacks the Bush administration decided that Saddam Hussein had to be overthrown to remove the threat of Iraqi weapons of mass destruction. During late 2002 and early 2003, the U.S. and British governments sought to obtain passage of the UN Security Council resolutions that would require Iraq to disarm on its own or to face disarmament by military force. When opposition from France and Russia blocked the resolution, Australia, Great Britain, and the United States, with more than forty other nations (the "Coalition of the Willing") invaded Iraq. After three weeks of fighting that began in mid-March 2003, the coalition removed Saddam Hussein from power. The announced goals of the invasion, in addition to toppling the Iraqi regime, were to destroy Iraq's capacity to manufacture or deploy weapons of mass destruction and to bring consensual government to the Iraqi people.

The invasion of Iraq occasioned considerable international opposition, most notably from France, Germany, and Russia, and provoked large antiwar demonstrations in the United States and other parts of the world. The war has created strains within the European Union and NATO and has begun a new era in international relations.

Currently, it remains difficult to ensure peace and stability in Iraq. Many Iraqis resisted the occupation by foreign forces, and historical factors militate against a unified government. The lack of preparation by the Americans and their allies for dealing with the chaos of postwar Iraq exacerbated matters. The complete failure to find weapons of mass destruction in Iraq led to wide questioning of the real rationale for the war. The

QUICK REVIEW

Iraq in the Early Twentieth Century

◆ Territory controlled by Britain after World War I

◆ Competing ethnic and religious groups

◆ Ruled by Arab Hashemite Dynasty, 1921–1958

•◆•–[Read the Document

Saddam Hussein's Invasion of Kuwait: (a) Saddam Hussein, "Victory Day" Speech; (b) Bishara A. Bahbah, "The Crisis in the Gulf: Why Iran Invaded Kuwait" at **myhistorylab.com** widespread destruction and suffering and the prolonged state of quasi-civil war that has only recently begun to diminish has left the American government open to criticism in the region and around the world.

Throughout Iraq an insurgency was launched against the Coalition forces and against Iraqis, particularly those in the security services, who had cooperated with the Coalition and the recently installed Iraqi government. In late January 2005, an election was held in Iraq under conditions of insurgent attacks to elect the Assembly that will write a new constitution. With voter turnout much higher than anticipated, the election succeeded. However, the challenges of securing internal support for the construction of democratic processes still confront the shaky Iraqi government and American policy makers. A "surge" policy increasing American troop presence in 2009 under U.S. President Obama seems to have helped internal stability somewhat, and the elections of 2010, while in dispute, seem as of March 2010 to hold promise of bringing a more democratic Iraqi government to power. Internal violence has not ended, but a 2009 American plan for phased withdrawal of American troops seems to have some possibility of success in the coming year or two.

Suicide Bomb Explosion, Iraq 2010. Iraqi civilians help rescue teams remove rubble at the site of a suicide bomb explosion that targeted a restaurant in the center of Baghdad. In 2010, suicide bombings continue to occur at an alarming rate, wounding and killing scores of civilians.

How is violence in Iraq transforming international relations?

SUMMARY

 WHAT ARE the two main developments that have occurred in the postcolonial world?

Beyond the Postcolonial Era. Since 1945, independent states have emerged from the European colonies of Africa and Asia. These states have had to adjust their political and economic relations first to the superpowers during the Cold War and, more recently, to the globalized economy and political structures. *page 867*

 WHERE IN Latin America did the major attempts to establish revolutionary governments occur?

Latin America since 1945. Most Latin American countries remain politically and economically dependent. Cuba was the only revolutionary movement to overturn the traditional structure of Latin American society, though socialist revolution was also attempted in Chile and Nicaragua. Despite social and economic problems, Argentina and Brazil have managed to move from military rule to stable democratic, civilian government. In Mexico, the PRI's long dominance ended in 2000. *page 869*

 WHAT ARE the most significant issues that Africa faces in the twenty-first century?

Postcolonial Africa. Independent Africa has faced arbitrary boundaries, disease, economic dependence, and political instability. While Nigeria has experienced ethnic and religious strife under a succession of military dictatorships, South Africa has emerged as a stable, multiethnic democracy. The challenge for Africa as a whole is to build a truly civil society and achieve economic health and political stability despite health, environmental, and other hurdles. *page 877*

 HOW HAS Islam affected politics in the developing world?

The Islamic Heartlands from North Africa to Indonesia. The vast area encompassing countries with large Muslim populations includes diverse national stories. Turkey straddles Europe and Central Asia geographically and culturally. India's politics have been significantly shaped by relations—generally antagonistic—with Muslim Pakistan. Indonesia has the world's largest population of Muslims. *page 882*

HOW DID the creation of the state of Israel affect the history of the modern Middle East?

The Postcolonial Middle East. Controversy surrounding the creation of the state of Israel has dominated the politics of the Middle East since the 1940s. Although efforts to negotiate an Israeli-Palestinian peace have sometimes progressed, the cycle of terror and retaliatory violence has persisted. Vast deposits of oil have made some Middle Eastern governments wealthy, yet they have not led to the creation of prosperous democratic societies. In the wake of the terrorist attacks of September 11, 2001, the United States overthrew Saddam Hussein in Iraq and became embroiled in a chaotic and unstable region of the world. *page 886*

KEY TERMS

apartheid (uh-PAHRT-heyed) (p. 878)

clash of civilizations (p. 869)

decolonization (p. 868)

globalization (p. 868)

HIV/AIDS (p. 881)

Intifadah **(IN-tuh-FAH-duh)** (p. 889)

liberation theology (p. 871)

occupied territories (p. 889)

peace process (p. 889)

Sandinistas (sahn-dihn-EES-tahs) (p. 873)

theocracy (p. 891)

Truth and Reconciliation Commission (TRC) (p. 879)

REVIEW QUESTIONS

1. Are the nations of Latin America still economically dependent on the United States and western Europe? If so, why? How did the superpower rivalry of the Cold War affect Latin America? How successful has the worldwide trend toward democratization been in Latin America? Describe the transition from military rule to civilian democracy in Brazil, Argentina, and Chile. Has Mexico made a similar transition?

2. What challenges did many newly independent states in Africa share? Has postcolonial Nigeria lived up to its potential? Why is Nigeria's record significant for Africa as a whole? Describe the apartheid regime in South Africa. Why was it dismantled in the 1990s? What problems does the Democratic Republic of the Congo face? What factors contributed to the 1994 genocide in Rwanda?

3. Compare and contrast the roles of social change, religion, and economics in Turkey, Iran, Pakistan, and Malaysia. How does the profound influence of Islam in this and other regions of the world suggest the power of religious tradition in modern politics and society?

4. What have been the major factors in the creation of the modern Middle East? How have interventions by European powers and the United States affected this region? Compare and contrast the roles of religion and nationalism in the Middle East.

5. Explain the origin and course of the Israeli-Palestinian conflict. What have been the major turning points? Have there been moments when the conflict might have reached a peaceful resolution?

6. Describe the origins and character of political and militant Islam. Why has it taken so radical a political course in the post–Iranian Revolution era (1979)? Why was the Soviet invasion of Afghanistan an important event in its development?

7. What is globalization? What are its costs and its benefits?

8. How has the legacy of European colonialism affected the Middle East, Asia, and Africa?

9. How and why was Iraq created? What influence does this early twentieth-century history have on current events in the region? What has happened in Iraq in the twenty-first century?

Note: To learn more about the topics in this chapter, please turn to the Suggested Readings at the end of the book. For additional sources related to this chapter please see www.myhistorylab.com

PEARSON

myhistorylab Connections

Reinforce what you learned in this chapter by studying the many documents, images, maps, review tools, and videos available at **www.myhistorylab.com**

Read and Review

✔•⌐Study and **Review** Chapter 33

••⌐Read the Document *Liberation Theology (1950s), p. 871*
Address before the Puebla Conference (1979), p. 871
Fidel Castro, History Will Absolve Me, 1953, p. 873
Juan Perón, excerpt from The Voice of Perón, p. 874
Brazil's Constitution of 1988, p. 874
Chico Mendes on the Rainforest (1980s), p. 875
Nelson Mandela, from Freedom, Justice and Dignity for All South Africa, p. 879
Alain Destexhe, excerpt from Rwanda and Genocide in the Twentieth Century, p. 880
Nelson Mandela, Closing Address at the 13th International AIDS Conference, July 200, p. 881
Jawaharlal Nehru, "Why India Is Non-Aligned" (India), 1956, p. 885
Jinnah, the "Father" of Pakistan, p. 886
Israel-PLO Declaration of Principles on Interim Self-Government Arrangements (1993), p. 889
Saddam Hussein's Invasion of Kuwait: (a) Saddam Hussein, "Victory Day" Speech; (b) Bishara A. Bahbah, "The Crisis in the Gulf: Why Iran Invaded Kuwait," p. 892

◉⌐See the Map *Africa, 2004, p. 878*
HIV Prevalence in Africa, p. 882
The Partition of Palestine after World War II, 1948, p. 888
The Modern Middle East, p. 890

●⌐View the Image *Voters Waiting to Vote in South Africa's First Open Election, 1994, p. 879*
Ayatollah Khomeini, p. 884
Rabin and Arafat Shake Hands at the White House, 1993, p. 889

((•⌐Hear the Audio *Decolonization 1, p. 868*

⌐Watch the Video *Creating Apartheid in South Africa, p. 878*

✔•⌐Study and Review
Soviet and Turkish Plans for Industrialization, p. 883
The Political Vision of Atatürk and Khomeini, p. 884

Research and Explore

◉⌐See the Map *Latin America, 2004, p. 875*

◉⌐See the Map *Map Discovery: Palestine*

((•⌐**Hear** the **Audio**

Hear the audio file for Chapter 33
at **www.myhistorylab.com**

Suggested Readings

Chapter 1

General Prehistory

P. Bogucki, The Origins of Human Society (1999). An excellent summary of recent scholarship on the earliest origins of human societies.

F. Bray, The Rice Economies: Technology and Development in Asian Societies (1986). Still the best authority on the origins of rice cultivation and its effect on the development of ancient Asia.

M. Ehrenberg, Women in Prehistory (1989). An account of the role of women in early times.

C. Freeman, Egypt, Greece and Rome: Civilizations of the Ancient Mediterranean (2004). Good comparative study of Egypt with Greece and Rome.

D.C. Johnson and M.R. Edey, Lucy: The Beginning of Mankind (1981). An account of the African origins of humans.

S.M. Nelson, ed., Ancient Queens: Archaeological Explorations (2003). Reassesses women rulers and female power in the ancient world.

S.M. Nelson and M. Rosen-Ayalon, In Pursuit of Gender: World-wide Archaeological Approaches (2002). Essays on gender and the archaeology of the ancient world.

D.L. Nichols and T.H. Charlton, eds., The Archaeology of City-States: Cross-cultural Approaches (1997). One of a growing body of books and essay collections employing cross-cultural and comparative approaches to world history and archaeology.

M. Oliphant, The Atlas of the Ancient World: Charting the Great Civilizations of the Past (1992). An excellent comprehensive atlas of the ancient world.

P.L. Shinnie, Ancient Nubia (1996). A study of the African state most influenced by Egyptian culture.

Near East

M.E. Auber, The Phoenicians and the West (1996). A new study of an important sea-going people who served as a conduit between East and West.

Ben-Tor, ed., The Archaeology of Ancient Israel (1992). A useful and up-to-date survey.

J. Bottéro, Everyday Life in Ancient Mesopotamia (2001). Interesting vignettes of ancient Mesopotamian life.

H. Crawford, Sumer and the Sumerians (1991). A discussion of the oldest Mesopotamian civilization.

I. Finkelstein and N.A. Silberman, The Bible Unearthed: Archaeology's New Vision of Ancient Israel and the Origin of Its Sacred Texts (2001). An interesting discussion of the insights of recent archaeological finds on the history of the Bible and ancient Israel.

G. Leick, Mesopotamia: The Invention of the City (2002). Good discussion of the urban history of ancient Mesopotamia.

J.N. Postgate, Early Mesopotamia (1992). An excellent study of Mesopotamian economy and society from the earliest times to about 1500 B.C.E., helpfully illustrated with drawings, photos, and translated documents.

D.B. Redford, Akhenaten (1987). A study of the controversial religious reformer.

W.F. Saggs, The Might That Was Assyria (1984). A history of the northern Mesopotamian Empire and a worthy companion to the author's account of the Babylonian Empire in the south.

M. Van de Mieroop, A History of the Ancient Near East, ca. 3000–323 B.C. (2004). An up-to-date comprehensive survey of ancient Near Eastern history.

India

D.P. Agrawal, The Archaeology of India (1982). A fine survey of the problems and data. Detailed, but with excellent summaries and brief discussions of major issues.

C. Chakraborty, Common Life in the Rigveda and Atharvaveda—An Account of the Folklore in the Vedic Period (1977). An interesting attempt to reconstruct everyday life in the Vedic period from the principal Vedic texts.

J.R. Mcintosh, A Peaceful Realm: The Rise and Fall of the Indus Civilization (2002). Discusses what archaeologists have managed to unearth so far regarding Harrapan civilization.

W.D. O'flaherty, The Rig Veda: An Anthology (1981). An excellent selection of Vedic texts in prosaic but very careful translation, with helpful notes on the texts.

J.E. Schwartzberg, ed., A Historical Atlas of South Asia (1978). The definitive reference work for historical geography. Includes chronological tables and substantive essays.

R. Thapar, Early India: From the Origins to A.D. 1300 (2003). A comprehensive introduction to the early history of India.

China

M. Loewe and E. Shaughnessy, eds., The Cambridge History of Ancient China: From the Origins of Civilization to 221 B.C. (1999). A comprehensive and authoritative history of ancient China.

K.C. Chang, The Archeology of Ancient China, 4th ed. (1986). The standard work on the subject.

K.C. Chang, Art, Myth, and Ritual: The Path to Political Authority in Ancient China (1984). A study of the relation between shamans, gods, agricultural production, and political authority during the Shang and Zhou dynasties.

N. Di Cosmo, Ancient China and Its Enemies: The Rise of Nomadic Power in East Asian History (2002). An excellent study of the relationship between China and nomadic peoples that was a powerful force in shaping Chinese and Central Asian history.

C.Y. Hsu, Western Chou Civilization (1988).

D.N. Keightley, The Origins of Chinese Civilization (1983).

M.E. Lewis, Sanctioned Violence in Early China (1990).

X.Q. Li, Eastern Zhou and Qin Civilizations (1986). Includes fresh interpretations based on archaeological finds.

Americas

R.L. Burger, Chavín and the Origins of Andean Civilization (1992). A lucid and detailed account of the rise of civilization in the Andes.

M.D. Coe and R. Koontz, Mexico: From the Olmecs to the Aztecs (2002). Good survey of ancient Mexico.

D. Drew, The Lost Chronicles of the Maya Kings (1999). Fine introduction to the history of Maya civilization.

V.W. Fitzhugh and A. Crowell, Crossroads of Continents: Cultures of Siberia and Alaska (1988). Covers the area where the immigration from Eurasia to the Americas began.

R. Ford, ed., Prehistoric Food Production in North America (1985). Examines the origins of agriculture in the Americas.

P.D. Hunt, Indian Agriculture in America: Prehistory to the Present (1987). Includes a discussion of preconquest agriculture.

A. Knight, Mexico: From the Beginning to the Spanish Conquest (2002). First of a three-volume comprehensive history of Mexico.

C. Morris and A. Von Hagen, The Inka Empire and Its Andean Origins (1993). An overview of Andean civilization with excellent illustrations.

M. Moseley, The Incas and Their Ancestors: The Archaeology of Ancient Peru (1992). An overview of Peruvian archaeology.

J.A. Sabloff, The New Archaeology and the Ancient Maya (1990). A lively account of recent research in Maya archaeology.

I. Silverblatt, Moon, Sun, and Witches: Gender Ideologies and Class in Inca and Colonial Peru (1987). A controversial but thought-provoking discussion of Incan ideas about gender.

Chapter 2

China

R. Bernstein, Ultimate Journey: Retracing the Path of an Ancient Buddhist Monk Who Crossed Asia in Search of Enlightenment (2001). Discusses the diffusion of Buddhism from India to China.

H.G. Creel, What Is Taoism? And Other Studies in Chinese Cultural History (1970).

W.T. de Bary et al., Sources of Chinese Tradition (1960). A reader in China's philosophical and historical literature. It should be consulted for the later periods as well as for the Zhou.

H. Fingarette, Confucius—The Secular as Sacred (1998).

Y.L. Fung, A Short History of Chinese Philosophy, ed. by D. Bodde (1948). A survey of Chinese philosophy from its origins down to recent times.

A. Graham, Disputers of the Tao (1989).

D. Hawkes, Ch'u Tz'u: The Songs of the South (1985).

D.C. Lau, trans., Lao-tzu, Tao Te Ching (1963).

D.C. Lau, trans., Confucius, The Analects (1979).

C. Li, ed., The Sage and the Second Sex: Confucianism, Ethics, and Gender (2000). A good introduction to gender and ethics in Confucian thought.

B.I. Schwartz, The World of Thought in Ancient China (1985).

A. Waley, Three Ways of Thought in Ancient China (1956). An easy yet sound introduction to Confucianism, Daoism, and Legalism.

A. Waley, The Book of Songs (1960).

B. Watson, trans., Basic Writings of Mo Tzu, Hsun Tzu, and Han Fei Tzu (1963).

B. Watson, trans., The Complete Works of Chuang Tzu (1968).

H. Welch, Taoism, The Parting of the Way (1967).

India

A.L. Basham, The Wonder That Was India, rev. ed. (1963). Still unsurpassed by more recent works. Chapter VII, "Religion," is a superb introduction to the Vedic Aryan, Brahmanic, Hindu, Jain, and Buddhist traditions of thought.

W.N. Brown, Man in the Universe: Some Continuities in Indian Thought (1970). A penetrating yet brief reflective summary of major patterns in Indian thinking.

W.T. de Bary et al., Sources of Indian Tradition (1958). 2 vols. Vol. I, From the Beginning to 1800, ed. and rev. by Ainslie T. Embree (1988). Excellent selections from a variety of Indian texts, with good introductions to chapters and individual selections.

P. Harvey, An Introduction to Buddhism (1990). Chapters 1–3 provide an excellent historical introduction.

T.J. Hopkins, The Hindu Religious Tradition (1971). A first-rate, thoughtful introduction to Hindu religious ideas and practice.

K. Klostermaier, Hinduism: A Short History (2000). A relatively compact survey of the history of Hinduism.

J.M. Koller, The Indian Way (1982). A useful, wide-ranging handbook of Indian thought and religion.

R.H. Robinson and W.L. Johnson, The Buddhist Religion, 3rd ed. (1982). An excellent first text on the Buddhist tradition, its thought and development.

R.C. Zaehner, Hinduism (1966). One of the best general introductions to central Indian religious and philosophical ideas.

Israel

A. Bach, ed., Women in the Hebrew Bible: A Reader (1999). Excellent introduction to the ways in which biblical scholars are exploring the role of women in the Bible.

Bright, A History of Israel (1968), 2nd ed. (1972). One of the standard scholarly introductions to biblical history and literature.

W.D. Davies and L. Finkelstein, eds., The Cambridge History of Judaism. Vol. I, Introduction: The Persian Period (1984). Excellent essays on diverse aspects of the exilic period and later.

J. Neusner, The Way of Torah: An Introduction to Judaism (1979). A sensitive introduction to the Judaic tradition and faith.

The Oxford History of the Biblical World, M. D. Coogan, ed. (1998).

Greece

The Cambridge Companion to Greek and Roman Philosophy, D. Sedley ed. (2003).

G.B. Kerferd, The Sophistic Movement (1981). An excellent description and analysis.

J. Lear, Aristotle: The Desire to Understand (1988). A brilliant yet comprehensible introduction to the work of the philosopher.

T.E. Rihil, Greek Science (1999). Good survey of Greek science incorporating recent reseach on the topic.

J.M. Robinson, An Introduction to Early Greek Philosophy (1968). A valuable collection of the main fragments and ancient testimony to the works of the early philosophers, with excellent commentary.

G. Vlastos, The Philosophy of Socrates (1971). A splendid collection of essays illuminating the problems presented by this remarkable man.

G. Vlastos, Platonic Studies, 2nd ed. (1981). A similar collection on the philosophy of Plato.

G. Vlastos, Socrates, Ironist and Moral Philosopher (1991). The results of a lifetime of study by the leading interpreter of Socrates in our time.

Comparative Studies

(Increasingly, world historians are looking at ancient civilizations in relationship to each other rather than as isolated entities to try to understand commonalities and differences in social and cultural development.)

W. Doniger, Splitting the Difference: Gender and Myth in Ancient Greece and India (1999).

G.E.R. Lloyd, The Ambitions of Curiosity: Understanding the World in Ancient Greece and China (2002).

G.E.R. Lloyd, The Way and the Word: Science and Medicine in Early China and Greece (2002).

T. McEvilley, The Shape of Ancient Thought: Comparative Studies of Greek and Indian Philosophies (2002).

Chapter 3

The Rise of Greek Civilization

P. Cartledge, The Spartans (2003). A readable account of this enigmatic people.

J. Chadwick, The Mycenaean World (1976). A readable account by a man who helped decipher Mycenaean writing.

R. Drews, The Coming of the Greeks (1988). A fine discussion of the Greeks' arrival as part of the movements of the Indo-European peoples.

J.V. Fine, The Ancient Greeks (1983). An excellent survey that discusses historical problems and the evidence that gives rise to them.

M.I. Finley, World of Odysseus, rev. ed. (1965). A fascinating attempt to reconstruct Homeric society.

P. Green, Xerxes at Salamis (1970). A lively and stimulating history of the Persian War.

D. Hamel, Trying Neaira (2003). A lively account of the events surrounding a famous jury trial that sheds interesting light on Athenian society in the fourth century B.C.E.

V.D. Hanson, The Western Way of War (1989). A brilliant and lively discussion of the rise and character of the hoplite phalanx and its influence on Greek society.

V.D. Hanson, The Other Greeks (1995). A revolutionary account of the Greek invention of the family farm and its centrality for the shaping of the polis.

D. Kagan, The Great Dialogue: A History of Greek Political Thought from Homer to Polybius (1965). A discussion of the relationship between the Greek historical experience and political theory.

W.K. Lacey, The Family in Ancient Greece (1984).

J.F. Lazenby, The Defense of Greece, 490–479 B.C. (1993). A new and valuable study of the Persian Wars.

J.F. McGlew, Tyranny and Political Culture in Ancient Greece (1993). A recent account of political developments in the Archaic period.

S.G. Miller, Ancient Greek Athletics (2004). The most complete and most useful account of the subject.

O. Murray, Early Greece (1980). A lively and imaginative account of the early history of Greece to the end of the Persian War.

A.M. Snodgrass, The Dark Age of Greece (1972). A good examination of the archaeological evidence.

B.S. Strauss, The Battle of Salamis: The Naval Encounter That Saved Greece and Western Civilization (2004). A lively account of the major naval battle of the Persian Wars and its setting.

A.G. Woodhead, Greeks in the West (1962). An account of the Greek settlements in Italy and Sicily.

W.J. Woodhouse, Solon the Liberator (1965). A discussion of the great Athenian reformer.

Classical and Hellenistic Greece

W. Burkert, Greek Religion (1987). An excellent study by an outstanding student of the subject.

J.R. Lane Fox, Alexander the Great (1973). An imaginative account that does more than the usual justice to the Persian side of the problem.

Y. Garlan, Slavery in Ancient Greece (1988). An up-to-date survey.

P. Green, Alexander to Actium: The Historical Evolution of the Hellenistic Age (1990). A remarkable synthesis of political and cultural history.

C.D. Hamilton, Agesilaus and the Failure of Spartan Hegemony (1991). An excellent biography of the king who was the central figure in Sparta during its domination in the fourth century B.C.E.

N.G.L. Hammond, Philip of Macedon (1994). A new biography of the founder of the Macedonian Empire.

N.G.L. Hammond and G.T. Griffith, A History of Macedonia, Vol. 2, 550–336 B.C. (1979). A thorough account of Macedonian history that focuses on the careers of Philip and Alexander.

R. Just, Women in Athenian Law and Life (1988). An account of women's place in Athenian society.

D. Kagan, The Peloponnesian War (2003). A narrative history of the war.

B.M.W. Knox, The Heroic Temper: Studies in Sophoclean Tragedy (1964). A brilliant analysis of tragic heroism.

D.M. Lewis, Sparta and Persia (1977). A valuable discussion of relations between Sparta and Persia in the fifth and fourth centuries B.C.E.

A.A. Long, Hellenistic Philosophy: Stoics, Epicureans, Sceptics (1974). An account of Greek science in the Hellenistic and Roman periods.

R. Meiggs, The Athenian Empire (1972). A fine study of the rise and fall of the empire, making excellent use of inscriptions.

J.J. Pollitt, Art and Experience in Classical Greece (1972). A scholarly and entertaining study of the relationship between art and history in classical Greece, with excellent illustrations.

J.J. Pollitt, Art in the Hellenistic Age (1986). An extraordinary analysis that places the art in its historical and intellectual context.

E.W. Robinson, Ancient Greek Democracy (2004). A stimulating collection of ancient sources and modern interpretations.

D.M. Schaps, Economic Rights of Women in Ancient Greece (1981).

B.S. Strauss, Athens after the Peloponnesian War (1987). An excellent discussion of Athens' recovery and of the nature of Athenian society and politics in the fourth century B.C.E.

B.S. Strauss, Fathers and Sons in Athens (1993). An unusual synthesis of social, political, and intellectual history.

V. Tcherikover, Hellenistic Civilization and the Jews (1970). A fine study of the impact of Hellenism on the Jews.

G. Vlastos, Socrates, Ironist and Moral Philosopher (1991). The results of a lifetime of study by the leading interpreter of Socrates in our time.

Chapter 4

Iran

M. Boyce, Zoroastrians: Their Religious Beliefs and Practices (1979). A detailed survey by the current authority on Zoroastrian religious history, organized historically and based on extensive research. See Chapters 7–9.

M. Boyce, ed. and trans., Textual Sources for the Study of Zoroastrianism (1984). Well-translated selections from a broad range of ancient Iranian materials and an important introduction that includes Boyce's arguments for a revision of the dates of Zoroaster's life (to between 1400 and 1200 B.C.E.).

J.M. Cook, The Persian Empire (1983). Survey of the Achaemenid period.

J. Curtis, Ancient Persia (1989). Excellent portfolio of photographs of artifacts and sites, with a clear historical survey of the arts and culture of ancient Iran.

W.D. Davies and L. Finklestein, ed., The Cambridge History of Judaism, Vol. 1, Introduction; "The Persian Period." Good articles on Iran and Iranian religion as well as Judaism.

J. Duchesne-Guillemin, trans., The Hymns of Zarathushtra, trans. by M. Henning (1952, 1963). The best short introduction to the original texts of the Zoroastrian hymns.

R.N. Frye, The Heritage of Persia (1963, 1966). A first-rate survey of Iranian history to Islamic times: readable but scholarly. Chapter 6 deals with the Sasanid era.

R. Ghirshman, Iran (1954). Good material on culture, society, and economy as well as politics and history.

R. Ghirshman, Persian Art: The Parthian and Sasanid Dynasties (1962). Superb photographs, and a very helpful glossary of places and names. The text is minimal.

W.W. Malandra, trans. and ed., An Introduction to Ancient Iranian Religion: Readings from the Avesta and Achaemenid Inscriptions (1983). Helpful especially for texts of inscriptions relevant to religion.

Geo Widengran, Mani and Manichaeism (1965). Still the standard introduction to Mani's life and the later spread and development of Manichaeism.

India

A.L. Basham, The Wonder That Was India, rev. ed. (1963). Excellent material on Mauryan religion, society, culture, and history.

A.L. Basham, ed., A Cultural History of India (1975). A fine collection of historical-survey essays by a variety of scholars. See Part I, "The Ancient Heritage" (Chapters 2–16).

N.N. Bhattacharyya, Ancient Indian History and Civilization: Trends and Perspectives (1988). Covers Mauryan and Gupta times as well as earlier periods, with chapters on political systems, cities and villages, ideology and religion, and art.

W.T. de Bary et al., comp., Sources of Indian Tradition, 2nd ed. (1958). Vol. I: From the Beginning to 1800, ed. and rev. by Ainslie T. Embree (1988). Excellent selections from a wide variety of Indian texts, with good introductions to chapters and selections.

S. Dutt, Buddhist Monks and Monasteries of India (1962). The standard work. See especially Chapters 3 ("Bhakti") and 4 ("Monasteries under the Gupta Kings").

D.G. Mandelbaum, Society in India (1972). 2 vols. The first two chapters in Volume I of this study of caste, family, and village relations are a good introduction to the caste system.

B. Rowland, The Art and Architecture of India: Buddhist/ Hindu/Jain, 3rd rev. ed. (1970). The standard work, lucid and easy to read. Note Part Three, "Romano-Indian Art in North-West India and Central Asia." See also the excellent chapters on Sungan, Andhran, and other early Buddhist art (6–8, 14), the Gupta period (15), and the Hindu Renaissance (17–19).

V.A. Smith, ed., The Oxford History of India, 4th rev. ed. by Percival Spear et al. (1981), pp. 71–163. A dry, occasionally dated historical survey. Includes useful reference chronologies. See especially pp. 164–229 (the Gupta period and following era to the Muslim invasions).

R. Thapar, A History of India, Part I (1966), pp. 50–108. Three chapters that provide a basic survey of the period.

R. Thapar, Ashoka and the Decline of the Mauryans (1973). The standard treatment of Ashoka's reign. Three chapters cover the rise of mercantilism, the Gupta "classical pattern," and the southern dynasties to ca. 900 C.E.

S. Wolpert, A New History of India, 2nd ed. (1982). A basic survey history. Chapters 5 and 6 cover the Mauryans, Guptas, and Kushans.

P. Younger, Introduction to Indian Religious Thought (1972). A sensitive attempt to delineate classical concerns of Indian religious thought and culture.

Greek and Asian Dynasties

A.K. Narain, The Indo-Greeks (1957. Reprinted with corrections, 1962). The most comprehensive account of the complex history of the various kings and kingdoms.

F.E. Peters, The Harvest of Hellenism (1970), pp. 222–308. Helpful chapters on Greek rulers of the Eastern world from Seleucus to the last Indo-Greeks.

J.W. Sedlar, India and the Greek World: A Study in the Transmission of Culture (1980). A basic work that provides a good overview.

D. Sinor, ed., The Cambridge History of Early Inner Asia (1990). See especially Chapters 6 and 7.

Chapter 5

R. Bates, V.Y. Mudimbe, and Jean O'Barr, eds., Africa and the Disciplines (1993). Explores how knowledge of Africa has shaped various fields of scholarship. The essay on history by Steven Feierman is particularly relevant to this chapter.

P. Bohannan and P. Curtin, Africa and Africans, rev. ed. (1995). An enjoyable and enlightening discussion of African history and prehistory and of major African institutions (e.g., arts, family life, religion).

R. Bulliet, The Camel and the Wheel (1990). Explains why the camel was chosen over the wheel as a means of transport in the Sahara.

P. Curtin, On the Fringes of History: A Memoir (2005). An engaging autobiography by one of the pioneers in African Studies in the United States; explores what it means to be a historian in the modern world.

P. Curtin, S. Feiermann, L. Thompson, and J. Vansina, African History, rev. ed . (1995). The classic survey history, written by four of the leaders in the field.

T.R.H. Davenport and Christopher Saunders, South Africa: A Modern History, rev. ed. (2000). A comprehensive survey, beginning with coverage of prehistoric southern Africa, the Khoisan peoples, and the Bantu migrations.

B. Davidson, Africa in History, rev. ed. (1995). A sweeping history of the diverse parts of Africa, emphasizing cultural exchange within the continent and beyond.

C.A. Diop, Precolonial Black Africa (1988). A seminal work by the pioneering Afrocentric scholar; his conclusions are controversial, but his writings are always provocative.

P.A. Ebron, Performing Africa (2002). Analyzes the role of performance in the creation and global circulation of African history and identity.

P. Garlake, Early Art and Architecture of Africa (2002). Highlights the diversity and sophistication of early African art and discusses the social context in which it was created.

E. Gilbert and J. Reynolds, Africa in World History, 2nd ed. (2008). The best new survey of African history, placing it in a global context. In conversational prose, the authors attend to environmental factors in African history and emphasize the roles of Western bias in shaping what we now know (and think we know) about Africa.

J. Iliffe, Africans: The History of a Continent (1995). A thematic survey of African history, from the paleontological record to the end of apartheid, with a focus on environment and demography.

E. Isichei, A History of Christianity in Africa: From Antiquity to the Present (1995). An amazing survey of Christianity's role on the African continent, from the time of Christ through European missionaries to the present popularity of Christian faith.

R. Oliver, The African Experience (1991). A masterly, balanced, and engaging sweep through African history.

I. Van Sertima, Black Women in Antiquity, rev. ed. (1988). From Lucy to Hatshepsut and beyond, essays explore the role and status of women in African societies of the past.

L. White et al., eds., African Words, African Voices: Critical Practices in Oral History (2001). A lively group of essays offer various perspectives on the uses of oral history in African research.

Chapter 6

From Republic to Empire

R. Baumann, Women and Politics in Ancient Rome (1995). A study of the role of women in Roman public life.

A.H. Bernstein, Tiberius Sempronius Gracchus: Tradition and Apostasy (1978). A new interpretation of Tiberius's place in Roman politics.

T.J. Cornell, The Beginnings of Rome: Italy and Rome from the Bronze Age to the Punic Wars, c. 1000–264 B.C. (1995). A consideration of the royal and early republican periods of Roman history.

T. Cornell and J. Matthews, Atlas of the Roman World (1982). Much more than the title indicates, this book presents a comprehensive view of the Roman world in its physical and cultural setting.

J-M. David, The Roman Conquest of Italy (1997). A good analysis of how Rome united Italy.

A. Goldsworthy, Roman Warfare (2002). A good military history of Rome.

A. Goldsworthy, In the Name of Rome: The Men Who Won the Roman Empire (2004). The story of Rome's greatest generals in the republican and imperial periods.

E.S. Gruen, Diaspora: Jews amidst Greeks and Romans (2002). A fine study of Jews in the Hellenistic and Roman world.

E.S. Gruen, The Hellenistic World and the Coming of Rome (1984). A new interpretation of Rome's conquest of the eastern Mediterranean.

W.V. Harris, War and Imperialism in Republican Rome, 327–70 B.C. (1975). An analysis of Roman attitudes and intentions concerning imperial expansion and war.

A. Keaveney, Rome and the Unification of Italy (1988). The story of how Rome organized its defeated opponents.

S. Lancel, Carthage, A History (1995). Includes a good account of Rome's dealings with Carthage.

J.F. Lazenby, Hannibal's War: A Military History of the Second Punic War (1978). A careful and thorough account.

F.G.B. Millar, The Crowd in Rome in the Late Republic (1999). A challenge to the view that only aristocrats counted in the late republic.

M. Pallottino, The Etruscans, 6th ed. (1974). Makes especially good use of archaeological evidence.

H.H. Scullard, A History of the Roman World, 753–146 B.C., 4th ed. (1980). An unusually fine narrative history with useful critical notes.

G. Williams, The Nature of Roman Poetry (1970). An unusually graceful and perceptive literary study.

Imperial Rome

W. Ball, Rome in the East: The Transformation of an Empire (2001). A thorough account of the influence of the East on Roman history.

T. Barnes, The New Empire of Diocletian and Constantine (1982).

K.R. Bradley, Slavery and Society at Rome (1994). A study of the role of slaves in Roman life.

P. Brown, The Rise of Western Christendom: Triumph and Diversity, 200–1000 (1996). A vivid picture of the spread of Christianity by a master of the field.

A. Ferrill, The Fall of the Roman Empire, The Military Explanation (1986). An interpretation that emphasizes the decline in the quality of the Roman army.

K. Galinsky, Augustan Culture (1996). A work that integrates art, literature, and politics.

A.H.M. Jones, The Later Roman Empire, 3 vols. (1964). A comprehensive study of the period.

D. Kagan, ed., The End of the Roman Empire: Decline or Transformation? 3rd ed. (1992). A collection of essays discussing the problem of the decline and fall of the Roman Empire.

J.E. Lendon, Empire of Honor, The Art of Government in the Roman World (1997). An original and path-breaking interpretation.

E.N. Luttwak, The Grand Strategy of the Roman Empire (1976). An original and fascinating analysis by a keen student of modern strategy.

R. MacMullen, Roman Social Relations, 50 B.C. to A.D. 284 (1981).

R. MacMullen, Corruption and the Decline of Rome (1988). A study that examines the importance of changes in ethical ideas and behavior.

R.W. Mathison, Roman Aristocrats in Barbarian Gaul: Strategies for Survival (1993). An unusual slant on the late empire.

J.F. Matthews, Laying Down the Law: A Study of the Theodosian Code (2000). A study of the importance of Roman law as a source for the understanding of Roman history and civilization.

W.A. Meeks, The Origins of Christian Morality: The First Two Centuries. An account of the shaping of Christianity in the Roman Empire.

F. Millar, The Emperor in the Roman World, 31 B.C.–A.D. 337 (1977). A study of Roman imperial government.

F. Millar, The Roman Empire and Its Neighbors, 2nd ed. (1981).

H.M.D. Parker, A History of the Roman World from A.D. 138 to 337 (1969). A good survey.

M.I. Rostovtzeff, Social and Economic History of the Roman Empire, 2nd ed. (1957). A masterpiece whose main thesis has been much disputed.

V. Rudich, Political Dissidence under Nero: The Price of Dissimulation (1993). A brilliant exposition of the lives and thoughts of political dissidents in the early empire.

E.T. Salmon, A History of the Roman World, 30 B.C. to A.D. 138 (1968). A good survey.

R. Syme, The Roman Revolution (1960). A brilliant study of Augustus, his supporters, and their rise to power.

R. Syme, The Augustan Aristocracy (1985). An examination of the new ruling class shaped by Augustus.

L.A. Thompson, Romans and Blacks (1989).

Chapter 7

D. Bodde, China's First Unifier (1938). A study of the Qin unification of China, viewed through the Legalist philosopher and statesman Li Si.

T.T. Ch'u, Law and Society in Traditional China (1961). Treats the sweep of Chinese history from 202 B.C.E. to 1911 C.E.

T.T. Ch'u, Han Social Structure (1972).

A. Cotterell, The First Emperor of China (1981). A study of the first Qin emperor.

R. Coulborn, Feudalism in History (1965). One chapter interestingly compares the quasi feudalism of the Zhou with that of the Six Dynasties period.

J.K. Fairbank, E.O. Reischauer, and A.M. Craig, East Asia: Tradition and Transformation (1989). A fairly detailed single-volume history covering China, Japan, and other countries in East Asia from antiquity to recent times.

J. Gernet, A History of Chinese Civilization (1982). A survey of Chinese history.

D.A. Graff and R. Higham, A Military History of China (2002).

C.Y. Hsu, Ancient China in Transition (1965). On social mobility during the Eastern Zhou era.

C.Y. Hsu, Han Agriculture (1980). A study of the agrarian economy of China during the Han Dynasty.

J. Levi, The Chinese Emperor (1987). A novel about the first Qin emperor based on scholarly sources.

M. Loewe, Everyday Life in Early Imperial China (1968). A social history of the Han Dynasty.

J. Needham, The Shorter Science and Civilization in China (1978). An abridgment of the multivolume work on the same subject with the same title—minus Shorter—by the same author.

S. Owen, ed., and Trans., An Anthology of Chinese Literature: Beginnings to 1911 (1996).

I. Robinet, Taoism: Growth of a Religion (1987).

M. Sullivan, The Arts of China (1967). An excellent survey history of Chinese art.

D. Twitchett and M. Loewe, eds., The Ch'in and Han Empires, 221 B.C.E.–C.E. 220 (1986). Vol. 1 of The Cambridge History of China.

Z. S. Wang, Han Civilization (1982).

B. Watson, Ssu-ma Ch'ien, Grand Historian of China (1958). A study of China's premier historian.

B. Watson, Records of the Grand Historian of China, Vols. 1 and 2 (1961). Selections from the Shiji by Sima Qian.

B. Watson, The Columbia Book of Chinese Poetry (1986).

F. Wood, The Silk Road: Two Thousand Years in the Heart of Asia (2003). A lively narrative combined with photographs and paintings.

A. Wright, Buddhism in Chinese History (1959).

Y.S. Yu, Trade and Expansion in Han China (1967). A study of economic relations between the Chinese and their neighbors.

Chapter 8

General

P. Bol, This Culture of Ours (1992). An insightful intellectual history of the Tang through the Song dynasties.

J. Cahill, Chinese Painting (1960). An excellent survey.

J.K. Fairbank and M. Goldman, China: A New History (1998). The summation of a lifetime engagement with Chinese history.

F.A. Kierman Jr., and J.K. Fairbank, eds., Chinese Ways in Warfare (1974). Chapters by different authors on the Chinese military experience from the Zhou to the Ming.

Sui and Tang

P.B. Ebrey, The Aristocratic Families of Early Imperial China (1978).

D. McMullen, State and Scholars in T'ang China (1988).

S. Owen, The Great Age of Chinese Poetry: The High T'ang (1980).

S. Owen, trans. and ed., An Anthology of Chinese Literature: Beginnings to 1911 (1996).

E.G. Pulleyblank, The Background of the Rebellion of An Lu-shan (1955). A study of the 755 rebellion that weakened the central authority of the Tang Dynasty.

E.O. Reischauer, Ennin's Travels in T'ang China (1955). China as seen through the eyes of a ninth-century Japanese Marco Polo.

E.H. Schafer, The Golden Peaches of Samarkand (1963). A study of Tang imagery.

So. Teiser, The Ghost Festival in Medieval China (1988). On Tang popular religion.

D. Twitchett, ed., The Cambridge History of China, Vol. III: Sui and T'ang China, 589–906 Part 1 (1979).

G. W. Wang, The Structure of Power in North China during the Five Dynasties (1963). A study of the interim period between the Tang and the Song dynasties.

A. F. Wright, The Sui Dynasty (1978).

Song

B. Birge, Women, Property, and Confucian Reaction in Song and Yuan China (960–1366) (2002). The rights of women to property—whether in the form of dowries or inheritances—were considerable during the Song but declined thereafter.

C.S. Chang and J. Smythe, South China in the Twelfth Century (1981). China as seen through the eyes of a twelfth-century Chinese poet, historian, and statesman.

E.L. Davis, Society and the Supernatural in Song China (2001).

J.W. Haeger, ed., Crisis and Prosperity in Song China (1975).

R. Hymes, Statesmen and Gentlemen (1987). On the transformation of officials into a local gentry elite during the twelfth and thirteenth centuries.

R. Hymes, Way and Byway: Taoism, Local Religion, and Models of Divinity in Sung and Modern China (2002).

M. Rossabi, China among Equals (1983). A study of the Liao, Qin, and Song empires and their relations.

W.M. Tu, Confucian Thought, Selfhood as Creative Transformation (1985).

K. Yoshikawa, An Introduction to Song Poetry, trans. by B. Watson (1967).

Yuan

T.T. Allsen, Mongol Imperialism (1987).

J.W. Dardess, Conquerors and Confucians: Aspects of Political Change in Late Yuan China (1973).

I. de Rachewiltz, Trans., The Secret History of the Mongols: A Mongolian Epic Chronicle of the Thirteenth Century (2003). A new translation of a key historical work on the life of Genghis.

H. Franke and D. Twitchett, eds., The Cambridge History of China, Vol. VI: Alien Regimes and Border States, 710–1368 (1994).

J.D. Langlois, China under Mongol Rule (1981).

R.Latham, trans., Travels of Marco Polo (1958).

H.D. Martin, The Rise of Chingis Khan and His Conquest of North China (1981).

D. Morgan, The Mongol Empire and Its Legacy (1999). Genghis, the several khanates, and the aftermath of empire.

P. Ratchnevsky, Genghis Khan, His Life and Legacy (1992). The rise to power of the Mongol leader, with a critical consideration of historical sources.

Chapter 9

M. Adolphson, The Gates of Power: Monks, Courtiers, and Warriors in Premodern Japan (2000). A new interpretation stressing the importance of temples in the political life of Heian and Kamakura Japan.

B.L. Batten, To the Ends of Japan: Premodern Frontiers, Boundaries, and Interactions. (2003). An interesting treatment of Heian Japan, topic by topic.

C. Blacker, The Catalpa Bow (1975). An insightful study of folk Shinto.

R. Borgen, Sugawara no Michizane and the Early Heian Court (1986). A study of a famous courtier and poet.

D.M. Brown, ed., The Cambridge History of Japan: Ancient Japan (1993). This series of six volumes sums up several decades of research on Japan.

D. Brown and E. Ishida, eds., The Future and the Past (1979). A translation of a history of Japan written in 1219.

The Cambridge History of Japan, D.M. Brown, ed.; Vol. 1, Ancient Japan, W. McCullough and D. H. Shively eds; Vol. 2, Heian Japan, K. Yamamura, ed. Vol. 3, Medieval Japan. Fine multi-author works.

M. Collcutt, Five Mountains (1980). A study of the monastic organization of medieval Zen.

T.D. Conlon, State of War: The Violent Order of Fourteenth Century Japan (2003). Compare Conlon's account with those of Souyri and Friday.

W.T. DeBary, D. Keene, G. Tanabe, and P. Varley, Comps., Sources of Japanese Tradition, 2nd ed. (2001).

P. Duus, Feudalism in Japan (1969). An easy survey of the subject.

W.W. Farris, Population, Disease, and Land in Early Japan, 645–900 (1985). An innovative reinterpretation of early history.

W.W. Farris, Heavenly Warriors: The Evolution of Japan's Military, 500–1300 (1992).

W.W. Farris, Sacred Texts and Buried Treasures (1998). Studies of Japan's prehistory and early history, based on recent Japanese research.

K.F. Friday, Samurai, Warfare and the State in Early Medieval Japan (2004). Weapons and warfare in Japan from the tenth to fourteenth centuries.

A.E. Goble, Go-Daigo's Revolution (1996). A provoking account of the 1331 revolt by an emperor who thought emperors should rule.

J.W. Hall, Government and Local Power in Japan, 500–1700: A Study Based on Bizen Province (1966). A splendid and insightful book.

J.W. Hall and T. Toyoda, Japan in the Muromachi Age (1977). Another collection of essays.

D. Keene, ed., Anthology of Japanese Literature from the Earliest Era to the Mid-Nineteenth Century (1955).

D. Keene, ed., Twenty Plays of the Nō Theatre (1970).

T. Lamarre, Uncovering Heian Japan: An Archeology of Sensation and Inscription (2000). The "archeology" in the title refers to digging into literature.

I.H. Levy, The Ten Thousand Leaves (1981). A fine translation of Japan's earliest collection of poetry.

J.P. Mass and W. Hauser, eds., The Bakufu in Japanese History (1985). Topics in Bakufu history from the twelfth to the nineteenth centuries.

I. Morris, trans., The Pillow Book of Sei Shōnagon (1967). Observations about the Heian court life by the Jane Austen of ancient Japan.

S. Murasaki, The Tale of Genji comparison of this translation with those of E. Seidensticker and R. Tyler.

S. Murasaki, The Tale of Genji, trans. by E.G. Seidensticker (1976). The world's first novel and the greatest work of Japanese fiction.

R.J. Pearson et al., eds., Windows on the Japanese Past: Studies in Archaeology and Prehistory (1986).

D.L. Philippi, trans., Kojiki (1968). Japan's ancient myths.

J. Piggot, The Emergence of Japanese Kingship (1997).

E.O. Reischauer, Ennin's Diary, the Record of a Pilgrimage to China in Search of the Law and Ennin's Travels in T'ang China (1955).

E.O. Reischauer and A.M. Craig, Japan: Tradition and Transformation (1989). A more detailed work covering the sweep of Japanese history from the early beginnings through the 1980s.

H. Sato, Legends of the Samurai (1995). Excerpts from various tales and writings.

D.H. Shively and W.H. McCullough, eds., The Cambridge History of Japan: Heian Japan (1999).

D.T. Suzuki, Zen and Japanese Culture (1959).

H. Tonomura, Community and Commerce in Late Medieval Japan (1992).

R. Tsunoda, W.T. de Bary, and D. Keene, comps., Sources of the Japanese Tradition (1958). A collection of original religious, political, and philosophical writings from each period of Japanese history. The best reader. A new edition was published in 2005.

H.P. Varley, Imperial Restoration in Medieval Japan (1971). A study of the 1331 attempt by an emperor to restore imperial power.

A. Waley, trans., The Nō Plays of Japan (1957). Medieval dramas.

K. Yamamura, ed., Cambridge History of Japan: Medieval Japan (1990).

Chapter 10

O. Grabar, The Formation of Islamic Art (1973). A critical and creative interpretation of major themes in the development of distinctively Islamic forms of art and architecture.

A. Hourani, A History of the Arab Peoples (1991). A masterly survey of the Arabs down through the centuries and a clear picture of many aspects of Islamic history and culture that extend beyond the Arab world.

H. Kennedy, The Prophet and the Age of the Caliphates: The Islamic Near East from the Sixth to the Eleventh Century (1986). The best survey of early Islamic history.

I. Lapidus, A History of Islamic Societies (1988). A comprehensive overview of the rise and development of Islam all over the world.

F.E. Peters, Muhammad and the Origins of Islam (1994). A balanced analysis of the life of Muhammad.

F. Rahman, Major Themes of the Qur'an (1980). The best introduction to the basic ideas of the Qur'an and Islam, seen through the eyes of a perceptive Muslim modernist scholar.

F. Schuon, Understanding Islam (1994). Compares the Islamic worldview with Catholic Christianity. A dense, but intellectually stimulating, discussion.

M. Sells, Approaching the Qur'an. The Early Revelations (1999). A fine introduction and new translations of some of the more common earlier Qur'anic revelations.

B. Stowasser, Women in the Qur'an, Traditions and Interpretation (1994). An outstanding systematic study of statements regarding women in the Qur'an.

Chapter 11

K. Armstrong, Muhammad: A Biography of the Prophet (1992). Strong on religion.

R. Bartlett, The Making of Europe, 950–1350 (1992). A study of the way immigration and colonial conquest shaped the Europe we know.

M. Bloch, Feudal Society, Vols. 1 and 2, trans. by L. A. Manyon (1971). A classic on the topic and as an example of historical study.

C.B. Brown, Singing the Gospel: Lutheran Hymns and the Success of the Reformation (2005). Outstanding study of Luther's hymns for children.

C.M. Brand, Byzantium Confronts the West, 1180–1204 (1968). Analyzes the internal and external pressures that Byzantium experienced during this quarter-century time period.

P. Brown, Augustine of Hippo: A Biography (1967). Late antiquity seen through the biography of its greatest Christian thinker.

J.H. Burns, The Cambridge History of Medieval Political Thought c. 350–c. 1450 (1991). The best scan.

R.H.C. Davis, A History of Medieval Europe: From Constantine to St. Louis (1972). Unsurpassed in clarity.

N.M. El-Cheikh, Byzantium Viewed by the Arabs (2004). Examines the Arabic-Islamic view of Byzantium.

R. Fletcher, The Barbarian Conversion: From Paganism to Christianity (1998). Up-to-date survey.

J.B. Glubb, The Great Arab Conquests (1995). Jihadists.

G. Guglielmo, ed., The Byzantines (1997). Updates key issues.

D. Gutas, Greek Thought, Arabic Culture (1998). A comparative intellectual history.

G. Holmes, ed., The Oxford History of Medieval Europe (1992). Overviews of Roman and northern Europe during the "Dark Ages."

B.J. Kaplan, Divided by Faith: Religious Conflict and the Practice of Toleration in Early Modern Europe (2007). How the Reformation created religious toleration and sowed the seeds of religious pluralism.

B. Lewis, The Middle East: A Brief History of the Last 2,000 Years (1995).

A.E. Laiou and H. Maguire, eds., Byzantium, a World Civilization (1992). Examines the centrality of Byzantium's role in world history.

C. Mango, Byzantium: The Empire of New Rome (1980).

J. Martin, Medieval Russia 980–1584 (1995). A concise narrative history.

R. Mckitterick, ed., Carolingian Culture: Emulation and Innovation (1994). Fresh essays.

J.J. Norwich, Byzantium: The Decline and Fall (1995).

J.J. Norwich, Byzantium: The Apogee (1997). The whole story in two volulmes.

G. Ostrogorsky, History of the Byzantine State (1999). Traces the thousand-year course of the Byzantine Empire.

R.I. Page, Chronicles of the Vikings: Records, Memorials, and Myths (1995). Sources galore.

F. Robinson, ed., The Cambridge Illustrated History of the Islamic World (1996). Spectacular.

S. Runciman, Byzantine Civilization (1970). Succinct, comprehensive account by a master.

P. Sawyer, The Age of the Vikings (1962). Old but solid account.

C. Stephenson, Medieval Feudalism (1969). Excellent short summary and introduction.

L. White Jr., Medieval Technology and Social Change (1962). Often fascinating account of how primitive technology changed life.

D. Whitford, Reformation and Early Modern Europe: A Guide to Research (2008). A goldmine of information on all aspects of the Reformation.

H. Wolfram, The Roman Empire and Its Germanic Peoples (1997). Challenging, but most rewarding.

Chapter 12

The Islamic Heartlands

L. Ahmed, Women and Gender in Islam: Historical Roots of a Modern Debate (1992). A good historical survey of the status of women in Middle Eastern societies.

J. Berkey, The Formation of Islam: Religion and Society in the Near East, 600–1800 (2002). An interesting new synthesis focusing on political and religious trends.

C.E. Bosworth, The Islamic Dynasties: A Chronological and Genealogical Handbook (1967). A handy reference work for dynasties and families important to Islamic history in all periods and places.

M.A. Cook, Commanding Right and Forbidding Wrong in Islamic Thought (2001). A masterful analysis of the development of Islamic law.

P.K. Hitti, History of the Arabs, 8th ed. (1964). Still a useful English resource, largely for factual detail. See especially Part IV, "The Arabs in Europe: Spain and Sicily."

A. Hourani, A History of the Arab Peoples (1991). The newest survey history and the best, at least for the Arab Islamic world.

S.K. Jayyusi, ed., The Legacy of Muslim Spain, 2 vols. (1994). A comprehensive survey of the arts, politics, literature, and society by experts in various fields.

B. Lewis, ed., Islam and the Arab World (1976). A large-format, heavily illustrated volume with many excellent articles on diverse aspects of Islamic (not simply Arab, as the misleading title indicates) civilization through the premodern period.

D. Morgan, The Mongols (1986). A recent and readable survey history.

J.J. Saunders, A History of Medieval Islam (1965). A brief and simple, if sketchy, introductory survey of Islamic history to the Mongol invasions.

India

W.T. de Bary et al., comp., Sources of Indian Tradition, 2nd ed. (1958), Vol. I, From the Beginning to 1800, ed. and rev. by Ainslie T. Embree (1988). Excellent selections from a wide variety of Indian texts, with good introductions to chapters and individual selections.

S.M. Ikram, Muslim Civilization in India (1964). The best short survey history, covering the period 711 to 1857.

R.C. Majumdar, gen. ed., The History and Culture of the Indian People, Vol. VI, The Delhi Sultanate, 3rd ed. (1980). A comprehensive political and cultural account of the period in India.

F. Robinson, ed., The Cambridge History of India, Pakistan, Bangladesh, Sri Lanka, Nepal, Bhutan, and the Maldives (1989). A very helpful quick reference source with brief but well-done survey essays on a wide range of topics relevant to South Asian history down to the present.

A. Wink, Al-Hind: The Making of the Indo-Islamic World, Vol. 1 (1991). The first of five promising volumes to be devoted to the Indo-Islamic world's history. This volume treats the seventh to eleventh centuries.

Southeast Asia

L. Andaya, The World of Maluku: Eastern Indonesia in the Early Modern Period (1993). A comprehensive view of the formation of what is now Indonesia.

B.W. Andaya and L. Andaya, A History of Malaysia (1982). A good overview of Indonesia's smaller but critical northern neighbor.

J. Siegel, Shadow and Sound: The Historical Thought of a Sumatran People (1979). An excellent analysis tracing the relation between foreign influences and local practice.

Chapter 13

B.S. Bauer, The Development of the Inca State (1992). Emphasizes archaeological evidence over the Spanish chronicles in accounting for the emergence of the Inca Empire.

B.S. Bauer, Ancient Cuzco: Heartland of the Inca (2004). Exploration of the ramifications of late-twentieth-century archaeological explorations of the ancient Inca capital

K.O. Bruhns, Ancient South America (1994). A clear discussion of the archaeology and civilization of the region with emphasis on the Andes.

E. M. Brumfiel, The Aztec World (2008). A well-illustrated work.

R.L. Burger, Chavín and the Origins of Andean Civilization (1992). A detailed study of early Andean prehistory by one of the leading authorities on Chavín.

R. L. Burger, Machu Picchu: Unveiling the Mystery of the Incas (2008). The best study of this famous site.

I. Clendinnen, Aztecs: An Interpretation (1995). A classic exploration of the Aztec world.

B. Cobo and R. Hamilton, History of the Inca Empire, rev. ed. (1983). A seventeenth-century account, with a modern translation and interpretation.

M.D. Coe, Breaking the Maya Code (1992). The story of the remarkable achievement of deciphering the ancient Mayalanguage.

M.D. Coe, Mexico from the Olmecs to the Aztecs (2008). A wide-ranging introductory discussion.

G. Conrad and A.A. Demarest, Religion and Empire: The Dynamics of Aztec and Inca Expansionism (1984). An interesting comparative study.

T. N. D'Altroy, The Incas (2004). A major study of all aspects of Inca civilization

A. Demarest, Ancient Maya: The Rise and Fall of a Rainforest Civilization (2004). Lively and engaged in recent scholarly debates.

S. T. Evans, Ancient Mexico & Central America: Archaeology and Culture History (2008). Now the best wide-ranging introduction.

S. Freidel, L. Schele, and J. Parker, Maya Cosmos: Three Thousand Years on the Shaman's Path (1995). The best account of the subject.

S.D. Gillespie, The Aztec Kings (1989).

R. Hassig, Aztec Warfare: Imperial Expansion and Political Control (1995). Explores the achievement of the Aztec Empire.

J. Hyslop, Inka Settlement Planning (1990). A detailed study.

M. León-Portilla, Fifteen Poets of the Aztec World (1992). An anthology of translations of Aztec poetry.

G. M. McEwan, The Incas: New Perspectives (2006). An excellent overview with fine reading lists for further exploration.

H. McKillop, The Ancient May: New Perspectives (2004). Clear presentations of recent research and debates.

M.E. Miller, The Art of Mesoamerica from Olmec to Aztec (2006). Most recent edition of a pioneering work.

C. Morris and A. Von Hagen, The Inka Empire and Its Andean Origins (1993). A clear overview of Andean prehistory by a leading authority. Beautifully illustrated.

M.E. Mosely, The Incas and Their Ancestors: The Archaeology of Peru (2001). Readable and thorough.

J.A. Sabloff, The Cities of Ancient Mexico (1989). Capsule summaries of ancient Mesoamerican cultures.

L. Schele and M.E. Miller, The Blood of Kings (1986). A rich and beautifully illustrated study of ancient Maya art and society.

H. Silverman, Andean Archaeology (2004). Overview of various Andean peoples.

M.E. Smith, The Aztecs (2002). Emphasizes impact of late-twentieth-century archaeological research.

R. Stone-Miller, Art of the Andes: From Chavin to Inca (2002). A well-illustrated overview.

Chapter 14

J. Abun-Nasr, A History of the Maghrib in the Islamic Period (1987). The most recent North African survey. Pages 59–247 are relevant to this chapter.

E.K. Akyeampyong, ed., Themes in West Africa's History (2006). A wide-ranging collection of essays by leading scholars.

I. Battuta, N. King, and S. Hamdun, Ibn Battuta in Black Africa, rev. ed. (2005). Well-selected excerpts from Battuta's extensive journals.

P. Ben-Amos, Art, Innovation and Politics in Eighteenth-Century Benin (1999). Offers insights into the many levels of meaning and authority in Benin's artworks.

I. Berger, E.F. White, and C. Skidmore-Hess, Women in Sub-Saharan Africa: Restoring Women to History (1999). A valuable resource on the role of women in African history.

D. Birmingham, Central Africa to 1870 (1981). Chapters from the Cambridge History of Africa that give a brief, lucid overview of developments in this region.

P. Bohannan and P. Curtin, Africa and Africans, rev. ed. (1995). Accessible, topical approach to African history, culture, society, politics, and economics.

P.D. Curtin, S. Feiermann, L. Thompson, and J. Vansina, African History, rev. ed. (1995). An older, but masterly survey. The relevant portions are Chapters 6–9.

B. Davidson, West Africa before the Colonial Era (1998). A typically readable survey by one of the great popularizers of African history.

R. Elphick, Kraal and Castle: Khoikhoi and the Founding of White South Africa (1977). An incisive, informative interpretation of the history of the Khoikhoi and their fateful interaction with European colonization.

R. Elphick and H. Giliomee, The Shaping of South African Society, 1652–1820 (1979). A superb, synthetic history of this crucial period.

J.D. Fage, A History of Africa, rev. ed., (2001). Still a readable survey history.

E. Gilbert and J. Reynolds, Africa in World History, 2nd ed. (2008). The best new survey of African history, placing it in a global context. See especially Chapters 6 and 7 on Islam, and Chapters 8 through 12 for the period leading to European colonization.

M. Hiskett, The Development of Islam in West Africa (1984). The standard survey study of the subject. Of the relevant sections (Chapters 1–10, 12, 15), that on Hausaland, which is treated only in passing in this text, is noteworthy.

M. Horton and J. Middleton, The Swahili (2000).

R.W. July, A History of the African People, 3rd ed. (1980). Chapters 3–6 treat Africa before about 1800 area by area; Chapter 7 deals with "The Coming of Europe."

N. Levtzion and R. Pouwels, eds. History of Islam in Africa (2000). A wide-ranging collection of essays.

N. Levtzion and D.T. Niani, eds., Africa from the Twelfth to the Sixteenth Century, UNESCO General History of Africa, Vol. IV (1984). Many survey articles cover the various regions and major states of Africa in the centuries noted in the title.

R. Oliver, The African Experience (1991). A masterly, balanced, and engaging survey, with outstanding syntheses and summaries of recent research.

C.A. Quinn and F. Quinn, Pride, Faith, and Fear: Islam in Sub-Saharan Africa (2005). A readable account of Islam in Africa, bringing the story almost to the present.

D. Robinson, Muslim Societies in African History (2004). A comprehensive overview.

A.F.C. Ryder, Benin and the Europeans: 1485–1897 (1969). A basic study.

John K. Thornton, The Kingdom of Kongo: Civil War and Transition, 1641–1718 (1983). A detailed and perceptive analysis for those who wish to delve into Kongo state and society in the seventeenth century.

M. Wilson and L. Thompson, eds., The Oxford History of South Africa, Vol. I., South Africa to 1870 (1969). Relatively detailed, if occasionally dated, treatment.

Chapter 15

M. Brecht, Martin Luther: His Road to Reformation, 1483–1521 (1985). Best on young Luther.

C. Brown et al., Rembrandt: The Master and His Workshop (1991). A great master's art and influence.

R. Briggs, Witches and Neighbors: A History of European Witchcraft (1996). A readable introduction.

E. Duffy, The Stripping of the Altars (1992). Strongest argument yet that there was no deep Reformation in England.

H.O. Evennett, The Spirit of the Counter Reformation (1968). The continuity and independence of Catholic reform.

Hans-Jürgen Goertz, The Anabaptists (1996). Best treatment of minority Protestants.

O.P. Grell and A. Cunningham, Health Care and Poor Relief in Protestant Europe (1997). The civic side of the Reformation.

M. Holt, The French Wars of Religion, 1562–1629 (1995). Scholarly appreciation of religious side of the story.

J.C. Hutchison, Albrecht Durer (1990). The life behind the art.

H. Jedin, A History of the Council of Trent, Vols. 1, 2 (1957–1961). Comprehensive, detailed, and authoritative.

M. Kitchen, The Cambridge Illustrated History of Germany (1996). Comprehensive and accessible.

A. Kors and E. Peters, eds., European Witchcraft, 1100–1700 (1972). Classics of witch belief.

W. Maccaffrey, Elizabeth I (1993). Magisterial study.

G. Mattingly, The Armada (1959). A masterpiece, novel-like in style.

D. Mcculloch, The Reformation (2004). No stone unturned, with English emphasis.

H.A. Oberman, Luther: Man between God and Devil (1989). Authoritative biography.

J.W. O'Malley, The First Jesuits (1993). Extremely detailed account of the creation of the Society of Jesus and its original purposes.

S. Ozment, The Age of Reform, 1250–1550: An Intellectual and Religious History of Late Medieval and Reformation Europe (1980). Broad, lucid survey.

S. Ozment, When Fathers Ruled: Family Life in Reformation Europe (1983). Effort to portray the constructive side of Protestant thinking about family relationships.

S. Ozment, The Bürgermeister's Daughter: Scandal in a Sixteenth-Century German Town (1996). What a woman could do at law in the sixteenth century.

G. Parker, The Thirty Years' War (1984). Large, lucid survey.

J.H. Parry, The Age of Reconnaissance (1964). A comprehensive account of explorations from 1450 to 1650.

W. Prinz, Durer (1998). Latest biography of Germany's greatest painter.

J.J. Scarisbrick, Henry VIII (1968). The best account of Henry's reign.

G. Strauss, ed. and trans., Manifestations of Discontent in Germany on the Eve of the Reformation (1971). A rich collection of sources for both rural and urban scenes.

H. Wunder, He Is the Sun, She Is the Moon: Women in Early Modern Germany (1998). Best study of early modern women.

Chapter 16

J. Abun-Nasr, A History of the Maghrib in the Islamic Period (1987). The essential North African survey. Pages 59–247 are relevant to this chapter.

D. Birminham, Central Africa to 1870 (1981). Chapters from the Cambridge History of Africa that give a brief, lucid overview of developments in this region.

P. Bohannan and P. Curtin, Africa and Africans, rev. ed. (1971). Accessible, topical approach to African history, culture, society, politics, and economics.

P.D. Curtin, S. Feiermann, L. Thompson, and J. Vansina, African History (1978). An older, but masterly survey. The relevant portions are Chapters 6–9.

R. Elphick, Kraal and Castle: Khoikhoi and the Founding of White South Africa (1977). An incisive, informative interpretation of the history of the Khoikhoi and their fateful interaction with European colonization.

R. Elphick and H. Giliomee, The Shaping of South African Society, 1652–1820 (1979). A superb, synthetic history of this crucial period.

J.D. Fage, A History of Africa (1978). Still a readable survey history.

M. Hiskett, The Development of Islam in West Africa (1984). The standard survey study of the subject. Of the relevant sections (Chapters 1–10, 12, 15), that on Hausaland, which is treated only in passing in this text, is noteworthy.

R.W. July, Precolonial Africa: An Economic and Social History (1975). Chapter 10 gives an interesting overall picture of slaving in African history.

R.W. July, A History of the African People, 3rd ed. (1980). Chapters 3–6 treat Africa before about 1800 area by area; Chapter 7 deals with "The Coming of Europe."

I.M. Lewis, ed., Islam in Tropical Africa (1966), pp. 4–96. Lewis's introduction is one of the best brief summaries of the role of Islam in West Africa and the Sudan.

D.T. Niani, ed., Africa from the Twelfth to the Sixteenth Century, UNESCO General History of Africa, Vol. IV (1984). Many survey articles cover the various regions and major states of Africa in the centuries noted in the title.

R. Oliver, The African Experience (1991). A masterly, balanced, and engaging survey, with outstanding syntheses and summaries of recent research.

J.A. Rawley, The Transatlantic Slave Trade: A History (1981). Impressively documented, detailed, and well-presented survey history of the Atlantic trade; little focus on African dimensions.

A.F.C. Ryder, Benin and the Europeans: 1485–1897 (1969). A basic study.

John K. Thornton, The Kingdom of Kongo: Civil War and Transition, 1641–1718 (1983). A detailed and perceptive analysis for those who wish to delve into Kongo state and society in the seventeenth century.

M. Wilson and L. Thompson, eds., The Oxford History of South Africa, Vol. I., South Africa to 1870 (1969). Relatively detailed, if occasionally dated, treatment.

Chapter 17

R. Adorno, The Polemics of Possession in Spanish American Narrative (2008). An exploration of the rhetoric used by the Spanish to assure their holding of their American empire.

A.C. Bailey, African Voices of the Atlantic Slave Trade: Beyond the Silence and the Shame (2006). Delivers just what the title promises.

B. Bailyn, Atlantic History: Concepts and Contours (2005). An essential overview to this burgeoning area of historical inquiry, written by a leader in the field.

I. Berlin, Many Thousands Gone: The First Two Centuries of Slavery in North America (1998); Generations of Captivity: A History of African American Slaves (2003). Two volumes representing the most extensive and important recent treatment of slavery in North America; highlights the diversity of slave experiences.

R. Blackburn, The Making of New World Slavery from the Baroque to the Modern 1492–1800 (1997). An extraordinary work.

V. Carretta, Equiano, the African: The Biography of a Self-Made Man (reprint 2007). Provides context and analysis of the renowned accounts of one-time slave Olaudah Equiano.

N.D. Cook, Born to Die: Disease and New World Conquest, 1492–1650 (1998). A survey of the devastating impact of previously unknown diseases on the native populations of the Americas.

M.S. Creighton and L. Norling, eds. Iron Men, Wooden Women: Gender and Seafaring in the Atlantic World, 1700–1920 (2006). Eye-opening accounts of life at sea, and how gender roles were shaped and challenged on the Atlantic.

P.D. Curtin, The Atlantic Slave Trade: A Census (1969). Remains a basic work.

P.D. Curtin, The Rise and Fall of the Plantation Complex (1998). Places the plantation economy in the context of world history.

D.B. Davis, Inhuman Bondage: The Rise and Fall of Slavery in the New World (2006). A splendid overview by a leading scholar.

J.H. Elliot, Empires of the Atlantic World: Britain and Spain in America 1492–1830 (2006). A brilliant, accessible comparative history.

D. Eltis, The Rise of African Slavery in the Americas (1999). Detailed discussion of the size and scope of the Atlantic market, with attention to the role of Africans on both sides of the Atlantic.

H.L. Gates Jr. and W.L. Andrews, eds., Pioneers of the Black Atlantic: Five Slave Narratives from the Enlightenment, 1772–1815 (1998). An anthology of autobiographical accounts.

S. Gruzinski, The Conquest of Mexico: The Incorporation of Indian Societies into the Western World, 16th–18th Centuries (1993). Interprets the experience of Native Americans, from their own point of view, during the time of the Spanish conquest.

L. Hanke, All Mankind Is One: A Study of the Disputation between Bartolome De Las Casas and Juan Gines De Sepulveda in 1550 on the Intellectual and Religious (1994). A study of the Spanish debate over the humanity of Native Americans in the Spanish Empire.

R. Harms, The Diligent: A Voyage through the Worlds of the Slave Trade (2002). A powerful narrative of the voyage of a French slave trader.

J. Hemming, The Conquest of the Incas, rev. ed., (2003). A lucid account of the conquest of the Inca Empire and its aftermath.

J. Hemming, Red Gold: The Conquest of the Brazilian Native Americans, 1500–1760 (1978). A careful account with excellent bibliography.

H. Kamen, Empire: How Spain Became a World Power, 1492–1763 (2005). An excellent overview by a major scholar.

H. Klein, The Atlantic Slave Trade (1999). A synthesis of scholarly knowledge.

W. Klooster and A. Padula, The Atlantic World: Essays on Slavery, Migration, and Imagination (2004). Essays by leading scholars examine important aspects of the creation of a new way of living—and a new way of thinking about the world.

P.E. Lovejoy, Transformations in Slavery: A History of Slavery in Africa (2000). An important new evaluation of slavery as it was practiced within Africa, and its relation to the Islamic and transatlantic slave trades.

K. Macquarrie, The Last Days of the Incas (2007). A fast-moving popular account.

K. Mann, Rethinking the African Diaspora: The Making of a Black Atlantic World in the Bight of Benin and Brazil (2005). This analysis of the dynamics of human and cultural migration and exchange on the busiest route of the slave trade is a significant addition to Atlantic World scholarship.

P. Manning, Slavery and African Life: Occidental, Oriental, and African Slave Trades (1990). An admirably concise economic-historical synthesis of the evidence, with multiple tables and statistics to supplement the magisterial analysis.

A. Pagden, Lords of All the World: Ideologies of Empire in Spain, Britain, and France c. 1500–c. 1800 (1995). An effort to explain the imperial thinking of the major European powers.

S. Peabody and K. Grinberg, Slavery, Freedom, and the Law in the Atlantic World: A Brief History with Documents (2007). Examines the legal frameworks through which slavery was institutionalized, and documents the many ways people challenged slavery.

M. Rediker, The Slave Ship: A Human History (2007). A exploration of the harrowing experience of slave transportation across the Atlantic.

M. Rediker, Villains of all Nations: Atlantic Pirates in the Golden Age (2008). A serious historical treatment of the subject.

D.K. Richter, Facing East from Indian Country: A Native History of Early America, new ed. (2003). Uses the biographies of three Native Americans to offer a fresh perspective on North American history from the time of Columbus to the American Revolution.

M. Russell, Seven Myths of the Spanish Conquest (2003). Challenges many long-held views of the event.

S.B. Schwartz, All Can Be Saved: Religious Tolerance and Salvation in the Iberian Atlantic World (2009). The most important recent study of the social and religious life of the Spanish Empire.

S.B. Schwartz, ed., Tropical Babylons: Sugar and the Making of the Atlantic World, 1450–1680 (2003). A comprehensive examination of the role of sugar in the plantation economy.

S.E. Smallwood, Saltwater Slavery: A Middle Passage from Africa to American Diaspora (2008). An intimate examination of the experience and economy of the slave trade.

H. Thomas, Conquest: Montezuma, Cortés, and the Fall of Old Mexico (1993). A splendid modern narrative of the event, with careful attention to the character of the participants.

J. Thornton, Africa and Africans in the Making of the Atlantic World, 1400–1680 (1992). A discussion of the role of Africans in the emergence of the transatlantic economy.

N. Wachtel, The Vision of the Vanquished: The Spanish Conquest of Peru through Indian Eyes, 1530–1570 (1977). A presentation of the Incan experience of conquest.

C.A. Williams, Bridging the Early Modern Atlantic World (2009). Explores the cultural and ethnic diversity of the transatlantic economy.

Chapter 18

China

D. Bodde and C. Morris, Law in Imperial China (1967). Focuses on the Qing Dynasty (1644–1911).

T. Brook, The Confusions of Pleasure: Commerce and Culture in Ming China (1988).

C.S. Chang and S.L.H. Chang, Crisis and Transformation in Seventeenth-century China: Society, Culture, and Modernity (1992).

P. Crossley, Translucent Mirror: History and Identity in Qing Imperial Ideology (1999).

W.T. De Bary, Learning for One's Self: Essays on the Individual in Neo-Confucian Thought (1991). A useful corrective to the view that Confucianism is simply a social ideology.

M.C. Elliott, The Manchu Way: The Eight Banners and Ethnic Identity in Late Imperial China (2001). The latest word; compare to Crossley above.

M. Elvin, The Pattern of the Chinese Past: A Social and Economic Interpretation (1973). A controversial but stimulating interpretation of Chinese economic history in terms of technology. It brings in earlier periods as well as the Ming, Qing, and modern China.

J.K. Fairbank, ed., The Chinese World Order: Traditional China's Foreign Relations (1968). An examination of the Chinese tribute system and its varying applications.

H.L. Kahn, Monarchy in the Emperor's Eyes: Image and Reality in the Ch'ien-lung Reign (1971). A study of the Chinese court during the mid-Qing period.

P. Kuhn, Soulstealers: The Chinese Sorcery Scare of 1768 (1990).

Li Yu, The Carnal Prayer Mat, trans. by P. Hanan (1990).

F. Mote and D. Twitchett, eds., The Cambridge History of China: The Ming Dynasty 1368–1644, Vols. VI (1988) and VII (1998).

S. Naquin, Peking Temples and City Life, 1400–1900 (2000).

S. Naquin and E.S. Rawski, Chinese Society in the Eighteenth Century (1987).

J.B. Parsons, The Peasant Rebellions of the Late Ming Dynasty (1970).

P.C. Perdue, Exhausting the Earth, State and Peasant in Hunan, 1500–1850 (1987).

D.H. Perkins, Agricultural Development in China, 1368–1968 (1969).

E. Rawski, The Last Emperors: A Social History of Qing Imperial Institutions (1998).

M. Ricci, China in the Sixteenth Century: The Journals of Matthew Ricci, 1583–1610 (1953).

W. Rowe, Hankow (1984). A study of a city in late imperial China.

G.W. Skinner, The City in Late Imperial China (1977).

J.D. Spence, Ts'ao Yin and the K'ang-hsi Emperor: Bondservant and Master (1966). An excellent study of the early Qing court.

J.D. Spence, Emperor of China: A Self-Portrait of K'ang-hsi (1974). The title of this readable book does not adequately convey the extent of the author's contribution to the study of the early Qing emperor.

J.D. Spence, Treason by the Book (2001). An account of the legal workings of the authoritarian Qing state that reads like a detective story.

L.A. Struve, trans. and ed., Voices from the Ming-Qing Cataclysm (1993). A reader with translations of Chinese sources.

F. Wakeman, The Great Enterprise (1985). On the founding of the Manchu Dynasty.

Japan

M.E. Berry, Hideyoshi (1982). A study of the sixteenth-century unifier of Japan.

M.E. Berry, The Culture of Civil War in Kyoto (1994). On the Warring States era.

H. Bolitho, Treasures among Men: The Fudai Daimyo in Tokugawa Japan (1974). A study in depth.

H. Bolitho, Bereavement and Consolation: Testimonies from Tokugawa Japan (2003). Instances of how Tokugawa Japanese handled the death of a child.

C.R. Boxer, The Christian Century in Japan, 1549–1650 (1951).

The Cambridge History of Japan; Vol. 4, J.W. Hall, ed., Early Modern Japan (1991). A multi-author work.

M. Chikamatsu, Major Plays of Chikamatsu, trans. by D. Keene (1961).

R.P. Dore, Education in Tokugawa Japan (1965).

G.S. Elison, Deus Destroyed: The Image of Christianity in Early Modern Japan (1973). A brilliant study of the persecutions of Christianity during the early Tokugawa period.

J.W. Hall and M. Jansen, eds., Studies in the Institutional History of Early Modern Japan (1968). A collection of articles on Tokugawa institutions.

J.W. Hall, K. Nagahara, and K. Yamamura, eds., Japan before Tokugawa (1981).

S. Hanley, Everyday Things in Premodern Japan: The Hidden Legacy of Material Culture (1997).

H.S. Hibbett, The Floating World in Japanese Fiction (1959). An eminently readable study of early Tokugawa literature.

M. Jansen, ed., The Nineteenth Century, Vol. 5 in The Cambridge History of Japan (1989).

K. Katsu, Musui's Story, trans. by T. Craig (1988). The life and adventures of a boisterous, no-good samurai of the early nineteenth century. Eminently readable.

D. Keene, trans., Chushingura, the Treasury of Loyal Retainers (1971). The puppet play about the forty-seven men who took revenge on the enemy of their former lord.

O.G. Lidin, Tanegashima: The Arrival of Europe in Japan (2002). The impact of the musket and Europeans on sixteenth-century Japan.

M. Maruyama, Studies in the Intellectual History of Tokugawa Japan, trans. by M. Hane (1974). A seminal work in this field by one of modern Japan's greatest scholars.

J.L. McClain et al., Edo and Paris: Urban Life and the State in the Early Modern Era (1994). Comparison of city life and government role in the capitals of Tokugawa Japan and France.

K.W. Nakai, Shogunal Politics (1988). A brilliant study of Arai Hakuseki's conceptualization of Tokugawa government.

P. Nosco, ed., Confucianism and Tokugawa Culture (1984). A lively collection of essays.

H. Ooms, Tokugawa Village Practice: Class, Status, Power, Law (1996).

A. Ravina, Land and Lordship in Early Modern Japan (1999). A sociopolitical study of three Tokugawa domains.

I. Saikaku, The Japanese Family Storehouse, trans. by G.W. Sargent (1959). A lively novel about merchant life in seventeenth-century Japan.

G.B. Sansom, The Western World and Japan (1950).

J.A. Sawada, Confucian Values and Popular Zen (1993). A study of Shingaku, a popular Tokugawa religious sect.

C.D. Sheldon, The Rise of the Merchant Class in Tokugawa Japan (1958).

T.C. Smith, The Agrarian Origins of Modern Japan (1959). On the evolution of farming and rural social organization in Tokugawa Japan.

P.F. Souyri, The World Turned Upside Down: Medieval Japanese Society (2001). After a running start from the late Heian period, an analysis of the overthrow of lords by their vassals.

R.P. Toby, State and Diplomacy in Early Modern Japan: Asia in the Development of the Tokugawa Bakufu (1984).

C. Totman, Tokugawa Ieyasu: Shōgun (1983).

C. Totman, Green Archipelago, Forestry in Preindustrial Japan (1989).

H.P. Varley, The Ōnin War: History of Its Origins and Background with a Selective Translation of the Chronicle of Ōnin (1967).

K. Yamamura and S.B. Hanley, Economic and Demographic Change in Preindustrial Japan, 1600–1868 (1977).

Korea

T. Hatada, A History of Korea (1969).

W.E. Henthorn, A History of Korea (1971).

Ki-Baik Lee, A New History of Korea (1984).

P. Lee, Sourcebook of Korean Civilization, Vol. I (1993).

Vietnam

J. Buttinger, A Dragon Defiant, a Short History of Vietnam (1972).

Nguyen Du, The Tale of Kieu (1983).

N. Tarling, ed., The Cambridge History of Southeast Asia (1992).

K. Taylor, The Birth of Vietnam (1983).

A.B. Woodside, Vietnam and the Chinese Model (1988).

Chapter 19

R.C. Allen, The British Industrial Revolution in Global Perspective (2009). A much needed addition to the study of the industrial revolution.

F. Anderson, The Crucible of War: The Seven Years' War and the Fate of Empire in British North America, 1754–1766 (2000). A splendid narrative and analysis.

W. Beik, Louis XIV and Absolutism: A Brief Study with Documents (2000). An excellent collection by a major scholar of absolutism.

T. Blanning, The Pursuit of Glory: Europe l648–l815 (2007). The best recent synthesis of the emergence of the modern European state system.

J. Blum, Lord and Peasant in Russia from the Ninth to the Nineteenth Century (1961). Remains a thorough and wide-ranging discussion.

P. Burke, The Fabrication of Louis XIV (1992). Examines the manner in which the public image of Louis XIV was forged in art.

J. Burnet, Gender, Work and Wages in Industrial Revolution Britain (2008). A major revisionist study of the wage structure for work by men and women.

P. Bushkovitch, Peter the Great: The Struggle for Power, 1671–1725 (2001). Replaces previous studies.

C. Clark, The Rise and Downfall of Prussia l600-l947 (2006). A stunning survey.

L. Colley, Britons: Forging the Nation, 1707–1837 (1992) A major study of the making of British nationhood.

P. Deane, The First Industrial Revolution (1999). A well-balanced and systematic treatment.

J. De Vries, The Industrious Revolution: Consumer Behavior and the Household Economy, 1650 to the Present (2008). Discusses the rise of development through the psychology and actions of consumers, thus presenting an important new perspective.

W. Doyle, The Old European Order, 1660–1800 (1992). Remains a classic study.

D. Fraser, Frederick the Great: King of Prussia (2001) Excellent on both Frederick and eighteenth-century Prussia.

T. Harris, Restoration: Charles II and His Kingdom, 1660–1685 (2006). A major exploration of the tumultuous years of the restoration of the English monarchy after the civil war.

E. Hobsbawm, Industry and Empire: The Birth of the Industrial Revolution (1999). A survey by a major historian of the subject.

K. Honeyman, Women, Gender and Industrialization in England, 1700–1850 (2000). Emphasizes how certain work or economic roles became associated with either men or women.

O.H. Hufton, The Poor of Eighteenth-Century France, 1750–1789 (1975). A brilliant classic study of poverty and the family economy.

L. Hughes, Russia in the Age of Peter the Great (1998). An excellent account.

C.J. Ingrao, The Habsburg Monarchy, 1618–1815 (2000). The best recent survey.

D.I. Kertzer and M. Barbagli, The History of the European Family: Family Life in Early Modern Times, 1500–1709 (2001). A series of broad-ranging essays covering the entire Continent.

S. King and G. Timmons, Making Sense of the Industrial Revolution: English Economy and Society, 1700–1850 (2001). Examines the industrial revolution through the social institutions that brought it about and were changed by it.

M. Kishlansky, A Monarchy Transformed: Britain 1603–1714 (1996) An excellent synthesis.

A. Lossky, Louis XIV and the French Monarchy (1994). The most recent major analysis.

F.E. Manuel, The Broken Staff: Judaism through Christian Eyes (1992). An important discussion of Christian interpretations of Judaism.

M.A. Meyer, The Origins of the Modern Jew: Jewish Identity and European Culture in Germany, 1749–1824 (1967). A general introduction organized around individual case studies.

S. Pincus, 1688: The First Modern Revolution (2009). The most important recent study.

G. Treasure, Louis XIV (2001). The best, most accessible recent study.

D. Valenze, The First Industrial Woman (1995). An elegant work exploring the manner in which industrialization transformed the work of women.

J. West, Gunpower, Government, and War in the Mid-Eighteenth Century (1991). A study of how warfare touched much government of the day.

Chapter 20

S.S. Blair and J. Bloom, The Art and Architecture of Islam, 1250–1800 (1994). A fine survey of the period for all parts of the Islamic world.

R. Canfield, ed., Turko-Persia in Historical Perspctive (1991). A good general collection of essays.

K. Chelebi, The Balance of Truth (1957). A marvelous volume of essays and reflections by probably the major intellectual of Ottoman times.

W.T. de Bary et al., comp., Sources of Indian Tradition, 2nd ed. (1958), Vol. I, From the Beginning to 1800, ed. and rev. by Ainslie T. Embree (1988). Excellent selections from a wide variety of Indian texts, with good introductions to chapters and individual selections.

S. Faroqi, Towns and Townsmen of Ottoman Anatolia (1984). Examines the changing balances of economic power between the urban and rural areas.

C.H. Fleischer, Bureaucrat and Intellectual in the Ottoman Empire: The Historian Mustafa Ali (1541–1600) (1986). A major study of Ottoman intellectual history.

G. Hambly, Central Asia (1966). Excellent survey chapters (9–13) on the Chaghatay and Uzbek (Shaybanid) Turks.

R.S. Hattox, Coffee and Coffee-Houses: The Origins of a Social Beverage in the Medieval Near East (1985). A fascinating piece of social history.

M.G.S. Hodgson, The Gunpowder Empires and Modern Times, Vol. 3 of The Venture of Islam, 3 vols. (1974). Less ample than Vols. 1 and 2 of Hodgson's monumental history, but a thoughtful survey of the great post–1500 empires.

S.M. Ikram, Muslim Civilization in India (1964). Still the best short survey history, covering the period from 711 to 1857.

H. Inalcik, The Ottoman Empire: The Classical Age, 1300–1600 (1973). An excellent, if dated, survey with solid treatment of Ottoman social, religious, and political institutions.

H. Inalcik, An Economic and Social History of the Ottoman Empire, 1300–1914 (1994). A masterly survey by the dean of Ottoman studies today.

C. Kafadar, Between Two Worlds: The Construction of the Ottoman State (1995). A readable analysis of theories of Ottoman origins and early development.

N.R. Keddie, ed., Scholars, Saints, and Sufis: Muslim Religious Institutions in the Middle East since 1500 (1972). A collection of interesting articles well worth reading.

M. Mujeeb, The Indian Muslims (1967). The best cultural study of Islamic civilization in India as a whole, from its origins onward.

G. Necipoglu, Architecture, Ceremonial, and Power: The Topkapi Palace in the Fifteenth and Sixteenth Centuries (1991). A superb analysis of the symbolism of Ottoman power and authority.

L. Pierce, The Imperial Harem: Women and Sex in the Ottoman Empire (1993). Ground-breaking study on the role of women in the Ottoman Empire.

D. Quatarert, An Economic and Social History of the Ottoman Empire, 1300–1914 (1994). The authoritative account of Ottoman economy and society.

J. Richards, The Mughal Empire, Vol. 5 of The New Cambridge History of India (1993). A impressive synthesis of the varying interpretations of Mughal India.

S.A.A. Rizvi, The Wonder That Was India, Vol. II (1987). A sequel to Basham's original The Wonder That Was India; treats Mughal life, culture, and history from 1200 to 1700.

F. Robinson, Atlas of the Islamic World since 1500 (1982). Brief, excellent historical essays, color illustrations with detailed accompanying text, and chronological tables, as well as precise maps, make this a refreshing general reference work.

R. Savory, Iran under the Safavids (1980). A solid and readable survey.

S.J. Shaw, Empire of the Gazis: The Rise and Decline of the Ottoman Empire, 1280–1808, Vol. I of History of the Ottoman Empire and Modern Turkey (1976). A solid historical survey with excellent bibliographic essays for each chapter and a good index.

Chapter 21

D. Beales, Joseph II, 2 Vols. (1987, 2009). The best treatment in English of the life of Joseph II.

M. Biagioli, Galileo Courtier: The Practice of Science in the Culture of Absolutism (1993). A major revisionist work that emphasizes the role of the political setting in Galileo's career and thought.

D.D. Bien, The Calas Affair: Persecution, Toleration, and Heresy in Eighteenth-Century Toulouse (1960). Classic treatment of the famous case.

T.C.W. Blanning, The Culture of Power and the Power of Culture: Old Regime Europe 1660–l789 (2002). The strongest treatment of the relationship of eighteenth-century cultural changes and politics.

P. Blom, Enlightening the World: Encyclopedie, The Book That Changed the Course of History (2005). A lively, accessible introduction.

J. Buchan, Crowded with Genius: The Scottish Enlightenment (2003). A lively, accessible introduction.

J.A. Conner, Kepler's Witch: An Astronomer's Discovery of Cosmic Order amid Religious War, Political Intrigue, and the Heresy Trial of His Mother (2005). Fascinating account of Kepler's effort to vindicate his mother against charges of witchcraft.

L. Damrosch, Rousseau: Restless Genius (2007). The best recent biography.

R. Darnton, The Literary Underground of the Old Regime (1982). Classic essays on the world of printers, publishers, and booksellers.

P. Dear, Revolutionizing the Sciences: European Knowledge and Its Ambitions, 1500–1700 (2001). A broad-ranging study of both the ideas and institutions of the new science.

I. De Madariaga, Catherine the Great: A Short History (1990). A good brief biography.

M. Feingold, The Newtonian Moment: Isaac Newton and the Making of Modern Culture (2004). A superb, well-illustrated volume.

S. Gaukroger, The Emergence of a Scientific Culture: Science and the Shaping of Modernity (2007). A challenging book exploring the differing understanding of natural knowledge in early modern European culture.

S. Gaukroger, Francis Bacon and the Transformation of Early-Modern Philosophy (2001). An excellent, accessible introduction.

J. Gleixk, Isaac Newton (2003). The best brief biography.

D. Goodman, The Republic of Letters: A Cultural History of the French Enlightenment (1994). Concentrates on the role of salons.

J.L. Heilbron, The Sun in the Church: Cathedrals as Solar Observatories (2000). A remarkable study of the manner in which Roman Catholic cathedrals were used to make astsronomical observations and calculations.

C. Hesse, The Other Enlightenment: How French Women Became Modern (2004). Explores the manner in which French women authors created their own sphere of thought and cultural activity.

K.J. Howell, God's Two Books: Copernican Cosmology and Biblical Interpretation in Early Modern Science (2003). Best introduction to early modern issues of science and religion.

J. Melton, The Rise of the Public in Enlightenmen Europe (2001). A superb overview of the emergence of new institutions that made the expression of a broad public opinion possible in Europe.

C. A. Kors, Encyclopedia of the Enlightenment (2002). A major reference work on all of the chief intellectual themes of the era.

J. Marshall, John Locke, Toleration and Early Enlightenment Culture (2006). A magisterial, challenging survey of seventeenth-century arguments for and against toleration.

T. Munck, The Enlightenment: A Comparative Social History 1721–1794 (2000). A clear introduction to the social background that made possible the spread of Enlightenment thought.

S. Muthu, Enlightenment against Empire (2003) A study of philosophes who criticized the European empires of their day.

D. Outram, The Enlightenment (1995). An excellent brief introduction.

R. Peason, Voltaire Almighty: A Life in Pursuit of Freedom (2005). An accessible biography.

R. Porter, The Creation of the Modern World: The Untold Story of the British Enlightenment (2001). A superb, lively overview.

J. Repcheck, Copernicus' Secret: How the Scientific Revolution Began (2007). A highly accessible biography of Copernicus.

E. Rothchild, Economic Sentiments: Adam Smith, Condorcet, and the Enlightenment (2001). A sensitive account of Smith's thought and its relationship to the social questions of the day.

S. Shapin, The Scientific Revolution (1996). An important revisionist survey emphasizing social factors.

J. Sheehan, The Enlightenment Bible (2007). Explores the Enlightenment treatment of the Bible.

D. Sorkin, The Religious Enlightenment: Protestants, Jews, and Catholics from London to Vienna (2008). Argues that important Enlightenment figures sought to protect religion.

L. Steinbrügge, The Moral Sex: Woman's Nature in the French Enlightenment (1995). Emphasizes the conservative nature of Enlightenment thought on women.

P. Zagorin, How the Idea of Religious Toleration Came to the West (2003). An excellent exploration of the rise of toleration.

Chapter 22

D. Andress, The Terror: The Merciless War for Freedom in Revolutionary France (2006). The best recent survey of the reign of terror.

R. Anstey, The Atlantic Slave Trade and British Abolition, 1760–1810 (1975). A standard overview that emphasizes the role of religious factors.

B. Bailyn, The Ideological Origins of the American Revolution (1967). An important work illustrating the role of English radical thought in the perceptions of the American colonists.

K.M. Baker, Inventing the French Revolution: Essays on French Political Culture in the Eighteenth Century (1990). Important essays on political thought before and during the revolution.

K.M. Baker and C. Lucas, eds., The French Revolution and the Creation of Modern Political Culture, 3 vols. (1987). A splendid collection of important original articles on all aspects of politics during the revolution.

R.J. Barman, Brazil: The Forging of a Nation, 1798–1852 (1988). The best coverage of this period.

D. Bell, The First Total War: Napoleon's Europe and the Birth of Warfare as We Know It (2007). A consideration of the Napoleonic conflicts and the culture of warfare.

M. S. Bell, Toussaint Louverture: A Biography (2007). An outstanding new biography.

J.F. Bernard, Talleyrand: A Biography (1973). A useful account.

L. Bethell, The Cambridge History of Latin America, Vol. 3 (1985). Contains an extensive treatment of independence.

R. Blackburn, The Overthrow of Colonial Slavery, 1776–1848 (1988). A major discussion quite skeptical of the humanitarian interpretation.

J. Brooke, King George III (1972). The best biography.

R. Cobb, The People's Armies (1987). The major treatment in English of the revolutionary army.

O. Connelly, Napoleon's Satellite Kingdoms (1965). The rule of Napoleon and his family in Europe.

D.B. Davis, The Problem of Slavery in the Age of Revolution, 1770–1823 (1975). A transatlantic perspective on the issue.

W. Doyle, The Oxford History of the French Revolution (2003). A broad, complex narrative with an excellent bibliography.

L. Dubois, Avengers of the New World: The Story of the Haitian Revolution (2004). An analytic narrative likely to replace others.

P. Dwyer, Napoleon: The Path to Power, l769–1799 (2008). A major study of the subject.

J. J. Ellis, His Excellency: George Washington (2004). A biography that explores the entire era of the American Revolution.

M. Glover, The Peninsular War, 1807–1814: A Concise Military History (1974). An interesting account of the military campaign that so drained Napoleon's resources in western Europe.

J. Godechot, The Counter-Revolution: Doctrine and Action, 1789–1804 (1971). An examination of opposition to the revolution.

A. Goodwin, The Friends of Liberty: The English Democratic Movement in the Age of the French Revolution (1979). A major work that explores the impact of the French Revolution on English radicalism.

L. Hunt, Politics, Culture, and Class in the French Revolution (1986). A series of essays that focus on the modes of expression of the revolutionary values and political ideas.

F. Kagan, The End of the old order: Napoleon and Europe, 1801–1805 (2006). A masterful narrative.

W.W. Kaufmann, British Policy and the Independence of Latin America, 1802–1828 (1951). A standard discussion of an important relationship.

E. Kennedy, A Cultural History of the French Revolution (1989). An important examination of the role of the arts, schools, clubs, and intellectual institutions.

M. Kennedy, The Jacobin Clubs in the French Revolution: The First Years (1982). A careful scrutiny of the organizations chiefly responsible for the radicalizing of the revolution.

M. Kennedy, The Jacobin Clubs in the French Revolution: The Middle Years (1988). A continuation of the previously listed study.

H. Kissinger, A World Restored: Metternich, Castlereagh and the Problems of Peace, 1812–1822 (1957). A provocative study by an author who became an American secretary of state.

G. Lefebvre, The Coming of the French Revolution (trans. 1947). A classic examination of the crisis of the French monarchy and the events of 1789.

G. Lefebvre, Napoleon, 2 vols., trans. by H. Stockhold (1969). The fullest and finest biography.

J. Lynch, Simon Bolivar: A Life (2006). Now the standard biography.

J. Lynch, The Spanish American Revolutions, 1808–1826 (1986). An excellent one-volume treatment.

P. Maier, American Scripture: Making the Declaration of Independence (1997). Stands as a major revision of our understanding of the Declaration.

S.E. Melzer and L.W. Rabine, eds., Rebel Daughters: Women and the French Revolution (1992). A collection of essays exploring various aspects of the role and image of women in the French Revolution.

M. Morris, The British Monarchy and the French Revolution (1998). Explores the manner in which the British monarchy saved itself from possible revolution.

R. Muir, Tactics and the Experience of Battle in the Age of Napoleon (1998). Examines the wars from the standpoint of the soldiers in combat.

H. Nicolson, The Congress of Vienna (1946). A good, readable account.

R.R. Palmer, Twelve Who Ruled: The Committee of Public Safety during the Terror (1941). A clear narrative and analysis of the policies and problems of the committee.

R.R. Palmer, The Age of the Democratic Revolution: A Political History of Europe and America, 1760–1800, 2 vols. (1959, 1964). An impressive survey of the political turmoil in the transatlantic world.

C. Proctor, Women, Equality, and the French Revolution (1990). An examination of how the ideas of the Enlightenment and the attitudes of revolutionaries affected the legal status of women.

A.J. Russell-Wood, ed., From Colony to Nation: Essays on the Independence of Brazil (1975). A series of important essays.

P. Schroeder, The Transformation of European Politics, 1763–1848 (1994). A fundamental treatment of the diplomacy of the era.

R. Scurr, Fatal Purity: Robespierre and the French Revolution (2007). A compelling analysis of a personality long difficult to understand.

A. Soboul, The Parisian Sans-Culottes and the French Revolution, 1793–94 (1964). The best work on the subject.

D.G. Sutherland, France, 1789–1825: Revolution and Counterrevolution (1986). A major synthesis based on recent scholarship in social history.

T. Tackett, Religion, Revolution, and Regional Culture in Eighteenth-Century France: The Ecclesiastical Oath of 1791 (1986). The most important study of this topic.

T. Tackett, Becoming a Revolutionary: The Deputies of the French National Assembly and the Emergence of a Revolutionary Culture (1789–1790) (1996). The best study of the early months of the revolution.

J.M. Thompson, Robespierre, 2 vols. (1935). The best biography.

D.K. Van Key, The Religious Origins of the French Revolution: From Calvin to the Civil Constitution, 1560–1791 (1996). Examines the manner in which debates within French Catholicism influenced the coming of the revolution.

M. Walzer, ed., Regicide and Revolution: Speeches at the Trial of Louis XVI (1974). An important and exceedingly interesting collection of documents with a useful introduction.

I. Woloch, The New Regime: Transformations of the French Civic Order, 1789–1820s (1994). An important overview of just what had and had not changed in France after the quarter century of revolution and war.

G. Wood, Empire of Liberty: A History of the Early Republic, 1789–1815 (2009) A major interpretation.

A. Zamoyski, Rites of Peace: The Fall of Napoleon and the Congress of Vienna (2007). A lively analysis and narrative.

Chapter 23

I. Berlin, Generations of Captivity: A History of African-American Slaves (2003). A major work.

P. Bew, Ireland: The Politics of Enmity 1789–2006 (2007). A major, new, outstanding survey of the sweep of modern Irish history.

D. Blackbourn, The Long Nineteenth Century: A History of Germany, 1780–1918 (1998). An outstanding survey.

D.G. Creighton, John A. MacDonald (1952, 1955). A major biography of the first Canadian prime minister.

D. Donald, Lincoln (1995). Now the standard biography.

R.B. Edgerton, Death or Glory: The Legacy of the Crimean War (2000). Multifaceted study of a badly mismanaged war that transformed many aspects of European domestic politics.

D.K. Goodwin, Team of Rivals: The Political Genius of Abraham Lincoln (2005). An accessible study of Lincoln's administration.

M. Holt, The Fate of Their Country: Politicians, Slavery Extension, and the Coming of the Civil War (2005). A brief introduction to the crucial decade of the 1850s in the United States.

M. Holt, The Rise and Fall of the American Whig Party: Jacksonian Politics and the Onset of the Civil War (2003). An extensive survey of the Jacksonian era.

R. Kee, The Green Flag: A History of Irish Nationalism (2001). A vast survey.

W. Lacquer, A History of Zionism (1989). The most extensive one-volume treatment.

M.B. Levinger, Enlightened Nationalism: The Transformation of Prussian Political Culture, 1806–1848 (2002). A major work.

J.M. McPherson, The Battle Cry of Freedom: The Civil War Era (1988). An excellent one-volume treatment.

D. Morton, A Short History of Canada (2001). Useful popular history.

J.P. Parry, The Rise and Fall of Liberal Government in Victorian Britain (1994). An outstanding study.

A. Plessis, The Rise and Fall of the Second Empire, 1852–1871 (1985). A useful survey of France under Napoleon III.

D.M. Potter, The Impending Crisis, 1848–1861 (1976) A penetrating study of the coming of the American Civil War.

L. Riall, Garibaldi: Invention of a Hero (2007). An exploration of a nationalist hero's reputation in his own day and later.

D. Shafer, The Paris Commune: French Politics, Culture, and Society at the Crossroads of the Revolutionary Tradition and Revolutionary Socialism (2005). Excellent in relating the Commune to previous and later revolutionary traditions.

A. Sked, Decline and Fall of the Habsburg Empire, 1815–1918 (2001). A major, accessible survey of a difficult subject.

A. Sked, Metternich and Austria: An Evaluation (2008). A thoughtful restoration of Metternich to the position of leading diplomat of his age.

D.M. Smith, Cavour (1984). An excellent biography.

C.P. Stacey, Canada and the Age of Conflict (1977, 1981). A study of Canadian foreign relations.

D. Wetzel, A Duel of Giants: Bismarck, Napoleon III, and the Origins of the Franco-Prussian War (2001). Broad study based on most recent scholarship.

Chapter 24

M. Adas, Machines as the Measure of Men: Science, Technology, and Ideologies of Western Dominance (1989). The best single volume on racial thinking and technological advances as forming ideologies of European colonial dominance.

A. Ascher and P.A. Stolypin, The Search for Stability in Late Imperial Russia (2000). A broad-ranging biography based on extensive research.

I. Berlin, Karl Marx: His Life and Environment, 4th ed. (1996). A classic volume that remains an excellent introduction.

P. Bowler, Evolution: The History of an Idea (2003). An outstanding survey.

Janet Browne, Charles Darwin, 2 vols. (2002). An eloquent, accessible biography.

J. Burrow, The Crisis of Reason: European Thought, 1848–1914 (2000). The best overview available.

A.D. Chandler Jr., The Visible Hand: Managerial Revolution in American Business (1977). Remains the best discussion of the innovative role of American business.

A. Clarke, The Struggle for the Breeches: Gender and the Making of the British Working Class (1995). An examination of the manner in which industrialization made problematical the relationships between men and women.

W. Cronin, Nature's Metropolis: Chicago and the Great West, 1848–1893 (1991). The best examination of any major American nineteenth-century city.

P. Gay, Freud: A Life for Our Time (1988). The new standard biography.

P. Gay, Modernism: The Lure of Heresy (2007). A broad interdisciplinary exploration.

R.F. Hamilton, Marxism, Revisionism, and Leninism: Explication, Assessment, and Commentary (2000). A contribution from the perspective of a historically minded sociologist.

S. Hahn, A Nation under Our Feet: Black Political Struggles in the Rural South from Slavery to the Great Migration (2003). A major synthesis.

A. Hourani, Arab Thought in the Liberal Age 1789–1939 (1967). A classic account, clearly written and accessible to the nonspecialist.

T. Hunt, Marx's General: The Revolutionary Life of Friedrich Engels (2009). A biography that also considers the general landscape of late nineteenth-century socialism.

D.I. Kertzer and M. Barbagli, eds., Family Life in the Long Nineteenth Century, 1789–1913: The History of the European Family (2002). Wide-ranging collection of essays.

J.T. Kloppenberg, Uncertain Victory: Social Democracy and Progressivism in European and American Thought (1986). An extremely important comparative study.

J. Köhler, Zarathustra's Secret: The Interior Life of Friedrich Nietzsche (2002). A controversial new biography.

L. Kolakowski, Main Currents of Marxism: Its Rise, Growth, and Dissolution, 3 vols. (1978). Especially good on the last years of the nineteenth century and the early years of the twentieth.

P. Krause, The Battle for Homestead, 1880–1892 (1992). Examines labor relations in the steel industry.

D. Landes, The Wealth and Poverty of Nations: Why Some Are So Rich and Some So Poor (1998). A major international discussion of the subject.

B. Lightman, Victorian Popularizers of Science: Designing Nature for New Audiences (2007). A study that adds numerous new dimensions to the subject.

G. Makari, Revolution in Mind: The Creation of Psychoanalysis (2008). A major, multidimensional survey.

M. McGerr, A Fierce Discontent: The Rise and Fall of the Progressive Moevement in America, 1870–1920 (2003). The best recent synthesis.

E. Morris, Theodore Rex (2002). Major survey of Theodore Roosevelt's presidency and personality.

A. Pais, Subtle Is the Lord: The Science and Life of Albert Einstein (1983). Remains the most accessible scientific biography.

J. Rendall, The Origins of Modern Feminism: Women in Britain, France and the United States, 1780–1860 (1985). A well-informed introduction.

R. Service, Lenin: A Biography (2002). Based on new sources and will no doubt become the standard biography.

R.M. Utley, The Indian Frontier and the American West, 1846–1890 (1984). A broad survey of the pressures of white civilization against Native Americans.

D. Vital, A People Apart: The Jews in Modern Europe, 1789–1939 (1999). A deeply informed survey.

Chapter 25

S. Arrom, The Women of Mexico City, 1790–1857 (1985). A pioneering study.

W. Baer, Brazilian Economy: Growth and Development (2007). An in-depth study of the subject.

L. Bethell, ed., The Cambridge History of Latin America, 8 vols. (1992). The single most authoritative coverage, with extensive bibliographical essays. This series has now been published in several smaller, nation-specific volumes edited by L. Bethell.

J.P. Brennan and M. Rougier, The Politics of National Capitalism: Peronism and the Argentine Bourgeoisie, 1946–1976 (2009). A challenging study of the relationship of Perón and business.

V. Bulmer-Thomas, The Economic History of Latin America since Independence (1994). Remains a major.

E.B. Burns, The Poverty of Progress: Latin America in the Nineteenth Century (1980). Remains a significant work arguing that the elites suppressed alternative modes of cultural and economic development.

D. Bushnell and N. Macaulay, The Emergence of Latin America in the Nineteenth Century (1994). A survey that examines the internal development of Latin America during the period.

R. Conrad, The Destruction of Brazilian Slavery, 1850–1889 (1971). Still a good survey of the most important problem in Brazil in the second half of the nineteenth century.

R. Conrad, World of Sorrow: The African Slave Trade to Brazil (1986). An excellent treatment of the subject.

N. Craske, Women and Politics in Latin America (1999). A useful overview.

E.V. Da Costa, The Brazilian Empire: Myths and Histories (1985). Essays that provide a thorough introduction to Brazil during the period of empire.

H.S. Ferns, Britain and Argentina in the Nineteenth Century (1968). Classic exploration of the intermeshing of the two economies.

M. Font, Coffee, Contention, and Change in the Making of Modern Brazil (1990). Extensive discussion of the problems of a single-commodity economy.

A. Gilly, The Mexican Revolution: A People's History (2005). Explores lesser known figures of the revolution.

R. Graham, Britain and the Onset of Modernization in Brazil (1968). Another study of British economic dominance.

S.H. Haber, Industry and Underdevelopment: The Industrialization of Mexico, 1890–1940 (1989). Examines the problem of industrialization before and after the revolution.

G. Hahner, Emancipating the Female Sex: The Struggle for Women's Rights in Brazil, 1850–1940 (1990). An extensive examination of a relatively understudied issue in Latin America.

C.H. Haring, Empire in Brazil: A New World Experiment with Monarchy (1958). Remains a useful overview.

J. Hemming, Amazon Frontier: The Defeat of the Brazilian Indians (1987). A brilliant survey of the experience of Native Americans in modern Brazil.

R.A. Humphreys, Latin America and the Second World War, 2 vols. (1981–1982). The standard work on the topic.

D. James, Resistance and Integration: Peronism and the Argentine Working Class, 1946–1976 (1994). Explores the complicated relationship of Perón and the working class over several decades.

M.B. Karush and O. Chamosa, The New Cultural History of Peronism: Power and Identity in Mid-Twentieth-Century Argentina (2010). Interdisciplinary collection of essays on the emergence of Peronism.

F. Katz, ed., Riot, Rebellion, and Revolution in Mexico: Social Base of Agrarian Violence, 1750–1940 (1988). Essays that put the violence of the revolution in a longer context.

F. Katz, The Life and Times of Pancho Villa (1998). An extensive critical biography

A. Knight, The Mexican Revolution, 2 vols. (1986). The best treatment of the subject.

C. M. MacLachlan, A History of Modern Brazil: The Past against the Future (2003). A basic brief introduction.

S. Mainwaring, The Catholic Church and Politics in Brazil, 1916–1985 (1986). An examination of a key institution in Brazilian life.

F. McLynn, Villa and Zapata: A History of the Mexican Revolution (2002). Examines the revolution through the lives and interrelationship of its two most important figures.

M. Morner, Adventurers and Proletarians: The Story of Migrants in Latin America (1985). Examines immigration to Latin America and migration within it.

A.D. Ortiz, Eva Perón: A Biography (1997) A biography of one of the most enigmatic figures of modern Latin America.

J. Page, Perón: A Biography (1983). The standard English treatment.

M. B. Plotkin, Manana Es San Perón: A Cultural History of Perón's Argentina (2003). Explores Argentina during the curious governance of Perón.

D. Rock, Politics in Argentina, 1890–1930: The Rise and Fall of Radicalism (2009). The major discussion of the Argentine Radical Party.

D. Rock, Argentina, 1516–1987: From Spanish Colonization to Alfonsin (1987). Now the standard survey.

D. Rock, ed., Latin America in the 1940s: War and Postwar Transitions (1994). Essays examining a very difficult decade for the continent.

R.M. Schneider, "Order and Progress": A Political History of Brazil (1991). A straightforward narrative with helpful notes for further reading.

R. Scott, The Abolition of Slavery and the Aftermath of Emancipation in Brazil (1988). A brief overview.

T.E. Skidmore, Black into White: Race and Nationality in Brazilian Thought (1993). Examines the role of racial theory in Brazil.

T.E. Skidmore, Politics in Brazil 1930–1964: An Experiment in Democracy (2007). An in-depth exploration of Brazilian politics before and after World War II.

S.J. Stein and B.H. Stein, The Colonial Heritage of Latin America: Essays on Economic Dependence in Perspective (1970). A classic statement of the dependence interpretation.

D. Tamarin, The Argentine Labor Movement, 1930–1945: A Study in the Origins of Perónism (1985). A useful introduction to a complex subject.

H.J. Wiarda, Politics and Social Change in Latin America: The Distinct Tradition (1974). Excellent essays that stress the ongoing role of Iberian traditions.

J.D. Wirth, ed., Latin American Oil Companies and the Politics of Energy (1985). A series of case studies.

J. Wolfe, Working Women, Working Men: São Paulo and the Rise of Brazil's Industrial Working Class, 1900–1955 (1993). Pays particular attention to the role of women.

J. Womack, Zapata and the Mexican Revolution (1968). A classic study.

Chapter 26

General Works

S. Cook, Colonial Encounters in the Age of High Imperialism (1996). A good introduction to the imperial enterprise in Africa and Asia.

D.K. Fieldhouse, The West and the Third World. Trade: Colonialism, Depedence and Development (1999). Addresses whether colonialism was detrimental or beneficial to colonized peoples.

D. Headrick, The Tentacles of Progress: Technology Transfer in the Age of Imperialism, 1850–1940 (1988). Discusses the roles of new methods of transportation (railroads, steamships), forms of expertise (doctors, botanists), and other types of "technology transfer" in European colonization, and post-independence development.

P. Hopkirk, The Great Game: The Struggle for Empire in Central Asia (1992). Focuses on the political and economic rivalries of the imperial powers.

India

A. Ahmad, Islamic Modernism in India and Pakistan, 1857–1964 (1967). The standard survey of Muslim thinkers and movements in India during the period.

C.A. Bayly, Indian Society and the Making of the British Empire, The New Cambridge History of India, II. 1 (1988). One of several major contributions of this author to the ongoing revision of our picture of modern Indian history since the eighteenth century.

A. Ghosh, In an Antique Land: History in the Guise of a Traveler's Tale (1992). An anthropologist traces the footsteps of a premodern slave traveling with his master from North Africa to India. A gripping tale of premodern life in the India Ocean basin and also of contemporary Egypt.

R. Guha, ed., Subaltern Studies: Writings on South Asian History and Society (1982). Essays on the colonial period that focus on the social, political, and economic history of "subaltern" groups and classes (hill tribes, peasants, etc.) rather than only the elites of India.

S.N. Hay, ed., "Modern India and Pakistan," Part VI of Wm. Theodore de Bary et al., eds., Sources of Indian Tradition, 2nd ed. (1988). A superb selection of primary-source documents, with brief introductions and helpful notes.

F. Robinson, ed., The Cambridge Encyclopedia of India, Pakistan, Bangladesh, Sri Lanka, Nepal, Bhutan, and the Maldives (1989). A fine collection of survey articles by various scholars, organized into topical chapters ranging from "Economies" to "Cultures."

Central Islamic Lands

W. Cleveland, A History of the Modern Middle East, 3rd ed. (2004). A balanced and well-organized overview of modern Middle Eastern history.

A. Dawisha, Arab Nationalism in the Twentieth Century, From Triumph to Despair (2003). A good overview of the development of Arab nationalism.

S. Deringil, The Well-Protected Domains: Ideology and the Legitimation of Power in the Ottoman Empire, 1876–1909 (1998). An impressive study on nationalism and reform in the Ottoman Empire.

J.J. Donahue and J.L. Esposito, eds., Islam in Transition: Muslim Perspectives (1982). An interesting selection of primary-source materials on Islamic thinking in this century.

D.F. Eickelman, Knowledge and Power in Morocco: The Education of a Twentieth-Century Notable (1985). A fascinating study of traditional Islamic education and society in the twentieth century through a social biography of a Moroccan religious scholar and judge.

A. Hourani, Arabic Thought in the Liberal Age, 1798–1939 (1967). The standard work, by which all subsequent scholarship on the topic is to be judged.

N.R. Keddie, An Islamic Response to Imperialism (1968). A brief study of al-Afghani, the great Muslim reformer, with translations of a number of his writings.

B. Lewis, The Emergence of Modern Turkey, 2nd ed. (1968). A concise but thorough history of the creation of the Turkish state, including nineteenth-century background.

J.O. Voll, Islam: Continuity and Change in the Modern World (1982). Chapters 1–6. An interpretive survey of the Islamic world since the eighteenth century. Its emphasis on eighteenth-century reform movements is especially noteworthy.

Africa

C. Achebe, Things Fall Apart (1959). Reading this classic novel may be the best way to get a profound sense of the ways African and European cultures interacted in the early colonial period.

D. Anderson, Histories of the Hanged: The Dirty War in Kenya and the End of Empire (2005). This account of the Kikuyu-led Mau Mau movement in Kenya emphasizes the way Mau Mau activities, and the British response, shaped and distorted Kenya's independence movement. (See also C. Elkins's Imperial Reckoning below.)

A.A. Boahen, Africa under Colonial Domination, 1880–1935 (1985). Vol. VII of the UNESCO General History of Africa. Excellent chapters on various regions of Africa in the period. Chapters 3–10 detail African resistance to European colonial intrusion in diverse regions.

W. Cartey and M. Kilson, eds., The Africa Reader: Colonial Africa (1970). Original source materials give a vivid picture of African resistance to colonial powers, adaptation to foreign rule, and the emergence of the African masses as a political force.

P. Curtin, S. Feiermann, L. Thompson, and J. Vansina, African History (1978). The relevant portions are Chapters 10–20.

B. Davidson, Modern Africa: A Social and Political History (1989). A very useful survey of African history.

C. Elkins, Imperial Reckoning: The Untold Story of Britain's Gulag in Kenya (2004). The Pulitzer Prize–winning account of Britain's appalling response to the Mau Mau movement in colonial Kenya; while Elkins focuses on the British, D. Anderson in Histories of the Hanged (see above) emphasizes the Kenyan side of the story.

J.D. Fage, A History of Africa (1978). The relevant chapters, which give a particularly clear overview of the colonial period, are 12–16.

B. Freund, The Making of Contemporary Africa: The Development of African Society since 1800 (1984). A refreshingly direct synthetic discussion and survey that take an avowedly, but not reductive, materialist approach to interpretation.

E. Gilbert and J.T. Reynolds, Africa in World History, 2nd ed. (2008). An engaging overview of the period, with attention to technology, economics, and ideologies, among other factors. See especially Chapters 13–15.

D. Headrick, Tools of Empire (1982). A provocative evaluation of the roles played by technology in the imperial venture.

A. Hochschild, King Leopold's Ghost: A Story of Greed, Terror, and Heroism in Colonial Africa (1998). A compelling, well-documented narrative of the atrocities committed in turn-of-the-twentieth-century Congo when it was held as the personal fiefdom of Belgium's monarch.

T. Pakenham, The Scramble for Africa (1991). An excellent analysis of the imperialist age in Africa.

A.D. Roberts, ed., The Colonial Moment in Africa: Essays on the Movement of Minds and Materials, 1900–1940 (1986). Chapters from The Cambridge History of Africa treating various aspects of the colonial period in Africa, including economics, politics, and religion.

Chapter 27

China

P.M. Coble, The Shanghai Capitalists and the Nationalist Government, 1927–1937 (1980).

L.E. Eastman, The Abortive Revolution: China under Nationalist Rule, 1927–1937 (1974).

L.E. Eastman, Seeds of Destruction: Nationalist China in War and Revolution, 1937–1949 (1984).

M. Elvin and G.W. Skinner, The Chinese City between Two Worlds (1974). A study of the late Qing and Republican eras.

J.W. Esherick, The Origins of the Boxer Rebellion (1987).

S. Et, China's Republican Revolution (1994).

J.K. Fairbank and M. Goldman, China, a New History (1998). A survey of the entire sweep of Chinese history; especially strong on the modern period.

J.K. Fairbank and D. Twitchett, eds., The Cambridge History of China. Like the premodern volumes in the same series, the volumes on modern China represent a survey of what is known. Volumes 10–15, which cover the history from the late Qing to the People's Republic, have been published, and the others will be available soon. The series is substantial. Each volume contains a comprehensive bibliography.

J. Fitzgerald, Awakening China: Politics, Culture, and Class in the Nationalist Revolution (1996).

C. Hao, Chinese Intellectuals in Crisis: Search for Order and Meaning, 1890–1911 (1987).

W.C. Kirby, ed., State and Economy in Republican China (2001).

P.A. Kuhn, Rebellion and Its Enemies in Late Imperial China: Militarization and Social Structure, 1796–1864 (1980). A study of how the Confucian gentry saved the Manchu Dynasty after the Taiping Rebellion.

P. Kuhn, Origins of the Modern Chinese State (2002).

J. Levenson, Liang Ch'i-ch'ao and the Mind of Modern China (1953). A classic study of a major Chinese reformer and thinker.

Lu Xun, Selected Works (1960). Novels, stories, and other writings by modern China's greatest writer.

S. Naquin, Peking: Temples and City Life, 1400–1900 (2000).

E.O. Reischauer, J.K. Fairbank, and A.M. Craig, East Asia: Tradition and Transformation (1989). A detailed text on East Asian history. Contains ample chapters on Japan and China and shorter chapters on Korea and Vietnam.

H.Z. Schiffrin, Sun Yat-sen, Reluctant Revolutionary (1980). A biography.

B.I. Schwartz, Chinese Communism and the Rise of Mao (1951). A classic study of Mao, his thought, and the Chinese Communist Party before 1949.

B.I. Schwartz, In Search of Wealth and Power: Yen Fu and the West (1964). A fine study of a late-nineteenth-century thinker who introduced Western ideas into China.

J.D. Spence, The Gate of Heavenly Peace: The Chinese and Their Revolution, 1895–1980 (1981). Historical reflections on twentieth-century China.

J.D. Spence, The Search for Modern China (1990). A thick text but well written.

M. Szonyi, Practicing Kinship: Lineage and Descent in Late Imperial China (2002).

S.Y. Teng and J.K. Fairbank, China's Response to the West (1954). A superb collection of translations from Chinese thinkers and political figures, with commentaries.

T.H. White and A. Jacoby, Thunder Out of China (1946). A view of China during World War II by two who were there.

Japan

G. Akita, Foundations of Constitutional Government in Modern Japan (1967). A study of Itō Hirobumi in the political process leading to the Meiji constitution.

G.C. Allen, A Short Economic History of Modern Japan (1958).

E. Barshay, The Social Sciences in Modern Japan: The Marxian and Modernist Traditions (2004). Different interpretations of history.

J.R. Bartholomew, The Formation of Science in Japan (1989). The pioneering English-language work on the subject.

W.G. Beasley, Japanese Imperialism, 1894–1945 (1987). Excellent short book on the subject.

G.M. Berger, Parties Out of Power in Japan, 1931–1941 (1977). An analysis of the condition of political parties during the militarist era.

G.L. Bernstein, ed., Recreating Japanese Women, 1600–1945 (1991).

The Cambridge History of Japan, The Nineteenth Century, M.B. Jansen, ed. (1989); The Twentieth Century, P. Duus, ed. (1988). Multi-author works.

A.M. Craig, Chōshū in the Meiji Restoration (2000). A study of the Chōshū domain, a Prussia of Japan, during the period 1840–1868.

A.M. Craig and D.H. Shively, eds., Personality in Japanese History (1970). An attempt to gauge the role of individuals and their personalities as factors explaining history.

P. Duus, Party Rivalry and Political Change in Taisho Japan (1968). A study of political change in Japan during the 1910s and 1920s.

P. Duus, The Abacus and the Sword: The Japanese Penetration of Korea, 1895–1910 (1995). A thoughtful analysis.

S. Ericson, The Sound of the Whistle: Railroads and the State in Meiji Japan (1996). An economic and social history of railroads, an engine of growth and popular symbol.

Y. Fukuzawa, Autobiography (1966). Japan's leading nineteenth-century thinker tells of his life and of the birth of modern Japan.

S. Garon, The State and Labor in Modern Japan (1987). A fine study of the subject.

C.N. Gluck, Japan's Modern Myths: Ideology in the Late Meiji Period (1988). A brilliant study of the complex weave of late Meiji thought.

A. Gordon, The Evolution of Labor Relations in Japan: Heavy Industry, 1853–1955 (1985). A seminal work.

B.R. Hackett, Yamagata Aritomo in the Rise of Modern Japan, 1932–1922 (1973). History as seen through the biography of a central figure.

I. Hall, Mori Arinori (1973). A biography of Japan's first minister of education.

T.R.H. Havens, The Valley of Darkness: The Japanese People and World War II (1978). Wartime society.

A. Iriye, After Imperialism: The Search for a New Order in the Far East, 1921–1931 (1965). (Also see other studies by this author.)

D.M.B. Jansen and G. Rozman, eds., Japan in Transition from Tokugawa to Meiji (1986). Contains fine essays.

W. Johnston, The Modern Epidemic: A History of Tuberculosis in Japan (1995). A social history of a disease.

D. Keene, ed., Modern Japanese Literature, An Anthology (1960). A collection of modern Japanese short stories and excerpts from novels.

Y.T. Matsusaka, The Making of Japanese Manchuria, 1904–1932 (2001). On railroad strategies in empire building.

J.W. Morley, ed., The China Quagmire (1983). A study of Japan's expansion on the continent between 1933 and 1941. (For diplomatic history, see also the many other works by this author.)

R.H. Myers and M.R. Peattie, eds., The Japanese Colonial Empire, 1895–1945 (1984).

T. Najita, Hara Kei in the Politics of Compromise, 1905–1915 (1967). A study of one of Japan's greatest party leaders.

K. Ohkawa and H. Rosovsky, Japanese Economic Growth: Trend Acceleration in the Twentieth Century (1973).

M. Ravina, The Last Samurai: The Life and Battles of Saigo Takamori (2004). Unlike the movie, this account of the Satsu-ma uprising is historical.

G. Shiba, Remembering Aizu (1999). A stirring autobiographical account of a samurai youth whose domain lost in the Meiji Restoration.

K. Smith, A Time of Crisis: The Great Depression and Rural Revitalization (2001). An intellectual history of village movements during the 1930s.

J.J. Stephan, Hawaii under the Rising Sun (1984). Japan's plans for rule in Hawaii.

R.H. Spector, Eagle against the Sun: The American War with Japan (1985). A narrative of World War II in the Pacific.

E.P. Tsurumi, Factory Girls: Women in the Thread Mills of Meiji Japan (1990). A sympathetic analysis of the key component of the Meiji labor force.

W. Wray, Mitsubishi and the N. Y. K., 1870–1914 (1984). The growth of a shipping zaibatsu, with analysis of business strategies, the role of government, and imperialist involvements.

Chapter 28

L. Albertini, The Origins of the War of 1914, 3 vols. (1952, 1957). Discursive but invaluable.

V.R. Berghahn, Germany and the Approach of War in 1914 (1973). A work similar in spirit to both of Fischer's (see below) but stressing the importance of Germany's naval program.

S.B. Fay, The Origins of the World War; 2 vols. (1928). The most influential of the revisionist accounts.

F. Fischer, Germany's Aims in the First World War (1967). An influential interpretation that stirred a great controversy in Germany and around the world by emphasizing Germany's role in bringing on the war.

D. Fromkin, Europe's Last Summer: Who Started the Great War in 1914? (2004). A lively account that fixes on the final crisis in July 1914.

J.N. Horne, Labour at War: France and Britain, 1914–1918 (1991). An examination of a major issue on the home fronts.

J. Keegan, The First World War (1999). A vivid and readable narrative.

P. Kennedy, The Rise of the Anglo-German Antagonism 1860–1914 (1980). An unusual and thorough analysis of the political, economic, and cultural roots of important diplomatic developments.

D.C.B. Lieven, Russia and the Origins of the First World War (1983). A good account of the forces that shaped Russian policy.

A. Mombauer, The Origins of the First World War. Controversies and Consensus (2002). A fascinating survey of the debate over the decades and the current state of the question.

R. Pipes, A Concise History of the Russian Revolution (1996). A one-volume version of a scholarly masterpiece.

Z. Steiner, Britain and the Origins of the First World War (1977). A perceptive and informed account of the way British foreign policy was made in the years before the war.

H. Strachan, The First World War (2004). A fine one-volume account of the war.

A.J.P. Taylor, The Struggle for Mastery in Europe, 1848–1918 (1954). Clever but controversial.

S.R. Williamson, Jr., Austria-Hungary and the Origins of the First World War (1991). A valuable study of a complex subject.

Chapter 29

W.S. Allen, The Nazi Seizure of Power: The Experience of a Single German Town, 1930–1935, rev. ed. (1984). A classic treatment of Nazism in a microcosmic setting.

A. Applebaum, Gulag: A History (2003). A superbly readable account of Stalin's system of persecution and resulting prison camps.

J. Barnard, Walter Reuther and the Rise of the Auto Workers (1983). A major introduction to the new American unions of the 1930s.

R.J. Bosworth, Mussolini (2002). A major new biography.

R.J.B. Bosworth, Mussolini's Italy: Life under the Fascist Dictatorship, 1915–1945 (2007) A broad-based study of both fascist politics and the impact of those politics on Italian life.

A. Brinkley, Voices of Protest: Huey Long, Father Coughlin, & the Great Depression (1983). An excellent study of Franklin Roosevelt's opponents.

M. Burleigh and W. Wipperman, The Racial State: Germany 1933–1945 (1991). Emphasizes the manner in which racial theory influenced numerous areas of policy.

R. Conquest, The Great Terror: Stalin's Purges of the Thirties (1968). Remains a major study.

B. Eichengreen, Golden Fetters: The Gold Standard and the Great Depression, 1919–1939 (1992). A remarkable study of the role of the gold standard in the economic policies of the interwar years.

R. Evans, The Coming of the Third Reich (2004) and The Third Reich in Power, 1933–1939 (2005) A superb narrative.

M.S. Fausold, The Presidency of Herbert Hoover (1985). An important treatment.

G. Feldman, The Great Disorder: Politics, Economics, and Society in the German Inflation, 1914–1924 (1993). The best work on the subject.

S. Fitzpatrick, Stalin's Peasants: Resistance and Survival in the Russian Village after Collectivization (1994). A pioneering study.

J.K. Galbraith, The Great Crash (1979). A well-known account by a leading economist.

R. Gellately, The Gestapo and German Society: Enforcing Racial Policy, 1933–1945 (1990). A discussion of how the police state supported Nazi racial policies.

R. Gellately and N. Stoltzfus, Social Outsiders in Nazi Germany (2001). Important essays on Nazi treatment of groups the party regarded as undesirables.

H.J. Gordon, Hitler and the Beer Hall Putsch (1972). An excellent account of the event and the political situation in the early Weimar Republic.

R. Hamilton, Who Voted for Hitler? (1982). An examination of voting patterns and sources of Nazi support.

P. Kenez, The Birth of the Propaganda State: Soviet Methods of Mass Mobilization, 1917–1929 (1985). An examination of the manner in which the communist government inculcated popular support.

D. Kennedy, Freedom from Fear: The American People in Depression and War, 1929–1945 (2001). The best one-volume study of the era.

B. Kent, The Spoils of War: The Politics, Economics, and Diplomacy of Reparations, 1918–1932 (1993). A comprehensive account of the intricacies of the reparations problem of the 1920s.

I. Kershaw, Hitler, 2 vols. (2001) Replaces all previous biographies.

D. Landes, The Unbound Prometheus: Technological Change and Industrial Development in Western Europe from 1750 to the Present (1969). Includes an excellent analysis of both the Great Depression and the few areas of economic growth.

W.E. Leuchtenburg, Franklin D. Roosevelt and the New Deal: 1932–1940 (2009). A superb one-volume treatment.

B. Lincoln, Red Victory: A History of the Russian Civil War (1989). An excellent narrative account.

D.J.K. Peukert, Inside Nazi Germany: Conformity, Opposition, and Racism in Everyday Life (1987). An excellent discussion of life under Nazi rule.

R. Pipes, The Unknown Lenin: From the Secret Archives (1996). A collection of previously unpublished documents that indicated the repressive character of Lenin's government.

P. Pulzer, Jews and the German State: The Political History of a Minority, 1848–1933 (1992). A detailed history by a major historian of European minorities.

L.J. Rupp, Mobilizing Women for War: German and America Propaganda, 1939–1945 (1978). Although concentrating on a later period, it includes an excellent discussion of general Nazi attitudes toward women.

R. Service, Stalin: A Biography (2005). The strongest of a host of recent biographical studies.

R. Service, Trotsky: A Biography (2009). A major new biography.

A. Solzhenitsyn, The Gulag Archipelago, 3 vols. (1974–1979). A major examination of the labor camps under Stalin by one of the most important late twentieth-century Russian writers.

A.J.P. Taylor, English History, 1914–1945 (1965). Lively and opinionated.

A. Tooze, The Wages of Destruction: The Making and Breaking of the Nazi Economy (2006). A wide-ranging, accessible study of the politics and ideology behind Nazi economic policy.

H.A. Turner Jr., German Big Business and the Rise of Hitler (1985). An important major study of the subject.

L. Yahil, The Holocaust: The Fate of European Jewry, 1932–1945 (1990). A major study of this fundamental subject in twentieth-century history.

Chapter 30

A. Adamthwaite, France and the Coming of the Second World War, 1936–1939 (1977). A careful account making good use of the French archives.

O. Bartov, Mirrors of Destruction: War, Genocide, and Modern Identity (2001). Remarkably penetrating essays.

E.R. Beck, Under the Bombs: The German Home Front, 1942–1945 (1986). An interesting examination of a generally unstudied subject.

P.M.H. Bell, The Origins of the Second World War in Europe, 3rd ed. (2007). A comprehensive study of the period and debates surrounding the European origins of World War II.

A. Beevor, The Spanish Civil War (2001). Particularly strong on the political issues.

C. Browning, The Origins of the Final Solution: The Evolution of the Nazi Jewish Policy (2004). The story of how Hitler's policy developed from discrimination to annihilation

A. Bullock, Hitler: A Study in Tyranny, rev. ed. (1964). A brilliant biography.

W.S. Churchill, The Second World War, 6 vols. (1948–1954). The memoirs of the great British leader.

A. Crozier, The Causes of the Second World War, 1997. An examination of what brought on the war.

R.B. Frank, Downfall: The End of the Imperial Japanese Empire (1998). A thorough, well-documented account of the last months of the Japanese Empire and the reasons for its surrender.

J.L. Gaddis, We Now Know: Rethinking Cold War History (1998). A fine account of the early years of the Cold War, making use of new evidence emerging since the collapse of the Soviet Union.

J.L. Gaddis, P.H. Gordon, E.May, eds., Cold War Statesmen Confront the Bomb: Nuclear Diplomacy since 1945 (1999). A collection of essays discussing the effect of atomic and nuclear weapons on diplomacy since World War II.

M. Gilbert, The Holocaust: A History of the Jews of Europe during the Second World War (1985). The best and most comprehensive treatment.

A. Iriye, Pearl Harbor and the Coming of the Pacific War (1999). Essays on how the Pacific war came about, including a selection of documents.

J. Keegan, The Second World War (1990). A lively and penetrating account by a master military historian.

I. Kershaw, Hitler: 1889–1936: Hubris (1999) and Hitler: 1936–1945: Nemesis (2001). An outstanding two-volume biography.

W.F. Kimball, Forged in War: Roosevelt, Churchill, and the Second World War (1998). A study of the collaboration between the two great leaders of the West based on a thorough knowledge of their correspondence.

W. Murray and A.R. Millett, A War to Be Won: Fighting the Second World War, (2000). A splendid account of the military operations in the war.

P. Neville, Hitler and Appeasement: The British Attempt to Prevent the Second World War (2005). A defense of the British appeasers of Hitler.

R. Overy, Why the Allies Won (1997). An anlysis of the reasons for the victory of the Allies, with special emphasis on technology.

N. Rich, Hitler War Aims, 2 vols. (1973–1974). The best study of the subject in English.

P. Wandycz, The Twilight of French Eastern Alliances, 1926–1936 (1988). A well-documented account of the diplomacy of central and eastern Europe in a crucial period.

G.L. Weinberg, A World at Arms: A Global History of World War II (1994). A thorough and excellent narrative account.

Chapter 31

B.S. Anderson and J.P. Pinsser, A History of Their Own: Women in Europe from Prehistory to the Present, Vol. 2 (1988). A broad-ranging survey.

R. Bernstein, Out of the Blue: The Story of September 11, 2001, from Jihad to Ground Zero (2002). An excellent account by a gifted journalist.

A. Brown, The Gorbachev Factor (1996). An important commentary by an English observer.

D. Calleo, Rethinking Europe's Future (2003). A daring book by an experienced commentator.

M. Cini, European Union Politics (2007). An authoritative guide.

J.F. Frieden, Global Capitalism: Its Fall and Rise in the Twentieth Century (2007). Background to the current financial crisis.

J.L. Gaddis, The Cold War: A New History (2006). An important overview.

D.J. Garrow, Bearing the Cross: Martin Luther King Jr. and the Southern Leadership Conference, 1955–1968 (1986). The best work on the subject.

M. I. Goldman, Petrostate: Putin, Power, and the New Russia (2008). A thoughtful, but critical analysis.

D. Halberstam, The Coldest Winter: America and the Korean War (2007). A superb narrative by a gifted journalist.

W. Hitchcock, Struggle for Europe: The Turbulent History of a Divided Continent, 1945–2002 (2003). The best overall narrative now available.

D. Kearns, Lyndon Johnson and the American Dream (1976). Remains a useful biography.

J. Keep, The Last of the Empires: A History of the Soviet Union, 1956–1991 (1995). A clear narrative.

M. Mandelbaum, The Ideas That Conquered the World: Peace, Democracy, and Free Markets (2002). An important analysis by a major commentator on international affairs.

J. Mann, The Rise of the Vulcans: The History of Bush's War Cabinet (2004). An account of the major foreign policy advisers behind the invasion of Iraq.

R. Mann, A Grand Delusion: America's Descent into Vietnam (2001). The best recent narrative.

J. McCormick, Understanding the European Union: A Concise Introduction (2002). Outlines the major features.

N. Naimark, Fires of Hatred: Ethnic Cleansing in Twentieth-Century Europe (2002). A remarkably sensitive treatment of a tragic subject.

T. R. Reid, The United States of Europe: The New Superpower and the End of American Supremacy (2004). A journalist's exploration of the impact of the European Union on American policy.

M.E. Sarotte, 1989: The Struggle to Create Post-Cold War Europe (2009). Explores paths taken and not taken at the time of the collapse of communism.

V. Sebestyen, Revolution 1989: The Fall of the Soviet Empire (2009). A masterful overview of the end of the Cold War Era.

L. Shevtsova, Russia—Lost in Transition: The Yelsin and Putin Legacies (2007). A major analysis and meditation on the past two decades.

R. Story, The Rise of Conservatism in America, 1945–2000: A Brief History with Documents (2007). A basic introductory overview.

M. Walker, The Cold War and the Making of the Modern World (1994). Remains a major survey.

Chapter 32

China

R. Baum, Burying Mao: Chinese Politics in the Age of Deng Xiaoping (1996).

A. Chan, R. Madsen, and J. Unger, Chen Village uunder Mao and Deng (1992).

J. Chang, Wild Swans: Three Daughters of China (1991). An intimate look at recent Chinese society through three generations of women. Immensely readable.

J. Feng, Ten Years of Madness: Oral Histories of China's Cultural Revolution (1996).

J. Fewsmith, China since Tiananmen: The Politics of Transition (2001). Focus is on the rise to power of Jiang Zemin and Chinese politics during the 1990s.

B.M. Frolic, Mao's People: Sixteen Portraits of Life in Revolutionary China (1987).

T. Gold, State and Society in the Taiwan Miracle (1986). The story of economic growth in postwar Taiwan.

M. Goldman, Sowing the Seeds of Democracy in China: Political Reform in the Deng Xiaoping Era (1994).

A. Iriye, China and Japan in the Global Setting (1992).

D.M. Lampton, Same Bed, Different Dreams: Managing U.S.–China Relations, 1989–2000 (2001).

H. Liang, Son of the Revolution (1983). An autobiographical account of a young man growing up in Mao's China.

K. Lieberthal, Governing China, from Revolution through Reform (2004).

B. Liu, People or Monsters? and Other Stories and Reportage from China After Mao (1983). Literary reflections on China.

R. MacFarquhar and J.K. Fairbank, eds., The Cambridge History of China, Vol. 14, Emergence of Revolutionary China (1987), and Vol. 15, Revolutions within the Chinese Revolution, 1966–1982 (1991).

L. Pan, Sons of the Yellow Emperor: A History of the Chinese Diaspora (1990). A pioneer study that treats not only Southeast Asia but the rest of the world as well.

M.R. Ristaino, Port of Last Resort: The Diaspora Communities of Shanghai (2001).

T. Saich, Governance and Politics of China (2004).

H. Wang, China's New Order (2003). Translation of a work by a Qinghua University professor, a liberal within the boundaries of what is permissible in China.

G. White, ed., In Search of Civil Society: Market Reform and Social Change in Contemporary China (1996).

M. Wolf, Revolution Postponed: Women in Contemporary China (1985).

Zhang X. and Sang Y., Chinese Lives: An Oral History of Contemporary China (1987).

Japan

A. Barshay, State and Intellectual in Imperial Japan (1988).

A. Barshay, The Social Sciences in Modern Japan (2007).

G.L. Bernstein, Haruko's World: A Japanese Farm Woman and Her Community (1983). A study of the changing life of a village woman in postwar Japan.

T. Bestor, Neighborhood Tokyo (1989). A portrait of contemporary urban life in Japan.

T. Bestor, Tsukiji (2003).

G.L. Curtis, The Logic of Japanese Politics: Leaders, Institutions, and the Limits of Change (1999).

G.L. Curtis, Policymaking in Japan: Defining the Role of Politicians (2002).

M.H. Cusumano, The Japanese Automobile Industry (1985). A neat study of the postwar business strategies of Toyota and Nissan.

W.T. DeBary, C. Gluck, and A. E. Tiedemann, Comps., Sources of the Japanese Tradition, 2nd ed. (2005).

R.P. Dore, Land Reform in Japan (1959). Another classic.

R.P. Dore, City Life in Japan (1999). A classic, reissued.

S. Garon, Molding Japanese Minds: The State in Everyday Life (1997).

S.M. Garon, The Evolution of Civil Society from Meiji to Heisei (2002). That is to say, from the mid-nineteenth century to the present day.

A. Gordon, ed., Postwar Japan as History (1993).

H. Hibbett, ed., Contemporary Japanese Literature: An Anthology of Fiction, Film, and Other Writing since 1945 (1977). Translations of postwar short stories.

Y. Kawabata, The Sound of the Mountain, trans. by E.G. Seidensticker (1970). Sensitive, moving novel by Nobel author.

J. Nathan, Sony, the Private Life (1999). A lively account of the human side of growth in the Sony Corporation.

D. Okimoto, Between MITI and the Market (1989). A discussion of the respective roles of government and private enterprise in Japan's postwar growth.

S. Pharr, Losing Face: Status Politics in Japan (1996).

E.F. Vogel, Japan as Number One: Lessons for America (1979). Though dated and somewhat sanguine, this remains an insightful classic.

Korea and Vietnam

B. Cumings, Korea: The Unknown War (1988).

B. Cumings, The Origins of the Korean War (Vol. 1, 1981; Vol. 2, 1991).

B. Cumings, The Two Koreas: On the Road to Reunification? (1990).

C.J. Eckert, Korea Old and New, A History (1990). The best short history of Korea, with extensive coverage of the postwar era.

C.J. Eckert, Offspring of Empire: The Koch'ang Kims and the Colonial Origins of Korean Capitalism, 1876–1945 (1991).

G.M.T. Kahin, Intervention: How America Became Involved in Vietnam (1986).

S. Karnow, Vietnam: A History, rev. ed., (1996).

L. Kendall, Shamans, Housewives, and Other Restless Spirits: Women in Korean Ritual and Life (1985).

K.B. Lee, A New History of Korea (1984). A translation by E. Wagner and others of an outstanding Korean work covering the full sweep of Korean history.

T. Li, Nguyen Cochinchina: South Vietnam in the Seventeenth and Eighteenth Centuries (1998).

D. Marr, Vietnam 1945: The Quest for Power (1995).

C.W. Sorensen, Over the Mountains Are Mountains (1988). How peasant households in Korea adapted to rapid industrialization.

A. Woodside, Vietnam and the Chinese Model (1988). Provides the background for Vietnam's relationship to China.

Chapter 33

General Works

P. Farmer, Pathologies of Power: Health, Human Rights, and the New War on the Poor (2003). Farmer, a physician, uses his experiences at Harvard and in the Caribbean to argue that inadequate health care in the Third World violates human rights and imperils us all.

J.H. Latham, Africa, Asia, and South America since 1800: A Bibliographic Guide (1995). A valuable tool for finding materials on the topics in this chapter.

S. Power, A Problem from Hell: America and the Age of Genocide (2002). A masterful analysis of genocides in the twentieth century (in Armenia, the Holocaust, the Khmer Rouge, Kurds, Rwanda, and Bosnia) and the U.S. response.

J.D. Sachs, The End of Poverty: Economic Possibilities for Our Time (2005). A renowned economist's plan to end extreme poverty around the world by 2025.

Latin America

S. Balfour, Castro (2008). A relatively brief survey of Castro's ability to hold power for half a century.

P. Brenner, A Contemporary Cuba Reader: Reinventing the Revolution (2007). A useful analysis of the developments in this century.

J. Dominguez and M. Shifter, Constructing Democratic Governance in Latin America (2008). Contains individual country studies.

G. W. Grayson, Mexico: Narco-Violence and a Failed State? (2009). Explores the impact of drug violence on Mexican politics.

G. Joseph et al., The Mexico Reader: History, Culture, Politics (2003). Excellent introduction to major issues.

P. Lowden, Moral Opposition to Authoritarian Rule in Chile (1996). A discussion of Chilean politics from the standpoint of human rights.

J. Preston and S. Dillon, Opening Mexico: The Making of a Democracy (2004). Excellent analysis of developments in Mexico prior to the outbreak of the drug wars.

H. Wiarda, Politics and Social Change in Latin America (2003). Attempts to examine the subject in light of long-standing historic trends in Latin America.

E. Williamson, The Penguin History of Latin America (2010). The best recent survey.

Africa

B. Davidson, Let Freedom Come (1978). Remains a thoughtful commentary of African independence.

P. Gourevitch, We Wish to Inform You that Tomorrow We Will Be Killed with Our Families (1999). An account of the Rwandan genocide that is beautifully written and almost unbearable to read.

J. Herbst, States and Power in Africa (2000). Relates current issues of African state-building to those before the colonial era.

R.W. July, A History of the African People, 5th ed. (1995). Provides a careful and clear survey of post–World War I history and consideration of nationalism.

N. Mandela, Long Walk to Freedom: The Autobiography of Nelson Mandela (1995). Autobiography of the African leader who transformed South Africa.

L. Thompson, A History of South Africa (2001). The best survey.

N. Van de Walle, African Economies and the Politics of Permanent Crisis, 1979–1999 (2001). Exploration of the difficulties of African economic development.

India and Pakistan

O.B. Jones, Pakistan: Eye of the Storm (2003). Best recent introduction.

R. Rashid, Taliban: Militant Islam, Oil and Fundamentalism in Central Asia (2001). Analysis of radical Isalmist regime in Afghanistan.

R.W. Stern, Changing India: Bourgeois Revolution on the Subcontinent (2003). Overview of forces now changing Indian society.

S. Wolpert, A New History of India (2003). The closing chapters of this fine survey history are particularly helpful in orienting the reader in postwar Indian history until the mid-1980s.

Islam and the Middle East

A. Ahmed, Discovering Islam: Making Sense of Muslim History and Society, rev. ed. (2003). An excellent and readable overview of Islamic–Western relations.

J. Esposito, The Islamic Threat: Myth or Reality, 2nd ed. (1992). A useful corrective to some of the polemics against Islam and Muslims today.

J.J. Esposito, ed., The Oxford Encyclopedia of Islam (1999). A thematic survey of Islamic history, particularly strong in the Modern Era.

D. Fromkin, A Peace to End All Peace: The Fall of the Ottoman Empire and the Creation of the Modern Middle East (2001). Very good on the impact of World War I on the region.

G. Fuller, The Future of Political Islam (2003). A very good overview of Islamist ideology by a former CIA staff member.

J. Keay, Sowing the Wind: The Seeds of Conflict in the Middle East (2003). A balanced account.

N.R. Keddie, Modern Iran: Roots and Results of Revolution (2003). Chapters 6–12 focus on Iran from 1941 through the first years of the 1978 revolution and provide a solid overview of history in this era.

G. Kepel, Jihad: The Trail of Political Islam (2002). An extensive treatment by a leading French scholar of the subject.

Credits

brary Ltd.; **page 680:** Courtesy of the Library of Congress; **page 681:** Caravan with Ivory, French Congo, (now the Republic of the Congo). Robert Visser (1882–1894). c. 1890–1900, postcard, collotype. Publisher unknown, c. 1900. Postcard 1912. Image No. EEPA 1985-140792. Eliot Elisofon Photographic Archives. National Museum of African Art, Smithsonian Institution; **page 683:** Getty Images Inc. - Hulton Archive Photos; **page 684:** Courtesy of the Library of Congress; **page 686:** Brown Brothers; **page 688:** © CORBIS All Rights Reserved; **page 688:** Getty Images Inc. - Hulton Archive Photos; **page 692:** Art Resource/Bildarchiv Preussischer Kulturbesitz; **page 693:** Courtesy of the Library of Congress. African and Middle Eastern Division; **page 693:** Photolibrary/Peter Arnold, Inc.

Chapter 27, page 694: Mita Arts Gallery CO., LTD; **page 698:** Courtesy United States Naval Academy Museum; **page 701:** Scala/Art Resource, NY; **page 701:** Adachi Ginko (active 1847–1894). View of the Issuance of the State Constitution in the State Chamber of the New Imperial Palace. Japan, Meiji period (1868–1912), March 2, 1889 (Meiji 22). Triptych of polychrome woodblock prints; ink and color on paper. The Metropolitan Museum of Art, Gift of Lincoln Kirstein, 1959 (JP3233-JP3225) Image © The Metropolitan Museum of Art/Art Resource, NY; **page 702:** ZUMA Press; **page 703:** Courtesy of the Library of Congress. Gift of Mrs. E. Crane Chadbourne; 1930; **page 704:** © Bettmann/CORBIS All Rights Reserved; **page 707:** National Archives and Records Administration; **page 710:** CORBIS - NY; **page 711:** The Art Archive/Picture Desk, Inc./Kobal Collection; **page 712:** Harvard-Yenching Library/Harvard University; **page 713:** Library of Congress; **page 713:** © Burton Holmes/CORBIS All Rights Reserved; **page 714:** Private Collection/The Bridgeman Art Library; **page 717:** IN/GEN/Camera Press/Retna Ltd; **page 720:** FPG/Getty Images Inc. - Hulton Archive Photos.

Chapter 28, page 724: Mary Evans Picture Library; **page 727:** Bettman/CORBIS/Bettman; **page 731:** Anti-Slavery International; **page 733:** German Information Center; **page 737:** Brown Brothers; **page 739:** National Archives and Records Administration; **page 741:** Photo Researchers; **page 742:** CORBIS - NY; **page 743:** Ria-Novosti/Sovfoto/Eastfoto; **page 745:** John Singer Sargent (1856–1925), "Gassed, an Oil Study". 1918-19 Oil on Canvas. Private Collection. Photo © Christie's Images. The Bridgeman Art Library; **page 748:** CORBIS - NY.

Chapter 29, page 752: Art Resource/Bildarchiv Preussischer Kulturbesitz; **page 755:** Getty Images Inc. - Hulton Archive Photos; **page 757:** Gemalde von A. M. Gerassimow, "Lenin als Agitator." Bildarchiv Preussischer Kulturbesitz; **page 758:** AP Wide World Photos; **page 760:** Poster concerning the 1st 5 Year Plan with a photograph of Joseph Stalin 1879–1953), 'At the end of the Plan, the basis of collectivisation must be completed', 1932 (colour litho) by Klutchis (fl.1932). Deutsches Plakat Museum, Essen, Germany/Archives Charmet/The Bridgeman Art Library; **page 760:** Itar-Tass/Sovfoto/Eastfoto; **page 762:** AP Wide World Photos; **page 764:** Library of Congress; **page 769:** Art Resource/Bildarchiv Preussischer Kulturbesitz; **page 770:** Art Resource/Bildarchiv Preussischer Kulturbesitz; **page 771:** Art Resource/Bildarchiv Preussischer Kulturbesitz; **page 773:** Ball State University Libraries, Archives & Special Collections, W.A. Swift Photo Collection; **page**

774: CORBIS - NY; **page 777:** Courtesy of the Library of Congress; **page 777:** Library of Congress.

Chapter 30, page 778: The Granger Collection; **page 782:** Pablo Picasso , 'Guernica' 1937, Oil on canvas. 11'5 1/2 × 25'5 3/4. Museo Nacional Centro de Arte Reina Sofia/© 2007 Estate of Pablo Picasso/Artists Rights Society (ARS), New York. **page 784:** Ullstein Bild, Berlin. The Granger Collection, New York. **page 786:** The Granger Collection; **page 788:** Photo by Bernhard Walter; source: National Archives and Records Administration; **page 789:** National Archives and Records Administration; **page 791:** courtesy of the Library of Congress; **page 793:** CORBIS - NY; **page 794:** Getty Images Inc. - Hulton Archive Photos; **page 794:** United States Signal Corps; **page 797:** Printed by permission of the Norman Rockwell Family Agency. Copyright © 1943 the Norman Rockwell Family Entities and © 1943 SEPS: Licensed by Curtis Publishing, Indianapolis, IN. All rghts reserved. *www.curtispublishing.com*; **page 798:** Getty Images Inc. - Hulton Archive Photos; **page 801:** Karlin/U.S. Army Photo.

Chapter 31, page 804: © CORBIS All Rights Reserved; **page 807:** Courtesy of the Library of Congress; **page 808:** Art Resource/Bildarchiv Preussischer Kulturbesitz; **page 811:** © CORBIS; **page 812:** AP Wide World Photos; **page 812:** AP Wide World Photos; **page 817:** Mike Schroeder/argus/Photolibrary/Peter Arnold, Inc.; **page 818:** Keystone_Paris/Getty Images Inc. - Hulton Archive Photos; **page 819:** CORBIS - NY; **page 820:** AP Wide World Photos; **page 821:** Magnum Photos, Inc.; **page 822:** Bernard Bisson/CORBIS - NY; **page 824:** Les Stone/CORBIS - NY; **page 825:** CORBIS - NY **page 830:** Gleb Garanich/CORBIS - NY; **page 831:** Reuters/CORBIS - NY; **page 833:** Igor Rodin/AFP/Getty Images; **page 834:** © Christinne Muschi/CORBIS All Rights Reserved.

Chapter 32, page 838: © Liu Liqun/CORBIS All Rights Reserved; **page 841:** CORBIS - NY; **page 845:** Reuters/Susumu Takahashi/Reuters Limited; **page 846:** Getty Images, Inc.; **page 847:** Clive Streeter © Dorling Kindersley; **page 848:** Nick Clements/Getty Images, Inc.; **page 849:** © Bettmann/CORBIS All Rights Reserved; **page 850:** © Bettmann/CORBIS All Rights Reserved; **page 852:** Reuters/Ed Nachtrieb/Reuters Limited; **page 853:** A. Ramey/PhotoEdit Inc.; **page 854:** Getty Images; **page 855:** © Imagemore Co., Ltd./CORBIS All Rights Reserved; **page 856:** © Reuters/CORBIS All Rights Reserved; **page 859:** Koren POOL/Yonhap/AP Wide World Photos; **page 860:** CORBIS - NY; **page 862:** AP Wide World Photos.

Chapter 33, page 866: © Nic Bothma/CORBIS All Rights Reserved; **page 868:** © Bettmann/CORBIS All Rights Reserved; **page 873:** Courtesy of the Library of Congress; **page 874:** © Douglas Engle/CORBIS All Rights Reserved; **page 875:** Newscom; **page 876:** Ronaldo Schemidt/AFP/Getty Images; **page 877:** UPI/CORBIS - NY; **page 878:** Getty Images Inc. - Hulton Archive Photos; **page 879:** © Peter Turnley/CORBIS; **page 880:** David Guttenfelder/AP Wide World Photos; **page 882:** Luc Gnago/CORBIS - NY; **page 883:** © Bettmann/CORBIS; **page 884:** © Micheline Pelletier/CORBIS All Rights Reserved; **page 885:** Sunil Malhotra/Reuters/CORBIS - NY; **page 888:** Getty Images, Inc. AFP; **page 889:** Getty Images, Inc. - Getty News; **page 893:** AFP/Getty Images.

Index

20° 40° 60° 80° 100° 120° 140° 160° 80°

OCEAN

RUSSIAN FEDERATION

60°

WAY

SWEDEN **FINLAND**

K

LITHUANIA
ESTONIA BELARUS
LATVIA CZECH REPUBLIC
SLOVAK REPUBLIC
SLOVENIA
KAZAKHSTAN **MONGOLIA**
GERMANY **POLAND** HUNGARY
CROATIA
UKRAINE
AUS. MOLDOVA
ROMANIA BOSNIA-HERZEGOVINA
ITALY SERBIA GEORGIA **UZBEKISTAN** **KYRGYZSTAN**
ALBANIA BULGARIA
MACEDONIA **TURKMENISTAN** **TAJIKISTAN**
GREECE TURKEY ARMENIA
MALTA **AZERBAIJAN** **PEOPLE'S REPUBLIC OF CHINA**
TUNISIA CYPRUS **SYRIA** IRAN **AFGHANISTAN** **NEPAL**
LEBANON IRAQ KUWAIT **BHUTAN**
ISRAEL JORDAN QATAR **PAKISTAN**
LIBYA BAHRAIN
EGYPT SAUDI **MYANMAR (BURMA)**
ARABIA OMAN **UNITED** **INDIA**
ARAB **TAIWAN**
NIGER ARAB EMIRATES **BANGLADESH** **LAOS**
CHAD ERITREA YEMEN **THAILAND**
SUDAN **VIETNAM** **PHILIPPINES**
GERIA DJIBOUTI **CAMBODIA**
CAMEROON ETHIOPIA **SRI LANKA** BRUNEI
UGANDA SOMALIA **MALDIVES** **MALAYSIA**
RWANDA **KENYA** **SINGAPORE**
BURUNDI
Democratic
Republic
of Congo TANZANIA SEYCHELLES **INDONESIA**
ANGOLA **MALAWI** COMOROS **INDIAN** **PAPUA**
ZAMBIA MOZAMBIQUE **OCEAN** **NEW GUINEA**
EAST TIMOR
NAMIBIA **BOTSWANA** MADAGASCAR MAURITIUS
Tropic of Capricorn
ZIMBABWE **AUSTRALIA**
SWAZILAND
SOUTH LESOTHO
AFRICA

NORTH
KOREA **JAPAN**
SOUTH
KOREA *PACIFIC*

40°

OCEAN Tropic of Cancer

20°

MARSHALL
ISLANDS

MICRONESIA
Equator KIRIBATI 0°
NAURU
SOLOMON
ISLANDS
TUVALU
VANUATU FIJI
20°
NEW CALEDONIA
(FRANCE)

40°

NEW ZEALAND

60°

Antarctic Circle

0   1,000   2,000 Miles

0   1,000 2,000 3,000 Kilometers

80°